101 Labs for the Cisco CCNP Exams

Hands on Practical Labs for the Cisco CCNP Exams

Paul Browning (LLB Hons) CCNP, MCSE
Farai Tafa dual CCIE

ISBN: 978-0-9569892-0-8

Published by:

Reality Press Ltd.

Midsummer Court

314 Midsummer Blvd.

Milton Keynes

MK9 2UB

help@reality-press.com

LEGAL NOTICE

The advice in this book is designed to help you achieve the standard of Cisco Certified Network Engineer which is Cisco's foundation internetworking examination. A CCNA is able to carry out basic router and switch installations and troubleshooting. Before you carry out more complex operations it is advisable to seek the advice of experts or Cisco Systems, Inc.

The practical scenarios in this book are meant to illustrate a technical point only and should be used on your privately owned equipment only and never on a live network.

INTRODUCTION

Cisco CCNP engineers are amongst the most highly paid and the most skilled network engineers in the IT industry. This is reflected by the fact that in order to pass the three challenging CCNP exams, you must be a master of a large number of topics, including configuring OSPF, EIGRP, BGP, VLANs, network security, IPv6, redistribution, and many other services and protocols. In addition, you must be able to devise and implement a troubleshooting strategy for a list of over 25 services and protocols that Cisco considers important in today's modern networks.

101 Labs for the Cisco CCNP Exams is designed to give you the skills and confidence to do all of the above, and much more. If you master these labs, we feel confident that you will not only perform well in the exam but also become a highly sought after network engineer or consultant. Of course, we speak from personal experience, having performed these roles ourselves for several years.

If you require more hands-on experience or theoretical input, then please check out our CCNP study manuals for ROUTE, SWITCH, and TSHOOT, which can be found via our Cisco training site www.howtonetwork.net.

One last note: we have refrained from dividing these labs into ROUTE, SWITCH, and TSHOOT exams because the TSHOOT exam, for example, requires knowledge of topics from both the SWITCH and the ROUTE labs. If you are taking just the ROUTE or the SWITCH exam, then concentrate on the relevant labs for these subjects, which are apparent from the lab titles.

Best of luck with your studies.

Paul Browning—CCNP
Farai Tafa—CCIE (RS & SP) 14811

ABOUT THE AUTHORS

Paul Browning

Paul Browning is the author of CCNA Simplified, which is one of the industry's leading CCNA study guides. Paul previously worked for Cisco TAC but left in 2002 to start his own Cisco training company in the UK. Paul has taught over 2,000 Cisco engineers with both his classroom-based courses and his online Cisco training site, www.howtonetwork.net. Paul lives in the UK with his wife and daughter.

Farai Tafa

Farai Tafa is a Dual CCIE in both Routing and Switching and Service Provider. Farai currently works for one of the world's largest telecoms companies as a network engineer. He has also written workbooks for the CCNA, CCNP, and Cisco Security exams. Farai lives in Washington, D.C. with his wife and daughter.

Table of Contents

CCNP Lab 1   VLANs, VTP, DTP and STP 1

CCNP Lab 2   VLANs, VTP, DTP and STP 11

CCNP Lab 3   LACP, PAgP, Multiple STP 23

CCNP Lab 4   MLS, EtherChannels and Security 37

CCNP Lab 5   DHCP, Source Guard and 802.1X 51

CCNP Lab 6   HSRP and Switch Security 60

CCNP Lab 7   HRRP and STP Convergence 72

CCNP Lab 8   SNMP, Logging and Management 84

CCNP Lab 9   QoS, Voice and Video Support 97

CCNP Lab 10   Router, Port and VLAN ACLs 111

CCNP Lab 11   EIGRP Multi-Technology 123

CCNP Lab 12   EIGRP Multi-Technology Lab 2 133

CCNP Lab 13   EIGRP Multi-Technology Lab 142

CCNP Lab 14   EIGRP Multi-Technology Lab 155

CCNP Lab 15   EIGRP Multi-Technology Lab 167

CCNP Lab 16   EIGRP Multi-Technology Lab 179

CCNP Lab 17   EIGRP Multi-Technology Lab 190

CCNP Lab 18   EIGRP Multi-Technology Lab 203

CCNP Lab 19   EIGRP Multi-Technology Lab 215

CCNP Lab 20   EIGRP Multi-Technology Lab 224

CCNP Lab 21   OSPF Multi-Technology Lab 235

CCNP Lab 22   OSPF Multi-Technology Lab 246

CCNP Lab 23   OSPF Multi-Technology Lab 259

CCNP Lab 24   OSPF Multi-Technology Lab 270

CCNP Lab 25   OSPF Multi-Technology Lab 284

CCNP Lab 26   OSPF Multi-Technology Lab 294

CCNP Lab 27   OSPF Multi-Technology Lab 305

CCNP Lab 28   OSPF Multi-Technology Lab 319

CCNP Lab 29   OSPF Multi-Technology Lab 333

CCNP Lab 30   OSPF Multi-Technology Lab 346

CCNP Lab 31   Border Gateway Protocol Lab 359

CCNP Lab 32   Border Gateway Protocol Lab 373

CCNP Lab 33   Border Gateway Protocol Lab 387

CCNP Lab 34   Border Gateway Protocol Lab 402

CCNP Lab 35   Border Gateway Protocol Lab 413

CCNP Lab 36   Border Gateway Protocol Lab 425

CCNP Lab 37   Border Gateway Protocol Lab 439

CCNP Lab 38	Border Gateway Protocol Lab	454
CCNP Lab 39	Border Gateway Protocol Lab	465
CCNP Lab 40	Border Gateway Protocol Lab	477
CCNP Lab 41	Internet Protocol Version 6 Lab	492
CCNP Lab 42	Internet Protocol Version 6 Lab	504
CCNP Lab 43	Internet Protocol Version 6 Lab	519
CCNP Lab 44	Internet Protocol Version 6 Lab	532
CCNP Lab 45	Internet Protocol Version 6 Lab	545
CCNP Lab 46	Internet Protocol Version 6 Lab	559
CCNP Lab 47	Internet Protocol Version 6 Lab	569
CCNP Lab 48	Internet Protocol Version 6 Lab	580
CCNP Lab 49	Internet Protocol Version 6 Lab	588
CCNP Lab 50	Internet Protocol Version 6 Lab	601
CCNP Lab 51	Cisco IOS IP SLA and FHRP Lab	611
CCNP Lab 52	Cisco IOS EOT and FHRP Lab	623
CCNP Lab 53	Cisco IOS IP SLA and BGP Lab	632
CCNP Lab 54	Cisco Policy Based Routing Lab	641
CCNP Lab 55	Cisco Policy Based Routing Lab	651
CCNP Lab 56	Cisco Policy Based Routing Lab	661
CCNP Lab 57	Cisco IOS PBR, SLA and EOT Lab	672
CCNP Lab 58	Cisco IOS GLBP Lab	685
CCNP Lab 59	Cisco IOS GLBP Lab	695
CCNP Lab 60	Cisco IOS IP SLA and GLBP Lab	706
CCNP Lab 61	Embedded Event Manager Lab	719
CCNP Lab 62	Embedded Event Manager Lab	724
CCNP Lab 63	Syslog and NTP Lab	729
CCNP Lab 64	SNMP Traps and Informs Lab	737
CCNP Lab 65	NetFlow and Accounting Lab	742
CCNP Lab 66	Cisco IOS NBAR Lab	749
CCNP Lab 67	Cisco Configuration Archive Lab	756
CCNP Lab 68	Cisco IOS RITE and SPAN Lab	760
CCNP Lab 69	Cisco IOS RITE and RSPAN Lab	767
CCNP Lab 70	Syslog and SNMP Lab	776
CCNP Lab 71	Multicast—PIM Dense Mode Lab	782
CCNP Lab 72	Multicast—PIM Sparse Mode Lab	790
CCNP Lab 73	Multicast—PIM Auto RP Lab	800
CCNP Lab 74	Branch Office Connectivity Lab	811
CCNP Lab 75	Branch Office Connectivity Lab	824
CCNP Lab 76	WAN IP Quality of Service Lab	835
CCNP Lab 77	WAN IP Quality of Service Lab	847
CCNP Lab 78	PPP over Ethernet (PPPoE) Lab	861
CCNP Lab 79	PPP over Ethernet (PPPoE) Lab	868
CCNP Lab 80	Branch Office Connectivity Lab	877
CCNP Lab 81	CCNP Multi-Technology Lab	886
CCNP Lab 82	CCNP Multi-Technology Lab	910

CCNP Lab 83   CCNP Multi-Technology Lab 937
CCNP Lab 84   CCNP Multi-Technology Lab 960
CCNP Lab 85   CCNP Multi-Technology Lab 987
CCNP Lab 86   Troubleshooting Lab 1019
CCNP Lab 87   Troubleshooting Lab 1032
CCNP Lab 88   Troubleshooting Lab 1046
CCNP Lab 89   Troubleshooting Lab 1059
CCNP Lab 90   Troubleshooting Lab 1076
CCNP Lab 91   Troubleshooting Lab 1092
CCNP Lab 92   Troubleshooting Lab 1101
CCNP Lab 93   Troubleshooting Lab 1110
CCNP Lab 94   Troubleshooting Lab 1117
CCNP Lab 95   Troubleshooting Lab 1124
CCNP Lab 96   Troubleshooting Lab 1131
CCNP Lab 97   Troubleshooting Lab 1138
CCNP Lab 98   Troubleshooting Lab 1145
CCNP Lab 99   Troubleshooting Lab 1152
CCNP Lab 100   Troubleshooting Lab 1159
CCNP Lab 101   EIGRP and OSPF VRF Lite Lab 1166

CCNP LAB 1

VLANs, VTP, DTP and STP

Lab Objective:

The focus of this lab is to understand basic VLAN, VTP, DTP and STP implementation and configuration in Cisco IOS Catalyst switches.

Lab Topology:

The lab network topology is illustrated below:

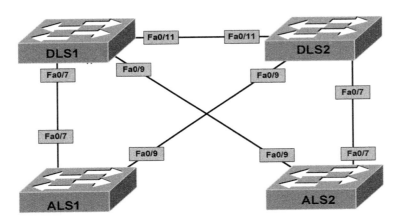

IMPORTANT NOTE: If you are using the www.howtonetwork.net racks, please begin each and every lab by shutting down all interfaces on all switches and then manually re-enabling only the interfaces that are illustrated in this topology.

Task 1

Enable and configure VTP on the switches illustrated in the topology as follows:

- All switches should reside in VTP domain 'SWITCH'
- All switches should run VTP version 2
- All switches should allow VLAN creation, deletion and modification
- All switches should use a VTP password of 'CCNP'

Task 2

Configure trunking on the switches as follows:

- Configure ALS1 so that its interfaces will only trunk if the upstream switch is trunking
- Configure ALS2 so that its interfaces will only trunk if the upstream switch is trunking
- Configure DLS1 so that its interfaces will actively attempt to become trunk links
- Configure DLS2 so that its interfaces will actively attempt to become trunk links

Task 3

Configure the following VLANs only on switch DLS1:
- VLAN 100 name USER-VLAN
- VLAN 200 name FILE-VLAN

Configure switch DLS1 so that Cisco IOS software automatically elects it as the root bridge for both VLANs without explicitly specifying a priority value. Ensure that switch DLS2 is also automatically elected backup root bridge for both VLANs.

Task 4

Configure Spanning Tree on switches ALS1 and ALS2 as follows:
- Port Fa0/7 on ALS1 and port Fa0/9 on ALS2 should be forwarding for VLAN 100
- Port Fa0/9 on ALS1 and port Fa0/7 on ALS2 should be forwarding for VLAN 200

Task 5

Configure your 802.1D network to improve convergence as follows:
- Backup ports on Access layer switches should transition to forwarding in 1 to 5 seconds following the failure of the primary link to the root bridge
- In the event of an indirect link failure, the network should converge within 30 seconds instead of the typical 50 seconds

LAB VALIDATION

Task 1

```
DLS1(config)#vtp domain SWITCH
Changing VTP domain name from null to SWITCH
DLS1(config)#vtp version 2
DLS1(config)#vtp password CCNP
Setting device VLAN database password to CCNP

DLS2(config)#vtp domain SWITCH
Changing VTP domain name from null to SWITCH
DLS2(config)#vtp version 2
DLS2(config)#vtp password CCNP
Setting device VLAN database password to CCNP

ALS1(config)#vtp domain SWITCH
Changing VTP domain name from null to SWITCH
ALS1(config)#vtp version 2
ALS1(config)#vtp password CCNP
Setting device VLAN database password to CCNP

ALS2(config)#vtp domain SWITCH
Changing VTP domain name from null to SWITCH
ALS2(config)#vtp version 2
ALS2(config)#vtp password CCNP
Setting device VLAN database password to CCNP
```

Task 2

```
ALS1(config)#interface range f0/7 , f0/9
ALS1(config-if-range)#switchport mode dynamic auto

ALS2(config)#interface range f0/7 , f0/9
ALS2(config-if-range)#switchport mode dynamic auto

DLS1(config)#int range f0/7 , f0/9 , f0/11
DLS1(config-if-range)#switchport mode dynamic desirable

DLS2(config)#int range f0/7 , f0/9 , f0/11
DLS2(config-if-range)#switchport mode dynamic desirable
```

Verify your configuration using the **show interfaces trunk** command as follows:

```
DLS2#show interfaces trunk

Port       Mode         Encapsulation   Status      Native vlan
Fa0/7      desirable    n-802.1q        trunking    1
Fa0/9      desirable    n-802.1q        trunking    1
Fa0/11     desirable    n-isl           trunking    1

DLS1#show interfaces trunk

Port       Mode         Encapsulation   Status      Native vlan
Fa0/7      desirable    n-802.1q        trunking    1
Fa0/9      desirable    n-802.1q        trunking    1
Fa0/11     desirable    n-isl           trunking    1

ALS1#show interfaces trunk

Port       Mode     Encapsulation   Status      Native vlan
Fa0/7      auto     802.1q          trunking    1
Fa0/9      auto     802.1q          trunking    1

ALS2#show interfaces trunk

Port       Mode     Encapsulation   Status      Native vlan
Fa0/7      auto     802.1q          trunking    1
Fa0/9      auto     802.1q          trunking    1
```

NOTE: Catalyst 3550 series switches (which are used in the H2N racks) support both ISL and 802.1Q and will attempt to negotiate an ISL trunk first. However, the modern Catalyst switches only support 802.1Q and will dynamically negotiate an 802.1Q trunk.

Task 3

```
DLS1(config)#vlan 100
DLS1(config-vlan)#name USER-VLAN
DLS1(config-vlan)#exit
DLS1(config)#vlan 200
DLS1(config-vlan)#name FILE-VLAN
DLS1(config-vlan)#exit
DLS1(config)#spanning-tree vlan 100 root primary
DLS1(config)#spanning-tree vlan 200 root primary

DLS2(config)#spanning-tree vlan 100 root secondary
DLS2(config)#spanning-tree vlan 200 root secondary
```

Verify your configuration using the **show spanning-tree root** command as follows:

```
DLS1#show spanning-tree root

                                    Root   Hello Max Fwd
Vlan                 Root ID        Cost   Time  Age Dly  Root Port
---------------      ----------------------  ---------  ----- --- ---  -------------
VLAN0100             24676 000f.2303.2d80       0     2    20  15
VLAN0200             24776 000f.2303.2d80       0     2    20  15

DLS2#show spanning-tree root

                                    Root   Hello Max Fwd
Vlan                 Root ID        Cost   Time  Age Dly  Root Port
---------------      ----------------------  ---------  ----- --- ---  -------------
VLAN0100             24676 000f.2303.2d80      19     2    20  15  Fa0/11
VLAN0200             24776 000f.2303.2d80      19     2    20  15  Fa0/11

ALS1#show spanning-tree root

                                   Root  Hello Max Fwd
Vlan                 Root ID       Cost  Time  Age Dly  Root Port
---------------      ----------------------  ------  ----- --- ---  ----------------
VLAN0100             24676 000f.2303.2d80      19     2    20  15  Fa0/7
VLAN0200             24776 000f.2303.2d80      19     2    20  15  Fa0/7
```

```
ALS2#show spanning-tree root
```

Vlan	Root ID	Root Cost	Hello Time	Max Age	Fwd Dly	Root Port
VLAN0100	24676 000f.2303.2d80	19	2	20	15	Fa0/9
VLAN0200	24776 000f.2303.2d80	19	2	20	15	Fa0/9

Task 4

```
ALS1(config)#interface fa 0/7
ALS1(config-if)#spanning-tree vlan 200 cost 40

ALS2(config)#interface fa 0/9
ALS2(config-if)#spanning-tree vlan 200 cost 40
```

NOTE: When selecting a root port, Spanning Tree considers the following:

- Lowest Root Bridge ID
- Lowest Root Path Cost to Root Bridge
- Lowest Sender Bridge ID
- Lowest Sender Port ID

By default, no additional configuration is required to ensure that Fa0/7 and Fa0/9 on switches ALS1 and ALS2, respectively, are the root ports (forwarding) for VLAN 100. However, to ensure that Fa0/9 and Fa0/7 on switches ALS1 and ALS2, respectively, are root ports (forwarding) for VLAN 200, you must increase the cost of the current root ports Fa0/7 and Fa0/9 on switches ALS1 and ALS2, respectively, to make these less desirable (blocking) for VLAN 200.

This value must be higher than the cumulative cost of 19 + 19, which is 38. Any cost value above number 38 on Fa0/7 and Fa0/9 on switches ALS1 and ALS2 for VLAN 200 will satisfy the requirements of this task. Before the change, the current STP status shows the following:

```
ALS1#show spanning-tree interface fastethernet 0/7
```

Vlan	Role	Sts	Cost	Prio.Nbr	Type
VLAN0001	Desg	FWD	19	128.7	P2p
VLAN0100	Root	FWD	19	128.7	P2p
VLAN0200	Root	FWD	19	128.7	P2p

```
ALS1#
ALS1#show spanning-tree interface fastethernet 0/9
```

Vlan	Role	Sts	Cost	Prio.Nbr	Type
VLAN0001	Desg	FWD	19	128.9	P2p
VLAN0100	Altn	BLK	19	128.9	P2p
VLAN0200	Altn	BLK	19	128.9	P2p

```
ALS2#show spanning-tree interface fastethernet 0/7
```

Vlan	Role	Sts	Cost	Prio.Nbr	Type
VLAN0001	Root	FWD	19	128.7	P2p
VLAN0100	Altn	BLK	19	128.7	P2p
VLAN0200	Altn	BLK	19	128.7	P2p

```
ALS2#
ALS2#show spanning-tree interface fastethernet 0/9
```

Vlan	Role	Sts	Cost	Prio.Nbr	Type
VLAN0001	Altn	BLK	19	128.9	P2p
VLAN0100	Root	FWD	19	128.9	P2p
VLAN0200	Root	FWD	19	128.9	P2p

Following the changing of the cost on the current root ports, the topology is now as follows:

```
ALS1#show spanning-tree interface fastethernet 0/7

Vlan               Role Sts Cost      Prio.Nbr Type
---------------    ---- --- --------- -------- --------------------------------
VLAN0001           Desg FWD 19        128.7    P2p
VLAN0100           Root FWD 19        128.7    P2p
VLAN0200           Altn BLK 40        128.7    P2p
ALS1#
ALS1#show spanning-tree interface fastethernet 0/9

Vlan               Role Sts Cost      Prio.Nbr Type
---------------    ---- --- --------- -------- --------------------------------
VLAN0001           Desg FWD 19        128.9    P2p
VLAN0100           Altn BLK 19        128.9    P2p
VLAN0200           Root FWD 19        128.9    P2p

ALS2#show spanning-tree interface fastethernet 0/7

Vlan               Role Sts Cost      Prio.Nbr Type
---------------    ---- --- --------- -------- --------------------------------
VLAN0001           Root FWD 19        128.7    P2p
VLAN0100           Altn BLK 19        128.7    P2p
VLAN0200           Root FWD 19        128.7    P2p
ALS2#
ALS2#show spanning-tree interface fastethernet 0/9

Vlan               Role Sts Cost      Prio.Nbr Type
---------------    ---- --- --------- -------- --------------------------------
VLAN0001           Altn BLK 19        128.9    P2p
VLAN0100           Root FWD 19        128.9    P2p
VLAN0200           Altn BLK 40        128.9    P2p
```

Task 5

This task requires the implementation of STP backbonefast and uplinkfast. Backbonefast is configured on ALL switches in the network as follows:

```
DLS1(config)#spanning-tree backbonefast
DLS2(config)#spanning-tree backbonefast
ALS1(config)#spanning-tree backbonefast
ALS2(config)#spanning-tree backbonefast
```

However, uplinkfast is configured only on access switches in the network as follows:

```
ALS1(config)#spanning-tree uplinkfast
ALS2(config)#spanning-tree uplinkfast
```

Verify backbonefast by shutting down the Fa0/11 link between DLS1 and DLS2. This will then generate RLQs which allow for the faster recovergence of the STP domain. You can verify backbonefast operation using the IOS **show spanning-tree backbonefast** command as follows:

```
DLS2(config)#int fastethernet 0/11
DLS2(config-if)#shut
DLS2(config-if)#end
DLS2#
DLS2#show spanning-tree backbonefast
BackboneFast is enabled

BackboneFast statistics
-----------------------
Number of transition via backboneFast (all VLANs)      : 0
Number of inferior BPDUs received (all VLANs)          : 0
Number of RLQ request PDUs received (all VLANs)        : 2
Number of RLQ response PDUs received (all VLANs)       : 0
Number of RLQ request PDUs sent (all VLANs)            : 0
Number of RLQ response PDUs sent (all VLANs)           : 2
```

On the downstream switch, for example ALS1, the same command shows the following:

```
ALS1#show spanning-tree backbonefast
BackboneFast is enabled

BackboneFast statistics
-----------------------
Number of transition via backboneFast (all VLANs)      : 3
Number of inferior BPDUs received (all VLANs)          : 3
Number of RLQ request PDUs received (all VLANs)        : 0
Number of RLQ response PDUs received (all VLANs)       : 3
Number of RLQ request PDUs sent (all VLANs)            : 3
Number of RLQ response PDUs sent (all VLANs)           : 0
```

Verify backbonefast by shutting down a trunk link on one of the access switches. This will then generate dummy frames, which are sent to the Multicast address 01-00.0C-CD-CD-CD. You can verify uplink-fast operation using the **show spanning-tree uplinkfast** command as follows:

```
ALS1(config)#int fastethernet 0/7
ALS1(config-if)#shut
ALS1(config-if)#end
ALS1#
ALS1#show spanning-tree uplinkfast
UplinkFast is enabled

Station update rate set to 150 packets/sec.

UplinkFast statistics
-----------------------
Number of transitions via uplinkFast (all VLANs)           : 2
Number of proxy multicast addresses transmitted (all VLANs) : 4

Name                    Interface List
------------------      ------------------------------------
VLAN0001                Fa0/9(fwd)
VLAN0100                Fa0/9(fwd)
VLAN0200                Fa0/9(fwd)
```

FINAL SWITCH CONFIGURATIONS

DLS1

```
DLS1#term len 0
DLS1#show run
Building configuration...

Current configuration : 3777 bytes
!
version 12.2
no service pad
service timestamps debug datetime msec
service timestamps log datetime msec
no service password-encryption
!
hostname DLS1
!
no logging console
!
no aaa new-model
ip subnet-zero
!
spanning-tree mode pvst
spanning-tree extend system-id
spanning-tree backbonefast
spanning-tree vlan 100,200 priority 24576
!
vlan internal allocation policy ascending
!
interface FastEthernet0/1
```

```
 switchport mode dynamic desirable
!
interface FastEthernet0/2
 switchport mode dynamic desirable
!
interface FastEthernet0/3
 switchport mode dynamic desirable
!
interface FastEthernet0/4
 switchport mode dynamic desirable
!
interface FastEthernet0/5
 switchport mode dynamic desirable
!
interface FastEthernet0/6
 switchport mode dynamic desirable
!
interface FastEthernet0/7
 switchport mode dynamic desirable
!
interface FastEthernet0/8
 switchport mode dynamic desirable
 shutdown
!
interface FastEthernet0/9
 switchport mode dynamic desirable
!
interface FastEthernet0/10
 switchport mode dynamic desirable
 shutdown
!
interface FastEthernet0/11
 switchport mode dynamic desirable
!
interface FastEthernet0/12
 switchport mode dynamic desirable
 shutdown
!
[Truncated Output]

interface Vlan1
 no ip address
 shutdown
!
ip classless
ip http server
ip http secure-server
!
control-plane
!
line con 0
line vty 5 15
!
end
DLS1#
```

DLS2

```
DLS2#term len 0
DLS2#show run
Building configuration...

Current configuration : 3777 bytes
!
version 12.2
no service pad
service timestamps debug datetime msec
service timestamps log datetime msec
no service password-encryption
!
hostname DLS2
!
no logging console
!
no aaa new-model
```

```
ip subnet-zero
!
spanning-tree mode pvst
spanning-tree extend system-id
spanning-tree backbonefast
spanning-tree vlan 100,200 priority 28672
!
vlan internal allocation policy ascending
!
interface FastEthernet0/1
 switchport mode dynamic desirable
!
interface FastEthernet0/2
 switchport mode dynamic desirable
!
interface FastEthernet0/3
 switchport mode dynamic desirable
!
interface FastEthernet0/4
 switchport mode dynamic desirable
!
interface FastEthernet0/5
 switchport mode dynamic desirable
!
interface FastEthernet0/6
 switchport mode dynamic desirable
!
interface FastEthernet0/7
 switchport mode dynamic desirable
!
interface FastEthernet0/8
 switchport mode dynamic desirable
 shutdown
!
interface FastEthernet0/9
 switchport mode dynamic desirable
!
interface FastEthernet0/10
 switchport mode dynamic desirable
 shutdown
!
interface FastEthernet0/11
 switchport mode dynamic desirable
!
interface FastEthernet0/12
 switchport mode dynamic desirable
 shutdown
!
[Truncated Output]

interface Vlan1
 no ip address
 shutdown
!
ip classless
ip http server
ip http secure-server
!
control-plane
!
line con 0
line vty 5 15
!
end

DLS2#
```

ALS1

```
ALS1#term len 0
ALS1#show run
Building configuration...

Current configuration : 906 bytes
!
```

```
version 12.1
no service pad
service timestamps debug uptime
service timestamps log uptime
no service password-encryption
!
hostname ALS1
!
no logging console
!
ip subnet-zero
!
spanning-tree mode pvst
no spanning-tree optimize bpdu transmission
spanning-tree extend system-id
spanning-tree uplinkfast
spanning-tree backbonefast
!
interface FastEthernet0/1
!
interface FastEthernet0/2
!
interface FastEthernet0/3
!
interface FastEthernet0/4
!
interface FastEthernet0/5
!
interface FastEthernet0/6
!
interface FastEthernet0/7
 switchport mode dynamic auto
 spanning-tree vlan 200 cost 40
!
interface FastEthernet0/8
!
interface FastEthernet0/9
 switchport mode dynamic auto
!
interface FastEthernet0/10
!
interface FastEthernet0/11
 shutdown
!
interface FastEthernet0/12
 shutdown
!
interface Vlan1
 no ip address
 no ip route-cache
 shutdown
!
ip http server
!
line con 0
line vty 5 15
!
end

ALS1#
```

ALS2

```
ALS2>en
ALS2#term len 0
ALS2#show run
Building configuration...

Current configuration : 906 bytes
!
version 12.1
no service pad
service timestamps debug uptime
service timestamps log uptime
no service password-encryption
!
```

```
hostname ALS2
!
no logging console
!
ip subnet-zero
!
spanning-tree mode pvst
no spanning-tree optimize bpdu transmission
spanning-tree extend system-id
spanning-tree uplinkfast
spanning-tree backbonefast
!
interface FastEthernet0/1
!
interface FastEthernet0/2
!
interface FastEthernet0/3
!
interface FastEthernet0/4
!
interface FastEthernet0/5
!
interface FastEthernet0/6
!
interface FastEthernet0/7
 switchport mode dynamic auto
!
interface FastEthernet0/8
!
interface FastEthernet0/9
 switchport mode dynamic auto
 spanning-tree vlan 200 cost 40
!
interface FastEthernet0/10
!
interface FastEthernet0/11
 shutdown
!
interface FastEthernet0/12
 shutdown
!
interface Vlan1
 no ip address
 no ip route-cache
 shutdown
!
ip http server
!
line con 0
line vty 5 15
!
end

ALS2#
```

CCNP LAB 2

VLANs, VTP, DTP and STP

Lab Objective:

The focus of this lab is to understand basic VLAN, VTP, DTP and STP implementation and configuration in Cisco IOS Catalyst switches.

Lab Topology:

The lab network topology is illustrated below:

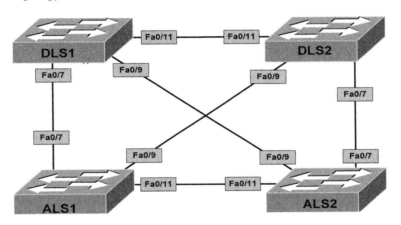

IMPORTANT NOTE: If you are using the www.howtonetwork.net racks, please begin each and every lab by shutting down all interfaces on all switches and then manually re-enabling only the interfaces that are illustrated in this topology.

Task 1

Disable VTP on all switches. All switches should support the configuration, modification and deletion of VLANs.

Task 2

Configure trunking on the switches so that all ports are explicitly trunking and DTP should never be used on any of these ports.

Task 3

Configure VLANs 100 and 200 on all switches and use the default IOS VLAN names. Explicitly configure switch DLS1 with a priority of 8192 so it is elected root for both of these VLANs. Additionally, also explicitly configure switch DLS2 so it is elected backup root for both VLANs.

Task 4

Configure Spanning Tree so that it will remain root bridge in the event that another switch is in advertently misconfigured with a lower priority for VLANs 100 and 200. Test and verify your configuration by specifying a priority of 0 for VLAN 100 on any switch within the STP network.

Task 5

Configure the trunk links on switch DLS2 so that they will be disabled automatically in the event that they do not receive BPDUs. Test and verify your configuration by disabling default BPDU transmission from one of the upstream switches.

Task 6

Ports FastEthernet0/1 through FastEthernet0/5 on switches ALS1 and ALS2 will be connected to hosts in the future. These hosts will reside in VLAN 100. Using only **TWO** commands, perform the following activities on these ports:

• Assign all of these individual ports to VLAN 100
• Configure the ports as static access port
• Enable PortFast for all the ports
• Disable bundling, i.e. EtherChannel, for these ports

LAB VALIDATION

Task 1

```
DLS1(config)#vtp mode transparent
Setting device to VTP TRANSPARENT mode.

DLS2(config)#vtp mode transparent
Setting device to VTP TRANSPARENT mode.

ALS1(config)#vtp mode transparent
Setting device to VTP TRANSPARENT mode.

ALS2(config)#vtp mode transparent
Setting device to VTP TRANSPARENT mode.
```

Task 2

```
DLS1(config)#interface range fa0/7, fa0/9, fa0/11
DLS1(config-if-range)#switchport trunk encapsulation dot1q
DLS1(config-if-range)#switchport mode trunk
DLS1(config-if-range)#switchport nonegotiate

DLS2(config)#interface range fa0/7, fa0/9, fa0/11
DLS2(config-if-range)#switchport trunk encapsulation dot1q
DLS2(config-if-range)#switchport mode trunk
DLS2(config-if-range)#switchport nonegotiate
```

NOTE: If using the H2N racks, the ALS switches are 2950 switches and therefore support only 802.1Q encapsulation. There is no need to specify trunk encapsulation.

```
ALS1(config)#interface range faste 0/7 , faste 0/9 , faste 0/11
ALS1(config-if-range)#switchport mode trunk
ALS1(config-if-range)#switchport nonegotiate

ALS2(config)#interface range faste 0/7 , faste 0/9 , faste 0/11
ALS2(config-if-range)#switchport mode trunk
ALS2(config-if-range)#switchport nonegotiate
```

Verify your configuration using the **show interfaces trunk** command:

```
DLS1#show interfaces trunk
Port            Mode            Encapsulation  Status          Native vlan
Fa0/7           on              802.1q         trunking        1
Fa0/9           on              802.1q         trunking        1
Fa0/11          on              802.1q         trunking        1

DLS2#show interfaces trunk

Port            Mode            Encapsulation  Status          Native vlan
Fa0/7           on              802.1q         trunking        1
Fa0/9           on              802.1q         trunking        1
Fa0/11          on              802.1q         trunking        1

ALS1#show interfaces trunk

Port            Mode            Encapsulation  Status          Native vlan
Fa0/7           on              802.1q         trunking        1
Fa0/9           on              802.1q         trunking        1
Fa0/11          on              802.1q         trunking        1

ALS2#show interfaces trunk

Port            Mode            Encapsulation  Status          Native vlan
Fa0/7           on              802.1q         trunking        1
Fa0/9           on              802.1q         trunking        1
Fa0/11          on              802.1q         trunking        1
```

Task 3

```
DLS1(config)#vlan 100
DLS1(config-vlan)#exit
DLS1(config)#vlan 200
DLS1(config-vlan)#exit
DLS1(config)#spanning-tree vlan 100 prior 8192
DLS1(config)#spanning-tree vlan 200 prior 8192

DLS2(config)#vlan 100
DLS2(config-vlan)#exit
DLS2(config)#vlan 200
DLS2(config-vlan)#exit
DLS2(config)#spanning-tree vlan 100 priority 16384
DLS2(config)#spanning-tree vlan 200 priority 16384

ALS1(config)#vlan 100
ALS1(config-vlan)#exit
ALS1(config)#vlan 200
ALS1(config-vlan)#exit

ALS2(config)#vlan 100
ALS2(config-vlan)#exit
ALS2(config)#vlan 200
ALS2(config-vlan)#exit
```

Verify your configuration using the **show spanning-tree root** command:

```
DLS1#show spanning-tree root

                                   Root   Hello Max Fwd
Vlan                   Root ID     Cost   Time  Age Dly  Root Port
----------------       ----------- -----  ----- --- ---  -----------
VLAN0100          8292 000f.2303.2d80    0    2    20  15
VLAN0200          8392 000f.2303.2d80    0    2    20  15

DLS2#show spanning-tree root

                                   Root   Hello Max Fwd
Vlan                   Root ID     Cost   Time  Age Dly  Root Port
----------------       ----------- -----  ----- --- ---  -----------
VLAN0100          8292 000f.2303.2d80   19    2    20  15  Fa0/11
```

```
VLAN0200            8392 000f.2303.2d80          19   2   20  15  Fa0/11
```

```
ALS1#show spanning-tree root

                                   Root Hello Max Fwd
Vlan                 Root ID       Cost Time  Age Dly  Root Port
---------------- -------------------- ------ ----- --- --- ----------------
VLAN0100         8292 000f.2303.2d80    19    2    20  15  Fa0/7
VLAN0200         8392 000f.2303.2d80    19    2    20  15  Fa0/7

ALS2#show spanning-tree root

                                   Root Hello Max Fwd
Vlan                 Root ID       Cost Time  Age Dly  Root Port
---------------- -------------------- ------ ----- --- --- ----------------
VLAN0100         8292 000f.2303.2d80    19    2    20  15  Fa0/9
VLAN0200         8392 000f.2303.2d80    19    2    20  15  Fa0/9
```

Task 4

This task requires identifying designated ports and configuring the root guard feature on them. The root guard feature prevents a designated port from becoming a root port.

If a port on which the root guard feature receives a superior BPDU, it moves the port into a root-inconsistent state, thus maintaining the current root bridge status quo. Use the **show spanning-tree vlan** command to determine the current Spanning Tree port states as follows:

```
DLS1#show spanning-tree vlan 100

VLAN0100
...

Interface        Role Sts Cost      Prio.Nbr Type
---------------- ---- --- --------- -------- --------------------------------
Fa0/7            Desg FWD 19        128.7    P2p
Fa0/9            Desg FWD 19        128.9    P2p
Fa0/11           Desg FWD 19        128.11   P2p

DLS2#show spanning-tree vlan 100

VLAN0100
...

Interface        Role Sts Cost      Prio.Nbr Type
---------------- ---- --- --------- -------- --------------------------------
Fa0/7            Desg FWD 19        128.7    P2p
Fa0/9            Desg FWD 19        128.9    P2p
Fa0/11           Root FWD 19        128.11   P2p

ALS1#show spanning-tree vlan 100

VLAN0100
...

Interface        Role Sts Cost      Prio.Nbr Type
---------------- ---- --- --------- -------- --------------------------------
Fa0/7            Root FWD 19        128.7    P2p
Fa0/9            Altn BLK 19        128.9    P2p
Fa0/11           Desg FWD 19        128.11   P2p

ALS2#show spanning-tree vlan 100

VLAN0100
...

Interface        Role Sts Cost      Prio.Nbr Type
---------------- ---- --- --------- -------- --------------------------------
Fa0/7            Altn BLK 19        128.7    P2p
Fa0/9            Root FWD 19        128.9    P2p
Fa0/11           Altn BLK 19        128.11   P2p
```

Following this, enable the root guard feature on all designated ports using the spanning-tree guard root interface configuration command. Referencing the list above, root guard would be enabled on the following interfaces or ports:

- Switch DSL1:   Fa0/7, Fa0/9, Fa0/11
- Switch DLS2:   Fa0/7, Fa0/9
- Switch ALS1:   Fa0/11
- Switch ALS2:   None - because this switch has no designated ports

This task is completed by enabling root guard on the ports above as follows:

```
DLS1(config)#interface range fa0/7, fa0/9, fa0/11
DLS1(config-if-range)#spanning-tree guard root

DLS2(config)#interface range fa0/7, fa0/9
DLS2(config-if-range)#spanning-tree guard root

ALS1(config)#interface fastethernet 0/11
ALS1(config-if)#spanning-tree guard root
```

Test your solution by setting the priority of a VLAN to 0 or 4096 and then verifying the port state on the adjacent segment designated bridge. For example, if you changed the priority of VLAN 100 on switch ALS2 to 0, all peer ports enabled for root guard with which this switch connects will be placed into a root inconsistent state as follows:

```
ALS2(config)#spanning-tree vlan 100 priority 0

DLS1#
*Mar  1 01:21:28.851: %SPANTREE-2-ROOTGUARD_BLOCK: Root guard blocking port
FastEthernet0/9 on VLAN0100.

DLS2#
*Mar  1 01:21:31.535: %SPANTREE-2-ROOTGUARD_BLOCK: Root guard blocking port
FastEthernet0/7 on VLAN0100.

ALS1#
*Mar  1 01:24:39.903: %SPANTREE-2-ROOTGUARD_BLOCK: Root guard blocking port
FastEthernet0/11 on VLAN0100.
```

Aside from the logged message, you can also use the **show spanning-tree inconsistentports** and the **show spanning-tree interface** commands to view root inconsistent ports:

```
DLS1#show spanning-tree inconsistentports

Name                    Interface               Inconsistency
--------------------    --------------------    ------------------
VLAN0001                FastEthernet0/7         Root Inconsistent
VLAN0001                FastEthernet0/9         Root Inconsistent
VLAN0001                FastEthernet0/11        Root Inconsistent
VLAN0100                FastEthernet0/9         Root Inconsistent

DLS1#show spanning-tree interface fastethernet 0/9

Vlan                 Role Sts Cost     Prio.Nbr Type
-------------------- ---- --- -------- -------- --------------------------------
VLAN0100             Desg BKN*19       128.9    P2p *ROOT_Inc
```

Task 5

This task requires the configuration of Loop Guard on switch DLS2. The Loop Guard detects root ports and blocked ports, and ensures they continue to receive BPDUs. When enabled, should one of these ports stop receiving BPDUs, it is moved into a loop-inconsistent state.

```
ALS2(config)#interface range faste 0/7 , faste 0/9 , faste 0/11
ALS2(config-if-range)#spanning-tree guard loop
```

NOTE: The Loop Guard feature can also be enabled globally as follows:

```
ALS2(config)#spanning-tree loopguard default
```

Test this configuration by filtering BPDUs from one of the connected switches as follows:

```
DLS1(config)#interface fastethernet 0/9
DLS1(config-if)#spanning-tree bpdufilter enable
```

After this configuration, the following log messages are printed on the console of ALS2:

```
ALS1#
01:41:26: %SPANTREE-2-LOOPGUARD_BLOCK: Loop guard blocking port FastEthernet0/9 on
VLAN0100.
01:41:28: %SPANTREE-2-LOOPGUARD_BLOCK: Loop guard blocking port FastEthernet0/9 on
VLAN0200.
```

Aside from the logged message, you can also use the **show spanning-tree inconsistentports** and the **show spanning-tree interface** commands to view root inconsistent ports:

```
ALS2#show spanning-tree inconsistentports

Name                     Interface               Inconsistency
-------------------      --------------------    ------------------
VLAN0100                 FastEthernet0/9         Loop Inconsistent
VLAN0200                 FastEthernet0/9         Loop Inconsistent

Number of inconsistent ports (segments) in the system : 2

ALS2#show spanning-tree interface fastethernet 0/9

Vlan                Role Sts Cost       Prio.Nbr Type
----------------    ---- --- ---------  -------- ----------------------------------
VLAN0100            Desg BKN*19         128.9    P2p *LOOP_Inc
VLAN0200            Desg BKN*19         128.9    P2p *LOOP_Inc
```

Task 6

While seemingly difficult, this task is actually very simple and requires the configuration of the **switchport access vlan** and **switchport host** commands. The **switchport host** command is an inbuilt Cisco IOS macro that performs three actions under the specified port(s):

- It configures the switchport for access mode
- It enables portfast
- It disables Etherchannel capabilities for the port

This task is completed as follows:

```
ALS1(config)#interface range fastethernet 0/1 - 5
ALS1(config-if-range)#switchport access vlan 100
ALS1(config-if-range)#switchport host
switchport mode will be set to access
spanning-tree portfast will be enabled
channel group will be disabled

ALS1(config-if-range)#end

ALS2(config)#interface range fastethernet 0/1 - 5
ALS2(config-if-range)#switchport access vlan 100
ALS2(config-if-range)#switchport host
switchport mode will be set to access
spanning-tree portfast will be enabled
```

```
channel group will be disabled
```

```
ALS2(config-if-range)#end
```

Verify your configuration by looking at the switch interface configuration or using **the show interfaces <interface> switchport** command:

```
ALS1#show running-config interface fastethernet 0/1
Building configuration...

Current configuration : 109 bytes
!
interface FastEthernet0/1
 switchport access vlan 100
 switchport mode access
 spanning-tree portfast
end

ALS1#show interfaces fastethernet 0/1 switchport
Name: Fa0/1
Switchport: Enabled
Administrative Mode: static access
Operational Mode: static access
Administrative Trunking Encapsulation: dot1q
Operational Trunking Encapsulation: native
Negotiation of Trunking: Off
Access Mode VLAN: 100 (VLAN0100)
Trunking Native Mode VLAN: 1 (default)
Voice VLAN: none
Administrative private-vlan host-association: none
Administrative private-vlan mapping: none
Administrative private-vlan trunk native VLAN: none
Administrative private-vlan trunk encapsulation: dot1q
Administrative private-vlan trunk normal VLANs: none
Administrative private-vlan trunk private VLANs: none
Operational private-vlan: none
Trunking VLANs Enabled: ALL
Pruning VLANs Enabled: 2-1001
Capture Mode Disabled
Capture VLANs Allowed: ALL
Protected: false
Appliance trust: none
```

FINAL SWITCH CONFIGURATIONS

DLS1

```
DLS1#term len 0
DLS1#show run
Building configuration...

Current configuration : 4013 bytes
!
version 12.2
no service pad
service timestamps debug datetime msec
service timestamps log datetime msec
no service password-encryption
!
hostname DLS1
!
no aaa new-model
ip subnet-zero
!
vtp domain SWITCH
vtp mode transparent
!
spanning-tree mode pvst
spanning-tree extend system-id
```

```
spanning-tree vlan 100,200 priority 8192
!
vlan internal allocation policy ascending
!
vlan 100,200
!
interface FastEthernet0/1
 switchport mode dynamic desirable
!
interface FastEthernet0/2
 switchport mode dynamic desirable
!
interface FastEthernet0/3
 switchport mode dynamic desirable
!
interface FastEthernet0/4
 switchport mode dynamic desirable
!
interface FastEthernet0/5
 switchport mode dynamic desirable
!
interface FastEthernet0/6
 switchport mode dynamic desirable
!
interface FastEthernet0/7
 switchport trunk encapsulation dot1q
 switchport mode trunk
 switchport nonegotiate
 spanning-tree guard root
!
interface FastEthernet0/8
 switchport mode dynamic desirable
 shutdown
!
interface FastEthernet0/9
 switchport trunk encapsulation dot1q
 switchport mode trunk
 switchport nonegotiate
 spanning-tree guard root
!
interface FastEthernet0/10
 switchport mode dynamic desirable
 shutdown
!
interface FastEthernet0/11
 switchport trunk encapsulation dot1q
 switchport mode trunk
 switchport nonegotiate
 spanning-tree guard root
!
interface FastEthernet0/12
 switchport mode dynamic desirable
 shutdown

[Truncated Output]

interface Vlan1
 no ip address
 shutdown
!
ip classless
ip http server
ip http secure-server
!
control-plane
!
line con 0
line vty 5 15
!
end

DLS1#
```

DLS2

```
DLS2#term len 0
DLS2#show run
Building configuration...

Current configuration : 3988 bytes
!
version 12.2
no service pad
service timestamps debug datetime msec
service timestamps log datetime msec
no service password-encryption
!
hostname DLS2
!
no aaa new-model
ip subnet-zero
!
vtp domain SWITCH
vtp mode transparent
!
spanning-tree mode pvst
spanning-tree extend system-id
spanning-tree vlan 100,200 priority 16384
!
vlan internal allocation policy ascending
!
vlan 100,200
!
interface FastEthernet0/1
 switchport mode dynamic desirable
!
interface FastEthernet0/2
 switchport mode dynamic desirable
!
interface FastEthernet0/3
 switchport mode dynamic desirable
!
interface FastEthernet0/4
 switchport mode dynamic desirable
!
interface FastEthernet0/5
 switchport mode dynamic desirable
!
interface FastEthernet0/6
 switchport mode dynamic desirable
!
interface FastEthernet0/7
 switchport trunk encapsulation dot1q
 switchport mode trunk
 switchport nonegotiate
 spanning-tree guard root
!
interface FastEthernet0/8
 switchport mode dynamic desirable
 shutdown
!
interface FastEthernet0/9
 switchport trunk encapsulation dot1q
 switchport mode trunk
 switchport nonegotiate
 spanning-tree guard root
!
interface FastEthernet0/10
 switchport mode dynamic desirable
 shutdown
!
interface FastEthernet0/11
 switchport trunk encapsulation dot1q
 switchport mode trunk
 switchport nonegotiate
!
interface FastEthernet0/12
```

```
 switchport mode dynamic desirable
 shutdown

[Truncated Output]

interface Vlan1
 no ip address
 shutdown
!
ip classless
ip http server
ip http secure-server
!
control-plane
!
line con 0
line vty 5 15
!
end

DLS2#
```

ALS1

```
ALS1#term len 0
ALS1#show run
Building configuration...

Current configuration : 1340 bytes
!
version 12.1
no service pad
service timestamps debug uptime
service timestamps log datetime msec
no service password-encryption
!
hostname ALS1
!
ip subnet-zero
!
vtp domain SWITCH
vtp mode transparent
!
spanning-tree mode pvst
no spanning-tree optimize bpdu transmission
spanning-tree extend system-id
!
vlan 100,200
!
interface FastEthernet0/1
 switchport access vlan 100
 switchport mode access
 spanning-tree portfast
!
interface FastEthernet0/2
 switchport access vlan 100
 switchport mode access
 spanning-tree portfast
!
interface FastEthernet0/3
 switchport access vlan 100
 switchport mode access
 spanning-tree portfast
!
interface FastEthernet0/4
 switchport access vlan 100
 switchport mode access
 spanning-tree portfast
!
interface FastEthernet0/5
 switchport access vlan 100
 switchport mode access
 spanning-tree portfast
```

```
!
interface FastEthernet0/6
!
interface FastEthernet0/7
 switchport mode trunk
 switchport nonegotiate
!
interface FastEthernet0/8
!
interface FastEthernet0/9
 switchport mode trunk
 switchport nonegotiate
!
interface FastEthernet0/10
!
interface FastEthernet0/11
 switchport mode trunk
 switchport nonegotiate
 spanning-tree guard root
!
interface FastEthernet0/12
 shutdown
!
interface Vlan1
 no ip address
 no ip route-cache
 shutdown
!
ip http server
!
line con 0
line vty 5 15
!
end
ALS1#
```

ALS2

```
ALS2#term len 0
ALS2#show run
Building configuration...

Current configuration : 1419 bytes
!
version 12.1
no service pad
service timestamps debug uptime
service timestamps log uptime
no service password-encryption
!
hostname ALS2
!
ip subnet-zero
!
vtp domain SWITCH
vtp mode transparent
!
spanning-tree mode pvst
spanning-tree loopguard default
no spanning-tree optimize bpdu transmission
spanning-tree extend system-id
!
vlan 100,200
!
interface FastEthernet0/1
 switchport access vlan 100
 switchport mode access
 spanning-tree portfast
!
interface FastEthernet0/2
 switchport access vlan 100
 switchport mode access
 spanning-tree portfast
```

```
!
interface FastEthernet0/3
 switchport access vlan 100
 switchport mode access
 spanning-tree portfast
!
interface FastEthernet0/4
 switchport access vlan 100
 switchport mode access
 spanning-tree portfast
!
interface FastEthernet0/5
 switchport access vlan 100
 switchport mode access
 spanning-tree portfast
!
interface FastEthernet0/6
!
interface FastEthernet0/7
 switchport mode trunk
 switchport nonegotiate
 spanning-tree guard loop
!
interface FastEthernet0/8
!
interface FastEthernet0/9
 switchport mode trunk
 switchport nonegotiate
 spanning-tree guard loop
!
interface FastEthernet0/10
!
interface FastEthernet0/11
 switchport mode trunk
 switchport nonegotiate
 spanning-tree guard loop
!
interface FastEthernet0/12
 shutdown
!
interface Vlan1
 no ip address
 no ip route-cache
 shutdown
!
ip http server
!
line con 0
line vty 5 15
!
end

ALS2#
```

CCNP LAB 3

LACP, PAgP, Multiple STP

Lab Objective:

The focus of this lab is to understand EtherChannel (LACP, PAgP) and Multiple Spanning Tree (MST) implementation and configuration in Cisco IOS Catalyst switches.

Lab Topology:

The lab network topology is illustrated below:

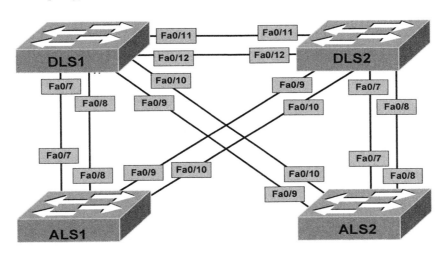

IMPORTANT NOTE: If you are using the www.howtonetwork.net racks, please begin each and every lab by shutting down all interfaces on all switches and then manually re-enabling only the interfaces that are illustrated in this topology.

Task 1

Disable VTP on all switches. All switches should support the configuration, modification and deletion of VLANs.

Task 2

Configure EtherChannel trunks on the switches illustrated in the topology. Only switches DLS1 and DLS2 should actively initiate channel establishment; switches ALS1 and ALS2 should be configured as passive links that will should not actively attempt to establish an EtherChannel. The EtherChannels should be configured as follows:

- The two ports between DLS1 and DLS2 belong to channel group 1 and use mode on
- The two ports between DLS1 and ALS1 belong to channel group 2 and use LACP
- The two ports between DLS1 and ALS2 belong to channel group 3 and use PAgP
- The two ports between DLS2 and ALS1 belong to channel group 4 and use LACP
- The two ports between DLS2 and ALS2 belong to channel group 5 and use PAgP

Task 3

Following the EtherChannel configuration, protect the switched network from any future misconfigurations by ensuring misconfigured EtherChannels are automatically disabled. Additionally, configure the switches to automatically bring up EtherChannels that were disabled due to misconfigurations after 10 minutes.

Task 4

Configure VLANs 100, 200, 300, 400, 500, 600, 700, and 800 all switches. Use the default VLAN names or specify your own names, if so desired.

Task 5

Selecting your own name and revision number, configure Multiple STP as follows:
- VLANs 100 and 200 will be mapped to MST Instance # 1: Switch DLS1 should be root
- VLANs 300 and 400 will be mapped to MST Instance # 2: Switch DLS2 should be root
- VLANs 500 and 600 will be mapped to MST Instance # 3: Switch ALS1 should be root
- VLANs 700 and 800 will be mapped to MST Instance # 4: Switch ALS2 should be root

Task 6

Configure Spanning Tree so that interface cost values appear to the 802.1t (long) version

LAB VALIDATION

Task 1

```
DLS1(config)#vtp mode transparent
Setting device to VTP TRANSPARENT mode.

DLS2(config)#vtp mode transparent
Setting device to VTP TRANSPARENT mode.

ALS1(config)#vtp mode transparent
Setting device to VTP TRANSPARENT mode.

ALS2(config)#vtp mode transparent
Setting device to VTP TRANSPARENT mode.
```

Task 2

```
DLS1(config)#interface range fa 0/11 - 12
DLS1(config-if-range)#switchport
DLS1(config-if-range)#switchport mode trunk
DLS1(config-if-range)#switchport trunk encapsulation dot1q
DLS1(config-if-range)#switchport mode trunk
DLS1(config-if-range)#channel-group 1 mode on
Creating a port-channel interface Port-channel 1
DLS1(config-if-range)#exit
DLS1(config)#interface range fa 0/7 - 8
DLS1(config-if-range)#switchport
DLS1(config-if-range)#switchport trunk encapsulation dot1q
DLS1(config-if-range)#switchport mode trunk
DLS1(config-if-range)#channel-group 2 mode active
Creating a port-channel interface Port-channel 2
DLS1(config-if-range)#exit
DLS1(config)#interface range fa 0/9 - 10
DLS1(config-if-range)#switchport
DLS1(config-if-range)#switchport trunk encapsulation dot1q
DLS1(config-if-range)#switchport mode trunk
DLS1(config-if-range)#channel-group 3 mode desirable
Creating a port-channel interface Port-channel 3
DLS1(config-if-range)#exit

DLS2(config)#interface range fa 0/11 - 12
DLS2(config-if-range)#switchport
```

```
DLS2(config-if-range)#switchport trunk encapsulation dot1q
DLS2(config-if-range)#switchport mode trunk
DLS2(config-if-range)#channel-group 1 mode on
Creating a port-channel interface Port-channel 1
DLS2(config-if-range)#exit
DLS2(config)#interface range fa 0/9 - 10
DLS2(config-if-range)#switchport
DLS2(config-if-range)#switchport trunk encapsulation dot1q
DLS2(config-if-range)#switchport mode trunk
DLS2(config-if-range)#channel-group 4 mode active
Creating a port-channel interface Port-channel 4
DLS2(config-if-range)#exit
DLS2(config)#interface range fa 0/7 - 8
DLS2(config-if-range)#switchport
DLS2(config-if-range)#switchport trunk encapsulation dot1q
DLS2(config-if-range)#switchport mode trunk
DLS2(config-if-range)#channel-group 5 mode desirable
Creating a port-channel interface Port-channel 5
DLS2(config-if-range)#exit

ALS1(config)#interface range f0/7 - 8
ALS1(config-if-range)#switchport mode trunk
ALS1(config-if-range)#channel-group 2 mode passive
Creating a port-channel interface Port-channel 2
ALS1(config-if-range)#exit
ALS1(config)#interface range fa 0/9 - 10
ALS1(config-if-range)#switchport mode trunk
ALS1(config-if-range)#channel-group 4 mode passive
Creating a port-channel interface Port-channel 4
ALS1(config-if-range)#exit

ALS2(config)#interface range f0/9 - 10
ALS2(config-if-range)#switchport mode trunk
ALS2(config-if-range)#channel-group 3 mode auto
Creating a port-channel interface Port-channel 3
ALS2(config-if-range)#exit
ALS2(config)#interface range f0/7 - 8
ALS2(config-if-range)#switchport mode trunk
ALS2(config-if-range)#channel-group 5 mode auto
Creating a port-channel interface Port-channel 5
ALS2(config-if-range)#exit
```

Verify your configuration using the **show etherchannel summary** and the **show interfaces trunk** Cisco IOS Catalyst switch commands

```
DLS1#show etherchannel summary
Flags:  D - down        P - bundled in port-channel
        I - stand-alone s - suspended
        H - Hot-standby (LACP only)
        R - Layer3       S - Layer2
        U - in use       f - failed to allocate aggregator

        M - not in use, minimum links not met
        u - unsuitable for bundling
        w - waiting to be aggregated
        d - default port


Number of channel-groups in use: 3
Number of aggregators:           3

Group  Port-channel  Protocol    Ports
------+-------------+-----------+----------------------------------------------
1      Po1(SD)          -        Fa0/11(D)   Fa0/12(D)
2      Po2(SU)        LACP       Fa0/7(P)    Fa0/8(P)
3      Po3(SU)        PAgP       Fa0/9(P)    Fa0/10(P)

DLS1#show interfaces trunk

Port     Mode      Encapsulation  Status      Native vlan
Po2      on        802.1q         trunking    1
Po3      on        802.1q         trunking    1
```

```
DLS2#show etherchannel summary
Flags:  D - down         P - bundled in port-channel
        I - stand-alone s - suspended
        H - Hot-standby (LACP only)
        R - Layer3       S - Layer2
        U - in use       f - failed to allocate aggregator

        M - not in use, minimum links not met
        u - unsuitable for bundling
        w - waiting to be aggregated
        d - default port


Number of channel-groups in use: 3
Number of aggregators:           3

Group  Port-channel  Protocol   Ports
------+-------------+----------+-----------------------------------------------
1      Po1(SD)          -        Fa0/11(D)   Fa0/12(D)
4      Po4(SU)        LACP       Fa0/9(P)    Fa0/10(P)
5      Po5(SU)        PAgP       Fa0/7(P)    Fa0/8(P)

DLS2#show interfaces trunk

Port        Mode        Encapsulation  Status     Native vlan
Po4         on          802.1q         trunking   1
Po5         on          802.1q         trunking   1


ALS1#show etherchannel summary
Flags:  D - down         P - in port-channel
        I - stand-alone s - suspended
        H - Hot-standby (LACP only)
        R - Layer3       S - Layer2
        u - unsuitable for bundling
        U - in use       f - failed to allocate aggregator
        d - default port

Number of channel-groups in use: 2
Number of aggregators:           2

Group  Port-channel  Protocol   Ports
------+-------------+----------+-----------------------------------------------
2      Po2(SU)        LACP       Fa0/7(Pd)   Fa0/8(P)
4      Po4(SU)        LACP       Fa0/9(Pd)   Fa0/10(P)

ALS1#show interfaces trunk

Port        Mode        Encapsulation  Status     Native vlan
Po2         on          802.1q         trunking   1
Po4         on          802.1q         trunking   1

ALS2#show etherchannel summary
Flags:  D - down         P - in port-channel
        I - stand-alone s - suspended
        H - Hot-standby (LACP only)
        R - Layer3       S - Layer2
        u - unsuitable for bundling
        U - in use       f - failed to allocate aggregator
        d - default port

Number of channel-groups in use: 2
Number of aggregators:           2

Group  Port-channel  Protocol   Ports
------+-------------+----------+-----------------------------------------------
3      Po3(SU)        PAgP       Fa0/9(P)    Fa0/10(Pd)
5      Po5(SU)        PAgP       Fa0/7(P)    Fa0/8(Pd)

ALS2#show interfaces trunk

Port        Mode        Encapsulation  Status     Native vlan
Po3         on          802.1q         trunking   1
Po5         on          802.1q         trunking   1
```

Task 3

This task calls for the configuration of the EtherChannel guard feature. This feature places the port(s) into an err-disabled state if EtherChannel configurations are mismatched, e.g. EtherChannel parameters are not the same, which can result in loops within the network.

The second part of this task requires the configuration of the errdisable recovery feature for EtherChannel misconfigurations. The feature's timer should be set to 600 seconds (10 mins).

```
DLS1(config)#spanning-tree etherchannel guard misconfig
DLS1(config)#errdisable recovery cause channel-misconfig
DLS1(config)#errdisable recovery interval 600

DLS2(config)#spanning-tree etherchannel guard misconfig
DLS2(config)#errdisable recovery cause channel-misconfig
DLS2(config)#errdisable recovery interval 600

ALS1(config)#spanning-tree etherchannel guard misconfig
ALS1(config)#errdisable recovery cause channel-misconfig
ALS1(config)#errdisable recovery interval 600

ALS2(config)#spanning-tree etherchannel guard misconfig
ALS2(config)#errdisable recovery cause channel-misconfig
ALS2(config)#errdisable recovery interval 600
```

You can use the **show spanning-tree summary** command to verify that the EtherChannel guard feature has been enabled. You can use the **show errdisable recovery** command to verify configured errdisable recovery feature settings:

```
DLS1#show spanning-tree summary
Switch is in pvst mode
Root bridge for: none
Extended system ID          is enabled
Portfast Default            is disabled
PortFast BPDU Guard Default is disabled
Portfast BPDU Filter Default is disabled
Loopguard Default           is disabled
EtherChannel misconfig guard is enabled
UplinkFast                  is disabled
BackboneFast                is disabled
Configured Pathcost method used is short

DLS1#show errdisable recovery
ErrDisable Reason     Timer Status
----------------      -------------
arp-inspection        Disabled
bpduguard             Disabled
channel-misconfig     Enabled
dhcp-rate-limit       Disabled
dtp-flap              Disabled
gbic-invalid          Disabled
l2ptguard             Disabled
link-flap             Disabled
mac-limit             Disabled
link-monitor-fail     Disabled
loopback              Disabled
oam-remote-failur     Disabled
pagp-flap             Disabled
port-mode-failure     Disabled
psecure-violation     Disabled
security-violatio     Disabled
sfp-config-mismat     Disabled
storm-control         Disabled
udld                  Disabled
unicast-flood         Disabled
vmps                  Disabled

Timer interval: 600 seconds

Interfaces that will be enabled at the next timeout:
```

Task 4

```
DLS1(config)#vlan 100
DLS1(config-vlan)#exit
DLS1(config)#vlan 200
DLS1(config-vlan)#exit
DLS1(config)#vlan 300
DLS1(config-vlan)#exit
DLS1(config)#vlan 400
DLS1(config-vlan)#exit
DLS1(config)#vlan 500
DLS1(config-vlan)#exit
DLS1(config)#vlan 600
DLS1(config-vlan)#exit
DLS1(config)#vlan 700
DLS1(config-vlan)#exit
DLS1(config)#vlan 800
DLS1(config-vlan)#exit

DLS2(config)#vlan 100
DLS2(config-vlan)#exit
DLS2(config)#vlan 200
DLS2(config-vlan)#exit
DLS2(config)#vlan 300
DLS2(config-vlan)#exit
DLS2(config)#vlan 400
DLS2(config-vlan)#exit
DLS2(config)#vlan 500
DLS2(config-vlan)#exit
DLS2(config)#vlan 600
DLS2(config-vlan)#exit
DLS2(config)#vlan 700
DLS2(config-vlan)#exit
DLS2(config)#vlan 800
DLS2(config-vlan)#exit

ALS1(config)#vlan 100
ALS1(config-vlan)#exit
ALS1(config)#vlan 200
ALS1(config-vlan)#exit
ALS1(config)#vlan 300
ALS1(config-vlan)#exit
ALS1(config)#vlan 400
ALS1(config-vlan)#exit
ALS1(config)#vlan 500
ALS1(config-vlan)#exit
ALS1(config)#vlan 600
ALS1(config-vlan)#exit
ALS1(config)#vlan 700
ALS1(config-vlan)#exit
ALS1(config)#vlan 800
ALS1(config-vlan)#exit


ALS2(config)#vlan 100
ALS2(config-vlan)#exit
ALS2(config)#vlan 200
ALS2(config-vlan)#exit
ALS2(config)#vlan 300
ALS2(config-vlan)#exit
ALS2(config)#vlan 400
ALS2(config-vlan)#exit
ALS2(config)#vlan 500
ALS2(config-vlan)#exit
ALS2(config)#vlan 600
ALS2(config-vlan)#exit
ALS2(config)#vlan 700
ALS2(config-vlan)#exit
ALS2(config)#vlan 800
ALS2(config-vlan)#exit
```

Task 5

```
DLS1(config)#spanning-tree mst configuration
DLS1(config-mst)#name CCNP
DLS1(config-mst)#revision 0
DLS1(config-mst)#instance 1 vlan 100, 200
DLS1(config-mst)#instance 2 vlan 300, 400
DLS1(config-mst)#instance 3 vlan 500, 600
DLS1(config-mst)#instance 4 vlan 700, 800
DLS1(config-mst)#show current
Current MST configuration
Name      [CCNP]
Revision   0      Instances configured 5

Instance  Vlans mapped
--------  -----------------------------------------------------------------
0         1-99,101-199,201-299,301-399,401-499,501-599,601-699,701-799
          801-4094
1         100,200
2         300,400
3         500,600
4         700,800
-------------------------------------------------------------------------
DLS1(config-mst)#exit
DLS1(config)#spanning-tree mst 1 priority 0
DLS1(config)#spanning-tree mode mst

DLS2(config)#spanning-tree mst configuration
DLS2(config-mst)#name CCNP
DLS2(config-mst)#revision 0
DLS2(config-mst)#instance 1 vlan 100, 200
DLS2(config-mst)#instance 2 vlan 300, 400
DLS2(config-mst)#instance 3 vlan 500, 600
DLS2(config-mst)#instance 4 vlan 700, 800
DLS2(config-mst)#show current
Current MST configuration
Name      [CCNP]
Revision   0      Instances configured 5

Instance  Vlans mapped
--------  -----------------------------------------------------------------
0         1-99,101-199,201-299,301-399,401-499,501-599,601-699,701-799
          801-4094
1         100,200
2         300,400
3         500,600
4         700,800
-------------------------------------------------------------------------
DLS2(config-mst)#exit
DLS2(config)#spanning-tree mst 2 priority 0
DLS2(config)#spanning-tree mode mst

ALS1(config)#spanning-tree mst configuration
ALS1(config-mst)#name CCNP
ALS1(config-mst)#revision 0
ALS1(config-mst)#instance 1 vlan 100, 200
ALS1(config-mst)#instance 2 vlan 300, 400
ALS1(config-mst)#instance 3 vlan 500, 600
ALS1(config-mst)#instance 4 vlan 700, 800
ALS1(config-mst)#show current
Current MST configuration
Name      [CCNP]
Revision   0      Instances configured 5

Instance  Vlans mapped
--------  -----------------------------------------------------------------
0         1-99,101-199,201-299,301-399,401-499,501-599,601-699,701-799
          801-4094
1         100,200
2         300,400
3         500,600
4         700,800
-------------------------------------------------------------------------
```

```
ALS1(config-mst)#exit
ALS1(config)#spanning-tree mst 3 priority 0
ALS1(config)#spanning-tree mode mst

ALS2(config)#spanning-tree mst configuration
ALS2(config-mst)#name CCNP
ALS2(config-mst)#revision 0
ALS2(config-mst)#instance 1 vlan 100, 200
ALS2(config-mst)#instance 2 vlan 300, 400
ALS2(config-mst)#instance 3 vlan 500, 600
ALS2(config-mst)#instance 4 vlan 700, 800
ALS2(config-mst)#show current
Current MST configuration
Name      [CCNP]
Revision  0       Instances configured 5

Instance  Vlans mapped
--------  -------------------------------------------------------------------
0         1-99,101-199,201-299,301-399,401-499,501-599,601-699,701-799
          801-4094
1         100,200
2         300,400
3         500,600
4         700,800
--------------------------------------------------------------------------
ALS2(config-mst)#exit
ALS2(config)#spanning-tree mst 4 priority 0
ALS2(config)#spanning-tree mode mst
```

Following this configuration, use the **show spanning-tree mst** command to verify MST:

```
DLS1#show spanning-tree mst 1

##### MST1      vlans mapped:   100,200
Bridge          address 000f.2303.2d80  priority    1    (0 sysid 1)
Root            this switch for MST1

Interface       Role Sts Cost      Prio.Nbr Type
--------------- ---- --- --------- -------- --------------------------------
Po1             Desg FWD 100000    128.68   P2p
Po2             Desg FWD 100000    128.69   P2p Pre-STD-Rx
Po3             Desg FWD 100000    128.70   P2p Pre-STD-Rx

DLS1#show spanning-tree mst 2

##### MST2      vlans mapped:   300,400
Bridge          address 000f.2303.2d80  priority    32770 (32768 sysid 2)
Root            address 000b.fd67.6500  priority    2    (0 sysid 2)
                port    Po1             cost        100000   rem hops 19

Interface       Role Sts Cost      Prio.Nbr Type
--------------- ---- --- --------- -------- --------------------------------
Po1             Root FWD 100000    128.68   P2p
Po2             Altn BLK 100000    128.69   P2p Pre-STD-Rx
Po3             Altn BLK 100000    128.70   P2p Pre-STD-Rx

DLS1#show spanning-tree mst 3

##### MST3      vlans mapped:   500,600
Bridge          address 000f.2303.2d80  priority    32771 (32768 sysid 3)
Root            address 0007.8432.dd00  priority    3    (0 sysid 3)
                port    Po2             cost        100000   rem hops 19

Interface       Role Sts Cost      Prio.Nbr Type
--------------- ---- --- --------- -------- --------------------------------
Po1             Altn BLK 100000    128.68   P2p
Po2             Root FWD 100000    128.69   P2p Pre-STD-Rx
Po3             Desg FWD 100000    128.70   P2p Pre-STD-Rx

DLS1#show spanning-tree mst 4

##### MST4      vlans mapped:   700,800
Bridge          address 000f.2303.2d80  priority    32772 (32768 sysid 4)
```

```
Root            address 0009.b79f.7d80  priority    4      (0 sysid 4)
                port    Po3             cost        100000    rem hops 19

Interface       Role Sts Cost      Prio.Nbr Type
--------------- ---- --- --------- -------- --------------------------------
Po1             Altn BLK 100000    128.68   P2p
Po2             Desg LRN 100000    128.69   P2p Pre-STD-Rx
Po3             Root FWD 100000    128.70   P2p Pre-STD-Rx
```

Task 6

By default, the 802.1D specification assigns a 16-bit (short) default port cost values to each port that is based on the bandwidth. The 802.1t standard assigns a 32-bit (long) default port cost values to each port using a formula that is based on the bandwidth of the port. The formula for obtaining default 32-bit port costs is to divide the bandwidth of the port by 200,000,000. To complete this task you will need to change the default 802.1D cost method as follows:

```
DLS1(config)#spanning-tree pathcost method long
```

```
DLS1(config)#spanning-tree pathcost method long
```

```
DLS1(config)#spanning-tree pathcost method long
```

```
DLS1(config)#spanning-tree pathcost method long
```

Verify the current cost method using the **show spanning-tree pathcost method** command

```
DLS1#show spanning-tree pathcost method
Spanning tree default pathcost method used is long
```

```
DLS1(config)#spanning-tree pathcost method long
```

FINAL SWITCH CONFIGURATIONS

DLS1

```
DLS1#term len 0
DLS1#show run
Building configuration...

Current configuration : 4639 bytes
!
version 12.2
no service pad
service timestamps debug datetime msec
service timestamps log datetime msec
no service password-encryption
!
hostname DLS1
!
no logging console
!
no aaa new-model
errdisable recovery cause channel-misconfig
errdisable recovery interval 600
ip subnet-zero
!
vtp domain SWITCH
vtp mode transparent
!
spanning-tree mode mst
spanning-tree extend system-id
spanning-tree pathcost method long
!
spanning-tree mst configuration
 name CCNP
 instance 1 vlan 100, 200
 instance 2 vlan 300, 400
 instance 3 vlan 500, 600
```

```
 instance 4 vlan 700, 800
!
spanning-tree mst 1 priority 0
!
vlan internal allocation policy ascending
!
vlan 100,200,300,400,500,600,700,800
!
interface Port-channel1
 switchport trunk encapsulation dot1q
 switchport mode trunk
!
interface Port-channel2
 switchport trunk encapsulation dot1q
 switchport mode trunk
!
interface Port-channel3
 switchport trunk encapsulation dot1q
 switchport mode trunk
!
interface FastEthernet0/1
 switchport mode dynamic desirable
!
interface FastEthernet0/2
 switchport mode dynamic desirable
!
interface FastEthernet0/3
 switchport mode dynamic desirable
!
interface FastEthernet0/4
 switchport mode dynamic desirable
!
interface FastEthernet0/5
 switchport mode dynamic desirable
!
interface FastEthernet0/6
 switchport mode dynamic desirable
!
interface FastEthernet0/7
 switchport trunk encapsulation dot1q
 switchport mode trunk
 channel-group 2 mode active
!
interface FastEthernet0/8
 switchport trunk encapsulation dot1q
 switchport mode trunk
 channel-group 2 mode active
!
interface FastEthernet0/9
 switchport trunk encapsulation dot1q
 switchport mode trunk
 channel-group 3 mode desirable
!
interface FastEthernet0/10
 switchport trunk encapsulation dot1q
 switchport mode trunk
 channel-group 3 mode desirable
!
interface FastEthernet0/11
 switchport trunk encapsulation dot1q
 switchport mode trunk
 channel-group 1 mode on
!
interface FastEthernet0/12
 switchport trunk encapsulation dot1q
 switchport mode trunk
 channel-group 1 mode on

[Truncated Output]

interface Vlan1
 no ip address
 shutdown
!
ip classless
ip http server
ip http secure-server
!
control-plane
!
line con 0
```

```
line vty 5 15
!
end
DLS1#
```

DLS2

```
DLS2#term len 0
DLS2#show run
Building configuration...

Current configuration : 4639 bytes
!
version 12.2
no service pad
service timestamps debug datetime msec
service timestamps log datetime msec
no service password-encryption
!
hostname DLS2
!
no logging console
!
no aaa new-model
errdisable recovery cause channel-misconfig
errdisable recovery interval 600
ip subnet-zero
!
vtp domain SWITCH
vtp mode transparent
!
spanning-tree mode mst
spanning-tree extend system-id
spanning-tree pathcost method long
!
spanning-tree mst configuration
 name CCNP
 instance 1 vlan 100, 200
 instance 2 vlan 300, 400
 instance 3 vlan 500, 600
 instance 4 vlan 700, 800
!
spanning-tree mst 2 priority 0
!
vlan internal allocation policy ascending
!
vlan 100,200,300,400,500,600,700,800
!
interface Port-channel1
 switchport trunk encapsulation dot1q
 switchport mode trunk
!
interface Port-channel4
 switchport trunk encapsulation dot1q
 switchport mode trunk
!
interface Port-channel5
 switchport trunk encapsulation dot1q
 switchport mode trunk
!
interface FastEthernet0/1
 switchport mode dynamic desirable
!
interface FastEthernet0/2
 switchport mode dynamic desirable
!
interface FastEthernet0/3
 switchport mode dynamic desirable
!
interface FastEthernet0/4
 switchport mode dynamic desirable
!
interface FastEthernet0/5
 switchport mode dynamic desirable
!
interface FastEthernet0/6
 switchport mode dynamic desirable
!
interface FastEthernet0/7
```

```
 switchport trunk encapsulation dot1q
 switchport mode trunk
 channel-group 5 mode desirable
!
interface FastEthernet0/8
 switchport trunk encapsulation dot1q
 switchport mode trunk
 channel-group 5 mode desirable
!
interface FastEthernet0/9
 switchport trunk encapsulation dot1q
 switchport mode trunk
 channel-group 4 mode active
!
interface FastEthernet0/10
 switchport trunk encapsulation dot1q
 switchport mode trunk
 channel-group 4 mode active
!
interface FastEthernet0/11
 switchport trunk encapsulation dot1q
 switchport mode trunk
 channel-group 1 mode on
!
interface FastEthernet0/12
 switchport trunk encapsulation dot1q
 switchport mode trunk
 channel-group 1 mode on

[Truncated Output]

interface Vlan1
 no ip address
 shutdown
!
ip classless
ip http server
ip http secure-server
!
control-plane
!
line con 0
line vty 5 15
!
end
DLS2#
```

ALS1

```
ALS1#term len 0
ALS1#show run
Building configuration...

Current configuration : 1488 bytes
!
version 12.1
no service pad
service timestamps debug uptime
service timestamps log uptime
no service password-encryption
!
hostname ALS1
!
no logging console
!
errdisable recovery cause channel-misconfig
errdisable recovery interval 600
ip subnet-zero
!
vtp domain SWITCH
vtp mode transparent
!
!
spanning-tree mode mst
no spanning-tree optimize bpdu transmission
spanning-tree extend system-id
spanning-tree pathcost method long
!
spanning-tree mst configuration
```

```
 name CCNP
 instance 1 vlan 100, 200
 instance 2 vlan 300, 400
 instance 3 vlan 500, 600
 instance 4 vlan 700, 800
!
spanning-tree mst 3 priority 0
!
vlan 100,200,300,400,500,600,700,800
!
interface Port-channel2
 switchport mode trunk
 flowcontrol send off
!
interface Port-channel4
 switchport mode trunk
 flowcontrol send off
!
interface FastEthernet0/1
!
interface FastEthernet0/2
!
interface FastEthernet0/3
!
interface FastEthernet0/4
!
interface FastEthernet0/5
!
interface FastEthernet0/6
!
interface FastEthernet0/7
 switchport mode trunk
 channel-group 2 mode passive
!
interface FastEthernet0/8
 switchport mode trunk
 channel-group 2 mode passive
!
interface FastEthernet0/9
 switchport mode trunk
 channel-group 4 mode passive
!
interface FastEthernet0/10
 switchport mode trunk
 channel-group 4 mode passive
!
interface FastEthernet0/11
 shutdown
!
interface FastEthernet0/12
 shutdown
!
interface Vlan1
 no ip address
 no ip route-cache
 shutdown
!
ip http server
!
line con 0
line vty 5 15
!
!
end
ALS1#
```

ALS2

```
ALS2#term len 0
ALS2#show run
Building configuration...

Current configuration : 1476 bytes
!
version 12.1
no service pad
service timestamps debug uptime
service timestamps log uptime
no service password-encryption
```

```
!
hostname ALS2
!
no logging console
!
errdisable recovery cause channel-misconfig
errdisable recovery interval 600
ip subnet-zero
!
vtp domain SWITCH
vtp mode transparent
!
!
spanning-tree mode mst
no spanning-tree optimize bpdu transmission
spanning-tree extend system-id
spanning-tree pathcost method long
!
spanning-tree mst configuration
 name CCNP
 instance 1 vlan 100, 200
 instance 2 vlan 300, 400
 instance 3 vlan 500, 600
 instance 4 vlan 700, 800
!
spanning-tree mst 4 priority 0
!
vlan 100,200,300,400,500,600,700,800
!
interface Port-channel3
 switchport mode trunk
 flowcontrol send off
!
interface Port-channel5
 switchport mode trunk
 flowcontrol send off
!
interface FastEthernet0/1
!
interface FastEthernet0/2
!
interface FastEthernet0/3
!
interface FastEthernet0/4
!
interface FastEthernet0/5
!
interface FastEthernet0/6
!
interface FastEthernet0/7
 switchport mode trunk
 channel-group 5 mode auto
!
interface FastEthernet0/8
 switchport mode trunk
 channel-group 5 mode auto
!
interface FastEthernet0/9
 switchport mode trunk
 channel-group 3 mode auto
!
interface FastEthernet0/10
 switchport mode trunk
 channel-group 3 mode auto
!
interface FastEthernet0/11
 shutdown
!
interface FastEthernet0/12
 shutdown
!
interface Vlan1
 no ip address
 no ip route-cache
 shutdown
!
ip http server
!
line con 0
line vty 5 15
!
end

ALS2#
```

CCNP LAB 4

MLS, EtherChannels and Security

Lab Objective:

The focus of this lab is to understand how to implement and verify MLS, routed EtherChannels as well as some of the different Cisco IOS Catalyst series switch security features.

Lab Topology:

The lab network topology is illustrated below:

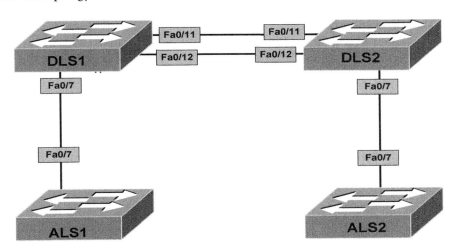

IMPORTANT NOTE: If you are using the www.howtonetwork.net racks, please begin each and every lab by shutting down all interfaces on all switches and then manually re-enabling only the interfaces that are illustrated in this topology.

Task 1

Disable VTP on all switches. All switches should support the configuration, modification and deletion of VLANs.

Task 2

Configure the following VLANs on the switches:
- DLS1 and ALS1: VLAN 100
- DLS2 and ALS2: VLAN 200

Configure the following SVIs on the switches:
- DLS1 SVI 100 - IP Address 100.1.1.1/30
- ALS1 SVI 100 - IP Address 100.1.1.2/30
- DLS2 SVI 200 - IP Address 200.1.1.1/30
- ALS2 SVI 200 - IP Address 200.1.1.2/30

Switches ALS1 and ALS2 should have their default gateway point to switches DLS1 and DLS2 respectively. There should be no default gateway configured on switches DLS1 and DLS2.

Task 3

Configure the ports between the access and distribution layer switches as static access ports. These should be assigned to the VLANs configured on the switches. Configure a routed EtherChannel between DLS1 and DLS2. Use any channel protocol. Assign switch DLS1 IP address 172.16.1.1/30 and switch DLS2 IP address 172.16.1.2/30.

Task 4

Using a routing protocol of your choice, configure switches DLS1 and DLS2 so that switches ALS1 and ALS2 have IP connectivity to each other. For efficiency, enable CEF. Verify your configuration and validate connectivity using PING and Telnet.

Task 5

At the VLAN level, implement filtering for VLAN 100 as follows:
- Drop all TCP packets
- Drop all UDP packets
- Forward all other non-IP packets
- Forward all other IP packets

At the VLAN level, implement filtering for VLAN 200 as follows:
- Forward all ICMP packets
- Forward all MAC packets from the MAC address of ALS2
- Drop all other IP packets
- Drop all other non-IP packets

Verify that you can still ping between switches ALS1 and ALS2; however, you should not be able to Telnet between switches ALS1 and ALS2. Verify your configuration.

Task 6

Configure Dynamic ARP Inspection for VLAN 100 such that the switch compares the ARP body for invalid and unexpected IP addresses, which includes 0.0.0.0, 255.255.255.255, all IP Multicast addresses, and a valid source MAC and explicitly denies them. Allow logging for DAI. Verify that switch ALS1 can still ping switch ALS2 after this configuration.

Task 7

In order to mitigate against Broadcast attacks, configure the access ports on switches DLS1 and DLS2 to monitor inbound packets and shut them down if Broadcast traffic exceeds 10% of the physical port bandwidth. Verify your configuration using relevant commands on the switches.

LAB VALIDATION

Task 1

```
DLS1(config)#vtp mode transparent
Setting device to VTP TRANSPARENT mode.

DLS2(config)#vtp mode transparent
Setting device to VTP TRANSPARENT mode.

ALS1(config)#vtp mode transparent
Setting device to VTP TRANSPARENT mode.
```

```
ALS2(config)#vtp mode transparent
Setting device to VTP TRANSPARENT mode.
```

Task 2

```
DLS1(config)#vlan 100
DLS1(config-vlan)#exit
DLS1(config)#interface vlan 100
DLS1(config-if)#ip address 100.1.1.1 255.255.255.252
DLS1(config-if)#exit

DLS2(config)#vlan 200
DLS2(config-vlan)#exit
DLS2(config)#interface vlan 200
DLS2(config-if)#ip address 200.1.1.1 255.255.255.252
DLS2(config-if)#exit

ALS1(config)#vlan 100
ALS1(config-vlan)#exit
ALS1(config)#interface vlan 100
ALS1(config-if)#ip address 100.1.1.1 255.255.255.252
ALS1(config-if)#exit
ALS1(config)#ip default-gateway 100.1.1.1

ALS2(config)#vlan 200
ALS2(config-vlan)#exit
ALS2(config)#interface vlan 200
ALS2(config-if)#ip address 200.1.1.2 255.255.255.252
ALS2(config-if)#exit
ALS2(config)#ip default-gateway 200.1.1.1
```

Task 3

```
DLS1(config)#interface fastethernet 0/7
DLS1(config-if)#switchport access vlan 100
DLS1(config-if)#switchport mode access
DLS1(config-if)#exit
DLS1(config)#interface range fastethernet 0/11 - 12
DLS1(config-if-range)#no switchport
DLS1(config-if-range)#channel-group 1 mode active
Creating a port-channel interface Port-channel 1

DLS1(config-if-range)#exit
DLS1(config)#interface port-channel 1
DLS1(config-if)#ip address 172.16.1.1 255.255.255.252
DLS1(config-if)#exit

DLS2(config)#interface fastethernet 0/7
DLS2(config-if)#switchport access vlan 200
DLS2(config-if)#switchport mode access
DLS2(config-if)#exit
DLS2(config)#interface range fastethernet 0/11 - 12
DLS2(config-if-range)#no switchport
DLS2(config-if-range)#channel-group 1 mode active
Creating a port-channel interface Port-channel 1

DLS2(config-if-range)#exit
DLS2(config)#interface port-channel 1
DLS2(config-if)#ip address 172.16.1.2 255.255.255.252
DLS2(config-if)#exit

ALS1(config)#interface fastethernet 0/7
ALS1(config-if)#switchport access vlan 100
ALS1(config-if)#switchport mode access
ALS1(config-if)#exit

ALS2(config)#interface fastethernet 0/7
ALS2(config-if)#switchport access vlan 200
ALS2(config-if)#switchport mode access
```

Verify your EtherChannel configuration using the **show etherchannel** suite of commands. You can also ping between the switches to verify configuration and connectivity:

```
DLS2#show etherchannel 1 summary
Flags:  D - down         P - bundled in port-channel
        I - stand-alone  s - suspended
        H - Hot-standby (LACP only)
        R - Layer3       S - Layer2
        U - in use       f - failed to allocate aggregator

        M - not in use, minimum links not met
        u - unsuitable for bundling
        w - waiting to be aggregated
        d - default port

Number of channel-groups in use: 1
Number of aggregators:           1

Group  Port-channel  Protocol    Ports
------+-------------+-----------+-----------------------------------------------
1      Po1(RU)        LACP        Fa0/11(P)   Fa0/12(P)

DLS2#ping 172.16.1.1

Type escape sequence to abort.
Sending 5, 100-byte ICMP Echos to 172.16.1.1, timeout is 2 seconds:
.!!!!
Success rate is 80 percent (4/5), round-trip min/avg/max = 1/3/4 ms
```

Task 4

```
DLS1(config)#ip routing
DLS1(config)#ip cef
DLS1(config)#router eigrp 1
DLS1(config-router)#network 0.0.0.0 255.255.255.255
DLS1(config-router)#no auto-summary
DLS1(config-router)#exit

DLS2(config)#ip routing
DLS2(config)#ip cef
DLS1(config)#router eigrp 1
DLS1(config-router)#network 0.0.0.0 255.255.255.255
DLS1(config-router)#no auto-summary
DLS1(config-router)#exit
```

Use the appropriate commands to verify correct operation for the routing protocol you selected.

```
DLS1#show ip eigrp neighbors
EIGRP-IPv4:(1) neighbors for process 1
H   Address                Interface       Hold Uptime   SRTT   RTO  Q   Seq
                                           (sec)         (ms)        Cnt Num
0   172.16.1.2             Po1             13 00:06:37    4      300  0   2

DLS1#show ip route eigrp
      200.1.1.0/30 is subnetted, 1 subnets
D        200.1.1.0 [90/15616] via 172.16.1.2, 00:01:15, Port-channel1
```

Use the show ip cef command to view FIB information and entries:

```
DLS1#show ip cef detail
IPv4 CEF is enabled and running
VRF Default:
 17 prefixes (17/0 fwd/non-fwd)
 Table id 0
 Database epoch:        0 (17 entries at this epoch)

0.0.0.0/0, epoch 0, flags default route handler
  no route
0.0.0.0/32, epoch 0, flags receive
```

```
 Special source: receive
 receive
100.1.1.0/30, epoch 0, flags attached, connected, cover dependents, need deagg
 Covered dependent prefixes: 4
   need deagg: 3
   notify cover updated: 1
 attached to Vlan100
100.1.1.0/32, epoch 0, flags receive
 Dependent covered prefix type cover need deagg cover 100.1.1.0/30
 Interface source: Vlan100
 receive for Vlan100
100.1.1.1/32, epoch 0, flags receive
 Dependent covered prefix type cover need deagg cover 100.1.1.0/30
 Interface source: Vlan100
 receive for Vlan100
100.1.1.2/32, epoch 0, flags attached
 Adj source: IP adj out of Vlan100, addr 100.1.1.2 01D83DC0
   Dependent covered prefix type adjfib cover 100.1.1.0/30
 attached to Vlan100
100.1.1.3/32, epoch 0, flags receive
 Dependent covered prefix type cover need deagg cover 100.1.1.0/30
 Interface source: Vlan100
 receive for Vlan100
172.16.1.0/30, epoch 0, flags attached, connected, cover dependents, need deagg
 Covered dependent prefixes: 4
   need deagg: 3
   notify cover updated: 1
 attached to Port-channel1
172.16.1.0/32, epoch 0, flags receive
 Dependent covered prefix type cover need deagg cover 172.16.1.0/30
 Interface source: Port-channel1
 receive for Port-channel1
172.16.1.1/32, epoch 0, flags receive
 Dependent covered prefix type cover need deagg cover 172.16.1.0/30
 Interface source: Port-channel1
 receive for Port-channel1
172.16.1.2/32, epoch 0, flags attached
 Adj source: IP adj out of Port-channel1, addr 172.16.1.2 01D83F40
   Dependent covered prefix type adjfib cover 172.16.1.0/30
 attached to Port-channel1
172.16.1.3/32, epoch 0, flags receive
 Dependent covered prefix type cover need deagg cover 172.16.1.0/30
 Interface source: Port-channel1
 receive for Port-channel1
200.1.1.0/30, epoch 0
 nexthop 172.16.1.2 Port-channel1
224.0.0.0/4, epoch 0
 Special source: drop
 drop
224.0.0.0/24, epoch 0, flags receive
 Special source: receive
 receive
240.0.0.0/4, epoch 0
 Special source: drop
 drop
255.255.255.255/32, epoch 0, flags receive
 Special source: receive
 receive
```

Finally, use a simple ping to verify connectivity between switches ALS1 and ALS2:

```
ALS1#ping 200.1.1.2

Type escape sequence to abort.
Sending 5, 100-byte ICMP Echos to 200.1.1.2, timeout is 2 seconds:
..!!!
Success rate is 60 percent (3/5), round-trip min/avg/max = 1/3/4 ms
```

And finally, Telnet between the switches:

```
ALS1#telnet 200.1.1.2
Trying 200.1.1.2 ... Open
```

```
Password required, but none set

[Connection to 200.1.1.2 closed by foreign host]
ALS1#
```

Task 5

This task requires a little thought. When configuring VACLs, if the configured VLAN map has a match clause for the type of packet, which can either be IP or MAC, and the packet does not match the type, the default is to drop the packet. However, if there is no match clause in the VLAN map for that type of packet, and no action specified, the packet is forwarded. This task is completed as follows:

```
DLS1(config)#ip access-list extended ALLOW-TCP
DLS1(config-ext-nacl)#permit tcp any any
DLS1(config-ext-nacl)#exit
DLS1(config)#ip access-list extended ALLOW-UDP
DLS1(config-ext-nacl)#permit udp any any
DLS1(config-ext-nacl)#exit
DLS1(config)#vlan access-map VLAN-100 10
DLS1(config-access-map)#match ip address ALLOW-TCP
DLS1(config-access-map)#action drop
DLS1(config-access-map)#exit
DLS1(config)#vlan access-map VLAN-100 20
DLS1(config-access-map)#match ip address ALLOW-UDP
DLS1(config-access-map)#action drop
DLS1(config-access-map)#exit
DLS1(config)#vlan access-map VLAN-100 30
DLS1(config-access-map)#action forward
DLS1(config-access-map)#exit
DLS1(config)#vlan filter VLAN-100 vlan-list 100
```

The configuration of the VACL on switch DLS2 follows similar logic. To determine the MAC address of switch ALS1, simply use the **show arp** command on switch DLS2.

```
DLS2(config)#ip access-list extended ALLOW-ICMP
DLS2(config-ext-nacl)#permit icmp any any
DLS2(config-ext-nacl)#exit
DLS2(config)#mac access-list extended SWITCH-ALS2
DLS2(config-ext-macl)#permit host 0009.b79f.7d80 any
DLS2(config-ext-macl)#exit
DLS2(config)#vlan access-map VLAN-200 10
DLS2(config-access-map)#match ip address ALLOW-ICMP
DLS2(config-access-map)#action forward
DLS2(config-access-map)#exit
DLS2(config)#vlan access-map VLAN-200 20
DLS2(config-access-map)#match mac address SWITCH-ALS2
DLS2(config-access-map)#action forward
DLS2(config-access-map)#exit
DLS2(config)#vlan filter VLAN-200 vlan-list 200
```

Following completion, verify the switch VACL configuration using the **show vlan access-map** and **show vlan filter** commands on switches DLS1 and DSL2. The output of the **show vlan access-map** command is shown below:

```
DLS2#show vlan filter
VLAN Map VLAN-200 is filtering VLANs:
  200
```

The output of the **show vlan filter** command is shown below:

```
DLS2#show vlan access-map
Vlan access-map "VLAN-200"  10
  Match clauses:
    ip  address: ALLOW-ICMP
  Action:
    forward
Vlan access-map "VLAN-200"  20
  Match clauses:
    mac address: SWITCH-ALS2
  Action:
    forward
```

Next, verify that Access layer switches ALS1 and ALS2 can still ping each other:

```
ALS1#ping 200.1.1.2

Type escape sequence to abort.
Sending 5, 100-byte ICMP Echos to 200.1.1.2, timeout is 2 seconds:
!!!!!
Success rate is 100 percent (5/5), round-trip min/avg/max = 1/2/4 ms
```

Finally, ensure that Telnet no longer works because of the applied VACL:

```
ALS1#telnet 200.1.1.2
Trying 200.1.1.2 ...
% Connection timed out; remote host not responding

ALS1#
```

Task 6

Dynamic ARP Inspection (DAI) depends on the entries in the DHCP Snooping binding database to verify IP-to-MAC address bindings in incoming ARP requests and ARP responses. However, when DHCP Snooping is disabled or in non-DHCP environments, you must use ARP ACLs to permit or to deny packets. The first part of this task entails configuring an ARP ACL for switch ALS1 in VLAN 100. This is completed as follows:

```
DLS1(config)#arp access-list VLAN-100-DAI-ACL
DLS1(config-arp-nacl)#permit ip host 100.1.1.2 mac host 0007.8432.dd00 log
DLS1(config-arp-nacl)#exit
DLS1(config)#ip arp inspection filter VLAN-100-DAI-ACL vlan 100 static
DLS1(config)#ip arp inspection vlan 100
DLS1(config)#ip arp inspection vlan 100 logging acl-match matchlog
```

NOTE: The additional static keyword is used to treat implicit denies in the ARP ACL as explicit denies and to drop packets that do not match any previous clauses in the ACL.

The second part of the task is to configure the interface on DLS1 that is connected to ALS1 as untrusted (which means packets are inspected by DAI). Additionally, the task calls for comparing invalid and unexpected IP addresses, which includes 0.0.0.0, 255.255.255.255, all IP Multicast addresses and source MACs. This task is completed as follows:

```
DLS1(config)#ip arp inspection validate ip src-mac
```

Use the **show ip arp inspection** commands to verify your configuration:

```
DLS1#show ip arp inspection vlan 100
```

```
Source Mac Validation      : Enabled
Destination Mac Validation : Disabled
IP Address Validation      : Enabled
```

Vlan	Configuration	Operation	ACL Match	Static ACL
100	Enabled	Active	VLAN-100-DAI-ACL	Yes

Vlan	ACL Logging	DHCP Logging	Probe Logging
100	Acl-Match	Deny	Off

Finally, verify that switch ALS1 can still ping switch ALS2 using a simple ping as follows:

```
ALS1#ping 200.1.1.2

Type escape sequence to abort.
Sending 5, 100-byte ICMP Echos to 200.1.1.2, timeout is 2 seconds:
!!!!!
```

You can test your configuration by changing the MAC address of SVI 100 on switch ALS1 and then attempting to ping switch ALS2. This is performed as follows:

```
ALS1(config)#int vlan 100
ALS1(config-if)#mac-address 0009.b79f.7d80
ALS1(config-if)#end
ALS1#sh run int vlan 100
Building configuration...

Current configuration : 110 bytes
!
interface Vlan100
 mac-address 0009.b79f.7d80
 ip address 100.1.1.2 255.255.255.252
 no ip route-cache
end

ALS1#ping 200.1.1.2

Type escape sequence to abort.
Sending 5, 100-byte ICMP Echos to 200.1.1.2, timeout is 2 seconds:
.....
Success rate is 0 percent (0/5)
```

On switch DLS1, use the **show ip arp inspection** command to see dropped packet statistics:

```
DLS1#show ip arp inspection

Source Mac Validation      : Enabled
Destination Mac Validation : Disabled
IP Address Validation      : Enabled
```

Vlan	Configuration	Operation	ACL Match	Static ACL
100	Enabled	Active	VLAN-100-DAI-ACL	Yes

Vlan	ACL Logging	DHCP Logging	Probe Logging
100	Acl-Match	Deny	Off

Vlan	Forwarded	Dropped	DHCP Drops	ACL Drops
100	0	12	0	12

Vlan	DHCP Permits	ACL Permits	Probe Permits	Source MAC Failures
100	0	0	0	0

Vlan	Dest MAC Failures	IP Validation Failures	Invalid Protocol Data

Vlan	Dest MAC Failures	IP Validation Failures	Invalid Protocol Data
100	0	0	0

When you change the MAC address of SVI 100 on ALS1 back to what it should be, you will see statistics for forwarded packets as well:

```
DLS1#show ip arp inspection

Source Mac Validation      : Enabled
Destination Mac Validation : Disabled
IP Address Validation      : Enabled
```

Vlan	Configuration	Operation	ACL Match	Static ACL
100	Enabled	Active	VLAN-100-DAI-ACL	Yes

Vlan	ACL Logging	DHCP Logging	Probe Logging
100	Acl-Match	Deny	Off

Vlan	Forwarded	Dropped	DHCP Drops	ACL Drops
100	2	18	0	18

Vlan	DHCP Permits	ACL Permits	Probe Permits	Source MAC Failures
100	0	2	0	0

Vlan	Dest MAC Failures	IP Validation Failures	Invalid Protocol Data

Vlan	Dest MAC Failures	IP Validation Failures	Invalid Protocol Data
100	0	0	0

FINAL SWITCH CONFIGURATIONS

DLS1

```
DLS1#term len 0
DLS1#show run
Building configuration...

Current configuration : 4591 bytes
!
version 12.2
no service pad
service timestamps debug datetime msec
service timestamps log datetime msec
no service password-encryption
!
hostname DLS1
!
no logging console
!
no aaa new-model
ip subnet-zero
ip routing
!
ip arp inspection vlan 100
ip arp inspection vlan 100 logging acl-match matchlog
ip arp inspection validate src-mac ip
ip arp inspection filter VLAN-100-DAI-ACL vlan  100 static
vtp domain hard
vtp mode transparent
!
spanning-tree mode pvst
spanning-tree extend system-id
!
vlan internal allocation policy ascending
!
vlan access-map VLAN-100 10
 action drop
 match ip address ALLOW-TCP
vlan access-map VLAN-100 20
 action drop
 match ip address ALLOW-UDP
vlan access-map VLAN-100 30
 action forward
!
vlan filter VLAN-100 vlan-list 100
!
vlan 100
!
interface Port-channel1
 no switchport
 ip address 172.16.1.1 255.255.255.252
!
interface FastEthernet0/1
 switchport mode dynamic desirable
!
interface FastEthernet0/2
 switchport mode dynamic desirable
```

```
!
interface FastEthernet0/3
 switchport mode dynamic desirable
!
interface FastEthernet0/4
 switchport mode dynamic desirable
!
interface FastEthernet0/5
 switchport mode dynamic desirable
!
interface FastEthernet0/6
 switchport mode dynamic desirable
!
interface FastEthernet0/7
 switchport access vlan 100
 switchport mode access
!
interface FastEthernet0/8
 switchport mode dynamic desirable
!
interface FastEthernet0/9
 switchport mode dynamic desirable
!
interface FastEthernet0/10
 switchport mode dynamic desirable
!
interface FastEthernet0/11
 no switchport
 no ip address
 channel-group 1 mode active
!
interface FastEthernet0/12
 no switchport
 no ip address
 channel-group 1 mode active

[Truncated Output]

interface Vlan1
 no ip address
 shutdown
!
interface Vlan100
 ip address 100.1.1.1 255.255.255.252
!
router eigrp 1
 no auto-summary
 network 0.0.0.0
!
ip classless
ip http server
ip http secure-server
!
ip access-list extended ALLOW-TCP
 permit tcp any any
ip access-list extended ALLOW-UDP
 permit udp any any
!
arp access-list VLAN-100-DAI-ACL
 permit ip host 100.1.1.2 mac host 0007.8432.dd00 log
!
control-plane
!
line con 0
line vty 5 15
!
end
DLS1#
```

DLS2

```
DLS2#term len 0
DLS2#sh run
Building configuration...

Current configuration : 4308 bytes
```

```
!
version 12.2
no service pad
service timestamps debug datetime msec
service timestamps log datetime msec
no service password-encryption
!
hostname DLS2
!
no logging console
!
no aaa new-model
ip subnet-zero
ip routing
!
vtp domain hard
vtp mode transparent
!
mac access-list extended SWITCH-ALS2
 permit host 0009.b79f.7d80 any
spanning-tree mode pvst
spanning-tree extend system-id
!
vlan internal allocation policy ascending
!
vlan access-map VLAN-200 10
 action forward
 match ip address ALLOW-ICMP
vlan access-map VLAN-200 20
 action forward
 match mac address SWITCH-ALS2
!
vlan filter VLAN-200 vlan-list 200
!
vlan 200
!
interface Port-channel1
 no switchport
 ip address 172.16.1.2 255.255.255.252
!
interface FastEthernet0/1
 switchport mode dynamic desirable
!
interface FastEthernet0/2
 switchport mode dynamic desirable
!
interface FastEthernet0/3
 switchport mode dynamic desirable
!
interface FastEthernet0/4
 switchport mode dynamic desirable
!
interface FastEthernet0/5
 switchport mode dynamic desirable
!
interface FastEthernet0/6
 switchport mode dynamic desirable
!
interface FastEthernet0/7
 switchport access vlan 200
 switchport mode access
!
interface FastEthernet0/8
 switchport mode dynamic desirable
!
interface FastEthernet0/9
 switchport mode dynamic desirable
!
interface FastEthernet0/10
 switchport mode dynamic desirable
!
interface FastEthernet0/11
 no switchport
 no ip address
 channel-group 1 mode active
!
interface FastEthernet0/12
```

```
 no switchport
 no ip address
 channel-group 1 mode active

[Truncated Output]

interface Vlan1
 no ip address
 shutdown
!
interface Vlan200
 ip address 200.1.1.1 255.255.255.252
!
router eigrp 1
 no auto-summary
 network 0.0.0.0
!
ip classless
ip http server
ip http secure-server
!
ip access-list extended ALLOW-ICMP
 permit icmp any any
!
control-plane
!
line con 0
line vty 5 15
!
end
DLS2#
```

ALS1

```
ALS1#term len 0
ALS1#sh run
Building configuration...

Current configuration : 997 bytes
!
version 12.1
no service pad
service timestamps debug uptime
service timestamps log uptime
no service password-encryption
!
hostname ALS1
!
no logging console
!
ip subnet-zero
!
vtp domain hard
vtp mode transparent
!
spanning-tree mode pvst
no spanning-tree optimize bpdu transmission
spanning-tree extend system-id
!
vlan 100
!
interface FastEthernet0/1
!
interface FastEthernet0/2
!
interface FastEthernet0/3
!
interface FastEthernet0/4
!
interface FastEthernet0/5
!
interface FastEthernet0/6
!
interface FastEthernet0/7
 switchport access vlan 100
 switchport mode access
```

```
!
interface FastEthernet0/8
 shutdown
!
interface FastEthernet0/9
 shutdown
!
interface FastEthernet0/10
 shutdown
!
interface FastEthernet0/11
 shutdown
!
interface FastEthernet0/12
 shutdown
!
interface Vlan1
 no ip address
 no ip route-cache
 shutdown
!
interface Vlan100
 ip address 100.1.1.2 255.255.255.252
 no ip route-cache
!
ip default-gateway 100.1.1.1
ip http server
!
line con 0
line vty 5 15
!
end

ALS1#
```

ALS2

```
ALS2#term len 0
ALS2#sh run
Building configuration...

Current configuration : 997 bytes
!
version 12.1
no service pad
service timestamps debug uptime
service timestamps log uptime
no service password-encryption
!
hostname ALS2
!
no logging console
!
ip subnet-zero
!
vtp domain hard
vtp mode transparent
!
spanning-tree mode pvst
no spanning-tree optimize bpdu transmission
spanning-tree extend system-id
!
vlan 200
!
interface FastEthernet0/1
!
interface FastEthernet0/2
!
interface FastEthernet0/3
!
interface FastEthernet0/4
!
interface FastEthernet0/5
!
interface FastEthernet0/6
!
```

```
interface FastEthernet0/7
 switchport access vlan 200
 switchport mode access
!
interface FastEthernet0/8
 shutdown
!
interface FastEthernet0/9
 shutdown
!
interface FastEthernet0/10
 shutdown
!
interface FastEthernet0/11
 shutdown
!
interface FastEthernet0/12
 shutdown
!
interface Vlan1
 no ip address
 no ip route-cache
 shutdown
!
interface Vlan200
 ip address 200.1.1.2 255.255.255.252
 no ip route-cache
!
ip default-gateway 200.1.1.1
ip http server
!
line con 0
line vty 5 15
!
end

ALS2#
```

CCNP LAB 5

DHCP, Source Guard and 802.1X

Lab Objective:

The focus of this lab is to understand how to implement and verify Cisco IOS DHCP features and security, IP Source Guard and IEEE 802.1X port-based security.

Lab Topology:

The lab network topology is illustrated below:

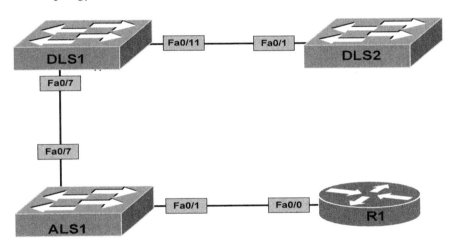

IMPORTANT NOTE: If you are using the www.howtonetwork.net racks, please begin each and every lab by shutting down all interfaces on all switches and then manually re-enabling only the interfaces that are illustrated in this topology.

Task 1

Disable VTP on all switches. All switches should support the configuration, modification and deletion of VLANs.

Task 2

Configure VLAN 100 on switches ALS1 and DLS1 and then configure SVI 100 on switch DLS1. This SVI should be assigned the address 100.1.1.1/24.

Configure VLAN 200 on switches DLS1 and DLS2 and then configure SVI 200 on switch DLS1 and DLS2. Assign these interfaces the IP addresses 200.1.1.1/30 and 200.1.1.2/30, respectively.

Task 3

Configure the ports between DLS1 and ALS1 and between ALS1 and R1 as access ports in VLAN 100. Next, configure the ports between the DLS1 and DLS2 as access ports in VLAN 100. Verify that DLS1 and DLS2 can ping each other across VLAN 200.

Task 4

Configure Cisco IOS DHCP Server functionality on switch DLS2 as follows:

- Network/Mask: 100.1.1.0/24
- Excluded Addresses: 100.1.1.1 - 100.1.1.5
- Default Gateway: 100.1.1.1
- Domain Name: howtonetwork.net
- Lease Expiration: 8 hours

Task 5

Configure Cisco IOS DHCP Relay Agent on switch DLS1. This should point to switch DLS2, which will be providing DHCP services for the 100.1.1.0/24 network.

Ensure that the network is appropriately configured so that the DHCP server can assign addresses to hosts on the 100.1.1.0/24 network.

Task 6

Configure DHCP Snooping on switch DLS1. The port connected to the DHCP server should be trusted. All other port should be considered untrusted. Enable IP Source Guard for VLAN 100.

Task 7

Configure router R1 to receive addressing via DHCP. Verify that DHCP Snooping and IP Source Guard are functioning correctly using the appropriate commands.

LAB VALIDATION

Task 1

```
DLS1(config)#vtp mode transparent
Setting device to VTP TRANSPARENT mode.

DLS2(config)#vtp mode transparent
Setting device to VTP TRANSPARENT mode.

ALS1(config)#vtp mode transparent
Setting device to VTP TRANSPARENT mode.

ALS2(config)#vtp mode transparent
Setting device to VTP TRANSPARENT mode.
```

Task 2

```
DLS1(config)#vlan 100
DLS1(config-vlan)#exit
DLS1(config)#vlan 200
DLS1(config-vlan)#exit
DLS1(config)#interface vlan 100
DLS1(config-if)#ip address 100.1.1.1 255.255.255.0
DLS1(config-if)#exit
DLS1(config)#interface vlan 200
DLS1(config-if)#ip address 200.1.1.1 255.255.255.252
DLS1(config-if)#exit
```

```
DLS2(config)#vlan 200
DLS2(config-vlan)#exit
DLS2(config)#interface vlan 200
DLS2(config-if)#ip address 200.1.1.2 255.255.255.252
DLS2(config-if)#exit

ALS1(config)#vlan 100
ALS1(config-vlan)#exit
```

Task 3

```
DLS1(config)#interface fastethernet 0/7
DLS1(config-if)#switchport mode access
DLS1(config-if)#switchport access vlan 100
DLS1(config-if)#exit
DLS1(config)#interface fastethernet0/11
DLS1(config-if)#switchport mode access
DLS1(config-if)#switchport access vlan 200
DLS1(config-if)#exit

DLS2(config)#interface fastethernet0/11
DLS2(config-if)#switchport mode access
DLS2(config-if)#switchport access vlan 200
DLS2(config-if)#exit

ALS1(config)#interface fastethernet 0/1
ALS1(config-if)#switchport mode access
ALS1(config-if)#switchport access vlan 100
ALS1(config-if)#exit
ALS1(config)#interface fastethernet 0/7
ALS1(config-if)#switchport mode access
ALS1(config-if)#switchport access vlan 100
ALS1(config-if)#exit
```

Finally, verify your configuration by pinging between switches DLS1 and DLS2:

```
DLS1#ping 200.1.1.2

Type escape sequence to abort.
Sending 5, 100-byte ICMP Echos to 200.1.1.2, timeout is 2 seconds:
.!!!!
Success rate is 80 percent (4/5), round-trip min/avg/max = 1/3/4 ms
```

Task 4

```
DLS2(config)#ip dhcp excluded-address 100.1.1.1 100.1.1.5
DLS2(config)#ip dhcp pool VLAN-100-POOL
DLS2(dhcp-config)#network 100.1.1.0 255.255.255.0
DLS2(dhcp-config)#default-router 100.1.1.1
DLS2(dhcp-config)#domain-name howtonetwork.net
DLS2(dhcp-config)#lease 0 8 0
DLS2(dhcp-config)#exit
```

Task 5

The first part of this task is straightforward and is completed as follows:

```
DLS1(config)#interface vlan 100
DLS1(config-if)#ip helper-address 200.1.1.2
DLS1(config-if)#exit
```

To complete the second part of the question, you need to ensure that switch DLS2 has IP reachability to the 100.1.1.0/24 subnet. Use either static routes or dynamic protocols. In this example, a simple default route pointing to switch DLS1 is configured on switch DLS2:

```
DLS2(config)#ip routing
DLS2(config)#ip route 0.0.0.0 0.0.0.0 vlan 200 200.1.1.1
```

Additionally, you need to enable IP routing on switch DLS1 (if not enabled by default)

```
DLS1(config)#ip routing
```

Following this, verify connectivity using a simple ping:

```
DLS2#ping 100.1.1.1

Type escape sequence to abort.
Sending 5, 100-byte ICMP Echos to 100.1.1.1, timeout is 2 seconds:
!!!!!
Success rate is 100 percent (5/5), round-trip min/avg/max = 4/4/4 ms
```

Task 6

This task requires a little thought. DHCP Snooping is required on VLANs 100 and 200. The port connected to switch DLS2 should be trusted because this is connected to the DHCP sever. All other ports should be considered untrusted. This task is completed on switch DLS1 as follows:

```
DLS1(config)#ip dhcp snooping
DLS1(config)#ip dhcp snooping vlan 100
DLS1(config)#ip dhcp snooping vlan 200
DLS1(config)#interface fastethernet 0/11
DLS1(config-if)#ip dhcp snooping trust
```

Verify DHCP Snooping configuration using the **show ip dhcp snooping** commands:

```
DLS1#show ip dhcp snooping
Switch DHCP snooping is enabled
DHCP snooping is configured on following VLANs:
100,200
DHCP snooping is operational on following VLANs:
100,200
DHCP snooping is configured on the following L3 Interfaces:

Insertion of option 82 is enabled
   circuit-id format: vlan-mod-port
    remote-id format: MAC
Option 82 on untrusted port is not allowed
Verification of hwaddr field is enabled
Verification of giaddr field is enabled
DHCP snooping trust/rate is configured on the following Interfaces:

Interface                   Trusted    Rate limit (pps)
-----------------------     -------    ----------------
FastEthernet0/11            yes        unlimited
```

The second part of this task is to enable IP Source Guard. IOS IP Source Guard is a feature that restricts IP traffic on untrusted Layer 2 ports by filtering the traffic based on the DHCP snooping binding database or manually configured IP source bindings.

This feature is used to prevent IP spoofing attacks. Any traffic coming into the interface with a source IP address other than that assigned via DHCP or static configuration will be filtered out on the untrusted Layer 2 ports. This task is completed as follows:

```
DLS1(config)#interface fastethernet 0/7
DLS1(config-if)#ip verify source
DLS1(config-if)#exit
```

Task 7

This task requires the router to be configured as DHCP client. This is completed as follows:

```
R1(config)#interface fastethernet 0/0
R1(config-if)#ip address dhcp
R1(config-if)#exit
```

```
R1(config)#
*Apr 10 01:33:28.183: %DHCP-6-ADDRESS_ASSIGN: Interface FastEthernet0/0 assigned DHCP
address 100.1.1.6, mask 255.255.255.0, hostname R1
```

Following successful DHCP assignment, verify DHCP Snooping configuration using the **show ip dhcp snooping** commands on switch DLS1:

```
DLS1#show ip dhcp snooping binding
MacAddress          IpAddress         Lease(sec)  Type           VLAN  Interface
------------------  ----------------  ----------  -------------  ----  ----------------
-----
00:0F:23:5E:EC:80   100.1.1.6         28602       dhcp-snooping  100
FastEthernet0/7
Total number of bindings: 1
```

Finally, verify IP Source Guard using the **show ip source binding** commands on switch DLS1:

```
DLS1#show ip source binding dhcp-snooping
MacAddress          IpAddress         Lease(sec)  Type           VLAN  Interface
------------------  ----------------  ----------  -------------  ----  ----------------
-----
00:0F:23:5E:EC:80   100.1.1.6         28421       dhcp-snooping  100
FastEthernet0/7
Total number of bindings: 1
```

FINAL SWITCH CONFIGURATIONS

DLS1

```
DLS1#term len 0
DLS1#sh run
Building configuration...

Current configuration : 4246 bytes
!
version 12.2
no service pad
service timestamps debug datetime msec
service timestamps log datetime msec
no service password-encryption
!
hostname DLS1
!
no logging console
!
no aaa new-model
ip subnet-zero
ip routing
no ip domain-lookup
!
ip dhcp snooping vlan 100,200
ip dhcp snooping
vtp domain hard
vtp mode transparent
!
spanning-tree mode pvst
spanning-tree extend system-id
!
vlan internal allocation policy ascending
!
vlan 100,200
!
interface FastEthernet0/1
 switchport mode dynamic desirable
 shutdown
!
interface FastEthernet0/2
 switchport mode dynamic desirable
 shutdown
!
interface FastEthernet0/3
```

```
 switchport mode dynamic desirable
 shutdown
!
interface FastEthernet0/4
 switchport mode dynamic desirable
 shutdown
!
interface FastEthernet0/5
 switchport mode dynamic desirable
 shutdown
!
interface FastEthernet0/6
 switchport mode dynamic desirable
 shutdown
!
interface FastEthernet0/7
 switchport access vlan 100
 switchport mode access
 ip verify source
!
interface FastEthernet0/8
 switchport mode dynamic desirable
 shutdown
!
interface FastEthernet0/9
 switchport mode dynamic desirable
 shutdown
!
interface FastEthernet0/10
 switchport mode dynamic desirable
 shutdown
!
interface FastEthernet0/11
 switchport access vlan 200
 switchport mode access
 ip dhcp snooping trust
!
interface FastEthernet0/12
 switchport mode dynamic desirable
 shutdown

[Truncated Output]

interface Vlan1
 no ip address
 shutdown
!
interface Vlan100
 ip address 100.1.1.1 255.255.255.0
 ip helper-address 200.1.1.2
!
interface Vlan200
 ip address 200.1.1.1 255.255.255.252
!
ip classless
ip http server
ip http secure-server
!
control-plane
!
line con 0
line vty 5 15
!
end

DLS1#
```

DLS2

```
DLS2#term len 0
DLS2#sh run
Building configuration...

Current configuration : 4287 bytes
!
version 12.2
no service pad
service timestamps debug datetime msec
service timestamps log datetime msec
```

```
no service password-encryption
!
hostname DLS2
!
no logging console
!
no aaa new-model
ip subnet-zero
ip routing
no ip domain-lookup
ip dhcp excluded-address 100.1.1.1 100.1.1.5
!
ip dhcp pool VLAN-100-POOL
   network 100.1.1.0 255.255.255.0
   default-router 100.1.1.1
   domain-name howtonetwork.net
   lease 0 8
!
vtp domain hard
vtp mode transparent
!
spanning-tree mode pvst
spanning-tree extend system-id
!
vlan internal allocation policy ascending
!
vlan 200
!
interface FastEthernet0/1
 switchport mode dynamic desirable
 shutdown
!
interface FastEthernet0/2
 switchport mode dynamic desirable
 shutdown
!
interface FastEthernet0/3
 switchport mode dynamic desirable
 shutdown
!
interface FastEthernet0/4
 switchport mode dynamic desirable
 shutdown
!
interface FastEthernet0/5
 switchport mode dynamic desirable
 shutdown
!
interface FastEthernet0/6
 switchport mode dynamic desirable
 shutdown
!
interface FastEthernet0/7
 switchport mode dynamic desirable
 shutdown
!
interface FastEthernet0/8
 switchport mode dynamic desirable
 shutdown
!
interface FastEthernet0/9
 switchport mode dynamic desirable
 shutdown
!
interface FastEthernet0/10
 switchport mode dynamic desirable
 shutdown
!
interface FastEthernet0/11
 switchport access vlan 200
 switchport mode access
!
interface FastEthernet0/12
 switchport mode dynamic desirable
 shutdown

[Truncated Output]

interface Vlan1
 no ip address
```

```
 shutdown
!
interface Vlan200
 ip address 200.1.1.2 255.255.255.252
!
ip classless
ip route 0.0.0.0 0.0.0.0 Vlan200 200.1.1.1
ip http server
ip http secure-server
!
control-plane
!
line con 0
line vty 5 15
!
end
DLS2#
```

ALS1

```
ALS1#term len 0
ALS1#sh run
Building configuration...

Current configuration : 993 bytes
!
version 12.1
no service pad
service timestamps debug uptime
service timestamps log uptime
no service password-encryption
!
hostname ALS1
!
no logging console
!
ip subnet-zero
!
vtp domain hard
vtp mode transparent
!
spanning-tree mode pvst
no spanning-tree optimize bpdu transmission
spanning-tree extend system-id
!
vlan 100
!
interface FastEthernet0/1
 switchport access vlan 100
 switchport mode access
!
interface FastEthernet0/2
 shutdown
!
interface FastEthernet0/3
 shutdown
!
interface FastEthernet0/4
 shutdown
!
interface FastEthernet0/5
 shutdown
!
interface FastEthernet0/6
 shutdown
!
interface FastEthernet0/7
 switchport access vlan 100
 switchport mode access
!
interface FastEthernet0/8
 shutdown
!
interface FastEthernet0/9
 shutdown
!
interface FastEthernet0/10
 shutdown
!
```

```
interface FastEthernet0/11
 shutdown
!
interface FastEthernet0/12
 shutdown
!
interface Vlan1
 no ip address
 no ip route-cache
 shutdown
!
ip http server
!
line con 0
line vty 5 15
!
end
ALS1#
```

FINAL ROUTER CONFIGURATIONS

R1

```
R1#term len 0
R1#sh run
Building configuration...

Current configuration : 742 bytes
!
version 12.4
service timestamps debug datetime msec
service timestamps log datetime msec
no service password-encryption
!
hostname R1
!
boot-start-marker
boot-end-marker
!
no aaa new-model
no network-clock-participate slot 1
no network-clock-participate wic 0
ip cef
!
no ip domain lookup
ip auth-proxy max-nodata-conns 3
ip admission max-nodata-conns 3
!
interface FastEthernet0/0
 ip address dhcp
 duplex auto
 speed auto
!
interface Serial0/0
 no ip address
 shutdown
!
interface Serial0/1
 no ip address
 shutdown
!
ip forward-protocol nd
!
no ip http server
no ip http secure-server
!
control-plane
!
line con 0
line aux 0
line vty 0 4
 login
!
end

R1#
```

CCNP LAB 6

HSRP and Switch Security

Lab Objective:

The focus of this lab is to understand basic HSRP and common security technology implementation and configuration in Cisco IOS Catalyst switches.

Lab Topology:

The lab network topology is illustrated below:

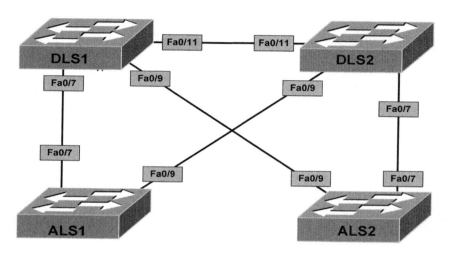

IMPORTANT NOTE: If you are using the www.howtonetwork.net racks, please begin each and every lab by shutting down all interfaces on all switches and then manually re-enabling only the interfaces that are illustrated in this topology.

Task 1

Disable VTP on all switches and create the following VLANs:
- DLS1: VLAN 100 and VLAN 200
- DLS2: VLAN 100 and VLAN 200
- ALS1: VLAN 100
- ALS2: VLAN 200

Task 2

Disable DTP and 802.1Q configure trunking on all switches as follows:
- The trunk links on switch DLS1 should only allow VLANs 1, 100 and 200
- The trunk links on switch DLS2 should only allow VLANs 1, 100 and 200
- The trunk links on switch ALS1 should only allow VLANs 1 and 100
- The trunk links on switch ALS2 should only allow VLANs 1 and 200

Task 3

Configure the following SVIs and interfaces on the switches in the topology:
- DLS1: Interface VLAN 100: IP address 100.1.1.1/24
- DLS1: Interface VLAN 200: IP address 200.1.1.1/24

- DLS2: Interface VLAN 100: IP address 100.1.1.2/24
- DLS2: Interface VLAN 200: IP address 200.1.1.2/24

- ALS1: Interface VLAN 100: IP address 100.1.1.3/24
- ALS2: Interface VLAN 100: IP address 200.1.1.3/24

Task 4

Configure Cisco HSRP version 1 with preemption on switches DLS1 and DLS2 as follows:
- DLS1: VLAN 100: HSRP IP address 100.1.1.254, group 1, priority 105, password HSRP1
- DLS1: VLAN 200: HSRP IP address 200.1.1.254, group 2, priority 100, password HSRP2

- DLS2: VLAN 100: HSRP IP address 100.1.1.254, group 1, priority 100, password HSRP1
- DLS2: VLAN 200: HSRP IP address 200.1.1.254, group 2, priority 105, password HSRP2

Task 5

To allow for faster convergence, enable RPVST+. In addition to this, ensure that your Layer 2 and Layer 3 topologies are consistent, i.e. the primary gateway should be the root for the corresponding VLAN. Finally, ensure that switches ALS1 and ALS2 can also ping each other.

Task 6

Configure port security on all trunk links on switches DLS1 and DLS2. The switch port security configuration should allow a maximum of 10 addresses. When this limit has been reached, the switch should drop packets with unknown MAC addresses, until the number is of MAC addresses is below the limit. Additionally, the switch should send out an SNMP trap and a Syslog message, and the violation counter should be incremented.

LAB VALIDATION

Task 1

```
DLS1(config)#vtp mode transparent
Setting device to VTP TRANSPARENT mode.
DLS1(config)#vlan 100
DLS1(config-vlan)#exit
DLS1(config)#vlan 200
DLS1(config-vlan)#exit

DLS2(config)#vtp mode transparent
Setting device to VTP TRANSPARENT mode.
DLS2(config)#vlan 100
DLS2(config-vlan)#exit
DLS2(config)#vlan 200
DLS2(config-vlan)#exit

ALS1(config)#vtp mode transparent
Setting device to VTP TRANSPARENT mode.
ALS1(config)#vlan 100
ALS1(config-vlan)#exit

ALS2(config)#vtp mode transparent
Setting device to VTP TRANSPARENT mode.
ALS2(config)#vlan 200
ALS2(config-vlan)#exit
```

Task 2

```
DLS1(config)#interface range fasteth 0/7 , fasteth 0/9 , fasteth 0/11
DLS1(config-if-range)#switchport
DLS1(config-if-range)#switchport trunk encapsulation dot1q
DLS1(config-if-range)#switchport mode trunk
DLS1(config-if-range)#switchport trunk allowed vlan 1,100,200
DLS1(config-if-range)#switchport nonegotiate
DLS1(config-if-range)#exit

DLS2(config)# interface range fasteth 0/7 , fasteth 0/9 , fasteth 0/11
DLS2(config-if-range)#switchport
DLS2(config-if-range)#switchport trunk encapsulation dot1q
DLS2(config-if-range)#switchport mode trunk
DLS2(config-if-range)#switchport trunk allowed vlan 1,100,200
DLS2(config-if-range)#switchport nonegotiate
DLS2(config-if-range)#exit

ALS1(config)#interface range fastethernet 0/7 , fastethernet 0/9
ALS1(config-if-range)#switchport mode trunk
ALS1(config-if-range)#switchport trunk allowed vlan 1,100
ALS1(config-if-range)#exit

ALS2(config)#interface range fastethernet 0/7 , fastethernet 0/9
ALS2(config-if-range)#switchport mode trunk
ALS2(config-if-range)#switchport trunk allowed vlan 1,200
ALS2(config-if-range)#exit
```

Verify your configuration using the **show interfaces trunk** command:

```
DLS1#show interfaces trunk
```

Port	Mode	Encapsulation	Status	Native vlan
Fa0/7	on	802.1q	trunking	1
Fa0/11	on	802.1q	trunking	1

Port	Vlans allowed on trunk
Fa0/7	1,100,200
Fa0/11	1,100,200

Port	Vlans allowed and active in management domain
Fa0/7	1,100,200
Fa0/11	1,100,200

Port	Vlans in spanning tree forwarding state and not pruned
Fa0/7	1,100,200
Fa0/11	200

Task 3

```
DLS1(config)#interface vlan 100
DLS1(config-if)#ip add 100.1.1.1 255.255.255.0
DLS1(config-if)#exit
DLS1(config)#interface vlan 200
DLS1(config-if)#ip add 200.1.1.1 255.255.255.0
DLS1(config-if)#exit

DLS2(config)#interface vlan 100
DLS2(config-if)#ip address 100.1.1.2 255.255.255.0
DLS2(config-if)#exit
DLS2(config)#interface vlan 200
DLS2(config-if)#ip address 200.1.1.2 255.255.255.0
DLS2(config-if)#exit

ALS1(config)#interface vlan 100
ALS1(config-if)#ip add 100.1.1.3 255.255.255.0
ALS1(config-if)#exit

ALS2(config)#interface vlan 200
ALS2(config-if)#ip address 200.1.1.3 255.255.255.0
ALS2(config-if)#exit
```

Task 4

When completing this task, keep in mind that the default priority value for HSRP is 100 and so no explicit configuration is required to specify this value. However, unlike VRRP, preemption for HSRP is disabled by default and must be explicitly configured. Additionally, by default, when HSRP is enabled, version 1 is enabled. This task is completed as follows:

```
DLS1(config)#interface vlan 100
DLS1(config-if)#standby 1 ip 100.1.1.254
DLS1(config-if)#standby 1 priority 105
DLS1(config-if)#standby 1 preempt
DLS1(config-if)#standby 1 authentication text HSRP1
DLS1(config-if)#exit
DLS1(config)#interface vlan 200
DLS1(config-if)#standby 2 ip 200.1.1.254
DLS1(config-if)#standby 2 preempt
DLS1(config-if)#standby 2 authentication text HSRP2
DLS1(config-if)#exit

DLS2(config)#interface vlan 100
DLS2(config-if)#standby 1 ip 100.1.1.254
DLS2(config-if)#standby 1 preempt
DLS2(config-if)#standby 1 authentication text HSRP1
DLS2(config-if)#exit
DLS2(config)#interface vlan 200
DLS2(config-if)#standby 2 ip 200.1.1.254
DLS2(config-if)#standby 2 priority 105
DLS2(config-if)#standby 2 preempt
DLS2(config-if)#standby 2 authentication text HSRP2
DLS2(config-if)#exit
```

Next, although not explicitly stated, configure the default gateway for switches ALS1 and ALS2 as the HSRP virtual IP (VIP) address so that they can reach other.

```
ALS1(config)#ip default-gateway 100.1.1.254

ALS2(config)#ip default-gateway 200.1.1.254
```

Verify your configuration using the **show standby** commands on switches DLS1 and DLS2:

```
DLS1#show stand brief
                  P indicates configured to preempt.
                  |
Interface Grp Prio P State    Active     Standby      Virtual IP
Vl100     1   105  P Active   local      100.1.1.2    100.1.1.254
Vl200     2   100  P Standby  200.1.1.2  local        200.1.1.254

DLS2#show standby
Vlan100 - Group 1
  State is Standby
    9 state changes, last state change 00:01:42
  Virtual IP address is 100.1.1.254
  Active virtual MAC address is 0000.0c07.ac01
    Local virtual MAC address is 0000.0c07.ac01 (v1 default)
  Hello time 3 sec, hold time 10 sec
    Next hello sent in 2.620 secs
  Authentication text "HSRP1"
  Preemption enabled
  Active router is 100.1.1.1, priority 105 (expires in 8.612 sec)
  Standby router is local
  Priority 100 (default 100)
  IP redundancy name is "hsrp-Vl100-1" (default)
Vlan200 - Group 2
  State is Active
    5 state changes, last state change 00:14:18
  Virtual IP address is 200.1.1.254
  Active virtual MAC address is 0000.0c07.ac02
    Local virtual MAC address is 0000.0c07.ac02 (v1 default)
  Hello time 3 sec, hold time 10 sec
    Next hello sent in 0.244 secs
```

```
Authentication text "HSRP2"
Preemption enabled
Active router is local
Standby router is 200.1.1.1, priority 100 (expires in 9.836 sec)
Priority 105 (configured 105)
IP redundancy name is "hsrp-Vl200-2" (default)
```

Task 5

The first part of this task is simple. RPVST+ is enabled on all switches as follows:

```
DLS1(config)#spanning-tree mode rapid-pvst
```

```
DLS2(config)#spanning-tree mode rapid-pvst
```

```
ALS1(config)#spanning-tree mode rapid-pvst
```

```
ALS2(config)#spanning-tree mode rapid-pvst
```

The second part of this task entails adjusting the default root bridges for the respective VLANs. Given that switch DLS1 is primary gateway for VLAN 100, it should be root for that VLAN. Given that switch DLS2 is primary gateway for VLAN 200, it should be root for that VLAN. These two switches should be configured as the secondary or backup root bridge for the other VLAN. This task is completed as follows:

```
DLS1(config)#spanning-tree vlan 100 priority 4096
DLS1(config)#spanning-tree vlan 200 priority 8192
```

```
DLS2(config)#spanning-tree vlan 100 priority 8192
DLS2(config)#spanning-tree vlan 200 priority 4096
```

Following this, verify your configuration using the **show spanning-tree** commands:

```
DLS1#show spanning-tree summary
Switch is in rapid-pvst mode
Root bridge for: VLAN0100
Extended system ID            is enabled
Portfast Default              is disabled
PortFast BPDU Guard Default   is disabled
Portfast BPDU Filter Default  is disabled
Loopguard Default             is disabled
EtherChannel misconfig guard  is enabled
UplinkFast                    is disabled
BackboneFast                  is disabled
Configured Pathcost method used is short

Name                  Blocking Listening Learning Forwarding STP Active
--------------------- -------- --------- -------- ---------- ----------
VLAN0001                 1         0         0         1          2
VLAN0100                 0         0         0         2          2
VLAN0200                 0         0         0         2          2
--------------------- -------- --------- -------- ---------- ----------
3 vlans                  1         0         0         5          6

DLS2#show spanning-tree summary
Switch is in rapid-pvst mode
Root bridge for: VLAN0200
Extended system ID            is enabled
Portfast Default              is disabled
PortFast BPDU Guard Default   is disabled
Portfast BPDU Filter Default  is disabled
Loopguard Default             is disabled
EtherChannel misconfig guard  is enabled
UplinkFast                    is disabled
BackboneFast                  is disabled
Configured Pathcost method used is short

Name                  Blocking Listening Learning Forwarding STP Active
--------------------- -------- --------- -------- ---------- ----------
```

```
VLAN0001                    0          0          0          2          2
VLAN0100                    0          0          0          2          2
VLAN0200                    0          0          0          2          2
----------------------  --------   --------   --------   ----------  ----------
3 vlans                     0          0          0          6          6
```

The final task calls for verifying that switches ALS1 and ALS2 can ping each other:

```
ALS1#ping 200.1.1.2

Type escape sequence to abort.
Sending 5, 100-byte ICMP Echos to 200.1.1.2, timeout is 2 seconds:
!!!!!
Success rate is 100 percent (5/5), round-trip min/avg/max = 1/1/4 ms

ALS2#ping 100.1.1.2

Type escape sequence to abort.
Sending 5, 100-byte ICMP Echos to 100.1.1.2, timeout is 2 seconds:
!!!!!
Success rate is 100 percent (5/5), round-trip min/avg/max = 4/4/4 ms
```

Task 6

```
DLS1(config)#interface range fasteth 0/7 , fasteth 0/9 , fasteth 0/11
DLS1(config-if-range)#switchport port-security
DLS1(config-if-range)#switchport port-security maximum 10
DLS1(config-if-range)#switchport port-security violation restrict
DLS1(config-if-range)#switchport port-security mac-address sticky
DLS1(config-if-range)#exit

DLS2(config)#interface range fasteth 0/7 , fasteth 0/9 , fasteth 0/11
DLS2(config-if-range)#switchport port-security
DLS2(config-if-range)#switchport port-security maximum 10
DLS2(config-if-range)#switchport port-security violation restrict
DLS2(config-if-range)#switchport port-security mac-address sticky
DLS2(config-if-range)#exit
```

Following this configuration, use the **show port-security** commands for verification:

```
DLS1#show port-security
Secure Port  MaxSecureAddr  CurrentAddr  SecurityViolation  Security Action
             (Count)        (Count)      (Count)
----------------------------------------------------------------------------
     Fa0/7        10             0                1              Restrict
     Fa0/9        10             0                1              Restrict
    Fa0/11        10             0                1              Restrict
----------------------------------------------------------------------------
Total Addresses in System (excluding one mac per port)    : 0
Max Addresses limit in System (excluding one mac per port) : 5120

DLS2#show port-security
Secure Port  MaxSecureAddr  CurrentAddr  SecurityViolation  Security Action
             (Count)        (Count)      (Count)
----------------------------------------------------------------------------
     Fa0/7        10             1                0              Restrict
     Fa0/9        10             1                0              Restrict
    Fa0/11        10             0                0              Restrict
----------------------------------------------------------------------------
Total Addresses in System (excluding one mac per port)    : 0
Max Addresses limit in System (excluding one mac per port) : 5120
```

FINAL SWITCH CONFIGURATIONS

DLS1

```
DLS1#term len 0
DLS1#show ru
Building configuration...

Current configuration : 5074 bytes
!
version 12.2
no service pad
service timestamps debug datetime msec
service timestamps log datetime msec
no service password-encryption
!
hostname DLS1
!
no logging console
!
no aaa new-model
ip subnet-zero
ip routing
no ip domain-lookup
!
vtp domain hard
vtp mode transparent
!
spanning-tree mode rapid-pvst
spanning-tree extend system-id
spanning-tree vlan 100 priority 4096
spanning-tree vlan 200 priority 8192
!
vlan internal allocation policy ascending
!
vlan 100,200
!
interface FastEthernet0/1
 switchport mode dynamic desirable
 shutdown
!
interface FastEthernet0/2
 switchport mode dynamic desirable
 shutdown
!
interface FastEthernet0/3
 switchport mode dynamic desirable
 shutdown
!
interface FastEthernet0/4
 switchport mode dynamic desirable
 shutdown
!
interface FastEthernet0/5
 switchport mode dynamic desirable
 shutdown
!
interface FastEthernet0/6
 switchport mode dynamic desirable
 shutdown
!
interface FastEthernet0/7
 switchport trunk encapsulation dot1q
 switchport trunk allowed vlan 1,100,200
 switchport mode trunk
 switchport nonegotiate
 switchport port-security maximum 10
 switchport port-security
 switchport port-security violation restrict
 switchport port-security mac-address sticky
!
interface FastEthernet0/8
 switchport mode dynamic desirable
 shutdown
!
interface FastEthernet0/9
 switchport trunk encapsulation dot1q
 switchport trunk allowed vlan 1,100,200
```

```
 switchport mode trunk
 switchport nonegotiate
 switchport port-security maximum 10
 switchport port-security
 switchport port-security violation restrict
 switchport port-security mac-address sticky
!
interface FastEthernet0/10
 switchport mode dynamic desirable
 shutdown
!
interface FastEthernet0/11
 switchport trunk encapsulation dot1q
 switchport trunk allowed vlan 1,100,200
 switchport mode trunk
 switchport nonegotiate
 switchport port-security maximum 10
 switchport port-security
 switchport port-security violation restrict
 switchport port-security mac-address sticky
!
interface FastEthernet0/12
 switchport mode dynamic desirable
 shutdown

[Truncated Output]

interface Vlan1
 no ip address
 shutdown
!
interface Vlan100
 ip address 100.1.1.1 255.255.255.0
 standby 1 ip 100.1.1.254
 standby 1 priority 105
 standby 1 preempt
 standby 1 authentication HSRP1
!
interface Vlan200
 ip address 200.1.1.1 255.255.255.0
 standby 2 ip 200.1.1.254
 standby 2 preempt
 standby 2 authentication HSRP2
!
ip classless
ip http server
ip http secure-server
!
control-plane
!
line con 0
line vty 5 15
!
end
DLS1#
```

DLS2

```
DLS2#term len 0
DLS2#sh run
Building configuration...

Current configuration : 5194 bytes
!
version 12.2
no service pad
service timestamps debug datetime msec
service timestamps log datetime msec
no service password-encryption
!
hostname DLS2
!
no logging console
!
no aaa new-model
ip subnet-zero
ip routing
no ip domain-lookup
```

```
!
vtp domain hard
vtp mode transparent
!
spanning-tree mode rapid-pvst
spanning-tree extend system-id
spanning-tree vlan 100 priority 8192
spanning-tree vlan 200 priority 4096
!
vlan internal allocation policy ascending
!
vlan 100,200
!
interface FastEthernet0/1
 switchport mode dynamic desirable
 shutdown
!
interface FastEthernet0/2
 switchport mode dynamic desirable
 shutdown
!
interface FastEthernet0/3
 switchport mode dynamic desirable
 shutdown
!
interface FastEthernet0/4
 switchport mode dynamic desirable
 shutdown
!
interface FastEthernet0/5
 switchport mode dynamic desirable
 shutdown
!
interface FastEthernet0/6
 switchport mode dynamic desirable
 shutdown
!
interface FastEthernet0/7
 switchport trunk encapsulation dot1q
 switchport trunk allowed vlan 1,100,200
 switchport mode trunk
 switchport nonegotiate
 switchport port-security maximum 10
 switchport port-security
 switchport port-security violation restrict
 switchport port-security mac-address sticky
 switchport port-security mac-address sticky 0009.b79f.7d87
!
interface FastEthernet0/8
 switchport mode dynamic desirable
 shutdown
!
interface FastEthernet0/9
 switchport trunk encapsulation dot1q
 switchport trunk allowed vlan 1,100,200
 switchport mode trunk
 switchport nonegotiate
 switchport port-security maximum 10
 switchport port-security
 switchport port-security violation restrict
 switchport port-security mac-address sticky
 switchport port-security mac-address sticky 0007.8432.dd09
!
interface FastEthernet0/10
 switchport mode dynamic desirable
 shutdown
!
interface FastEthernet0/11
 switchport trunk encapsulation dot1q
 switchport trunk allowed vlan 1,100,200
 switchport mode trunk
 switchport nonegotiate
 switchport port-security maximum 10
 switchport port-security
 switchport port-security violation restrict
 switchport port-security mac-address sticky
!
interface FastEthernet0/12
 switchport mode dynamic desirable
```

```
 shutdown
!

[Truncated Output]

interface Vlan1
 no ip address
 shutdown
!
interface Vlan100
 ip address 100.1.1.2 255.255.255.0
 standby 1 ip 100.1.1.254
 standby 1 preempt
 standby 1 authentication HSRP1
!
interface Vlan200
 ip address 200.1.1.2 255.255.255.0
 standby 2 ip 200.1.1.254
 standby 2 priority 105
 standby 2 preempt
 standby 2 authentication HSRP2
!
ip classless
ip http server
ip http secure-server
!
control-plane
!
line con 0
line vty 5 15
!
end
DLS2#
```

ALS1

```
ALS1>en
ALS1#term len 0
ALS1#sh run
Building configuration...

Current configuration : 1143 bytes
!
version 12.1
no service pad
service timestamps debug uptime
service timestamps log uptime
no service password-encryption
!
hostname ALS1
!
no logging console
!
ip subnet-zero
!
no ip domain-lookup
vtp domain hard
vtp mode transparent
!
!
spanning-tree mode rapid-pvst
no spanning-tree optimize bpdu transmission
spanning-tree extend system-id
!
vlan 100
!
interface FastEthernet0/1
 shutdown
!
interface FastEthernet0/2
 shutdown
!
interface FastEthernet0/3
 shutdown
!
interface FastEthernet0/4
 shutdown
!
```

```
interface FastEthernet0/5
 shutdown
!
interface FastEthernet0/6
 shutdown
!
interface FastEthernet0/7
 switchport trunk allowed vlan 1,100
 switchport mode trunk
!
interface FastEthernet0/8
 shutdown
!
interface FastEthernet0/9
 switchport trunk allowed vlan 1,100
 switchport mode trunk
!
interface FastEthernet0/10
 shutdown
!
interface FastEthernet0/11
 shutdown
!
interface FastEthernet0/12
 shutdown
!
interface Vlan1
 no ip address
 no ip route-cache
 shutdown
!
interface Vlan100
 ip address 100.1.1.3 255.255.255.0
 no ip route-cache
!
ip default-gateway 100.1.1.254
ip http server
!
line con 0
line vty 5 15
!
end

ALS1#
```

ALS2

```
ALS2>en
ALS2#term len 0
ALS2#sh run
Building configuration...

Current configuration : 1143 bytes
!
version 12.1
no service pad
service timestamps debug uptime
service timestamps log uptime
no service password-encryption
!
hostname ALS2
!
no logging console
!
ip subnet-zero
!
no ip domain-lookup
vtp domain hard
vtp mode transparent
!
!
spanning-tree mode rapid-pvst
no spanning-tree optimize bpdu transmission
spanning-tree extend system-id
!
vlan 200
!
interface FastEthernet0/1
```

```
 shutdown
!
interface FastEthernet0/2
 shutdown
!
interface FastEthernet0/3
 shutdown
!
interface FastEthernet0/4
 shutdown
!
interface FastEthernet0/5
 shutdown
!
interface FastEthernet0/6
 shutdown
!
interface FastEthernet0/7
 switchport trunk allowed vlan 1,200
 switchport mode trunk
!
interface FastEthernet0/8
 shutdown
!
interface FastEthernet0/9
 switchport trunk allowed vlan 1,200
 switchport mode trunk
!
interface FastEthernet0/10
 shutdown
!
interface FastEthernet0/11
 shutdown
!
interface FastEthernet0/12
 shutdown
!
interface Vlan1
 no ip address
 no ip route-cache
 shutdown
!
interface Vlan200
 ip address 200.1.1.3 255.255.255.0
 no ip route-cache
!
ip default-gateway 200.1.1.254
ip http server
!
line con 0
line vty 5 15
!
end

ALS2#
```

CCNP LAB 7

HRRP and STP Convergence

Lab Objective:

The focus of this lab is to understand basic HSRP and STP convergence tweaking implementation and configuration in Cisco IOS Catalyst switches.

Lab Topology:

The lab network topology is illustrated below:

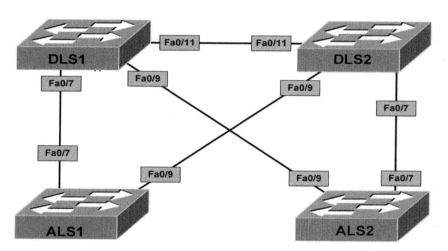

IMPORTANT NOTE: If you are using the www.howtonetwork.net racks, please begin each and every lab by shutting down all interfaces on all switches and then manually re-enabling only the interfaces that are illustrated in this topology.

Task 1

Disable VTP on all switches and create the following VLANs:
- DLS1: VLAN 100 and VLAN 200
- DLS2: VLAN 100 and VLAN 200
- ALS1: VLAN 100
- ALS2: VLAN 200

Task 2

Disable DTP and configure trunking on all switches as follows:
- The trunk links on switch DLS1 should only allow VLANs 1, 100 and 200
- The trunk links on switch DLS2 should only allow VLANs 1, 100 and 200
- The trunk links on switch ALS1 should only allow VLANs 1 and 100
- The trunk links on switch ALS2 should only allow VLANs 1 and 200

Task 3

Configure the following SVIs and interfaces on the switches in the topology:
- DLS1: Interface VLAN 100: IP address 100.1.1.1/24
- DLS1: Interface VLAN 200: IP address 200.1.1.1/24
- DLS1: Interface Loopback0: IP address 192.1.1.1/24

- DLS2: Interface VLAN 100: IP address 100.1.1.2/24
- DLS2: Interface VLAN 200: IP address 200.1.1.2/24

- ALS1: Interface VLAN 100: IP address 100.1.1.3/24
- ALS2: Interface VLAN 100: IP address 200.1.1.3/24

Task 4

Configure HSRP with preemption and MD5 authentication on DLS1 and DLS2 as follows:
- DLS1: VLAN 100: HSRP IP address 100.1.1.254, group 1, priority 200, MD5 password: ONE
- DLS1: VLAN 200: HSRP IP address 200.1.1.254, group 2, priority 200, MD5 password: TWO

- DLS2: VLAN 100: HSRP IP address 100.1.1.254, group 1, priority 150, MD5 password: ONE
- DLS2: VLAN 200: HSRP IP address 200.1.1.254, group 2, priority 150 MD5 password: TWO

Task 5

In the future, switch DLS1 will be configured to track an uplink port to the WAN routers. To test this solution, configure HSRP on switch DLS1 to track the Loopback0 interface. Should Loopback0 be shut down, ensure switch DLS2 becomes the active gateway for both groups.

Task 6

To allow for faster 802.1D convergence, configure the lowest possible diameter that will allow all devices in the network to communicate. In addition to this, ensure that your Layer 2 and Layer 3 topologies are consistent, i.e. the primary gateway should be the root for the corresponding VLAN. Finally, ensure that switches ALS1 and ALS2 can also ping each other.

LAB VALIDATION

Task 1

```
DLS1(config)#vtp mode transparent
Setting device to VTP TRANSPARENT mode.
DLS1(config)#vlan 100
DLS1(config-vlan)#exit
DLS1(config)#vlan 200
DLS1(config-vlan)#exit

DLS2(config)#vtp mode transparent
Setting device to VTP TRANSPARENT mode.
DLS2(config)#vlan 100
DLS2(config-vlan)#exit
DLS2(config)#vlan 200
DLS2(config-vlan)#exit

ALS1(config)#vtp mode transparent
Setting device to VTP TRANSPARENT mode.
ALS1(config)#vlan 100
ALS1(config-vlan)#exit

ALS2(config)#vtp mode transparent
Setting device to VTP TRANSPARENT mode.
ALS2(config)#vlan 200
ALS2(config-vlan)#exit
```

Task 2

```
DLS1(config)#interface range fasteth 0/7 , fasteth 0/9 , fasteth 0/11
DLS1(config-if-range)#switchport
DLS1(config-if-range)#switchport trunk encapsulation dot1q
DLS1(config-if-range)#switchport mode trunk
DLS1(config-if-range)#switchport trunk allowed vlan 1,100,200
DLS1(config-if-range)#switchport nonegotiate
DLS1(config-if-range)#exit

DLS2(config)# interface range fasteth 0/7 , fasteth 0/9 , fasteth 0/11
DLS2(config-if-range)#switchport
DLS2(config-if-range)#switchport trunk encapsulation dot1q
DLS2(config-if-range)#switchport mode trunk
DLS2(config-if-range)#switchport trunk allowed vlan 1,100,200
DLS2(config-if-range)#switchport nonegotiate
DLS2(config-if-range)#exit

ALS1(config)#interface range fastethernet 0/7 , fastethernet 0/9
ALS1(config-if-range)#switchport mode trunk
ALS1(config-if-range)#switchport trunk allowed vlan 1,100
ALS1(config-if-range)#exit

ALS2(config)#interface range fastethernet 0/7 , fastethernet 0/9
ALS2(config-if-range)#switchport mode trunk
ALS2(config-if-range)#switchport trunk allowed vlan 1,200
ALS2(config-if-range)#exit
```

Verify your configuration using the **show interfaces trunk** command:

```
ALS2#show interfaces trunk

Port        Mode          Encapsulation   Status      Native vlan
Fa0/7       on            802.1q          trunking    1
Fa0/9       on            802.1q          trunking    1

Port        Vlans allowed on trunk
Fa0/7       1,200
Fa0/9       1,200

Port        Vlans allowed and active in management domain
Fa0/7       1,200
Fa0/9       1,200

Port        Vlans in spanning tree forwarding state and not pruned
Fa0/7       1,200
Fa0/9       200
```

Task 3

```
DLS1(config)#interface vlan 100
DLS1(config-if)#ip add 100.1.1.1 255.255.255.0
DLS1(config-if)#exit
DLS1(config)#interface vlan 200
DLS1(config-if)#ip add 200.1.1.1 255.255.255.0
DLS1(config-if)#exit
DLS1(config)#int  loopback 0
DLS1(config-if)#ip add 192.1.1.1 255.255.255.0
DLS1(config-if)#exit

DLS2(config)#interface vlan 100
DLS2(config-if)#ip address 100.1.1.2 255.255.255.0
DLS2(config-if)#exit
DLS2(config)#interface vlan 200
DLS2(config-if)#ip address 200.1.1.2 255.255.255.0
DLS2(config-if)#exit

ALS1(config)#interface vlan 100
ALS1(config-if)#ip add 100.1.1.3 255.255.255.0
ALS1(config-if)#exit
```

```
ALS2(config)#interface vlan 200
ALS2(config-if)#ip address 200.1.1.3 255.255.255.0
ALS2(config-if)#exit
```

Task 4

When configuring HSRP MD5 authentication, you can reference a key chain, which contains the keys and key strings, or specify the key string directly with the HSRP configuration. Both methods are illustrated. The configuration on switch DLS1 has been implemented as follows:

```
DLS1(config)#key chain HSRP-GROUP-ONE
DLS1(config-keychain)#key 1
DLS1(config-keychain-key)#key-string ONE
DLS1(config-keychain-key)#exit
DLS1(config)#interface vlan 100
DLS1(config-if)#standby 1 ip 100.1.1.254
DLS1(config-if)#standby 1 priority 200
DLS1(config-if)#standby 1 preempt
DLS1(config-if)#standby 1 authentication md5 key-chain HSRP-GROUP-ONE
DLS1(config-if)#exit
DLS1(config)#interface vlan 200
DLS1(config-if)#standby 2 ip 200.1.1.254
DLS1(config-if)#standby 2  priority 200
DLS1(config-if)#standby 2 preempt
DLS1(config-if)#standby 2 authentication md5 key-string TWO
DLS1(config-if)#exit
```

The configuration on switch DLS1 has been implemented as follows:

```
DLS2(config)#key chain HSRP-GROUP-ONE
DLS2(config-keychain)#key 1
DLS2(config-keychain-key)#key-string ONE
DLS2(config-keychain-key)#exit
DLS2(config)#interface vlan 100
DLS2(config-if)#standby 1 ip 100.1.1.254
DLS2(config-if)#standby 1 preempt
DLS2(config-if)#standby 1 priority 150
DLS2(config-if)#standby 1 authentication md5 key-chain HSRP-GROUP-ONE
DLS2(config-if)#exit
DLS2(config)#interface vlan 200
DLS2(config-if)#standby 2 ip 200.1.1.254
DLS2(config-if)#standby 2 preempt
DLS2(config-if)#standby 2 priority 150
DLS2(config-if)#standby 2 authentication md5 key-string TWO
DLS2(config-if)#exit
```

Following this configuration, use the **show standby** commands to verify HSRP:

```
DLS1#show standby brief
                     P indicates configured to preempt.
                     |
Interface   Grp Prio P State    Active      Standby       Virtual IP
Vl100       1   200  P Active   local       100.1.1.2     100.1.1.254
Vl200       2   200  P Active   local       200.1.1.2     200.1.1.254

DLS2#show standby
Vlan100 - Group 1
  State is Standby
    4 state changes, last state change 00:01:46
  Virtual IP address is 100.1.1.254
  Active virtual MAC address is 0000.0c07.ac01
    Local virtual MAC address is 0000.0c07.ac01 (v1 default)
  Hello time 3 sec, hold time 10 sec
    Next hello sent in 1.776 secs
  Authentication MD5, key-chain "HSRP-GROUP-ONE"
  Preemption enabled
  Active router is 100.1.1.1, priority 200 (expires in 7.776 sec)
  Standby router is local
  Priority 150 (configured 150)
  IP redundancy name is "hsrp-Vl100-1" (default)
Vlan200 - Group 2
```

```
   State is Standby
     4 state changes, last state change 00:03:23
   Virtual IP address is 200.1.1.254
   Active virtual MAC address is 0000.0c07.ac02
     Local virtual MAC address is 0000.0c07.ac02 (v1 default)
   Hello time 3 sec, hold time 10 sec
     Next hello sent in 0.828 secs
   Authentication MD5, key-string "TWO"
   Preemption enabled
   Active router is 200.1.1.1, priority 200 (expires in 8.452 sec)
   Standby router is local
   Priority 150 (configured 150)
   IP redundancy name is "hsrp-Vl200-2" (default)
```

Task 5

To complete this task, you need to configure HSRP tracking so that the priority of switch DLS1 is decremented to a value less than 150 when Loopback0 is disabled - allowing switch DLS2 to assume primary gateway functionality. This task is completed as follows:

```
DLS1(config)#track 500 interface loopback 0 line-protocol
DLS1(config-track)#exit
DLS1(config)#interface vlan 100
DLS1(config-if)#standby 1 track 500 decrement 51
DLS1(config-if)#exit
DLS1(config)#interface vlan 200
DLS1(config-if)#standby 2 track 500 decrement 51
DLS1(config-if)#exit
```

Following this configuration, use the show track command to verify object tracking:

```
DLS1#show track 500
Track 500
   Interface Loopback0 line-protocol
   Line protocol is Up
     1 change, last change 00:01:51
   Tracked by:
     HSRP Vlan100 1
     HSRP Vlan200 2
```

Additionally, use the **show standby** commands to verify HSRP tracking configuration:

```
DLS1#show standby vlan 100
Vlan100 - Group 1
   State is Active
     2 state changes, last state change 00:22:23
   Virtual IP address is 100.1.1.254
   Active virtual MAC address is 0000.0c07.ac01
     Local virtual MAC address is 0000.0c07.ac01 (v1 default)
   Hello time 3 sec, hold time 10 sec
     Next hello sent in 0.908 secs
   Authentication MD5, key-chain "HSRP-GROUP-ONE"
   Preemption enabled
   Active router is local
   Standby router is 100.1.1.2, priority 150 (expires in 8.900 sec)
   Priority 200 (configured 200)
     Track object 500 state Up decrement 51
   IP redundancy name is "hsrp-Vl100-1" (default)
```

Test the configuration by shutting down the Loopback0 interface on switch DLS1:

```
DLS1(config)#interface loopback 0
DLS1(config-if)#shutdown
DLS1(config-if)#
*Mar  1 00:51:16.799: %HSRP-5-STATECHANGE: Vlan200 Grp 2 state Active -> Speak
*Mar  1 00:51:17.159: %HSRP-5-STATECHANGE: Vlan100 Grp 1 state Active -> Speak
*Mar  1 00:51:18.627: %LINK-5-CHANGED: Interface Loopback0, changed state to
administratively down
*Mar  1 00:51:19.627: %LINEPROTO-5-UPDOWN: Line protocol on Interface Loopback0,
changed state to down
*Mar  1 00:51:26.799: %HSRP-5-STATECHANGE: Vlan200 Grp 2 state Speak -> Standby
*Mar  1 00:51:27.159: %HSRP-5-STATECHANGE: Vlan100 Grp 1 state Speak -> Standby
```

Again, the **show standby** commands can be used to verify HSRP tracking configuration:

```
DLS1#show standby vlan 100
Vlan100 - Group 1
  State is Standby
    4 state changes, last state change 00:01:07
  Virtual IP address is 100.1.1.254
  Active virtual MAC address is 0000.0c07.ac01
    Local virtual MAC address is 0000.0c07.ac01 (v1 default)
  Hello time 3 sec, hold time 10 sec
    Next hello sent in 1.716 secs
  Authentication MD5, key-chain "HSRP-GROUP-ONE"
  Preemption enabled
  Active router is 100.1.1.2, priority 150 (expires in 7.720 sec)
  Standby router is local
  Priority 149 (configured 200)
    Track object 500 state Down decrement 51
  IP redundancy name is "hsrp-Vl100-1" (default)
```

The **show track** command can be used to determine the state of the tracked object:

```
DLS1#show track
Track 500
  Interface Loopback0 line-protocol
  Line protocol is Down (hw admin-down)
    2 changes, last change 00:01:42
  Tracked by:
    HSRP Vlan100 1
    HSRP Vlan200 2
```

Task 6

Given the topology, the maximum diameter in any given situation would be 4. There are two ways the diameter can be influenced. These two methods are:

- Manually configuring STP parameters to force a diameter of 4
- Using the Cisco IOS macro to specify the diameter

The first method entails performing manual calculations using one of the following formulas:
Diameter = (Max Age + 2 - (4 * Hello)) / 2 or **Diameter = ((2 * Forward Delay) - (4 * Hello)) / 3**

The second method entails using the Cisco IOS macro, enabled by issuing the **spanning-tree vlan <number> root primary diameter <2-7>** global configuration command. The simplest method is to use the IOS macro on switch DLS1 which will be the root bridge for both VLANs.

```
DLS1(config)#spanning-tree vlan 100 root primary diameter 4
DLS1(config)#spanning-tree vlan 200 root primary diameter 4
```

When the diameter is changed, default STP timers are also adjusted. Use the **show spanning-tree** commands to verify the configuration:

```
DLS1#show spanning-tree vlan 100

VLAN0100
  Spanning tree enabled protocol ieee
  Root ID    Priority    24676
             Address     000f.2303.2d80
             This bridge is the root
             Hello Time   2 sec  Max Age 14 sec  Forward Delay 10 sec

  Bridge ID  Priority    24676  (priority 24576 sys-id-ext 100)
             Address     000f.2303.2d80
             Hello Time   2 sec  Max Age 14 sec  Forward Delay 10 sec
             Aging Time 300

Interface           Role Sts Cost      Prio.Nbr Type
------------------- ---- --- --------- -------- ----------------------------
Fa0/7               Desg FWD 19        128.7    P2p
```

```
Fa0/9          Desg FWD 19        128.9    P2p
Fa0/11         Desg FWD 19        128.11   P2p
```

Using the manual method, we could confirm this calculation as follows:
- Diameter = (Max Age + 2 - (4 * Hello)) / 2
- Diameter = (14 + 2 - (4 * 2)) / 2
- Diameter = (16 - 8)) / 2
- Diameter = (8)) / 2
- Diameter = 4

The same result would be obtained using the alternate formula.

The final task is to ensure that switches ALS1 and ALS2 can ping each other. This requires that both switches be configured with default gateways (HSRP VIPs).

```
ALS1(config)#ip default-gateway 100.1.1.254

ALS2(config)#ip default-gateway 200.1.1.254
```

Finally, verify connectivity using a simple ping:

```
ALS1#ping 200.1.1.2

Type escape sequence to abort.
Sending 5, 100-byte ICMP Echos to 200.1.1.2, timeout is 2 seconds:
..!!!
Success rate is 60 percent (3/5), round-trip min/avg/max = 1/3/4 ms

ALS2#ping 100.1.1.2

Type escape sequence to abort.
Sending 5, 100-byte ICMP Echos to 100.1.1.2, timeout is 2 seconds:
..!!!
Success rate is 60 percent (3/5), round-trip min/avg/max = 1/3/4 ms
```

FINAL SWITCH CONFIGURATIONS

DLS1

```
DLS1#term len 0
DLS1#sh run
Building configuration...

Current configuration : 4851 bytes
!
version 12.2
no service pad
service timestamps debug datetime msec
service timestamps log datetime msec
no service password-encryption
!
hostname DLS1
!
no aaa new-model
!
track 500 interface Loopback0 line-protocol
ip subnet-zero
ip routing
no ip domain-lookup
!
vtp domain hard
vtp mode transparent
!
key chain HSRP-GROUP-ONE
 key 1
```

```
    key-string ONE
!
spanning-tree mode pvst
spanning-tree extend system-id
spanning-tree vlan 100,200 priority 24576
spanning-tree vlan 100,200 forward-time 10
spanning-tree vlan 100,200 max-age 14
!
vlan internal allocation policy ascending
!
vlan 100,200
!
interface Loopback0
 ip address 192.1.1.1 255.255.255.0
!
interface FastEthernet0/1
 switchport mode dynamic desirable
 shutdown
!
interface FastEthernet0/2
 switchport mode dynamic desirable
 shutdown
!
interface FastEthernet0/3
 switchport mode dynamic desirable
 shutdown
!
interface FastEthernet0/4
 switchport mode dynamic desirable
 shutdown
!
interface FastEthernet0/5
 switchport mode dynamic desirable
 shutdown
!
interface FastEthernet0/6
 switchport mode dynamic desirable
 shutdown
!
interface FastEthernet0/7
 switchport trunk encapsulation dot1q
 switchport trunk allowed vlan 1,100,200
 switchport mode trunk
!
interface FastEthernet0/8
 switchport mode dynamic desirable
 shutdown
!
interface FastEthernet0/9
 switchport trunk encapsulation dot1q
 switchport trunk allowed vlan 1,100,200
 switchport mode trunk
!
interface FastEthernet0/10
 switchport mode dynamic desirable
 shutdown
!
interface FastEthernet0/11
 switchport trunk encapsulation dot1q
 switchport trunk allowed vlan 1,100,200
 switchport mode trunk
!
interface FastEthernet0/12
 switchport mode dynamic desirable
 shutdown

[Truncated Output]

interface Vlan1
 no ip address
 shutdown
!
interface Vlan100
 ip address 100.1.1.1 255.255.255.0
 standby 1 ip 100.1.1.254
 standby 1 priority 200
 standby 1 preempt
 standby 1 authentication md5 key-chain HSRP-GROUP-ONE
 standby 1 track 500 decrement 51
```

```
!
interface Vlan200
 ip address 200.1.1.1 255.255.255.0
 standby 2 ip 200.1.1.254
 standby 2 priority 200
 standby 2 preempt
 standby 2 authentication md5 key-string TWO
 standby 2 track 500 decrement 51
!
ip classless
ip http server
ip http secure-server
!
control-plane
!
line con 0
line vty 5 15
!
end
DLS1#
```

DLS2

```
DLS2#term len 0
DLS2#sh run
Building configuration...

Current configuration : 4573 bytes
!
version 12.2
no service pad
service timestamps debug datetime msec
service timestamps log datetime msec
no service password-encryption
!
hostname DLS2
!
no logging console
!
no aaa new-model
ip subnet-zero
ip routing
no ip domain-lookup
!
vtp domain hard
vtp mode transparent
!
!
key chain HSRP-GROUP-ONE
 key 1
   key-string ONE
!
spanning-tree mode pvst
spanning-tree extend system-id
!
vlan internal allocation policy ascending
!
vlan 100,200
!
interface FastEthernet0/1
 switchport mode dynamic desirable
 shutdown
!
interface FastEthernet0/2
 switchport mode dynamic desirable
 shutdown
!
interface FastEthernet0/3
 switchport mode dynamic desirable
 shutdown
!
interface FastEthernet0/4
 switchport mode dynamic desirable
 shutdown
!
interface FastEthernet0/5
 switchport mode dynamic desirable
 shutdown
```

```
!
interface FastEthernet0/6
 switchport mode dynamic desirable
 shutdown
!
interface FastEthernet0/7
 switchport trunk encapsulation dot1q
 switchport trunk allowed vlan 1,100,200
 switchport mode trunk
!
interface FastEthernet0/8
 switchport mode dynamic desirable
 shutdown
!
interface FastEthernet0/9
 switchport trunk encapsulation dot1q
 switchport trunk allowed vlan 1,100,200
 switchport mode trunk
!
interface FastEthernet0/10
 switchport mode dynamic desirable
 shutdown
!
interface FastEthernet0/11
 switchport trunk encapsulation dot1q
 switchport trunk allowed vlan 1,100,200
 switchport mode trunk
!
interface FastEthernet0/12
 switchport mode dynamic desirable
 shutdown

[Truncated Output]

interface Vlan1
 no ip address
 shutdown
!
interface Vlan100
 ip address 100.1.1.2 255.255.255.0
 standby 1 ip 100.1.1.254
 standby 1 priority 150
 standby 1 preempt
 standby 1 authentication md5 key-chain HSRP-GROUP-ONE
!
interface Vlan200
 ip address 200.1.1.2 255.255.255.0
 standby 2 ip 200.1.1.254
 standby 2 priority 150
 standby 2 preempt
 standby 2 authentication md5 key-string TWO
!
ip classless
ip http server
ip http secure-server
!
control-plane
!
line con 0
line vty 5 15
!
end

DLS2#
```

ALS1

```
ALS1#term len 0
ALS1#sh run
Building configuration...

Current configuration : 1139 bytes
!
version 12.1
no service pad
service timestamps debug uptime
service timestamps log uptime
no service password-encryption
```

```
!
hostname ALS1
!
no logging console
!
ip subnet-zero
!
no ip domain-lookup
vtp domain hard
vtp mode transparent
!
spanning-tree mode pvst
no spanning-tree optimize bpdu transmission
spanning-tree extend system-id
!
vlan 100,200
!
interface FastEthernet0/1
 shutdown
!
interface FastEthernet0/2
 shutdown
!
interface FastEthernet0/3
 shutdown
!
interface FastEthernet0/4
 shutdown
!
interface FastEthernet0/5
 shutdown
!
interface FastEthernet0/6
 shutdown
!
interface FastEthernet0/7
 switchport trunk allowed vlan 1,100
 switchport mode trunk
!
interface FastEthernet0/8
 shutdown
!
interface FastEthernet0/9
 switchport trunk allowed vlan 1,100
 switchport mode trunk
!
interface FastEthernet0/10
 shutdown
!
interface FastEthernet0/11
 shutdown
!
interface FastEthernet0/12
 shutdown
!
interface Vlan1
 no ip address
 no ip route-cache
 shutdown
!
interface Vlan100
 ip address 100.1.1.3 255.255.255.0
 no ip route-cache
!
ip default-gateway 100.1.1.254
ip http server
!
line con 0
line vty 5 15
!
end
ALS1#
```

ALS2

```
ALS2#term len 0
ALS2#sh ru
Building configuration...
```

```
Current configuration : 1135 bytes
!
version 12.1
no service pad
service timestamps debug uptime
service timestamps log uptime
no service password-encryption
!
hostname ALS2
!
no logging console
!
ip subnet-zero
!
no ip domain-lookup
vtp domain hard
vtp mode transparent
!
spanning-tree mode pvst
no spanning-tree optimize bpdu transmission
spanning-tree extend system-id
!
vlan 200
!
interface FastEthernet0/1
 shutdown
!
interface FastEthernet0/2
 shutdown
!
interface FastEthernet0/3
 shutdown
!
interface FastEthernet0/4
 shutdown
!
interface FastEthernet0/5
 shutdown
!
interface FastEthernet0/6
 shutdown
!
interface FastEthernet0/7
 switchport trunk allowed vlan 1,200
 switchport mode trunk
!
interface FastEthernet0/8
 shutdown
!
interface FastEthernet0/9
 switchport trunk allowed vlan 1,200
 switchport mode trunk
!
interface FastEthernet0/10
 shutdown
!
interface FastEthernet0/11
 shutdown
!
interface FastEthernet0/12
 shutdown
!
interface Vlan1
 no ip address
 no ip route-cache
 shutdown
!
interface Vlan200
 ip address 200.1.1.3 255.255.255.0
 no ip route-cache
!
ip default-gateway 200.1.1.254
ip http server
!
line con 0
line vty 5 15
!
end
ALS2#
```

CCNP LAB 8

SNMP, Logging and Management

Lab Objective:

The focus of this lab is to understand basic SNMP, logging and switch management implementation and configuration in Cisco IOS Catalyst switches.

Lab Topology:

The lab network topology is illustrated below:

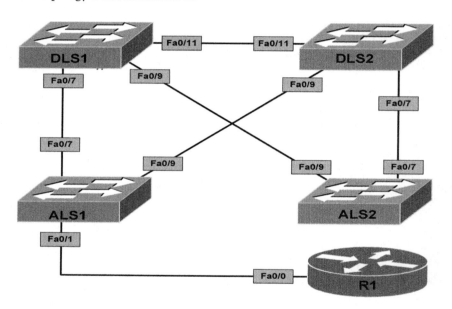

IMPORTANT NOTE: If you are using the www.howtonetwork.net racks, please begin each and every lab by shutting down all interfaces on all switches and then manually re-enabling only the interfaces that are illustrated in this topology.

Task 1

Configure VTP as following on the switches illustrated in the topology:
- Switches DLS1 and DLS2 should be VTP servers
- Switches ALS1 and ALS2 should be VTP clients
- The switches should reside in VTP domain 'CCNP'
- The VTP domain should be secured using the password 'CCNP'
- All switches should run VTP version 2

Task 2

Configure trunking on all switches and allow DTP to negotiate the trunking protocol. Assign the FastEthernet0/1 interface on switch ALS1 to VLAN 100.

Task 3

Configure switch DLS1 as the root bridge for VLAN 100, with switch DLS2 as the secondary (backup) root bridge. Next, configure the following SVIs and interfaces on the switches:

- DLS1: Interface VLAN 100: IP address 100.1.1.1/24
- DLS2: Interface VLAN 100: IP address 100.1.1.2/24
- ALS1: Interface VLAN 100: IP address 100.1.1.3/24
- ALS2: Interface VLAN 100: IP address 100.1.1.4/24

Finally, configure R1s FastEthernet 0/0 interface with the IP address 100.1.1.254.

Task 4

Configure SNMP on switches ALS1 and ALS2 as follows:

- Community string LEVEL1 should provide read only access from 192.168.1.0/24
- Community string LEVEL2 should provide read write access from 192.168.2.0/24
- SNMP traps for VTP should be sent to 10.1.1.253 using community LEVEL1
- SNMP traps for STP should be sent to 10.1.1.254 using community LEVEL2

Task 5

Configure logging on switches DLS1 and DLS2 as follows:

- Informational log messages should be sent to hosts 10.1.1.253 and 10.1.1.254
- Debugging log messages should be stored in the local buffer
- Log messages should include the date, time, millisecond values and local time zone
- Log messages should include a sequence number
- The local switch buffer size should be restricted to 10, 000

Task 6

For effective time management, configure Network Time Protocol as follows:

- Router RI should be configured as the NTP server
- All switches should synchronize their time with router R1
- All network devices should reside in the EST (GMT -5) time zone
- All network devices should adjust time for daylight saving

Task 7

For effective configuration management, configure the Cisco IOS Command Scheduler to automatically save the configurations on switches DLS1 and DLS2 every 8 hours.

LAB VALIDATION

Task 1

```
DLS1(config)#vtp mode server
DLS1(config)#vtp domain CCNP
DLS1(config)#vtp password CCNP
DLS1(config)#vtp version 2

DLS2(config)#vtp mode server
DLS2(config)#vtp domain CCNP
DLS2(config)#vtp password CCNP
DLS2(config)#vtp version 2

ALS1(config)#vtp version 2
ALS1(config)#vtp mode client
ALS1(config)#vtp domain CCNP
ALS1(config)#vtp password CCNP
ALS2(config)#vtp version 2
```

```
ALS2(config)#vtp mode client
ALS2(config)#vtp domain CCNP
ALS2(config)#vtp password CCNP
```

NOTE: It is important to change the VTP version prior to configuring a switch as a VTP client. When the switch is in client mode, you cannot change the VTP version as shown below:

```
ALS2(config)#vtp version 2
Cannot modify version in VTP client mode
```

Task 2

```
DLS1(config)#interface range fasteth 0/7, fasteth 0/9, fasteth 0/11
DLS1(config-if-range)#switchport
DLS1(config-if-range)#no shutdown
DLS2(config-if-range)#exit

DLS2(config)#interface range fasteth 0/7, fasteth 0/9, fasteth 0/11
DLS2(config-if-range)#switchport
DLS2(config-if-range)#no shutdown
DLS2(config-if-range)#exit

ALS1(config)#interface range fastethernet 0/7 , fastethernet 0/9
ALS1(config-if-range)#no shutdown
ALS1(config)#interface fastethernet 0/1
ALS1(config-if)#switchport mode access
ALS1(config-if)#switchport access vlan 100
ALS1(config-if)#no shutdown

ALS2(config)#interface range fastethernet 0/7 , fastethernet 0/9
ALS2(config-if-range)#no shutdown
```

Following this, verify your configuration using the **show interfaces trunk** command:

```
DLS1#show interfaces trunk
```

Port	Mode	Encapsulation	Status	Native vlan
Fa0/7	desirable	n-802.1q	trunking	1
Fa0/9	desirable	n-802.1q	trunking	1
Fa0/11	desirable	n-isl	trunking	1

```
ALS1#show interfaces trunk
```

Port	Mode	Encapsulation	Status	Native vlan
Fa0/7	desirable	802.1q	trunking	1
Fa0/9	desirable	802.1q	trunking	1

Task 3

To complete this task, you first need to configure VLAN 100 on the VTP server devices prior to configuring the VLAN interfaces (SVIs) on the switches. This task is completed as follows:

```
DLS1(config)#vlan 100
DLS1(config-vlan)#exit
DLS1(config)#spanning-tree vlan 100 priority 4096
DLS1(config)#interface vlan 100
DLS1(config-if)#ip address 100.1.1.1 255.255.255.0
DLS1(config-if)#exit

DLS2(config)#vlan 100
DLS2(config-vlan)#exit
DLS2(config)#spanning-tree vlan 100 priority 8192
DLS2(config)#interface vlan 100
DLS2(config-if)#ip address 100.1.1.2 255.255.255.0
DLS2(config-if)#exit

ALS1(config)#interface vlan 100
```

```
ALS1(config-if)#ip address 100.1.1.3 255.255.255.0
ALS1(config-if)#exit

R1(config)#interface fastethernet 0/0
R1(config-if)#ip address 100.1.1.254 255.255.255.0
R1(config-if)#exit
```

Next, verify your STP configuration using the **show spanning-tree** commands:

```
ALS2#show spanning-tree vlan 100

VLAN0100
  Spanning tree enabled protocol ieee
  Root ID    Priority    4196
             Address     000f.2303.2d80
             Cost        19
             Port        9 (FastEthernet0/9)
             Hello Time   2 sec  Max Age 20 sec  Forward Delay 15 sec

  Bridge ID  Priority    32868  (priority 32768 sys-id-ext 100)
             Address     0009.b79f.7d80
             Hello Time   2 sec  Max Age 20 sec  Forward Delay 15 sec
             Aging Time 300

Interface        Role Sts Cost      Prio.Nbr Type
---------------- ---- --- --------- -------- --------------------------------
Fa0/7            Altn BLK 19        128.7    P2p
Fa0/9            Root FWD 19        128.9    P2p
```

Finally, verify IP connectivity between the switches using a simple ping:

```
R1#ping 100.1.1.0

Type escape sequence to abort.
Sending 5, 100-byte ICMP Echos to 100.1.1.0, timeout is 2 seconds:
.
Reply to request 1 from 100.1.1.1, 1 ms
Reply to request 1 from 100.1.1.4, 1 ms
Reply to request 1 from 100.1.1.3, 1 ms
Reply to request 1 from 100.1.1.2, 1 ms
Reply to request 2 from 100.1.1.1, 1 ms
Reply to request 2 from 100.1.1.4, 4 ms
Reply to request 2 from 100.1.1.3, 4 ms
Reply to request 2 from 100.1.1.2, 4 ms
Reply to request 3 from 100.1.1.1, 1 ms
Reply to request 3 from 100.1.1.4, 4 ms
Reply to request 3 from 100.1.1.3, 4 ms
Reply to request 3 from 100.1.1.2, 4 ms
Reply to request 4 from 100.1.1.1, 1 ms
Reply to request 4 from 100.1.1.4, 4 ms
Reply to request 4 from 100.1.1.3, 4 ms
Reply to request 4 from 100.1.1.2, 4 ms
```

Task 4

```
ALS1(config)#access-list 1 permit 192.168.1.0 0.0.0.255
ALS1(config)#access-list 2 permit 192.168.2.0 0.0.0.255
ALS1(config)#snmp-server community LEVEL1 ro 1
ALS1(config)#snmp-server community LEVEL2 rw 2
ALS1(config)#snmp-server enable traps vtp
ALS1(config)#snmp-server enable traps stp
ALS1(config)#snmp-server host 10.1.1.253 traps version 2c LEVEL1 vtp
ALS1(config)# snmp-server host 10.1.1.254 traps version 2c LEVEL2 stp


ALS2(config)#access-list 1 permit 192.168.1.0 0.0.0.255
ALS2(config)#access-list 2 permit 192.168.2.0 0.0.0.255
ALS2(config)#snmp-server community LEVEL1 ro 1
ALS2(config)#snmp-server community LEVEL2 rw 2
ALS2(config)#snmp-server enable traps vtp
ALS2(config)#snmp-server enable traps stp
ALS2(config)#snmp-server host 10.1.1.253 traps version 2c LEVEL1 vtp
ALS2(config)# snmp-server host 10.1.1.254 traps version 2c LEVEL2 stp
```

Verify your SNMP configuration using the **show snmp** commands:

```
ALS1#show snmp
Chassis: FAB0540Y20Z
0 SNMP packets input
    0 Bad SNMP version errors
    0 Unknown community name
    0 Illegal operation for community name supplied
    0 Encoding errors
    0 Number of requested variables
    0 Number of altered variables
    0 Get-request PDUs
    0 Get-next PDUs
    0 Set-request PDUs
0 SNMP packets output
    0 Too big errors (Maximum packet size 1500)
    0 No such name errors
    0 Bad values errors
    0 General errors
    0 Response PDUs
    0 Trap PDUs
SNMP global trap: disabled
SNMP logging: enabled
    Logging to 10.1.1.253.162, 0/10, 0 sent, 0 dropped.
    Logging to 10.1.1.254.162, 0/10, 0 sent, 0 dropped.
```

Task 5

```
DLS1(config)#logging on
DLS1(config)#logging host 10.1.1.253
DLS1(config)#logging host 10.1.1.254
DLS1(config)#logging trap informational
DLS1(config)#logging buffered debugging
DLS1(config)#logging buffered 10000
DLS1(config)#service timestamps log datetime msec localtime
DLS1(config)#service sequence-numbers
DLS1(config)#exit

DLS2(config)#logging on
DLS2(config)#logging host 10.1.1.253
DLS2(config)#logging host 10.1.1.254
DLS2(config)#logging trap informational
DLS2(config)#logging buffered debugging
DLS2(config)#logging buffered 10000
DLS2(config)#service timestamps log datetime msec localtime
DLS2(config)#service sequence-numbers
DLS2(config)#exit
```

Verify your configuration using the **show logging** commands:

```
DLS2#show logging
Syslog logging: enabled (0 messages dropped, 14 messages rate-limited, 0 flushes, 0
overruns, xml disabled, filtering disabled)

No Active Message Discriminator.

No Inactive Message Discriminator.

    Console logging: disabled
    Monitor logging: level debugging, 0 messages logged, xml disabled,
                    filtering disabled
    Buffer logging:  level debugging, 3 messages logged, xml disabled,
                    filtering disabled
    Exception Logging: size (4096 bytes)
    Count and timestamp logging messages: disabled
    File logging: disabled
    Persistent logging: disabled
    Trap logging: level informational, 87 message lines logged
        Logging to 10.1.1.253 (udp port 514, audit disabled,
            authentication disabled, encryption disabled, link up),
            3 message lines logged.
```

```
            O message lines rate-limited,
            O message lines dropped-by-MD,
            xml disabled, sequence number disabled
            filtering disabled
        Logging to 10.1.1.254 (udp port 514, audit disabled,
            authentication disabled, encryption disabled, link up),
            3 message lines logged,
            O message lines rate-limited,
            O message lines dropped-by-MD,
            xml disabled, sequence number disabled
            filtering disabled

Log Buffer (10000 bytes):

000082: *Mar  1 00:51:56.759: %SYS-5-CONFIG_I: Configured from console by console
000083: *Mar  1 00:51:57.759: %SYS-6-LOGGINGHOST_STARTSTOP: Logging to host
10.1.1.253 Port 514 started - CLI initiated
000084: *Mar  1 00:52:00.759: %SYS-6-LOGGINGHOST_STARTSTOP: Logging to host
10.1.1.254 Port 514 started - CLI initiated
```

Task 6

```
R1(config)#ntp master
R1(config)#clock summer-time EST recurring
R1(config)#clock timezone EST -5
May  1 01:40:00.000: %SYS-6-CLOCKUPDATE: System clock has been updated from 03:34:46
EST Wed Apr 10 2002 to 21:40:00 EST Sat Apr 30 2011

DLS1(config)#ntp server 100.1.1.254
DLS1(config)#clock summer-time EST recurring
DLS1(config)#clock timezone EST -5

DLS2(config)#ntp server 100.1.1.254
DLS2(config)#clock summer-time EST recurring
DLS2(config)#clock timezone EST -5

ALS1(config)#ntp server 100.1.1.254
ALS1(config)#clock summer-time EST recurring
ALS1(config)#clock timezone EST -5

ALS2(config)#ntp server 100.1.1.254
ALS2(config)#clock summer-time EST recurring
ALS2(config)#clock timezone EST -5
```

Following this configuration, use the **show ntp status** and **show ntp associations** commands to validate NTP. The **show ntp status** command shows whether or not the device is synchronized with the specified NTP server, the server stratum and server IP address. This command also includes the time received from the server. On the NTP master, the local Loopback address 127.127.7.1 is used as the NTP server IP address. This can be viewed below:

```
R1#show ntp status
Clock is synchronized, stratum 8, reference is 127.127.7.1
nominal freq is 250.0000 Hz, actual freq is 250.0000 Hz, precision is 2**16
reference time is D1673875.D60DC757 (21:40:05.836 EST Sat Apr 30 2011)
clock offset is 0.0000 msec, root delay is 0.00 msec
root dispersion is 15875.02 msec, peer dispersion is 15875.02 msec
```

All other devices show the IP address of the NTP server, which is 100.1.1.254, as shown below:

```
DLS1#show ntp status
Clock is synchronized, stratum 9, reference is 100.1.1.254
nominal freq is 250.0000 Hz, actual freq is 249.9999 Hz, precision is 2**18
reference time is D167397B.173143D3 (21:44:27.090 EST Sat Apr 30 2011)
clock offset is 0.0928 msec, root delay is 2.50 msec
root dispersion is 1750.17 msec, peer dispersion is 875.05 msec
```

The **show ntp associations [detail]** command provides information about each NTP server, including the stratum information as shown below:

```
DLS1#show ntp associations detail
100.1.1.254 configured, our_master, sane, valid, stratum 8
ref ID 127.127.7.1, time D16739B5.D60C5557 (21:45:25.836 EST Sat Apr 30 2011)
our mode client, peer mode server, our poll intvl 64, peer poll intvl 64
root delay 0.00 msec, root disp 375.03, reach 77, sync dist 752.274
delay 2.50 msec, offset 1.0837 msec, dispersion 375.99
precision 2**16, version 3
org time D16739BB.172AB9E9 (21:45:31.090 EST Sat Apr 30 2011)
rcv time D16739BB.173610D7 (21:45:31.090 EST Sat Apr 30 2011)
xmt time D16739BB.168E92A1 (21:45:31.088 EST Sat Apr 30 2011)
filtdelay =    2.50     2.50    2.50    2.52    2.52    2.50    0.00     0.00
filtoffset =   1.08     0.09    0.08    0.06    0.04    0.02    0.00     0.00
filterror =    0.02     0.99    1.01    1.02    1.04    1.05 16000.0 16000.0
```

Task 7

```
DLS1(config)#kron policy-list Save-Configuration
DLS1(config-kron-policy)#cli write memory
DLS1(config-kron-policy)#exit
DLS1(config)#kron occurrence Auto-Management in 8:00 recurring
DLS1(config-kron-occurrence)#policy-list Save-Configuration
DLS1(config-kron-occurrence)#exit
```

Following this configuration, use the **show kron schedule** command for validation:

```
DLS1#show kron schedule
Kron Occurrence Schedule
Auto-Management inactive, will run again in 0 days 07:58:25
```

FINAL SWITCH CONFIGURATIONS

DLS1

```
DLS1#term len 0
DLS1#sh run
Building configuration...

Current configuration : 4401 bytes
!
! Last configuration change at 21:57:52 EST Sat Apr 30 2011
!
version 12.2
no service pad
service timestamps debug datetime msec
service timestamps log datetime msec localtime
no service password-encryption
service sequence-numbers
!
hostname DLS1
!
logging buffered 10000
no logging console
!
no aaa new-model
clock timezone EST -5
clock summer-time EST recurring
ip subnet-zero
no ip domain-lookup
!
spanning-tree mode pvst
spanning-tree extend system-id
spanning-tree vlan 100 priority 4096
!
vlan internal allocation policy ascending
!
interface FastEthernet0/1
 switchport mode dynamic desirable
 shutdown
!
interface FastEthernet0/2
 switchport mode dynamic desirable
 shutdown
```

```
!
interface FastEthernet0/3
 switchport mode dynamic desirable
 shutdown
!
interface FastEthernet0/4
 switchport mode dynamic desirable
 shutdown
!
interface FastEthernet0/5
 switchport mode dynamic desirable
 shutdown
!
interface FastEthernet0/6
 switchport mode dynamic desirable
 shutdown
!
interface FastEthernet0/7
 switchport mode dynamic desirable
!
interface FastEthernet0/8
 switchport mode dynamic desirable
 shutdown
!
interface FastEthernet0/9
 switchport mode dynamic desirable
!
interface FastEthernet0/10
 switchport mode dynamic desirable
 shutdown
!
interface FastEthernet0/11
 switchport mode dynamic desirable
!
interface FastEthernet0/12
 switchport mode dynamic desirable
 shutdown

[Truncated Output]

interface Vlan1
 no ip address
 shutdown
!
interface Vlan100
 ip address 100.1.1.1 255.255.255.0
!
ip classless
ip http server
ip http secure-server
!
!
kron occurrence Auto-Management in 8:0 recurring
 policy-list Save-Configuration
!
kron policy-list Save-Configuration
 cli write memory
!
logging 10.1.1.253
logging 10.1.1.254
!
control-plane
!
line con 0
line vty 5 15
!
ntp clock-period 17179919
ntp server 100.1.1.254
end
DLS1#
```

DLS2

```
DLS2#term len 0
DLS2#sh run
Building configuration...

Current configuration : 4262 bytes
```

```
!
! Last configuration change at 21:44:40 EST Sat Apr 30 2011
!
version 12.2
no service pad
service timestamps debug datetime msec
service timestamps log datetime msec localtime
no service password-encryption
service sequence-numbers
!
hostname DLS2
!
logging buffered 10000
no logging console
!
no aaa new-model
clock timezone EST -5
clock summer-time EST recurring
ip subnet-zero
no ip domain-lookup
!
spanning-tree mode pvst
spanning-tree extend system-id
spanning-tree vlan 100 priority 8192
!
vlan internal allocation policy ascending
!
!
interface FastEthernet0/1
 switchport mode dynamic desirable
 shutdown
!
interface FastEthernet0/2
 switchport mode dynamic desirable
 shutdown
!
interface FastEthernet0/3
 switchport mode dynamic desirable
 shutdown
!
interface FastEthernet0/4
 switchport mode dynamic desirable
 shutdown
!
interface FastEthernet0/5
 switchport mode dynamic desirable
 shutdown
!
interface FastEthernet0/6
 switchport mode dynamic desirable
 shutdown
!
interface FastEthernet0/7
 switchport mode dynamic desirable
!
interface FastEthernet0/8
 switchport mode dynamic desirable
 shutdown
!
interface FastEthernet0/9
 switchport mode dynamic desirable
!
interface FastEthernet0/10
 switchport mode dynamic desirable
 shutdown
!
interface FastEthernet0/11
 switchport mode dynamic desirable
!
interface FastEthernet0/12
 switchport mode dynamic desirable
 shutdown

[Truncated Output]

interface Vlan1
 no ip address
 shutdown
!
```

```
interface Vlan100
 ip address 100.1.1.2 255.255.255.0
!
ip classless
ip http server
ip http secure-server
!
logging 10.1.1.253
logging 10.1.1.254
!
control-plane
!
line con 0
line vty 5 15
!
ntp clock-period 17179889
ntp server 100.1.1.254
end

DLS2#
```

ALS1

```
ALS1#term len 0
ALS1#sh run
Building configuration...

Current configuration : 1458 bytes
!
! Last configuration change at 03:39:39 EST Wed Apr 10 2002
!
version 12.1
no service pad
service timestamps debug uptime
service timestamps log uptime
no service password-encryption
!
hostname ALS1
!
no logging console
!
clock timezone EST -5
clock summer-time EST recurring
ip subnet-zero
!
no ip domain-lookup
!
spanning-tree mode pvst
no spanning-tree optimize bpdu transmission
spanning-tree extend system-id
!
interface FastEthernet0/1
 switchport access vlan 100
 switchport mode access
!
interface FastEthernet0/2
 shutdown
!
interface FastEthernet0/3
 shutdown
!
interface FastEthernet0/4
 shutdown
!
interface FastEthernet0/5
 shutdown
!
interface FastEthernet0/6
 shutdown
!
interface FastEthernet0/7
!
interface FastEthernet0/8
 shutdown
!
interface FastEthernet0/9
!
interface FastEthernet0/10
```

```
 shutdown
!
interface FastEthernet0/11
 shutdown
!
interface FastEthernet0/12
 shutdown
!
interface Vlan1
 no ip address
 no ip route-cache
 shutdown
!
interface Vlan100
 ip address 100.1.1.3 255.255.255.0
 no ip route-cache
!
ip http server
access-list 1 permit 192.168.1.0 0.0.0.255
access-list 2 permit 192.168.2.0 0.0.0.255
snmp-server community LEVEL1 RO 1
snmp-server community LEVEL2 RW 2
snmp-server enable traps stpx
snmp-server enable traps vtp
snmp-server host 10.1.1.253 version 2c LEVEL1  vtp
snmp-server host 10.1.1.254 version 2c LEVEL2  stpx
!
line con 0
line vty 5 15
!
ntp clock-period 17179847
ntp server 100.1.1.254
!
end
ALS1#
```

ALS2

```
ALS2#term len 0
ALS2#sh run
Building configuration...

Current configuration : 1390 bytes
!
! Last configuration change at 21:47:21 EST Sat Apr 30 2011
!
version 12.1
no service pad
service timestamps debug uptime
service timestamps log uptime
no service password-encryption
!
hostname ALS2
!
no logging console
!
clock timezone EST -5
clock summer-time EST recurring
ip subnet-zero
!
no ip domain-lookup
!
spanning-tree mode pvst
no spanning-tree optimize bpdu transmission
spanning-tree extend system-id
!
interface FastEthernet0/1
 shutdown
!
interface FastEthernet0/2
 shutdown
!
interface FastEthernet0/3
 shutdown
!
interface FastEthernet0/4
 shutdown
!
```

```
interface FastEthernet0/5
 shutdown
!
interface FastEthernet0/6
 shutdown
!
interface FastEthernet0/7
!
interface FastEthernet0/8
 shutdown
!
interface FastEthernet0/9
!
interface FastEthernet0/10
 shutdown
!
interface FastEthernet0/11
 shutdown
!
interface FastEthernet0/12
 shutdown
!
interface Vlan1
 no ip address
 no ip route-cache
 shutdown
!
interface Vlan100
 ip address 100.1.1.4 255.255.255.0
 no ip route-cache
!
ip http server
access-list 1 permit 192.168.1.0 0.0.0.255
access-list 2 permit 192.168.2.0 0.0.0.255
snmp-server community LEVEL1 RO 1
snmp-server community LEVEL2 RW 2
snmp-server enable traps stpx
snmp-server enable traps vtp
snmp-server host 10.1.1.253 version 2c LEVEL1  vtp
snmp-server host 10.1.1.254 version 2c LEVEL2  stpx
!
line con 0
line vty 5 15
!
ntp server 100.1.1.254
!
end

ALS2#
```

FINAL ROUTER CONFIGURATIONS

R1

```
R1#term len 0
R1#sh run
Building configuration...

Current configuration : 890 bytes
!
! Last configuration change at 03:31:26 EST Wed Apr 10 2002
!
version 12.4
service timestamps debug datetime msec
service timestamps log datetime msec
no service password-encryption
!
hostname R1
!
boot-start-marker
boot-end-marker
!
no aaa new-model
clock timezone EST -5
clock summer-time EST recurring
no network-clock-participate slot 1
```

```
no network-clock-participate wic 0
ip cef
!
no ip domain lookup
ip auth-proxy max-nodata-conns 3
ip admission max-nodata-conns 3
!
interface FastEthernet0/0
 ip address 100.1.1.254 255.255.255.0
 duplex auto
 speed auto
!
interface Serial0/0
 no ip address
 shutdown
!
interface Serial0/1
 no ip address
 shutdown
!
ip forward-protocol nd
!
no ip http server
no ip http secure-server
!
control-plane
!
line con 0
line aux 0
line vty 0 4
 login
!
ntp master
!
end

R1#
```

CCNP LAB 9

QoS, Voice and Video Support

Lab Objective:

The focus of this lab is to understand Quality of Service (QoS) implementation and configuration for voice and video services in Cisco IOS Catalyst switches.

Lab Topology:

The lab network topology is illustrated below:

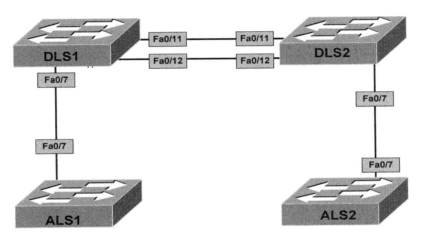

IMPORTANT NOTE: If you are using the www.howtonetwork.net racks, please begin each and every lab by shutting down all interfaces on all switches and then manually re-enabling only the interfaces that are illustrated in this topology.

Task 1

Configure VTP on all switches illustrated in the network topology as follows:

- Switches DLS1 and ALS1 should reside in VTP domain ONE
- Switch DLS1 should be configured as a VTP server and ALS1 as a VTP client
- Switches DLS1 and ALS1 should secure VTP using a password of ONE
- Both switches should run VTP version 2

- Switches DLS2 and ALS2 should reside in VTP domain TWO
- Switch DLS2 should be configured as a VTP server and ALS2 as a VTP client
- Switches DLS2 and ALS2 should secure VTP using a password of TWO
- Both switches should run VTP version 2

Task 2

Configure an 802.1Q trunk between DLS1 and ALS1 as well as between DLS2 and ALS2. Next, configure a PAgP Layer 3 EtherChannel between switches DLS1 and DLS2. Use the 192.168.0.0/30 subnet for the EtherChannel.

Task 3

Configure VLANs and the following SVIs and interfaces on the switches in the topology:
- DLS1: VLAN 100 - name DATA; VLAN 101 - name VOICE
- DLS1: Interface VLAN 100: IP address 100.1.1.1/24
- DLS1: Interface VLAN 101: IP address 101.1.1.1/24

- DLS2: VLAN 200 - name DATA; VLAN 201 - name VOICE
- DLS2: Interface VLAN 200: IP address 200.1.1.1/24
- DLS2: Interface VLAN 201: IP address 201.1.1.1/24

Task 4

Configure Cisco IOS DHCP on switch DLS1 to provide IP addressing information to both the DATA and VOICE VLANs. The first 5 addresses should be excluded from the DHCP scopes. The Cisco IP phones that will be assigned to the VOICE VLANs on the switches will need to communicate with a Cisco Unified Communications Manager with the IP address 192.168.0.254. This address should be included in the VOICE DHCP scopes. The DHCP scopes should be configured for a lease time of 5 days, use the domain name howtonetwork.net and use servers 172.16.1.253 and 172.16.2.254 for name resolution.

Configure switch DLS2 to forward DHCP requests to servers 192.168.1.254 and 192.168.2.254

Task 5

Configure OSPF on switches DLS1 and DLS2 so that switches ALS1 and ALS2 have IP reachability to each other.

Task 6

Configure Quality of Service on switches DLS1 and DLS2 as follows:
- All markings for packets received across the Layer 3 EtherChannel should be trusted
- All markings for packets received from their access switches should be trusted

Task 7

Configure voice support and Quality of Service on switch ALS1. Ports FastEthernet0/1- 0/5 will be connected to Cisco IP phones. The phones will should use VLAN 101 and the users connected to the phone LAN port should use VLAN 100. The switch should trust QoS markings from the phones only.

Configure voice support and Quality of Service on switch ALS2. Ports FastEthernet0/1 - 0/5 will be connected to Cisco IP phones. The phones will should use VLAN 201 and the users connected to the phone LAN port should use VLAN 200. The switch should trust QoS markings from both the phones as well as the user devices connected to the phones.

Task 8

On switches ALS1 and ALS2, ports FastEthernet0/10 - 12 will be connected to non-trusted video endpoints. To ensure that these do not affect other services, e.g. voice, configure the switches to ignore any CoS values in frames received on these ports and assign a default CoS value of 3.

LAB VALIDATION

Task 1

```
DLS1(config)#vtp domain ONE
DLS1(config)#vtp password ONE
DLS1(config)#vtp version 2
```

```
DLS2(config)#vtp domain TWO
DLS2(config)#vtp password TWO
DLS2(config)#vtp version 2

ALS1(config)#vtp version 2
ALS1(config)#vtp domain ONE
ALS1(config)#vtp password ONE
ALS1(config)#vtp mode client

ALS2(config)#vtp domain TWO
ALS2(config)#vtp password TWO
ALS2(config)#vtp version 2
ALS2(config)#vtp mode client
```

Task 2

```
DLS1(config)#interface fastethernet 0/7
DLS1(config-if)#switchport
DLS1(config-if)#switchport trunk encapsulation dot1q
DLS1(config-if)#switchport mode trunk
DLS1(config-if)#no shutdown
DLS1(config-if)#exit
DLS1(config)#interface range fastethernet 0/11 - 12
DLS1(config-if-range)#no switchport
DLS1(config-if-range)#channel-group 1 mode desirable
Creating a port-channel interface Port-channel 1

DLS1(config-if-range)#no shutdown
DLS1(config-if-range)#exit
DLS1(config)#interface port-channel 1
DLS1(config-if)#ip address 192.168.0.1 255.255.255.252
DLS1(config-if)#exit

DLS2(config)#interface fastethernet 0/7
DLS2(config-if)#switchport
DLS2(config-if)#switchport trunk encapsulation dot1q
DLS2(config-if)#switchport mode trunk
DLS2(config-if)#no shutdown
DLS2(config-if)#exit
DLS2(config)#interface range fastethernet 0/11 - 12
DLS2(config-if-range)#no switchport
DLS2(config-if-range)#channel-group 1 mode desirable
Creating a port-channel interface Port-channel 1

DLS2(config-if-range)#no shutdown
DLS2(config-if-range)#exit
DLS2(config)#interface port-channel 1
DLS2(config-if)#ip address 192.168.0.2 255.255.255.252
DLS2(config-if)#exit

ALS1(config)#interface fastethernet 0/7
ALS1(config-if)#no shutdown
ALS1(config-if)#switchport mode trunk
ALS1(config-if)#exit

ALS2(config)#interface fastethernet 0/7
ALS2(config-if)#no shutdown
ALS2(config-if)#switchport mode trunk
ALS2(config-if)#exit
```

Verify trunking status and configuration using the **show interfaces trunk** command:

```
ALS1#show interfaces trunk

Port        Mode        Encapsulation  Status      Native vlan
Fa0/7       on          802.1q         trunking    1

ALS2#show interfaces trunk

Port        Mode        Encapsulation  Status      Native vlan
Fa0/7       on          802.1q         trunking    1
```

Verify EtherChannel status and configuration using the **show etherchannel** commands:

```
DLS1#show etherchannel summary
Flags:  D - down         P - bundled in port-channel
        I - stand-alone  s - suspended
        H - Hot-standby (LACP only)
        R - Layer3       S - Layer2
        U - in use       f - failed to allocate aggregator

        M - not in use, minimum links not met
        u - unsuitable for bundling
        w - waiting to be aggregated
        d - default port

Number of channel-groups in use: 1
Number of aggregators:           1

Group  Port-channel  Protocol    Ports
------+-------------+-----------+----------------------------------------------
1      Po1(RU)       PAgP        Fa0/11(P)   Fa0/12(P)
```

And finally, verify IP connectivity between switches DLS1 and DLS2 using a simple ping:

```
DLS1#ping 192.168.0.2

Type escape sequence to abort.
Sending 5, 100-byte ICMP Echos to 192.168.0.2, timeout is 2 seconds:
.!!!!
Success rate is 80 percent (4/5), round-trip min/avg/max = 1/3/4 ms
```

Task 3

```
DLS1(config)#vlan 100
DLS1(config-vlan)#name DATA
DLS1(config-vlan)#exit
DLS1(config)#vlan 101
DLS1(config-vlan)#name VOICE
DLS1(config-vlan)#exit
DLS1(config)#interface vlan 100
DLS1(config-if)#ip address 100.1.1.1 255.255.255.0
DLS1(config-if)#exit
DLS1(config)#interface vlan 101
DLS1(config-if)#ip address 101.1.1.1 255.255.255.0
DLS1(config-if)#exit

DLS2(config)#vlan 200
DLS2(config-vlan)#name DATA
DLS2(config-vlan)#exit
DLS2(config)#vlan 201
DLS2(config-vlan)#name VOICE
DLS2(config-vlan)#exit
DLS2(config)#interface vlan 200
DLS2(config-if)#ip address 200.1.1.1 255.255.255.0
DLS2(config-if)#exit
DLS2(config)#interface vlan 201
DLS2(config-if)#ip address 201.1.1.1 255.255.255.0
DLS2(config-if)#exit
```

Task 4

While the other DHCP configuration tasks are simple, when configuring the Cisco Unified Communications Manager (CUCM) address in DHCP, you can use either DHCP option 66 (name) or DHCP option 150 (IP address). This task is completed as follows on switch DLS1:

```
DLS1(config)#ip dhcp excluded-address 100.1.1.1 100.1.1.4
DLS1(config)#ip dhcp excluded-address 101.1.1.1 101.1.1.4
DLS1(config)#ip dhcp pool DATA
DLS1(dhcp-config)#network 100.1.1.0 255.255.255.0
DLS1(dhcp-config)#default-router 100.1.1.1
DLS1(dhcp-config)#lease 5 0 0
```

```
DLS1(dhcp-config)#domain-name howtonetwork.net
DLS1(dhcp-config)#dns-server 172.16.1.254 172.16.2.254
DLS1(dhcp-config)#exit
DLS1(config)#ip dhcp pool VOICE
DLS1(dhcp-config)#network 101.1.1.0 255.255.255.0
DLS1(dhcp-config)#lease 5 0 0
DLS1(dhcp-config)#domain-name howtonetwork.net
DLS1(dhcp-config)#lease 5 0 0
DLS1(dhcp-config)#dns-server 172.16.1.254 172.16.2.254
DLS1(dhcp-config)#option 150 ip 192.168.0.254
DLS1(dhcp-config)#exit
```

The second part of this task calls for the configuration of the Cisco IOS DHCP Relay Agent, configured using
the ip helper-address command. This task is completed as follows:

```
DLS2(config)#interface vlan 200
DLS2(config-if)#ip helper-address 192.168.1.254
DLS2(config-if)#ip helper-address 192.168.2.254
DLS2(config-if)#exit
DLS2(config)#interface vlan 201
DLS2(config-if)#ip helper-address 192.168.1.254
DLS2(config-if)#ip helper-address 192.168.2.254
DLS2(config-if)#exit
```

You can verify the helper addresses configured on a per-interface basis by looking at the device configuration
or using the **show ip interface** command:

```
DLS2#show ip interface vlan 200
Vlan200 is up, line protocol is up
  Internet address is 200.1.1.1/24
  Broadcast address is 255.255.255.255
  Address determined by setup command
  MTU is 1500 bytes
  Helper addresses are 192.168.1.254
                       192.168.2.254
  Directed broadcast forwarding is disabled
  Outgoing access list is not set
  Inbound  access list is not set
```

Task 5

```
DLS1(config)#ip routing
DLS1(config)#router ospf 1
DLS1(config-router)#network 100.1.1.0 0.0.0.255 area 0
DLS1(config-router)#network 101.1.1.0 0.0.0.255 area 0
DLS1(config-router)#network 192.168.0.0 0.0.0.3 area 0
DLS1(config-router)#exit

DLS2(config)#ip routing
DLS2(config)#router ospf 2
DLS2(config-router)#network 200.1.1.0 0.0.0.255 area 0
DLS2(config-router)#network 201.1.1.0 0.0.0.255 area 0
DLS2(config-router)#network 192.168.0.0 0.0.0.3 area 0
DLS2(config-router)#exit
```

Verify your configuration using the **show ip ospf** and **show ip route** commands:

```
DLS1#show ip ospf neighbor

Neighbor ID  Pri State    Dead Time  Address      Interface
201.1.1.1    1   FULL/BDR 00:00:32   192.168.0.2  Port-channel1

DLS1#show ip route ospf
O  201.1.1.0/24 [110/2] via 192.168.0.2, 00:01:47, Port-channel1
O  200.1.1.0/24 [110/2] via 192.168.0.2, 00:01:47, Port-channel1
```

Task 6

When configuring QoS on Catalyst switches, first QoS must be enabled globally. When this is done, by default, all interfaces are untrusted and a trust state must be explicitly configured. When configuring trust states, configure the switch to trust CoS only on trunks or ports connected to Cisco IP phones; and to trust DSCP or IP Precedence on Layer 3 (routed) ports or ports connected to non-Cisco IP phones, e.g. ports connected to workstations only.

```
DLS1(config)#mls qos
DLS1(config-if)#interface fastethernet 0/7
DLS1(config-if)#mls qos trust cos
DLS1(config-if)#exit
DLS1(config)#interface range fastethernet 0/11 - 12
DLS1(config-if-range)#mls qos trust dscp
DLS1(config-if-range)#exit
```

NOTE: Depending on the switch platform, when configuring QoS for EtherChannels, you must configure it on a per-port basis. It is imperative to ensure that all ports have the same configuration, otherwise, some of the ports will not be included in the EtherChannel bundle.

```
DLS2(config)#mls qos
DLS2(config)#interface fastethernet 0/7
DLS2(config-if)#mls qos trust cos
DLS2(config-if)#exit
DLS2(config)#interface range fastethernet 0/11 - 12
DLS2(config-if-range)#mls qos trust dscp
DLS2(config-if-range)#exit
```

Verify your configuration using the **show mls qos** commands:

```
DLS2#show mls qos
QoS is enabled

DLS2#show mls qos interface fastethernet 0/7
FastEthernet0/7
QoS is disabled. pass-through mode
When QoS is enabled, following settings will be applied
trust state: trust cos
trust mode: trust cos
COS override: dis
default COS: 0
DSCP Mutation Map: Default DSCP Mutation Map
Trust device: none
```

Task 7

```
ALS1(config)#interface range fastethernet 0/1 - 5
ALS1(config-if-range)#switchport mode access
ALS1(config-if-range)#switchport access vlan 100
ALS1(config-if-range)#switchport voice vlan 100
ALS1(config-if-range)#mls qos trust cos
ALS1(config-if-range)#mls qos trust device cisco-phone
ALS1(config-if-range)#exit
```

By default, the Cisco IP phone does not trust traffic received from its LAN port and resets the QoS values to 0 (default). To allow the Cisco IP phone to trust the connected devices QoS settings, the trust boundary must be extended to the device. This task is completed as follows:

```
ALS2(config)#interface range fastethernet 0/1 - 5
ALS2(config-if-range)#switchport mode access
ALS2(config-if-range)#switchport access vlan 200
ALS2(config-if-range)#switchport voice vlan 201
ALS2(config-if-range)#mls qos trust cos
ALS2(config-if-range)#switchport priority extend trust
ALS2(config-if-range)#exit
```

Verify the configuration using the **show mls qos** commands:

```
ALS1#show mls qos interface fastethernet 0/1
FastEthernet0/1
trust state: not trusted
trust mode: trust cos
COS override: dis
default COS: 0
pass-through: none
trust device: cisco-phone
```

NOTE: The port trust state will be 'not trusted' until a Cisco IP phone is connected to the port.

```
ALS2#show mls qos interface fastethernet 0/1
FastEthernet0/1
trust state: trust cos
trust mode: trust cos
COS override: dis
default COS: 0
pass-through: none
trust device: none
```

You can also use the **show interfaces switchport** command to verify QoS configuration:

```
ALS1#show interfaces fastethernet 0/1 switchport
Name: Fa0/1
Switchport: Enabled
Administrative Mode: static access
Operational Mode: down
Administrative Trunking Encapsulation: dot1q
Negotiation of Trunking: Off
Access Mode VLAN: 100 (DATA)
Trunking Native Mode VLAN: 1 (default)
Voice VLAN: 100 (DATA)
Administrative private-vlan host-association: none
Administrative private-vlan mapping: none
Administrative private-vlan trunk native VLAN: none
Administrative private-vlan trunk encapsulation: dot1q
Administrative private-vlan trunk normal VLANs: none
Administrative private-vlan trunk private VLANs: none
Operational private-vlan: none
Trunking VLANs Enabled: ALL
Pruning VLANs Enabled: 2-1001
Capture Mode Disabled
Capture VLANs Allowed: ALL
Protected: false
Appliance trust: none

ALS2#show interfaces fastethernet 0/1 switchport
Name: Fa0/1
Switchport: Enabled
Administrative Mode: static access
Operational Mode: down
Administrative Trunking Encapsulation: dot1q
Negotiation of Trunking: Off
Access Mode VLAN: 200 (DATA)
Trunking Native Mode VLAN: 1 (default)
Voice VLAN: 201 (VOICE)
Administrative private-vlan host-association: none
Administrative private-vlan mapping: none
Administrative private-vlan trunk native VLAN: none
Administrative private-vlan trunk encapsulation: dot1q
Administrative private-vlan trunk normal VLANs: none
Administrative private-vlan trunk private VLANs: none
Operational private-vlan: none
Trunking VLANs Enabled: ALL
Pruning VLANs Enabled: 2-1001
Capture Mode Disabled
Capture VLANs Allowed: ALL
Protected: false
Appliance trust: trusted
```

Task 8

By default, Cisco IOS Catalyst switches uses a default CoS value of 0. To specify a default CoS value other than 0, you must explicitly configure the switch port using the **mls qos cos [override]** command. The [**override**] keyword overrides the configured trust state and assigns all traffic the configured CoS value.

```
ALS1(config)#interface range fastethernet 0/10 - 12
ALS1(config-if-range)#switchport mode access
ALS1(config-if-range)#mls qos cos 3
ALS1(config-if-range)#mls qos cos override
ALS1(config-if-range)#exit

ALS2(config)#interface range fastethernet 0/10 - 12
ALS2(config-if-range)#switchport mode access
ALS2(config-if-range)#mls qos cos 3
ALS2(config-if-range)#mls qos cos override
ALS2(config-if-range)#exit
```

Again, use the **show mls qos** commands to verify this configuration:

```
ALS2#show mls qos interface fastethernet 0/12
FastEthernet0/12
trust state: not trusted
trust mode: not trusted
COS override: ena
default COS: 3
pass-through: none
trust device: none
```

FINAL SWITCH CONFIGURATIONS

DLS1

```
DLS1#term len 0
DLS1#sh run
Building configuration...

Current configuration : 4834 bytes
!
version 12.2
no service pad
service timestamps debug datetime msec
service timestamps log datetime msec
no service password-encryption
!
hostname DLS1
!
no logging console
!
no aaa new-model
mls qos
ip subnet-zero
ip routing
no ip domain-lookup
ip dhcp excluded-address 100.1.1.1 100.1.1.4
ip dhcp excluded-address 101.1.1.1 101.1.1.4
!
ip dhcp pool DATA
   network 100.1.1.0 255.255.255.0
   default-router 100.1.1.1
   domain-name howtonetwork.net
   dns-server 172.16.1.254 172.16.2.254
   lease 5
!
ip dhcp pool VOICE
   network 101.1.1.0 255.255.255.0
   domain-name howtonetwork.net
   dns-server 172.16.1.254 172.16.2.254
   option 150 ip 192.168.0.254
   lease 5
!
spanning-tree mode pvst
```

```
spanning-tree extend system-id
!
vlan internal allocation policy ascending
!
interface Port-channel1
 no switchport
 ip address 192.168.0.1 255.255.255.252
!
interface FastEthernet0/1
 switchport mode dynamic desirable
 shutdown
!
interface FastEthernet0/2
 switchport mode dynamic desirable
 shutdown
!
interface FastEthernet0/3
 switchport mode dynamic desirable
 shutdown
!
interface FastEthernet0/4
 switchport mode dynamic desirable
 shutdown
!
interface FastEthernet0/5
 switchport mode dynamic desirable
 shutdown
!
interface FastEthernet0/6
 switchport mode dynamic desirable
 shutdown
!
interface FastEthernet0/7
 switchport trunk encapsulation dot1q
 switchport mode trunk
 mls qos trust cos
!
interface FastEthernet0/8
 switchport mode dynamic desirable
 shutdown
!
interface FastEthernet0/9
 switchport mode dynamic desirable
 shutdown
!
interface FastEthernet0/10
 switchport mode dynamic desirable
 shutdown
!
interface FastEthernet0/11
 no switchport
 no ip address
 mls qos trust dscp
 channel-group 1 mode desirable
!
interface FastEthernet0/12
 no switchport
 no ip address
 mls qos trust dscp
 channel-group 1 mode desirable

[Truncated Output]

interface Vlan1
 no ip address
 shutdown
!
interface Vlan100
 ip address 100.1.1.1 255.255.255.0
!
interface Vlan101
 ip address 101.1.1.1 255.255.255.0
!
router ospf 1
 log-adjacency-changes
 network 100.1.1.0 0.0.0.255 area 0
 network 101.1.1.0 0.0.0.255 area 0
 network 192.168.0.0 0.0.0.3 area 0
!
```

```
ip classless
ip http server
ip http secure-server
!
control-plane
!
line con 0
line vty 5 15
!
end

DLS1#
```

DLS2

```
DLS2#term len 0
DLS2#sh run
Building configuration...

Current configuration : 4536 bytes
!
version 12.2
no service pad
service timestamps debug datetime msec
service timestamps log datetime msec
no service password-encryption
!
hostname DLS2
!
no logging console
!
no aaa new-model
mls qos
ip subnet-zero
ip routing
no ip domain-lookup
!
spanning-tree mode pvst
spanning-tree extend system-id
!
vlan internal allocation policy ascending
!
interface Port-channel1
 no switchport
 ip address 192.168.0.2 255.255.255.252
!
interface FastEthernet0/1
 switchport mode dynamic desirable
 shutdown
!
interface FastEthernet0/2
 switchport mode dynamic desirable
 shutdown
!
interface FastEthernet0/3
 switchport mode dynamic desirable
 shutdown
!
interface FastEthernet0/4
 switchport mode dynamic desirable
 shutdown
!
interface FastEthernet0/5
 switchport mode dynamic desirable
 shutdown
!
interface FastEthernet0/6
 switchport mode dynamic desirable
 shutdown
!
interface FastEthernet0/7
 switchport trunk encapsulation dot1q
 switchport mode trunk
 mls qos trust cos
!
interface FastEthernet0/8
 switchport mode dynamic desirable
 shutdown
```

```
!
interface FastEthernet0/9
 switchport mode dynamic desirable
 shutdown
!
interface FastEthernet0/10
 switchport mode dynamic desirable
 shutdown
!
interface FastEthernet0/11
 no switchport
 no ip address
 mls qos trust dscp
 channel-group 1 mode desirable
!
interface FastEthernet0/12
 no switchport
 no ip address
 mls qos trust dscp
 channel-group 1 mode desirable

[Truncated Output]

interface Vlan1
 no ip address
 shutdown
!
interface Vlan200
 ip address 200.1.1.1 255.255.255.0
 ip helper-address 192.168.1.254
 ip helper-address 192.168.2.254
!
interface Vlan201
 ip address 201.1.1.1 255.255.255.0
 ip helper-address 192.168.1.254
 ip helper-address 192.168.2.254
!
router ospf 2
 log-adjacency-changes
 network 192.168.0.0 0.0.0.3 area 0
 network 200.1.1.0 0.0.0.255 area 0
 network 201.1.1.0 0.0.0.255 area 0
!
ip classless
ip http server
ip http secure-server
!
control-plane
!
line con 0
line vty 5 15
!
end

DLS2#
```

ALS1

```
ALS1#term len 0
ALS1#sh run
Building configuration...

Current configuration : 1856 bytes
!
version 12.1
no service pad
service timestamps debug uptime
service timestamps log uptime
no service password-encryption
!
hostname ALS1
!
no logging console
!
ip subnet-zero
!
no ip domain-lookup
!
```

```
spanning-tree mode pvst
no spanning-tree optimize bpdu transmission
spanning-tree extend system-id
!
interface FastEthernet0/1
 switchport access vlan 100
 switchport mode access
 switchport voice vlan 100
 shutdown
 mls qos trust device cisco-phone
 mls qos trust cos
 spanning-tree portfast
!
interface FastEthernet0/2
 switchport access vlan 100
 switchport mode access
 switchport voice vlan 100
 shutdown
 mls qos trust device cisco-phone
 mls qos trust cos
 spanning-tree portfast
!
interface FastEthernet0/3
 switchport access vlan 100
 switchport mode access
 switchport voice vlan 100
 shutdown
 mls qos trust device cisco-phone
 mls qos trust cos
 spanning-tree portfast
!
interface FastEthernet0/4
 switchport access vlan 100
 switchport mode access
 switchport voice vlan 100
 shutdown
 mls qos trust device cisco-phone
 mls qos trust cos
 spanning-tree portfast
!
interface FastEthernet0/5
 switchport access vlan 100
 switchport mode access
 switchport voice vlan 100
 shutdown
 mls qos trust device cisco-phone
 mls qos trust cos
 spanning-tree portfast
!
interface FastEthernet0/6
 shutdown
!
interface FastEthernet0/7
 switchport mode trunk
!
interface FastEthernet0/8
 shutdown
!
interface FastEthernet0/9
 shutdown
!
interface FastEthernet0/10
 switchport mode access
 shutdown
 mls qos cos 3
 mls qos cos override
!
interface FastEthernet0/11
 switchport mode access
 shutdown
 mls qos cos 3
 mls qos cos override
!
interface FastEthernet0/12
 switchport mode access
 shutdown
 mls qos cos 3
 mls qos cos override
!
```

```
interface Vlan1
 no ip address
 no ip route-cache
 shutdown
!
ip http server
!
line con 0
line vty 5 15
!
end
ALS1#
```

ALS2

```
ALS2#term len 0
ALS2#sh run
Building configuration...

Current configuration : 1856 bytes
!
version 12.1
no service pad
service timestamps debug uptime
service timestamps log uptime
no service password-encryption
!
hostname ALS2
!
no logging console
!
ip subnet-zero
!
no ip domain-lookup
!
spanning-tree mode pvst
no spanning-tree optimize bpdu transmission
spanning-tree extend system-id
!
interface FastEthernet0/1
 switchport access vlan 200
 switchport mode access
 switchport voice vlan 201
 switchport priority extend trust
 shutdown
 mls qos trust cos
 spanning-tree portfast
!
interface FastEthernet0/2
 switchport access vlan 200
 switchport mode access
 switchport voice vlan 201
 switchport priority extend trust
 shutdown
 mls qos trust cos
 spanning-tree portfast
!
interface FastEthernet0/3
 switchport access vlan 200
 switchport mode access
 switchport voice vlan 201
 switchport priority extend trust
 shutdown
 mls qos trust cos
 spanning-tree portfast
!
interface FastEthernet0/4
 switchport access vlan 200
 switchport mode access
 switchport voice vlan 201
 switchport priority extend trust
 shutdown
 mls qos trust cos
 spanning-tree portfast
!
interface FastEthernet0/5
 switchport access vlan 200
 switchport mode access
```

```
 switchport voice vlan 201
 switchport priority extend trust
 shutdown
 mls qos trust cos
 spanning-tree portfast
!
interface FastEthernet0/6
 shutdown
!
interface FastEthernet0/7
 switchport mode trunk
!
interface FastEthernet0/8
 shutdown
!
interface FastEthernet0/9
 shutdown
!
interface FastEthernet0/10
 switchport mode access
 shutdown
 mls qos cos 3
 mls qos cos override
!
interface FastEthernet0/11
 switchport mode access
 shutdown
 mls qos cos 3
 mls qos cos override
!
interface FastEthernet0/12
 switchport mode access
 shutdown
 mls qos cos 3
 mls qos cos override
!
interface Vlan1
 no ip address
 no ip route-cache
 shutdown
!
ip http server
!
line con 0
line vty 5 15
!
end

ALS2#
```

CCNP LAB 10

Router, Port and VLAN ACLs

Lab Objective:

The focus of this lab is to understand basic RACL, PACL, and VACL implementation and configuration in Cisco IOS Catalyst switches.

Lab Topology:

The lab network topology is illustrated below:

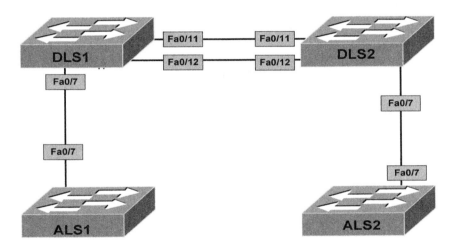

IMPORTANT NOTE: If you are using the www.howtonetwork.net racks, please begin each and every lab by shutting down all interfaces on all switches and then manually re-enabling only the interfaces that are illustrated in this topology.

Task 1

Disable VTP on all switches and configure VLAN 100 on switches DLS1 and ALS1 and VLAN 200 on switches DLS2 and ALS2.

Task 2

Configure 802.1Q trunks between DLS1 and ALS1 as well as between DLS2 and ALS2. Ensure that DTP is disabled on all trunk links.

Next, configure an LACP Layer 3 EtherChannel between switches DLS1 and DLS2. Use the 192.168.0.0/30 subnet for the EtherChannel.

Task 3

Configure the following SVIs and interfaces on the switches in the topology:

- DLS1: Interface VLAN 100: IP address 100.1.1.1/24
- ALS1: Interface VLAN 100: IP address 100.1.1.2/24

- DLS2: Interface VLAN 200: IP address 200.1.1.1/24
- ALS2: Interface VLAN 200: IP address 200.1.1.2/24

Task 4

Configure OSPF on switches DLS1 and DLS2 so that switches ALS1 and ALS2 have IP reachability to each other. Verify that switches ALS1 and ALS2 can ping each other.

Task 5

Configure an inbound RACL on switch DLS1s EtherChannel that allows OSPF and PING traffic anywhere. The RACL should also only allow TCP traffic if the session was initiated by any host residing on VLAN 100. In other words, switches DLS2 and ALS2 should not be able to initiate a Telnet (for example) connection to switches ALS1 and DLS1. However, switches ALS1 and DLS1 can Telnet to them. Test your configuration.

Task 6

Configure an inbound PACL on the trunk link between DLS1 and ALS1 that allows frames only sent by switch ALS1 to be forwarded. Verify that you can still ping ALS2 from ALS1. Additionally, in the event that routing fails on switch DLS1, ensure that non-IP packets can be bridged between VLAN 100 and switch DLS2.

Task 7

Configure a VACL on switch DLS2 for VLAN 200 that performs the following:
- It permits all non-IP traffic
- It denies all UDP traffic
- It permits all TCP traffic
- It permits all ICMP traffic
- It denies all other traffic

LAB VALIDATION

Task 1

```
DLS1(config)#vtp mode transparent
Setting device to VTP TRANSPARENT mode.

DLS2(config)#vtp mode transparent
Setting device to VTP TRANSPARENT mode.

ALS1(config)#vtp mode transparent
Setting device to VTP TRANSPARENT mode.

ALS2(config)#vtp mode transparent
Setting device to VTP TRANSPARENT mode.
```

Task 2

```
DLS1(config)#interface fastethernet 0/7
DLS1(config-if)#switchport
DLS1(config-if)#switchport trunk encapsulation dot1q
DLS1(config-if)#switchport mode trunk
DLS1(config-if)#switchport nonegotiate
DLS1(config-if)#exit
DLS1(config)#interface range fastethernet 0/11 - 12
```

```
DLS1(config-if-range)#no switchport
DLS1(config-if-range)#channel-group 1 mode active
Creating a port-channel interface Port-channel 1

DLS1(config-if-range)#exit
DLS1(config)#interface port-channel 1
DLS1(config-if)#ip address 192.168.0.1 255.255.255.252
DLS1(config-if)#exit

DLS2(config)#interface fastethernet 0/7
DLS2(config-if)#switchport
DLS2(config-if)#switchport trunk encapsulation dot1q
DLS2(config-if)#switchport mode trunk
DLS2(config-if)#switchport nonegotiate
DLS2(config-if)#exit
DLS2(config)#interface range fastethernet 0/11 - 12
DLS2(config-if-range)#no switchport
DLS2(config-if-range)#channel-group 1 mode active
Creating a port-channel interface Port-channel 1

DLS2(config-if-range)#exit
DLS2(config)#interface port-channel 1
DLS2(config-if)#ip address 192.168.0.2 255.255.255.252
DLS2(config-if)#exit

ALS1(config)#interface fastethernet 0/7
ALS1(config-if)#switchport mode trunk
ALS1(config-if)#switchport nonegotiate
ALS1(config-if)#exit

ALS2(config)#interface fastethernet 0/7
ALS2(config-if)#switchport mode trunk
ALS2(config-if)#switchport nonegotiate
ALS2(config-if)#exit
```

Verify your trunking configuration using the **show interfaces trunk** command:

```
ALS1#show interfaces trunk

Port        Mode          Encapsulation Status        Native vlan
Fa0/7       on            802.1q        trunking      1

Port        Vlans allowed on trunk
Fa0/7       1-4094

Port        Vlans allowed and active in management domain
Fa0/7       1,101

Port        Vlans in spanning tree forwarding state and not pruned
Fa0/7       1,101
```

Use the show **etherchannel** commands to verify EtherChannel configuration:

```
DLS1#show etherchannel summary
Flags:  D - down         P - bundled in port-channel
        I - stand-alone s - suspended
        H - Hot-standby (LACP only)
        R - Layer3        S - Layer2
        U - in use        f - failed to allocate aggregator

        M - not in use, minimum links not met
        u - unsuitable for bundling
        w - waiting to be aggregated
        d - default port

Number of channel-groups in use: 1
Number of aggregators:           1

Group  Port-channel  Protocol    Ports
------+-------------+-----------+-----------------------------------------
1      Po1(RU)       LACP        Fa0/11(P)   Fa0/12(P)
```

Finally, use a simple ping test to verify connectivity between switches DLS1 and DLS2:

```
DLS1#ping 192.168.0.2 repeat 10

Type escape sequence to abort.
Sending 10, 100-byte ICMP Echos to 192.168.0.2, timeout is 2 seconds:
..!!!!!!!!
Success rate is 80 percent (8/10), round-trip min/avg/max = 4/4/4 ms
```

Task 3

```
DLS1(config)#vlan 100
DLS1(config-vlan)#exit
DLS1(config)#interface vlan 100
DLS1(config-if)#ip address 100.1.1.1 255.255.255.0
DLS1(config-if)#exit

DLS2(config)#vlan 200
DLS2(config-vlan)#exit
DLS2(config)#interface vlan 200
DLS2(config-if)#ip address 200.1.1.1 255.255.255.0
DLS2(config-if)#exit

ALS1(config)#vlan 100
ALS1(config-vlan)#exit
ALS1(config)#interface vlan 100
ALS1(config-if)#ip address 100.1.1.2 255.255.255.0
ALS1(config-if)#exit

ALS2(config)#vlan 200
ALS2(config-vlan)#exit
ALS2(config)#interface vlan 200
ALS2(config-if)#ip address 200.1.1.2 255.255.255.0
ALS2(config-if)#exit
```

Verify connectivity between switches DLS1 and ALS1 using a simple ping:

```
ALS1#ping 100.1.1.1

Type escape sequence to abort.
Sending 5, 100-byte ICMP Echos to 100.1.1.1, timeout is 2 seconds:
.!!!!
Success rate is 80 percent (4/5), round-trip min/avg/max = 1/3/4 ms
```

Verify connectivity between switches DLS1 and ALS1 using a simple ping:

```
ALS2#ping 200.1.1.1

Type escape sequence to abort.
Sending 5, 100-byte ICMP Echos to 200.1.1.1, timeout is 2 seconds:
.!!!!
Success rate is 80 percent (4/5), round-trip min/avg/max = 1/3/4 ms
```

Task 4

The first part of this task is straightforward and is completed as follows:

```
DLS1(config)#ip routing
DLS1(config)#router ospf 1
DLS1(config-router)#network 0.0.0.0 255.255.255.255 area 0
DLS1(config-router)#exit

DLS2(config)#ip routing
DLS2(config)#router ospf 2
DLS2(config-router)#network 0.0.0.0 255.255.255.255 area 0
DLS2(config-router)#exit
```

Verify OSPF configuration using the **show ip ospf** and **show ip route** commands:

```
DLS2#show ip ospf neighbor

Neighbor ID   Pri State    Dead Time   Address       Interface
192.168.0.1   1   FULL/DR  00:00:31    192.168.0.1   Port-channel1

DLS2#show ip route ospf
     100.0.0.0/24 is subnetted, 1 subnets
0        100.1.1.0 [110/2] via 192.168.0.1, 00:02:21, Port-channel1
```

In order to allow ALS1 and ALS2 to ping each other, both switches need a default gateway:

```
ALS1(config)#ip default-gateway 100.1.1.1

ALS2(config)#ip default-gateway 200.1.1.1
```

Finally, verify connectivity using a simple ping:

```
ALS2#ping 100.1.1.1

Type escape sequence to abort.
Sending 5, 100-byte ICMP Echos to 100.1.1.1, timeout is 2 seconds:
!!!!!
Success rate is 100 percent (5/5), round-trip min/avg/max = 4/4/4 ms
```

Task 5

The first two requirements are straightforward; however, the third; however, requires the use of the established keyword. This keyword matches on both the TCP ACK and RST bits. These bits are sent in response to an original SYN (hence are sent in response to an initiated connection). This task is completed as follows:

```
DLS1(config)#ip access-list extended INBOUND
DLS1(config-ext-nacl)#permit ospf any any
DLS1(config-ext-nacl)#permit icmp any any
DLS1(config-ext-nacl)#permit tcp any any established
DLS1(config-ext-nacl)#exit
DLS1(config)#interface port-channel 1
DLS1(config-if)#ip access-group INBOUND in
DLS1(config-if)#exit
```

To verify your configuration, attempt to Telnet from switch ALS2 to switch ALS1:

```
ALS2#ping 100.1.1.2

Type escape sequence to abort.
Sending 5, 100-byte ICMP Echos to 100.1.1.1, timeout is 2 seconds:
!!!!!
Success rate is 100 percent (5/5), round-trip min/avg/max = 1/3/4 ms
ALS2#
ALS2#telnet 100.1.1.2
Trying 100.1.1.2 ...
% Destination unreachable; gateway or host down
```

Next, attempt to Telnet from switch ALS1 to switch ALS2:

```
ALS1#ping 200.1.1.2

Type escape sequence to abort.
Sending 5, 100-byte ICMP Echos to 200.1.1.2, timeout is 2 seconds:
!!!!!
Success rate is 100 percent (5/5), round-trip min/avg/max = 1/2/4 ms
ALS1#
ALS1#telnet 200.1.1.2
Trying 200.1.1.2 ... Open

Password required, but none set

[Connection to 200.1.1.2 closed by foreign host]
ALS1#
```

Task 6

The first part of this task requires the use of a MAC ACL. This is completed as follows:

```
DLS1(config)#mac access-list extended HOST-ALS1-ONLY
DLS1(config-ext-macl)#permit host 0007.8432.dd00 any
DLS1(config-ext-macl)#exit
DLS1(config)#interface fastethernet 0/7
DLS1(config-if)#mac access-group HOST-ALS1-ONLY in
DLS1(config-if)#exit
```

NOTE: You can use the show arp command to acquire the MAC address of switch ALS1.

Next, verify that following the PACL configuration, switch ALS1 can reach DLS2 and ALS2:

```
ALS1#ping 200.1.1.2

Type escape sequence to abort.
Sending 5, 100-byte ICMP Echos to 200.1.1.2, timeout is 2 seconds:
!!!!!
Success rate is 100 percent (5/5), round-trip min/avg/max = 4/4/4 ms
```

The second part of this task requires the configuration of fallback bridging. Fallback bridging allows the bridging together of two or more VLANs or routed ports, allowing the switch to forward non-routable traffic within the bridge group. This task is completed as follows:

```
DLS1(config)#bridge 1 protocol vlan-bridge
DLS1(config)#interface vlan 100
DLS1(config-if)#bridge-group 1
DLS1(config-if)#exit
DLS1(config)#interface port-channel 1
DLS1(config-if)#bridge-group 1
DLS1(config-if)#exit
```

Verify your configuration using the **show bridge** commands:

```
DLS1#show bridge group

Bridge Group 1 is running the VLAN Bridge compatible Spanning Tree protocol

    Port 57 (Vlan100) of bridge group 1 is forwarding
    Port 56 (Port-channel1) of bridge group 1 is forwarding
```

Task 7

When configuring VACLs, if the VLAN map has at least one match clause for the type of packet (IP or MAC) and the packet does not match any of these match clauses, the default is to drop the packet. If there is no match clause for that type of packet in the VLAN map, the default is to forward the packet. This task is completed as follows:

```
DLS2(config)#ip access-list extended ALLOW-ICMP-ONLY
DLS2(config-ext-nacl)#permit icmp any any
DLS2(config-ext-nacl)#exit
DLS2(config)#ip access-list extended ALLOW-TCP-ONLY
DLS2(config-ext-nacl)#permit tcp any any
DLS2(config-ext-nacl)#exit
DLS2(config)#vlan access-map VLAN-200-FILTER 10
DLS2(config-access-map)#match ip address ALLOW-ICMP-ONLY
DLS2(config-access-map)#action forward
DLS2(config-access-map)#exit
DLS2(config)#vlan access-map VLAN-200-FILTER 20
DLS2(config-access-map)#match ip address ALLOW-TCP-ONLY
DLS2(config-access-map)#action forward
DLS2(config-access-map)#exit
DLS2(config)#vlan filter VLAN-200-FILTER vlan-list 200
```

Use the **show vlan access-map** and **show vlan filter** commands to verify your configuration:

```
DLS2#show vlan access-map
Vlan access-map "VLAN-200-FILTER" 10
  Match clauses:
    ip address: ALLOW-ICMP ALLOW-ICMP-ONLY
  Action:
    forward
Vlan access-map "VLAN-200-FILTER" 20
  Match clauses:
    ip address: ALLOW-TCP ALLOW-TCP-ONLY
  Action:
    forward

DLS2#show vlan filter
VLAN Map VLAN-200-FILTER is filtering VLANs:
  200
```

Finally, test your configuration using PING and Telnet from ALS1 to ALS2:

```
ALS1#ping 200.1.1.2

Type escape sequence to abort.
Sending 5, 100-byte ICMP Echos to 200.1.1.2, timeout is 2 seconds:
!!!!!
Success rate is 100 percent (5/5), round-trip min/avg/max = 1/2/4 ms
ALS1#
ALS1#telnet 200.1.1.2
Trying 200.1.1.2 ... Open


Password required, but none set

[Connection to 200.1.1.2 closed by foreign host]
```

FINAL SWITCH CONFIGURATIONS

DLS1

```
DLS1#term len 0
DLS1#sh run
Building configuration...

Current configuration : 4587 bytes
!
version 12.2
no service pad
service timestamps debug datetime msec
service timestamps log datetime msec
no service password-encryption
!
hostname DLS1
!
no logging console
!
no aaa new-model
ip subnet-zero
ip routing
no ip domain-lookup
!
vtp domain ONE
vtp mode transparent
!
mac access-list extended HOST-ALS1-ONLY
 permit host 0007.8432.dd00 any
spanning-tree mode pvst
spanning-tree extend system-id
!
vlan internal allocation policy ascending
!
vlan 100
!
interface Port-channel1
```

```
  no switchport
  ip address 192.168.0.1 255.255.255.252
  ip access-group INBOUND in
  bridge-group 1
!
interface FastEthernet0/1
 switchport mode dynamic desirable
 shutdown
!
interface FastEthernet0/2
 switchport mode dynamic desirable
 shutdown
!
interface FastEthernet0/3
 switchport mode dynamic desirable
 shutdown
!
interface FastEthernet0/4
 switchport mode dynamic desirable
 shutdown
!
interface FastEthernet0/5
 switchport mode dynamic desirable
 shutdown
!
interface FastEthernet0/6
 switchport mode dynamic desirable
 shutdown
!
interface FastEthernet0/7
 switchport trunk encapsulation dot1q
 switchport mode trunk
 switchport nonegotiate
 mac access-group HOST-ALS1-ONLY in
!
interface FastEthernet0/8
 switchport mode dynamic desirable
 shutdown
!
interface FastEthernet0/9
 switchport mode dynamic desirable
 shutdown
!
interface FastEthernet0/10
 switchport mode dynamic desirable
 shutdown
!
interface FastEthernet0/11
 no switchport
 no ip address
 channel-group 1 mode active
!
interface FastEthernet0/12
 no switchport
 no ip address
 channel-group 1 mode active

[Truncated Output]

interface Vlan1
 no ip address
 shutdown
!
interface Vlan100
 ip address 100.1.1.1 255.255.255.0
 bridge-group 1
!
router ospf 1
 log-adjacency-changes
 network 0.0.0.0 255.255.255.255 area 0
!
ip classless
ip http server
ip http secure-server
!
ip access-list extended INBOUND
 permit ospf any any
 permit icmp any any
 permit tcp any any established
```

```
!
bridge 1 protocol vlan-bridge
!
control-plane
!
line con 0
line vty 5 15
!
end

DLS1#
```

DLS2

```
DLS2#term len 0
DLS2#sh run
Building configuration...

Current configuration : 4637 bytes
!
version 12.2
no service pad
service timestamps debug datetime msec
service timestamps log datetime msec
no service password-encryption
!
hostname DLS2
!
no logging console
!
no aaa new-model
ip subnet-zero
ip routing
no ip domain-lookup
!
vtp domain TWO
vtp mode transparent
!
spanning-tree mode pvst
spanning-tree extend system-id
!
vlan internal allocation policy ascending
!
vlan access-map VLAN-200-FILTER 10
 action forward
 match ip address ALLOW-ICMP ALLOW-ICMP-ONLY
vlan access-map VLAN-200-FILTER 20
 action forward
 match ip address ALLOW-TCP ALLOW-TCP-ONLY
!
vlan filter VLAN-200-FILTER vlan-list 200
!
vlan 200
!
interface Port-channel1
 no switchport
 ip address 192.168.0.2 255.255.255.252
!
interface FastEthernet0/1
 switchport mode dynamic desirable
 shutdown
!
interface FastEthernet0/2
 switchport mode dynamic desirable
 shutdown
!
interface FastEthernet0/3
 switchport mode dynamic desirable
 shutdown
!
interface FastEthernet0/4
 switchport mode dynamic desirable
 shutdown
!
interface FastEthernet0/5
 switchport mode dynamic desirable
 shutdown
!
interface FastEthernet0/6
```

```
 switchport mode dynamic desirable
 shutdown
!
interface FastEthernet0/7
 switchport trunk encapsulation dot1q
 switchport mode trunk
 switchport nonegotiate
!
interface FastEthernet0/8
 switchport mode dynamic desirable
 shutdown
!
interface FastEthernet0/9
 switchport mode dynamic desirable
 shutdown
!
interface FastEthernet0/10
 switchport mode dynamic desirable
 shutdown
!
interface FastEthernet0/11
 no switchport
 no ip address
 channel-group 1 mode active
!
interface FastEthernet0/12
 no switchport
 no ip address
 channel-group 1 mode active

[Truncated Output]

interface Vlan1
 no ip address
 shutdown
!
interface Vlan200
 ip address 200.1.1.1 255.255.255.0
!
router ospf 2
 log-adjacency-changes
 network 0.0.0.0 255.255.255.255 area 0
!
ip classless
ip http server
ip http secure-server
!
!
ip access-list extended ALLOW-ICMP-ONLY
 permit icmp any any
ip access-list extended ALLOW-TCP-ONLY
 permit tcp any any
!
control-plane
!
line con 0
line vty 5 15
!
end

DLS2#
```

ALS1

```
ALS1#term len 0
ALS1#sh run
Building configuration...

Current configuration : 1069 bytes
!
version 12.1
no service pad
service timestamps debug uptime
service timestamps log uptime
no service password-encryption
!
hostname ALS1
!
```

```
no logging console
!
ip subnet-zero
!
no ip domain-lookup
vtp domain ONE
vtp mode transparent
!
spanning-tree mode pvst
no spanning-tree optimize bpdu transmission
spanning-tree extend system-id
!
vlan 100
!
interface FastEthernet0/1
 shutdown
!
interface FastEthernet0/2
 shutdown
!
interface FastEthernet0/3
 shutdown
!
interface FastEthernet0/4
 shutdown
!
interface FastEthernet0/5
 shutdown
!
interface FastEthernet0/6
 shutdown
!
interface FastEthernet0/7
 switchport mode trunk
 switchport nonegotiate
!
interface FastEthernet0/8
 shutdown
!
interface FastEthernet0/9
 shutdown
!
interface FastEthernet0/10
 shutdown
!
interface FastEthernet0/11
 shutdown
!
interface FastEthernet0/12
 shutdown
!
interface Vlan1
 no ip address
 no ip route-cache
 shutdown
!
interface Vlan100
 ip address 100.1.1.2 255.255.255.0
 no ip route-cache
!
ip default-gateway 100.1.1.1
ip http server
!
line con 0
line vty 5 15
!
end

ALS1#
```

ALS2

```
ALS2#term len 0
ALS2#sh run
Building configuration...

Current configuration : 1069 bytes
!
```

```
version 12.1
no service pad
service timestamps debug uptime
service timestamps log uptime
no service password-encryption
!
hostname ALS2
!
no logging console
!
ip subnet-zero
!
no ip domain-lookup
vtp domain TWO
vtp mode transparent
!
spanning-tree mode pvst
no spanning-tree optimize bpdu transmission
spanning-tree extend system-id
!
vlan 200
!
interface FastEthernet0/1
 shutdown
!
interface FastEthernet0/2
 shutdown
!
interface FastEthernet0/3
 shutdown
!
interface FastEthernet0/4
 shutdown
!
interface FastEthernet0/5
 shutdown
!
interface FastEthernet0/6
 shutdown
!
interface FastEthernet0/7
 switchport mode trunk
 switchport nonegotiate
!
interface FastEthernet0/8
 shutdown
!
interface FastEthernet0/9
 shutdown
!
interface FastEthernet0/10
 shutdown
!
interface FastEthernet0/11
 shutdown
!
interface FastEthernet0/12
 shutdown
!
interface Vlan1
 no ip address
 no ip route-cache
 shutdown
!
interface Vlan200
 ip address 200.1.1.2 255.255.255.0
 no ip route-cache
!
ip default-gateway 200.1.1.1
ip http server
!
line con 0
line vty 5 15
!
end

ALS2#
```

CCNP LAB 11

EIGRP Multi-Technology

Lab Objective:

The focus of this lab is to understand EIGRP implementation and configuration in Cisco IOS routers. Additional technologies tested include redistribution and path control. In addition, basic ODR implementation and configuration is also tested.

Lab Topology:

The lab network topology is illustrated below:

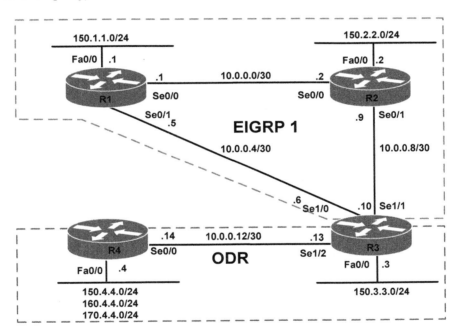

IMPORTANT NOTE: If you are using the www.howtonetwork.net racks, please bring up the LAN interfaces connected to the routers by issuing the no shutdown command on the connected switches. If you are using a home lab with no Switches, you can bring up the LAN interfaces using the following configurations on your routers:

```
interface fastethernet 0/0
  no keepalive
  loopback
  no shutdown
```

Alternately, you can simply connect the interfaces to a hub or switch if you have one available in your own lab.

Task 1

Configure hostnames and IP addressing on all routers as illustrated in the network topology.

Task 2

Configure EIGRP for AS 1as is illustrated in the topology; however, you should NOT advertise the 10.0.0.12/30 subnet between routers R3 and R4 or the 150.3.3.0/24 LAN subnet connected to R3 via EIGRP. Ensure that no EIGRP packets are sent or received on any interfaces for which EIGRP is enabled but which will have no EIGRP neighbors. Verify your configuration.

Task 3

Configure ODR between R3 and R4. Verify that R3 receives the 150.4.4.0/24, 160.4.4.0/24, and 170.4.4.0/24 subnets connected to R4s LAN interface via ODR.

Task 4

Configure your network so that all the other routers can reach the 150.4.4.0/24, 160.4.4.0/24, and 170.4.4.4.0/24 subnets configured on R4. These prefixes should be assigned a route tag of 150, 160, and 170, respectively. Ensure all routers can ping each other following this configuration. Verify your configuration using the appropriate commands.

Task 5

Configure your network so R1 prefers the path via R2 to reach the 150.3.3.0/24 and 150.4.4.0/24 subnets. All other routes should follow the best path. Do NOT modify EIGRP metrics in any manner to complete this task. Verify your configuration.

LAB VALIDATION

Task 1

```
Router(config)#hostname R1
R1(config)#interface fastethernet 0/0
R1(config-if)#no shutdown
R1(config-if)#ip address 150.1.1.1 255.255.255.0
R1(config-if)#exit
R1(config)#interface serial 0/0
R1(config-if)#no shutdown
R1(config-if)#ip address 10.0.0.1 255.255.255.252
R1(config-if)#clock rate 2000000
R1(config-if)#exit
R1(config)#interface serial 0/1
R1(config-if)#no shutdown
R1(config-if)#ip address 10.0.0.5 255.255.255.252
R1(config-if)#exit

Router(config)#hostname R2
R2(config)#interface fastethernet 0/0
R2(config-if)#no shutdown
R2(config-if)#ip address 150.2.2.2 255.255.255.0
R2(config-if)#exit
R2(config)#interface serial 0/0
R2(config-if)#no shutdown
R2(config-if)#ip address 10.0.0.2 255.255.255.252
R2(config-if)#exit
R2(config)#interface serial 0/0
R2(config-if)#no shutdown
R2(config-if)#ip address 10.0.0.9 255.255.255.252
R2(config-if)#exit

Router(config)#hostname R3
R3(config)#interface fastethernet 0/0
R3(config-if)#no shutdown
R3(config-if)#ip address 150.3.3.3 255.255.255.0
R3(config-if)#exit
R3(config)#interface serial 1/0
R3(config-if)#no shutdown
R3(config-if)#ip address 10.0.0.6 255.255.255.252
```

```
R3(config-if)#clock rate 128000
R3(config-if)#exit
R3(config)#interface serial 1/1
R3(config-if)#no shutdown
R3(config-if)#ip address 10.0.0.10 255.255.255.252
R3(config-if)#clock rate 128000
R3(config-if)#exit
R3(config)#interface serial 1/2
R3(config-if)#no shutdown
R3(config-if)#ip address 10.0.0.13 255.255.255.252
R3(config-if)#clock rate 128000
R2(config-if)#exit

Router(config)#hostname R4
R4(config)#interface fastethernet 0/0
R4(config-if)#no shutdown
R4(config-if)#ip address 150.4.4.4 255.255.255.0
R4(config-if)#ip address 160.4.4.4 255.255.255.0 secondary
R4(config-if)#ip address 170.4.4.4 255.255.255.0 secondary
R4(config-if)#exit
R4(config)#interface serial 0/0
R4(config-if)#no shutdown
R4(config-if)#ip address 10.0.0.14 255.255.255.252
R4(config-if)#exit
```

Task 2

```
R1(config)#router eigrp 1
R1(config-router)#network 150.1.1.0 0.0.0.255
R1(config-router)#network 10.0.0.0 0.0.0.3
R1(config-router)#network 10.0.0.4 0.0.0.3
R1(config-router)#passive-interface fastethernet 0/0
R1(config-router)#no auto-summary
R1(config-router)#exit

R2(config)#router eigrp 1
R2(config-router)#network 150.2.2.0 0.0.0.255
R2(config-router)#network 10.0.0.0 0.0.0.3
R2(config-router)#network 10.0.0.8 0.0.0.3
R2(config-router)#passive-interface fastethernet 0/0
R2(config-router)#no auto-summary
R2(config-router)#exit

R3(config)#router eigrp 1
R3(config-router)#network 10.0.0.4 0.0.0.3
R3(config-router)#network 10.0.0.8 0.0.0.3
R3(config-router)#no auto-summary
R3(config-router)#exit
```

Verify your configuration using the show ip eigrp neighbors command:

```
R1#show ip eigrp neighbors
IP-EIGRP neighbors for process 1
H   Address               Interface      Hold Uptime    SRTT   RTO   Q   Seq
                                         (sec)          (ms)         Cnt Num
1   10.0.0.6              Se0/1          13 00:00:06    14     200   0   21
0   10.0.0.2              Se0/0          12 00:00:07    5      200   0   25

R2#show ip eigrp neighbors
IP-EIGRP neighbors for process 1
H   Address               Interface      Hold Uptime    SRTT   RTO   Q   Seq
                                         (sec)          (ms)         Cnt Num
1   10.0.0.1              Se0/0          11 00:00:03    3      200   0   31
0   10.0.0.10             Se0/1          14 00:00:05    24     200   0   30

R3#show ip eigrp neighbors
IP-EIGRP neighbors for process 1
H   Address               Interface      Hold Uptime    SRTT   RTO   Q   Seq
                                         (sec)          (ms)         Cnt Num
1   10.0.0.9              Se1/1          11 00:00:03    15     1140  0   38
0   10.0.0.5              Se1/0          14 00:00:05    11     1140  0   35
```

You can view passive interfaces using the show ip protocols command:

```
R1#show ip protocols
Routing Protocol is "eigrp 1"
  Outgoing update filter list for all interfaces is not set
  Incoming update filter list for all interfaces is not set
  Default networks flagged in outgoing updates
  Default networks accepted from incoming updates
  EIGRP metric weight K1=1, K2=0, K3=1, K4=0, K5=0
  EIGRP maximum hopcount 100
  EIGRP maximum metric variance 1
  Redistributing: eigrp 1
  EIGRP NSF-aware route hold timer is 240s
  Automatic network summarization is not in effect
  Maximum path: 4
  Routing for Networks:
    10.0.0.0/30
    10.0.0.4/30
    150.1.1.0/24
  Passive Interface(s):
    FastEthernet0/0
  Routing Information Sources:
    Gateway          Distance      Last Update
    (this router)          90      00:00:27
    10.0.0.2               90      00:00:22
    10.0.0.6               90      00:00:22
  Distance: internal 90 external 170
```

Task 3

In order to run ODR, CDP must be enabled. By default, CDP is enabled on LAN and point-to-point WAN interfaces. If CDP is disabled, it can be globally enabled using the cdp run command. Alternatively, CDP can be enabled on a per-interface basis using the cdp enable command. Use the show cdp interface command to see the interfaces running CDP.

```
R4#show cdp interface
FastEthernet0/0 is up, line protocol is up
  Encapsulation ARPA
  Sending CDP packets every 60 seconds
  Holdtime is 180 seconds
Serial0/0 is up, line protocol is up
  Encapsulation HDLC
  Sending CDP packets every 60 seconds
  Holdtime is 180 seconds
Serial0/1 is administratively down, line protocol is down
  Encapsulation HDLC
  Sending CDP packets every 60 seconds
  Holdtime is 180 seconds
```

The second requirement is that ODR routing is enabled only on the hub using the router odr command. This command should not be enabled on the spoke router. Additionally, there should be no other routing protocols enabled on the spoke router. If a routing protocol has been enabled, ODR will not run on the spoke router. Complete the first part of this task as follows:

```
R3(config)#router odr
R3(config-router)#exit
```

Verify your configuration using the show ip route command:

```
R3#show ip route odr
     170.4.0.0/24 is subnetted, 1 subnets
o       170.4.4.0 [160/1] via 10.0.0.14, 00:00:09, Serial1/2
     160.4.0.0/24 is subnetted, 1 subnets
o       160.4.4.0 [160/1] via 10.0.0.14, 00:00:09, Serial1/2
     150.4.0.0/24 is subnetted, 1 subnets
o       150.4.4.0 [160/1] via 10.0.0.14, 00:00:09, Serial1/2
```

By default, the hub will advertise the spoke router(s) a default route when ODR is enabled:

```
R4#show ip route
Codes: C - connected, S - static, R - RIP, M - mobile, B - BGP
       D - EIGRP, EX - EIGRP external, O - OSPF, IA - OSPF inter area
       N1 - OSPF NSSA external type 1, N2 - OSPF NSSA external type 2
       E1 - OSPF external type 1, E2 - OSPF external type 2
       i - IS-IS, su - IS-IS summary, L1 - IS-IS level-1, L2 - IS-IS level-2
       ia - IS-IS inter area, * - candidate default, U - per-user static route
       o - ODR, P - periodic downloaded static route

Gateway of last resort is 10.0.0.13 to network 0.0.0.0

     170.4.0.0/24 is subnetted, 1 subnets
C       170.4.4.0 is directly connected, FastEthernet0/0
     160.4.0.0/24 is subnetted, 1 subnets
C       160.4.4.0 is directly connected, FastEthernet0/0
     10.0.0.0/30 is subnetted, 1 subnets
C       10.0.0.12 is directly connected, Serial0/0
     150.4.0.0/24 is subnetted, 1 subnets
C       150.4.4.0 is directly connected, FastEthernet0/0
o*   0.0.0.0/0 [160/1] via 10.0.0.13, 00:00:48, Serial0/0
```

Task 4

There are multiple ways in which this task can be completed. The first overall requirement is to complete this task are to redistribute ODR routes into EIGRP via a route map using IP prefix list or ACL matching. Because EIGRP does not assign a default metric to ODR routes, you must specify the metric in the route map, when using the redistribute command, or by configuring a seed metric for EIGRP using the default-metric command. The second overall requirement is to complete this task is to redistribute the connected ODR subnets into EIGRP. This will allow R4 to ping all other routers and vice-versa.

```
R3(config)#ip prefix-list NET-150 seq 5 permit 150.4.4.0/24
R3(config)#ip prefix-list NET-160 seq 5 permit 160.4.4.0/24
R3(config)#ip prefix-list NET-170 seq 5 permit 170.4.4.0/24
R3(config)#route-map ODR-2-EIGRP permit 10
R3(config-route-map)#match ip address prefix-list NET-150
R3(config-route-map)#set tag 150
R3(config-route-map)#exit
R3(config)#route-map ODR-2-EIGRP permit 20
R3(config-route-map)#match ip address prefix-list NET-160
R3(config-route-map)#set tag 160
R3(config-route-map)#exit
R3(config)#route-map ODR-2-EIGRP permit 30
R3(config-route-map)#match ip address prefix-list NET-170
R3(config-route-map)#set tag 170
R3(config-route-map)#exit
R3(config)#router eigrp 1
R3(config-router)#redistribute odr route-map ODR-2-EIGRP
R3(config-router)#redistribute connected
R3(config-router)#default-metric 100000 100 255 1 1500
R3(config-router)#exit
```

Verify the EIGRP redistribution configuration using the show ip eigrp topology command on the local router:

```
R3#show ip eigrp topology | include (tag|Redistributed)
P 150.4.4.0/24, 1 successors, FD is 51200, tag is 150
        via Redistributed (51200/0)
P 160.4.4.0/24, 1 successors, FD is 51200, tag is 160
        via Redistributed (51200/0)
P 170.4.4.0/24, 1 successors, FD is 51200, tag is 170
        via Redistributed (51200/0)
```

NOTE: When routes are redistributed into EIGRP from ODR, the routing protocol is listed as 'Unknown'. This can be verified by looking at specific route entries in the topology table:

```
R3#show ip eigrp topology 150.4.4.0/24
IP-EIGRP (AS 1): Topology entry for 150.4.4.0/24
  State is Passive, Query origin flag is 1, 1 Successor(s), FD is 51200
```

```
Routing Descriptor Blocks:
10.0.0.14, from Redistributed, Send flag is 0x0
    Composite metric is (51200/0), Route is External
    Vector metric:
        Minimum bandwidth is 100000 Kbit
        Total delay is 1000 microseconds
        Reliability is 255/255
        Load is 1/255
        Minimum MTU is 1500
        Hop count is 0
    External data:
        Originating router is 150.3.3.3 (this system)
        AS number of route is 0
        External protocol is Unknown protocol, external metric is 1
        Administrator tag is 150 (0x00000096)
```

Complete this task by pinging between the routers as required in the task:

```
R1#ping 10.0.0.14 source 150.1.1.1

Type escape sequence to abort.
Sending 5, 100-byte ICMP Echos to 10.0.0.14, timeout is 2 seconds:
Packet sent with a source address of 150.1.1.1
!!!!!
Success rate is 100 percent (5/5), round-trip min/avg/max = 28/28/32 ms

R1#ping 150.3.3.3 source 150.1.1.1

Type escape sequence to abort.
Sending 5, 100-byte ICMP Echos to 150.3.3.3, timeout is 2 seconds:
Packet sent with a source address of 150.1.1.1
!!!!!
Success rate is 100 percent (5/5), round-trip min/avg/max = 16/16/16 ms

R1#ping 150.2.2.2 source 150.1.1.1

Type escape sequence to abort.
Sending 5, 100-byte ICMP Echos to 150.2.2.2, timeout is 2 seconds:
Packet sent with a source address of 150.1.1.1
!!!!!
Success rate is 100 percent (5/5), round-trip min/avg/max = 1/2/4 ms
```

Task 5

Before completing this task, the RIB on R1 should show the following external route entries:

```
R1#show ip route eigrp | include EX
D EX    170.4.4.0 [170/2195456] via 10.0.0.6, 00:21:13, Serial0/1
D EX    160.4.4.0 [170/2195456] via 10.0.0.6, 00:21:13, Serial0/1
D EX    10.0.0.12 [170/21024000] via 10.0.0.6, 00:21:27, Serial0/1
D EX    150.3.3.0 [170/2172416] via 10.0.0.6, 00:21:27, Serial0/1
D EX    150.4.4.0 [170/2195456] via 10.0.0.6, 00:21:13, Serial0/1
```

Complete this task my modifying the metrics with an offset list as follows:

```
R1(config)#access-list 1 permit 150.3.3.0 0.0.0.255
R1(config)#access-list 1 permit 150.4.4.0 0.0.0.255
R1(config)#router eigrp 1
R1(config-router)# offset-list 1 in 123456789 serial 0/1
R1(config-router)#exit
```

Following this change, the RIB on R1 should show the following external route entries:

```
R1#show ip route eigrp | include EX
D EX    170.4.4.0 [170/2195456] via 10.0.0.6, 00:02:16, Serial0/1
D EX    160.4.4.0 [170/2195456] via 10.0.0.6, 00:02:16, Serial0/1
D EX    10.0.0.12 [170/21024000] via 10.0.0.6, 00:02:16, Serial0/1
D EX    150.3.3.0 [170/2684416] via 10.0.0.2, 00:01:36, Serial0/0
D EX    150.4.4.0 [170/2707456] via 10.0.0.2, 00:01:36, Serial0/0
```

FINAL ROUTER CONFIGURATIONS

R1

```
R1#term len 0
R1#sh run
Building configuration...

Current configuration : 1094 bytes
!
version 12.4
service timestamps debug datetime msec
service timestamps log datetime msec
no service password-encryption
!
hostname R1
!
boot-start-marker
boot-end-marker
!
no logging console
!
no aaa new-model
no network-clock-participate slot 1
no network-clock-participate wic 0
ip cef
!
no ip domain lookup
ip auth-proxy max-nodata-conns 3
ip admission max-nodata-conns 3
!
interface FastEthernet0/0
 ip address 150.1.1.1 255.255.255.0
 duplex auto
 speed auto
!
interface Serial0/0
 ip address 10.0.0.1 255.255.255.252
 clock rate 2000000
!
interface Serial0/1
 ip address 10.0.0.5 255.255.255.252
!
router eigrp 1
 passive-interface FastEthernet0/0
 offset-list 1 in 123456789 Serial0/1
 network 10.0.0.0 0.0.0.3
 network 10.0.0.4 0.0.0.3
 network 150.1.1.0 0.0.0.255
 no auto-summary
!
ip forward-protocol nd
!
no ip http server
no ip http secure-server
!
access-list 1 permit 150.3.3.0 0.0.0.255
access-list 1 permit 150.4.4.0 0.0.0.255
!
control-plane
!
line con 0
line aux 0
line vty 0 4
 login
!
end

R1#
```

R2

```
R2#term len 0
R2#sh run
Building configuration...
```

```
Current configuration : 954 bytes
!
version 12.4
service timestamps debug datetime msec
service timestamps log datetime msec
no service password-encryption
!
hostname R2
!
boot-start-marker
boot-end-marker
!
no logging console
!
no aaa new-model
no network-clock-participate slot 1
no network-clock-participate wic 0
ip cef
!
no ip domain lookup
ip auth-proxy max-nodata-conns 3
ip admission max-nodata-conns 3
!
interface FastEthernet0/0
 ip address 150.2.2.2 255.255.255.0
 duplex auto
 speed auto
!
interface Serial0/0
 ip address 10.0.0.2 255.255.255.252
!
interface Serial0/1
 ip address 10.0.0.9 255.255.255.252
!
router eigrp 1
 passive-interface FastEthernet0/0
 network 10.0.0.0 0.0.0.3
 network 10.0.0.8 0.0.0.3
 network 150.2.2.0 0.0.0.255
 no auto-summary
!
ip forward-protocol nd
!
no ip http server
no ip http secure-server
!
control-plane
!
line con 0
line aux 0
line vty 0 4
 login
!
end

R2#
```

R3

```
R3#term len 0
R3#sh run
Building configuration...

Current configuration : 1766 bytes
!
version 12.4
service timestamps debug datetime msec
service timestamps log datetime msec
no service password-encryption
!
hostname R3
!
boot-start-marker
boot-end-marker
```

```
!
no logging console
!
no aaa new-model
no network-clock-participate slot 1
no network-clock-participate wic 0
ip cef
!
no ip domain lookup
ip auth-proxy max-nodata-conns 3
ip admission max-nodata-conns 3
!
interface FastEthernet0/0
 ip address 150.3.3.3 255.255.255.0
 duplex auto
 speed auto
!
interface Serial1/0
 ip address 10.0.0.6 255.255.255.252
 clock rate 128000
!
interface Serial1/1
 ip address 10.0.0.10 255.255.255.252
 clock rate 128000
!
interface Serial1/2
 ip address 10.0.0.13 255.255.255.252
 clock rate 128000
!
interface Serial1/3
 no ip address
 shutdown
!
interface Serial1/4
 no ip address
 shutdown
!
interface Serial1/5
 no ip address
 shutdown
!
interface Serial1/6
 no ip address
 shutdown
!
interface Serial1/7
 no ip address
 shutdown
!
router odr
!
router eigrp 1
 redistribute connected
 redistribute odr route-map ODR-2-EIGRP
 network 10.0.0.4 0.0.0.3
 network 10.0.0.8 0.0.0.3
 default-metric 100000 100 255 1 1500
 no auto-summary
!
ip forward-protocol nd
!
no ip http server
no ip http secure-server
!
ip prefix-list NET-150 seq 5 permit 150.4.4.0/24
!
ip prefix-list NET-160 seq 5 permit 160.4.4.0/24
!
ip prefix-list NET-170 seq 5 permit 170.4.4.0/24
!
route-map ODR-2-EIGRP permit 10
 match ip address prefix-list NET-150
 set tag 150
!
route-map ODR-2-EIGRP permit 20
 match ip address prefix-list NET-160
```

```
 set tag 160
!
route-map ODR-2-EIGRP permit 30
 match ip address prefix-list NET-170
 set tag 170
!
control-plane
!
line con 0
line aux 0
line vty 0 4
 login
!
end

R3#
```

R4

```
R4#term len 0
R4#sh run
Building configuration...

Current configuration : 885 bytes
!
version 12.4
service timestamps debug datetime msec
service timestamps log datetime msec
no service password-encryption
!
hostname R4
!
boot-start-marker
boot-end-marker
!
no logging console
!
no aaa new-model
no network-clock-participate slot 1
no network-clock-participate wic 0
ip cef
!
no ip domain lookup
ip auth-proxy max-nodata-conns 3
ip admission max-nodata-conns 3
!
interface FastEthernet0/0
 ip address 160.4.4.4 255.255.255.0 secondary
 ip address 170.4.4.4 255.255.255.0 secondary
 ip address 150.4.4.4 255.255.255.0
 duplex auto
 speed auto
!
interface Serial0/0
 ip address 10.0.0.14 255.255.255.252
!
interface Serial0/1
 no ip address
 shutdown
!
ip forward-protocol nd
!
no ip http server
no ip http secure-server
!
control-plane
!
line con 0
line aux 0
line vty 0 4
 login
!
end
R4#
```

CCNP LAB 12

EIGRP Multi-Technology Lab 2

Lab Objective:

The focus of this lab is to understand EIGRP implementation and configuration in Cisco IOS routers. Additional technologies tested include path control and stub routing.

Lab Topology:

The lab network topology is illustrated below:

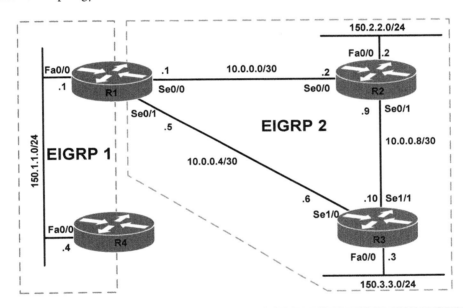

IMPORTANT NOTE: If you are using the www.howtonetwork.net racks, please bring up the LAN interfaces connected to the routers by issuing the no shutdown command on the connected switches. If you are using a home lab with no Switches, you can bring up the LAN interfaces using the following configurations on your routers:

```
interface fastethernet 0/0
  no keepalive
  loopback
  no shutdown
```

Alternately, you can simply connect the interfaces to a hub or switch if you have one available in your own lab.

Task 1

Configure hostnames and IP addressing on all routers as illustrated in the network topology.

Task 2

Configure EIGRP for AS 1 as shown in the topology. R4 should be configured as an EIGRP stub router. R4 should NEVER advertise any routes. In addition to this, ensure that router R4 will only ever receive a default route from R1 even if external routes are redistributed into EIGRP 1.

Task 3

Configure EIGRP for AS 2 as illustrated in the topology. Verify your configuration using the appropriate commands for EIGRP.

Task 4

Configure EIGRP so that R4 can reach all other routers in the network and vice-versa. Ensure that only the 150.1.1.0/24 is allowed into the topology table for EIGRP 2. Verify your configuration and also ping to and from R4 from the 150.2.2.0/24 and 150.3.3.0/24 subnets.

Task 5

Assume that the WAN link between R1 and R3 is unreliable and should only be used when the WAN link between R1 and R2 is down. However, an EIGRP neighbor relationship should still be maintained across this link. Configure EIGRP so that neither routers R1 nor R3 use this link unless the WAN link between R1 and R2 is down. You are only allowed to configure R3. Do NOT issue any configuration commands on R1 to complete this task.

LAB VALIDATION

Task 1

```
Router(config)#hostname R1
R1(config)#interface fastethernet 0/0
R1(config-if)#no shutdown
R1(config-if)#ip address 150.1.1.1 255.255.255.0
R1(config-if)#exit
R1(config)#interface serial 0/0
R1(config-if)#no shutdown
R1(config-if)#ip address 10.0.0.1 255.255.255.252
R1(config-if)#clock rate 2000000
R1(config-if)#exit
R1(config)#interface serial 0/1
R1(config-if)#no shutdown
R1(config-if)#ip address 10.0.0.5 255.255.255.252
R1(config-if)#exit

Router(config)#hostname R2
R2(config)#interface fastethernet 0/0
R2(config-if)#no shutdown
R2(config-if)#ip address 150.2.2.2 255.255.255.0
R2(config-if)#exit
R2(config)#interface serial 0/0
R2(config-if)#no shutdown
R2(config-if)#ip address 10.0.0.2 255.255.255.252
R2(config-if)#exit
R2(config)#interface serial 0/0
R2(config-if)#no shutdown
R2(config-if)#ip address 10.0.0.9 255.255.255.252
R2(config-if)#exit

Router(config)#hostname R3
R3(config)#interface fastethernet 0/0
R3(config-if)#no shutdown
R3(config-if)#ip address 150.3.3.3 255.255.255.0
R3(config-if)#exit
R3(config)#interface serial 1/0
R3(config-if)#no shutdown
R3(config-if)#ip address 10.0.0.6 255.255.255.252
R3(config-if)#clock rate 128000
R3(config-if)#exit
```

```
R3(config)#interface serial 1/1
R3(config-if)#no shutdown
R3(config-if)#ip address 10.0.0.10 255.255.255.252
R3(config-if)#clock rate 128000
R3(config-if)#exit

Router(config)#hostname R4
R4(config)#interface fastethernet 0/0
R4(config-if)#no shutdown
R4(config-if)#ip address 150.4.4.4 255.255.255.0
R4(config-if)#exit
```

Task 2

```
R1(config)#ip prefix-list DEFAULT-ONLY seq 5 permit 0.0.0.0/0
R1(config)#router eigrp 1
R1(config-router)#network 150.1.1.0 0.0.0.255
R1(config-router)#distribute-list prefix DEFAULT-ONLY out fastethernet 0/0
R1(config-router)#exit
R1(config)#interface fastethernet 0/0
R1(config-if)#ip summary-address eigrp 1 0.0.0.0 0.0.0.0
R1(config-if)#exit
```

NOTE: You can also configure a static default route to Null0 and redistribute into EIGRP. For example, you could complete this task as follows:

```
R1(config)#ip prefix-list DEFAULT-ONLY seq 5 permit 0.0.0.0/0
R1(config)#ip route 0.0.0.0 0.0.0.0 null 0
R1(config)#router eigrp 1
R1(config-router)#redistribute static
R1(config-router)#distribute-list prefix DEFAULT-ONLY out fastethernet 0/0
R1(config-router)#exit
```

Complete the configuration on R4 as follows:

```
R4(config)#router eigrp 1
R4(config-router)#network 150.1.1.0 0.0.0.255
R4(config-router)#eigrp stub receive-only
R4(config-router)#exit
```

Verify your EIGRP configuration using the show ip eigrp neighbors [detail] and the show ip route [eigrp] commands:

```
R1#show ip eigrp neighbors detail
IP-EIGRP neighbors for process 1
H   Address              Interface      Hold Uptime   SRTT   RTO  Q  Seq
                                        (sec)         (ms)        Cnt Num
0   150.1.1.4            Fa0/0          12 00:05:24   653   3918  0  6
    Restart time 00:01:18
    Version 12.4/1.2, Retrans: 0, Retries: 0
    Receive-Only Peer Advertising ( No ) Routes
    Suppressing queries

R4#show ip route
Codes: C - connected, S - static, R - RIP, M - mobile, B - BGP
       D - EIGRP, EX - EIGRP external, O - OSPF, IA - OSPF inter area
       N1 - OSPF NSSA external type 1, N2 - OSPF NSSA external type 2
       E1 - OSPF external type 1, E2 - OSPF external type 2
       i - IS-IS, su - IS-IS summary, L1 - IS-IS level-1, L2 - IS-IS level-2
       ia - IS-IS inter area, * - candidate default, U - per-user static route
       o - ODR, P - periodic downloaded static route

Gateway of last resort is 150.1.1.1 to network 0.0.0.0

     150.1.0.0/24 is subnetted, 1 subnets
C       150.1.1.0 is directly connected, FastEthernet0/0
D*   0.0.0.0/0 [90/30720] via 150.1.1.1, 00:01:49, FastEthernet0/0
```

Task 3

```
R1(config)#router eigrp 2
R1(config-router)#no auto-summary
R1(config-router)#network 10.0.0.0 0.0.0.3
R1(config-router)#network 10.0.0.4 0.0.0.3
R1(config-router)#exit

R2(config)#router eigrp 2
R2(config-router)#no auto-summary
R2(config-router)#network 150.2.2.2 0.0.0.0
R2(config-router)#network 10.0.0.2 0.0.0.0
R2(config-router)#network 10.0.0.9 0.0.0.0
R2(config-router)#exit

R3(config)#router eigrp 2
R3(config-router)#network 150.3.3.3 0.0.0.0
R3(config-router)#network 10.0.0.6 0.0.0.0
R3(config-router)#network 10.0.0.10 0.0.0.0
R3(config-router)#no auto-summary
R3(config-router)#exit
```

Task 4

To complete this task, you need to redistribute between EIGRP for AS 1 and EIGRP for AS 2. It is important to remember that a seed metric is not required when redistributing between different EIGRP processes. Additionally, configure filtering when redistributing so that only the 150.1.1.0/24 subnet is allowed into EIGRP 2. Complete this task as follows:

```
R1(config)#router eigrp 1
R1(config-router)#redistribute eigrp 2
R1(config-router)#exit
R1(config)#ip prefix-list NET-150-ONLY seq 5 permit 150.1.1.0/24
R1(config)#route-map EIGRP1-2-EIGRP2 permit 10
R1(config-route-map)#match ip address prefix-list NET-150-ONLY
R1(config-route-map)#exit
R1(config)#route-map EIGRP1-2-EIGRP2 deny 20
R1(config-route-map)#exit
R1(config)#router eigrp 2
R1(config-router)#redistribute eigrp 1 route-map EIGRP1-2-EIGRP2
R1(config-router)#exit
```

Following this configuration, verify that external routes exist in the topology tables for both of the autonomous systems. Use the `show ip eigrp topology` command. Next, verify the routing tables of all the other routers in the topology following the redistribution configuration:

```
R2#show ip route eigrp
     10.0.0.0/30 is subnetted, 3 subnets
D       10.0.0.4 [90/2681856] via 10.0.0.1, 00:16:15, Serial0/0
     150.1.0.0/24 is subnetted, 1 subnets
D EX    150.1.1.0 [170/2172416] via 10.0.0.1, 00:14:33, Serial0/0
     150.3.0.0/24 is subnetted, 1 subnets
D       150.3.3.0 [90/2172416] via 10.0.0.10, 00:16:11, Serial0/1

R3#show ip route eigrp
     10.0.0.0/30 is subnetted, 3 subnets
D       10.0.0.0 [90/21024000] via 10.0.0.9, 00:15:46, Serial1/1
                 [90/21024000] via 10.0.0.5, 00:15:46, Serial1/0
     150.1.0.0/24 is subnetted, 1 subnets
D EX    150.1.1.0 [170/20514560] via 10.0.0.5, 00:14:04, Serial1/0
     150.2.0.0/24 is subnetted, 1 subnets
D       150.2.2.0 [90/20514560] via 10.0.0.9, 00:15:46, Serial1/1

R4#show ip route
Codes: C - connected, S - static, R - RIP, M - mobile, B - BGP
       D - EIGRP, EX - EIGRP external, O - OSPF, IA - OSPF inter area
       N1 - OSPF NSSA external type 1, N2 - OSPF NSSA external type 2
       E1 - OSPF external type 1, E2 - OSPF external type 2
```

```
      i - IS-IS, su - IS-IS summary, L1 - IS-IS level-1, L2 - IS-IS level-2
      ia - IS-IS inter area, * - candidate default, U - per-user static route
      o - ODR, P - periodic downloaded static route
Gateway of last resort is 150.1.1.1 to network 0.0.0.0

     150.1.0.0/24 is subnetted, 1 subnets
C         150.1.1.0 is directly connected, FastEthernet0/0
D*   0.0.0.0/0 [90/30720] via 150.1.1.1, 00:06:21, FastEthernet0/0
```

Finally, ping between R4 and 150.2.2.0/24 and 150.3.3.0/24 subnets:

```
R4#ping 150.2.2.2 source 150.1.1.4 repeat 10

Type escape sequence to abort.
Sending 10, 100-byte ICMP Echos to 150.2.2.2, timeout is 2 seconds:
Packet sent with a source address of 150.1.1.4
!!!!!!!!!!
Success rate is 100 percent (10/10), round-trip min/avg/max = 1/3/4 ms

R4#ping 150.3.3.3 source 150.1.1.4 repeat 10

Type escape sequence to abort.
Sending 10, 100-byte ICMP Echos to 150.3.3.3, timeout is 2 seconds:
Packet sent with a source address of 150.1.1.4
!!!!!!!!!!
Success rate is 100 percent (10/10), round-trip min/avg/max = 16/16/16 ms
```

Task 5

To complete this task, you need to configure an inbound AND outbound offset list on R3 so that routes received or sent via the WAN link between R1 and R3 are undesirable:

```
R3(config)#router eigrp 2
R3(config-router)#offset-list 0 in 1234567890 serial 1/0
R3(config-router)#offset-list 0 out 123456789 serial 1/0
R3(config-router)#exit
```

Following this, R3 should prefer the path via R2 - even for the 150.1.1.0/24 subnet:

```
R3#show ip route eigrp
     10.0.0.0/30 is subnetted, 3 subnets
D        10.0.0.0 [90/21024000] via 10.0.0.9, 00:00:04, Serial1/1
     150.1.0.0/24 is subnetted, 1 subnets
D EX    150.1.1.0 [170/21026560] via 10.0.0.9, 00:00:04, Serial1/1
     150.2.0.0/24 is subnetted, 1 subnets
D        150.2.2.0 [90/20514560] via 10.0.0.9, 00:00:04, Serial1/1
```

The same applies to R1, which prefers the path via R2 - even for the 150.3.3.0/24 subnet:

```
R1#show ip route eigrp
     10.0.0.0/30 is subnetted, 3 subnets
D        10.0.0.8 [90/2681856] via 10.0.0.2, 00:01:24, Serial0/0
     150.2.0.0/24 is subnetted, 1 subnets
D        150.2.2.0 [90/2172416] via 10.0.0.2, 00:01:24, Serial0/0
     150.3.0.0/24 is subnetted, 1 subnets
D        150.3.3.0 [90/2684416] via 10.0.0.2, 00:01:24, Serial0/0
D*   0.0.0.0/0 is a summary, 00:29:25, Null0
```

In the event that the link to R2 fails, the WAN link between R1 and R2 is used:

```
R3#configure terminal
Enter configuration commands, one per line.  End with CNTL/Z.
R3(config)#interface serial 1/1
R3(config-if)#shutdown
R3(config-if)#do ping 150.1.1.4 source 150.3.3.3

Type escape sequence to abort.
Sending 5, 100-byte ICMP Echos to 150.1.1.4, timeout is 2 seconds:
Packet sent with a source address of 150.3.3.3
```

```
!!!!!
Success rate is 100 percent (5/5), round-trip min/avg/max = 16/16/16 ms
R3(config-if)#do show ip route eigrp
     10.0.0.0/30 is subnetted, 2 subnets
D       10.0.0.0 [90/1255591890] via 10.0.0.5, 00:00:05, Serial1/0
     150.1.0.0/24 is subnetted, 1 subnets
D EX    150.1.1.0 [170/1255082450] via 10.0.0.5, 00:00:05, Serial1/0
     150.2.0.0/24 is subnetted, 1 subnets
D       150.2.2.0 [90/1255594450] via 10.0.0.5, 00:00:05, Serial1/0
```

FINAL ROUTER CONFIGURATIONS

R1

```
R1#term len 0
R1#sh run
Building configuration...

Current configuration : 1369 bytes
!
version 12.4
service timestamps debug datetime msec
service timestamps log datetime msec
no service password-encryption
!
hostname R1
!
boot-start-marker
boot-end-marker
!
no logging console
!
no aaa new-model
no network-clock-participate slot 1
no network-clock-participate wic 0
ip cef
!
no ip domain lookup
ip auth-proxy max-nodata-conns 3
ip admission max-nodata-conns 3
!
interface FastEthernet0/0
 ip address 150.1.1.1 255.255.255.0
 ip summary-address eigrp 1 0.0.0.0 0.0.0.0 5
 duplex auto
 speed auto
!
interface Serial0/0
 ip address 10.0.0.1 255.255.255.252
 clock rate 2000000
!
interface Serial0/1
 ip address 10.0.0.5 255.255.255.252
!
router eigrp 1
 redistribute eigrp 2
 network 150.1.1.0 0.0.0.255
 distribute-list prefix DEFAULT-ONLY out FastEthernet0/0
 auto-summary
!
router eigrp 2
 redistribute eigrp 1 route-map EIGRP1-2-EIGRP2
 network 10.0.0.0 0.0.0.3
 network 10.0.0.4 0.0.0.3
 no auto-summary
!
ip forward-protocol nd
!
no ip http server
no ip http secure-server
!
ip prefix-list DEFAULT-ONLY seq 5 permit 0.0.0.0/0
!
ip prefix-list NET-150-ONLY seq 5 permit 150.1.1.0/24
!
```

```
route-map EIGRP1-2-EIGRP2 permit 10
 match ip address prefix-list NET-150-ONLY
!
route-map EIGRP1-2-EIGRP2 deny 20
!
control-plane
!
line con 0
line aux 0
line vty 0 4
 login
!
end

R1#
```

R2

```
R2#term len 0
R2#sh run
Building configuration...

Current configuration : 917 bytes
!
version 12.4
service timestamps debug datetime msec
service timestamps log datetime msec
no service password-encryption
!
hostname R2
!
boot-start-marker
boot-end-marker
!
no logging console
!
no aaa new-model
no network-clock-participate slot 1
no network-clock-participate wic 0
ip cef
!
no ip domain lookup
ip auth-proxy max-nodata-conns 3
ip admission max-nodata-conns 3
!
interface FastEthernet0/0
 ip address 150.2.2.2 255.255.255.0
 duplex auto
 speed auto
!
interface Serial0/0
 ip address 10.0.0.2 255.255.255.252
!
interface Serial0/1
 ip address 10.0.0.9 255.255.255.252
!
router eigrp 2
 network 10.0.0.2 0.0.0.0
 network 10.0.0.9 0.0.0.0
 network 150.2.2.2 0.0.0.0
 no auto-summary
!
ip forward-protocol nd
!
no ip http server
no ip http secure-server
!
control-plane
!
line con 0
line aux 0
line vty 0 4
 login
!
end

 R2#
```

R3

```
R3#term len 0
R3#sh run
Building configuration...

Current configuration : 1346 bytes
!
version 12.4
service timestamps debug datetime msec
service timestamps log datetime msec
no service password-encryption
!
hostname R3
!
boot-start-marker
boot-end-marker
!
no logging console
!
no aaa new-model
no network-clock-participate slot 1
no network-clock-participate wic 0
ip cef
!
no ip domain lookup
ip auth-proxy max-nodata-conns 3
ip admission max-nodata-conns 3
!
interface FastEthernet0/0
 ip address 150.3.3.3 255.255.255.0
 duplex auto
 speed auto
!
interface Serial1/0
 ip address 10.0.0.6 255.255.255.252
 clock rate 128000
!
interface Serial1/1
 ip address 10.0.0.10 255.255.255.252
 shutdown
 clock rate 128000
!
interface Serial1/2
 no ip address
 shutdown
 clock rate 128000
!
interface Serial1/3
 no ip address
 shutdown
!
interface Serial1/4
 no ip address
 shutdown
!
interface Serial1/5
 no ip address
 shutdown
!
interface Serial1/6
 no ip address
 shutdown
!
interface Serial1/7
 no ip address
 shutdown
!
router eigrp 2
 offset-list 0 in 1234567890 Serial1/0
 offset-list 0 out 123456789 Serial1/0
 network 10.0.0.6 0.0.0.0
 network 10.0.0.10 0.0.0.0
 network 150.3.3.3 0.0.0.0
 no auto-summary
!
ip forward-protocol nd
!
```

```
no ip http server
no ip http secure-server
!
control-plane
!
line con 0
line aux 0
line vty 0 4
 login
!
end

R3#
```

R4

```
R4#term len 0
R4#sh run
Building configuration...

Current configuration : 865 bytes
!
version 12.4
service timestamps debug datetime msec
service timestamps log datetime msec
no service password-encryption
!
hostname R4
!
boot-start-marker
boot-end-marker
!
no logging console
!
no aaa new-model
no network-clock-participate slot 1
no network-clock-participate wic 0
ip cef
!
no ip domain lookup
ip auth-proxy max-nodata-conns 3
ip admission max-nodata-conns 3
!
interface FastEthernet0/0
 ip address 150.1.1.4 255.255.255.0
 duplex auto
 speed auto
!
interface Serial0/0
 no ip address
 shutdown
!
interface Serial0/1
 no ip address
 shutdown
!
router eigrp 1
 network 150.1.1.0 0.0.0.255
 auto-summary
 eigrp stub receive-only
!
ip forward-protocol nd
!
no ip http server
no ip http secure-server
!
control-plane
!
line con 0
line aux 0
line vty 0 4
 login
!
end

R4#
```

CCNP LAB 13

EIGRP Multi-Technology Lab

Lab Objective:

The focus of this lab is to understand EIGRP implementation and configuration in Cisco IOS routers. Additional technologies tested include summarization and authentication.

Lab Topology:

The lab network topology is illustrated below:

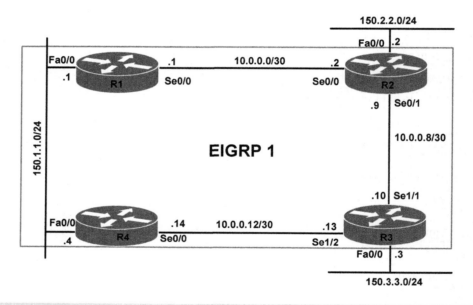

IMPORTANT NOTE: If you are using the www.howtonetwork.net racks, please bring up the LAN interfaces connected to the routers by issuing the no shutdown command on the connected switches. If you are using a home lab with no Switches, you can bring up the LAN interfaces using the following configurations on your routers:

```
interface fastethernet 0/0
  no keepalive
  loopback
  no shutdown
```

Alternately, you can simply connect the interfaces to a hub or switch if you have one available in your own lab.

Task 1

Configure hostnames and IP addressing on all routers as illustrated in the network topology.

Task 2

Configure EIGRP for AS 1 as illustrated in the topology. However, do NOT advertise the 150.2.2.0/24 and

150.3.3.0/24 subnets connected to R2 and R3 via EIGRP. Additionally, authenticate EIGRP protocol updates using the password 'CCNP'.

Task 3

Configure routers R2 and R3 to advertise ONLY the default route to R1 and R4. Ensure that R2 and R3 can ping each others' 150.x.x.x/24 subnets. Verify that R1 and R4 can reach the 150.2.2.0/24 and 150.3.3.0/24 subnets even if their own WAN links are down or unavailable.

Task 4

Configure the following secondary subnets on the LAN segment between R1 and R4:
*   Network: 192.168.0.0/24 - Assign 192.168.0.1/24 to R1 and 192.168.0.4/24 to R4
*   Network: 192.168.1.0/24 - Assign 192.168.1.1/24 to R1 and 192.168.1.4/24 to R4
*   Network: 192.168.2.0/24 - Assign 192.168.2.1/24 to R1 and 192.168.2.4/24 to R4
*   Network: 192.168.3.0/24 - Assign 192.168.3.1/24 to R1 and 192.168.3.4/24 to R4

Next, configure R1 and R4 to advertise only a single route for these subnets to R2 and R3.

Task 5

Management has decided that packets sourced from the LAN interface of R2 (150.2.2.2) should use the R2-R3-R4 path to reach the 150.1.1.0/24 and 192.168.1.0/24 subnets. This should be completed without performing any modifications on any other router except for R2. Verify your configuration using the appropriate commands. Corporate IT policy states that NO static routes are allowed. Complete this solution while adhering to this policy.

LAB VALIDATION

Task 1

```
Router(config)#hostname R1
R1(config)#interface fastethernet 0/0
R1(config-if)#no shutdown
R1(config-if)#ip address 150.1.1.1 255.255.255.0
R1(config-if)#exit
R1(config)#interface serial 0/0
R1(config-if)#no shutdown
R1(config-if)#ip address 10.0.0.1 255.255.255.252
R1(config-if)#clock rate 2000000
R1(config-if)#exit

Router(config)#hostname R2
R2(config)#interface fastethernet 0/0
R2(config-if)#no shutdown
R2(config-if)#ip address 150.2.2.2 255.255.255.0
R2(config-if)#exit
R2(config)#interface serial 0/0
R2(config-if)#no shutdown
R2(config-if)#ip address 10.0.0.2 255.255.255.252
R2(config-if)#exit
R2(config)#interface serial 0/0
R2(config-if)#no shutdown
R2(config-if)#ip address 10.0.0.9 255.255.255.252
R2(config-if)#exit

Router(config)#hostname R3
R3(config)#interface fastethernet 0/0
R3(config-if)#no shutdown
R3(config-if)#ip address 150.3.3.3 255.255.255.0
R3(config-if)#exit
R3(config)#interface serial 1/1
R3(config-if)#no shutdown
```

```
R3(config-if)#ip address 10.0.0.10 255.255.255.252
R3(config-if)#clock rate 128000
R3(config-if)#exit
R3(config)#interface serial 1/2
R3(config-if)#no shutdown
R3(config-if)#ip address 10.0.0.13 255.255.255.252
R3(config-if)#clock rate 128000
R3(config-if)#exit

Router(config)#hostname R4
R4(config)#interface fastethernet 0/0
R4(config-if)#no shutdown
R4(config-if)#ip address 150.4.4.4 255.255.255.0
R4(config-if)#exit
R4(config)#interface serial 0/0
R4(config-if)#no shutdown
R4(config-if)#ip address 10.0.0.14 255.255.255.252
R4(config-if)#exit
```

Task 2

```
R1(config)#key chain EIGRP-AUTH
R1(config-keychain)#key 1
R1(config-keychain-key)#key-string CCNP
R1(config-keychain-key)#exit
R1(config-keychain)#exit
R1(config)#router eigrp 1
R1(config-router)#network 150.1.1.1 0.0.0.0
R1(config-router)#network 10.0.0.1 0.0.0.0
R1(config-router)#no auto-summary
R1(config-router)#exit
R1(config)#interface fastethernet 0/0
R1(config-if)#ip authentication mode eigrp 1 md5
R1(config-if)#ip authentication key-chain eigrp 1 EIGRP-AUTH
R1(config-if)#exit
R1(config)#interface serial 0/0
R1(config-if)#ip authentication mode eigrp 1 md5
R1(config-if)#ip authentication key-chain eigrp 1 EIGRP-AUTH
R1(config-if)#exit

R2(config)#key chain EIGRP-AUTH
R2(config-keychain)#key 1
R2(config-keychain-key)#key-string CCNP
R2(config-keychain-key)#exit
R2(config)#router eigrp 1
R2(config-router)#network 10.0.0.2 0.0.0.0
R2(config-router)#network 10.0.0.9 0.0.0.0
R2(config-router)#no auto-summary
R2(config-router)#exit
R2(config)#interface serial 0/0
R2(config-if)#ip authentication mode eigrp 1 md5
R2(config-if)#ip authentication key-chain eigrp 1 EIGRP-AUTH
R2(config-if)#exit
R2(config)#interface serial 0/1
R2(config-if)#ip authentication mode eigrp 1 md5
R2(config-if)#ip authentication key-chain eigrp 1 EIGRP-AUTH
R2(config-if)#exit

R3(config)#key chain EIGRP-AUTH
R3(config-keychain)#key 1
R3(config-keychain-key)#key-string CCNP
R3(config-keychain-key)#exit
R3(config-keychain)#exit
R3(config router eigrp 1
R3(config-router)#no auto-summary
R3(config-router)#network 10.0.0.10 0.0.0.0
R3(config-router)#network 10.0.0.13 0.0.0.0
R3(config-router)#exit
R3(config)#interface serial 1/1
R3(config-if)#ip authentication mode eigrp 1 md5
R3(config-if)#ip authentication key-chain eigrp 1 EIGRP-AUTH
R3(config-if)#exit
```

```
R3(config)#interface serial 1/2
R3(config-if)#ip authentication mode eigrp 1 md5
R3(config-if)#ip authentication key-chain eigrp 1 EIGRP-AUTH
R3(config-if)#exit

R4(config)#key chain EIGRP-AUTH
R4(config-keychain)#key 1
R4(config-keychain-key)#key-string CCNP
R4(config-keychain-key)#exit
R4(config-keychain)#exit
R4(config)#router eigrp 1
R4(config-router)#no auto-summary
R4(config-router)#network 150.1.1.4 0.0.0.0
R4(config-router)#network 10.0.0.14 0.0.0.0
R4(config-router)#exit
R4(config)#interface fastethernet 0/0
R4(config-if)#ip authentication mode eigrp 1 md5
R4(config-if)#ip authentication key-chain eigrp 1 EIGRP-AUTH
R4(config-if)#exit
R4(config)#interface serial 0/0
R4(config-if)#ip authentication mode eigrp 1 md5
R4(config-if)#ip authentication key-chain eigrp 1 EIGRP-AUTH
R4(config-if)#exit
```

Verify your configuration using the show ip eigrp neighbors command:

```
R1#show ip eigrp neighbors
IP-EIGRP neighbors for process 1
H   Address              Interface       Hold Uptime    SRTT   RTO   Q   Seq
                                         (sec)          (ms)         Cnt Num
1   150.1.1.4            Fa0/0           10 00:01:22      3    200   0   4
0   10.0.0.2             Se0/0           14 00:06:40      3    200   0   11

R2#show ip eigrp neighbors
IP-EIGRP neighbors for process 1
H   Address              Interface       Hold Uptime    SRTT   RTO   Q   Seq
                                         (sec)          (ms)         Cnt Num
1   10.0.0.10            Se0/1           14 00:04:30     15    200   0   8
0   10.0.0.1             Se0/0           11 00:06:52      4    200   0   10

R3#show ip  eigrp neighbors
IP-EIGRP neighbors for process 1
H   Address              Interface       Hold Uptime    SRTT   RTO   Q   Seq
                                         (sec)          (ms)         Cnt Num
1   10.0.0.14            Se1/2           10 00:01:36     21   1140   0   7
0   10.0.0.9             Se1/1           11 00:04:42     19   1140   0   10

R4#show ip eigrp neighbors
IP-EIGRP neighbors for process 1
H   Address              Interface       Hold Uptime    SRTT   RTO   Q   Seq
                                         (sec)          (ms)         Cnt Num
1   10.0.0.13            Se0/0           14 00:01:59     21    200   0   9
0   150.1.1.1            Fa0/0           12 00:02:10   1022   5000   0   9
```

Verify configured key chains using the **show key chain [name]** command:

```
R1#show key chain EIGRP-AUTH
Key-chain EIGRP-AUTH:
    key 1 -- text "CCNP"
        accept lifetime (always valid) - (always valid) [valid now]
        send lifetime (always valid) - (always valid) [valid now]
```

Verify authentication using the show ip eigrp interfaces detail [name] command:

```
R1#show ip eigrp interfaces detail
IP-EIGRP interfaces for process 1
                      Xmit Queue    Mean   Pacing Time   Multicast    Pending
Interface      Peers  Un/Reliable   SRTT   Un/Reliable   Flow Timer   Routes
Fa0/0          1       0/0          3       0/1          50           0
   Hello interval is 5 sec
   Next xmit serial <none>
   Un/reliable mcasts: 0/2  Un/reliable ucasts: 1/4
   Mcast exceptions: 1  CR packets: 1  ACKs suppressed: 1
```

```
        Retransmissions sent: 1  Out-of-sequence rcvd: 0
        Authentication mode is md5,  key-chain is "EIGRP-AUTH"
        Use multicast
Se0/0            1         0/0        3       0/15       50        0
        Hello interval is 5 sec
        Next xmit serial <none>
        Un/reliable mcasts: 0/0  Un/reliable ucasts: 2/6
        Mcast exceptions: 0  CR packets: 0  ACKs suppressed: 3
        Retransmissions sent: 0  Out-of-sequence rcvd: 0
        Authentication mode is md5,  key-chain is "EIGRP-AUTH"
        Use unicast
```

Task 3

```
R2(config)#ip prefix-list DEFAULT-ONLY seq 5 permit 0.0.0.0/0
R2(config)#router eigrp 1
R2(config-router)#redistribute connected
R2(config-router)#distribute-list prefix DEFAULT-ONLY out serial 0/0
R2(config-router)#exit
R2(config)#interface serial 0/0
R2(config-if)#ip summary-address eigrp 1 0.0.0.0 0.0.0.0
R2(config-if)#exit

R3(config)#ip prefix-list DEFAULT-ONLY seq 5 permit 0.0.0.0/0
R3(config)#router eigrp 1
R3(config-router)#redistribute connected
R3(config-router)#distribute-list prefix DEFAULT-ONLY out serial 1/2
R3(config-router)#exit
R3(config)#interface serial 1/2
R3(config-if)#ip summary-address eigrp 1 0.0.0.0 0.0.0.0
R3(config-if)#exit
```

NOTE: You can also configure a static default route to Null0 and redistribute into EIGRP. For example, you could complete this task as follows:

```
R2(config)#ip prefix-list DEFAULT-ONLY seq 5 permit 0.0.0.0/0
R2(config)#ip route 0.0.0.0 0.0.0.0 null 0
R2(config)#router eigrp 1
R2(config-router)#redistribute connected
R2(config-router)#redistribute static
R2(config-router)#distribute-list prefix DEFAULT-ONLY out serial 0/0
R2(config-router)#exit
```

Verify your configurations by looking at the routing tables of all routers:

```
R1#show ip route eigrp
     10.0.0.0/30 is subnetted, 2 subnets
D       10.0.0.12 [90/2172416] via 150.1.1.4, 00:14:57, FastEthernet0/0
D*   0.0.0.0/0 [90/2172416] via 10.0.0.2, 00:05:17, Serial0/0

R2#show ip route eigrp
     10.0.0.0/30 is subnetted, 3 subnets
D       10.0.0.12 [90/2684416] via 10.0.0.1, 00:15:15, Serial0/0
     150.1.0.0/24 is subnetted, 1 subnets
D       150.1.1.0 [90/2172416] via 10.0.0.1, 00:15:05, Serial0/0
     150.3.0.0/24 is subnetted, 1 subnets
D EX    150.3.3.0 [170/2172416] via 10.0.0.10, 00:06:05, Serial0/1
D*   0.0.0.0/0 is a summary, 00:05:35, Null0

R3#show ip route eigrp
     10.0.0.0/30 is subnetted, 3 subnets
D       10.0.0.0 [90/21024000] via 10.0.0.9, 00:15:22, Serial1/1
     150.1.0.0/24 is subnetted, 1 subnets
D       150.1.1.0 [90/20514560] via 10.0.0.14, 00:15:22, Serial1/2
     150.2.0.0/24 is subnetted, 1 subnets
D EX    150.2.2.0 [170/20514560] via 10.0.0.9, 00:08:15, Serial1/1
D*   0.0.0.0/0 is a summary, 00:05:51, Null0
```

```
R4#show ip route eigrp
     10.0.0.0/30 is subnetted, 2 subnets
D       10.0.0.0 [90/2172416] via 150.1.1.1, 00:06:14, FastEthernet0/0
D*   0.0.0.0/0 [90/2172416] via 10.0.0.13, 00:06:07, Serial0/0
```

Test R1 or R4 failover by shutting down the WAN interface and pinging R2 and R3:

```
R1(config)#interface serial 0/0
R1(config-if)#shutdown
R1(config-if)#do ping 150.2.2.2 source 150.1.1.1

Type escape sequence to abort.
Sending 5, 100-byte ICMP Echos to 150.2.2.2, timeout is 2 seconds:
Packet sent with a source address of 150.1.1.1
!!!!!
Success rate is 100 percent (5/5), round-trip min/avg/max = 28/30/32 ms
R1(config-if)#do ping 150.3.3.3 source 150.1.1.1

Type escape sequence to abort.
Sending 5, 100-byte ICMP Echos to 150.3.3.3, timeout is 2 seconds:
Packet sent with a source address of 150.1.1.1
!!!!!
Success rate is 100 percent (5/5), round-trip min/avg/max = 16/16/16 ms
R1(config-if)#do show ip route eigrp
     10.0.0.0/30 is subnetted, 1 subnets
D       10.0.0.12 [90/2172416] via 150.1.1.4, 00:17:20, FastEthernet0/0
D*   0.0.0.0/0 [90/2174976] via 150.1.1.4, 00:00:47, FastEthernet0/0
```

Task 4

```
R1(config)#interface fastethernet 0/0
R1(config-if)#ip address 192.168.0.1 255.255.255.0 secondary
R1(config-if)#ip address 192.168.1.1 255.255.255.0 secondary
R1(config-if)#ip address 192.168.2.1 255.255.255.0 secondary
R1(config-if)#ip address 192.168.3.1 255.255.255.0 secondary
R1(config-if)#exit
R1(config)#router eigrp 1
R1(config-router)#network 192.168.0.0 0.0.3.255
R1(config-router)#exit
R1(config)#interface serial 0/0
R1(config-if)#ip summary-address eigrp 1 192.168.0.0 255.255.252.0
R1(config-if)#exit

R4(config)#interface fastethernet 0/0
R4(config-if)#ip address 192.168.0.4 255.255.255.0 secondary
R4(config-if)#ip address 192.168.1.4 255.255.255.0 secondary
R4(config-if)#ip address 192.168.2.4 255.255.255.0 secondary
R4(config-if)#ip address 192.168.3.4 255.255.255.0 secondary
R4(config-if)#exit
R4(config)#router eigrp 1
R4(config-router)#network 192.168.0.0 0.0.3.255
R4(config-router)#exit
R4(config)#interface serial 0/0
R4(config-if)#ip summary-address eigrp 1 192.168.0.0 255.255.252.0
R4(config-if)#exit
```

Verify your configuration by looking at the routing tables of all routers:

```
R1#show ip route eigrp
     10.0.0.0/30 is subnetted, 2 subnets
D       10.0.0.12 [90/2172416] via 150.1.1.4, 00:26:41, FastEthernet0/0
D*   0.0.0.0/0 [90/2172416] via 10.0.0.2, 00:03:13, Serial0/0
D    192.168.0.0/22 is a summary, 00:02:43, Null0

R2#show ip route eigrp
     10.0.0.0/30 is subnetted, 3 subnets
D       10.0.0.12 [90/2684416] via 10.0.0.1, 00:03:47, Serial0/0
     150.1.0.0/24 is subnetted, 1 subnets
D       150.1.1.0 [90/2172416] via 10.0.0.1, 00:03:47, Serial0/0
     150.3.0.0/24 is subnetted, 1 subnets
```

```
D EX    150.3.3.0 [170/2172416] via 10.0.0.10, 00:18:06, Serial0/1
D*      0.0.0.0/0 is a summary, 00:03:50, Null0
D       192.168.0.0/22 [90/2172416] via 10.0.0.1, 00:01:44, Serial0/0

R3#show ip route eigrp
        10.0.0.0/30 is subnetted, 3 subnets
D          10.0.0.0 [90/21024000] via 10.0.0.9, 00:03:57, Serial1/1
        150.1.0.0/24 is subnetted, 1 subnets
D          150.1.1.0 [90/20514560] via 10.0.0.14, 00:03:53, Serial1/2
        150.2.0.0/24 is subnetted, 1 subnets
D EX       150.2.2.0 [170/20514560] via 10.0.0.9, 00:20:06, Serial1/1
D*      0.0.0.0/0 is a summary, 00:17:42, Null0
D       192.168.0.0/22 [90/20514560] via 10.0.0.14, 00:01:51, Serial1/2

R4#show ip route eigrp
        10.0.0.0/30 is subnetted, 2 subnets
D          10.0.0.0 [90/2172416] via 150.1.1.1, 00:04:00, FastEthernet0/0
D*      0.0.0.0/0 [90/2172416] via 10.0.0.13, 00:03:57, Serial0/0
D       192.168.0.0/22 is a summary, 00:01:54, Null0
```

Additionally, test connectivity to these subnets using a simple ping:

```
R2#ping 192.168.0.0

Type escape sequence to abort.
Sending 5, 100-byte ICMP Echos to 192.168.0.0, timeout is 2 seconds:
!!!!!
Success rate is 100 percent (5/5), round-trip min/avg/max = 1/3/4 ms

R2#ping 192.168.1.0

Type escape sequence to abort.
Sending 5, 100-byte ICMP Echos to 192.168.1.0, timeout is 2 seconds:
!!!!!
Success rate is 100 percent (5/5), round-trip min/avg/max = 1/3/4 ms

R2#ping 192.168.2.0

Type escape sequence to abort.
Sending 5, 100-byte ICMP Echos to 192.168.2.0, timeout is 2 seconds:
!!!!!
Success rate is 100 percent (5/5), round-trip min/avg/max = 1/2/4 ms

R2#ping 192.168.3.0

Type escape sequence to abort.
Sending 5, 100-byte ICMP Echos to 192.168.3.0, timeout is 2 seconds:
!!!!!
Success rate is 100 percent (5/5), round-trip min/avg/max = 1/3/4 ms

R3#ping 192.168.0.0

Type escape sequence to abort.
Sending 5, 100-byte ICMP Echos to 192.168.0.0, timeout is 2 seconds:
!!!!!
Success rate is 100 percent (5/5), round-trip min/avg/max = 16/16/16 ms

R3#ping 192.168.1.0

Type escape sequence to abort.
Sending 5, 100-byte ICMP Echos to 192.168.1.0, timeout is 2 seconds:
!!!!!
Success rate is 100 percent (5/5), round-trip min/avg/max = 16/16/16 ms

R3#ping 192.168.2.0

Type escape sequence to abort.
Sending 5, 100-byte ICMP Echos to 192.168.2.0, timeout is 2 seconds:
!!!!!
Success rate is 100 percent (5/5), round-trip min/avg/max = 16/16/16 ms

R3#ping 192.168.3.0
```

```
Type escape sequence to abort.
Sending 5, 100-byte ICMP Echos to 192.168.3.0, timeout is 2 seconds:
!!!!!
Success rate is 100 percent (5/5), round-trip min/avg/max = 12/16/20 ms
```

Task 5

This task requires that PBR be configured on R2 as it cannot be completed with routing alone:

```
R2(config)#access-list 100 permit ip host 150.2.2.2 150.1.1.0 0.0.0.255
R2(config)#access-list 100 permit ip host 150.2.2.2 192.168.1.0 0.0.0.255
R2(config)#route-map R2-FA-0/0-PBR permit 10
R2(config-route-map)#match ip address 100
R2(config-route-map)#set ip next-hop 10.0.0.10
R2(config-route-map)#exit
R2(config)#route-map R2-FA-0/0-PBR deny 20
R2(config-route-map)#exit
R2(config)#ip local policy route-map R2-FA-0/0-PBR
R2(config)#exit
```

Verify your configuration for the 150.1.1.0/24 subnet by debugging PBR on R2:

```
R2#debug ip policy
Policy routing debugging is on
R2#ping 150.1.1.1 source 150.2.2.2 repeat 1

Type escape sequence to abort.
Sending 1, 100-byte ICMP Echos to 150.1.1.1, timeout is 2 seconds:
Packet sent with a source address of 150.2.2.2
!
Success rate is 100 percent (1/1), round-trip min/avg/max = 16/18/20 ms
R2#
*May  6 00:03:23.379: IP: s=150.2.2.2 (local), d=150.1.1.1, len 100, policy match
*May  6 00:03:23.379: IP: route map R2-FA-0/0-PBR, item 10, permit
*May  6 00:03:23.379: IP: s=150.2.2.2 (local), d=150.1.1.1 (Serial0/1), len 100,
policy routed
*May  6 00:03:23.383: IP: local to Serial0/1 10.0.0.10
```

Verify your configuration for the 12.168.1.0/24 subnet by debugging PBR on R2:

```
R2#ping 192.168.1.0 source 150.2.2.2 repeat 1

Type escape sequence to abort.
Sending 1, 100-byte ICMP Echos to 192.168.1.0, timeout is 2 seconds:
Packet sent with a source address of 150.2.2.2
!
Success rate is 100 percent (1/1), round-trip min/avg/max = 32/32/32 ms
R2#
*May  6 00:04:46.951: IP: s=150.2.2.2 (local), d=192.168.1.0, len 100, policy match
*May  6 00:04:46.951: IP: route map R2-FA-0/0-PBR, item 10, permit
*May  6 00:04:46.951: IP: s=150.2.2.2 (local), d=192.168.1.0 (Serial0/1), len 100,
policy routed
*May  6 00:04:46.951: IP: local to Serial0/1 10.0.0.10
```

You can also use the show route-map [name] command to view matches against the configured statement(s) within the route map:

```
R2#show route-map R2-FA-0/0-PBR
route-map R2-FA-0/0-PBR, permit, sequence 10
  Match clauses:
    ip address (access-lists): 100
  Set clauses:
    ip next-hop 10.0.0.10
  Policy routing matches: 2 packets, 200 bytes
route-map R2-FA-0/0-PBR, deny, sequence 20
  Match clauses:
  Set clauses:
  Policy routing matches: 0 packets, 0 bytes
```

FINAL ROUTER CONFIGURATIONS

R1

```
R1#term len 0
R1#sh run
Building configuration...

Current configuration : 1395 bytes
!
version 12.4
service timestamps debug datetime msec
service timestamps log datetime msec
no service password-encryption
!
hostname R1
!
boot-start-marker
boot-end-marker
!
no logging console
!
no aaa new-model
no network-clock-participate slot 1
no network-clock-participate wic 0
ip cef
!
no ip domain lookup
ip auth-proxy max-nodata-conns 3
ip admission max-nodata-conns 3
!
key chain EIGRP-AUTH
 key 1
   key-string CCNP
!
interface FastEthernet0/0
 ip address 192.168.0.1 255.255.255.0 secondary
 ip address 192.168.1.1 255.255.255.0 secondary
 ip address 192.168.2.1 255.255.255.0 secondary
 ip address 192.168.3.1 255.255.255.0 secondary
 ip address 150.1.1.1 255.255.255.0
 ip authentication mode eigrp 1 md5
 ip authentication key-chain eigrp 1 EIGRP-AUTH
 duplex auto
 speed auto
!
interface Serial0/0
 ip address 10.0.0.1 255.255.255.252
 ip authentication mode eigrp 1 md5
 ip authentication key-chain eigrp 1 EIGRP-AUTH
 ip summary-address eigrp 1 192.168.0.0 255.255.252.0 5
 clock rate 2000000
!
interface Serial0/1
 no ip address
 shutdown
!
router eigrp 1
 network 10.0.0.1 0.0.0.0
 network 150.1.1.1 0.0.0.0
 network 192.168.0.0 0.0.3.255
 no auto-summary
!
ip forward-protocol nd
!
no ip http server
no ip http secure-server
!
control-plane
!
line con 0
line aux 0
line vty 0 4
 login
```

```
!
end

R1#
```

R2

```
R2#term len 0
R2#sh run
Building configuration...

Current configuration : 1564 bytes
!
version 12.4
service timestamps debug datetime msec
service timestamps log datetime msec
no service password-encryption
!
hostname R2
!
boot-start-marker
boot-end-marker
!
no logging console
!
no aaa new-model
no network-clock-participate slot 1
no network-clock-participate wic 0
ip cef
!
no ip domain lookup
ip auth-proxy max-nodata-conns 3
ip admission max-nodata-conns 3
!
key chain EIGRP-AUTH
 key 1
   key-string CCNP
!
interface FastEthernet0/0
 ip address 150.2.2.2 255.255.255.0
 duplex auto
 speed auto
!
interface Serial0/0
 ip address 10.0.0.2 255.255.255.252
 ip authentication mode eigrp 1 md5
 ip authentication key-chain eigrp 1 EIGRP-AUTH
 ip summary-address eigrp 1 0.0.0.0 0.0.0.0 5
!
interface Serial0/1
 ip address 10.0.0.9 255.255.255.252
 ip authentication mode eigrp 1 md5
 ip authentication key-chain eigrp 1 EIGRP-AUTH
!
router eigrp 1
 redistribute connected
 network 10.0.0.2 0.0.0.0
 network 10.0.0.9 0.0.0.0
 distribute-list prefix DEFAULT-ONLY out Serial0/0
 no auto-summary
!
ip local policy route-map R2-FA-0/0-PBR
ip forward-protocol nd
!
no ip http server
no ip http secure-server
!
ip prefix-list DEFAULT-ONLY seq 5 permit 0.0.0.0/0
access-list 100 permit ip host 150.2.2.2 150.1.1.0 0.0.0.255
access-list 100 permit ip host 150.2.2.2 192.168.1.0 0.0.0.255
!
route-map R2-FA-0/0-PBR permit 10
 match ip address 100
 set ip next-hop 10.0.0.10
```

```
!
route-map R2-FA-0/0-PBR deny 20
!
control-plane
!
line con 0
line aux 0
line vty 0 4
 login
!
end

R2#
```

R3

```
R3#term len 0
R3#sh run
Building configuration...

Current configuration : 1624 bytes
!
version 12.4
service timestamps debug datetime msec
service timestamps log datetime msec
no service password-encryption
!
hostname R3
!
boot-start-marker
boot-end-marker
!
no logging console
!
no aaa new-model
no network-clock-participate slot 1
no network-clock-participate wic 0
ip cef
!
no ip domain lookup
ip auth-proxy max-nodata-conns 3
ip admission max-nodata-conns 3
!
key chain EIGRP-AUTH
 key 1
   key-string CCNP
!
interface FastEthernet0/0
 ip address 150.3.3.3 255.255.255.0
 duplex auto
 speed auto
!
interface Serial1/0
 no ip address
 shutdown
 clock rate 128000
!
interface Serial1/1
 ip address 10.0.0.10 255.255.255.252
 ip authentication mode eigrp 1 md5
 ip authentication key-chain eigrp 1 EIGRP-AUTH
 clock rate 128000
!
interface Serial1/2
 ip address 10.0.0.13 255.255.255.252
 ip authentication mode eigrp 1 md5
 ip authentication key-chain eigrp 1 EIGRP-AUTH
 ip summary-address eigrp 1 0.0.0.0 0.0.0.0 5
 clock rate 128000
!
interface Serial1/3
 no ip address
 shutdown
!
```

```
interface Serial1/4
 no ip address
 shutdown
!
interface Serial1/5
 no ip address
 shutdown
!
interface Serial1/6
 no ip address
 shutdown
!
interface Serial1/7
 no ip address
 shutdown
!
router eigrp 1
 redistribute connected
 network 10.0.0.10 0.0.0.0
 network 10.0.0.13 0.0.0.0
 distribute-list prefix DEFAULT-ONLY out Serial1/2
 no auto-summary
!
ip forward-protocol nd
!
no ip http server
no ip http secure-server
!
ip prefix-list DEFAULT-ONLY seq 5 permit 0.0.0.0/0
!
control-plane
!
line con 0
line aux 0
line vty 0 4
 login
!
end

R3#
```

R4

```
R4#term len 0
R4#sh run
Building configuration...

Current configuration : 1377 bytes
!
version 12.4
service timestamps debug datetime msec
service timestamps log datetime msec
no service password-encryption
!
hostname R4
!
boot-start-marker
boot-end-marker
!
no logging console
!
no aaa new-model
no network-clock-participate slot 1
no network-clock-participate wic 0
ip cef
!
no ip domain lookup
ip auth-proxy max-nodata-conns 3
ip admission max-nodata-conns 3
!
key chain EIGRP-AUTH
 key 1
   key-string CCNP
!
```

```
interface FastEthernet0/0
 ip address 192.168.0.4 255.255.255.0 secondary
 ip address 192.168.1.4 255.255.255.0 secondary
 ip address 192.168.2.4 255.255.255.0 secondary
 ip address 192.168.3.4 255.255.255.0 secondary
 ip address 150.1.1.4 255.255.255.0
 ip authentication mode eigrp 1 md5
 ip authentication key-chain eigrp 1 EIGRP-AUTH
 duplex auto
 speed auto
!
interface Serial0/0
 ip address 10.0.0.14 255.255.255.252
 ip authentication mode eigrp 1 md5
 ip authentication key-chain eigrp 1 EIGRP-AUTH
 ip summary-address eigrp 1 192.168.0.0 255.255.252.0 5
!
interface Serial0/1
 no ip address
 shutdown
!
router eigrp 1
 network 10.0.0.14 0.0.0.0
 network 150.1.1.4 0.0.0.0
 network 192.168.0.0 0.0.3.255
 no auto-summary
!
ip forward-protocol nd
!
no ip http server
no ip http secure-server
!
control-plane
!
line con 0
line aux 0
line vty 0 4
 login
!
end

R4#
```

CCNP LAB 14

EIGRP Multi-Technology Lab

Lab Objective:

The focus of this lab is to understand EIGRP implementation and configuration in Cisco IOS routers. Additional technologies tested include stub routing, filtering, and authentication.

Lab Topology:

The lab network topology is illustrated below:

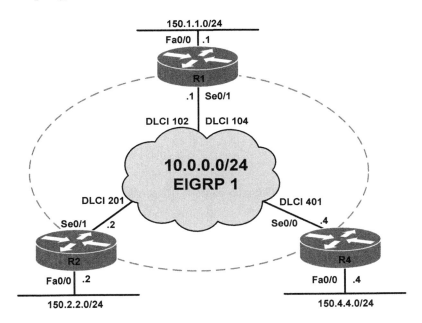

IMPORTANT NOTE: If you are using the www.howtonetwork.net racks, please bring up the LAN interfaces connected to the routers by issuing the `no shutdown` command on the connected switches. If you are using a home lab with no Switches, you can bring up the LAN interfaces using the following configurations on your routers:

```
interface fastethernet 0/0
 no keepalive
 loopback
 no shutdown
```

Alternately, you can simply connect the interfaces to a hub or switch if you have one available in your own lab. Also, if you are using the www.howtonetwork.net racks, configure R3 as the Frame Relay switch using the following configuration commands:

```
hostname R3-Frame-Relay-Switch
!
frame-relay switching
!
```

```
interface serial 1/0
 description 'Connected To R1 Serial 0/1'
 encapsulation frame-relay
 no ip address
 clock rate 128000
 frame-relay intf-type dce
 frame-relay route 102 interface serial 1/1 201
 frame-relay route 104 interface serial 1/2 401
 no shutdown
!
interface serial 1/1
 description 'Connected To R2 Serial 0/1'
 encapsulation frame-relay
 no ip address
 clock rate 128000
 frame-relay intf-type dce
 frame-relay route 201 interface serial 1/0 102
 no shutdown
!
interface serial 1/2
 description 'Connected To R4 Serial 0/0'
 encapsulation frame-relay
 no ip address
 clock rate 128000
 frame-relay intf-type dce
 frame-relay route 401 interface serial 1/0 104
 no shutdown
!
end
```

Task 1

Configure hostnames and IP addressing on all routers as illustrated in the network topology.

Task 2

Configure EIGRP for AS 1 as illustrated in the topology. However, do NOT advertise the 150.x.x.x subnets on any router via EIGRP.

Task 3

Configure routers R2 and R4 to as EIGRP stub routers. These routers should advertise their 150.x.x.x/24 subnets as Internal EIGRP routes to R1.

Task 4

Configure R1 so that it advertises ONLY a default route to both R2 and R4 as an External EIGRP route. Next, verify your configuration using the appropriate commands. Additionally, also verify that R2 and R4 can ping each others' 150.x.x.x/24 subnets from their LAN interfaces, as well as the 150.1.1.0/24 subnet on R1s LAN.

Task 5

Configure EIGRP authentication for AS 1 so that all the routers use the password CCNP-2010; however, after 15 minutes, the routers should stop using this password and begin using the password CCNP-2011. The password CCNP-2011 should be used by all routers indefinitely. Verify your configuration using the appropriate commands.

LAB VALIDATION

Task 1

```
Router(config)#hostname R1
R1(config)#interface fastethernet 0/0
R1(config-if)#no shutdown
R1(config-if)#ip address 150.1.1.1 255.255.255.0
```

```
R1(config-if)#exit
R1(config)#interface serial 0/1
R1(config-if)#ip address 10.0.0.1 255.255.255.0
R1(config-if)#no shutdown
R1(config-if)#encapsulation frame-relay
R1(config-if)#exit

Router(config)#hostname R2
R2(config)#interface fastethernet 0/0
R2(config-if)#no shutdown
R2(config-if)#ip address 150.2.2.2 255.255.255.0
R2(config-if)#exit
R2(config)#interface serial 0/1
R2(config-if)#ip address 10.0.0.2 255.255.255.0
R2(config-if)#no shutdown
R2(config-if)#encapsulation frame-relay
R2(config-if)#exit
Router(config)#hostname R4
R4(config)#interface fastethernet 0/0
R4(config-if)#no shutdown
R4(config-if)#ip address 150.4.4.4 255.255.255.0
R4(config-if)#exit
R4(config)#interface serial 0/0
R4(config-if)#ip address 10.0.0.4 255.255.255.0
R4(config-if)#no shutdown
R4(config-if)#encapsulation frame-relay
R4(config-if)#exit
```

Task 2

```
R1(config)#router eigrp 1
R1(config-router)#no auto-summary
R1(config-router)#network 10.0.0.1 0.0.0.0
R1(config-router)#exit

R2(config)#router eigrp 1
R2(config-router)#no auto-summary
R2(config-router)#network 10.0.0.2 0.0.0.0
R2(config-router)#exit

R4(config)#router eigrp 1
R4(config-router)#no auto-summary
R4(config-router)#network 10.0.0.4 0.0.0.0
R4(config-router)#exit
```

Use the show ip eigrp neighbors command to verify your configuration:

```
R1#show ip eigrp neighbors
IP-EIGRP neighbors for process 1
H   Address          Interface    Hold Uptime   SRTT  RTO  Q   Seq
                                  (sec)         (ms)       Cnt Num
1   10.0.0.4         Se0/1        135 00:00:46   16   200  0   3
0   10.0.0.2         Se0/1        157 00:01:20   15   200  0   3

R2#show ip eigrp neighbors
IP-EIGRP neighbors for process 1
H   Address          Interface    Hold Uptime   SRTT  RTO  Q   Seq
                                  (sec)         (ms)       Cnt Num
0   10.0.0.1         Se0/1        166 00:01:39 1264  5000  0   3

R4#show ip eigrp neighbors
IP-EIGRP neighbors for process 1
H   Address          Interface    Hold Uptime   SRTT  RTO  Q   Seq
                                  (sec)         (ms)       Cnt Num
0   10.0.0.1         Se0/0        151 00:01:19 1219  5000  0   5
```

Task 3

By default, EIGRP stub routers advertise connected and summary routes. Therefore, no explicit configuration other than enabling EIGRP for the 150.x.x.x/24 subnets is required:

```
R2(config)#router eigrp 1
R2(config-router)#network 150.2.2.2 0.0.0.0
R2(config-router)#eigrp stub
R2(config-router)#exit

R4(config)#router eigrp 1
R4(config-router)#network 150.4.4.4 0.0.0.0
R4(config-router)#eigrp stub
R4(config-router)#exit
```

Verify your configuration using the show ip eigrp neighbors detail command on R1:

```
R1#show ip eigrp neighbors detail
IP-EIGRP neighbors for process 1
H   Address             Interface        Hold Uptime   SRTT   RTO  Q  Seq
                                         (sec)         (ms)        Cnt Num
1   10.0.0.4            Se0/1            160 00:00:21 1253   5000  0  8
    Version 12.4/1.2, Retrans: 0, Retries: 0, Prefixes: 1
    Stub Peer Advertising ( CONNECTED SUMMARY ) Routes
    Suppressing queries

0   10.0.0.2            Se0/1            161 00:02:15  654   3924  0  7
    Version 12.4/1.2, Retrans: 0, Retries: 0, Prefixes: 1
    Stub Peer Advertising ( CONNECTED SUMMARY ) Routes
    Suppressing queries
```

Alternatively, you can use the show ip protocols command on the stub routers:

```
R2#show ip protocols
Routing Protocol is "eigrp 1"
  Outgoing update filter list for all interfaces is not set
  Incoming update filter list for all interfaces is not set
  Default networks flagged in outgoing updates
  Default networks accepted from incoming updates
  EIGRP metric weight K1=1, K2=0, K3=1, K4=0, K5=0
  EIGRP maximum hopcount 100
  EIGRP maximum metric variance 1
  EIGRP stub, connected, summary
  Redistributing: eigrp 1
  EIGRP NSF-aware route hold timer is 240s
  Automatic network summarization is not in effect
  Maximum path: 4
  Routing for Networks:
    10.0.0.2/32
    150.2.2.2/32
  Routing Information Sources:
    Gateway         Distance      Last Update
    10.0.0.1             90       00:01:39
  Distance: internal 90 external 170

R4#show ip protocols
Routing Protocol is "eigrp 1"
  Outgoing update filter list for all interfaces is not set
  Incoming update filter list for all interfaces is not set
  Default networks flagged in outgoing updates
  Default networks accepted from incoming updates
  EIGRP metric weight K1=1, K2=0, K3=1, K4=0, K5=0
  EIGRP maximum hopcount 100
  EIGRP maximum metric variance 1
  EIGRP stub, connected, summary
  Redistributing: eigrp 1
  EIGRP NSF-aware route hold timer is 240s
  Automatic network summarization is not in effect
  Maximum path: 4
  Routing for Networks:
    10.0.0.4/32
    150.4.4.4/32
  Routing Information Sources:
    Gateway         Distance      Last Update
    10.0.0.1             90       00:00:48
  Distance: internal 90 external 170
```

Verify that the routes are received on R1 using the show ip route [eigrp] command:

```
R1#show ip route eigrp
     150.2.0.0/24 is subnetted, 1 subnets
D       150.2.2.0 [90/2172416] via 10.0.0.2, 00:05:26, Serial0/1
     150.4.0.0/24 is subnetted, 1 subnets
D       150.4.4.0 [90/2172416] via 10.0.0.4, 00:03:32, Serial0/1
```

Task 4

The task is to advertise an external default route to R2 and R4. Because split horizon is enabled by default, R1 will not advertise the 150.2.2.0/24 and 150.3.3.0/24 subnets out the same interface via which they were received, so no explicit filtering configuration for EIGRP is required on R1. This task is completed as follows:

```
R1(config)#ip route 0.0.0.0 0.0.0.0 null 0
R1(config)#router eigrp 1
R1(config-router)#redistribute static
R1(config-router)#exit
```

Verify your configuration by looking at the routing tables on R2 and R4:

```
R2#show ip route eigrp
D*EX 0.0.0.0/0 [170/2169856] via 10.0.0.1, 00:00:35, Serial0/1

R4#show ip route eigrp
D*EX 0.0.0.0/0 [170/2169856] via 10.0.0.1, 00:00:53, Serial0/0
```

Verify IP connectivity using simple pings:

```
R1#ping 150.2.2.2 source 150.1.1.1

Type escape sequence to abort.
Sending 5, 100-byte ICMP Echos to 150.2.2.2, timeout is 2 seconds:
Packet sent with a source address of 150.1.1.1
!!!!!
Success rate is 100 percent (5/5), round-trip min/avg/max = 28/29/32 ms

R1#ping 150.4.4.4 source 150.1.1.1

Type escape sequence to abort.
Sending 5, 100-byte ICMP Echos to 150.4.4.4, timeout is 2 seconds:
Packet sent with a source address of 150.1.1.1
!!!!!
Success rate is 100 percent (5/5), round-trip min/avg/max = 28/30/32 ms

R2#ping 150.1.1.1 source 150.2.2.2

Type escape sequence to abort.
Sending 5, 100-byte ICMP Echos to 150.1.1.1, timeout is 2 seconds:
Packet sent with a source address of 150.2.2.2
!!!!!
Success rate is 100 percent (5/5), round-trip min/avg/max = 28/30/32 ms

R2#ping 150.4.4.4 source 150.2.2.2

Type escape sequence to abort.
Sending 5, 100-byte ICMP Echos to 150.4.4.4, timeout is 2 seconds:
Packet sent with a source address of 150.2.2.2
!!!!!
Success rate is 100 percent (5/5), round-trip min/avg/max = 56/57/60 ms

R4#ping 150.1.1.1 source 150.4.4.4

Type escape sequence to abort.
Sending 5, 100-byte ICMP Echos to 150.1.1.1, timeout is 2 seconds:
Packet sent with a source address of 150.4.4.4
!!!!!
Success rate is 100 percent (5/5), round-trip min/avg/max = 28/30/32 ms

R4#ping 150.2.2.2 source 150.4.4.4
```

```
Type escape sequence to abort.
Sending 5, 100-byte ICMP Echos to 150.2.2.2, timeout is 2 seconds:
Packet sent with a source address of 150.4.4.4
!!!!!
Success rate is 100 percent (5/5), round-trip min/avg/max = 56/57/60 ms
```

Task 5

There are several ways in which this task can be completed. One way would be to synchronize the router clocks by manually setting the system clock using the clock set command or using Network Time Protocol (NTP). If this solution is used, this task is completed as follows:

```
R1(config)#clock timezone CST -6
R1(config)#clock summer-time CST recurring
R1(config)#ntp master
R1(config)#exit

R2(config)#clock timezone CST -6
R2(config)#clock summer-time CST recurring
R2(config)#ntp server 10.0.0.1
R2(config)#exit

R4(config)#clock timezone CST -6
R4(config)#clock summer-time CST recurring
R4(config)#ntp server 10.0.0.1
R4(config)#exit
```

Verify Network Time Protocol and clock settings using the show ntp status command:

```
R4#show ntp status
Clock is synchronized, stratum 9, reference is 10.0.0.1
nominal freq is 250.0000 Hz, actual freq is 250.0000 Hz, precision is 2**18
reference time is D170B71D.82C8E0A7 (01:30:53.510 CST Sun May 8 2011)
clock offset is -0.0292 msec, root delay is 24.98 msec
root dispersion is 125.11 msec, peer dispersion is 125.05 msec
```

Following this configuration, you can then configure EIGRP authentication as follows:

```
R1(config)#key chain EIGRP-AUTH
R1(config-keychain)#key 1
R1(config-keychain-key)#key-string CCNP-2010
R1(config-keychain-key)#accept local 01:45:00 May 8 2011 02:00:00 May 8 2011
R1(config-keychain-key)#send local 01:45:00 May 8 2011 02:00:00 May 8 2011
R1(config-keychain-key)#exit
R1(config-keychain)#key 2
R1(config-keychain-key)#key-string CCNP-2011
R1(config-keychain-key)#accept-lifetime local 02:00:00 May 8 2011 infinite
R1(config-keychain-key)#send-lifetime local 02:00:00 May 8 2011 infinite
R1(config-keychain-key)#exit
R1(config-keychain)#exit
R1(config)#interface serial 0/0
R1(config-if)#ip authentication mode eigrp 1 md5
R1(config-if)#ip authentication key-chain eigrp 1 EIGRP-AUTH
R1(config-if)#exit

R2(config)#key chain EIGRP-AUTH
R2(config-keychain)#key 1
R2(config-keychain-key)#key-string CCNP-2010
R2(config-keychain-key)#accept local 01:45:00 May 8 2011 02:00:00 May 8 2011
R2(config-keychain-key)#send local 01:45:00 May 8 2011 02:00:00 May 8 2011
R2(config-keychain-key)#exit
R2(config-keychain)#key 2
R2(config-keychain-key)#key-string CCNP-2011
R2(config-keychain-key)#accept-lifetime local 02:00:00 May 8 2011 infinite
R2(config-keychain-key)#send-lifetime local 02:00:00 May 8 2011 infinite
R2(config-keychain-key)#exit
R2(config-keychain)#exit
R2(config)#interface serial 0/1
R2(config-if)#ip authentication mode eigrp 1 md5
R2(config-if)#ip authentication key-chain eigrp 1 EIGRP-AUTH
```

```
R2(config-if)#exit

R4(config)#key chain EIGRP-AUTH
R4(config-keychain)#key 1
R4(config-keychain-key)#key-string CCNP-2010
R4(config-keychain-key)#accept local 01:45:00 May 8 2011 02:00:00 May 8 2011
R4(config-keychain-key)#send local 01:45:00 May 8 2011 02:00:00 May 8 2011
R4(config-keychain-key)#exit
R4(config-keychain)#key 2
R4(config-keychain-key)#key-string CCNP-2011
R4(config-keychain-key)#accept-lifetime local 02:00:00 May 8 2011 infinite
R4(config-keychain-key)#send-lifetime local 02:00:00 May 8 2011 infinite
R4(config-keychain-key)#exit
R4(config-keychain)#exit
R4(config)#interface serial 0/0
R4(config-if)#ip authentication mode eigrp 1 md5
R4(config-if)#ip authentication key-chain eigrp 1 EIGRP-AUTH
R4(config-if)#exit
```

Following this, verify key chain configuring using the show key chain command:

```
R1#show clock
01:54:36.175 CST Sun May 8 2011

R1#show key chain EIGRP-AUTH
Key-chain EIGRP-AUTH:
    key 1 -- text "CCNP-2010"
        accept lifetime (01:45:00 CST May 8 2011) - (02:00:00 CST May 8 2011) [valid
now]
        send lifetime (01:45:00 CST May 8 2011) - (02:00:00 CST May 8 2011) [valid
now]
    key 2 -- text "CCNP-2011"
        accept lifetime (02:00:00 CST May 8 2011) - (infinite)
        send lifetime (02:00:00 CST May 8 2011) - (infinite)
```

After the configured time interval has elapsed, the second key is used and the first invalidated:

```
R1#show key chain EIGRP-AUTH
Key-chain EIGRP-AUTH:
    key 1 -- text "CCNP-2010"
        accept lifetime (01:45:00 CST May 8 2011) - (02:00:00 CST May 8 2011)
        send lifetime (01:45:00 CST May 8 2011) - (02:00:00 CST May 8 2011)
    key 2 -- text "CCNP-2011"
        accept lifetime (02:00:00 CST May 8 2011) - (infinite) [valid now]
        send lifetime (02:00:00 CST May 8 2011) - (infinite) [valid now]
```

The second method would simply be to specify the duration in the key chain. To do this, you will need to know the local time on each router, which is why the synchronized time, i.e. NTP, method is better - especially if you have multiple routers. This is completed as follows:

```
R1(config)#key chain EIGRP-AUTH
R1(config-keychain)#key 1
R1(config-keychain-key)#key-string CCNP-2010
R1(config-keychain-key)#send-lifetime 01:45:00 May 8 2011 duration 900
R1(config-keychain-key)#accept-lifetime 01:45:00 May 8 2011 duration 900
R1(config-keychain-key)#exit
R1(config-keychain)#exit
R1(config)#key chain EIGRP-AUTH
R1(config-keychain)#key 2
R1(config-keychain-key)#key-string CCNP-2011
R1(config-keychain-key)#accept 02:00:00 May 8 2011 infinite
R1(config-keychain-key)#exit
```

NOTE: The duration is specified in seconds. 15 minutes = 900 seconds.

```
R1#show key chain EIGRP-AUTH
Key-chain EIGRP-AUTH:
    key 1 -- text "CCNP-2010"
```

```
        accept lifetime (01:45:00 UTC May 8 2011) - (900 seconds) [valid now]
        send lifetime (01:45:00 UTC May 8 2011) - (900 seconds) [valid now]
   key 2 -- text "CCNP-2011"
        accept lifetime (02:00:00 UTC May 8 2011) - (infinite)
        send lifetime (02:00:00 UTC May 8 2011) - (infinite)
```

After the configured time interval has elapsed, the second key is used and the first invalidated:

```
R1#show key chain EIGRP-AUTH
Key-chain EIGRP-AUTH:
   key 1 -- text "CCNP-2010"
        accept lifetime (01:45:00 UTC May 8 2011) - (900 seconds)
        send lifetime (01:45:00 UTC May 8 2011) - (900 seconds)
   key 2 -- text "CCNP-2011"
        accept lifetime (02:00:00 UTC May 8 2011) - (infinite) [valid now]
        send lifetime (02:00:00 UTC May 8 2011) - (infinite) [valid now]
```

FINAL ROUTER CONFIGURATIONS

R1

```
R1#term len 0
R1#sh run
Building configuration...

Current configuration : 1478 bytes
!
! Last configuration change at 01:52:43 CST Sun May 8 2011
!
version 12.4
service timestamps debug datetime msec
service timestamps log datetime msec
no service password-encryption
!
hostname R1
!
boot-start-marker
boot-end-marker
!
no logging console
!
no aaa new-model
clock timezone CST -6
clock summer-time CST recurring
no network-clock-participate slot 1
no network-clock-participate wic 0
ip cef
!
no ip domain lookup
ip auth-proxy max-nodata-conns 3
ip admission max-nodata-conns 3
!
key chain EIGRP-AUTH
 key 1
   key-string CCNP-2010
   accept-lifetime local 01:45:00 May 8 2011 02:00:00 May 8 2011
   send-lifetime local 01:45:00 May 8 2011 02:00:00 May 8 2011
 key 2
   key-string CCNP-2011
   accept-lifetime local 02:00:00 May 8 2011 infinite
   send-lifetime local 02:00:00 May 8 2011 infinite
!
interface FastEthernet0/0
 ip address 150.1.1.1 255.255.255.0
 duplex auto
 speed auto
!
interface Serial0/0
 no ip address
```

```
 ip authentication mode eigrp 1 md5
 ip authentication key-chain eigrp 1 EIGRP-AUTH
 shutdown
 clock rate 2000000
!
interface Serial0/1
 ip address 10.0.0.1 255.255.255.0
 encapsulation frame-relay
!
router eigrp 1
 redistribute static
 network 10.0.0.1 0.0.0.0
 no auto-summary
!
ip forward-protocol nd
ip route 0.0.0.0 0.0.0.0 Null0
!
no ip http server
no ip http secure-server
!
control-plane
!
line con 0
line aux 0
line vty 0 4
 login
!
ntp master
!
end

R1#
```

R2

```
R2#term len 0
R2#sh run
Building configuration...

Current configuration : 1414 bytes
!
! Last configuration change at 02:02:25 CST Sun May 8 2011
!
version 12.4
service timestamps debug datetime msec
service timestamps log datetime msec
no service password-encryption
!
hostname R2
!
boot-start-marker
boot-end-marker
!
no logging console
!
no aaa new-model
clock timezone CST -6
clock summer-time CST recurring
no network-clock-participate slot 1
no network-clock-participate wic 0
ip cef
!
no ip domain lookup
ip auth-proxy max-nodata-conns 3
ip admission max-nodata-conns 3
!
key chain EIGRP-AUTH
 key 1
  key-string CCNP-2010
  accept-lifetime local 01:45:00 May 8 2011 02:00:00 May 8 2011
  send-lifetime local 01:45:00 May 8 2011 02:00:00 May 8 2011
 key 2
  key-string CCNP-2011
  accept-lifetime local 02:00:00 May 8 2011 infinite
```

```
     send-lifetime local 02:00:00 May 8 2011 infinite
!
interface FastEthernet0/0
 ip address 150.2.2.2 255.255.255.0
 duplex auto
 speed auto
!
interface Serial0/0
 no ip address
 shutdown
!
interface Serial0/1
 ip address 10.0.0.2 255.255.255.0
 encapsulation frame-relay
!
router eigrp 1
 network 10.0.0.2 0.0.0.0
 network 150.2.2.2 0.0.0.0
 no auto-summary
 eigrp stub connected summary
!
ip forward-protocol nd
!
no ip http server
no ip http secure-server
!
control-plane
!
line con 0
line aux 0
line vty 0 4
 login
!
ntp clock-period 17179893
ntp server 10.0.0.1
!
end

R2#
```

R3

```
R3-Frame-Relay-Switch#term len 0
R3-Frame-Relay-Switch#sh run
Building configuration...

Current configuration : 1656 bytes
!
! Last configuration change at 02:03:34 UTC Sun May 8 2011
!
version 12.4
service timestamps debug datetime msec
service timestamps log datetime msec
no service password-encryption
!
hostname R3-Frame-Relay-Switch
!
boot-start-marker
boot-end-marker
!
no logging console
!
no aaa new-model
no network-clock-participate slot 1
no network-clock-participate wic 0
ip cef
!
no ip domain lookup
ip auth-proxy max-nodata-conns 3
ip admission max-nodata-conns 3
!
frame-relay switching
!
interface FastEthernet0/0
```

```
 no ip address
 shutdown
 duplex auto
 speed auto
!
interface Serial1/0
 description 'Connected To R1 Serial 0/1'
 no ip address
 encapsulation frame-relay
 clock rate 128000
 frame-relay intf-type dce
 frame-relay route 102 interface Serial1/1 201
 frame-relay route 104 interface Serial1/2 401
!
interface Serial1/1
 description 'Connected To R2 Serial 0/1'
 no ip address
 encapsulation frame-relay
 clock rate 128000
 frame-relay intf-type dce
 frame-relay route 201 interface Serial1/0 102
!
interface Serial1/2
 description 'Connected To R4 Serial 0/0'
 no ip address
 encapsulation frame-relay
 clock rate 128000
 frame-relay intf-type dce
 frame-relay route 401 interface Serial1/0 104
!
interface Serial1/3
 no ip address
 shutdown
!
interface Serial1/4
 no ip address
 shutdown
!
interface Serial1/5
 no ip address
 shutdown
!
interface Serial1/6
 no ip address
 shutdown
!
interface Serial1/7
 no ip address
 shutdown
!
ip forward-protocol nd
!
no ip http server
no ip http secure-server
!
control-plane
!
line con 0
line aux 0
line vty 0 4
 login
!
!
end

R3-Frame-Relay-Switch#
```

R4

```
R4#term len 0
R4#sh run
Building configuration...

Current configuration : 1414 bytes
```

```
!
! Last configuration change at 01:52:40 CST Sun May 8 2011
!
version 12.4
service timestamps debug datetime msec
service timestamps log datetime msec
no service password-encryption
!
hostname R4
!
boot-start-marker
boot-end-marker
!
no logging console
!
no aaa new-model
clock timezone CST -6
clock summer-time CST recurring
no network-clock-participate slot 1
no network-clock-participate wic 0
ip cef
!
no ip domain lookup
ip auth-proxy max-nodata-conns 3
ip admission max-nodata-conns 3
!
key chain EIGRP-AUTH
 key 1
   key-string CCNP-2010
   accept-lifetime local 01:45:00 May 8 2011 02:00:00 May 8 2011
   send-lifetime local 01:45:00 May 8 2011 02:00:00 May 8 2011
 key 2
   key-string CCNP-2011
   accept-lifetime local 02:00:00 May 8 2011 infinite
   send-lifetime local 02:00:00 May 8 2011 infinite
!
interface FastEthernet0/0
 ip address 150.4.4.4 255.255.255.0
 duplex auto
 speed auto
!
interface Serial0/0
 ip address 10.0.0.4 255.255.255.0
 encapsulation frame-relay
!
interface Serial0/1
 no ip address
 shutdown
!
router eigrp 1
 network 10.0.0.4 0.0.0.0
 network 150.4.4.4 0.0.0.0
 no auto-summary
 eigrp stub connected summary
!
ip forward-protocol nd
!
no ip http server
no ip http secure-server
!
control-plane
!
line con 0
line aux 0
line vty 0 4
 login
!
ntp clock-period 17179872
ntp server 10.0.0.1
!
end

R4#
```

CCNP LAB 15

EIGRP Multi-Technology Lab

Lab Objective:

The focus of this lab is to understand EIGRP implementation and configuration in Cisco IOS routers. Additional technologies tested include authentication and default routing.

Lab Topology:

The lab network topology is illustrated below:

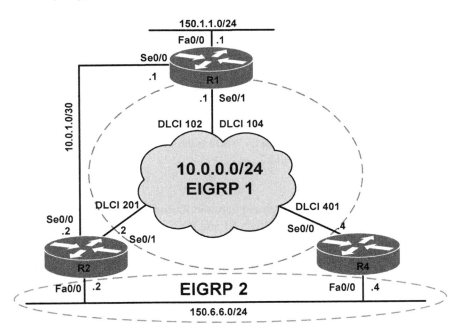

IMPORTANT NOTE: If you are using the www.howtonetwork.net racks, please bring up the LAN interfaces connected to the routers by issuing the no shutdown command on the connected switches. If you are using a home lab with no Switches, you can bring up the LAN interfaces using the following configurations on your routers:

```
interface fastethernet 0/0
  no keepalive
  loopback
  no shutdown
```

Alternately, you can simply connect the interfaces to a hub or switch if you have one available in your own lab. Also, if you are using the www.howtonetwork.net racks, configure R3 as the Frame Relay switch using the following configuration commands:

```
hostname R3-Frame-Relay-Switch
!
frame-relay switching
!
```

```
interface serial 1/0
 description 'Connected To R1 Serial 0/1'
 encapsulation frame-relay
 no ip address
 clock rate 128000
 frame-relay intf-type dce
 frame-relay route 102 interface serial 1/1 201
 frame-relay route 104 interface serial 1/2 401
 no shutdown
!
interface serial 1/1
 description 'Connected To R2 Serial 0/1'
 encapsulation frame-relay
 no ip address
 clock rate 128000
 frame-relay intf-type dce
 frame-relay route 201 interface serial 1/0 102
 no shutdown
!
interface serial 1/2
 description 'Connected To R4 Serial 0/0'
 encapsulation frame-relay
 no ip address
 clock rate 128000
 frame-relay intf-type dce
 frame-relay route 401 interface serial 1/0 104
 no shutdown
!
end
```

Task 1

Configure hostnames and IP addressing on all routers as illustrated in the network topology.

Task 2

Configure EIGRP for AS 1 across the Frame Relay WAN as illustrated in the topology. Do NOT enable EIGRP for the point-to-point link between R1 and R2.

Task 3

Configure EIGRP for AS 2 over the LAN segment between R2 and R4 as illustrated in the topology. Do NOT enable EIGRP for the point-to-point link between R1 and R2.

Task 4

Advertise the 150.1.1.0/24 via EIGRP as an External EIGRP route. This route should be injected into EIGRP with a metric of 100,000 - 100 - 255 - 1 - 1500 and administrative route tag of 1111.

Additionally, advertise the 150.6.6.0/24 subnet via EIGRP 1. The route advertised by R2 should include the administrator tag 2222 and the route advertised by R4 should include the administrative tag 4444. Ensure that R1 prefers the path via R2 to reach this subnet. In the event that this path is unavailable, R1 should prefer the path via R4. In the event that the Frame Relay WAN is down, R1 should use the point-to-point link between R1 and R2. Verify your configuration using the appropriate commands.

Task 5

Configure EIGRP AS 2 so that the 150.6.6.0/24 subnet uses R2s Frame Relay connection to reach the 150.1.1.0/24 subnet. In the event that R2s Frame Relay connection is down, R4s Frame Relay connection should be used.

In the event that both R2 and R4 Frame Relay connections are down, then the point-to-point link between R1 and R2 should be used. You are NOT allowed to use offset lists or modify interface bandwidth values in your solution. Verify and test your configuration.

LAB VALIDATION

Task 1

```
Router(config)#hostname R1
R1(config)#interface fastethernet 0/0
R1(config-if)#no shutdown
R1(config-if)#ip address 150.1.1.1 255.255.255.0
R1(config-if)#exit
R1(config)#interface serial 0/0
R1(config-if)#ip address 10.0.1.1 255.255.255.252
R1(config-if)#no shutdown
R1(config-if)#clock rate 2000000
R1(config-if)#exit
R1(config)#interface serial 0/1
R1(config-if)#ip address 10.0.0.1 255.255.255.0
R1(config-if)#no shutdown
R1(config-if)#encapsulation frame-relay
R1(config-if)#exit

Router(config)#hostname R2
R2(config)#interface fastethernet 0/0
R2(config-if)#no shutdown
R2(config-if)#ip address 150.6.6.2 255.255.255.0
R2(config-if)#exit
R2(config)#interface serial 0/0
R2(config-if)#ip address 10.0.1.2 255.255.255.252
R2(config-if)#no shutdown
R2(config-if)#exit
R2(config)#interface serial 0/1
R2(config-if)#ip address 10.0.0.2 255.255.255.0
R2(config-if)#no shutdown
R2(config-if)#encapsulation frame-relay
R2(config-if)#exit

Router(config)#hostname R4
R4(config)#interface fastethernet 0/0
R4(config-if)#no shutdown
R4(config-if)#ip address 150.6.6.4 255.255.255.0
R4(config-if)#exit
R4(config)#interface serial 0/0
R4(config-if)#ip address 10.0.0.4 255.255.255.0
R4(config-if)#no shutdown
R4(config-if)#encapsulation frame-relay
R4(config-if)#exit
```

Task 2

```
R1(config)#router eigrp 1
R1(config-router)#no auto-summary
R1(config-router)#network 10.0.0.1 0.0.0.0
R1(config-router)#exit

R2(config)#router eigrp 1
R2(config-router)#no auto-summary
R2(config-router)#network 10.0.0.2 0.0.0.0
R2(config-router)#exit

R4(config)#router eigrp 1
R4(config-router)#no auto-summary
R4(config-router)#network 10.0.0.4 0.0.0.0
R4(config-router)#exit
```

Verify your configuration using the show ip eigrp neighbors command:

```
R1#show ip eigrp neighbors
IP-EIGRP neighbors for process 1
H   Address          Interface    Hold Uptime   SRTT   RTO  Q   Seq
                                  (sec)         (ms)        Cnt Num
1   10.0.0.4         Se0/1        145 00:00:36  1561   5000 0   3
0   10.0.0.2         Se0/1        144 00:02:30  20     200  0   3
```

```
R2#show ip eigrp neighbors
IP-EIGRP neighbors for process 1
H   Address                Interface     Hold Uptime   SRTT   RTO  Q  Seq
                                         (sec)         (ms)        Cnt Num
0   10.0.0.1               Se0/1         163 00:03:09 1240  5000  0  3

R4#show ip eigrp neighbors
IP-EIGRP neighbors for process 1
H   Address                Interface     Hold Uptime   SRTT   RTO  Q  Seq
                                         (sec)         (ms)        Cnt Num
0   10.0.0.1               Se0/0         160 00:01:18   15   200  0  5
```

Task 3

```
R2(config)#router eigrp 2
R2(config-router)#no auto-summary
R2(config-router)#network 150.6.6.2 0.0.0.0
R2(config-router)#exit

R4(config)#router eigrp 2
R4(config-router)#no auto-summary
R4(config-router)#network 150.6.6.4 0.0.0.0
R4(config-router)#exit
```

Verify your configuration using the show ip eigrp neighbors command:

```
R2#show ip eigrp neighbors
IP-EIGRP neighbors for process 1
H   Address                Interface     Hold Uptime   SRTT   RTO  Q  Seq
                                         (sec)         (ms)        Cnt Num
0   10.0.0.1               Se0/1         152 00:06:09 1240  5000  0  3

IP-EIGRP neighbors for process 2
H   Address                Interface     Hold Uptime   SRTT   RTO  Q  Seq
                                         (sec)         (ms)        Cnt Num
0   150.6.6.4              Fa0/0          14 00:00:48    3   200  0  3

R4#show ip eigrp neighbors
IP-EIGRP neighbors for process 1
H   Address                Interface     Hold Uptime   SRTT   RTO  Q  Seq
                                         (sec)         (ms)        Cnt Num
0   10.0.0.1               Se0/0         171 00:03:57   15   200  0  5

IP-EIGRP neighbors for process 2
H   Address                Interface     Hold Uptime   SRTT   RTO  Q  Seq
                                         (sec)         (ms)        Cnt Num
0   150.6.6.2              Fa0/0          14 00:00:29    5   200  0  3
```

Task 4

The first part of this task is completed by redistributing the 150.1.1.0/24 subnet into EIGRP using a route map to administrative tag. The metric can also be specified in the route map, or alternatively, you can specify the metric using the redistribute command. Either option is acceptable to complete this task:

```
R1(config)#route-map CONNECTED permit 10
R1(config-route-map)#match interface fastethernet 0/0
R1(config-route-map)#set metric 100000 100 255 1 1500
R1(config-route-map)#set tag 1111
R1(config-route-map)#exit
R1(config)#route-map CONNECTED deny 20
R1(config-route-map)#exit
R1(config)#router eigrp 1
R1(config-router)#redistribute connected route-map CONNECTED
R1(config-router)#exit
```

The second part of this task requires redistribution metric manipulation and floating static route configuration. The 150.6.6.0/24 subnet must be redistributed into EIGRP 1 with a better route metric on R2 than on R4. Next, a floating static route is required to ensure that if the Frame Relay WAN is down, R1 will send packets to the 150.6.6.0/24 subnet via the point-to-point link to R2. The floating static route is should be configured with an administrative distance greater than 170 (external EIGRP administrative distance) but less than 255 (discard route). This task is completed by specifying an administrative distance between 171 and 254:

```
R1(config)#ip route 150.6.6.0 255.255.255.0 serial 0/0 200
```

The redistribution section of this task is completed as follows:

```
R2(config)#route-map CONNECTED permit 10
R2(config-route-map)#match interface fastethernet 0/0
R2(config-route-map)#set metric 100000 100 255 1 1500
R2(config-route-map)#set tag 2222
R2(config-route-map)#exit
R2(config)#route-map CONNECTED deny 20
R2(config-route-map)#exit
R2(config)#router eigrp 1
R2(config-router)#redistribute connected route-map CONNECTED
R2(config-router)#exit

R4(config)#route-map CONNECTED permit 10
R4(config-route-map)#match interface fastethernet 0/0
R4(config-route-map)#set metric 10000 1000 255 1 1500
R4(config-route-map)#set tag 4444
R4(config-route-map)#exit
R4(config)#route-map CONNECTED deny 20
R4(config-route-map)#exit
R4(config)#router eigrp 1
R4(config-router)#redistribute connected route-map CONNECTED
R4(config-router)#exit
```

Verify your configuration by looking at the topology table on R1:

```
R1#show ip eigrp topology 150.6.6.0 255.255.255.0
IP-EIGRP (AS 1): Topology entry for 150.6.6.0/24
  State is Passive, Query origin flag is 1, 1 Successor(s), FD is 2195456
  Routing Descriptor Blocks:
  10.0.0.2 (Serial0/1), from 10.0.0.2, Send flag is 0x0
      Composite metric is (2195456/51200), Route is External
      Vector metric:
        Minimum bandwidth is 1544 Kbit
        Total delay is 21000 microseconds
        Reliability is 255/255
        Load is 1/255
        Minimum MTU is 1500
        Hop count is 1
      External data:
        Originating router is 150.6.6.2
        AS number of route is 0
        External protocol is Connected, external metric is 0
        Administrator tag is 2222 (0x000008AE)

  10.0.0.4 (Serial0/1), from 10.0.0.4, Send flag is 0x0
      Composite metric is (2425856/512000), Route is External
      Vector metric:
        Minimum bandwidth is 1544 Kbit
        Total delay is 30000 microseconds
        Reliability is 255/255
        Load is 1/255
        Minimum MTU is 1500
        Hop count is 1
      External data:
        Originating router is 150.6.6.4
        AS number of route is 0
        External protocol is Connected, external metric is 0
        Administrator tag is 4444 (0x0000115C)
```

Verify the floating static route configuration by shutting down the Frame Relay WAN:

```
R1(config)#interface serial 0/1
R1(config-if)#shutdown
R1(config-if)#exit
```

```
R1(config)#do show ip route 150.6.6.0 255.255.255.0
Routing entry for 150.6.6.0/24
  Known via "static", distance 200, metric 0 (connected)
  Routing Descriptor Blocks:
  * directly connected, via Serial0/0
      Route metric is 0, traffic share count is 1
```

Task 5

The first requirement of this task is that the 150.1.1.0/24 subnet should known within EIGRP AS 2. This requires that EIGRP 1 be redistributed into EIGRP 2 on R2 and R4:

```
R2(config)#router eigrp 2
R2(config-router)#redistribute eigrp 1
R2(config-router)#exit

R4(config)#router eigrp 2
R4(config-router)#redistribute eigrp 1
R4(config-router)#exit
```

The second requirement is completed by modifying the default interface delay values so that routes received via R4 are less preferable to those received via R2.

To influence path selection, increase the delay on R4s Frame Relay interface OR decrease the delay on R2s Frame Relay interface. Either solution is acceptable.

```
R2(config)#int s 0/1
R2(config-if)#delay 100
R2(config-if)#exit
```

Following this change, R2 and R4 show the following route entries for the 150.1.1.0/24 subnet:

```
R2#show ip route 150.1.1.0 255.255.255.0
Routing entry for 150.1.1.0/24
  Known via "eigrp 1", distance 170, metric 1709056
  Tag 1111, type external
  Redistributing via eigrp 1, eigrp 2
  Advertised by eigrp 2
  Last update from 10.0.0.1 on Serial0/1, 00:00:42 ago
  Routing Descriptor Blocks:
  * 10.0.0.1, from 10.0.0.1, 00:00:42 ago, via Serial0/1
      Route metric is 1709056, traffic share count is 1
      Total delay is 2000 microseconds, minimum bandwidth is 1544 Kbit
      Reliability 255/255, minimum MTU 1500 bytes
      Loading 1/255, Hops 1
      Route tag 1111

R4#show ip route 150.1.1.0 255.255.255.0
Routing entry for 150.1.1.0/24
  Known via "eigrp 2", distance 170, metric 1711616
  Tag 1111, type external
  Redistributing via eigrp 2
  Last update from 150.6.6.2 on FastEthernet0/0, 00:01:04 ago
  Routing Descriptor Blocks:
  * 150.6.6.2, from 150.6.6.2, 00:01:04 ago, via FastEthernet0/0
      Route metric is 1711616, traffic share count is 1
      Total delay is 2100 microseconds, minimum bandwidth is 1544 Kbit
      Reliability 255/255, minimum MTU 1500 bytes
      Loading 1/255, Hops 2
      Route tag 1111
```

The third required requires a floating static route to be configured on R2 for the 150.1.1.0/24 subnet. This floating static will also need to be redistributed into EIGRP 2 so that R4 receives this route when the Frame Relay WAN in down. This task is completed as follows:

```
R2(config)#ip route 150.1.1.0 255.255.255.0 serial 0/0 200 name R1-BACKUP
R2(config)#router eigrp 2
R2(config-router)#redistribute static metric 5000 5000 255 1 1500
R2(config-router)#exit
```

Finally, verify that routing works as required. Shut down the Frame Relay WAN link on R2 and ensure that this router can still reach the 150.1.1.0/24 subnet and vice-versa across the Frame Relay network, i.e. via R4:

```
R2(config)#int s0/1
R2(config-if)#shutdown
R2(config-if)#exit
R2(config)#do show ip route 150.1.1.0 255.255.255.0
Routing entry for 150.1.1.0/24
  Known via "eigrp 2", distance 170, metric 2198016
  Tag 1111, type external
  Redistributing via eigrp 2
  Last update from 150.6.6.4 on FastEthernet0/0, 00:00:14 ago
  Routing Descriptor Blocks:
  * 150.6.6.4, from 150.6.6.4, 00:00:14 ago, via FastEthernet0/0
      Route metric is 2198016, traffic share count is 1
      Total delay is 21100 microseconds, minimum bandwidth is 1544 Kbit
      Reliability 255/255, minimum MTU 1500 bytes
      Loading 1/255, Hops 2
      Route tag 1111

R2(config)#do ping 150.1.1.1 source 150.6.6.2

Type escape sequence to abort.
Sending 5, 100-byte ICMP Echos to 150.1.1.1, timeout is 2 seconds:
Packet sent with a source address of 150.6.6.2
!!!!!
Success rate is 100 percent (5/5), round-trip min/avg/max = 28/31/32 ms
```

Next, shut down the Frame Relay WAN link on R4 and ensure that both R2 and R4 can still reach the 150.1.1.0/24 subnet and vice-versa:

```
R2(config)#int s0/1
R2(config-if)#shutdown
R2(config-if)#exit

R4(config)#int s0/0
R4(config-if)#shutdown
R4(config-if)#exit

R1#show ip route 150.6.6.0 255.255.255.0
Routing entry for 150.6.6.0/24
  Known via "static", distance 200, metric 0 (connected)
  Routing Descriptor Blocks:
  * directly connected, via Serial0/0
      Route metric is 0, traffic share count is 1

R2#show ip route 150.1.1.0 255.255.255.0
Routing entry for 150.1.1.0/24
  Known via "static", distance 200, metric 0 (connected)
  Redistributing via eigrp 2
  Advertised by eigrp 2 metric 5000 5000 255 1 1500
  Routing Descriptor Blocks:
  * directly connected, via Serial0/0
      Route metric is 0, traffic share count is 1

R4#show ip route 150.1.1.0 255.255.255.0
Routing entry for 150.1.1.0/24
  Known via "eigrp 2", distance 170, metric 1794560, type external
  Redistributing via eigrp 2
  Last update from 150.6.6.2 on FastEthernet0/0, 00:00:47 ago
  Routing Descriptor Blocks:
  * 150.6.6.2, from 150.6.6.2, 00:00:47 ago, via FastEthernet0/0
      Route metric is 1794560, traffic share count is 1
      Total delay is 50100 microseconds, minimum bandwidth is 5000 Kbit
      Reliability 255/255, minimum MTU 1500 bytes
      Loading 1/255, Hops 1

R1#ping 150.6.6.0 source 150.1.1.1

Type escape sequence to abort.
Sending 5, 100-byte ICMP Echos to 150.6.6.0, timeout is 2 seconds:
```

```
Packet sent with a source address of 150.1.1.1
!!!!!
Success rate is 100 percent (5/5), round-trip min/avg/max = 1/2/4 ms

R2#ping 150.1.1.0 source 150.6.6.2

Type escape sequence to abort.
Sending 5, 100-byte ICMP Echos to 150.1.1.0, timeout is 2 seconds:
Packet sent with a source address of 150.6.6.2
!!!!!
Success rate is 100 percent (5/5), round-trip min/avg/max = 1/3/4 ms

R4#ping 150.1.1.0 source 150.6.6.4

Type escape sequence to abort.
Sending 5, 100-byte ICMP Echos to 150.1.1.0, timeout is 2 seconds:
Packet sent with a source address of 150.6.6.4
!!!!!
Success rate is 100 percent (5/5), round-trip min/avg/max = 1/3/4 ms
```

FINAL ROUTER CONFIGURATIONS

R1

```
R1#term len 0
R1#sh run
Building configuration...

Current configuration : 1143 bytes
!
version 12.4
service timestamps debug datetime msec
service timestamps log datetime msec
no service password-encryption
!
hostname R1
!
boot-start-marker
boot-end-marker
!
no logging console
!
no aaa new-model
no network-clock-participate slot 1
no network-clock-participate wic 0
ip cef
!
no ip domain lookup
ip auth-proxy max-nodata-conns 3
ip admission max-nodata-conns 3
!
interface FastEthernet0/0
 ip address 150.1.1.1 255.255.255.0
 duplex auto
 speed auto
!
interface Serial0/0
 ip address 10.0.1.1 255.255.255.252
 clock rate 2000000
!
interface Serial0/1
 ip address 10.0.0.1 255.255.255.0
 encapsulation frame-relay
!
router eigrp 1
 redistribute connected route-map CONNECTED
 network 10.0.0.1 0.0.0.0
 no auto-summary
!
ip forward-protocol nd
ip route 150.6.6.0 255.255.255.0 Serial0/0 200
!
```

```
no ip http server
no ip http secure-server
!
route-map CONNECTED permit 10
 match interface FastEthernet0/0
 set metric 100000 100 255 1 1500
 set tag 1111
!
route-map CONNECTED deny 20
!
control-plane
!
line con 0
line aux 0
line vty 0 4
 login
!
end

R1#
```

R2

```
R2#term len 0
R2#sh run
Building configuration...

Current configuration : 1281 bytes
!
version 12.4
service timestamps debug datetime msec
service timestamps log datetime msec
no service password-encryption
!
hostname R2
!
boot-start-marker
boot-end-marker
!
no logging console
!
no aaa new-model
no network-clock-participate slot 1
no network-clock-participate wic 0
ip cef
!
no ip domain lookup
ip auth-proxy max-nodata-conns 3
ip admission max-nodata-conns 3
!
interface FastEthernet0/0
 ip address 150.6.6.2 255.255.255.0
 duplex auto
 speed auto
!
interface Serial0/0
 ip address 10.0.1.2 255.255.255.252
!
interface Serial0/1
 ip address 10.0.0.2 255.255.255.0
 encapsulation frame-relay
 delay 100
!
router eigrp 1
 redistribute connected route-map CONNECTED
 network 10.0.0.2 0.0.0.0
 no auto-summary
!
router eigrp 2
 redistribute static metric 5000 5000 255 1 1500
 redistribute eigrp 1
 network 150.6.6.2 0.0.0.0
 no auto-summary
!
```

```
ip forward-protocol nd
ip route 150.1.1.0 255.255.255.0 Serial0/0 200 name R1-BACKUP
!
no ip http server
no ip http secure-server
!
route-map CONNECTED permit 10
 match interface FastEthernet0/0
 set metric 100000 100 255 1 1500
 set tag 2222
!
route-map CONNECTED deny 20
!
control-plane
!
line con 0
line aux 0
line vty 0 4
 login
!
end

R2#
```

R3

```
R3-Frame-Relay-Switch#term len 0
R3-Frame-Relay-Switch#sh run
Building configuration...

Current configuration : 1556 bytes
!
version 12.4
service timestamps debug datetime msec
service timestamps log datetime msec
no service password-encryption
!
hostname R3-Frame-Relay-Switch
!
boot-start-marker
boot-end-marker
!
no aaa new-model
no network-clock-participate slot 1
no network-clock-participate wic 0
ip cef
!
ip auth-proxy max-nodata-conns 3
ip admission max-nodata-conns 3
!
frame-relay switching
!
interface FastEthernet0/0
 no ip address
 shutdown
 duplex auto
 speed auto
!
interface Serial1/0
 description 'Connected To R1 Serial 0/1'
 no ip address
 encapsulation frame-relay
 clock rate 128000
 frame-relay intf-type dce
 frame-relay route 102 interface Serial1/1 201
 frame-relay route 104 interface Serial1/2 401
!
interface Serial1/1
 description 'Connected To R2 Serial 0/1'
 no ip address
 encapsulation frame-relay
 clock rate 128000
 frame-relay intf-type dce
 frame-relay route 201 interface Serial1/0 102
```

```
!
interface Serial1/2
 description 'Connected To R4 Serial 0/0'
 no ip address
 encapsulation frame-relay
 clock rate 128000
 frame-relay intf-type dce
 frame-relay route 401 interface Serial1/0 104
!
interface Serial1/3
 no ip address
 shutdown
!
interface Serial1/4
 no ip address
 shutdown
!
interface Serial1/5
 no ip address
 shutdown
!
interface Serial1/6
 no ip address
 shutdown
!
interface Serial1/7
 no ip address
 shutdown
!
ip forward-protocol nd
!
no ip http server
no ip http secure-server
!
control-plane
!
line con 0
line aux 0
line vty 0 4
 login
!
end

R3-Frame-Relay-Switch#
```

R4

```
R4#term len 0
R4#sh run
Building configuration...

Current configuration : 1137 bytes
!
version 12.4
service timestamps debug datetime msec
service timestamps log datetime msec
no service password-encryption
!
hostname R4
!
boot-start-marker
boot-end-marker
!
no logging console
!
no aaa new-model
no network-clock-participate slot 1
no network-clock-participate wic 0
ip cef
!
no ip domain lookup
ip auth-proxy max-nodata-conns 3
ip admission max-nodata-conns 3
```

```
!
interface FastEthernet0/0
 ip address 150.6.6.4 255.255.255.0
 duplex auto
 speed auto
!
interface Serial0/0
 ip address 10.0.0.4 255.255.255.0
 encapsulation frame-relay
!
interface Serial0/1
 no ip address
!
router eigrp 1
 redistribute connected route-map CONNECTED
 network 10.0.0.4 0.0.0.0
 no auto-summary
!
router eigrp 2
 redistribute eigrp 1
 network 150.6.6.4 0.0.0.0
 no auto-summary
!
ip forward-protocol nd
!
no ip http server
no ip http secure-server
!
route-map CONNECTED permit 10
 match interface FastEthernet0/0
 set metric 10000 1000 255 1 1500
 set tag 4444
!
route-map CONNECTED deny 20
!
control-plane
!
line con 0
line aux 0
line vty 0 4
 login
!
end

R4#
```

CCNP LAB 16

EIGRP Multi-Technology Lab

Lab Objective:

The focus of this lab is to understand EIGRP implementation and configuration in Cisco IOS routers. Additional technologies tested include split horizon and next-hop processing.

Lab Topology:

The lab network topology is illustrated below:

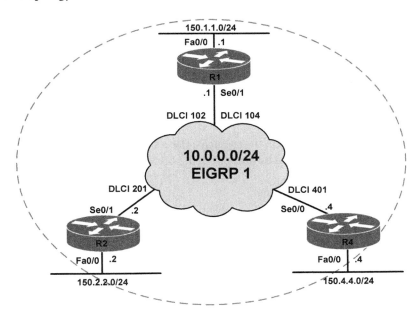

IMPORTANT NOTE: If you are using the www.howtonetwork.net racks, please bring up the LAN interfaces connected to the routers by issuing the `no shutdown` command on the connected switches. If you are using a home lab with no Switches, you can bring up the LAN interfaces using the following configurations on your routers:

```
interface fastethernet 0/0
  no keepalive
  loopback
  no shutdown
```

Alternately, you can simply connect the interfaces to a hub or switch if you have one available in your own lab. Also, if you are using the www.howtonetwork.net racks, configure R3 as the Frame Relay switch using the following configuration commands:

```
hostname R3-Frame-Relay-Switch
!
frame-relay switching
!
```

```
interface serial 1/0
 description 'Connected To R1 Serial 0/1'
 encapsulation frame-relay
 no ip address
 clock rate 128000
 frame-relay intf-type dce
 frame-relay route 102 interface serial 1/1 201
 frame-relay route 104 interface serial 1/2 401
 no shutdown
!
interface serial 1/1
 description 'Connected To R2 Serial 0/1'
 encapsulation frame-relay
 no ip address
 clock rate 128000
 frame-relay intf-type dce
 frame-relay route 201 interface serial 1/0 102
 no shutdown
!
interface serial 1/2
 description 'Connected To R4 Serial 0/0'
 encapsulation frame-relay
 no ip address
 clock rate 128000
 frame-relay intf-type dce
 frame-relay route 401 interface serial 1/0 104
 no shutdown
!
end
```

Task 1

Configure hostnames and IP addressing on all routers as illustrated in the network topology.

Task 2

Configure EIGRP for AS 1 as illustrated in the topology. Use a single 'network' command to enable EIGRP for all interfaces. No EIGRP packets should be sent out of the LAN interfaces.

Task 3

Configure EIGRP so that routers R2 and R4 are able to ping each others' 150.x.x.x/24 subnets, as well as the 150.1.1.0/24 subnet connected to R1. Do NOT use default or static routing to do this.

Task 4

Additional spoke routers will be added to the Frame Relay network in the future. In order to easily identify which spoke router is advertising which 150.x.x.x subnet, configure EIGRP so that the next hop IP address for each 150.x.x.x is the WAN IP address of the router that advertised it instead of the IP address of the hub router (R1). For example, on R2, the next hop IP address of the 150.4.4.0/24 subnet should be 10.0.0.4.

Task 5

Configure the network so that spoke R2 and R4 routers can ping each others' 150.x.x.x/24 subnets. Test your configuration by pinging LAN-to-LAN between the spoke routers.

LAB VALIDATION

Task 1

```
Router(config)#hostname R1
R1(config)#interface fastethernet 0/0
R1(config-if)#no shutdown
R1(config-if)#ip address 150.1.1.1 255.255.255.0
R1(config-if)#exit
R1(config)#interface serial 0/1
```

```
R1(config-if)#ip address 10.0.0.1 255.255.255.0
R1(config-if)#no shutdown
R1(config-if)#encapsulation frame-relay
R1(config-if)#exit

Router(config)#hostname R2
R2(config)#interface fastethernet 0/0
R2(config-if)#no shutdown
R2(config-if)#ip address 150.2.2.2 255.255.255.0
R2(config-if)#exit
R2(config)#interface serial 0/1
R2(config-if)#ip address 10.0.0.2 255.255.255.0
R2(config-if)#no shutdown
R2(config-if)#encapsulation frame-relay
R2(config-if)#exit

Router(config)#hostname R4
R4(config)#interface fastethernet 0/0
R4(config-if)#no shutdown
R4(config-if)#ip address 150.4.4.4 255.255.255.0
R4(config-if)#exit
R4(config)#interface serial 0/0
R4(config-if)#ip address 10.0.0.4 255.255.255.0
R4(config-if)#no shutdown
R4(config-if)#encapsulation frame-relay
R4(config-if)#exit
```

Task 2

```
R1(config)#router eigrp 1
R1(config-router)#no auto-summary
R1(config-router)#passive-interface fastethernet 0/0
R1(config-router)#network 0.0.0.0 255.255.255.255
R1(config-router)#exit

R2(config)#router eigrp 1
R2(config-router)#no auto-summary
R4(config-router)#passive-interface fastethernet 0/0
R2(config-router)#network 0.0.0.0 255.255.255.255
R2(config-router)#exit

R4(config)#router eigrp 1
R4(config-router)#no auto-summary
R4(config-router)#passive-interface fastethernet 0/0
R4(config-router)#network 0.0.0.0 255.255.255.255
R4(config-router)#exit
```

Verify your configuration using the show ip eigrp neighbors command:

```
R1#show ip eigrp neighbors
IP-EIGRP neighbors for process 1
H   Address              Interface      Hold Uptime    SRTT   RTO  Q   Seq
                                        (sec)          (ms)        Cnt Num
2   10.0.0.4             Se0/1          141 00:02:32   20     200  0   11
0   10.0.0.2             Se0/1          159 00:03:02   23     200  0   3

R2#show ip eigrp neighbors
IP-EIGRP neighbors for process 1
H   Address              Interface      Hold Uptime    SRTT   RTO  Q   Seq
                                        (sec)          (ms)        Cnt Num
0   10.0.0.1             Se0/1          138 00:03:06   1215   5000 0   12

R4#show ip eigrp neighbors
IP-EIGRP neighbors for process 1
H   Address              Interface      Hold Uptime    SRTT   RTO  Q   Seq
                                        (sec)          (ms)        Cnt Num
1   10.0.0.1             Se0/0          147 00:02:26   20     200  0   12
```

Task 3

By default, EIGRP will not advertise routes out the same interface via which they were learned due to split horizon. Prior to any changes, the routing tables of all three routers are as follows:

```
R1#show ip route eigrp
      150.2.0.0/24 is subnetted, 1 subnets
D        150.2.2.0 [90/2172416] via 10.0.0.2, 00:04:21, Serial0/1
      150.4.0.0/24 is subnetted, 1 subnets
D        150.4.4.0 [90/2172416] via 10.0.0.4, 00:02:29, Serial0/1

R2#show ip route eigrp
      150.1.0.0/24 is subnetted, 1 subnets
D        150.1.1.0 [90/2172416] via 10.0.0.1, 00:04:58, Serial0/1

R4#show ip route eigrp
      150.1.0.0/24 is subnetted, 1 subnets
D        150.1.1.0 [90/2172416] via 10.0.0.1, 00:02:37, Serial0/0
```

To complete this task, split horizon should be disabled on the WAN interface on R1 (hub):

```
R1(config)#interface serial 0/1
R1(config-if)#no ip split-horizon eigrp 1
R1(config-if)#exit
```

Following this change, the routing tables on all three routers show the following:

```
R1#show ip route eigrp
      150.2.0.0/24 is subnetted, 1 subnets
D        150.2.2.0 [90/2172416] via 10.0.0.2, 00:06:42, Serial0/1
      150.4.0.0/24 is subnetted, 1 subnets
D        150.4.4.0 [90/2172416] via 10.0.0.4, 00:04:50, Serial0/1

R2#show ip route eigrp
      150.1.0.0/24 is subnetted, 1 subnets
D        150.1.1.0 [90/2172416] via 10.0.0.1, 00:07:37, Serial0/1
      150.4.0.0/24 is subnetted, 1 subnets
D        150.4.4.0 [90/2684416] via 10.0.0.1, 00:01:19, Serial0/1

R4#show ip route eigrp
      150.1.0.0/24 is subnetted, 1 subnets
D        150.1.1.0 [90/2172416] via 10.0.0.1, 00:05:38, Serial0/0
      150.2.0.0/24 is subnetted, 1 subnets
D        150.2.2.0 [90/2684416] via 10.0.0.1, 00:01:43, Serial0/0
```

Verify connectivity between the LAN subnets using a simple ping:

```
R1#ping 150.2.2.2 source 150.1.1.1

Type escape sequence to abort.
Sending 5, 100-byte ICMP Echos to 150.2.2.2, timeout is 2 seconds:
Packet sent with a source address of 150.1.1.1
!!!!!
Success rate is 100 percent (5/5), round-trip min/avg/max = 28/29/32 ms

R1#ping 150.4.4.4 source 150.1.1.1

Type escape sequence to abort.
Sending 5, 100-byte ICMP Echos to 150.4.4.4, timeout is 2 seconds:
Packet sent with a source address of 150.1.1.1
!!!!!
Success rate is 100 percent (5/5), round-trip min/avg/max = 28/30/32 ms

R2#ping 150.1.1.1 source 150.2.2.2

Type escape sequence to abort.
Sending 5, 100-byte ICMP Echos to 150.1.1.1, timeout is 2 seconds:
Packet sent with a source address of 150.2.2.2
```

```
!!!!!
Success rate is 100 percent (5/5), round-trip min/avg/max = 28/31/32 ms

R2#ping 150.4.4.4 source 150.2.2.2

Type escape sequence to abort.
Sending 5, 100-byte ICMP Echos to 150.4.4.4, timeout is 2 seconds:
Packet sent with a source address of 150.2.2.2
!!!!!
Success rate is 100 percent (5/5), round-trip min/avg/max = 56/58/60 ms

R4#ping 150.1.1.1 source 150.4.4.4

Type escape sequence to abort.
Sending 5, 100-byte ICMP Echos to 150.1.1.1, timeout is 2 seconds:
Packet sent with a source address of 150.4.4.4
!!!!!
Success rate is 100 percent (5/5), round-trip min/avg/max = 28/30/32 ms

R4#ping 150.2.2.2 source 150.4.4.4

Type escape sequence to abort.
Sending 5, 100-byte ICMP Echos to 150.2.2.2, timeout is 2 seconds:
Packet sent with a source address of 150.4.4.4
!!!!!
Success rate is 100 percent (5/5), round-trip min/avg/max = 56/70/120 ms
```

Task 4

EIGRP does not set the NEXT HOP field in EIGRP packets by default. Therefore, on a multi-access network, such as an NBMA or Ethernet network, a router receiving routes from an EIGRP router assumes that the next hop of these routes is the router sending the updates, even though it might actually be another router on the same subnet, as illustrated below:

```
R2#show ip route 150.4.4.0 255.255.255.0
Routing entry for 150.4.4.0/24
  Known via "eigrp 1", distance 90, metric 2684416, type internal
  Redistributing via eigrp 1
  Last update from 10.0.0.1 on Serial0/1, 00:08:43 ago
  Routing Descriptor Blocks:
  * 10.0.0.1, from 10.0.0.1, 00:08:43 ago, via Serial0/1
      Route metric is 2684416, traffic share count is 1
      Total delay is 40100 microseconds, minimum bandwidth is 1544 Kbit
      Reliability 255/255, minimum MTU 1500 bytes
      Loading 1/255, Hops 2

R4#show ip route 150.2.2.0 255.255.255.0
Routing entry for 150.2.2.0/24
  Known via "eigrp 1", distance 90, metric 2684416, type internal
  Redistributing via eigrp 1
  Last update from 10.0.0.1 on Serial0/0, 00:09:23 ago
  Routing Descriptor Blocks:
  * 10.0.0.1, from 10.0.0.1, 00:09:23 ago, via Serial0/0
      Route metric is 2684416, traffic share count is 1
      Total delay is 40100 microseconds, minimum bandwidth is 1544 Kbit
      Reliability 255/255, minimum MTU 1500 bytes
      Loading 1/255, Hops 2
```

The first part of this task is completed by using the **no ip next-hop-self eigrp <ASN>** command on the hub router interface. When this command is issued, R1 will begin to set the NEXT HOP field in outgoing routing updates only if the IP next hop in its EIGRP topology table belongs to the IP subnet of the outgoing interface. The NEXT HOP field is set in internal as well as external EIGRP routing updates, optimizing traffic flow in route redistribution scenarios.

```
R1(config)#interface serial 0/1
R1(config-if)#no ip next-hop-self eigrp 1
R1(config-if)#exit
```

Following this configuration, the routing tables for the spoke routers show the following:

```
R2#show ip route 150.4.4.0 255.255.255.0
Routing entry for 150.4.4.0/24
  Known via "eigrp 1", distance 90, metric 2684416, type internal
  Redistributing via eigrp 1
  Last update from 10.0.0.4 on Serial0/1, 00:00:20 ago
  Routing Descriptor Blocks:
  * 10.0.0.4, from 10.0.0.1, 00:00:20 ago, via Serial0/1
      Route metric is 2684416, traffic share count is 1
      Total delay is 40100 microseconds, minimum bandwidth is 1544 Kbit
      Reliability 255/255, minimum MTU 1500 bytes
      Loading 1/255, Hops 2

R4#show ip route 150.2.2.0 255.255.255.0
Routing entry for 150.2.2.0/24
  Known via "eigrp 1", distance 90, metric 2684416, type internal
  Redistributing via eigrp 1
  Last update from 10.0.0.2 on Serial0/0, 00:01:03 ago
  Routing Descriptor Blocks:
  * 10.0.0.2, from 10.0.0.1, 00:01:03 ago, via Serial0/0
      Route metric is 2684416, traffic share count is 1
      Total delay is 40100 microseconds, minimum bandwidth is 1544 Kbit
      Reliability 255/255, minimum MTU 1500 bytes
      Loading 1/255, Hops 2
```

Notice that the NEXT HOP has changed for each spoke LAN subnet and it reflects the interface address of the actual spoke router. However, because there is no direct Frame Relay PVC between the two spoke routers, you will not be able to ping between the LAN interfaces:

```
R4#show frame-relay map
Serial0/0 (up): ip 10.0.0.1 dlci 401(0x191,0x6410), dynamic,
                broadcast,, status defined, active

R4#ping 150.2.2.2 source 150.4.4.4

Type escape sequence to abort.
Sending 5, 100-byte ICMP Echos to 150.2.2.2, timeout is 2 seconds:
Packet sent with a source address of 150.4.4.4
.....
Success rate is 0 percent (0/5)
```
Task 5

In the previous task, following the changing of the NEXT HOP, we observed that we were still unable to ping between the LAN routers. This task is required to allow this connectivity:

```
R2(config)#interface serial 0/1
R2(config-if)#frame-relay map ip 10.0.0.1 201 broadcast
R2(config-if)#frame-relay map ip 10.0.0.4 201 broadcast
R2(config-if)#exit
R2(config)#
R2(config)#do show frame-relay map
Serial0/1 (up): ip 10.0.0.1 dlci 201(0xC9,0x3090), static,
                broadcast,
                CISCO, status defined, active
Serial0/1 (up): ip 10.0.0.4 dlci 201(0xC9,0x3090), static,
                broadcast,
                CISCO, status defined, active

R4(config)#interface serial 0/0
R4(config-if)#frame-relay map ip 10.0.0.1 401 broadcast
R4(config-if)#frame-relay map ip 10.0.0.2 401 broadcast
R4(config-if)#exit
R4(config)#
R4(config)#do show frame-relay map
Serial0/0 (up): ip 10.0.0.1 dlci 401(0x191,0x6410), static,
                broadcast,
                CISCO, status defined, active
Serial0/0 (up): ip 10.0.0.2 dlci 401(0x191,0x6410), static,
                broadcast,
                CISCO, status defined, active
```

Following this configuration, the spokes are again able to ping LAN to LAN:

```
R4#ping 150.2.2.2 source 150.4.4.4 repeat 10 size 1500 df-bit timeout 1

Type escape sequence to abort.
Sending 10, 1500-byte ICMP Echos to 150.2.2.2, timeout is 1 seconds:
Packet sent with a source address of 150.4.4.4
Packet sent with the DF bit set
!!!!!!!!!!
Success rate is 100 percent (10/10), round-trip min/avg/max = 760/760/760 ms
```

It should be noted that simply creating the static Frame Relay map statement does not mean that an EIGRP neighbor relationship is established between the spokes. The spoke routing information will not change. In other words the NEXT HOP will still be the spoke router that originated the route, but the route will still be received from R1:

```
R4#show ip route 150.2.2.0 255.255.255.0
Routing entry for 150.2.2.0/24
  Known via "eigrp 1", distance 90, metric 2684416, type internal
  Redistributing via eigrp 1
  Last update from 10.0.0.2 on Serial0/0, 00:24:56 ago
  Routing Descriptor Blocks:
  * 10.0.0.2, from 10.0.0.1, 00:24:56 ago, via Serial0/0
      Route metric is 2684416, traffic share count is 1
      Total delay is 40100 microseconds, minimum bandwidth is 1544 Kbit
      Reliability 255/255, minimum MTU 1500 bytes
      Loading 1/255, Hops 2
```

FINAL ROUTER CONFIGURATIONS

R1

```
R1#term len 0
R1#sh run
Building configuration...

Current configuration : 981 bytes
!
version 12.4
service timestamps debug datetime msec
service timestamps log datetime msec
no service password-encryption
!
hostname R1
!
boot-start-marker
boot-end-marker
!
no logging console
!
no aaa new-model
no network-clock-participate slot 1
no network-clock-participate wic 0
ip cef
!
no ip domain lookup
ip auth-proxy max-nodata-conns 3
ip admission max-nodata-conns 3
!
interface FastEthernet0/0
 ip address 150.1.1.1 255.255.255.0
 duplex auto
 speed auto
!
interface Serial0/0
 no ip address
 shutdown
 clock rate 2000000
!
interface Serial0/1
```

```
 ip address 10.0.0.1 255.255.255.0
 no ip next-hop-self eigrp 1
 encapsulation frame-relay
 no ip split-horizon eigrp 1
!
router eigrp 1
 passive-interface FastEthernet0/0
 network 0.0.0.0
 no auto-summary
!
ip forward-protocol nd
!
no ip http server
no ip http secure-server
!
control-plane
!
line con 0
line aux 0
line vty 0 4
 login
!
end

R1#
```

R2

```
R2#term len 0
R2#sh run
Building configuration...

Current configuration : 989 bytes
!
version 12.4
service timestamps debug datetime msec
service timestamps log datetime msec
no service password-encryption
!
hostname R2
!
boot-start-marker
boot-end-marker
!
no logging console
!
no aaa new-model
no network-clock-participate slot 1
no network-clock-participate wic 0
ip cef
!
no ip domain lookup
ip auth-proxy max-nodata-conns 3
ip admission max-nodata-conns 3
!
interface FastEthernet0/0
 ip address 150.2.2.2 255.255.255.0
 duplex auto
 speed auto
!
interface Serial0/0
 no ip address
 shutdown
!
interface Serial0/1
 ip address 10.0.0.2 255.255.255.0
 encapsulation frame-relay
 frame-relay map ip 10.0.0.1 201 broadcast
 frame-relay map ip 10.0.0.4 201 broadcast
!
router eigrp 1
 passive-interface FastEthernet0/0
 network 0.0.0.0
 no auto-summary
!
```

```
ip forward-protocol nd
!
no ip http server
no ip http secure-server
!
control-plane
!
line con 0
line aux 0
line vty 0 4
 login
!
end

R2#
```

R3

```
R3-Frame-Relay-Switch#term len 0
R3-Frame-Relay-Switch#sh run
Building configuration...

Current configuration : 1556 bytes
!
version 12.4
service timestamps debug datetime msec
service timestamps log datetime msec
no service password-encryption
!
hostname R3-Frame-Relay-Switch
!
boot-start-marker
boot-end-marker
!
no aaa new-model
no network-clock-participate slot 1
no network-clock-participate wic 0
ip cef
!
ip auth-proxy max-nodata-conns 3
ip admission max-nodata-conns 3
!
frame-relay switching
!
interface FastEthernet0/0
 no ip address
 shutdown
 duplex auto
 speed auto
!
interface Serial1/0
 description 'Connected To R1 Serial 0/1'
 no ip address
 encapsulation frame-relay
 clock rate 128000
 frame-relay intf-type dce
 frame-relay route 102 interface Serial1/1 201
 frame-relay route 104 interface Serial1/2 401
!
interface Serial1/1
 description 'Connected To R2 Serial 0/1'
 no ip address
 encapsulation frame-relay
 clock rate 128000
 frame-relay intf-type dce
 frame-relay route 201 interface Serial1/0 102
!
interface Serial1/2
 description 'Connected To R4 Serial 0/0'
 no ip address
 encapsulation frame-relay
 clock rate 128000
 frame-relay intf-type dce
```

```
 frame-relay route 401 interface Serial1/0 104
!
interface Serial1/3
 no ip address
 shutdown
!
interface Serial1/4
 no ip address
 shutdown
!
interface Serial1/5
 no ip address
 shutdown
!
interface Serial1/6
 no ip address
 shutdown
!
interface Serial1/7
 no ip address
 shutdown
!
ip forward-protocol nd
!
no ip http server
no ip http secure-server
!
control-plane
!
line con 0
line aux 0
line vty 0 4
 login
!
end

R3-Frame-Relay-Switch#
```

R4

```
R4#term len 0
R4#sh run
Building configuration...

Current configuration : 989 bytes
!
version 12.4
service timestamps debug datetime msec
service timestamps log datetime msec
no service password-encryption
!
hostname R4
!
boot-start-marker
boot-end-marker
!
no logging console
!
no aaa new-model
no network-clock-participate slot 1
no network-clock-participate wic 0
ip cef
!
no ip domain lookup
ip auth-proxy max-nodata-conns 3
ip admission max-nodata-conns 3
!
interface FastEthernet0/0
 ip address 150.4.4.4 255.255.255.0
 duplex auto
 speed auto
!
interface Serial0/0
```

```
 ip address 10.0.0.4 255.255.255.0
 encapsulation frame-relay
 frame-relay map ip 10.0.0.1 401 broadcast
 frame-relay map ip 10.0.0.2 401 broadcast
!
interface Serial0/1
 no ip address
 shutdown
!
router eigrp 1
 passive-interface FastEthernet0/0
 network 0.0.0.0
 no auto-summary
!
ip forward-protocol nd
!
no ip http server
no ip http secure-server
!
control-plane
!
line con 0
line aux 0
line vty 0 4
 login
!
end

R4#
```

CCNP LAB 17

EIGRP Multi-Technology Lab

Lab Objective:

The focus of this lab is to understand EIGRP implementation and configuration in Cisco IOS routers. Additional technologies tested include path control and summarization.

Lab Topology:

The lab network topology is illustrated below:

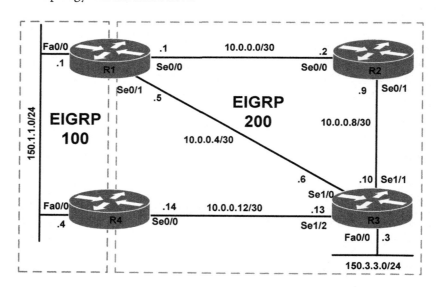

IMPORTANT NOTE: If you are using the www.howtonetwork.net racks, please bring up the LAN interfaces connected to the routers by issuing the no shutdown command on the connected switches. If you are using a home lab with no Switches, you can bring up the LAN interfaces using the following configurations on your routers:

```
interface fastethernet 0/0
 no keepalive
 loopback
 no shutdown
```

Alternately, you can simply connect the interfaces to a hub or switch if you have one available in your own lab.

Task 1

Configure hostnames and IP addressing on all routers as illustrated in the network topology.

Task 2

Configure EIGRP AS 100 for the 150.1.1.0/24 subnet between R1 and R4. Configure EIGRP AS 200 as illustrated in the topology.

Task 3

Redistribute between EIGRP 100 and EIGRP 200. Use default metrics in your configuration. Verify that R1 has three paths to the 150.3.3.0/24 subnet.

Task 4

Without modifying interface bandwidth or delay values, configure routing and path control for EIGRP on R1 as shown below. Use the most simple configuration in your solution:
- R1 should first prefer the path via R4 (FastEthernet 0/0) to reach the 150.3.3.0/24 subnet
- If the path via R4 is down, R1 should prefer the path via R2 (Serial 0/0)
- If the path via R4 and via R2 is down, R1 should use the direct path to R3 (Serial 0/1)

Task 5

Without modifying interface bandwidth or delay values, configure routing and path control for EIGRP on R1 as shown below. Use the most simple configuration in your solution:
- R3 should first prefer the path via R4 (Serial 1/2) to reach the 150.1.1.0/24 subnet
- If the path via R4 is down, R3 should prefer the path via R2 (Serial 1/1)
- If the paths via R4 R2 are down, R3 should use the direct path to R1 (Serial 1/0)

Task 6

Configure routing on R3 so that all three paths are installed into the routing table; however, ONLY a single path - the path via R4 - should actually be used to forward packets destined to that subnet. The other two paths should not be used while this path is up. The path with the next-best route metric should then be used when the primary path is unavailable.

LAB VALIDATION

Task 1

```
Router(config)#hostname R1
R1(config)#interface fastethernet 0/0
R1(config-if)#no shutdown
R1(config-if)#ip address 150.1.1.1 255.255.255.0
R1(config-if)#exit
R1(config)#interface serial 0/0
R1(config-if)#no shutdown
R1(config-if)#ip address 10.0.0.1 255.255.255.252
R1(config-if)#clock rate 2000000
R1(config-if)#exit
R1(config)#interface serial 0/1
R1(config-if)#no shutdown
R1(config-if)#ip address 10.0.0.5 255.255.255.252
R1(config-if)#exit

Router(config)#hostname R2
R2(config)#interface serial 0/0
R2(config-if)#no shutdown
R2(config-if)#ip address 10.0.0.2 255.255.255.252
R2(config-if)#exit
R2(config)#interface serial 0/0
R2(config-if)#no shutdown
R2(config-if)#ip address 10.0.0.9 255.255.255.252
R2(config-if)#exit

Router(config)#hostname R3
R3(config)#interface fastethernet 0/0
R3(config-if)#no shutdown
R3(config-if)#ip address 150.3.3.3 255.255.255.0
R3(config-if)#exit
R3(config)#interface serial 1/0
R3(config-if)#no shutdown
```

```
R3(config-if)#ip address 10.0.0.6 255.255.255.252
R3(config-if)#clock rate 128000
R3(config-if)#exit
R3(config)#interface serial 1/1
R3(config-if)#no shutdown
R3(config-if)#ip address 10.0.0.10 255.255.255.252
R3(config-if)#clock rate 128000
R3(config-if)#exit
R3(config)#interface serial 1/2
R3(config-if)#no shutdown
R3(config-if)#ip address 10.0.0.13 255.255.255.252
R3(config-if)#clock rate 128000
R3(config-if)#exit

Router(config)#hostname R4
R4(config)#interface fastethernet 0/0
R4(config-if)#no shutdown
R4(config-if)#ip address 150.4.4.4 255.255.255.0
R4(config-if)#exit
R3(config)#interface serial 0/0
R3(config-if)#no shutdown
R3(config-if)#ip address 10.0.0.14 255.255.255.252
R3(config-if)#exit
```

Task 2

```
R1(config)#router eigrp 100
R1(config-router)#no auto-summary
R1(config-router)#network 150.1.1.1 0.0.0.0
R1(config-router)#exit
R1(config)#router eigrp 200
R1(config-router)#network 10.0.0.1 0.0.0.0
R1(config-router)#network 10.0.0.5 0.0.0.0
R1(config-router)#exit

R2(config)#router eigrp 200
R2(config-router)#no auto-summary
R2(config-router)#network 10.0.0.2 0.0.0.0
R2(config-router)#network 10.0.0.9 0.0.0.0
R2(config-router)#exit

R3(config)#router eigrp 200
R3(config-router)#no auto-summary
R3(config-router)#network 150.3.3.3 0.0.0.0
R3(config-router)#network 10.0.0.6 0.0.0.0
R3(config-router)#network 10.0.0.10 0.0.0.0
R3(config-router)#network 10.0.0.13 0.0.0.0
R3(config-router)#exit

R4(config)#router eigrp 100
R4(config-router)#no auto-summary
R4(config-router)#network 150.1.1.4 0.0.0.0
R4(config-router)#exit
R4(config)#router eigrp 200
R4(config-router)#no auto-summary
R4(config-router)#network 10.0.0.14 0.0.0.0
R4(config-router)#exit
```

Verify your configuration using the show ip eigrp neighbors command:

```
R1#show ip eigrp neighbors
IP-EIGRP neighbors for process 100
H   Address              Interface    Hold Uptime   SRTT  RTO  Q   Seq
                                      (sec)         (ms)       Cnt Num
0   150.1.1.4            Fa0/0        11 00:09:19     5   200  0   3

IP-EIGRP neighbors for process 200
H   Address              Interface    Hold Uptime   SRTT  RTO  Q   Seq
                                      (sec)         (ms)       Cnt Num
1   10.0.0.6             Se0/1        13 00:05:52    10   200  0   13
0   10.0.0.2             Se0/0        12 00:07:13     2   200  0   11
```

```
R2#show ip eigrp neighbors
IP-EIGRP neighbors for process 200
H   Address                 Interface        Hold Uptime    SRTT    RTO   Q    Seq
                                             (sec)          (ms)          Cnt  Num
1   10.0.0.10               Se0/1            11 00:05:49    10      200   0    14
0   10.0.0.1                Se0/0            11 00:07:18    1       200   0    11

R3#show ip eigrp neighbors
IP-EIGRP neighbors for process 200
H   Address                 Interface        Hold Uptime    SRTT    RTO   Q    Seq
                                             (sec)          (ms)          Cnt  Num
2   10.0.0.14               Se1/2            11 00:01:46    14      1140  0    3
1   10.0.0.9                Se1/1            11 00:05:53    10      1140  0    12
0   10.0.0.5                Se1/0            11 00:06:00    9       1140  0    12

R4#show ip eigrp neighbors
IP-EIGRP neighbors for process 100
H   Address                 Interface        Hold Uptime    SRTT    RTO   Q    Seq
                                             (sec)          (ms)          Cnt  Num
0   150.1.1.1               Fa0/0            14 00:09:32    4       200   0    3

IP-EIGRP neighbors for process 200
H   Address                 Interface        Hold Uptime    SRTT    RTO   Q    Seq
                                             (sec)          (ms)          Cnt  Num
0   10.0.0.13               Se0/0            13 00:01:50    14      200   0    17
```

Task 3

```
R1(config)#router eigrp 100
R1(config-router)#redistribute eigrp 200
R1(config-router)#exit
R1(config)#router eigrp 200
R1(config-router)#redistribute eigrp 100
R1(config-router)#exit

R4(config)#router eigrp 100
R4(config-router)#redistribute eigrp 200
R4(config-router)#exit
R4(config)#router eigrp 200
R4(config-router)#redistribute eigrp 100
R4(config-router)#exit
```

Verify that R1 has three routes to 150.3.3.0/24 by looking at the EIGRP topology table:

```
R1#show ip eigrp topology 150.3.3.0 255.255.255.0
IP-EIGRP (AS 100): Topology entry for 150.3.3.0/24
  State is Passive, Query origin flag is 1, 1 Successor(s), FD is 2172416
  Routing Descriptor Blocks:
  10.0.0.6, from Redistributed, Send flag is 0x0
      Composite metric is (2172416/0), Route is External
      Vector metric:
        Minimum bandwidth is 1544 Kbit
        Total delay is 20100 microseconds
        Reliability is 255/255
        Load is 1/255
        Minimum MTU is 1500
        Hop count is 1
      External data:
        Originating router is 150.1.1.1 (this system)
        AS number of route is 200
        External protocol is EIGRP, external metric is 2172416
        Administrator tag is 0 (0x00000000)
  150.1.1.4 (FastEthernet0/0), from 150.1.1.4, Send flag is 0x0
      Composite metric is (2174976/2172416), Route is External
      Vector metric:
        Minimum bandwidth is 1544 Kbit
        Total delay is 20200 microseconds
        Reliability is 255/255
        Load is 1/255
        Minimum MTU is 1500
        Hop count is 2
```

```
      External data:
          Originating router is 150.1.1.4
          AS number of route is 200
          External protocol is EIGRP, external metric is 2172416
          Administrator tag is 0 (0x00000000)
  IP-EIGRP (AS 200): Topology entry for 150.3.3.0/24
    State is Passive, Query origin flag is 1, 1 Successor(s), FD is 2172416
    Routing Descriptor Blocks:
    10.0.0.6 (Serial0/1), from 10.0.0.6, Send flag is 0x0
        Composite metric is (2172416/28160), Route is Internal
        Vector metric:
        Minimum bandwidth is 1544 Kbit
        Total delay is 20100 microseconds
        Reliability is 255/255
        Load is 1/255
        Minimum MTU is 1500
        Hop count is 1
    10.0.0.2 (Serial0/0), from 10.0.0.2, Send flag is 0x0
        Composite metric is (2684416/2172416), Route is Internal
        Vector metric:
        Minimum bandwidth is 1544 Kbit
        Total delay is 40100 microseconds
        Reliability is 255/255
        Load is 1/255
        Minimum MTU is 1500
        Hop count is 2
```

Task 4

This task requires a little thought. First, the path via R4 is external, which means that this route has a higher administrative distance than the paths via R2 and directly to R3 and is therefore less preferred. The first task is therefore to 'level the playing field' by adjusting the default administrative distance values. In this case, the better administrative distance values, i.e. those for EIGRP AS 200 should be modified so that they are numerically higher than those of EIGRP for AS 100. Before any changes are made, R1s routing table shows the following entry:

```
R1#show ip route 150.3.3.0 255.255.255.0
Routing entry for 150.3.3.0/24
  Known via "eigrp 200", distance 90, metric 2172416, type internal
  Redistributing via eigrp 100, eigrp 200
  Advertised by eigrp 100
  Last update from 10.0.0.6 on Serial0/1, 00:02:33 ago
  Routing Descriptor Blocks:
  * 10.0.0.6, from 10.0.0.6, 00:02:33 ago, via Serial0/1
      Route metric is 2172416, traffic share count is 1
      Total delay is 20100 microseconds, minimum bandwidth is 1544 Kbit
      Reliability 255/255, minimum MTU 1500 bytes
      Loading 1/255, Hops 1
```

The first part of this task is completed by increasing the administrative distance of EIGRP 200. Use any acceptable values between 171 and 254 to complete this task.

```
R1(config)#router eigrp 200
R1(config-router)#distance eigrp 180 200
R1(config-router)#exit
```

Following this change, verify your configuration using the **show ip route** command:

```
R1#show ip route 150.3.3.0 255.255.255.0
Routing entry for 150.3.3.0/24
  Known via "eigrp 100", distance 170, metric 2174976, type external
  Redistributing via eigrp 100, eigrp 200
  Advertised by eigrp 200
  Last update from 150.1.1.4 on FastEthernet0/0, 00:01:29 ago
  Routing Descriptor Blocks:
  * 150.1.1.4, from 150.1.1.4, 00:01:29 ago, via FastEthernet0/0
      Route metric is 2174976, traffic share count is 1
      Total delay is 20200 microseconds, minimum bandwidth is 1544 Kbit
      Reliability 255/255, minimum MTU 1500 bytes
      Loading 1/255, Hops 2
```

NOTE: There is no need to configure a filter for EIGRP 200 on R1 so that it doesn't re-advertise this route back to R3 because even if it does, the route will not meet the Feasibility Condition on R3 and will never be considered a feasible successor. The Feasibility Condition is met when the Reported or Advertised Distance (RD or AD) is less than the Feasible Distance (FD). This can be verified by looking at the entry for the 150.3.3.0/24 subnet in R3s topology table:

```
R3#show ip eigrp 200 topology 150.3.3.0 255.255.255.0
IP-EIGRP (AS 200): Topology entry for 150.3.3.0/24
  State is Passive, Query origin flag is 1, 1 Successor(s), FD is 28160
  Routing Descriptor Blocks:
  0.0.0.0 (FastEthernet0/0), from Connected, Send flag is 0x0
      Composite metric is (28160/0), Route is Internal
      Vector metric:
        Minimum bandwidth is 100000 Kbit
        Total delay is 100 microseconds
        Reliability is 255/255
        Load is 1/255
        Minimum MTU is 1500
        Hop count is 0
  10.0.0.5 (Serial1/0), from 10.0.0.5, Send flag is 0x0
      Composite metric is (21029120/2174976), Route is External
      Vector metric:
        Minimum bandwidth is 128 Kbit
        Total delay is 40200 microseconds
        Reliability is 255/255
        Load is 1/255
        Minimum MTU is 1500
        Hop count is 3
      External data:
        Originating router is 150.1.1.1
        AS number of route is 100
        External protocol is EIGRP, external metric is 2174976
        Administrator tag is 0 (0x00000000)
```

The second part of this task requires the use of an inbound offset list to ensure that the path via R2 is preferred over the path via R3. Prior to any changes the topology table on R1 shows:

```
R1#show ip eigrp 200 topology 150.3.3.0 255.255.255.0
IP-EIGRP (AS 200): Topology entry for 150.3.3.0/24
  State is Passive, Query origin flag is 1, 1 Successor(s), FD is 2174976
  Routing Descriptor Blocks:
  150.1.1.4, from Redistributed, Send flag is 0x0
      Composite metric is (2174976/0), Route is External
      Vector metric:
        Minimum bandwidth is 1544 Kbit
        Total delay is 20200 microseconds
        Reliability is 255/255
        Load is 1/255
        Minimum MTU is 1500
        Hop count is 2
      External data:
        Originating router is 150.1.1.1 (this system)
        AS number of route is 100
        External protocol is EIGRP, external metric is 2174976
        Administrator tag is 0 (0x00000000)
  10.0.0.6 (Serial0/1), from 10.0.0.6, Send flag is 0x0
      Composite metric is (2172416/28160), Route is Internal
      Vector metric:
        Minimum bandwidth is 1544 Kbit
        Total delay is 20100 microseconds
        Reliability is 255/255
        Load is 1/255
        Minimum MTU is 1500
        Hop count is 1
  10.0.0.2 (Serial0/0), from 10.0.0.2, Send flag is 0x0
      Composite metric is (2684416/2172416), Route is Internal
      Vector metric:
        Minimum bandwidth is 1544 Kbit
        Total delay is 40100 microseconds
        Reliability is 255/255
```

```
Load is 1/255
Minimum MTU is 1500
Hop count is 2
```

This task is completed by modifying the metric using as offset list for Serial 0/1. Use any acceptable value to complete this task:

```
R1(config)#router eigrp 200
R1(config-router)#offset-list 0 in 1234567890 serial 0/1
R1(config-router)#exit
```

Following the offset list configuration, the topology table on R1 shows the following:

```
R1#show ip eigrp 200 topology 150.3.3.0 255.255.255.0
IP-EIGRP (AS 200): Topology entry for 150.3.3.0/24
  State is Passive, Query origin flag is 1, 1 Successor(s), FD is 2174976
  Routing Descriptor Blocks:
  150.1.1.4, from Redistributed, Send flag is 0x0
      Composite metric is (2174976/0), Route is External
      Vector metric:
        Minimum bandwidth is 1544 Kbit
        Total delay is 20200 microseconds
        Reliability is 255/255
        Load is 1/255
        Minimum MTU is 1500
        Hop count is 2
      External data:
        Originating router is 150.1.1.1 (this system)
        AS number of route is 100
        External protocol is EIGRP, external metric is 2174976
        Administrator tag is 0 (0x00000000)
  10.0.0.2 (Serial0/0), from 10.0.0.2, Send flag is 0x0
      Composite metric is (2684416/2172416), Route is Internal
      Vector metric:
        Minimum bandwidth is 1544 Kbit
        Total delay is 40100 microseconds
        Reliability is 255/255
        Load is 1/255
        Minimum MTU is 1500
        Hop count is 2
  10.0.0.6 (Serial0/1), from 10.0.0.6, Send flag is 0x0
      Composite metric is (1236740306/1234596050), Route is Internal
      Vector metric:
        Minimum bandwidth is 1544 Kbit
        Total delay is 48245408 microseconds
        Reliability is 255/255
        Load is 1/255
        Minimum MTU is 1500
        Hop count is 1
```

Task 5

To complete this task, you only need to configure a single offset-list. By default, the paths via R4 and R1 are equal cost. The only thing that needs to be done is that the path via R1 be assigned a worse metric than that via R2. This automatically makes it the least preferred path, completing the requirements stipulated in the task. Prior to any changes, the R3 topology table shows:

```
R3#show ip eigrp 200 topology 150.1.1.0 255.255.255.0
IP-EIGRP (AS 200): Topology entry for 150.1.1.0/24
  State is Passive, Query origin flag is 1, 2 Successor(s), FD is 20258560
  Routing Descriptor Blocks:
  10.0.0.5 (Serial1/0), from 10.0.0.5, Send flag is 0x0
      Composite metric is (20514560/28160), Route is External
      Vector metric:
        Minimum bandwidth is 128 Kbit
        Total delay is 20100 microseconds
        Reliability is 255/255
        Load is 1/255
        Minimum MTU is 1500
        Hop count is 1
```

```
      External data:
        Originating router is 150.1.1.1
        AS number of route is 100
        External protocol is EIGRP, external metric is 0
        Administrator tag is 0 (0x00000000)
    10.0.0.14 (Serial1/2), from 10.0.0.14, Send flag is 0x0
        Composite metric is (20514560/28160), Route is External
        Vector metric:
          Minimum bandwidth is 128 Kbit
          Total delay is 20100 microseconds
          Reliability is 255/255
          Load is 1/255
          Minimum MTU is 1500
          Hop count is 1
        External data:
          Originating router is 150.1.1.4
          AS number of route is 100
          External protocol is EIGRP, external metric is 0
          Administrator tag is 0 (0x00000000)
    10.0.0.9 (Serial1/1), from 10.0.0.9, Send flag is 0x0
        Composite metric is (20770560/2172416), Route is External
        Vector metric:
          Minimum bandwidth is 128 Kbit
          Total delay is 30100 microseconds
          Reliability is 255/255
          Load is 1/255
          Minimum MTU is 1500
          Hop count is 2
        External data:
          Originating router is 150.1.1.1
          AS number of route is 100
          External protocol is EIGRP, external metric is 0
          Administrator tag is 0 (0x00000000)
```

This task is completed by off-setting the metric routes received via the current best path. Use any acceptable value to complete this task.

```
R3(config)#router eigrp 200
R3(config-router)# offset-list 0 in 300000 serial 1/0
R3(config-router)#exit
```

Following this change, the topology table on R3 shows the following:

```
R3#show ip eigrp 200 topology 150.1.1.0 255.255.255.0
IP-EIGRP (AS 200): Topology entry for 150.1.1.0/24
  State is Passive, Query origin flag is 1, 1 Successor(s), FD is 20258560
  Routing Descriptor Blocks:
    10.0.0.14 (Serial1/2), from 10.0.0.14, Send flag is 0x0
        Composite metric is (20514560/28160), Route is External
        Vector metric:
          Minimum bandwidth is 128 Kbit
          Total delay is 20100 microseconds
          Reliability is 255/255
          Load is 1/255
          Minimum MTU is 1500
          Hop count is 1
        External data:
          Originating router is 150.1.1.4
          AS number of route is 100
          External protocol is EIGRP, external metric is 0
          Administrator tag is 0 (0x00000000)
    10.0.0.9 (Serial1/1), from 10.0.0.9, Send flag is 0x0
        Composite metric is (20770560/2172416), Route is External
        Vector metric:
          Minimum bandwidth is 128 Kbit
          Total delay is 30100 microseconds
          Reliability is 255/255
          Load is 1/255
          Minimum MTU is 1500
          Hop count is 2
        External data:
          Originating router is 150.1.1.1
```

```
                AS number of route is 100
                External protocol is EIGRP, external metric is 0
                Administrator tag is 0 (0x00000000)
        10.0.0.5 (Serial1/0), from 10.0.0.5, Send flag is 0x0
          Composite metric is (20814560/328160), Route is External
          Vector metric:
              Minimum bandwidth is 128 Kbit
              Total delay is 31818 microseconds
              Reliability is 255/255
              Load is 1/255
              Minimum MTU is 1500
              Hop count is 1
          External data:
              Originating router is 150.1.1.1
              AS number of route is 100
              External protocol is EIGRP, external metric is 0
              Administrator tag is 0 (0x00000000)
```

Task 6

The requirements of this task are two-fold. First, to install more than one path into the routing table, when multiple paths with multiple metrics exist, you need to configure unequal-cost load-sharing for EIGRP using the `variance <multiplier>` command.

To complete the second part of this task, it is important to remember that, by default, when the unequal-cost load sharing feature is enabled, all paths installed into the routing table will be used to forward packets. To prevent this default behavior, , the `traffic-share min across-interfaces` command is required under the EIGRP configuration. The requirements in this task are completed as follows:

```
R3(config)#router eigrp 200
R3(config-router)#variance 2
R3(config-router)#traffic-share min across-interfaces
R3(config-router)#exit
```

Following this configuration, the RIB on R3 shows the following for the 150.1.1.0/24 subnet:

```
R3#show ip route 150.1.1.1 255.255.255.0
Routing entry for 150.1.1.0/24
  Known via "eigrp 200", distance 170, metric 20514560, type external
  Redistributing via eigrp 200
  Last update from 10.0.0.5 on Serial1/0, 00:00:18 ago
  Routing Descriptor Blocks:
  * 10.0.0.14, from 10.0.0.14, 00:00:18 ago, via Serial1/2
      Route metric is 20514560, traffic share count is 1
      Total delay is 20100 microseconds, minimum bandwidth is 128 Kbit
      Reliability 255/255, minimum MTU 1500 bytes
      Loading 1/255, Hops 1
    10.0.0.9, from 10.0.0.9, 00:00:18 ago, via Serial1/1
      Route metric is 20770560, traffic share count is 0
      Total delay is 30100 microseconds, minimum bandwidth is 128 Kbit
      Reliability 255/255, minimum MTU 1500 bytes
      Loading 1/255, Hops 2
    10.0.0.5, from 10.0.0.5, 00:00:18 ago, via Serial1/0
      Route metric is 20814560, traffic share count is 0
      Total delay is 31818 microseconds, minimum bandwidth is 128 Kbit
      Reliability 255/255, minimum MTU 1500 bytes
      Loading 1/255, Hops 1
```

FINAL ROUTER CONFIGURATIONS

R1

```
R1#term len 0
R1#sh run
Building configuration...

Current configuration : 1083 bytes
!
version 12.4
service timestamps debug datetime msec
service timestamps log datetime msec
no service password-encryption
!
hostname R1
!
boot-start-marker
boot-end-marker
!
no logging console
!
no aaa new-model
no network-clock-participate slot 1
no network-clock-participate wic 0
ip cef
!
no ip domain lookup
ip auth-proxy max-nodata-conns 3
ip admission max-nodata-conns 3
!
interface FastEthernet0/0
 ip address 150.1.1.1 255.255.255.0
 duplex auto
 speed auto
!
interface Serial0/0
 ip address 10.0.0.1 255.255.255.252
 clock rate 2000000
!
interface Serial0/1
 ip address 10.0.0.5 255.255.255.252
!
router eigrp 100
 redistribute eigrp 200
 network 150.1.1.1 0.0.0.0
 no auto-summary
!
router eigrp 200
 redistribute eigrp 100
 offset-list 0 in 1234567890 Serial0/1
 network 10.0.0.1 0.0.0.0
 network 10.0.0.5 0.0.0.0
 distance eigrp 180 200
 auto-summary
!
ip forward-protocol nd
!
no ip http server
no ip http secure-server
!
control-plane
!
line con 0
line aux 0
line vty 0 4
 login
!
end

R1#
```

R2

```
R2#term len 0
R2#sh run
Building configuration...

Current configuration : 881 bytes
!
version 12.4
service timestamps debug datetime msec
service timestamps log datetime msec
no service password-encryption
!
hostname R2
!
boot-start-marker
boot-end-marker
!
no logging console
!
no aaa new-model
no network-clock-participate slot 1
no network-clock-participate wic 0
ip cef
!
no ip domain lookup
ip auth-proxy max-nodata-conns 3
ip admission max-nodata-conns 3
!
interface FastEthernet0/0
 no ip address
 shutdown
 duplex auto
 speed auto
!
interface Serial0/0
 ip address 10.0.0.2 255.255.255.252
!
interface Serial0/1
 ip address 10.0.0.9 255.255.255.252
!
router eigrp 200
 network 10.0.0.2 0.0.0.0
 network 10.0.0.9 0.0.0.0
 no auto-summary
!
ip forward-protocol nd
!
no ip http server
no ip http secure-server
!
control-plane
!
line con 0
line aux 0
line vty 0 4
 login
!
end

R2#
```

R3

```
R3#term len 0
R3#sh run
Building configuration...

Current configuration : 1396 bytes
!
version 12.4
service timestamps debug datetime msec
service timestamps log datetime msec
```

```
no service password-encryption
!
hostname R3
!
boot-start-marker
boot-end-marker
!
no logging console
!
no aaa new-model
no network-clock-participate slot 1
no network-clock-participate wic 0
ip cef
!
no ip domain lookup
ip auth-proxy max-nodata-conns 3
ip admission max-nodata-conns 3
!
interface FastEthernet0/0
 ip address 150.3.3.3 255.255.255.0
 duplex auto
 speed auto
!
interface Serial1/0
 ip address 10.0.0.6 255.255.255.252
 clock rate 128000
!
interface Serial1/1
 ip address 10.0.0.10 255.255.255.252
 delay 1000
 clock rate 128000
!
interface Serial1/2
 ip address 10.0.0.13 255.255.255.252
 clock rate 128000
!
interface Serial1/3
 no ip address
 shutdown
!
interface Serial1/4
 no ip address
 shutdown
!
interface Serial1/5
 no ip address
 shutdown
!
interface Serial1/6
 no ip address
 shutdown
!
interface Serial1/7
 no ip address
 shutdown
!
router eigrp 200
 variance 2
 traffic-share min across-interfaces
 offset-list 0 in 300000 Serial1/0
 network 10.0.0.6 0.0.0.0
 network 10.0.0.10 0.0.0.0
 network 10.0.0.13 0.0.0.0
 network 150.3.3.3 0.0.0.0
 no auto-summary
!
ip forward-protocol nd
!
no ip http server
no ip http secure-server
!
control-plane
!
line con 0
line aux 0
```

```
 line vty 0 4
  login
 !
 end

 R3#
```

R4

```
R4#term len 0
R4#sh run
Building configuration...

Current configuration : 967 bytes
!
version 12.4
service timestamps debug datetime msec
service timestamps log datetime msec
no service password-encryption
!
hostname R4
!
boot-start-marker
boot-end-marker
!
no logging console
!
no aaa new-model
no network-clock-participate slot 1
no network-clock-participate wic 0
ip cef
!
no ip domain lookup
ip auth-proxy max-nodata-conns 3
ip admission max-nodata-conns 3
!
interface FastEthernet0/0
 ip address 150.1.1.4 255.255.255.0
 duplex auto
 speed auto
!
interface Serial0/0
 ip address 10.0.0.14 255.255.255.252
!
interface Serial0/1
 no ip address
 shutdown
!
router eigrp 100
 redistribute eigrp 200
 network 150.1.1.4 0.0.0.0
 no auto-summary
!
router eigrp 200
 redistribute eigrp 100
 network 10.0.0.14 0.0.0.0
 no auto-summary
!
ip forward-protocol nd
!
no ip http server
no ip http secure-server
!
control-plane
!
line con 0
line aux 0
line vty 0 4
 login
!
end

R4#
```

CCNP LAB 18

EIGRP Multi-Technology Lab

Lab Objective:

The focus of this lab is to understand EIGRP implementation and configuration in Cisco IOS routers. Additional technologies tested include path control, summarization and optimization.

Lab Topology:

The lab network topology is illustrated below:

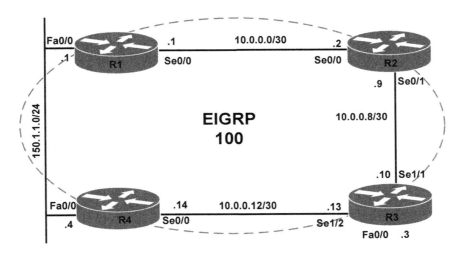

IMPORTANT NOTE: If you are using the **www.howtonetwork.net racks**, please bring up the LAN interfaces connected to the routers by issuing the no shutdown command on the connected switches. If you are using a home lab with no Switches, you can bring up the LAN interfaces using the following configurations on your routers:

```
interface fastethernet 0/0
 no keepalive
 loopback
 no shutdown
```

Alternately, you can simply connect the interfaces to a hub or switch if you have one available in your own lab.

Task 1

Configure hostnames and IP addressing on all routers as illustrated in the network topology.

Task 2

Configure EIGRP for AS 100 as illustrated in the topology. Ensure that the 150.1.1.0/24 subnet is advertised as an external EIGRP route with a route tag of 111 from R1 and 444 from R4. Verify your configuration using the appropriate commands.

Ensure that neither R1 nor R4 has a duplicate entry for this subnet in the EIGRP topology table. You are NOT allowed to use IP ACLs or IP prefix lists to implement this solution. Verify your configuration using the appropriate commands.

Task 3

Configure the 10.5.0.0/24, 10.5.1.0/24, 10.5.2.0/24, and 10.5.3.0/24 secondary subnets on the LAN segment between R1 and R4. Use the .1 address for R1 and the .4 address for R4. These should be advertised via EIGRP as internal EIGRP routes.

Task 4

Configure EIGRP on routers R1 and R4 to advertise a single summary route for the 10.5.0.0/24, 10.5.1.0/24, 10.5.2.0/24, and 10.5.3.0/24 secondary subnets. Verify this on R2 and R3.

Task 5

Without removing the summary configuration on routers R1 and R4, adding any static routes, or using PBR; configure your network so that R2 and R3 prefer the path via R1 to reach the 10.5.0.0/24 subnet; and the path via R4 to reach the 10.5.3.0/24 subnet. As a hint, use an EIGRP feature to complete this task. Verify your configuration using the appropriate commands.

Task 6

Management has advised that within the next year, the EIGRP network will scale to at least 200 routers and switches. These routers will be comprised of Cisco 2900 series routers running IOS Software 15.3. The switches will be Cisco Catalyst 6500 series switches, ranging from Catalyst 6504 through Catalyst 6513 switches. These will all be Multilayer switches. The future network will run both IPv4 and IPv6Configure the current EIGRP implementation to support the future EIGRP network. Verify your configuration using the appropriate commands.

LAB VALIDATION

Task 1

```
Router(config)#hostname R1
R1(config)#interface fastethernet 0/0
R1(config-if)#no shutdown
R1(config-if)#ip address 150.1.1.1 255.255.255.0
R1(config-if)#exit
R1(config)#interface serial 0/0
R1(config-if)#no shutdown
R1(config-if)#ip address 10.0.0.1 255.255.255.252
R1(config-if)#clock rate 2000000
R1(config-if)#exit

Router(config)#hostname R2
R2(config)#interface serial 0/0
R2(config-if)#no shutdown
R2(config-if)#ip address 10.0.0.2 255.255.255.252
R2(config-if)#exit
R2(config)#interface serial 0/0
R2(config-if)#no shutdown
R2(config-if)#ip address 10.0.0.9 255.255.255.252
R2(config-if)#exit

Router(config)#hostname R3
R3(config)#interface serial 1/1
R3(config-if)#no shutdown
R3(config-if)#ip address 10.0.0.10 255.255.255.252
R3(config-if)#clock rate 128000
R3(config-if)#exit
R3(config)#interface serial 1/2
R3(config-if)#no shutdown
R3(config-if)#ip address 10.0.0.13 255.255.255.252
```

```
R3(config-if)#clock rate 128000
R3(config-if)#exit

Router(config)#hostname R4
R4(config)#interface fastethernet 0/0
R4(config-if)#no shutdown
R4(config-if)#ip address 150.4.4.4 255.255.255.0
R4(config-if)#exit
R4(config)#interface serial 0/0
R4(config-if)#no shutdown
R4(config-if)#ip address 10.0.0.14 255.255.255.252
R4(config-if)#exit
```

Task 2

```
R1(config)#route-map CONNECTED permit 10
R1(config-route-map)#match interface fastethernet 0/0
R1(config-route-map)#set tag 111
R1(config-route-map)#exit
R1(config)#router eigrp 100
R1(config-router)#network 10.0.0.1 0.0.0.0
R1(config-router)#no auto-summary
R1(config-router)#redistribute connected route-map CONNECTED
R1(config-router)#exit

R2(config)#router eigrp 100
R2(config-router)#no auto-summary
R2(config-router)#network 10.0.0.2 0.0.0.0
R2(config-router)#network 10.0.0.9 0.0.0.0
R2(config-router)#exit

R3(config)#router eigrp 100
R3(config-router)#no auto-summary
R3(config-router)#network 10.0.0.10 0.0.0.0
R3(config-router)#network 10.0.0.13 0.0.0.0
R3(config-router)#exit

R4(config)#route-map CONNECTED permit 10
R4(config-route-map)#match interface fastethernet 0/0
R4(config-route-map)#set tag 444
R4(config-route-map)#exit
R4(config)#route-map CONNECTED deny 20
R4(config-route-map)#exit
R4(config)#router eigrp 100
R4(config-router)#no auto-summary
R4(config-router)#network 10.0.0.14 0.0.0.0
R4(config-router)#no auto-summary
R4(config-router)#redistribute connected route-map CONNECTED
R4(config-router)#exit
```

Verify your base EIGRP configuration by verifying EIGRP neighbor relationships:

```
R1#show ip eigrp neighbors
IP-EIGRP neighbors for process 100
H   Address              Interface        Hold Uptime    SRTT   RTO   Q   Seq
                                          (sec)          (ms)         Cnt Num
0   10.0.0.2             Se0/0            12 00:03:53     6    200   0   10


R2#show ip eigrp neighbors
IP-EIGRP neighbors for process 100
H   Address              Interface        Hold Uptime    SRTT   RTO   Q   Seq
                                          (sec)          (ms)         Cnt Num
1   10.0.0.10            Se0/1            14 00:03:18    10    200   0   10
0   10.0.0.1             Se0/0            11 00:03:59     3    200   0   3


R3#show ip eigrp neighbors
IP-EIGRP neighbors for process 100
H   Address              Interface        Hold Uptime    SRTT   RTO   Q   Seq
                                          (sec)          (ms)         Cnt Num
1   10.0.0.14            Se1/2            13 00:01:27    12   1140   0   5
0   10.0.0.9             Se1/1            10 00:03:21    10   1140   0   9
```

```
R4#show ip eigrp neighbors
IP-EIGRP neighbors for process 100
H   Address                Interface        Hold Uptime    SRTT   RTO  Q  Seq
                                            (sec)          (ms)        Cnt Num
0   10.0.0.13              Se0/0            11  00:01:31   12     200  0  9
```

After configuring redistribution, the EIGRP topology tables on the routers show the following:

```
R1#show ip eigrp topology 150.1.1.0 255.255.255.0
IP-EIGRP (AS 100): Topology entry for 150.1.1.0/24
  State is Passive, Query origin flag is 1, 1 Successor(s), FD is 28160
  Routing Descriptor Blocks:
  0.0.0.0, from Rconnected, Send flag is 0x0
      Composite metric is (28160/0), Route is External
      Vector metric:
        Minimum bandwidth is 100000 Kbit
        Total delay is 100 microseconds
        Reliability is 255/255
        Load is 1/255
        Minimum MTU is 1500
        Hop count is 0
      External data:
        Originating router is 150.1.1.1 (this system)
        AS number of route is 0
        External protocol is Connected, external metric is 0
        Administrator tag is 111 (0x0000006F)
```

```
R4#show ip eigrp topology 150.1.1.0 255.255.255.0
IP-EIGRP (AS 100): Topology entry for 150.1.1.0/24
  State is Passive, Query origin flag is 1, 1 Successor(s), FD is 28160
  Routing Descriptor Blocks:
  0.0.0.0, from Rconnected, Send flag is 0x0
      Composite metric is (28160/0), Route is External
      Vector metric:
        Minimum bandwidth is 100000 Kbit
        Total delay is 100 microseconds
        Reliability is 255/255
        Load is 1/255
        Minimum MTU is 1500
        Hop count is 0
      External data:
        Originating router is 150.1.1.4 (this system)
        AS number of route is 0
        External protocol is Connected, external metric is 0
        Administrator tag is 444 (0x000001BC)
  10.0.0.13 (Serial0/0), from 10.0.0.13, Send flag is 0x0
      Composite metric is (21538560/21026560), Route is External
      Vector metric:
        Minimum bandwidth is 128 Kbit
        Total delay is 60100 microseconds
        Reliability is 255/255
        Load is 1/255
        Minimum MTU is 1500
        Hop count is 3
      External data:
        Originating router is 150.1.1.1
        AS number of route is 0
        External protocol is Connected, external metric is 0
        Administrator tag is 111 (0x0000006F)
```

In the output above, we can see that R4 has a duplicate entry for the 150.1.1.0/24 subnet. This is the entry received from R1 with an administrative route tag of 111. To prevent either router from receiving or accepting the other routers' advertisement, a distribute list used with a route map is required. The route map should perform filtering based on route tags:

```
R1(config)#route-map NOT-TAG-444 deny 10
R1(config-route-map)#match tag 444
R1(config-route-map)#exit
R1(config)#route-map NO-TAG-444 permit 20
R1(config-route-map)#exit
R1(config)#router eigrp 100
```

```
R1(config-router)#distribute-list route-map NO-TAG-444 in
R1(config-router)#exit

R4(config)#route-map NO-TAG-111 deny 10
R4(config-route-map)#match tag 111
R4(config-route-map)#exit
R4(config)#route-map NO-TAG-11 permit 20
R4(config-route-map)#exit
R4(config)#router eigrp 100
R4(config-router)#distribute-list route-map NO-TAG-111 in
R4(config-router)#exit
```

Following this configuration, the topology tables on R1 and R4 show the following:

```
R1#show ip eigrp topology 150.1.1.0 255.255.255.0
IP-EIGRP (AS 100): Topology entry for 150.1.1.0/24
  State is Passive, Query origin flag is 1, 1 Successor(s), FD is 28160
  Routing Descriptor Blocks:
  0.0.0.0, from Rconnected, Send flag is 0x0
      Composite metric is (28160/0), Route is External
      Vector metric:
        Minimum bandwidth is 100000 Kbit
        Total delay is 100 microseconds
        Reliability is 255/255
        Load is 1/255
        Minimum MTU is 1500
        Hop count is 0
      External data:
        Originating router is 150.1.1.1 (this system)
        AS number of route is 0
        External protocol is Connected, external metric is 0
        Administrator tag is 111 (0x0000006F)

R4#show ip eigrp topology 150.1.1.0 255.255.255.0
IP-EIGRP (AS 100): Topology entry for 150.1.1.0/24
  State is Passive, Query origin flag is 1, 1 Successor(s), FD is 28160
  Routing Descriptor Blocks:
  0.0.0.0, from Rconnected, Send flag is 0x0
      Composite metric is (28160/0), Route is External
      Vector metric:
        Minimum bandwidth is 100000 Kbit
        Total delay is 100 microseconds
        Reliability is 255/255
        Load is 1/255
        Minimum MTU is 1500
        Hop count is 0
      External data:
        Originating router is 150.1.1.4 (this system)
        AS number of route is 0
        External protocol is Connected, external metric is 0
        Administrator tag is 444 (0x000001BC)
```

Task 3

```
R1(config)#interface fastethernet 0/0
R1(config-if)#ip address 10.5.0.1 255.255.255.0 secondary
R1(config-if)#ip address 10.5.1.1 255.255.255.0 secondary
R1(config-if)#ip address 10.5.2.1 255.255.255.0 secondary
R1(config-if)#ip address 10.5.3.1 255.255.255.0 secondary
R1(config-if)#exit
R1(config)#router eigrp 100
R1(config-router)#network 10.5.0.0 0.0.3.255
R1(config-router)#exit

R4(config)#interface fastethernet 0/0
R4(config-if)#ip address 10.5.0.4 255.255.255.0 secondary
R4(config-if)#ip address 10.5.1.4 255.255.255.0 secondary
R4(config-if)#ip address 10.5.2.4 255.255.255.0 secondary
R4(config-if)#ip address 10.5.3.4 255.255.255.0 secondary
R4(config-if)#exit
R4(config)#router eigrp 100
R4(config-router)#network 10.5.0.0 0.0.3.255
R4(config-router)#exit
```

Verify that the prefixes are advertised to R2 and R3 using the show ip route command:

```
R2#show ip route eigrp
     10.0.0.0/8 is variably subnetted, 7 subnets, 2 masks
D       10.0.0.12/30 [90/2684416] via 10.0.0.1, 00:02:30, Serial0/0
D       10.5.3.0/24 [90/2172416] via 10.0.0.1, 00:02:32, Serial0/0
D       10.5.2.0/24 [90/2172416] via 10.0.0.1, 00:02:32, Serial0/0
D       10.5.1.0/24 [90/2172416] via 10.0.0.1, 00:02:32, Serial0/0
D       10.5.0.0/24 [90/2172416] via 10.0.0.1, 00:02:32, Serial0/0
     150.1.0.0/24 is subnetted, 1 subnets
D EX    150.1.1.0 [170/2172416] via 10.0.0.1, 00:21:51, Serial0/0

R3#show ip route eigrp
     10.0.0.0/8 is variably subnetted, 7 subnets, 2 masks
D       10.0.0.0/30 [90/21024000] via 10.0.0.9, 00:24:19, Serial1/1
D       10.5.3.0/24 [90/20514560] via 10.0.0.14, 00:02:51, Serial1/2
D       10.5.2.0/24 [90/20514560] via 10.0.0.14, 00:02:51, Serial1/2
D       10.5.1.0/24 [90/20514560] via 10.0.0.14, 00:02:51, Serial1/2
D       10.5.0.0/24 [90/20514560] via 10.0.0.14, 00:02:51, Serial1/2
     150.1.0.0/24 is subnetted, 1 subnets
D EX    150.1.1.0 [170/20514560] via 10.0.0.14, 00:22:10, Serial1/2
```

Task 4

```
R1(config)#interface serial 0/0
R1(config-if)#ip summary-address eigrp 100 10.5.0.0 255.255.252.0
R1(config-if)#exit

R4(config)#interface serial 0/0
R4(config-if)#ip summary-address eigrp 100 10.5.0.0 255.255.252.0
R4(config-if)#exit
```

Verify that the summaries are advertised to R2 and R3 using the show ip route command:

```
R2#show ip route eigrp
     10.0.0.0/8 is variably subnetted, 4 subnets, 2 masks
D       10.0.0.12/30 [90/2684416] via 10.0.0.1, 00:05:10, Serial0/0
D       10.5.0.0/22 [90/2172416] via 10.0.0.1, 00:00:48, Serial0/0
     150.1.0.0/24 is subnetted, 1 subnets
D EX    150.1.1.0 [170/2172416] via 10.0.0.1, 00:24:31, Serial0/0

R3#show ip route eigrp
     10.0.0.0/8 is variably subnetted, 4 subnets, 2 masks
D       10.0.0.0/30 [90/21024000] via 10.0.0.9, 00:27:12, Serial1/1
D       10.5.0.0/22 [90/20514560] via 10.0.0.14, 00:01:20, Serial1/2
     150.1.0.0/24 is subnetted, 1 subnets
D EX    150.1.1.0 [170/20514560] via 10.0.0.14, 00:25:03, Serial1/2
```

Task 5

EIGRP supports route leaking when summarizing, which allows for greater flexibility as far as path control is concerned. When summarizing, EIGRP allows you to 'leak' or advertise more specific routes encompassed by that summary, ensuring that traffic destined to the leaked subnet is sent to the router that leaked the route by virtue of the longest-match rule. This task is completed on R1 and R4 as follows:

```
R1(config)#access-list 1 permit 10.5.0.0 0.0.0.255
R1(config)#route-map LEAK permit 10
R1(config-route-map)#match ip address 1
R1(config-route-map)#exit
R1(config)#route-map LEAK deny 20
R1(config-route-map)#exit
R1(config)#interface serial 0/0
R1(config-if)#ip summary-a eigrp 100 10.5.0.0 255.255.252.0 leak-map LEAK
R1(config-if)#exit

R4(config)#access-list 4 permit 10.5.3.0 0.0.0.255
R4(config)#route-map LEAK permit 10
R4(config-route-map)#match ip address 4
R4(config-route-map)#exit
R4(config)#route-map LEAK deny 20
```

```
R4(config-route-map)#exit
R4(config)#interface serial 0/0
R4(config-if)#ip summary- eigrp 100 10.5.0.0 255.255.252.0 leak-map LEAK
R4(config-if)#exit
```

Following this configuration, the routing tables on R2 and R3 show the following entries:

```
R2#show ip route eigrp
     10.0.0.0/8 is variably subnetted, 6 subnets, 3 masks
D       10.0.0.12/30 [90/2684416] via 10.0.0.1, 00:17:43, Serial0/0
D       10.5.3.0/24 [90/21026560] via 10.0.0.10, 00:01:12, Serial0/1
D       10.5.0.0/24 [90/2172416] via 10.0.0.1, 00:04:02, Serial0/0
D       10.5.0.0/22 [90/2172416] via 10.0.0.1, 00:13:21, Serial0/0
     150.1.0.0/24 is subnetted, 1 subnets
D EX    150.1.1.0 [170/2172416] via 10.0.0.1, 00:37:04, Serial0/0

R3#show ip route eigrp
     10.0.0.0/8 is variably subnetted, 6 subnets, 3 masks
D       10.0.0.0/30 [90/21024000] via 10.0.0.9, 00:39:19, Serial1/1
D       10.5.3.0/24 [90/20514560] via 10.0.0.14, 00:01:18, Serial1/2
D       10.5.0.0/24 [90/21026560] via 10.0.0.9, 00:04:08, Serial1/1
D       10.5.0.0/22 [90/20514560] via 10.0.0.14, 00:13:27, Serial1/2
     150.1.0.0/24 is subnetted, 1 subnets
D EX    150.1.1.0 [170/20514560] via 10.0.0.14, 00:37:10, Serial1/2
```

When using route leaking (leak maps) in conjunction with EIGRP manual summarization, it is important to ensure that you remember the following considerations:

If the leak-map keyword is configured to reference a nonexistent route map, the configuration of this keyword has no effect. In other words, the configured summary will still be advertised, based on the stipulated rules of advertisement, and the component routes remain suppressed.

However, if the leak-map keyword is configured, but the access list does not exist or the route map does not reference the access list, the summary address and all component routes are sent.

Task 6

This task is straightforward. If you ignore the 'fluff' and pay attention to detail you will see that the task simply calls for increasing the default EIGRP hop count limitation of 100 to 200 to accommodate devices in the new network. The default hop count is printed in the output of the show ip protocols command:

```
R1#show ip protocols
Routing Protocol is "eigrp 100"
  Outgoing update filter list for all interfaces is not set
  Incoming update filter list for all interfaces is (route-map) NO-TAG-444
  Default networks flagged in outgoing updates
  Default networks accepted from incoming updates
  EIGRP metric weight K1=1, K2=0, K3=1, K4=0, K5=0
  EIGRP maximum hopcount 100
  EIGRP maximum metric variance 1
  Redistributing: connected, eigrp 100
  EIGRP NSF-aware route hold timer is 240s
  Automatic network summarization is not in effect
  Address Summarization:
    10.5.0.0/22 for Serial0/0
      Summarizing with metric 28160
  Maximum path: 4
  Routing for Networks:
    10.0.0.1/32
    10.5.0.0/22
  Routing Information Sources:
    Gateway         Distance      Last Update
    (this router)         90      00:22:13
    10.0.0.2              90      00:09:33
    150.1.1.4            90      00:21:41
  Distance: internal 90 external 170
```

This task is completed by configuring a hop count limit of 200 or greater on ALL routers:

```
R1(config)#router eigrp 100
R1(config-router)#metric maximum-hops 200
R1(config-router)#exit

R2(config)#router eigrp 100
R2(config-router)#metric maximum-hops 200
R2(config-router)#exit

R3(config)#router eigrp 100
R3(config-router)#metric maximum-hops 200
R3(config-router)#exit

R4(config)#router eigrp 100
R4(config-router)#metric maximum-hops 200
R4(config-router)#exit
```

Following this change, the `show ip protocols` command reflects the configuration:

```
R1#show ip protocols
Routing Protocol is "eigrp 100"
  Outgoing update filter list for all interfaces is not set
  Incoming update filter list for all interfaces is (route-map) NO-TAG-444
  Default networks flagged in outgoing updates
  Default networks accepted from incoming updates
  EIGRP metric weight K1=1, K2=0, K3=1, K4=0, K5=0
  EIGRP maximum hopcount 200
  EIGRP maximum metric variance 1
  Redistributing: connected, eigrp 100
  EIGRP NSF-aware route hold timer is 240s
  Automatic network summarization is not in effect
  Address Summarization:
    10.5.0.0/22 for Serial0/0
      Summarizing with metric 28160
  Maximum path: 4
  Routing for Networks:
    10.0.0.1/32
    10.5.0.0/22
  Routing Information Sources:
    Gateway         Distance      Last Update
    (this router)         90      00:01:20
    10.0.0.2              90      00:00:24
    150.1.1.4             90      00:00:24
  Distance: internal 90 external 170
```

FINAL ROUTER CONFIGURATIONS

R1

```
R1#term len 0
R1#sh run
Building configuration...

Current configuration : 1561 bytes
!
version 12.4
service timestamps debug datetime msec
service timestamps log datetime msec
no service password-encryption
!
hostname R1
!
boot-start-marker
boot-end-marker
!
no logging console
!
no aaa new-model
no network-clock-participate slot 1
```

```
no network-clock-participate wic 0
ip cef
!
no ip domain lookup
ip auth-proxy max-nodata-conns 3
ip admission max-nodata-conns 3
!
interface FastEthernet0/0
 ip address 10.5.0.1 255.255.255.0 secondary
 ip address 10.5.1.1 255.255.255.0 secondary
 ip address 10.5.2.1 255.255.255.0 secondary
 ip address 10.5.3.1 255.255.255.0 secondary
 ip address 150.1.1.1 255.255.255.0
 duplex auto
 speed auto
!
interface Serial0/0
 ip address 10.0.0.1 255.255.255.252
 ip summary-address eigrp 100 10.5.0.0 255.255.252.0 5 leak-map LEAK
 clock rate 2000000
!
interface Serial0/1
 no ip address
 shutdown
!
router eigrp 100
 redistribute connected route-map CONNECTED
 network 10.0.0.1 0.0.0.0
 network 10.5.0.0 0.0.3.255
 metric maximum-hops 200
 distribute-list route-map NO-TAG-444 in
 no auto-summary
!
ip forward-protocol nd
!
no ip http server
no ip http secure-server
!
access-list 1 permit 10.5.0.0 0.0.0.255
!
route-map LEAK permit 10
 match ip address 1
!
route-map LEAK deny 20
!
route-map NOT-TAG-444 deny 10
 match tag 444
!
route-map CONNECTED permit 10
 match interface FastEthernet0/0
 set tag 111
!
route-map CONNECTED deny 20
!
route-map NO-TAG-444 permit 20
!
control-plane
!
line con 0
line aux 0
line vty 0 4
 login
!
end

R1#
```

R2

```
R2#term len 0
R2#sh run
Building configuration...

Current configuration : 906 bytes
!
version 12.4
service timestamps debug datetime msec
```

```
service timestamps log datetime msec
no service password-encryption
!
hostname R2
!
boot-start-marker
boot-end-marker
!
no logging console
!
no aaa new-model
no network-clock-participate slot 1
no network-clock-participate wic 0
ip cef
!
no ip domain lookup
ip auth-proxy max-nodata-conns 3
ip admission max-nodata-conns 3
!
interface FastEthernet0/0
 no ip address
 shutdown
 duplex auto
 speed auto
!
interface Serial0/0
 ip address 10.0.0.2 255.255.255.252
!
interface Serial0/1
 ip address 10.0.0.9 255.255.255.252
!
router eigrp 100
 network 10.0.0.2 0.0.0.0
 network 10.0.0.9 0.0.0.0
 metric maximum-hops 200
 no auto-summary
!
ip forward-protocol nd
!
no ip http server
no ip http secure-server
!
control-plane
!
line con 0
line aux 0
line vty 0 4
 login
!
end

R2#
```

R3

```
R3#term len 0
R3#sh run
Building configuration...

Current configuration : 1249 bytes
!
version 12.4
service timestamps debug datetime msec
service timestamps log datetime msec
no service password-encryption
!
hostname R3
!
boot-start-marker
boot-end-marker
!
no logging console
!
no aaa new-model
no network-clock-participate slot 1
no network-clock-participate wic 0
```

```
ip cef
!
no ip domain lookup
ip auth-proxy max-nodata-conns 3
ip admission max-nodata-conns 3
!
interface FastEthernet0/0
 no ip address
 shutdown
 duplex auto
 speed auto
!
interface Serial1/0
 no ip address
 shutdown
 clock rate 128000
!
interface Serial1/1
 ip address 10.0.0.10 255.255.255.252
 clock rate 128000
!
interface Serial1/2
 ip address 10.0.0.13 255.255.255.252
 clock rate 128000
!
interface Serial1/3
 no ip address
 shutdown
!
interface Serial1/4
 no ip address
 shutdown
!
interface Serial1/5
 no ip address
 shutdown
!
interface Serial1/6
 no ip address
 shutdown
!
interface Serial1/7
 no ip address
 shutdown
!
router eigrp 100
 network 10.0.0.10 0.0.0.0
 network 10.0.0.13 0.0.0.0
 metric maximum-hops 200
 no auto-summary
!
ip forward-protocol nd
!
no ip http server
no ip http secure-server
!
control-plane
!
line con 0
line aux 0
line vty 0 4
 login
!
end

R3#
```

R4

```
R4#term len 0
R4#sh run
Building configuration...

Current configuration : 1541 bytes
!
version 12.4
service timestamps debug datetime msec
```

```
service timestamps log datetime msec
no service password-encryption
!
hostname R4
!
boot-start-marker
boot-end-marker
!
no logging console
!
no aaa new-model
no network-clock-participate slot 1
no network-clock-participate wic 0
ip cef
!
no ip domain lookup
ip auth-proxy max-nodata-conns 3
ip admission max-nodata-conns 3
!
interface FastEthernet0/0
 ip address 10.5.0.4 255.255.255.0 secondary
 ip address 10.5.1.4 255.255.255.0 secondary
 ip address 10.5.2.4 255.255.255.0 secondary
 ip address 10.5.3.4 255.255.255.0 secondary
 ip address 150.1.1.4 255.255.255.0
 duplex auto
 speed auto
!
interface Serial0/0
 ip address 10.0.0.14 255.255.255.252
 ip summary-address eigrp 100 10.5.0.0 255.255.252.0 5 leak-map LEAK
!
interface Serial0/1
 no ip address
 shutdown
!
router eigrp 100
 redistribute connected route-map CONNECTED
 network 10.0.0.14 0.0.0.0
 network 10.5.0.0 0.0.3.255
 metric maximum-hops 200
 distribute-list route-map NO-TAG-111 in
 no auto-summary
!
ip forward-protocol nd
!
no ip http server
no ip http secure-server
!
access-list 4 permit 10.5.3.0 0.0.0.255
!
route-map LEAK permit 10
 match ip address 4
!
route-map LEAK deny 20
!
route-map NO-TAG-11 permit 20
!
route-map CONNECTED permit 10
 match interface FastEthernet0/0
 set tag 444
!
route-map CONNECTED deny 20
!
route-map NO-TAG-111 deny 10
 match tag 111
!
control-plane
!
line con 0
line aux 0
line vty 0 4
 login
!
end

R4#
```

CCNP LAB 19

EIGRP Multi-Technology Lab

Lab Objective:

The focus of this lab is to understand EIGRP implementation and configuration in Cisco IOS routers. Additional technologies tested include authentication and default routing.

Lab Topology:

The lab network topology is illustrated below:

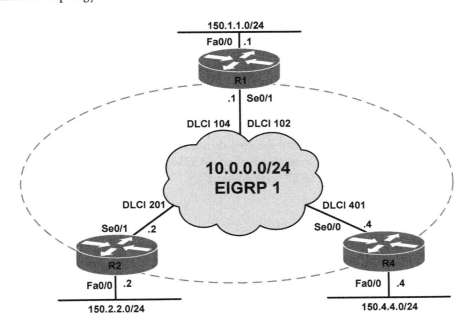

IMPORTANT NOTE: If you are using the www.howtonetwork.net racks, please bring up the LAN interfaces connected to the routers by issuing the no shutdown command on the connected switches. If you are using a home lab with no Switches, you can bring up the LAN interfaces using the following configurations on your routers:

```
interface fastethernet 0/0
  no keepalive
  loopback
  no shutdown
```

Alternately, you can simply connect the interfaces to a hub or switch if you have one available in your own lab. Also, if you are using the www.howtonetwork.net racks, configure R3 as the Frame Relay switch using the following configuration commands:

```
hostname R3-Frame-Relay-Switch
!
frame-relay switching
!
```

```
interface serial 1/0
 description 'Connected To R1 Serial 0/1'
 encapsulation frame-relay
 no ip address
 clock rate 128000
 frame-relay intf-type dce
 frame-relay route 102 interface serial 1/1 201
 frame-relay route 104 interface serial 1/2 401
 no shutdown
!
interface serial 1/1
 description 'Connected To R2 Serial 0/1'
 encapsulation frame-relay
 no ip address
 clock rate 128000
 frame-relay intf-type dce
 frame-relay route 201 interface serial 1/0 102
 no shutdown
!
interface serial 1/2
 description 'Connected To R4 Serial 0/0'
 encapsulation frame-relay
 no ip address
 clock rate 128000
 frame-relay intf-type dce
 frame-relay route 401 interface serial 1/0 104
 no shutdown
!
end
```

Task 1

Configure hostnames and IP addressing on all routers as illustrated in the network topology.

Task 2

The Frame Relay Service Provider has stated that they do not support Multicast traffic across the Frame Relay network. Configure EIGRP for AS 1 to use Unicast instead of Multicast to adhere to the Frame Relay Service Provider requirements. Verify your EIGRP configuration.

Task 3

Redistribute the 150.x.x.x/24 subnets into EIGRP on all routers. These subnets should be redistributed using the following values: 100 000 - 100 - 255 - 1 - 1500. In the future, if any other connected routes are redistributed into EIGRP, they should be injected using the following values: 50 000 - 1250 - 255 - 1 - 1500.

Finally, ensure and verify that all routers can ping each others' 150.x.x.x/24 subnets.

Task 4

Configure EIGRP so that no more than 5 % of the WAN link bandwidth may be used by EIGRP on all routers in the network.

Task 5

In order to avoid possible SIA issues, configure the routing wait time to be 10 minutes.

LAB VALIDATION

Task 1

```
Router(config)#hostname R1
R1(config)#interface fastethernet 0/0
R1(config-if)#no shutdown
R1(config-if)#ip address 150.1.1.1 255.255.255.0
R1(config-if)#exit
```

```
R1(config)#interface serial 0/1
R1(config-if)#ip address 10.0.0.1 255.255.255.0
R1(config-if)#no shutdown
R1(config-if)#encapsulation frame-relay
R1(config-if)#exit

Router(config)#hostname R2
R2(config)#interface fastethernet 0/0
R2(config-if)#no shutdown
R2(config-if)#ip address 150.2.2.2 255.255.255.0
R2(config-if)#exit
R2(config)#interface serial 0/1
R2(config-if)#ip address 10.0.0.2 255.255.255.0
R2(config-if)#no shutdown
R2(config-if)#encapsulation frame-relay
R2(config-if)#exit

Router(config)#hostname R4
R4(config)#interface fastethernet 0/0
R4(config-if)#no shutdown
R4(config-if)#ip address 150.4.4.4 255.255.255.0
R4(config-if)#exit
R4(config)#interface serial 0/0
R4(config-if)#ip address 10.0.0.4 255.255.255.0
R4(config-if)#no shutdown
R4(config-if)#encapsulation frame-relay
R4(config-if)#exit
```

Task 2

By default, EIGRP uses Multicast to send packets. To configure EIGRP to use Unicast packets, you must configure static EIGRP neighbor statements. When a static neighbor is configured, EIGRP stops sending and processing received any EIGRP Multicast packets via the interface(s).

```
R1(config)#router eigrp 1
R1(config-router)#no auto-summary
R1(config-router)#neighbor 10.0.0.2 serial 0/1
R1(config-router)#neighbor 10.0.0.4 serial 0/1
R1(config-router)#network 10.0.0.1 0.0.0.0
R1(config-router)#exit

R2(config)#router eigrp 1
R2(config-router)#no auto-summary
R2(config-router)#neighbor 10.0.0.1 serial 0/1
R2(config-router)#network 10.0.0.2 0.0.0.0
R2(config-router)#exit

R4(config)#router eigrp 1
R4(config-router)#no auto-summary
R4(config-router)#neighbor 10.0.0.1 serial 0/0
R4(config-router)#network 10.0.0.4 0.0.0.0
R4(config-router)#exit
```

Verify your configuration using the show ip eigrp neighbors [detail] command:

```
R1#show ip eigrp neighbors detail
IP-EIGRP neighbors for process 1
H   Address                 Interface      Hold Uptime    SRTT   RTO  Q   Seq
                                           (sec)          (ms)        Cnt Num
1   10.0.0.4                Se0/1          131 00:01:39    20   200  0   3
    Static neighbor
    Version 12.4/1.2, Retrans: 0, Retries: 0

0   10.0.0.2                Se0/1          132 00:02:39    23   200  0   3
    Static neighbor
    Version 12.4/1.2, Retrans: 0, Retries: 0

R2#show ip eigrp neighbors detail
IP-EIGRP neighbors for process 1
H   Address                 Interface      Hold Uptime    SRTT   RTO  Q   Seq
```

```
                                            (sec)      (ms)       Cnt Num
0   10.0.0.1                 Se0/1          158 00:03:07  18   200  0  3
      Static neighbor
      Version 12.4/1.2, Retrans: 0, Retries: 0

R4#show ip eigrp neighbors detail
IP-EIGRP neighbors for process 1
H   Address                  Interface      Hold Uptime   SRTT  RTO  Q  Seq
                                            (sec)         (ms)      Cnt Num
0   10.0.0.1                 Se0/0          169 00:01:04  23   200  0  5
      Static neighbor
      Version 12.4/1.2, Retrans: 0, Retries: 0
```

Task 3

```
R1(config)#route-map CONNECTED permit 10
R1(config-route-map)#match interface fastethernet 0/0
R1(config-route-map)#set metric 100000 100 255 1 1500
R1(config-route-map)#exit
R1(config)#route-map CONNECTED permit 20
R1(config-route-map)#set metric 50000 1250 255 1 1500
R1(config-route-map)#exit
R1(config)#router eigrp 1
R1(config-router)#redistribute connected route-map CONNECTED
R1(config-router)#exit
R1(config)#interface serial 0/1
R1(config-if)#no ip split-horizon eigrp 1
R1(config-if)#exit
```

> **NOTE:** The default split horizon rules still apply even when using static neighbor relationships. Therefore, you must disable split horizon on R1 otherwise it will not advertise the 150.2.2.0/24 and 150.4.4.0/24 subnets received from either spoke back out the Serial 0/1 interface. The result in that the spoke routers will not be able to ping each others' 150.x.x.x/24 subnets.

```
R2(config)#route-map CONNECTED permit 10
R2(config-route-map)#match interface fastethernet 0/0
R2(config-route-map)#set metric 100000 100 255 1 1500
R2(config-route-map)#exit
R2(config)#route-map CONNECTED permit 20
R2(config-route-map)#set metric 50000 1250 255 1 1500
R2(config-route-map)#exit
R2(config)#router eigrp 1
R2(config-router)#redistribute connected route-map CONNECTED
R2(config-router)#exit

R4(config)#route-map CONNECTED permit 10
R4(config-route-map)#match interface fastethernet 0/0
R4(config-route-map)#set metric 100000 100 255 1 1500
R4(config-route-map)#exit
R4(config)#route-map CONNECTED permit 20
R4(config-route-map)#set metric 50000 1250 255 1 1500
R4(config-route-map)#exit
R4(config)#router eigrp 1
R4(config-router)#redistribute connected route-map CONNECTED
R4(config-router)#exit
```

Following this configuration, verify the routing table using the show ip route command:

```
R1#show ip route eigrp
     150.2.0.0/24 is subnetted, 1 subnets
D EX    150.2.2.0 [170/2195456] via 10.0.0.2, 00:07:51, Serial0/1
     150.4.0.0/24 is subnetted, 1 subnets
D EX    150.4.4.0 [170/2195456] via 10.0.0.4, 00:06:30, Serial0/1

R2#show ip route eigrp
     150.1.0.0/24 is subnetted, 1 subnets
D EX    150.1.1.0 [170/2195456] via 10.0.0.1, 00:24:52, Serial0/1
```

```
         150.4.0.0/24 is subnetted, 1 subnets
 D EX     150.4.4.0 [170/2707456] via 10.0.0.1, 00:03:16, Serial0/1

 R4#show ip route eigrp
         150.1.0.0/24 is subnetted, 1 subnets
 D EX     150.1.1.0 [170/2195456] via 10.0.0.1, 00:07:03, Serial0/0
         150.2.0.0/24 is subnetted, 1 subnets
 D EX     150.2.2.0 [170/2707456] via 10.0.0.1, 00:03:32, Serial0/0
```

Task 4

By default, EIGRP can use up to 50% of the link bandwidth. This is not desirable when using a low bandwidth link. This task is completed as follows:

```
R1(config)#interface serial 0/1
R1(config-if)#ip bandwidth-percent eigrp 1 5
R1(config-if)#exit

R2(config)#interface serial 0/1
R2(config-if)#ip bandwidth-percent eigrp 1 5
R2(config-if)#exit

R4(config)#interface serial 0/1
R4(config-if)#ip bandwidth-percent eigrp 1 5
R4(config-if)#exit
```

Task 5

The default route-waiting timer is set to 3 minutes. The configured timer value must be similar on all routers in the network. Complete this task as follows:

```
R1(config)#router eigrp 1
R1(config-router)#timers active-time 10
R1(config-router)#exit

R2(config)#router eigrp 1
R2(config-router)#timers active-time 10
R2(config-router)#exit

R4(config)#router eigrp 1
R4(config-router)#timers active-time 10
R4(config-router)#exit
```

FINAL ROUTER CONFIGURATIONS

R1

```
R1#term len 0
R1#sh run
Building configuration...

Current configuration : 1248 bytes
!
version 12.4
service timestamps debug datetime msec
service timestamps log datetime msec
no service password-encryption
!
hostname R1
!
boot-start-marker
boot-end-marker
!
no logging console
!
no aaa new-model
no network-clock-participate slot 1
```

```
 no network-clock-participate wic 0
 ip cef
 !
 no ip domain lookup
 ip auth-proxy max-nodata-conns 3
 ip admission max-nodata-conns 3
 !
 interface FastEthernet0/0
  ip address 150.1.1.1 255.255.255.0
  duplex auto
  speed auto
 !
 interface Serial0/0
  no ip address
  shutdown
  clock rate 2000000
 !
 interface Serial0/1
  ip address 10.0.0.1 255.255.255.0
  ip bandwidth-percent eigrp 1 5
  encapsulation frame-relay
  no ip split-horizon eigrp 1
 !
 router eigrp 1
  timers active-time 10
  redistribute connected route-map CONNECTED
  network 10.0.0.1 0.0.0.0
  no auto-summary
  neighbor 10.0.0.4 Serial0/1
  neighbor 10.0.0.2 Serial0/1
 !
 ip forward-protocol nd
 !
 no ip http server
 no ip http secure-server
 !
 route-map CONNECTED permit 10
  match interface FastEthernet0/0
  set metric 100000 100 255 1 1500
 !
 route-map CONNECTED permit 20
  set metric 50000 1250 255 1 1500
 !
 control-plane
 !
 line con 0
 line aux 0
 line vty 0 4
  login
 !
 end

 R1#
```

R2

```
R2#term len 0
R2#sh run
Building configuration...

Current configuration : 1170 bytes
!
version 12.4
service timestamps debug datetime msec
service timestamps log datetime msec
no service password-encryption
!
hostname R2
!
boot-start-marker
boot-end-marker
!
no logging console
!
```

```
no aaa new-model
no network-clock-participate slot 1
no network-clock-participate wic 0
ip cef
!
no ip domain lookup
ip auth-proxy max-nodata-conns 3
ip admission max-nodata-conns 3
!
interface FastEthernet0/0
 ip address 150.2.2.2 255.255.255.0
 duplex auto
 speed auto
!
interface Serial0/0
 no ip address
 shutdown
!
interface Serial0/1
 ip address 10.0.0.2 255.255.255.0
 ip bandwidth-percent eigrp 1 5
 encapsulation frame-relay
!
router eigrp 1
 timers active-time 10
 redistribute connected route-map CONNECTED
 network 10.0.0.2 0.0.0.0
 no auto-summary
 neighbor 10.0.0.1 Serial0/1
!
ip forward-protocol nd
!
no ip http server
no ip http secure-server
!
route-map CONNECTED permit 10
 match interface FastEthernet0/0
 set metric 100000 100 255 1 1500
!
route-map CONNECTED permit 20
 set metric 50000 1250 255 1 1500
!
control-plane
!
line con 0
line aux 0
line vty 0 4
 login
!
end

R2#
```

R3

```
R3-Frame-Relay-Switch#term len 0
R3-Frame-Relay-Switch#sh run
Building configuration...

Current configuration : 1616 bytes
!
version 12.4
service timestamps debug datetime msec
service timestamps log datetime msec
no service password-encryption
!
hostname R3-Frame-Relay-Switch
!
boot-start-marker
boot-end-marker
!
no logging console
!
no aaa new-model
```

```
 no network-clock-participate slot 1
 no network-clock-participate wic 0
 ip cef
 !
 no ip domain lookup
 ip auth-proxy max-nodata-conns 3
 ip admission max-nodata-conns 3
 !
 frame-relay switching
 !
 interface FastEthernet0/0
  ip address 150.3.3.3 255.255.255.0
  shutdown
  duplex auto
  speed auto
 !
 interface Serial1/0
  description 'Connected To R1 Serial 0/1'
  no ip address
  encapsulation frame-relay
  clock rate 128000
  frame-relay intf-type dce
  frame-relay route 102 interface Serial1/1 201
  frame-relay route 104 interface Serial1/2 401
 !
 interface Serial1/1
  description 'Connected To R2 Serial 0/1'
  no ip address
  encapsulation frame-relay
  clock rate 128000
  frame-relay intf-type dce
  frame-relay route 201 interface Serial1/0 102
 !
 interface Serial1/2
  description 'Connected To R4 Serial 0/0'
  no ip address
  encapsulation frame-relay
  clock rate 128000
  frame-relay intf-type dce
  frame-relay route 401 interface Serial1/0 104
 !
 interface Serial1/3
  no ip address
  shutdown
 !
 interface Serial1/4
  no ip address
  shutdown
 !
 interface Serial1/5
  no ip address
  shutdown
 !
 interface Serial1/6
  no ip address
  shutdown
 !
 interface Serial1/7
  no ip address
  shutdown
 !
 ip forward-protocol nd
 !
 no ip http server
 no ip http secure-server
 !
 control-plane
 !
 line con 0
 line aux 0
 line vty 0 4
  login
 !
 end

 R3-Frame-Relay-Switch#
```

R4

```
R4#term len 0
R4#sh run
Building configuration...

Current configuration : 1170 bytes
!
version 12.4
service timestamps debug datetime msec
service timestamps log datetime msec
no service password-encryption
!
hostname R4
!
boot-start-marker
boot-end-marker
!
no logging console
!
no aaa new-model
no network-clock-participate slot 1
no network-clock-participate wic 0
ip cef
!
no ip domain lookup
ip auth-proxy max-nodata-conns 3
ip admission max-nodata-conns 3
!
interface FastEthernet0/0
 ip address 150.4.4.4 255.255.255.0
 duplex auto
 speed auto
!
interface Serial0/0
 ip address 10.0.0.4 255.255.255.0
 ip bandwidth-percent eigrp 1 5
 encapsulation frame-relay
!
interface Serial0/1
 no ip address
 shutdown
!
router eigrp 1
 timers active-time 10
 redistribute connected route-map CONNECTED
 network 10.0.0.4 0.0.0.0
 no auto-summary
 neighbor 10.0.0.1 Serial0/0
!
ip forward-protocol nd
!
no ip http server
no ip http secure-server
!
route-map CONNECTED permit 10
 match interface FastEthernet0/0
 set metric 100000 100 255 1 1500
!
route-map CONNECTED permit 20
 set metric 50000 1250 255 1 1500
!
control-plane
!
line con 0
line aux 0
line vty 0 4
 login
!
end

R4#
```

CCNP LAB 20

EIGRP Multi-Technology Lab

Lab Objective:

The focus of this lab is to understand EIGRP implementation and configuration in Cisco IOS routers. Additional technologies tested include advanced route filtering and manipulation.

Lab Topology:

The lab network topology is illustrated below:

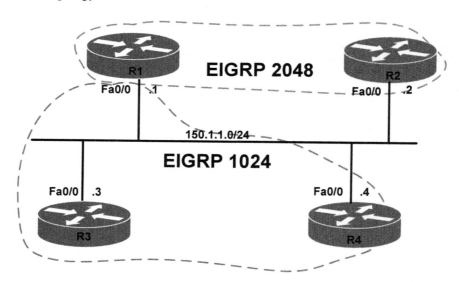

IMPORTANT NOTE: If you are using the www.howtonetwork.net racks, please bring up the LAN interfaces connected to the routers by issuing the no shutdown command on the connected switches. If you are using a home lab with no Switches, you can bring up the LAN interfaces using the following configurations on your routers:

```
interface fastethernet 0/0
  no keepalive
  loopback
  no shutdown
```

Alternately, you can simply connect the interfaces to a hub or switch if you have one available in your own lab.

Task 1

Configure hostnames and IP addressing on all routers as illustrated in the network topology.

Task 2

Configure EIGRP for AS 1024 on R1, R3, and R4 as illustrated in the topology. EIGRP should be configured to use Unicast packets instead of Multicast packets. Verify your configuration using the appropriate commands.

Task 3

Configure EIGRP for AS 2048 on R1 and R2 as illustrated in the topology. EIGRP should be configured to use Unicast packets instead of Multicast packets. Verify your configuration using the appropriate commands.

Task 4

Configure and advertise the following subnets via EIGRP using the following metrics:
- R2: Loopback192 - 192.1.1.1/32: Redistribution Metric - 100,000 - 1,000 - 255 - 1 - 1500
- R2: Loopback193 - 193.1.1.1/32: Redistribution Metric - 10,000 - 500 - 255 - 1 - 1500

- R3: Loopback12 - 12.1.1.1/32: Redistribution Metric - 30,000 - 300 - 255 - 1 - 1500
- R3: Loopback13 - 13.1.1./32: Redistribution Metric - 40,000 - 400 - 255 - 1 - 1500

- R4: Loopback12 - 12.1.1.1/32: Redistribution Metric - Default
- R4: Loopback13 - 13.1.1.1/32: Redistribution Metric - Default

Task 5

Redistribute between EIGRP 1024 and EIGRP 2048. Ensure that the next hop IP address for the redistributed routes is the IP address of the router that originated the route and NOT the IP address of R1. Verify your configuration.

Task 6

Configure route filtering on R4 so that the router only accepts routes with a metric between 200,000 and 300,000. Verify your configuration using the appropriate commands.

LAB VALIDATION

Task 1

```
Router(config)#hostname R1
R1(config)#interface fastethernet 0/0
R1(config-if)#no shutdown
R1(config-if)#ip address 150.1.1.1 255.255.255.0
R1(config-if)#exit

Router(config)#hostname R2
R2(config)#interface fastethernet 0/0
R2(config-if)#no shutdown
R2(config-if)#ip address 150.1.1.2 255.255.255.0
R2(config-if)#exit

Router(config)#hostname R3
R3(config)#interface fastethernet 0/0
R3(config-if)#no shutdown
R3(config-if)#ip address 150.1.1.3 255.255.255.0
R3(config-if)#exit

Router(config)#hostname R4
R4(config)#interface fastethernet 0/0
R4(config-if)#no shutdown
R4(config-if)#ip address 150.1.1.4 255.255.255.0
R4(config-if)#exit
```

Task 2

```
R1(config)#router eirgp 1024
R1(config-router)#no auto-summary
R1(config-router)#neighbor 150.1.1.3 fastethernet 0/0
R1(config-router)#neighbor 150.1.1.4 fastethernet 0/0
R1(config-router)#network 150.1.1.1 0.0.0.0
```

```
R1(config-router)#exit

R3(config)#router eigrp 1024
R3(config-router)#no auto-summary
R3(config-router)#neighbor 150.1.1.1 fastethernet 0/0
R3(config-router)#neighbor 150.1.1.4 fastethernet 0/0
R3(config-router)#network 150.1.1.3 0.0.0.0
R3(config-router)#exit

R4(config)#router eigrp 1024
R4(config-router)#no auto-summary
R4(config-router)#neighbor 150.1.1.1 fastethernet 0/0
R4(config-router)#neighbor 150.1.1.3 fastethernet 0/0
R4(config-router)#network 150.1.1.4 0.0.0.0
R4(config-router)#exit
```

Verify your configuration using the **show ip eigrp neighbors** command:

```
R1#show ip eigrp neighbors
IP-EIGRP neighbors for process 1024
H   Address              Interface     Hold Uptime    SRTT    RTO  Q   Seq
                                       (sec)          (ms)         Cnt Num
1   150.1.1.4            Fa0/0          14 00:01:32      5    200  0   4
0   150.1.1.3            Fa0/0          14 00:04:52      4    200  0   3

R3#show ip eigrp neighbors
IP-EIGRP neighbors for process 1024
H   Address              Interface     Hold Uptime    SRTT    RTO  Q   Seq
                                       (sec)          (ms)         Cnt Num
1   150.1.1.4            Fa0/0          12 00:01:48      4    200  0   5
0   150.1.1.1            Fa0/0          12 00:05:08      4    200  0   3

R4#show ip eigrp neighbors
IP-EIGRP neighbors for process 1024
H   Address              Interface     Hold Uptime    SRTT    RTO  Q   Seq
                                       (sec)          (ms)         Cnt Num
1   150.1.1.1            Fa0/0          13 00:02:09      4    200  0   5
0   150.1.1.3            Fa0/0          14 00:02:09      8    200  0   5
```

Task 3

```
R1(config)#router eigrp 2048
R1(config-router)#no auto-summary
R1(config-router)#neighbor 150.1.1.2 fastethernet 0/0
R1(config-router)#network 150.1.1.1 0.0.0.0
R1(config-router)#exit

R2(config)#router eigrp 2048
R2(config-router)#no auto-summary
R2(config-router)#neighbor 150.1.1.1 fastethernet 0/0
R2(config-router)#network 150.1.1.2 0.0.0.0
R2(config-router)#exit
```

Verify your configuration using the show ip eigrp neighbors command:

```
R1#show ip eigrp neighbors
IP-EIGRP neighbors for process 1024
H   Address              Interface     Hold Uptime    SRTT    RTO  Q   Seq
                                       (sec)          (ms)         Cnt Num
1   150.1.1.4            Fa0/0          12 00:04:42      5    200  0   4
0   150.1.1.3            Fa0/0          14 00:08:01      4    200  0   3

IP-EIGRP neighbors for process 2048
H   Address              Interface     Hold Uptime    SRTT    RTO  Q   Seq
                                       (sec)          (ms)         Cnt Num
0   150.1.1.2            Fa0/0          12 00:00:39      4    200  0   3

R2#show ip eigrp neighbors
IP-EIGRP neighbors for process 2048
H   Address              Interface     Hold Uptime    SRTT    RTO  Q   Seq
```

```
                                    (sec)          (ms)       Cnt Num
0   150.1.1.1              Fa0/0      12 00:00:35    2   200   0  3
```

Task 4

```
R2(config)#interface loopback 192
R2(config-if)#ip address 192.1.1.1 255.255.255.255
R2(config-if)#exit
R2(config)#interface loopback 193
R2(config-if)#ip address 193.1.1.1 255.255.255.255
R2(config-if)#exit
R2(config)#route-map LOOPBACK permit 10
R2(config-route-map)#match interface loopback 192
R2(config-route-map)#set metric 100000 1000 255 1 1500
R2(config-route-map)#exit
R2(config)#route-map LOOPBACK permit 20
R2(config-route-map)#set metric 10000 500 255 1 1500
R2(config-route-map)#exit
R2(config)#router eigrp 2048
R2(config-router)#redistribute connected route-map LOOPBACK
R2(config-router)#exit


R3(config)#interface loopback 12
R3(config-if)#ip address 12.1.1.1 255.255.255.255
R3(config-if)#exit
R3(config)#interface loopback 13
R3(config-if)#ip address 13.1.1.1 255.255.255.255
R3(config-if)#exit
R3(config)#route-map LOOPBACK permit 10
R3(config-route-map)#match interface loopback 12
R3(config-route-map)#set metric 30000 300 255 1 1500
R3(config-route-map)#exit
R3(config)#route-map LOOPBACK permit 20
R3(config-route-map)#match interface loopback 13
R3(config-route-map)#set metric 40000 400 255 1 1500
R3(config-route-map)#exit
R3(config)#router eigrp 1024
R3(config-router)#redistribute connected route-map LOOPBACK
R3(config-router)#exit


R4(config)#interface loopback 12
R4(config-if)#ip address 12.1.1.1 255.255.255.255
R4(config-if)#exit
R4(config)#interface loopback 13
R4(config-if)#ip address 13.1.1.1 255.255.255.255
R4(config-if)#exit
R4(config)#router eigrp 1024
R4(config-router)#redistribute connected
R4(config-router)#exit
```

Verify your configuration by looking at the EIGRP topology tables of all routers using the show ip eigrp topology all-links command because of the different redistribution metrics:

```
R1#show ip eigrp topology all-links
IP-EIGRP Topology Table for AS(1024)/ID(150.1.1.1)
Codes: P - Passive, A - Active, U - Update, Q - Query, R - Reply,
       r - reply Status, s - sia Status

P 13.1.1.1/32, 1 successors, FD is 156160, serno 7
        via 150.1.1.4 (156160/128256), FastEthernet0/0
        via 150.1.1.3 (168960/166400), FastEthernet0/0
P 12.1.1.1/32, 1 successors, FD is 156160, serno 6
        via 150.1.1.4 (156160/128256), FastEthernet0/0
        via 150.1.1.3 (164608/162048), FastEthernet0/0
P 150.1.1.0/24, 1 successors, FD is 28160, serno 1
        via Connected, FastEthernet0/0
IP-EIGRP Topology Table for AS(2048)/ID(150.1.1.1)
Codes: P - Passive, A - Active, U - Update, Q - Query, R - Reply,
       r - reply Status, s - sia Status
```

```
P 150.1.1.0/24, 1 successors, FD is 28160, serno 1
        via Connected, FastEthernet0/0
P 193.1.1.1/32, 1 successors, FD is 386560, serno 2
        via 150.1.1.2 (386560/384000), FastEthernet0/0
P 192.1.1.1/32, 1 successors, FD is 284160, serno 3
        via 150.1.1.2 (284160/281600), FastEthernet0/0

R2#show ip eigrp topology all-links
IP-EIGRP Topology Table for AS(2048)/ID(150.1.1.2)
Codes: P - Passive, A - Active, U - Update, Q - Query, R - Reply,
       r - reply Status, s - sia Status

P 150.1.1.0/24, 1 successors, FD is 28160, serno 1
        via Connected, FastEthernet0/0
P 193.1.1.1/32, 1 successors, FD is 384000, serno 2
        via Rconnected (384000/0)
P 192.1.1.1/32, 1 successors, FD is 281600, serno 3
        via Rconnected (281600/0)

R3#show ip eigrp topology all-links
IP-EIGRP Topology Table for AS(1024)/ID(150.1.1.3)
Codes: P - Passive, A - Active, U - Update, Q - Query, R - Reply,
       r - reply Status, s - sia Status

P 13.1.1.1/32, 1 successors, FD is 166400, serno 3
        via Rconnected (166400/0)
        via 150.1.1.4 (156160/128256), FastEthernet0/0
P 12.1.1.1/32, 1 successors, FD is 162048, serno 2
        via Rconnected (162048/0)
        via 150.1.1.4 (156160/128256), FastEthernet0/0
P 150.1.1.0/24, 1 successors, FD is 28160, serno 1
        via Connected, FastEthernet0/0

R4#show ip eigrp topology all-links
IP-EIGRP Topology Table for AS(1024)/ID(150.1.1.4)
Codes: P - Passive, A - Active, U - Update, Q - Query, R - Reply,
       r - reply Status, s - sia Status

P 13.1.1.1/32, 1 successors, FD is 128256, serno 7
        via Rconnected (128256/0)
        via 150.1.1.3 (168960/166400), FastEthernet0/0
P 12.1.1.1/32, 1 successors, FD is 128256, serno 6
        via Rconnected (128256/0)
        via 150.1.1.3 (164608/162048), FastEthernet0/0
P 150.1.1.0/24, 1 successors, FD is 28160, serno 1
        via Connected, FastEthernet0/0
```

Task 5

The first part of this task is straightforward. This task is completed as follows:

```
R1(config)#router eigrp 1024
R1(config-router)#redistribute eigrp 2048
R1(config-router)#exit
R1(config)#router eigrp 2048
R1(config-router)#redistribute eigrp 1024
R1(config-router)#exit
```

The second part of this task requires that default NEXT HOP behavior for EIGRP be modified. EIGRP does not set the NEXT HOP field in EIGRP packets by default. Therefore, on a multi-access network, such as an NBMA or Ethernet network, a router receiving routes from an EIGRP router assumes that the next hop of these routes is the router sending the updates, even though it might actually be another router on the same subnet. For example, R2 assumes that the NEXT HOP address for the 12.1.1.1/32 and 13.1.1.32 is R1 (150.1.1.1) as shown below:

```
R2#show ip route eigrp
     12.0.0.0/32 is subnetted, 1 subnets
D EX    12.1.1.1 [170/158720] via 150.1.1.1, 00:18:59, FastEthernet0/0
     13.0.0.0/32 is subnetted, 1 subnets
D EX    13.1.1.1 [170/158720] via 150.1.1.1, 00:18:59, FastEthernet0/0
```

To complete this task, disable the default EIGRP NEXT HOP behavior:

```
R1(config)#interface fastethernet 0/0
R1(config-if)#no ip next-hop-self eigrp 1024
R1(config-if)#no ip next-hop-self eigrp 2048
R1(config-if)#exit
```

Following this change, verify the IP routing tables using the show ip route command:

```
R2#show ip route eigrp
     12.0.0.0/32 is subnetted, 1 subnets
D EX    12.1.1.1 [170/158720] via 150.1.1.4, 00:01:23, FastEthernet0/0
     13.0.0.0/32 is subnetted, 1 subnets
D EX    13.1.1.1 [170/158720] via 150.1.1.4, 00:01:23, FastEthernet0/0

R3#show ip route eigrp
     193.1.1.0/32 is subnetted, 1 subnets
D EX    193.1.1.1 [170/389120] via 150.1.1.2, 00:01:44, FastEthernet0/0
     192.1.1.0/32 is subnetted, 1 subnets
D EX    192.1.1.1 [170/286720] via 150.1.1.2, 00:01:44, FastEthernet0/0

R4#show ip route eigrp
     193.1.1.0/32 is subnetted, 1 subnets
D EX    193.1.1.1 [170/389120] via 150.1.1.2, 00:01:58, FastEthernet0/0
     192.1.1.0/32 is subnetted, 1 subnets
D EX    192.1.1.1 [170/286720] via 150.1.1.2, 00:01:58, FastEthernet0/0
```

Task 6

This task requires the implementation of route map filtering. Cisco IOS route maps allow you to specify a valid metric range using standard deviation via the +- keyword. When you specify a metric deviation with the + and - keywords, the router will match any metric that falls inclusively in that range. For example, if you issue the command match metric 100 +- 10 within the route map, the router will match routes with a metric that is 10 less than 100 (90) or 10 more than 100 (110) and anything in between. Prior to any changes, R4s EIGRP routing table shows the following entries for routes received from R1:

```
R4#show ip route eigrp
     193.1.1.0/32 is subnetted, 1 subnets
D EX    193.1.1.1 [170/389120] via 150.1.1.2, 00:02:35, FastEthernet0/0
     192.1.1.0/32 is subnetted, 1 subnets
D EX    192.1.1.1 [170/286720] via 150.1.1.2, 00:02:35, FastEthernet0/0
```

Notice that the 192.1.1.1/32 prefix has a route metric of 286,720 and the 193.1.1.1/32 prefix has a route metric of 389,120. To complete this task, think logically. Given the required metric range, i.e. 200,000 to 300,000; simply match a metric of 250,000 and allow for a deviation of 50,000 in either direction. This task is completed as follows:

```
R4(config)#route-map EIGRP-FILTER permit 10
R4(config-route-map)#match metric 250000 +- 50000
R4(config-route-map)#exit
R4(config)#route-map EIGRP-FILTER deny 20
R4(config-route-map)#exit
R4(config)#router eigrp 1024
R4(config-router)#distribute-list route-map EIGRP-FILTER in
R4(config-router)#exit
```

Following the implementation of the route map, the routing table on R1 shows the following:

```
R4#show ip route eigrp
     192.1.1.0/32 is subnetted, 1 subnets
D EX    192.1.1.1 [170/286720] via 150.1.1.2, 00:05:33, FastEthernet0/0
```

Notice that the 193.1.1.1/32 prefix, which had a route metric of 389,120 is no longer present in the routing table because this metric falls outside the permitted range of 200,000 to 300,000.

FINAL ROUTER CONFIGURATIONS

R1

```
R1#term len 0
R1#sh run
Building configuration...

Current configuration : 1177 bytes
!
version 12.4
service timestamps debug datetime msec
service timestamps log datetime msec
no service password-encryption
!
hostname R1
!
boot-start-marker
boot-end-marker
!
no logging console
!
no aaa new-model
no network-clock-participate slot 1
no network-clock-participate wic 0
ip cef
!
no ip domain lookup
ip auth-proxy max-nodata-conns 3
ip admission max-nodata-conns 3
!
interface FastEthernet0/0
 ip address 150.1.1.1 255.255.255.0
 no ip next-hop-self eigrp 1024
 no ip next-hop-self eigrp 2048
 duplex auto
 speed auto
!
interface Serial0/0
 no ip address
 shutdown
 clock rate 2000000
!
interface Serial0/1
 no ip address
 shutdown
!
router eigrp 1024
 redistribute eigrp 2048
 network 150.1.1.1 0.0.0.0
 no auto-summary
 neighbor 150.1.1.4 FastEthernet0/0
 neighbor 150.1.1.3 FastEthernet0/0
!
router eigrp 2048
 redistribute eigrp 1024
 network 150.1.1.1 0.0.0.0
 no auto-summary
 neighbor 150.1.1.2 FastEthernet0/0
!
ip forward-protocol nd
!
no ip http server
no ip http secure-server
!
control-plane
!
line con 0
line aux 0
line vty 0 4
 login
!
end

R1#
```

R2

```
R2#term len 0
R2#sh run
Building configuration...

Current configuration : 1230 bytes
!
version 12.4
service timestamps debug datetime msec
service timestamps log datetime msec
no service password-encryption
!
hostname R2
!
boot-start-marker
boot-end-marker
!
no logging console
!
no aaa new-model
no network-clock-participate slot 1
no network-clock-participate wic 0
ip cef
!
no ip domain lookup
ip auth-proxy max-nodata-conns 3
ip admission max-nodata-conns 3
!
interface Loopback192
 ip address 192.1.1.1 255.255.255.255
!
interface Loopback193
 ip address 193.1.1.1 255.255.255.255
!
interface FastEthernet0/0
 ip address 150.1.1.2 255.255.255.0
 duplex auto
 speed auto
!
interface Serial0/0
 ip address 10.0.0.2 255.255.255.252
!
interface Serial0/1
 ip address 10.0.0.9 255.255.255.252
!
router eigrp 2048
 redistribute connected route-map LOOPBACK
 network 150.1.1.2 0.0.0.0
 no auto-summary
 neighbor 150.1.1.1 FastEthernet0/0
!
ip forward-protocol nd
!
no ip http server
no ip http secure-server
!
route-map LOOPBACK permit 10
 match interface Loopback192
 set metric 100000 1000 255 1 1500
!
route-map LOOPBACK permit 20
 set metric 10000 500 255 1 1500
!
control-plane
!
line con 0
line aux 0
line vty 0 4
 login
!
end

R2#
```

R3

```
R3#term len 0
R3#sh run
Building configuration...

Current configuration : 1602 bytes
!
version 12.4
service timestamps debug datetime msec
service timestamps log datetime msec
no service password-encryption
!
hostname R3
!
boot-start-marker
boot-end-marker
!
no logging console
!
no aaa new-model
no network-clock-participate slot 1
no network-clock-participate wic 0
ip cef
!
no ip domain lookup
ip auth-proxy max-nodata-conns 3
ip admission max-nodata-conns 3
!
interface Loopback12
 ip address 12.1.1.1 255.255.255.255
!
interface Loopback13
 ip address 13.1.1.1 255.255.255.255
!
interface FastEthernet0/0
 ip address 150.1.1.3 255.255.255.0
 duplex auto
 speed auto
!
interface Serial1/0
 no ip address
 shutdown
 clock rate 128000
!
interface Serial1/1
 no ip address
 shutdown
 clock rate 128000
!
interface Serial1/2
 no ip address
 shutdown
 clock rate 128000
!
interface Serial1/3
 no ip address
 shutdown
!
interface Serial1/4
 no ip address
 shutdown
!
interface Serial1/5
 no ip address
 shutdown
!
interface Serial1/6
 no ip address
 shutdown
!
interface Serial1/7
 no ip address
 shutdown
!
router eigrp 1024
 redistribute connected route-map LOOPBACK
 network 150.1.1.3 0.0.0.0
 no auto-summary
```

```
 neighbor 150.1.1.4 FastEthernet0/0
 neighbor 150.1.1.1 FastEthernet0/0
!
ip forward-protocol nd
!
no ip http server
no ip http secure-server
!
route-map LOOPBACK permit 10
 match interface Loopback12
 set metric 30000 300 255 1 1500
!
route-map LOOPBACK permit 20
 match interface Loopback13
 set metric 40000 400 255 1 1500
!
control-plane
!
line con 0
line aux 0
line vty 0 4
 login
!
end

R3#
```

R4

```
R4#term len 0
R4#sh run
Building configuration...

Current configuration : 1201 bytes
!
version 12.4
service timestamps debug datetime msec
service timestamps log datetime msec
no service password-encryption
!
hostname R4
!
boot-start-marker
boot-end-marker
!
no logging console
!
no aaa new-model
no network-clock-participate slot 1
no network-clock-participate wic 0
ip cef
!
no ip domain lookup
ip auth-proxy max-nodata-conns 3
ip admission max-nodata-conns 3
!
interface Loopback12
 ip address 12.1.1.1 255.255.255.255
!
interface Loopback13
 ip address 13.1.1.1 255.255.255.255
!
interface FastEthernet0/0
 ip address 150.1.1.4 255.255.255.0
 duplex auto
 speed auto
!
interface Serial0/0
 no ip address
 shutdown
!
interface Serial0/1
 no ip address
 shutdown
!
router eigrp 1024
 redistribute connected
 network 150.1.1.4 0.0.0.0
```

```
 distribute-list route-map EIGRP-FILTER in
 no auto-summary
 neighbor 150.1.1.3 FastEthernet0/0
 neighbor 150.1.1.1 FastEthernet0/0
!
ip forward-protocol nd
!
no ip http server
no ip http secure-server
!
route-map EIGRP-FILTER permit 10
 match metric 250000 +- 50000
!
route-map EIGRP-FILTER deny 20
!
control-plane
!
line con 0
line aux 0
line vty 0 4
 login
!
end

R4#
```

CCNP LAB 21

OSPF Multi-Technology Lab

Lab Objective:

The focus of this lab is to understand OSPF implementation and configuration in Cisco IOS routers. Additional technologies tested include authentication and route and LSA filtering.

Lab Topology:

The lab network topology is illustrated below:

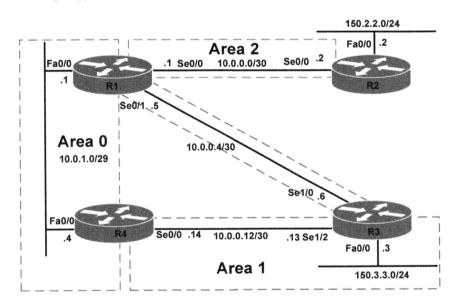

IMPORTANT NOTE: If you are using the www.howtonetwork.net racks, please bring up the LAN interfaces connected to the routers by issuing the `no shutdown` command on the connected switches. If you are using a home lab with no Switches, you can bring up the LAN interfaces using the following configurations on your routers:

```
interface fastethernet 0/0
  no keepalive
  loopback
  no shutdown
```

Alternately, you can simply connect the interfaces to a hub or switch if you have one available in your own lab.

Task 1

Configure hostnames and IP addressing on all routers as illustrated in the network topology.

Task 2

Using interface-based configuration, configure the OSPF backbone (area 0) on the LAN segment between R1 and R4. In the future, additional routers may be added to this segment. Ensure that no DR/BDR election is held on this segment; however, ensure that multiple routers can exist on the same segment. Do NOT modify any OSPF priority values.

Task 3

Using interface-based configuration, configure OSPF area 1 between R1, R3 and R4. Configure MD5 authentication for area 1 using the password 'CCNP'. Verify your configuration.

Task 4

Using interface-based configuration, configure OSPF area 2 between R1 and R2. R1 should not advertise any inter-area routes into area 2; however, a default route should be advertised by default. This default route should be advertised into area 2 so that it appears in the routing table of R2 with a route metric of 500. Do NOT modify interface bandwidth or cost values when completing this task. Verify the configuration.

Task 5

R2 should inject the 150.2.2.0/24 subnet into area 2 as an External N1 route with a route tag of 2222. Verify your configuration.

Task 6

Configure a secondary subnet of 150.1.1.0/29 on the LAN segment between R1 and R4. Assign the 150.1.1.1/29 address to R1 and 150.1.1.4/29 address to R4. This subnet should not be advertised into area 1; however, R2 should be able to reach it. You are NOT allowed to use any distribute lists or other forms of filters to complete this task. In addition to this, you are NOT allowed to configure any static routes. Verify your OSPF configuration.

LAB VALIDATION

Task 1

```
Router(config)#hostname R1
R1(config)#interface fastethernet 0/0
R1(config-if)#no shutdown
R1(config-if)#ip address 10.0.1.1 255.255.255.248
R1(config-if)#exit
R1(config)#interface serial 0/0
R1(config-if)#no shutdown
R1(config-if)#ip address 10.0.0.1 255.255.255.252
R1(config-if)#clock rate 2000000
R1(config-if)#exit
R1(config)#interface serial 0/1
R1(config-if)#ip address 10.0.0.5 255.255.255.252
R1(config-if)#exit

Router(config)#hostname R2
R2(config)#interface fastethernet 0/0
R2(config-if)#no shutdown
R2(config-if)#ip address 150.2.2.2 255.255.255.0
R2(config-if)#exit
R2(config)#interface serial 0/0
R2(config-if)#no shutdown
R2(config-if)#ip address 10.0.0.2 255.255.255.252
R2(config-if)#exit

Router(config)#hostname R3
R3(config)#interface fastethernet 0/0
R3(config-if)#no shutdown
R3(config-if)#ip address 150.3.3.3 255.255.255.0
R3(config-if)#exit
R3(config)#interface serial 1/0
R3(config-if)#no shutdown
R3(config-if)#ip address 10.0.0.6 255.255.255.252
```

```
R3(config-if)#clock rate 128000
R3(config-if)#exit
R3(config)#interface serial 1/2
R3(config-if)#no shutdown
R3(config-if)#ip address 10.0.0.13 255.255.255.252
R3(config-if)#clock rate 128000
R3(config-if)#exit

Router(config)#hostname R4
R4(config)#interface fastethernet 0/0
R4(config-if)#no shutdown
R4(config-if)# ip add 10.0.1.4 255.255.255.248
R4(config-if)#exit
R4(config)#interface serial 0/0
R4(config-if)#no shutdown
R4(config-if)#ip address 10.0.0.14 255.255.255.252
R4(config-if)#exit
```

Task 2

This task requires that the default OSPF network type be changed from Broadcast to point-to-multipoint, which allows multiple routers on the same segment, but requires no DR/BDR election. This task is completed as follows:

```
R1(config)#router ospf 1
R1(config-router)#router-id 1.1.1.1
R1(config-router)#exit
R1(config)#interface fastethernet 0/0
R1(config-if)#ip ospf network point-to-multipoint
R1(config-if)#ip ospf 1 area 0
R1(config-if)#exit

R4(config)#router ospf 4
R4(config-router)#router-id 4.4.4.4
R4(config-router)#exit
R4(config)#interface fastethernet 0/0
R4(config-if)#ip ospf network point-to-multipoint
R4(config-if)#ip ospf 4 area 0
R4(config-if)#exit
```

Verify your configuration using the show ip ospf neighbor command:

```
R1#show ip ospf neighbor

Neighbor ID    Pri    State       Dead Time    Address      Interface
4.4.4.4          0    FULL/   -   00:01:56     10.0.1.4     FastEthernet0/0

R4#show ip ospf neighbor

Neighbor ID    Pri    State       Dead Time    Address      Interface
1.1.1.1          0    FULL/   -   00:01:49     10.0.1.1     FastEthernet0/0
```

Task 3

```
R1(config)#router ospf 1
R1(config-router)#area 1 authentication message-digest
R1(config-router)#exit
R1(config)#interface serial 0/1
R1(config-if)#ip ospf 1 area 1
R1(config-if)#ip ospf message-digest-key 1 md5 CCNP
R1(config-if)#exit

R4(config)#router ospf 4
R4(config-router)#area 1 authentication message-digest
R4(config-router)#exit
R4(config)#interface serial 0/0
R4(config-if)#ip ospf 4 area 1
R4(config-if)#ip ospf message-digest-key 1 md5 CCNP
R4(config-if)#exit
```

```
R3(config)#router ospf 3
R3(config-router)#router-id 3.3.3.3
R3(config-router)#area 1 authentication message-digest
R3(config-router)#exit
Enter configuration commands, one per line.  End with CNTL/Z.
R3(config)#interface fastethernet 0/0
R3(config-if)#ip ospf 3 area 1
R3(config-if)#ip ospf message-digest 1 md5 CCNP
R3(config-if)#exit
R3(config)#interface serial 1/0
R3(config-if)#ip ospf 3 area 1
R3(config-if)#ip ospf message-digest 1 md5 CCNP
R3(config-if)#exit
R3(config)#interface serial 1/2
R3(config-if)#ip ospf 3 area 1
R3(config-if)#ip ospf message-digest 1 md5 CCNP
R3(config-if)#exit
```

Verify your configuration using the show ip ospf neighbor command:

```
R3#show ip ospf neighbor

Neighbor ID     Pri   State           Dead Time   Address         Interface
4.4.4.4           0   FULL/  -        00:00:38    10.0.0.14       Serial1/2
1.1.1.1           0   FULL/  -        00:00:36    10.0.0.5        Serial1/0
```

You can verify area authentication using the show ip ospf <process> command:

```
R3#show ip ospf 3 | begin Area 1
    Area 1
        Number of interfaces in this area is 3
        Area has message digest authentication
        SPF algorithm last executed 00:00:58.140 ago
        SPF algorithm executed 6 times
        Area ranges are
        Number of LSA 11. Checksum Sum 0x143DCC
        Number of opaque link LSA 0. Checksum Sum 0x000000
        Number of DCbitless LSA 0
        Number of indication LSA 0
        Number of DoNotAge LSA 0
        Flood list length 0
```

Use the show ip ospf interface <name> to view interface authentication configuration:

```
R3#show ip ospf interface serial 1/0
Serial1/0 is up, line protocol is up
  Internet Address 10.0.0.6/30, Area 1
  Process ID 3, Router ID 3.3.3.3, Network Type POINT_TO_POINT, Cost: 781
  Enabled by interface config, including secondary ip addresses
  Transmit Delay is 1 sec, State POINT_TO_POINT
  Timer intervals configured, Hello 10, Dead 40, Wait 40, Retransmit 5
    oob-resync timeout 40
    Hello due in 00:00:00
  Supports Link-local Signaling (LLS)
  Index 1/1, flood queue length 0
  Next 0x0(0)/0x0(0)
  Last flood scan length is 1, maximum is 3
  Last flood scan time is 0 msec, maximum is 0 msec
  Neighbor Count is 1, Adjacent neighbor count is 1
    Adjacent with neighbor 1.1.1.1
  Suppress hello for 0 neighbor(s)
  Message digest authentication enabled
    Youngest key id is 1
```

Task 4

To complete this task you need to configure R1 as a NSSA totally stubby ABR so that R1 will automatically advertise the default route into area 2. To complete the second part of the task, the area <> default-cost <cost> command is required to specify the default cost of the default route that is advertised into the stub or NSSA area.

Because OSPF cost is cumulative, you need to calculate the cost of 500 by subtracting the cost of the link between R1 and R2 from this number and specifying the remainder using the `area <> default-cost <cost>` command. Assuming the default cost of 64 for the WAN link between R1 and R2, to configure a cost of 500 perform the following: 500 - 64 = 436. This task is completed as follows:

```
R1(config)#router ospf 1
R1(config-router)#area 2 nssa no-summary
R1(config-router)#area 2 default-cost 436
R1(config-router)#exit
R1(config)#interface serial 0/0
R1(config-if)#ip ospf 1 area 2
R1(config-if)#exit

R2(config)#router ospf 2
R2(config-router)#router-id 2.2.2.2
R2(config-router)#area 2 nssa
R2(config-router)#exit
R2(config)#interface serial 0/0
R2(config-if)#ip ospf 2 area 2
```

Verify your configuration using the `show ip ospf neighbor` command:

```
R2#show ip ospf neighbor

Neighbor ID     Pri   State          Dead Time   Address      Interface
1.1.1.1           0   FULL/   -      00:00:36    10.0.0.1     Serial0/0
```

Verify the cost of the default route on R2 by looking at the routing table:

```
R2#show ip route ospf
O*IA 0.0.0.0/0 [110/500] via 10.0.0.1, 00:00:15, Serial0/0
```

The advertised cost can also be viewed by looking at the entry in the LSDB:

```
R2#show ip ospf database summary 0.0.0.0

            OSPF Router with ID (2.2.2.2) (Process ID 2)

                Summary Net Link States (Area 2)

    Routing Bit Set on this LSA
    LS age: 64
    Options: (No TOS-capability, DC, Upward)
    LS Type: Summary Links(Network)
    Link State ID: 0.0.0.0 (summary Network Number)
    Advertising Router: 1.1.1.1
    LS Seq Number: 80000003
    Checksum: 0x2556
    Length: 28
    Network Mask: /0
        TOS: 0  Metric: 436
```

Task 5

Because only a single interface exists, this can be completed using a single configuration line:

```
R2(config)#router ospf 2
R2(config-router)#redistribute connected subnets tag 2222 metric-type 1
R2(config-router)#exit
```

Verify your configuration by looking at the entry for this prefix in the Link State Database:

```
R1#show ip ospf database external 150.2.2.0

            OSPF Router with ID (1.1.1.1) (Process ID 1)

                Type-5 AS External Link States
```

```
LS age: 63
Options: (No TOS-capability, DC)
LS Type: AS External Link
Link State ID: 150.2.2.0 (External Network Number )
Advertising Router: 1.1.1.1
LS Seq Number: 80000001
Checksum: 0xCDF1
Length: 36
Network Mask: /24
        Metric Type: 1 (Comparable directly to link state metric)
        TOS: 0
        Metric: 20
        Forward Address: 10.0.0.2
        External Route Tag: 2222
```

Task 6

The requirements of this task are two-fold. To complete the first part of this task, you need to prevent the secondary subnet configured on R1 and R4 from being advertised by OSPF. By default, OSPF will advertise all secondary subnets as can be seen in the LSDB on R3:

```
R3#show ip ospf database | include 150.
150.1.1.1         1.1.1.1         142         0x80000001 0x00A4FA
150.1.1.1         4.4.4.4         153         0x80000001 0x00543E
150.1.1.4         1.1.1.1         142         0x80000001 0x00900B
150.1.1.4         4.4.4.4         153         0x80000001 0x002C64
150.2.2.0         1.1.1.1         723         0x80000001 0x00CDF1 2222
```

Complete this task by preventing OSPF from advertising secondary subnets as follows:

```
R1(config)#interface fastethernet 0/0
R1(config-if)#ip ospf 1 area 0 secondaries none
R1(config-if)#exit

R4(config)#interface fastethernet 0/0
R4(config-if)#ip ospf 4 area 0 secondaries none
R4(config-if)#exit
```

Following this configuration, the secondary subnet is no longer advertised by OSPF and is no longer present in the LSDB on R3:

```
R3#show ip ospf database | include 150
150.2.2.0         1.1.1.1         1188        0x80000002 0x00CBF2 2222
```

To complete the second part of this task, you need to configure R1 and R4 to advertise a default route to R3 using the `default-information originate always` command. This allows OSPF to advertise a default route without one existing in the RIB:

```
R1(config)#router ospf 1
R1(config-router)#default-information originate always
R1(config-router)#exit

R4(config)#router ospf 4
R4(config-router)#default-information originate always
R4(config-router)#exit
```

Following this configuration, R3s RIB contains two default routes: one from R1 and one from R4. This is verified by looking at either the RIB or LSDB on R3:

```
R3#show ip route ospf
      10.0.0.0/8 is variably subnetted, 5 subnets, 2 masks
O IA    10.0.1.1/32 [110/781] via 10.0.0.5, 00:00:52, Serial1/0
O IA    10.0.0.0/30 [110/845] via 10.0.0.5, 00:00:52, Serial1/0
O IA    10.0.1.4/32 [110/781] via 10.0.0.14, 00:00:52, Serial1/2
      150.2.0.0/24 is subnetted, 1 subnets
O E1    150.2.2.0 [110/865] via 10.0.0.5, 00:00:42, Serial1/0
```

```
O*E2 0.0.0.0/0 [110/1] via 10.0.0.14, 00:00:42, Serial1/2
                [110/1] via 10.0.0.5, 00:00:43, Serial1/0
```

Finally, verify that R3 can ping the 150.1.1.1 and 150.1.1.4 addresses:

```
R3#ping 150.1.1.1 repeat 10 source fastethernet 0/0

Type escape sequence to abort.
Sending 10, 100-byte ICMP Echos to 150.1.1.1, timeout is 2 seconds:
Packet sent with a source address of 150.3.3.3
!!!!!!!!!!
Success rate is 100 percent (10/10), round-trip min/avg/max = 16/16/16 ms

R3#ping 150.1.1.4 repeat 10 source fastethernet 0/0

Type escape sequence to abort.
Sending 10, 100-byte ICMP Echos to 150.1.1.4, timeout is 2 seconds:
Packet sent with a source address of 150.3.3.3
!!!!!!!!!!
Success rate is 100 percent (10/10), round-trip min/avg/max = 16/16/16 ms
```

FINAL ROUTER CONFIGURATIONS

R1

```
R1#term len 0
R1#sh run
Building configuration...

Current configuration : 1204 bytes
!
version 12.4
service timestamps debug datetime msec
service timestamps log datetime msec
no service password-encryption
!
hostname R1
!
boot-start-marker
boot-end-marker
!
no logging console
!
no aaa new-model
no network-clock-participate slot 1
no network-clock-participate wic 0
ip cef
!
no ip domain lookup
ip auth-proxy max-nodata-conns 3
ip admission max-nodata-conns 3
!
interface FastEthernet0/0
 ip address 150.1.1.1 255.255.255.248 secondary
 ip address 10.0.1.1 255.255.255.248
 ip ospf network point-to-multipoint
 ip ospf 1 area 0 secondaries none
 duplex auto
 speed auto
!
interface Serial0/0
 ip address 10.0.0.1 255.255.255.252
 ip ospf 1 area 2
 clock rate 2000000
!
interface Serial0/1
 ip address 10.0.0.5 255.255.255.252
 ip ospf message-digest-key 1 md5 CCNP
 ip ospf 1 area 1
!
```

```
 router ospf 1
  router-id 1.1.1.1
  log-adjacency-changes
  area 1 authentication message-digest
  area 2 nssa no-summary
  area 2 default-cost 436
  default-information originate always
 !
 ip forward-protocol nd
 !
 no ip http server
 no ip http secure-server
 !
 control-plane
 !
 line con 0
 line aux 0
 line vty 0 4
  login
 !
 end

 R1#
```

R2

```
R2#term len 0
R2#sh run
Building configuration...

Current configuration : 936 bytes
!
version 12.4
service timestamps debug datetime msec
service timestamps log datetime msec
no service password-encryption
!
hostname R2
!
boot-start-marker
boot-end-marker
!
no logging console
!
no aaa new-model
no network-clock-participate slot 1
no network-clock-participate wic 0
ip cef
!
no ip domain lookup
ip auth-proxy max-nodata-conns 3
ip admission max-nodata-conns 3
!
interface FastEthernet0/0
 ip address 150.2.2.2 255.255.255.0
 duplex auto
 speed auto
!
interface Serial0/0
 ip address 10.0.0.2 255.255.255.252
 ip ospf 2 area 2
!
interface Serial0/1
 no ip address
 shutdown
!
router ospf 2
 router-id 2.2.2.2
 log-adjacency-changes
 area 2 nssa
 redistribute connected metric-type 1 subnets tag 2222
!
ip forward-protocol nd
!
```

```
!
no ip http server
no ip http secure-server
!
control-plane
!
line con 0
line aux 0
line vty 0 4
 login
!
end

R2#
```

R3

```
R3#term len 0
R3#sh run
Building configuration...

Current configuration : 1411 bytes
!
version 12.4
service timestamps debug datetime msec
service timestamps log datetime msec
no service password-encryption
!
hostname R3
!
boot-start-marker
boot-end-marker
!
no logging console
!
no aaa new-model
no network-clock-participate slot 1
no network-clock-participate wic 0
ip cef
!
no ip domain lookup
ip auth-proxy max-nodata-conns 3
ip admission max-nodata-conns 3
!
interface FastEthernet0/0
 ip address 150.3.3.3 255.255.255.0
 ip ospf message-digest-key 1 md5 CCNP
 ip ospf 3 area 1
 duplex auto
 speed auto
!
interface Serial1/0
 ip address 10.0.0.6 255.255.255.252
 ip ospf message-digest-key 1 md5 CCNP
 ip ospf 3 area 1
 clock rate 128000
!
interface Serial1/1
 no ip address
 shutdown
 clock rate 128000
!
interface Serial1/2
 ip address 10.0.0.13 255.255.255.252
 ip ospf message-digest-key 1 md5 CCNP
 ip ospf 3 area 1
 clock rate 128000
!
interface Serial1/3
 no ip address
 shutdown
!
interface Serial1/4
 no ip address
```

```
 shutdown
!
interface Serial1/5
 no ip address
 shutdown
!
interface Serial1/6
 no ip address
 shutdown
!
interface Serial1/7
 no ip address
 shutdown
!
router ospf 3
 router-id 3.3.3.3
 log-adjacency-changes
 area 1 authentication message-digest
!
ip forward-protocol nd
!
no ip http server
no ip http secure-server
!
control-plane
!
line con 0
line aux 0
line vty 0 4
 login
!
end

R3#
```

R4

```
R4#term len 0
R4#sh run
Building configuration...

Current configuration : 1105 bytes
!
version 12.4
service timestamps debug datetime msec
service timestamps log datetime msec
no service password-encryption
!
hostname R4
!
boot-start-marker
boot-end-marker
!
no logging console
!
no aaa new-model
no network-clock-participate slot 1
no network-clock-participate wic 0
ip cef
!
no ip domain lookup
ip auth-proxy max-nodata-conns 3
ip admission max-nodata-conns 3
!
interface FastEthernet0/0
 ip address 150.1.1.4 255.255.255.248 secondary
 ip address 10.0.1.4 255.255.255.248
 ip ospf network point-to-multipoint
 ip ospf 4 area 0 secondaries none
 duplex auto
 speed auto
!
interface Serial0/0
```

```
 ip address 10.0.0.14 255.255.255.252
 ip ospf message-digest-key 1 md5 CCNP
 ip ospf 4 area 1
!
interface Serial0/1
 no ip address
 shutdown
!
router ospf 4
 router-id 4.4.4.4
 log-adjacency-changes
 area 1 authentication message-digest
 default-information originate always
!
ip forward-protocol nd
!
no ip http server
no ip http secure-server
!
control-plane
!
line con 0
line aux 0
line vty 0 4
 login
!
end

R4#
```

CCNP LAB 22

OSPF Multi-Technology Lab

Lab Objective:

The focus of this lab is to understand OSPF implementation and configuration in Cisco IOS routers. Additional technologies tested include authentication and backbone connectivity.

Lab Topology:

The lab network topology is illustrated below:

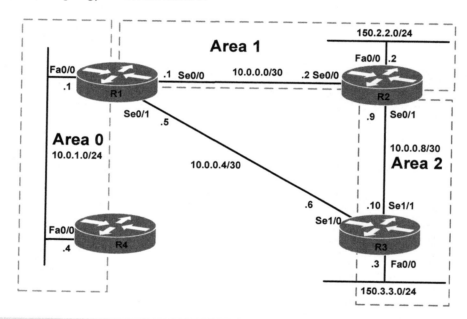

IMPORTANT NOTE: If you are using the www.howtonetwork.net racks, please bring up the LAN interfaces connected to the routers by issuing the no shutdown command on the connected switches. If you are using a home lab with no Switches, you can bring up the LAN interfaces using the following configurations on your routers:

```
interface fastethernet 0/0
  no keepalive
  loopback
  no shutdown
```

Alternately, you can simply connect the interfaces to a hub or switch if you have one available in your own lab.

Task 1

Configure hostnames and IP addressing on all routers as illustrated in the network topology.

Task 2

Using interface-based configuration, configure OSPF area 0 on the LAN segment connecting R1 and R4. To allow for faster convergence, configure OSPF to detect neighbor failure within one second. The OSPF Dead Interval should be set to 1 second. The routers should send four Hellos every second. Verify your configuration using the appropriate commands.

Task 3

Using interface-based configuration, configure OSPF area 1 between R1 and R2. This area should be configured as a Totally Stubby area. Verify your configuration.

Task 4

Using interface-based configuration, configure OSPF area 2 between R2 and R3. Ensure that this area is able to communicate with the OSPF backbone. Verify your configuration.

Task 5

To allow for area 2 resiliency, configure your network so that the WAN link between R1 and R3 is used to allow reachability to and from R3 as well as to the 150.3.3.0/24 subnet should the WAN link between R2 and R3 fail. You are permitted to use TWO static routes to complete this task. Test your solution by shutting down the WAN link between R2 and R3.

Task 6

Configure plain text authentication for the OSPF backbone area. Ensure that all routing still works following your configuration. Use the password 'CCNP' for authentication.

LAB VALIDATION

Task 1

```
Router(config)#hostname R1
R1(config)#interface fastethernet 0/0
R1(config-if)#no shutdown
R1(config-if)#ip address 10.0.1.1 255.255.255.0
R1(config-if)#exit
R1(config)#interface serial 0/0
R1(config-if)#no shutdown
R1(config-if)#ip address 10.0.0.1 255.255.255.252
R1(config-if)#clock rate 2000000
R1(config-if)#exit
R1(config)#interface serial 0/1
R1(config-if)#ip address 10.0.0.5 255.255.255.252
R1(config-if)#exit

Router(config)#hostname R2
R2(config)#interface fastethernet 0/0
R2(config-if)#no shutdown
R2(config-if)#ip address 150.2.2.2 255.255.255.0
R2(config-if)#exit
R2(config)#interface serial 0/0
R2(config-if)#no shutdown
R2(config-if)#ip address 10.0.0.2 255.255.255.252
R2(config-if)#exit
R2(config)#interface serial 0/1
R2(config-if)#no shutdown
R2(config-if)#ip address 10.0.0.9 255.255.255.252
R2(config-if)#exit

Router(config)#hostname R3
R3(config)#interface fastethernet 0/0
R3(config-if)#no shutdown
R3(config-if)#ip address 150.3.3.3 255.255.255.0
R3(config-if)#exit
```

```
R3(config)#interface serial 1/0
R3(config-if)#no shutdown
R3(config-if)#ip address 10.0.0.6 255.255.255.252
R3(config-if)#clock rate 128000
R3(config-if)#exit
R3(config)#interface serial 1/1
R3(config-if)#no shutdown
R3(config-if)#ip address 10.0.0.10 255.255.255.252
R3(config-if)#clock rate 128000
R3(config-if)#exit

Router(config)#hostname R4
R4(config)#interface fastethernet 0/0
R4(config-if)#no shutdown
R4(config-if)#ip add 10.0.1.4 255.255.255.0
R4(config-if)#exit
```

Task 2

The requirements of this task are two-fold. The first part entails enabling OSPF using interface-based configuration. This is completed as follows:

```
R1(config)#router ospf 1
R1(config-router)#router-id 1.1.1.1
R1(config-router)#exit
R1(config)#interface fastethernet 0/0
R1(config-if)#ip ospf 1 area 0
R1(config-if)#exit

R4(config)#router ospf 4
R4(config-router)#router-id 4.4.4.4
R4(config-router)#exit
R4(config)#interface fastethernet 0/0
R4(config-if)#ip ospf 4 area 0
R4(config-if)#exit
```

When complete, verify your configuration using the show ip ospf neighbor command:

```
R1#show ip ospf neighbor

Neighbor ID   Pri   State      Dead Time   Address    Interface
4.4.4.4        1    FULL/BDR   00:00:32    10.0.1.4   FastEthernet0/0

R4#show ip ospf neighbor

Neighbor ID   Pri   State      Dead Time   Address    Interface
1.1.1.1        1    FULL/DR    00:00:31    10.0.1.1   FastEthernet0/0
```

The second part of this task requires enabling OSPF Fast Hellos. The OSPF Fast Hello feature provides a way to configure the sending of hello packets in intervals less than 1 second, thus allowing for faster convergence of the OSPF network. This feature is enabled using the ip ospf dead-interval minimal hello-multiplier <3-20> interface configuration command. The ip ospf dead-interval minimal portion of this command tells OSPF to advertise a dead interval of 1 second.

The hello-multiplier <3-20> portion of the command specifies the number of Hellos that should be sent every second. The valid range is 3 to 20 - although this will vary depending on Cisco IOS Software version and platform. For example, to configure OSPF to send 15 Hello packets every second, you would issue the ip ospf dead-interval minimal hello-multiplier 15 OSPF interface configuration command. This task is completed as follows:

```
R1(config)#interface fastethernet 0/0
R1(config-if)#ip ospf dead-interval minimal hello-multiplier 4
R1(config-if)#exit

R4(config)#interface fastethernet 0/0
R4(config-if)#ip ospf dead-interval minimal hello-multiplier 4
R4(config-if)#exit
```

Verify your configuration using the show ip ospf interface <name> command:

```
R4#show ip ospf interface fastethernet 0/0
FastEthernet0/0 is up, line protocol is up
  Internet Address 10.0.1.4/24, Area 0
  Process ID 4, Router ID 4.4.4.4, Network Type BROADCAST, Cost: 1
  Enabled by interface config, including secondary ip addresses
  Transmit Delay is 1 sec, State BDR, Priority 1
  Designated Router (ID) 1.1.1.1, Interface address 10.0.1.1
  Backup Designated router (ID) 4.4.4.4, Interface address 10.0.1.4
  Timer intervals configured, Hello 250 msec, Dead 1, Wait 1, Retransmit 5
    oob-resync timeout 40
    Hello due in 166 msec
  Supports Link-local Signaling (LLS)
  Index 1/1, flood queue length 0
  Next 0x0(0)/0x0(0)
  Last flood scan length is 1, maximum is 1
  Last flood scan time is 0 msec, maximum is 0 msec
  Neighbor Count is 1, Adjacent neighbor count is 1
    Adjacent with neighbor 1.1.1.1  (Designated Router)
  Suppress hello for 0 neighbor(s)
```

You can also determine that Fast Hellos have been enabled if the dead timer value in the output of the show ip ospf neighbor [detail] command is in milliseconds versus seconds:

```
R1#show ip ospf neighbor detail
 Neighbor 4.4.4.4, interface address 10.0.1.4
    In the area 0 via interface FastEthernet0/0
    Neighbor priority is 1, State is FULL, 6 state changes
    DR is 10.0.1.1 BDR is 10.0.1.4
    Options is 0x12 in Hello (E-bit L-bit )
    Options is 0x52 in DBD (E-bit L-bit O-bit)
    LLS Options is 0x1 (LR)
    Dead timer due in 848 msec
    Neighbor is up for 00:14:50
    Index 1/1, retransmission queue length 0, number of retransmission 0
    First 0x0(0)/0x0(0) Next 0x0(0)/0x0(0)
    Last retransmission scan length is 0, maximum is 0
    Last retransmission scan time is 0 msec, maximum is 0 msec
```

Task 3

```
R1(config)#router ospf 1
R1(config-router)#area 1 stub no-summary
R1(config-router)#exit
R1(config)#interface serial 0/0
R1(config-if)#ip ospf 1 area 1
R1(config-if)#exit

R2(config)#router ospf 2
R2(config-router)#router-id 2.2.2.2
R2(config-router)#area 1 stub
R2(config-router)#exit
R2(config)#interface fastethernet 0/0
R2(config-if)#ip ospf 2 area 1
R2(config-if)#exit
R2(config)#interface serial 0/0
R2(config-if)#ip ospf 2 area 1
R2(config-if)#exit
```

When complete, verify your configuration using the show ip ospf neighbor command:

```
R1#show ip ospf neighbor

Neighbor ID    Pri   State        Dead Time   Address    Interface
4.4.4.4         1    FULL/BDR     824 msec    10.0.1.4   FastEthernet0/0
2.2.2.2         0    FULL/  -     00:00:37    10.0.0.2   Serial0/0
```

```
R2#show ip ospf neighbor

Neighbor ID  Pri  State      Dead Time   Address    Interface
1.1.1.1        0  FULL/  -   00:00:37    10.0.0.1   Serial0/0
```

Additionally, use the show ip ospf commands to verify totally stub area configuration:

```
R1#show ip ospf
 Routing Process "ospf 1" with ID 1.1.1.1

[Truncated Output]

 Number of areas in this router is 2. 1 normal 1 stub 0 nssa

[Truncated Output]

    Area BACKBONE(0)
        Number of interfaces in this area is 1
        Area has no authentication
        SPF algorithm last executed 00:04:03.140 ago
        SPF algorithm executed 6 times

[Truncated Output]

    Area 1
        Number of interfaces in this area is 1
        It is a stub area, no summary LSA in this area
          generates stub default route with cost 1
        Area has no authentication
        SPF algorithm last executed 00:02:59.252 ago
        SPF algorithm executed 5 times

[Truncated Output]

R2#show ip ospf database

            OSPF Router with ID (2.2.2.2) (Process ID 2)

            Router Link States (Area 1)

Link ID       ADV Router     Age     Seq#        Checksum Link count
1.1.1.1       1.1.1.1        333     0x80000002 0x004A38 2
2.2.2.2       2.2.2.2        319     0x80000002 0x00CF03 3

            Summary Net Link States (Area 1)

Link ID       ADV Router     Age     Seq#        Checksum
0.0.0.0       1.1.1.1        386     0x80000001 0x0093A6
```

Task 4

The requirements of this task are two-fold. The first requirement is to enable OSPF for area 2. This requirement is completed as follows:

```
R2(config)#interface serial 0/1
R2(config-if)#ip ospf 2 area 2
R2(config-if)#exit

R3(config)#router ospf 3
R3(config-router)#router-id 3.3.3.3
R3(config-router)#exit
R3(config)#interface serial 1/1
R3(config-if)#ip ospf 3 area 2
R3(config-if)#exit
R3(config)#interface fastethernet 0/0
R3(config-if)#ip ospf 3 area 2
R3(config-if)#exit
```

When complete, verify your configuration using the show ip ospf neighbor command:

```
R2#show ip ospf neighbor

Neighbor ID     Pri   State       Dead Time   Address     Interface
1.1.1.1           0   FULL/  -    00:00:30    10.0.0.1    Serial0/0
3.3.3.3           0   FULL/  -    00:00:31    10.0.0.10   Serial0/1

R3#show ip ospf neighbor

Neighbor ID     Pri   State       Dead Time   Address     Interface
2.2.2.2           0   FULL/  -    00:00:30    10.0.0.9    Serial1/1
```

Following this configuration, the routes from area 2 are not advertised into the OSPF backbone because the area is not connected to the backbone. OSPF areas are typically connected to the backbone using virtual links. However, in this case, a virtual cannot be used because a virtual link cannot be configured over a stub area. The next alternative is to use a GRE tunnel.

Prior to any changes being made, there will no entries in the LSDB of the backbone routers for the area 2 networks. This can be validated by looking at the LSDB via the show ip ospf database command, or looking at the routing table using the show ip route command:

```
R1#show ip route ospf
      150.2.0.0/24 is subnetted, 1 subnets
O        150.2.2.0 [110/65] via 10.0.0.2, 00:07:15, Serial0/0
```

To complete this task, configure a GRE tunnel and assign it to the OSPF backbone (area 0):

```
R1(config)#interface tunnel 0
R1(config-if)#ip address 11.0.0.1 255.255.255.252
R1(config-if)#tunnel source serial 0/0
R1(config-if)#tunnel destination 10.0.0.2
R1(config-if)#ip ospf 1 area 0
R1(config-if)#exit

R2(config)#interface tunnel 0
R2(config-if)#ip address 11.0.0.2 255.255.255.252
R2(config-if)#tunnel source serial 0/0
R2(config-if)#tunnel destination 10.0.0.1
R2(config-if)#ip ospf 2 area 0
R2(config-if)#exit
```

When complete, verify your configuration using the show ip ospf neighbor command:

```
R1#show ip ospf neighbor

Neighbor ID     Pri   State       Dead Time   Address     Interface
2.2.2.2           0   FULL/  -    00:00:34    11.0.0.2    Tunnel0
4.4.4.4           1   FULL/BDR    744 msec    10.0.1.4    FastEthernet0/0
2.2.2.2           0   FULL/  -    00:00:33    10.0.0.2    Serial0/0
```

Next, verify that the routes exist by looking at either the LSDB or RIB on the backbone routers:

```
R1#show ip route ospf
      10.0.0.0/8 is variably subnetted, 4 subnets, 2 masks
O IA    10.0.0.8/30 [110/11175] via 11.0.0.2, 00:00:41, Tunnel0
      150.2.0.0/24 is subnetted, 1 subnets
O        150.2.2.0 [110/65] via 10.0.0.2, 00:10:58, Serial0/0
      150.3.0.0/24 is subnetted, 1 subnets
O IA    150.3.3.0 [110/11176] via 11.0.0.2, 00:00:41, Tunnel0

R4#show ip route ospf
      10.0.0.0/8 is variably subnetted, 3 subnets, 2 masks
O IA    10.0.0.8/30 [110/11176] via 10.0.1.1, 00:00:10, FastEthernet0/0
O IA    10.0.0.0/30 [110/65] via 10.0.1.1, 00:00:10, FastEthernet0/0
      11.0.0.0/30 is subnetted, 1 subnets
O        11.0.0.0 [110/11112] via 10.0.1.1, 00:00:10, FastEthernet0/0
      150.2.0.0/24 is subnetted, 1 subnets
O IA    150.2.2.0 [110/66] via 10.0.1.1, 00:00:10, FastEthernet0/0
```

```
       150.3.0.0/24 is subnetted, 1 subnets
  O IA    150.3.3.0 [110/11177] via 10.0.1.1, 00:00:10, FastEthernet0/0
```

Finally, verify end-to-end connectivity using simple pings:

```
R4#ping 150.2.2.2 repeat 10 size 1500

Type escape sequence to abort.
Sending 10, 1500-byte ICMP Echos to 150.2.2.2, timeout is 2 seconds:
!!!!!!!!!!
Success rate is 100 percent (10/10), round-trip min/avg/max = 16/17/20 ms

R4#ping 150.3.3.3 repeat 10 size 1500

Type escape sequence to abort.
Sending 10, 1500-byte ICMP Echos to 150.3.3.3, timeout is 2 seconds:
!!!!!!!!!!
Success rate is 100 percent (10/10), round-trip min/avg/max = 208/208/212 ms
```

Task 5

To complete this task, you need to configure a default route on R3 that points towards R1. You do NOT need to specify a non-default administrative distance because of the longest-match rules. The default route will therefore only be used when there are no other more specific routes in the routing table, i.e. when the WAN link between R2 and R3 fails.

The second configuration requirement is that you need to a) configure a static route on R1 that points to R3 for the 150.3.3.0/24 subnet and b) redistribute the WAN link between R1 and R3 into OSPF. The static route needs to be configured with an administrative distance higher than 110 so that the route via the tunnel is preferred instead. In addition to this, the static route also needs to be redistributed into OSPF so that it is advertised to R4. Redistributing the WAN link between R1 and R3 will allow other devices to ping R4. This task is completed as follows:

```
R3(config)#ip route 0.0.0.0 0.0.0.0 serial 1/0

R1(config)#ip route 150.3.3.0 255.255.255.0 serial 0/1 150
R1(config)#router ospf 1
R1(config-router)#redistribute connected subnets
R1(config-router)#redistribute static subnets
R1(config-router)#exit
```

After this configuration, test the solution by shutting down the WAN link between R2 and R3:

```
R3(config)#interface serial 1/1
R3(config-if)#shutdown
R3(config-if)#exit
R3(config)#do show ip route
Codes: C - connected, S - static, R - RIP, M - mobile, B - BGP
       D - EIGRP, EX - EIGRP external, O - OSPF, IA - OSPF inter area
       N1 - OSPF NSSA external type 1, N2 - OSPF NSSA external type 2
       E1 - OSPF external type 1, E2 - OSPF external type 2
       i - IS-IS, su - IS-IS summary, L1 - IS-IS level-1, L2 - IS-IS level-2
       ia - IS-IS inter area, * - candidate default, U - per-user static route
       o - ODR, P - periodic downloaded static route

Gateway of last resort is 0.0.0.0 to network 0.0.0.0

     10.0.0.0/30 is subnetted, 1 subnets
  C     10.0.0.4 is directly connected, Serial1/0
     150.3.0.0/24 is subnetted, 1 subnets
  C     150.3.3.0 is directly connected, FastEthernet0/0
  S*  0.0.0.0/0 is directly connected, Serial1/0
```

Following this, verify that all other routers can ping the WAN interface of R3 as well as the connected 150.3.3.0/24 subnet:

```
R1#ping 150.3.3.3 repeat 10 size 1500 source fastethernet 0/0

Type escape sequence to abort.
Sending 10, 1500-byte ICMP Echos to 150.3.3.3, timeout is 2 seconds:
Packet sent with a source address of 10.0.1.1
!!!!!!!!!!
Success rate is 100 percent (10/10), round-trip min/avg/max = 188/191/192 ms
R1#
R1#ping 10.0.0.6 repeat 10 size 1500 source fastethernet 0/0

Type escape sequence to abort.
Sending 10, 1500-byte ICMP Echos to 10.0.0.6, timeout is 2 seconds:
Packet sent with a source address of 10.0.1.1
!!!!!!!!!!
Success rate is 100 percent (10/10), round-trip min/avg/max = 188/191/192 ms

R2#ping 10.0.0.6 repeat 10 size 1500 source fastethernet 0/0

Type escape sequence to abort.
Sending 10, 1500-byte ICMP Echos to 10.0.0.6, timeout is 2 seconds:
Packet sent with a source address of 150.2.2.2
!!!!!!!!!!
Success rate is 100 percent (10/10), round-trip min/avg/max = 204/206/208 ms
R2#
R2#ping 150.3.3.3 repeat 10 size 1500 source fastethernet 0/0

Type escape sequence to abort.
Sending 10, 1500-byte ICMP Echos to 150.3.3.3, timeout is 2 seconds:
Packet sent with a source address of 150.2.2.2
!!!!!!!!!!
Success rate is 100 percent (10/10), round-trip min/avg/max = 204/206/208 ms

R4#ping 150.3.3.3 size 1500 repeat 10

Type escape sequence to abort.
Sending 10, 1500-byte ICMP Echos to 150.3.3.3, timeout is 2 seconds:
!!!!!!!!!!
Success rate is 100 percent (10/10), round-trip min/avg/max = 192/193/196 ms
R4#
R4#ping 10.0.0.6 size 1500 repeat 10

Type escape sequence to abort.
Sending 10, 1500-byte ICMP Echos to 10.0.0.6, timeout is 2 seconds:
!!!!!!!!!!
Success rate is 100 percent (10/10), round-trip min/avg/max = 192/193/196 ms
```

Task 6

```
R1(config)#router ospf 1
R1(config-router)#area 0 authentication
R1(config-router)#exit
R1(config)#interface tunnel 0
R1(config-if)#ip ospf authentication-key CCNP
R1(config-if)#exit
R1(config)#interface fastethernet 0/0
R1(config-if)#ip ospf authentication-key CCNP
R1(config-if)#exit

R2(config)#router ospf 2
R2(config-router)#area 0 authentication
R2(config-router)#exit
R2(config)#interface tunnel 0
R2(config-if)#ip ospf authentication-key CCNP
R2(config-if)#exit

R4(config)#router ospf 4
R4(config-router)#area 0 authentication
R4(config-router)#exit
R4(config)#interface fastethernet 0/0
R4(config-if)#ip ospf authentication-key CCNP
R4(config-if)#exit
```

Verify the solution using the `show ip ospf` and `show ip ospf interface` commands:

```
R1#show ip ospf
 Routing Process "ospf 1" with ID 1.1.1.1

[Truncated Output]

    Area BACKBONE(0)
        Number of interfaces in this area is 2
        Area has simple password authentication

[Truncated Output]

    Area 1
        Number of interfaces in this area is 1
        It is a stub area, no summary LSA in this area
          generates stub default route with cost 1
        Area has no authentication

[Truncated Output]

R1#show ip ospf interface | section  Tunnel|FastEthernet
Tunnel0 is up, line protocol is up
  Internet Address 11.0.0.1/30, Area 0
  Process ID 1, Router ID 1.1.1.1, Network Type POINT_TO_POINT, Cost: 11111
  Enabled by interface config, including secondary ip addresses
  Transmit Delay is 1 sec, State POINT_TO_POINT

[Truncated Output]

  Simple password authentication enabled

FastEthernet0/0 is up, line protocol is up
  Internet Address 10.0.1.1/24, Area 0
  Process ID 1, Router ID 1.1.1.1, Network Type BROADCAST, Cost: 1
  Enabled by interface config, including secondary ip addresses
  Transmit Delay is 1 sec, State BDR, Priority 1
  Designated Router (ID) 4.4.4.4, Interface address 10.0.1.4
  Backup Designated router (ID) 1.1.1.1, Interface address 10.0.1.1
  Timer intervals configured, Hello 250 msec, Dead 1, Wait 1, Retransmit 5
    oob-resync timeout 40

[Truncated Output]

  Simple password authentication enabled
```

Finally, verify connectivity is still present by pinging end-to-end from R4 to R3 for example:

```
R3#ping 10.0.1.4 size 1500 repeat 10 source fastethernet 0/0

Type escape sequence to abort.
Sending 10, 1500-byte ICMP Echos to 10.0.1.4, timeout is 2 seconds:
Packet sent with a source address of 150.3.3.3
!!!!!!!!!!
Success rate is 100 percent (10/10), round-trip min/avg/max = 204/206/212 ms
```

FINAL ROUTER CONFIGURATIONS

R1

```
R1#term len 0
R1#sh run
Building configuration...

Current configuration : 1317 bytes
!
version 12.4
service timestamps debug datetime msec
service timestamps log datetime msec
```

```
no service password-encryption
!
hostname R1
!
boot-start-marker
boot-end-marker
!
no logging console
!
no aaa new-model
no network-clock-participate slot 1
no network-clock-participate wic 0
ip cef
!
no ip domain lookup
ip auth-proxy max-nodata-conns 3
ip admission max-nodata-conns 3
!
interface Tunnel0
 ip address 11.0.0.1 255.255.255.252
 ip ospf authentication-key CCNP
 ip ospf 1 area 0
 tunnel source Serial0/0
 tunnel destination 10.0.0.2
!
interface FastEthernet0/0
 ip address 10.0.1.1 255.255.255.0
 ip ospf authentication-key CCNP
 ip ospf dead-interval minimal hello-multiplier 4
 ip ospf 1 area 0
 duplex auto
 speed auto
!
interface Serial0/0
 ip address 10.0.0.1 255.255.255.252
 ip ospf 1 area 1
 clock rate 2000000
!
interface Serial0/1
 ip address 10.0.0.5 255.255.255.252
!
router ospf 1
 router-id 1.1.1.1
 log-adjacency-changes
 area 0 authentication
 area 1 stub no-summary
 redistribute connected subnets
 redistribute static subnets
!
ip forward-protocol nd
ip route 150.3.3.0 255.255.255.0 Serial0/1 150
!
no ip http server
no ip http secure-server
!
control-plane
!
line con 0
line aux 0
line vty 0 4
 login
!
end

R1#
```

R2

```
R2#term len 0
R2#sh run
Building configuration...

Current configuration : 1114 bytes
!
```

```
version 12.4
service timestamps debug datetime msec
service timestamps log datetime msec
no service password-encryption
!
hostname R2
!
boot-start-marker
boot-end-marker
!
no logging console
!
no aaa new-model
no network-clock-participate slot 1
no network-clock-participate wic 0
ip cef
!
no ip domain lookup
ip auth-proxy max-nodata-conns 3
ip admission max-nodata-conns 3
!
interface Tunnel0
 ip address 11.0.0.2 255.255.255.252
 ip ospf authentication-key CCNP
 ip ospf 2 area 0
 tunnel source Serial0/0
 tunnel destination 10.0.0.1
!
interface FastEthernet0/0
 ip address 150.2.2.2 255.255.255.0
 ip ospf 2 area 1
 duplex auto
 speed auto
!
interface Serial0/0
 ip address 10.0.0.2 255.255.255.252
 ip ospf 2 area 1
!
interface Serial0/1
 ip address 10.0.0.9 255.255.255.252
 ip ospf 2 area 2
!
router ospf 2
 router-id 2.2.2.2
 log-adjacency-changes
 area 0 authentication
 area 1 stub
!
ip forward-protocol nd
!
no ip http server
no ip http secure-server
!
control-plane
!
line con 0
line aux 0
line vty 0 4
 login
!
end

R2#
```

R3

```
R3#term len 0
R3#sh run
Building configuration...

Current configuration : 1273 bytes
!
version 12.4
```

```
service timestamps debug datetime msec
service timestamps log datetime msec
no service password-encryption
!
hostname R3
!
boot-start-marker
boot-end-marker
!
no logging console
!
no aaa new-model
no network-clock-participate slot 1
no network-clock-participate wic 0
ip cef
!
no ip domain lookup
ip auth-proxy max-nodata-conns 3
ip admission max-nodata-conns 3
!
interface FastEthernet0/0
 ip address 150.3.3.3 255.255.255.0
 ip ospf 3 area 2
 duplex auto
 speed auto
!
interface Serial1/0
 ip address 10.0.0.6 255.255.255.252
 clock rate 128000
!
interface Serial1/1
 ip address 10.0.0.10 255.255.255.252
 ip ospf 3 area 2
 clock rate 128000
!
interface Serial1/2
 no ip address
 shutdown
 clock rate 128000
!
interface Serial1/3
 no ip address
 shutdown
!
interface Serial1/4
 no ip address
 shutdown
!
interface Serial1/5
 no ip address
 shutdown
!
interface Serial1/6
 no ip address
 shutdown
!
interface Serial1/7
 no ip address
 shutdown
!
router ospf 3
 router-id 3.3.3.3
 log-adjacency-changes
!
ip forward-protocol nd
ip route 0.0.0.0 0.0.0.0 Serial1/0
!
no ip http server
no ip http secure-server
!
control-plane
!
line con 0
line aux 0
line vty 0 4
```

```
 login
 !
 end

 R3#
```

R4

```
 R4#term len 0
 R4#sh run
 Building configuration...

 Current configuration : 961 bytes
 !
 version 12.4
 service timestamps debug datetime msec
 service timestamps log datetime msec
 no service password-encryption
 !
 hostname R4
 !
 boot-start-marker
 boot-end-marker
 !
 no logging console
 !
 no aaa new-model
 no network-clock-participate slot 1
 no network-clock-participate wic 0
 ip cef
 !
 no ip domain lookup
 ip auth-proxy max-nodata-conns 3
 ip admission max-nodata-conns 3
 !
 interface FastEthernet0/0
  ip address 10.0.1.4 255.255.255.0
  ip ospf authentication-key CCNP
  ip ospf dead-interval minimal hello-multiplier 4
  ip ospf 4 area 0
  duplex auto
  speed auto
 !
 interface Serial0/0
  no ip address
  shutdown
 !
 interface Serial0/1
  no ip address
  shutdown
 !
 router ospf 4
  router-id 4.4.4.4
  log-adjacency-changes
  area 0 authentication
 !
 ip forward-protocol nd
 !
 no ip http server
 no ip http secure-server
 !
 control-plane
 !
 line con 0
 line aux 0
 line vty 0 4
  login
 !
 end

 R4#
```

CCNP LAB 23

OSPF Multi-Technology Lab

Lab Objective:

The focus of this lab is to understand OSPF implementation and configuration in Cisco IOS routers. Additional technologies tested include summarization and path control.

Lab Topology:

The lab network topology is illustrated below:

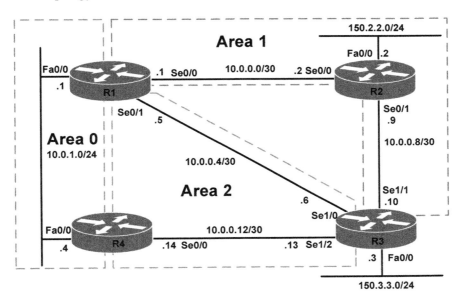

IMPORTANT NOTE: If you are using the www.howtonetwork.net racks, please bring up the LAN interfaces connected to the routers by issuing the `no shutdown` command on the connected switches. If you are using a home lab with no Switches, you can bring up the LAN interfaces using the following configurations on your routers:

```
interface fastethernet 0/0
  no keepalive
  loopback
  no shutdown
```

Alternately, you can simply connect the interfaces to a hub or switch if you have one available in your own lab.

Task 1

Configure hostnames and IP addressing on all routers as illustrated in the network topology.

Task 2

Using either inter-based or legacy 'network' statement configuration, configure the OSPF backbone on the LAN segment between R1 and R4.

Task 3

Using either inter-based or legacy 'network' statement configuration, configure OSPF area 1 between R1, R2 and R3. Do NOT advertise the 150.3.3.0/24 subnet on R3 via OSPF.

Task 4

Using either inter-based or legacy 'network' statement configuration, configure OSPF area 2 between R1, R3 and R4. Do NOT advertise the 150.3.3.0/24 subnet on R3 via OSPF.

Task 5

Configure the following secondary subnets on the LAN interface of R3:
* 172.16.12.0/24
* 172.16.13.0/24
* 172.16.14.0/24
* 172.16.15.0/24

Next, inject the 150.3.3.0/24 subnet as a Type 2 External LSA. The 172.16.x.x/24 subnets should be injected into OSPF as Type 1 External LSAs. You can use only ONE prefix list or ACL in your solution. Verify your configuration using the appropriate commands.

Task 6

Advertise a single route for the 172.16.x.x/24 subnets connected to the LAN interface on R3. This single route should be assigned a route tag of 3333. This summary address should NOT be present in OSPF area 0; however, it should be in OSPF areas 1 and 2. Verify your configuration.

Task 7

Configure OSPF so that R3 prefers the path via R2 to reach the OSPF backbone, i.e. 10.0.1.0/24. R1 should also be configured to prefer the path via R2 to reach the 150.3.3.0/24 subnet. This should be completed without modifying interface bandwidths. Verify this configuration using the appropriate commands.

LAB VALIDATION

Task 1

```
Router(config)#hostname R1
R1(config)#interface fastethernet 0/0
R1(config-if)#no shutdown
R1(config-if)#ip address 10.0.1.1 255.255.255.0
R1(config-if)#exit
R1(config)#interface serial 0/0
R1(config-if)#no shutdown
R1(config-if)#ip address 10.0.0.1 255.255.255.252
R1(config-if)#clock rate 2000000
R1(config-if)#exit
R1(config)#interface serial 0/1
R1(config-if)#no shutdown
R1(config-if)#ip address 10.0.0.5 255.255.255.252
R1(config-if)#exit

Router(config)#hostname R2
R2(config)#interface fastethernet 0/0
R2(config-if)#no shutdown
R2(config-if)#ip address 150.2.2.2 255.255.255.0
R2(config-if)#exit
R2(config)#interface serial 0/0
R2(config-if)#no shutdown
R2(config-if)#ip address 10.0.0.2 255.255.255.252
R2(config-if)#exit
R2(config)#interface serial 0/0
```

```
R2(config-if)#no shutdown
R2(config-if)#ip address 10.0.0.9 255.255.255.252
R2(config-if)#exit

Router(config)#hostname R3
R3(config)#interface fastethernet 0/0
R3(config-if)#no shutdown
R3(config-if)#ip address 150.3.3.3 255.255.255.0
R3(config-if)#exit
R3(config)#interface serial 1/0
R3(config-if)#no shutdown
R3(config-if)#ip address 10.0.0.6 255.255.255.252
R3(config-if)#clock rate 128000
R3(config-if)#exit
R3(config)#interface serial 1/1
R3(config-if)#no shutdown
R3(config-if)#ip address 10.0.0.10 255.255.255.252
R3(config-if)#clock rate 128000
R3(config-if)#exit
R3(config)#interface serial 1/2
R3(config-if)#no shutdown
R3(config-if)#ip address 10.0.0.13 255.255.255.252
R3(config-if)#clock rate 128000
R2(config-if)#exit

Router(config)#hostname R4
R4(config)#interface fastethernet 0/0
R4(config-if)#no shutdown
R4(config-if)#ip address 10.0.1.4 255.255.255.0
R4(config-if)#exit
R4(config)#interface serial 0/0
R4(config-if)#no shutdown
R4(config-if)#ip address 10.0.0.14 255.255.255.252
R4(config-if)#exit
```

Task 2

```
R1(config)#router ospf 1
R1(config-router)#router-id 1.1.1.1
R1(config-router)#network 10.0.1.1 0.0.0.0 area 0
R1(config-router)#exit

R4(config)#router ospf 4
R4(config-router)#router-id 4.4.4.4
R4(config-router)#network 10.0.1.4 0.0.0.0 area 0
R4(config-router)#exit
```

Verify your configuration using the show ip ospf neighbor command:

```
R4#show ip ospf neighbor

Neighbor ID     Pri   State      Dead Time   Address      Interface
1.1.1.1           1   FULL/DR    00:00:37    10.0.1.1     FastEthernet0/0
```

Task 3

```
R1(config)#interface serial 0/0
R1(config-if)#ip ospf 1 area 0
R1(config-if)#exit

R2(config)#router ospf 2
R2(config-router)#router-id 2.2.2.2
R2(config-router)#exit
R2(config)#interface fastethernet 0/0
R2(config-if)#ip ospf 2 area 1
R2(config-if)#exit
R2(config)#interface serial 0/0
R2(config-if)#ip ospf 2 area 1
R2(config-if)#exit
R2(config)#interface serial 0/1
R2(config-if)#ip ospf 2 area 1
R2(config-if)#exit
```

```
R3(config-if)#router ospf 3
R3(config-router)#router-id 3.3.3.3
R3(config-router)#network 10.0.0.10 0.0.0.0 area 1
R3(config-router)#exit
```

Verify your configuration using the show ip ospf neighbor command:

```
R1#show ip ospf neighbor

Neighbor ID     Pri   State        Dead Time    Address      Interface
4.4.4.4           1   FULL/BDR     00:00:36     10.0.1.4     FastEthernet0/0
2.2.2.2           0   FULL/  -     00:00:30     10.0.0.2     Serial0/0

R2#show ip ospf neighbor

Neighbor ID     Pri   State        Dead Time    Address      Interface
3.3.3.3           0   FULL/  -     00:00:33     10.0.0.10    Serial0/1
1.1.1.1           0   FULL/  -     00:00:38     10.0.0.1     Serial0/0

R3#show ip ospf neighbor

Neighbor ID     Pri   State        Dead Time    Address      Interface
2.2.2.2           0   FULL/  -     00:00:39     10.0.0.9     Serial1/1
```

Task 4

```
R1(config)#interface serial 0/1
R1(config-if)#ip ospf 1 area 2
R1(config-if)#exit

R3(config)#interface serial 1/0
R3(config-if)#ip ospf 3 area 2
R3(config-if)#exit
R3(config)#interface serial 1/2
R3(config-if)#ip ospf 3 area 2
R3(config-if)#exit

R4(config)#router ospf 4
R4(config-router)#network 10.0.0.14 0.0.0.0 area 2
R4(config-router)#exit
```

Verify your configuration using the show ip ospf neighbor command:

```
R1#show ip ospf neighbor

Neighbor ID     Pri   State        Dead Time    Address      Interface
4.4.4.4           1   FULL/BDR     00:00:34     10.0.1.4     FastEthernet0/0
2.2.2.2           0   FULL/  -     00:00:37     10.0.0.2     Serial0/0
3.3.3.3           0   FULL/  -     00:00:35     10.0.0.6     Serial0/1

R2#show ip ospf neighbor

Neighbor ID     Pri   State        Dead Time    Address      Interface
3.3.3.3           0   FULL/  -     00:00:38     10.0.0.10    Serial0/1
1.1.1.1           0   FULL/  -     00:00:32     10.0.0.1     Serial0/0

R3#show ip ospf neighbor

Neighbor ID     Pri   State        Dead Time    Address      Interface
2.2.2.2           0   FULL/  -     00:00:31     10.0.0.9     Serial1/1
4.4.4.4           0   FULL/  -     00:00:32     10.0.0.14    Serial1/2
1.1.1.1           0   FULL/  -     00:00:39     10.0.0.5     Serial1/0

R4#show ip ospf neighbor

Neighbor ID     Pri   State        Dead Time    Address      Interface
1.1.1.1           1   FULL/DR      00:00:31     10.0.1.1     FastEthernet0/0
3.3.3.3           0   FULL/  -     00:00:38     10.0.0.13    Serial0/0
```

Task 5

This task has two requirements. The first requirement is simple and entails configuring the LAN interface with the specified secondary subnets. This is completed as follows:

```
R3(config)#interface fastethernet 0/0
R3(config-if)#ip address 172.16.12.3 255.255.255.0 secondary
R3(config-if)#ip address 172.16.13.3 255.255.255.0 secondary
R3(config-if)#ip address 172.16.14.3 255.255.255.0 secondary
R3(config-if)#ip address 172.16.15.3 255.255.255.0 secondary
R3(config-if)#exit
```

The second part of this task requires redistribution into OSPF using a route map. This route map can match against an ACL or IP prefix list. This task is completed as follows:

```
R3(config)#ip prefix-list PRIMARY seq 5 permit 150.3.3.0/24
R3(config)#route-map CONNECTED permit 10
R3(config-route-map)#match ip address prefix-list PRIMARY
R3(config-route-map)#exit
R3(config)#route-map CONNECTED permit 20
R3(config-route-map)#set metric-type type-1
R3(config-route-map)#exit
R3(config)#router ospf 3
R3(config-router)#redistribute connected subnets route-map CONNECTED
R3(config-router)#exit
```

Verify your configuration by looking at the Link State Database or simply by looking at the IP routing tables of any other routers in the domain:

```
R4#show ip route ospf | include E1|E2
O E1    172.16.12.0 [110/84] via 10.0.0.13, 00:01:56, Serial0/0
O E1    172.16.13.0 [110/84] via 10.0.0.13, 00:01:56, Serial0/0
O E1    172.16.14.0 [110/84] via 10.0.0.13, 00:01:56, Serial0/0
O E1    172.16.15.0 [110/84] via 10.0.0.13, 00:01:56, Serial0/0
O E2    150.3.3.0 [110/20] via 10.0.0.13, 00:01:56, Serial0/0
```

Task 6

The first part of this task requires summarization. Because the 172.16.x.x/24 subnets have been redistributed into OSPF, the summary-address command must be used on the ASBR to generate the summary route for these subnets. The first part of the task is completed as follows:

```
R3(config)#router ospf 3
R3(config-router)#summary-address 172.16.12.0 255.255.252.0 tag 3333
R3(config-router)#exit
```

Verify your configuration using the show ip ospf database command:

```
R3#show ip ospf database external self-originate

            OSPF Router with ID (3.3.3.3) (Process ID 3)

                Type-5 AS External Link States
[Truncated Output]

   LS age: 66
   Options: (No TOS-capability, DC)
   LS Type: AS External Link
   Link State ID: 172.16.12.0 (External Network Number )
   Advertising Router: 3.3.3.3
   LS Seq Number: 80000002
   Checksum: 0x2715
   Length: 36
   Network Mask: /22
        Metric Type: 1 (Comparable directly to link state metric)
        TOS: 0
        Metric: 20
        Forward Address: 0.0.0.0
        External Route Tag: 3333
```

To complete the second part of this task, you need to configure distribute lists so that the prefix will not be present in area 0. This task is completed as follows:

```
R1(config)#route-map TAG-3333 deny 10
R1(config-route-map)#match tag 3333
R1(config-route-map)#exit
R1(config)#route-map TAG-3333 permit 20
R1(config-route-map)#exit
R1(config)#router ospf 1
R1(config-router)#distribute-list route-map TAG-3333 in
R1(config-router)#exit

R4(config)#route-map TAG-3333 deny 10
R4(config-route-map)#match tag 3333
R4(config-route-map)#exit
R4(config)#route-map TAG-3333 permit 20
R4(config-route-map)#exit
R4(config)#router ospf 4
R4(config-router)#distribute-list route-map TAG-3333 in
R4(config-router)#exit
```

Verify your configuration by looking at the routing tables on R1, R2 and R4. Only R2 should have a route for the 172.16.12.0/22 prefix:

```
R4#show ip route ospf
      10.0.0.0/8 is variably subnetted, 5 subnets, 2 masks
O IA    10.0.0.8/30 [110/129] via 10.0.1.1, 00:00:52, FastEthernet0/0
O IA    10.0.0.0/30 [110/65] via 10.0.1.1, 00:00:52, FastEthernet0/0
O       10.0.0.4/30 [110/845] via 10.0.0.13, 00:00:52, Serial0/0
      150.2.0.0/24 is subnetted, 1 subnets
O IA    150.2.2.0 [110/66] via 10.0.1.1, 00:00:52, FastEthernet0/0
      150.3.0.0/24 is subnetted, 1 subnets
O E2    150.3.3.0 [110/20] via 10.0.0.13, 00:00:52, Serial0/0

R2#show ip route ospf
      172.16.0.0/22 is subnetted, 1 subnets
O E1    172.16.12.0 [110/84] via 10.0.0.10, 00:12:01, Serial0/1
      10.0.0.0/8 is variably subnetted, 5 subnets, 2 masks
O IA    10.0.0.12/30 [110/909] via 10.0.0.1, 00:20:02, Serial0/0
O IA    10.0.1.0/24 [110/65] via 10.0.0.1, 00:20:02, Serial0/0
O IA    10.0.0.4/30 [110/128] via 10.0.0.1, 00:20:02, Serial0/0
      150.3.0.0/24 is subnetted, 1 subnets
O E2    150.3.3.0 [110/20] via 10.0.0.10, 00:19:52, Serial0/1

R4#show ip route ospf
      10.0.0.0/8 is variably subnetted, 5 subnets, 2 masks
O IA    10.0.0.8/30 [110/129] via 10.0.1.1, 00:00:52, FastEthernet0/0
O IA    10.0.0.0/30 [110/65] via 10.0.1.1, 00:00:52, FastEthernet0/0
O       10.0.0.4/30 [110/845] via 10.0.0.13, 00:00:52, Serial0/0
      150.2.0.0/24 is subnetted, 1 subnets
O IA    150.2.2.0 [110/66] via 10.0.1.1, 00:00:52, FastEthernet0/0
      150.3.0.0/24 is subnetted, 1 subnets
O E2    150.3.3.0 [110/20] via 10.0.0.13, 00:00:52, Serial0/0
```

NOTE: As described in the ROUTE guide, filtering using distribute lists prevents the prefix from being accepted by the router and installed into the RIB; however, the Link State Advertisement (LSA) for the prefix will still be present in the Link State Database (LSDB). Consider, for example, the LSDB on R1, which still shows the LSA for the 172.16.12.0/22 prefix even though the prefix itself is filtered via the distribute list:

```
R1#show ip ospf database external

        OSPF Router with ID (1.1.1.1) (Process ID 1)

        Type-5 AS External Link States

Routing Bit Set on this LSA
LS age: 1484
Options: (No TOS-capability, DC)
```

```
LS Type: AS External Link
Link State ID: 150.3.3.0 (External Network Number )
Advertising Router: 3.3.3.3
LS Seq Number: 80000001
Checksum: 0xA255
Length: 36
Network Mask: /24
        Metric Type: 2 (Larger than any link state path)
        TOS: 0
        Metric: 20
        Forward Address: 0.0.0.0
        External Route Tag: 0

Routing Bit Set on this LSA
LS age: 999
Options: (No TOS-capability, DC)
LS Type: AS External Link
Link State ID: 172.16.12.0 (External Network Number )
Advertising Router: 3.3.3.3
LS Seq Number: 80000002
Checksum: 0x2715
Length: 36
Network Mask: /22
        Metric Type: 1 (Comparable directly to link state metric)
        TOS: 0
        Metric: 20
        Forward Address: 0.0.0.0
        External Route Tag: 3333
```

Task 7

This task is completed by modifying the default interface OSPF costs using the `ip ospf cost` interface configuration command. You can complete this task by increasing the cost of the R3-R1 and R3-R4 links OR lowering the cost of the R1-R2 and R2-R3 links. Either option will be ok:

```
R1(config)#interface serial 0/0
R1(config-if)#ip ospf cost 1
R1(config-if)#exit

R2(config)#interface serial 0/0
R2(config-if)#ip ospf cost 1
R2(config-if)#exit
R2(config)#interface serial 0/1
R2(config-if)#ip ospf cost 1
R2(config-if)#exit

R3(config)#interface serial 1/1
R3(config-if)#ip ospf cost 1
R3(config-if)#exit
```

Verify your configuration by looking at the routing tables of R1 and R3:

```
R1#show ip route ospf
     10.0.0.0/8 is variably subnetted, 5 subnets, 2 masks
O       10.0.0.8/30 [110/2] via 10.0.0.2, 00:00:35, Serial0/0
O       10.0.0.12/30 [110/845] via 10.0.0.6, 00:15:05, Serial0/1
     150.2.0.0/24 is subnetted, 1 subnets
O       150.2.2.0 [110/2] via 10.0.0.2, 00:00:35, Serial0/0
     150.3.0.0/24 is subnetted, 1 subnets
O E2    150.3.3.0 [110/20] via 10.0.0.2, 00:00:35, Serial0/0

R3#show ip route ospf
     172.16.0.0/16 is variably subnetted, 5 subnets, 2 masks
O       172.16.12.0/22 is a summary, 00:23:36, Null0
     10.0.0.0/8 is variably subnetted, 5 subnets, 2 masks
O       10.0.0.0/30 [110/2] via 10.0.0.9, 00:00:42, Serial1/1
O IA    10.0.1.0/24 [110/3] via 10.0.0.9, 00:00:42, Serial1/1
     150.2.0.0/24 is subnetted, 1 subnets
O       150.2.2.0 [110/2] via 10.0.0.9, 00:00:42, Serial1/1
```

FINAL ROUTER CONFIGURATIONS

R1

```
R1#term len 0
R1#sh run
Building configuration...

Current configuration : 1081 bytes
!
version 12.4
service timestamps debug datetime msec
service timestamps log datetime msec
no service password-encryption
!
hostname R1
!
boot-start-marker
boot-end-marker
!
no logging console
!
no aaa new-model
no network-clock-participate slot 1
no network-clock-participate wic 0
ip cef
!
no ip domain lookup
ip auth-proxy max-nodata-conns 3
ip admission max-nodata-conns 3
!
interface FastEthernet0/0
 ip address 10.0.1.1 255.255.255.0
 duplex auto
 speed auto
!
interface Serial0/0
 ip address 10.0.0.1 255.255.255.252
 ip ospf cost 1
 ip ospf 1 area 1
 clock rate 2000000
!
interface Serial0/1
 ip address 10.0.0.5 255.255.255.252
 ip ospf 1 area 2
!
router ospf 1
 router-id 1.1.1.1
 log-adjacency-changes
 network 10.0.1.1 0.0.0.0 area 0
 distribute-list route-map TAG-3333 in
!
ip forward-protocol nd
!
no ip http server
no ip http secure-server
!
route-map TAG-3333 deny 10
 match tag 3333
!
route-map TAG-3333 permit 20
!
control-plane
!
line con 0
line aux 0
line vty 0 4
 login
!
end

R1#
```

R2

```
R2#term len 0
R2#sh run
Building configuration...

Current configuration : 948 bytes
!
version 12.4
service timestamps debug datetime msec
service timestamps log datetime msec
no service password-encryption
!
hostname R2
!
boot-start-marker
boot-end-marker
!
no logging console
!
no aaa new-model
no network-clock-participate slot 1
no network-clock-participate wic 0
ip cef
!
no ip domain lookup
ip auth-proxy max-nodata-conns 3
ip admission max-nodata-conns 3
!
interface FastEthernet0/0
 ip address 150.2.2.2 255.255.255.0
 ip ospf 2 area 1
 duplex auto
 speed auto
!
interface Serial0/0
 ip address 10.0.0.2 255.255.255.252
 ip ospf cost 1
 ip ospf 2 area 1
!
interface Serial0/1
 ip address 10.0.0.9 255.255.255.252
 ip ospf cost 1
 ip ospf 2 area 1
!
router ospf 2
 router-id 2.2.2.2
 log-adjacency-changes
!
ip forward-protocol nd
!
no ip http server
no ip http secure-server
!
control-plane
!
line con 0
line aux 0
line vty 0 4
 login
!
end

R2#
```

R3

```
R3#term len 0
R3#sh run
Building configuration...

Current configuration : 1774 bytes
!
version 12.4
service timestamps debug datetime msec
service timestamps log datetime msec
no service password-encryption
!
```

```
hostname R3
!
boot-start-marker
boot-end-marker
!
no logging console
!
no aaa new-model
no network-clock-participate slot 1
no network-clock-participate wic 0
ip cef
!
no ip domain lookup
ip auth-proxy max-nodata-conns 3
ip admission max-nodata-conns 3
!
interface FastEthernet0/0
 ip address 172.16.12.3 255.255.255.0 secondary
 ip address 172.16.13.3 255.255.255.0 secondary
 ip address 172.16.14.3 255.255.255.0 secondary
 ip address 172.16.15.3 255.255.255.0 secondary
 ip address 150.3.3.3 255.255.255.0
 duplex auto
 speed auto
!
interface Serial1/0
 ip address 10.0.0.6 255.255.255.252
 ip ospf 3 area 2
 clock rate 128000
!
interface Serial1/1
 ip address 10.0.0.10 255.255.255.252
 ip ospf cost 1
 clock rate 128000
!
interface Serial1/2
 ip address 10.0.0.13 255.255.255.252
 ip ospf 3 area 2
 clock rate 128000
!
interface Serial1/3
 no ip address
 shutdown
!
interface Serial1/4
 no ip address
 shutdown
!
interface Serial1/5
 no ip address
 shutdown
!
interface Serial1/6
 no ip address
 shutdown
!
interface Serial1/7
 no ip address
 shutdown
!
router ospf 3
 router-id 3.3.3.3
 log-adjacency-changes
 summary-address 172.16.12.0 255.255.252.0 tag 3333
 redistribute connected subnets route-map CONNECTED
 network 10.0.0.10 0.0.0.0 area 1
!
ip forward-protocol nd
!
no ip http server
no ip http secure-server
!
ip prefix-list PRIMARY seq 5 permit 150.3.3.0/24
!
route-map CONNECTED permit 10
 match ip address prefix-list PRIMARY
!
route-map CONNECTED permit 20
 set metric-type type-1
```

```
!
control-plane
!
line con 0
line aux 0
line vty 0 4
 login
!
end

R3#
```

R4

```
R4#term len 0
R4#sh run
Building configuration...

Current configuration : 1032 bytes
!
version 12.4
service timestamps debug datetime msec
service timestamps log datetime msec
no service password-encryption
!
hostname R4
!
boot-start-marker
boot-end-marker
!
no logging console
!
no aaa new-model
no network-clock-participate slot 1
no network-clock-participate wic 0
ip cef
!
no ip domain lookup
ip auth-proxy max-nodata-conns 3
ip admission max-nodata-conns 3
!
interface FastEthernet0/0
 ip address 10.0.1.4 255.255.255.0
 duplex auto
 speed auto
!
interface Serial0/0
 ip address 10.0.0.14 255.255.255.252
!
interface Serial0/1
 no ip address
 shutdown
!
router ospf 4
 router-id 4.4.4.4
 log-adjacency-changes
 network 10.0.0.14 0.0.0.0 area 2
 network 10.0.1.4 0.0.0.0 area 0
 distribute-list route-map TAG-3333 in
!
ip forward-protocol nd
!
no ip http server
no ip http secure-server
!
route-map TAG-3333 deny 10
 match tag 3333
!
route-map TAG-3333 permit 20
!
control-plane
!
line con 0
line aux 0
line vty 0 4
 login
!
end

R4#
```

CCNP LAB 24

OSPF Multi-Technology Lab

Lab Objective:

The focus of this lab is to understand OSPF implementation and configuration in Cisco IOS routers. Additional technologies tested include Frame Relay connectivity and redistribution.

Lab Topology:

The lab network topology is illustrated below:

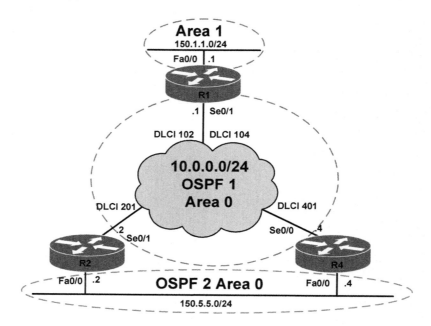

IMPORTANT NOTE: If you are using the www.howtonetwork.net racks, please bring up the LAN interfaces connected to the routers by issuing the no shutdown command on the connected switches. If you are using a home lab with no Switches, you can bring up the LAN interfaces using the following configurations on your routers:

```
interface fastethernet 0/0
 no keepalive
 loopback
 no shutdown
```

Alternately, you can simply connect the interfaces to a hub or switch if you have one available in your own lab. Also, if you are using the www.howtonetwork.net racks, configure R3 as the Frame Relay switch using the following configuration commands:

```
hostname R3-Frame-Relay-Switch
!
frame-relay switching
!
```

```
interface serial 1/0
  description 'Connected To R1 Serial 0/1'
  encapsulation frame-relay
  no ip address
  clock rate 128000
  frame-relay intf-type dce
  frame-relay route 102 interface serial 1/1 201
  frame-relay route 104 interface serial 1/2 401
  no shutdown
!
interface serial 1/1
  description 'Connected To R2 Serial 0/1'
  encapsulation frame-relay
  no ip address
  clock rate 128000
  frame-relay intf-type dce
  frame-relay route 201 interface serial 1/0 102
  no shutdown
!
interface serial 1/2
  description 'Connected To R4 Serial 0/0'
  encapsulation frame-relay
  no ip address
  clock rate 128000
  frame-relay intf-type dce
  frame-relay route 401 interface serial 1/0 104
  no shutdown
!
end
```

Task 1

Configure hostnames and IP addressing on all routers as illustrated in the network topology.

Task 2

Configure the Frame Relay network so that all routers can ping each others' WAN interfaces. Verify your configuration by pinging the WAN interfaces of all routers from each other.

Task 3

Using interface-based configuration, configure OSPF using process ID number 1 on all routers for the Frame Relay WAN connecting routers R1, R2, and R4. Use the default network type and ensure that R1 is always elected DR even if it fails and comes back up. Verify your configuration.

Task 4

Using interface-based configuration, enable OSPF for the LAN segment connected to R1. This LAN segment should reside on OSPF area 1. No Hellos should be sent on this segment.

Task 5

Using interface-based configuration, configure OSPF using process ID number 2 on the LAN segment connected to R2 and R4. Ensure that no DR/BDR election takes place on this segment; however, ensure that multiple routers can still exist on the segment.

Task 6

Configure and perform mutual redistribution between OSPF process 1 and OSPF process 2 on routers R2 and R4. Ensure that routes from one process are not re-advertised back to the same process. You are NOT allowed to use any ACLs or IP prefix lists in your solution. Verify the configuration using the appropriate commands.

Task 7

Configure your network so that R1 prefers the path via R2 to reach the 150.5.5.0/24 subnet. In the event that R2 is down, the path via R4 should be used. Additionally, configure R4 so that it prefers the path via R2 to reach the 150.1.1.0/24 subnet. In the event that R2 is down, it should use the Frame Relay WAN connection to R1. Verify your configuration.

LAB VALIDATION

Task 1

```
Router(config)#hostname R1
R1(config)#interface fastethernet 0/0
R1(config-if)#no shutdown
R1(config-if)#ip address 150.1.1.1 255.255.255.0
R1(config-if)#exit
R1(config)#interface serial 0/1
R1(config-if)#ip address 10.0.0.1 255.255.255.0
R1(config-if)#no shutdown
R1(config-if)#encapsulation frame-relay
R1(config-if)#exit

Router(config)#hostname R2
R2(config)#interface fastethernet 0/0
R2(config-if)#no shutdown
R2(config-if)#ip address 150.5.5.2 255.255.255.0
R2(config-if)#exit
R2(config)#interface serial 0/1
R2(config-if)#ip address 10.0.0.2 255.255.255.0
R2(config-if)#no shutdown
R2(config-if)#encapsulation frame-relay
R2(config-if)#exit

Router(config)#hostname R4
R4(config)#interface fastethernet 0/0
R4(config-if)#no shutdown
R4(config-if)#ip address 150.5.5.4 255.255.255.0
R4(config-if)#exit
R4(config)#interface serial 0/0
R4(config-if)#ip address 10.0.0.4 255.255.255.0
R4(config-if)#no shutdown
R4(config-if)#encapsulation frame-relay
R4(config-if)#exit
```

Task 2

Although Frame Relay configuration is not a CCNP topic, per se, it is still important that you remember your Frame Relay configurations from the CCNA. The task is completed as follows:

```
R1(config)#interface serial 0/1
R1(config-if)#frame-relay map ip 10.0.0.2 102 broadcast
R1(config-if)#frame-relay map ip 10.0.0.4 104 broadcast
R1(config-if)#exit
```

On the spoke routers, because the same DLCI is being used, the broadcast keyword should only be specified once to avoid duplicate Broadcast packets across the Frame Relay WAN. This task is completed as follows:

```
R2(config)#interface serial 0/1
R2(config-if)#frame-relay map ip 10.0.0.1 201 broadcast
R2(config-if)#frame-relay map ip 10.0.0.4 201
R2(config-if)#exit

R4(config)#interface serial 0/0
R4(config-if)#frame-relay map ip 10.0.0.1 401 broadcast
R4(config-if)#frame-relay map ip 10.0.0.2 401
R4(config-if)#exit
```

Verify your Frame Relay configuration using the show frame-relay map command:
```
R1#show frame-relay map
Serial0/1 (up): ip 10.0.0.2 dlci 102(0x66,0x1860), static,
                broadcast,
                CISCO, status defined, active
Serial0/1 (up): ip 10.0.0.4 dlci 104(0x68,0x1880), static,
                broadcast,
                CISCO, status defined, active
```

```
R2#show frame-relay map
Serial0/1 (up): ip 10.0.0.1 dlci 201(0xC9,0x3090), static,
                broadcast,
                CISCO, status defined, active
Serial0/1 (up): ip 10.0.0.4 dlci 201(0xC9,0x3090), static,
                CISCO, status defined, active

R4#show frame-relay map
Serial0/0 (up): ip 10.0.0.1 dlci 401(0x191,0x6410), static,
                broadcast,
                CISCO, status defined, active
Serial0/0 (up): ip 10.0.0.2 dlci 401(0x191,0x6410), static,
                CISCO, status defined, active
```

Finally, verify that you can ping between all routers across the Frame Relay WAN:

```
R1#ping 10.0.0.2 repeat 10

Type escape sequence to abort.
Sending 10, 100-byte ICMP Echos to 10.0.0.2, timeout is 2 seconds:
!!!!!!!!!!
Success rate is 100 percent (10/10), round-trip min/avg/max = 28/29/32 ms
R1#
R1#ping 10.0.0.4 repeat 10

Type escape sequence to abort.
Sending 10, 100-byte ICMP Echos to 10.0.0.4, timeout is 2 seconds:
!!!!!!!!!!
Success rate is 100 percent (10/10), round-trip min/avg/max = 28/29/32 ms

R2#ping 10.0.0.1 repeat 10

Type escape sequence to abort.
Sending 10, 100-byte ICMP Echos to 10.0.0.1, timeout is 2 seconds:
!!!!!!!!!!
Success rate is 100 percent (10/10), round-trip min/avg/max = 28/30/32 ms
R2#
R2#ping 10.0.0.4 repeat 10

Type escape sequence to abort.
Sending 10, 100-byte ICMP Echos to 10.0.0.4, timeout is 2 seconds:
!!!!!!!!!!
Success rate is 100 percent (10/10), round-trip min/avg/max = 56/59/64 ms

R4#ping 10.0.0.1 repeat 10

Type escape sequence to abort.
Sending 10, 100-byte ICMP Echos to 10.0.0.1, timeout is 2 seconds:
!!!!!!!!!!
Success rate is 100 percent (10/10), round-trip min/avg/max = 28/34/52 ms
R4#
R4#ping 10.0.0.2 repeat 10

Type escape sequence to abort.
Sending 10, 100-byte ICMP Echos to 10.0.0.2, timeout is 2 seconds:
!!!!!!!!!!
Success rate is 100 percent (10/10), round-trip min/avg/max = 56/58/60 ms
```

Task 3

In order to ensure that R1 is always elected DR even if it fails and comes back up, you need to disable DR/BDR election on R2 and R4 by assigning them an OSPF priority of 0. Also, when configuring OSPF on NBMA networks, you need to manually specify neighbors, even though the broadcast keyword has been specified for the static Frame Relay map statements:

```
R1(config)#router ospf 1
R1(config-router)#router-id 1.1.1.1
R1(config-router)#neighbor 10.0.0.2
R1(config-router)#neighbor 10.0.0.4
R1(config-router)#exit
R1(config)#interface serial 0/1
```

```
R1(config-if)#ip ospf 1 area 0
R1(config-if)#exit

R2(config)#router ospf 1
R2(config-router)#router-id 2.2.2.2
R2(config-router)#neighbor 10.0.0.1
R2(config-router)#exit
R2(config)#interface serial 0/1
R2(config-if)#ip ospf 1 area 0
R2(config-if)#ip ospf priority 0
R2(config-if)#exit

R4(config)#router ospf 1
R4(config-router)#router-id 4.4.4.4
R4(config-router)#exit
R4(config)#interface serial 0/0
R4(config-if)#ip ospf 1 area 0
R4(config-if)#ip ospf priority 0
R4(config-if)#exit
```

Verify your configuration using the show ip ospf neighbor command:

```
R1#show ip ospf neighbor

Neighbor ID    Pri   State           Dead Time   Address     Interface
2.2.2.2         0    FULL/DROTHER    00:01:46    10.0.0.2    Serial0/1
4.4.4.4         0    FULL/DROTHER    00:01:57    10.0.0.4    Serial0/1

R2#show ip ospf neighbor

Neighbor ID    Pri   State           Dead Time   Address     Interface
1.1.1.1         1    FULL/DR         00:01:39    10.0.0.1    Serial0/1

R4#show ip ospf neighbor

Neighbor ID    Pri   State           Dead Time   Address     Interface
1.1.1.1         1    FULL/DR         00:01:31    10.0.0.1    Serial0/0
```

Task 4

```
R1(config)#router ospf 1
R1(config-router)#passive-interface fastethernet 0/0
R1(config-router)#exit
R1(config)#interface fastethernet 0/0
R1(config-if)#ip ospf 1 area 1
R1(config-if)#exit
```

Verify your configuration using the show ip ospf <options> commands:

```
R1#show ip ospf
 Routing Process "ospf 1" with ID 1.1.1.1
 Start time: 03:04:16.984, Time elapsed: 00:10:22.164

[Truncated Output]

Number of areas in this router is 2. 2 normal 0 stub 0 nssa
 Number of areas transit capable is 0
 External flood list length 0
    Area BACKBONE(0)
        Number of interfaces in this area is 1
        Area has no authentication
        SPF algorithm last executed 00:00:48.304 ago
        SPF algorithm executed 11 times
        Area ranges are
        Number of LSA 6. Checksum Sum 0x033F51
        Number of opaque link LSA 0. Checksum Sum 0x000000
        Number of DCbitless LSA 0
        Number of indication LSA 0
        Number of DoNotAge LSA 0
```

```
          Flood list length 0
     Area 1
          Number of interfaces in this area is 1
          Area has no authentication
          SPF algorithm last executed 00:00:48.304 ago
          SPF algorithm executed 2 times
          Area ranges are
          Number of LSA 2. Checksum Sum 0x014C32
          Number of opaque link LSA 0. Checksum Sum 0x000000
          Number of DCbitless LSA 0
          Number of indication LSA 0
          Number of DoNotAge LSA 0
          Flood list length 0

R1#show ip ospf interface brief
Interface    PID   Area        IP Address/Mask    Cost   State Nbrs F/C
Se0/1        1     0           10.0.0.1/24        64     DR    2/2
Fa0/0        1     1           150.1.1.1/24       1      DR    0/0
```

Task 5

To prevent DR/BDR election but allow multiple routers to exist on the same multi-access segment, you need to configure a point-to-multipoint network type:

```
R2(config)#router ospf 2
R2(config-router)#router-id 22.22.22.22
R2(config-router)#exit
R2(config)#interface fastethernet 0/0
R2(config-if)#ip ospf network point-to-multipoint
R2(config-if)#ip ospf 2 area 0
R2(config-if)#exit

R4(config)#router ospf 2
R4(config-router)#router-id 44.44.44.44
R4(config-router)#exit
R4(config)#interface fastethernet 0/0
R4(config-if)#ip ospf network point-to-multipoint
R4(config-if)#ip ospf 2 area 0
R4(config-if)#exit
```

Verify your configuration using the show ip ospf neighbor command:

```
R4#show ip ospf neighbor

Neighbor ID     Pri   State       Dead Time   Address      Interface
22.22.22.22     0     FULL/  -    00:01:48    150.5.5.2    FastEthernet0/0
1.1.1.1         1     FULL/DR     00:01:47    10.0.0.1     Serial0/0

R2#show ip ospf neighbor

Neighbor ID     Pri   State       Dead Time   Address      Interface
44.44.44.44     0     FULL/  -    00:01:49    150.5.5.4    FastEthernet0/0
1.1.1.1         1     FULL/DR     00:01:57    10.0.0.1     Serial0/1
```

Task 6

To complete this task you need to use route tags. This task is completed as follows:

```
R2(config)#route-map OSPF1-INTO-OSPF2 deny 10
R2(config-route-map)#match tag 444
R2(config-route-map)#exit
R2(config)#route-map OSPF1-INTO-OSPF2 permit 20
R2(config-route-map)#set tag 222
R2(config-route-map)#exit
R2(config)#route-map OSPF2-INTO-OSPF1 deny 10
R2(config-route-map)#match tag 444
R2(config-route-map)#exit
R2(config)#route-map OSPF2-INTO-OSPF1 permit 20
R2(config-route-map)#set tag 222
```

```
R2(config-route-map)#exit
R2(config)#router ospf 1
R2(config-router)#redistribute ospf 2 subnets route-map OSPF2-INTO-OSPF1
R2(config-router)#exit
R2(config)#router ospf 2
R2(config-router)#redistribute ospf 1 subnets route-map OSPF1-INTO-OSPF2
R2(config-router)#exit

R4(config)#route-map OSPF1-INTO-OSPF2 deny 10
R4(config-route-map)#match tag 222
R4(config-route-map)#exit
R4(config)#route-map OSPF1-INTO-OSPF2 permit 20
R4(config-route-map)#set tag 444
R4(config-route-map)#exit
R4(config)#route-map OSPF2-INTO-OSPF1 deny 10
R4(config-route-map)#match tag 222
R4(config-route-map)#exit
R4(config)#route-map OSPF2-INTO-OSPF1 permit 20
R4(config-route-map)#set tag 444
R4(config-route-map)#exit
R4(config)#router ospf 1
R4(config-router)#redistribute ospf 2 subnets route-map OSPF2-INTO-OSPF1
R4(config-router)#exit
R4(config)#router ospf 2
R4(config-router)#redistribute ospf 1 subnets route-map OSPF1-INTO-OSPF2
R4(config-router)#exit
```

While this configuration seems complex, it is actually quite simple. The logic is as follows:

When OSPF process ID 1 on R2 redistributes routes from OSPF process ID 2, it denies all routes with an administrative route tag of 444. This tag is specified when OSPF process ID 2 on R4 redistributes OSPF process ID 1 routes. This prevents R2 from re-advertising these same routes back across the Frame Relay WAN. After denying these routes, OSPF process ID 1 on R2 accepts all other routes and sets an administrative tag of 222 for those routes.

When those routes are received by R4 via the Frame Relay WAN, they are denied by OSPF process ID 2 on R4, again preventing those same routes from being re-advertised across the LAN between R2 and R4. The same logic works in the reverse direction.

Verify your configuration by looking at the Link State Database on all routers in the network:

```
R1#show ip ospf database
            OSPF Router with ID (1.1.1.1) (Process ID 1)

                Router Link States (Area 0)
```

Link ID	ADV Router	Age	Seq#	Checksum	Link count
1.1.1.1	1.1.1.1	89	0x80000004	0x00DBF5	1
2.2.2.2	2.2.2.2	900	0x80000003	0x00A226	1
4.4.4.4	4.4.4.4	191	0x80000004	0x002491	1
150.5.5.2	150.5.5.2	2459	0x80000002	0x00672F	1

```
                Net Link States (Area 0)
```

Link ID	ADV Router	Age	Seq#	Checksum
10.0.0.1	1.1.1.1	341	0x80000008	0x007E85

```
                Summary Net Link States (Area 0)
```

Link ID	ADV Router	Age	Seq#	Checksum
150.1.1.0	1.1.1.1	89	0x80000002	0x00B6E7

```
                Router Link States (Area 1)
```

Link ID	ADV Router	Age	Seq#	Checksum	Link count
1.1.1.1	1.1.1.1	89	0x80000002	0x00DEB0	1

```
                Summary Net Link States (Area 1)
```

```
Link ID          ADV Router       Age        Seq#         Checksum
10.0.0.0         1.1.1.1          91         0x80000002 0x006984

                 Summary ASB Link States (Area 1)

Link ID          ADV Router       Age        Seq#         Checksum
2.2.2.2          1.1.1.1          896        0x80000001 0x00836C
4.4.4.4          1.1.1.1          299        0x80000001 0x0027C0

                 Type-5 AS External Link States

Link ID          ADV Router       Age        Seq#         Checksum Tag
150.5.5.0        2.2.2.2          558        0x80000002 0x007DAD 222
150.5.5.0        4.4.4.4          304        0x80000001 0x00ED57 444
150.5.5.2        4.4.4.4          304        0x80000001 0x00D969 444
150.5.5.4        2.2.2.2          558        0x80000002 0x0055D1 222

R2#show ip ospf database

           OSPF Router with ID (22.22.22.22) (Process ID 2)

                 Router Link States (Area 0)

Link ID          ADV Router       Age        Seq#         Checksum Link count
22.22.22.22      22.22.22.22      916        0x80000003 0x00D6A2 2
44.44.44.44      44.44.44.44      336        0x80000003 0x00A17B 2

                 Type-5 AS External Link States

Link ID          ADV Router       Age        Seq#         Checksum Tag
10.0.0.0         22.22.22.22      597        0x80000002 0x0032FF 222
10.0.0.0         44.44.44.44      336        0x80000001 0x0048B3 444
150.1.1.0        22.22.22.22      597        0x80000002 0x0002A0 222
150.1.1.0        44.44.44.44      336        0x80000001 0x001854 444

           OSPF Router with ID (2.2.2.2) (Process ID 1)

                 Router Link States (Area 0)

Link ID          ADV Router       Age        Seq#         Checksum Link count
1.1.1.1          1.1.1.1          123        0x80000004 0x00DBF5 1
2.2.2.2          2.2.2.2          933        0x80000003 0x00A226 1
4.4.4.4          4.4.4.4          228        0x80000004 0x002491 1
150.5.5.2        150.5.5.2        2495       0x80000002 0x00672F 1

                 Net Link States (Area 0)

Link ID          ADV Router       Age        Seq#         Checksum
10.0.0.1         1.1.1.1          377        0x80000008 0x007E85

                 Summary Net Link States (Area 0)

Link ID          ADV Router       Age        Seq#         Checksum
150.1.1.0        1.1.1.1          125        0x80000002 0x00B6E7

                 Type-5 AS External Link States

Link ID          ADV Router       Age        Seq#         Checksum Tag
150.5.5.0        2.2.2.2          590        0x80000002 0x007DAD 222
150.5.5.0        4.4.4.4          339        0x80000001 0x00ED57 444
150.5.5.2        4.4.4.4          339        0x80000001 0x00D969 444
150.5.5.4        2.2.2.2          590        0x80000002 0x0055D1 222

R4#show ip ospf database

           OSPF Router with ID (44.44.44.44) (Process ID 2)

                 Router Link States (Area 0)

Link ID          ADV Router       Age        Seq#         Checksum Link count
22.22.22.22      22.22.22.22      942        0x80000003 0x00D6A2 2
44.44.44.44      44.44.44.44      361        0x80000003 0x00A17B 2

                 Type-5 AS External Link States

Link ID          ADV Router       Age        Seq#         Checksum Tag
10.0.0.0         22.22.22.22      624        0x80000002 0x0032FF 222
```

```
10.0.0.0          44.44.44.44       360        0x80000001 0x0048B3 444
150.1.1.0         22.22.22.22       623        0x80000002 0x0002A0 222
150.1.1.0         44.44.44.44       360        0x80000001 0x001854 444

                OSPF Router with ID (4.4.4.4) (Process ID 1)

                  Router Link States (Area 0)

Link ID           ADV Router        Age        Seq#       Checksum Link count
1.1.1.1           1.1.1.1           149        0x80000004 0x00DBF5 1
2.2.2.2           2.2.2.2           960        0x80000003 0x00A226 1
4.4.4.4           4.4.4.4           252        0x80000004 0x002491 1
150.5.5.2         150.5.5.2         2520       0x80000002 0x00672F 1

                  Net Link States (Area 0)

Link ID           ADV Router        Age        Seq#       Checksum
10.0.0.1          1.1.1.1           403        0x80000008 0x007E85

                  Summary Net Link States (Area 0)

Link ID           ADV Router        Age        Seq#       Checksum
150.1.1.0         1.1.1.1           151        0x80000002 0x00B6E7

                  Type-5 AS External Link States

Link ID           ADV Router        Age        Seq#       Checksum Tag
150.5.5.0         2.2.2.2           618        0x80000002 0x007DAD 222
150.5.5.0         4.4.4.4           362        0x80000001 0x00ED57 444
150.5.5.2         4.4.4.4           362        0x80000001 0x00D969 444
150.5.5.4         2.2.2.2           618        0x80000002 0x0055D1 222
```

Task 7

While the first option that might come to mind might be specifying costs using the **neighbor** command, keep in mind that you cannot specify cost when using the default NBMA network type. If you do attempt to do so, you will receive the following error message:

```
R1(config)#router ospf 1
R1(config-router)#neighbor 10.0.0.2 cost 10
R1(config-router)#
*May 10 06:59:25.183: %OSPF-4-CFG_NBR_INVAL_NBMA_OPT: Can not use configured
neighbor: cost and database-filter options are allowed only for a point-to-multipoint
network
```

Prior to any configuration changes, the routing table on R1 shows the following entries:

```
R1#show ip route ospf
        150.5.0.0/16 is variably subnetted, 3 subnets, 2 masks
O E2    150.5.5.4/32 [110/1] via 10.0.0.2, 00:24:53, Serial0/1
O E2    150.5.5.2/32 [110/1] via 10.0.0.4, 00:24:53, Serial0/1
O E2    150.5.5.0/24 [110/1] via 10.0.0.4, 00:24:53, Serial0/1
                     [110/1] via 10.0.0.2, 00:24:53, Serial0/1
```

To complete this task, you need to modify redistribution metrics. The most simple way is to increment the redistribution metric configured on R4:

```
R4(config)#router ospf 1
R4(config-router)#redis ospf 2 su route-ma OSPF2-INTO-OSPF1 met 4
R4(config-router)#end
R4#clear ip ospf redistribution
```

Following this change, the routing table on R1 now shows the following entries:

```
R1#show ip route ospf
        150.5.0.0/16 is variably subnetted, 3 subnets, 2 masks
O E2    150.5.5.4/32 [110/1] via 10.0.0.2, 00:27:18, Serial0/1
O E2    150.5.5.2/32 [110/4] via 10.0.0.4, 00:00:19, Serial0/1
O E2    150.5.5.0/24 [110/1] via 10.0.0.2, 00:00:19, Serial0/1
```

To complete the second part of this task, you need to modify default administrative distance values. You cannot use the cost because the route via the Frame Relay WAN is internal and while the route via the LAN is external. Internal will always be preferred over external. This task is completed by modifying OSPF process ID 2s administrative distance on R4. Prior to configuration changes, the routing table on R4 shows the following entries:

```
R4#show ip route ospf
     150.1.0.0/24 is subnetted, 1 subnets
O IA    150.1.1.0 [110/65] via 10.0.0.1, 00:04:41, Serial0/0
     150.5.0.0/16 is variably subnetted, 2 subnets, 2 masks
O       150.5.5.2/32 [110/1] via 150.5.5.2, 00:29:22, FastEthernet0/0
```

This task is completed as follows:

```
R4(config)#router ospf 2
R4(config-router)#distance ospf external 100
R4(config-router)#exit
```

Following this change, the routing table on R4 shows the following entries:

```
R4#show ip route ospf
     150.1.0.0/24 is subnetted, 1 subnets
O E2    150.1.1.0 [100/65] via 150.5.5.2, 00:00:42, FastEthernet0/0
     150.5.0.0/16 is variably subnetted, 2 subnets, 2 masks
O       150.5.5.2/32 [110/1] via 150.5.5.2, 00:00:42, FastEthernet0/0
```

FINAL ROUTER CONFIGURATIONS

R1

```
R1#term len 0
R1#sh run
Building configuration...

Current configuration : 1090 bytes
!
version 12.4
service timestamps debug datetime msec
service timestamps log datetime msec
no service password-encryption
!
hostname R1
!
boot-start-marker
boot-end-marker
!
no logging console
!
no aaa new-model
no network-clock-participate slot 1
no network-clock-participate wic 0
ip cef
!
no ip domain lookup
ip auth-proxy max-nodata-conns 3
ip admission max-nodata-conns 3
!
interface FastEthernet0/0
 ip address 150.1.1.1 255.255.255.0
 ip ospf 1 area 1
 duplex auto
 speed auto
!
interface Serial0/0
 no ip address
 shutdown
```

```
 clock rate 2000000
!
interface Serial0/1
 ip address 10.0.0.1 255.255.255.0
 encapsulation frame-relay
 ip ospf 1 area 0
 frame-relay map ip 10.0.0.2 102 broadcast
 frame-relay map ip 10.0.0.4 104 broadcast
!
router ospf 1
 router-id 1.1.1.1
 log-adjacency-changes
 passive-interface FastEthernet0/0
 neighbor 10.0.0.2
 neighbor 10.0.0.4
!
ip forward-protocol nd
!
no ip http server
no ip http secure-server
!
control-plane
!
line con 0
line aux 0
line vty 0 4
 login
!
end

R1#
```

R2

```
R2#term len 0
R2#sh run
Building configuration...

Current configuration : 1426 bytes
!
version 12.4
service timestamps debug datetime msec
service timestamps log datetime msec
no service password-encryption
!
hostname R2
!
boot-start-marker
boot-end-marker
!
no logging console
!
no aaa new-model
no network-clock-participate slot 1
no network-clock-participate wic 0
ip cef
!
no ip domain lookup
ip auth-proxy max-nodata-conns 3
ip admission max-nodata-conns 3
!
interface FastEthernet0/0
 ip address 150.5.5.2 255.255.255.0
 ip ospf network point-to-multipoint
 ip ospf 2 area 0
 duplex auto
 speed auto
!
interface Serial0/0
 no ip address
 shutdown
!
interface Serial0/1
 ip address 10.0.0.2 255.255.255.0
 encapsulation frame-relay
```

```
 ip ospf priority 0
 ip ospf 1 area 0
 frame-relay map ip 10.0.0.1 201 broadcast
 frame-relay map ip 10.0.0.4 201
!
router ospf 1
 router-id 2.2.2.2
 log-adjacency-changes
 redistribute ospf 2 subnets route-map OSPF2-INTO-OSPF1
!
router ospf 2
 router-id 22.22.22.22
 log-adjacency-changes
 redistribute ospf 1 subnets route-map OSPF1-INTO-OSPF2
!
ip forward-protocol nd
!
no ip http server
no ip http secure-server
!
route-map OSPF1-INTO-OSPF2 deny 10
 match tag 444
!
route-map OSPF1-INTO-OSPF2 permit 20
 set tag 222
!
route-map OSPF2-INTO-OSPF1 deny 10
 match tag 444
!
route-map OSPF2-INTO-OSPF1 permit 20
 set tag 222
!
control-plane
!
line con 0
line aux 0
line vty 0 4
 login
!
end

R2#
```

R3

```
R3-Frame-Relay-Switch#term len 0
R3-Frame-Relay-Switch#sh run
Building configuration...

Current configuration : 1556 bytes
!
version 12.4
service timestamps debug datetime msec
service timestamps log datetime msec
no service password-encryption
!
hostname R3-Frame-Relay-Switch
!
boot-start-marker
boot-end-marker
!
no aaa new-model
no network-clock-participate slot 1
no network-clock-participate wic 0
ip cef
!
ip auth-proxy max-nodata-conns 3
ip admission max-nodata-conns 3
!
frame-relay switching
!
interface FastEthernet0/0
 no ip address
 shutdown
```

```
  duplex auto
  speed auto
 !
 interface Serial1/0
  description 'Connected To R1 Serial 0/1'
  no ip address
  encapsulation frame-relay
  clock rate 128000
  frame-relay intf-type dce
  frame-relay route 102 interface Serial1/1 201
  frame-relay route 104 interface Serial1/2 401
 !
 interface Serial1/1
  description 'Connected To R2 Serial 0/1'
  no ip address
  encapsulation frame-relay
  clock rate 128000
  frame-relay intf-type dce
  frame-relay route 201 interface Serial1/0 102
 !
 interface Serial1/2
  description 'Connected To R4 Serial 0/0'
  no ip address
  encapsulation frame-relay
  clock rate 128000
  frame-relay intf-type dce
  frame-relay route 401 interface Serial1/0 104
 !
 interface Serial1/3
  no ip address
  shutdown
 !
 interface Serial1/4
  no ip address
  shutdown
 !
 interface Serial1/5
  no ip address
  shutdown
 !
 interface Serial1/6
  no ip address
  shutdown
 !
 interface Serial1/7
  no ip address
  shutdown
 !
ip forward-protocol nd
 !
no ip http server
no ip http secure-server
 !
control-plane
 !
line con 0
line aux 0
line vty 0 4
 login
 !
end

R3-Frame-Relay-Switch#
```

R4

```
R4#term len 0
R4#sh run
Building configuration...

Current configuration : 1463 bytes
!
version 12.4
service timestamps debug datetime msec
```

```
service timestamps log datetime msec
no service password-encryption
!
hostname R4
!
boot-start-marker
boot-end-marker
!
no logging console
!
no aaa new-model
no network-clock-participate slot 1
no network-clock-participate wic 0
ip cef
!
no ip domain lookup
ip auth-proxy max-nodata-conns 3
ip admission max-nodata-conns 3
!
interface FastEthernet0/0
 ip address 150.5.5.4 255.255.255.0
 ip ospf network point-to-multipoint
 ip ospf 2 area 0
 duplex auto
 speed auto
!
interface Serial0/0
 ip address 10.0.0.4 255.255.255.0
 encapsulation frame-relay
 ip ospf priority 0
 ip ospf 1 area 0
 frame-relay map ip 10.0.0.1 401 broadcast
 frame-relay map ip 10.0.0.2 401
!
interface Serial0/1
 no ip address
 shutdown
!
router ospf 1
 router-id 4.4.4.4
 log-adjacency-changes
 redistribute ospf 2 metric 4 subnets route-map OSPF2-INTO-OSPF1
!
router ospf 2
 router-id 44.44.44.44
 log-adjacency-changes
 redistribute ospf 1 subnets route-map OSPF1-INTO-OSPF2
 distance ospf external 100
!
ip forward-protocol nd
!
no ip http server
no ip http secure-server
!
route-map OSPF1-INTO-OSPF2 deny 10
 match tag 222
!
route-map OSPF1-INTO-OSPF2 permit 20
 set tag 444
!
route-map OSPF2-INTO-OSPF1 deny 10
 match tag 222
!
route-map OSPF2-INTO-OSPF1 permit 20
 set tag 444
!
control-plane
!
line con 0
line aux 0
line vty 0 4
 login
!
end

R4#
```

CCNP LAB 25

OSPF Multi-Technology Lab

Lab Objective:

The focus of this lab is to understand OSPF implementation and configuration in Cisco IOS routers. Additional technologies tested include Frame Relay connectivity and path control.

Lab Topology:

The lab network topology is illustrated below:

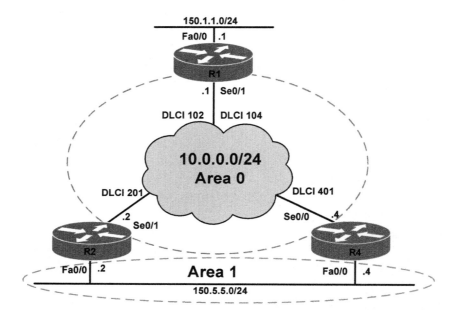

IMPORTANT NOTE: If you are using the www.howtonetwork.net racks, please bring up the LAN interfaces connected to the routers by issuing the `no shutdown` command on the connected switches. If you are using a home lab with no Switches, you can bring up the LAN interfaces using the following configurations on your routers:

```
interface fastethernet 0/0
 no keepalive
 loopback
 no shutdown
```

Alternately, you can simply connect the interfaces to a hub or switch if you have one available in your own lab. Also, if you are using the www.howtonetwork.net racks, configure R3 as the Frame Relay switch using the following configuration commands:

```
hostname R3-Frame-Relay-Switch
!
frame-relay switching
!
```

```
interface serial 1/0
 description 'Connected To R1 Serial 0/1'
 encapsulation frame-relay
 no ip address
 clock rate 128000
 frame-relay intf-type dce
 frame-relay route 102 interface serial 1/1 201
 frame-relay route 104 interface serial 1/2 401
 no shutdown
!
interface serial 1/1
 description 'Connected To R2 Serial 0/1'
 encapsulation frame-relay
 no ip address
 clock rate 128000
 frame-relay intf-type dce
 frame-relay route 201 interface serial 1/0 102
 no shutdown
!
interface serial 1/2
 description 'Connected To R4 Serial 0/0'
 encapsulation frame-relay
 no ip address
 clock rate 128000
 frame-relay intf-type dce
 frame-relay route 401 interface serial 1/0 104
 no shutdown
!
end
```

Task 1

Configure hostnames and IP addressing on all routers as illustrated in the network topology.

Task 2

Configure the Frame Relay network so that all routers can ping each others' WAN interfaces.

Task 3

Using interface-based configuration, configure OSPF area 0 on the Frame Relay WAN between R1, R2, and R4. Configure OSPF so that there is no DR/BDR election held over the Frame Relay WAN. Ensure that OSPF uses ONLY Unicast packets and not Multicast packets over the Frame Relay WAN. Verify your configuration using the appropriate commands.

Task 4

Advertise the 150.1.1.0/24 subnet connected to the LAN segment on R1 via OSPF. This subnet should be advertised as a Type 1 External LSA with a route tag of 111 and metric of 111.

Task 5

Using interface-based configuration, configure OSPF area 1 on the LAN between R2 and R4. In your configuration, ensure that R2 is elected master during the DBD exchange; however, R4 should be elected as the DR for the segment. Verify your configuration using the appropriate commands and debugs.

Task 6

Configure OSPF so that R1 prefers the path via R2 to reach the 150.5.5.0/24 subnet. If this path is unavailable, the path via R4 should be used. Verify your configuration.

LAB VALIDATION

Task 1

```
Router(config)#hostname R1
R1(config)#interface fastethernet 0/0
R1(config-if)#no shutdown
```

```
R1(config-if)#ip address 150.1.1.1 255.255.255.0
R1(config-if)#exit
R1(config)#interface serial 0/1
R1(config-if)#ip address 10.0.0.1 255.255.255.0
R1(config-if)#no shutdown
R1(config-if)#encapsulation frame-relay
R1(config-if)#exit

Router(config)#hostname R2
R2(config)#interface fastethernet 0/0
R2(config-if)#no shutdown
R2(config-if)#ip address 150.5.5.2 255.255.255.0
R2(config-if)#exit
R2(config)#interface serial 0/1
R2(config-if)#ip address 10.0.0.2 255.255.255.0
R2(config-if)#no shutdown
R2(config-if)#encapsulation frame-relay
R2(config-if)#exit

Router(config)#hostname R4
R4(config)#interface fastethernet 0/0
R4(config-if)#no shutdown
R4(config-if)#ip address 150.5.5.4 255.255.255.0
R4(config-if)#exit
R4(config)#interface serial 0/0
R4(config-if)#ip address 10.0.0.4 255.255.255.0
R4(config-if)#no shutdown
R4(config-if)#encapsulation frame-relay
R4(config-if)#exit
```

Task 2

Although Frame Relay configuration is not a CCNP topic, per se, it is still important that you remember your Frame Relay configurations from the CCNA. The task is completed as follows:

```
R1(config)#interface serial 0/1
R1(config-if)#frame-relay map ip 10.0.0.2 102 broadcast
R1(config-if)#frame-relay map ip 10.0.0.4 104 broadcast
R1(config-if)#exit
```

On the spoke routers, because the same DLCI is being used, the broadcast keyword should only be specified once to avoid duplicate Broadcast packets across the Frame Relay WAN. This task is completed as follows:

```
R2(config)#interface serial 0/1
R2(config-if)#frame-relay map ip 10.0.0.1 201 broadcast
R2(config-if)#frame-relay map ip 10.0.0.4 201
R2(config-if)#exit

R4(config)#interface serial 0/0
R4(config-if)#frame-relay map ip 10.0.0.1 401 broadcast
R4(config-if)#frame-relay map ip 10.0.0.2 401
R4(config-if)#exit
```

Verify your Frame Relay configuration using the show frame-relay map command:

```
R1#show frame-relay map
Serial0/1 (up): ip 10.0.0.2 dlci 102(0x66,0x1860), static,
             broadcast,
             CISCO, status defined, active
Serial0/1 (up): ip 10.0.0.4 dlci 104(0x68,0x1880), static,
             broadcast,
             CISCO, status defined, active

R2#show frame-relay map
Serial0/1 (up): ip 10.0.0.1 dlci 201(0xC9,0x3090), static,
             broadcast,
             CISCO, status defined, active
Serial0/1 (up): ip 10.0.0.4 dlci 201(0xC9,0x3090), static,
             CISCO, status defined, active
```

```
R4#show frame-relay map
Serial0/0 (up): ip 10.0.0.1 dlci 401(0x191,0x6410), static,
               broadcast,
               CISCO, status defined, active
Serial0/0 (up): ip 10.0.0.2 dlci 401(0x191,0x6410), static,
               CISCO, status defined, active
```

Finally, verify that you can ping between all routers across the Frame Relay WAN:

```
R1#ping 10.0.0.2 repeat 10

Type escape sequence to abort.
Sending 10, 100-byte ICMP Echos to 10.0.0.2, timeout is 2 seconds:
!!!!!!!!!!
Success rate is 100 percent (10/10), round-trip min/avg/max = 28/29/32 ms
R1#
R1#ping 10.0.0.4 repeat 10

Type escape sequence to abort.
Sending 10, 100-byte ICMP Echos to 10.0.0.4, timeout is 2 seconds:
!!!!!!!!!!
Success rate is 100 percent (10/10), round-trip min/avg/max = 28/29/32 ms

R2#ping 10.0.0.1 repeat 10

Type escape sequence to abort.
Sending 10, 100-byte ICMP Echos to 10.0.0.1, timeout is 2 seconds:
!!!!!!!!!!
Success rate is 100 percent (10/10), round-trip min/avg/max = 28/30/32 ms
R2#
R2#ping 10.0.0.4 repeat 10

Type escape sequence to abort.
Sending 10, 100-byte ICMP Echos to 10.0.0.4, timeout is 2 seconds:
!!!!!!!!!!
Success rate is 100 percent (10/10), round-trip min/avg/max = 56/59/64 ms

R4#ping 10.0.0.1 repeat 10

Type escape sequence to abort.
Sending 10, 100-byte ICMP Echos to 10.0.0.1, timeout is 2 seconds:
!!!!!!!!!!
Success rate is 100 percent (10/10), round-trip min/avg/max = 28/34/52 ms
R4#
R4#ping 10.0.0.2 repeat 10

Type escape sequence to abort.
Sending 10, 100-byte ICMP Echos to 10.0.0.2, timeout is 2 seconds:
!!!!!!!!!!
Success rate is 100 percent (10/10), round-trip min/avg/max = 56/58/60 ms
```

Task 3

To ensure that there is no DR/BDR election and allow OSPF to use Unicast and not Multicast packets, you need to specify a point-to-multipoint non-broadcast network type. This network type requires the static configuration of neighbors, which exchange updates using Unicast versus Multicast. This task is completed as follows:

```
R1(config)#router ospf 1
R1(config-router)#router-id 1.1.1.1
R1(config-router)#neighbor 10.0.0.2
R1(config-router)#neighbor 10.0.0.4
R1(config-router)#exit
R1(config)#interface serial 0/1
R1(config-if)#ip ospf network point-to-multipoint non-broadcast
R1(config-if)#ip ospf 1 area 0
R1(config-if)#exit

R2(config)#router ospf 2
R2(config-router)#router-id 2.2.2.2
R2(config-router)#neighbor 10.0.0.1
R2(config-router)#exit
```

```
R2(config)#interface serial 0/1
R2(config-if)#ip ospf network point-to-multipoint non-broadcast
R2(config-if)#ip ospf 2 area 0
R2(config-if)#exit

R4(config)#router ospf 4
R4(config-router)#router-id 4.4.4.4
R4(config-router)#neighbor 10.0.0.1
R4(config-router)#exit
R4(config)#interface serial 0/0
R4(config-if)#ip ospf network point-to-multipoint non-broadcast
R4(config-if)#ip ospf 4 area 0
R4(config-if)#exit
```

Verify your configuration using the show ip ospf neighbor command:

```
R1#show ip ospf neighbor

Neighbor ID     Pri   State         Dead Time   Address     Interface
4.4.4.4           0   FULL/  -      00:01:59    10.0.0.4    Serial0/1
2.2.2.2           0   FULL/  -      00:01:54    10.0.0.2    Serial0/1

R2#show ip ospf neighbor

Neighbor ID     Pri   State         Dead Time   Address     Interface
1.1.1.1           0   FULL/  -      00:01:57    10.0.0.1    Serial0/1

R4#show ip ospf neighbor

Neighbor ID     Pri   State         Dead Time   Address     Interface
1.1.1.1           0   FULL/  -      00:01:54    10.0.0.1    Serial0/0
```

Task 4

```
R1(config)#router ospf 1
R1(config-router)#redis connected subnets metric-type 1 metric 111 tag 111
R1(config-router)#exit
```

Verify your configuration by looking at the external LSA for the 150.1.1.0/24 subnet:

```
R1#show ip ospf database external 150.1.1.0

            OSPF Router with ID (1.1.1.1) (Process ID 1)

            Type-5 AS External Link States

  LS age: 37
  Options: (No TOS-capability, DC)
  LS Type: AS External Link
  Link State ID: 150.1.1.0 (External Network Number )
  Advertising Router: 1.1.1.1
  LS Seq Number: 80000001
  Checksum: 0xF0C8
  Length: 36
  Network Mask: /24
        Metric Type: 1 (Comparable directly to link state metric)
        TOS: 0
        Metric: 111
        Forward Address: 0.0.0.0
        External Route Tag: 111
```

Task 5

The OSPF master/slave election process is based solely on IP address (the highest wins), while the DR/BDR election process is based on priority or IP address. To ensure that R2 is elected master during the database exchange process, it needs to be configured with a higher IP address. To ensure that R4 is elected DR, it needs to be configured with a higher priority. This task is completed as follows:

```
R2(config)#router ospf 2
R2(config-router)#router-id 22.22.22.22
Reload or use "clear ip ospf process" command, for this to take effect
R2(config-router)#exit
R2(config)#interface fastethernet 0/0
R2(config-if)#ip ospf 2 area 1
R2(config-if)#end
R2#clear ip ospf process
Reset ALL OSPF processes? [no]: yes

R4(config)#interface fastethernet 0/0
R4(config-if)#ip ospf 4 area 1
R4(config-if)#ip ospf priority 4
R4(config-if)#end
R4#clear ip ospf process
Reset ALL OSPF processes? [no]: yes
```

You can verify the master/slave and DR/BDR election process using the debug ip ospf adj command on either R2 or R4 after resetting the adjacency:

```
R2#debug ip ospf adj
OSPF adjacency events debugging is on
R2#clear ip ospf process
Reset ALL OSPF processes? [no]: yes
R2#
R2#
R2#
R2#

[Truncated Output]

*May 10 08:24:58.678: OSPF: DR/BDR election on FastEthernet0/0
*May 10 08:24:58.678: OSPF: Elect BDR 22.22.22.22
*May 10 08:24:58.678: OSPF: Elect DR 4.4.4.4
*May 10 08:24:58.678: OSPF: Elect BDR 22.22.22.22
*May 10 08:24:58.678: OSPF: Elect DR 4.4.4.4
*May 10 08:24:58.678:        DR: 4.4.4.4 (Id)    BDR: 22.22.22.22 (Id)
*May 10 08:24:58.678: OSPF: Send DBD to 4.4.4.4 on FastEthernet0/0 seq 0x7B5 opt 0x52
flag 0x7 len 32
*May 10 08:24:58.686: OSPF: Rcv DBD from 4.4.4.4 on FastEthernet0/0 seq 0x3C6 opt
0x52 flag 0x7 len 32   mtu 1500 state EXSTART
*May 10 08:24:58.686: OSPF: First DBD and we are not SLAVE
*May 10 08:24:58.686: OSPF: Rcv DBD from 4.4.4.4 on FastEthernet0/0 seq 0x7B5 opt
0x52 flag 0x2 len 172  mtu 1500 state EXSTART
*May 10 08:24:58.686: OSPF: NBR Negotiation Done. We are the MASTER

[Truncated Output]
```

Task 6

Unlike in the previous lab, in this lab you can specify a per-neighbor cost because of the point-to-multipoint non-broadcast network type. Prior to any changes being made to the current OSPF routing configuration, the routing table on router R1 shows the following route entries:

```
R1#show ip ro ospf
      10.0.0.0/8 is variably subnetted, 3 subnets, 2 masks
O        10.0.0.2/32 [110/64] via 10.0.0.2, 00:05:13, Serial0/1
O        10.0.0.4/32 [110/64] via 10.0.0.4, 00:05:13, Serial0/1
      150.5.0.0/24 is subnetted, 1 subnets
O IA     150.5.5.0 [110/65] via 10.0.0.4, 00:05:13, Serial0/1
                   [110/65] via 10.0.0.2, 00:05:13, Serial0/1
```

Complete this task by either decreasing the cost of neighbor R2 to a value less than 64:

```
R1(config)#router ospf 1
R1(config-router)#neighbor 10.0.0.2 cost 1
R1(config-router)#exit
```

Following this change, the routing table on R1 now shows the following route entries:

```
R1#show ip route ospf
     10.0.0.0/8 is variably subnetted, 3 subnets, 2 masks
O       10.0.0.2/32 [110/1] via 10.0.0.2, 00:00:47, Serial0/1
O       10.0.0.4/32 [110/64] via 10.0.0.4, 00:00:47, Serial0/1
     150.5.0.0/24 is subnetted, 1 subnets
O IA    150.5.5.0 [110/2] via 10.0.0.2, 00:00:47, Serial0/1
```

FINAL ROUTER CONFIGURATIONS

R1

```
R1#term len 0
R1#sh run
Building configuration...

Current configuration : 1141 bytes
!
version 12.4
service timestamps debug datetime msec
service timestamps log datetime msec
no service password-encryption
!
hostname R1
!
boot-start-marker
boot-end-marker
!
no logging console
!
no aaa new-model
no network-clock-participate slot 1
no network-clock-participate wic 0
ip cef
!
no ip domain lookup
ip auth-proxy max-nodata-conns 3
ip admission max-nodata-conns 3
!
interface FastEthernet0/0
 ip address 150.1.1.1 255.255.255.0
 duplex auto
 speed auto
!
interface Serial0/0
 no ip address
 shutdown
 clock rate 2000000
!
interface Serial0/1
 ip address 10.0.0.1 255.255.255.0
 encapsulation frame-relay
 ip ospf network point-to-multipoint non-broadcast
 ip ospf 1 area 0
 frame-relay map ip 10.0.0.2 102 broadcast
 frame-relay map ip 10.0.0.4 104 broadcast
!
router ospf 1
 router-id 1.1.1.1
 log-adjacency-changes
 redistribute connected metric 111 metric-type 1 subnets tag 111
 neighbor 10.0.0.2 cost 1
!
ip forward-protocol nd
!
no ip http server
no ip http secure-server
!
control-plane
!
line con 0
line aux 0
line vty 0 4
 login
!
end
```

R2

```
R2#term len 0
R2#sh run
Building configuration...

Current configuration : 1042 bytes
!
version 12.4
service timestamps debug datetime msec
service timestamps log datetime msec
no service password-encryption
!
hostname R2
!
boot-start-marker
boot-end-marker
!
no aaa new-model
no network-clock-participate slot 1
no network-clock-participate wic 0
ip cef
!
no ip domain lookup
ip auth-proxy max-nodata-conns 3
ip admission max-nodata-conns 3
!
interface FastEthernet0/0
 ip address 150.5.5.2 255.255.255.0
 ip ospf 2 area 1
 duplex auto
 speed auto
!
interface Serial0/0
 no ip address
 shutdown
!
interface Serial0/1
 ip address 10.0.0.2 255.255.255.0
 encapsulation frame-relay
 ip ospf network point-to-multipoint non-broadcast
 ip ospf 2 area 0
 frame-relay map ip 10.0.0.1 201 broadcast
 frame-relay map ip 10.0.0.4 201
!
router ospf 2
 router-id 22.22.22.22
 log-adjacency-changes
 neighbor 10.0.0.1
!
ip forward-protocol nd
!
no ip http server
no ip http secure-server
!
control-plane
!
line con 0
line aux 0
line vty 0 4
 login
!
end
```

R3

```
R3-Frame-Relay-Switch#term len 0
R3-Frame-Relay-Switch#sh run
Building configuration...

Current configuration : 1556 bytes
!
version 12.4
service timestamps debug datetime msec
```

```
service timestamps log datetime msec
no service password-encryption
!
hostname R3-Frame-Relay-Switch
!
boot-start-marker
boot-end-marker
!
no aaa new-model
no network-clock-participate slot 1
no network-clock-participate wic 0
ip cef
!
ip auth-proxy max-nodata-conns 3
ip admission max-nodata-conns 3
!
frame-relay switching
!
interface FastEthernet0/0
 no ip address
 shutdown
 duplex auto
 speed auto
!
interface Serial1/0
 description 'Connected To R1 Serial 0/1'
 no ip address
 encapsulation frame-relay
 clock rate 128000
 frame-relay intf-type dce
 frame-relay route 102 interface Serial1/1 201
 frame-relay route 104 interface Serial1/2 401
!
interface Serial1/1
 description 'Connected To R2 Serial 0/1'
 no ip address
 encapsulation frame-relay
 clock rate 128000
 frame-relay intf-type dce
 frame-relay route 201 interface Serial1/0 102
!
interface Serial1/2
 description 'Connected To R4 Serial 0/0'
 no ip address
 encapsulation frame-relay
 clock rate 128000
 frame-relay intf-type dce
 frame-relay route 401 interface Serial1/0 104
!
interface Serial1/3
 no ip address
 shutdown
!
interface Serial1/4
 no ip address
 shutdown
!
interface Serial1/5
 no ip address
 shutdown
!
interface Serial1/6
 no ip address
 shutdown
!
interface Serial1/7
 no ip address
 shutdown
!
ip forward-protocol nd
!
no ip http server
no ip http secure-server
!
control-plane
!
line con 0
```

```
line aux 0
line vty 0 4
 login
!
end
```

R4

```
R4#term len 0
R4#sh run
Building configuration...

Current configuration : 1077 bytes
!
version 12.4
service timestamps debug datetime msec
service timestamps log datetime msec
no service password-encryption
!
hostname R4
!
boot-start-marker
boot-end-marker
!
no logging console
!
no aaa new-model
no network-clock-participate slot 1
no network-clock-participate wic 0
ip cef
!
no ip domain lookup
ip auth-proxy max-nodata-conns 3
ip admission max-nodata-conns 3
!
interface FastEthernet0/0
 ip address 150.5.5.4 255.255.255.0
 ip ospf priority 4
 ip ospf 4 area 1
 duplex auto
 speed auto
!
interface Serial0/0
 ip address 10.0.0.4 255.255.255.0
 encapsulation frame-relay
 ip ospf network point-to-multipoint non-broadcast
 ip ospf 4 area 0
 frame-relay map ip 10.0.0.1 401 broadcast
 frame-relay map ip 10.0.0.2 401
!
interface Serial0/1
 no ip address
 shutdown
!
router ospf 4
 router-id 4.4.4.4
 log-adjacency-changes
 neighbor 10.0.0.1
!
ip forward-protocol nd
!
no ip http server
no ip http secure-server
!
control-plane
!
line con 0
line aux 0
line vty 0 4
 login
!
end
```

CCNP LAB 26

OSPF Multi-Technology Lab

Lab Objective:

The focus of this lab is to understand OSPF implementation and configuration in Cisco IOS routers. Additional technologies tested include path control and backbone connectivity.

Lab Topology:

The lab network topology is illustrated below:

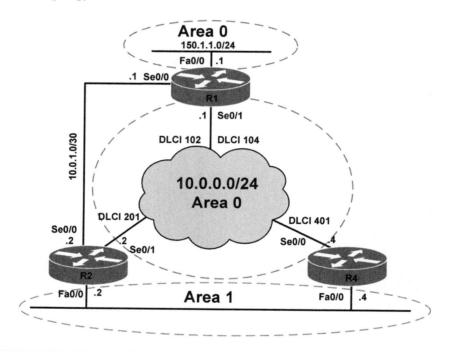

IMPORTANT NOTE: If you are using the www.howtonetwork.net racks, please bring up the LAN interfaces connected to the routers by issuing the no shutdown command on the connected switches. If you are using a home lab with no Switches, you can bring up the LAN interfaces using the following configurations on your routers:

```
interface fastethernet 0/0
 no keepalive
 loopback
 no shutdown
```

Alternately, you can simply connect the interfaces to a hub or switch if you have one available in your own lab. Also, if you are using the www.howtonetwork.net racks, configure R3 as the Frame Relay switch using the following configuration commands:

```
hostname R3-Frame-Relay-Switch
!
frame-relay switching
!
```

```
interface serial 1/0
  description 'Connected To R1 Serial 0/1'
  encapsulation frame-relay
  no ip address
  clock rate 128000
  frame-relay intf-type dce
  frame-relay route 102 interface serial 1/1 201
  frame-relay route 104 interface serial 1/2 401
  no shutdown
!
interface serial 1/1
  description 'Connected To R2 Serial 0/1'
  encapsulation frame-relay
  no ip address
  clock rate 128000
  frame-relay intf-type dce
  frame-relay route 201 interface serial 1/0 102
  no shutdown
!
interface serial 1/2
  description 'Connected To R4 Serial 0/0'
  encapsulation frame-relay
  no ip address
  clock rate 128000
  frame-relay intf-type dce
  frame-relay route 401 interface serial 1/0 104
  no shutdown
!
end
```

Task 1

Configure hostnames and IP addressing on all routers as illustrated in the network topology.

Task 2

Configure the Frame Relay network so that all routers can ping each others' WAN interfaces.

Task 3

Using interface-based configuration, configure OSPF over the Frame Relay WAN connectivity R1, R2, and R4, as well as on the LAN segment connected to R1. Ensure that there is no DR/BDR election on the WAN segment. Also, ensure that no Hellos or LSAs are flooded out of the LAN segment. Finally, ensure that OSPF uses Multicast packets when sending updates over the WAN. Verify your configuration using the appropriate commands.

Task 4

Configure the 192.168.0.0/24 subnet on the LAN segment between R2 and R4. In addition, also configure a secondary IP subnet of 192.168.1.0/24 on the LAN segment between R2 and R4. Using interface-based configuration, configure OSPF area 1 on the LAN segment between R1 and R2. Ensure that both the primary 192.168.0.0/24 and secondary 192.168.1.0/24 subnets are advertised as internal OSPF routes. Verify that R1 can ping both subnets.

Task 5

Without modifying any interface bandwidth or cost values, or default administrative distance values, configure OSPF so that R1 prefers the path via R2 to reach the 192.168.0.0/24 and prefers the path via R4 to reach the 192.168.1.0/24 subnet. Verify your path control configuration using the appropriate commands.

Task 6

Configure OSPF so that R1 and R2 establish an OSPF adjacency in area 5. Do NOT enable OSPF for the point-to-point link, i.e. the 10.0.1.0/30 subnet, between R1 and R2. Implement your configuration so that when the Frame Relay network is unavailable, the 192.168.0.0/24 and the 192.168.1.0/24 subnets can still communicate with the 150.1.1.0/24 subnet. Verify your OSPF configuration using the appropriate commands.

LAB VALIDATION

Task 1

```
Router(config)#hostname R1
R1(config)#interface fastethernet 0/0
R1(config-if)#no shutdown
R1(config-if)#ip address 150.1.1.1 255.255.255.0
R1(config-if)#exit
R1(config)#interface serial 0/0
R1(config-if)#no shutdown
R1(config-if)#ip address 10.0.1.1 255.255.255.252
R1(config-if)#clock rate 2000000
R1(config-if)#exit
R1(config)#interface serial 0/1
R1(config-if)#ip address 10.0.0.1 255.255.255.0
R1(config-if)#no shutdown
R1(config-if)#encapsulation frame-relay
R1(config-if)#exit

Router(config)#hostname R2
R2(config)#interface fastethernet 0/0
R2(config-if)#no shutdown
R2(config-if)#ip address 150.5.5.2 255.255.255.0
R2(config-if)#exit
R2(config)#interface serial 0/0
R2(config-if)#no shutdown
R2(config-if)#ip address 10.0.1.2 255.255.255.252
R2(config-if)#exit
R2(config)#interface serial 0/1
R2(config-if)#ip address 10.0.0.2 255.255.255.0
R2(config-if)#no shutdown
R2(config-if)#encapsulation frame-relay
R2(config-if)#exit

Router(config)#hostname R4
R4(config)#interface fastethernet 0/0
R4(config-if)#ip address 150.5.5.4 255.255.255.0
R4(config-if)#exit
R4(config)#interface serial 0/0
R4(config-if)#ip address 10.0.0.4 255.255.255.0
R4(config-if)#no shutdown
R4(config-if)#encapsulation frame-relay
R4(config-if)#exit
```

Task 2

Although Frame Relay configuration is not a CCNP topic, per se, it is still important that you remember your Frame Relay configurations from the CCNA. The task is completed as follows:

```
R1(config)#interface serial 0/1
R1(config-if)#frame-relay map ip 10.0.0.2 102 broadcast
R1(config-if)#frame-relay map ip 10.0.0.4 104 broadcast
R1(config-if)#exit
```

On the spoke routers, because the same DLCI is being used, the broadcast keyword should only be specified once to avoid duplicate Broadcast packets across the Frame Relay WAN. This task is completed as follows:

```
R2(config)#interface serial 0/1
R2(config-if)#frame-relay map ip 10.0.0.1 201 broadcast
R2(config-if)#frame-relay map ip 10.0.0.4 201
R2(config-if)#exit

R4(config)#interface serial 0/0
R4(config-if)#frame-relay map ip 10.0.0.1 401 broadcast
R4(config-if)#frame-relay map ip 10.0.0.2 401
R4(config-if)#exit
```

Verify your Frame Relay configuration using the show frame-relay map command:

```
R1#show frame-relay map
Serial0/1 (up): ip 10.0.0.2 dlci 102(0x66,0x1860), static,
                broadcast,
                CISCO, status defined, active
Serial0/1 (up): ip 10.0.0.4 dlci 104(0x68,0x1880), static,
                broadcast,
                CISCO, status defined, active

R2#show frame-relay map
Serial0/1 (up): ip 10.0.0.1 dlci 201(0xC9,0x3090), static,
                broadcast,
                CISCO, status defined, active
Serial0/1 (up): ip 10.0.0.4 dlci 201(0xC9,0x3090), static,
                CISCO, status defined, active

R4#show frame-relay map
Serial0/0 (up): ip 10.0.0.1 dlci 401(0x191,0x6410), static,
                broadcast,
                CISCO, status defined, active
Serial0/0 (up): ip 10.0.0.2 dlci 401(0x191,0x6410), static,
                CISCO, status defined, active
```

Finally, verify that you can ping between all routers across the Frame Relay WAN:

```
R1#ping 10.0.0.2 repeat 10

Type escape sequence to abort.
Sending 10, 100-byte ICMP Echos to 10.0.0.2, timeout is 2 seconds:
!!!!!!!!!!
Success rate is 100 percent (10/10), round-trip min/avg/max = 28/29/32 ms
R1#
R1#ping 10.0.0.4 repeat 10

Type escape sequence to abort.
Sending 10, 100-byte ICMP Echos to 10.0.0.4, timeout is 2 seconds:
!!!!!!!!!!
Success rate is 100 percent (10/10), round-trip min/avg/max = 28/29/32 ms

R2#ping 10.0.0.1 repeat 10

Type escape sequence to abort.
Sending 10, 100-byte ICMP Echos to 10.0.0.1, timeout is 2 seconds:
!!!!!!!!!!
Success rate is 100 percent (10/10), round-trip min/avg/max = 28/30/32 ms
R2#
R2#ping 10.0.0.4 repeat 10

Type escape sequence to abort.
Sending 10, 100-byte ICMP Echos to 10.0.0.4, timeout is 2 seconds:
!!!!!!!!!!
Success rate is 100 percent (10/10), round-trip min/avg/max = 56/59/64 ms

R4#ping 10.0.0.1 repeat 10

Type escape sequence to abort.
Sending 10, 100-byte ICMP Echos to 10.0.0.1, timeout is 2 seconds:
!!!!!!!!!!
Success rate is 100 percent (10/10), round-trip min/avg/max = 28/34/52 ms
R4#
R4#ping 10.0.0.2 repeat 10

Type escape sequence to abort.
Sending 10, 100-byte ICMP Echos to 10.0.0.2, timeout is 2 seconds:
!!!!!!!!!!
Success rate is 100 percent (10/10), round-trip min/avg/max = 56/58/60 ms
```

Task 3

To complete this task, you need to configure a point-to-multipoint network type. This will allow OSPF to use Multicast but prevent DR/BDR election. This task is completed as follows:

```
R1(config)#router ospf 1
R1(config-router)#router-id 1.1.1.1
```

```
R1(config-router)#passive-interface fastethernet 0/0
R1(config-router)#exit
R1(config)#interface fastethernet 0/0
R1(config-if)#ip ospf 1 area 0
R1(config-if)#exit
R1(config)#interface serial 0/1
R1(config-if)#ip ospf network point-to-multipoint
R1(config-if)#ip ospf 1 area 0
R1(config-if)#exit

R2(config)#router ospf 2
R2(config-router)#router-id 2.2.2.2
R2(config-router)#exit
R2(config)#interface serial 0/1
R2(config-if)#ip ospf network point-to-multipoint
R2(config-if)#ip ospf 2 area 0
R2(config-if)#exit

R4(config)#router ospf 4
R4(config-router)#router-id 4.4.4.4
R4(config-router)#exit
R4(config)#interface serial 0/0
R4(config-if)#ip ospf network point-to-multipoint
R4(config-if)#ip ospf 4 area 0
R4(config-if)#exit
```

Verify your configuration using the show ip ospf neighbor command:

```
R1#show ip ospf neighbor

Neighbor ID     Pri   State        Dead Time   Address      Interface
4.4.4.4          0    FULL/    -   00:01:59    10.0.0.4     Serial0/1
2.2.2.2          0    FULL/    -   00:01:40    10.0.0.2     Serial0/1

R2#show ip ospf neighbor

Neighbor ID     Pri   State        Dead Time   Address      Interface
1.1.1.1          0    FULL/    -   00:01:33    10.0.0.1     Serial0/1

R4#show ip ospf neighbor

Neighbor ID     Pri   State        Dead Time   Address      Interface
1.1.1.1          0    FULL/    -   00:01:40    10.0.0.1     Serial0/0
```

Task 4

```
R2(config)#interface fastethernet 0/0
R2(config-if)#ip address 192.168.0.2 255.255.255.0
R2(config-if)#ip address 192.168.1.2 255.255.255.0 secondary
R2(config-if)#ip ospf 2 area 1
R2(config-if)#exit

R4(config)#interface fastethernet 0/0
R4(config-if)#ip address 192.168.0.4 255.255.255.0
R4(config-if)#ip address 192.168.1.4 255.255.255.0 secondary
R4(config-if)#ip ospf 4 area 1
R4(config-if)#exit
```

Verify OSPF configuration using the show ip ospf neighbor command:

```
R2#show ip ospf neighbor

Neighbor ID     Pri   State        Dead Time   Address         Interface
1.1.1.1          0    FULL/    -   00:01:34    10.0.0.1        Serial0/1
4.4.4.4          1    FULL/BDR     00:00:34    192.168.0.4     FastEthernet0/0

R4#show ip ospf neighbor

Neighbor ID     Pri   State        Dead Time   Address         Interface
```

```
1.1.1.1          0   FULL/  -   00:01:58   10.0.0.1    Serial0/0
2.2.2.2          1   FULL/DR    00:00:38   192.168.0.2 FastEthernet0/0
```

Finally, verify that R1 has two routes to these subnets and can ping them both:

```
R1#show ip route ospf
       10.0.0.0/8 is variably subnetted, 3 subnets, 2 masks
O         10.0.0.2/32 [110/64] via 10.0.0.2, 00:01:03, Serial0/1
O         10.0.0.4/32 [110/64] via 10.0.0.4, 00:01:03, Serial0/1
O IA  192.168.0.0/24 [110/65] via 10.0.0.4, 00:01:03, Serial0/1
                      [110/65] via 10.0.0.2, 00:01:03, Serial0/1
O IA  192.168.1.0/24 [110/65] via 10.0.0.4, 00:01:03, Serial0/1
                      [110/65] via 10.0.0.2, 00:01:03, Serial0/1

R1#ping 192.168.0.0

Type escape sequence to abort.
Sending 5, 100-byte ICMP Echos to 192.168.0.0, timeout is 2 seconds:
!!!!!
Success rate is 100 percent (5/5), round-trip min/avg/max = 28/30/32 ms

R1#ping 192.168.1.0

Type escape sequence to abort.
Sending 5, 100-byte ICMP Echos to 192.168.1.0, timeout is 2 seconds:
!!!!!
Success rate is 100 percent (5/5), round-trip min/avg/max = 28/30/32 ms
```

Task 5

To complete this task you need to think outside the box and use the area <area> range command. This command allows you to directly specify the cost of the advertised summary route. Prior to any routing changes, R1 shows the following route entries:

```
R1#show ip route ospf
       10.0.0.0/8 is variably subnetted, 3 subnets, 2 masks
O         10.0.0.2/32 [110/64] via 10.0.0.2, 00:01:03, Serial0/1
O         10.0.0.4/32 [110/64] via 10.0.0.4, 00:01:03, Serial0/1
O IA  192.168.0.0/24 [110/65] via 10.0.0.4, 00:01:03, Serial0/1
                      [110/65] via 10.0.0.2, 00:01:03, Serial0/1
O IA  192.168.1.0/24 [110/65] via 10.0.0.4, 00:01:03, Serial0/1
                      [110/65] via 10.0.0.2, 00:01:03, Serial0/1
```

This task is completed as follows:

```
R2(config)#router ospf 2
R2(config-router)#area 1 range 192.168.0.0 255.255.255.0 cost 1
R2(config-router)#area 1 range 192.168.1.0 255.255.255.0 cost 5
R2(config-router)#exit

R4(config)#router ospf 4
R4(config-router)#area 1 range 192.168.0.0 255.255.255.0 cost 5
R4(config-router)#area 1 range 192.168.1.0 255.255.255.0 cost 1
R4(config-router)#exit
```

Following this configuration, the routing table on R1 shows the following entries:

```
R1#show ip route ospf
       10.0.0.0/8 is variably subnetted, 3 subnets, 2 masks
O         10.0.0.2/32 [110/64] via 10.0.0.2, 00:01:58, Serial0/1
O         10.0.0.4/32 [110/64] via 10.0.0.4, 00:01:58, Serial0/1
O IA  192.168.0.0/24 [110/65] via 10.0.0.2, 00:01:58, Serial0/1
O IA  192.168.1.0/24 [110/65] via 10.0.0.4, 00:01:35, Serial0/1
```

Task 6

The requirements of this task are two-fold. First, you must enable OSPF across the WAN link between R1 and R2 without explicitly enabling it for the 10.0.1.0/30 subnet. To do so, you should configure a GRE tunnel between the two routers. This task is completed as follows:

```
R1(config)#interface tunnel 0
R1(config-if)#ip address 200.0.0.1 255.255.255.252
R1(config-if)#ip ospf 1 area 5
R1(config-if)#tunnel source serial 0/0
R1(config-if)#tunnel destination 10.0.1.2
R1(config-if)#exit

R2(config)#interface tunnel 0
R2(config-if)#ip address 200.0.0.2 255.255.255.252
R2(config-if)#ip ospf 2 area 5
R2(config-if)#tunnel source serial 0/0
R2(config-if)#tunnel destination 10.0.1.1
R2(config-if)#exit
```

Verify your configuration using the show ip ospf neighbor command:

```
R1#show ip ospf neighbor

Neighbor ID     Pri    State        Dead Time   Address       Interface
4.4.4.4          0     FULL/  -     00:01:58    10.0.0.4      Serial0/1
2.2.2.2          0     FULL/  -     00:01:57    10.0.0.2      Serial0/1
2.2.2.2          0     FULL/  -     00:00:34    200.0.0.2     Tunnel0

R2#show ip ospf neighbor

Neighbor ID     Pri    State        Dead Time   Address       Interface
1.1.1.1          0     FULL/  -     00:01:54    10.0.0.1      Serial0/1
4.4.4.4          1     FULL/BDR     00:00:38    192.168.0.4   FastEthernet0/0
1.1.1.1          0     FULL/  -     00:00:32    200.0.0.1     Tunnel0
```

The second part of this task requires that you configure a virtual link so that when the Frame Relay WAN is down, area 1 still has a logical connection to the backbone. If you do not configure a virtual link, routing will 'break' when the Frame Relay WAN fails. This task is completed as follows:

```
R1(config)#router ospf 1
R1(config-router)#area 5 virtual-link 2.2.2.2
R1(config-router)#exit

R2(config)#router ospf 2
R2(config-router)#area 5 virtual-link 1.1.1.1
R2(config-router)#exit
```

Verify your configuration using the show ip ospf virtual-links command:

```
R1#show ip ospf virtual-links
Virtual Link OSPF_VL0 to router 2.2.2.2 is up
  Run as demand circuit
  DoNotAge LSA allowed.
  Transit area 5, via interface Tunnel0, Cost of using 11111
  Transmit Delay is 1 sec, State POINT_TO_POINT,
  Timer intervals configured, Hello 10, Dead 40, Wait 40, Retransmit 5
    Hello due in 00:00:02
    Adjacency State FULL (Hello suppressed)
    Index 3/4, retransmission queue length 0, number of retransmission 0
    First 0x0(0)/0x0(0) Next 0x0(0)/0x0(0)
    Last retransmission scan length is 0, maximum is 0
    Last retransmission scan time is 0 msec, maximum is 0 msec
```

Finally, test your configuration by shutting down the Frame Relay interface on R1:

```
R1(config)#interface serial 0/1
R1(config-if)#shutdown
R1(config-if)#exit
R1(config)#do show ip route ospf
     10.0.0.0/8 is variably subnetted, 2 subnets, 2 masks
O       10.0.0.2/32 [110/11111] via 200.0.0.2, 00:00:03, Tunnel0
O IA 192.168.0.0/24 [110/11112] via 200.0.0.2, 00:00:03, Tunnel0
O IA 192.168.1.0/24 [110/11116] via 200.0.0.2, 00:00:03, Tunnel0
```

FINAL ROUTER CONFIGURATIONS

R1

```
R1#term len 0
R1#sh run
Building configuration...

Current configuration : 1260 bytes
!
version 12.4
service timestamps debug datetime msec
service timestamps log datetime msec
no service password-encryption
!
hostname R1
!
boot-start-marker
boot-end-marker
!
no logging console
!
no aaa new-model
no network-clock-participate slot 1
no network-clock-participate wic 0
ip cef
!
no ip domain lookup
ip auth-proxy max-nodata-conns 3
ip admission max-nodata-conns 3
!
interface Tunnel0
 ip address 200.0.0.1 255.255.255.252
 ip ospf 1 area 5
 tunnel source Serial0/0
 tunnel destination 10.0.1.2
!
interface FastEthernet0/0
 ip address 150.1.1.1 255.255.255.0
 ip ospf 1 area 0
 duplex auto
 speed auto
!
interface Serial0/0
 ip address 10.0.1.1 255.255.255.252
 clock rate 2000000
!
interface Serial0/1
 ip address 10.0.0.1 255.255.255.0
 encapsulation frame-relay
 ip ospf network point-to-multipoint
 ip ospf 1 area 0
 frame-relay map ip 10.0.0.2 102 broadcast
 frame-relay map ip 10.0.0.4 104 broadcast
!
router ospf 1
 router-id 1.1.1.1
 log-adjacency-changes
 area 5 virtual-link 2.2.2.2
 passive-interface FastEthernet0/0
!
ip forward-protocol nd
!
no ip http server
no ip http secure-server
!
control-plane
!
line con 0
line aux 0
line vty 0 4
 login
!
end

R1#
```

R2

```
R2#term len 0
R2#sh run
Building configuration...

Current configuration : 1339 bytes
!
version 12.4
service timestamps debug datetime msec
service timestamps log datetime msec
no service password-encryption
!
hostname R2
!
boot-start-marker
boot-end-marker
!
no logging console
!
no aaa new-model
no network-clock-participate slot 1
no network-clock-participate wic 0
ip cef
!
no ip domain lookup
ip auth-proxy max-nodata-conns 3
ip admission max-nodata-conns 3
!
interface Tunnel0
 ip address 200.0.0.2 255.255.255.252
 ip ospf 2 area 5
 tunnel source Serial0/0
 tunnel destination 10.0.1.1
!
interface FastEthernet0/0
 ip address 192.168.1.2 255.255.255.0 secondary
 ip address 192.168.0.2 255.255.255.0
 ip ospf 2 area 1
 duplex auto
 speed auto
!
interface Serial0/0
 ip address 10.0.1.2 255.255.255.252
!
interface Serial0/1
 ip address 10.0.0.2 255.255.255.0
 encapsulation frame-relay
 ip ospf network point-to-multipoint
 ip ospf 2 area 0
 frame-relay map ip 10.0.0.1 201 broadcast
 frame-relay map ip 10.0.0.4 201
!
router ospf 2
 router-id 2.2.2.2
 log-adjacency-changes
 area 1 range 192.168.0.0 255.255.255.0 cost 1
 area 1 range 192.168.1.0 255.255.255.0 cost 5
 area 5 virtual-link 1.1.1.1
!
ip forward-protocol nd
!
no ip http server
no ip http secure-server
!
control-plane
!
line con 0
line aux 0
line vty 0 4
 login
!
end

R2#
```

R3

```
R3-Frame-Relay-Switch#term len 0
R3-Frame-Relay-Switch#sh run
```

```
Building configuration...

Current configuration : 1556 bytes
!
version 12.4
service timestamps debug datetime msec
service timestamps log datetime msec
no service password-encryption
!
hostname R3-Frame-Relay-Switch
!
boot-start-marker
boot-end-marker
!
no aaa new-model
no network-clock-participate slot 1
no network-clock-participate wic 0
ip cef
!
ip auth-proxy max-nodata-conns 3
ip admission max-nodata-conns 3
!
frame-relay switching
!
interface FastEthernet0/0
 no ip address
 shutdown
 duplex auto
 speed auto
!
interface Serial1/0
 description 'Connected To R1 Serial 0/1'
 no ip address
 encapsulation frame-relay
 clock rate 128000
 frame-relay intf-type dce
 frame-relay route 102 interface Serial1/1 201
 frame-relay route 104 interface Serial1/2 401
!
interface Serial1/1
 description 'Connected To R2 Serial 0/1'
 no ip address
 encapsulation frame-relay
 clock rate 128000
 frame-relay intf-type dce
 frame-relay route 201 interface Serial1/0 102
!
interface Serial1/2
 description 'Connected To R4 Serial 0/0'
 no ip address
 encapsulation frame-relay
 clock rate 128000
 frame-relay intf-type dce
 frame-relay route 401 interface Serial1/0 104
!
interface Serial1/3
 no ip address
 shutdown
!
interface Serial1/4
 no ip address
 shutdown
!
interface Serial1/5
 no ip address
 shutdown
!
interface Serial1/6
 no ip address
 shutdown
!
interface Serial1/7
 no ip address
 shutdown
!
ip forward-protocol nd
!
no ip http server
no ip http secure-server
!
```

```
control-plane
!
line con 0
line aux 0
line vty 0 4
 login
!
end
R3-Frame-Relay-Switch#
```

R4

```
R4#term len 0
R4#sh run
Building configuration...

Current configuration : 1168 bytes
!
version 12.4
service timestamps debug datetime msec
service timestamps log datetime msec
no service password-encryption
!
hostname R4
!
boot-start-marker
boot-end-marker
!
no logging console
!
no aaa new-model
no network-clock-participate slot 1
no network-clock-participate wic 0
ip cef
!
no ip domain lookup
ip auth-proxy max-nodata-conns 3
ip admission max-nodata-conns 3
!
interface FastEthernet0/0
 ip address 192.168.1.4 255.255.255.0 secondary
 ip address 192.168.0.4 255.255.255.0
 ip ospf 4 area 1
 duplex auto
 speed auto
!
interface Serial0/0
 ip address 10.0.0.4 255.255.255.0
 encapsulation frame-relay
 ip ospf network point-to-multipoint
 ip ospf 4 area 0
 frame-relay map ip 10.0.0.1 401 broadcast
 frame-relay map ip 10.0.0.2 401
!
interface Serial0/1
 no ip address
 shutdown
!
router ospf 4
 router-id 4.4.4.4
 log-adjacency-changes
 area 1 range 192.168.0.0 255.255.255.0 cost 5
 area 1 range 192.168.1.0 255.255.255.0 cost 1
!
ip forward-protocol nd
!
no ip http server
no ip http secure-server
!
control-plane
!
line con 0
line aux 0
line vty 0 4
 login
!
end
R4#
```

CCNP LAB 27

OSPF Multi-Technology Lab

Lab Objective:

The focus of this lab is to understand OSPF implementation and configuration in Cisco IOS routers. Additional technologies tested include Stub/NSSA areas and route and LSA filtering.

Lab Topology:

The lab network topology is illustrated below:

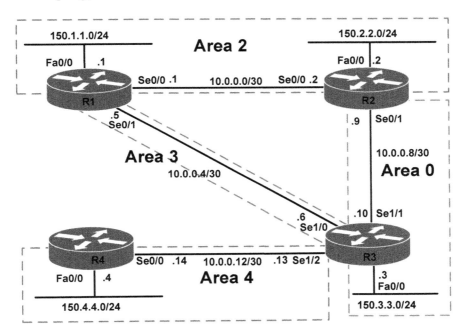

IMPORTANT NOTE: If you are using the www.howtonetwork.net racks, please bring up the LAN interfaces connected to the routers by issuing the no shutdown command on the connected switches. If you are using a home lab with no Switches, you can bring up the LAN interfaces using the following configurations on your routers:

```
interface fastethernet 0/0
  no keepalive
  loopback
  no shutdown
```

Alternately, you can simply connect the interfaces to a hub or switch if you have one available in your own lab.

Task 1

Configure hostnames and IP addressing on all routers as illustrated in the network topology.

Task 2

Using legacy `network x.x.x.x y.y.y.y area <area>` OSPF configuration commands, configure OSPF as illustrated in the topology. All areas should be configured as normal OSPF areas EXCEPT for area 4, which should be configured as an NSSA. Verify your configuration using the appropriate commands.

Task 3

Configure the following static routes on R4 and redistribute them as Type 1 External routes:
- 192.168.1.0/24 via 150.4.4.254
- 192.168.2.0/24 via 150.4.4.254

Next, configure your OSPF network so that the forward address in the Type 5 LSAs indicates that traffic should be sent to R3 (ASBR Type 5 LSAs) and NOT to R4 (ASBR Type 7 LSAs). In other words, ensure that the forward address of the Type 5 LSAs is set to 0.0.0.0. Verify your configuration using the appropriate commands.

Task 4

Configure a Loopback11 interface on R1 with the IP address 11.11.11.11/32. Redistribute this interface into OSPF using default metric type and metric values. Following the route redistribution, configure OSPF so that all routers are able to ping this subnet from their LAN subnets, i.e. from their 150.x.x.x addresses. Verify your configuration.

Task 5

Configure OSPF so that the 150.3.3.0/24 subnet connected to R3s LAN segment and as well as the 150.4.4.0/24 subnet connected to R4s LAN segment are not advertised to any other area. Do NOT use any ACL or prefix-list based filtering methods when implementing this solution. However, ensure that R1 and R2 are still able to ping 150.3.3.3 as well as 150.4.4.4. Verify your configuration using the appropriate commands.

Task 6

Configure OSPF so that the 150.1.1.0/24 and 150.2.2.0/24 subnets are NOT advertised only to area 3. They should still be advertised to other areas. Do NOT use any distribute lists when completing this task. Verify your configuration using the appropriate commands.

LAB VALIDATION

Task 1

```
Router(config)#hostname R1
R1(config)#interface fastethernet 0/0
R1(config-if)#no shutdown
R1(config-if)#ip address 150.1.1.1 255.255.255.0
R1(config-if)#exit
R1(config)#interface serial 0/0
R1(config-if)#no shutdown
R1(config-if)#ip address 10.0.1.1 255.255.255.252
R1(config-if)#clock rate 2000000
R1(config-if)#exit
R1(config)#interface serial 0/1
R1(config-if)#ip address 10.0.0.5 255.255.255.252
R1(config-if)#no shutdown
R1(config-if)#exit

Router(config)#hostname R2
R2(config)#interface fastethernet 0/0
R2(config-if)#no shutdown
R2(config-if)#ip address 150.2.2.2 255.255.255.0
R2(config-if)#exit
R2(config)#interface serial 0/0
R2(config-if)#no shutdown
R2(config-if)#ip address 10.0.1.2 255.255.255.252
```

```
R2(config-if)#exit
R2(config)#interface serial 0/1
R2(config-if)#ip address 10.0.0.9 255.255.255.252
R2(config-if)#no shutdown
R2(config-if)#exit

Router(config)#hostname R3
R3(config)#interface fastethernet 0/0
R3(config-if)#ip address 150.3.3.3 255.255.255.0
R3(config-if)#exit
R3(config)#interface serial 1/0
R3(config-if)#ip address 10.0.0.6 255.255.255.252
R3(config-if)#no shutdown
R3(config-if)# clock rate 128000
R3(config-if)#exit
R3(config)#interface serial 1/1
R3(config-if)#ip address 10.0.0.10 255.255.255.252
R3(config-if)#no shutdown
R3(config-if)# clock rate 128000
R3(config-if)#exit
R3(config)#interface serial 1/2
R3(config-if)#ip address 10.0.0.13 255.255.255.252
R3(config-if)#no shutdown
R3(config-if)# clock rate 128000
R3(config-if)#exit

Router(config)#hostname R4
R4(config)#interface fastethernet 0/0
R4(config-if)#ip address 150.4.4.4 255.255.255.0
R4(config-if)#exit
R4(config)#interface serial 0/0
R4(config-if)#ip address 10.0.0.14 255.255.255.252
R4(config-if)#no shutdown
R4(config-if)#exit
```

Task 2

```
R1(config)#router ospf 1
R1(config-router)#router-id 1.1.1.1
R1(config-router)#network 10.0.0.1 0.0.0.0 area 2
R1(config-router)#network 10.0.0.5 0.0.0.0 area 3
R1(config-router)#network 150.1.1.1 0.0.0.0 area 2
R1(config-router)#exit

R2(config)#router ospf 2
R2(config-router)#router-id 2.2.2.2
R2(config-router)#network 10.0.0.2 0.0.0.0 area 2
R2(config-router)#network 10.0.0.9 0.0.0.0 area 0
R2(config-router)#network 150.2.2.2 0.0.0.0 area 2
R2(config-router)#exit

R3(config)#router ospf 3
R3(config-router)#router-id 3.3.3.3
R3(config-router)#network 10.0.0.6 0.0.0.0 area 3
R3(config-router)#network 10.0.0.10 0.0.0.0 area 0
R3(config-router)#network 10.0.0.13 0.0.0.0 area 4
R3(config-router)#network 150.3.3.3 0.0.0.0 area 0
R3(config-router)#area 4 nssa
R3(config-router)#exit

R4(config)#router ospf 4
R4(config-router)#router-id 4.4.4.4
R4(config-router)#network 150.4.4.4 0.0.0.0 area 4
R4(config-router)#network 10.0.0.14 0.0.0.0 area 4
R4(config-router)#area 4 nssa
R4(config-router)#exit
```

Verify your configuration using the show ip ospf neighbor command:

```
R1#show ip ospf neighbor

Neighbor ID    Pri   State      Dead Time   Address      Interface
```

```
2.2.2.2           0    FULL/  -   00:00:30   10.0.0.2    Serial0/0
3.3.3.3           0    FULL/  -   00:00:29   10.0.0.6    Serial0/1

R2#show ip ospf neighbor

Neighbor ID    Pri   State       Dead Time   Address     Interface
3.3.3.3          0    FULL/  -   00:00:36   10.0.0.10   Serial0/1
1.1.1.1          0    FULL/  -   00:00:37   10.0.0.1    Serial0/0

R3#show ip ospf neighbor

Neighbor ID    Pri   State       Dead Time   Address     Interface
2.2.2.2          0    FULL/  -   00:00:38   10.0.0.9    Serial1/1
1.1.1.1          0    FULL/  -   00:00:38   10.0.0.5    Serial1/0
4.4.4.4          0    FULL/  -   00:00:33   10.0.0.14   Serial1/2

R4#show ip ospf neighbor

Neighbor ID    Pri   State       Dead Time   Address     Interface
3.3.3.3          0    FULL/  -   00:00:36   10.0.0.13   Serial0/0
```

Task 3

The first part of this task is straightforward and is completed as follows:

```
R4(config)#ip route 192.168.1.0 255.255.255.255 150.4.4.254
R4(config)#ip route 192.168.2.0 255.255.255.255 150.4.4.254
R4(config)#router ospf 4
R4(config-router)#redistribute static subnets metric-type 1
R4(config-router)#exit
```

The second part of this task requires some additional thought. By default, the forward address of the external LSAs will be set to 0.0.0.0, meaning traffic should be forwarded to the ASBR, unless the next hop IP address is included in network statement configuration, i.e. is advertised by OSPF. This can be verified by checking the Link State Database (LSDB) on R1, R3 or R3:

```
R1#show ip ospf database external

              OSPF Router with ID (1.1.1.1) (Process ID 1)

              Type-5 AS External Link States

  Routing Bit Set on this LSA
  LS age: 839
  Options: (No TOS-capability, DC)
  LS Type: AS External Link
  Link State ID: 192.168.1.0 (External Network Number )
  Advertising Router: 3.3.3.3
  LS Seq Number: 80000001
  Checksum: 0x1CF0
  Length: 36
  Network Mask: /32
        Metric Type: 1 (Comparable directly to link state metric)
        TOS: 0
        Metric: 20
        Forward Address: 150.4.4.254
        External Route Tag: 0

  Routing Bit Set on this LSA
  LS age: 839
  Options: (No TOS-capability, DC)
  LS Type: AS External Link
  Link State ID: 192.168.2.0 (External Network Number )
  Advertising Router: 3.3.3.3
  LS Seq Number: 80000001
  Checksum: 0x11FA
  Length: 36
  Network Mask: /32
        Metric Type: 1 (Comparable directly to link state metric)
        TOS: 0
```

```
Metric: 20
Forward Address: 150.4.4.254
External Route Tag: 0
```

To modify this default behavior, you have to configure R3, the ABR, to suppress the forward address. This task is completed as follows:

```
R3(config)#router ospf 3
R3(config-router)#area 4 nssa translate type7 suppress-fa
R3(config-router)#exit
```

Following this configuration change, the LSDB on R1 now shows the following entries:

```
R1#show ip ospf database external

          OSPF Router with ID (1.1.1.1) (Process ID 1)

             Type-5 AS External Link States

    Routing Bit Set on this LSA
    LS age: 39
    Options: (No TOS-capability, DC)
    LS Type: AS External Link
    Link State ID: 192.168.1.0 (External Network Number )
    Advertising Router: 3.3.3.3
    LS Seq Number: 80000002
    Checksum: 0x4B5E
    Length: 36
    Network Mask: /32
          Metric Type: 1 (Comparable directly to link state metric)
          TOS: 0
          Metric: 20
          Forward Address: 0.0.0.0
          External Route Tag: 0

    Routing Bit Set on this LSA
    LS age: 39
    Options: (No TOS-capability, DC)
    LS Type: AS External Link
    Link State ID: 192.168.2.0 (External Network Number )
    Advertising Router: 3.3.3.3
    LS Seq Number: 80000002
    Checksum: 0x4068
    Length: 36
    Network Mask: /32
          Metric Type: 1 (Comparable directly to link state metric)
          TOS: 0
          Metric: 20
          Forward Address: 0.0.0.0
          External Route Tag: 0
```

The forward address of 0.0.0.0 indicates that the traffic should be sent to the ASBR. By default, R3 will be designated ASBR because it translates the Type 3 LSAs to Type 5 LSAs, which are then flooded throughout the OSPF domain. You can verify that the Type 4 LSA for the ASBR exists using the `show ip ospf database asbr-summary` command:

```
R1#show ip ospf database asbr-summary

          OSPF Router with ID (1.1.1.1) (Process ID 1)

             Summary ASB Link States (Area 2)

    LS age: 67
    Options: (No TOS-capability, DC, Upward)
    LS Type: Summary Links(AS Boundary Router)
    Link State ID: 3.3.3.3 (AS Boundary Router address)
    Advertising Router: 2.2.2.2
    LS Seq Number: 80000002
    Checksum: 0x35B1
    Length: 28
```

```
Network Mask: /0
        TOS: 0 Metric: 64
```

Task 4

The first part of this task is straightforward and requires route redistribution configuration:

```
R1(config)#interface loopback 11
R1(config-if)#ip address 11.11.11.11 255.255.255.255
R1(config-if)#exit
R1(config)#router ospf 1
R1(config-router)#redistribute connected subnets
R1(config-router)#exit
```

To complete the second part of this task, we have to remember that by default, a Type 5 LSA has a domain-flooding scope; however, it is NOT advertised into stub or NSSA areas. As a result of this default behavior, all other routers in the network will have an LSA for this subnet, except for R4. Validate this by looking at the Link State Database on R4:

R4#show ip ospf database

```
        OSPF Router with ID (4.4.4.4) (Process ID 4)

            Router Link States (Area 4)

Link ID         ADV Router      Age       Seq#       Checksum Link count
3.3.3.3         3.3.3.3         1937      0x80000004 0x002284 2
4.4.4.4         4.4.4.4         1788      0x80000006 0x00C8C7 3

            Summary Net Link States (Area 4)

Link ID         ADV Router      Age       Seq#       Checksum
10.0.0.0        3.3.3.3         424       0x80000004 0x005A76
10.0.0.4        3.3.3.3         424       0x80000004 0x00AF5D
10.0.0.8        3.3.3.3         424       0x80000004 0x008781
150.1.1.0       3.3.3.3         424       0x80000004 0x003C02
150.2.2.0       3.3.3.3         424       0x80000004 0x00A2D9
150.3.3.0       3.3.3.3         424       0x80000003 0x00EF9B

            Type-7 AS External Link States (Area 4)

Link ID         ADV Router      Age       Seq#       Checksum Tag
192.168.1.0     4.4.4.4         1788      0x80000002 0x006796 0
192.168.2.0     4.4.4.4         1788      0x80000002 0x005CA0 0
```

Because the Type 5 LSA will not be flooded into area 4, you need to configure the ABR (R3) to advertise a default route to R4. This is completed as follows:

```
R3(config)#router ospf 3
R3(config-router)#area 4 nssa default-information-originate
R3(config-router)#exit
```

Following this configuration, the LSDB on R4 shows the following entries:

R4#show ip ospf database

```
        OSPF Router with ID (4.4.4.4) (Process ID 4)

            Router Link States (Area 4)

Link ID         ADV Router      Age       Seq#       Checksum Link count
3.3.3.3         3.3.3.3         57        0x80000005 0x002085 2
4.4.4.4         4.4.4.4         1927      0x80000006 0x00C8C7 3

            Summary Net Link States (Area 4)

Link ID         ADV Router      Age       Seq#       Checksum
10.0.0.0        3.3.3.3         564       0x80000004 0x005A76
10.0.0.4        3.3.3.3         564       0x80000004 0x00AF5D
```

```
10.0.0.8          3.3.3.3          564          0x80000004 0x008781
150.1.1.0         3.3.3.3          564          0x80000004 0x003C02
150.2.2.0         3.3.3.3          564          0x80000004 0x00A2D9
150.3.3.0         3.3.3.3          564          0x80000003 0x00EF9B

                  Type-7 AS External Link States (Area 4)

Link ID           ADV Router       Age          Seq#       Checksum Tag
0.0.0.0           3.3.3.3          47           0x80000001 0x00B2F2 0
192.168.1.0       4.4.4.4          1927         0x80000002 0x006796 0
192.168.2.0       4.4.4.4          1929         0x80000002 0x005CA0 0
```

Finally, verify that all routers can ping the 11.11.11.11/32 address from their LAN interfaces:

```
R2#ping 11.11.11.11 repeat 10 source fastethernet 0/0

Type escape sequence to abort.
Sending 10, 100-byte ICMP Echos to 11.11.11.11, timeout is 2 seconds:
Packet sent with a source address of 150.2.2.2
!!!!!!!!!!
Success rate is 100 percent (10/10), round-trip min/avg/max = 1/2/4 ms

R3#ping 11.11.11.11 repeat 10 source fastethernet 0/0

Type escape sequence to abort.
Sending 10, 100-byte ICMP Echos to 11.11.11.11, timeout is 2 seconds:
Packet sent with a source address of 150.3.3.3
!!!!!!!!!!
Success rate is 100 percent (10/10), round-trip min/avg/max = 16/16/16 ms

R4#ping 11.11.11.11 repeat 10 source fastethernet 0/0

Type escape sequence to abort.
Sending 10, 100-byte ICMP Echos to 11.11.11.11, timeout is 2 seconds:
Packet sent with a source address of 150.4.4.4
!!!!!!!!!!
Success rate is 100 percent (10/10), round-trip min/avg/max = 28/30/32 ms
```

Task 5

This task requires the use of the area <area> range command, which can also be used for route filtering.
Prior to any changes, R1 and R2s routing tables show the following entries:

```
R1#show ip route ospf | include 150.
      150.2.0.0/24 is subnetted, 1 subnets
O        150.2.2.0 [110/65] via 10.0.0.2, 00:09:46, Serial0/0
      150.3.0.0/24 is subnetted, 1 subnets
O IA     150.3.3.0 [110/65] via 10.0.0.6, 00:09:46, Serial0/1
      150.4.0.0/24 is subnetted, 1 subnets
O IA     150.4.4.0 [110/846] via 10.0.0.6, 00:09:46, Serial0/1

R2#show ip route ospf | include 150.
      150.1.0.0/24 is subnetted, 1 subnets
O        150.1.1.0 [110/65] via 10.0.0.1, 00:09:53, Serial0/0
      150.3.0.0/24 is subnetted, 1 subnets
O        150.3.3.0 [110/65] via 10.0.0.10, 01:19:47, Serial0/1
      150.4.0.0/24 is subnetted, 1 subnets
O IA     150.4.4.0 [110/846] via 10.0.0.10, 00:09:53, Serial0/1
```

Complete this task by configuring both R3 and R2 as follows:

```
R2(config)#router ospf 2
R2(config-router)#area 0 range 150.3.3.0 255.255.255.0 not-advertise
R2(config-router)#exit

R3(config)#router ospf 3
R3(config-router)#area 0 range 150.3.3.0 255.255.255.0 not-advertise
R3(config-router)#area 4 range 150.4.4.0 255.255.255.0 not-advertise
R3(config-router)#exit
```

Following this configuration change, the routing tables on R1 and R2 show the following:

```
R1#show ip route ospf | include 150.
       150.2.0.0/24 is subnetted, 1 subnets
O         150.2.2.0 [110/65] via 10.0.0.2, 00:02:34, Serial0/0

R2#show ip route ospf | include 150.
       150.1.0.0/24 is subnetted, 1 subnets
O         150.1.1.0 [110/65] via 10.0.0.1, 00:01:01, Serial0/0
       150.3.0.0/24 is subnetted, 1 subnets
O         150.3.3.0 [110/65] via 10.0.0.10, 00:01:01, Serial0/1
```

NOTE: The 150.3.3.0/24 prefix will show up in R2s routing table because this router also resides in area 0 along with R3. The configuration of the area <area> range command on BOTH routers, i.e. R2 and R3 prevents this from being advertised outside of area 0 to any other area as required in the task.

To ensure that R1 and R2 are still able to ping both the 150.3.3.0/24 and 150.4.4.0/24 subnets, you need to advertise a default route via OSPF on R3. This is completed as follows:

```
R3(config)#router ospf 3
R3(config-router)#default-information originate always
R3(config-router)#exit
```

Following this change, the routing tables on R1 and R2 show the following entries:

```
R1#show ip route ospf
        10.0.0.0/30 is subnetted, 4 subnets
O IA    10.0.0.8 [110/128] via 10.0.0.2, 00:11:04, Serial0/0
O IA    10.0.0.12 [110/845] via 10.0.0.6, 00:11:04, Serial0/1
        192.168.1.0/32 is subnetted, 1 subnets
O E1    192.168.1.0 [110/84] via 10.0.0.6, 00:11:04, Serial0/1
        192.168.2.0/32 is subnetted, 1 subnets
O E1    192.168.2.0 [110/84] via 10.0.0.6, 00:11:04, Serial0/1
        150.2.0.0/24 is subnetted, 1 subnets
O       150.2.2.0 [110/65] via 10.0.0.2, 00:11:04, Serial0/0
O*E2 0.0.0.0/0 [110/1] via 10.0.0.6, 00:00:38, Serial0/1

R2#show ip route ospf
        10.0.0.0/30 is subnetted, 4 subnets
O IA    10.0.0.12 [110/845] via 10.0.0.10, 00:09:42, Serial0/1
O IA    10.0.0.4 [110/845] via 10.0.0.10, 00:09:42, Serial0/1
        11.0.0.0/32 is subnetted, 1 subnets
O E2    11.11.11.11 [110/20] via 10.0.0.1, 00:09:42, Serial0/0
        192.168.1.0/32 is subnetted, 1 subnets
O E1    192.168.1.0 [110/84] via 10.0.0.10, 00:09:42, Serial0/1
        192.168.2.0/32 is subnetted, 1 subnets
O E1    192.168.2.0 [110/84] via 10.0.0.10, 00:09:42, Serial0/1
        150.1.0.0/24 is subnetted, 1 subnets
O       150.1.1.0 [110/65] via 10.0.0.1, 00:09:42, Serial0/0
        150.3.0.0/24 is subnetted, 1 subnets
O       150.3.3.0 [110/65] via 10.0.0.10, 00:09:42, Serial0/1
O*E2 0.0.0.0/0 [110/1] via 10.0.0.10, 00:00:54, Serial0/1
```

Finally, verify that R1 and R2 can still ping the 150.3.3.0/24 and 150.4.4.0/24 subnets:

```
R1#ping 150.3.3.3 source fastethernet 0/0 repeat 10

Type escape sequence to abort.
Sending 10, 100-byte ICMP Echos to 150.3.3.3, timeout is 2 seconds:
Packet sent with a source address of 150.1.1.1
!!!!!!!!!!
Success rate is 100 percent (10/10), round-trip min/avg/max = 16/16/20 ms
R1#
R1#ping 150.4.4.4 source fastethernet 0/0 repeat 10

Type escape sequence to abort.
Sending 10, 100-byte ICMP Echos to 150.4.4.4, timeout is 2 seconds:
```

```
Packet sent with a source address of 150.1.1.1
!!!!!!!!!!
Success rate is 100 percent (10/10), round-trip min/avg/max = 28/29/32 ms

R2#ping 150.3.3.3 source fastethernet 0/0 repeat 10

Type escape sequence to abort.
Sending 10, 100-byte ICMP Echos to 150.3.3.3, timeout is 2 seconds:
Packet sent with a source address of 150.2.2.2
!!!!!!!!!!
Success rate is 100 percent (10/10), round-trip min/avg/max = 16/16/16 ms
R2#
R2#ping 150.4.4.4 source fastethernet 0/0 repeat 10

Type escape sequence to abort.
Sending 10, 100-byte ICMP Echos to 150.4.4.4, timeout is 2 seconds:
Packet sent with a source address of 150.2.2.2
!!!!!!!!!!
Success rate is 100 percent (10/10), round-trip min/avg/max = 28/29/32 ms
```

Task 6

To complete this task, use the `area <area> filter-list prefix <name> in` command on R1 and R3 to prevent Type 3 LSAs for the 150.1.1.0/24 and 150.2.2.0/24 subnets from being advertised into area 3. For verification, prior to filtering changes, the LSDBs on R1 and R3 show:

```
R1#show ip ospf database

        OSPF Router with ID (1.1.1.1) (Process ID 1)

[Truncated Output]

            Summary Net Link States (Area 3)

Link ID          ADV Router       Age       Seq#        Checksum
10.0.0.0         3.3.3.3          403       0x80000004 0x00B422
10.0.0.8         3.3.3.3          403       0x80000004 0x00E12D
10.0.0.12        3.3.3.3          403       0x80000004 0x00B951
150.1.1.0        3.3.3.3          403       0x80000004 0x0096AD
150.2.2.0        3.3.3.3          403       0x80000004 0x00FC85

[Truncated Output]

R3#show ip ospf database

        OSPF Router with ID (3.3.3.3) (Process ID 3)

[Truncated Output]

            Summary Net Link States (Area 3)

Link ID          ADV Router       Age       Seq#        Checksum
10.0.0.0         3.3.3.3          453       0x80000004 0x00B422
10.0.0.8         3.3.3.3          453       0x80000004 0x00E12D
10.0.0.12        3.3.3.3          453       0x80000004 0x00B951
150.1.1.0        3.3.3.3          453       0x80000004 0x0096AD
150.2.2.0        3.3.3.3          453       0x80000004 0x00FC85

[Truncated Output]
```

Complete this task by filtering the Type 3 LSAs for the 150.1.1.0/24 and 150.2.2.0/24 from being advertised into area 3. The `area <area> filter-list prefix <name> out` command prevents Type 3 LSAs from being advertised out of the specified area(s):

```
R1(config)#ip prefix-list FILTER seq 5 deny 150.1.1.0/24
R1(config)#ip prefix-list FILTER seq 7 deny 150.2.2.0/24
R1(config)#ip prefix-list FILTER seq 9 permit 0.0.0.0/0 le 32
R1(config)#router ospf 1
R1(config-router)#area 1 filter-list prefix FILTER in
R1(config-router)#exit
R3(config)#ip prefix-list FILTER seq 5 deny 150.1.1.0/24
```

```
R3(config)#ip prefix-list FILTER seq 7 deny 150.2.2.0/24
R3(config)#ip prefix-list FILTER seq 9 permit 0.0.0.0/0 le 32
R3(config)#router ospf 3
R3(config-router)#area 1 filter-list prefix FILTER in
R3(config-router)#exit
```

Following this configuration, the LSDBs on R1 and R3 show:

```
R1#show ip ospf database

            OSPF Router with ID (1.1.1.1) (Process ID 1)

            Router Link States (Area 2)

[Truncated Output]

            Summary Net Link States (Area 3)

Link ID        ADV Router       Age       Seq#        Checksum
10.0.0.0       3.3.3.3          859       0x80000004  0x00B422
10.0.0.8       3.3.3.3          859       0x80000004  0x00E12D
10.0.0.12      3.3.3.3          859       0x80000004  0x00B951

[Truncated Output]

R3#show ip ospf database

            OSPF Router with ID (3.3.3.3) (Process ID 3)

[Truncated Output]

            Summary Net Link States (Area 3)

Link ID        ADV Router       Age       Seq#        Checksum
10.0.0.0       3.3.3.3          887       0x80000004  0x00B422
10.0.0.8       3.3.3.3          887       0x80000004  0x00E12D
10.0.0.12      3.3.3.3          887       0x80000004  0x00B951

[Truncated Output]
```

FINAL ROUTER CONFIGURATIONS

R1

```
R1#term len 0
R1#sh run
Building configuration...

Current configuration : 1259 bytes
!
version 12.4
service timestamps debug datetime msec
service timestamps log datetime msec
no service password-encryption
!
hostname R1
!
boot-start-marker
boot-end-marker
!
no logging console
!
no aaa new-model
no network-clock-participate slot 1
no network-clock-participate wic 0
ip cef
!
no ip domain lookup
ip auth-proxy max-nodata-conns 3
ip admission max-nodata-conns 3
!
```

```
interface Loopback11
 ip address 11.11.11.11 255.255.255.255
!
interface FastEthernet0/0
 ip address 150.1.1.1 255.255.255.0
 duplex auto
 speed auto
!
interface Serial0/0
 ip address 10.0.0.1 255.255.255.252
 clock rate 2000000
!
interface Serial0/1
 ip address 10.0.0.5 255.255.255.252
!
router ospf 1
 router-id 1.1.1.1
 log-adjacency-changes
 area 3 filter-list prefix FILTER in
 redistribute connected subnets
 network 10.0.0.1 0.0.0.0 area 2
 network 10.0.0.5 0.0.0.0 area 3
 network 150.1.1.1 0.0.0.0 area 2
!
ip forward-protocol nd
!
no ip http server
no ip http secure-server
!
ip prefix-list FILTER seq 5 deny 150.1.1.0/24
ip prefix-list FILTER seq 7 deny 150.2.2.0/24
ip prefix-list FILTER seq 9 permit 0.0.0.0/0 le 32
!
control-plane
!
line con 0
line aux 0
line vty 0 4
 login
!
end

R1#
```

R2

```
R2#term len 0
R2#sh run
Building configuration...

Current configuration : 1014 bytes
!
version 12.4
service timestamps debug datetime msec
service timestamps log datetime msec
no service password-encryption
!
hostname R2
!
boot-start-marker
boot-end-marker
!
no logging console
!
no aaa new-model
no network-clock-participate slot 1
no network-clock-participate wic 0
ip cef
!
no ip domain lookup
ip auth-proxy max-nodata-conns 3
ip admission max-nodata-conns 3
!
interface FastEthernet0/0
 ip address 150.2.2.2 255.255.255.0
 duplex auto
```

```
 speed auto
!
interface Serial0/0
 ip address 10.0.0.2 255.255.255.252
!
interface Serial0/1
 ip address 10.0.0.9 255.255.255.252
!
router ospf 2
 router-id 2.2.2.2
 log-adjacency-changes
 area 0 range 150.3.3.0 255.255.255.0 not-advertise
 network 10.0.0.2 0.0.0.0 area 2
 network 10.0.0.9 0.0.0.0 area 0
 network 150.2.2.2 0.0.0.0 area 2
!
ip forward-protocol nd
!
no ip http server
no ip http secure-server
!
control-plane
!
line con 0
line aux 0
line vty 0 4
 login
!
end

R2#
```

R3

```
R3#term len 0
R3#sh run
Building configuration...

Current configuration : 1758 bytes
!
version 12.4
service timestamps debug datetime msec
service timestamps log datetime msec
no service password-encryption
!
hostname R3
!
boot-start-marker
boot-end-marker
!
no logging console
!
no aaa new-model
no network-clock-participate slot 1
no network-clock-participate wic 0
ip cef
!
no ip domain lookup
ip auth-proxy max-nodata-conns 3
ip admission max-nodata-conns 3
!
interface FastEthernet0/0
 ip address 150.3.3.3 255.255.255.0
 duplex auto
 speed auto
!
interface Serial1/0
 ip address 10.0.0.6 255.255.255.252
 clock rate 128000
!
interface Serial1/1
 ip address 10.0.0.10 255.255.255.252
 clock rate 128000
!
interface Serial1/2
```

```
 ip address 10.0.0.13 255.255.255.252
 clock rate 128000
!
interface Serial1/3
 no ip address
 shutdown
!
interface Serial1/4
 no ip address
 shutdown
!
interface Serial1/5
 no ip address
 shutdown
!
interface Serial1/6
 no ip address
 shutdown
!
interface Serial1/7
 no ip address
 shutdown
!
router ospf 3
 router-id 3.3.3.3
 log-adjacency-changes
 area 0 range 150.3.3.0 255.255.255.0 not-advertise
 area 3 filter-list prefix FILTER in
 area 4 nssa default-information-originate
 area 4 nssa translate type7 suppress-fa
 area 4 range 150.4.4.0 255.255.255.0 not-advertise
 network 10.0.0.6 0.0.0.0 area 3
 network 10.0.0.10 0.0.0.0 area 0
 network 10.0.0.13 0.0.0.0 area 4
 network 150.3.3.3 0.0.0.0 area 0
 default-information originate always
!
ip forward-protocol nd
!
no ip http server
no ip http secure-server
!
ip prefix-list FILTER seq 5 deny 150.1.1.0/24
ip prefix-list FILTER seq 7 deny 150.2.2.0/24
ip prefix-list FILTER seq 9 permit 0.0.0.0/0 le 32
!
control-plane
!
line con 0
line aux 0
line vty 0 4
 login
!
end

R3#
```

R4

```
R4#term len 0
R4#sh run
Building configuration...

Current configuration : 1073 bytes
!
version 12.4
service timestamps debug datetime msec
service timestamps log datetime msec
no service password-encryption
!
hostname R4
!
boot-start-marker
boot-end-marker
```

```
!
no logging console
!
no aaa new-model
no network-clock-participate slot 1
no network-clock-participate wic 0
ip cef
!
no ip domain lookup
ip auth-proxy max-nodata-conns 3
ip admission max-nodata-conns 3
!
interface FastEthernet0/0
 ip address 150.4.4.4 255.255.255.0
 duplex auto
 speed auto
!
interface Serial0/0
 ip address 10.0.0.14 255.255.255.252
!
interface Serial0/1
 no ip address
 shutdown
!
router ospf 4
 router-id 4.4.4.4
 log-adjacency-changes
 area 4 nssa
 redistribute static metric-type 1 subnets
 network 10.0.0.14 0.0.0.0 area 4
 network 150.4.4.4 0.0.0.0 area 4
!
ip forward-protocol nd
ip route 192.168.1.0 255.255.255.255 150.4.4.254
ip route 192.168.2.0 255.255.255.255 150.4.4.254
!
no ip http server
no ip http secure-server
!
control-plane
!
line con 0
line aux 0
line vty 0 4
 login
!
end

R4#
```

CCNP LAB 28

OSPF Multi-Technology Lab

Lab Objective:

The focus of this lab is to understand OSPF implementation and configuration in Cisco IOS routers. Additional technologies tested include authentication, optimization and resiliency.

Lab Topology:

The lab network topology is illustrated below:

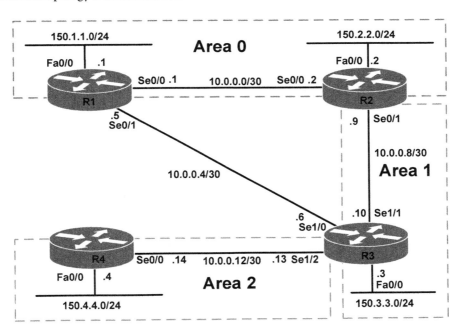

IMPORTANT NOTE: If you are using the www.howtonetwork.net racks, please bring up the LAN interfaces connected to the routers by issuing the no shutdown command on the connected switches. If you are using a home lab with no Switches, you can bring up the LAN interfaces using the following configurations on your routers:

```
interface fastethernet 0/0
 no keepalive
 loopback
 no shutdown
```

Alternately, you can simply connect the interfaces to a hub or switch if you have one available in your own lab.

Task 1

Configure hostnames and IP addressing on all routers as illustrated in the network topology.

Task 2

Using legacy `network x.x.x.x y.y.y.y area <area>` OSPF configuration commands, configure OSPF as illustrated in the topology. Ensure that all routers are able to reach each other. Do NOT enable OSPF over the point-to-point link between R1 and R3. Additionally, ensure that no OSPF packets are sent out of the LAN interfaces on any routers. Verify the OSPF configuration using the appropriate commands.

Task 3

Authenticate the OSPF backbone using MD5 authentication with a secret of 'CCNP'. Verify that all routing is still functional following this change.

Task 4

Management is concerned about how a large Link State Database can cause adverse issues, such as performance issues, on a router. They would link to see if the LSDB on all routers can be restricted to no more than 100 LSAs. As a test, configure your network so that OSPF will limit the size of the LSDB to 100 non self-generated LSAs. For the time being, OSPF should only log a warning message when 80% of this number has been reached.

In addition to this, configure the network so that if any router is rebooted, it will send router LSAs with a metric of infinity for 5 minutes after it has come back up. Verify your configuration using the appropriate commands.

Task 5

Management has stated that the network will grow to significant amount of routers in the near future. This deployment will include numerous OSPF areas. They are worried about convergence and would like you to ensure that only minimal SPF calculations are performed when changes to router or network LSAs occur within an area. Given this, configure your network so that and full SPF calculation is NOT performed, unless these changes are local to the router in question. Verify your configuration using the appropriate commands.

Task 6

The R2-to-R3 link has had a bad history of failures and management is afraid that they might lose connectivity to parts of the network when this goes down. They have therefore decided to get a point-to-point link between R1 and R3 for backup purposes should the link between R2 and R3 fail. They request that you use EIGRP to ensure that R3 and R4 can still communicate with R1 and R2 when the R2-to-R3 link fails.

However, they have made it explicitly clear that when the R2-to-R3 link is up, only OSPF routes should exist in the network. Management is fine with both internal and external OSPF and EIGRP routes when using the backup link. Additionally, you are allowed to make basic modifications to OSPF to get this solution to work. Given this information, implement a routing solution to meet these requirements. Verify your configuration by shutting down the R2-to-R3 point-to-point link and pinging LAN-to-LAN between R4 and R2.

LAB VALIDATION

Task 1

```
Router(config)#hostname R1
R1(config)#interface fastethernet 0/0
R1(config-if)#no shutdown
R1(config-if)#ip address 150.1.1.1 255.255.255.0
R1(config-if)#exit
R1(config)#interface serial 0/0
R1(config-if)#no shutdown
R1(config-if)#ip address 10.0.1.1 255.255.255.252
R1(config-if)#clock rate 2000000
R1(config-if)#exit
R1(config)#interface serial 0/1
R1(config-if)#ip address 10.0.0.5 255.255.255.252
```

```
R1(config-if)#no shutdown
R1(config-if)#exit

Router(config)#hostname R2
R2(config)#interface fastethernet 0/0
R2(config-if)#no shutdown
R2(config-if)#ip address 150.2.2.2 255.255.255.0
R2(config-if)#exit
R2(config)#interface serial 0/0
R2(config-if)#no shutdown
R2(config-if)#ip address 10.0.1.2 255.255.255.252
R2(config-if)#exit
R2(config)#interface serial 0/1
R2(config-if)#ip address 10.0.0.9 255.255.255.252
R2(config-if)#no shutdown
R2(config-if)#exit

Router(config)#hostname R3
R3(config)#interface fastethernet 0/0
R3(config-if)#ip address 150.3.3.3 255.255.255.0
R3(config-if)#exit
R3(config)#interface serial 1/0
R3(config-if)#ip address 10.0.0.6 255.255.255.252
R3(config-if)#no shutdown
R3(config-if)# clock rate 128000
R3(config-if)#exit
R3(config)#interface serial 1/1
R3(config-if)#ip address 10.0.0.10 255.255.255.252
R3(config-if)#no shutdown
R3(config-if)# clock rate 128000
R3(config-if)#exit
R3(config)#interface serial 1/2
R3(config-if)#ip address 10.0.0.13 255.255.255.252
R3(config-if)#no shutdown
R3(config-if)# clock rate 128000
R3(config-if)#exit

Router(config)#hostname R4
R4(config)#interface fastethernet 0/0
R4(config-if)#ip address 150.4.4.4 255.255.255.0
R4(config-if)#exit
R4(config)#interface serial 0/0
R4(config-if)#ip address 10.0.0.14 255.255.255.252
R4(config-if)#no shutdown
R4(config-if)#exit
```

Task 2

In order to complete this task, you need to ensure that you configure a virtual link across area 1, otherwise area 2 routes will not be reachable from R1 and R2. This is completed as follows:

```
R1(config)#router ospf 1
R1(config-router)#router-id 1.1.1.1
R1(config-router)#network 150.1.1.1 0.0.0.0 area 0
R1(config-router)#network 10.0.0.1 0.0.0.0 area 0
R1(config-router)#passive-interface fastethernet 0/0
R1(config-router)#exit

R2(config)#router ospf 2
R2(config-router)#router-id 2.2.2.2
R2(config-router)#area 1 virtual-link 3.3.3.3
R2(config-router)#network 150.2.2.2 0.0.0.0 area 0
R2(config-router)#network 10.0.0.2 0.0.0.0 area 0
R2(config-router)#network 10.0.0.9 0.0.0.0 area 1
R2(config-router)#passive-interface fastethernet 0/0
R2(config-router)#exit

R3(config)#router ospf 3
R3(config-router)#router-id 3.3.3.3
R3(config-router)#area 1 virtual-link 2.2.2.2
R3(config-router)#network 150.3.3.3 0.0.0.0 area 1
R3(config-router)#network 10.0.0.10 0.0.0.0 area 1
```

```
R3(config-router)#network 10.0.0.13 0.0.0.0 area 2
R3(config-router)#passive-interface fastethernet 0/0
R3(config-router)#exit

R4(config)#router ospf 4
R4(config-router)#router-id 4.4.4.4
R4(config-router)#network 150.4.4.4 0.0.0.0 area 2
R4(config-router)#network 10.0.0.14 0.0.0.0 area 2
R4(config-router)#passive-interface fastethernet 0/0
R4(config-router)#exit
```

Verify your OSPF configuration using the show ip ospf neighbor command:

```
R1#show ip ospf neighbor

Neighbor ID     Pri   State       Dead Time   Address     Interface
2.2.2.2           0   FULL/  -    00:00:36    10.0.0.2    Serial0/0

R2#show ip ospf neighbor

Neighbor ID     Pri   State       Dead Time   Address     Interface
3.3.3.3           0   FULL/  -    -           10.0.0.10   OSPF_VL0
1.1.1.1           0   FULL/  -    00:00:31    10.0.0.1    Serial0/0
3.3.3.3           0   FULL/  -    00:00:37    10.0.0.10   Serial0/1

R3#show ip ospf neighbor

Neighbor ID     Pri   State       Dead Time   Address     Interface
2.2.2.2           0   FULL/  -    -           10.0.0.9    OSPF_VL0
2.2.2.2           0   FULL/  -    00:00:39    10.0.0.9    Serial1/1
4.4.4.4           0   FULL/  -    00:00:31    10.0.0.14   Serial1/2

R4#show ip ospf neighbor

Neighbor ID     Pri   State       Dead Time   Address     Interface
3.3.3.3           0   FULL/  -    00:00:34    10.0.0.13   Serial0/0
```

Task 3

This task is straightforward; however, you must remember that the virtual link is a logical extension of area 0 (the backbone) and this needs authentication configuration as well. This means that area 0 authentication must also be configured on R3 even though no interfaces actually reside within the backbone area. This task is completed as follows:

```
R1(config)#router ospf 1
R1(config-router)#area 0 authentication message-digest
R1(config-router)#exit
R1(config)#interface serial 0/0
R1(config-if)#ip ospf message-digest-key 1 md5 CCNP
R1(config-if)#exit

R2(config)#router ospf 2
R2(config-router)#area 0 authentication message-digest
R2(config-router)#area 1 virtual-link 3.3.3.3 message-digest-key 1 md5 CCNP
R2(config-router)#exit
R2(config)#interface serial 0/0
R2(config-if)#ip ospf message-digest-key 1 md5 CCNP
R2(config-if)#exit

R3(config)#router ospf 3
R3(config-router)#area 0 authentication message-digest
R3(config-router)#area 1 virtual-link 2.2.2.2 message-digest-key 1 md5 CCNP
R3(config-router)#exit
```

Following OSPF backbone authentication configuration, verify the backbone area adjacencies:

```
R1#show ip ospf neighbor
```

```
Neighbor ID      Pri   State          Dead Time   Address      Interface
2.2.2.2            0   FULL/  -        00:00:39    10.0.0.2     Serial0/0

R2#show ip ospf neighbor

Neighbor ID      Pri   State          Dead Time   Address      Interface
3.3.3.3            0   FULL/  -           -        10.0.0.10    OSPF_VL0
1.1.1.1            0   FULL/  -        00:00:36    10.0.0.1     Serial0/0
3.3.3.3            0   FULL/  -        00:00:32    10.0.0.10    Serial0/1

R3#show ip ospf neighbor

Neighbor ID      Pri   State          Dead Time   Address      Interface
2.2.2.2            0   FULL/  -           -        10.0.0.9     OSPF_VL0
2.2.2.2            0   FULL/  -        00:00:39    10.0.0.9     Serial1/1
4.4.4.4            0   FULL/  -        00:00:31    10.0.0.14    Serial1/2
```

NOTE: Use the `show ip ospf neighbor detail` command for additional detail. To view information about the virtual links, use the show ip ospf virtual-links command:

```
R2#show ip ospf virtual-links
Virtual Link OSPF_VL0 to router 3.3.3.3 is up
  Run as demand circuit
  DoNotAge LSA allowed.
  Transit area 1, via interface Serial0/1, Cost of using 64
  Transmit Delay is 1 sec, State POINT_TO_POINT,
  Timer intervals configured, Hello 10, Dead 40, Wait 40, Retransmit 5
    Hello due in 00:00:06
    Adjacency State FULL (Hello suppressed)
    Index 2/3, retransmission queue length 0, number of retransmission 0
    First 0x0(0)/0x0(0) Next 0x0(0)/0x0(0)
    Last retransmission scan length is 0, maximum is 0
    Last retransmission scan time is 0 msec, maximum is 0 msec
  Message digest authentication enabled
    Youngest key id is 1
```

Task 4

The OSPF Link-State Database Overload Protection feature allows you to limit the number of non self-generated LSAs for a given OSPF process. Excessive LSAs generated by other routers in the OSPF domain can substantially drain the CPU and memory resources of the router. To complete the first part of this task, you need to enable this feature using the `max-lsa <maximum> [threshold-percentage] [warning-only] [ignore-time minutes] [ignore-count count-number] [reset-time minutes]` command.

To complete the second part of this task, you will need to enable the Stub Router Advertisement feature which allows a router to advertise infinity metric (0xFFFF) for its connected links in Router LSAs, and advertise normal interface cost if the link is a stub network. The `max-metric router-lsa on-startup <seconds>` command is used to enable this feature. Be careful when performing such activities in production networks because OSPF adjacencies will be reset.

This task is completed as follows:

```
R1(config)#router ospf 1
R1(config-router)#max-lsa 100 80 warning-only
R1(config-router)#max-metric router-lsa on-startup 300
R1(config-router)#exit

R2(config)#router ospf 2
R2(config-router)#max-lsa 100 80 warning-only
R2(config-router)#max-metric router-lsa on-startup 300
R2(config-router)#exit

R3(config)#router ospf 3
R3(config-router)#max-lsa 100 80 warning-only
R3(config-router)#max-metric router-lsa on-startup 300
```

```
R3(config-router)#exit

R4(config)#router ospf 4
R4(config-router)#max-lsa 100 80 warning-only
R4(config-router)#max-metric router-lsa on-startup 300
R4(config-router)#exit
```

Verify your configurations using the show ip ospf command:

```
R4#show ip ospf
 Routing Process "ospf 4" with ID 4.4.4.4
 Start time: 02:45:57.136, Time elapsed: 00:52:38.132
 Supports only single TOS(TOS0) routes
 Supports opaque LSA
 Supports Link-local Signaling (LLS)
 Supports area transit capability
 Maximum number of non self-generated LSA allowed 100 (warning-only)
    Threshold for warning message 80%
 Originating router-LSAs with maximum metric
    Condition: on startup for 300 seconds, State: inactive
 Initial SPF schedule delay 5000 msecs
 Minimum hold time between two consecutive SPFs 10000 msecs
 Maximum wait time between two consecutive SPFs 10000 msecs

[Truncated Output]
```

Task 5

To complete this task, you need to enable the incremental SPF feature. When this feature is enabled, the router will run a partial SPF to recompute the parts of the tree that have been affected, instead of running a full or complete SPF recomputation. This feature saves router resources, such as processor (CPU) and allows for faster OSPF convergence.

When incremental SPF is enabled, the local router will run a full or complete SPF recomputation is when the changes to the router and network LSAs occurred on the local router itself. Incremental SPF is scheduled in the same way as the full SPF. Routers enabled with incremental SPF and routers not enabled with incremental SPF can function in the same internetwork. This task is completed as follows:

```
R1(config)#router ospf 1
R1(config-router)#ispf
R1(config-router)#exit

R2(config)#router ospf 2
R2(config-router)#ispf
R2(config-router)#exit

R3(config)#router ospf 3
R3(config-router)#ispf
R3(config-router)#exit

R4(config)#router ospf 4
R4(config-router)#ispf
R4(config-router)#exit
```

Verify your configuration using the show ip ospf command:

```
R1#show ip ospf
 Routing Process "ospf 1" with ID 1.1.1.1
 Start time: 02:42:17.444, Time elapsed: 01:08:22.652

[Truncated Output]

 Initial SPF schedule delay 5000 msecs
 Minimum hold time between two consecutive SPFs 10000 msecs
 Maximum wait time between two consecutive SPFs 10000 msecs
 Incremental-SPF enabled
 Minimum LSA interval 5 secs
```

```
Minimum LSA arrival 1000 msecs
LSA group pacing timer 240 secs

[Truncated Output]
```

Task 6

This task may initially seem daunting but after further observation, it is pretty straightforward. The solution is to enable EIGRP on the point-to-point link between R1 and R3 and then redistribute between EIGRP and OSPF on both routers. Because external EIGRP routes have an administrative distance of 170, only OSPF routes will be installed into the routing tables.

The only caveat here is understanding multi-area OSPF behavior. By default, inter-area routes will not be advertised when there is no backbone area. This means that when the R2-to-R3 point-to-point link fails, R4 will not receive the 150.3.3.0/24 route because it resides in area 1. You cannot redistribute this into OSPF on R3 because that results in a Type 5 LSA. Again, without a backbone area, this LSA is not flooded into area 2. The only solution is to reconfigure your OSPF network so that this interface resides in area 2. This task is completed as follows:

```
R1(config)#router eigrp 1
R1(config-router)#no auto-summary
R1(config-router)#network 10.0.0.5 0.0.0.0
R1(config-router)#redistribute ospf 1 metric 100000 100 255 1 1500
R1(config-router)#exit
R1(config)#router ospf 1
R1(config-router)#redistribute eigrp 1 subnets
R1(config-router)#exit

R3(config)#router eigrp 1
R3(config-router)#no auto-summary
R3(config-router)#network 10.0.0.6 0.0.0.0
R3(config-router)#redistribute ospf 3 metric 100000 100 255 1 1500
R3(config-router)#exit
R3(config)#router ospf 3
R3(config-router)#network 150.3.3.3 0.0.0.0 area 2
R3(config-router)#redistribute eigrp 1 subnets
R3(config-router)#exit
```

Following your configuration, first verify EIGRP neighbor relationships:

```
R1#show ip eigrp neighbors
IP-EIGRP neighbors for process 1
H   Address          Interface      Hold Uptime   SRTT   RTO  Q  Seq
                                    (sec)         (ms)        Cnt Num

0   10.0.0.6         Se0/1          10 00:00:56    14    200  0  5


R3#show ip eigrp neighbors
IP-EIGRP neighbors for process 1
H   Address          Interface      Hold Uptime   SRTT   RTO  Q  Seq
                                    (sec)         (ms)        Cnt Num

0   10.0.0.5         Se1/0          10 00:01:23    18    1140 0  3
```

Next, verify the routing tables and ensure that all routes are known via OSPF as required:

```
R1#show ip route
Codes: C - connected, S - static, R - RIP, M - mobile, B - BGP
       D - EIGRP, EX - EIGRP external, O - OSPF, IA - OSPF inter area
       N1 - OSPF NSSA external type 1, N2 - OSPF NSSA external type 2
       E1 - OSPF external type 1, E2 - OSPF external type 2
       i - IS-IS, su - IS-IS summary, L1 - IS-IS level-1, L2 - IS-IS level-2
       ia - IS-IS inter area, * - candidate default, U - per-user static route
       o - ODR, P - periodic downloaded static route

Gateway of last resort is not set

     10.0.0.0/30 is subnetted, 4 subnets
```

```
O IA    10.0.0.8 [110/128] via 10.0.0.2, 00:00:03, Serial0/0
O IA    10.0.0.12 [110/909] via 10.0.0.2, 00:00:03, Serial0/0
C       10.0.0.0 is directly connected, Serial0/0
C       10.0.0.4 is directly connected, Serial0/1
        150.1.0.0/24 is subnetted, 1 subnets
C       150.1.1.0 is directly connected, FastEthernet0/0
        150.2.0.0/24 is subnetted, 1 subnets
O       150.2.2.0 [110/65] via 10.0.0.2, 00:00:03, Serial0/0
        150.3.0.0/24 is subnetted, 1 subnets
O IA    150.3.3.0 [110/129] via 10.0.0.2, 00:00:04, Serial0/0

R2#show ip route
Codes: C - connected, S - static, R - RIP, M - mobile, B - BGP
       D - EIGRP, EX - EIGRP external, O - OSPF, IA - OSPF inter area
       N1 - OSPF NSSA external type 1, N2 - OSPF NSSA external type 2
       E1 - OSPF external type 1, E2 - OSPF external type 2
       i - IS-IS, su - IS-IS summary, L1 - IS-IS level-1, L2 - IS-IS level-2
       ia - IS-IS inter area, * - candidate default, U - per-user static route
       o - ODR, P - periodic downloaded static route

Gateway of last resort is not set

        10.0.0.0/30 is subnetted, 4 subnets
C       10.0.0.8 is directly connected, Serial0/1
O IA    10.0.0.12 [110/845] via 10.0.0.10, 00:00:09, Serial0/1
C       10.0.0.0 is directly connected, Serial0/0
O E2    10.0.0.4 [110/20] via 10.0.0.10, 00:00:09, Serial0/1
                   [110/20] via 10.0.0.1, 00:00:09, Serial0/0
        150.1.0.0/24 is subnetted, 1 subnets
O       150.1.1.0 [110/65] via 10.0.0.1, 00:00:09, Serial0/0
        150.2.0.0/24 is subnetted, 1 subnets
C       150.2.2.0 is directly connected, FastEthernet0/0
        150.3.0.0/24 is subnetted, 1 subnets
O       150.3.3.0 [110/65] via 10.0.0.10, 00:00:11, Serial0/1

R3#show ip route
Codes: C - connected, S - static, R - RIP, M - mobile, B - BGP
       D - EIGRP, EX - EIGRP external, O - OSPF, IA - OSPF inter area
       N1 - OSPF NSSA external type 1, N2 - OSPF NSSA external type 2
       E1 - OSPF external type 1, E2 - OSPF external type 2
       i - IS-IS, su - IS-IS summary, L1 - IS-IS level-1, L2 - IS-IS level-2
       ia - IS-IS inter area, * - candidate default, U - per-user static route
       o - ODR, P - periodic downloaded static route

Gateway of last resort is not set

        10.0.0.0/30 is subnetted, 4 subnets
C       10.0.0.8 is directly connected, Serial1/1
C       10.0.0.12 is directly connected, Serial1/2
O       10.0.0.0 [110/845] via 10.0.0.9, 00:00:20, Serial1/1
C       10.0.0.4 is directly connected, Serial1/0
        150.1.0.0/24 is subnetted, 1 subnets
O       150.1.1.0 [110/782] via 10.0.0.14, 00:00:30, Serial1/2
        150.2.0.0/24 is subnetted, 1 subnets
O       150.2.2.0 [110/782] via 10.0.0.9, 00:00:20, Serial1/1
        150.3.0.0/24 is subnetted, 1 subnets
C       150.3.3.0 is directly connected, FastEthernet0/0

R4#show ip route
Codes: C - connected, S - static, R - RIP, M - mobile, B - BGP
       D - EIGRP, EX - EIGRP external, O - OSPF, IA - OSPF inter area
       N1 - OSPF NSSA external type 1, N2 - OSPF NSSA external type 2
       E1 - OSPF external type 1, E2 - OSPF external type 2
       i - IS-IS, su - IS-IS summary, L1 - IS-IS level-1, L2 - IS-IS level-2
       ia - IS-IS inter area, * - candidate default, U - per-user static route
       o - ODR, P - periodic downloaded static route

Gateway of last resort is not set

        10.0.0.0/30 is subnetted, 4 subnets
O IA    10.0.0.8 [110/845] via 10.0.0.13, 00:00:36, Serial0/0
C       10.0.0.12 is directly connected, Serial0/0
O IA    10.0.0.0 [110/909] via 10.0.0.13, 00:00:26, Serial0/0
O E2    10.0.0.4 [110/20] via 10.0.0.13, 00:00:26, Serial0/0
```

```
        150.1.0.0/24 is subnetted, 1 subnets
C          150.1.1.0 is directly connected, FastEthernet0/0
        150.2.0.0/24 is subnetted, 1 subnets
O IA       150.2.2.0 [110/846] via 10.0.0.13, 00:00:26, Serial0/0
        150.3.0.0/24 is subnetted, 1 subnets
O IA       150.3.3.0 [110/65] via 10.0.0.13, 00:00:37, Serial0/0
```

Finally, test your solution by shutting down the link between R2 and R3:

```
R3(config)#interface serial 1/1
R3(config-if)#shutdown
```

After shutting down the R2-to-R3 link, check the routing tables on all routers again:

```
R1#show ip route
Codes: C - connected, S - static, R - RIP, M - mobile, B - BGP
       D - EIGRP, EX - EIGRP external, O - OSPF, IA - OSPF inter area
       N1 - OSPF NSSA external type 1, N2 - OSPF NSSA external type 2
       E1 - OSPF external type 1, E2 - OSPF external type 2
       i - IS-IS, su - IS-IS summary, L1 - IS-IS level-1, L2 - IS-IS level-2
       ia - IS-IS inter area, * - candidate default, U - per-user static route
       o - ODR, P - periodic downloaded static route

Gateway of last resort is not set

        10.0.0.0/30 is subnetted, 3 subnets
D EX    10.0.0.12 [170/2195456] via 10.0.0.6, 00:06:31, Serial0/1
C       10.0.0.0 is directly connected, Serial0/0
C       10.0.0.4 is directly connected, Serial0/1
        150.1.0.0/24 is subnetted, 1 subnets
C          150.1.1.0 is directly connected, FastEthernet0/0
        150.2.0.0/24 is subnetted, 1 subnets
O          150.2.2.0 [110/65] via 10.0.0.2, 00:06:31, Serial0/0
        150.3.0.0/24 is subnetted, 1 subnets
D EX       150.3.3.0 [170/2195456] via 10.0.0.6, 00:06:31, Serial0/1
        150.4.0.0/24 is subnetted, 1 subnets
D EX       150.4.4.0 [170/2195456] via 10.0.0.6, 00:06:32, Serial0/1

R2#show ip route
Codes: C - connected, S - static, R - RIP, M - mobile, B - BGP
       D - EIGRP, EX - EIGRP external, O - OSPF, IA - OSPF inter area
       N1 - OSPF NSSA external type 1, N2 - OSPF NSSA external type 2
       E1 - OSPF external type 1, E2 - OSPF external type 2
       i - IS-IS, su - IS-IS summary, L1 - IS-IS level-1, L2 - IS-IS level-2
       ia - IS-IS inter area, * - candidate default, U - per-user static route
       o - ODR, P - periodic downloaded static route

Gateway of last resort is not set

        10.0.0.0/30 is subnetted, 3 subnets
O E2    10.0.0.12 [110/20] via 10.0.0.1, 00:07:39, Serial0/0
C       10.0.0.0 is directly connected, Serial0/0
O E2    10.0.0.4 [110/20] via 10.0.0.1, 00:07:39, Serial0/0
        150.1.0.0/24 is subnetted, 1 subnets
O          150.1.1.0 [110/65] via 10.0.0.1, 00:07:39, Serial0/0
        150.2.0.0/24 is subnetted, 1 subnets
C          150.2.2.0 is directly connected, FastEthernet0/0
        150.3.0.0/24 is subnetted, 1 subnets
O E2       150.3.3.0 [110/20] via 10.0.0.1, 00:07:40, Serial0/0
        150.4.0.0/24 is subnetted, 1 subnets
O E2       150.4.4.0 [110/20] via 10.0.0.1, 00:07:40, Serial0/0

R3#show ip route
Codes: C - connected, S - static, R - RIP, M - mobile, B - BGP
       D - EIGRP, EX - EIGRP external, O - OSPF, IA - OSPF inter area
       N1 - OSPF NSSA external type 1, N2 - OSPF NSSA external type 2
       E1 - OSPF external type 1, E2 - OSPF external type 2
       i - IS-IS, su - IS-IS summary, L1 - IS-IS level-1, L2 - IS-IS level-2
       ia - IS-IS inter area, * - candidate default, U - per-user static route
       o - ODR, P - periodic downloaded static route
```

```
Gateway of last resort is not set

      10.0.0.0/30 is subnetted, 3 subnets
C        10.0.0.12 is directly connected, Serial1/2
D EX     10.0.0.0 [170/20537600] via 10.0.0.5, 00:08:16, Serial1/0
C        10.0.0.4 is directly connected, Serial1/0
      150.1.0.0/24 is subnetted, 1 subnets
D EX      150.1.1.0 [170/20537600] via 10.0.0.5, 00:08:16, Serial1/0
      150.2.0.0/24 is subnetted, 1 subnets
D EX      150.2.2.0 [170/20537600] via 10.0.0.5, 00:08:16, Serial1/0
      150.3.0.0/24 is subnetted, 1 subnets
C         150.3.3.0 is directly connected, FastEthernet0/0
      150.4.0.0/24 is subnetted, 1 subnets
O         150.4.4.0 [110/782] via 10.0.0.14, 00:03:57, Serial1/2

R4#show ip route
Codes: C - connected, S - static, R - RIP, M - mobile, B - BGP
       D - EIGRP, EX - EIGRP external, O - OSPF, IA - OSPF inter area
       N1 - OSPF NSSA external type 1, N2 - OSPF NSSA external type 2
       E1 - OSPF external type 1, E2 - OSPF external type 2
       i - IS-IS, su - IS-IS summary, L1 - IS-IS level-1, L2 - IS-IS level-2
       ia - IS-IS inter area, * - candidate default, U - per-user static route
       o - ODR, P - periodic downloaded static route

Gateway of last resort is not set

      10.0.0.0/30 is subnetted, 3 subnets
C        10.0.0.12 is directly connected, Serial0/0
O E2     10.0.0.0 [110/20] via 10.0.0.13, 00:04:11, Serial0/0
O E2     10.0.0.4 [110/20] via 10.0.0.13, 00:04:11, Serial0/0
      150.1.0.0/24 is subnetted, 1 subnets
O E2      150.1.1.0 [110/20] via 10.0.0.13, 00:04:11, Serial0/0
      150.2.0.0/24 is subnetted, 1 subnets
O E2      150.2.2.0 [110/20] via 10.0.0.13, 00:04:11, Serial0/0
      150.3.0.0/24 is subnetted, 1 subnets
O         150.3.3.0 [110/65] via 10.0.0.13, 00:04:12, Serial0/0
      150.4.0.0/24 is subnetted, 1 subnets
C         150.4.4.0 is directly connected, FastEthernet0/0
```

Finally, verify your solution by pinging LAN-to-LAN between R4 and the other routers:

```
R4#ping 150.1.1.1 source fastethernet 0/0 repeat 10 size 100

Type escape sequence to abort.
Sending 10, 100-byte ICMP Echos to 150.1.1.1, timeout is 2 seconds:
Packet sent with a source address of 150.4.4.4
!!!!!!!!!!
Success rate is 100 percent (10/10), round-trip min/avg/max = 28/30/32 ms

R4#ping 150.2.2.2 source fastethernet 0/0 repeat 10 size 100

Type escape sequence to abort.
Sending 10, 100-byte ICMP Echos to 150.2.2.2, timeout is 2 seconds:
Packet sent with a source address of 150.4.4.4
!!!!!!!!!!
Success rate is 100 percent (10/10), round-trip min/avg/max = 28/30/32 ms

R4#ping 150.3.3.3 source fastethernet 0/0 repeat 10 size 100

Type escape sequence to abort.
Sending 10, 100-byte ICMP Echos to 150.3.3.3, timeout is 2 seconds:
Packet sent with a source address of 150.4.4.4
!!!!!!!!!!
Success rate is 100 percent (10/10), round-trip min/avg/max = 16/16/16 ms
```

FINAL ROUTER CONFIGURATIONS

R1

```
R1#term len 0
R1#sh run
Building configuration...

Current configuration : 1274 bytes
!
version 12.4
service timestamps debug datetime msec
service timestamps log datetime msec
no service password-encryption
!
hostname R1
!
boot-start-marker
boot-end-marker
!
no logging console
!
no aaa new-model
no network-clock-participate slot 1
no network-clock-participate wic 0
ip cef
!
no ip domain lookup
ip auth-proxy max-nodata-conns 3
ip admission max-nodata-conns 3
!
interface FastEthernet0/0
 ip address 150.1.1.1 255.255.255.0
 duplex auto
 speed auto
!
interface Serial0/0
 ip address 10.0.0.1 255.255.255.252
 ip ospf message-digest-key 1 md5 CCNP
 clock rate 2000000
!
interface Serial0/1
 ip address 10.0.0.5 255.255.255.252
!
router eigrp 1
 redistribute ospf 1 metric 100000 100 255 1 1500
 network 10.0.0.5 0.0.0.0
 no auto-summary
!
router ospf 1
 router-id 1.1.1.1
 max-metric router-lsa on-startup 300
 ispf
 log-adjacency-changes
 max-lsa 100 80 warning-only
 area 0 authentication message-digest
 redistribute eigrp 1 subnets
 passive-interface FastEthernet0/0
 network 10.0.0.1 0.0.0.0 area 0
 network 150.1.1.1 0.0.0.0 area 0
!
ip forward-protocol nd
!
no ip http server
no ip http secure-server
!
control-plane
!
line con 0
line aux 0
line vty 0 4
 login
!
end

R1#
```

R2

```
R2#term len 0
R2#sh run
Building configuration...

Current configuration : 1206 bytes
!
version 12.4
service timestamps debug datetime msec
service timestamps log datetime msec
no service password-encryption
!
hostname R2
!
boot-start-marker
boot-end-marker
!
no logging console
!
no aaa new-model
no network-clock-participate slot 1
no network-clock-participate wic 0
ip cef
!
no ip domain lookup
ip auth-proxy max-nodata-conns 3
ip admission max-nodata-conns 3
!
interface FastEthernet0/0
 ip address 150.2.2.2 255.255.255.0
 duplex auto
 speed auto
!
interface Serial0/0
 ip address 10.0.0.2 255.255.255.252
 ip ospf message-digest-key 1 md5 CCNP
!
interface Serial0/1
 ip address 10.0.0.9 255.255.255.252
!
router ospf 2
 router-id 2.2.2.2
 max-metric router-lsa on-startup 300
 ispf
 log-adjacency-changes
 max-lsa 100 80 warning-only
 area 0 authentication message-digest
 area 1 virtual-link 3.3.3.3 message-digest-key 1 md5 CCNP
 passive-interface FastEthernet0/0
 network 10.0.0.2 0.0.0.0 area 0
 network 10.0.0.9 0.0.0.0 area 1
 network 150.2.2.2 0.0.0.0 area 0
!
ip forward-protocol nd
!
no ip http server
no ip http secure-server
!
control-plane
!
line con 0
line aux 0
line vty 0 4
 login
!
end

R2#
```

R3

```
R3#term len 0
R3#sh run
Building configuration...

Current configuration : 1672 bytes
!
version 12.4
```

```
service timestamps debug datetime msec
service timestamps log datetime msec
no service password-encryption
!
hostname R3
!
boot-start-marker
boot-end-marker
!
no logging console
!
no aaa new-model
no network-clock-participate slot 1
no network-clock-participate wic 0
ip cef
!
no ip domain lookup
ip auth-proxy max-nodata-conns 3
ip admission max-nodata-conns 3
!
interface FastEthernet0/0
 ip address 150.3.3.3 255.255.255.0
 duplex auto
 speed auto
!
interface Serial1/0
 ip address 10.0.0.6 255.255.255.252
 clock rate 128000
!
interface Serial1/1
 ip address 10.0.0.10 255.255.255.252
 shutdown
 clock rate 128000
!
interface Serial1/2
 ip address 10.0.0.13 255.255.255.252
 clock rate 128000
!
interface Serial1/3
 no ip address
 shutdown
!
interface Serial1/4
 no ip address
 shutdown
!
interface Serial1/5
 no ip address
 shutdown
!
interface Serial1/6
 no ip address
 shutdown
!
interface Serial1/7
 no ip address
 shutdown
!
router eigrp 1
 redistribute ospf 3 metric 100000 100 255 1 1500
 network 10.0.0.6 0.0.0.0
 no auto-summary
!
router ospf 3
 router-id 3.3.3.3
 max-metric router-lsa on-startup 300
 ispf
 log-adjacency-changes
 max-lsa 100 80 warning-only
 area 0 authentication message-digest
 area 1 virtual-link 2.2.2.2 message-digest-key 1 md5 CCNP
 redistribute eigrp 1 subnets
 passive-interface FastEthernet0/0
 network 10.0.0.10 0.0.0.0 area 1
 network 10.0.0.13 0.0.0.0 area 2
 network 150.3.3.3 0.0.0.0 area 2
!
ip forward-protocol nd
!
no ip http server
no ip http secure-server
```

```
!
control-plane
!
line con 0
line aux 0
line vty 0 4
 login
!
end

R3#
```

R4

```
R4#term len 0
R4#sh run
Building configuration...

Current configuration : 1027 bytes
!
version 12.4
service timestamps debug datetime msec
service timestamps log datetime msec
no service password-encryption
!
hostname R4
!
boot-start-marker
boot-end-marker
!
no logging console
!
no aaa new-model
no network-clock-participate slot 1
no network-clock-participate wic 0
ip cef
!
no ip domain lookup
ip auth-proxy max-nodata-conns 3
ip admission max-nodata-conns 3
!
interface FastEthernet0/0
 ip address 150.4.4.4 255.255.255.0
 duplex auto
 speed auto
!
interface Serial0/0
 ip address 10.0.0.14 255.255.255.252
!
interface Serial0/1
 no ip address
 shutdown
!
router ospf 4
 router-id 4.4.4.4
 max-metric router-lsa on-startup 300
 ispf
 log-adjacency-changes
 max-lsa 100 80 warning-only
 passive-interface FastEthernet0/0
 network 10.0.0.14 0.0.0.0 area 2
 network 150.4.4.4 0.0.0.0 area 2
!
ip forward-protocol nd
!
no ip http server
no ip http secure-server
!
control-plane
!
line con 0
line aux 0
line vty 0 4
 login
!
end

R4#
```

CCNP LAB 29

OSPF Multi-Technology Lab

Lab Objective:

The focus of this lab is to understand OSPF implementation and configuration in Cisco IOS routers. Additional technologies tested include authentication, metrics and .

Lab Topology:

The lab network topology is illustrated below:

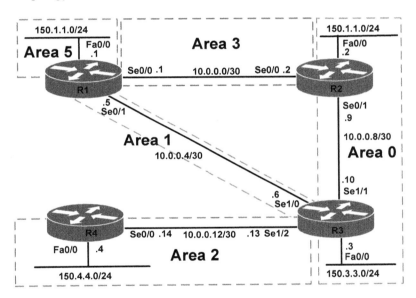

IMPORTANT NOTE: If you are using the www.howtonetwork.net racks, please bring up the LAN interfaces connected to the routers by issuing the no shutdown command on the connected switches. If you are using a home lab with no Switches, you can bring up the LAN interfaces using the following configurations on your routers:

```
interface fastethernet 0/0
  no keepalive
  loopback
  no shutdown
```

Alternately, you can simply connect the interfaces to a hub or switch if you have one available in your own lab.

Task 1

Configure hostnames and IP addressing on all routers as illustrated in the network topology.

Task 2

Using legacy network x.x.x.x y.y.y.y area <area> OSPF configuration commands, configure OSPF area 0 as illustrated in the topology. Ensure that no OSPF Hellos are sent out of the LAN interfaces on R2 and R3. Verify your configuration using the appropriate commands.

Task 3

Using legacy network x.x.x.x y.y.y.y area <area> OSPF configuration commands, configure OSPF area 2 as illustrated in the topology. This area should not allow any inter-area LSAs (except for the default route) or any external LSAs.

Additionally, the router should not send log messages when Type 6 LSAs are received. Ensure that the default route shows up in the routing table of R4 with a route metric of 222. You are NOT allowed to modify any interface bandwidth or cost values to complete this task. Ensure that no OSPF packets are sent out of the LAN interface on R4. Verify your configuration using the appropriate commands.

Task 4

Using legacy network x.x.x.x y.y.y.y area <area> OSPF configuration commands, configure OSPF area 3 as illustrated in the topology. Authenticate OSPF messages between R1 and R2 using the plain text password 'CCNP'. Authentication should be performed only at the interface level. Verify your configuration using the appropriate commands.

Task 5

Using legacy network x.x.x.x y.y.y.y area <area> OSPF configuration commands, configure OSPF area 1 as illustrated in the topology. Configure MD5 authentication for area 1 using the password 'CCNP'. Verify your configuration.

Task 6

Using legacy network x.x.x.x y.y.y.y area <area> OSPF configuration commands, configure OSPF for area 5 as illustrated in the topology. In the future, an additional router will be added to this segment. This router will be redistributing external routes from business partner routers. Configure area 5 so that these routes can be imported into OSPF as Type 7 routes. No inter-area or Type 5 LSAs should be allowed into this area. Finally, ensure that all other routers in the network are able to ping R1s LAN (and any future area 5 subnets).Verify your configuration using the appropriate commands.

Task 7

Configure R1 so that the virtual link going to R2 is assigned a cost of 2 and the virtual link going to R3 is assigned a cost of 3. Verify your configuration.

Task 8

In the future, the FastEthernet link on R2 will be replaced with a GigabitEthernet link. Configure R2 so that OSPF accurately calculates route metrics when this is performed.

LAB VALIDATION

Task 1

```
Router(config)#hostname R1
R1(config)#interface fastethernet 0/0
R1(config-if)#no shutdown
R1(config-if)#ip address 150.1.1.1 255.255.255.0
R1(config-if)#exit
R1(config)#interface serial 0/0
R1(config-if)#no shutdown
R1(config-if)#ip address 10.0.1.1 255.255.255.252
R1(config-if)#clock rate 2000000
R1(config-if)#exit
R1(config)#interface serial 0/1
```

```
R1(config-if)#ip address 10.0.0.5 255.255.255.252
R1(config-if)#no shutdown
R1(config-if)#exit

Router(config)#hostname R2
R2(config)#interface fastethernet 0/0
R2(config-if)#no shutdown
R2(config-if)#ip address 150.2.2.2 255.255.255.0
R2(config-if)#exit
R2(config)#interface serial 0/0
R2(config-if)#no shutdown
R2(config-if)#ip address 10.0.1.2 255.255.255.252
R2(config-if)#exit
R2(config)#interface serial 0/1
R2(config-if)#ip address 10.0.0.9 255.255.255.252
R2(config-if)#no shutdown
R2(config-if)#exit

Router(config)#hostname R3
R3(config)#interface fastethernet 0/0
R3(config-if)#ip address 150.3.3.3 255.255.255.0
R3(config-if)#exit
R3(config)#interface serial 1/0
R3(config-if)#ip address 10.0.0.6 255.255.255.252
R3(config-if)#no shutdown
R3(config-if)# clock rate 128000
R3(config-if)#exit
R3(config)#interface serial 1/1
R3(config-if)#ip address 10.0.0.10 255.255.255.252
R3(config-if)#no shutdown
R3(config-if)# clock rate 128000
R3(config-if)#exit
R3(config)#interface serial 1/2
R3(config-if)#ip address 10.0.0.13 255.255.255.252
R3(config-if)#no shutdown
R3(config-if)# clock rate 128000
R3(config-if)#exit

Router(config)#hostname R4
R4(config)#interface fastethernet 0/0
R4(config-if)#ip address 150.4.4.4 255.255.255.0
R4(config-if)#exit
R4(config)#interface serial 0/0
R4(config-if)#ip address 10.0.0.14 255.255.255.252
R4(config-if)#no shutdown
R4(config-if)#exit
```

Task 2

```
R2(config)#router ospf 2
R2(config-router)#router-id 2.2.2.2
R2(config-router)#network 150.2.2.2 0.0.0.0 area 0
R2(config-router)#network 10.0.0.9 0.0.0.0 area 0
R2(config-router)#passive-interface fastethernet 0/0
R2(config-router)#exit

R3(config-if)#router ospf 3
R3(config-router)#router-id 3.3.3.3
R3(config-router)#network 150.3.3.3 0.0.0.0 area 0
R3(config-router)#network 10.0.0.10 0.0.0.0 area 0
R3(config-router)#passive-interface fastethernet 0/0
```

Verify your configuration using the show ip ospf neighbor command:

```
R2#show ip ospf neighbor

Neighbor ID    Pri   State     Dead Time   Address      Interface
3.3.3.3          0   FULL/  -  00:00:38    10.0.0.10    Serial0/1

R3#show ip ospf neighbor

Neighbor ID    Pri   State     Dead Time   Address      Interface
2.2.2.2          0   FULL/  -  00:00:32    10.0.0.9     Serial1/1
```

Task 3

This task requires that a totally stubby area be configured. To ensure that the default route shows up in R4s routing table with a metric of 222, you need to specify a cost value that is derived by subtracting the default interface cost of 64 from 222. The is completed as follows:

```
R3(config)#router ospf 3
R3(config-router)#network 10.0.0.13 0.0.0.0 area 2
R3(config-router)#area 2 stub no-summary
R3(config-router)#area 2 default-cost 158
R3(config-router)#exit

R4(config)#router ospf 4
R4(config-router)#router-id 4.4.4.4
R4(config-router)#network 150.4.4.4 0.0.0.0 area 2
R4(config-router)#network 10.0.0.14 0.0.0.0 area 2
R4(config-router)#passive-interface fastethernet 0/0
R4(config-router)#area 2 stub
R4(config-router)#exit
```

Verify your configuration using the show ip ospf neighbor command:

```
R3#show ip ospf neighbor

Neighbor ID     Pri   State          Dead Time   Address         Interface
2.2.2.2           0   FULL/   -      00:00:31    10.0.0.9        Serial1/1
4.4.4.4           0   FULL/   -      00:00:39    10.0.0.14       Serial1/2

R4#show ip ospf neighbor

Neighbor ID     Pri   State          Dead Time   Address         Interface
3.3.3.3           0   FULL/   -      00:00:30    10.0.0.13       Serial0/0
```

Next, verify that the default route has a route metric of 222 as required in the task:

```
R4#show ip route ospf
O*IA 0.0.0.0/0 [110/222] via 10.0.0.13, 00:01:50, Serial0/0
```

You can verify the cost value specified for the default route by looking at the LSA in the LSDB:

```
R4#show ip ospf database summary 0.0.0.0

            OSPF Router with ID (4.4.4.4) (Process ID 4)

              Summary Net Link States (Area 2)

  Routing Bit Set on this LSA
  LS age: 226
  Options: (No TOS-capability, DC, Upward)
  LS Type: Summary Links(Network)
  Link State ID: 0.0.0.0 (summary Network Number)
  Advertising Router: 3.3.3.3
  LS Seq Number: 80000003
  Checksum: 0x7B17
  Length: 28
  Network Mask: /0
        TOS: 0  Metric: 158
```

Task 4

```
R1(config)#router ospf 1
R1(config-router)#router-id 1.1.1.1
R1(config-router)#network 10.0.0.1 0.0.0.0 area 2
R1(config-router)#exit
R1(config)#interface serial 0/0
R1(config-if)#ip ospf authentication
R1(config-if)#ip ospf authentication-key CCNP
R1(config-if)#exit
```

```
R2(config)#router ospf 2
R2(config-router)#network 10.0.0.2 0.0.0.0 area 2
R2(config-router)#exit
R2(config)#interface serial 0/0
R2(config-if)#ip ospf authentication
R2(config-if)#ip ospf authentication-key CCNP
R2(config-if)#exit
```

Verify your configuration using the show ip ospf neighbor command:

```
R1#show ip ospf neighbor

Neighbor ID     Pri   State          Dead Time   Address      Interface
2.2.2.2           0   FULL/   -      00:00:34    10.0.0.2     Serial0/0

R2#show ip ospf neighbor

Neighbor ID     Pri   State          Dead Time   Address      Interface
3.3.3.3           0   FULL/   -      00:00:33    10.0.0.10    Serial0/1
1.1.1.1           0   FULL/   -      00:00:36    10.0.0.1     Serial0/0
```

Verify authentication configuration using the show ip ospf interface command:

```
R1#show ip ospf interface serial 0/0
Serial0/0 is up, line protocol is up
  Internet Address 10.0.0.1/30, Area 2
  Process ID 1, Router ID 1.1.1.1, Network Type POINT_TO_POINT, Cost: 64
  Transmit Delay is 1 sec, State POINT_TO_POINT
  Timer intervals configured, Hello 10, Dead 40, Wait 40, Retransmit 5
    oob-resync timeout 40
    Hello due in 00:00:02
  Supports Link-local Signaling (LLS)
  Index 1/1, flood queue length 0
  Next 0x0(0)/0x0(0)
  Last flood scan length is 1, maximum is 1
  Last flood scan time is 0 msec, maximum is 0 msec
  Neighbor Count is 1, Adjacent neighbor count is 1
    Adjacent with neighbor 2.2.2.2
  Suppress hello for 0 neighbor(s)
  Simple password authentication enabled
```

Task 5

```
R1(config)#router ospf 1
R1(config-router)#network 10.0.0.5 0.0.0.0 area 1
R1(config-router)#area 1 authentication message-digest
R1(config-router)#exit
R1(config)#interface serial 0/1
R1(config-if)#ip ospf message-digest-key 1 md5 CCNP
R1(config-if)#exit

R3(config)#router ospf 3
R3(config-router)#network 10.0.0.6 0.0.0.0 area 1
R3(config-router)#area 1 authentication message-digest
R3(config-router)#exit
R3(config)#interface serial 1/0
R3(config-if)#ip ospf message-digest-key 1 md5 CCNP
R3(config-if)#exit
```

Verify your configuration using the show ip ospf neighbor command:

```
R1#show ip ospf neighbor

Neighbor ID     Pri   State          Dead Time   Address      Interface
3.3.3.3           0   FULL/   -      00:00:30    10.0.0.6     Serial0/1
2.2.2.2           0   FULL/   -      00:00:39    10.0.0.2     Serial0/0

R3#show ip ospf neighbor
```

```
Neighbor ID      Pri   State        Dead Time   Address       Interface
2.2.2.2            0   FULL/ -      00:00:38    10.0.0.9      Serial1/1
1.1.1.1            0   FULL/ -      00:00:39    10.0.0.5      Serial1/0
4.4.4.4            0   FULL/ -      00:00:36    10.0.0.14     Serial1/2
```

Verify area authentication configuration using the show ip ospf command:

```
R3#show ip ospf | begin Area 1
    Area 1
        Number of interfaces in this area is 1
        Area has message digest authentication
        SPF algorithm last executed 00:03:18.600 ago
        SPF algorithm executed 2 times
        Area ranges are
        Number of LSA 8. Checksum Sum 0x03AA2E
        Number of opaque link LSA 0. Checksum Sum 0x000000
        Number of DCbitless LSA 0
        Number of indication LSA 0
        Number of DoNotAge LSA 0
        Flood list length 0
```

Verify interface authentication using the show ip ospf interface command:

```
R3#show ip ospf interface serial 1/0
Serial1/0 is up, line protocol is up
  Internet Address 10.0.0.6/30, Area 1
  Process ID 3, Router ID 3.3.3.3, Network Type POINT_TO_POINT, Cost: 781
  Transmit Delay is 1 sec, State POINT_TO_POINT
  Timer intervals configured, Hello 10, Dead 40, Wait 40, Retransmit 5
    oob-resync timeout 40
    Hello due in 00:00:08
  Supports Link-local Signaling (LLS)
  Index 1/4, flood queue length 0
  Next 0x0(0)/0x0(0)
  Last flood scan length is 1, maximum is 1
  Last flood scan time is 0 msec, maximum is 0 msec
  Neighbor Count is 1, Adjacent neighbor count is 1
    Adjacent with neighbor 1.1.1.1
  Suppress hello for 0 neighbor(s)
  Message digest authentication enabled
    Youngest key id is 1
```

Task 6

This task requires the implementation of area 5 as a totally stubby NSSA. This configuration will allow a default route to be advertised into the area. It will also allow the external routes from the business partners to be advertised to the rest of the domain. Finally, you need to configure two virtual links to connect area 5 to the OSPF backbone. One virtual link will use area 1 as the transit area and the other will use area 3. This task is completed as follows:

```
R1(config)#router ospf 1
R1(config-router)#network 150.1.1.1 0.0.0.0 area 5
R1(config-router)#area 5 nssa no-summary
R1(config-router)#area 1 virtual-link 3.3.3.3
R1(config-router)#area 2 virtual-link 2.2.2.2
R1(config-router)#exit

R2(config)#router ospf 2
R2(config-router)#area 2 virtual-link 1.1.1.1
R2(config-router)#exit

R3(config)#router ospf 3
R3(config-router)#area 1 virtual-link 1.1.1.1
R3(config-router)#exit
```

Verify OSPF virtual link states using the show ip ospf neighbor command:

```
R1#show ip ospf neighbor
```

```
Neighbor ID      Pri    State        Dead Time    Address        Interface
2.2.2.2            0    FULL/ -          -         10.0.0.2       OSPF_VL1
3.3.3.3            0    FULL/ -          -         10.0.0.6       OSPF_VL0
3.3.3.3            0    FULL/ -      00:00:35      10.0.0.6       Serial0/1
2.2.2.2            0    FULL/ -      00:00:34      10.0.0.2       Serial0/0
```

View detailed virtual link information using the show ip ospf virtual-links command:

```
R1#show ip ospf virtual-links
Virtual Link OSPF_VL1 to router 2.2.2.2 is up
  Run as demand circuit
  DoNotAge LSA allowed.
  Transit area 2, via interface Serial0/0, Cost of using 64
  Transmit Delay is 1 sec, State POINT_TO_POINT,
  Timer intervals configured, Hello 10, Dead 40, Wait 40, Retransmit 5
    Hello due in 00:00:02
    Adjacency State FULL (Hello suppressed)
    Index 1/3, retransmission queue length 0, number of retransmission 0
    First 0x0(0)/0x0(0) Next 0x0(0)/0x0(0)
    Last retransmission scan length is 0, maximum is 0
    Last retransmission scan time is 0 msec, maximum is 0 msec
Virtual Link OSPF_VL0 to router 3.3.3.3 is up
  Run as demand circuit
  DoNotAge LSA allowed.
  Transit area 1, via interface Serial0/1, Cost of using 64
  Transmit Delay is 1 sec, State POINT_TO_POINT,
  Timer intervals configured, Hello 10, Dead 40, Wait 40, Retransmit 5
    Hello due in 00:00:05
    Adjacency State FULL (Hello suppressed)
    Index 2/4, retransmission queue length 0, number of retransmission 0
    First 0x0(0)/0x0(0) Next 0x0(0)/0x0(0)
    Last retransmission scan length is 0, maximum is 0
    Last retransmission scan time is 0 msec, maximum is 0 msec
```

Finally, verify that the 150.1.1.0/24 subnet exist in the routing table of all routers. For example, on R3, you should see the following route entry:

```
R3#show ip route ospf
      10.0.0.0/30 is subnetted, 4 subnets
O IA    10.0.0.0 [110/845] via 10.0.0.9, 00:03:26, Serial1/1
                 [110/845] via 10.0.0.5, 00:03:26, Serial1/0
      150.1.0.0/24 is subnetted, 1 subnets
O        150.1.1.0 [110/782] via 10.0.0.14, 00:10:45, Serial1/2
      150.2.0.0/24 is subnetted, 1 subnets
O        150.2.2.0 [110/782] via 10.0.0.9, 00:03:26, Serial1/1
```

Additionally, verify connectivity by pinging LAN-to-LAN between R1 and R4:

```
R4#ping 150.1.1.1 source 150.4.4.4 repeat 10 size 1500

Type escape sequence to abort.
Sending 10, 1500-byte ICMP Echos to 150.1.1.1, timeout is 2 seconds:
Packet sent with a source address of 150.4.4.4
!!!!!!!!!!
Success rate is 100 percent (10/10), round-trip min/avg/max = 380/381/384 ms
```

Task 7

By default, the virtual link cost is derived from the interface cost. To modify the virtual link cost, you need to modify the cost of the interface the virtual link is established across. Before any changes are made to the network, the virtual links on R1 show the following costs:

```
R1#show ip ospf virtual-links
Virtual Link OSPF_VL1 to router 2.2.2.2 is up
  Run as demand circuit
  DoNotAge LSA allowed.
  Transit area 2, via interface Serial0/0, Cost of using 64
  Transmit Delay is 1 sec, State POINT_TO_POINT,
  Timer intervals configured, Hello 10, Dead 40, Wait 40, Retransmit 5
```

```
Hello due in 00:00:02
Adjacency State FULL (Hello suppressed)
Index 1/3, retransmission queue length 0, number of retransmission 0
First 0x0(0)/0x0(0) Next 0x0(0)/0x0(0)
Last retransmission scan length is 0, maximum is 0
Last retransmission scan time is 0 msec, maximum is 0 msec
Virtual Link OSPF_VL0 to router 3.3.3.3 is up
  Run as demand circuit
  DoNotAge LSA allowed.
  Transit area 1, via interface Serial0/1, Cost of using 64
  Transmit Delay is 1 sec, State POINT_TO_POINT,
  Timer intervals configured, Hello 10, Dead 40, Wait 40, Retransmit 5
    Hello due in 00:00:05
    Adjacency State FULL (Hello suppressed)
    Index 2/4, retransmission queue length 0, number of retransmission 0
    First 0x0(0)/0x0(0) Next 0x0(0)/0x0(0)
    Last retransmission scan length is 0, maximum is 0
    Last retransmission scan time is 0 msec, maximum is 0 msec
```

To complete this task, implement the following configuration:

```
R1(config)#interface serial 0/0
R1(config-if)#ip ospf cost 2
R1(config-if)#exit
R1(config)#interface serial 0/1
R1(config-if)#ip ospf cost 3
R1(config-if)#exit
```

Verify the new costs using the show ip ospf virtual-links command:

```
R1#show ip ospf virtual-links
Virtual Link OSPF_VL1 to router 2.2.2.2 is up
  Run as demand circuit
  DoNotAge LSA allowed.
  Transit area 2, via interface Serial0/0, Cost of using 2
  Transmit Delay is 1 sec, State POINT_TO_POINT,
  Timer intervals configured, Hello 10, Dead 40, Wait 40, Retransmit 5
    Hello due in 00:00:08
    Adjacency State FULL (Hello suppressed)
    Index 1/3, retransmission queue length 0, number of retransmission 0
    First 0x0(0)/0x0(0) Next 0x0(0)/0x0(0)
    Last retransmission scan length is 0, maximum is 0
    Last retransmission scan time is 0 msec, maximum is 0 msec
Virtual Link OSPF_VL0 to router 3.3.3.3 is up
  Run as demand circuit
  DoNotAge LSA allowed.
  Transit area 1, via interface Serial0/1, Cost of using 3
  Transmit Delay is 1 sec, State POINT_TO_POINT,
  Timer intervals configured, Hello 10, Dead 40, Wait 40, Retransmit 5
    Hello due in 00:00:01
    Adjacency State FULL (Hello suppressed)
    Index 2/4, retransmission queue length 0, number of retransmission 0
    First 0x0(0)/0x0(0) Next 0x0(0)/0x0(0)
    Last retransmission scan length is 0, maximum is 0
    Last retransmission scan time is 0 msec, maximum is 0 msec
```

Task 8

By default, OSPF uses a reference bandwidth of 100Mbps when calculating cost values for links. If you change this value on one router - change it on every other router otherwise this could result in inconsistent routing information. Complete this task by implementing the following:

```
R1(config)#router ospf 1
R1(config-router)#auto-cost reference-bandwidth 1000
% OSPF: Reference bandwidth is changed.
        Please ensure reference bandwidth is consistent across all routers.
R1(config-router)#exit

R2(config)#router ospf 2
R2(config-router)#auto-cost reference-bandwidth 1000
```

```
% OSPF: Reference bandwidth is changed.
        Please ensure reference bandwidth is consistent across all routers.
R2(config-router)#exit

R3(config)#router ospf 3
R3(config-router)#auto-cost reference-bandwidth 1000
% OSPF: Reference bandwidth is changed.
        Please ensure reference bandwidth is consistent across all routers.
R3(config-router)#exit

R4(config)#router ospf 1
R4(config-router)#auto-cost reference-bandwidth 1000
% OSPF: Reference bandwidth is changed.
        Please ensure reference bandwidth is consistent across all routers.
R4(config-router)#exit
```

Verify the default reference bandwidth using the show ip protocols command:

```
R4#show ip protocols
Routing Protocol is "ospf 4"
  Outgoing update filter list for all interfaces is not set
  Incoming update filter list for all interfaces is not set
  Router ID 4.4.4.4
  Number of areas in this router is 1. 0 normal 1 stub 0 nssa
  Maximum path: 4
  Routing for Networks:
    10.0.0.14 0.0.0.0 area 2
    150.4.4.4 0.0.0.0 area 2
  Reference bandwidth unit is 1000 mbps
  Passive Interface(s):
    FastEthernet0/0
  Routing Information Sources:
    Gateway         Distance      Last Update
    3.3.3.3              110      00:02:15
  Distance: (default is 110)
```

FINAL ROUTER CONFIGURATIONS

R1

```
R1#term len 0
R1#sh run
Building configuration...

Current configuration : 1266 bytes
!
version 12.4
service timestamps debug datetime msec
service timestamps log datetime msec
no service password-encryption
!
hostname R1
!
boot-start-marker
boot-end-marker
!
no logging console
!
no aaa new-model
no network-clock-participate slot 1
no network-clock-participate wic 0
ip cef
!
no ip domain lookup
ip auth-proxy max-nodata-conns 3
ip admission max-nodata-conns 3
!
interface FastEthernet0/0
 ip address 150.1.1.1 255.255.255.0
```

```
  duplex auto
  speed auto
 !
 interface Serial0/0
  ip address 10.0.0.1 255.255.255.252
  ip ospf authentication
  ip ospf authentication-key CCNP
  ip ospf cost 2
  clock rate 2000000
 !
 interface Serial0/1
  ip address 10.0.0.5 255.255.255.252
  ip ospf message-digest-key 1 md5 CCNP
  ip ospf cost 3
 !
 router ospf 1
  router-id 1.1.1.1
  log-adjacency-changes
  auto-cost reference-bandwidth 1000
  area 1 authentication message-digest
  area 1 virtual-link 3.3.3.3
  area 2 virtual-link 2.2.2.2
  area 5 nssa no-summary
  network 10.0.0.1 0.0.0.0 area 2
  network 10.0.0.5 0.0.0.0 area 1
  network 150.1.1.1 0.0.0.0 area 5
 !
 ip forward-protocol nd
 !
 no ip http server
 no ip http secure-server
 !
 control-plane
 !
 line con 0
 line aux 0
 line vty 0 4
  login
 !
 end

 R1#
```

R2

```
R2#term len 0
R2#sh run
Building configuration...

Current configuration : 1119 bytes
!
version 12.4
service timestamps debug datetime msec
service timestamps log datetime msec
no service password-encryption
!
hostname R2
!
boot-start-marker
boot-end-marker
!
no logging console
!
no aaa new-model
no network-clock-participate slot 1
no network-clock-participate wic 0
ip cef
!
no ip domain lookup
ip auth-proxy max-nodata-conns 3
ip admission max-nodata-conns 3
!
interface FastEthernet0/0
 ip address 150.2.2.2 255.255.255.0
```

```
 duplex auto
 speed auto
!
interface Serial0/0
 ip address 10.0.0.2 255.255.255.252
 ip ospf authentication
 ip ospf authentication-key CCNP
!
interface Serial0/1
 ip address 10.0.0.9 255.255.255.252
!
router ospf 2
 router-id 2.2.2.2
 log-adjacency-changes
 auto-cost reference-bandwidth 1000
 area 2 virtual-link 1.1.1.1
 passive-interface FastEthernet0/0
 network 10.0.0.2 0.0.0.0 area 2
 network 10.0.0.9 0.0.0.0 area 0
 network 150.2.2.2 0.0.0.0 area 0
!
ip forward-protocol nd
!
no ip http server
no ip http secure-server
!
control-plane
!
line con 0
line aux 0
line vty 0 4
 login
!
end

R2#
```

R3

```
R3#term len 0
R3#sh run
Building configuration...

Current configuration : 1577 bytes
!
version 12.4
service timestamps debug datetime msec
service timestamps log datetime msec
no service password-encryption
!
hostname R3
!
boot-start-marker
boot-end-marker
!
no logging console
!
no aaa new-model
no network-clock-participate slot 1
no network-clock-participate wic 0
ip cef
!
no ip domain lookup
ip auth-proxy max-nodata-conns 3
ip admission max-nodata-conns 3
!
!
interface FastEthernet0/0
 ip address 150.3.3.3 255.255.255.0
 duplex auto
 speed auto
!
interface Serial1/0
 ip address 10.0.0.6 255.255.255.252
```

```
 ip ospf message-digest-key 1 md5 CCNP
 clock rate 128000
!
interface Serial1/1
 ip address 10.0.0.10 255.255.255.252
 clock rate 128000
!
interface Serial1/2
 ip address 10.0.0.13 255.255.255.252
 clock rate 128000
!
interface Serial1/3
 no ip address
 shutdown
!
interface Serial1/4
 no ip address
 shutdown
!
interface Serial1/5
 no ip address
 shutdown
!
interface Serial1/6
 no ip address
 shutdown
!
interface Serial1/7
 no ip address
 shutdown
!
router ospf 3
 router-id 3.3.3.3
 log-adjacency-changes
 auto-cost reference-bandwidth 1000
 area 1 authentication message-digest
 area 1 virtual-link 1.1.1.1
 area 2 stub no-summary
 area 2 default-cost 158
 passive-interface FastEthernet0/0
 network 10.0.0.6 0.0.0.0 area 1
 network 10.0.0.10 0.0.0.0 area 0
 network 10.0.0.13 0.0.0.0 area 2
 network 150.3.3.3 0.0.0.0 area 0
!
ip forward-protocol nd
!
no ip http server
no ip http secure-server
!
control-plane
!
line con 0
line aux 0
line vty 0 4
 login
!
end

R3#
```

R4

```
R4#term len 0
R4#sh run
Building configuration...

Current configuration : 1003 bytes
!
version 12.4
service timestamps debug datetime msec
service timestamps log datetime msec
no service password-encryption
```

```
!
hostname R4
!
boot-start-marker
boot-end-marker
!
no logging console
!
no aaa new-model
no network-clock-participate slot 1
no network-clock-participate wic 0
ip cef
!
no ip domain lookup
ip auth-proxy max-nodata-conns 3
ip admission max-nodata-conns 3
!
interface FastEthernet0/0
 ip address 150.4.4.4 255.255.255.0
 duplex auto
 speed auto
!
interface Serial0/0
 ip address 10.0.0.14 255.255.255.252
!
interface Serial0/1
 no ip address
 shutdown
!
router ospf 4
 router-id 4.4.4.4
 log-adjacency-changes
 auto-cost reference-bandwidth 1000
 area 2 stub
 passive-interface FastEthernet0/0
 network 10.0.0.14 0.0.0.0 area 2
 network 150.4.4.4 0.0.0.0 area 2
!
ip forward-protocol nd
!
no ip http server
no ip http secure-server
!
control-plane
!
line con 0
line aux 0
line vty 0 4
 login
!
end

R4#
```

CCNP LAB 30

OSPF Multi-Technology Lab

Lab Objective:

The focus of this lab is to understand OSPF implementation and configuration in Cisco IOS routers. Additional technologies tested include management and convergence.

Lab Topology:

The lab network topology is illustrated below:

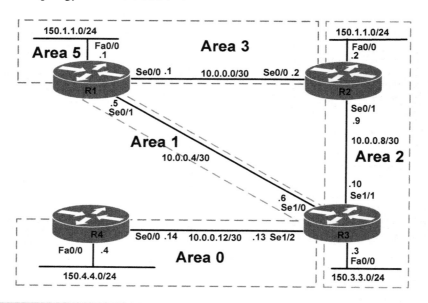

IMPORTANT NOTE: If you are using the www.howtonetwork.net racks, please bring up the LAN interfaces connected to the routers by issuing the no shutdown command on the connected switches. If you are using a home lab with no Switches, you can bring up the LAN interfaces using the following configurations on your routers:

```
interface fastethernet 0/0
  no keepalive
  loopback
  no shutdown
```

Alternately, you can simply connect the interfaces to a hub or switch if you have one available in your own lab.

Task 1

Configure hostnames and IP addressing on all routers as illustrated in the network topology.

Task 2

Using legacy network x.x.x.x y.y.y.y area <area> OSPF configuration commands, configure OSPF area 0 between R3 and R4. Configure MD5 area authentication using a secret password of 'CCNP'. Verify your configuration using the appropriate commands.

Task 3

Using legacy network x.x.x.x y.y.y.y area <area> OSPF configuration commands, configure OSPF area 1 between R1 and R3. Area 1 should be configured as a totally stub OSPF area wherein R3 advertises a default route only to R1. Verify your configuration using the appropriate commands.

Task 4

Using legacy network x.x.x.x y.y.y.y area <area> OSPF configuration commands, configure OSPF area 2 between R2 and R3. Ensure that OSPF Hellos are not sent out the LAN interfaces connected to R2 or R3. Verify your configuration using the appropriate commands.

Task 5

Using legacy network x.x.x.x y.y.y.y area <area> OSPF configuration commands, configure OSPF area 3 between R1 and R2. No OSPF packets should be sent out the LAN interfaces on R1 and R2. Additionally, ensure that this area has connectivity to all the other OSPF areas in the event that either the R1-R2 or R1-R3 links fail. Verify your configuration using the appropriate commands.

Task 6

Users in the NOC has complained that it is difficult to identify all routers based on IP addresses when they are troubleshooting. They ask if it is possible to identify OSPF neighbors by the hostnames versus IP addresses. Configure your network to provide this capability. Test your solution using the show ip ospf neighbor and show ip ospf database commands. If you have configured OSPF in the correct manner, all RIDs should be replaced by hostnames.

LAB VALIDATION

Task 1

```
Router(config)#hostname R1
R1(config)#interface fastethernet 0/0
R1(config-if)#no shutdown
R1(config-if)#ip address 150.1.1.1 255.255.255.0
R1(config-if)#exit
R1(config)#interface serial 0/0
R1(config-if)#no shutdown
R1(config-if)#ip address 10.0.1.1 255.255.255.252
R1(config-if)#clock rate 2000000
R1(config-if)#exit
R1(config)#interface serial 0/1
R1(config-if)#ip address 10.0.0.5 255.255.255.252
R1(config-if)#no shutdown
R1(config-if)#exit

Router(config)#hostname R2
R2(config)#interface fastethernet 0/0
R2(config-if)#no shutdown
R2(config-if)#ip address 150.2.2.2 255.255.255.0
R2(config-if)#exit
R2(config)#interface serial 0/0
R2(config-if)#no shutdown
R2(config-if)#ip address 10.0.1.2 255.255.255.252
R2(config-if)#exit
R2(config)#interface serial 0/1
R2(config-if)#ip address 10.0.0.9 255.255.255.252
R2(config-if)#no shutdown
R2(config-if)#exit
```

```
Router(config)#hostname R3
R3(config)#interface fastethernet 0/0
R3(config-if)#ip address 150.3.3.3 255.255.255.0
R3(config-if)#exit
R3(config)#interface serial 1/0
R3(config-if)#ip address 10.0.0.6 255.255.255.252
R3(config-if)#no shutdown
R3(config-if)# clock rate 128000
R3(config-if)#exit
R3(config)#interface serial 1/1
R3(config-if)#ip address 10.0.0.10 255.255.255.252
R3(config-if)#no shutdown
R3(config-if)# clock rate 128000
R3(config-if)#exit
R3(config)#interface serial 1/2
R3(config-if)#ip address 10.0.0.13 255.255.255.252
R3(config-if)#no shutdown
R3(config-if)# clock rate 128000
R3(config-if)#exit

Router(config)#hostname R4
R4(config)#interface fastethernet 0/0
R4(config-if)#ip address 150.4.4.4 255.255.255.0
R4(config-if)#exit
R4(config)#interface serial 0/0
R4(config-if)#ip address 10.0.0.14 255.255.255.252
R4(config-if)#no shutdown
R4(config-if)#exit
```

Task 2

```
R3(config)#router ospf 3
R3(config-router)#router-id 3.3.3.3
R3(config-router)#network 10.0.0.13 0.0.0.0 area 0
R3(config-router)#area 0 authentication message-digest
R3(config-router)#exit
R3(config)#interface serial 1/2
R3(config-if)#ip ospf message-digest-key 1 md5 CCNP
R3(config-router)#exit

R4(config)#router ospf 4
R4(config-router)#router-id 4.4.4.4
R4(config-router)#network 150.4.4.4 0.0.0.0 area 0
R4(config-router)#network 10.0.0.14 0.0.0.0 area 0
R4(config-router)#area 0 authentication message-digest
R4(config-router)#exit
R4(config)#interface serial 0/0
R4(config-if)#ip ospf message-digest-key 1 md5 CCNP
R4(config-if)#exit
```

Verify your configuration using the show ip ospf neighbor command:

```
R3#show ip ospf neighbor

Neighbor ID     Pri    State       Dead Time    Address        Interface
4.4.4.4           0    FULL/   -   00:00:32     10.0.0.14      Serial1/2

R4#show ip ospf neighbor

Neighbor ID     Pri    State       Dead Time    Address        Interface
3.3.3.3           0    FULL/   -   00:00:39     10.0.0.13      Serial0/0
```

Verify area authentication using the show ip ospf command:

```
R3#show ip ospf | begin Area BACKBONE
    Area BACKBONE(0)
        Number of interfaces in this area is 1
        Area has message digest authentication
        SPF algorithm last executed 00:01:23.648 ago
        SPF algorithm executed 2 times
        Area ranges are
        Number of LSA 2. Checksum Sum 0x009D60
        Number of opaque link LSA 0. Checksum Sum 0x000000
```

```
        Number of DCbitless LSA 0
        Number of indication LSA 0
        Number of DoNotAge LSA 0
        Flood list length 0
```

Finally, verify interface configuration using the show ip ospf interface command:

```
R3#show ip ospf interface serial 1/2
Serial1/2 is up, line protocol is up
  Internet Address 10.0.0.13/30, Area 0
  Process ID 3, Router ID 3.3.3.3, Network Type POINT_TO_POINT, Cost: 781
  Transmit Delay is 1 sec, State POINT_TO_POINT
  Timer intervals configured, Hello 10, Dead 40, Wait 40, Retransmit 5
    oob-resync timeout 40
    Hello due in 00:00:05
  Supports Link-local Signaling (LLS)
  Index 1/1, flood queue length 0
  Next 0x0(0)/0x0(0)
  Last flood scan length is 1, maximum is 1
  Last flood scan time is 0 msec, maximum is 0 msec
  Neighbor Count is 1, Adjacent neighbor count is 1
    Adjacent with neighbor 4.4.4.4
  Suppress hello for 0 neighbor(s)
  Message digest authentication enabled
    Youngest key id is 1
```

Task 3

```
R1(config)#router ospf 1
R1(config-router)#router-id 1.1.1.1
R1(config-router)#network 10.0.0.5 0.0.0.0 area 1
R1(config-router)#area 1 stub
R1(config-router)#exit

R3(config)#router ospf 3
R3(config-router)#network 10.0.0.6 0.0.0.0 area 1
R3(config-router)#area 1 stub no-summary
R3(config-router)#exit
```

Verify your configuration using the show ip ospf neighbor command:

```
R1#show ip ospf neighbor

Neighbor ID     Pri   State         Dead Time   Address     Interface
3.3.3.3           0   FULL/  -      00:00:32    10.0.0.6    Serial0/1

R3#show ip ospf neighbor

Neighbor ID     Pri   State         Dead Time   Address     Interface
4.4.4.4           0   FULL/  -      00:00:33    10.0.0.14   Serial1/2
1.1.1.1           0   FULL/  -      00:00:31    10.0.0.5    Serial1/0
```

Verify stub router configuration by looking at either the LSDB or routing table on R1:

```
R1#show ip ospf database

            OSPF Router with ID (1.1.1.1) (Process ID 1)

                Router Link States (Area 1)

Link ID         ADV Router      Age         Seq#        Checksum Link count
1.1.1.1         1.1.1.1         117         0x80000002 0x00F97D 2
3.3.3.3         3.3.3.3         118         0x80000002 0x001FAE 2

                Summary Net Link States (Area 1)

Link ID         ADV Router      Age         Seq#        Checksum
0.0.0.0         3.3.3.3         190         0x80000001 0x0057DA
```

Additionally, you can also verify stub configuration using the `show ip ospf` command:

```
R1#show ip ospf
 Routing Process "ospf 1" with ID 1.1.1.1
 Start time: 00:30:16.176, Time elapsed: 00:03:00.312
 Supports only single TOS(TOS0) routes
 Supports opaque LSA
 Supports Link-local Signaling (LLS)
 Supports area transit capability
 Router is not originating router-LSAs with maximum metric
 Initial SPF schedule delay 5000 msecs
 Minimum hold time between two consecutive SPFs 10000 msecs
 Maximum wait time between two consecutive SPFs 10000 msecs
 Incremental-SPF disabled
 Minimum LSA interval 5 secs
 Minimum LSA arrival 1000 msecs
 LSA group pacing timer 240 secs
 Interface flood pacing timer 33 msecs
 Retransmission pacing timer 66 msecs
 Number of external LSA 0. Checksum Sum 0x000000
 Number of opaque AS LSA 0. Checksum Sum 0x000000
 Number of DCbitless external and opaque AS LSA 0
 Number of DoNotAge external and opaque AS LSA 0
 Number of areas in this router is 1. 0 normal 1 stub 0 nssa
 Number of areas transit capable is 0
 External flood list length 0
    Area 1
        Number of interfaces in this area is 1
        It is a stub area
        Area has no authentication
        SPF algorithm last executed 00:02:40.196 ago
        SPF algorithm executed 2 times
        Area ranges are
        Number of LSA 3. Checksum Sum 0x017105
        Number of opaque link LSA 0. Checksum Sum 0x000000
        Number of DCbitless LSA 0
        Number of indication LSA 0
        Number of DoNotAge LSA 0
        Flood list length 0
```

Task 4

```
R2(config)#router ospf 2
R2(config-router)#router-id 2.2.2.2
R2(config-router)#network 150.2.2.2 0.0.0.0 area 2
R2(config-router)#network 10.0.0.9 0.0.0.0 area 2
R2(config-router)#passive-interface fastethernet 0/0
R2(config-router)#exit

R3(config)#router ospf 3
R3(config-router)#network 10.0.0.10 0.0.0.0 area 2
R3(config-router)#exit
```

Verify your configuration using the `show ip ospf neighbor` command:

```
R2#show ip ospf neighbor

Neighbor ID     Pri   State           Dead Time   Address         Interface
3.3.3.3           0   FULL/  -        00:00:31    10.0.0.10       Serial0/1

R3#show ip ospf neighbor

Neighbor ID     Pri   State           Dead Time   Address         Interface
4.4.4.4           0   FULL/  -        00:00:31    10.0.0.14       Serial1/2
1.1.1.1           0   FULL/  -        00:00:39    10.0.0.5        Serial1/0
2.2.2.2           0   FULL/  -        00:00:36    10.0.0.9        Serial1/1
```

Task 5

To complete this task, you need to configure a virtual link across area 2. This virtual link must also be configured for MD5 authentication, which is being used in the backbone. However, because area 1 is a stub area, you cannot configure a virtual link. Instead, you need to configure a tunnel between R1 and R3. Because this tunnel will need to be assigned to area 0, you need to configure the OSPF password on this interface as well. This task is completed as follows:

```
R1(config)#router ospf 1
R1(config-router)#area 0 authentication message-digest
R1(config-router)#network 10.0.0.1 0.0.0.0 area 3
R1(config-router)#network 11.0.0.1 0.0.0.0 area 0
R1(config-router)#network 150.1.1.1 0.0.0.0 area 3
R1(config-router)#exit
R1(config)#interface tunnel 0
R1(config-if)#ip address 11.0.0.1 255.255.255.252
R1(config-if)#tunnel source serial 0/1
R1(config-if)#tunnel destination 10.0.0.6
R1(config-if)#ip ospf message-digest-key 1 md5 CCNP
R1(config-if)#exit

R2(config)#router ospf 2
R2(config-router)#area 0 authentication message-digest
R2(config-router)#network 10.0.0.2 0.0.0.0 area 3
R2(config-router)#area 2 virtual-link 3.3.3.3 message-digest-key 1 md5 CCNP
R2(config-router)#exit

R3(config)#router ospf 3
R3(config-router)#area 2 virtual-link 2.2.2.2 message-digest-key 1 md5 CCNP
R3(config-router)#network 11.0.0.2 0.0.0.0 area 0
R3(config-router)#exit
R3(config)#interface tunnel 0
R3(config-if)#ip address 11.0.0.2 255.255.255.252
R3(config-if)#tunnel source serial 1/0
R3(config-if)#tunnel destination 10.0.0.5
R3(config-if)#ip ospf message-digest-key 1 md5 CCNP
R3(config-if)#exit
```

Verify your configuration using the show ip ospf neighbor command:

```
R1#show ip ospf neighbor

Neighbor ID     Pri   State       Dead Time   Address     Interface
3.3.3.3           0   FULL/   -   00:00:32    11.0.0.2    Tunnel0
3.3.3.3           0   FULL/   -   00:00:39    10.0.0.6    Serial0/1
2.2.2.2           0   FULL/   -   00:00:36    10.0.0.2    Serial0/0

R3#show ip ospf neighbor

Neighbor ID     Pri   State       Dead Time   Address     Interface
1.1.1.1           0   FULL/   -   00:00:31    11.0.0.1    Tunnel0
2.2.2.2           0   FULL/   -   -           10.0.0.9    OSPF_VL0
1.1.1.1           0   FULL/   -   00:00:35    10.0.0.5    Serial1/0
2.2.2.2           0   FULL/   -   00:00:38    10.0.0.9    Serial1/1
```

Test your configuration by disabling the R1-to-R2 link and pinging from R4 to R1:

```
R1(config)#interface serial 0/0
R1(config-if)#shutdown

R3#show ip route 150.1.1.0 255.255.255.0
Routing entry for 150.1.1.0/24
  Known via "ospf 3", distance 110, metric 11112, type inter area
  Last update from 11.0.0.1 on Tunnel0, 00:00:00 ago
  Routing Descriptor Blocks:
  * 11.0.0.1, from 1.1.1.1, 00:00:00 ago, via Tunnel0
      Route metric is 11112, traffic share count is 1
```

```
R4#ping 150.1.1.1 source 150.4.4.4 repeat 10 size 1500

Type escape sequence to abort.
Sending 10, 1500-byte ICMP Echos to 150.1.1.1, timeout is 2 seconds:
Packet sent with a source address of 150.4.4.4
!!!!!!!!!!
Success rate is 100 percent (10/10), round-trip min/avg/max = 388/388/392 ms
```

Test failover using the tunnel by shutting down the R1-to-R3 link:

```
R2(config)#interface serial 0/1
R2(config-if)#shutdown

R3#show ip route 150.1.1.0 255.255.255.0
Routing entry for 150.1.1.0/24
  Known via "ospf 3", distance 110, metric 846, type inter area
  Last update from 10.0.0.9 on Serial1/1, 00:00:46 ago
  Routing Descriptor Blocks:
  * 10.0.0.9, from 2.2.2.2, 00:00:46 ago, via Serial1/1
      Route metric is 846, traffic share count is 1

R4#ping 150.1.1.1 source 150.4.4.4 repeat 10 size 1500

Type escape sequence to abort.
Sending 10, 1500-byte ICMP Echos to 150.1.1.1, timeout is 2 seconds:
Packet sent with a source address of 150.4.4.4
!!!!!!!!!!
Success rate is 100 percent (10/10), round-trip min/avg/max = 388/388/392 ms
```

Task 6

By default, OSPF uses IP addresses to identify neighbors. To configure Open Shortest Path First (OSPF) to look up Domain Name System (DNS) names for use in all OSPF `show` EXEC command displays, you need to enable OSPF name lookup. Because there are no DNS servers in this lab, you need to statically configure host entries on all routers. Prior to any changes, the `show ip ospf neighbor` command on all routers shows the following entries:

```
R1#show ip ospf neighbor

Neighbor ID     Pri   State          Dead Time    Address         Interface
3.3.3.3           0   FULL/  -       00:00:38     11.0.0.2        Tunnel0
3.3.3.3           0   FULL/  -       00:00:39     10.0.0.6        Serial0/1
2.2.2.2           0   FULL/  -       00:00:30     10.0.0.2        Serial0/0

R2#show ip ospf neighbor

Neighbor ID     Pri   State          Dead Time    Address         Interface
3.3.3.3           0   FULL/  -          -         10.0.0.10       OSPF_VL0
3.3.3.3           0   FULL/  -       00:00:32     10.0.0.10       Serial0/1
1.1.1.1           0   FULL/  -       00:00:36     10.0.0.1        Serial0/0

R3#show ip ospf neighbor

Neighbor ID     Pri   State          Dead Time    Address         Interface
1.1.1.1           0   FULL/  -       00:00:37     11.0.0.1        Tunnel0
4.4.4.4           0   FULL/  -       00:00:37     10.0.0.14       Serial1/2
2.2.2.2           0   FULL/  -          -         10.0.0.9        OSPF_VL0
1.1.1.1           0   FULL/  -       00:00:31     10.0.0.5        Serial1/0
2.2.2.2           0   FULL/  -       00:00:30     10.0.0.9        Serial1/1

R4#show ip ospf neighbor

Neighbor ID     Pri   State          Dead Time    Address         Interface
3.3.3.3           0   FULL/  -       00:00:34     10.0.0.13       Serial0/0
```

This task is completed using the `ip ospf name-lookup` and `ip host` commands:

```
R1(config)#ip host R1 1.1.1.1
R1(config)#ip host R2 2.2.2.2
R1(config)#ip host R3 3.3.3.3
```

```
R1(config)#ip host R4 4.4.4.4
R1(config)#ip ospf name-lookup

R2(config)#ip host R1 1.1.1.1
R2(config)#ip host R2 2.2.2.2
R2(config)#ip host R3 3.3.3.3
R2(config)#ip host R4 4.4.4.4
R2(config)#ip ospf name-lookup

R3(config)#ip host R1 1.1.1.1
R3(config)#ip host R2 2.2.2.2
R3(config)#ip host R3 3.3.3.3
R3(config)#ip host R4 4.4.4.4
R3(config)#ip ospf name-lookup

R4(config)#ip host R1 1.1.1.1
R4(config)#ip host R2 2.2.2.2
R4(config)#ip host R3 3.3.3.3
R4(config)#ip host R4 4.4.4.4
R4(config)#ip ospf name-lookup
```

After this configuration, the show ip ospf neighbor command now shows hostnames:

```
R1#show ip ospf neighbor

Neighbor ID    Pri    State      Dead Time    Address      Interface
R3              0     FULL/  -   00:00:35     11.0.0.2     Tunnel0
R3              0     FULL/  -   00:00:35     10.0.0.6     Serial0/1
R2              0     FULL/  -   00:00:37     10.0.0.2     Serial0/0

R2#show ip ospf neighbor

Neighbor ID    Pri    State      Dead Time    Address      Interface
R3              0     FULL/  -   -            10.0.0.10    OSPF_VL0
R3              0     FULL/  -   00:00:35     10.0.0.10    Serial0/1
R1              0     FULL/  -   00:00:39     10.0.0.1     Serial0/0

R3#show ip ospf neighbor

Neighbor ID    Pri    State      Dead Time    Address      Interface
R1              0     FULL/  -   00:00:35     11.0.0.1     Tunnel0
R4              0     FULL/  -   00:00:35     10.0.0.14    Serial1/2
R2              0     FULL/  -   -            10.0.0.9     OSPF_VL0
R1              0     FULL/  -   00:00:39     10.0.0.5     Serial1/0
R2              0     FULL/  -   00:00:38     10.0.0.9     Serial1/1

R4#show ip ospf neighbor

Neighbor ID    Pri    State      Dead Time    Address      Interface
R3              0     FULL/  -   00:00:33     10.0.0.13    Serial0/0
```

The same is also applicable to entries that are stored in the Link State Database. The hostname replaces the IP address in the 'ADV Router' field of the show ip ospf database command:

```
R3#show ip ospf database

            OSPF Router with ID (3.3.3.3) (Process ID 3)

                Router Link States (Area 0)

Link ID        ADV Router     Age        Seq#          Checksum Link count
1.1.1.1        R1             824              0x80000006 0x007D54 2
2.2.2.2        R2             1     (DNA)      0x8000000B 0x002691 1
3.3.3.3        R3             771              0x8000000F 0x00F613 5
4.4.4.4        R4             1109             0x80000009 0x00A4F0 3

                Summary Net Link States (Area 0)

Link ID        ADV Router     Age        Seq#          Checksum
10.0.0.0       R1             829              0x80000001 0x005998
10.0.0.0       R2             1     (DNA)      0x80000001 0x003BB2
10.0.0.4       R1             829              0x80000001 0x0031BC
10.0.0.4       R3             829              0x80000001 0x001006
```

```
10.0.0.8       R2            10    (DNA) 0x80000001 0x00EAFA
10.0.0.8       R3            782         0x80000001 0x00E72A
150.1.1.0      R1            1729        0x80000001 0x00B8E6
150.1.1.0      R2            1     (DNA) 0x80000001 0x001D3E
150.2.2.0      R2            10    (DNA) 0x80000001 0x008316
150.2.2.0      R3            773         0x80000001 0x000382

              Router Link States (Area 1)

Link ID        ADV Router    Age         Seq#       Checksum Link count
1.1.1.1        R1            831         0x80000007 0x00F27E 2
3.3.3.3        R3            836         0x80000003 0x001DAF 2

              Summary Net Link States (Area 1)

Link ID        ADV Router    Age         Seq#       Checksum
0.0.0.0        R1            826         0x80000003 0x008FA8
0.0.0.0        R3            1720        0x80000001 0x0057DA
10.0.0.0       R1            832         0x80000001 0x00777C
10.0.0.8       R1            785         0x80000001 0x00D0B8
10.0.0.12      R1            817         0x80000001 0x00A8DC
11.0.0.0       R1            827         0x80000001 0x00762A
150.1.1.0      R1            826         0x80000003 0x00D2CC
150.2.2.0      R1            775         0x80000001 0x00EB11
150.4.4.0      R1            817         0x80000001 0x00BD3B

              Router Link States (Area 2)

Link ID        ADV Router    Age         Seq#       Checksum Link count
2.2.2.2        R2            776         0x80000017 0x00039C 3
3.3.3.3        R3            776         0x8000000D 0x00A907 2

              Summary Net Link States (Area 2)

Link ID        ADV Router    Age         Seq#       Checksum
10.0.0.0       R2            781         0x80000003 0x0037B4
10.0.0.4       R3            834         0x80000001 0x001006
10.0.0.12      R3            1718        0x80000001 0x00BF4E
11.0.0.0       R3            824         0x80000001 0x001C7A
150.1.1.0      R2            781         0x80000003 0x001940
150.4.4.0      R3            1108        0x80000001 0x00D4AC
```

This is also applicable when looking at specific LSAs in the Link State Database:

```
R1#show ip ospf database summary 0.0.0.0

          OSPF Router with ID (1.1.1.1) (Process ID 1)

          Summary Net Link States (Area 1)

  LS age: 997
  Options: (No TOS-capability, DC, Upward)
  LS Type: Summary Links(Network)
  Link State ID: 0.0.0.0 (summary Network Number)
  Advertising Router: R1
  LS Seq Number: 80000003
  Checksum: 0x8FA8
  Length: 28
  Network Mask: /0
        TOS: 0  Metric: 1

  LS age: 1892
  Options: (No TOS-capability, DC, Upward)
  LS Type: Summary Links(Network)
  Link State ID: 0.0.0.0 (summary Network Number)
  Advertising Router: R3
  LS Seq Number: 80000001
  Checksum: 0x57DA
  Length: 28
  Network Mask: /0
        TOS: 0  Metric: 1
```

FINAL ROUTER CONFIGURATIONS

R1

```
R1#term len 0
R1#sh run
Building configuration...

Current configuration : 1312 bytes
!
version 12.4
service timestamps debug datetime msec
service timestamps log datetime msec
no service password-encryption
!
hostname R1
!
boot-start-marker
boot-end-marker
!
no logging console
!
no aaa new-model
no network-clock-participate slot 1
no network-clock-participate wic 0
ip cef
!
no ip domain lookup
ip host R2 2.2.2.2
ip host R3 3.3.3.3
ip host R1 1.1.1.1
ip host R4 4.4.4.4
ip auth-proxy max-nodata-conns 3
ip admission max-nodata-conns 3
!
interface Tunnel0
 ip address 11.0.0.1 255.255.255.252
 ip ospf message-digest-key 1 md5 CCNP
 tunnel source Serial0/1
 tunnel destination 10.0.0.6
!
interface FastEthernet0/0
 ip address 150.1.1.1 255.255.255.0
 duplex auto
 speed auto
!
interface Serial0/0
 ip address 10.0.0.1 255.255.255.252
 clock rate 2000000
!
interface Serial0/1
 ip address 10.0.0.5 255.255.255.252
!
router ospf 1
 router-id 1.1.1.1
 log-adjacency-changes
 area 0 authentication message-digest
 area 1 stub
 network 10.0.0.1 0.0.0.0 area 3
 network 10.0.0.5 0.0.0.0 area 1
 network 11.0.0.1 0.0.0.0 area 0
 network 150.1.1.1 0.0.0.0 area 3
!
ip forward-protocol nd
!
no ip http server
no ip http secure-server
ip ospf name-lookup
!
control-plane
!
line con 0
line aux 0
line vty 0 4
 login
!
end

R1#
```

R2

```
R2#term len 0
R2#sh run
Building configuration...

Current configuration : 1190 bytes
!
version 12.4
service timestamps debug datetime msec
service timestamps log datetime msec
no service password-encryption
!
hostname R2
!
boot-start-marker
boot-end-marker
!
no logging console
!
no aaa new-model
no network-clock-participate slot 1
no network-clock-participate wic 0
ip cef
!
no ip domain lookup
ip host R1 1.1.1.1
ip host R2 2.2.2.2
ip host R3 3.3.3.3
ip host R4 4.4.4.4
ip auth-proxy max-nodata-conns 3
ip admission max-nodata-conns 3
!
interface FastEthernet0/0
 ip address 150.2.2.2 255.255.255.0
 duplex auto
 speed auto
!
interface Serial0/0
 ip address 10.0.0.2 255.255.255.252
!
interface Serial0/1
 ip address 10.0.0.9 255.255.255.252
!
router ospf 2
 router-id 2.2.2.2
 log-adjacency-changes
 area 0 authentication message-digest
 area 2 virtual-link 3.3.3.3 message-digest-key 1 md5 CCNP
 passive-interface FastEthernet0/0
 network 10.0.0.2 0.0.0.0 area 3
 network 10.0.0.9 0.0.0.0 area 2
 network 150.2.2.2 0.0.0.0 area 2
!
ip forward-protocol nd
!
no ip http server
no ip http secure-server
ip ospf name-lookup
!
control-plane
!
line con 0
line aux 0
line vty 0 4
 login
!
end

R2#
```

R3

```
% Type "show ?" for a list of subcommands
R3#term len 0
R3#sh run
Building configuration...

Current configuration : 1755 bytes
!
version 12.4
service timestamps debug datetime msec
service timestamps log datetime msec
no service password-encryption
!
hostname R3
!
boot-start-marker
boot-end-marker
!
no logging console
!
no aaa new-model
no network-clock-participate slot 1
no network-clock-participate wic 0
ip cef
!
no ip domain lookup
ip host R1 1.1.1.1
ip host R2 2.2.2.2
ip host R3 3.3.3.3
ip host R4 4.4.4.4
ip auth-proxy max-nodata-conns 3
ip admission max-nodata-conns 3
!
interface Tunnel0
 ip address 11.0.0.2 255.255.255.252
 ip ospf message-digest-key 1 md5 CCNP
 tunnel source Serial1/0
 tunnel destination 10.0.0.5
!
interface FastEthernet0/0
 ip address 150.3.3.3 255.255.255.0
 duplex auto
 speed auto
!
interface Serial1/0
 ip address 10.0.0.6 255.255.255.252
 clock rate 128000
!
interface Serial1/1
 ip address 10.0.0.10 255.255.255.252
 clock rate 128000
!
interface Serial1/2
 ip address 10.0.0.13 255.255.255.252
 ip ospf message-digest-key 1 md5 CCNP
 clock rate 128000
!
interface Serial1/3
 no ip address
 shutdown
!
interface Serial1/4
 no ip address
 shutdown
!
interface Serial1/5
 no ip address
 shutdown
!
interface Serial1/6
 no ip address
 shutdown
!
interface Serial1/7
 no ip address
 shutdown
!
router ospf 3
```

```
   router-id 3.3.3.3
   log-adjacency-changes
   area 0 authentication message-digest
   area 1 stub no-summary
   area 2 virtual-link 2.2.2.2 message-digest-key 1 md5 CCNP
   network 10.0.0.6 0.0.0.0 area 1
   network 10.0.0.10 0.0.0.0 area 2
   network 10.0.0.13 0.0.0.0 area 0
   network 11.0.0.2 0.0.0.0 area 0
!
ip forward-protocol nd
!
no ip http server
no ip http secure-server
ip ospf name-lookup
!
control-plane
!
line con 0
line aux 0
line vty 0 4
 login
!
end

R3#
```

R4

```
no aaa new-model
no network-clock-participate slot 1
no network-clock-participate wic 0
ip cef
!
no ip domain lookup
ip host R1 1.1.1.1
ip host R2 2.2.2.2
ip host R3 3.3.3.3
ip host R4 4.4.4.4
ip auth-proxy max-nodata-conns 3
ip admission max-nodata-conns 3
!
interface FastEthernet0/0
 ip address 150.4.4.4 255.255.255.0
 duplex auto
 speed auto
!
interface Serial0/0
 ip address 10.0.0.14 255.255.255.252
 ip ospf message-digest-key 1 md5 CCNP
!
interface Serial0/1
 no ip address
 shutdown
!
router ospf 4
 router-id 4.4.4.4
 log-adjacency-changes
 area 0 authentication message-digest
 network 10.0.0.14 0.0.0.0 area 0
 network 150.4.4.4 0.0.0.0 area 0
!
ip forward-protocol nd
!
no ip http server
no ip http secure-server
ip ospf name-lookup
!
control-plane
!
line con 0
line aux 0
line vty 0 4
 login
!
end

R4#
```

CCNP LAB 31

Border Gateway Protocol Lab

Lab Objective:

The focus of this lab is to understand BGP implementation and configuration in Cisco IOS routers. Additional technologies tested include route reflectors, route-maps, and security.

Lab Topology:

The lab network topology is illustrated below:

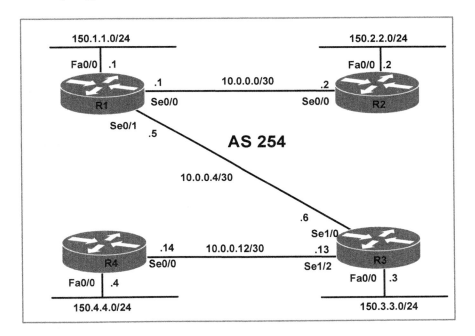

IMPORTANT NOTE: If you are using the www.howtonetwork.net racks, please bring up the LAN interfaces connected to the routers by issuing the `no shutdown` command on the connected switches. If you are using a home lab with no Switches, you can bring up the LAN interfaces using the following configurations on your routers:

```
interface fastethernet 0/0
  no keepalive
  loopback
  no shutdown
```

Alternately, you can simply connect the interfaces to a hub or switch if you have one available in your own lab.

Task 1

Configure hostnames and IP addressing on all routers as illustrated in the network topology.

Task 2

Without using peer groups, configure internal BGP on R1, R2, R3, and R4 as follows:
- Statically configure a BGP router ID using the router number, e.g. 1.1.1.1 for R1, etc.
- All routers should peer using their physical interface addresses
- R1 should peer to R2 and R3
- R2 should peer to R1
- R3 should peer to R1 and R4
- R4 should peer to R3
- All routers should use the TCP MD5 authentication password 'CCNP'
- BGP Hellos should be sent out every 5 seconds
- All of the BGP speakers should advertise a Hold Time of 15 seconds
- The COMMUNITIES attribute (standard) should be supported

Task 3

Advertise the 150.1.1.0/24, 150.2.2.0, and 150.3.3.0/24 subnets on R1, R2, and R3 via BGP. These prefixes must be advertised with the standard community values listed below. You are NOT allowed to redistribute these prefixes into BGP. Additionally, you are NOT allowed to use outbound or inbound route-maps when completing this task. Ensure that the community values are displayed in ASN:*nn* (RFC 1997 - BGP Communities Attribute) format. Verify your configuration using the appropriate commands.

- The 150.1.1.0/24: community value of 254:111
- The 150.2.2.0/24: community value of 254:222
- The 150.3.3.0/24: community value of 254:333

Task 4

Configure your network so that all 150.x.x.x/24 subnets can reach each other. You are NOT allowed to use any static routes in your solution. Additionally, you are NOT allowed to advertise or redistribute the 150.4.4.0/24 subnet into BGP on R4. Instead, consider other BGP features to complete this task. You are NOT allowed to configure R2 or R4. Additionally, you are NOT allowed to configure a dynamic routing protocol to complete this task.

Next, verify your configuration using the appropriate commands as well as the extended ping function. For example, on R1 use the extended ping function to send a ping to 150.2.2.2 sourced from 150.1.1.1, etc, etc. All pings should work when the task is completed correctly.

LAB VALIDATION

Task 1

Please refer to previous tasks for basic IP addressing and hostname configuration. This will not be included in this section to avoid being redundant.

Task 2

The requirements of this task are straightforward and are completed as follows:

```
R1(config)#router bgp 254
R1(config-router)#bgp router-id 1.1.1.1
R1(config-router)#neighbor 10.0.0.2 remote-as 254
R1(config-router)#neighbor 10.0.0.2 timers 5 15
% Warning: A hold time of less than 20 seconds increases
  the chances of peer flapping
R1(config-router)#neighbor 10.0.0.2 password CCNP
R1(config-router)#neighbor 10.0.0.2 send-community standard
R1(config-router)#neighbor 10.0.0.6 remote-as 254
R1(config-router)#neighbor 10.0.0.6 timers 5 15
% Warning: A hold time of less than 20 seconds increases
```

```
  the chances of peer flapping
R1(config-router)#neighbor 10.0.0.6 password CCNP
R1(config-router)#neighbor 10.0.0.6 send-community standard
R1(config-router)#exit

R2(config)#router bgp 254
R2(config-router)#bgp router-id 2.2.2.2
R2(config-router)#neighbor 10.0.0.1 remote-as 254
R2(config-router)#neighbor 10.0.0.1 timers 5 15
% Warning: A hold time of less than 20 seconds increases
  the chances of peer flapping
R2(config-router)#neighbor 10.0.0.1 password CCNP
R2(config-router)#neighbor 10.0.0.1 send-community standard
R2(config-router)#exit

R3(config)#router bgp 254
R3(config-router)#bgp router-id 3.3.3.3
R3(config-router)#neighbor 10.0.0.5 remote-as 254
R3(config-router)#neighbor 10.0.0.5 timers 5 15
% Warning: A hold time of less than 20 seconds increases
  the chances of peer flapping
R3(config-router)#neighbor 10.0.0.5 password CCNP
R3(config-router)#neighbor 10.0.0.5 send-community standard
R3(config-router)#neighbor 10.0.0.14 remote-as 254
R3(config-router)#neighbor 10.0.0.14 timers 5 15
% Warning: A hold time of less than 20 seconds increases
  the chances of peer flapping
R3(config-router)#neighbor 10.0.0.14 password CCNP
R3(config-router)#neighbor 10.0.0.14 send-community standard
R3(config-router)#exit

R4(config)#router bgp 254
R4(config-router)#bgp router-id 4.4.4.4
R4(config-router)#neighbor 10.0.0.13 remote-as 254
R4(config-router)#neighbor 10.0.0.13 timers 5 15
% Warning: A hold time of less than 20 seconds increases
  the chances of peer flapping
R4(config-router)#neighbor 10.0.0.13 password CCNP
R4(config-router)#neighbor 10.0.0.13 send-community standard
R4(config-router)#exit
```

Verify your configuration using the show ip bgp summary command:

```
R1#show ip bgp summary
BGP router identifier 1.1.1.1, local AS number 254
BGP table version is 1, main routing table version 1

Neighbor     V    AS MsgRcvd MsgSent   TblVer  InQ OutQ Up/Down  State/PfxRcd
10.0.0.2     4   254      32      32        1    0    0 00:02:27           0
10.0.0.6     4   254      20      21        1    0    0 00:01:25           0

R2#show ip bgp summary
BGP router identifier 2.2.2.2, local AS number 254
BGP table version is 1, main routing table version 1

Neighbor     V    AS MsgRcvd MsgSent   TblVer  InQ OutQ Up/Down  State/PfxRcd
10.0.0.1     4   254      33      33        1    0    0 00:02:31           0

R3#show ip bgp summary
BGP router identifier 3.3.3.3, local AS number 254
BGP table version is 1, main routing table version 1

Neighbor     V    AS MsgRcvd MsgSent   TblVer  InQ OutQ Up/Down  State/PfxRcd
10.0.0.5     4   254      22      21        1    0    0 00:01:33           0
10.0.0.14    4   254       8       8        1    0    0 00:00:22           0

R4#show ip bgp summary
BGP router identifier 4.4.4.4, local AS number 254
BGP table version is 1, main routing table version 1

Neighbor     V    AS MsgRcvd MsgSent   TblVer  InQ OutQ Up/Down  State/PfxRcd
10.0.0.13    4   254       9       9        1    0    0 00:00:25           0
```

Task 3

BGP allows you to set attributes for prefixes advertised via the `network <network> mask <mask>` command by appending a route map to this command. The route map can be used to set or modify different BGP attributes for the network. This is completed as follows:

```
R1(config)#route-map COMMUNITY permit 10
R1(config-route-map)#set community 254:111
R1(config-route-map)#exit
R1(config)#router bgp 254
R1(config-router)#network 150.1.1.0 mask 255.255.255.0 route-map COMMUNITY
R1(config-router)#exit

R2(config)#route-map COMMUNITY permit 10
R2(config-route-map)#set community 254:222
R2(config-route-map)#exit
R2(config)#router bgp 254
R2(config-router)#network 150.2.2.0 mask 255.255.255.0 route-map COMMUNITY
R2(config-router)#exit

R3(config)#route-map COMMUNITY permit 10
R3(config-route-map)#set community 254:333
R3(config-route-map)#exit
R3(config)#router bgp 254
R3(config-router)#network 150.3.3.0 mask 255.255.255.0 route-map COMMUNITY
R3(config-router)#exit
```

Verify your configuration using the `show ip bgp` command on all routers:

```
R1#show ip bgp 150.1.1.0 255.255.255.0
BGP routing table entry for 150.1.1.0/24, version 2
Paths: (1 available, best #1, table Default-IP-Routing-Table)
Flag: 0x820
  Advertised to update-groups:
     1
  Local
    0.0.0.0 from 0.0.0.0 (1.1.1.1)
      Origin IGP, metric 0, localpref 100, weight 32768, valid, sourced, local, best
      Community: 16646255
```

By default, the Cisco default community format is one 32-bit number (as seen above). To ensure that the community conforms to RFC 1997 (BGP Communities Attribute), you need to issue the `ip bgp-community new-format` command on all routers. This task is completed as follows:

```
R1(config)#ip bgp-community new-format
```
```
R2(config)#ip bgp-community new-format
```
```
R3(config)#ip bgp-community new-format
```
```
R4(config)#ip bgp-community new-format
```

Verify these changes using the `show ip bgp` command on all routers:

```
R1#show ip bgp 150.1.1.0 255.255.255.0
BGP routing table entry for 150.1.1.0/24, version 2
Paths: (1 available, best #1, table Default-IP-Routing-Table)
Flag: 0x820
  Advertised to update-groups:
     1
  Local
    0.0.0.0 from 0.0.0.0 (1.1.1.1)
      Origin IGP, metric 0, localpref 100, weight 32768, valid, sourced, local, best
      Community: 254:111

R2#show ip bgp 150.2.2.0 255.255.255.0
BGP routing table entry for 150.2.2.0/24, version 3
Paths: (1 available, best #1, table Default-IP-Routing-Table)
Flag: 0x820
  Advertised to update-groups:
     1
```

```
Local
   0.0.0.0 from 0.0.0.0 (2.2.2.2)
      Origin IGP, metric 0, localpref 100, weight 32768, valid, sourced, local, best
      Community: 254:222

R3#show ip bgp 150.3.3.0 255.255.255.0
BGP routing table entry for 150.3.3.0/24, version 3
Paths: (1 available, best #1, table Default-IP-Routing-Table)
Flag: 0x820
  Advertised to update-groups:
     1
  Local
   0.0.0.0 from 0.0.0.0 (3.3.3.3)
      Origin IGP, metric 0, localpref 100, weight 32768, valid, sourced, local, best
      Community: 254:333
```

You can verify that the COMMUNITY attribute is being sent to peers using the `show ip bgp neighbors <address>` command:

```
R1#show ip bgp neighbors 10.0.0.2
BGP neighbor is 10.0.0.2,  remote AS 254, internal link
  BGP version 4, remote router ID 10.0.0.2
  BGP state = Established, up for 00:34:11
  Last read 00:00:00, last write 00:00:00, hold time is 15, keepalive interval is 5
seconds
  Configured hold time is 15,keepalive interval is 5 seconds  Minimum holdtime from
neighbor is 0 seconds
  Neighbor capabilities:
    Route refresh: advertised and received(old & new)
    Address family IPv4 Unicast: advertised and received
  Message statistics:
    InQ depth is 0
    OutQ depth is 0
                       Sent       Rcvd
    Opens:                1          1
    Notifications:        0          0
    Updates:              5          1
    Keepalives:         413        413
    Route Refresh:        0          0
    Total:              419        415
  Default minimum time between advertisement runs is 0 seconds

 For address family: IPv4 Unicast
  BGP table version 6, neighbor version 6/0
 Output queue size : 0
  Index 1, Offset 0, Mask 0x2
  1 update-group member
  Community attribute sent to this neighbor
```

Task 4

The requirements of this final task are three-fold. Because we cannot advertise the 150.4.4.0/24 subnet connected to R4 via BGP, we need to configure this router to advertise a default route to the rest of the domain, allowing all other routers to reach this subnet.

Therefore, the first part of this task is completed by advertising a default route from R4 so that all other routers can reach the 150.4.4.0/24 subnet since this cannot be advertised or redistributed into BGP. To advertise a default route without one existing in the routing table, use the `neighbor <address> default-originate` command under BGP. This task is completed by executing this command on R4 as follows:

```
R4(config)#router bgp 254
R4(config-router)#neighbor 10.0.0.13 default-originate
R4(config-router)#exit
```

Following this, verify that there is NO default route locally on R4:

```
R4#show ip bgp 0.0.0.0 0.0.0.0
% Network not in table
```

However, based on the configuration, a BGP-originated default route is now advertised to R3:

```
R3#show ip bgp 0.0.0.0 0.0.0.0
BGP routing table entry for 0.0.0.0/0, version 4
Paths: (1 available, best #1, table Default-IP-Routing-Table)
Flag: 0x820
  Not advertised to any peer
  Local
    10.0.0.14 from 10.0.0.14 (4.4.4.4)
      Origin IGP, metric 0, localpref 100, valid, internal, best
```

The second part of this task is to ensure that routes are advertised between all routers. Since we cannot configure R2 or R4, we need to configure R1 and R3 as route reflectors. This is because, by default, internal BGP (iBGP) speakers will NOT advertise routes received from one iBGP speaker to another iBGP speaker.

Because of this default rule, the BGP tables on all routers are incomplete and do not contain all the prefixes. Verify using the show ip bgp command. For example, R1 will not have the default route advertised by R4 in its BGP Table because this default route is received by R3 from another iBGP peer:

```
R1#show ip bgp
BGP table version is 4, local router ID is 1.1.1.1
Status codes: s suppressed, d damped, h history, * valid, > best, i - internal,
              r RIB-failure, S Stale
Origin codes: i - IGP, e - EGP, ? - incomplete

   Network          Next Hop         Metric LocPrf Weight Path
*> 150.1.1.0/24     0.0.0.0               0          32768 i
*>i150.2.2.0/24     10.0.0.2              0    100       0 i
*>i150.3.3.0/24     10.0.0.6              0    100       0 i
```

Likewise, R2 will not show an entry for the 150.3.3.0/24 (R3) and 0.0.0.0/0 (R4) prefixes in its BGP Table because the 150.3.3.0/24 prefix is advertised to R1 from an iBGP peer. Likewise, because R1 never receives the default route from R3, this will never show up in R2s BGP Table.

```
R2#show ip bgp
BGP table version is 3, local router ID is 2.2.2.2
Status codes: s suppressed, d damped, h history, * valid, > best, i - internal,
              r RIB-failure, S Stale
Origin codes: i - IGP, e - EGP, ? - incomplete

   Network          Next Hop         Metric LocPrf Weight Path
*>i150.1.1.0/24     10.0.0.1              0    100       0 i
*> 150.2.2.0/24     0.0.0.0               0          32768 i
```

The same concept is also applicable to R3 and R4. To address this issue, you need to configure R1 and R3 as route reflectors. When doing so, you do NOT need to configure R1 and R3 as clients of each other. This is because, by default, a route reflector will advertise routes received from a client to a non-client and vice versa. This task is completed as follows:

```
R1(config)#router bgp 254
R1(config-router)#neighbor 10.0.0.2 route-reflector-client
R1(config-router)#exit

R3(config)#router bgp 254
R3(config-router)#neighbor 10.0.0.14 route-reflector-client
R3(config-router)#exit
```

However, you will still notice that the routers still cannot ping each others' 150.x.x.x/24 subnets. This is because the NEXT_HOP attribute is NOT changed when these prefixes are advertised between the iBGP peers. For example, on R1, the NEXT_HOP for the 0.0.0.0/0 prefix reflects the IP address of R1 (10.0.0.14). Because there is no route for this prefix, it is considered inaccessible and is not advertised to R2:

```
R1#show ip bgp 0.0.0.0 0.0.0.0
BGP routing table entry for 0.0.0.0/0, version 12
Paths: (1 available, no best path)
  Not advertised to any peer
  Local
    10.0.0.14 (inaccessible) from 10.0.0.6 (3.3.3.3)
      Origin IGP, metric 0, localpref 100, valid, internal
      Originator: 4.4.4.4, Cluster list: 3.3.3.3
```

To resolve this issue, you need to either run an IGP or use static routes, which is forbidden in this task, or modify the BGP NEXT_HOP. However, because these updates are from iBGP neighbors, you cannot use the the `neighbor <address> next-hop-self` command. The reason you need to modify the NEXT_HOP using a route-map is because the `neighbor <address> next-hop-self` command should not be used to modify the NEXT_HOP attribute for a route reflector when this feature is enabled for a route reflector client.

It will not work because this command will modify next hop attributes only for routes that are learned from eBGP peers and not the intended routes that are being reflected from the route reflector clients. This means that the NEXT_HOP for all routes received from the iBGP peers will be inaccessible since we are not running an IGP or using static routes in the network. For example, on R1, the NEXT_HOP for the default advertised by R4 shows the IP address of the Serial0/0 interface on R4, which is 10.0.0.14, as illustrated or shown in the previous output.

Because the `neighbor <address> next-hop-self` command will not work due to the route reflector configuration, the only other way to modify the next NEXT_HOP attribute is using an outbound route map. This task is completed as follows:

```
R1(config)#route-map R2-NEXT-HOP permit 10
R1(config-route-map)#set ip next-hop 10.0.0.1
% Warning: Next hop address is our address
R1(config-route-map)#exit
R1(config)#route-map R3-NEXT-HOP permit 10
R1(config-route-map)#set ip next-hop 10.0.0.5
% Warning: Next hop address is our address
R1(config-route-map)#exit
R1(config)#router bgp 254
R1(config-router)#neighbor 10.0.0.2 route-map R2-NEXT-HOP out
R1(config-router)#neighbor 10.0.0.6 route-map R3-NEXT-HOP out
R1(config-router)#exit

R3(config)#route-map R1-NEXT-HOP permit 10
R3(config-route-map)#set ip next-hop 10.0.0.6
% Warning: Next hop address is our address
R3(config-route-map)#exit
R3(config)#route-map R4-NEXT-HOP permit 10
R3(config-route-map)#set ip next-hop 10.0.0.13
% Warning: Next hop address is our address
R3(config-route-map)#exit
R3(config)#router bgp 254
R3(config-router)#neighbor 10.0.0.14 route-map R4-NEXT-HOP out
R3(config-router)#neighbor 10.0.0.5 route-map R1-NEXT-HOP out
R3(config-router)#exit
```

Following this configuration, the BGP RIBs on all routers show the following entries:

```
R1#show ip bgp
BGP table version is 7, local router ID is 1.1.1.1
Status codes: s suppressed, d damped, h history, * valid, > best, i - internal,
              r RIB-failure, S Stale
Origin codes: i - IGP, e - EGP, ? - incomplete

   Network          Next Hop            Metric LocPrf Weight Path
*>i0.0.0.0          10.0.0.6                 0    100      0 i
*>  150.1.1.0/24    0.0.0.0                  0         32768 i
*>i150.2.2.0/24     10.0.0.2                 0    100      0 i
*>i150.3.3.0/24     10.0.0.6                 0    100      0 i
```

```
R2#show ip bgp
BGP table version is 7, local router ID is 2.2.2.2
Status codes: s suppressed, d damped, h history, * valid, > best, i - internal,
              r RIB-failure, S Stale
Origin codes: i - IGP, e - EGP, ? - incomplete

   Network          Next Hop          Metric LocPrf Weight Path
*>i0.0.0.0          10.0.0.1               0    100      0 i
*>i150.1.1.0/24     10.0.0.1               0    100      0 i
*> 150.2.2.0/24     0.0.0.0                0          32768 i
*>i150.3.3.0/24     10.0.0.1               0    100      0 i

R3#show ip bgp
BGP table version is 4, local router ID is 3.3.3.3
Status codes: s suppressed, d damped, h history, * valid, > best, i - internal,
              r RIB-failure, S Stale
Origin codes: i - IGP, e - EGP, ? - incomplete

   Network          Next Hop          Metric LocPrf Weight Path
*>i0.0.0.0          10.0.0.14              0    100      0 i
*>i150.1.1.0/24     10.0.0.5               0    100      0 i
*>i150.2.2.0/24     10.0.0.5               0    100      0 i

R4#show ip bgp
BGP table version is 7, local router ID is 4.4.4.4
Status codes: s suppressed, d damped, h history, * valid, > best, i - internal,
              r RIB-failure, S Stale
Origin codes: i - IGP, e - EGP, ? - incomplete

   Network          Next Hop          Metric LocPrf Weight Path
*>i150.1.1.0/24     10.0.0.13              0    100      0 i
*>i150.2.2.0/24     10.0.0.13              0    100      0 i
*>i150.3.3.0/24     10.0.0.13              0    100      0 i
```

Finally, complete this task by issuing extended pings, LAN-to-LAN, between the routers:

```
R1#ping 150.2.2.2 source fastethernet 0/0 repeat 10

Type escape sequence to abort.
Sending 10, 100-byte ICMP Echos to 150.2.2.2, timeout is 2 seconds:
Packet sent with a source address of 150.1.1.1
!!!!!!!!!!
Success rate is 100 percent (10/10), round-trip min/avg/max = 1/3/4 ms

R1#ping 150.3.3.3 source fastethernet 0/0 repeat 10

Type escape sequence to abort.
Sending 10, 100-byte ICMP Echos to 150.3.3.3, timeout is 2 seconds:
Packet sent with a source address of 150.1.1.1
!!!!!!!!!!
Success rate is 100 percent (10/10), round-trip min/avg/max = 16/16/16 ms

R1#ping 150.4.4.4 source fastethernet 0/0 repeat 10

Type escape sequence to abort.
Sending 10, 100-byte ICMP Echos to 150.4.4.4, timeout is 2 seconds:
Packet sent with a source address of 150.1.1.1
!!!!!!!!!!
Success rate is 100 percent (10/10), round-trip min/avg/max = 28/30/32 ms

R2#ping 150.1.1.1 source fastethernet 0/0 repeat 10

Type escape sequence to abort.
Sending 10, 100-byte ICMP Echos to 150.1.1.1, timeout is 2 seconds:
Packet sent with a source address of 150.2.2.2
!!!!!!!!!!
Success rate is 100 percent (10/10), round-trip min/avg/max = 1/2/4 ms

R2#ping 150.3.3.3 source fastethernet 0/0 repeat 10

Type escape sequence to abort.
Sending 10, 100-byte ICMP Echos to 150.3.3.3, timeout is 2 seconds:
```

```
Packet sent with a source address of 150.2.2.2
!!!!!!!!!!
Success rate is 100 percent (10/10), round-trip min/avg/max = 16/16/20 ms

R2#ping 150.4.4.4 source fastethernet 0/0 repeat 10

Type escape sequence to abort.
Sending 10, 100-byte ICMP Echos to 150.4.4.4, timeout is 2 seconds:
Packet sent with a source address of 150.2.2.2
!!!!!!!!!!
Success rate is 100 percent (10/10), round-trip min/avg/max = 28/31/40 ms

R3#ping 150.1.1.1 source fastethernet 0/0 repeat 10

Type escape sequence to abort.
Sending 10, 100-byte ICMP Echos to 150.1.1.1, timeout is 2 seconds:
Packet sent with a source address of 150.3.3.3
!!!!!!!!!!
Success rate is 100 percent (10/10), round-trip min/avg/max = 12/14/16 ms

R3#ping 150.2.2.2 source fastethernet 0/0 repeat 10

Type escape sequence to abort.
Sending 10, 100-byte ICMP Echos to 150.2.2.2, timeout is 2 seconds:
Packet sent with a source address of 150.3.3.3
!!!!!!!!!!
Success rate is 100 percent (10/10), round-trip min/avg/max = 16/16/20 ms

R3#ping 150.4.4.4 source fastethernet 0/0 repeat 10

Type escape sequence to abort.
Sending 10, 100-byte ICMP Echos to 150.4.4.4, timeout is 2 seconds:
Packet sent with a source address of 150.3.3.3
!!!!!!!!!!
Success rate is 100 percent (10/10), round-trip min/avg/max = 16/16/16 ms

R4#ping 150.1.1.1 source fastethernet 0/0 repeat 10

Type escape sequence to abort.
Sending 10, 100-byte ICMP Echos to 150.1.1.1, timeout is 2 seconds:
Packet sent with a source address of 150.4.4.4
!!!!!!!!!!
Success rate is 100 percent (10/10), round-trip min/avg/max = 28/30/32 ms

R4#ping 150.2.2.2 source fastethernet 0/0 repeat 10

Type escape sequence to abort.
Sending 10, 100-byte ICMP Echos to 150.2.2.2, timeout is 2 seconds:
Packet sent with a source address of 150.4.4.4
!!!!!!!!!!
Success rate is 100 percent (10/10), round-trip min/avg/max = 28/30/32 ms

R4#ping 150.3.3.3 source fastethernet 0/0 repeat 10

Type escape sequence to abort.
Sending 10, 100-byte ICMP Echos to 150.3.3.3, timeout is 2 seconds:
Packet sent with a source address of 150.4.4.4
!!!!!!!!!!
Success rate is 100 percent (10/10), round-trip min/avg/max = 16/16/16 ms
```

FINAL ROUTER CONFIGURATIONS

R1

```
R1#term len 0
R1#sh run
Building configuration...

Current configuration : 1582 bytes
!
version 12.4
service timestamps debug datetime msec
```

```
service timestamps log datetime msec
no service password-encryption
!
hostname R1
!
boot-start-marker
boot-end-marker
!
no logging console
!
no aaa new-model
no network-clock-participate slot 1
no network-clock-participate wic 0
ip cef
!
no ip domain lookup
ip auth-proxy max-nodata-conns 3
ip admission max-nodata-conns 3
!
interface FastEthernet0/0
 ip address 150.1.1.1 255.255.255.0
 duplex auto
 speed auto
!
interface Serial0/0
 ip address 10.0.0.1 255.255.255.252
 clock rate 2000000
!
interface Serial0/1
 ip address 10.0.0.5 255.255.255.252
!
router bgp 254
 no synchronization
 bgp router-id 1.1.1.1
 bgp log-neighbor-changes
 network 150.1.1.0 mask 255.255.255.0 route-map COMMUNITY
 neighbor 10.0.0.2 remote-as 254
 neighbor 10.0.0.2 password CCNP
 neighbor 10.0.0.2 timers 5 15
 neighbor 10.0.0.2 route-reflector-client
 neighbor 10.0.0.2 send-community
 neighbor 10.0.0.2 route-map R2-NEXT-HOP out
 neighbor 10.0.0.6 remote-as 254
 neighbor 10.0.0.6 password CCNP
 neighbor 10.0.0.6 timers 5 15
 neighbor 10.0.0.6 send-community
 neighbor 10.0.0.6 route-map R3-NEXT-HOP out
 no auto-summary
!
ip forward-protocol nd
!
ip bgp-community new-format
!
no ip http server
no ip http secure-server
!
route-map R2-NEXT-HOP permit 10
 set ip next-hop 10.0.0.1
!
route-map R3-NEXT-HOP permit 10
 set ip next-hop 10.0.0.5
!
route-map COMMUNITY permit 10
 set community 254:111
!
control-plane
!
line con 0
line aux 0
line vty 0 4
 login
!
end

R1#
```

R2

```
R2#term len 0
R2#sh run
Building configuration...

Current configuration : 1167 bytes
!
version 12.4
service timestamps debug datetime msec
service timestamps log datetime msec
no service password-encryption
!
hostname R2
!
boot-start-marker
boot-end-marker
!
no logging console
!
no aaa new-model
no network-clock-participate slot 1
no network-clock-participate wic 0
ip cef
!
no ip domain lookup
ip auth-proxy max-nodata-conns 3
ip admission max-nodata-conns 3
!
interface FastEthernet0/0
 ip address 150.2.2.2 255.255.255.0
 duplex auto
 speed auto
!
interface Serial0/0
 ip address 10.0.0.2 255.255.255.252
!
interface Serial0/1
 no ip address
 shutdown
!
router bgp 254
 no synchronization
 bgp router-id 2.2.2.2
 bgp log-neighbor-changes
 network 150.2.2.0 mask 255.255.255.0 route-map COMMUNITY
 neighbor 10.0.0.1 remote-as 254
 neighbor 10.0.0.1 password CCNP
 neighbor 10.0.0.1 timers 5 15
 neighbor 10.0.0.1 send-community
 no auto-summary
!
ip forward-protocol nd
!
ip bgp-community new-format
!
no ip http server
no ip http secure-server
!
route-map COMMUNITY permit 10
 set community 254:222
!
control-plane
!
line con 0
line aux 0
line vty 0 4
 login
!
end

R2#
```

R3

```
R3#term len 0
R3#sh run
Building configuration...

Current configuration : 1909 bytes
!
version 12.4
service timestamps debug datetime msec
service timestamps log datetime msec
no service password-encryption
!
hostname R3
!
boot-start-marker
boot-end-marker
!
no logging console
!
no aaa new-model
no network-clock-participate slot 1
no network-clock-participate wic 0
ip cef
!
no ip domain lookup
ip auth-proxy max-nodata-conns 3
ip admission max-nodata-conns 3
!
interface FastEthernet0/0
 ip address 150.3.3.3 255.255.255.0
 duplex auto
 speed auto
!
interface Serial1/0
 ip address 10.0.0.6 255.255.255.252
 clock rate 128000
!
interface Serial1/1
 no ip address
 shutdown
 clock rate 128000
!
interface Serial1/2
 ip address 10.0.0.13 255.255.255.252
 clock rate 128000
!
interface Serial1/3
 no ip address
 shutdown
!
interface Serial1/4
 no ip address
 shutdown
!
interface Serial1/5
 no ip address
 shutdown
!
interface Serial1/6
 no ip address
 shutdown
!
interface Serial1/7
 no ip address
 shutdown
!
router bgp 254
 no synchronization
 bgp router-id 3.3.3.3
 bgp log-neighbor-changes
 network 150.3.3.0 mask 255.255.255.0 route-map COMMUNITY
 neighbor 10.0.0.5 remote-as 254
 neighbor 10.0.0.5 password CCNP
```

```
 neighbor 10.0.0.5 timers 5 15
 neighbor 10.0.0.5 send-community
 neighbor 10.0.0.5 route-map R1-NEXT-HOP out
 neighbor 10.0.0.14 remote-as 254
 neighbor 10.0.0.14 password CCNP
 neighbor 10.0.0.14 timers 5 15
 neighbor 10.0.0.14 route-reflector-client
 neighbor 10.0.0.14 send-community
 neighbor 10.0.0.14 route-map R4-NEXT-HOP out
 no auto-summary
!
ip forward-protocol nd
!
ip bgp-community new-format
!
no ip http server
no ip http secure-server
!
route-map R1-NEXT-HOP permit 10
 set ip next-hop 10.0.0.6
!
route-map R4-NEXT-HOP permit 10
 set ip next-hop 10.0.0.13
!
route-map COMMUNITY permit 10
 set community 254:333
!
control-plane
!
line con 0
line aux 0
line vty 0 4
 login
!
end

R3#
```

R4

```
R4#term len 0
R4#sh run
Building configuration...

Current configuration : 1097 bytes
!
version 12.4
service timestamps debug datetime msec
service timestamps log datetime msec
no service password-encryption
!
hostname R4
!
boot-start-marker
boot-end-marker
!
no logging console
!
no aaa new-model
no network-clock-participate slot 1
no network-clock-participate wic 0
ip cef
!
no ip domain lookup
ip auth-proxy max-nodata-conns 3
ip admission max-nodata-conns 3
!
interface FastEthernet0/0
 ip address 150.4.4.4 255.255.255.0
 duplex auto
 speed auto
!
interface Serial0/0
```

```
 ip address 10.0.0.14 255.255.255.252
!
interface Serial0/1
 no ip address
 shutdown
!
router bgp 254
 no synchronization
 bgp router-id 4.4.4.4
 bgp log-neighbor-changes
 neighbor 10.0.0.13 remote-as 254
 neighbor 10.0.0.13 password CCNP
 neighbor 10.0.0.13 timers 5 15
 neighbor 10.0.0.13 send-community
 neighbor 10.0.0.13 default-originate
 no auto-summary
!
ip forward-protocol nd
!
ip bgp-community new-format
!
no ip http server
no ip http secure-server
!
control-plane
!
line con 0
line aux 0
line vty 0 4
 login
!
end

R4#
```

CCNP LAB 32

Border Gateway Protocol Lab

Lab Objective:

The focus of this lab is to understand BGP implementation and configuration in Cisco IOS routers. Additional technologies tested include route reflection and path control.

Lab Topology:

The lab network topology is illustrated below:

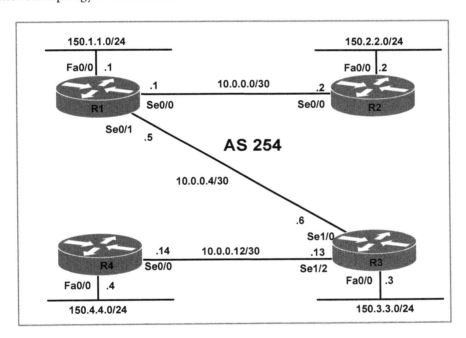

IMPORTANT NOTE: If you are using the www.howtonetwork.net racks, please bring up the LAN interfaces connected to the routers by issuing the no shutdown command on the connected switches. If you are using a home lab with no Switches, you can bring up the LAN interfaces using the following configurations on your routers:

```
interface fastethernet 0/0
  no keepalive
  loopback
  no shutdown
```

Alternately, you can simply connect the interfaces to a hub or switch if you have one available in your own lab.

Task 1

Configure hostnames and IP addressing on all routers as illustrated in the network topology.

Task 2

Configure the following Loopback 0 interfaces on all routers:
- R1 - Loopback 0: IP Address 1.1.1.1/32
- R2 - Loopback 0: IP Address 2.2.2.2/32
- R3 - Loopback 0: IP Address 3.3.3.3/32
- R4 - Loopback 0: IP Address 4.4.4.4/32

Next, configure EIGRP, using AS 254, on all routers and enable EIGRP for all interfaces EXCEPT for the 150.x.x.x/24 LAN subnets connected to R1, R2, R3, and R4. Verify your configuration.

Task 3

Configure internal BGP on R1, R2, R3, and R4 shown below. Use peer-group configuration on R2 and R4 but NOT on R1 and R3:
- All routers should use their Loopback 0 interface addresses as their router IDs
- All routers should peer using their Loopback 0 interface addresses
- R1 and R3 should be configured as Route Reflectors
- R2 should peer with R1 and R3
- R4 should peer with R1 and R3
- R1 and R3 belong to the same cluster to reduce the size of the RIB
- All routers should use TCP MD5 authentication with a password of 'CCNP'
- BGP Hellos should be sent every 5 seconds and the Hold Time should be set to 15 seconds

Verify your configuration using the appropriate commands.

Task 4

Advertise the 150.x.x.x/24 subnets on all routers via BGP. These prefixes should be redistributed into BGP on every router. In the future, there will be external BGP connections to one or more ISPs. Management has decided that the 150.x.x.x/24 subnets should never be advertised to these ISPs. Ensure that these prefixes are NEVER advertised out of AS 254. You are NOT allowed to use prefix lists or any type of filters. Verify your configuration using the appropriate commands. Verify that each router can also ping every other routers' 150.x.x.x/24 LAN subnet.

Task 5

Ensure that R2 and R4 always prefer routes received from R3 to those received from R1 for each others' 150.x.x.x/24 prefixes. You are only allowed to configure ONE router. Your solution should be globally significant; however, you are NOT allowed to modify any of the BGP default administrative distance values. You can modify BGP attributes as you see fit. Verify the configuration using the appropriate commands.

LAB VALIDATION

Task 1

Please refer to previous labs for basic IP addressing and hostname configuration. This will not be included in this section to avoid being redundant.

Task 2

Please refer to previous labs for basic EIGRP configuration. This will not be included in this section to avoid being redundant. Following completion, the routing tables on your routers should show the following EIGRP route entries:

```
R1#show ip route eigrp
     2.0.0.0/32 is subnetted, 1 subnets
D       2.2.2.2 [90/2297856] via 10.0.0.2, 00:01:21, Serial0/0
```

```
       3.0.0.0/32 is subnetted, 1 subnets
D        3.3.3.3 [90/2297856] via 10.0.0.6, 00:00:46, Serial0/1
       4.0.0.0/32 is subnetted, 1 subnets
D        4.4.4.4 [90/21152000] via 10.0.0.6, 00:00:15, Serial0/1
       10.0.0.0/30 is subnetted, 3 subnets
D        10.0.0.12 [90/21024000] via 10.0.0.6, 00:01:01, Serial0/1

R2#show ip route eigrp
       1.0.0.0/32 is subnetted, 1 subnets
D        1.1.1.1 [90/2297856] via 10.0.0.1, 00:01:42, Serial0/0
       3.0.0.0/32 is subnetted, 1 subnets
D        3.3.3.3 [90/2809856] via 10.0.0.1, 00:01:00, Serial0/0
       4.0.0.0/32 is subnetted, 1 subnets
D        4.4.4.4 [90/21664000] via 10.0.0.1, 00:00:30, Serial0/0
       10.0.0.0/30 is subnetted, 3 subnets
D        10.0.0.12 [90/21536000] via 10.0.0.1, 00:01:15, Serial0/0
D        10.0.0.4 [90/2681856] via 10.0.0.1, 00:01:42, Serial0/0

R3#show ip route eigrp
       1.0.0.0/32 is subnetted, 1 subnets
D        1.1.1.1 [90/20640000] via 10.0.0.5, 00:01:34, Serial1/0
       2.0.0.0/32 is subnetted, 1 subnets
D        2.2.2.2 [90/21152000] via 10.0.0.5, 00:01:34, Serial1/0
       4.0.0.0/32 is subnetted, 1 subnets
D        4.4.4.4 [90/20640000] via 10.0.0.14, 00:00:44, Serial1/2
       10.0.0.0/30 is subnetted, 3 subnets
D        10.0.0.0 [90/21024000] via 10.0.0.5, 00:01:34, Serial1/0

R4#show ip route eigrp
       1.0.0.0/32 is subnetted, 1 subnets
D        1.1.1.1 [90/21152000] via 10.0.0.13, 00:01:06, Serial0/0
       2.0.0.0/32 is subnetted, 1 subnets
D        2.2.2.2 [90/21664000] via 10.0.0.13, 00:01:06, Serial0/0
       3.0.0.0/32 is subnetted, 1 subnets
D        3.3.3.3 [90/2297856] via 10.0.0.13, 00:01:06, Serial0/0
       10.0.0.0/30 is subnetted, 3 subnets
D        10.0.0.0 [90/21536000] via 10.0.0.13, 00:01:06, Serial0/0
D        10.0.0.4 [90/21024000] via 10.0.0.13, 00:01:06, Serial0/0
```

Task 3

This task is straightforward. By default, the BGP RID will be derived from the highest address of all physical interfaces or the highest address of all Loopback interfaces. Given that the Loopback0 interfaces are configured on all routers, there is NO need to manually configure the RID using the bgp router-id <address> command.

Additionally, when configuring the route reflectors, it is important to understand that they do not need to be clients of each other. Instead, in environments where there are multiple route reflectors being used for redundancy, you should configure route reflectors in the same cluster, i.e. serving the same clients, using the bgp cluster-id <cluster ID> command. This prevents multiple entries in the BGP Table because the route reflectors recognize updates from each other based on the CLUSTER_LIST attribute. The CLUSTER_LIST attribute is an optional, non-transitive BGP attribute of Type Code 10.

It is a sequence of CLUSTER_ID values representing the route reflection path that the prefix has traversed. When the RR reflects a route, it must prepend the local CLUSTER_ID to the CLUSTER_LIST. If the UPDATE has an empty CLUSTER_LIST, the RR must create a new one. Like the ORIGINATOR_ID attribute, the CLUSTER_LIST attribute is also used for to prevent loops in iBGP implementations.

Finally, remember that when you are configuring multiple BGP peers, you can also configure peer groups to minimize the number of commands that are issued. Both the long version and peer group configuration are illustrated in this example. You may use either method to complete this task. In this example, the task is completed using both of the methods as follows:

```
R1(config)#router bgp 254
R1(config-router)#bgp cluster-id 55.55.55.55
R1(config-router)#neighbor 2.2.2.2 remote-as 254
```

```
R1(config-router)#neighbor 2.2.2.2 update-source loopback 0
R1(config-router)#neighbor 2.2.2.2 route-reflector-client
R1(config-router)#neighbor 2.2.2.2 password CCNP
R1(config-router)#neighbor 2.2.2.2 timers 5 15
% Warning: A hold time of less than 20 seconds increases
  the chances of peer flapping
R1(config-router)#neighbor 3.3.3.3 remote-as 254
R1(config-router)#neighbor 3.3.3.3 update-source loopback 0
R1(config-router)#neighbor 3.3.3.3 password CCNP
R1(config-router)#neighbor 3.3.3.3 timers 5 15
% Warning: A hold time of less than 20 seconds increases
  the chances of peer flapping
R1(config-router)#neighbor 4.4.4.4 remote-as 254
R1(config-router)#neighbor 4.4.4.4 update-source loopback 0
R1(config-router)#neighbor 4.4.4.4 route-reflector-client
R1(config-router)#neighbor 4.4.4.4 password CCNP
R1(config-router)#neighbor 4.4.4.4 timers 5 15
% Warning: A hold time of less than 20 seconds increases
  the chances of peer flapping
R1(config-router)#exit

R2(config)#router bgp 254
R2(config-router)#neighbor INTERNAL peer-group
R2(config-router)#neighbor INTERNAL remote-as 254
R2(config-router)#neighbor INTERNAL update-source loopback 0
R2(config-router)#neighbor INTERNAL password CCNP
R2(config-router)#neighbor INTERNAL timers 5 15
% Warning: A hold time of less than 20 seconds increases
  the chances of peer flapping
R2(config-router)#neighbor 1.1.1.1 peer-group INTERNAL
R2(config-router)#neighbor 3.3.3.3 peer-group INTERNAL
R2(config-router)#exit

R3(config)#router bgp 254
R3(config-router)#bgp cluster-id 55.55.55.55
R3(config-router)#neighbor 1.1.1.1 remote-as 254
R3(config-router)#neighbor 1.1.1.1 update-source loopback 0
R3(config-router)#neighbor 1.1.1.1 password CCNP
R3(config-router)#neighbor 1.1.1.1 timers 5 15
% Warning: A hold time of less than 20 seconds increases
  the chances of peer flapping
R3(config-router)#neighbor 2.2.2.2 remote-as 254
R3(config-router)#neighbor 2.2.2.2 update-source loopback 0
R3(config-router)#neighbor 2.2.2.2 password CCNP
R3(config-router)#neighbor 2.2.2.2 timers 5 15
% Warning: A hold time of less than 20 seconds increases
  the chances of peer flapping
R3(config-router)#neighbor 2.2.2.2 route-reflector-client
R3(config-router)#neighbor 3.3.3.3 remote-as 254
% Cannot configure the local system as neighbor
R3(config-router)#neighbor 4.4.4.4 remote-as 254
R3(config-router)#neighbor 4.4.4.4 update-source loopback 0
R3(config-router)#neighbor 4.4.4.4 password CCNP
R3(config-router)#neighbor 4.4.4.4 timers 5 15
% Warning: A hold time of less than 20 seconds increases
  the chances of peer flapping
R3(config-router)#neighbor 4.4.4.4 route-reflector-client
R3(config-router)#exit

R4(config)#router bgp 254
R4(config-router)#neighbor INTERNAL peer-group
R4(config-router)#neighbor INTERNAL update-source loopback 0
R4(config-router)#neighbor INTERNAL remote-as 254
R4(config-router)#neighbor INTERNAL timers 5 15
% Warning: A hold time of less than 20 seconds increases
  the chances of peer flapping
R4(config-router)#neighbor INTERNAL password CCNP
R4(config-router)#neighbor 1.1.1.1 peer-group INTERNAL
R4(config-router)#neighbor 3.3.3.3 peer-group INTERNAL
R4(config-router)#exit
```

Verify your configuration using the show ip bgp summary command:

```
R1#show ip bgp summary
BGP router identifier 1.1.1.1, local AS number 254
BGP table version is 1, main routing table version 1

Neighbor      V    AS MsgRcvd MsgSent   TblVer  InQ OutQ Up/Down   State/PfxRcd
2.2.2.2       4   254      70      70        1    0    0 00:05:32         0
3.3.3.3       4   254      53      53        1    0    0 00:04:09         0
4.4.4.4       4   254      12      13        1    0    0 00:00:45         0

R2#show ip bgp summary
BGP router identifier 2.2.2.2, local AS number 254
BGP table version is 1, main routing table version 1

Neighbor      V    AS MsgRcvd MsgSent   TblVer  InQ OutQ Up/Down   State/PfxRcd
1.1.1.1       4   254      71      71        1    0    0 00:05:37         0
3.3.3.3       4   254      40      40        1    0    0 00:03:00         0

R3#show ip bgp summary
BGP router identifier 3.3.3.3, local AS number 254
BGP table version is 1, main routing table version 1

Neighbor      V    AS MsgRcvd MsgSent   TblVer  InQ OutQ Up/Down   State/PfxRcd
1.1.1.1       4   254      55      55        1    0    0 00:04:17         0
2.2.2.2       4   254      40      40        1    0    0 00:03:04         0
4.4.4.4       4   254      12      12        1    0    0 00:00:41         0

R4#show ip bgp summary
BGP router identifier 4.4.4.4, local AS number 254
BGP table version is 1, main routing table version 1

Neighbor      V    AS MsgRcvd MsgSent   TblVer  InQ OutQ Up/Down   State/PfxRcd
1.1.1.1       4   254      15      14        1    0    0 00:00:57         0
3.3.3.3       4   254      12      12        1    0    0 00:00:44         0
```

Task 4

To complete this task, you need to use the COMMUNITY attribute. This attribute, Attribute Type Code 8, is an optional transitive attribute that is used to group destinations, called communities. Once the destination prefixes have been grouped, routing decisions, such as acceptance, preference, and redistribution, can be applied. Cisco IOS route maps are to set the community attribute.

Well-known communities are communities that have predefined meanings. Cisco IOS software supports four well-known communities which are NO_EXPORT, NO_ADVERTISE, INTERNET, and LOCAL_AS. The NO_EXPORT well-known community prevents BGP prefixes that are specifically assigned this predefined community attribute value from being advertised to any eBGP peers. The prefixes, however, will continue to be advertised to all other BGP speakers within the local AS. In other words, prefixes assigned this community value will remain local to the Autonomous System (AS).

The NO_ADVERTISE community prevents any prefixes that are assigned this predefined community attribute from being advertised to any peer – internal or external. The INTERNET community allows all prefixes assigned to this community to be advertised to any and all BGP peers (assuming no filtering, etc, is in place). In Cisco IOS software, all BGP prefixes belong to the INTERNET community by default.
And finally, the LOCAL_AS community is used in a somewhat similar manner to another of the previously described communities: the NO_EXPORT community. If used in a Confederation, the LOCAL_AS community prevents all prefixes assigned this community from being advertised out of the local sub autonomous system. When Confederations are not implemented, the LOCAL_AS community is applied in the same manner as the NO_EXPORT community.

To complete this task, use either the LOCAL_AS or NO_EXPORT communities. In order to use the COMMUNITY attribute, you need to configure the neighbor <address> send-community command for all peers. This task is completed as follows:

```
R1(config)#route-map CONNECTED permit 10
R1(config-route-map)#match interface fastethernet 0/0
R1(config-route-map)#set community local-as
R1(config-route-map)#exit
R1(config)#route-map CONNECTED deny 20
R1(config-route-map)#exit
R1(config)#router bgp 254
R1(config-router)#redistribute connected route-map CONNECTED
R1(config-router)#neighbor 2.2.2.2 send-community standard
R1(config-router)#neighbor 3.3.3.3 send-community standard
R1(config-router)#neighbor 4.4.4.4 send-community standard

R2(config)#route-map CONNECTED permit 10
R2(config-route-map)#match interface fastethernet 0/0
R2(config-route-map)#set community local-as
R2(config-route-map)#exit
R2(config)#route-map CONNECTED deny 20
R2(config-route-map)#exit
R2(config)#router bgp 254
R2(config-router)#redistribute connected route-map CONNECTED
R2(config-router)#neighbor INTERNAL send-community standard
R2(config-router)#exit

R3(config-router)#route-map CONNECTED permit 10
R3(config-route-map)#match interface fastethernet 0/0
R3(config-route-map)#set community local-as
R3(config-route-map)#exit
R3(config)#route-map CONNECTED deny 20
R3(config-route-map)#exit
R3(config)#router bgp 254
R3(config-router)#redistribute connected route-map CONNECTED
R3(config-router)#neighbor 1.1.1.1 send-community standard
R3(config-router)#neighbor 2.2.2.2 send-community standard
R3(config-router)#neighbor 4.4.4.4 send-community standard

R4(config)#route-map CONNECTED permit 10
R4(config-route-map)#match interface fastethernet 0/0
R4(config-route-map)#set community local-as
R4(config-route-map)#exit
R4(config)#route-map CONNECTED deny 20
R4(config-route-map)#exit
R4(config)#router bgp 254
R4(config-router)#redistribute connected route-map CONNECTED
R4(config-router)#neighbor INTERNAL send-community standard
R4(config-router)#exit
```

Following this configuration, verify your configuration using the show ip bgp command:

```
R1#show ip bgp 150.1.1.0 255.255.255.0
BGP routing table entry for 150.1.1.0/24, version 2
Paths: (1 available, best #1, table Default-IP-Routing-Table, not advertised outside
local AS)
  Advertised to update-groups:
     1          2
  Local
    0.0.0.0 from 0.0.0.0 (1.1.1.1)
      Origin incomplete, metric 0, localpref 100, weight 32768, valid, sourced, best
      Community: local-AS

R2#show ip bgp 150.2.2.0 255.255.255.0
BGP routing table entry for 150.2.2.0/24, version 3
Paths: (1 available, best #1, table Default-IP-Routing-Table, not advertised outside
local AS)
Flag: 0x820
  Advertised to update-groups:
     1
  Local
    0.0.0.0 from 0.0.0.0 (2.2.2.2)
      Origin incomplete, metric 0, localpref 100, weight 32768, valid, sourced, best
      Community: local-AS

R3#show ip bgp 150.3.3.0 255.255.255.0
BGP routing table entry for 150.3.3.0/24, version 4
```

```
Paths: (1 available, best #1, table Default-IP-Routing-Table, not advertised outside
local AS)
  Advertised to update-groups:
     1          2
  Local
     0.0.0.0 from 0.0.0.0 (3.3.3.3)
       Origin incomplete, metric 0, localpref 100, weight 32768, valid, sourced, best
       Community: local-AS

R4#show ip bgp 150.4.4.0 255.255.255.0
BGP routing table entry for 150.4.4.0/24, version 6
Paths: (1 available, best #1, table Default-IP-Routing-Table, not advertised outside
local AS)
Flag: 0x820
  Advertised to update-groups:
     1
  Local
     0.0.0.0 from 0.0.0.0 (4.4.4.4)
       Origin incomplete, metric 0, localpref 100, weight 32768, valid, sourced, best
       Community: local-AS
```

You can verify that the COMMUNITY attribute is being sent to peers using the show ip bgp neighbors
<address> command:

```
R1#show ip bgp neighbors 2.2.2.2
BGP neighbor is 2.2.2.2,  remote AS 254, internal link
  BGP version 4, remote router ID 2.2.2.2
  BGP state = Established, up for 00:34:11
  Last read 00:00:00, last write 00:00:00, hold time is 15, keepalive interval is 5
seconds
  Configured hold time is 15,keepalive interval is 5 seconds  Minimum holdtime from
neighbor is 0 seconds
  Neighbor capabilities:
     Route refresh: advertised and received(old & new)
     Address family IPv4 Unicast: advertised and received
  Message statistics:
    InQ depth is 0
    OutQ depth is 0
                          Sent       Rcvd
    Opens:                 1          1
    Notifications:         0          0
    Updates:               5          1
    Keepalives:          413        413
    Route Refresh:         0          0
    Total:               419        415
  Default minimum time between advertisement runs is 0 seconds

 For address family: IPv4 Unicast
  BGP table version 6, neighbor version 6/0
 Output queue size : 0
  Index 1, Offset 0, Mask 0x2
  Route-Reflector Client
  1 update-group member
  Community attribute sent to this neighbor
                          Sent       Rcvd
                          ----       ----
  Prefix activity:
    Prefixes Current:       4          1 (Consumes 52 bytes)
    Prefixes Total:         5          1
    Implicit Withdraw:      1          0
    Explicit Withdraw:      0          0
    Used as bestpath:     n/a          1
    Used as multipath:    n/a          0

                        Outbound   Inbound
                        --------   -------
  Local Policy Denied Prefixes:
    Total:                  0          0
  Number of NLRIs in the update sent: max 1, min 1
```

Task 5

Prior to any configuration changes, the BGP tables on R2 and R4 show the following entries for each others'
150.x.x.x/24 subnets:

```
R2#show ip bgp 150.4.4.0 255.255.255.0
BGP routing table entry for 150.4.4.0/24, version 13
Paths: (2 available, best #1, table Default-IP-Routing-Table, not advertised outside
local AS)
  Not advertised to any peer
  Local
    4.4.4.4 (metric 21664000) from 1.1.1.1 (1.1.1.1)
      Origin incomplete, metric 0, localpref 100, valid, internal, best
      Community: local-AS
      Originator: 4.4.4.4, Cluster list: 55.55.55.55
  Local
    4.4.4.4 (metric 21664000) from 3.3.3.3 (3.3.3.3)
      Origin incomplete, metric 0, localpref 100, valid, internal
      Community: local-AS
      Originator: 4.4.4.4, Cluster list: 55.55.55.55

R4#show ip bgp 150.2.2.0 255.255.255.0
BGP routing table entry for 150.2.2.0/24, version 11
Paths: (2 available, best #1, table Default-IP-Routing-Table, not advertised outside
local AS)
  Not advertised to any peer
  Local
    2.2.2.2 (metric 21664000) from 1.1.1.1 (1.1.1.1)
      Origin incomplete, metric 0, localpref 100, valid, internal, best
      Community: local-AS
      Originator: 2.2.2.2, Cluster list: 55.55.55.55
  Local
    2.2.2.2 (metric 21664000) from 3.3.3.3 (3.3.3.3)
      Origin incomplete, metric 0, localpref 100, valid, internal
      Community: local-AS
      Originator: 2.2.2.2, Cluster list: 55.55.55.55
```

Given that all else is equal, the route received from R1 is preferred because it is comes from the lowest neighbor address. To complete this task, it is most simple to use LOCAL_PREF:

```
R3(config-router)#route-map LOCAL-PREF permit 10
R3(config-route-map)#set local-preference 200
R3(config)#router bgp 254
R3(config-router)#neighbor 2.2.2.2 route-map LOCAL-PREF in
R3(config-router)#neighbor 4.4.4.4 route-map LOCAL-PREF in
R3(config-router)#exit
```

Following this change, the BGP RIBs show the following for the LAN subnets:

```
R2#show ip bgp 150.4.4.0 255.255.255.0
BGP routing table entry for 150.4.4.0/24, version 20
Paths: (2 available, best #2, table Default-IP-Routing-Table, not advertised outside
local AS)
Flag: 0x800
  Not advertised to any peer
  Local
    4.4.4.4 (metric 21664000) from 1.1.1.1 (1.1.1.1)
      Origin incomplete, metric 0, localpref 100, valid, internal
      Community: local-AS
      Originator: 4.4.4.4, Cluster list: 55.55.55.55
  Local
    4.4.4.4 (metric 21664000) from 3.3.3.3 (3.3.3.3)
      Origin incomplete, metric 0, localpref 200, valid, internal, best
      Community: local-AS
      Originator: 4.4.4.4, Cluster list: 55.55.55.55

R4#show ip bgp 150.2.2.0 255.255.255.0
BGP routing table entry for 150.2.2.0/24, version 17
Paths: (2 available, best #2, table Default-IP-Routing-Table, not advertised outside
local AS)
Flag: 0x800
  Not advertised to any peer
  Local
    2.2.2.2 (metric 21664000) from 1.1.1.1 (1.1.1.1)
      Origin incomplete, metric 0, localpref 100, valid, internal
      Community: local-AS
      Originator: 2.2.2.2, Cluster list: 55.55.55.55
```

```
Local
    2.2.2.2 (metric 21664000) from 3.3.3.3 (3.3.3.3)
      Origin incomplete, metric 0, localpref 200, valid, internal, best
      Community: local-AS
      Originator: 2.2.2.2, Cluster list: 55.55.55.55
```

NOTE: Setting the route map INBOUND allows the R3 to essentially 're-set' the LOCAL_PREF of all received prefixes to the specified value. Because LOCAL_PREF is included in updates to iBGP peers, this value is propagated to all other routers in the domain. If you sent LOCAL_PREF in the outbound direction, this is applicable only to routes originated by and advertised by R3. In other words, it would only apply to the 150.3.3.0/24 prefix. Again, it is very important to understand the direction in which attributes are applied.

FINAL ROUTER CONFIGURATIONS

R1

```
R1#term len 0
R1#sh run
Building configuration...

Current configuration : 1855 bytes
!
version 12.4
service timestamps debug datetime msec
service timestamps log datetime msec
no service password-encryption
!
hostname R1
!
boot-start-marker
boot-end-marker
!
no logging console
!
no aaa new-model
no network-clock-participate slot 1
no network-clock-participate wic 0
ip cef
!
no ip domain lookup
ip auth-proxy max-nodata-conns 3
ip admission max-nodata-conns 3
!
interface Loopback0
 ip address 1.1.1.1 255.255.255.255
!
interface FastEthernet0/0
 ip address 150.1.1.1 255.255.255.0
 duplex auto
 speed auto
!
interface Serial0/0
 ip address 10.0.0.1 255.255.255.252
 clock rate 2000000
!
interface Serial0/1
 ip address 10.0.0.5 255.255.255.252
!
router eigrp 254
 network 1.1.1.1 0.0.0.0
 network 10.0.0.1 0.0.0.0
 network 10.0.0.5 0.0.0.0
 no auto-summary
!
router bgp 254
 no synchronization
 bgp cluster-id 55.55.55.55
 bgp log-neighbor-changes
```

```
  redistribute connected route-map CONNECTED
  neighbor 2.2.2.2 remote-as 254
  neighbor 2.2.2.2 password CCNP
  neighbor 2.2.2.2 update-source Loopback0
  neighbor 2.2.2.2 timers 5 15
  neighbor 2.2.2.2 route-reflector-client
  neighbor 2.2.2.2 send-community
  neighbor 3.3.3.3 remote-as 254
  neighbor 3.3.3.3 password CCNP
  neighbor 3.3.3.3 update-source Loopback0
  neighbor 3.3.3.3 timers 5 15
  neighbor 3.3.3.3 send-community
  neighbor 4.4.4.4 remote-as 254
  neighbor 4.4.4.4 password CCNP
  neighbor 4.4.4.4 update-source Loopback0
  neighbor 4.4.4.4 timers 5 15
  neighbor 4.4.4.4 route-reflector-client
  neighbor 4.4.4.4 send-community
 no auto-summary
!
ip forward-protocol nd
!
no ip http server
no ip http secure-server
!
route-map CONNECTED permit 10
 match interface FastEthernet0/0
 set community local-AS
!
route-map CONNECTED deny 20
!
control-plane
!
line con 0
line aux 0
line vty 0 4
 login
!
end

R1#
```

R2

```
R2#term len 0
R2#sh run
Building configuration...

Current configuration : 1460 bytes
!
version 12.4
service timestamps debug datetime msec
service timestamps log datetime msec
no service password-encryption
!
hostname R2
!
boot-start-marker
boot-end-marker
!
no logging console
!
no aaa new-model
no network-clock-participate slot 1
no network-clock-participate wic 0
ip cef
!
no ip domain lookup
ip auth-proxy max-nodata-conns 3
ip admission max-nodata-conns 3
!
interface Loopback0
 ip address 2.2.2.2 255.255.255.255
```

```
!
interface FastEthernet0/0
 ip address 150.2.2.2 255.255.255.0
 duplex auto
 speed auto
!
interface Serial0/0
 ip address 10.0.0.2 255.255.255.252
!
interface Serial0/1
 no ip address
 shutdown
!
router eigrp 254
 network 2.2.2.2 0.0.0.0
 network 10.0.0.2 0.0.0.0
 no auto-summary
!
router bgp 254
 no synchronization
 bgp log-neighbor-changes
 redistribute connected route-map CONNECTED
 neighbor INTERNAL peer-group
 neighbor INTERNAL remote-as 254
 neighbor INTERNAL password CCNP
 neighbor INTERNAL update-source Loopback0
 neighbor INTERNAL timers 5 15
 neighbor INTERNAL send-community
 neighbor 1.1.1.1 peer-group INTERNAL
 neighbor 3.3.3.3 peer-group INTERNAL
 no auto-summary
!
ip forward-protocol nd
!
no ip http server
no ip http secure-server
!
route-map CONNECTED permit 10
 match interface FastEthernet0/0
 set community local-AS
!
route-map CONNECTED deny 20
!
control-plane
!
line con 0
line aux 0
line vty 0 4
 login
!
end

R2#
```

R3

```
R3#term len 0
R3#sh run
Building configuration...

Current configuration : 2319 bytes
!
version 12.4
service timestamps debug datetime msec
service timestamps log datetime msec
no service password-encryption
!
hostname R3
!
boot-start-marker
boot-end-marker
!
no logging console
!
```

```
no aaa new-model
no network-clock-participate slot 1
no network-clock-participate wic 0
ip cef
!
no ip domain lookup
ip auth-proxy max-nodata-conns 3
ip admission max-nodata-conns 3
!
interface Loopback0
 ip address 3.3.3.3 255.255.255.255
!
interface FastEthernet0/0
 ip address 150.3.3.3 255.255.255.0
 duplex auto
 speed auto
!
interface Serial1/0
 ip address 10.0.0.6 255.255.255.252
 clock rate 128000
!
interface Serial1/1
 no ip address
 shutdown
 clock rate 128000
!
interface Serial1/2
 ip address 10.0.0.13 255.255.255.252
 clock rate 128000
!
interface Serial1/3
 no ip address
 shutdown
!
interface Serial1/4
 no ip address
 shutdown
!
interface Serial1/5
 no ip address
 shutdown
!
interface Serial1/6
 no ip address
 shutdown
!
interface Serial1/7
 no ip address
 shutdown
!
router eigrp 254
 network 3.3.3.3 0.0.0.0
 network 10.0.0.6 0.0.0.0
 network 10.0.0.13 0.0.0.0
 no auto-summary
!
router bgp 254
 no synchronization
 bgp cluster-id 55.55.55.55
 bgp log-neighbor-changes
 redistribute connected route-map CONNECTED
 neighbor 1.1.1.1 remote-as 254
 neighbor 1.1.1.1 password CCNP
 neighbor 1.1.1.1 update-source Loopback0
 neighbor 1.1.1.1 timers 5 15
 neighbor 1.1.1.1 send-community
 neighbor 2.2.2.2 remote-as 254
 neighbor 2.2.2.2 password CCNP
 neighbor 2.2.2.2 update-source Loopback0
 neighbor 2.2.2.2 timers 5 15
 neighbor 2.2.2.2 route-reflector-client
 neighbor 2.2.2.2 send-community
 neighbor 2.2.2.2 route-map LOCAL-PREF in
 neighbor 4.4.4.4 remote-as 254
 neighbor 4.4.4.4 password CCNP
```

```
 neighbor 4.4.4.4 update-source Loopback0
 neighbor 4.4.4.4 timers 5 15
 neighbor 4.4.4.4 route-reflector-client
 neighbor 4.4.4.4 send-community
 neighbor 4.4.4.4 route-map LOCAL-PREF in
 no auto-summary
!
ip forward-protocol nd
!
no ip http server
no ip http secure-server
!
route-map CONNECTED permit 10
 match interface FastEthernet0/0
 set community local-AS
!
route-map CONNECTED deny 20
!
route-map LOCAL-PREF permit 10
 set local-preference 200
!
control-plane
!
line con 0
line aux 0
line vty 0 4
 login
!
end

R3#
```

R4

```
R4#term len 0
R4#sh run
Building configuration...

Current configuration : 1462 bytes
!
version 12.4
service timestamps debug datetime msec
service timestamps log datetime msec
no service password-encryption
!
hostname R4
!
boot-start-marker
boot-end-marker
!
no logging console
!
no aaa new-model
no network-clock-participate slot 1
no network-clock-participate wic 0
ip cef
!
no ip domain lookup
ip auth-proxy max-nodata-conns 3
ip admission max-nodata-conns 3
!
interface Loopback0
 ip address 4.4.4.4 255.255.255.255
!
interface FastEthernet0/0
 ip address 150.4.4.4 255.255.255.0
 duplex auto
 speed auto
!
interface Serial0/0
 ip address 10.0.0.14 255.255.255.252
!
interface Serial0/1
```

```
 no ip address
 shutdown
!
router eigrp 254
 network 4.4.4.4 0.0.0.0
 network 10.0.0.14 0.0.0.0
 no auto-summary
!
router bgp 254
 no synchronization
 bgp log-neighbor-changes
 redistribute connected route-map CONNECTED
 neighbor INTERNAL peer-group
 neighbor INTERNAL remote-as 254
 neighbor INTERNAL password CCNP
 neighbor INTERNAL update-source Loopback0
 neighbor INTERNAL timers 5 15
 neighbor INTERNAL send-community
 neighbor 1.1.1.1 peer-group INTERNAL
 neighbor 3.3.3.3 peer-group INTERNAL
 no auto-summary
!
ip forward-protocol nd
!
no ip http server
no ip http secure-server
!
route-map CONNECTED permit 10
 match interface FastEthernet0/0
 set community local-AS
!
route-map CONNECTED deny 20
!
control-plane
!
line con 0
line aux 0
line vty 0 4
 login
!
end

R4#
```

CCNP LAB 33

Border Gateway Protocol Lab

Lab Objective:

The focus of this lab is to understand BGP implementation and configuration in Cisco IOS routers. Additional technologies include confederations, summarization and path control.

Lab Topology:

The lab network topology is illustrated below:

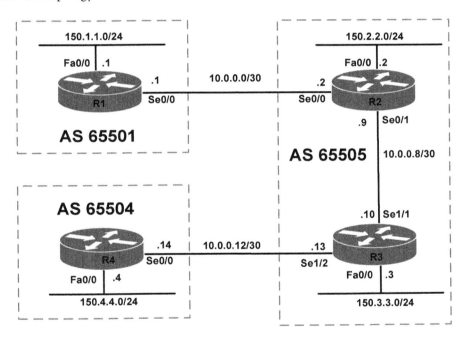

IMPORTANT NOTE: If you are using the www.howtonetwork.net racks, please bring up the LAN interfaces connected to the routers by issuing the no shutdown command on the connected switches. If you are using a home lab with no Switches, you can bring up the LAN interfaces using the following configurations on your routers:

```
interface fastethernet 0/0
  no keepalive
  loopback
  no shutdown
```

Alternately, you can simply connect the interfaces to a hub or switch if you have one available in your own lab.

Task 1

Configure hostnames and IP addressing on all routers as illustrated in the network topology.

Task 2

Configure the following the following Loopback 0 interfaces on all routers and then enable OSPF using area 0 (backbone) on all routers. OSPF should only be enabled for the Loopback and 10.x.x.x/30 WAN subnets. Do NOT enable OSPF for the 150.x.x.x/24 LAN subnets.
- R1: Loopback 0: IP Address 1.1.1.1/32
- R2: Loopback 0: IP Address 2.2.2.2/32
- R3: Loopback 0: IP Address 3.3.3.3/32
- R4: Loopback 0: IP Address 4.4.4.4/32

Task 3

Configure BGP confederations as illustrated in the network topology. Use Loopback interface IP addresses for BGP peering. To the outside world, all routers should appear to be in BGP AS 254. Verify your configuration using the appropriate commands.

Task 4

Advertise the 150.x.x.x/24 subnets on R1, R2, R3, and R4 via BGP. Ensure that all routers can ping each others' LAN subnet from their own LAN subnet. For example, from R1 ping the 150.4.4.4 address using an extended ping sourced from the routers FastEthernet0/0 interface.

Task 5

In the future, a link will be provisioned between R1 and R4. However, management has decided that R1 and R2 should ALWAYS prefer the path through sub-AS 65505 to reach each others' LAN subnets ONLY. Any other subnets that may be added to additional sub-ASes in the future should be affected by this configuration. For example, if another sub-AS is connected to R4, then R1 should prefer the path directly through R4 to reach this sub-AS since it will have a shorter AS_PATH list than going through sub-AS 65505. You are NOT allowed to use IP ACLs or prefix lists to complete this task. Verify the solution using the appropriate commands.

Task 6

Configure sub-AS 65505 to advertise a single prefix instead of the two 150.2.2.0/24 as well as the 150.3.3./24 prefixes connected to R2 and R3s LAN interfaces to R1 and R4.

> **HINT:** Use the `neighbor <address> unsuppress-map <route-map-name>` command on R2 and R3 to allow these prefixes to be advertised within sub AS 65505 so that R2 and R3 still have LAN-to-LAN connectivity.

Verify your configuration and ensure that R1 and R2 can still reach the LAN that are connected to R2 and R3. Use extended pings to verify your configuration.

LAB VALIDATION

Task 1

Please refer to previous labs for basic IP addressing and hostname configuration. This will not be included in this section to avoid being redundant.

Task 2

Please refer to previous labs for basic OSPF configuration. This will not be included in this section to avoid being redundant. Following completion, the routing tables on your routers should show the following OSPF route entries:

```
R1#show ip route ospf
     2.0.0.0/32 is subnetted, 1 subnets
O       2.2.2.2 [110/65] via 10.0.0.2, 00:00:05, Serial0/0
```

```
          3.0.0.0/32 is subnetted, 1 subnets
O           3.3.3.3 [110/129] via 10.0.0.2, 00:00:05, Serial0/0
          4.0.0.0/32 is subnetted, 1 subnets
O           4.4.4.4 [110/910] via 10.0.0.2, 00:00:05, Serial0/0
          10.0.0.0/30 is subnetted, 3 subnets
O           10.0.0.8 [110/128] via 10.0.0.2, 00:00:05, Serial0/0
O           10.0.0.12 [110/909] via 10.0.0.2, 00:00:05, Serial0/0

R2#show ip route ospf
          1.0.0.0/32 is subnetted, 1 subnets
O           1.1.1.1 [110/65] via 10.0.0.1, 00:00:11, Serial0/0
          3.0.0.0/32 is subnetted, 1 subnets
O           3.3.3.3 [110/65] via 10.0.0.10, 00:00:11, Serial0/1
          4.0.0.0/32 is subnetted, 1 subnets
O           4.4.4.4 [110/846] via 10.0.0.10, 00:00:11, Serial0/1
          10.0.0.0/30 is subnetted, 3 subnets
O           10.0.0.12 [110/845] via 10.0.0.10, 00:00:11, Serial0/1

R3#show ip route ospf
          1.0.0.0/32 is subnetted, 1 subnets
O           1.1.1.1 [110/846] via 10.0.0.9, 00:00:14, Serial1/1
          2.0.0.0/32 is subnetted, 1 subnets
O           2.2.2.2 [110/782] via 10.0.0.9, 00:00:14, Serial1/1
          4.0.0.0/32 is subnetted, 1 subnets
O           4.4.4.4 [110/782] via 10.0.0.14, 00:00:14, Serial1/2
          10.0.0.0/30 is subnetted, 3 subnets
O           10.0.0.0 [110/845] via 10.0.0.9, 00:00:14, Serial1/1

R4#show ip route ospf
          1.0.0.0/32 is subnetted, 1 subnets
O           1.1.1.1 [110/910] via 10.0.0.13, 00:00:12, Serial0/0
          2.0.0.0/32 is subnetted, 1 subnets
O           2.2.2.2 [110/846] via 10.0.0.13, 00:00:12, Serial0/0
          3.0.0.0/32 is subnetted, 1 subnets
O           3.3.3.3 [110/65] via 10.0.0.13, 00:00:12, Serial0/0
          10.0.0.0/30 is subnetted, 3 subnets
O           10.0.0.8 [110/845] via 10.0.0.13, 00:00:12, Serial0/0
O           10.0.0.0 [110/909] via 10.0.0.13, 00:00:12, Serial0/0
```

Task 3

The configuration of confederations is a little more complex than that required to configure and implement Route Reflectors. In Cisco IOS software, the following sequence of steps is required to configure and implement BGP confederations:

- Configure the local BGP speaker with the desired private AS number using the router bgp [private AS number] global configuration command
- Configure the local BGP speaker with the public AS using the bgp confederation identifier [public AS number] router configuration command
- Specify one or more sub-AS peers that this local BGP speaker will peer to using the bgp confederation peers [sub-AS] router configuration command. If the local BGP speaker will not peer to any other sub-AS, this command must be omitted
- Configure the BGP neighbor relationships following the standard steps. However, if a local BGP speaker will be peered to another BGP speaker in a different sub-AS, you must use the neighbor [address] ebgp-multihop command if you will be using Loopback interfaces for the BGP session

Following the sequence of steps illustrated above, this task is completed as follows:

```
R1(config)#router bgp 65501
R1(config-router)#bgp confederation identifier 254
R1(config-router)#bgp confederation peers 65505
R1(config-router)#neighbor 2.2.2.2 remote-as 65505
R1(config-router)#neighbor 2.2.2.2 update-source loopback 0
R1(config-router)#neighbor 2.2.2.2 ebgp-multihop
R1(config-router)#exit

R2(config)#router bgp 65505
R2(config-router)#bgp confederation identifier 254
R2(config-router)#bgp confederation peers 65501
```

```
R2(config-router)#neighbor 1.1.1.1 remote-as 65501
R2(config-router)#neighbor 1.1.1.1 update-source loopback 0
R2(config-router)#neighbor 1.1.1.1 ebgp-multihop
R2(config-router)#neighbor 3.3.3.3 remote-as 65505
R2(config-router)#neighbor 3.3.3.3 update-source loopback 0
R2(config-router)#neighbor 3.3.3.3 ebgp-multihop
R2(config-router)#exit

R3(config)#router bgp 65505
R3(config-router)#bgp confederation identifier 254
R3(config-router)#bgp confederation peers 65504
R3(config-router)#neighbor 2.2.2.2 remote-as 65505
R3(config-router)#neighbor 2.2.2.2 update-source loopback 0
R3(config-router)#neighbor 2.2.2.2 ebgp-multihop
R3(config-router)#neighbor 4.4.4.4 remote-as 65504
R3(config-router)#neighbor 4.4.4.4 update-source loopback 0
R3(config-router)#neighbor 4.4.4.4 ebgp-multihop
R3(config-router)#exit

R4(config)#router bgp 65504
R4(config-router)#bgp confederation identifier 254
R4(config-router)#bgp confederation peers 65505
R4(config-router)#neighbor 3.3.3.3 remote-as 65505
R4(config-router)#neighbor 3.3.3.3 update-source loopback 0
R4(config-router)#neighbor 3.3.3.3 ebgp-multihop
R4(config-router)#exit
```

Verify your configuration using the **show ip bgp summary** command:

```
R1#show ip bgp summary
BGP router identifier 1.1.1.1, local AS number 65501
BGP table version is 1, main routing table version 1

Neighbor     V    AS MsgRcvd MsgSent   TblVer  InQ OutQ Up/Down  State/PfxRcd
2.2.2.2      4 65505     22      22        1    0    0 00:00:04           0

R2#show ip bgp summary
BGP router identifier 2.2.2.2, local AS number 65505
BGP table version is 1, main routing table version 1

Neighbor     V    AS MsgRcvd MsgSent   TblVer  InQ OutQ Up/Down  State/PfxRcd
1.1.1.1      4 65501     22      22        1    0    0 00:00:13           0
3.3.3.3      4 65505      6       6        1    0    0 00:03:53           0

R3#show ip bgp summary
BGP router identifier 3.3.3.3, local AS number 65505
BGP table version is 1, main routing table version 1

Neighbor     V    AS MsgRcvd MsgSent   TblVer  InQ OutQ Up/Down  State/PfxRcd
2.2.2.2      4 65505      6       6        1    0    0 00:03:57           0
4.4.4.4      4 65504      6       6        1    0    0 00:02:22           0

R4#show ip bgp summary
BGP router identifier 4.4.4.4, local AS number 65504
BGP table version is 1, main routing table version 1

Neighbor     V    AS MsgRcvd MsgSent   TblVer  InQ OutQ Up/Down  State/PfxRcd
3.3.3.3      4 65505      6       6        1    0    0 00:02:26           0
```

Task 4

This is a straightforward task that is completed using the network command under BGP:

```
R1(config)#router bgp 65501
R1(config-router)#network 150.1.1.0 mask 255.255.255.0
R1(config-router)#exit

R2(config)#router bgp 65505
R2(config-router)#network 150.2.2.0 mask 255.255.255.0
R2(config-router)#exit
```

```
R3(config)#router bgp 65505
R3(config-router)#network 150.3.3.0 mask 255.255.255.0
R3(config-router)#exit

R4(config)#router bgp 65504
R4(config-router)#network 150.4.4.0 mask 255.255.255.0
R4(config-router)#exit
```

Verify your configuration using the **show ip bgp** command on all routers:

```
R1#show ip bgp
BGP table version is 5, local router ID is 1.1.1.1
Status codes: s suppressed, d damped, h history, * valid, > best, i - internal,
              r RIB-failure, S Stale
Origin codes: i - IGP, e - EGP, ? - incomplete

   Network          Next Hop        Metric LocPrf Weight Path
*> 150.1.1.0/24     0.0.0.0              0          32768 i
*> 150.2.2.0/24     2.2.2.2              0    100       0 (65505) i
*> 150.3.3.0/24     3.3.3.3              0    100       0 (65505) i
*> 150.4.4.0/24     4.4.4.4              0    100       0 (65505 65504) i

R2#show ip bgp
BGP table version is 5, local router ID is 2.2.2.2
Status codes: s suppressed, d damped, h history, * valid, > best, i - internal,
              r RIB-failure, S Stale
Origin codes: i - IGP, e - EGP, ? - incomplete

   Network          Next Hop        Metric LocPrf Weight Path
*> 150.1.1.0/24     1.1.1.1              0    100       0 (65501) i
*> 150.2.2.0/24     0.0.0.0              0          32768 i
*>i150.3.3.0/24     3.3.3.3              0    100       0 i
*>i150.4.4.0/24     4.4.4.4              0    100       0 (65504) i

R3#show ip bgp
BGP table version is 5, local router ID is 3.3.3.3
Status codes: s suppressed, d damped, h history, * valid, > best, i - internal,
              r RIB-failure, S Stale
Origin codes: i - IGP, e - EGP, ? - incomplete

   Network          Next Hop        Metric LocPrf Weight Path
*>i150.1.1.0/24     1.1.1.1              0    100       0 (65501) i
*>i150.2.2.0/24     2.2.2.2              0    100       0 i
*> 150.3.3.0/24     0.0.0.0              0          32768 i
*> 150.4.4.0/24     4.4.4.4              0    100       0 (65504) i

R4#show ip bgp
BGP table version is 4, local router ID is 4.4.4.4
Status codes: s suppressed, d damped, h history, * valid, > best, i - internal,
              r RIB-failure, S Stale
Origin codes: i - IGP, e - EGP, ? - incomplete

   Network          Next Hop        Metric LocPrf Weight Path
*> 150.1.1.0/24     1.1.1.1              0    100       0 (65505 65501) i
*> 150.2.2.0/24     2.2.2.2              0    100       0 (65505) i
*> 150.4.4.0/24     0.0.0.0              0          32768 i
```

Finally, use the extended ping function to verify LAN-to-LAN connectivity between subnets:

```
R1#ping 150.2.2.2 source fastethernet 0/0 repeat 10

Type escape sequence to abort.
Sending 10, 100-byte ICMP Echos to 150.2.2.2, timeout is 2 seconds:
Packet sent with a source address of 150.1.1.1
!!!!!!!!!!
Success rate is 100 percent (10/10), round-trip min/avg/max = 1/3/4 ms

R1#ping 150.3.3.3 source fastethernet 0/0 repeat 10

Type escape sequence to abort.
```

```
Sending 10, 100-byte ICMP Echos to 150.3.3.3, timeout is 2 seconds:
Packet sent with a source address of 150.1.1.1
!!!!!!!!!!
Success rate is 100 percent (10/10), round-trip min/avg/max = 16/16/20 ms

R1#ping 150.4.4.4 source fastethernet 0/0 repeat 10

Type escape sequence to abort.
Sending 10, 100-byte ICMP Echos to 150.4.4.4, timeout is 2 seconds:
Packet sent with a source address of 150.1.1.1
!!!!!!!!!!
Success rate is 100 percent (10/10), round-trip min/avg/max = 28/30/32 ms

R2#ping 150.1.1.1 source fastethernet 0/0 repeat 10

Type escape sequence to abort.
Sending 10, 100-byte ICMP Echos to 150.1.1.1, timeout is 2 seconds:
Packet sent with a source address of 150.2.2.2
!!!!!!!!!!
Success rate is 100 percent (10/10), round-trip min/avg/max = 1/3/4 ms

R2#ping 150.3.3.3 source fastethernet 0/0 repeat 10

Type escape sequence to abort.
Sending 10, 100-byte ICMP Echos to 150.3.3.3, timeout is 2 seconds:
Packet sent with a source address of 150.2.2.2
!!!!!!!!!!
Success rate is 100 percent (10/10), round-trip min/avg/max = 12/15/16 ms

R2#ping 150.4.4.4 source fastethernet 0/0 repeat 10

Type escape sequence to abort.
Sending 10, 100-byte ICMP Echos to 150.4.4.4, timeout is 2 seconds:
Packet sent with a source address of 150.2.2.2
!!!!!!!!!!
Success rate is 100 percent (10/10), round-trip min/avg/max = 28/32/48 ms

R3#ping 150.1.1.1 source fastethernet 0/0 repeat 10

Type escape sequence to abort.
Sending 10, 100-byte ICMP Echos to 150.1.1.1, timeout is 2 seconds:
Packet sent with a source address of 150.3.3.3
!!!!!!!!!!
Success rate is 100 percent (10/10), round-trip min/avg/max = 16/16/20 ms

R3#ping 150.2.2.2 source fastethernet 0/0 repeat 10

Type escape sequence to abort.
Sending 10, 100-byte ICMP Echos to 150.2.2.2, timeout is 2 seconds:
Packet sent with a source address of 150.3.3.3
!!!!!!!!!!
Success rate is 100 percent (10/10), round-trip min/avg/max = 12/15/16 ms

R3#ping 150.3.3.3 source fastethernet 0/0 repeat 10

Type escape sequence to abort.
Sending 10, 100-byte ICMP Echos to 150.3.3.3, timeout is 2 seconds:
Packet sent with a source address of 150.3.3.3
!!!!!!!!!!
Success rate is 100 percent (10/10), round-trip min/avg/max = 1/1/4 ms

R4#ping 150.1.1.1 source fastethernet 0/0 repeat 10

Type escape sequence to abort.
Sending 10, 100-byte ICMP Echos to 150.1.1.1, timeout is 2 seconds:
Packet sent with a source address of 150.4.4.4
!!!!!!!!!!
Success rate is 100 percent (10/10), round-trip min/avg/max = 28/30/32 ms

R4#ping 150.2.2.2 source fastethernet 0/0 repeat 10

Type escape sequence to abort.
Sending 10, 100-byte ICMP Echos to 150.2.2.2, timeout is 2 seconds:
```

```
Packet sent with a source address of 150.4.4.4
!!!!!!!!!!
Success rate is 100 percent (10/10), round-trip min/avg/max = 28/30/32 ms

R4#ping 150.3.3.3 source fastethernet 0/0 repeat 10

Type escape sequence to abort.
Sending 10, 100-byte ICMP Echos to 150.3.3.3, timeout is 2 seconds:
Packet sent with a source address of 150.4.4.4
!!!!!!!!!!
Success rate is 100 percent (10/10), round-trip min/avg/max = 16/16/16 ms
```

Task 5

To complete this task, you need to use either the WEIGHT or LOCAL_PREF attributes along with a regular expression (since using IP ACLs and prefix lists is forbidden). In Cisco IOS software, AS path filters are used to perform BGP filtering policy control based on the AS_PATH attribute. The AS path attribute pattern used in these filters is defined by a regular expression string that is configured using the ip as-path access-list [number] [permit | deny] <regexp> global configuration command. The configured filter list may then be applied directly on a per-neighbor basis using the neighbor [address] filter-list <as_path_acl_number> router configuration command or indirectly on a per-neighbor basis by referencing an route map which matches one or more AS path filters using the match as-path <as_path_acl_number> route map match clause.

The table below shows some basic regular expression configuration and what they match:

Regular Expression	Matches
.*	This regular expression is used to match all prefixes
^$	This regular expression matches only prefixes local to the AS
_254$	This regular expression matches only prefixes that originate in AS 254
^254_ [0-9]*$	This regular expression matches prefixes received from directly connected AS 254 and any ASes directly attached to AS 254
_254_	This regular expression matches prefixes that have traversed AS 254
^254$	This regular expression matches prefixes only originated from directly connected AS 254

This task is completed using regular expressions and the Cisco proprietary WEIGHT attribute. However, keep in mind that you may also use LOCAL_PREF. Either attribute is acceptable. Match on prefixes originated from sub-AS 65501 and sub-AS 65504 to complete this task. You can verify which prefixes will match your AS_PATH ACL Filter beforehand using the show ip bgp regexp <regular expression> command as follows:

```
R1#show ip bgp regexp _\(65505 65504\)$
BGP table version is 5, local router ID is 1.1.1.1
Status codes: s suppressed, d damped, h history, * valid, > best, i - internal,
              r RIB-failure, S Stale
Origin codes: i - IGP, e - EGP, ? - incomplete

   Network          Next Hop         Metric LocPrf Weight Path
*> 150.4.4.0/24     4.4.4.4               0    100      0 (65505 65504) i

R4#show ip bgp regexp _\(65505 65501\)$
BGP table version is 5, local router ID is 4.4.4.4
Status codes: s suppressed, d damped, h history, * valid, > best, i - internal,
              r RIB-failure, S Stale
Origin codes: i - IGP, e - EGP, ? - incomplete

   Network          Next Hop         Metric LocPrf Weight Path
*> 150.1.1.0/24     1.1.1.1               0    100      0 (65505 65501) i
```

This task is completed as follows:

```
R1(config)#ip as-path access-list 1 permit _\(65505 65504\)$
R1(config)#route-map WEIGHT permit 10
R1(config-route-map)#match as-path 1
R1(config-route-map)#set weight 50000
R1(config-route-map)#exit
R1(config)#route-map WEIGHT permit 20
R1(config-route-map)#exit
R1(config)#router bgp 65501
R1(config-router)#neighbor 2.2.2.2 route-map WEIGHT in
R1(config-router)#exit

R4(config)#ip as-path access-list 1 permit _\(65505 65501\)$
R4(config)#route-map WEIGHT permit 10
R4(config-route-map)#match as-path 1
R4(config-route-map)#set weight 50000
R4(config-route-map)#exit
R4(config)#route-map WEIGHT permit 20
R4(config-route-map)#exit
R4(config)#router bgp 65504
R4(config-router)#neighbor 3.3.3.3 route-map WEIGHT in
R4(config-router)#exit
```

Verify your configuration using the show ip bgp command on routers R1 and R4 as follows:

```
R1#show ip bgp
BGP table version is 6, local router ID is 1.1.1.1
Status codes: s suppressed, d damped, h history, * valid, > best, i - internal,
              r RIB-failure, S Stale
Origin codes: i - IGP, e - EGP, ? - incomplete

    Network          Next Hop          Metric LocPrf Weight Path
*>  150.1.1.0/24     0.0.0.0                0          32768 i
*>  150.2.2.0/24     2.2.2.2                0    100       0 (65505) i
*>  150.3.3.0/24     3.3.3.3                0    100       0 (65505) i
*>  150.4.4.0/24     4.4.4.4                0    100   50000 (65505 65504) i

R4#show ip bgp
BGP table version is 10, local router ID is 4.4.4.4
Status codes: s suppressed, d damped, h history, * valid, > best, i - internal,
              r RIB-failure, S Stale
Origin codes: i - IGP, e - EGP, ? - incomplete

    Network          Next Hop          Metric LocPrf Weight Path
*>  150.1.1.0/24     1.1.1.1                0    100   50000 (65505 65501) i
*>  150.2.2.0/24     2.2.2.2                0    100       0 (65505) i
*>  150.3.3.0/24     3.3.3.3                0    100       0 (65505) i
*>  150.4.4.0/24     0.0.0.0                0          32768 i
```

NOTE: Additional information on regular expressions is available in the ROUTE guide.

Task 6

This task is completed using the aggregate-address command. By default, this command will advertise BOTH the aggregate (summary) and the more specific prefixes. To advertise only the summary, you need to append the summary-only keyword. This keyword instructs the router to advertise the aggregate only and suppress the more specific routes that are covered by the summary. This task is completed as follows:

```
R2(config)#router bgp 65505
R2(config-router)#aggregate-address 150.2.0.0 255.254.0.0 summary-only
R2(config-router)#exit

R3(config)#router bgp 65505
R3(config-router)#aggregate-address 150.2.0.0 255.254.0.0 summary-only
R3(config-router)#exit
```

Next, verify that the more specific 150.2.2.0/24 and 150.3.3.0/24 prefixes are suppressed:

```
R2#show ip bgp
BGP table version is 9, local router ID is 2.2.2.2
Status codes: s suppressed, d damped, h history, * valid, > best, i - internal,
              r RIB-failure, S Stale
Origin codes: i - IGP, e - EGP, ? - incomplete

   Network          Next Hop         Metric LocPrf Weight Path
*> 150.1.1.0/24     1.1.1.1               0    100      0 (65501) i
*  i150.2.0.0/15    3.3.3.3               0    100      0 i
*>                  0.0.0.0                         32768 i
s> 150.2.2.0/24     0.0.0.0               0         32768 i
*>i150.4.4.0/24     4.4.4.4               0    100      0 (65504) i

R3#show ip bgp
BGP table version is 9, local router ID is 3.3.3.3
Status codes: s suppressed, d damped, h history, * valid, > best, i - internal,
              r RIB-failure, S Stale
Origin codes: i - IGP, e - EGP, ? - incomplete

   Network          Next Hop         Metric LocPrf Weight Path
*>i150.1.1.0/24     1.1.1.1               0    100      0 (65501) i
*> 150.2.0.0/15     0.0.0.0                         32768 i
*  i                2.2.2.2               0    100      0 i
s> 150.3.3.0/24     0.0.0.0               0         32768 i
*> 150.4.4.0/24     4.4.4.4               0    100      0 (65504) i
```

You will notice that neither R2 nor R3 has a route to the other routers' LAN subnet. Therefore, as was hinted in the task, use the neighbor <address> unsuppress-map <route-map-name> command to unsuppress (leak) these routes between the routers. This is similar to route leaking with EIGRP. This task is completed as follows:

```
R2(config)#ip prefix-list LAN-SUBNET seq 5 permit 150.2.2.0/24
R2(config)#route-map UNSUPRESS permit 10
R2(config-route-map)#match ip addres prefix-list LAN-SUBNET
R2(config-route-map)#exit
R2(config)#router bgp 65505
R2(config-router)#neighbor 3.3.3.3 unsuppress-map UNSUPRESS
R2(config-router)#exit

R3(config)#ip prefix-list LAN-SUBNET seq 5 permit 150.3.3.0/24
R3(config)#route-map UNSUPRESS permit 10
R3(config-route-map)#match ip addres prefix-list LAN-SUBNET
R3(config-route-map)#exit
R3(config)#router bgp 65505
R3(config-router)#neighbor 2.2.2.2 unsuppress-map UNSUPRESS
R3(config-router)#exit
```

Following this configuration, you will notice that the LAN prefixes are now present as well:

```
R2#show ip bgp
BGP table version is 11, local router ID is 2.2.2.2
Status codes: s suppressed, d damped, h history, * valid, > best, i - internal,
              r RIB-failure, S Stale
Origin codes: i - IGP, e - EGP, ? - incomplete

   Network          Next Hop         Metric LocPrf Weight Path
*> 150.1.1.0/24     1.1.1.1               0    100      0 (65501) i
*  i150.2.0.0/15    3.3.3.3               0    100      0 i
*>                  0.0.0.0                         32768 i
s> 150.2.2.0/24     0.0.0.0               0         32768 i
s>i150.3.3.0/24     3.3.3.3               0    100      0 i
*>i150.4.4.0/24     4.4.4.4               0    100      0 (65504) i

R3#show ip bgp
BGP table version is 11, local router ID is 3.3.3.3
Status codes: s suppressed, d damped, h history, * valid, > best, i - internal,
              r RIB-failure, S Stale
Origin codes: i - IGP, e - EGP, ? - incomplete
```

```
      Network          Next Hop          Metric LocPrf Weight Path
 *>i150.1.1.0/24       1.1.1.1                0    100      0 (65501) i
 *> 150.2.0.0/15       0.0.0.0                         32768 i
 *  i                  2.2.2.2                0    100      0 i
 s>i150.2.2.0/24       2.2.2.2                0    100      0 i
 s> 150.3.3.0/24       0.0.0.0                0         32768 i
 *> 150.4.4.0/24       4.4.4.4                0    100      0 (65504) i
```

Although the specific LAN subnets are advertised within sub-AS 65505, verify that only a single prefix is received by routers R1 and R4 from peers R2 and R3, respectively:

```
R1#show ip bgp
BGP table version is 9, local router ID is 1.1.1.1
Status codes: s suppressed, d damped, h history, * valid, > best, i - internal,
              r RIB-failure, S Stale
Origin codes: i - IGP, e - EGP, ? - incomplete

      Network          Next Hop          Metric LocPrf Weight Path
 *> 150.1.1.0/24       0.0.0.0                0         32768 i
 *> 150.2.0.0/15       2.2.2.2                0    100      0 (65505) i
 *> 150.4.4.0/24       4.4.4.4                0    100  50000 (65505 65504) i

R4#show ip bgp
BGP table version is 14, local router ID is 4.4.4.4
Status codes: s suppressed, d damped, h history, * valid, > best, i - internal,
              r RIB-failure, S Stale
Origin codes: i - IGP, e - EGP, ? - incomplete

      Network          Next Hop          Metric LocPrf Weight Path
 *> 150.1.1.0/24       1.1.1.1                0    100  50000 (65505 65501) i
 *> 150.2.0.0/15       3.3.3.3                0    100      0 (65505) i
 *> 150.4.4.0/24       0.0.0.0                0         32768 i
```

Finally, verify that R1 and R4 can still ping the R2 and R3 LAN subnets using an extended ping:

```
R4#ping 150.2.2.2 source fastethernet 0/0 repeat 10

Type escape sequence to abort.
Sending 10, 100-byte ICMP Echos to 150.2.2.2, timeout is 2 seconds:
Packet sent with a source address of 150.4.4.4
!!!!!!!!!!
Success rate is 100 percent (10/10), round-trip min/avg/max = 28/30/36 ms

R4#ping 150.3.3.3 source fastethernet 0/0 repeat 10

Type escape sequence to abort.
Sending 10, 100-byte ICMP Echos to 150.3.3.3, timeout is 2 seconds:
Packet sent with a source address of 150.4.4.4
!!!!!!!!!!
Success rate is 100 percent (10/10), round-trip min/avg/max = 16/16/16 ms

R1#ping 150.2.2.2 source fastethernet 0/0 repeat 10

Type escape sequence to abort.
Sending 10, 100-byte ICMP Echos to 150.2.2.2, timeout is 2 seconds:
Packet sent with a source address of 150.1.1.1
!!!!!!!!!!
Success rate is 100 percent (10/10), round-trip min/avg/max = 1/3/4 ms

R1#ping 150.3.3.3 source fastethernet 0/0 repeat 10

Type escape sequence to abort.
Sending 10, 100-byte ICMP Echos to 150.3.3.3, timeout is 2 seconds:
Packet sent with a source address of 150.1.1.1
!!!!!!!!!!
Success rate is 100 percent (10/10), round-trip min/avg/max = 16/17/20 ms
```

FINAL ROUTER CONFIGURATIONS

R1

```
R1#term len 0
R1#sh run
Building configuration...

Current configuration : 1424 bytes
!
version 12.4
service timestamps debug datetime msec
service timestamps log datetime msec
no service password-encryption
!
hostname R1
!
boot-start-marker
boot-end-marker
!
no logging console
!
no aaa new-model
no network-clock-participate slot 1
no network-clock-participate wic 0
ip cef
!
no ip domain lookup
ip auth-proxy max-nodata-conns 3
ip admission max-nodata-conns 3
!
interface Loopback0
 ip address 1.1.1.1 255.255.255.255
 ip ospf 1 area 0
!
interface FastEthernet0/0
 ip address 150.1.1.1 255.255.255.0
 duplex auto
 speed auto
!
interface Serial0/0
 ip address 10.0.0.1 255.255.255.252
 ip ospf 1 area 0
 clock rate 2000000
!
interface Serial0/1
 no ip address
 shutdown
!
router ospf 1
 log-adjacency-changes
!
router bgp 65501
 no synchronization
 bgp log-neighbor-changes
 bgp confederation identifier 254
 bgp confederation peers 65505
 network 150.1.1.0 mask 255.255.255.0
 neighbor 2.2.2.2 remote-as 65505
 neighbor 2.2.2.2 ebgp-multihop 255
 neighbor 2.2.2.2 update-source Loopback0
 neighbor 2.2.2.2 route-map WEIGHT in
 no auto-summary
!
ip forward-protocol nd
!
ip as-path access-list 1 permit _\(65505 65504\)$
!
no ip http server
no ip http secure-server
!
route-map WEIGHT permit 10
 match as-path 1
```

```
 set weight 50000
!
route-map WEIGHT permit 20
!
control-plane
!
line con 0
line aux 0
line vty 0 4
 login
!
end

R1#
```

R2

```
R2#term len 0
R2#sh run
Building configuration...

Current configuration : 1589 bytes
!
version 12.4
service timestamps debug datetime msec
service timestamps log datetime msec
no service password-encryption
!
hostname R2
!
boot-start-marker
boot-end-marker
!
no logging console
!
no aaa new-model
no network-clock-participate slot 1
no network-clock-participate wic 0
ip cef
!
no ip domain lookup
ip auth-proxy max-nodata-conns 3
ip admission max-nodata-conns 3
!
interface Loopback0
 ip address 2.2.2.2 255.255.255.255
 ip ospf 2 area 0
!
interface FastEthernet0/0
 ip address 150.2.2.2 255.255.255.0
 duplex auto
 speed auto
!
interface Serial0/0
 ip address 10.0.0.2 255.255.255.252
 ip ospf 2 area 0
!
interface Serial0/1
 ip address 10.0.0.9 255.255.255.252
 ip ospf 2 area 0
!
router ospf 2
 log-adjacency-changes
!
router bgp 65505
 no synchronization
 bgp log-neighbor-changes
 bgp confederation identifier 254
 bgp confederation peers 65501
 network 150.2.2.0 mask 255.255.255.0
 aggregate-address 150.2.0.0 255.254.0.0 summary-only
 neighbor 1.1.1.1 remote-as 65501
 neighbor 1.1.1.1 ebgp-multihop 255
 neighbor 1.1.1.1 update-source Loopback0
```

```
 neighbor 3.3.3.3 remote-as 65505
 neighbor 3.3.3.3 ebgp-multihop 255
 neighbor 3.3.3.3 update-source Loopback0
 neighbor 3.3.3.3 unsuppress-map UNSUPRESS
 no auto-summary
!
ip forward-protocol nd
!
no ip http server
no ip http secure-server
!
ip prefix-list LAN-SUBNET seq 5 permit 150.2.2.0/24
!
route-map UNSUPRESS permit 10
 match ip address prefix-list LAN-SUBNET
!
control-plane
!
line con 0
line aux 0
line vty 0 4
 login
!
end

R2#
```

R3

```
R3#term len 0
R3#sh run
Building configuration...

Current configuration : 1930 bytes
!
version 12.4
service timestamps debug datetime msec
service timestamps log datetime msec
no service password-encryption
!
hostname R3
!
boot-start-marker
boot-end-marker
!
no logging console
!
no aaa new-model
no network-clock-participate slot 1
no network-clock-participate wic 0
ip cef
!
no ip domain lookup
ip auth-proxy max-nodata-conns 3
ip admission max-nodata-conns 3
!
interface Loopback0
 ip address 3.3.3.3 255.255.255.255
 ip ospf 3 area 0
!
interface FastEthernet0/0
 ip address 150.3.3.3 255.255.255.0
 duplex auto
 speed auto
!
interface Serial1/0
 no ip address
 shutdown
 clock rate 128000
!
interface Serial1/1
 ip address 10.0.0.10 255.255.255.252
 ip ospf 3 area 0
 clock rate 128000
```

```
!
interface Serial1/2
 ip address 10.0.0.13 255.255.255.252
 ip ospf 3 area 0
 clock rate 128000
!
interface Serial1/3
 no ip address
 shutdown
!
interface Serial1/4
 no ip address
 shutdown
!
interface Serial1/5
 no ip address
 shutdown
!
interface Serial1/6
 no ip address
 shutdown
!
interface Serial1/7
 no ip address
 shutdown
!
router ospf 3
 log-adjacency-changes
!
router bgp 65505
 no synchronization
 bgp log-neighbor-changes
 bgp confederation identifier 254
 bgp confederation peers 65504
 network 150.3.3.0 mask 255.255.255.0
 aggregate-address 150.2.0.0 255.254.0.0 summary-only
 neighbor 2.2.2.2 remote-as 65505
 neighbor 2.2.2.2 ebgp-multihop 255
 neighbor 2.2.2.2 update-source Loopback0
 neighbor 2.2.2.2 unsuppress-map UNSUPRESS
 neighbor 4.4.4.4 remote-as 65504
 neighbor 4.4.4.4 ebgp-multihop 255
 neighbor 4.4.4.4 update-source Loopback0
 no auto-summary
!
ip forward-protocol nd
!
no ip http server
no ip http secure-server
!
ip prefix-list LAN-SUBNET seq 5 permit 150.3.3.0/24
!
route-map UNSUPRESS permit 10
 match ip address prefix-list LAN-SUBNET
!
control-plane
!
line con 0
line aux 0
line vty 0 4
 login
!
end

R3#
```

R4

```
R4#term len 0
R4#sh run
Building configuration...

Current configuration : 1405 bytes
!
```

```
version 12.4
service timestamps debug datetime msec
service timestamps log datetime msec
no service password-encryption
!
hostname R4
!
boot-start-marker
boot-end-marker
!
no logging console
!
no aaa new-model
no network-clock-participate slot 1
no network-clock-participate wic 0
ip cef
!
no ip domain lookup
ip auth-proxy max-nodata-conns 3
ip admission max-nodata-conns 3
!
interface Loopback0
 ip address 4.4.4.4 255.255.255.255
 ip ospf 4 area 0
!
interface FastEthernet0/0
 ip address 150.4.4.4 255.255.255.0
 duplex auto
 speed auto
!
interface Serial0/0
 ip address 10.0.0.14 255.255.255.252
 ip ospf 4 area 0
!
interface Serial0/1
 no ip address
 shutdown
!
router ospf 4
 log-adjacency-changes
!
router bgp 65504
 no synchronization
 bgp log-neighbor-changes
 bgp confederation identifier 254
 bgp confederation peers 65505
 network 150.4.4.0 mask 255.255.255.0
 neighbor 3.3.3.3 remote-as 65505
 neighbor 3.3.3.3 ebgp-multihop 255
 neighbor 3.3.3.3 update-source Loopback0
 neighbor 3.3.3.3 route-map WEIGHT in
 no auto-summary
!
ip forward-protocol nd
!
ip as-path access-list 1 permit _\(65505 65501\)$
!
no ip http server
no ip http secure-server
!
route-map WEIGHT permit 10
 match as-path 1
 set weight 50000
!
route-map WEIGHT permit 20
!
control-plane
!
line con 0
line aux 0
line vty 0 4
 login
!
end

R4#
```

CCNP LAB 34

Border Gateway Protocol Lab

Lab Objective:

The focus of this lab is to understand BGP implementation and configuration in Cisco IOS routers. Additional technologies include BGP and OSPF route redistribution .

Lab Topology:

The lab network topology is illustrated below:

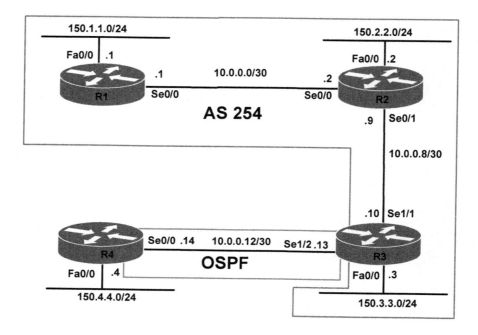

IMPORTANT NOTE: If you are using the www.howtonetwork.net racks, please bring up the LAN interfaces connected to the routers by issuing the `no shutdown` command on the connected switches. If you are using a home lab with no Switches, you can bring up the LAN interfaces using the following configurations on your routers:

```
interface fastethernet 0/0
  no keepalive
  loopback
  no shutdown
```

Alternately, you can simply connect the interfaces to a hub or switch if you have one available in your own lab.

Task 1

Configure hostnames and IP addressing on all routers as illustrated in the network topology.

Task 2

Configure EIGRP using AS 254 only for the R1-to-R2 link and for the R2-to-R3 link. Do NOT enable EIGRP for any other subnets. Verify your configuration.

Task 3

Configure BGP in AS 254 as illustrated in the topology. Use physical interfaces for peering. R1 should peer with R2 and R2 should peer with R3. Verify your configuration.

Task 4

Redistribute the 150.1.1.0/24, 150.2.2.0/24 and 150.3.3.0/24 subnets on R1, R2 and R3 into BGP. There should be no 10.x.x.x prefixes in the BGP Table. You are required to use a route map in conjunction with an EXTENDED IP ACL to complete this task. Ensure that all three routers can ping each others' 150.x.x.x/24 subnets from their own LAN subnet. Use the extended ping feature to verify your configuration.

Task 5

Configure OSPF area 0 between R3 and R4. Advertise the 150.4.4.0/24 subnet via OSPF as an Type 1 External LSA. Verify your configuration using the appropriate commands.

Task 6

Redistribute between BGP and OSPF on R3. BGP should only redistribute EXTERNAL Type 5 routes from OSPF. Do NOT redistribute anything into or out of EIGRP. Ensure that the 150.4.4.0/24 subnet is able to reach all other 150.x.x.x/24 subnets and vice-versa. Verify your configuration using extended ping.

LAB VALIDATION

Task 1

Please refer to previous labs for basic IP addressing and hostname configuration. This will not be included in this section to avoid being redundant.

Task 2

Please refer to previous labs for basic EIGRP configuration. This will not be included in this section to avoid being redundant. Following completion, the routing tables on your routers should show the following EIGRP route entries:

```
R1#show ip route eigrp
     10.0.0.0/30 is subnetted, 2 subnets
D       10.0.0.8 [90/2681856] via 10.0.0.2, 00:01:05, Serial0/0

R3#show ip route eigrp
     10.0.0.0/30 is subnetted, 3 subnets
D       10.0.0.0 [90/21024000] via 10.0.0.9, 00:00:38, Serial1/1
```

NOTE: R2 will not have EIGRP routes because the two WAN subnets are directly connected.

Task 3

```
R1(config)#router bgp 254
R1(config-router)#bgp router-id 1.1.1.1
R1(config-router)#neighbor 10.0.0.2 remote-as 254
R1(config-router)#exit

R2(config)#router bgp 254
R2(config-router)#bgp router-id 2.2.2.2
R2(config-router)#neighbor 10.0.0.1 remote-as 254
R2(config-router)#neighbor 10.0.0.10 remote-as 254
R2(config-router)#exit
```

```
R3(config)#router bgp 254
R3(config-router)#bgp router-id 3.3.3.3
R3(config-router)#neighbor 10.0.0.9 remote-as 254
R3(config-router)#exit
```

Verify your configuration using the show ip bgp summary command:

```
R1#show ip bgp summary
BGP router identifier 1.1.1.1, local AS number 254
BGP table version is 1, main routing table version 1

Neighbor     V    AS MsgRcvd MsgSent   TblVer  InQ OutQ Up/Down  State/PfxRcd
10.0.0.2     4   254       4       4        1    0    0 00:01:11           0

R2#show ip bgp summary
BGP router identifier 2.2.2.2, local AS number 254
BGP table version is 1, main routing table version 1

Neighbor     V    AS MsgRcvd MsgSent   TblVer  InQ OutQ Up/Down  State/PfxRcd
10.0.0.1     4   254       4       4        1    0    0 00:01:15           0
10.0.0.10    4   254       4       4        1    0    0 00:00:33           0

R3#show ip bgp summary
BGP router identifier 3.3.3.3, local AS number 254
BGP table version is 1, main routing table version 1

Neighbor     V    AS MsgRcvd MsgSent   TblVer  InQ OutQ Up/Down  State/PfxRcd
10.0.0.9     4   254       4       4        1    0    0 00:00:35           0
```

Task 4

This task requires that a route-map be used for route redistribution. The route map can be used to match the interface or address (IP ACL and prefix list). Because the task requirements stipulate that an only an extended IP ACL can be used, you can use either named or numbered extended ACLs to complete. The configuration below shows how to use both named and numbered (standard and expanded range) extended IP ACLs. This task is completed as follows:

```
R1(config)#access-list 100 permit ip host 150.1.1.0 host 255.255.255.0
R1(config)#route-map CONNECTED permit 10
R1(config-route-map)#match ip address 100
R1(config-route-map)#exit
R1(config)#route-map CONNECTED deny 20
R1(config-route-map)#exit
R1(config)#router bgp 254
R1(config-router)#redistribute connected route-map CONNECTED
R1(config-router)#exit

R2(config)#ip access-list extended CONNECTED
R2(config-ext-nacl)#permit ip host 150.2.2.0 host 255.255.255.0
R2(config-ext-nacl)#exit
R2(config)#route-map CONNECTED permit 10
R2(config-route-map)#match ip address CONNECTED
R2(config-route-map)#exit
R2(config)#route-map CONNECTED deny 20
R2(config-route-map)#exit
R2(config)#router bgp 254
R2(config-router)#redistribute connected route-map CONNECTED
R2(config-router)#exit

R3(config)#access-list 2000 permit ip host 150.3.3.0 host 255.255.255.0
R3(config)#route-map CONNECTED permit 10
R3(config-route-map)#match ip address 2000
R3(config-route-map)#exit
R3(config)#route-map CONNECTED deny 20
R3(config-route-map)#exit
R3(config)#router bgp 254
R3(config-router)#redistribute connected route-map CONNECTED
R3(config-router)#exit
```

Following the redistribution, we have to remember the default iBGP advertisement rules. In this topology, R2 will not advertise the R1 or R3 subnets to R3 and R1 respectively because they are received from iBGP peers. To work around this limitation, then R2 should also be configured as a route reflector. This is completed as follows:

```
R2(config)#router bgp 254
R2(config-router)#neighbor 10.0.0.1 route-reflector-client
R2(config-router)#neighbor 10.0.0.10 route-reflector-client
R2(config-router)#exit
```

Next, verify your configuration using the show ip bgp command on all three routers:

```
R1#show ip bgp
BGP table version is 8, local router ID is 1.1.1.1
Status codes: s suppressed, d damped, h history, * valid, > best, i - internal,
              r RIB-failure, S Stale
Origin codes: i - IGP, e - EGP, ? - incomplete

   Network          Next Hop          Metric LocPrf Weight Path
*> 150.1.1.0/24     0.0.0.0                0         32768 ?
*>i150.2.2.0/24     10.0.0.2               0    100      0 ?
*>i150.3.3.0/24     10.0.0.10              0    100      0 ?

R2#show ip bgp
BGP table version is 8, local router ID is 2.2.2.2
Status codes: s suppressed, d damped, h history, * valid, > best, i - internal,
              r RIB-failure, S Stale
Origin codes: i - IGP, e - EGP, ? - incomplete

   Network          Next Hop          Metric LocPrf Weight Path
*>i150.1.1.0/24     10.0.0.1               0    100      0 ?
*> 150.2.2.0/24     0.0.0.0                0         32768 ?
*>i150.3.3.0/24     10.0.0.10              0    100      0 ?

R3#show ip bgp
BGP table version is 8, local router ID is 3.3.3.3
Status codes: s suppressed, d damped, h history, * valid, > best, i - internal,
              r RIB-failure, S Stale
Origin codes: i - IGP, e - EGP, ? - incomplete

   Network          Next Hop          Metric LocPrf Weight Path
*>i150.1.1.0/24     10.0.0.1               0    100      0 ?
*>i150.2.2.0/24     10.0.0.9               0    100      0 ?
*> 150.3.3.0/24     0.0.0.0                0         32768 ?
```

Finally, verify that all LAN subnets can ping each other using the extended ping feature:

```
R1#ping 150.2.2.2 source 150.1.1.1 repeat 10

Type escape sequence to abort.
Sending 10, 100-byte ICMP Echos to 150.2.2.2, timeout is 2 seconds:
Packet sent with a source address of 150.1.1.1
!!!!!!!!!!
Success rate is 100 percent (10/10), round-trip min/avg/max = 1/3/4 ms

R1#ping 150.3.3.3 source 150.1.1.1 repeat 10

Type escape sequence to abort.
Sending 10, 100-byte ICMP Echos to 150.3.3.3, timeout is 2 seconds:
Packet sent with a source address of 150.1.1.1
!!!!!!!!!!
Success rate is 100 percent (10/10), round-trip min/avg/max = 16/16/20 ms

R2#ping 150.1.1.1 source 150.2.2.2 repeat 10

Type escape sequence to abort.
Sending 10, 100-byte ICMP Echos to 150.1.1.1, timeout is 2 seconds:
Packet sent with a source address of 150.2.2.2
!!!!!!!!!!
Success rate is 100 percent (10/10), round-trip min/avg/max = 1/3/4 ms
```

```
R2#ping 150.3.3.3 source 150.2.2.2 repeat 10

Type escape sequence to abort.
Sending 10, 100-byte ICMP Echos to 150.3.3.3, timeout is 2 seconds:
Packet sent with a source address of 150.2.2.2
!!!!!!!!!!
Success rate is 100 percent (10/10), round-trip min/avg/max = 16/16/16 ms

R3#ping 150.1.1.1 source 150.3.3.3 repeat 10

Type escape sequence to abort.
Sending 10, 100-byte ICMP Echos to 150.1.1.1, timeout is 2 seconds:
Packet sent with a source address of 150.3.3.3
!!!!!!!!!!
Success rate is 100 percent (10/10), round-trip min/avg/max = 16/16/20 ms

R3#ping 150.2.2.2 source 150.3.3.3 repeat 10

Type escape sequence to abort.
Sending 10, 100-byte ICMP Echos to 150.2.2.2, timeout is 2 seconds:
Packet sent with a source address of 150.3.3.3
!!!!!!!!!!
Success rate is 100 percent (10/10), round-trip min/avg/max = 16/16/16 ms
```

Task 5

```
R3(config)#router ospf 3
R3(config-router)#router-id 3.3.3.3
R3(config-router)#network 10.0.0.13 0.0.0.0 area 0
R3(config-router)#exit

R4(config)#interface serial 0/0
R4(config-if)#ip ospf 4 area 0
R4(config-if)#exit
R4(config)#router ospf 4
R4(config-router)#router-id 4.4.4.4
R4(config-router)#redistribute connected subnet metric-type 1
R4(config-router)#exit
```

Verify your basic OSPF configuration using the show ip ospf neighbor command:

```
R3#show ip ospf neighbor

Neighbor ID    Pri    State        Dead Time    Address      Interface
4.4.4.4          0    FULL/   -    00:00:38     10.0.0.14    Serial1/2

R4#show ip ospf neighbor

Neighbor ID    Pri    State        Dead Time    Address      Interface
3.3.3.3          0    FULL/   -    00:00:34     10.0.0.13    Serial0/0
```

Finally, verify your OSPF redistribution using the show ip ospf database command:

```
R4#show ip ospf database external 150.4.4.0

            OSPF Router with ID (4.4.4.4) (Process ID 4)

            Type-5 AS External Link States

  LS age: 132
  Options: (No TOS-capability, DC)
  LS Type: AS External Link
  Link State ID: 150.4.4.0 (External Network Number )
  Advertising Router: 4.4.4.4
  LS Seq Number: 80000001
  Checksum: 0xE988
  Length: 36
  Network Mask: /24
        Metric Type: 1 (Comparable directly to link state metric)
        TOS: 0
        Metric: 20
        Forward Address: 0.0.0.0
        External Route Tag: 0
```

Task 6

There are four caveats to be aware of when completing this task. The first is that, by default, when BGP routes are redistributed into an IGP, only EXTERNAL routes are redistributed.

The second caveat is that when OSPF routes are redistributed into BGP, only INTERNAL routes are redistributed. Explicit configuration is required to redistribute internal BGP routes and external OSPF routes when performing OSPF-to-BGP redistribution and vice-versa.

The third caveat is that by default, an iBGP speaker does not change the NEXT_HOP attribute for an external route when advertising it to another iBGP speaker. Therefore, the NEXT_HOP attribute must be changed after redistributing OSPF into BGP. The other alternative would be to redistribute the R3-to-R4 WAN link into EIGRP; however, this is not permitted.

The fourth caveat is that while the 150.3.3.0/24 subnet is advertised by BGP, it is redistributed into BGP. Therefore, it will not automatically be redistributed into OSPF when BGP is redistributed into OSPF. Instead, a route map must be used to redistribute this subnet into OSPF as was performed earlier for BGP. This task is completed as follows:

```
R3(config)#router bgp 254
R3(config-router)#redistribute ospf 3 match external 1 external 2
R3(config-router)#bgp redistribute-internal
R3(config-router)#neighbor 10.0.0.9 next-hop-self
R3(config-router)#exit
R3(config)#router ospf 3
R3(config-router)#redistribute connected subnets route-map CONNECTED
R3(config-router)#redistribute bgp 254 subnets
R3(config-router)#exit
```

Following this configuration, verify the LSDB and BGP Table on R3 using the show ip ospf database and the show ip bgp commands, respectively:

```
R3#show ip ospf database

            OSPF Router with ID (3.3.3.3) (Process ID 3)

                Router Link States (Area 0)

Link ID         ADV Router      Age         Seq#        Checksum Link count
3.3.3.3         3.3.3.3         1012        0x80000004 0x007934 2
4.4.4.4         4.4.4.4         1356        0x80000001 0x002E1D 2
150.4.4.4       150.4.4.4       1385        0x80000001 0x008F98 2

                Type-5 AS External Link States

Link ID         ADV Router      Age         Seq#        Checksum Tag
150.1.1.0       3.3.3.3         1012        0x80000001 0x0012FC 0
150.2.2.0       3.3.3.3         1012        0x80000001 0x00FA12 0
150.3.3.0       3.3.3.3         16          0x80000001 0x00A255 0
150.4.4.0       4.4.4.4         1355        0x80000001 0x00E988 0
```

```
R3#show ip bgp
BGP table version is 9, local router ID is 3.3.3.3
Status codes: s suppressed, d damped, h history, * valid, > best, i - internal,
              r RIB-failure, S Stale
Origin codes: i - IGP, e - EGP, ? - incomplete

   Network          Next Hop         Metric LocPrf Weight Path
*>i150.1.1.0/24     10.0.0.1              0    100      0 ?
*>i150.2.2.0/24     10.0.0.9              0    100      0 ?
*> 150.3.3.0/24     0.0.0.0               0          32768 ?
*> 150.4.4.0/24     10.0.0.14           801          32768 ?
```

To verify the redistributed route in BGP, use the show ip bgp command on R1 or R2:

```
R1#show ip bgp 150.4.4.0 255.255.255.0
BGP routing table entry for 150.4.4.0/24, version 9
```

```
Paths: (1 available, best #1, table Default-IP-Routing-Table)
Flag: 0x820
  Not advertised to any peer
  Local
    10.0.0.10 (metric 2681856) from 10.0.0.2 (2.2.2.2)
      Origin incomplete, metric 801, localpref 100, valid, internal, best
      Originator: 3.3.3.3, Cluster list: 2.2.2.2
```

Finally, verify your configuration using the extended ping feature on R4:

```
R4#ping 150.1.1.1 source 150.4.4.4 repeat 10

Type escape sequence to abort.
Sending 10, 100-byte ICMP Echos to 150.1.1.1, timeout is 2 seconds:
Packet sent with a source address of 150.4.4.4
!!!!!!!!!!
Success rate is 100 percent (10/10), round-trip min/avg/max = 28/30/32 ms

R4#ping 150.2.2.2 source 150.4.4.4 repeat 10

Type escape sequence to abort.
Sending 10, 100-byte ICMP Echos to 150.2.2.2, timeout is 2 seconds:
Packet sent with a source address of 150.4.4.4
!!!!!!!!!!
Success rate is 100 percent (10/10), round-trip min/avg/max = 28/30/32 ms

R4#ping 150.3.3.3 source 150.4.4.4 repeat 10

Type escape sequence to abort.
Sending 10, 100-byte ICMP Echos to 150.3.3.3, timeout is 2 seconds:
Packet sent with a source address of 150.4.4.4
!!!!!!!!!!
Success rate is 100 percent (10/10), round-trip min/avg/max = 12/14/16 ms
```

FINAL ROUTER CONFIGURATIONS

R1

```
R1#term len 0
R1#
R1#sh run
Building configuration...

Current configuration : 1198 bytes
!
version 12.4
service timestamps debug datetime msec
service timestamps log datetime msec
no service password-encryption
!
hostname R1
!
boot-start-marker
boot-end-marker
!
no logging console
!
no aaa new-model
no network-clock-participate slot 1
no network-clock-participate wic 0
ip cef
!
no ip domain lookup
ip auth-proxy max-nodata-conns 3
ip admission max-nodata-conns 3
!
interface FastEthernet0/0
 ip address 150.1.1.1 255.255.255.0
 duplex auto
```

```
 speed auto
!
interface Serial0/0
 ip address 10.0.0.1 255.255.255.252
 clock rate 2000000
!
interface Serial0/1
 no ip address
 shutdown
!
router eigrp 254
 network 10.0.0.1 0.0.0.0
 no auto-summary
!
router bgp 254
 no synchronization
 bgp router-id 1.1.1.1
 bgp log-neighbor-changes
 redistribute connected route-map CONNECTED
 neighbor 10.0.0.2 remote-as 254
 no auto-summary
!
ip forward-protocol nd
!
no ip http server
no ip http secure-server
!
access-list 100 permit ip host 150.1.1.0 host 255.255.255.0
!
route-map CONNECTED permit 10
 match ip address 100
!
route-map CONNECTED deny 20
!
control-plane
!
line con 0
line aux 0
line vty 0 4
 login
!
end

R1#
```

R2

```
R2#term len 0
R2#sh run
Building configuration...

Current configuration : 1362 bytes
!
version 12.4
service timestamps debug datetime msec
service timestamps log datetime msec
no service password-encryption
!
hostname R2
!
boot-start-marker
boot-end-marker
!
no logging console
!
no aaa new-model
no network-clock-participate slot 1
no network-clock-participate wic 0
ip cef
!
no ip domain lookup
ip auth-proxy max-nodata-conns 3
ip admission max-nodata-conns 3
!
```

```
interface FastEthernet0/0
 ip address 150.2.2.2 255.255.255.0
 duplex auto
 speed auto
!
interface Serial0/0
 ip address 10.0.0.2 255.255.255.252
!
interface Serial0/1
 ip address 10.0.0.9 255.255.255.252
!
router eigrp 254
 network 10.0.0.2 0.0.0.0
 network 10.0.0.9 0.0.0.0
 no auto-summary
!
router bgp 254
 no synchronization
 bgp router-id 2.2.2.2
 bgp log-neighbor-changes
 redistribute connected route-map CONNECTED
 neighbor 10.0.0.1 remote-as 254
 neighbor 10.0.0.1 route-reflector-client
 neighbor 10.0.0.10 remote-as 254
 neighbor 10.0.0.10 route-reflector-client
 no auto-summary
!
ip forward-protocol nd
!
no ip http server
no ip http secure-server
!
ip access-list extended CONNECTED
 permit ip host 150.2.2.0 host 255.255.255.0
!
route-map CONNECTED permit 10
 match ip address CONNECTED
!
route-map CONNECTED deny 20
!
control-plane
!
line con 0
line aux 0
line vty 0 4
 login
!
end

R2#
```

R3

```
R3#term len 0
R3#sh run
Building configuration...

Current configuration : 1817 bytes
!
version 12.4
service timestamps debug datetime msec
service timestamps log datetime msec
no service password-encryption
!
hostname R3
!
boot-start-marker
boot-end-marker
!
no logging console
!
no aaa new-model
no network-clock-participate slot 1
no network-clock-participate wic 0
ip cef
!
no ip domain lookup
```

```
ip auth-proxy max-nodata-conns 3
ip admission max-nodata-conns 3
!
interface FastEthernet0/0
 ip address 150.3.3.3 255.255.255.0
 duplex auto
 speed auto
!
interface Serial1/0
 no ip address
 shutdown
 clock rate 128000
!
interface Serial1/1
 ip address 10.0.0.10 255.255.255.252
 clock rate 128000
!
interface Serial1/2
 ip address 10.0.0.13 255.255.255.252
 clock rate 128000
!
interface Serial1/3
 no ip address
 shutdown
!
interface Serial1/4
 no ip address
 shutdown
!
interface Serial1/5
 no ip address
 shutdown
!
interface Serial1/6
 no ip address
 shutdown
!
interface Serial1/7
 no ip address
 shutdown
!
router eigrp 254
 network 10.0.0.10 0.0.0.0
 no auto-summary
!
router ospf 3
 router-id 3.3.3.3
 log-adjacency-changes
 redistribute connected subnets route-map CONNECTED
 redistribute bgp 254 subnets
 network 10.0.0.13 0.0.0.0 area 0
!
router bgp 254
 no synchronization
 bgp router-id 3.3.3.3
 bgp log-neighbor-changes
 bgp redistribute-internal
 redistribute connected route-map CONNECTED
 redistribute ospf 3 match external 1 external 2
 neighbor 10.0.0.9 remote-as 254
 neighbor 10.0.0.9 next-hop-self
 no auto-summary
!
ip forward-protocol nd
!
no ip http server
no ip http secure-server
!
access-list 2000 permit ip host 150.3.3.0 host 255.255.255.0
!
route-map CONNECTED permit 10
 match ip address 2000
!
route-map CONNECTED deny 20
!
control-plane
!
```

```
line con 0
line aux 0
line vty 0 4
 login
!
end

R3#
```

R4

```
R4#term len 0
R4#sh run
Building configuration...

Current configuration : 915 bytes
!
version 12.4
service timestamps debug datetime msec
service timestamps log datetime msec
no service password-encryption
!
hostname R4
!
boot-start-marker
boot-end-marker
!
no logging console
!
no aaa new-model
no network-clock-participate slot 1
no network-clock-participate wic 0
ip cef
!
no ip domain lookup
ip auth-proxy max-nodata-conns 3
ip admission max-nodata-conns 3
!
interface FastEthernet0/0
 ip address 150.4.4.4 255.255.255.0
 duplex auto
 speed auto
!
interface Serial0/0
 ip address 10.0.0.14 255.255.255.252
 ip ospf 4 area 0
!
interface Serial0/1
 no ip address
 shutdown
!
router ospf 4
 router-id 4.4.4.4
 log-adjacency-changes
 redistribute connected metric-type 1 subnets
!
ip forward-protocol nd
!
no ip http server
no ip http secure-server
!
control-plane
!
line con 0
line aux 0
line vty 0 4
 login
!
end

R4#
```

CCNP LAB 35

Border Gateway Protocol Lab

Lab Objective:

The focus of this lab is to understand BGP implementation and configuration in Cisco IOS routers. Additional technologies include confederations and path control.

Lab Topology:

The lab network topology is illustrated below:

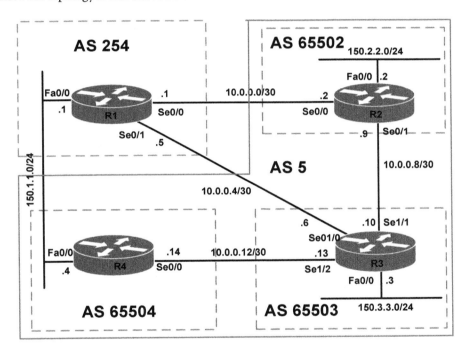

IMPORTANT NOTE: If you are using the www.howtonetwork.net racks, please bring up the LAN interfaces connected to the routers by issuing the no shutdown command on the connected switches. If you are using a home lab with no Switches, you can bring up the LAN interfaces using the following configurations on your routers:

```
interface fastethernet 0/0
 no keepalive
 loopback
 no shutdown
```

Alternately, you can simply connect the interfaces to a hub or switch if you have one available in your own lab.

Task 1

Configure hostnames and IP addressing on all routers as illustrated in the network topology.

Task 2

Configure BGP on R1 as illustrated in the topology. R1 will peer to R2, R3, and R4 using directly connected IP addresses. From R1s perspective, all these routers reside in AS 5. R1 should advertise the 150.1.1.0/24 prefix via BGP. Verify your configuration using relevant commands.

Task 3

Configure BGP on R2, R3, and R4 as illustrated in the topology. All routers will reside in AS 5 to the outside world. Internally, R2 will reside in AS 65502, R3 will reside in AS 65503, and R4 will reside in AS 65504. R2 will peer to R3, which in turn will peer to R4. R2 and R4 will not peer to each other. Ensure that R1, R2, and R3 routers peer with R1 is AS 254. Next, configure R2, R3, and R4 to advertise their respective 150.x.x.x/24 subnets. Ensure that all of the routers can ping the LAN IP address of every other router.

Task 4

Configure AS 5 so that R2 and R3 prefer the path via R1 to reach the 150.1.1.0/24 prefix. Ensure that this is ONLY applicable to this single prefix. Verify your configuration.

Task 5

R1 has three paths to the 150.3.3.0/24 subnet advertised by R3. Configure your network so that R1 prefers the path via R2 first, the path via R4 second and then path via R3 last. You are not allowed to make any changes on R1 to complete this task. Additionally, you are NOT allowed to modify the AS_PATH or MED attributes or administrative distance in any manner. Verify your configuration using the appropriate commands.

LAB VALIDATION

Task 1

Please refer to previous labs for basic IP addressing and hostname configuration. This will not be included in this section to avoid being redundant.

Task 2

```
R1(config)#router bgp 254
R1(config-router)#bgp router-id 1.1.1.1
R1(config-router)#neighbor 150.1.1.4 remote-as 5
R1(config-router)#neighbor 10.0.0.2 remote-as 5
R1(config-router)#neighbor 10.0.0.6 remote-as 5
R1(config-router)#network 150.1.1.0 mask 255.255.255.0
R1(config-router)#exit
```

Because no BGP adjacencies will be present, at this point, verify that the 150.1.1.0/24 prefix has been injected into BGP as requested in this task using the `show ip bgp` command:

```
R1#show ip bgp
BGP table version is 1, local router ID is 1.1.1.1
Status codes: s suppressed, d damped, h history, * valid, > best, i - internal,
              r RIB-failure, S Stale
Origin codes: i - IGP, e - EGP, ? - incomplete

   Network          Next Hop            Metric LocPrf Weight Path
*  150.1.1.0/24     0.0.0.0                  0         32768 i
```

Task 3

To complete this task, you need to configure BGP confederations. When configuring the routers, keep in mind that external confederation peers (in a way) also behave in a manner similar to external BGP peers. For example, just as you would need to use the `neighbor <address> ebgp-multihop` command when peering using Loopback interfaces; you still need to modify the NEXT_HOP attribute using the `neighbor <address>`

next-hop-self command just as you would when receiving routes from an eBGP peer in an environment that is not using confederederations. Alternatively, you can use static routes or advertise routes using a dynamic routing protocol to ensure that the NEXT_HOP is reachable. This task is completed as follows:

```
R2(config)#router bgp 65502
R2(config-router)#bgp router-id 2.2.2.2
R2(config-router)#bgp confederation identifier 5
R2(config-router)#bgp confederation peers 65503
R2(config-router)#network 150.2.2.0 mask 255.255.255.0
R2(config-router)#neighbor 10.0.0.1 remote-as 254
R2(config-router)#neighbor 10.0.0.10 remote-as 65503
R2(config-router)#neighbor 10.0.0.10 next-hop-self
R2(config-router)#exit

R3(config)#router bgp 65503
R3(config-router)#bgp router-id 3.3.3.3
R3(config-router)#bgp confederation identifier 5
R3(config-router)#bgp confederation peers 65502 65504
R3(config-router)#neighbor 10.0.0.5 remote-as 254
R3(config-router)#neighbor 10.0.0.9 remote-as 65502
R3(config-router)#neighbor 10.0.0.9 next-hop-self
R3(config-router)#neighbor 10.0.0.14 remote-as 65504
R3(config-router)#neighbor 10.0.0.14  next-hop-self
R3(config-router)#network 150.3.3.0 mask 255.255.255.0
R3(config-router)#exit

R4(config)#router bgp 65504
R4(config-router)#bgp router-id 4.4.4.4
R4(config-router)#network 150.1.1.0 mask 255.255.255.0
R4(config-router)#bgp confederation identifier 5
R4(config-router)#bgp confederation peers 65503
R4(config-router)#neighbor 150.1.1.1 remote-as 254
R4(config-router)#neighbor 10.0.0.13 remote-as 65503
R4(config-router)#neighbor 10.0.0.13  next-hop-self
R4(config-router)#exit
```

Next, verify BGP peering configuration using the show ip bgp summary command:

```
R1#show ip bgp summary
BGP router identifier 1.1.1.1, local AS number 254
BGP table version is 4, main routing table version 4
3 network entries using 351 bytes of memory
8 path entries using 416 bytes of memory
4/2 BGP path/bestpath attribute entries using 496 bytes of memory
1 BGP AS-PATH entries using 24 bytes of memory
0 BGP route-map cache entries using 0 bytes of memory
0 BGP filter-list cache entries using 0 bytes of memory
BGP using 1287 total bytes of memory
BGP activity 3/0 prefixes, 8/0 paths, scan interval 60 secs

Neighbor     V    AS MsgRcvd MsgSent   TblVer  InQ OutQ Up/Down  State/PfxRcd
10.0.0.2     4     5      13      14        4    0    0 00:07:52        2
10.0.0.6     4     5      10      10        4    0    0 00:03:39        3
150.1.1.4    4     5       8       8        4    0    0 00:02:02        2

R2#show ip bgp summary
BGP router identifier 2.2.2.2, local AS number 65502
BGP table version is 4, main routing table version 4
3 network entries using 351 bytes of memory
4 path entries using 208 bytes of memory
5/3 BGP path/bestpath attribute entries using 620 bytes of memory
3 BGP AS-PATH entries using 72 bytes of memory
0 BGP route-map cache entries using 0 bytes of memory
0 BGP filter-list cache entries using 0 bytes of memory
BGP using 1251 total bytes of memory
BGP activity 3/0 prefixes, 4/0 paths, scan interval 60 secs

Neighbor     V     AS MsgRcvd MsgSent   TblVer  InQ OutQ Up/Down  State/PfxRcd
10.0.0.1     4    254      14      13        4    0    0 00:07:57        1
10.0.0.10    4  65503      11       9        4    0    0 00:03:51        2
```

```
R3#show ip bgp summary
BGP router identifier 3.3.3.3, local AS number 65503
BGP table version is 6, main routing table version 6
3 network entries using 351 bytes of memory
5 path entries using 260 bytes of memory
6/3 BGP path/bestpath attribute entries using 744 bytes of memory
4 BGP AS-PATH entries using 96 bytes of memory
0 BGP route-map cache entries using 0 bytes of memory
0 BGP filter-list cache entries using 0 bytes of memory
BGP using 1451 total bytes of memory
BGP activity 3/0 prefixes, 5/0 paths, scan interval 60 secs

Neighbor       V    AS MsgRcvd MsgSent   TblVer  InQ OutQ Up/Down  State/PfxRcd
10.0.0.5       4   254      10      10        6    0    0 00:03:48           1
10.0.0.9       4 65502       9      11        6    0    0 00:03:55           2
10.0.0.14      4 65504       8      10        6    0    0 00:02:14           1

R4#show ip bgp summary
BGP router identifier 4.4.4.4, local AS number 65504
BGP table version is 6, main routing table version 6
3 network entries using 351 bytes of memory
4 path entries using 208 bytes of memory
5/3 BGP path/bestpath attribute entries using 620 bytes of memory
3 BGP AS-PATH entries using 72 bytes of memory
0 BGP route-map cache entries using 0 bytes of memory
0 BGP filter-list cache entries using 0 bytes of memory
BGP using 1251 total bytes of memory
BGP activity 3/0 prefixes, 5/1 paths, scan interval 60 secs

Neighbor       V    AS MsgRcvd MsgSent   TblVer  InQ OutQ Up/Down  State/PfxRcd
10.0.0.13      4 65503      10       8        6    0    0 00:02:17           2
150.1.1.1      4   254       8       8        6    0    0 00:02:14           1
```

Finally, verify the BGP Tables on all routers using the `show ip bgp` command:

```
R1#show ip bgp
BGP table version is 4, local router ID is 1.1.1.1
Status codes: s suppressed, d damped, h history, * valid, > best, i - internal,
              r RIB-failure, S Stale
Origin codes: i - IGP, e - EGP, ? - incomplete

   Network          Next Hop            Metric LocPrf Weight Path
*  150.1.1.0/24     10.0.0.2                               0 5 i
*                   10.0.0.6                               0 5 i
*                   150.1.1.4                0             0 5 i
*>                  0.0.0.0                  0         32768 i
*  150.2.2.0/24     150.1.1.4                              0 5 i
*                   10.0.0.6                               0 5 i
*>                  10.0.0.2                 0             0 5 i
*  150.3.3.0/24     150.1.1.4                              0 5 i
*                   10.0.0.2                               0 5 i
*>                  10.0.0.6                 0             0 5 i

R2#show ip bgp
BGP table version is 7, local router ID is 2.2.2.2
Status codes: s suppressed, d damped, h history, * valid, > best, i - internal,
              r RIB-failure, S Stale
Origin codes: i - IGP, e - EGP, ? - incomplete

   Network          Next Hop            Metric LocPrf Weight Path
*> 150.1.1.0/24     10.0.0.10                0    100      0 (65503 65504) i
*                   10.0.0.1                 0             0 254 i
*> 150.2.2.0/24     0.0.0.0                  0         32768 i
*> 150.3.3.0/24     10.0.0.10                0    100      0 (65503) i

R3#show ip bgp
BGP table version is 8, local router ID is 3.3.3.3
Status codes: s suppressed, d damped, h history, * valid, > best, i - internal,
              r RIB-failure, S Stale
Origin codes: i - IGP, e - EGP, ? - incomplete

   Network          Next Hop            Metric LocPrf Weight Path
```

```
*> 150.1.1.0/24    10.0.0.14                 0    100      0 (65504) i
*                  10.0.0.5                  0             0 254 i
*> 150.2.2.0/24    10.0.0.9                  0    100      0 (65502) i
*> 150.3.3.0/24    0.0.0.0                   0         32768 i

R4#show ip bgp
BGP table version is 6, local router ID is 4.4.4.4
Status codes: s suppressed, d damped, h history, * valid, > best, i - internal,
              r RIB-failure, S Stale
Origin codes: i - IGP, e - EGP, ? - incomplete

   Network          Next Hop          Metric LocPrf Weight Path
*> 150.1.1.0/24    0.0.0.0                0         32768 i
*                  150.1.1.1              0             0 254 i
*> 150.2.2.0/24    10.0.0.13              0    100      0 (65503 65502) i
*> 150.3.3.0/24    10.0.0.13              0    100      0 (65503) i
```

Finally, verify that all routers can ping each others' LAN subnets using an extended ping:

```
R1#ping 150.2.2.2 source 150.1.1.1 repeat 10

Type escape sequence to abort.
Sending 10, 100-byte ICMP Echos to 150.2.2.2, timeout is 2 seconds:
Packet sent with a source address of 150.1.1.1
!!!!!!!!!!
Success rate is 100 percent (10/10), round-trip min/avg/max = 16/16/20 ms

R1#ping 150.3.3.3 source 150.1.1.1 repeat 10

Type escape sequence to abort.
Sending 10, 100-byte ICMP Echos to 150.3.3.3, timeout is 2 seconds:
Packet sent with a source address of 150.1.1.1
!!!!!!!!!!
Success rate is 100 percent (10/10), round-trip min/avg/max = 16/16/16 ms

R2#ping 150.1.1.1 source 150.2.2.2 repeat 10

Type escape sequence to abort.
Sending 10, 100-byte ICMP Echos to 150.1.1.1, timeout is 2 seconds:
Packet sent with a source address of 150.2.2.2
!!!!!!!!!!
Success rate is 100 percent (10/10), round-trip min/avg/max = 16/16/16 ms

R2#ping 150.1.1.4 source 150.2.2.2 repeat 10

Type escape sequence to abort.
Sending 10, 100-byte ICMP Echos to 150.1.1.4, timeout is 2 seconds:
Packet sent with a source address of 150.2.2.2
!!!!!!!!!!
Success rate is 100 percent (10/10), round-trip min/avg/max = 28/30/32 ms

R2#ping 150.3.3.3 source 150.2.2.2 repeat 10

Type escape sequence to abort.
Sending 10, 100-byte ICMP Echos to 150.3.3.3, timeout is 2 seconds:
Packet sent with a source address of 150.2.2.2
!!!!!!!!!!
Success rate is 100 percent (10/10), round-trip min/avg/max = 16/16/16 ms

3#ping 150.1.1.1 source 150.3.3.3 repeat 10

Type escape sequence to abort.
Sending 10, 100-byte ICMP Echos to 150.1.1.1, timeout is 2 seconds:
Packet sent with a source address of 150.3.3.3
!!!!!!!!!!
Success rate is 100 percent (10/10), round-trip min/avg/max = 16/16/16 ms

R3#ping 150.1.1.4 source 150.3.3.3 repeat 10

Type escape sequence to abort.
Sending 10, 100-byte ICMP Echos to 150.1.1.4, timeout is 2 seconds:
```

```
Packet sent with a source address of 150.3.3.3
!!!!!!!!!!
Success rate is 100 percent (10/10), round-trip min/avg/max = 12/15/16 ms

R3#ping 150.2.2.2 source 150.3.3.3 repeat 10

Type escape sequence to abort.
Sending 10, 100-byte ICMP Echos to 150.2.2.2, timeout is 2 seconds:
Packet sent with a source address of 150.3.3.3
!!!!!!!!!!
Success rate is 100 percent (10/10), round-trip min/avg/max = 16/16/16 ms

R4#ping 150.2.2.2 source 150.1.1.4 repeat 10

Type escape sequence to abort.
Sending 10, 100-byte ICMP Echos to 150.2.2.2, timeout is 2 seconds:
Packet sent with a source address of 150.1.1.4
!!!!!!!!!!
Success rate is 100 percent (10/10), round-trip min/avg/max = 28/29/32 ms

R4#ping 150.3.3.3 source 150.1.1.4 repeat 10

Type escape sequence to abort.
Sending 10, 100-byte ICMP Echos to 150.3.3.3, timeout is 2 seconds:
Packet sent with a source address of 150.1.1.4
!!!!!!!!!!
Success rate is 100 percent (10/10), round-trip min/avg/max = 16/16/16 ms
```

Task 4

To complete this task, you need to modify either the WEIGHT or the LOCAL_PREF attributes for the 150.1.1.0/24 prefix received from R1 on routers R2 and R3. Prior to any configuration changes, both routers R2 and R3 show the following BGP RIB entries for the 150.1.1.0/24 prefix:

```
R2#show ip bgp 150.1.1.0 255.255.255.0
BGP routing table entry for 150.1.1.0/24, version 9
Paths: (2 available, best #1, table Default-IP-Routing-Table)
  Advertised to update-groups:
     1
  (65503 65504)
    10.0.0.10 from 10.0.0.10 (3.3.3.3)
      Origin IGP, metric 0, localpref 100, valid, confed-external, best
  254
    10.0.0.1 from 10.0.0.1 (1.1.1.1)
      Origin IGP, metric 0, localpref 100, valid, external

R3#show ip bgp 150.1.1.0 255.255.255.0
BGP routing table entry for 150.1.1.0/24, version 10
Paths: (2 available, best #1, table Default-IP-Routing-Table)
  Advertised to update-groups:
     1        3
  (65504)
    10.0.0.14 from 10.0.0.14 (4.4.4.4)
      Origin IGP, metric 0, localpref 100, valid, confed-external, best
  254
    10.0.0.5 from 10.0.0.5 (1.1.1.1)
      Origin IGP, metric 0, localpref 100, valid, external
```

To complete this task, use either LOCAL_PREF or WEIGHT as follows:

```
R2(config)#ip prefix-list NET-ONE seq 5 permit 150.1.1.0/24
R2(config)#route-map WEIGHT permit 10
R2(config-route-map)#match ip address prefix-list NET-ONE
R2(config-route-map)#set weight 50000
R2(config-route-map)#exit
R2(config)#route-map WEIGHT permit 20
R2(config-route-map)#exit
R2(config)#router bgp 65502
R2(config-router)#neighbor 10.0.0.1 route-map WEIGHT in
R2(config-router)#exit
```

```
R3(config)#ip prefix-list NET-ONE seq 5 permit 150.1.1.0/24
R3(config)#route-map WEIGHT permit 10
R3(config-route-map)#match ip address prefix-list NET-ONE
R3(config-route-map)#set weight 50000
R3(config-route-map)#exit
R3(config)#router bgp 65503
R3(config-router)#neighbor 10.0.0.5 route-map WEIGHT in
R3(config-router)#exit
R3(config)#route-map WEIGHT permit 20
R3(config-route-map)#exit
```

Following this change, the BGP RIB on R2 and R3 now shows the following:

```
R2#show ip bgp 150.1.1.0 255.255.255.0
BGP routing table entry for 150.1.1.0/24, version 10
Paths: (2 available, best #2, table Default-IP-Routing-Table)
Flag: 0x820
  Advertised to update-groups:
     2
  (65503 65504)
    10.0.0.10 from 10.0.0.10 (3.3.3.3)
      Origin IGP, metric 0, localpref 100, valid, confed-external
  254
    10.0.0.1 from 10.0.0.1 (1.1.1.1)
      Origin IGP, metric 0, localpref 100, weight 50000, valid, external, best

R3#show ip bgp 150.1.1.0 255.255.255.0
BGP routing table entry for 150.1.1.0/24, version 10
Paths: (2 available, best #1, table Default-IP-Routing-Table)
  Advertised to update-groups:
     1          3
  (65504)
    10.0.0.14 from 10.0.0.14 (4.4.4.4)
      Origin IGP, metric 0, localpref 100, valid, confed-external, best
  254
    10.0.0.5 from 10.0.0.5 (1.1.1.1)
      Origin IGP, metric 0, localpref 100, valid, external
```

Task 5

This task requires a little thought. In addition to the AS_PATH and MED attributes, there is yet another BGP attribute that can be used to influence path selection: ORIGIN. During the BGP best path selection process, if all paths have the same AS_PATH length, then prefer the path with the lowest ORIGIN. An ORIGIN of IGP (I) is more preferred (lower) than EGP (E) , which in turn in more preferred (lower) than Incomplete (?). In mathematical terms, IGP < EGP < Incomplete. Because all routers are advertising this prefix with an ORIGIN of IGP, because it was injected into BGP on R3 using the network command, you only need to modify this attribute on R2 and R3. Prior to any attribute changes, the BGP RIB on R1 shows as follows:

```
R1#show ip bgp 150.3.3.0 255.255.255.0
BGP routing table entry for 150.3.3.0/24, version 4
Paths: (3 available, best #3, table Default-IP-Routing-Table)
  Advertised to update-groups:
     1
  5
    150.1.1.4 from 150.1.1.4 (4.4.4.4)
      Origin IGP, localpref 100, valid, external
  5
    10.0.0.2 from 10.0.0.2 (2.2.2.2)
      Origin IGP, localpref 100, valid, external
  5
    10.0.0.6 from 10.0.0.6 (3.3.3.3)
      Origin IGP, metric 0, localpref 100, valid, external, best
```

This task is completed as follows:

```
R4(config)#ip prefix-list NET-THREE seq 5 permit 150.3.3.0/24
R4(config)#route-map ORIGIN permit 10
```

```
R4(config-route-map)#match ip address prefix-list NET-THREE
R4(config-route-map)#set origin egp 1
R4(config-route-map)#exit
R4(config)#route-map ORIGIN permit 20
R4(config-route-map)#exit
R4(config)#router bgp 65504
R4(config-router)#neighbor 150.1.1.1 route-map ORIGIN out
R4(config-router)#exit

R3(config)#ip prefix-list NET-THREE seq 5 permit 150.3.3.0/24
R3(config)#route-map ORIGIN permit 10
R3(config-route-map)#match ip address prefix-list NET-THREE
R3(config-route-map)#set origin incomplete
R3(config-route-map)#exit
R3(config)#route-map ORIGIN permit 20
R3(config-route-map)#exit
R3(config)#router bgp 65503
R3(config-router)#neighbor 10.0.0.5 route-map ORIGIN out
R3(config-router)#exit
```

Following these changes, the BGP RIB on R1 shows the following for the 150.3.3.0/24 prefix:

```
R1#show ip bgp 150.3.3.0 255.255.255.0
BGP routing table entry for 150.3.3.0/24, version 5
Paths: (3 available, best #2, table Default-IP-Routing-Table)
Flag: 0x840
  Advertised to update-groups:
     1
  5
    150.1.1.4 from 150.1.1.4 (4.4.4.4)
      Origin EGP, localpref 100, valid, external
  5
    10.0.0.2 from 10.0.0.2 (2.2.2.2)
      Origin IGP, localpref 100, valid, external, best
  5
    10.0.0.6 from 10.0.0.6 (3.3.3.3)
      Origin incomplete, metric 0, localpref 100, valid, external
```

FINAL ROUTER CONFIGURATIONS

R1

```
R1#term len 0
R1#sh run
Building configuration...

Current configuration : 1059 bytes
!
version 12.4
service timestamps debug datetime msec
service timestamps log datetime msec
no service password-encryption
!
hostname R1
!
boot-start-marker
boot-end-marker
!
no logging console
!
no aaa new-model
no network-clock-participate slot 1
no network-clock-participate wic 0
ip cef
!
no ip domain lookup
ip auth-proxy max-nodata-conns 3
ip admission max-nodata-conns 3
!
interface FastEthernet0/0
```

```
 ip address 150.1.1.1 255.255.255.0
 duplex auto
 speed auto
!
interface Serial0/0
 ip address 10.0.0.1 255.255.255.252
 clock rate 2000000
!
interface Serial0/1
 ip address 10.0.0.5 255.255.255.252
!
router bgp 254
 no synchronization
 bgp router-id 1.1.1.1
 bgp log-neighbor-changes
 network 150.1.1.0 mask 255.255.255.0
 neighbor 10.0.0.2 remote-as 5
 neighbor 10.0.0.6 remote-as 5
 neighbor 150.1.1.4 remote-as 5
 no auto-summary
!
ip forward-protocol nd
!
no ip http server
no ip http secure-server
!
control-plane
!
line con 0
line aux 0
line vty 0 4
 login
!
end

R1#
```

R2

```
R2#term len 0
R2#sh run
Building configuration...

Current configuration : 1318 bytes
!
version 12.4
service timestamps debug datetime msec
service timestamps log datetime msec
no service password-encryption
!
hostname R2
!
boot-start-marker
boot-end-marker
!
no logging console
!
no aaa new-model
no network-clock-participate slot 1
no network-clock-participate wic 0
ip cef
!
no ip domain lookup
ip auth-proxy max-nodata-conns 3
ip admission max-nodata-conns 3
!
interface FastEthernet0/0
 ip address 150.2.2.2 255.255.255.0
 duplex auto
 speed auto
!
interface Serial0/0
 ip address 10.0.0.2 255.255.255.252
!
interface Serial0/1
 ip address 10.0.0.9 255.255.255.252
!
```

```
router bgp 65502
 no synchronization
 bgp router-id 2.2.2.2
 bgp log-neighbor-changes
 bgp confederation identifier 5
 bgp confederation peers 65503
 network 150.2.2.0 mask 255.255.255.0
 neighbor 10.0.0.1 remote-as 254
 neighbor 10.0.0.1 route-map WEIGHT in
 neighbor 10.0.0.10 remote-as 65503
 neighbor 10.0.0.10 next-hop-self
 no auto-summary
!
ip forward-protocol nd
!
no ip http server
no ip http secure-server
!
ip prefix-list NET-ONE seq 5 permit 150.1.1.0/24
!
route-map WEIGHT permit 10
 match ip address prefix-list NET-ONE
 set weight 50000
!
route-map WEIGHT permit 20
!
control-plane
!
line con 0
line aux 0
line vty 0 4
 login
!
end

R2#
```

R3

```
R3#term len 0
R3#sh run
Building configuration...

Current configuration : 1959 bytes
!
version 12.4
service timestamps debug datetime msec
service timestamps log datetime msec
no service password-encryption
!
hostname R3
!
boot-start-marker
boot-end-marker
!
no logging console
!
no aaa new-model
no network-clock-participate slot 1
no network-clock-participate wic 0
ip cef
!
no ip domain lookup
ip auth-proxy max-nodata-conns 3
ip admission max-nodata-conns 3
!
interface FastEthernet0/0
 ip address 150.3.3.3 255.255.255.0
 duplex auto
 speed auto
!
interface Serial1/0
 ip address 10.0.0.6 255.255.255.252
 clock rate 128000
!
```

```
interface Serial1/1
 ip address 10.0.0.10 255.255.255.252
 clock rate 128000
!
interface Serial1/2
 ip address 10.0.0.13 255.255.255.252
 clock rate 128000
!
interface Serial1/3
 no ip address
 shutdown
!
interface Serial1/4
 no ip address
 shutdown
!
interface Serial1/5
 no ip address
 shutdown
!
interface Serial1/6
 no ip address
 shutdown
!
interface Serial1/7
 no ip address
 shutdown
!
router bgp 65503
 no synchronization
 bgp router-id 3.3.3.3
 bgp log-neighbor-changes
 bgp confederation identifier 5
 bgp confederation peers 65502 65504
 network 150.3.3.0 mask 255.255.255.0
 neighbor 10.0.0.5 remote-as 254
 neighbor 10.0.0.5 route-map WEIGHT in
 neighbor 10.0.0.5 route-map ORIGIN out
 neighbor 10.0.0.9 remote-as 65502
 neighbor 10.0.0.9 next-hop-self
 neighbor 10.0.0.14 remote-as 65504
 neighbor 10.0.0.14 next-hop-self
 no auto-summary
!
ip forward-protocol nd
!
no ip http server
no ip http secure-server
!
ip prefix-list NET-ONE seq 5 permit 150.1.1.0/24
!
ip prefix-list NET-THREE seq 5 permit 150.3.3.0/24
!
route-map WEIGHT permit 10
 match ip address prefix-list NET-ONE
 set weight 50000
!
route-map WEIGHT permit 20
!
route-map ORIGIN permit 10
 match ip address prefix-list NET-THREE
 set origin incomplete
!
route-map ORIGIN permit 20
!
control-plane
!
line con 0
line aux 0
line vty 0 4
 login
!
end

R3#
```

R4

```
R4#term len 0
R4#sh run
Building configuration...

Current configuration : 1314 bytes
!
version 12.4
service timestamps debug datetime msec
service timestamps log datetime msec
no service password-encryption
!
hostname R4
!
boot-start-marker
boot-end-marker
!
no logging console
!
no aaa new-model
no network-clock-participate slot 1
no network-clock-participate wic 0
ip cef
!
no ip domain lookup
ip auth-proxy max-nodata-conns 3
ip admission max-nodata-conns 3
!
interface FastEthernet0/0
 ip address 150.1.1.4 255.255.255.0
 duplex auto
 speed auto
!
interface Serial0/0
 ip address 10.0.0.14 255.255.255.252
!
interface Serial0/1
 no ip address
 shutdown
!
router bgp 65504
 no synchronization
 bgp router-id 4.4.4.4
 bgp log-neighbor-changes
 bgp confederation identifier 5
 bgp confederation peers 65503
 network 150.1.1.0 mask 255.255.255.0
 neighbor 10.0.0.13 remote-as 65503
 neighbor 10.0.0.13 next-hop-self
 neighbor 150.1.1.1 remote-as 254
 neighbor 150.1.1.1 route-map ORIGIN out
 no auto-summary
!
ip forward-protocol nd
!
no ip http server
no ip http secure-server
!
ip prefix-list NET-THREE seq 5 permit 150.3.3.0/24
!
route-map ORIGIN permit 10
 match ip address prefix-list NET-THREE
 set origin egp 1
!
route-map ORIGIN permit 20
!
control-plane
!
line con 0
line aux 0
line vty 0 4
 login
!
end

R4#
```

CCNP LAB 36

Border Gateway Protocol Lab

Lab Objective:

The focus of this lab is to understand BGP implementation and configuration in Cisco IOS routers. Additional technologies include route filtering, summarization and path control.

Lab Topology:

The lab network topology is illustrated below:

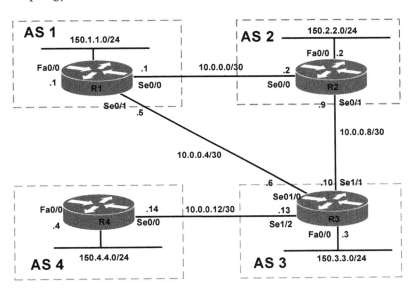

IMPORTANT NOTE: If you are using the www.howtonetwork.net racks, please bring up the LAN interfaces connected to the routers by issuing the no shutdown command on the connected switches. If you are using a home lab with no Switches, you can bring up the LAN interfaces using the following configurations on your routers:

```
interface fastethernet 0/0
  no keepalive
  loopback
  no shutdown
```

Alternately, you can simply connect the interfaces to a hub or switch if you have one available in your own lab.

Task 1

Configure hostnames and IP addressing on all routers as illustrated in the network topology.

Task 2

Configure BGP as illustrated in the topology. R1 will peer with R2 and R3. R2 will peer with R1 and R3. R3 will peer with R1, R2 and R4. R4 will peer only with R3. The routers should all use their physical interface addresses for BGP peering. Verify your configuration.

Task 3

Advertise the 150.x.x.x LAN subnets on all routers via BGP. These should be injected using the `network` command on all routers. Verify that all routers' LAN subnets can ping every other routers LAN subnet. Use an extended ping to perform this verification.

Task 4

Configure R1 with the following Loopback interfaces:
- Loopback 1920: IP Address 192.0.0.1/32
- Loopback 1921: IP Address 192.0.1.1/32

These prefixes should be advertised only to R2. Next, configure R2 to advertise a single route for these prefixes to R3. Ensure that this aggregate route ONLY appears in the BGP Table of R4 but not in the BGP Table of R1. Adhere to the following restrictions when completing this task:
- You can NOT use an outbound route map on R1
- You can NOT use any outbound filters or route maps on R2 or R3
- You can NOT use any inbound filters or route maps on R1 or R3
- You can NOT modify administrative distance values

Verify your configuration using the appropriate commands. Verify that R2, R3, and R4 can ping these prefixes from their LAN subnets, i.e. the 150.x.x.x/24 addresses.

Task 5

To support a future Anycast solution, configure R2 and R4 with a Loopback 200 interface with the IP address 200.8.8.8/32. Next, redistribute this prefix into BGP on R2 and R4 and configure BGP path control so that R1 prefers the prefix originated by R4 over the prefix originated by R1. However, you must adhere to the following restrictions when completing this task:
- You can NOT modify the AS_PATH length for this prefix on ANY router
- You can NOT modify default administrative distance values
- You can NOT modify the WEIGHT or LOCAL_PREF attributes on R1
- You can only issue ONE single command on R1, i.e. one line of code
- You MUST use route maps when redistributing this interface on R2 and R4

Verify your configuration using the appropriate commands. Ensure that R1 can ping this address from its LAN IP address of 150.1.1.1/24.

LAB VALIDATION

Task 1

Please refer to previous labs for basic IP addressing and hostname configuration. This will not be included in this section to avoid being redundant.

Task 2

```
R1(config)#router bgp 1
R1(config-router)#bgp router-id 1.1.1.1
R1(config-router)#neighbor 10.0.0.2 remote-as 2
R1(config-router)#neighbor 10.0.0.6 remote-as 3
R1(config-router)#exit

R2(config)#router bgp 2
R2(config-router)#bgp router-id 2.2.2.2
R2(config-router)#neighbor 10.0.0.1 remote-as 1
R2(config-router)#neighbor 10.0.0.10 remote-as 3
R2(config-router)#exit
```

```
R3(config)#router bgp 3
R3(config-router)#bgp router-id 3.3.3.3
R3(config-router)#neighbor 10.0.0.5 remote-as 5
R3(config-router)#neighbor 10.0.0.9 remote-as 2
R3(config-router)#neighbor 10.0.0.14 remote-as 4
R3(config-router)#exit

R4(config)#router bgp 4
R4(config-router)#bgp router-id 4.4.4.4
R4(config-router)#neighbor 10.0.0.13 remote-as 3
R4(config-router)#exit
```

Verify your configuration using the show ip bgp summary command on all routers:

```
R1#show ip bgp summary
BGP router identifier 1.1.1.1, local AS number 1
BGP table version is 1, main routing table version 1

Neighbor     V   AS MsgRcvd MsgSent   TblVer  InQ OutQ Up/Down  State/PfxRcd
10.0.0.2     4    2       5       5        1    0    0 00:02:52         0
10.0.0.6     4    3       5       6        1    0    0 00:01:16         0

R2#show ip bgp summary
BGP router identifier 2.2.2.2, local AS number 2
BGP table version is 1, main routing table version 1

Neighbor     V   AS MsgRcvd MsgSent   TblVer  InQ OutQ Up/Down  State/PfxRcd
10.0.0.1     4    1       5       5        1    0    0 00:02:58         0
10.0.0.10    4    3       4       5        1    0    0 00:01:24         0

R3#show ip bgp summary
BGP router identifier 3.3.3.3, local AS number 3
BGP table version is 1, main routing table version 1

Neighbor     V   AS MsgRcvd MsgSent   TblVer  InQ OutQ Up/Down  State/PfxRcd
10.0.0.5     4    1       6       5        1    0    0 00:01:25         0
10.0.0.9     4    2       5       4        1    0    0 00:01:26         0
10.0.0.14    4    4       4       4        1    0    0 00:00:21         0

R4#show ip bgp summary
BGP router identifier 4.4.4.4, local AS number 4
BGP table version is 1, main routing table version 1

Neighbor     V   AS MsgRcvd MsgSent   TblVer  InQ OutQ Up/Down  State/PfxRcd
10.0.0.13    4    3       4       4        1    0    0 00:00:24         0
```

Task 3

```
R1(config)#router bgp 1
R1(config-router)#network 150.1.1.0 mask 255.255.255.0
R1(config-router)#exit

R2(config)#router bgp 2
R2(config-router)#network 150.2.2.0 mask 255.255.255.0
R2(config-router)#exit

R3(config)#router bgp 3
R3(config-router)#network 150.3.3.0 mask 255.255.255.0
R3(config-router)#exit

R4(config)#router bgp 4
R4(config-router)#network 150.4.4.0 mask 255.255.255.0
R4(config-router)#exit
```

Verify that all routers have the 150.x.x.x/24 subnets in their BGP Tables:

```
R1#show ip bgp
BGP table version is 5, local router ID is 1.1.1.1
Status codes: s suppressed, d damped, h history, * valid, > best, i - internal,
              r RIB-failure, S Stale
```

```
Origin codes: i - IGP, e - EGP, ? - incomplete

     Network          Next Hop         Metric LocPrf Weight Path
*>   150.1.1.0/24     0.0.0.0               0         32768 i
*    150.2.2.0/24     10.0.0.6                            0 3 2 i
*>                    10.0.0.2              0               0 2 i
*    150.3.3.0/24     10.0.0.2                            0 2 3 i
*>                    10.0.0.6              0               0 3 i
*    150.4.4.0/24     10.0.0.2                            0 2 3 4 i
*>                    10.0.0.6                            0 3 4 i

R2#show ip bgp
BGP table version is 5, local router ID is 2.2.2.2
Status codes: s suppressed, d damped, h history, * valid, > best, i - internal,
              r RIB-failure, S Stale
Origin codes: i - IGP, e - EGP, ? - incomplete

     Network          Next Hop         Metric LocPrf Weight Path
*    150.1.1.0/24     10.0.0.10                           0 3 1 i
*>                    10.0.0.1              0               0 1 i
*>   150.2.2.0/24     0.0.0.0               0         32768 i
*    150.3.3.0/24     10.0.0.1                            0 1 3 i
*>                    10.0.0.10             0               0 3 i
*    150.4.4.0/24     10.0.0.1                            0 1 3 4 i
*>                    10.0.0.10                           0 3 4 i

R3#show ip bgp
BGP table version is 5, local router ID is 3.3.3.3
Status codes: s suppressed, d damped, h history, * valid, > best, i - internal,
              r RIB-failure, S Stale
Origin codes: i - IGP, e - EGP, ? - incomplete

     Network          Next Hop         Metric LocPrf Weight Path
*    150.1.1.0/24     10.0.0.9                            0 2 1 i
*>                    10.0.0.5              0               0 1 i
*    150.2.2.0/24     10.0.0.5                            0 1 2 i
*>                    10.0.0.9              0               0 2 i
*>   150.3.3.0/24     0.0.0.0               0         32768 i
*>   150.4.4.0/24     10.0.0.14             0               0 4 i

R4#show ip bgp
BGP table version is 5, local router ID is 4.4.4.4
Status codes: s suppressed, d damped, h history, * valid, > best, i - internal,
              r RIB-failure, S Stale
Origin codes: i - IGP, e - EGP, ? - incomplete

     Network          Next Hop         Metric LocPrf Weight Path
*>   150.1.1.0/24     10.0.0.13                           0 3 1 i
*>   150.2.2.0/24     10.0.0.13                           0 3 2 i
*>   150.3.3.0/24     10.0.0.13             0               0 3 i
*>   150.4.4.0/24     0.0.0.0               0         32768 i
```

Finally, verify that each router can ping every other routers' LAN interface from its own:

```
R1#ping 150.2.2.2 source fastethernet 0/0 repeat 10

Type escape sequence to abort.
Sending 10, 100-byte ICMP Echos to 150.2.2.2, timeout is 2 seconds:
Packet sent with a source address of 150.1.1.1
!!!!!!!!!!
Success rate is 100 percent (10/10), round-trip min/avg/max = 1/3/4 ms

R1#ping 150.3.3.3 source fastethernet 0/0 repeat 10

Type escape sequence to abort.
Sending 10, 100-byte ICMP Echos to 150.3.3.3, timeout is 2 seconds:
Packet sent with a source address of 150.1.1.1
!!!!!!!!!!
Success rate is 100 percent (10/10), round-trip min/avg/max = 12/15/16 ms

R1#ping 150.4.4.4 source fastethernet 0/0 repeat 10

Type escape sequence to abort.
Sending 10, 100-byte ICMP Echos to 150.4.4.4, timeout is 2 seconds:
```

```
Packet sent with a source address of 150.1.1.1
!!!!!!!!!!
Success rate is 100 percent (10/10), round-trip min/avg/max = 28/30/32 ms

R2#ping 150.1.1.1 source fastethernet 0/0 repeat 10

Type escape sequence to abort.
Sending 10, 100-byte ICMP Echos to 150.1.1.1, timeout is 2 seconds:
Packet sent with a source address of 150.2.2.2
!!!!!!!!!!
Success rate is 100 percent (10/10), round-trip min/avg/max = 1/3/4 ms

R2#ping 150.3.3.3 source fastethernet 0/0 repeat 10

Type escape sequence to abort.
Sending 10, 100-byte ICMP Echos to 150.3.3.3, timeout is 2 seconds:
Packet sent with a source address of 150.2.2.2
!!!!!!!!!!
Success rate is 100 percent (10/10), round-trip min/avg/max = 16/16/16 ms

R2#ping 150.4.4.4 source fastethernet 0/0 repeat 10

Type escape sequence to abort.
Sending 10, 100-byte ICMP Echos to 150.4.4.4, timeout is 2 seconds:
Packet sent with a source address of 150.2.2.2
!!!!!!!!!!
Success rate is 100 percent (10/10), round-trip min/avg/max = 28/29/32 ms

R3#ping 150.1.1.1 source fastethernet 0/0 repeat 10

Type escape sequence to abort.
Sending 10, 100-byte ICMP Echos to 150.1.1.1, timeout is 2 seconds:
Packet sent with a source address of 150.3.3.3
!!!!!!!!!!
Success rate is 100 percent (10/10), round-trip min/avg/max = 16/16/16 ms

R3#ping 150.2.2.2 source fastethernet 0/0 repeat 10

Type escape sequence to abort.
Sending 10, 100-byte ICMP Echos to 150.2.2.2, timeout is 2 seconds:
Packet sent with a source address of 150.3.3.3
!!!!!!!!!!
Success rate is 100 percent (10/10), round-trip min/avg/max = 16/16/16 ms

R3#ping 150.3.3.3 source fastethernet 0/0 repeat 10

Type escape sequence to abort.
Sending 10, 100-byte ICMP Echos to 150.3.3.3, timeout is 2 seconds:
Packet sent with a source address of 150.3.3.3
!!!!!!!!!!
Success rate is 100 percent (10/10), round-trip min/avg/max = 1/1/4 ms

R4#ping 150.1.1.1 source fastethernet 0/0 repeat 10

Type escape sequence to abort.
Sending 10, 100-byte ICMP Echos to 150.1.1.1, timeout is 2 seconds:
Packet sent with a source address of 150.4.4.4
!!!!!!!!!!
Success rate is 100 percent (10/10), round-trip min/avg/max = 28/30/32 ms

R4#ping 150.2.2.2 source fastethernet 0/0 repeat 10

Type escape sequence to abort.
Sending 10, 100-byte ICMP Echos to 150.2.2.2, timeout is 2 seconds:
Packet sent with a source address of 150.4.4.4
!!!!!!!!!!
Success rate is 100 percent (10/10), round-trip min/avg/max = 28/30/32 ms

R4#ping 150.3.3.3 source fastethernet 0/0 repeat 10

Type escape sequence to abort.
Sending 10, 100-byte ICMP Echos to 150.3.3.3, timeout is 2 seconds:
Packet sent with a source address of 150.4.4.4
!!!!!!!!!!
Success rate is 100 percent (10/10), round-trip min/avg/max = 12/15/16 ms
```

Task 4

The requirements of this task are three-fold. First, configure the Loopback interfaces on R1 and then advertise them via BGP but ONLY to R2. This is done using an outbound prefix list that prevents the prefixes from
being advertised to R3. The first part is completed on R1 as follows:

```
R1(config)#interface loopback 1920
R1(config-if)#ip add 192.0.0.1 255.255.255.255
R1(config-if)#exit
R1(config)#interface loopback 1921
R1(config-if)#ip add 192.0.1.1 255.255.255.255
R1(config-if)#exit
R1(config)#ip prefix-list FILTER seq 1 deny 192.0.0.1/32
R1(config)#ip prefix-list FILTER seq 2 deny 192.0.1.1/32
R1(config)#ip prefix-list FILTER seq 3 permit 0.0.0.0/0 le 32
R1(config)#router bgp 1
R1(config-router)#network 192.0.0.1 mask 255.255.255.255
R1(config-router)#network 192.0.1.1 mask 255.255.255.255
R1(config-router)#exit
```

Verify your configuration using **show ip bgp neighbor <address> advertised**-routes command on R1 to see
which prefixes are advertised to R2 and R3:

```
R1#show ip bgp neighbors 10.0.0.2 advertised-routes
BGP table version is 7, local router ID is 1.1.1.1
Status codes: s suppressed, d damped, h history, * valid, > best, i - internal,
              r RIB-failure, S Stale
Origin codes: i - IGP, e - EGP, ? - incomplete

   Network          Next Hop            Metric LocPrf Weight Path
*> 150.1.1.0/24     0.0.0.0                  0         32768 i
*> 150.2.2.0/24     10.0.0.2                 0             0 2 i
*> 150.3.3.0/24     10.0.0.6                 0             0 3 i
*> 150.4.4.0/24     10.0.0.6                               0 3 4 i
*> 192.0.0.1/32     0.0.0.0                  0         32768 i
*> 192.0.1.1/32     0.0.0.0                  0         32768 i

Total number of prefixes 6

R1#show ip bgp neighbors 10.0.0.6 advertised-routes
BGP table version is 7, local router ID is 1.1.1.1
Status codes: s suppressed, d damped, h history, * valid, > best, i - internal,
              r RIB-failure, S Stale
Origin codes: i - IGP, e - EGP, ? - incomplete

   Network          Next Hop            Metric LocPrf Weight Path
*> 150.1.1.0/24     0.0.0.0                  0         32768 i
*> 150.2.2.0/24     10.0.0.2                 0             0 2 i

Total number of prefixes 2
```

The second part of this task requires that you summarize these prefixes and ensure that they are NOT advertised back to R1 by R3. Given the restrictions, which prevent the manipulation of attributes, administrative
distance values, or using inbound or outbound filters, we need to use another solution. When summarizing
with BGP, if you use the aggregate-address command, the router that performs the aggregation removes,
by default, any other AS_PATH information (AS_SET). The summarized route is therefore originated from
the AS of the router that generated the summary. This means that if the routes that are summarized were
received from another AS, as is our case, the aggregate can be re-advertised back to that AS, causing all sorts
of issues. For example, assume the following command was issued on R2:

```
R2(config)#router bgp 2
R2(config-router)#aggregate-address 192.0.0.0 255.255.254.0 summary-only
R2(config-router)#exit
```

Given this configuration, R2 suppresses the specific 192.0.0.1/32 and 192.0.1.1/32 prefixes and advertises
only a single route to R3. This route appears on R3 as follows:

```
R3#show ip bgp 192.0.0.0 255.255.254.0
BGP routing table entry for 192.0.0.0/23, version 10
Paths: (2 available, best #2, table Default-IP-Routing-Table)
Flag: 0x820
  Advertised to update-groups:
    1
  1 2, (aggregated by 2 2.2.2.2)
    10.0.0.5 from 10.0.0.5 (1.1.1.1)
      Origin IGP, localpref 100, valid, external, atomic-aggregate
  2, (aggregated by 2 2.2.2.2)
    10.0.0.9 from 10.0.0.9 (2.2.2.2)
      Origin IGP, metric 0, localpref 100, valid, external, atomic-aggregate, best
```

Notice that the AS_PATH shows that this aggregate originates in AS 2, even though it is based on prefixes originated in AS 1. Given this, R1 will accept this same prefix from both R2 an R3:

```
R1#show ip bgp 192.0.0.0 255.255.254.0
BGP routing table entry for 192.0.0.0/23, version 8
Paths: (2 available, best #2, table Default-IP-Routing-Table)
  Advertised to update-groups:
    2
  3 2, (aggregated by 2 2.2.2.2)
    10.0.0.6 from 10.0.0.6 (3.3.3.3)
      Origin IGP, localpref 100, valid, external, atomic-aggregate
  2, (aggregated by 2 2.2.2.2)
    10.0.0.2 from 10.0.0.2 (2.2.2.2)
      Origin IGP, metric 0, localpref 100, valid, external, atomic-aggregate, best
```

To complete this task, we need append the as-set keyword to the BGP aggregate-address command. The as-set argument creates an aggregate address with a mathematical set of autonomous systems. In other words, it includes all ASes of the specific prefixes from which the aggregate is generated. This prevents the aggregate from being advertised back to those ASes; i.e. the routers receiving this UPDATE will see their own AS_PATH in the string and drop it. To complete this task, configure R2 as follows:

```
R2(config)#router bgp 2
R2(config-router)#aggregate-add 192.0.0.0 255.255.254.0 summary-only as-set
R2(config-router)#exit
```

Following this change, the aggregate now reflects an origin of AS 1 when seen on R3:

```
R3#show ip bgp 192.0.0.0 255.255.254.0
BGP routing table entry for 192.0.0.0/23, version 13
Paths: (1 available, best #1, table Default-IP-Routing-Table)
  Advertised to update-groups:
    1
  2 1, (aggregated by 2 2.2.2.2)
    10.0.0.9 from 10.0.0.9 (2.2.2.2)
      Origin IGP, metric 0, localpref 100, valid, external, best
```

Because R1 sees its own AS_PATH in the list, it does NOT accept the aggregate:

```
R1#show ip bgp 192.0.0.0 255.255.254.0
% Network not in table
```

However, the aggregate is still advertised to R4:

```
R4#show ip bgp 192.0.0.0 255.255.254.0
BGP routing table entry for 192.0.0.0/23, version 13
Paths: (1 available, best #1, table Default-IP-Routing-Table)
  Not advertised to any peer
  3 2 1, (aggregated by 2 2.2.2.2)
    10.0.0.13 from 10.0.0.13 (3.3.3.3)
      Origin IGP, localpref 100, valid, external, best
```

The final task is to verify that R1, R2 and R3 can all ping the 192.0.0.1/32 and 192.0.1.1/32 prefixes from their LAN interfaces. This last part is completed as follows:

```
R2#ping 192.0.0.1 source fastethernet 0/0 repeat 10

Type escape sequence to abort.
Sending 10, 100-byte ICMP Echos to 192.0.0.1, timeout is 2 seconds:
Packet sent with a source address of 150.2.2.2
!!!!!!!!!!
Success rate is 100 percent (10/10), round-trip min/avg/max = 1/3/4 ms

R2#ping 192.0.1.1 source fastethernet 0/0 repeat 10

Type escape sequence to abort.
Sending 10, 100-byte ICMP Echos to 192.0.1.1, timeout is 2 seconds:
Packet sent with a source address of 150.2.2.2
!!!!!!!!!!
Success rate is 100 percent (10/10), round-trip min/avg/max = 1/3/4 ms

R3#ping 192.0.0.1 source fastethernet 0/0 repeat 10

Type escape sequence to abort.
Sending 10, 100-byte ICMP Echos to 192.0.0.1, timeout is 2 seconds:
Packet sent with a source address of 150.3.3.3
!!!!!!!!!!
Success rate is 100 percent (10/10), round-trip min/avg/max = 16/16/16 ms

R3#ping 192.0.1.1 source fastethernet 0/0 repeat 10

Type escape sequence to abort.
Sending 10, 100-byte ICMP Echos to 192.0.1.1, timeout is 2 seconds:
Packet sent with a source address of 150.3.3.3
!!!!!!!!!!
Success rate is 100 percent (10/10), round-trip min/avg/max = 16/16/20 ms

R4#ping 192.0.0.1 source fastethernet 0/0 repeat 10

Type escape sequence to abort.
Sending 10, 100-byte ICMP Echos to 192.0.0.1, timeout is 2 seconds:
Packet sent with a source address of 150.4.4.4
!!!!!!!!!!
Success rate is 100 percent (10/10), round-trip min/avg/max = 28/30/32 ms

R4#ping 192.0.1.1 source fastethernet 0/0 repeat 10

Type escape sequence to abort.
Sending 10, 100-byte ICMP Echos to 192.0.1.1, timeout is 2 seconds:
Packet sent with a source address of 150.4.4.4
!!!!!!!!!!
Success rate is 100 percent (10/10), round-trip min/avg/max = 28/30/32 ms
```

Task 5

While seemingly very difficult, this task is quite simple IF you have read the BGP path selection process in the ROUTE guide. Because we cannot use WEIGHT or LOCAL_PREF, those two attributes are ruled out. Because both prefixes are not originated on the local router, we can skip this step of the path selection process.

The next attribute to consider then would be the AS_PATH length. However, the task says that we cannot MODIFY the AS_PATH length; however, it says nothing about ignoring the AS_PATH. In the ROUTE guide, in the BGP path selection process section, it reads as follows:

> If no route was originated, prefer the route that has the shortest AS_PATH. However, if the bgp best-path as-path ignore command is issued on the router, the AS_PATH attribute is not used in BGP best path selection. Also, when comparing this attribute, an AS_SET is counted once, regardless of the number of autonomous systems in the set. And, finally, the AS_CONFED_SEQUENCE is not included in the AS_PATH length

Therefore, we can configure R1 to IGNORE the AS_PATH attribute in best path selection and look at the next attribute in the best path selection process, which is ORIGIN, we can influence the path selection by configuring R1 to ignore the AS_PATH attribute in the path selection process and advertising the prefix from R4 with a better ORIGIN code than that on R2. This task is completed as follows:

```
R1(config)#router bgp 1
R1(config-router)#bgp bestpath as-path  ignore
R1(config-router)#exit
```

NOTE: The bgp bestpath as-path ignore command is a hidden command. It will not show up when you hit the question mark (?). Simply type it in and is shows up in the config.

```
R1(config)#router bgp 1
R1(config-router)#bgp bestpath ?
  compare-routerid  Compare router-id for identical EBGP paths
  cost-community    cost community
  med               MED attribute
```

Complete your configuration on routers R2 and R4 as follows:

```
R2(config)#interface loopback 200
R2(config-if)#ip address 200.8.8.8 255.255.255.255
R2(config-if)#exit
R2(config)#route-map LOOPBACK permit 10
R2(config-route-map)#match interface loopback 200
R2(config-route-map)#exit
R2(config)#router bgp 2
R2(config-router)#redistribute connected route-map LOOPBACK
R2(config-router)#exit

R4(config)#interface loopback 200
R4(config-if)#ip address 200.8.8.8 255.255.255.255
R4(config-if)#exit
R4(config)#route-map LOOPBACK permit 10
R4(config-route-map)#match interface loopback 200
R4(config-route-map)#set origin igp
R4(config-route-map)#exit
R4(config)#router bgp 4
R4(config-router)#redistribute connected route-map LOOPBACK
R4(config-router)#exit
```

Following this change, the BGP Table on R1 reflects the following for the 200.8.8.8/32 prefix:

```
R1#show ip bgp 200.8.8.8 255.255.255.255
BGP routing table entry for 200.8.8.8/32, version 8
Paths: (2 available, best #2, table Default-IP-Routing-Table)
Flag: 0x820
  Advertised to update-groups:
    1
  2
    10.0.0.2 from 10.0.0.2 (2.2.2.2)
      Origin incomplete, metric 0, localpref 100, valid, external
  3 4
    10.0.0.6 from 10.0.0.6 (3.3.3.3)
      Origin IGP, localpref 100, valid, external, best
```

Because the AS_PATH attribute is ignored in best path selection on R1, it is omitted in the path selection process and the next valid attribute, ORIGIN, is used instead. Given that an ORIGIN of IGP > EGP > Incomplete, the path from R4 wins and is used instead. The same logic is also applicable to R3, which prefers this same path because of the ORIGIN:

```
R3#show ip bgp 200.8.8.8 255.255.255.255
BGP routing table entry for 200.8.8.8/32, version 15
Paths: (2 available, best #1, table Default-IP-Routing-Table)
  Advertised to update-groups:
    1
  4
    10.0.0.14 from 10.0.0.14 (4.4.4.4)
      Origin IGP, metric 0, localpref 100, valid, external, best
  2
    10.0.0.9 from 10.0.0.9 (2.2.2.2)
      Origin incomplete, metric 0, localpref 100, valid, external
```

Finally, complete this task by pinging from R1s LAN to the 192.8.8.8/32 address:

```
R1#ping 200.8.8.8 source 150.1.1.1 repeat 10

Type escape sequence to abort.
Sending 10, 100-byte ICMP Echos to 200.8.8.8, timeout is 2 seconds:
Packet sent with a source address of 150.1.1.1
!!!!!!!!!!
Success rate is 100 percent (10/10), round-trip min/avg/max = 28/30/32 ms
```

FINAL ROUTER CONFIGURATIONS

R1

```
R1#term len 0
R1#sh run
Building configuration...

Current configuration : 1447 bytes
!
version 12.4
service timestamps debug datetime msec
service timestamps log datetime msec
no service password-encryption
!
hostname R1
!
boot-start-marker
boot-end-marker
!
no logging console
!
no aaa new-model
no network-clock-participate slot 1
no network-clock-participate wic 0
ip cef
!
no ip domain lookup
ip auth-proxy max-nodata-conns 3
ip admission max-nodata-conns 3
!
interface Loopback1920
 ip address 192.0.0.1 255.255.255.255
!
interface Loopback1921
 ip address 192.0.1.1 255.255.255.255
!
interface FastEthernet0/0
 ip address 150.1.1.1 255.255.255.0
 duplex auto
 speed auto
!
interface Serial0/0
 ip address 10.0.0.1 255.255.255.252
 clock rate 2000000
!
interface Serial0/1
 ip address 10.0.0.5 255.255.255.252
!
router bgp 1
 no synchronization
 bgp router-id 1.1.1.1
 bgp log-neighbor-changes
 bgp bestpath as-path ignore
 network 150.1.1.0 mask 255.255.255.0
 network 192.0.0.1 mask 255.255.255.255
 network 192.0.1.1 mask 255.255.255.255
 neighbor 10.0.0.2 remote-as 2
 neighbor 10.0.0.6 remote-as 3
 neighbor 10.0.0.6 prefix-list FILTER out
```

```
 no auto-summary
!
ip forward-protocol nd
!
no ip http server
no ip http secure-server
!
ip prefix-list FILTER seq 1 deny 192.0.0.1/32
ip prefix-list FILTER seq 2 deny 192.0.1.1/32
ip prefix-list FILTER seq 3 permit 0.0.0.0/0 le 32
!
control-plane
!
line con 0
line aux 0
line vty 0 4
 login
!
end

R1#
```

R2

```
R2#sh run
Building configuration...

Current configuration : 1234 bytes
!
version 12.4
service timestamps debug datetime msec
service timestamps log datetime msec
no service password-encryption
!
hostname R2
!
boot-start-marker
boot-end-marker
!
no logging console
!
no aaa new-model
no network-clock-participate slot 1
no network-clock-participate wic 0
ip cef
!
no ip domain lookup
ip auth-proxy max-nodata-conns 3
ip admission max-nodata-conns 3
!
interface Loopback200
 ip address 200.8.8.8 255.255.255.255
!
interface FastEthernet0/0
 ip address 150.2.2.2 255.255.255.0
 duplex auto
 speed auto
!
interface Serial0/0
 ip address 10.0.0.2 255.255.255.252
!
interface Serial0/1
 ip address 10.0.0.9 255.255.255.252
!
router bgp 2
 no synchronization
 bgp router-id 2.2.2.2
 bgp log-neighbor-changes
 network 150.2.2.0 mask 255.255.255.0
 aggregate-address 192.0.0.0 255.255.254.0 as-set summary-only
 redistribute connected route-map LOOPBACK
 neighbor 10.0.0.1 remote-as 1
 neighbor 10.0.0.10 remote-as 3
```

```
 no auto-summary
!
ip forward-protocol nd
!
no ip http server
no ip http secure-server
!
route-map LOOPBACK permit 10
 match interface Loopback200
!
control-plane
!
line con 0
line aux 0
line vty 0 4
 login
!
end

R2#
```

R3

```
R3#term len 0
R3#sh run
Building configuration...

Current configuration : 1390 bytes
!
version 12.4
service timestamps debug datetime msec
service timestamps log datetime msec
no service password-encryption
!
hostname R3
!
boot-start-marker
boot-end-marker
!
no logging console
!
no aaa new-model
no network-clock-participate slot 1
no network-clock-participate wic 0
ip cef
!
no ip domain lookup
ip auth-proxy max-nodata-conns 3
ip admission max-nodata-conns 3
!
interface FastEthernet0/0
 ip address 150.3.3.3 255.255.255.0
 duplex auto
 speed auto
!
interface Serial1/0
 ip address 10.0.0.6 255.255.255.252
 clock rate 128000
!
interface Serial1/1
 ip address 10.0.0.10 255.255.255.252
 clock rate 128000
!
interface Serial1/2
 ip address 10.0.0.13 255.255.255.252
 clock rate 128000
!
interface Serial1/3
 no ip address
 shutdown
!
interface Serial1/4
 no ip address
 shutdown
```

```
!
interface Serial1/5
 no ip address
 shutdown
!
interface Serial1/6
 no ip address
 shutdown
!
interface Serial1/7
 no ip address
 shutdown
!
router bgp 3
 no synchronization
 bgp router-id 3.3.3.3
 bgp log-neighbor-changes
 network 150.3.3.0 mask 255.255.255.0
 neighbor 10.0.0.5 remote-as 1
 neighbor 10.0.0.9 remote-as 2
 neighbor 10.0.0.14 remote-as 4
 no auto-summary
!
ip forward-protocol nd
!
no ip http server
no ip http secure-server
!
control-plane
!
line con 0
line aux 0
line vty 0 4
 login
!
end

R3#
```

R4

```
R4#term len 0
R4#sh run
Building configuration...

Current configuration : 1145 bytes
!
version 12.4
service timestamps debug datetime msec
service timestamps log datetime msec
no service password-encryption
!
hostname R4
!
boot-start-marker
boot-end-marker
!
no logging console
!
no aaa new-model
no network-clock-participate slot 1
no network-clock-participate wic 0
ip cef
!
no ip domain lookup
ip auth-proxy max-nodata-conns 3
ip admission max-nodata-conns 3
!
interface Loopback200
 ip address 200.8.8.8 255.255.255.255
!
interface FastEthernet0/0
 ip address 150.4.4.4 255.255.255.0
 duplex auto
```

```
 speed auto
!
interface Serial0/0
 ip address 10.0.0.14 255.255.255.252
!
interface Serial0/1
 no ip address
 shutdown
!
router bgp 4
 no synchronization
 bgp router-id 4.4.4.4
 bgp log-neighbor-changes
 network 150.4.4.0 mask 255.255.255.0
 redistribute connected route-map LOOPBACK
 neighbor 10.0.0.13 remote-as 3
 no auto-summary
!
ip forward-protocol nd
!
no ip http server
no ip http secure-server
!
route-map LOOPBACK permit 10
 match interface Loopback200
 set origin igp
!
control-plane
!
line con 0
line aux 0
line vty 0 4
 login
!
end

R4#
```

CCNP LAB 37

Border Gateway Protocol Lab

Lab Objective:

The focus of this lab is to understand BGP implementation and configuration in Cisco IOS routers. Additional technologies include route filtering and path control.

Lab Topology:

The lab network topology is illustrated below:

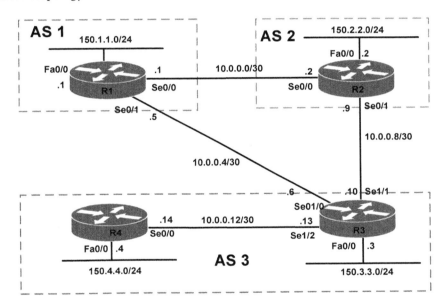

IMPORTANT NOTE: If you are using the www.howtonetwork.net racks, please bring up the LAN interfaces connected to the routers by issuing the no shutdown command on the connected switches. If you are using a home lab with no Switches, you can bring up the LAN interfaces using the following configurations on your routers:

```
interface fastethernet 0/0
  no keepalive
  loopback
  no shutdown
```

Alternately, you can simply connect the interfaces to a hub or switch if you have one available in your own lab.

Task 1

Configure hostnames and IP addressing on all routers as illustrated in the network topology.

Task 2

Configure BGP as illustrated in the topology. R1 will peer with R2 and R3. R2 will peer with R1 and R3. R3 will peer with R1, R2 and R4. R4 will peer only with R3. The routers should all use their physical interface addresses for BGP peering. Verify your configuration.

Task 3

Advertise the 150.x.x.x LAN subnets on all routers via BGP. These should be injected using the `network` command on all routers. Verify that all routers' LAN subnets can ping every other routers LAN subnet. Use an extended ping to perform this verification.

Task 4

Configure BGP so that R1 prefers the path via R2 to reach the 150.4.4.0/24 subnet. You are NOT allowed to make any changes on R1 or R2 when completing this task. Ensure that when R2 is down, R1 can still reach the 150.4.4.0/24 subnet. Verify your configuration using the appropriate commands and simulating a R2 failure.

Task 5

Configure the following Loopback interfaces on R1:
*   Loopback 192: IP Address 192.1.1.1/32
*   Loopback 193: IP Address 193.1.1.1/32

Advertise the 192.1.1.1/32 subnet only to R2. Ensure that this is NOT re-advertised to R3. Next, advertise the 193.1.1.1/32 subnet only to R3. Ensure that this is NOT re-advertised to R2 or R4.

Task 6

Configure BGP in such a way that R4 can reach the 192.1.1.1/32 and 193.1.1.1/32 from its local LAN subnet. You are allowed to configure on R1 to complete this task; however, do NOT modify the existing configuration. You are NOT allowed to configure any static routes when completing this task. Ensure that R4 can always reach these prefixes even if the R1-R3 or R2-R3 link is down. Verify your configuration by pinging from the 150.4.4.0/24 subnet to the 193.1.1.1/32 host address on R1.

LAB VALIDATION

Task 1

Please refer to previous labs for basic IP addressing and hostname configuration. This will not be included in this section to avoid being redundant.

Task 2

```
R1(config)#router bgp 1
R1(config-router)#bgp router-id 1.1.1.1
R1(config-router)#neighbor 10.0.0.2 remote-as 2
R1(config-router)#neighbor 10.0.0.6 remote-as 3
R1(config-router)#exit

R2(config)#router bgp 2
R2(config-router)#bgp router-id 2.2.2.2
R2(config-router)#neighbor 10.0.0.1 remote-as 1
R2(config-router)#neighbor 10.0.0.10 remote-as 3
R2(config-router)#exit

R3(config)#router bgp 3
R3(config-router)#bgp router-id 3.3.3.3
R3(config-router)#neighbor 10.0.0.5 remote-as 1
R3(config-router)#neighbor 10.0.0.9 remote-as 2
R3(config-router)#neighbor 10.0.0.14 remote-as 3
R3(config-router)#exit

R4(config)#router bgp 3
```

```
R4(config-router)#bgp router-id 4.4.4.4
R4(config-router)#neighbor 10.0.0.13 remote-as 3
R4(config-router)#exit
```

Verify your configuration using the show ip bgp summary command:

```
R1#show ip bgp summary
BGP router identifier 1.1.1.1, local AS number 1
BGP table version is 1, main routing table version 1

Neighbor      V   AS MsgRcvd MsgSent   TblVer  InQ OutQ Up/Down  State/PfxRcd
10.0.0.2      4    2     12      12        1    0    0 00:09:27         0
10.0.0.6      4    3     11      12        1    0    0 00:08:44         0

R2#show ip bgp summary
BGP router identifier 2.2.2.2, local AS number 2
BGP table version is 1, main routing table version 1

Neighbor      V   AS MsgRcvd MsgSent   TblVer  InQ OutQ Up/Down  State/PfxRcd
10.0.0.1      4    1     12      12        1    0    0 00:09:31         0
10.0.0.10     4    3     11      12        1    0    0 00:08:43         0

R3#show ip bgp summary
BGP router identifier 3.3.3.3, local AS number 3
BGP table version is 1, main routing table version 1

Neighbor      V   AS MsgRcvd MsgSent   TblVer  InQ OutQ Up/Down  State/PfxRcd
10.0.0.5      4    1     12      11        1    0    0 00:08:51         0
10.0.0.9      4    2     12      11        1    0    0 00:08:45         0
10.0.0.14     4    3     11      11        1    0    0 00:07:17         0

R4#show ip bgp summary
BGP router identifier 4.4.4.4, local AS number 3
BGP table version is 1, main routing table version 1

Neighbor      V   AS MsgRcvd MsgSent   TblVer  InQ OutQ Up/Down  State/PfxRcd
10.0.0.13     4    3     11      11        1    0    0 00:07:06         0
```

Task 3

```
R1(config)#router bgp 1
R1(config-router)#network 150.1.1.0 mask 255.255.255.0
R1(config-router)#exit

R2(config)#router bgp 2
R2(config-router)#network 150.2.2.0 mask 255.255.255.0
R2(config-router)#exit
```

Because R3 will be receiving prefixes from external peers (R1 and R2) and advertising those same prefixes to an internal peer (R4), you need to change the NEXT_HOP for the prefixes, otherwise R4 will not be able to reach them. The configuration to be implemented is as follows:

```
R3(config)#router bgp 3
R3(config-router)#network 150.3.3.0 mask 255.255.255.0
R3(config-router)#neighbor 10.0.0.14 next-hop-self
R3(config-router)#exit

R4(config)#router bgp 3
R4(config-router)#network 150.4.4.0 mask 255.255.255.0
R4(config-router)#exit
```

Verify your configuration using the show ip bgp command:

```
R1#show ip bgp
BGP table version is 5, local router ID is 1.1.1.1
Status codes: s suppressed, d damped, h history, * valid, > best, i - internal,
              r RIB-failure, S Stale
Origin codes: i - IGP, e - EGP, ? - incomplete
```

```
        Network          Next Hop          Metric LocPrf Weight Path
  *>  150.1.1.0/24     0.0.0.0                0            32768 i
  *   150.2.2.0/24     10.0.0.6                              0 3 2 i
  *>                   10.0.0.2               0              0 2 i
  *   150.3.3.0/24     10.0.0.2                              0 2 3 i
  *>                   10.0.0.6               0              0 3 i
  *   150.4.4.0/24     10.0.0.2                              0 2 3 i
  *>                   10.0.0.6                              0 3 i

R2#show ip bgp
BGP table version is 5, local router ID is 2.2.2.2
Status codes: s suppressed, d damped, h history, * valid, > best, i - internal,
              r RIB-failure, S Stale
Origin codes: i - IGP, e - EGP, ? - incomplete

        Network          Next Hop          Metric LocPrf Weight Path
  *   150.1.1.0/24     10.0.0.10                              0 3 1 i
  *>                   10.0.0.1               0              0 1 i
  *>  150.2.2.0/24     0.0.0.0                0            32768 i
  *   150.3.3.0/24     10.0.0.1                              0 1 3 i
  *>                   10.0.0.10              0              0 3 i
  *   150.4.4.0/24     10.0.0.1                              0 1 3 i
  *>                   10.0.0.10                              0 3 i

R3#show ip bgp
BGP table version is 5, local router ID is 3.3.3.3
Status codes: s suppressed, d damped, h history, * valid, > best, i - internal,
              r RIB-failure, S Stale
Origin codes: i - IGP, e - EGP, ? - incomplete

        Network          Next Hop          Metric LocPrf Weight Path
  *   150.1.1.0/24     10.0.0.9                               0 2 1 i
  *>                   10.0.0.5               0              0 1 i
  *   150.2.2.0/24     10.0.0.5                              0 1 2 i
  *>                   10.0.0.9               0              0 2 i
  *>  150.3.3.0/24     0.0.0.0                0            32768 i
  *>i150.4.4.0/24      10.0.0.14              0      100      0 i

R4#show ip bgp
BGP table version is 5, local router ID is 4.4.4.4
Status codes: s suppressed, d damped, h history, * valid, > best, i - internal,
              r RIB-failure, S Stale
Origin codes: i - IGP, e - EGP, ? - incomplete

        Network          Next Hop          Metric LocPrf Weight Path
  *>i150.1.1.0/24      10.0.0.13              0      100      0 1 i
  *>i150.2.2.0/24      10.0.0.13              0      100      0 2 i
  *>i150.3.3.0/24      10.0.0.13              0      100      0 i
  *>  150.4.4.0/24     0.0.0.0                0            32768 i
```

Finally, verify that you have LAN-to-LAN connectivity on all routers using extended pings:

```
1#ping 150.2.2.2 source fastethernet 0/0 repeat 10

Type escape sequence to abort.
Sending 10, 100-byte ICMP Echos to 150.2.2.2, timeout is 2 seconds:
Packet sent with a source address of 150.1.1.1
!!!!!!!!!!
Success rate is 100 percent (10/10), round-trip min/avg/max = 1/3/4 ms

R1#ping 150.3.3.3 source fastethernet 0/0 repeat 10

Type escape sequence to abort.
Sending 10, 100-byte ICMP Echos to 150.3.3.3, timeout is 2 seconds:
Packet sent with a source address of 150.1.1.1
!!!!!!!!!!
Success rate is 100 percent (10/10), round-trip min/avg/max = 16/16/16 ms

R1#ping 150.4.4.4 source fastethernet 0/0 repeat 10

Type escape sequence to abort.
Sending 10, 100-byte ICMP Echos to 150.4.4.4, timeout is 2 seconds:
```

```
Packet sent with a source address of 150.1.1.1
!!!!!!!!!!
Success rate is 100 percent (10/10), round-trip min/avg/max = 28/29/32 ms

R2#ping 150.1.1.1 source fastethernet 0/0 repeat 10

Type escape sequence to abort.
Sending 10, 100-byte ICMP Echos to 150.1.1.1, timeout is 2 seconds:
Packet sent with a source address of 150.2.2.2
!!!!!!!!!!
Success rate is 100 percent (10/10), round-trip min/avg/max = 1/3/4 ms

R2#ping 150.3.3.3 source fastethernet 0/0 repeat 10

Type escape sequence to abort.
Sending 10, 100-byte ICMP Echos to 150.3.3.3, timeout is 2 seconds:
Packet sent with a source address of 150.2.2.2
!!!!!!!!!!
Success rate is 100 percent (10/10), round-trip min/avg/max = 12/15/16 ms

R2#ping 150.4.4.4 source fastethernet 0/0 repeat 10

Type escape sequence to abort.
Sending 10, 100-byte ICMP Echos to 150.4.4.4, timeout is 2 seconds:
Packet sent with a source address of 150.2.2.2
!!!!!!!!!!
Success rate is 100 percent (10/10), round-trip min/avg/max = 28/29/32 ms

R3#ping 150.1.1.1 source fastethernet 0/0 repeat 10

Type escape sequence to abort.
Sending 10, 100-byte ICMP Echos to 150.1.1.1, timeout is 2 seconds:
Packet sent with a source address of 150.3.3.3
!!!!!!!!!!
Success rate is 100 percent (10/10), round-trip min/avg/max = 16/16/16 ms

R3#ping 150.2.2.2 source fastethernet 0/0 repeat 10

Type escape sequence to abort.
Sending 10, 100-byte ICMP Echos to 150.2.2.2, timeout is 2 seconds:
Packet sent with a source address of 150.3.3.3
!!!!!!!!!!
Success rate is 100 percent (10/10), round-trip min/avg/max = 16/16/16 ms

R3#ping 150.4.4.4 source fastethernet 0/0 repeat 10

Type escape sequence to abort.
Sending 10, 100-byte ICMP Echos to 150.4.4.4, timeout is 2 seconds:
Packet sent with a source address of 150.3.3.3
!!!!!!!!!!
Success rate is 100 percent (10/10), round-trip min/avg/max = 16/16/16 ms

R4#ping 150.1.1.1 source fastethernet 0/0 repeat 10

Type escape sequence to abort.
Sending 10, 100-byte ICMP Echos to 150.1.1.1, timeout is 2 seconds:
Packet sent with a source address of 150.4.4.4
!!!!!!!!!!
Success rate is 100 percent (10/10), round-trip min/avg/max = 28/30/32 ms

R4#ping 150.2.2.2 source fastethernet 0/0 repeat 10

Type escape sequence to abort.
Sending 10, 100-byte ICMP Echos to 150.2.2.2, timeout is 2 seconds:
Packet sent with a source address of 150.4.4.4
!!!!!!!!!!
Success rate is 100 percent (10/10), round-trip min/avg/max = 28/29/32 ms

R4#ping 150.3.3.3 source fastethernet 0/0 repeat 10

Type escape sequence to abort.
Sending 10, 100-byte ICMP Echos to 150.3.3.3, timeout is 2 seconds:
Packet sent with a source address of 150.4.4.4
!!!!!!!!!!
Success rate is 100 percent (10/10), round-trip min/avg/max = 12/15/16 ms
```

Task 4

Because the MED attribute is not compared when routes are received from multiple ASes, unless the `bgp always-compare-med` command is used, use AS_PATH prepending to complete this task. Prior to any changes, the BGP RIB on R1 shows the following entries:

```
R1#show ip bgp
BGP table version is 5, local router ID is 1.1.1.1
Status codes: s suppressed, d damped, h history, * valid, > best, i - internal,
              r RIB-failure, S Stale
Origin codes: i - IGP, e - EGP, ? - incomplete

     Network          Next Hop         Metric LocPrf Weight Path
*>   150.1.1.0/24     0.0.0.0               0         32768 i
*    150.2.2.0/24     10.0.0.6                            0 3 2 i
*>                    10.0.0.2              0             0 2 i
*    150.3.3.0/24     10.0.0.2                            0 2 3 i
*>                    10.0.0.6              0             0 3 i
*    150.4.4.0/24     10.0.0.2                            0 2 3 i
*>                    10.0.0.6                            0 3 i
```

NOTE: The greater than sign (>) indicates the current best path in the BGP RIB.

The current best path for 150.4.4.0/24 is via R3 because of the shorter AS_PATH. To complete this task, prepend the AS_PATH for this prefix on R3 for the neighbor relationship to R1:

```
R3(config)#ip prefix-list R4-LAN seq 5 permit 150.4.4.0/24
R3(config)#route-map PATH-CONTROL permit 10
R3(config-route-map)#match ip address prefix list R4-LAN
R3(config-route-map)#set as-path prepend 3 3
R3(config-route-map)#exit
R3(config)#route-map PATH-CONTROL permit 20
R3(config-route-map)#exit
R3(config)#router bgp 3
R3(config-router)#neighbor 10.0.0.5 route-map PATH-CONTROL out
R3(config-router)#exit
```

Following this configuration, the BGP Table on R1 shows the following for 150.4.4.0/24:

```
R1#show ip bgp
BGP table version is 7, local router ID is 1.1.1.1
Status codes: s suppressed, d damped, h history, * valid, > best, i - internal,
              r RIB-failure, S Stale
Origin codes: i - IGP, e - EGP, ? - incomplete

     Network          Next Hop         Metric LocPrf Weight Path
*>   150.1.1.0/24     0.0.0.0               0         32768 i
*    150.2.2.0/24     10.0.0.6                            0 3 3 3 2 i
*>                    10.0.0.2              0             0 2 i
*>   150.3.3.0/24     10.0.0.2                            0 2 3 i
*                     10.0.0.6              0             0 3 3 3 i
*>   150.4.4.0/24     10.0.0.2                            0 2 3 i
*                     10.0.0.6                            0 3 3 3 i
```

Next, verify that R1 and R4 can still ping each other LAN-to-LAN using an extended ping:

```
R1#ping 150.4.4.4 source fastethernet 0/0 repeat 10

Type escape sequence to abort.
Sending 10, 100-byte ICMP Echos to 150.4.4.4, timeout is 2 seconds:
Packet sent with a source address of 150.1.1.1
!!!!!!!!!!
Success rate is 100 percent (10/10), round-trip min/avg/max = 28/35/84 ms
```

Finally, test the redundancy by disabling the R1-R2 WAN link and ensuring that R1 can still ping the 150.4.4.0/24 subnet:

```
R1(config)#interface serial 0/0
R1(config-if)#shutdown
R1(config-if)#exit
R1(config)#do show ip bgp 150.4.4.0 255.255.255.0
BGP routing table entry for 150.4.4.0/24, version 10
Paths: (1 available, best #1, table Default-IP-Routing-Table)
  Advertised to update-groups:
     1
  3 3 3
    10.0.0.6 from 10.0.0.6 (3.3.3.3)
      Origin IGP, localpref 100, valid, external, best
R1(config)#
R1(config)#do ping 150.4.4.4 source fastethernet 0/0 repeat 10

Type escape sequence to abort.
Sending 10, 100-byte ICMP Echos to 150.4.4.4, timeout is 2 seconds:
Packet sent with a source address of 150.1.1.1
!!!!!!!!!!
Success rate is 100 percent (10/10), round-trip min/avg/max = 28/29/32 ms
```

Task 5

This task requires some thought and is three-fold. The configuration of the Loopback interfaces on router R1 is straightforward. The second part of the task is to advertise the 192.1.1.1/32 address to R2 only and then the 193.1.1.1/32 address to R3 only. This requires the use of route maps in conjunction with IP ACLs or prefix lists. The reason route maps are used in because of the third required, which will be illustrated later. This second part is completed as follows:

```
R1(config)#interface loopback 192
R1(config-if)#ip address 192.1.1.1 255.255.255.255
R1(config-if)#exit
R1(config)#interface loopback 193
R1(config-if)#ip addres 193.1.1.1 255.255.255.255
R1(config-if)#exit
R1(config)#ip prefix-list LOOPBACK192 seq 5 permit 192.1.1.1/32
R1(config)#ip prefix-list LOOPBACK193 seq 5 permit 193.1.1.1/32
R1(config)#route-map R2-OUTBOUND deny 10
R1(config-route-map)#match ip address prefix-list LOOPBACK193
R1(config-route-map)#exit
R1(config)#route-map R2-OUTBOUND permit 20
R1(config-route-map)#exit
R1(config)#route-map R3-OUTBOUND deny 10
R1(config-route-map)#match ip address prefix-list LOOPBACK192
R1(config-route-map)#exit
R1(config)#route-map R3-OUTBOUND permit 20
R1(config-route-map)#exit
R1(config)#router bgp 1
R1(config-router)#network 192.1.1.1 mask 255.255.255.255
R1(config-router)#network 193.1.1.1 mask 255.255.255.255
R1(config-router)#neighbor 10.0.0.2 route-map R2-OUTBOUND out
R1(config-router)#neighbor 10.0.0.6 route-map R3-OUTBOUND out
R1(config-router)#exit
```

Verify the configuration using the show ip bgp neighbors <address> advertised-routes command on R1 to see the prefixes advertised to R2 and R3:

```
R1#show ip bgp neighbors 10.0.0.2 advertised-routes
BGP table version is 15, local router ID is 1.1.1.1
Status codes: s suppressed, d damped, h history, * valid, > best, i - internal,
              r RIB-failure, S Stale
Origin codes: i - IGP, e - EGP, ? - incomplete

   Network          Next Hop            Metric LocPrf Weight Path
*> 150.1.1.0/24     0.0.0.0                  0         32768 i
*> 192.1.1.1/32     0.0.0.0                  0         32768 i

Total number of prefixes 2

R1#show ip bgp neighbor 10.0.0.6 advertised-routes
BGP table version is 15, local router ID is 1.1.1.1
Status codes: s suppressed, d damped, h history, * valid, > best, i - internal,
              r RIB-failure, S Stale
```

```
Origin codes: i - IGP, e - EGP, ? - incomplete

    Network          Next Hop          Metric LocPrf Weight Path
*>  150.1.1.0/24     0.0.0.0               0          32768 i
*>  150.2.2.0/24     10.0.0.2              0              0 2 i
*>  150.3.3.0/24     10.0.0.2                            0 2 3 i
*>  150.4.4.0/24     10.0.0.2                            0 2 3 i
*>  193.1.1.1/32     0.0.0.0               0          32768 i
```

The third part of this task requires the use of the COMMUNITY attribute. The BGP well-known communities are communities that have predefined meanings. Cisco IOS software supports four well-known communities which are:

- NO_EXPORT
- NO_ADVERTISE
- INTERNET
- LOCAL_AS

The NO_EXPORT well-known community prevents BGP prefixes that are specifically assigned this predefined community attribute value from being advertised to any eBGP peers. The prefixes, however, will continue to be advertised to all other BGP speakers within the local AS. In other words, prefixes assigned this community value will remain local to the AS.

The NO_ADVERTISE community prevents any prefixes that are assigned this predefined community attribute from being advertised to any peer – internal or external.

The INTERNET community allows all prefixes assigned to this community to be advertised to any and all BGP peers (assuming no filtering, etc, is in place). In Cisco IOS software, all BGP prefixes belong to the INTERNET community by default.

And finally, the LOCAL_AS community is used in a somewhat similar manner to another of the previously described communities: the NO_EXPORT community. If used in a Confederation, the LOCAL_AS community prevents all prefixes assigned this community from being advertised out of the local sub autonomous system. When Confederations are not implemented, the LOCAL_AS community is applied in the same manner as the NO_EXPORT community.

This task is therefore completed by modifying the existing configuration as follows:

```
R1(config)#route-map R2-OUTBOUND permit 20
R1(config-route-map)#match ip address prefix-list LOOPBACK192
R1(config-route-map)#set community no-advertise
R1(config-route-map)#exit
R1(config)#route-map R2-OUTBOUND permit 30
R1(config-route-map)#exit
R1(config)#route-map R3-OUTBOUND permit 20
R1(config-route-map)#match ip address prefix-list LOOPBACK193
R1(config-route-map)#set community no-advertise
R1(config-route-map)#exit
R1(config)#route-map R3-OUTBOUND permit 30
R1(config-route-map)#exit
R1(config)#router bgp 1
R1(config-router)#neighbor 10.0.0.2 send-community standard
R1(config-router)#neighbor 10.0.0.6 send-community standard
R1(config-router)#end
R1#
R1#clear ip bgp * soft out
```

Next, verify that these prefixes are received by R2 and R3 and are not re-advertised as required:

```
R2#show ip bgp
BGP table version is 11, local router ID is 2.2.2.2
Status codes: s suppressed, d damped, h history, * valid, > best, i - internal,
```

```
              r RIB-failure, S Stale
Origin codes: i - IGP, e - EGP, ? - incomplete

      Network         Next Hop      Metric LocPrf Weight Path
*>  150.1.1.0/24      10.0.0.1         0              0 1 i
*                     10.0.0.10                       0 3 1 i
*>  150.2.2.0/24      0.0.0.0          0          32768 i
*>  150.3.3.0/24      10.0.0.10        0              0 3 i
*>  150.4.4.0/24      10.0.0.10                       0 3 i
*>  192.1.1.1/32      10.0.0.1         0              0 1 i
```

Use the **show ip bgp <network> <mask>** command to view all attribute information:

```
R2#show ip bgp 192.1.1.1 255.255.255.255
BGP routing table entry for 192.1.1.1/32, version 10
Paths: (1 available, best #1, table Default-IP-Routing-Table, not advertised to any
peer)
  Not advertised to any peer
  1
    10.0.0.1 from 10.0.0.1 (1.1.1.1)
      Origin IGP, metric 0, localpref 100, valid, external, best
      Community: no-advertise
```

The BGP RIB on R3 shows the following entries:

```
R3#show ip bgp
BGP table version is 9, local router ID is 3.3.3.3
Status codes: s suppressed, d damped, h history, * valid, > best, i - internal,
              r RIB-failure, S Stale
Origin codes: i - IGP, e - EGP, ? - incomplete

      Network         Next Hop      Metric LocPrf Weight Path
*   150.1.1.0/24      10.0.0.9                        0 2 1 i
*>                    10.0.0.5         0              0 1 i
*   150.2.2.0/24      10.0.0.5         0              0 1 2 i
*>                    10.0.0.9         0              0 2 i
*>  150.3.3.0/24      0.0.0.0          0          32768 i
*>i 150.4.4.0/24      10.0.0.14        0    100       0 i
*>  193.1.1.1/32      10.0.0.5         0              0 1 i
```

Use the show ip bgp <network> <mask> command to view all attribute information:

```
R3#show ip bgp 193.1.1.1 255.255.255.255
BGP routing table entry for 193.1.1.1/32, version 9
Paths: (1 available, best #1, table Default-IP-Routing-Table, not advertised to any
peer)
  Not advertised to any peer
  1
    10.0.0.5 from 10.0.0.5 (1.1.1.1)
      Origin IGP, metric 0, localpref 100, valid, external, best
      Community: no-advertise
```

The BGP RIB on R4 should have NO entries for the 192.1.1.1/32 or 193.1.1.1/32 prefixes:

```
R4#show ip bgp
BGP table version is 9, local router ID is 4.4.4.4
Status codes: s suppressed, d damped, h history, * valid, > best, i - internal,
              r RIB-failure, S Stale
Origin codes: i - IGP, e - EGP, ? - incomplete

      Network         Next Hop      Metric LocPrf Weight Path
*>i 150.1.1.0/24      10.0.0.13        0    100       0 1 i
*>i 150.2.2.0/24      10.0.0.13        0    100       0 2 i
*>i 150.3.3.0/24      10.0.0.13        0    100       0 i
*>  150.4.4.0/24      0.0.0.0          0          32768 i
```

Task 6

To complete this task, configure R1 to advertise a default route to R2 and R3. This will allow R4 to always reach these two prefixes when either the R1-R3 or R2-R3 link is down:

```
R1(config)#router bgp 1
R1(config-router)#neighbor 10.0.0.2 default-originate
R1(config-router)#neighbor 10.0.0.6 default-originate
R1(config-router)#exit
```

Verify that the default route exists in R4s BGP RIB using the show ip bgp command:

```
4#show ip bgp 0.0.0.0 0.0.0.0
BGP routing table entry for 0.0.0.0/0, version 11
Paths: (1 available, best #1, table Default-IP-Routing-Table)
Flag: 0x820
  Not advertised to any peer
  1
    10.0.0.13 from 10.0.0.13 (3.3.3.3)
      Origin IGP, metric 0, localpref 100, valid, internal, best
```

Next, ping the 192.1.1.1/32 and 193.1.1.1/32 prefixes from R4s LAN subnet address:

```
R4#ping 192.1.1.1 source fastethernet 0/0 repeat 10

Type escape sequence to abort.
Sending 10, 100-byte ICMP Echos to 192.1.1.1, timeout is 2 seconds:
Packet sent with a source address of 150.4.4.4
!!!!!!!!!!
Success rate is 100 percent (10/10), round-trip min/avg/max = 28/30/32 ms

R4#ping 193.1.1.1 source fastethernet 0/0 repeat 10

Type escape sequence to abort.
Sending 10, 100-byte ICMP Echos to 193.1.1.1, timeout is 2 seconds:
Packet sent with a source address of 150.4.4.4
!!!!!!!!!!
Success rate is 100 percent (10/10), round-trip min/avg/max = 28/30/32 ms
```

Finally, test BGP redundancy by shutting down the R1-R3 link and performing the same test:

```
R4#show ip bgp 0.0.0.0 0.0.0.0
BGP routing table entry for 0.0.0.0/0, version 13
Paths: (1 available, best #1, table Default-IP-Routing-Table)
Flag: 0x820
  Not advertised to any peer
  2 1
    10.0.0.13 from 10.0.0.13 (3.3.3.3)
      Origin IGP, metric 0, localpref 100, valid, internal, best

R4#ping 192.1.1.1 source fastethernet 0/0 repeat 10

Type escape sequence to abort.
Sending 10, 100-byte ICMP Echos to 192.1.1.1, timeout is 2 seconds:
Packet sent with a source address of 150.4.4.4
!!!!!!!!!!
Success rate is 100 percent (10/10), round-trip min/avg/max = 28/30/32 ms

R4#ping 193.1.1.1 source fastethernet 0/0 repeat 10

Type escape sequence to abort.
Sending 10, 100-byte ICMP Echos to 193.1.1.1, timeout is 2 seconds:
Packet sent with a source address of 150.4.4.4
!!!!!!!!!!
Success rate is 100 percent (10/10), round-trip min/avg/max = 28/31/32 ms
```

FINAL ROUTER CONFIGURATIONS

R1

```
R1#term len 0
R1#sh run
Building configuration...

Current configuration : 1995 bytes
!
version 12.4
service timestamps debug datetime msec
service timestamps log datetime msec
no service password-encryption
!
hostname R1
!
boot-start-marker
boot-end-marker
!
no logging console
!
no aaa new-model
no network-clock-participate slot 1
no network-clock-participate wic 0
ip cef
!
no ip domain lookup
ip auth-proxy max-nodata-conns 3
ip admission max-nodata-conns 3
!
interface Loopback192
 ip address 192.1.1.1 255.255.255.255
!
interface Loopback193
 ip address 193.1.1.1 255.255.255.255
!
interface FastEthernet0/0
 ip address 150.1.1.1 255.255.255.0
 duplex auto
 speed auto
!
interface Serial0/0
 ip address 10.0.0.1 255.255.255.252
 clock rate 2000000
!
interface Serial0/1
 ip address 10.0.0.5 255.255.255.252
!
router bgp 1
 no synchronization
 bgp router-id 1.1.1.1
 bgp log-neighbor-changes
 network 150.1.1.0 mask 255.255.255.0
 network 192.1.1.1 mask 255.255.255.255
 network 193.1.1.1 mask 255.255.255.255
 neighbor 10.0.0.2 remote-as 2
 neighbor 10.0.0.2 send-community
 neighbor 10.0.0.2 default-originate
 neighbor 10.0.0.2 route-map R2-OUTBOUND out
 neighbor 10.0.0.6 remote-as 3
 neighbor 10.0.0.6 send-community
 neighbor 10.0.0.6 default-originate
 neighbor 10.0.0.6 route-map R3-OUTBOUND out
 no auto-summary
!
ip forward-protocol nd
!
no ip http server
no ip http secure-server
!
ip prefix-list LOOPBACK192 seq 5 permit 192.1.1.1/32
!
```

```
ip prefix-list LOOPBACK193 seq 5 permit 193.1.1.1/32
!
route-map R3-OUTBOUND deny 10
 match ip address prefix-list LOOPBACK192
!
route-map R3-OUTBOUND permit 20
 match ip address prefix-list LOOPBACK193
 set community no-advertise
!
route-map R3-OUTBOUND permit 30
!
route-map R2-OUTBOUND deny 10
 match ip address prefix-list LOOPBACK193
!
route-map R2-OUTBOUND permit 20
 match ip address prefix-list LOOPBACK192
 set community no-advertise
!
route-map R2-OUTBOUND permit 30
!
control-plane
!
line con 0
line aux 0
line vty 0 4
 login
!
end

R1#
```

R2

```
R2#term len 0
R2#sh run
Building configuration...

Current configuration : 1006 bytes
!
version 12.4
service timestamps debug datetime msec
service timestamps log datetime msec
no service password-encryption
!
hostname R2
!
boot-start-marker
boot-end-marker
!
no logging console
!
no aaa new-model
no network-clock-participate slot 1
no network-clock-participate wic 0
ip cef
!
no ip domain lookup
ip auth-proxy max-nodata-conns 3
ip admission max-nodata-conns 3
!
!
interface FastEthernet0/0
 ip address 150.2.2.2 255.255.255.0
 duplex auto
 speed auto
!
interface Serial0/0
 ip address 10.0.0.2 255.255.255.252
!
interface Serial0/1
 ip address 10.0.0.9 255.255.255.252
!
router bgp 2
```

```
 no synchronization
 bgp router-id 2.2.2.2
 bgp log-neighbor-changes
 network 150.2.2.0 mask 255.255.255.0
 neighbor 10.0.0.1 remote-as 1
 neighbor 10.0.0.10 remote-as 3
 no auto-summary
!
ip forward-protocol nd
!
no ip http server
no ip http secure-server
!
control-plane
!
line con 0
line aux 0
line vty 0 4
 login
!
end

R2#
```

R3

```
R3#term len 0
R3#sh run
Building configuration...

Current configuration : 1667 bytes
!
version 12.4
service timestamps debug datetime msec
service timestamps log datetime msec
no service password-encryption
!
hostname R3
!
boot-start-marker
boot-end-marker
!
no logging console
!
no aaa new-model
no network-clock-participate slot 1
no network-clock-participate wic 0
ip cef
!
no ip domain lookup
ip auth-proxy max-nodata-conns 3
ip admission max-nodata-conns 3
!
interface FastEthernet0/0
 ip address 150.3.3.3 255.255.255.0
 duplex auto
 speed auto
!
interface Serial1/0
 ip address 10.0.0.6 255.255.255.252
 shutdown
 clock rate 128000
!
interface Serial1/1
 ip address 10.0.0.10 255.255.255.252
 clock rate 128000
!
interface Serial1/2
 ip address 10.0.0.13 255.255.255.252
 clock rate 128000
!
interface Serial1/3
 no ip address
 shutdown
```

```
!
interface Serial1/4
 no ip address
 shutdown
!
interface Serial1/5
 no ip address
 shutdown
!
interface Serial1/6
 no ip address
 shutdown
!
interface Serial1/7
 no ip address
 shutdown
!
router bgp 3
 no synchronization
 bgp router-id 3.3.3.3
 bgp log-neighbor-changes
 network 150.3.3.0 mask 255.255.255.0
 neighbor 10.0.0.5 remote-as 1
 neighbor 10.0.0.5 route-map PATH-CONTROL out
 neighbor 10.0.0.9 remote-as 2
 neighbor 10.0.0.14 remote-as 3
 neighbor 10.0.0.14 next-hop-self
 no auto-summary
!
ip forward-protocol nd
!
no ip http server
no ip http secure-server
!
ip prefix-list R4-LAN seq 5 permit 150.4.4.0/24
!
route-map PATH-CONTROL permit 10
 match ip address prefix-list list R4-LAN
 set as-path prepend 3 3
!
route-map PATH-CONTROL permit 20
!
control-plane
!
line con 0
line aux 0
line vty 0 4
 login
!
end

R3#
```

R4

```
R4#term len 0
R4#sh run
Building configuration...

Current configuration : 964 bytes
!
version 12.4
service timestamps debug datetime msec
service timestamps log datetime msec
no service password-encryption
!
hostname R4
!
boot-start-marker
boot-end-marker
!
no logging console
!
no aaa new-model
```

```
no network-clock-participate slot 1
no network-clock-participate wic 0
ip cef
!
no ip domain lookup
ip auth-proxy max-nodata-conns 3
ip admission max-nodata-conns 3
!
interface FastEthernet0/0
 ip address 150.4.4.4 255.255.255.0
 duplex auto
 speed auto
!
interface Serial0/0
 ip address 10.0.0.14 255.255.255.252
!
interface Serial0/1
 no ip address
 shutdown
!
router bgp 3
 no synchronization
 bgp router-id 4.4.4.4
 bgp log-neighbor-changes
 network 150.4.4.0 mask 255.255.255.0
 neighbor 10.0.0.13 remote-as 3
 no auto-summary
!
ip forward-protocol nd
!
no ip http server
no ip http secure-server
!
control-plane
!
line con 0
line aux 0
line vty 0 4
 login
!
end

R4#
```

CCNP LAB 38

Border Gateway Protocol Lab

Lab Objective:

The focus of this lab is to understand BGP implementation and configuration in Cisco IOS routers. Additional technologies include route filtering and path control.

Lab Topology:

The lab network topology is illustrated below:

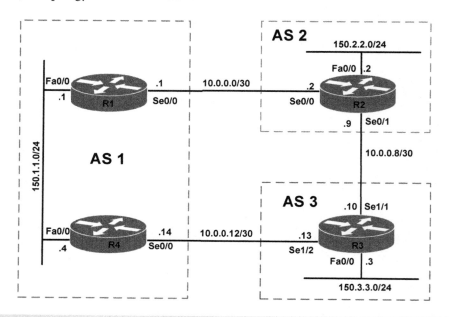

IMPORTANT NOTE: If you are using the www.howtonetwork.net racks, please bring up the LAN interfaces connected to the routers by issuing the no shutdown command on the connected switches. If you are using a home lab with no Switches, you can bring up the LAN interfaces using the following configurations on your routers:

```
interface fastethernet 0/0
  no keepalive
  loopback
  no shutdown
```

Alternately, you can simply connect the interfaces to a hub or switch if you have one available in your own lab.

Task 1

Configure hostnames and IP addressing on all routers as illustrated in the network topology.

Task 2

Configure BGP as illustrated in the topology. R1 will peer with R2. R2 will peer with R1 and R3. R3 will peer with R4. Do NOT peer R1 and R4 even though they exist in the same AS. Verify the configuration using the appropriate commands.

Task 3

Advertise the 150.2.2.0/24 and 150.3.3.0/24 prefixes connected to R2 and R3, respectively, using BGP. Do NOT advertise the 150.1.1.0/24 subnet connected to R1 and R4. However, ensure that both R2 and R3 can still ping this subnet. You are NOT allowed to use static routes. Verify your configuration using an extended ping from the LAN subnets connected to R2 and R3 to the 150.1.1.0/24 subnet connected to R1 and R4.

Task 4

Configure BGP so that R3 prefers the path via R2 to reach the 150.1.1.0/24 subnet. You are only allowed to configure a device in AS 1. You are NOT allowed to advertise the 150.1.1.0/24 prefix when completing this task. Verify your configuration and ensure that R2 and R3 can still ping the 150.1.1.1/24 and 150.1.1.4/24 addresses when complete. Use an extended ping that is sourced from R3s LAN IP address.

Task 5

Configure OSPF on the LAN subnet between R1 and R4. Next, configure AS 1 so that R4 will prefer the path via R1 to reach the 150.2.2.0/24 or 150.3.3.0/24 subnets. In the event that the WAN link between R1 and R2 is down, the path via R4 should be used instead. You are NOT allowed to establish an iBGP neighbor relationship between R1 and R4 to complete this task. Additionally, you are not allowed to use the distance command to modify any protocol administrative distance values. Instead, use a BGP feature when completing this task. Verify your configuration using the appropriate commands. Ensure R4 can still ping the 150.2.2.0/24 and the 150.3.3.0/24 subnets when complete.

HINT: Use the BGP network command to complete this task.

LAB VALIDATION

Task 1

Please refer to previous labs for basic IP addressing and hostname configuration. This will not be included in this section to avoid being redundant.

Task 2

```
R1(config)#router bgp 1
R1(config-router)#bgp router-id 1.1.1.1
R1(config-router)#neighbor 10.0.0.2 remote-as 2
R1(config-router)#exit

R2(config)#router bgp 2
R2(config-router)#bgp router-id 2.2.2.2
R2(config-router)#neighbor 10.0.0.1 remote-as 1
R2(config-router)#neighbor 10.0.0.10 remote-as 3
R2(config-router)#exit

R3(config)#router bgp 3
R3(config-router)#bgp router-id 3.3.3.3
R3(config-router)#neighbor 10.0.0.9 remote-as 2
R3(config-router)#neighbor 10.0.0.14 remote-as 1
R3(config-router)#exit

R4(config)#router bgp 1
R4(config-router)#bgp router-id 4.4.4.4
R4(config-router)#neighbor 10.0.0.13 remote-as 3
R4(config-router)#exit
```

Verify your configuration using the `show ip bgp summary` command:

```
R1#show ip bgp summary
BGP router identifier 1.1.1.1, local AS number 1
BGP table version is 1, main routing table version 1

Neighbor      V     AS MsgRcvd MsgSent    TblVer  InQ OutQ Up/Down  State/PfxRcd
10.0.0.2      4      2       7       7         1    0    0 00:05:00            0

R2#show ip bgp summary
BGP router identifier 2.2.2.2, local AS number 2
BGP table version is 1, main routing table version 1

Neighbor      V     AS MsgRcvd MsgSent    TblVer  InQ OutQ Up/Down  State/PfxRcd
10.0.0.1      4      1       8       8         1    0    0 00:05:03            0
10.0.0.10     4      3       6       7         1    0    0 00:03:31            0

R3#show ip bgp summary
BGP router identifier 3.3.3.3, local AS number 3
BGP table version is 1, main routing table version 1

Neighbor      V     AS MsgRcvd MsgSent    TblVer  InQ OutQ Up/Down  State/PfxRcd
10.0.0.9      4      2       7       6         1    0    0 00:03:35            0
10.0.0.14     4      1       6       6         1    0    0 00:02:41            0

R4#show ip bgp summary
BGP router identifier 4.4.4.4, local AS number 1
BGP table version is 1, main routing table version 1

Neighbor      V     AS MsgRcvd MsgSent    TblVer  InQ OutQ Up/Down  State/PfxRcd
10.0.0.13     4      3       6       6         1    0    0 00:02:30            0
```

Task 3

To complete this task, you need to configure R1 and R4 to advertise defaults to R2 and R3:

```
R2(config)#router bgp 2
R2(config-router)#network 150.2.2.0 mask 255.255.255.0
R2(config-router)#exit

R3(config)#router bgp 3
R3(config-router)#network 150.3.3.0 mask 255.255.255.0
R3(config-router)#exit

R1(config)#router bgp 1
R1(config-router)#neighbor 10.0.0.2 default-originate
R1(config-router)#exit

R4(config)#router bgp 1
R4(config-router)#neighbor 10.0.0.13 default-originate
R4(config-router)#exit
```

Next, verify your configuration using the **show ip bgp** command:

```
R1#show ip bgp
BGP table version is 3, local router ID is 1.1.1.1
Status codes: s suppressed, d damped, h history, * valid, > best, i - internal,
              r RIB-failure, S Stale
Origin codes: i - IGP, e - EGP, ? - incomplete

   Network          Next Hop            Metric LocPrf Weight Path
*> 150.2.2.0/24     10.0.0.2                 0             0 2 i
*> 150.3.3.0/24     10.0.0.2                               0 2 3 i

R2#show ip bgp
BGP table version is 4, local router ID is 2.2.2.2
Status codes: s suppressed, d damped, h history, * valid, > best, i - internal,
              r RIB-failure, S Stale
Origin codes: i - IGP, e - EGP, ? - incomplete
```

```
     Network          Next Hop         Metric LocPrf Weight Path
*    0.0.0.0          10.0.0.10                         0 3 1 i
*>                    10.0.0.1          0                0 1 i
*>   150.2.2.0/24     0.0.0.0           0            32768 i
*>   150.3.3.0/24     10.0.0.10         0                0 3 i

R3#show ip bgp
BGP table version is 5, local router ID is 3.3.3.3
Status codes: s suppressed, d damped, h history, * valid, > best, i - internal,
              r RIB-failure, S Stale
Origin codes: i - IGP, e - EGP, ? - incomplete

     Network          Next Hop         Metric LocPrf Weight Path
*>   0.0.0.0          10.0.0.14         0                0 1 i
*                     10.0.0.9                           0 2 1 i
*>   150.2.2.0/24     10.0.0.9          0                0 2 i
*>   150.3.3.0/24     0.0.0.0           0            32768 i

R4#show ip bgp
BGP table version is 3, local router ID is 4.4.4.4
Status codes: s suppressed, d damped, h history, * valid, > best, i - internal,
              r RIB-failure, S Stale
Origin codes: i - IGP, e - EGP, ? - incomplete

     Network          Next Hop         Metric LocPrf Weight Path
*>   150.2.2.0/24     10.0.0.13                         0 3 2 i
*>   150.3.3.0/24     10.0.0.13         0                0 3 i
```

Finally, verify that R2 and R3 can ping the 150.1.1.1/24 and 150.1.1.4/24 addresses from their respective LAN addresses using an extended ping:

```
R2#ping 150.1.1.1 source fastethernet 0/0 repeat 10

Type escape sequence to abort.
Sending 10, 100-byte ICMP Echos to 150.1.1.1, timeout is 2 seconds:
Packet sent with a source address of 150.2.2.2
!!!!!!!!!!
Success rate is 100 percent (10/10), round-trip min/avg/max = 1/2/4 ms

R2#ping 150.1.1.4 source fastethernet 0/0 repeat 10

Type escape sequence to abort.
Sending 10, 100-byte ICMP Echos to 150.1.1.4, timeout is 2 seconds:
Packet sent with a source address of 150.2.2.2
!!!!!!!!!!
Success rate is 100 percent (10/10), round-trip min/avg/max = 16/16/20 ms

R3#ping 150.1.1.1 source fastethernet 0/0 repeat 10

Type escape sequence to abort.
Sending 10, 100-byte ICMP Echos to 150.1.1.1, timeout is 2 seconds:
Packet sent with a source address of 150.3.3.3
!!!!!!!!!!
Success rate is 100 percent (10/10), round-trip min/avg/max = 16/16/20 ms

R3#ping 150.1.1.4 source fastethernet 0/0 repeat 10

Type escape sequence to abort.
Sending 10, 100-byte ICMP Echos to 150.1.1.4, timeout is 2 seconds:
Packet sent with a source address of 150.3.3.3
!!!!!!!!!!
Success rate is 100 percent (10/10), round-trip min/avg/max = 16/16/16 ms
```

Task 4

To complete this task, you need to use a route map and AS_PATH prepending to make the default route advertised by R4 longer than that advertised by R1. This route-map should be applied to the default route advertised to R3. This task is completed as follows:

```
R4(config)#route-map PREPEND permit 10
R4(config-route-map)#set as-path prepend 1 1 1 1
```

```
R4(config-route-map)#exit
R4(config)#router bgp 1
R4(config-router)#neighbor 10.0.0.13 default-originate route-map PREPEND
R4(config-router)#exit
```

Following this change, verify the BGP Table on R3 to ensure the preferred default is via R2:

```
R3#show ip bgp
BGP table version is 6, local router ID is 3.3.3.3
Status codes: s suppressed, d damped, h history, * valid, > best, i - internal,
              r RIB-failure, S Stale
Origin codes: i - IGP, e - EGP, ? - incomplete

     Network          Next Hop            Metric LocPrf Weight Path
 *   0.0.0.0          10.0.0.14                0             0 1 1 1 1 1 i
 *>                   10.0.0.9                               0 2 1 i
 *>  150.2.2.0/24     10.0.0.9                 0             0 2 i
 *>  150.3.3.0/24     0.0.0.0                  0         32768 i
```

Finally, verify that R3 can still ping the 150.1.1.1/24 and 150.1.1.4/24 addresses after the change:

```
R3#ping 150.1.1.1 source fastethernet 0/0 repeat 10

Type escape sequence to abort.
Sending 10, 100-byte ICMP Echos to 150.1.1.1, timeout is 2 seconds:
Packet sent with a source address of 150.3.3.3
!!!!!!!!!!
Success rate is 100 percent (10/10), round-trip min/avg/max = 16/18/28 ms

R3#ping 150.1.1.4 source fastethernet 0/0 repeat 10

Type escape sequence to abort.
Sending 10, 100-byte ICMP Echos to 150.1.1.4, timeout is 2 seconds:
Packet sent with a source address of 150.3.3.3
!!!!!!!!!!
Success rate is 100 percent (10/10), round-trip min/avg/max = 16/16/16 ms
```

Task 5

The requirements of this task are threefold. First, you need to enable OSPF between R1 and R4 across their directly connected LAN segment. Following this configuration, verify the OSPF adjacency between the routers using the show ip ospf neighbor command. You can refer to previous labs for OSPF configuration basics.

```
R1#show ip ospf neighbor

Neighbor ID   Pri   State     Dead Time   Address      Interface
4.4.4.4         1   FULL/BDR  00:00:37    150.1.1.4    FastEthernet0/0

R4#show ip ospf neighbor

Neighbor ID   Pri   State     Dead Time   Address      Interface
1.1.1.1         1   FULL/DR   00:00:39    150.1.1.1    FastEthernet0/0
```

The second part of this task entails redistribution between OSPF and BGP. This allows the LAN subnets connected to R2 and R4 to be advertised across the LAN link connecting R1 and R2. You do NOT need to redistribute OSPF routes into BGP, otherwise you will advertise the LAN subnet between R1 and R4, which is NOT permitted as stated in previous tasks:

```
R1(config)#router ospf 1
R1(config-router)#redistribute bgp 1 subnets
R1(config-router)#exit

R4(config)#router ospf 4
R4(config-router)#redistribute bgp 1 subnets
R4(config-router)#exit
```

Following this configuration, verify that the routing tables on both routers show all routes:

```
R1#show ip route
Codes: C - connected, S - static, R - RIP, M - mobile, B - BGP
       D - EIGRP, EX - EIGRP external, O - OSPF, IA - OSPF inter area
       N1 - OSPF NSSA external type 1, N2 - OSPF NSSA external type 2
       E1 - OSPF external type 1, E2 - OSPF external type 2
       i - IS-IS, su - IS-IS summary, L1 - IS-IS level-1, L2 - IS-IS level-2
       ia - IS-IS inter area, * - candidate default, U - per-user static route
       o - ODR, P - periodic downloaded static route

Gateway of last resort is not set

     10.0.0.0/30 is subnetted, 1 subnets
C       10.0.0.0 is directly connected, Serial0/0
     150.1.0.0/24 is subnetted, 1 subnets
C       150.1.1.0 is directly connected, FastEthernet0/0
     150.2.0.0/24 is subnetted, 1 subnets
B       150.2.2.0 [20/0] via 10.0.0.2, 00:28:43
     150.3.0.0/24 is subnetted, 1 subnets
B       150.3.3.0 [20/0] via 10.0.0.2, 00:29:14

R4#show ip route
Codes: C - connected, S - static, R - RIP, M - mobile, B - BGP
       D - EIGRP, EX - EIGRP external, O - OSPF, IA - OSPF inter area
       N1 - OSPF NSSA external type 1, N2 - OSPF NSSA external type 2
       E1 - OSPF external type 1, E2 - OSPF external type 2
       i - IS-IS, su - IS-IS summary, L1 - IS-IS level-1, L2 - IS-IS level-2
       ia - IS-IS inter area, * - candidate default, U - per-user static route
       o - ODR, P - periodic downloaded static route

Gateway of last resort is not set

     10.0.0.0/30 is subnetted, 1 subnets
C       10.0.0.12 is directly connected, Serial0/0
     150.1.0.0/24 is subnetted, 1 subnets
C       150.1.1.0 is directly connected, FastEthernet0/0
     150.2.0.0/24 is subnetted, 1 subnets
B       150.2.2.0 [20/0] via 10.0.0.13, 00:07:07
     150.3.0.0/24 is subnetted, 1 subnets
B       150.3.3.0 [20/0] via 10.0.0.13, 00:29:10
```

As illustrated in the output above, both routers prefer the BGP routes because of the lower administrative distance of external BGP (20) versus OSPF (110). To complete this task, use the hint provided in the lab, which states that you should use the BGP network command.

The correct command to use in this case would be network <address> <mask> backdoor command. The backdoor keyword configures the router to change the administrative distance of the specified external BGP route from 20 to 200. This allows IGP routes to be preferred instead. When the IGP routes are no longer present in the routing table, the BGP route is again used. This task is completed as follows:

```
R4(config)#router bgp 1
R4(config-router)#network 150.2.2.0 mask 255.255.255.0 backdoor
R4(config-router)#network 150.3.3.0 mask 255.255.255.0 backdoor
R4(config-router)#exit
```

Following this change, the routing table on R4 shows the following route entries:

```
R4#show ip route
Codes: C - connected, S - static, R - RIP, M - mobile, B - BGP
       D - EIGRP, EX - EIGRP external, O - OSPF, IA - OSPF inter area
       N1 - OSPF NSSA external type 1, N2 - OSPF NSSA external type 2
       E1 - OSPF external type 1, E2 - OSPF external type 2
       i - IS-IS, su - IS-IS summary, L1 - IS-IS level-1, L2 - IS-IS level-2
       ia - IS-IS inter area, * - candidate default, U - per-user static route
       o - ODR, P - periodic downloaded static route

Gateway of last resort is not set
```

```
        10.0.0.0/30 is subnetted, 1 subnets
C         10.0.0.12 is directly connected, Serial0/0
        150.1.0.0/24 is subnetted, 1 subnets
C         150.1.1.0 is directly connected, FastEthernet0/0
        150.2.0.0/24 is subnetted, 1 subnets
O E2      150.2.2.0 [110/1] via 150.1.1.1, 00:00:43, FastEthernet0/0
        150.3.0.0/24 is subnetted, 1 subnets
O E2      150.3.3.0 [110/1] via 150.1.1.1, 00:00:35, FastEthernet0/0
```

Next, complete this task by ensuring that R4 can still ping the 150.2.2.0/24 and the 150.3.3.0/24 subnets when complete. Because the routes are known via the FastEthernet0/0 interface, you do NOT need to use an extended ping as the ping will be sourced from the egress interface:

```
R4#ping 150.2.2.2 repeat 10

Type escape sequence to abort.
Sending 10, 100-byte ICMP Echos to 150.2.2.2, timeout is 2 seconds:
!!!!!!!!!!
Success rate is 100 percent (10/10), round-trip min/avg/max = 1/3/4 ms

R4#ping 150.3.3.3 repeat 10

Type escape sequence to abort.
Sending 10, 100-byte ICMP Echos to 150.3.3.3, timeout is 2 seconds:
!!!!!!!!!!
Success rate is 100 percent (10/10), round-trip min/avg/max = 16/17/20 ms
```

Finally, verify redundancy by shutting down the R1-R2 link and ensuring that R1 can still reach the 150.2.2.0/24 and 150.3.3.0/24 subnets. This is completed as follows:

```
R1(config)#interface serial 0/0
R1(config-if)#shutdown
R1(config-if)#exit
R1(config)#do show ip route
Codes: C - connected, S - static, R - RIP, M - mobile, B - BGP
       D - EIGRP, EX - EIGRP external, O - OSPF, IA - OSPF inter area
       N1 - OSPF NSSA external type 1, N2 - OSPF NSSA external type 2
       E1 - OSPF external type 1, E2 - OSPF external type 2
       i - IS-IS, su - IS-IS summary, L1 - IS-IS level-1, L2 - IS-IS level-2
       ia - IS-IS inter area, * - candidate default, U - per-user static route
       o - ODR, P - periodic downloaded static route

Gateway of last resort is not set

        150.1.0.0/24 is subnetted, 1 subnets
C         150.1.1.0 is directly connected, FastEthernet0/0
        150.2.0.0/24 is subnetted, 1 subnets
O E2      150.2.2.0 [110/1] via 150.1.1.4, 00:00:08, FastEthernet0/0
        150.3.0.0/24 is subnetted, 1 subnets
O E2      150.3.3.0 [110/1] via 150.1.1.4, 00:00:08, FastEthernet0/0
R1(config)#
R1(config)#do ping 150.2.2.2 repeat 10

Type escape sequence to abort.
Sending 10, 100-byte ICMP Echos to 150.2.2.2, timeout is 2 seconds:
!!!!!!!!!!
Success rate is 100 percent (10/10), round-trip min/avg/max = 28/30/32 ms
R1(config)#
R1(config)#do ping 150.3.3.3 repeat 10

Type escape sequence to abort.
Sending 10, 100-byte ICMP Echos to 150.3.3.3, timeout is 2 seconds:
!!!!!!!!!!
Success rate is 100 percent (10/10), round-trip min/avg/max = 16/16/16 ms
```

FINAL ROUTER CONFIGURATIONS

R1

```
R1#term len 0
R1#sh run
Building configuration...

Current configuration : 1135 bytes
!
version 12.4
service timestamps debug datetime msec
service timestamps log datetime msec
no service password-encryption
!
hostname R1
!
boot-start-marker
boot-end-marker
!
no logging console
!
no aaa new-model
no network-clock-participate slot 1
no network-clock-participate wic 0
ip cef
!
no ip domain lookup
ip auth-proxy max-nodata-conns 3
ip admission max-nodata-conns 3
!
interface FastEthernet0/0
 ip address 150.1.1.1 255.255.255.0
 ip ospf 1 area 0
 duplex auto
 speed auto
!
interface Serial0/0
 ip address 10.0.0.1 255.255.255.252
 shutdown
 clock rate 2000000
!
interface Serial0/1
 no ip address
 shutdown
!
router ospf 21
 log-adjacency-changes
!
router ospf 1
 router-id 1.1.1.1
 log-adjacency-changes
 redistribute bgp 1 subnets
!
router bgp 1
 no synchronization
 bgp router-id 1.1.1.1
 bgp log-neighbor-changes
 neighbor 10.0.0.2 remote-as 2
 neighbor 10.0.0.2 default-originate
 no auto-summary
!
ip forward-protocol nd
!
no ip http server
no ip http secure-server
!
control-plane
!
line con 0
line aux 0
line vty 0 4
 login
!
end

R1#
```

R2

```
R2#term len 0
R2#sh run
Building configuration...

Current configuration : 1006 bytes
!
version 12.4
service timestamps debug datetime msec
service timestamps log datetime msec
no service password-encryption
!
hostname R2
!
boot-start-marker
boot-end-marker
!
no logging console
!
no aaa new-model
no network-clock-participate slot 1
no network-clock-participate wic 0
ip cef
!
no ip domain lookup
ip auth-proxy max-nodata-conns 3
ip admission max-nodata-conns 3
!
interface FastEthernet0/0
 ip address 150.2.2.2 255.255.255.0
 duplex auto
 speed auto
!
interface Serial0/0
 ip address 10.0.0.2 255.255.255.252
!
interface Serial0/1
 ip address 10.0.0.9 255.255.255.252
!
router bgp 2
 no synchronization
 bgp router-id 2.2.2.2
 bgp log-neighbor-changes
 network 150.2.2.0 mask 255.255.255.0
 neighbor 10.0.0.1 remote-as 1
 neighbor 10.0.0.10 remote-as 3
 no auto-summary
!
ip forward-protocol nd
!
no ip http server
no ip http secure-server
!
control-plane
!
line con 0
line aux 0
line vty 0 4
 login
!
end

R2#
```

R3

```
R3#term len 0
R3#sh run
Building configuration...

Current configuration : 1347 bytes
!
version 12.4
service timestamps debug datetime msec
service timestamps log datetime msec
no service password-encryption
!
```

```
hostname R3
!
boot-start-marker
boot-end-marker
!
no logging console
!
no aaa new-model
no network-clock-participate slot 1
no network-clock-participate wic 0
ip cef
!
no ip domain lookup
ip auth-proxy max-nodata-conns 3
ip admission max-nodata-conns 3
!
interface FastEthernet0/0
 ip address 150.3.3.3 255.255.255.0
 duplex auto
 speed auto
!
interface Serial1/0
 no ip address
 shutdown
 clock rate 128000
!
interface Serial1/1
 ip address 10.0.0.10 255.255.255.252
 clock rate 128000
!
interface Serial1/2
 ip address 10.0.0.13 255.255.255.252
 clock rate 128000
!
interface Serial1/3
 no ip address
 shutdown
!
interface Serial1/4
 no ip address
 shutdown
!
interface Serial1/5
 no ip address
 shutdown
!
interface Serial1/6
 no ip address
 shutdown
!
interface Serial1/7
 no ip address
 shutdown
!
router bgp 3
 no synchronization
 bgp router-id 3.3.3.3
 bgp log-neighbor-changes
 network 150.3.3.0 mask 255.255.255.0
 neighbor 10.0.0.9 remote-as 2
 neighbor 10.0.0.14 remote-as 1
 no auto-summary
!
ip forward-protocol nd
!
no ip http server
no ip http secure-server
!
control-plane
!
line con 0
line aux 0
line vty 0 4
 login
!
end

R3#
```

R4

```
R4#term len 0
R4#sh run
Building configuration...

Current configuration : 1239 bytes
!
version 12.4
service timestamps debug datetime msec
service timestamps log datetime msec
no service password-encryption
!
hostname R4
!
boot-start-marker
boot-end-marker
!
no logging console
!
no aaa new-model
no network-clock-participate slot 1
no network-clock-participate wic 0
ip cef
!
no ip domain lookup
ip auth-proxy max-nodata-conns 3
ip admission max-nodata-conns 3
!
interface FastEthernet0/0
 ip address 150.1.1.4 255.255.255.0
 ip ospf 4 area 0
 duplex auto
 speed auto
!
interface Serial0/0
 ip address 10.0.0.14 255.255.255.252
!
interface Serial0/1
 no ip address
 shutdown
!
router ospf 4
 router-id 4.4.4.4
 log-adjacency-changes
 redistribute bgp 1 subnets
!
router bgp 1
 no synchronization
 bgp router-id 4.4.4.4
 bgp log-neighbor-changes
 network 150.2.2.0 mask 255.255.255.0 backdoor
 network 150.3.3.0 mask 255.255.255.0 backdoor
 neighbor 10.0.0.13 remote-as 3
 neighbor 10.0.0.13 default-originate route-map PREPEND
 no auto-summary
!
ip forward-protocol nd
!
no ip http server
no ip http secure-server
!
route-map PREPEND permit 10
 set as-path prepend 1 1 1 1
!
control-plane
!
line con 0
line aux 0
line vty 0 4
 login
!
end

R4#
```

CCNP LAB 39

Border Gateway Protocol Lab

Lab Objective:

The focus of this lab is to understand BGP implementation and configuration in Cisco IOS routers. Additional technologies include route filtering and path control.

Lab Topology:

The lab network topology is illustrated below:

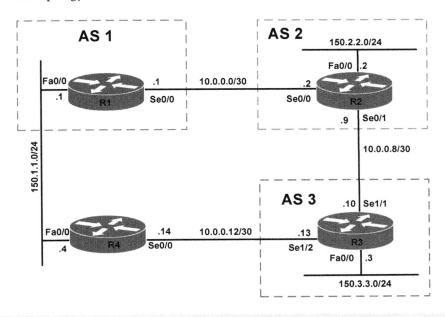

IMPORTANT NOTE: If you are using the **www.howtonetwork.net racks**, please bring up the LAN interfaces connected to the routers by issuing the `no shutdown` command on the connected switches. If you are using a home lab with no Switches, you can bring up the LAN interfaces using the following configurations on your routers:

```
interface fastethernet 0/0
  no keepalive
  loopback
  no shutdown
```

Alternately, you can simply connect the interfaces to a hub or switch if you have one available in your own lab.

Task 1

Configure hostnames and IP addressing on all routers as illustrated in the network topology.

Task 2

Configure BGP as illustrated in the topology. R1 will peer with R2. R2 will peer with R1 and R3. R3 will peer with R2. Verify the configuration using the appropriate commands.

Task 3

Configure R2 and R3 to advertise their 150.2.2.0/24 and 150.3.3.0/24 prefixes via BGP. Do NOT advertise the 150.1.1.0/24 subnet via BGP; however, ensure that both R2 and R3 can ping R1s LAN IP address. They do NOT need to be able to ping the LAN address of R4. Finally, verify your configuration using the appropriate commands and as Cisco IOS extended ping functions.

Task 4

Management has decided that they would like BGP neighbor relationship between R1 and R3. This should transit R4. Configure a BGP peer relationship between R1s Fa0/0 interface and R3s Se1/2 interface. You are NOT allowed to enable an IGP on R1, R3 or R4; you are NOT allowed to configure BGP or static routing on R4; however, you are allowed to configure a single /32 host route on both R1 and R3. Ensure that when the R1-R2 WAN link is up, R1 prefers the path via R2 to reach the 150.2.2.0/24 and 150.3.3.0/24 prefixes. YOU are NOT allowed to use route maps as part of your solution. Verify your configuration using the appropriate commands.

Task 5

Configure your network so that when the R1-R2 link is down, R1s LAN address can still reach the 150.2.2.0/24 and 150.3.3.0/24 subnets and vice-versa. You are NOT allowed to configure static routes or an IGP on R1, R3, or R4. Do NOT configure BGP on R4. You can NOT use PBR on any routers, or create a tunnel between R1 and R3. And finally, do NOT advertise the 150.1.1.0/24 prefix via BGP. Your solution should ensure that when the R1-R2 link is up, R3 will use the path via R2 to reach the 150.1.1.0/24 subnet.

When complete, verify your configuration by shutting down the R1-R2 WAN link. After this, verify that R1s LAN interface can ping both the 150.2.2.0/24 and 150.3.3.0/24 subnets and vice-versa. All your pings should be successful.

LAB VALIDATION

Task 1

Please refer to previous labs for basic IP addressing and hostname configuration. This will not be included in this section to avoid being redundant.

Task 2

```
R1(config)#router bgp 1
R1(config-router)#bgp router-id 1.1.1.1
R1(config-router)#neighbor 10.0.0.2 remote-as 2
R1(config-router)#exit

R2(config)#router bgp 2
R2(config-router)#bgp router-id 2.2.2.2
R2(config-router)#neighbor 10.0.0.1 remote-as 1
R2(config-router)#neighbor 10.0.0.10 remote-as 10
R2(config-router)#exit

R3(config)#router bgp 3
R3(config-router)#bgp router-id 3.3.3.3
R3(config-router)#neighbor 10.0.0.9 remote-as 2
R3(config-router)#exit
```

Verify your configuration using the show ip bgp summary command:

```
R1#show ip bgp summary
BGP router identifier 1.1.1.1, local AS number 1
BGP table version is 1, main routing table version 1

Neighbor      V    AS MsgRcvd MsgSent   TblVer   InQ OutQ Up/Down   State/PfxRcd
10.0.0.2      4     2       4       5        1     0    0 00:01:55             0
```

```
R2#show ip bgp summary
BGP router identifier 2.2.2.2, local AS number 2
BGP table version is 1, main routing table version 1

Neighbor     V    AS MsgRcvd MsgSent   TblVer   InQ OutQ Up/Down   State/PfxRcd
10.0.0.1     4    1      6       5        1     0    0 00:02:12       0
10.0.0.10    4    3      8       8        1     0    0 00:00:20       0

R3#show ip bgp summary
BGP router identifier 3.3.3.3, local AS number 3
BGP table version is 1, main routing table version 1

Neighbor     V    AS MsgRcvd MsgSent   TblVer   InQ OutQ Up/Down   State/PfxRcd
10.0.0.9     4    2      8       8        1     0    0 00:00:46       0
```

Task 3

The requirements of this task are three-fold. First, simply advertise the LAN subnets connected to R2 and R3 using the network command. Second, to allow R2 and R3 to ping the LAN interface address of R1, configure R1 to advertise a default route to R2, which will then advertise it to R3. The first two steps of this task are completed on R1, R2, and R3 as follows:

```
R1(config)#router bgp 1
R1(config-router)#neighbor 10.0.0.2 default-originate
R1(config-router)#exit

R2(config)#router bgp 2
R2(config-router)#network 150.2.2.0 mask 255.255.255.0
R2(config-router)#exit

R3(config)#router bgp 3
R3(config-router)#network 150.3.3.0 mask 255.255.255.0
R3(config-router)#exit
```

Verify your configuration using the show ip bgp command on all three routers:

```
R1#show ip bgp
BGP table version is 3, local router ID is 1.1.1.1
Status codes: s suppressed, d damped, h history, * valid, > best, i - internal,
              r RIB-failure, S Stale
Origin codes: i - IGP, e - EGP, ? - incomplete

   Network          Next Hop        Metric LocPrf Weight Path
*> 150.2.2.0/24     10.0.0.2             0            0 2 i
*> 150.3.3.0/24     10.0.0.2                          0 2 3 i

R2#show ip bgp
BGP table version is 4, local router ID is 2.2.2.2
Status codes: s suppressed, d damped, h history, * valid, > best, i - internal,
              r RIB-failure, S Stale
Origin codes: i - IGP, e - EGP, ? - incomplete

   Network          Next Hop        Metric LocPrf Weight Path
*> 0.0.0.0          10.0.0.1             0            0 1 i
*> 150.2.2.0/24     0.0.0.0              0        32768 i
*> 150.3.3.0/24     10.0.0.10            0            0 3 i

R3#show ip bgp
BGP table version is 4, local router ID is 3.3.3.3
Status codes: s suppressed, d damped, h history, * valid, > best, i - internal,
              r RIB-failure, S Stale
Origin codes: i - IGP, e - EGP, ? - incomplete

   Network          Next Hop        Metric LocPrf Weight Path
*> 0.0.0.0          10.0.0.9                          0 2 1 i
*> 150.2.2.0/24     10.0.0.9             0            0 2 i
*> 150.3.3.0/24     0.0.0.0              0        32768 i
```

Finally, verify your configuration using extended pings between R1, R2, and R3:

```
R1#ping 150.2.2.2 source fastethernet 0/0 repeat 10

Type escape sequence to abort.
Sending 10, 100-byte ICMP Echos to 150.2.2.2, timeout is 2 seconds:
Packet sent with a source address of 150.1.1.1
!!!!!!!!!!
Success rate is 100 percent (10/10), round-trip min/avg/max = 1/3/4 ms

R1#ping 150.3.3.3 source fastethernet 0/0 repeat 10

Type escape sequence to abort.
Sending 10, 100-byte ICMP Echos to 150.3.3.3, timeout is 2 seconds:
Packet sent with a source address of 150.1.1.1
!!!!!!!!!!
Success rate is 100 percent (10/10), round-trip min/avg/max = 16/17/20 ms

R2#ping 150.1.1.1 source fastethernet 0/0 repeat 10

Type escape sequence to abort.
Sending 10, 100-byte ICMP Echos to 150.1.1.1, timeout is 2 seconds:
Packet sent with a source address of 150.2.2.2
!!!!!!!!!!
Success rate is 100 percent (10/10), round-trip min/avg/max = 1/2/4 ms

R2#ping 150.3.3.3 source fastethernet 0/0 repeat 10

Type escape sequence to abort.
Sending 10, 100-byte ICMP Echos to 150.3.3.3, timeout is 2 seconds:
Packet sent with a source address of 150.2.2.2
!!!!!!!!!!
Success rate is 100 percent (10/10), round-trip min/avg/max = 16/16/16 ms

R3#ping 150.1.1.1 source fastethernet 0/0 repeat 10

Type escape sequence to abort.
Sending 10, 100-byte ICMP Echos to 150.1.1.1, timeout is 2 seconds:
Packet sent with a source address of 150.3.3.3
!!!!!!!!!!
Success rate is 100 percent (10/10), round-trip min/avg/max = 16/16/20 ms

R3#ping 150.2.2.2 source fastethernet 0/0 repeat 10

Type escape sequence to abort.
Sending 10, 100-byte ICMP Echos to 150.2.2.2, timeout is 2 seconds:
Packet sent with a source address of 150.3.3.3
!!!!!!!!!!
Success rate is 100 percent (10/10), round-trip min/avg/max = 16/16/16 ms
```

Task 4

The requirements of this task are two-fold. The first is that you need to enable BGP between R1 and R3. This should be done across R4 and is completed using two static routes, one on R1 and the other on R3 to establish an external BGP adjacency. This task is completed as follows:

```
R1(config)#router bgp 1
R1(config-router)#neighbor 10.0.0.13 remote-as 3
R1(config-router)#neighbor 10.0.0.13 update-source fastethernet 0/0
R1(config-router)#neighbor 10.0.0.13 ebgp-multihop
R1(config-router)#exit

R3(config)#router bgp 3
R3(config-router)#neighbor 150.1.1.1 remote-as 1
R3(config-router)#neighbor 150.1.1.1 ebgp-multihop
R3(config-router)#neighbor 150.1.1.1 update-source serial 1/2
R3(config-router)#exit
```

Verify your configuration using the show ip bgp summary command on R1 and R3:

```
R1#show ip bgp summary
BGP router identifier 1.1.1.1, local AS number 1
BGP table version is 4, main routing table version 4
2 network entries using 234 bytes of memory
```

```
4 path entries using 208 bytes of memory
5/2 BGP path/bestpath attribute entries using 620 bytes of memory
4 BGP AS-PATH entries using 96 bytes of memory
0 BGP route-map cache entries using 0 bytes of memory
0 BGP filter-list cache entries using 0 bytes of memory
BGP using 1158 total bytes of memory
BGP activity 2/0 prefixes, 4/0 paths, scan interval 60 secs

Neighbor     V    AS MsgRcvd MsgSent   TblVer  InQ OutQ Up/Down   State/PfxRcd
10.0.0.2     4     2     65      66        4    0    0 00:59:35         2
10.0.0.13    4     3      8       9        0    0    0 00:01:08         2


R3#show ip bgp summary
BGP router identifier 3.3.3.3, local AS number 3
BGP table version is 7, main routing table version 7
3 network entries using 351 bytes of memory
4 path entries using 208 bytes of memory
6/3 BGP path/bestpath attribute entries using 744 bytes of memory
4 BGP AS-PATH entries using 96 bytes of memory
0 BGP route-map cache entries using 0 bytes of memory
0 BGP filter-list cache entries using 0 bytes of memory
BGP using 1399 total bytes of memory
BGP activity 3/0 prefixes, 7/3 paths, scan interval 60 secs

Neighbor     V    AS MsgRcvd MsgSent   TblVer  InQ OutQ Up/Down   State/PfxRcd
10.0.0.9     4     2     74      74        6    0    0 01:01:23         2
150.1.1.1    4     1     20      19        6    0    0 00:00:44         1
```

The second requirement is that R1 should prefer the path via R2 to reach the 150.2.2.0/24 prefix as well as the 150.3.3.0/24 prefix. By default, R1 will prefer the path via R2 to reach the 150.2.2.0/24 prefix because of the shorter AS_PATH. However, now that an external BGP peer session has been established between R1 and R3, R1 will prefer the path via R3 to reach the 150.3.3.0/24 prefix. Prior to changes on R1, the BGP RIB entry for this prefix shows as follows:

```
R1#show ip bgp 150.3.3.0 255.255.255.0
BGP routing table entry for 150.3.3.0/24, version 4
Paths: (2 available, best #1, table Default-IP-Routing-Table)
  Advertised to update-groups:
     1
  3
    10.0.0.13 from 10.0.0.13 (3.3.3.3)
      Origin IGP, metric 0, localpref 100, valid, external, best
  2 3
    10.0.0.2 from 10.0.0.2 (2.2.2.2)
      Origin IGP, localpref 100, valid, external
```

Because we cannot use route maps to set the LOCAL_PREF, we must instead use the neighbor <address> weight <value> command to assign all prefixes received via R1 a higher WEIGHT value. This will ensure that R1 prefers the path via R2 to reach the 150.3.3.0/24 prefix:

```
R1(config)#router bgp 1
R1(config-router)#neighbor 10.0.0.2 weight 1
R1(config-router)#exit
```

Following this change, R1 shows the following BGP Table entry for the 150.3.3.0/24 prefix:

```
R1#show ip bgp 150.3.3.0 255.255.255.0
BGP routing table entry for 150.3.3.0/24, version 6
Paths: (2 available, best #2, table Default-IP-Routing-Table)
Flag: 0x820
  Advertised to update-groups:
     2
  3
    10.0.0.13 from 10.0.0.13 (3.3.3.3)
      Origin IGP, metric 0, localpref 100, valid, external
  2 3
    10.0.0.2 from 10.0.0.2 (2.2.2.2)
      Origin IGP, localpref 100, weight 1, valid, external, best
```

Task 5

This task requires a little bit of thought and has two core requirements. The first requirement is that router R2 and R3 should be able to reach the 150.1.1.0/24 when the R1-R2 link is down. This must be performed in such a manner that router R3 still prefers the path via R2 to reach the 150.1.1.0/24 subnet. Because routers will not compare MED values for prefixes received from different ASes, the AS_PATH attribute must be used instead. This part is completed as follows:

```
R1(config)#route-map PREPEND permit 10
R1(config-route-map)#set as-path prepend 1 1
R1(config-route-map)#exit
R1(config)#router bgp 1
R1(config-router)#neighbor 10.0.0.13 default-originate route-map PREPEND
R1(config-router)#exit
```

Following this change, the BGP Tables on R2 and R3 show the following for the default route:

```
R2#show ip bgp 0.0.0.0 0.0.0.0
BGP routing table entry for 0.0.0.0/0, version 6
Paths: (1 available, best #1, table Default-IP-Routing-Table)
  Advertised to update-groups:
     1
  1
    10.0.0.1 from 10.0.0.1 (1.1.1.1)
      Origin IGP, metric 0, localpref 100, valid, external, best

R3#show ip bgp 0.0.0.0 0.0.0.0
BGP routing table entry for 0.0.0.0/0, version 7
Paths: (2 available, best #2, table Default-IP-Routing-Table)
  Advertised to update-groups:
     1
  1 1 1
    150.1.1.1 from 150.1.1.1 (1.1.1.1)
      Origin IGP, metric 0, localpref 100, valid, external
  2 1
    10.0.0.9 from 10.0.0.9 (2.2.2.2)
      Origin IGP, localpref 100, valid, external, best
```

The second requirement, or part, of this task is that R1s LAN interface be able to ping the R2 and R3 LAN addresses and vice-versa. From a routing perspective, when the WAN link between R1 and R2 is shut down, the routes are received via R3. This is demonstrated below:

```
R1(config)#interface serial 0/0
R1(config-if)#shutdown
R1(config-if)#exit
R1(config)#do show ip bgp
BGP table version is 8, local router ID is 1.1.1.1
Status codes: s suppressed, d damped, h history, * valid, > best, i - internal,
              r RIB-failure, S Stale
Origin codes: i - IGP, e - EGP, ? - incomplete

   Network          Next Hop            Metric LocPrf Weight Path
*> 150.2.2.0/24     10.0.0.13                           0 3 2 i
*> 150.3.3.0/24     10.0.0.13                0          0 3 i
```

The issue, however, exists on R4. This router is a transit router between R1 and R3; however, it has no routing information for the 150.2.2.0/24 or 150.3.3.0/24 prefixes. Therefore, when a ping from R1 is initiated to either of these subnets, it is dropped by R4 because this router has no routing information for the destination. This is demonstrated by initiating a ping to 150.2.2.2 from R1 while running the debug ip packet [detail] command on R4:

```
R1#ping 150.2.2.2 source fastethernet 0/0 repeat 10
Type escape sequence to abort.
Sending 10, 100-byte ICMP Echos to 150.2.2.2, timeout is 2 seconds:
Packet sent with a source address of 150.1.1.1
U.U.U.U.U.
Success rate is 0 percent (0/10)
```

The debug ip packet detail command output on R4 shows the following:

```
R4#debug ip pack detail
IP packet debugging is on (detailed)
R4#
R4#
R4#
*May 12 19:49:29.067: IP: s=150.1.1.1 (FastEthernet0/0), d=150.2.2.2, len 100,
unroutable
*May 12 19:49:29.067:     ICMP type=8, code=0
*May 12 19:49:29.067: IP: tableid=0, s=150.1.1.4 (local), d=150.1.1.1
(FastEthernet0/0), routed via FIB
*May 12 19:49:29.067: IP: s=150.1.1.4 (local), d=150.1.1.1 (FastEthernet0/0), len 56,
sending
*May 12 19:49:29.067:     ICMP type=3, code=1
*May 12 19:49:31.067: IP: s=150.1.1.1 (FastEthernet0/0), d=150.2.2.2, len 100,
unroutable
*May 12 19:49:31.067:     ICMP type=8, code=0
*May 12 19:49:31.067: IP: tableid=0, s=150.1.1.4 (local), d=150.1.1.1
(FastEthernet0/0), routed via FIB
*May 12 19:49:31.071: IP: s=150.1.1.4 (local), d=150.1.1.1 (FastEthernet0/0), len 56,
sending
*May 12 19:49:31.071:     ICMP type=3, code=1
*May 12 19:49:33.071: IP: s=150.1.1.1 (FastEthernet0/0), d=150.2.2.2, len 100,
unroutable
*May 12 19:49:33.071:     ICMP type=8, code=0
*May 12 19:49:33.071: IP: tableid=0, s=150.1.1.4 (local), d=150.1.1.1
(FastEthernet0/0), routed via FIB
*May 12 19:49:33.075: IP: s=150.1.1.4 (local), d=150.1.1.1 (FastEthernet0/0), len 56,
sending
*May 12 19:49:33.075:     ICMP type=3, code=1

[Truncated Output]
```

The difficulty level of this task is further increased because we are not allowed to configure any additional static routes or enable a dynamic routing protocol on R1, R3, and R4. Additionally, the task requirements stipulate that we cannot use PBR or a tunnel to complete this task. With such stringent requirements, we must think outside the box and consider other Cisco IOS software features. In essence, based on the debug output, we know that all we need is routing information on R4 pointing to R3 for the 150.2.2.0/24 and 150.3.3.0/24 prefixes. While we cannot use static routes or enable a dynamic routing protocol, there is NO stipulation against using ODR. This is because ODR is NOT a routing protocol, but rather a CDP extension. Therefore, to complete this task, simply configure R3 to advertise a default route via ODR to R1.

Because R1 will automatically advertise the 150.1.1.0/24 prefix, we need to filter from R3 so that this path is NOT used to forward traffic to the 150.1.1.0/24 prefix when the R1-R2 link is up. This task is completed by implementing the following configuration on R3:

```
R3(config)#access-list 1 deny any
R3(config)#router odr
R3(config-router)#distribute-list 1 in
R3(config-router)#exit
```

Following this configuration R3s routing table still shows only BGP routes:

```
R3#show ip route
Codes: C - connected, S - static, R - RIP, M - mobile, B - BGP
       D - EIGRP, EX - EIGRP external, O - OSPF, IA - OSPF inter area
       N1 - OSPF NSSA external type 1, N2 - OSPF NSSA external type 2
       E1 - OSPF external type 1, E2 - OSPF external type 2
       i - IS-IS, su - IS-IS summary, L1 - IS-IS level-1, L2 - IS-IS level-2
       ia - IS-IS inter area, * - candidate default, U - per-user static route
       o - ODR, P - periodic downloaded static route

Gateway of last resort is 150.1.1.1 to network 0.0.0.0

     10.0.0.0/30 is subnetted, 2 subnets
C       10.0.0.8 is directly connected, Serial1/1
```

```
C        10.0.0.12 is directly connected, Serial1/2
         150.1.0.0/32 is subnetted, 1 subnets
S         150.1.1.1 is directly connected, Serial1/2
         150.2.0.0/24 is subnetted, 1 subnets
B         150.2.2.0 [20/0] via 10.0.0.9, 00:01:17
         150.3.0.0/24 is subnetted, 1 subnets
C         150.3.3.0 is directly connected, FastEthernet0/0
B*      0.0.0.0/0 [20/0] via 150.1.1.1, 00:01:17
```

The same is also applicable to R2s routing table which only shows BGP routes:

```
R2#show ip route
Codes: C - connected, S - static, R - RIP, M - mobile, B - BGP
       D - EIGRP, EX - EIGRP external, O - OSPF, IA - OSPF inter area
       N1 - OSPF NSSA external type 1, N2 - OSPF NSSA external type 2
       E1 - OSPF external type 1, E2 - OSPF external type 2
       i - IS-IS, su - IS-IS summary, L1 - IS-IS level-1, L2 - IS-IS level-2
       ia - IS-IS inter area, * - candidate default, U - per-user static route
       o - ODR, P - periodic downloaded static route

Gateway of last resort is 10.0.0.10 to network 0.0.0.0

         10.0.0.0/30 is subnetted, 1 subnets
C         10.0.0.8 is directly connected, Serial0/1
         150.2.0.0/24 is subnetted, 1 subnets
C         150.2.2.0 is directly connected, FastEthernet0/0
         150.3.0.0/24 is subnetted, 1 subnets
B         150.3.3.0 [20/0] via 10.0.0.10, 04:42:47
B*      0.0.0.0/0 [20/0] via 10.0.0.10, 03:01:52
```

R4s routing table, however, now includes a default route received via ODR pointing to R3. This will allow R4 to forward packets sent from R1 destined to 150.2.2.0/24 and 150.3.3.0/24. There is no need to configure any static routes on R3 for R1s LAN IP address because a static route already exists and is pointing to R4. This is the static route used to establish the eBGP neighbor relationship with R1 that was configured earlier in this lab:

```
R4#show ip route
Codes: C - connected, S - static, R - RIP, M - mobile, B - BGP
       D - EIGRP, EX - EIGRP external, O - OSPF, IA - OSPF inter area
       N1 - OSPF NSSA external type 1, N2 - OSPF NSSA external type 2
       E1 - OSPF external type 1, E2 - OSPF external type 2
       i - IS-IS, su - IS-IS summary, L1 - IS-IS level-1, L2 - IS-IS level-2
       ia - IS-IS inter area, * - candidate default, U - per-user static route
       o - ODR, P - periodic downloaded static route

Gateway of last resort is 10.0.0.13 to network 0.0.0.0

         10.0.0.0/30 is subnetted, 1 subnets
C         10.0.0.12 is directly connected, Serial0/0
         150.1.0.0/24 is subnetted, 1 subnets
C         150.1.1.0 is directly connected, FastEthernet0/0
o*      0.0.0.0/0 [160/1] via 10.0.0.13, 00:00:44, Serial0/0
```

Following this change, R1 is now able to ping the 150.2.2.0/24 and 150.3.3.0/24 subnets:

```
1#ping 150.2.2.2 repeat 10

Type escape sequence to abort.
Sending 10, 100-byte ICMP Echos to 150.2.2.2, timeout is 2 seconds:
!!!!!!!!!!
Success rate is 100 percent (10/10), round-trip min/avg/max = 28/30/32 ms

R1#ping 150.3.3.3 repeat 10

Type escape sequence to abort.
Sending 10, 100-byte ICMP Echos to 150.3.3.3, timeout is 2 seconds:
!!!!!!!!!!
Success rate is 100 percent (10/10), round-trip min/avg/max = 16/18/20 ms
```

FINAL ROUTER CONFIGURATIONS

R1

```
R1#term len 0
R1#sh run
Building configuration...

Current configuration : 1311 bytes
!
version 12.4
service timestamps debug datetime msec
service timestamps log datetime msec
no service password-encryption
!
hostname R1
!
boot-start-marker
boot-end-marker
!
no logging console
!
no aaa new-model
no network-clock-participate slot 1
no network-clock-participate wic 0
ip cef
!
no ip domain lookup
ip auth-proxy max-nodata-conns 3
ip admission max-nodata-conns 3
!
interface FastEthernet0/0
 ip address 150.1.1.1 255.255.255.0
 duplex auto
 speed auto
!
interface Serial0/0
 ip address 10.0.0.1 255.255.255.252
 shutdown
 clock rate 2000000
!
interface Serial0/1
 no ip address
 shutdown
!
router bgp 1
 no synchronization
 bgp router-id 1.1.1.1
 bgp log-neighbor-changes
 neighbor 10.0.0.2 remote-as 2
 neighbor 10.0.0.2 default-originate
 neighbor 10.0.0.2 weight 1
 neighbor 10.0.0.13 remote-as 3
 neighbor 10.0.0.13 ebgp-multihop 255
 neighbor 10.0.0.13 update-source FastEthernet0/0
 neighbor 10.0.0.13 default-originate route-map PREPEND
 no auto-summary
!
ip forward-protocol nd
ip route 10.0.0.13 255.255.255.255 FastEthernet0/0 150.1.1.4
!
no ip http server
no ip http secure-server
!
route-map PREPEND permit 10
 set as-path prepend 1 1
!
control-plane
!
line con 0
line aux 0
line vty 0 4
 login
!
end

R1#
```

R2

```
R2#term len 0
R2#sh run
Building configuration...

Current configuration : 1006 bytes
!
version 12.4
service timestamps debug datetime msec
service timestamps log datetime msec
no service password-encryption
!
hostname R2
!
boot-start-marker
boot-end-marker
!
no logging console
!
no aaa new-model
no network-clock-participate slot 1
no network-clock-participate wic 0
ip cef
!
no ip domain lookup
ip auth-proxy max-nodata-conns 3
ip admission max-nodata-conns 3
!
interface FastEthernet0/0
 ip address 150.2.2.2 255.255.255.0
 duplex auto
 speed auto
!
interface Serial0/0
 ip address 10.0.0.2 255.255.255.252
!
interface Serial0/1
 ip address 10.0.0.9 255.255.255.252
!
router bgp 2
 no synchronization
 bgp router-id 2.2.2.2
 bgp log-neighbor-changes
 network 150.2.2.0 mask 255.255.255.0
 neighbor 10.0.0.1 remote-as 1
 neighbor 10.0.0.10 remote-as 3
 no auto-summary
!
ip forward-protocol nd
!
no ip http server
no ip http secure-server
!
control-plane
!
line con 0
line aux 0
line vty 0 4
 login
!
end

R2#
```

R3

```
R3#term len 0
R3#sh run
Building configuration...

Current configuration : 1534 bytes
!
version 12.4
service timestamps debug datetime msec
service timestamps log datetime msec
```

```
no service password-encryption
!
hostname R3
!
boot-start-marker
boot-end-marker
!
no logging console
!
no aaa new-model
no network-clock-participate slot 1
no network-clock-participate wic 0
ip cef
!
no ip domain lookup
ip auth-proxy max-nodata-conns 3
ip admission max-nodata-conns 3
!
interface FastEthernet0/0
 ip address 150.3.3.3 255.255.255.0
 duplex auto
 speed auto
!
interface Serial1/0
 no ip address
 shutdown
 clock rate 128000
!
interface Serial1/1
 ip address 10.0.0.10 255.255.255.252
 clock rate 128000
!
interface Serial1/2
 ip address 10.0.0.13 255.255.255.252
 clock rate 128000
!
interface Serial1/3
 no ip address
 shutdown
!
interface Serial1/4
 no ip address
 shutdown
!
interface Serial1/5
 no ip address
 shutdown
!
interface Serial1/6
 no ip address
 shutdown
!
interface Serial1/7
 no ip address
 shutdown
!
router odr
 distribute-list 1 in
!
router bgp 3
 no synchronization
 bgp router-id 3.3.3.3
 bgp log-neighbor-changes
 network 150.3.3.0 mask 255.255.255.0
 neighbor 10.0.0.9 remote-as 2
 neighbor 150.1.1.1 remote-as 1
 neighbor 150.1.1.1 ebgp-multihop 255
 neighbor 150.1.1.1 update-source Serial1/2
 no auto-summary
!
ip forward-protocol nd
ip route 150.1.1.1 255.255.255.255 Serial1/2
!
no ip http server
no ip http secure-server
```

```
!
access-list 1 deny    any
!
control-plane
!
line con 0
line aux 0
line vty 0 4
 login
!
end

R3#
```

R4

```
R4#term len 0
R4#sh run
Building configuration...

Current configuration : 793 bytes
!
version 12.4
service timestamps debug datetime msec
service timestamps log datetime msec
no service password-encryption
!
hostname R4
!
boot-start-marker
boot-end-marker
!
no logging console
!
no aaa new-model
no network-clock-participate slot 1
no network-clock-participate wic 0
ip cef
!
no ip domain lookup
ip auth-proxy max-nodata-conns 3
ip admission max-nodata-conns 3
!
interface FastEthernet0/0
 ip address 150.1.1.4 255.255.255.0
 duplex auto
 speed auto
!
interface Serial0/0
 ip address 10.0.0.14 255.255.255.252
!
interface Serial0/1
 no ip address
 shutdown
!
ip forward-protocol nd
!
no ip http server
no ip http secure-server
!
control-plane
!
line con 0
line aux 0
line vty 0 4
 login
!
end

R4#
```

CCNP LAB 40

Border Gateway Protocol Lab

Lab Objective:

The focus of this lab is to understand BGP implementation and configuration in Cisco IOS routers. Additional technologies include summarization, route filtering and path control.

Lab Topology:

The lab network topology is illustrated below:

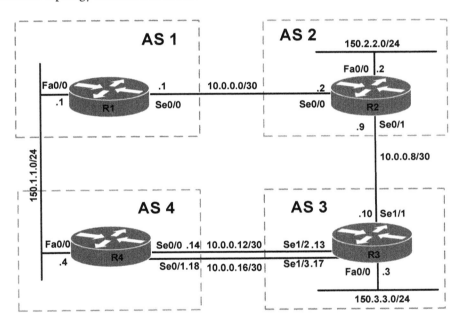

IMPORTANT NOTE: If you are using the **www.howtonetwork.net racks**, please bring up the LAN interfaces connected to the routers by issuing the `no shutdown` command on the connected switches. If you are using a home lab with no Switches, you can bring up the LAN interfaces using the following configurations on your routers:

```
interface fastethernet 0/0
  no keepalive
  loopback
  no shutdown
```

Alternately, you can simply connect the interfaces to a hub or switch if you have one available in your own lab.

Task 1

Configure hostnames and IP addressing on all routers as illustrated in the network topology. Additionally, configure a Loopback 0 interface on all routers using the router number and a host mask. For example, on R1, configure Loopback 0 with the IP address 1.1.1.1/32, on R2 configure interface Loopback 0 with the IP address 2.2.2.2/32 and so forth for R3 and also R4.

Task 2

Configure BGP as illustrated in the topology. Use the Loopback 0 addresses for peering. Do NOT configure any IGPs. Instead, use static routes only. R1 should peer with R2 and R4. R2 should peer with R1 and R3. R3 should peer with R2 and R4. R4 should peer with R1 and R3. On R3 and R4, ensure that packets are load balanced between the two WAN links. Do NOT configure PPP Multilink. Verify the configuration using the appropriate commands.

Task 3

Configure all routers to advertise their LAN subnet addresses via BGP. These should appear in the BGP RIBs of all other routers with an ORIGIN code of INCOMPLETE, by default. Verify the configuration using the appropriate commands.

Task 4

Configure BGP so that R4 prefers the path via R3 to reach any subnet. You are NOT allowed to implement any configuration on R4 itself. Verify your BGP configuration using the appropriate commands.

Task 5

Configure R4 so that it sends all updates to R3 with a MED of 4. Configure R2 so that it sends all updates to R3 with a MED of 2. Ensure that R3 prefers all routes with the better (lower) MED value. Do NOT modify any other BGP attributes or default administrative distance values when completing this task. Verify your configuration using the appropriate commands.

Task 6

Configure the following Loopback interfaces on R2:
* Loopback 192: IP Address 192.1.1.1/24
* Loopback 193: IP Address 193.1.1.1/24
* Loopback 194: IP Address 194.1.1.1/24
* Loopback 195: IP Address 195.1.1.1/24

The 192.1.1.1/24 subnet should appear to have originated in AS 192. The 193.1.1.1/24 subnet should appear to have originated in AS 193. The 194.1.1.1/24 subnet should appear to have originated in AS 194. And finally, the 195.1.1.1/24 subnet should appear to have originated in AS 195. These prefixes should be advertised using the network command. Verify your configuration using the appropriate commands.

Task 7

Configure R1 so that it only accepts prefixes originated in AS 192, 193, 194 and 195 from R4. It should never have any entries in its BGP RIB for any prefixes originating in these ASes directly from R2. Use an AS_PATH filter. This should only have TWO lines. Verify your configuration using the appropriate commands.

LAB VALIDATION

Task 1

Please refer to previous labs for basic IP addressing and hostname configuration. This will not be included in this section to avoid being redundant.

Task 2

The most simple way to complete this task is to use BGP peer group configuration to minimize the number of commands that you need to specify. However, the task specifically states that peer groups should not be used. Additionally, in order to establish the BGP adjacencies using peer groups, you need to configure static routes on all routers because you are not allowed to enable an IGP of any kind. This task is completed as follows:

```
R1(config)#ip route 2.2.2.2 255.255.255.255 serial 0/0
R1(config)#ip route 4.4.4.4 255.255.255.255 fastethernet 0/0 150.1.1.4
R1(config)#router bgp 1
R1(config-router)#neighbor 2.2.2.2 remote-as 2
R1(config-router)#neighbor 2.2.2.2 update-source loopback 0
R1(config-router)#neighbor 2.2.2.2 ebgp-multihop
R1(config-router)#neighbor 4.4.4.4 remote-as 4
R1(config-router)#neighbor 4.4.4.4 update-source loopback 0
R1(config-router)#neighbor 4.4.4.4 ebgp-multihop
R1(config-router)#exit

R2(config)#ip route 1.1.1.1 255.255.255.255 serial 0/0
R2(config)#ip route 3.3.3.3 255.255.255.255 serial 0/1
R2(config)#router bgp 2
R2(config-router)#neighbor 1.1.1.1 remote-as 1
R2(config-router)#neighbor 1.1.1.1 update-source loopback 0
R2(config-router)#neighbor 1.1.1.1 ebgp-multihop
R2(config-router)#neighbor 3.3.3.3 remote-as 3
R2(config-router)#neighbor 3.3.3.3 update-source loopback 0
R2(config-router)#neighbor 3.3.3.3 ebgp-multihop
R2(config-router)#exit

R3(config)#ip route 2.2.2.2 255.255.255.255 serial 1/1
R3(config)#ip route 4.4.4.4 255.255.255.255 serial 1/2
R3(config)#ip route 4.4.4.4 255.255.255.255 serial 1/3
R3(config)#router bgp 3
R3(config-router)#neighbor 2.2.2.2 remote-as 2
R3(config-router)#neighbor 2.2.2.2 update-source loopback 0
R3(config-router)#neighbor 2.2.2.2 ebgp-multihop
R3(config-router)#neighbor 4.4.4.4 remote-as 4
R3(config-router)#neighbor 4.4.4.4 update-source loopback 0
R3(config-router)#neighbor 4.4.4.4 ebgp-multihop
R3(config-router)#exit

R4(config)#ip route 1.1.1.1 255.255.255.255 fastethernet 0/0 150.1.1.1
R4(config)#ip route 3.3.3.3 255.255.255.255 serial 0/0
R4(config)#ip route 3.3.3.3 255.255.255.255 serial 0/1
R4(config)#router bgp 4
R4(config-router)#neighbor 1.1.1.1 remote-as 1
R4(config-router)#neighbor 1.1.1.1 update-source loopback 0
R4(config-router)#neighbor 1.1.1.1 ebgp-multihop
R4(config-router)#neighbor 3.3.3.3 remote-as 3
R4(config-router)#neighbor 3.3.3.3 update-source loopback 0
R4(config-router)#neighbor 3.3.3.3 ebgp-multihop
R4(config-router)#exit
```

Verify your configuration using the show ip bgp summary command on all routers:

```
R1#show ip bgp summary
BGP router identifier 1.1.1.1, local AS number 1
BGP table version is 1, main routing table version 1

Neighbor     V    AS MsgRcvd MsgSent   TblVer  InQ OutQ Up/Down  State/PfxRcd
2.2.2.2      4     2      11      12        1    0    0 00:08:30            0
4.4.4.4      4     4       5       5        1    0    0 00:01:30            0

R2#show ip bgp summary
BGP router identifier 2.2.2.2, local AS number 2
BGP table version is 1, main routing table version 1

Neighbor     V    AS MsgRcvd MsgSent   TblVer  InQ OutQ Up/Down  State/PfxRcd
1.1.1.1      4     1      12      11        1    0    0 00:08:33            0
3.3.3.3      4     3       7       8        1    0    0 00:04:03            0

R3#show ip bgp summary
BGP router identifier 3.3.3.3, local AS number 3
BGP table version is 1, main routing table version 1

Neighbor     V    AS MsgRcvd MsgSent   TblVer  InQ OutQ Up/Down  State/PfxRcd
2.2.2.2      4     2       8       7        1    0    0 00:04:06            0
4.4.4.4      4     4       4       4        1    0    0 00:00:57            0

R4#show ip bgp summary
BGP router identifier 4.4.4.4, local AS number 4
```

```
BGP table version is 1, main routing table version 1

Neighbor     V    AS MsgRcvd MsgSent    TblVer   InQ OutQ Up/Down  State/PfxRcd
1.1.1.1      4     1       5       5         1     0    0 00:01:40           0
3.3.3.3      4     3       5       5         1     0    0 00:01:00           0
```

Task 3

In order to ensure that the ORIGIN code is INCOMPLETE, you need to redistribute the LAN subnets into BGP. However, you can also use the network statement in conjunction with a route map and set the ORIGIN code within the route map. Either option is acceptable when completing this task. This task is completed as follows when using the redistribution method:

```
R1(config)#route-map CONNECTED permit 10
R1(config-route-map)#match interface fastethernet 0/0
R1(config-route-map)#exit
R1(config)#route-map CONNECTED deny 20
R1(config-route-map)#exit
R1(config)#router bgp 1
R1(config-router)#redistribute connected route-map CONNECTED
R1(config-router)#exit

R2(config)#route-map CONNECTED permit 10
R2(config-route-map)#match interface fastethernet 0/0
R2(config-route-map)#exit
R2(config)#route-map CONNECTED deny 20
R2(config-route-map)#exit
R2(config)#router bgp 2
R2(config-router)#redistribute connected route-map CONNECTED
R2(config-router)#exit

R3(config)#route-map CONNECTED permit 10
R3(config-route-map)#match interface fastethernet 0/0
R3(config-route-map)#exit
R3(config)#route-map CONNECTED deny 20
R3(config-route-map)#exit
R3(config)#router bgp 3
R3(config-router)#redistribute connected route-map CONNECTED
R3(config-router)#exit

R4(config)#route-map CONNECTED permit 10
R4(config-route-map)#match interface fastethernet 0/0
R4(config-route-map)#exit
R4(config)#route-map CONNECTED deny 20
R4(config-route-map)#exit
R4(config)#router bgp 4
R4(config-router)#redistribute connected route-map CONNECTED
R4(config-router)#exit
```

You can verify the ORIGIN code by looking at the prefix entry in the BGP Tables. The ORIGIN code of IN-COMPLETE is denoted by a question mark (?) in the output of the show ip bgp command. You can view additional detail on a per-prefix basis also when using this command.

```
R1#show ip bgp
BGP table version is 4, local router ID is 1.1.1.1
Status codes: s suppressed, d damped, h history, * valid, > best, i - internal,
              r RIB-failure, S Stale
Origin codes: i - IGP, e - EGP, ? - incomplete

   Network          Next Hop          Metric LocPrf Weight Path
*  150.1.1.0/24     4.4.4.4                0           0 4 ?
*>                  0.0.0.0                0       32768 ?
*> 150.2.2.0/24     2.2.2.2                0           0 2 ?
*  150.3.3.0/24     2.2.2.2                            0 2 3 ?
*>                  4.4.4.4                            0 4 3 ?

R2#show ip bgp
BGP table version is 4, local router ID is 2.2.2.2
```

```
Status codes: s suppressed, d damped, h history, * valid, > best, i - internal,
              r RIB-failure, S Stale
Origin codes: i - IGP, e - EGP, ? - incomplete

     Network          Next Hop          Metric LocPrf Weight Path
*    150.1.1.0/24     3.3.3.3                               0 3 4 ?
*>                    1.1.1.1                0              0 1 ?
*>   150.2.2.0/24     0.0.0.0                0          32768 ?
*    150.3.3.0/24     1.1.1.1                               0 1 4 3 ?
*>                    3.3.3.3                0              0 3 ?
```

```
R3#show ip bgp
BGP table version is 5, local router ID is 3.3.3.3
Status codes: s suppressed, d damped, h history, * valid, > best, i - internal,
              r RIB-failure, S Stale
Origin codes: i - IGP, e - EGP, ? - incomplete

     Network          Next Hop          Metric LocPrf Weight Path
*>   150.1.1.0/24     4.4.4.4                0              0 4 ?
*                     2.2.2.2                               0 2 1 ?
*    150.2.2.0/24     4.4.4.4                               0 4 1 2 ?
*>                    2.2.2.2                0              0 2 ?
*>   150.3.3.0/24     0.0.0.0                0          32768 ?
```

```
R4#show ip bgp
BGP table version is 6, local router ID is 4.4.4.4
Status codes: s suppressed, d damped, h history, * valid, > best, i - internal,
              r RIB-failure, S Stale
Origin codes: i - IGP, e - EGP, ? - incomplete

     Network          Next Hop          Metric LocPrf Weight Path
*>   150.1.1.0/24     0.0.0.0                0          32768 ?
*                     1.1.1.1                0              0 1 ?
*    150.2.2.0/24     3.3.3.3                               0 3 2 ?
*>                    1.1.1.1                               0 1 2 ?
*>   150.3.3.0/24     3.3.3.3                0              0 3 ?
```

Task 4

This task requires a little thought. Because we cannot implement any configuration on R4 itself, we have to think outside the box. The current BGP RIB on R4 shows the following entries:

```
R4#show ip bgp
BGP table version is 6, local router ID is 4.4.4.4
Status codes: s suppressed, d damped, h history, * valid, > best, i - internal,
              r RIB-failure, S Stale
Origin codes: i - IGP, e - EGP, ? - incomplete

     Network          Next Hop          Metric LocPrf Weight Path
*>   150.1.1.0/24     0.0.0.0                0          32768 ?
*                     1.1.1.1                0              0 1 ?
*    150.2.2.0/24     3.3.3.3                               0 3 2 ?
*>                    1.1.1.1                               0 1 2 ?
*>   150.3.3.0/24     3.3.3.3                0              0 3 ?
```

In the output above, the path via R3 is preferred for the 150.3.3.0/24 prefix; however, the router prefers the path via R1 for the 150.2.2.0/24 prefix because, all else being equal, it is the router with the lower IP address. To influence path selection in this case, we need to configure BGP on R1 to advertise all prefixes with a longer AS_PATH. The MED will not work because this attribute is not, by default, considered when prefixes are received from multiple ASes. This task is completed by configuring R1 as follows:

```
R1(config)#route-map PREPEND permit 10
R1(config-route-map)#set as-path prepend 1 1 1 1
R1(config-route-map)#exit
R1(config)#router bgp 1
R1(config-router)#neighbor 4.4.4.4 route-map PREPEND out
R1(config-router)#exit
```

Following this configuration, the BGP Table on R4 shows the following:

```
R4#show ip bgp
BGP table version is 14, local router ID is 4.4.4.4
Status codes: s suppressed, d damped, h history, * valid, > best, i - internal,
              r RIB-failure, S Stale
Origin codes: i - IGP, e - EGP, ? - incomplete

      Network          Next Hop            Metric LocPrf Weight Path
 *    150.1.1.0/24     1.1.1.1                  0              0 1 1 1 1 1 ?
 *>                    0.0.0.0                  0          32768 ?
 *>   150.2.2.0/24     3.3.3.3                                 0 3 2 ?
 *                     1.1.1.1                                 0 1 1 1 1 1 2 ?
 *>   150.3.3.0/24     3.3.3.3                  0              0 3 ?
 *                     1.1.1.1                                 0 1 1 1 1 1 2 3 ?
```

Task 5

The requirements of this task are two-fold. The first requirement is that R4 and R2 advertise all prefixes to R3 with a MED of 4 and 2, respectively. This is completed using an outbound route map on these two routers. Before any BGP configuration changes, the BGP RIB on R3 shows the following route entries:

```
R3#show ip bgp
BGP table version is 11, local router ID is 3.3.3.3
Status codes: s suppressed, d damped, h history, * valid, > best, i - internal,
              r RIB-failure, S Stale
Origin codes: i - IGP, e - EGP, ? - incomplete

      Network          Next Hop            Metric LocPrf Weight Path
 *>   150.1.1.0/24     4.4.4.4                  0              0 4 ?
 *                     2.2.2.2                                 0 2 1 ?
 *>   150.2.2.0/24     2.2.2.2                  0              0 2 ?
 *>   150.3.3.0/24     0.0.0.0                  0          32768 ?
```

The first part of this task is completed as follows:

```
R4(config)#route-map MED permit 10
R4(config-route-map)#set metric 4
R4(config-route-map)#exit
R4(config)#router bgp 4
R4(config-router)#neighbor 3.3.3.3 route-map MED out
R4(config-router)#exit

R2(config)#route-map MED permit 10
R2(config-route-map)#set metric 2
R2(config-route-map)#exit
R2(config)#router bgp 2
R2(config-router)#neighbor 3.3.3.3 route-map MED out
R2(config-router)#exit
```

Following these changes, the BGP RIB on R3 shows the following:

```
R3#show ip bgp
BGP table version is 13, local router ID is 3.3.3.3
Status codes: s suppressed, d damped, h history, * valid, > best, i - internal,
              r RIB-failure, S Stale
Origin codes: i - IGP, e - EGP, ? - incomplete

      Network          Next Hop            Metric LocPrf Weight Path
 *>   150.1.1.0/24     4.4.4.4                  4              0 4 ?
 *                     2.2.2.2                  2              0 2 1 ?
 *>   150.2.2.0/24     2.2.2.2                  2              0 2 ?
 *>   150.3.3.0/24     0.0.0.0                  0          32768 ?
```

The second part of this task has two caveats. The first is that the MED attribute should be used in the path selection process. The issue here is that, by default, the MED is only compared for path received from the same AS. In order to allow BGP to compare MED values from prefixes received from multiple ASes, this default behavior needs to be modified. The second caveat is that the MED is compared AFTER the AS_PATH. This means that, for example, BGP will select the path via R4 as the best path to the 150.1.1.0/24 prefix because of the shorter AS_PATH length. Again, this default behavior has to be modified to complete this task. The second part of this task is therefore completed as follows:

```
R3(config)#router bgp 3
R3(config-router)#bgp bestpath as-path ignore
R3(config-router)#bgp always-compare-med
R3(config-router)#exit
```

Following this configuration, the BGP Table on R3 now shows the following:

```
R3#show ip bgp
BGP table version is 14, local router ID is 3.3.3.3
Status codes: s suppressed, d damped, h history, * valid, > best, i - internal,
              r RIB-failure, S Stale
Origin codes: i - IGP, e - EGP, ? - incomplete

     Network          Next Hop          Metric LocPrf Weight Path
*    150.1.1.0/24     4.4.4.4                4          0 4 ?
*>                    2.2.2.2                2          0 2 1 ?
*>   150.2.2.0/24     2.2.2.2                2          0 2 ?
*>   150.3.3.0/24     0.0.0.0                0      32768 ?
```

A more detailed look reveals that the path with the longer AS_PATH sequence, but LOWER metric (MED) value is now preferred because of the configuration implemented on R3:

```
R3#show ip bgp 150.1.1.0 255.255.255.0
BGP routing table entry for 150.1.1.0/24, version 14
Paths: (2 available, best #2, table Default-IP-Routing-Table)
Flag: 0x820
  Advertised to update-groups:
     1
  4
    4.4.4.4 from 4.4.4.4 (4.4.4.4)
      Origin incomplete, metric 4, localpref 100, valid, external
  2 1
    2.2.2.2 from 2.2.2.2 (2.2.2.2)
      Origin incomplete, metric 2, localpref 100, valid, external, best
```

Task 6

While seemingly difficult, this task is very straightforward and requires the use of AS_PATH prepending when advertising these prefixes via BGP on R2. This is completed as follows:

```
R2(config)#interface loopback 192
R2(config-if)#ip address 192.1.1.1 255.255.255.0
R2(config-if)#exit
R2(config)#interface loopback 193
R2(config-if)#ip address 193.1.1.1 255.255.255.0
R2(config-if)#exit
R2(config)#interface loopback 194
R2(config-if)#ip address 194.1.1.1 255.255.255.0
R2(config-if)#exit
R2(config)#interface loopback 195
R2(config-if)#ip address 195.1.1.1 255.255.255.0
R2(config-if)#exit
R2(config)#ip prefix-list LOOPBACK192 seq 5 permit 192.1.1.0/24
R2(config)#ip prefix-list LOOPBACK193 seq 5 permit 193.1.1.0/24
R2(config)#ip prefix-list LOOPBACK194 seq 5 permit 194.1.1.0/24
R2(config)#ip prefix-list LOOPBACK195 seq 5 permit 195.1.1.0/24
R2(config)#route-map PREPEND permit 10
R2(config-route-map)#match ip address prefix-list LOOPBACK192
R2(config-route-map)#set as-path prepend 192
R2(config-route-map)#exit
R2(config)#route-map PREPEND permit 20
R2(config-route-map)#match ip address prefix-list LOOPBACK193
R2(config-route-map)#set as-path prepend 193
R2(config-route-map)#exit
R2(config)#route-map PREPEND permit 30
R2(config-route-map)#match ip address prefix-list LOOPBACK194
```

```
R2(config-route-map)#set as-path prepend 194
R2(config-route-map)#exit
R2(config)#route-map PREPEND permit 40
R2(config-route-map)#match ip address prefix-list LOOPBACK195
R2(config-route-map)#set as-path prepend 195
R2(config-route-map)#exit
R2(config)#route-map PREPEND permit 50
R2(config-route-map)#exit
R2(config)#router bgp 2
R2(config-router)#network 192.1.1.0
R2(config-router)#network 193.1.1.0
R2(config-router)#network 194.1.1.0
R2(config-router)#network 195.1.1.0
R2(config-router)#neighbor 1.1.1.1 route-map PREPEND out
R2(config-router)#neighbor 3.3.3.3 route-map PREPEND out
R2(config-router)#exit
```

Following this configuration, verify the BGP RIB entries for these prefixes are correct:

```
R1#show ip bgp
BGP table version is 29, local router ID is 1.1.1.1
Status codes: s suppressed, d damped, h history, * valid, > best, i - internal,
              r RIB-failure, S Stale
Origin codes: i - IGP, e - EGP, ? - incomplete

     Network          Next Hop         Metric LocPrf Weight Path
*    150.1.1.0/24     4.4.4.4               0           0 4 ?
*>                    0.0.0.0               0       32768 ?
*    150.2.2.0/24     4.4.4.4                           0 4 3 2 ?
*>                    2.2.2.2               0           0 2 ?
*    150.3.3.0/24     4.4.4.4                           0 4 3 ?
*>                    2.2.2.2               0           0 2 3 ?
*    192.1.1.0        4.4.4.4                           0 4 3 2 192 i
*>                    2.2.2.2               0           0 2 192 i
*    193.1.1.0        4.4.4.4                           0 4 3 2 193 i
*>                    2.2.2.2               0           0 2 193 i
*    194.1.1.0        4.4.4.4                           0 4 3 2 194 i
*>                    2.2.2.2               0           0 2 194 i
*    195.1.1.0        4.4.4.4                           0 4 3 2 195 i
*>                    2.2.2.2               0           0 2 195 i

R3#show ip bgp
BGP table version is 44, local router ID is 3.3.3.3
Status codes: s suppressed, d damped, h history, * valid, > best, i - internal,
              r RIB-failure, S Stale
Origin codes: i - IGP, e - EGP, ? - incomplete

     Network          Next Hop         Metric LocPrf Weight Path
*    150.1.1.0/24     4.4.4.4               4           0 4 ?
*>                    2.2.2.2                           0 2 1 ?
*>   150.2.2.0/24     2.2.2.2               0           0 2 ?
*>   150.3.3.0/24     0.0.0.0               0       32768 ?
*>   192.1.1.0        2.2.2.2               0           0 2 192 i
*>   193.1.1.0        2.2.2.2               0           0 2 193 i
*>   194.1.1.0        2.2.2.2               0           0 2 194 i
*>   195.1.1.0        2.2.2.2               0           0 2 195 i

R4#show ip bgp
BGP table version is 38, local router ID is 4.4.4.4
Status codes: s suppressed, d damped, h history, * valid, > best, i - internal,
              r RIB-failure, S Stale
Origin codes: i - IGP, e - EGP, ? - incomplete

     Network          Next Hop         Metric LocPrf Weight Path
*    150.1.1.0/24     3.3.3.3                           0 3 2 1 ?
*                     1.1.1.1               0           0 1 1 1 1 1 ?
*>                    0.0.0.0               0       32768 ?
*>   150.2.2.0/24     3.3.3.3                           0 3 2 ?
*                     1.1.1.1                           0 1 1 1 1 1 2 ?
*>   150.3.3.0/24     3.3.3.3               0           0 3 ?
*                     1.1.1.1                           0 1 1 1 1 1 2 3 ?
*>   192.1.1.0        3.3.3.3                           0 3 2 192 i
*                     1.1.1.1                           0 1 1 1 1 1 2 192 i
```

```
*> 193.1.1.0        3.3.3.3                              0 3 2 193 i
*                   1.1.1.1                              0 1 1 1 1 1 2 193 i
*> 194.1.1.0        3.3.3.3                              0 3 2 194 i
*                   1.1.1.1                              0 1 1 1 1 1 2 194 i
*> 195.1.1.0        3.3.3.3                              0 3 2 195 i
*                   1.1.1.1                              0 1 1 1 1 1 2 195 i
```

Task 7

To complete this task, we need to use a two-line AS_PATH filter. Prior to any configuration changes, the BGP Table on R1 shows the following entries:

```
R1#show ip bgp
BGP table version is 29, local router ID is 1.1.1.1
Status codes: s suppressed, d damped, h history, * valid, > best, i - internal,
              r RIB-failure, S Stale
Origin codes: i - IGP, e - EGP, ? - incomplete

      Network          Next Hop        Metric LocPrf Weight Path
*     150.1.1.0/24     4.4.4.4              0             0 4 ?
*>                     0.0.0.0              0         32768 ?
*     150.2.2.0/24     4.4.4.4                            0 4 3 2 ?
*>                     2.2.2.2              0             0 2 ?
*     150.3.3.0/24     4.4.4.4                            0 4 3 ?
*>                     2.2.2.2              0             0 2 3 ?
*     192.1.1.0        4.4.4.4                            0 4 3 2 192 i
*>                     2.2.2.2              0             0 2 192 i
*     193.1.1.0        4.4.4.4                            0 4 3 2 193 i
*>                     2.2.2.2              0             0 2 193 i
*     194.1.1.0        4.4.4.4                            0 4 3 2 194 i
*>                     2.2.2.2              0             0 2 194 i
*     195.1.1.0        4.4.4.4                            0 4 3 2 195 i
*>                     2.2.2.2              0             0 2 195 i
```

To complete this task, you need to have a good understanding of basic regular expressions and how they are configured. A regular expression comprises four main parts. These four main parts, which are described in the following sections, are:

- A Range
- An Atom
- A Piece
- A Branch

A range is a sequence of characters within left and right square brackets. Examples of ranges are [abcd] or [1-9] or [0,4-7]. An atom is a single character. A Piece or Multiplier is a symbol that follows an Atom. Examples include the plus sign (+) and the question mark (?).branch is 0 or more concatenated pieces, i.e. 0 or more pieces used together in a regular expression, for example ^[0-9]+ [0-9]+?$. Before configuring and then applying AS_PATH filters, you should always use the show ip bgp regexp <regular expression> command to ensure that you are matching the desired routes. For example, prior to R1s configuration change, this command, used with the appropriate regular expression, confirms that the AS_PATH filter will match the desired prefixes:

```
R1#show ip bgp regexp _19[2-5]$
BGP table version is 29, local router ID is 1.1.1.1
Status codes: s suppressed, d damped, h history, * valid, > best, i - internal,
              r RIB-failure, S Stale
Origin codes: i - IGP, e - EGP, ? - incomplete

      Network          Next Hop        Metric LocPrf Weight Path
*     192.1.1.0        4.4.4.4                            0 4 3 2 192 i
*>                     2.2.2.2              0             0 2 192 i
*     193.1.1.0        4.4.4.4                            0 4 3 2 193 i
*>                     2.2.2.2              0             0 2 193 i
*     194.1.1.0        4.4.4.4                            0 4 3 2 194 i
*>                     2.2.2.2              0             0 2 194 i
*     195.1.1.0        4.4.4.4                            0 4 3 2 195 i
*>                     2.2.2.2              0             0 2 195 i
```

To complete this task, implement the following configuration on R1:

```
R1(config)#ip as-path access-list 1 deny _19[2-5]$
R1(config)#ip as-path access-list 1 permit .*
R1(config)#router bgp 1
R1(config-router)#neighbor 2.2.2.2 filter-list 1 in
R1(config-router)#exit
```

Following this change, the BGP Table on R1 shows the following entries:

```
R1#show ip bgp
BGP table version is 33, local router ID is 1.1.1.1
Status codes: s suppressed, d damped, h history, * valid, > best, i - internal,
              r RIB-failure, S Stale
Origin codes: i - IGP, e - EGP, ? - incomplete

     Network          Next Hop          Metric LocPrf Weight Path
 *   150.1.1.0/24     4.4.4.4               0             0 4 ?
 *>                   0.0.0.0               0         32768 ?
 *   150.2.2.0/24     4.4.4.4                             0 4 3 2 ?
 *>                   2.2.2.2               0             0 2 ?
 *   150.3.3.0/24     4.4.4.4                             0 4 3 ?
 *>                   2.2.2.2                             0 2 3 ?
 *>  192.1.1.0        4.4.4.4                             0 4 3 2 192 i
 *>  193.1.1.0        4.4.4.4                             0 4 3 2 193 i
 *>  194.1.1.0        4.4.4.4                             0 4 3 2 194 i
 *>  195.1.1.0        4.4.4.4                             0 4 3 2 195 i
```

NOTE: You can also complete this task by matching the configured AS_PATH ACL in a route map and applying that inbound. Either solution is acceptable.

FINAL ROUTER CONFIGURATIONS

R1

```
R1#term len 0
R1#sh run
Building configuration...

Current configuration : 1614 bytes
!
version 12.4
service timestamps debug datetime msec
service timestamps log datetime msec
no service password-encryption
!
hostname R1
!
boot-start-marker
boot-end-marker
!
no logging console
!
no aaa new-model
no network-clock-participate slot 1
no network-clock-participate wic 0
ip cef
!
no ip domain lookup
ip auth-proxy max-nodata-conns 3
ip admission max-nodata-conns 3
!
interface Loopback0
 ip address 1.1.1.1 255.255.255.255
!
interface FastEthernet0/0
 ip address 150.1.1.1 255.255.255.0
 duplex auto
```

```
 speed auto
!
interface Serial0/0
 ip address 10.0.0.1 255.255.255.252
 clock rate 2000000
!
interface Serial0/1
 no ip address
 shutdown
!
router bgp 1
 no synchronization
 bgp log-neighbor-changes
 redistribute connected route-map CONNECTED
 neighbor 2.2.2.2 remote-as 2
 neighbor 2.2.2.2 ebgp-multihop 255
 neighbor 2.2.2.2 update-source Loopback0
 neighbor 2.2.2.2 filter-list 1 in
 neighbor 4.4.4.4 remote-as 4
 neighbor 4.4.4.4 ebgp-multihop 255
 neighbor 4.4.4.4 update-source Loopback0
 neighbor 4.4.4.4 route-map PREPEND out
 no auto-summary
!
ip forward-protocol nd
ip route 2.2.2.2 255.255.255.255 Serial0/0
ip route 4.4.4.4 255.255.255.255 FastEthernet0/0 150.1.1.4
!
ip as-path access-list 1 deny _19[2-5]$
ip as-path access-list 1 permit .*
!
no ip http server
no ip http secure-server
!
route-map PREPEND permit 10
 set as-path prepend 1 1 1 1
!
route-map CONNECTED permit 10
 match interface FastEthernet0/0
!
route-map CONNECTED deny 20
!
control-plane
!
line con 0
line aux 0
line vty 0 4
 login
!
end

R1#
```

R2

```
R2#term len 0
R2#sh run
Building configuration...

Current configuration : 2455 bytes
!
version 12.4
service timestamps debug datetime msec
service timestamps log datetime msec
no service password-encryption
!
hostname R2
!
boot-start-marker
boot-end-marker
!
no logging console
!
no aaa new-model
```

```
no network-clock-participate slot 1
no network-clock-participate wic 0
ip cef
!
no ip domain lookup
ip auth-proxy max-nodata-conns 3
ip admission max-nodata-conns 3
!
interface Loopback0
 ip address 2.2.2.2 255.255.255.255
!
interface Loopback192
 ip address 192.1.1.1 255.255.255.0
!
interface Loopback193
 ip address 193.1.1.1 255.255.255.0
!
interface Loopback194
 ip address 194.1.1.1 255.255.255.0
!
interface Loopback195
 ip address 195.1.1.1 255.255.255.0
!
interface FastEthernet0/0
 ip address 150.2.2.2 255.255.255.0
 duplex auto
 speed auto
!
interface Serial0/0
 ip address 10.0.0.2 255.255.255.252
!
interface Serial0/1
 ip address 10.0.0.9 255.255.255.252
!
router bgp 2
 no synchronization
 bgp log-neighbor-changes
 network 192.1.1.0
 network 193.1.1.0
 network 194.1.1.0
 network 195.1.1.0
 redistribute connected route-map CONNECTED
 neighbor 1.1.1.1 remote-as 1
 neighbor 1.1.1.1 ebgp-multihop 255
 neighbor 1.1.1.1 update-source Loopback0
 neighbor 1.1.1.1 route-map PREPEND out
 neighbor 3.3.3.3 remote-as 3
 neighbor 3.3.3.3 ebgp-multihop 255
 neighbor 3.3.3.3 update-source Loopback0
 neighbor 3.3.3.3 route-map PREPEND out
 no auto-summary
!
ip forward-protocol nd
ip route 1.1.1.1 255.255.255.255 Serial0/0
ip route 3.3.3.3 255.255.255.255 Serial0/1
!
no ip http server
no ip http secure-server
!
ip prefix-list LOOPBACK192 seq 5 permit 192.1.1.0/24
!
ip prefix-list LOOPBACK193 seq 5 permit 193.1.1.0/24
!
ip prefix-list LOOPBACK194 seq 5 permit 194.1.1.0/24
!
ip prefix-list LOOPBACK195 seq 5 permit 195.1.1.0/24
!
route-map MED permit 10
 set metric 2
!
route-map PREPEND permit 10
 match ip address prefix-list LOOPBACK192
 set as-path prepend 192
!
route-map PREPEND permit 20
```

```
 match ip address prefix-list LOOPBACK193
 set as-path prepend 193
!
route-map PREPEND permit 30
 match ip address prefix-list LOOPBACK194
 set as-path prepend 194
!
route-map PREPEND permit 40
 match ip address prefix-list LOOPBACK195
 set as-path prepend 195
!
route-map PREPEND permit 50
!
route-map CONNECTED permit 10
 match interface FastEthernet0/0
!
route-map CONNECTED deny 20
!
control-plane
!
line con 0
line aux 0
line vty 0 4
 login
!
end

R2#
```

R3

```
R3#term len 0
R3#sh run
Building configuration...

Current configuration : 1850 bytes
!
version 12.4
service timestamps debug datetime msec
service timestamps log datetime msec
no service password-encryption
!
hostname R3
!
boot-start-marker
boot-end-marker
!
no logging console
!
no aaa new-model
no network-clock-participate slot 1
no network-clock-participate wic 0
ip cef
!
no ip domain lookup
ip auth-proxy max-nodata-conns 3
ip admission max-nodata-conns 3
!
interface Loopback0
 ip address 3.3.3.3 255.255.255.255
!
interface FastEthernet0/0
 ip address 150.3.3.3 255.255.255.0
 duplex auto
 speed auto
!
interface Serial1/0
 no ip address
 shutdown
 clock rate 128000
!
interface Serial1/1
 ip address 10.0.0.10 255.255.255.252
 clock rate 128000
!
```

```
interface Serial1/2
 ip address 10.0.0.13 255.255.255.252
 clock rate 128000
!
interface Serial1/3
 ip address 10.0.0.17 255.255.255.252
 clock rate 128000
!
interface Serial1/4
 no ip address
 shutdown
!
interface Serial1/5
 no ip address
 shutdown
!
interface Serial1/6
 no ip address
 shutdown
!
interface Serial1/7
 no ip address
 shutdown
!
router bgp 3
 no synchronization
 bgp always-compare-med
 bgp log-neighbor-changes
 bgp bestpath as-path ignore
 redistribute connected route-map CONNECTED
 neighbor 2.2.2.2 remote-as 2
 neighbor 2.2.2.2 ebgp-multihop 255
 neighbor 2.2.2.2 update-source Loopback0
 neighbor 4.4.4.4 remote-as 4
 neighbor 4.4.4.4 ebgp-multihop 255
 neighbor 4.4.4.4 update-source Loopback0
 no auto-summary
!
ip forward-protocol nd
ip route 2.2.2.2 255.255.255.255 Serial1/1
ip route 4.4.4.4 255.255.255.255 Serial1/2
ip route 4.4.4.4 255.255.255.255 Serial1/3
!
no ip http server
no ip http secure-server
!
route-map CONNECTED permit 10
 match interface FastEthernet0/0
!
route-map CONNECTED deny 20
!
control-plane
!
line con 0
line aux 0
line vty 0 4
 login
!
end

R3#
```

R4

```
R4#term len 0
R4#sh run
Building configuration...

Current configuration : 1518 bytes
!
version 12.4
service timestamps debug datetime msec
service timestamps log datetime msec
no service password-encryption
```

```
!
hostname R4
!
boot-start-marker
boot-end-marker
!
no logging console
!
no aaa new-model
no network-clock-participate slot 1
no network-clock-participate wic 0
ip cef
!
no ip domain lookup
ip auth-proxy max-nodata-conns 3
ip admission max-nodata-conns 3
!
!
interface Loopback0
 ip address 4.4.4.4 255.255.255.255
!
interface FastEthernet0/0
 ip address 150.1.1.4 255.255.255.0
 duplex auto
 speed auto
!
interface Serial0/0
 ip address 10.0.0.14 255.255.255.252
!
interface Serial0/1
 ip address 10.0.0.18 255.255.255.252
!
router bgp 4
 no synchronization
 bgp log-neighbor-changes
 redistribute connected route-map CONNECTED
 neighbor 1.1.1.1 remote-as 1
 neighbor 1.1.1.1 ebgp-multihop 255
 neighbor 1.1.1.1 update-source Loopback0
 neighbor 3.3.3.3 remote-as 3
 neighbor 3.3.3.3 ebgp-multihop 255
 neighbor 3.3.3.3 update-source Loopback0
 neighbor 3.3.3.3 route-map MED out
 no auto-summary
!
ip forward-protocol nd
ip route 1.1.1.1 255.255.255.255 FastEthernet0/0 150.1.1.1
ip route 3.3.3.3 255.255.255.255 Serial0/0
ip route 3.3.3.3 255.255.255.255 Serial0/1
!
no ip http server
no ip http secure-server
!
route-map MED permit 10
 set metric 4
!
route-map CONNECTED permit 10
 match interface FastEthernet0/0
!
route-map CONNECTED deny 20
!
control-plane
!
line con 0
line aux 0
line vty 0 4
 login
!
end

R4#
```

CCNP LAB 41

Internet Protocol Version 6 Lab

Lab Objective:

The focus of this lab is to understand RIPng implementation and configuration in Cisco IOS routers. Additional technologies include stateless auto-configuration and summarization.

Lab Topology:

The lab network topology is illustrated below:

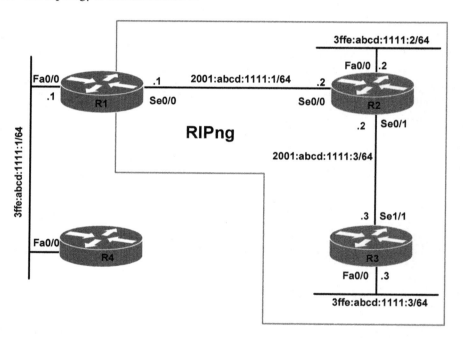

IMPORTANT NOTE: If you are using the www.howtonetwork.net racks, please bring up the LAN interfaces connected to the routers by issuing the no shutdown command on the connected switches. If you are using a home lab with no Switches, you can bring up the LAN interfaces using the following configurations on your routers:

```
interface fastethernet 0/0
 no keepalive
 loopback
 no shutdown
```

Alternately, you can simply connect the interfaces to a hub or switch if you have one available in your own lab.

Task 1

Configure hostnames and IPv6 addressing on all routers as illustrated in the network topology. Do NOT configure an IPv6 address on R4s FastEthernet 0/0 interface.

Task 2

Configure R4 so that it uses stateless auto-configuration to dynamically provision its address. Ensure that this router also has a default route in its routing table. Verify your configuration.

Task 3

Configure RIPng on R1, R2, and R3. RIPng messages should be exchanged using UDP port 520. Do NOT enable RIPng for the LAN subnet connected to R1. Next configure your network so that R2 is able to reach R4; however, R3 should NOT be able to reach R4. You are NOT allowed to use redistribution, any types of route filters on any router in the network, or static routes. Verify your configuration using the appropriate commands.

Task 4

Configure the following Loopback interfaces on R3 and redistribute them via RIPng:
* Loopback 1: IPv6 address 2002:abcd:1234:a::4/128
* Loopback 2: IPv6 address 2002:abcd:1234:b::4/128
* Loopback 3: IPv6 address 2002:abcd:1234:c::4/128
* Loopback 4: IPv6 address 2002:abcd:1234:d::4/128
* Loopback 5: IPv6 address 2002:abcd:1234:e::4/128

Next, configure RIPng to advertise a SINGLE route for these 5 Loopback interfaces. Ensure that this single route is advertised to R1 and R2 and the specific prefixes are suppressed. Verify your configuration using the appropriate commands as well as standard or extended pings.

Task 5

Configure RIPng so that all routes that R2 receives from R3 have a route metric of 10. Verify your configuration using the appropriate commands.

LAB VALIDATION

Task 1

```
Router(config)#hostname R1
R1(config)#ipv6 unicast-routing
R1(config)#ipv6 cef
R1(config)#interface fastethernet 0/0
R1(config-if)#ipv6 address 3ffe:abcd:1111:1::1/64
R1(config-if)#no shutdown
R1(config-if)#exit
R1(config)#interface serial 0/0
R1(config-if)#ipv6 address 2001:abcd:1111:1::1/64
R1(config-if)#clock rate 2000000
R1(config-if)#no shutdown
R1(config-if)#exit

Router(config)#hostname R2
R2(config)#ipv6 unicast-routing
R2(config)#ipv6 cef
R2(config)#interface fastethernet 0/0
R2(config-if)#ipv6 address 3ffe:abcd:1111:2::2/64
R2(config-if)#no shutdown
R2(config)#interface serial 0/0
R2(config-if)#ipv6 address 2001:abcd:1111:1::2/64
R2(config-if)#no shutdown
R2(config-if)#exit
R2(config)#interface serial 0/1
R2(config-if)#ipv6 address 2001:abcd:1111:3::2/64
R2(config-if)#no shutdown
R2(config-if)#exit

Router(config)#hostname R3
R3(config)#ipv6 unicast-routing
```

```
R3(config)#ipv6 cef
R3(config)#interface fastethernet 0/0
R3(config-if)#ipv6 address 3ffe:abcd:1111:3::3/64
R3(config-if)#no shutdown
R3(config-if)#exit
R3(config)#interface serial 1/1
R3(config-if)#ipv6 address 2001:abcd:1111:3::3/64
R3(config-if)#clock rate 128000
R3(config-if)#no shutdown
R3(config-if)#exit

Router(config)#hostname R4
R4(config)#ipv6 unicast-routing
R4(config)#ipv6 cef
```

Task 2

To complete this task, append the default keyword to the ipv6 address autoconfig interface configuration command. If the default keyword keyword is omitted, a default route will not be installed into the local routers IPv6 RIB. This task is completed as follows:

```
R4(config)#interface fastethernet 0/0
R4(config-if)#no shutdown
R4(config-if)#ipv6 address autoconfig default
R4(config-if)#exit
```

Verify stateless auto-configuration using the show ipv6 interface command:

```
R4#show ipv6 interface fastethernet 0/0
FastEthernet0/0 is up, line protocol is up
  IPv6 is enabled, link-local address is FE80::20F:23FF:FE5E:F120
  Global unicast address(es):
    3FFE:ABCD:1111:1:20F:23FF:FE5E:F120, subnet is 3FFE:ABCD:1111:1::/64 [PRE]
      valid lifetime 2591989 preferred lifetime 604789
  Joined group address(es):
    FF02::1
    FF02::2
    FF02::1:FF5E:F120
  MTU is 1500 bytes
  ICMP error messages limited to one every 100 milliseconds
  ICMP redirects are enabled
  ND DAD is enabled, number of DAD attempts: 1
  ND reachable time is 30000 milliseconds
  ND advertised reachable time is 0 milliseconds
  ND advertised retransmit interval is 0 milliseconds
  ND router advertisements are sent every 200 seconds
  ND router advertisements live for 1800 seconds
  Hosts use stateless autoconfig for addresses.
```

Verify that the default route has been installed using the show ipv6 route command. This will point to the Link Local address of R1, rather than the global Unicast address:

```
R4#show ipv6 route
IPv6 Routing Table - 5 entries
Codes: C - Connected, L - Local, S - Static, R - RIP, B - BGP
       U - Per-user Static route
       I1 - ISIS L1, I2 - ISIS L2, IA - ISIS interarea, IS - ISIS summary
       O - OSPF intra, OI - OSPF inter, OE1 - OSPF ext 1, OE2 - OSPF ext 2
       ON1 - OSPF NSSA ext 1, ON2 - OSPF NSSA ext 2
S   ::/0 [1/0]
     via FE80::20F:23FF:FE5E:EC80, FastEthernet0/0
C   3FFE:ABCD:1111:1::/64 [0/0]
     via ::, FastEthernet0/0
L   3FFE:ABCD:1111:1:20F:23FF:FE5E:F120/128 [0/0]
     via ::, FastEthernet0/0
L   FE80::/10 [0/0]
     via ::, Null0
L   FF00::/8 [0/0]
     via ::, Null0
```

Task 3

The requirements of this task are two-fold. The first requirement is to configure RIPng as stated in the requirements. This is a straightforward task; however, because the task requires RIPng to use UDP port 520 instead of the default port 521, some additional configuration is required. The first part of this task is completed as follows:

```
R1(config)#ipv6 router rip CCNP
R1(config-rtr)#port 520 multicast-group ff02::9
R1(config-rtr)#exit
R1(config)#interface serial 0/0
R1(config-if)#ipv6 rip CCNP enable
R1(config-if)#exit

R2(config)#ipv6 router rip CCNP
R2(config-rtr)#port 520 multicast-group ff02::9
R2(config-rtr)#exit
R2(config)#interface fastethernet 0/0
R2(config-if)#ipv6 rip CCNP enable
R2(config-if)#exit
R2(config)#interface serial 0/0
R2(config-if)#ipv6 rip CCNP enable
R2(config-if)#exit
R2(config)#interface serial 0/1
R2(config-if)#ipv6 rip CCNP enable
R2(config-if)#exit

R3(config)#ipv6 router rip CCNP
R3(config-rtr)#port 520 multicast-group ff02::9
R3(config-rtr)#exit
R3(config)#interface fastethernet 0/0
R3(config-if)#ipv6 rip CCNP enable
R3(config-if)#exit
R3(config)#interface serial 1/1
R3(config-if)#ipv6 rip CCNP enable
R3(config-if)#exit
```

Verify your configuration using the show ipv6 route command:

```
R1#show ipv6 route rip
IPv6 Routing Table - 9 entries
Codes: C - Connected, L - Local, S - Static, R - RIP, B - BGP
       U - Per-user Static route
       I1 - ISIS L1, I2 - ISIS L2, IA - ISIS interarea, IS - ISIS summary
       O - OSPF intra, OI - OSPF inter, OE1 - OSPF ext 1, OE2 - OSPF ext 2
       ON1 - OSPF NSSA ext 1, ON2 - OSPF NSSA ext 2
R   2001:ABCD:1111:3::/64 [120/2]
     via FE80::20D:28FF:FE9E:F940, Serial0/0
R   3FFE:ABCD:1111:2::/64 [120/2]
     via FE80::20D:28FF:FE9E:F940, Serial0/0
R   3FFE:ABCD:1111:3::/64 [120/3]
     via FE80::20D:28FF:FE9E:F940, Serial0/0

R2#show ipv6 route rip
IPv6 Routing Table - 8 entries
Codes: C - Connected, L - Local, S - Static, R - RIP, B - BGP
       U - Per-user Static route
       I1 - ISIS L1, I2 - ISIS L2, IA - ISIS interarea, IS - ISIS summary
       O - OSPF intra, OI - OSPF inter, OE1 - OSPF ext 1, OE2 - OSPF ext 2
       ON1 - OSPF NSSA ext 1, ON2 - OSPF NSSA ext 2
R   3FFE:ABCD:1111:3::/64 [120/2]
     via FE80::213:7FFF:FEAF:3E00, Serial0/1

R3#show ipv6 route rip
IPv6 Routing Table - 7 entries
Codes: C - Connected, L - Local, S - Static, R - RIP, B - BGP
       U - Per-user Static route
       I1 - ISIS L1, I2 - ISIS L2, IA - ISIS interarea, IS - ISIS summary
       O - OSPF intra, OI - OSPF inter, OE1 - OSPF ext 1, OE2 - OSPF ext 2
       ON1 - OSPF NSSA ext 1, ON2 - OSPF NSSA ext 2
R   2001:ABCD:1111:1::/64 [120/2]
     via FE80::20D:28FF:FE9E:F940, Serial1/1
R   3FFE:ABCD:1111:2::/64 [120/2]
     via FE80::20D:28FF:FE9E:F940, Serial1/1
```

The second part of this task requires that R2 and R3 be able to ping R4 and vice-versa without enabling RIPng on the R1-R4 LAN segment. To do so, you need to advertise a default route from R1; however, to ensure that this is not advertised to R4, you need to set a metric of 14 for this route. This means that when R2 receives it, the metric will be 15, which is the maximum allowed metric for RIP. If advertised to R3, this route will have a metric of 16 - which is unreachable for RIP - and will therefore not be installed into the routing table. The second part of this task is completed as follows:

```
R1(config)#interface serial 0/0
R1(config-if)#ipv6 rip CCNP default-information originate metric 14
R1(config-if)#exit
```

Verify your configuration by looking at the routings of R2 and R3:

```
R2#show ipv6 route rip
IPv6 Routing Table - 9 entries
Codes: C - Connected, L - Local, S - Static, R - RIP, B - BGP
       U - Per-user Static route
       I1 - ISIS L1, I2 - ISIS L2, IA - ISIS interarea, IS - ISIS summary
       O - OSPF intra, OI - OSPF inter, OE1 - OSPF ext 1, OE2 - OSPF ext 2
       ON1 - OSPF NSSA ext 1, ON2 - OSPF NSSA ext 2
R    ::/0 [120/15]
     via FE80::20F:23FF:FE5E:EC80, Serial0/0
R    3FFE:ABCD:1111:3::/64 [120/2]
     via FE80::213:7FFF:FEAF:3E00, Serial0/1

R3#show ipv6 route rip
IPv6 Routing Table - 7 entries
Codes: C - Connected, L - Local, S - Static, R - RIP, B - BGP
       U - Per-user Static route
       I1 - ISIS L1, I2 - ISIS L2, IA - ISIS interarea, IS - ISIS summary
       O - OSPF intra, OI - OSPF inter, OE1 - OSPF ext 1, OE2 - OSPF ext 2
       ON1 - OSPF NSSA ext 1, ON2 - OSPF NSSA ext 2
R    2001:ABCD:1111:1::/64 [120/2]
     via FE80::20D:28FF:FE9E:F940, Serial1/1
R    3FFE:ABCD:1111:2::/64 [120/2]
     via FE80::20D:28FF:FE9E:F940, Serial1/1
```

Finally, verify that R2 and R4 can reach each other using a standard or extended ping:

```
R2#show ipv6 route 3FFE:ABCD:1111:1:20F:23FF:FE5E:F120
IPv6 Routing Table - 9 entries
Codes: C - Connected, L - Local, S - Static, R - RIP, B - BGP
       U - Per-user Static route
       I1 - ISIS L1, I2 - ISIS L2, IA - ISIS interarea, IS - ISIS summary
       O - OSPF intra, OI - OSPF inter, OE1 - OSPF ext 1, OE2 - OSPF ext 2
       ON1 - OSPF NSSA ext 1, ON2 - OSPF NSSA ext 2
R    ::/0 [120/15]
     via FE80::20F:23FF:FE5E:EC80, Serial0/0

R2#ping 3FFE:ABCD:1111:1:20F:23FF:FE5E:F120 source fastethernet 0/0

Type escape sequence to abort.
Sending 5, 100-byte ICMP Echos to 3FFE:ABCD:1111:1:20F:23FF:FE5E:F120, timeout is 2
seconds:
Packet sent with a source address of 3FFE:ABCD:1111:2::2
!!!!!
Success rate is 100 percent (5/5), round-trip min/avg/max = 0/1/4 ms
```

Task 4

The requirements of this task are two-fold. The first requirement is that you configure Loopback interfaces on R3 and advertise them via RIPng. This is completed as follows:

```
R3(config)#interface loopback 1
R3(config-if)#ipv6 address 2002:abcd:1234:a::4/128
R3(config-if)#exit
R3(config)#interface loopback 2
```

```
R3(config-if)#ipv6 address 2002:abcd:1234:b::4/128
R3(config-if)#exit
R3(config)#interface loopback 3
R3(config-if)#ipv6 address 2002:abcd:1234:c::4/128
R3(config-if)#exit
R3(config)#interface loopback 4
R3(config-if)#ipv6 address 2002:abcd:1234:d::4/128
R3(config-if)#exit
R3(config)#interface loopback 5
R3(config-if)#ipv6 address 2002:abcd:1234:e::4/128
R3(config-if)#exit
R3(config)#ipv6 router rip CCNP
R3(config-rtr)#redistribute connected
R3(config-rtr)#exit
```

Verify your configuration by checking the routing tables on R2 and R1:

```
R1#show ipv6 route rip | include 2002
R   2002:ABCD:1234:A::4/128 [120/3]
R   2002:ABCD:1234:B::4/128 [120/3]
R   2002:ABCD:1234:C::4/128 [120/3]
R   2002:ABCD:1234:D::4/128 [120/3]
R   2002:ABCD:1234:E::4/128 [120/3]

R2#show ipv6 route rip | include 2002
R   2002:ABCD:1234:A::4/128 [120/2]
R   2002:ABCD:1234:B::4/128 [120/2]
R   2002:ABCD:1234:C::4/128 [120/2]
R   2002:ABCD:1234:D::4/128 [120/2]
R   2002:ABCD:1234:E::4/128 [120/2]
```

The second part of this task requires route summarization, i.e. summarizing the 5 Loopback interface addresses and advertise only a single route using RIPng. IPv6 summarization is not as complex as one would think. It is also performed in a manner similar to IPv4 route summarization. First, identify and locate the first different 16-bit field. In our example, it is the fourth field, which contains the values a, b, c, d, and e. Next, convert these values to binary as illustrated in the following table:

Hexadecimal Value	Binary Representation	Matching Bit Values
A	0000 0000 0000 1010	0000 0000 0000 1
B	0000 0000 0000 1011	0000 0000 0000 1
C	0000 0000 0000 1100	0000 0000 0000 1
D	0000 0000 0000 1101	0000 0000 0000 1
E	0000 0000 0000 1110	0000 0000 0000 1

Referencing the table above, the first thirteen bits match. To complete the address, we simply input zeros for the non-matching bits, resulting in the Binary address: 0000 0000 0000 1000. In Hexadecimal, the same address would be written as 8.

Next, we need to calculate the mask. This is simple and entails just counting the number of matching bits in the address, which would be 61. This task is completed as follows:

```
R3(config)#interface serial 1/1
R3(config-if)#ipv6 rip CCNP summary-address 2002:abcd:1234:8::/61
R3(config-if)#exit
```

Verify your configuration by checking the routing tables on R2 and R1:

```
R1#show ipv6 route rip | include 2002
R   2002:ABCD:1234:8::/61 [120/3]

R2#show ipv6 route rip | include 2002
R   2002:ABCD:1234:8::/61 [120/2]
```

Verify your configuration using a simple ping from R1 and R2:

```
1#ping 2002:ABCD:1234:A::4 repeat 10

Type escape sequence to abort.
Sending 10, 100-byte ICMP Echos to 2002:ABCD:1234:A::4, timeout is 2 seconds:
!!!!!!!!!!
Success rate is 100 percent (10/10), round-trip min/avg/max = 16/22/76 ms

R1#ping 2002:ABCD:1234:B::4 repeat 10

Type escape sequence to abort.
Sending 10, 100-byte ICMP Echos to 2002:ABCD:1234:B::4, timeout is 2 seconds:
!!!!!!!!!!
Success rate is 100 percent (10/10), round-trip min/avg/max = 16/16/20 ms

R1#ping 2002:ABCD:1234:C::4 repeat 10

Type escape sequence to abort.
Sending 10, 100-byte ICMP Echos to 2002:ABCD:1234:C::4, timeout is 2 seconds:
!!!!!!!!!!
Success rate is 100 percent (10/10), round-trip min/avg/max = 16/16/20 ms

R1#ping 2002:ABCD:1234:D::4 repeat 10

Type escape sequence to abort.
Sending 10, 100-byte ICMP Echos to 2002:ABCD:1234:D::4, timeout is 2 seconds:
!!!!!!!!!!
Success rate is 100 percent (10/10), round-trip min/avg/max = 16/16/16 ms

R1#ping 2002:ABCD:1234:E::4 repeat 10

Type escape sequence to abort.
Sending 10, 100-byte ICMP Echos to 2002:ABCD:1234:E::4, timeout is 2 seconds:
!!!!!!!!!!
Success rate is 100 percent (10/10), round-trip min/avg/max = 16/16/16 ms

R2#ping 2002:ABCD:1234:A::4 repeat 10

Type escape sequence to abort.
Sending 10, 100-byte ICMP Echos to 2002:ABCD:1234:A::4, timeout is 2 seconds:
!!!!!!!!!!
Success rate is 100 percent (10/10), round-trip min/avg/max = 16/16/16 ms

R2#ping 2002:ABCD:1234:B::4 repeat 10

Type escape sequence to abort.
Sending 10, 100-byte ICMP Echos to 2002:ABCD:1234:B::4, timeout is 2 seconds:
!!!!!!!!!!
Success rate is 100 percent (10/10), round-trip min/avg/max = 16/22/76 ms

R2#ping 2002:ABCD:1234:C::4 repeat 10

Type escape sequence to abort.
Sending 10, 100-byte ICMP Echos to 2002:ABCD:1234:C::4, timeout is 2 seconds:
!!!!!!!!!!
Success rate is 100 percent (10/10), round-trip min/avg/max = 12/14/16 ms

R2#ping 2002:ABCD:1234:D::4 repeat 10

Type escape sequence to abort.
Sending 10, 100-byte ICMP Echos to 2002:ABCD:1234:D::4, timeout is 2 seconds:
!!!!!!!!!!
Success rate is 100 percent (10/10), round-trip min/avg/max = 16/16/16 ms

R2#ping 2002:ABCD:1234:E::4 repeat 10

Type escape sequence to abort.
Sending 10, 100-byte ICMP Echos to 2002:ABCD:1234:E::4, timeout is 2 seconds:
!!!!!!!!!!
Success rate is 100 percent (10/10), round-trip min/avg/max = 12/14/16 ms
```

Task 5

This last task requires RIPng metric offsetting. With RIPng, this functionality is performed on a per-interface basis and can be performed in the inbound direction only. Prior to any changes, R2s routing table shows the following entries:

```
R2#show ipv6 route rip
IPv6 Routing Table - 10 entries
Codes: C - Connected, L - Local, S - Static, R - RIP, B - BGP
       U - Per-user Static route
       I1 - ISIS L1, I2 - ISIS L2, IA - ISIS interarea, IS - ISIS summary
       O - OSPF intra, OI - OSPF inter, OE1 - OSPF ext 1, OE2 - OSPF ext 2
       ON1 - OSPF NSSA ext 1, ON2 - OSPF NSSA ext 2
R    ::/0 [120/15]
     via FE80::20F:23FF:FE5E:EC80, Serial0/0
R    2002:ABCD:1234:8::/61 [120/2]
     via FE80::213:7FFF:FEAF:3E00, Serial0/1
R    3FFE:ABCD:1111:3::/64 [120/2]
     via FE80::213:7FFF:FEAF:3E00, Serial0/1
```

To ensure that the routes are received on R2 with a route-metric of 10, you have to offset the metric on R2s Serial 0/1 interface by a value of 9. This task is completed as follows:

```
R2(config)#interface serial 0/1
R2(config-if)#ipv6 rip CCNP metric-offset 9
R2(config-if)#exit
```

Following this configuration, the same prefixes on R2 now show a route metric of 10:

```
R2#show ipv6 route rip
IPv6 Routing Table - 11 entries
Codes: C - Connected, L - Local, S - Static, R - RIP, B - BGP
       U - Per-user Static route
       I1 - ISIS L1, I2 - ISIS L2, IA - ISIS interarea, IS - ISIS summary
       O - OSPF intra, OI - OSPF inter, OE1 - OSPF ext 1, OE2 - OSPF ext 2
       ON1 - OSPF NSSA ext 1, ON2 - OSPF NSSA ext 2
R    ::/0 [120/15]
     via FE80::20F:23FF:FE5E:EC80, Serial0/0
R    2002:ABCD:1234:8::/61 [120/10]
     via FE80::213:7FFF:FEAF:3E00, Serial0/1
R    3FFE:ABCD:1111:3::/64 [120/10]
     via FE80::213:7FFF:FEAF:3E00, Serial0/1
```

FINAL ROUTER CONFIGURATIONS

R1

```
R1#term len 0
R1#sh run
Building configuration...

Current configuration : 1008 bytes
!
version 12.4
service timestamps debug datetime msec
service timestamps log datetime msec
no service password-encryption
!
hostname R1
!
boot-start-marker
boot-end-marker
!
no logging console
!
no aaa new-model
no network-clock-participate slot 1
no network-clock-participate wic 0
ip cef
!
no ip domain lookup
ip auth-proxy max-nodata-conns 3
ip admission max-nodata-conns 3
!
ipv6 unicast-routing
```

```
 ipv6 cef
 !
 interface FastEthernet0/0
  no ip address
  duplex auto
  speed auto
  ipv6 address 3FFE:ABCD:1111:1::1/64
 !
 interface Serial0/0
  no ip address
  ipv6 address 2001:ABCD:1111:1::1/64
  ipv6 rip CCNP enable
  ipv6 rip CCNP default-information originate metric 14
  clock rate 2000000
 !
 interface Serial0/1
  no ip address
  shutdown
 !
 ip forward-protocol nd
 !
 no ip http server
 no ip http secure-server
 !
 ipv6 router rip CCNP
   port 520 multicast-group FF02::9
 !
 control-plane
 !
 line con 0
 line aux 0
 line vty 0 4
  login
 !
 end

 R1#
```

R2

```
 R2#term len 0
 R2#sh run
 Building configuration...

 Current configuration : 1059 bytes
 !
 version 12.4
 service timestamps debug datetime msec
 service timestamps log datetime msec
 no service password-encryption
 !
 hostname R2
 !
 boot-start-marker
 boot-end-marker
 !
 no logging console
 !
 no aaa new-model
 no network-clock-participate slot 1
 no network-clock-participate wic 0
 ip cef
 !
 no ip domain lookup
 ip auth-proxy max-nodata-conns 3
 ip admission max-nodata-conns 3
 !
 ipv6 unicast-routing
 ipv6 cef
 !
 interface FastEthernet0/0
  no ip address
  loopback
  duplex auto
```

```
 speed auto
 ipv6 address 3FFE:ABCD:1111:2::2/64
 ipv6 rip CCNP enable
 no keepalive
!
interface Serial0/0
 no ip address
 ipv6 address 2001:ABCD:1111:1::2/64
 ipv6 rip CCNP enable
!
interface Serial0/1
 no ip address
 ipv6 address 2001:ABCD:1111:3::2/64
 ipv6 rip CCNP enable
 ipv6 rip CCNP metric-offset 9
!
ip forward-protocol nd
!
no ip http server
no ip http secure-server
!
ipv6 router rip CCNP
  port 520 multicast-group FF02::9
!
control-plane
!
line con 0
line aux 0
line vty 0 4
 login
!
end

R2#
```

R3

```
R3#term len 0
R3#sh run
Building configuration...

Current configuration : 1770 bytes
!
version 12.4
service timestamps debug datetime msec
service timestamps log datetime msec
no service password-encryption
!
hostname R3
!
boot-start-marker
boot-end-marker
!
no logging console
!
no aaa new-model
no network-clock-participate slot 1
no network-clock-participate wic 0
ip cef
!
no ip domain lookup
ip auth-proxy max-nodata-conns 3
ip admission max-nodata-conns 3
!
ipv6 unicast-routing
ipv6 cef
!
interface Loopback1
 no ip address
 ipv6 address 2002:ABCD:1234:A::4/128
!
interface Loopback2
 no ip address
 ipv6 address 2002:ABCD:1234:B::4/128
!
interface Loopback3
```

```
 no ip address
 ipv6 address 2002:ABCD:1234:C::4/128
!
interface Loopback4
 no ip address
 ipv6 address 2002:ABCD:1234:D::4/128
!
interface Loopback5
 no ip address
 ipv6 address 2002:ABCD:1234:E::4/128
!
interface FastEthernet0/0
 no ip address
 loopback
 duplex auto
 speed auto
 ipv6 address 3FFE:ABCD:1111:3::3/64
 ipv6 rip CCNP enable
 no keepalive
!
interface Serial1/0
 no ip address
 shutdown
 clock rate 128000
!
interface Serial1/1
 no ip address
 ipv6 address 2001:ABCD:1111:3::3/64
 ipv6 rip CCNP enable
 ipv6 rip CCNP summary-address 2002:ABCD:1234:8::/61
 clock rate 128000
!
interface Serial1/2
 no ip address
 shutdown
 clock rate 128000
!
interface Serial1/3
 no ip address
 shutdown
!
interface Serial1/4
 no ip address
 shutdown
!
interface Serial1/5
 no ip address
 shutdown
!
interface Serial1/6
 no ip address
 shutdown
!
interface Serial1/7
 no ip address
 shutdown
!
ip forward-protocol nd
!
no ip http server
no ip http secure-server
!
ipv6 router rip CCNP
 redistribute connected
 port 520 multicast-group FF02::9
!
control-plane
!
line con 0
line aux 0
line vty 0 4
 login
!
end

R3#
```

R4

```
R4#term len 0
R4#sh run
Building configuration...

Current configuration : 822 bytes
!
version 12.4
service timestamps debug datetime msec
service timestamps log datetime msec
no service password-encryption
!
hostname R4
!
boot-start-marker
boot-end-marker
!
no logging console
!
no aaa new-model
no network-clock-participate slot 1
no network-clock-participate wic 0
ip cef
!
no ip domain lookup
ip auth-proxy max-nodata-conns 3
ip admission max-nodata-conns 3
!
ipv6 unicast-routing
ipv6 cef
!
interface FastEthernet0/0
 no ip address
 duplex auto
 speed auto
 ipv6 address autoconfig default
!
interface Serial0/0
 no ip address
 shutdown
!
interface Serial0/1
 no ip address
 shutdown
!
ip forward-protocol nd
!
!
no ip http server
no ip http secure-server
!
control-plane
!
line con 0
line aux 0
line vty 0 4
 login
!
end

R4#
```

CCNP LAB 42

Internet Protocol Version 6 Lab

Lab Objective:

The focus of this lab is to understand OSPFv3 and RIPng implementation and configuration in Cisco IOS routers. Additional technologies include redistribution, path control, and security.

Lab Topology:

The lab network topology is illustrated below:

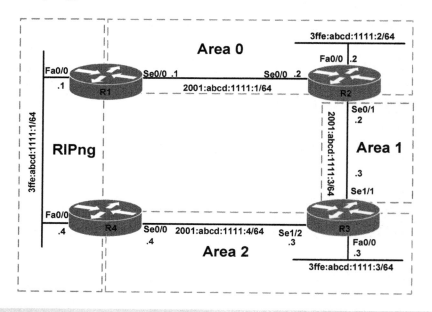

IMPORTANT NOTE: If you are using the www.howtonetwork.net racks, please bring up the LAN interfaces connected to the routers by issuing the no shutdown command on the connected switches. If you are using a home lab with no Switches, you can bring up the LAN interfaces using the following configurations on your routers:

```
interface fastethernet 0/0
  no keepalive
  loopback
  no shutdown
```

Alternately, you can simply connect the interfaces to a hub or switch if you have one available in your own lab.

Task 1

Configure hostnames and IPv6 addressing on all routers as illustrated in the network topology.

Task 2

Configure RIPng on the LAN segment between R1 and R4.

Task 3

Configure OSPFv3 as illustrated in the topology. Area 1 should be configured as a totally stub OSPF area, wherein R2 generates and advertises a default route to R3. Ensure that OSPF area 2 is still connected to the backbone. Ensure that no Hellos are sent out the LAN interfaces. Verify your configuration using the appropriate commands.

Task 4

Configure redistribution on routers R1 and R4.Use the most simple solution that negates the need to filter routes when redistributing. Verify your configuration using the appropriate commands.

Task 5

Configure R4 so that it prefers the path via R1 to reach all other subnets. In the event that this path is unavailable, the path via R3 should be used instead. Verify the configuration using the appropriate commands on R4.

Task 6

For security, configure area authentication for the OSPF backbone. Use the following parameters when you are configuring the authentication parameters:
- Use a Security Parameters Index (SPI) of 678
- Use Message Digest 5 (MD5) authentication
- Use a key of 1234567890abcdef1234567890abcdef

Verify your configuration using the appropriate commands.

Task 7

For security, configure interface authentication on the OSPF interfaces residing in area 2. Use the following parameters when you are configuring the
- Use a Security Parameters Index (SPI) of 500
- Use Message Digest 5 (MD5) authentication
- Use a key of 1234567890abcdef1234567890abcdef

Verify your configuration using the appropriate commands.

LAB VALIDATION

Task 1

```
Router(config)#hostname R1
R1(config)#ipv6 unicast-routing
R1(config)#ipv6 cef
R1(config)#interface fastethernet 0/0
R1(config-if)#ipv6 address 3ffe:abcd:1111:1::1/64
R1(config-if)#no shutdown
R1(config-if)#exit
R1(config)#interface serial 0/0
R1(config-if)#ipv6 address 2001:abcd:1111:1::1/64
R1(config-if)#clock rate 2000000
R1(config-if)#no shutdown
R1(config-if)#exit

Router(config)#hostname R2
R2(config)#ipv6 unicast-routing
R2(config)#ipv6 cef
R2(config)#interface fastethernet 0/0
R2(config-if)#ipv6 address 3ffe:abcd:1111:2::2/64
R2(config-if)#no shutdown
R2(config)#interface serial 0/0
R2(config-if)#ipv6 address 2001:abcd:1111:1::2/64
```

```
R2(config-if)#no shutdown
R2(config-if)#exit
R2(config)#interface serial 0/1
R2(config-if)#ipv6 address 2001:abcd:1111:3::2/64
R2(config-if)#no shutdown
R2(config-if)#exit

Router(config)#hostname R3
R3(config)#ipv6 unicast-routing
R3(config)#ipv6 cef
R3(config)#interface fastethernet 0/0
R3(config-if)#ipv6 address 3ffe:abcd:1111:3::3/64
R3(config-if)#no shutdown
R3(config-if)#exit
R3(config)#interface serial 1/1
R3(config-if)#ipv6 address 2001:abcd:1111:3::3/64
R3(config-if)#clock rate 128000
R3(config-if)#no shutdown
R3(config-if)#exit
R3(config)#interface serial 1/2
R3(config-if)#ipv6 address 2001:abcd:1111:4::3/64
R3(config-if)#clock rate 128000
R3(config-if)#no shutdown
R3(config-if)#exit

Router(config)#hostname R4
R4(config)#ipv6 unicast-routing
R4(config)#ipv6 cef
R4(config)#interface fastethernet 0/0
R4(config-if)#ipv6 address 3ffe:abcd:1111:1::4/64
R4(config-if)#no shutdown
R4(config-if)#interface serial 0/0
R4(config-if)#ipv6 address 2001:abcd:1111:4::4/64
R4(config-if)#no shutdown
R4(config-if)#exit
```

Task 2

```
R1(config)#ipv6 router rip CCNP
R1(config-rtr)#exit
R1(config)#interface fastethernet 0/0
R1(config-if)#ipv6 rip CCNP enable
R1(config-if)#exit

R4(config)#ipv6 router rip CCNP
R4(config-rtr)#exit
R4(config)#interface fastethernet 0/0
R4(config-if)#ipv6 rip CCNP enable
R4(config-if)#exit
```

Verify your configuration using the show ipv6 rip <tag> database command:

```
R1#show ipv6 rip CCNP database
RIP process "CCNP", local RIB
 3FFE:ABCD:1111:1::/64, metric 2
    FastEthernet0/0/FE80::20F:23FF:FE5E:F120, expires in 157 secs

R4#show ipv6 rip CCNP database
RIP process "CCNP", local RIB
 3FFE:ABCD:1111:1::/64, metric 2
    FastEthernet0/0/FE80::20F:23FF:FE5E:EC80, expires in 167 secs
```

Task 3

The basic OSPF requirements are simple. However, to ensure that area 2 is connected to area 0 we need to configure a GRE Tunnel, since a virtual link cannot be established across a stub area. The encapsulation for this tunnel should be gre ipv6 because IPv6 will be the transport protocol. If you specify gre, the configuration will not work, because IPv4 is not the transport protocol. This task is completed as follows:

```
R1(config)#ipv6 router ospf 1
R1(config-rtr)#router-id 1.1.1.1
R1(config-rtr)#exit
R1(config)#interface serial 0/0
R1(config-if)#ipv6 ospf 1 area 0
R1(config-if)#exit

R2(config)#ipv6 router ospf 2
R2(config-rtr)#router-id 2.2.2.2
R2(config-rtr)#passive-interface fastethernet 0/0
R2(config-rtr)#area 1 stub no-summary
R2(config-rtr)#exit
R2(config)#interface fastethernet 0/0
R2(config-if)#ipv6 ospf 2 area 0
R2(config-if)#exit
R2(config)#interface serial 0/0
R2(config-if)#ipv6 ospf 2 area 0
R2(config-if)#exit
R2(config)#interface serial 0/1
R2(config-if)#ipv6 ospf 2 area 1
R2(config-if)#exit
R2(config)#interface tunnel 0
R2(config-if)#tunnel source serial 0/1
R2(config-if)#tunnel destination 2001:abcd:1111:3::3
R2(config-if)#tunnel mode gre ipv6
R2(config-if)#ipv6 address 2001:abcd:1111:8::2/64
R2(config-if)#ipv6 ospf 2 area 0
R2(config-if)#exit

R3(config)#ipv6 router ospf 3
R3(config-rtr)#router-id 3.3.3.3
R3(config-rtr)#area 1 stub
R3(config-rtr)#passive-interface fastethernet 0/0
R3(config-rtr)#exit
R3(config)#interface serial 1/1
R3(config-if)#ipv6 ospf 3 area 1
R3(config-if)#exit
R3(config)#interface fastethernet 0/0
R3(config-if)#ipv6 ospf 3 area 2
R3(config-if)#exit
R3(config)#interface serial 1/2
R3(config-if)#ipv6 ospf 3 area 2
R3(config-if)#exit
R3(config)#interface tunnel 0
R3(config-if)#tunnel source serial 1/1
R3(config-if)#tunnel destination 2001:abcd:1111:3::3
R3(config-if)#tunnel mode gre ipv6
R3(config-if)#ipv6 address 2001:abcd:1111:8::3/64
R3(config-if)#ipv6 ospf 3 area 0
R3(config-if)#exit

R4(config)#ipv6 router ospf 4
R4(config-rtr)#router-id 4.4.4.4
R4(config-rtr)#exit
R4(config)#interface serial 0/0
R4(config-if)#ipv6 ospf 4 area 2
R4(config-if)#exit
```

Verify your OSPF configuration using the show ipv6 ospf neighbor command:

```
R1#show ipv6 ospf neighbor

Neighbor ID     Pri   State         Dead Time   Interface ID   Interface
2.2.2.2           1   FULL/  -      00:00:37    5              Serial0/0

R2#show ipv6 ospf neighbor

Neighbor ID     Pri   State         Dead Time   Interface ID   Interface
3.3.3.3           1   FULL/  -      00:00:32    23             Tunnel0
1.1.1.1           1   FULL/  -      00:00:39    5              Serial0/0
3.3.3.3           1   FULL/  -      00:00:38    6              Serial0/1

R3#show ipv6 ospf neighbor

Neighbor ID     Pri   State         Dead Time   Interface ID   Interface
```

```
2.2.2.2          1    FULL/  -    00:00:33    9              Tunnel0
2.2.2.2          1    FULL/  -    00:00:39    6              Serial1/1
4.4.4.4          1    FULL/  -    00:00:35    5              Serial1/2

R4#show ipv6 ospf neighbor

Neighbor ID    Pri   State        Dead Time   Interface ID   Interface
3.3.3.3          1    FULL/  -    00:00:37    7              Serial0/0
```

Next, verify routing information using the show ipv6 route command:

```
R1#show ipv6 route ospf
IPv6 Routing Table - 11 entries
Codes: C - Connected, L - Local, S - Static, R - RIP, B - BGP
       U - Per-user Static route
       I1 - ISIS L1, I2 - ISIS L2, IA - ISIS interarea, IS - ISIS summary
       O - OSPF intra, OI - OSPF inter, OE1 - OSPF ext 1, OE2 - OSPF ext 2
       ON1 - OSPF NSSA ext 1, ON2 - OSPF NSSA ext 2
OI  2001:ABCD:1111:3::/64 [110/128]
     via FE80::20D:28FF:FE9E:F940, Serial0/0
OI  2001:ABCD:1111:4::/64 [110/11956]
     via FE80::20D:28FF:FE9E:F940, Serial0/0
O   2001:ABCD:1111:8::/64 [110/11175]
     via FE80::20D:28FF:FE9E:F940, Serial0/0
O   3FFE:ABCD:1111:2::/64 [110/65]
     via FE80::20D:28FF:FE9E:F940, Serial0/0
OI  3FFE:ABCD:1111:3::/64 [110/11176]
     via FE80::20D:28FF:FE9E:F940, Serial0/0

R2#show ipv6 route ospf
IPv6 Routing Table - 12 entries
Codes: C - Connected, L - Local, S - Static, R - RIP, B - BGP
       U - Per-user Static route
       I1 - ISIS L1, I2 - ISIS L2, IA - ISIS interarea, IS - ISIS summary
       O - OSPF intra, OI - OSPF inter, OE1 - OSPF ext 1, OE2 - OSPF ext 2
       ON1 - OSPF NSSA ext 1, ON2 - OSPF NSSA ext 2
OI  2001:ABCD:1111:4::/64 [110/11892]
     via FE80::213:7FFF:FEAF:3E00, Tunnel0
OI  3FFE:ABCD:1111:3::/64 [110/11112]
     via FE80::213:7FFF:FEAF:3E00, Tunnel0

R3#show ipv6 route ospf
IPv6 Routing Table - 12 entries
Codes: C - Connected, L - Local, S - Static, R - RIP, B - BGP
       U - Per-user Static route
       I1 - ISIS L1, I2 - ISIS L2, IA - ISIS interarea, IS - ISIS summary
       O - OSPF intra, OI - OSPF inter, OE1 - OSPF ext 1, OE2 - OSPF ext 2
       ON1 - OSPF NSSA ext 1, ON2 - OSPF NSSA ext 2
O   2001:ABCD:1111:1::/64 [110/11175]
     via FE80::20D:28FF:FE9E:F940, Tunnel0
O   3FFE:ABCD:1111:2::/64 [110/11112]
     via FE80::20D:28FF:FE9E:F940, Tunnel0

R4#show ipv6 route ospf
IPv6 Routing Table - 11 entries
Codes: C - Connected, L - Local, S - Static, R - RIP, B - BGP
       U - Per-user Static route
       I1 - ISIS L1, I2 - ISIS L2, IA - ISIS interarea, IS - ISIS summary
       O - OSPF intra, OI - OSPF inter, OE1 - OSPF ext 1, OE2 - OSPF ext 2
       ON1 - OSPF NSSA ext 1, ON2 - OSPF NSSA ext 2
OI  2001:ABCD:1111:1::/64 [110/11239]
     via FE80::213:7FFF:FEAF:3E00, Serial0/0
OI  2001:ABCD:1111:3::/64 [110/845]
     via FE80::213:7FFF:FEAF:3E00, Serial0/0
OI  2001:ABCD:1111:8::/64 [110/11175]
     via FE80::213:7FFF:FEAF:3E00, Serial0/0
OI  3FFE:ABCD:1111:2::/64 [110/11176]
     via FE80::213:7FFF:FEAF:3E00, Serial0/0
O   3FFE:ABCD:1111:3::/64 [110/65]
     via FE80::213:7FFF:FEAF:3E00, Serial0/0
```

Task 4

The most simple solution that can be used to complete this task is to redistribute the connected RIPng subnet into OSPFv3 and then redistribute OSPFv3 into RIP. This negates the need to implement any filters preventing routes from being re-advertised back to into the same protocol and potentially causing a routing information loop. This task is completed as follows:

```
R1(config)#ipv6 router rip CCNP
R1(config-rtr)#redistribute connected metric 1
R1(config-rtr)#redistribute ospf 1 metric 1
R1(config-rtr)#exit
R1(config)#ipv6 router ospf 1
R1(config-rtr)#redistribute rip CCNP
R1(config-rtr)#redistribute connected
R1(config-rtr)#exit

R4(config)#ipv6 router rip CCNP
R4(config-rtr)#redistribute connected metric 1
R4(config-rtr)#redistribute ospf 4 metric 1
R4(config-rtr)#exit
R4(config)#ipv6 router ospf 4
R4(config-rtr)#redistribute connected
R4(config-rtr)#redistribute rip CCNP
R4(config-rtr)#exit
```

Verify RIPng redistributed routes by verifying the entries in the RIPng database:

```
R1#show ipv6 rip CCNP database
RIP process "CCNP", local RIB
 2001:ABCD:1111:1::/64, metric 2
    FastEthernet0/0/FE80::20F:23FF:FE5E:F120, expires in 178 secs
 2001:ABCD:1111:3::/64, metric 2
    FastEthernet0/0/FE80::20F:23FF:FE5E:F120, expires in 178 secs
 2001:ABCD:1111:4::/64, metric 2
    FastEthernet0/0/FE80::20F:23FF:FE5E:F120, expires in 178 secs
 2001:ABCD:1111:8::/64, metric 2
    FastEthernet0/0/FE80::20F:23FF:FE5E:F120, expires in 178 secs
 3FFE:ABCD:1111:1::/64, metric 2
    FastEthernet0/0/FE80::20F:23FF:FE5E:F120, expires in 178 secs
 3FFE:ABCD:1111:2::/64, metric 2
    FastEthernet0/0/FE80::20F:23FF:FE5E:F120, expires in 178 secs
 3FFE:ABCD:1111:3::/64, metric 2
    FastEthernet0/0/FE80::20F:23FF:FE5E:F120, expires in 178 secs

R4#show ipv6 rip CCNP database
RIP process "CCNP", local RIB
 2001:ABCD:1111:1::/64, metric 2
    FastEthernet0/0/FE80::20F:23FF:FE5E:EC80, expires in 162 secs
 2001:ABCD:1111:3::/64, metric 2
    FastEthernet0/0/FE80::20F:23FF:FE5E:EC80, expires in 162 secs
 2001:ABCD:1111:4::/64, metric 2
    FastEthernet0/0/FE80::20F:23FF:FE5E:EC80, expires in 162 secs
 2001:ABCD:1111:8::/64, metric 2
    FastEthernet0/0/FE80::20F:23FF:FE5E:EC80, expires in 162 secs
 3FFE:ABCD:1111:1::/64, metric 2
    FastEthernet0/0/FE80::20F:23FF:FE5E:EC80, expires in 162 secs
 3FFE:ABCD:1111:2::/64, metric 2
    FastEthernet0/0/FE80::20F:23FF:FE5E:EC80, expires in 162 secs
 3FFE:ABCD:1111:3::/64, metric 2
    FastEthernet0/0/FE80::20F:23FF:FE5E:EC80, expires in 162 secs
```

Verify OSPFv3 redistributed routes by verifying Type 5 LSAs in the LSDB:

```
R1#show ipv6 ospf database external

            OSPFv3 Router with ID (1.1.1.1) (Process ID 1)

              Type-5 AS External Link States

  LS age: 158
```

```
LS Type: AS External Link
Link State ID: 0
Advertising Router: 1.1.1.1
LS Seq Number: 80000001
Checksum: 0xA934
Length: 36
Prefix Address: 3FFE:ABCD:1111:1::
Prefix Length: 64, Options: None
Metric Type: 2 (Larger than any link state path)
Metric: 20

Routing Bit Set on this LSA
LS age: 79
LS Type: AS External Link
Link State ID: 0
Advertising Router: 4.4.4.4
LS Seq Number: 80000001
Checksum: 0x4F82
Length: 36
Prefix Address: 3FFE:ABCD:1111:1::
Prefix Length: 64, Options: None
Metric Type: 2 (Larger than any link state path)
Metric: 20
```

```
R4#show ipv6 ospf database external

            OSPFv3 Router with ID (4.4.4.4) (Process ID 4)

               Type-5 AS External Link States

Routing Bit Set on this LSA
LS age: 168
LS Type: AS External Link
Link State ID: 0
Advertising Router: 1.1.1.1
LS Seq Number: 80000001
Checksum: 0xA934
Length: 36
Prefix Address: 3FFE:ABCD:1111:1::
Prefix Length: 64, Options: None
Metric Type: 2 (Larger than any link state path)
Metric: 20

LS age: 83
LS Type: AS External Link
Link State ID: 0
Advertising Router: 4.4.4.4
LS Seq Number: 80000001
Checksum: 0x4F82
Length: 36
Prefix Address: 3FFE:ABCD:1111:1::
Prefix Length: 64, Options: None
Metric Type: 2 (Larger than any link state path)
Metric: 20
```

Task 5

To complete this task, simply raise the default administrative distance for OSPF internal routes, since there are no external OSPF routes, to a value higher than 120, which is the RIPng default administrative distance. Any value between 1 and 254 can be used to complete this task. This task is completed as follows:

```
R4(config)#ipv6 router ospf 4
R4(config-rtr)#distance ospf intra-area 150 inter-area 150
R4(config-rtr)#exit
```

Following this configuration, verify the contents of the routing table on R4:

```
R4# Verify RIPng redistributed routes by verifying the entries in the RIPng database:

IPv6 Routing Table - 11 entries
Codes: C - Connected, L - Local, S - Static, R - RIP, B - BGP
       U - Per-user Static route
       I1 - ISIS L1, I2 - ISIS L2, IA - ISIS interarea, IS - ISIS summary
```

```
      O - OSPF intra, OI - OSPF inter, OE1 - OSPF ext 1, OE2 - OSPF ext 2
      ON1 - OSPF NSSA ext 1, ON2 - OSPF NSSA ext 2
R   2001:ABCD:1111:1::/64 [120/2]
      via FE80::20F:23FF:FE5E:EC80, FastEthernet0/0
R   2001:ABCD:1111:3::/64 [120/2]
      via FE80::20F:23FF:FE5E:EC80, FastEthernet0/0
C   2001:ABCD:1111:4::/64 [0/0]
      via ::, Serial0/0
L   2001:ABCD:1111:4::4/128 [0/0]
      via ::, Serial0/0
R   2001:ABCD:1111:8::/64 [120/2]
      via FE80::20F:23FF:FE5E:EC80, FastEthernet0/0
C   3FFE:ABCD:1111:1::/64 [0/0]
      via ::, FastEthernet0/0
L   3FFE:ABCD:1111:1::4/128 [0/0]
      via ::, FastEthernet0/0
R   3FFE:ABCD:1111:2::/64 [120/2]
      via FE80::20F:23FF:FE5E:EC80, FastEthernet0/0
R   3FFE:ABCD:1111:3::/64 [120/2]
      via FE80::20F:23FF:FE5E:EC80, FastEthernet0/0
L   FE80::/10 [0/0]
      via ::, Null0
L   FF00::/8 [0/0]
      via ::, Null0
```

Task 6

OSPFv3 supports both authentication and encryption for security. To configure OSPFv3 area authentication, you need to use the `area <area> authentication ipsec spi <size> [md5|sha1] <key>` OSPFv3 configuration command. This task is completed as follows:

```
R1(config)#ipv6 router ospf 1
R1(config-rtr)#$ication ipsec spi 678 md5 1234567890abcdef1234567890abcdef
R2(config-rtr)#exit

R2(config)#ipv6 router ospf 2
R2(config-rtr)#$ication ipsec spi 678 md5 1234567890abcdef1234567890abcdef
R2(config-rtr)#exit

R3(config)#ipv6 router ospf 3
R3(config-rtr)#$ication ipsec spi 678 md5 1234567890abcdef1234567890abcdef
R3(config-rtr)#exit
```

Verify OSPFv3 area authentication using the `show ipv6 ospf` command:

```
R2#show ipv6 ospf
 Routing Process "ospfv3 2" with ID 2.2.2.2
 It is an area border router
 SPF schedule delay 5 secs, Hold time between two SPFs 10 secs
 Minimum LSA interval 5 secs. Minimum LSA arrival 1 secs
 LSA group pacing timer 240 secs
 Interface flood pacing timer 33 msecs
 Retransmission pacing timer 66 msecs
 Number of external LSA 7. Checksum Sum 0x020EF4
 Number of areas in this router is 2. 1 normal 1 stub 0 nssa
 Reference bandwidth unit is 100 mbps
    Area BACKBONE(0)
        Number of interfaces in this area is 3
        MD5 Authentication, SPI 678
        SPF algorithm executed 17 times
        Number of LSA 16. Checksum Sum 0x07AE65
        Number of DCbitless LSA 0
        Number of indication LSA 0
        Number of DoNotAge LSA 0
        Flood list length 0
    Area 1
        Number of interfaces in this area is 1
        It is a stub area, no summary LSA in this area
          generates stub default route with cost 1
        SPF algorithm executed 15 times
        Number of LSA 13. Checksum Sum 0x04EB52
```

```
Number of DCbitless LSA 0
Number of indication LSA 0
Number of DoNotAge LSA 0
Flood list length 0
```

By default, because IPv6 uses built-in IPsec functions, Cisco IOS software automatically creates IPsec policies for the configured authentication. The policy can be viewed using the show crypto ipsec sa [interface <name>] command on the router(s). Authentication Header (AH) is used. If you configure encryption, then Encapsulating Security Payload (ESP) will be used instead. Check the relevant SA states based on your configuration:

```
R2#show crypto ipsec sa interface serial 0/0

interface: Serial0/0
    Crypto map tag: (none), local addr FE80::20D:28FF:FE9E:F940

    IPsecv6 policy name: OSPFv3-2-678
    IPsecv6-created ACL name: Serial0/0-ipsecv6-ACL

    protected vrf: (none)
    local  ident (addr/mask/prot/port): (FE80::/10/89/0)
    remote ident (addr/mask/prot/port): (::/0/89/0)
    current_peer :: port 500
      PERMIT, flags={origin_is_acl,}
    #pkts encaps: 20, #pkts encrypt: 0, #pkts digest: 20
    #pkts decaps: 23, #pkts decrypt: 0, #pkts verify: 23
    #pkts compressed: 0, #pkts decompressed: 0
    #pkts not compressed: 0, #pkts compr. failed: 0
    #pkts not decompressed: 0, #pkts decompress failed: 0
    #send errors 0, #recv errors 0

     local crypto endpt.: FE80::20D:28FF:FE9E:F940, remote crypto endpt.: ::
     path mtu 1500, ip mtu 1500, ip mtu idb Serial0/0
     current outbound spi: 0x2A6(678)

     inbound esp sas:

     inbound ah sas:
      spi: 0x2A6(678)
        transform: ah-md5-hmac ,
        in use settings ={Transport, }
        conn id: 2005, flow_id: SW:5, crypto map: (none)
        no sa timing
        replay detection support: N
        Status: ACTIVE

     inbound pcp sas:

     outbound esp sas:

     outbound ah sas:
      spi: 0x2A6(678)
        transform: ah-md5-hmac ,
        in use settings ={Transport, }
        conn id: 2006, flow_id: SW:6, crypto map: (none)
        no sa timing
        replay detection support: N
        Status: ACTIVE

     outbound pcp sas:
```

Additionally, you can also view the configuration parameters for the applied policy using the show crypto ipsec policy command on the router. The policy name, by default, will be OSPFv3-<process ID>-<SPI>. For example, on R1, the applied policy name will be OSPFv3-R1-678. This is validated and illustrated in the following output:

```
R1#show crypto ipsec policy
Crypto IPsec client security policy data
```

```
Policy name:       OSPFv3-1-678
Policy refcount:   1
Inbound  AH SPI:   678 (0x2A6)
Outbound AH SPI:   678 (0x2A6)
Inbound  AH Key:   1234567890ABCDEF1234567890ABCDEF
Outbound AH Key:   1234567890ABCDEF1234567890ABCDEF
Transform set:     ah-md5-hmac
```

Task 7

Interface authentication is applied at the interface using the `ipv6 ospf authentication   ipsec spi <spi> [md5|sha1] <key>` interface configuration command. This task is completed by applying the specified configuration parameters on all interfaces within area 2:

```
R3(config)#interface serial 1/2
R3(config-if)#$ion  ipsec spi 500 md5   1234567890abcdef1234567890abcdef
R3(config-if)#exit

R4(config)#interface serial 0/0
R4(config-if)#$ion  ipsec spi 500 md5   1234567890abcdef1234567890abcdef
R4(config-if)#exit
```

Verify OSPFv3 interface authentication using the `show ipv6 ospf interface` command:

```
R4#show ipv6 ospf interface serial 0/0
Serial0/0 is up, line protocol is up
  Link Local Address FE80::20F:23FF:FE5E:F120, Interface ID 5
  Area 2, Process ID 4, Instance ID 0, Router ID 4.4.4.4
  Network Type POINT_TO_POINT, Cost: 64
  MD5 Authentication SPI 500, secure socket state UP (errors: 0)
  Transmit Delay is 1 sec, State POINT_TO_POINT,
  Timer intervals configured, Hello 10, Dead 40, Wait 40, Retransmit 5
    Hello due in 00:00:02
  Index 1/1/1, flood queue length 0
  Next 0x0(0)/0x0(0)/0x0(0)
  Last flood scan length is 1, maximum is 5
  Last flood scan time is 0 msec, maximum is 0 msec
  Neighbor Count is 1, Adjacent neighbor count is 1
    Adjacent with neighbor 3.3.3.3
  Suppress hello for 0 neighbor(s)
```

NOTE: You should have NO errors (as illustrated above). If you do, check the configuration.

As is the case with area authentication, a policy is dynamically created and applied by the Cisco IOS software. This can be viewed using the `show crypto ipsec sa [interface <name>]` command on the router on which interface authentication has been implemented. The policy name, by default, will be OSPFv3-<process ID>-<SPI> as illustrated below:

```
R4#show crypto ipsec sa interface serial 0/0

interface: Serial0/0
    Crypto map tag: (none), local addr FE80::20F:23FF:FE5E:F120

   IPsecv6 policy name: OSPFv3-4-500
   IPsecv6-created ACL name: Serial0/0-ipsecv6-ACL

   protected vrf: (none)
   local  ident (addr/mask/prot/port): (FE80::/10/89/0)
   remote ident (addr/mask/prot/port): (::/0/89/0)
   current_peer :: port 500
     PERMIT, flags={origin_is_acl,}
    #pkts encaps: 29, #pkts encrypt: 0, #pkts digest: 29
    #pkts decaps: 31, #pkts decrypt: 0, #pkts verify: 31
    #pkts compressed: 0, #pkts decompressed: 0
    #pkts not compressed: 0, #pkts compr. failed: 0
    #pkts not decompressed: 0, #pkts decompress failed: 0
    #send errors 0, #recv errors 0
```

```
      local crypto endpt.: FE80::20F:23FF:FE5E:F120, remote crypto endpt.: ::
      path mtu 1500, ip mtu 1500, ip mtu idb Serial0/0
      current outbound spi: 0x1F4(500)

      inbound esp sas:

      inbound ah sas:
       spi: 0x1F4(500)
         transform: ah-md5-hmac ,
         in use settings ={Transport, }
         conn id: 2001, flow_id: SW:1, crypto map: (none)
         no sa timing
         replay detection support: N
         Status: ACTIVE

      inbound pcp sas:

      outbound esp sas:

      outbound ah sas:
       spi: 0x1F4(500)
         transform: ah-md5-hmac ,
         in use settings ={Transport, }
         conn id: 2002, flow_id: SW:2, crypto map: (none)
         no sa timing
         replay detection support: N
         Status: ACTIVE

      outbound pcp sas:
```

FINAL ROUTER CONFIGURATIONS

R1

```
R1#term len 0
R1#sh run
Building configuration...

Current configuration : 1185 bytes
!
version 12.4
service timestamps debug datetime msec
service timestamps log datetime msec
no service password-encryption
!
hostname R1
!
boot-start-marker
boot-end-marker
!
no logging console
!
no aaa new-model
no network-clock-participate slot 1
no network-clock-participate wic 0
ip cef
!
no ip domain lookup
ip auth-proxy max-nodata-conns 3
ip admission max-nodata-conns 3
!
ipv6 unicast-routing
ipv6 cef
!
interface FastEthernet0/0
 no ip address
 duplex auto
 speed auto
 ipv6 address 3FFE:ABCD:1111:1::1/64
 ipv6 rip CCNP enable
!
```

```
interface Serial0/0
 no ip address
 ipv6 address 2001:ABCD:1111:1::1/64
 ipv6 ospf 1 area 0
 clock rate 2000000
!
interface Serial0/1
 no ip address
 shutdown
!
ip forward-protocol nd
!
no ip http server
no ip http secure-server
!
ipv6 router ospf 1
 router-id 1.1.1.1
 log-adjacency-changes
 area 0 authentication ipsec spi 678 md5 1234567890ABCDEF1234567890ABCDEF
 redistribute connected
 redistribute rip CCNP
!
ipv6 router rip CCNP
 redistribute connected metric 1
 redistribute ospf 1 metric 1
!
control-plane
!
line con 0
line aux 0
line vty 0 4
 login
!
end

R1#
```

R2

```
R2#term len 0
R2#sh run
Building configuration...

Current configuration : 1315 bytes
!
version 12.4
service timestamps debug datetime msec
service timestamps log datetime msec
no service password-encryption
!
hostname R2
!
boot-start-marker
boot-end-marker
!
no logging console
!
no aaa new-model
no network-clock-participate slot 1
no network-clock-participate wic 0
ip cef
!
no ip domain lookup
ip auth-proxy max-nodata-conns 3
ip admission max-nodata-conns 3
!
ipv6 unicast-routing
ipv6 cef
!
interface Tunnel0
 no ip address
 ipv6 address 2001:ABCD:1111:8::2/64
 ipv6 ospf 2 area 0
 tunnel source Serial0/1
```

```
 tunnel destination 2001:ABCD:1111:3::3
 tunnel mode gre ipv6
!
interface FastEthernet0/0
 no ip address
 duplex auto
 speed auto
 ipv6 address 3FFE:ABCD:1111:2::2/64
 ipv6 ospf 2 area 0
!
interface Serial0/0
 no ip address
 ipv6 address 2001:ABCD:1111:1::2/64
 ipv6 ospf 2 area 0
!
interface Serial0/1
 no ip address
 ipv6 address 2001:ABCD:1111:3::2/64
 ipv6 ospf 2 area 1
!
ip forward-protocol nd
!
no ip http server
no ip http secure-server
!
ipv6 router ospf 2
 router-id 2.2.2.2
 log-adjacency-changes
 area 0 authentication ipsec spi 678 md5 1234567890ABCDEF1234567890ABCDEF
 area 1 stub no-summary
 passive-interface FastEthernet0/0
!
control-plane
!
line con 0
line aux 0
line vty 0 4
 login
!
end

R2#
```

R3

```
R3#term len 0
R3#sh run
Building configuration...

Current configuration : 1720 bytes
!
version 12.4
service timestamps debug datetime msec
service timestamps log datetime msec
no service password-encryption
!
hostname R3
!
boot-start-marker
boot-end-marker
!
no logging console
!
no aaa new-model
no network-clock-participate slot 1
no network-clock-participate wic 0
ip cef
!
no ip domain lookup
ip auth-proxy max-nodata-conns 3
ip admission max-nodata-conns 3
!
ipv6 unicast-routing
ipv6 cef
```

```
!
interface Tunnel0
 no ip address
 ipv6 address 2001:ABCD:1111:8::3/64
 ipv6 ospf 3 area 0
 tunnel source Serial1/1
 tunnel destination 2001:ABCD:1111:3::2
 tunnel mode gre ipv6
!
interface FastEthernet0/0
 no ip address
 duplex auto
 speed auto
 ipv6 address 3FFE:ABCD:1111:3::3/64
 ipv6 ospf 3 area 2
!
interface Serial1/0
 no ip address
 shutdown
 clock rate 128000
!
interface Serial1/1
 no ip address
 ipv6 address 2001:ABCD:1111:3::3/64
 ipv6 ospf 3 area 1
 clock rate 128000
!
interface Serial1/2
 no ip address
 ipv6 address 2001:ABCD:1111:4::3/64
 ipv6 ospf 3 area 2
 ipv6 ospf authentication ipsec spi 500 md5 1234567890ABCDEF1234567890ABCDEF
 clock rate 128000
!
interface Serial1/3
 no ip address
 shutdown
!
interface Serial1/4
 no ip address
 shutdown
!
interface Serial1/5
 no ip address
 shutdown
!
interface Serial1/6
 no ip address
 shutdown
!
interface Serial1/7
 no ip address
 shutdown
!
ip forward-protocol nd
!
no ip http server
no ip http secure-server
!
ipv6 router ospf 3
 router-id 3.3.3.3
 log-adjacency-changes
 area 0 authentication ipsec spi 678 md5 1234567890ABCDEF1234567890ABCDEF
 area 1 stub
 passive-interface FastEthernet0/0
!
control-plane
!
line con 0
line aux 0
line vty 0 4
 login
!
end

R3#
```

R4

```
R4#term len 0
R4#sh run
Building configuration...

Current configuration : 1214 bytes
!
version 12.4
service timestamps debug datetime msec
service timestamps log datetime msec
no service password-encryption
!
hostname R4
!
boot-start-marker
boot-end-marker
!
no logging console
!
no aaa new-model
no network-clock-participate slot 1
no network-clock-participate wic 0
ip cef
!
no ip domain lookup
ip auth-proxy max-nodata-conns 3
ip admission max-nodata-conns 3
!
ipv6 unicast-routing
ipv6 cef
!
interface FastEthernet0/0
 no ip address
 duplex auto
 speed auto
 ipv6 address 3FFE:ABCD:1111:1::4/64
 ipv6 rip CCNP enable
!
interface Serial0/0
 no ip address
 ipv6 address 2001:ABCD:1111:4::4/64
 ipv6 ospf 4 area 2
 ipv6 ospf authentication ipsec spi 500 md5 1234567890ABCDEF1234567890ABCDEF
!
interface Serial0/1
 no ip address
 shutdown
!
ip forward-protocol nd
!
no ip http server
no ip http secure-server
!
ipv6 router ospf 4
 router-id 4.4.4.4
 log-adjacency-changes
 distance ospf intra-area 150 inter-area 150
 redistribute connected
 redistribute rip CCNP
!
ipv6 router rip CCNP
 redistribute connected metric 1
 redistribute ospf 4 metric 1
!
control-plane
!
line con 0
line aux 0
line vty 0 4
 login
!
end

R4#
```

CCNP LAB 43

Internet Protocol Version 6 Lab

Lab Objective:

The focus of this lab is to understand OSPFv3 implementation and configuration in Cisco IOS routers. Additional technologies include Frame Relay, summarization and path control.

Lab Topology:

The lab network topology is illustrated below:

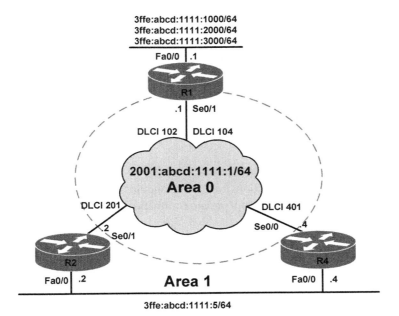

IMPORTANT NOTE: If you are using the www.howtonetwork.net racks, please bring up the LAN interfaces connected to the routers by issuing the no shutdown command on the connected switches. If you are using a home lab with no Switches, you can bring up the LAN interfaces using the following configurations on your routers:

```
interface fastethernet 0/0
 no keepalive
 loopback
 no shutdown
```

Alternately, you can simply connect the interfaces to a hub or switch if you have one available in your own lab. Also, if you are using the www.howtonetwork.net racks, configure R3 as the Frame Relay switch using the following configuration commands:

```
hostname R3-Frame-Relay-Switch
!
frame-relay switching
!
```

```
interface serial 1/0
 description 'Connected To R1 Serial 0/1'
 encapsulation frame-relay
 no ip address
 clock rate 128000
 frame-relay intf-type dce
 frame-relay route 102 interface serial 1/1 201
 frame-relay route 104 interface serial 1/2 401
 no shutdown
!
interface serial 1/1
 description 'Connected To R2 Serial 0/1'
 encapsulation frame-relay
 no ip address
 clock rate 128000
 frame-relay intf-type dce
 frame-relay route 201 interface serial 1/0 102
 no shutdown
!
interface serial 1/2
 description 'Connected To R4 Serial 0/0'
 encapsulation frame-relay
 no ip address
 clock rate 128000
 frame-relay intf-type dce
 frame-relay route 401 interface serial 1/0 104
 no shutdown
!
end
```

Task 1

Configure hostnames and IP addressing on all routers as illustrated in the network topology.

Task 2

Configure the Frame Relay network so that all routers can ping each others' WAN interfaces. This connectivity should be for Link Local addresses only. Verify the configuration.

Task 3

Configure OSPF over the Frame Relay WAN connectivity R1, R2, and R4. Ensure that there is no DR/BDR election held on the WAN segment. Additionally, OSPFv3 should use Unicast packets to send protocol messages. Verify your configuration using the appropriate commands.

Task 4

Redistribute the LAN subnets connected to R1 into OSPF. Configure R1 so that only a single route is advertised to R2 and R4. Verify that these routers can ping the three LAN subnets connected to R1 although they have only a single route for the subnets in their routing tables.

Task 5

Advertise the subnet connected to R2 and R4s LAN interfaces via OSPF. Do NOT redistribute this subnet into OSPF. These routes should be received as inter-area routes on R1. Ensure that no OSPFv3 messages are sent out these interfaces. Verify your configuration.

Task 6

Configure OSPF so that R1 prefers the path via R2 to reach the 3ffe:abcd:1111:5/64 IPv6 subnet connected to R2 and R4. You are NOT allowed to implement any configurations on R1 to complete this task. Additionally, you are NOT allowed to modify interface bandwidth or cost values, or default administrative distance values. Finally, you can NOT use any static routes or redistribution to complete this task. Verify your configuration using the appropriate commands.

LAB VALIDATION

Task 1

```
Router(config)#hostname R1
R1(config)#ipv6 unicast-routing
R1(config)#ipv6 cef
R1(config)#interface fastethernet 0/0
R1(config-if)#no shutdown
R1(config-if)#ipv6 address 3ffe:abcd:1111:1000::1/64
R1(config-if)#ipv6 address 3ffe:abcd:1111:2000::1/64
R1(config-if)#ipv6 address 3ffe:abcd:1111:3000::1/64
R1(config-if)#exit
R1(config)#interface serial 0/1
R1(config-if)#ipv6 address 2001:abcd:1111:1::1/64
R1(config-if)#no shutdown
R1(config-if)#encapsulation frame-relay
R1(config-if)#exit

Router(config)#hostname R2
R2(config)#ipv6 unicast-routing
R2(config)#ipv6 cef
R2(config)#interface fastethernet 0/0
R2(config-if)#no shutdown
R2(config-if)#ipv6 address 3ffe:abcd:1111:5::2/64
R2(config-if)#exit
R2(config)#interface serial 0/1
R2(config-if)# ipv6 address 2001:abcd:1111:1::2/64
R2(config-if)#no shutdown
R2(config-if)#encapsulation frame-relay
R2(config-if)#exit

Router(config)#hostname R4
R4(config)#ipv6 unicast-routing
R4(config)#ipv6 cef
R4(config)#interface fastethernet 0/0
R4(config-if)#ipv6 address 3ffe:abcd:1111:5::4/64
R4(config-if)#exit
R4(config)#interface serial 0/0
R4(config-if)#ipv6 address 2001:abcd:1111:1::4/64
R4(config-if)#no shutdown
R4(config-if)#encapsulation frame-relay
R4(config-if)#exit
```

Task 2

To complete this task, you need to use the `frame-relay map ipv6 [address] [dlci] [broadcast]` command on all routers. This task is completed as follows:

```
R1(config)#interface serial 0/1
R1(config-if)#frame-relay map ipv6 FE80::20D:28FF:FE9E:F940 102 broadcast
R1(config-if)#frame-relay map ipv6 FE80::20F:23FF:FE5E:F120 104 broadcast
R1(config-if)#exit

R2(config)#interface serial 0/1
R2(config-if)#frame-relay map ipv6 FE80::20F:23FF:FE5E:EC80 201 broadcast
R2(config-if)#frame-relay map ipv6 FE80::20F:23FF:FE5E:F120 201
R2(config-if)#exit

R4(config)#interface serial 0/0
R4(config-if)#frame-relay map ipv6 FE80::20F:23FF:FE5E:EC80 401 broadcast
R4(config-if)#frame-relay map ipv6 FE80::20D:28FF:FE9E:F940 401
R4(config-if)#exit
```

Verify your configuration using the `show frame-relay map` command on all routers:

```
1#show frame-relay map
Serial0/1 (up): ipv6 FE80::20D:28FF:FE9E:F940 dlci 102(0x66,0x1860), static,
          broadcast,
```

```
                    CISCO, status defined, active
Serial0/1 (up): ipv6 FE80::20F:23FF:FE5E:F120 dlci 104(0x68,0x1880), static,
                    broadcast,
                    CISCO, status defined, active


R2#show frame-relay map
Serial0/1 (up): ipv6 FE80::20F:23FF:FE5E:F120 dlci 201(0xC9,0x3090), static,
                    CISCO, status defined, active
Serial0/1 (up): ipv6 FE80::20F:23FF:FE5E:EC80 dlci 201(0xC9,0x3090), static,
                    broadcast,
                    CISCO, status defined, active


R4#show frame-relay map
Serial0/0 (up): ipv6 FE80::20D:28FF:FE9E:F940 dlci 401(0x191,0x6410), static,
                    CISCO, status defined, active
Serial0/0 (up): ipv6 FE80::20F:23FF:FE5E:EC80 dlci 401(0x191,0x6410), static,
                    broadcast,
                    CISCO, status defined, active
```

Finally, complete the task by pinging between all three routers across the Frame Relay WAN:

```
R1#ping FE80::20D:28FF:FE9E:F940
Output Interface: serial0/1
Type escape sequence to abort.
Sending 5, 100-byte ICMP Echos to FE80::20D:28FF:FE9E:F940, timeout is 2 seconds:
Packet sent with a source address of FE80::20F:23FF:FE5E:EC80
!!!!!
Success rate is 100 percent (5/5), round-trip min/avg/max = 28/29/32 ms


R1#ping FE80::20F:23FF:FE5E:F120
Output Interface: serial0/1
Type escape sequence to abort.
Sending 5, 100-byte ICMP Echos to FE80::20F:23FF:FE5E:F120, timeout is 2 seconds:
Packet sent with a source address of FE80::20F:23FF:FE5E:EC80
!!!!!
Success rate is 100 percent (5/5), round-trip min/avg/max = 28/29/32 ms


R2#ping FE80::20F:23FF:FE5E:F120
Output Interface: serial0/1
Type escape sequence to abort.
Sending 5, 100-byte ICMP Echos to FE80::20F:23FF:FE5E:F120, timeout is 2 seconds:
Packet sent with a source address of FE80::20D:28FF:FE9E:F940
!!!!!
Success rate is 100 percent (5/5), round-trip min/avg/max = 84/84/88 ms


R2#ping FE80::20F:23FF:FE5E:EC80
Output Interface: serial0/1
Type escape sequence to abort.
Sending 5, 100-byte ICMP Echos to FE80::20F:23FF:FE5E:EC80, timeout is 2 seconds:
Packet sent with a source address of FE80::20D:28FF:FE9E:F940
!!!!!
Success rate is 100 percent (5/5), round-trip min/avg/max = 28/29/32 ms


R4#ping FE80::20D:28FF:FE9E:F940
Output Interface: serial0/0
Type escape sequence to abort.
Sending 5, 100-byte ICMP Echos to FE80::20D:28FF:FE9E:F940, timeout is 2 seconds:
Packet sent with a source address of FE80::20F:23FF:FE5E:F120
!!!!!
Success rate is 100 percent (5/5), round-trip min/avg/max = 84/84/88 ms


R4#ping FE80::20F:23FF:FE5E:EC80
Output Interface: serial0/0
Type escape sequence to abort.
Sending 5, 100-byte ICMP Echos to FE80::20F:23FF:FE5E:EC80, timeout is 2 seconds:
Packet sent with a source address of FE80::20F:23FF:FE5E:F120
!!!!!
Success rate is 100 percent (5/5), round-trip min/avg/max = 28/29/32 ms
```

Task 3

To prevent DR/BDR election on the Frame Relay WAN and allow OSPF to use Unicast packets to send protocol messages, you must configure a point-to-multipoint non-broadcast network type, which requires static neighbor configuration. Unlike OSPFv2, OSPFv3 neighbors are configured using the Link Local address and under the interface. Complete this task as follows:

```
R1(config)#ipv6 router ospf 1
R1(config-rtr)#router-id 1.1.1.1
R1(config-rtr)#exit
R1(config)#interface serial 0/1
R1(config-if)#ipv6 ospf network point-to-multipoint non-broadcast
R1(config-if)#ipv6 ospf 1 area 0
R1(config-if)#ipv6 ospf neighbor FE80::20D:28FF:FE9E:F940
R1(config-if)#ipv6 ospf neighbor FE80::20F:23FF:FE5E:F120
R1(config-if)#exit

R2(config)#ipv6 router ospf 2
R2(config-rtr)#router-id 2.2.2.2
R2(config-rtr)#exit
R2(config)#interface serial 0/0
R2(config-if)#exit
R2(config)#interface serial 0/1
R2(config-if)#ipv6 ospf network point-to-multipoint non-broadcast
R2(config-if)#ipv6 ospf 2 area 0
R2(config-if)#ipv6 ospf neighbor FE80::20F:23FF:FE5E:EC80
R2(config-if)#exit

R4(config)#ipv6 router ospf 4
R4(config-rtr)#router-id 4.4.4.4
R4(config-rtr)#exit
R4(config)#interface serial 0/0
R4(config-if)#ipv6 ospf network point-to-multipoint non-broadcast
R4(config-if)#ipv6 ospf 4 area 0
R4(config-if)#ipv6 ospf neighbor FE80::20F:23FF:FE5E:EC80
R4(config-if)#exit
```

Verify your configuration using the show ipv6 ospf neighbor command on all routers:

```
R1#show ipv6 ospf neighbor

Neighbor ID     Pri   State         Dead Time    Interface ID    Interface
2.2.2.2           1   FULL/   -     00:01:58     6               Serial0/1
4.4.4.4           1   FULL/   -     00:01:30     5               Serial0/1

R2#show ipv6 ospf neighbor

Neighbor ID     Pri   State         Dead Time    Interface ID    Interface
1.1.1.1           1   FULL/   -     00:01:44     6               Serial0/1

R4#show ipv6 ospf neighbor

Neighbor ID     Pri   State         Dead Time    Interface ID    Interface
1.1.1.1           1   FULL/   -     00:01:41     6               Serial0/0
```

Task 4

The first part of this task simply requires that you redistribute the connected prefixes into OSPF. This first part is completed as follows:

```
R1(config)#ipv6 router ospf 1
R1(config-rtr)#redistribute connected
R1(config-rtr)#exit
```

Verify your configuration by looking at the Link State Database entries on R1:

```
R1#show ipv6 ospf database external
```

```
        OSPFv3 Router with ID (1.1.1.1) (Process ID 1)

            Type-5 AS External Link States
  LS age: 101
  LS Type: AS External Link
  Link State ID: 0
  Advertising Router: 1.1.1.1
  LS Seq Number: 80000001
  Checksum: 0xA826
  Length: 36
  Prefix Address: 3FFE:ABCD:1111:1000::
  Prefix Length: 64, Options: None
  Metric Type: 2 (Larger than any link state path)
  Metric: 20

  LS age: 101
  LS Type: AS External Link
  Link State ID: 1
  Advertising Router: 1.1.1.1
  LS Seq Number: 80000001
  Checksum: 0xAF0E
  Length: 36
  Prefix Address: 3FFE:ABCD:1111:2000::
  Prefix Length: 64, Options: None
  Metric Type: 2 (Larger than any link state path)
  Metric: 20

  LS age: 103
  LS Type: AS External Link
  Link State ID: 2
  Advertising Router: 1.1.1.1
  LS Seq Number: 80000001
  Checksum: 0xB6F5
  Length: 36
  Prefix Address: 3FFE:ABCD:1111:3000::
  Prefix Length: 64, Options: None
  Metric Type: 2 (Larger than any link state path)
  Metric: 20
```

Additionally, you can also verify the configuration by looking at R2 and R4s routing tables:

```
R2#show ipv6 route ospf | include OE2
      O - OSPF intra, OI - OSPF inter, OE1 - OSPF ext 1, OE2 - OSPF ext 2
OE2  3FFE:ABCD:1111:1000::/64 [110/20]
OE2  3FFE:ABCD:1111:2000::/64 [110/20]
OE2  3FFE:ABCD:1111:3000::/64 [110/20]

R4#show ipv6 route ospf | include OE2
      O - OSPF intra, OI - OSPF inter, OE1 - OSPF ext 1, OE2 - OSPF ext 2
OE2  3FFE:ABCD:1111:1000::/64 [110/20]
OE2  3FFE:ABCD:1111:2000::/64 [110/20]
OE2  3FFE:ABCD:1111:3000::/64 [110/20]
```

The second part of this task requires route summarization, i.e. summarizing the 3 FastEthernet interface addresses and advertise only a single route using OSPFv3. IPv6 summarization is not as complex as one would think. It is also performed in a manner similar to IPv4 route summarization. First, identify and locate the first different 16-bit field. In our example, it is the fourth field, which contains the values 1000, 2000 and 3000. Next, convert these values to binary as illustrated in the following table:

Hexadecimal Value	Binary Representation	Matching Bit Values
1000	0001 0000 0000 0000	00
2000	0010 0000 0000 0000	00
3000	0011 0000 0000 0000	00

Referencing the table above, the first two bits match. To complete the address, we simply input zeros for the non-matching bits, resulting in the Binary address: 0000 0000 0000 0000. In Hexadecimal, the same address would be written as 0.

Next, we need to calculate the mask. This is simple and entails just counting the number of matching bits in the address, which would be 50. This task is completed as follows:

```
R1(config)#ipv6 router ospf 1
R1(config-rtr)#summary-prefix 3ffe:abcd:1111::/50
R1(config-rtr)#exit
```

Following your configuration, verify the summary prefix in the LSDB on R1:

```
R1#show ipv6 ospf database external 3ffe:abcd:1111::/50

            OSPFv3 Router with ID (1.1.1.1) (Process ID 1)

            Type-5 AS External Link States

  LS age: 67
  LS Type: AS External Link
  Link State ID: 3
  Advertising Router: 1.1.1.1
  LS Seq Number: 80000001
  Checksum: 0x17D2
  Length: 36
  Prefix Address: 3FFE:ABCD:1111::
  Prefix Length: 50, Options: None
  Metric Type: 2 (Larger than any link state path)
  Metric: 20
```

The same can also be verified by looking at the LSDBs on R2 and R4. Additionally, you can also just simply check the IPv6 routing tables on these routers. Only a single external prefix should exist following the implemented route summarization on R1:

```
R2#show ipv6 route ospf | include OE2
       O - OSPF intra, OI - OSPF inter, OE1 - OSPF ext 1, OE2 - OSPF ext 2
OE2  3FFE:ABCD:1111::/50 [110/20]

R4#show ipv6 route ospf | include OE2
       O - OSPF intra, OI - OSPF inter, OE1 - OSPF ext 1, OE2 - OSPF ext 2
OE2  3FFE:ABCD:1111::/50 [110/20]
```

Finally, complete the task by verifying that R2 and R4 can ping all three R1 LAN prefixes:

```
R2#ping 3FFE:ABCD:1111:1000::1

Type escape sequence to abort.
Sending 5, 100-byte ICMP Echos to 3FFE:ABCD:1111:1000::1, timeout is 2 seconds:
!!!!!
Success rate is 100 percent (5/5), round-trip min/avg/max = 28/28/32 ms

R2#ping 3FFE:ABCD:1111:2000::1

Type escape sequence to abort.
Sending 5, 100-byte ICMP Echos to 3FFE:ABCD:1111:2000::1, timeout is 2 seconds:
!!!!!
Success rate is 100 percent (5/5), round-trip min/avg/max = 28/28/32 ms

R2#ping 3FFE:ABCD:1111:3000::1

Type escape sequence to abort.
Sending 5, 100-byte ICMP Echos to 3FFE:ABCD:1111:3000::1, timeout is 2 seconds:
!!!!!
Success rate is 100 percent (5/5), round-trip min/avg/max = 28/29/32 ms

R4#ping 3FFE:ABCD:1111:1000::1

Type escape sequence to abort.
Sending 5, 100-byte ICMP Echos to 3FFE:ABCD:1111:1000::1, timeout is 2 seconds:
!!!!!
Success rate is 100 percent (5/5), round-trip min/avg/max = 28/29/32 ms
```

```
R4#ping 3FFE:ABCD:1111:2000::1

Type escape sequence to abort.
Sending 5, 100-byte ICMP Echos to 3FFE:ABCD:1111:2000::1, timeout is 2 seconds:
!!!!!
Success rate is 100 percent (5/5), round-trip min/avg/max = 28/29/32 ms

R4#ping 3FFE:ABCD:1111:3000::1

Type escape sequence to abort.
Sending 5, 100-byte ICMP Echos to 3FFE:ABCD:1111:3000::1, timeout is 2 seconds:
!!!!!
Success rate is 100 percent (5/5), round-trip min/avg/max = 28/29/32 ms
```

Task 5

Inter-area routes are routes received from another area. To complete this task, simply assign the LAN subnets connected to R2 and R4 to a different OSPF area. This is completed as follows:

```
R2(config)#ipv6 router ospf 2
R2(config-rtr)#passive-interface fastethernet 0/0
R2(config-rtr)#exit
R2(config)#interface fastethernet 0/0
R2(config-if)#ipv6 ospf 2 area 2
R2(config-if)#exit

R4(config)#ipv6 router ospf 4
R4(config-rtr)#passive-interface fastethernet 0/0
R4(config-rtr)#exit
R4(config)#interface fastethernet 0/0
R4(config-if)#ipv6 ospf 4 area 4
R4(config-if)#exit
```

Verify your configuration by looking at the IPv6 routing table entries on R1:

```
R1#show ipv6 route 3FFE:ABCD:1111:5::/64
IPv6 Routing Table - 17 entries
Codes: C - Connected, L - Local, S - Static, R - RIP, B - BGP
       U - Per-user Static route
       I1 - ISIS L1, I2 - ISIS L2, IA - ISIS interarea, IS - ISIS summary
       O - OSPF intra, OI - OSPF inter, OE1 - OSPF ext 1, OE2 - OSPF ext 2
       ON1 - OSPF NSSA ext 1, ON2 - OSPF NSSA ext 2
OI  3FFE:ABCD:1111:5::/64 [110/65]
     via FE80::20D:28FF:FE9E:F940, Serial0/1
     via FE80::20F:23FF:FE5E:F120, Serial0/1
```

Task 6

This task requires a little thought based on the imposed restrictions. By default, R1 will load-balance between R2 and R4 for the LAN prefix these routers are connected to as follows:

```
R1#show ipv6 route 3FFE:ABCD:1111:5::/64
IPv6 Routing Table - 17 entries
Codes: C - Connected, L - Local, S - Static, R - RIP, B - BGP
       U - Per-user Static route
       I1 - ISIS L1, I2 - ISIS L2, IA - ISIS interarea, IS - ISIS summary
       O - OSPF intra, OI - OSPF inter, OE1 - OSPF ext 1, OE2 - OSPF ext 2
       ON1 - OSPF NSSA ext 1, ON2 - OSPF NSSA ext 2
OI  3FFE:ABCD:1111:5::/64 [110/65]
     via FE80::20D:28FF:FE9E:F940, Serial0/1
     via FE80::20F:23FF:FE5E:F120, Serial0/1
```

The most simple method of ensuring that R1 prefers the path via R2 would be to use the `ipv6 ospf neighbor <address> cost <cost>` interface configuration command under the Serial0/1 interface; however, we are NOT allowed to make any modifications to R1. Therefore, consideration must be given to another OSPF feature. The only other feature that allows us to assign costs directly to OSPF prefixes is the `area <are>`

range <prefix> cost <cost> cost command. The task is completed by implementing different summary costs on R2 and R4:

```
R2(config)#ipv6 router ospf 2
R2(config-rtr)#area 2 range 3FFE:ABCD:1111:5::/64 cost 2
R2(config-rtr)#exit

R4(config)#ipv6 router ospf 4
R4(config-rtr)#area 4 range 3FFE:ABCD:1111:5::/64 cost 4
R4(config-rtr)#exit
```

NOTE: You could simply increment the cost on R4 to achieve the same result. As long as that value is higher than 1, the path via R2 will be preferred by R1.

Following this configuration, R1 prefers the path via R2 because of the lower cost value.

```
R1#show ipv6 route 3FFE:ABCD:1111:5::/64
IPv6 Routing Table - 17 entries
Codes: C - Connected, L - Local, S - Static, R - RIP, B - BGP
       U - Per-user Static route
       I1 - ISIS L1, I2 - ISIS L2, IA - ISIS interarea, IS - ISIS summary
       O - OSPF intra, OI - OSPF inter, OE1 - OSPF ext 1, OE2 - OSPF ext 2
       ON1 - OSPF NSSA ext 1, ON2 - OSPF NSSA ext 2
OI  3FFE:ABCD:1111:5::/64 [110/66]
     via FE80::20D:28FF:FE9E:F940, Serial0/1
```

Finally, verify that R1 can ping both R2 and R4s LAN addresses when complete:

```
R1#ping 3FFE:ABCD:1111:5::2

Type escape sequence to abort.
Sending 5, 100-byte ICMP Echos to 3FFE:ABCD:1111:5::2, timeout is 2 seconds:
!!!!!
Success rate is 100 percent (5/5), round-trip min/avg/max = 28/29/32 ms

R1#ping 3FFE:ABCD:1111:5::4

Type escape sequence to abort.
Sending 5, 100-byte ICMP Echos to 3FFE:ABCD:1111:5::4, timeout is 2 seconds:
!!!!!
Success rate is 100 percent (5/5), round-trip min/avg/max = 28/30/32 ms
```

FINAL ROUTER CONFIGURATIONS

R1

```
R1#term len 0
R1#sh run
Building configuration...

Current configuration : 1428 bytes
!
version 12.4
service timestamps debug datetime msec
service timestamps log datetime msec
no service password-encryption
!
hostname R1
!
boot-start-marker
boot-end-marker
!
no logging console
!
no aaa new-model
no network-clock-participate slot 1
no network-clock-participate wic 0
ip cef
!
```

```
no ip domain lookup
ip auth-proxy max-nodata-conns 3
ip admission max-nodata-conns 3
!
ipv6 unicast-routing
ipv6 cef
!
interface FastEthernet0/0
 no ip address
 duplex auto
 speed auto
 ipv6 address 3FFE:ABCD:1111:1000::1/64
 ipv6 address 3FFE:ABCD:1111:2000::1/64
 ipv6 address 3FFE:ABCD:1111:3000::1/64
!
interface Serial0/0
 no ip address
 shutdown
 clock rate 2000000
!
interface Serial0/1
 no ip address
 encapsulation frame-relay
 ipv6 address 2001:ABCD:1111:1::1/64
 ipv6 ospf network point-to-multipoint non-broadcast
 ipv6 ospf neighbor FE80::20D:28FF:FE9E:F940
 ipv6 ospf neighbor FE80::20F:23FF:FE5E:F120
 ipv6 ospf 1 area 0
 frame-relay map ipv6 FE80::20D:28FF:FE9E:F940 102 broadcast
 frame-relay map ipv6 FE80::20F:23FF:FE5E:F120 104 broadcast
!
ip forward-protocol nd
!
no ip http server
no ip http secure-server
!
ipv6 router ospf 1
 router-id 1.1.1.1
 log-adjacency-changes
 summary-prefix 3FFE:ABCD:1111::/50
 redistribute connected
!
control-plane
!
line con 0
line aux 0
line vty 0 4
 login
!
end

R1#
```

R2

```
R2#term len 0
R2#sh run
Building configuration...

Current configuration : 1308 bytes
!
version 12.4
service timestamps debug datetime msec
service timestamps log datetime msec
no service password-encryption
!
hostname R2
!
boot-start-marker
boot-end-marker
!
no logging console
!
no aaa new-model
no network-clock-participate slot 1
no network-clock-participate wic 0
ip cef
!
```

```
no ip domain lookup
ip auth-proxy max-nodata-conns 3
ip admission max-nodata-conns 3
!
ipv6 unicast-routing
ipv6 cef
!
interface FastEthernet0/0
 no ip address
 duplex auto
 speed auto
 ipv6 address 3FFE:ABCD:1111:5::2/64
 ipv6 ospf 2 area 2
!
interface Serial0/0
 no ip address
 shutdown
!
interface Serial0/1
 no ip address
 encapsulation frame-relay
 ipv6 address 2001:ABCD:1111:1::2/64
 ipv6 ospf network point-to-multipoint non-broadcast
 ipv6 ospf neighbor FE80::20F:23FF:FE5E:EC80
 ipv6 ospf 2 area 0
 frame-relay map ipv6 FE80::20F:23FF:FE5E:F120 201
 frame-relay map ipv6 FE80::20F:23FF:FE5E:EC80 201 broadcast
!
ip forward-protocol nd
!
no ip http server
no ip http secure-server
!
ipv6 router ospf 2
 router-id 2.2.2.2
 log-adjacency-changes
 area 2 range 3FFE:ABCD:1111:5::/64 cost 2
 passive-interface FastEthernet0/0
!
control-plane
!
line con 0
line aux 0
line vty 0 4
 login
!
end

R2#
```

R3

```
R3-Frame-Relay-Switch#term len 0
R3-Frame-Relay-Switch#sh run
Building configuration...

Current configuration : 1766 bytes
!
version 12.4
service timestamps debug datetime msec
service timestamps log datetime msec
no service password-encryption
!
hostname R3-Frame-Relay-Switch
!
boot-start-marker
boot-end-marker
!
no aaa new-model
no network-clock-participate slot 1
no network-clock-participate wic 0
no ip routing
no ip cef
!
ip auth-proxy max-nodata-conns 3
ip admission max-nodata-conns 3
!
frame-relay switching
```

```
!
interface FastEthernet0/0
 no ip address
 no ip route-cache
 speed auto
 half-duplex
 no mop enabled
!
interface Serial1/0
 description 'Connected To R1 Serial 0/1'
 no ip address
 encapsulation frame-relay
 no ip route-cache
 clock rate 128000
 frame-relay intf-type dce
 frame-relay route 102 interface Serial1/1 201
 frame-relay route 104 interface Serial1/2 401
!
interface Serial1/1
 description 'Connected To R2 Serial 0/1'
 no ip address
 encapsulation frame-relay
 no ip route-cache
 clock rate 128000
 frame-relay intf-type dce
 frame-relay route 201 interface Serial1/0 102
!
interface Serial1/2
 description 'Connected To R4 Serial 0/0'
 no ip address
 encapsulation frame-relay
 no ip route-cache
 clock rate 128000
 frame-relay intf-type dce
 frame-relay route 401 interface Serial1/0 104
!
interface Serial1/3
 no ip address
 no ip route-cache
 shutdown
!
interface Serial1/4
 no ip address
 no ip route-cache
 shutdown
!
interface Serial1/5
 no ip address
 no ip route-cache
 shutdown
!
interface Serial1/6
 no ip address
 no ip route-cache
 shutdown
!
interface Serial1/7
 no ip address
 no ip route-cache
 shutdown
!
ip forward-protocol nd
!
no ip http server
no ip http secure-server
!
control-plane
!
line con 0
line aux 0
line vty 0 4
 password cisco
 login
!
end

R3-Frame-Relay-Switch#
```

R4

```
R4#term len 0
R4#sh run
Building configuration...

Current configuration : 1377 bytes
!
version 12.4
service timestamps debug datetime msec
service timestamps log datetime msec
no service password-encryption
!
hostname R4
!
boot-start-marker
boot-end-marker
!
no logging console
!
no aaa new-model
no network-clock-participate slot 1
no network-clock-participate wic 0
no ip routing
no ip cef
!
no ip domain lookup
ip auth-proxy max-nodata-conns 3
ip admission max-nodata-conns 3
!
ipv6 unicast-routing
ipv6 cef
!
interface FastEthernet0/0
 no ip address
 no ip route-cache
 duplex auto
 speed auto
 ipv6 address 3FFE:ABCD:1111:5::4/64
 ipv6 ospf 4 area 4
 no mop enabled
!
interface Serial0/0
 no ip address
 encapsulation frame-relay
 no ip route-cache
 ipv6 address 2001:ABCD:1111:1::4/64
 ipv6 ospf network point-to-multipoint non-broadcast
 ipv6 ospf neighbor FE80::20F:23FF:FE5E:EC80
 ipv6 ospf 4 area 0
 frame-relay map ipv6 FE80::20D:28FF:FE9E:F940 401
 frame-relay map ipv6 FE80::20F:23FF:FE5E:EC80 401 broadcast
!
interface Serial0/1
 no ip address
 no ip route-cache
 shutdown
!
ip forward-protocol nd
!
no ip http server
no ip http secure-server
!
ipv6 router ospf 4
 router-id 4.4.4.4
 log-adjacency-changes
 area 4 range 3FFE:ABCD:1111:5::/64 cost 4
 passive-interface FastEthernet0/0
!
control-plane
!
line con 0
line aux 0
line vty 0 4
 password cisco
 login
!
end

R4#
```

CCNP LAB 44

Internet Protocol Version 6 Lab

Lab Objective:

The focus of this lab is to understand MP-BGP implementation and configuration in Cisco IOS routers. Additional technologies include path control, attribute manipulation and filtering.

Lab Topology:

The lab network topology is illustrated below:

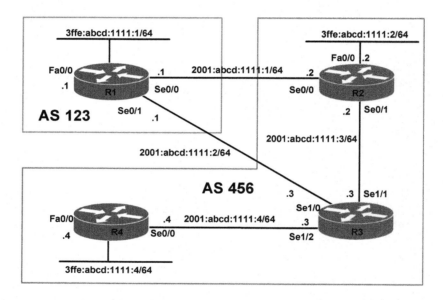

> **IMPORTANT NOTE:** If you are using the www.howtonetwork.net racks, please bring up the LAN interfaces connected to the routers by issuing the `no shutdown` command on the connected switches. If you are using a home lab with no Switches, you can bring up the LAN interfaces using the following configurations on your routers:
>
> ```
> interface fastethernet 0/0
>   no keepalive
>   loopback
>   no shutdown
> ```
>
> Alternately, you can simply connect the interfaces to a hub or switch if you have one available in your own lab.

Task 1

Configure hostnames and IPv6 addressing on all routers as illustrated in the network topology.

Task 2

Configure MP-BGP on R1. This router will reside in AS 1 and will peer with R2 and R3. Use the global Unicast IPv6 addresses for peering.

Task 3

Configure MP-BGP on R2, R3, and R4. R2 and R3 will peer with R1. R2 will peer with R1 and R3. R3 will peer with R1, R2, and R4. R4 will peer only with R3. Use the global Unicast IPv6 addresses for peering. Verify your configuration.

Task 4

Advertise the 3ffe:abcd:1111:1/64 prefix connected to R1 using MP-BGP. This prefix should have an ORIGIN code of IGP and should be assigned the community 123:1. Verify your configuration using the appropriate commands.

Task 5

Advertise the 3ffe:abcd:1111:2/64 prefix as well as the 3ffe:abcd:1111:4/64 prefix connected to the LAN interfaces of R2 and R4, respectively, via MP-BGP. Ensure that R2 and R4 can ping each other LAN to LAN following this configuration. You are NOT allowed to configure R3 as a route-reflector, or use confederations. Instead, use BGP default routing. However, ensure that a default route is NEVER advertised to AS 123. Do NOT use any type of filters to complete this task. Verify your configuration.

Task 6

In the future, AS 123 will be advertising thousands of prefixes to AS 456. Configure AS 456 so that R2 prefers the path via R3 to reach all prefixes originated in AS 123 only.

The direct path to AS 123 via R2 should only be used in the event that the R2-R3 link is down. As 123 should therefore also prefer the R1-R3 for all traffic destined to AS 456.

This configuration should have no impact on any other router in the network and should be implemented on R3 and R1. Verify your configuration using the appropriate commands.

If you have completed all previous requirements correctly, R1, R2 and R4 will be able to ping each other LAN-to-LAN. Verify this using extended pings.

LAB VALIDATION

Task 1

```
Router(config)#hostname R1
R1(config)#ipv6 unicast-routing
R1(config)#ipv6 cef
R1(config)#interface fastethernet 0/0
R1(config-if)#ipv6 address 3ffe:abcd:1111:1::1/64
R1(config-if)#no shutdown
R1(config-if)#exit
R1(config)#interface serial 0/0
R1(config-if)#ipv6 address 2001:abcd:1111:1::1/64
R1(config-if)#clock rate 2000000
R1(config-if)#no shutdown
R1(config-if)#exit
R1(config)#interface serial 0/1
R1(config-if)#ipv6 address 2001:abcd:1111:2::1/64
R1(config-if)#no shutdown
R1(config-if)#exit

Router(config)#hostname R2
R2(config)#ipv6 unicast-routing
R2(config)#ipv6 cef
R2(config)#interface fastethernet 0/0
R2(config-if)#ipv6 address 3ffe:abcd:1111:2::2/64
R2(config-if)#no shutdown
R2(config)#interface serial 0/0
```

```
R2(config-if)#ipv6 address 2001:abcd:1111:1::2/64
R2(config-if)#no shutdown
R2(config-if)#exit
R2(config)#interface serial 0/1
R2(config-if)#ipv6 address 2001:abcd:1111:3::2/64
R2(config-if)#no shutdown
R2(config-if)#exit

Router(config)#hostname R3
R3(config)#ipv6 unicast-routing
R3(config)#ipv6 cef
R3(config)#interface serial 1/0
R3(config-if)#ipv6 address 2001:abcd:1111:2::3/64
R3(config-if)#clock rate 128000
R3(config-if)#no shutdown
R3(config-if)#exit
R3(config)#interface serial 1/1
R3(config-if)#ipv6 address 2001:abcd:1111:3::3/64
R3(config-if)#clock rate 128000
R3(config-if)#no shutdown
R3(config-if)#exit
R3(config)#interface serial 1/2
R3(config-if)#ipv6 address 2001:abcd:1111:4::3/64
R3(config-if)#clock rate 128000
R3(config-if)#no shutdown
R3(config-if)#exit

Router(config)#hostname R4
R4(config)#ipv6 unicast-routing
R4(config)#ipv6 cef
R3(config)#interface fastethernet 0/0
R3(config-if)#ipv6 address 3ffe:abcd:1111:4::4/64
R3(config-if)#no shutdown
R3(config-if)#exit
R4(config)#interface serial 0/0
R4(config-if)#ipv6 address 2001:abcd:1111:4::4/64
R4(config-if)#clock rate 128000
R4(config-if)#no shutdown
R4(config-if)#exit
```

Task 2

```
R1(config)#router bgp 123
R1(config-router)#bgp router-id 1.1.1.1
R1(config-router)#address-family ipv6 unicast
R1(config-router-af)#neighbor 2001:abcd:1111:1::2 remote-as 456
R1(config-router-af)#neighbor 2001:abcd:1111:2::3 remote-as 456
R1(config-router-af)#exit
R1(config-router)#exit
```

Task 3

```
R2(config)#router bgp 456
R2(config-router)#bgp router-id 2.2.2.2
R2(config-router)#address-family ipv6 unicast
R2(config-router-af)#neighbor 2001:abcd:1111:1::1 remote-as 123
R2(config-router-af)#neighbor 2001:abcd:1111:3::3 remote-as 456
R2(config-router-af)#exit
R2(config-router)#exit

R3(config)#router bgp 456
R3(config-router)#bgp router-id 3.3.3.3
R3(config-router)#address-family ipv6 unicast
R3(config-router-af)#neighbor 2001:abcd:1111:2::1 remote-as 123
R3(config-router-af)#neighbor 2001:abcd:1111:3::2 remote-as 456
R3(config-router-af)#neighbor 2001:abcd:1111:4::4 remote-as 456
R3(config-router-af)#exit
R3(config-router)#exit

R4(config)#router bgp 456
R4(config-router)#bgp router-id 4.4.4.4
```

```
R4(config-router)#address-family ipv6 unicast
R4(config-router-af)#neighbor 2001:abcd:1111:4::3 remote-as 456
R4(config-router-af)#exit
R4(config-router)#exit
```

Verify your configuration using the show bgp ipv6 unicast summary command on all MP-BGP speakers.

```
R1#show bgp ipv6 unicast summary
BGP router identifier 1.1.1.1, local AS number 123
BGP table version is 1, main routing table version 1

Neighbor        V    AS MsgRcvd MsgSent   TblVer  InQ OutQ Up/Down  State/PfxRcd
2001:ABCD:1111:1::2
                4   456     12      12        1    0    0 00:03:02        0
2001:ABCD:1111:2::3
                4   456     13      13        1    0    0 00:01:26        0

R2#show bgp ipv6 unicast summary
BGP router identifier 2.2.2.2, local AS number 456
BGP table version is 1, main routing table version 1

Neighbor        V    AS MsgRcvd MsgSent   TblVer  InQ OutQ Up/Down  State/PfxRcd
2001:ABCD:1111:1::1
                4   123      6       6        1    0    0 00:03:06        0
2001:ABCD:1111:3::3
                4   456      7       7        1    0    0 00:01:52        0

R3#show bgp ipv6 unicast summary
BGP router identifier 3.3.3.3, local AS number 456
BGP table version is 1, main routing table version 1

Neighbor        V    AS MsgRcvd MsgSent   TblVer  InQ OutQ Up/Down  State/PfxRcd
2001:ABCD:1111:2::1
                4   123      5       5        1    0    0 00:01:33        0
2001:ABCD:1111:3::2
                4   456      5       5        1    0    0 00:01:55        0
2001:ABCD:1111:4::4
                4   456      5       5        1    0    0 00:00:50        0

R4#show bgp ipv6 unicast summary
BGP router identifier 4.4.4.4, local AS number 456
BGP table version is 1, main routing table version 1

Neighbor        V    AS MsgRcvd MsgSent   TblVer  InQ OutQ Up/Down  State/PfxRcd
2001:ABCD:1111:4::3
                4   456      4       4        1    0    0 00:00:53        0
```

Task 4

By default, all prefixes injected into MP-BGP using the network statement will be assigned an ORIGIN code of IGP. To complete the second requirement of this task, we need to use a route-map to assign this prefix the specified COMMUNITY attribute. In addition to this, we need to configure MP-BGP so that this attribute is included in updates to peers:

```
R1(config)#route-map COMMUNITY permit 10
R1(config-route-map)#set community 123:1
R1(config-route-map)#exit
R1(config)#ip bgp-community new-format
R1(config)#router bgp 123
R1(config-router)#address-family ipv6 unicast
R1(config-router-af)#network 3FFE:abcd:1111:1::/64 route-map COMMUNITY
R1(config-router-af)#neighbor 2001:ABCD:1111:1::2 send-community standard
R1(config-router-af)#neighbor 2001:ABCD:1111:2::3 send-community standard
R1(config-router-af)#exit
R1(config-router)#exit
```

NOTE: The ip bgp-community new-format command is required to display a configured COMMUNITY value in ASN:nn notation. The Cisco default community format is one 32-bit number. The ip bgp-community new-format command changes the community format to AA:NN to conform to RFC 1997.

If this command is issued, the configured COMMUNITY would be displayed as follows:

```
R1#show bgp ipv6 unicast 3FFE:abcd:1111:1::/64
BGP routing table entry for 3FFE:ABCD:1111:1::/64, version 3
Paths: (1 available, best #1, table Global-IPv6-Table)
  Advertised to update-groups:
     1
  Local
    :: from 0.0.0.0 (1.1.1.1)
       Origin IGP, metric 0, localpref 100, weight 32768, valid, sourced, local, best
       Community: 8060929
```

However, with this command enabled, the COMMUNITY is displayed in RFC 1997 format:

```
R1#show bgp ipv6 unicast 3FFE:abcd:1111:1::/64
BGP routing table entry for 3FFE:ABCD:1111:1::/64, version 3
Paths: (1 available, best #1, table Global-IPv6-Table)
  Advertised to update-groups:
     1
  Local
    :: from 0.0.0.0 (1.1.1.1)
       Origin IGP, metric 0, localpref 100, weight 32768, valid, sourced, local, best
       Community: 123:1
```

To complete this task, we also therefore need to issue this command on R2, R3, and R4. Also, we need to ensure that the COMMUNITY attribute is sent to all internal MP-BGP peers. In other words, this attribute should be included in updates from R2 to R3, and in updates from R3 to R2 and R4. Since R4 is not receiving and advertising any prefixes with this attribute, it does not need to include it in updates sent to R3. This part of the task is completed as follows:

```
R2(config)#router bgp 456
R2(config-router)#address-family ipv6 unicast
R2(config-router-af)#neighbor 2001:abcd:1111:3::3 send-community standard
R2(config-router-af)#exit
R2(config-router)#exit
R2(config)#ip bgp-community new-format
R2(config)#exit

R3(config)#router bgp 456
R3(config-router)#address-family ipv6 unicast
R3(config-router-af)#neighbor 2001:abcd:1111:3::2 send-community standard
R3(config-router-af)#neighbor 2001:abcd:1111:4::4 send-community standard
R3(config-router-af)#exit
R3(config-router)#exit
R3(config)#ip bgp-community new-format
R3(config)#exit

R4(config)#ip bgp-community new-format
```

Finally, verify that the prefix is received by R2 and R4 with the assigned COMMUNITY:

```
R2#show bgp ipv6 unicast 3FFE:abcd:1111:1::/64
BGP routing table entry for 3FFE:ABCD:1111:1::/64, version 4
Paths: (2 available, best #2, table Global-IPv6-Table)
  Advertised to update-groups:
     2
  123
    2001:ABCD:1111:2::1 (inaccessible) from 2001:ABCD:1111:3::3 (3.3.3.3)
       Origin IGP, metric 0, localpref 100, valid, internal
       Community: 123:1
  123
    2001:ABCD:1111:1::1 (FE80::20F:23FF:FE5E:EC80) from 2001:ABCD:1111:1::1 (1.1.1.1)
       Origin IGP, metric 0, localpref 100, valid, external, best
       Community: 123:1

R3#show bgp ipv6 unicast 3FFE:abcd:1111:1::/64
BGP routing table entry for 3FFE:ABCD:1111:1::/64, version 4
Paths: (2 available, best #2, table Global-IPv6-Table)
  Advertised to update-groups:
```

```
      2
   123
      2001:ABCD:1111:1::1 (inaccessible) from 2001:ABCD:1111:3::2 (2.2.2.2)
         Origin IGP, metric 0, localpref 100, valid, internal
         Community: 123:1
   123
      2001:ABCD:1111:2::1 (FE80::20F:23FF:FE5E:EC80) from 2001:ABCD:1111:2::1 (1.1.1.1)
         Origin IGP, metric 0, localpref 100, valid, external, best
         Community: 123:1

R4#show bgp ipv6 unicast 3FFE:abcd:1111:1::/64
BGP routing table entry for 3FFE:ABCD:1111:1::/64, version 0
Paths: (1 available, no best path)
  Not advertised to any peer
  123
      2001:ABCD:1111:2::1 (inaccessible) from 2001:ABCD:1111:4::3 (3.3.3.3)
         Origin IGP, metric 0, localpref 100, valid, internal
         Community: 123:1
```

Task 5

The requirements of this task are two-fold. First, we need to advertise the LAN subnets that are connected to R2 and R4 via MP-BGP. This first part is completed as follows:

```
R2(config)#router bgp 456
R2(config-router)#address-family ipv6 unicast
R2(config-router-af)#network 3ffe:abcd:1111:2::/64
R2(config-router-af)#exit
R2(config-router)#exit

R4(config)#router bgp 456
R4(config-router)#address-family ipv6 unicast
R4(config-router-af)#network 3ffe:abcd:1111:4::/64
R4(config-router-af)#exit
R4(config-router)#exit
```

Verify your configuration using the show bgp ipv6 unicast command on R2 and R4:

```
R2#show bgp ipv6 unicast 3ffe:abcd:1111:2::/64
BGP routing table entry for 3FFE:ABCD:1111:2::/64, version 5
Paths: (1 available, best #1, table Global-IPv6-Table)
  Advertised to update-groups:
     1           2
  Local
     :: from 0.0.0.0 (2.2.2.2)
        Origin IGP, metric 0, localpref 100, weight 32768, valid, sourced, local, best

R4#show bgp ipv6 unicast 3ffe:abcd:1111:4::/64
BGP routing table entry for 3FFE:ABCD:1111:4::/64, version 2
Paths: (1 available, best #1, table Global-IPv6-Table)
  Advertised to update-groups:
     1
  Local
     :: from 0.0.0.0 (4.4.4.4)
        Origin IGP, metric 0, localpref 100, weight 32768, valid, sourced, local, best
```

The second part of this task requires some thought. In a typical BGP implementation, router R3 would be configured as a route reflector, allowing these prefixes to be advertised to its clients R2 and R4; however the task states that this is forbidden. To complete this task, we need to use BGP default routing as stated. However, to ensure that the default route is not advertised to AS 123, we need to use the COMMUNITY attribute (LOCAL_AS or NO_EXPORT) since we are forbidden from using any types of filters. The second part of this task is completed as follows:

```
R3(config)#route-map LOCAL permit 10
R3(config-route-map)#set community local-AS
R3(config-route-map)#exit
R3(config)#router bgp 456
```

```
R3(config-router)#address-family ipv6 unicast
R3(config-router-af)#$01:abcd:1111:3::2 default-originate route-map LOCAL
R3(config-router-af)#neighbor 2001:abcd:1111:4::4 default-originate
R3(config-router-af)#exit
```

Following this configuration, verify the default routes received by R2 and R4:

```
R2#show bgp ipv6 unicast ::/0
BGP routing table entry for ::/0, version 7
Paths: (1 available, best #1, table Global-IPv6-Table, not advertised outside local
AS)
Flag: 0x880
  Not advertised to any peer
  Local
    2001:ABCD:1111:3::3 from 2001:ABCD:1111:3::3 (3.3.3.3)
      Origin IGP, metric 0, localpref 100, valid, internal, best
      Community: local-AS
```

NOTE: You do NOT have to specify the NO_EXPORT or LOCAL_AS for the default route that is advertised to R4 because this BGP speaker is not peered with AS 123.

```
R4#show bgp ipv6 unicast ::/0
BGP routing table entry for ::/0, version 6
Paths: (1 available, best #1, table Global-IPv6-Table)
  Not advertised to any peer
  Local
    2001:ABCD:1111:4::3 from 2001:ABCD:1111:4::3 (3.3.3.3)
      Origin IGP, metric 0, localpref 100, valid, internal, best
```

Finally, complete this task by ensuring that R2 and R4 can ping each other LAN to LAN:

```
R2#ping 3FFE:ABCD:1111:4::4 source fastethernet 0/0 repeat 10 size 1500

Type escape sequence to abort.
Sending 10, 1500-byte ICMP Echos to 3FFE:ABCD:1111:4::4, timeout is 2 seconds:
Packet sent with a source address of 3FFE:ABCD:1111:2::2
!!!!!!!!!!
Success rate is 100 percent (10/10), round-trip min/avg/max = 384/384/384 ms

R4#ping 3FFE:ABCD:1111:2::2 source fastethernet 0/0 repeat 10 size 1500

Type escape sequence to abort.
Sending 10, 1500-byte ICMP Echos to 3FFE:ABCD:1111:2::2, timeout is 2 seconds:
Packet sent with a source address of 3FFE:ABCD:1111:4::4
!!!!!!!!!!
Success rate is 100 percent (10/10), round-trip min/avg/max = 388/388/388 ms
```

Task 6

To complete this task, you can use the LOCAL_PREF attributes on R3 so that it sends updates for prefixes originated in AS 123 with a higher value than the default LOCAL_PREF value. Because there will be a lot of prefixes from AS 123, use an AS_PATH filter on R3. This task is completed by implementing the following configuration on R3:

```
R3(config)#ip as-path access-list 1 permit ^123$
R3(config)#route-map PREF permit 10
R3(config-route-map)#match as-path 1
R3(config-route-map)#set local-preference 200
R3(config-route-map)#exit
R3(config-router)#route-map PREF permit 20
R3(config-route-map)#exit
R3(config)#router bgp 456
R3(config-router)#address-family ipv6
R3(config-router-af)#neighbor 2001:abcd:1111:3::2 route-map PREF out
R3(config-router-af)#exit
R3(config-router)#exit
```

Following this configuration, the MP-BGP RIB shows the following entry for the R1 prefix:

```
R2#show bgp ipv6 unicast 3FFE:ABCD:1111:1::/64
BGP routing table entry for 3FFE:ABCD:1111:1::/64, version 8
Paths: (2 available, best #1, table Global-IPv6-Table)
  Advertised to update-groups:
    1
  123
    2001:ABCD:1111:2::1 from 2001:ABCD:1111:3::3 (3.3.3.3)
      Origin IGP, metric 0, localpref 200, valid, internal, best
      Community: 123:1
  123
    2001:ABCD:1111:1::1 (FE80::20F:23FF:FE5E:EC80) from 2001:ABCD:1111:1::1 (1.1.1.1)
      Origin IGP, metric 0, localpref 100, valid, external
      Community: 123:1
```

To complete the second part of this task, you can use either LOCAL_PREF or WEIGHT to ensure that R1 prefers the path via R3 for all prefixes originated in AS 456:

```
R1(config)#ip as-path access-list 1 permit ^456$
R1(config)#route-map WEIGHT permit 10
R1(config-route-map)#match as-path 1
R1(config-route-map)#set weight 1
R1(config-route-map)#exit
R1(config)#route-map WEIGHT permit 20
R1(config-route-map)#exit
R1(config)#router bgp 123
R1(config-router)#address-family ipv6
R1(config-router-af)#neighbor 2001:ABCD:1111:2::3 route-map WEIGHT in
R1(config-router-af)#exit
R1(config-router)#exit
```

Following this configuration, the MP-BGP RIB shows the following entry for the R2 prefix:

```
R1#show bgp ipv6 unicast 3FFE:ABCD:1111:2::/64
BGP routing table entry for 3FFE:ABCD:1111:2::/64, version 10
Paths: (2 available, best #1, table Global-IPv6-Table)
Flag: 0x840
  Advertised to update-groups:
    1
  456
    2001:ABCD:1111:2::3 (FE80::213:7FFF:FEAF:3E00) from 2001:ABCD:1111:2::3 (3.3.3.3)
      Origin IGP, localpref 100, weight 1, valid, external, best
  456
    2001:ABCD:1111:1::2 (FE80::20D:28FF:FE9E:F940) from 2001:ABCD:1111:1::2 (2.2.2.2)
      Origin IGP, metric 0, localpref 100, valid, external
```

Finally, verify your configurations using extended pings LAN-to-LAN between R1, R2, and R4:

```
R1#ping 3FFE:ABCD:1111:2::2 source fastethernet 0/0 repeat 10 size 1500

Type escape sequence to abort.
Sending 10, 1500-byte ICMP Echos to 3FFE:ABCD:1111:2::2, timeout is 2 seconds:
Packet sent with a source address of 3FFE:ABCD:1111:1::1
!!!!!!!!!!
Success rate is 100 percent (10/10), round-trip min/avg/max = 384/384/384 ms

R1#ping 3FFE:ABCD:1111:4::4 source fastethernet 0/0 repeat 10 size 1500

Type escape sequence to abort.
Sending 10, 1500-byte ICMP Echos to 3FFE:ABCD:1111:4::4, timeout is 2 seconds:
Packet sent with a source address of 3FFE:ABCD:1111:1::1
!!!!!!!!!!
Success rate is 100 percent (10/10), round-trip min/avg/max = 384/384/384 ms

R2#ping 3FFE:ABCD:1111:1::1 source fastethernet 0/0 repeat 10 size 1500

Type escape sequence to abort.
Sending 10, 1500-byte ICMP Echos to 3FFE:ABCD:1111:1::1, timeout is 2 seconds:
Packet sent with a source address of 3FFE:ABCD:1111:2::2
```

```
!!!!!!!!!!
Success rate is 100 percent (10/10), round-trip min/avg/max = 384/384/384 ms

R4#ping 3FFE:ABCD:1111:1::1 source fastethernet 0/0 repeat 10 size 1500

Type escape sequence to abort.
Sending 10, 1500-byte ICMP Echos to 3FFE:ABCD:1111:1::1, timeout is 2 seconds:
Packet sent with a source address of 3FFE:ABCD:1111:4::4
!!!!!!!!!!
Success rate is 100 percent (10/10), round-trip min/avg/max = 384/384/384 ms
```

FINAL ROUTER CONFIGURATIONS

R1

```
R1#term len 0
R1#sh run
Building configuration...

Current configuration : 1703 bytes
!
version 12.4
service timestamps debug datetime msec
service timestamps log datetime msec
no service password-encryption
!
hostname R1
!
boot-start-marker
boot-end-marker
!
no logging console
!
no aaa new-model
no network-clock-participate slot 1
no network-clock-participate wic 0
ip cef
!
no ip domain lookup
ip auth-proxy max-nodata-conns 3
ip admission max-nodata-conns 3
!
ipv6 unicast-routing
ipv6 cef
!
interface FastEthernet0/0
 no ip address
 duplex auto
 speed auto
 ipv6 address 3FFE:ABCD:1111:1::1/64
!
interface Serial0/0
 no ip address
 ipv6 address 2001:ABCD:1111:1::1/64
 clock rate 2000000
!
interface Serial0/1
 no ip address
 ipv6 address 2001:ABCD:1111:2::1/64
!
router bgp 123
 no synchronization
 bgp router-id 1.1.1.1
 bgp log-neighbor-changes
 neighbor 2001:ABCD:1111:1::2 remote-as 456
 no neighbor 2001:ABCD:1111:1::2 activate
 neighbor 2001:ABCD:1111:2::3 remote-as 456
 no neighbor 2001:ABCD:1111:2::3 activate
 no auto-summary
 !
 address-family ipv6
  neighbor 2001:ABCD:1111:1::2 activate
  neighbor 2001:ABCD:1111:1::2 send-community
  neighbor 2001:ABCD:1111:2::3 activate
  neighbor 2001:ABCD:1111:2::3 send-community
```

```
  neighbor 2001:ABCD:1111:2::3 route-map WEIGHT in
  network 3FFE:ABCD:1111:1::/64 route-map COMMUNITY
 exit-address-family
!
ip forward-protocol nd
!
ip bgp-community new-format
ip as-path access-list 1 permit ^456$
!
no ip http server
no ip http secure-server
!
route-map WEIGHT permit 10
 match as-path 1
 set weight 1
!
route-map WEIGHT permit 20
!
route-map COMMUNITY permit 10
 set community 123:1
!
control-plane
!
line con 0
line aux 0
line vty 0 4
 login
!
end

R1#
```

R2

```
R2#term len 0
R2#sh run
Building configuration...

Current configuration : 1386 bytes
!
version 12.4
service timestamps debug datetime msec
service timestamps log datetime msec
no service password-encryption
!
hostname R2
!
boot-start-marker
boot-end-marker
!
no logging console
!
no aaa new-model
no network-clock-participate slot 1
no network-clock-participate wic 0
ip cef
!
no ip domain lookup
ip auth-proxy max-nodata-conns 3
ip admission max-nodata-conns 3
!
ipv6 unicast-routing
ipv6 cef
!
interface FastEthernet0/0
 no ip address
 duplex auto
 speed auto
 ipv6 address 3FFE:ABCD:1111:2::2/64
!
interface Serial0/0
 no ip address
 ipv6 address 2001:ABCD:1111:1::2/64
!
interface Serial0/1
 no ip address
 ipv6 address 2001:ABCD:1111:3::2/64
!
router bgp 456
```

```
 no synchronization
 bgp router-id 2.2.2.2
 bgp log-neighbor-changes
 neighbor 2001:ABCD:1111:1::1 remote-as 123
 no neighbor 2001:ABCD:1111:1::1 activate
 neighbor 2001:ABCD:1111:3::3 remote-as 456
 no neighbor 2001:ABCD:1111:3::3 activate
 no auto-summary
 !
 address-family ipv6
  neighbor 2001:ABCD:1111:1::1 activate
  neighbor 2001:ABCD:1111:3::3 activate
  neighbor 2001:ABCD:1111:3::3 send-community
  network 3FFE:ABCD:1111:2::/64
 exit-address-family
!
ip forward-protocol nd
!
ip bgp-community new-format
!
no ip http server
no ip http secure-server
!
control-plane
!
line con 0
line aux 0
line vty 0 4
 login
!
end
R2#
```

R3

```
R3#term len 0
R3#sh run
Building configuration...

Current configuration : 2297 bytes
!
version 12.4
service timestamps debug datetime msec
service timestamps log datetime msec
no service password-encryption
!
hostname R3
!
boot-start-marker
boot-end-marker
!
no logging console
!
no aaa new-model
no network-clock-participate slot 1
no network-clock-participate wic 0
ip cef
!
no ip domain lookup
ip auth-proxy max-nodata-conns 3
ip admission max-nodata-conns 3
!
ipv6 unicast-routing
ipv6 cef
!
interface FastEthernet0/0
 no ip address
 shutdown
 duplex auto
 speed auto
 no mop enabled
!
interface Serial1/0
 no ip address
 ipv6 address 2001:ABCD:1111:2::3/64
 clock rate 128000
!
interface Serial1/1
 no ip address
```

```
 ipv6 address 2001:ABCD:1111:3::3/64
 clock rate 128000
!
interface Serial1/2
 no ip address
 ipv6 address 2001:ABCD:1111:4::3/64
 clock rate 128000
!
interface Serial1/3
 no ip address
 shutdown
!
interface Serial1/4
 no ip address
 shutdown
!
interface Serial1/5
 no ip address
 shutdown
!
interface Serial1/6
 no ip address
 shutdown
!
interface Serial1/7
 no ip address
 shutdown
!
router bgp 456
 no synchronization
 bgp router-id 3.3.3.3
 bgp log-neighbor-changes
 neighbor 2001:ABCD:1111:2::1 remote-as 123
 no neighbor 2001:ABCD:1111:2::1 activate
 neighbor 2001:ABCD:1111:3::2 remote-as 456
 no neighbor 2001:ABCD:1111:3::2 activate
 neighbor 2001:ABCD:1111:4::4 remote-as 456
 no neighbor 2001:ABCD:1111:4::4 activate
 no auto-summary
 !
 address-family ipv6
  neighbor 2001:ABCD:1111:2::1 activate
  neighbor 2001:ABCD:1111:3::2 activate
  neighbor 2001:ABCD:1111:3::2 send-community
  neighbor 2001:ABCD:1111:3::2 default-originate route-map LOCAL
  neighbor 2001:ABCD:1111:3::2 route-map PREF out
  neighbor 2001:ABCD:1111:4::4 activate
  neighbor 2001:ABCD:1111:4::4 send-community
  neighbor 2001:ABCD:1111:4::4 default-originate
 exit-address-family
!
ip forward-protocol nd
!
ip bgp-community new-format
ip as-path access-list 1 permit ^123$
!
no ip http server
no ip http secure-server
!
snmp-server community public RO
!
route-map PREF permit 10
 match as-path 1
 set local-preference 200
!
route-map PREF permit 20
!
route-map LOCAL permit 10
 set community local-AS
!
control-plane
!
line con 0
line aux 0
line vty 0 4
 password config-register 0x2142
 login
!
end
R3#
```

R4

```
R4#term len 0
R4#sh run
Building configuration...

Current configuration : 1187 bytes
!
version 12.4
service timestamps debug datetime msec
service timestamps log datetime msec
no service password-encryption
!
hostname R4
!
boot-start-marker
boot-end-marker
!
no logging console
!
no aaa new-model
no network-clock-participate slot 1
no network-clock-participate wic 0
ip cef
!
no ip domain lookup
ip auth-proxy max-nodata-conns 3
ip admission max-nodata-conns 3
!
ipv6 unicast-routing
ipv6 cef
!
interface FastEthernet0/0
 no ip address
 duplex auto
 speed auto
 ipv6 address 3FFE:ABCD:1111:4::4/64
!
interface Serial0/0
 no ip address
 ipv6 address 2001:ABCD:1111:4::4/64
!
interface Serial0/1
 no ip address
 shutdown
!
router bgp 456
 no synchronization
 bgp router-id 4.4.4.4
 bgp log-neighbor-changes
 neighbor 2001:ABCD:1111:4::3 remote-as 456
 no neighbor 2001:ABCD:1111:4::3 activate
 no auto-summary
 !
 address-family ipv6
  neighbor 2001:ABCD:1111:4::3 activate
  network 3FFE:ABCD:1111:4::/64
 exit-address-family
!
ip forward-protocol nd
!
ip bgp-community new-format
!
no ip http server
no ip http secure-server
!
control-plane
!
line con 0
line aux 0
line vty 0 4
 login
!
end

R4#
```

CCNP LAB 45

Internet Protocol Version 6 Lab

Lab Objective:

The focus of this lab is to understand MP-BGP implementation and configuration in Cisco IOS routers. Additional technologies include attribute manipulation and route redistribution.

Lab Topology:

The lab network topology is illustrated below:

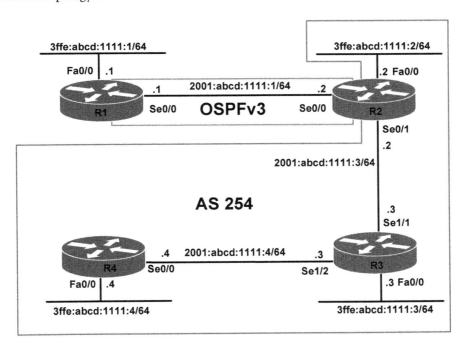

IMPORTANT NOTE: If you are using the www.howtonetwork.net racks, please bring up the LAN interfaces connected to the routers by issuing the no shutdown command on the connected switches. If you are using a home lab with no Switches, you can bring up the LAN interfaces using the following configurations on your routers:

```
interface fastethernet 0/0
 no keepalive
 loopback
 no shutdown
```

Alternately, you can simply connect the interfaces to a hub or switch if you have one available in your own lab.

Task 1

Configure hostnames and IPv6 addressing on all routers as illustrated in the network topology.

Task 2

Configure OSPFv3 on R1 and R2. Enable OSPFv3 for the WAN interfaces of R1 and R2. Do NOT advertise R1 or R2s LAN subnet using OSPFv3. Ensure that R1s LAN subnet is advertised as an external Type 1 LSA. Verify the configuration using the appropriate commands.

Task 3

Configure MP-BGP on R2, R3 and R4. All routers should use Link Local addresses for peering and establishing MP-BGP sessions. Verify your configuration

Task 4

Advertise the LAN subnets of R1, R2, and R3 via MP-BGP. Verify your configuration.

Task 5

Redistribute between MP-BGP and OSPFv3 on R2. Ensure that ONLY the LAN subnets are redistributed. Verify your configuration using the appropriate commands.

Task 6

Configure your network so that all routers can ping each others' LAN subnets from their own local LAN subnet, i.e. LAN-to-LAN pings. Verify your configuration using extended ping. When completing this task, adhere to the following restrictions:
- You are NOT allowed to enable an IGP within AS 254
- You are NOT allowed to configure static routes on R2, R3 and R4
- You are NOT allowed to create any tunnels
- You are NOT allowed to advertise the WAN prefixes via BGP
- You are NOT allowed to use MP-BGP default routing

LAB VALIDATION

Task 1

Please refer to previous labs for basic IPv6 addressing and hostname configuration. This will not be included in this section to avoid being redundant.

Task 2

```
R1(config)#ipv6 router ospf 1
R1(config-rtr)#router-id 1.1.1.1
R1(config-rtr)#redistribute connected metric-type 1
R1(config-rtr)#exit
R1(config)#interface serial 0/0
R1(config-if)#ipv6 ospf 1 area 0
R1(config-if)#exit

R2(config)#ipv6 router ospf 2
R2(config-rtr)#router-id 2.2.2.2
R2(config-rtr)#exit
R2(config)#interface serial 0/0
R2(config-if)#ipv6 ospf 2 area 0
R2(config-if)#exit
```

Verify basic OSPFv3 configuration using the show ipv6 ospf neighbor command:

```
R1#show ipv6 ospf neighbor

Neighbor ID     Pri   State       Dead Time   Interface ID   Interface
2.2.2.2           1   FULL/  -    00:00:35    5              Serial0/0
```

```
R2#show ipv6 ospf neighbor

Neighbor ID      Pri   State         Dead Time   Interface ID   Interface
1.1.1.1            1   FULL/  -      00:00:32    5              Serial0/0
```

Next, verify OSPFv3 redistribution by looking at the external LSA entry in the LSDB:

```
R1#show ipv6 ospf database external

            OSPFv3 Router with ID (1.1.1.1) (Process ID 1)

            Type-5 AS External Link States

  LS age: 127
  LS Type: AS External Link
  Link State ID: 0
  Advertising Router: 1.1.1.1
  LS Seq Number: 80000001
  Checksum: 0x9D44
  Length: 36
  Prefix Address: 3FFE:ABCD:1111:1::
  Prefix Length: 64, Options: None
  Metric Type: 1 (Comparable directly to link state metric)
  Metric: 20

R2#show ipv6 ospf database external

            OSPFv3 Router with ID (2.2.2.2) (Process ID 2)

            Type-5 AS External Link States

  Routing Bit Set on this LSA
  LS age: 135
  LS Type: AS External Link
  Link State ID: 0
  Advertising Router: 1.1.1.1
  LS Seq Number: 80000001
  Checksum: 0x9D44
  Length: 36
  Prefix Address: 3FFE:ABCD:1111:1::
  Prefix Length: 64, Options: None
  Metric Type: 1 (Comparable directly to link state metric)
  Metric: 20
```

Task 3

This task is relatively straightforward; however, it is important to remember that when using a Link Local address for peering, you must use the neighbor [address] update-source [interface] command to ensure that the session will be established because Link-Local addresses are specific to interfaces. This is required only when using Link-Local addresses for peering. This task is completed as follows:

```
R2(config)#router bgp 254
R2(config-router)#bgp router-id 2.2.2.2
R2(config-router)#address-family ipv6
R2(config-router-af)#neighbor FE80::213:7FFF:FEAF:3E00 remote-as 254
R2(config-router-af)#$80::213:7FFF:FEAF:3E00 update-source serial 0/1
R2(config-router-af)#exit

R3(config)#router bgp 254
R3(config-router)#bgp router-id 3.3.3.3
R3(config-router)#address-family ipv6
R3(config-router-af)#neighbor FE80::20D:28FF:FE9E:F940 remote-as 254
R3(config-router-af)#$80::20D:28FF:FE9E:F940 update-source serial 1/1
R3(config-router-af)#neighbor FE80::20F:23FF:FE5E:F120 remote-as 254
R3(config-router-af)#$80::20F:23FF:FE5E:F120 update-source serial 1/2
R3(config-router-af)#exit

R4(config)#router bgp 254
R4(config-router)#bgp router-id 4.4.4.4
R4(config-router)#address-family ipv6
```

```
R4(config-router-af)#neighbor FE80::213:7FFF:FEAF:3E00 remote-as 254
R4(config-router-af)#$80::213:7FFF:FEAF:3E00 update-source serial 0/0
R4(config-router-af)#exit
```

Verify your configuration using the show bgp ipv6 unicast summary command:

```
R2#show bgp ipv6 unicast summary
BGP router identifier 2.2.2.2, local AS number 254
BGP table version is 1, main routing table version 1

Neighbor        V    AS MsgRcvd MsgSent  TblVer  InQ OutQ Up/Down  State/PfxRcd
FE80::213:7FFF:FEAF:3E00
                4   254       5       5       1    0    0 00:01:47           0

R3#show bgp ipv6 unicast summary
BGP router identifier 3.3.3.3, local AS number 254
BGP table version is 1, main routing table version 1

Neighbor        V    AS MsgRcvd MsgSent  TblVer  InQ OutQ Up/Down  State/PfxRcd
FE80::20D:28FF:FE9E:F940
                4   254       4       4       1    0    0 00:01:51           0
FE80::20F:23FF:FE5E:F120
                4   254       4       4       1    0    0 00:00:28           0

R4#show bgp ipv6 unicast summary
BGP router identifier 4.4.4.4, local AS number 254
BGP table version is 1, main routing table version 1

Neighbor        V    AS MsgRcvd MsgSent  TblVer  InQ OutQ Up/Down  State/PfxRcd
FE80::213:7FFF:FEAF:3E00
                4   254       4       4       1    0    0 00:00:31           0
```

Task 4

The advertisement of the LAN subnets via BGP is straightforward. To ensure that R2 and R4 do see each others' LAN subnets in their respective BGP RIBs, R3 must be configured as a route reflector. This task is completed as follows:

```
R2(config)#router bgp 254
R2(config-router)#address-family ipv6
R2(config-router-af)#network 3FFE:ABCD:1111:2::/64
R2(config-router-af)#exit
R2(config-router)#exit

R3(config)#router bgp 254
R3(config-router)#address-family ipv6
R3(config-router-af)#network 3FFE:ABCD:1111:3::/64
R3(config-router-af)#exit
R3(config-router)#exit

R4(config)#router bgp 254
R4(config-router)#address-family ipv6
R4(config-router-af)#network 3FFE:ABCD:1111:4::/64
R4(config-router-af)#exit
R4(config-router)#exit
```

Verify your configuration using the show bgp ipv6 unicast command on all routers:

```
R2#show bgp ipv6 unicast 3FFE:ABCD:1111:2::2/64
BGP routing table entry for 3FFE:ABCD:1111:2::/64, version 2
Paths: (1 available, best #1, table Global-IPv6-Table)
  Advertised to update-groups:
     1
  Local
    :: from 0.0.0.0 (2.2.2.2)
      Origin IGP, metric 0, localpref 100, weight 32768, valid, sourced, local, best

R3#show bgp ipv6 unicast 3FFE:ABCD:1111:3::3/64
BGP routing table entry for 3FFE:ABCD:1111:3::/64, version 5
```

```
Paths: (1 available, best #1, table Global-IPv6-Table)
  Advertised to update-groups:
      2
  Local
    :: from 0.0.0.0 (3.3.3.3)
       Origin IGP, metric 0, localpref 100, weight 32768, valid, sourced, local, best

R4#show bgp ipv6 unicast 3FFE:ABCD:1111:4::4/64
BGP routing table entry for 3FFE:ABCD:1111:4::/64, version 3
Paths: (1 available, best #1, table Global-IPv6-Table)
  Advertised to update-groups:
      1
  Local
    :: from 0.0.0.0 (4.4.4.4)
       Origin IGP, metric 0, localpref 100, weight 32768, valid, sourced, local, best
```

Task 5

By default, when redistributing between IPv6 routing protocols, connected subnets will not be included. Therefore, you must explicitly redistribute the connected R2 LAN subnet into OSPF using a route map so that only this subnet is redistributed.

When redistributing between OSPFv3 and MP-BGP, the same OSPF-to-BGP rules apply, i.e. only internal prefixes are accepted. This default behavior must be modified to complete this task. This task is completed by implementing the following configuration on R2:

```
R2(config)#route-map LAN-ONLY permit 10
R2(config-route-map)#match interface fastethernet 0/0
R2(config-route-map)#exit
R2(config)#route-map LAN-ONLY deny 20
R2(config-route-map)#exit
R2(config)#ipv6 router ospf 2
R2(config-rtr)#redistribute connected route-map LAN-ONLY
R2(config-rtr)#redistribute bgp 254
R2(config-rtr)#exit
R2(config)#router bgp 254
R2(config-router)#address-family ipv6
R2(config-router-af)#redistribute ospf 2 match external 1
R2(config-router-af)#bgp redistribute-internal
R2(config-router-af)#exit
R2(config-router)#exit
```

Verify your configuration by looking at the LSDB on either R1 or R2 for BGP-to-OSPF route redistribution. At this point in time, not all prefixes will be present. This is normal given the implemented configuration up to this point:

```
R2#show ipv6 ospf database external

            OSPFv3 Router with ID (2.2.2.2) (Process ID 2)

            Type-5 AS External Link States

  Routing Bit Set on this LSA
  LS age: 1760
  LS Type: AS External Link
  Link State ID: 0
  Advertising Router: 1.1.1.1
  LS Seq Number: 80000001
  Checksum: 0x9D44
  Length: 36
  Prefix Address: 3FFE:ABCD:1111:1::
  Prefix Length: 64, Options: None
  Metric Type: 1 (Comparable directly to link state metric)
  Metric: 20

  LS age: 272
  LS Type: AS External Link
  Link State ID: 0
  Advertising Router: 2.2.2.2
```

```
LS Seq Number: 80000001
Checksum: 0x3DAD
Length: 36
Prefix Address: 3FFE:ABCD:1111:3::
Prefix Length: 64, Options: None
Metric Type: 2 (Larger than any link state path)
Metric: 1

LS age: 56
LS Type: AS External Link
Link State ID: 1
Advertising Router: 2.2.2.2
LS Seq Number: 80000001
Checksum: 0x9344
Length: 36
Prefix Address: 3FFE:ABCD:1111:2::
Prefix Length: 64, Options: None
Metric Type: 2 (Larger than any link state path)
Metric: 20
```

Similarly, verify OSPF-to-BGP redistribution by looking at the MP-BGP RIB:

```
R2#show bgp ipv6 unicast
BGP table version is 4, local router ID is 2.2.2.2
Status codes: s suppressed, d damped, h history, * valid, > best, i - internal,
              r RIB-failure, S Stale
Origin codes: i - IGP, e - EGP, ? - incomplete

   Network          Next Hop            Metric LocPrf Weight Path
*> 3FFE:ABCD:1111:1::/64
                    ::                      84         32768 ?
*> 3FFE:ABCD:1111:2::/64
                    ::                       0         32768 i
*>i3FFE:ABCD:1111:3::/64
                    FE80::213:7FFF:FEAF:3E00
                                             0    100     0 i
```

Task 6

This task requires some considerable thought and is two-fold. First, it is important to recall that when peering using Link Local addresses, you must use a route map to specify the global Unicast address as the next hop address for the UPDATE messages sent by the local router. To complete this first part, implement the following configuration on R1, R2 and R3:

```
R2(config)#route-map NEXT-HOP permit 10
R2(config-route-map)#set ipv6 next-hop 2001:ABCD:1111:3::2
R2(config-route-map)#exit
R2(config)#router bgp 254
R2(config-router)#address-family ipv6
R2(config-router-af)#neighbor FE80::213:7FFF:FEAF:3E00 route-map NEXT-HOP out
R2(config-router-af)#exit
R2(config-router)#exit

R3(config)#route-map R2-NEXT-HOP permit 10
R3(config-route-map)#set ipv6 next-hop 2001:ABCD:1111:3::3
R3(config-route-map)#exit
R3(config)#route-map R4-NEXT-HOP permit 10
R3(config-route-map)#set ipv6 next-hop 2001:ABCD:1111:4::3
R3(config-route-map)#exit
R3(config)#router bgp 254
R3(config-router)#address-family ipv6
R3(config-router-af)#$80::20D:28FF:FE9E:F940 route-map R2-NEXT-HOP out
R3(config-router-af)#$80::20F:23FF:FE5E:F120 route-map R4-NEXT-HOP out
R3(config-router-af)#exit
R3(config-router)#exit

R4(config)#router bgp 254
R4(config-router)#address-family ipv6
R4(config-router-af)#neighbor FE80::213:7FFF:FEAF:3E00 route-map NEXT-HOP out
R4(config-router-af)#exit
R4(config-router)#exit
```

Following NEXT_HOP modification, the second part of this task is to ensure that you remember the normal iB-GP-to-iBGP advertisement rules. By default, R3 will not advertise prefixes received from R2 to R4 and vice-versa. To work around this issue, R3 must be configured as a route reflector. This second part is completed as follows:

```
R3(config)#router bgp 254
R3(config-router)#address-family ipv6
R3(config-router-af)#neighbor FE80::20D:28FF:FE9E:F940 route-reflector-client
R3(config-router-af)#neighbor FE80::20F:23FF:FE5E:F120 route-reflector-client
R3(config-router-af)#network 3FFE:ABCD:1111:3::/64
R3(config-router-af)#exit
R3(config-router)#exit
```

Following this configuration, verify the appropriate prefix entries in the relevant protocol data structures, i.e. the LSDB on R1 and the MP-BGP RIBs on R2, R3, and R4 as follows::

```
R1#show ipv6 ospf database

            OSPFv3 Router with ID (1.1.1.1) (Process ID 1)

            Router Link States (Area 0)

ADV Router      Age         Seq#        Fragment ID  Link count  Bits
1.1.1.1         1004        0x80000007  0            1           E
2.2.2.2         1152        0x80000004  0            1           E

            Link (Type-8) Link States (Area 0)

ADV Router      Age         Seq#        Link ID   Interface
1.1.1.1         1505        0x80000002  5         Se0/0
2.2.2.2         1152        0x80000002  5         Se0/0

            Intra Area Prefix Link States (Area 0)

ADV Router      Age         Seq#        Link ID   Ref-lstype  Ref-LSID
1.1.1.1         1004        0x80000004  0         0x2001      0
2.2.2.2         1152        0x80000002  0         0x2001      0

            Type-5 AS External Link States

ADV Router      Age         Seq#        Prefix
1.1.1.1         1004        0x80000002  3FFE:ABCD:1111:1::/64
2.2.2.2         1455        0x80000001  3FFE:ABCD:1111:3::/64
2.2.2.2         1237        0x80000001  3FFE:ABCD:1111:2::/64
2.2.2.2         375         0x80000001  3FFE:ABCD:1111:4::/64

R2#show bgp ipv6 unicast
BGP table version is 7, local router ID is 2.2.2.2
Status codes: s suppressed, d damped, h history, * valid, > best, i - internal,
              r RIB-failure, S Stale
Origin codes: i - IGP, e - EGP, ? - incomplete

   Network          Next Hop            Metric LocPrf Weight Path
*> 3FFE:ABCD:1111:1::/64
                    ::                      84         32768 ?
*> 3FFE:ABCD:1111:2::/64
                    ::                       0         32768 i
*>i3FFE:ABCD:1111:3::/64
                    2001:ABCD:1111:3::3
                                             0    100     0 i
*>i3FFE:ABCD:1111:4::/64
                    2001:ABCD:1111:3::3
                                             0    100     0 i

R3#show bgp ipv6 unicast
BGP table version is 12, local router ID is 3.3.3.3
Status codes: s suppressed, d damped, h history, * valid, > best, i - internal,
              r RIB-failure, S Stale
Origin codes: i - IGP, e - EGP, ? - incomplete

   Network          Next Hop            Metric LocPrf Weight Path
```

```
*>i3FFE:ABCD:1111:1::/64
                2001:ABCD:1111:3::2
                                        84    100      0 ?
*>i3FFE:ABCD:1111:2::/64
                2001:ABCD:1111:3::2
                                         0    100      0 i
*> 3FFE:ABCD:1111:3::/64
                ::
                                         0          32768 i
*>i3FFE:ABCD:1111:4::/64
                2001:ABCD:1111:4::4
                                         0    100      0 i

R4#show bgp ipv6 unicast
BGP table version is 6, local router ID is 4.4.4.4
Status codes: s suppressed, d damped, h history, * valid, > best, i - internal,
              r RIB-failure, S Stale
Origin codes: i - IGP, e - EGP, ? - incomplete

   Network          Next Hop         Metric LocPrf Weight Path
*>i3FFE:ABCD:1111:1::/64
                2001:ABCD:1111:4::3
                                        84    100      0 ?
*>i3FFE:ABCD:1111:2::/64
                2001:ABCD:1111:4::3
                                         0    100      0 i
*>i3FFE:ABCD:1111:3::/64
                2001:ABCD:1111:4::3
                                         0    100      0 i
*> 3FFE:ABCD:1111:4::/64
                ::
                                         0          32768 i
```

Finally, complete this task by pinging LAN-to-LAN between all routers:

```
R1#ping 3FFE:ABCD:1111:2::2 source fastethernet 0/0

Type escape sequence to abort.
Sending 5, 100-byte ICMP Echos to 3FFE:ABCD:1111:2::2, timeout is 2 seconds:
Packet sent with a source address of 3FFE:ABCD:1111:1::1
!!!!!
Success rate is 100 percent (5/5), round-trip min/avg/max = 0/1/4 ms

R1#ping 3FFE:ABCD:1111:3::3 source fastethernet 0/0

Type escape sequence to abort.
Sending 5, 100-byte ICMP Echos to 3FFE:ABCD:1111:3::3, timeout is 2 seconds:
Packet sent with a source address of 3FFE:ABCD:1111:1::1
!!!!!
Success rate is 100 percent (5/5), round-trip min/avg/max = 16/16/16 ms

R1#ping 3FFE:ABCD:1111:4::4 source fastethernet 0/0

Type escape sequence to abort.
Sending 5, 100-byte ICMP Echos to 3FFE:ABCD:1111:4::4, timeout is 2 seconds:
Packet sent with a source address of 3FFE:ABCD:1111:1::1
!!!!!
Success rate is 100 percent (5/5), round-trip min/avg/max = 28/29/32 ms

R2#ping 3FFE:ABCD:1111:1::1 source fastethernet 0/0

Type escape sequence to abort.
Sending 5, 100-byte ICMP Echos to 3FFE:ABCD:1111:1::1, timeout is 2 seconds:
Packet sent with a source address of 3FFE:ABCD:1111:2::2
!!!!!
Success rate is 100 percent (5/5), round-trip min/avg/max = 0/2/4 ms

R2#ping 3FFE:ABCD:1111:3::3 source fastethernet 0/0

Type escape sequence to abort.
Sending 5, 100-byte ICMP Echos to 3FFE:ABCD:1111:3::3, timeout is 2 seconds:
Packet sent with a source address of 3FFE:ABCD:1111:2::2
!!!!!
Success rate is 100 percent (5/5), round-trip min/avg/max = 12/14/16 ms
```

```
R2#ping 3FFE:ABCD:1111:4::4 source fastethernet 0/0

Type escape sequence to abort.
Sending 5, 100-byte ICMP Echos to 3FFE:ABCD:1111:4::4, timeout is 2 seconds:
Packet sent with a source address of 3FFE:ABCD:1111:2::2
!!!!!
Success rate is 100 percent (5/5), round-trip min/avg/max = 28/28/32 ms

R3#ping 3FFE:ABCD:1111:1::1 source fastethernet 0/0

Type escape sequence to abort.
Sending 5, 100-byte ICMP Echos to 3FFE:ABCD:1111:1::1, timeout is 2 seconds:
Packet sent with a source address of 3FFE:ABCD:1111:3::3
!!!!!
Success rate is 100 percent (5/5), round-trip min/avg/max = 16/16/16 ms

R3#ping 3FFE:ABCD:1111:2::2 source fastethernet 0/0

Type escape sequence to abort.
Sending 5, 100-byte ICMP Echos to 3FFE:ABCD:1111:2::2, timeout is 2 seconds:
Packet sent with a source address of 3FFE:ABCD:1111:3::3
!!!!!
Success rate is 100 percent (5/5), round-trip min/avg/max = 12/14/16 ms

R3#ping 3FFE:ABCD:1111:4::4 source fastethernet 0/0

Type escape sequence to abort.
Sending 5, 100-byte ICMP Echos to 3FFE:ABCD:1111:4::4, timeout is 2 seconds:
Packet sent with a source address of 3FFE:ABCD:1111:3::3
!!!!!
Success rate is 100 percent (5/5), round-trip min/avg/max = 16/16/16 ms

4#ping 3FFE:ABCD:1111:1::1 source fastethernet 0/0

Type escape sequence to abort.
Sending 5, 100-byte ICMP Echos to 3FFE:ABCD:1111:1::1, timeout is 2 seconds:
Packet sent with a source address of 3FFE:ABCD:1111:4::4
!!!!!
Success rate is 100 percent (5/5), round-trip min/avg/max = 28/29/32 ms

R4#ping 3FFE:ABCD:1111:2::2 source fastethernet 0/0

Type escape sequence to abort.
Sending 5, 100-byte ICMP Echos to 3FFE:ABCD:1111:2::2, timeout is 2 seconds:
Packet sent with a source address of 3FFE:ABCD:1111:4::4
!!!!!
Success rate is 100 percent (5/5), round-trip min/avg/max = 28/29/32 ms

R4#ping 3FFE:ABCD:1111:3::3 source fastethernet 0/0

Type escape sequence to abort.
Sending 5, 100-byte ICMP Echos to 3FFE:ABCD:1111:3::3, timeout is 2 seconds:
Packet sent with a source address of 3FFE:ABCD:1111:4::4
!!!!!
Success rate is 100 percent (5/5), round-trip min/avg/max = 12/13/16 ms
```

FINAL ROUTER CONFIGURATIONS

R1

```
R1#term len 0
R1#sh run
Building configuration...

Current configuration : 994 bytes
!
version 12.4
service timestamps debug datetime msec
service timestamps log datetime msec
no service password-encryption
```

```
!
hostname R1
!
boot-start-marker
boot-end-marker
!
no logging console
!
no aaa new-model
no network-clock-participate slot 1
no network-clock-participate wic 0
ip cef
!
no ip domain lookup
ip auth-proxy max-nodata-conns 3
ip admission max-nodata-conns 3
!
ipv6 unicast-routing
ipv6 cef
!
interface FastEthernet0/0
 no ip address
 duplex auto
 speed auto
 ipv6 address 3FFE:ABCD:1111:1::1/64
!
interface Serial0/0
 no ip address
 ipv6 address 2001:ABCD:1111:1::1/64
 ipv6 ospf 1 area 0
 clock rate 2000000
!
interface Serial0/1
 no ip address
 shutdown
!
ip forward-protocol nd
!
no ip http server
no ip http secure-server
!
ipv6 router ospf 1
 router-id 1.1.1.1
 log-adjacency-changes
 redistribute connected metric-type 1
!
control-plane
!
line con 0
line aux 0
line vty 0 4
 login
!
end

R1#
```

R2

```
R2#term len 0
R2#sh run
Building configuration...

Current configuration : 1718 bytes
!
version 12.4
service timestamps debug datetime msec
service timestamps log datetime msec
no service password-encryption
!
hostname R2
!
boot-start-marker
boot-end-marker
```

```
!
no logging console
!
no aaa new-model
no network-clock-participate slot 1
no network-clock-participate wic 0
ip cef
!
no ip domain lookup
ip auth-proxy max-nodata-conns 3
ip admission max-nodata-conns 3
!
ipv6 unicast-routing
ipv6 cef
!
interface FastEthernet0/0
 no ip address
 duplex auto
 speed auto
 ipv6 address 3FFE:ABCD:1111:2::2/64
!
interface Serial0/0
 no ip address
 ipv6 address 2001:ABCD:1111:1::2/64
 ipv6 ospf 2 area 0
!
interface Serial0/1
 no ip address
 ipv6 address 2001:ABCD:1111:3::2/64
!
router bgp 254
 no synchronization
 bgp router-id 2.2.2.2
 bgp log-neighbor-changes
 neighbor FE80::213:7FFF:FEAF:3E00 remote-as 254
 neighbor FE80::213:7FFF:FEAF:3E00 update-source Serial0/1
 no neighbor FE80::213:7FFF:FEAF:3E00 activate
 no auto-summary
 !
 address-family ipv6
  neighbor FE80::213:7FFF:FEAF:3E00 activate
  neighbor FE80::213:7FFF:FEAF:3E00 route-map NEXT-HOP out
  bgp redistribute-internal
  network 3FFE:ABCD:1111:2::/64
  redistribute ospf 2 match external 1
  no synchronization
 exit-address-family
!
ip forward-protocol nd
!
no ip http server
no ip http secure-server
!
ipv6 router ospf 2
 router-id 2.2.2.2
 log-adjacency-changes
 redistribute connected route-map LAN-ONLY
 redistribute bgp 254
!
route-map LAN-ONLY permit 10
 match interface FastEthernet0/0
!
route-map LAN-ONLY deny 20
!
route-map NEXT-HOP permit 10
 set ipv6 next-hop 2001:ABCD:1111:3::2
!
control-plane
!
line con 0
line aux 0
line vty 0 4
 login
!
end

R2#
```

R3

```
R3#term len 0
R3#sh run
Building configuration...

Current configuration : 2187 bytes
!
version 12.4
service timestamps debug datetime msec
service timestamps log datetime msec
no service password-encryption
!
hostname R3
!
boot-start-marker
boot-end-marker
!
no logging console
!
no aaa new-model
no network-clock-participate slot 1
no network-clock-participate wic 0
ip cef
!
no ip domain lookup
ip auth-proxy max-nodata-conns 3
ip admission max-nodata-conns 3
!
ipv6 unicast-routing
ipv6 cef
!
interface FastEthernet0/0
 no ip address
 duplex auto
 speed auto
 ipv6 address 3FFE:ABCD:1111:3::3/64
!
interface Serial1/0
 no ip address
 shutdown
 clock rate 128000
!
interface Serial1/1
 no ip address
 ipv6 address 2001:ABCD:1111:3::3/64
 clock rate 128000
!
interface Serial1/2
 no ip address
 ipv6 address 2001:ABCD:1111:4::3/64
 clock rate 128000
!
interface Serial1/3
 no ip address
 shutdown
!
interface Serial1/4
 no ip address
 shutdown
!
interface Serial1/5
 no ip address
 shutdown
!
interface Serial1/6
 no ip address
 shutdown
!
interface Serial1/7
 no ip address
 shutdown
!
router bgp 254
```

```
no synchronization
bgp router-id 3.3.3.3
bgp log-neighbor-changes
neighbor FE80::20D:28FF:FE9E:F940 remote-as 254
neighbor FE80::20D:28FF:FE9E:F940 update-source Serial1/1
no neighbor FE80::20D:28FF:FE9E:F940 activate
neighbor FE80::20F:23FF:FE5E:F120 remote-as 254
neighbor FE80::20F:23FF:FE5E:F120 update-source Serial1/2
no neighbor FE80::20F:23FF:FE5E:F120 activate
no auto-summary
!
address-family ipv6
 neighbor FE80::20D:28FF:FE9E:F940 activate
 neighbor FE80::20D:28FF:FE9E:F940 route-reflector-client
 neighbor FE80::20D:28FF:FE9E:F940 route-map R2-NEXT-HOP out
 neighbor FE80::20F:23FF:FE5E:F120 activate
 neighbor FE80::20F:23FF:FE5E:F120 route-reflector-client
 neighbor FE80::20F:23FF:FE5E:F120 route-map R4-NEXT-HOP out
 network 3FFE:ABCD:1111:3::/64
exit-address-family
!
ip forward-protocol nd
!
no ip http server
no ip http secure-server
!
route-map R2-NEXT-HOP permit 10
 set ipv6 next-hop 2001:ABCD:1111:3::3
!
route-map R4-NEXT-HOP permit 10
 set ipv6 next-hop 2001:ABCD:1111:4::3
!
control-plane
!
line con 0
line aux 0
line vty 0 4
 login
!
end

R3#
```

R4

```
R4#term len 0
R4#sh run
Building configuration...

Current configuration : 1362 bytes
!
version 12.4
service timestamps debug datetime msec
service timestamps log datetime msec
no service password-encryption
!
hostname R4
!
boot-start-marker
boot-end-marker
!
no logging console
!
no aaa new-model
no network-clock-participate slot 1
no network-clock-participate wic 0
ip cef
!
no ip domain lookup
ip auth-proxy max-nodata-conns 3
ip admission max-nodata-conns 3
!
ipv6 unicast-routing
ipv6 cef
```

```
!
interface FastEthernet0/0
 no ip address
 duplex auto
 speed auto
 ipv6 address 3FFE:ABCD:1111:4::4/64
!
interface Serial0/0
 no ip address
 ipv6 address 2001:ABCD:1111:4::4/64
!
interface Serial0/1
 no ip address
 shutdown
!
router bgp 254
 no synchronization
 bgp router-id 4.4.4.4
 bgp log-neighbor-changes
 neighbor FE80::213:7FFF:FEAF:3E00 remote-as 254
 neighbor FE80::213:7FFF:FEAF:3E00 update-source Serial0/0
 no neighbor FE80::213:7FFF:FEAF:3E00 activate
 no auto-summary
 !
 address-family ipv6
  neighbor FE80::213:7FFF:FEAF:3E00 activate
  neighbor FE80::213:7FFF:FEAF:3E00 route-map NEXT-HOP out
  network 3FFE:ABCD:1111:4::/64
 exit-address-family
!
ip forward-protocol nd
!
no ip http server
no ip http secure-server
!
route-map NEXT-HOP permit 10
 set ipv6 next-hop 2001:ABCD:1111:4::4
!
control-plane
!
line con 0
line aux 0
line vty 0 4
 login
!
end

R4#
```

CCNP LAB 46

Internet Protocol Version 6 Lab

Lab Objective:

The focus of this lab is to understand tunneling implementation and configuration in Cisco IOS routers. Additional technologies include OSPFv3 authentication and security.

Lab Topology:

The lab network topology is illustrated below:

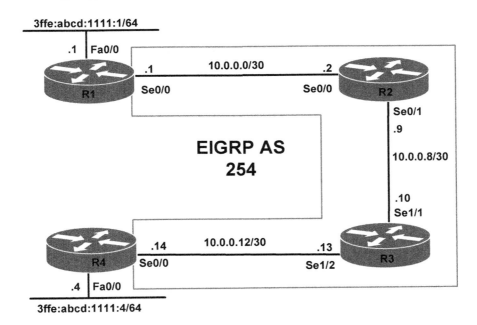

IMPORTANT NOTE: If you are using the www.howtonetwork.net racks, please bring up the LAN interfaces connected to the routers by issuing the no shutdown command on the connected switches. If you are using a home lab with no Switches, you can bring up the LAN interfaces using the following configurations on your routers:

```
interface fastethernet 0/0
   no keepalive
   loopback
   no shutdown
```

Alternately, you can simply connect the interfaces to a hub or switch if you have one available in your own lab.

Task 1

Configure hostnames, IP addressing on all routers as illustrated in the network topology.

Task 2

Enable EIGRP on all routers as illustrated in the topology. Verify your EIGRP configuration.

Task 3

Configure a static IPv6 tunnel between R1 and R4. Ensure that you can ping across the tunnel. Verify your configuration using the appropriate commands.

Task 4

Configure OSPFv3 across the R1-R4 tunnel. Use OSPF area 0. Advertise the LAN subnets on R1 and R4 as inter-area OSPF routes. Verify that R1 and R4 can ping each other LAN-to-LAN.

Task 5

For security, configure area authentication for the OSPF backbone. Use the following parameters when you are configuring the authentication parameters:

- Use a Security Parameters Index (SPI) of 256
- Use Secure Hash Algorithm (SHA) authentication
- Use a key of 1234567890abcdef1234567890abcdef12345678

Verify your configuration using the appropriate commands.

LAB VALIDATION

Task 1

Please refer to previous labs for basic IPv4, IPv6 addressing and hostname configuration. This will not be included in this section to avoid being redundant.

Task 2

```
R1(config)#router eigrp 254
R1(config-router)#no auto-summary
R1(config-router)#network 10.0.0.0
R1(config-router)#exit

R2(config)#router eigrp 254
R2(config-router)#no auto-summary
R2(config-router)#network 10.0.0.0
R2(config-router)#exit

R3(config)#router eigrp 254
R3(config-router)#no auto-summary
R3(config-router)#network 10.0.0.0
R3(config-router)#exit

R4(config)#router eigrp 254
R4(config-router)#no auto-summary
R4(config-router)#network 10.0.0.0
R4(config-router)#exit
```

Verify your EIGRP configuration using the `show ip eigrp neighbors` command:

```
R1#show ip eigrp neighbors
IP-EIGRP neighbors for process 254
H   Address                 Interface       Hold Uptime    SRTT   RTO  Q   Seq
                                            (sec)          (ms)        Cnt  Num
0   10.0.0.2                Se0/0           12 00:01:31      5    200  0    8

R2#show ip eigrp neighbors
IP-EIGRP neighbors for process 254
H   Address                 Interface       Hold Uptime    SRTT   RTO  Q    Seq
```

			(sec)	(ms)		Cnt	Num
1	10.0.0.10	Se0/1	10 00:01:28	9	300	0	3
0	10.0.0.1	Se0/0	12 00:01:34	2	200	0	3

```
R3#show ip eigrp neighbors
IP-EIGRP neighbors for process 254
```

H	Address	Interface	Hold Uptime	SRTT	RTO	Q	Seq
			(sec)	(ms)		Cnt	Num
1	10.0.0.14	Se1/2	13 00:01:26	12	1140	0	3
0	10.0.0.9	Se1/1	12 00:01:31	12	1140	0	7

```
R4#show ip eigrp neighbors
IP-EIGRP neighbors for process 254
```

H	Address	Interface	Hold Uptime	SRTT	RTO	Q	Seq
			(sec)	(ms)		Cnt	Num
0	10.0.0.13	Se0/0	14 00:01:29	14	200	0	7

Task 3

When you are configuring static (manual) IPv6 tunnels, you must specify IPv6 as the passenger protocol and IPv4 as both the encapsulation and transport protocol for the manual IPv6 tunnel using the tunnel mode ipv6ip interface configuration command. The requirements of this task are straightforward and are completed as follows:

```
R1(config)#interface tunnel 0
R1(config-if)#ipv6 address 2001:abcd:1111:a::1/64
R1(config-if)#tunnel source serial 0/0
R1(config-if)#tunnel destination 10.0.0.14
R1(config-if)#tunnel mode ipv6ip
R1(config-if)#exit

R4(config)#interface tunnel 0
R4(config-if)#ipv6 address 2001:abcd:1111:a::4/64
R4(config-if)#tunnel source serial 0/0
R4(config-if)#tunnel destination 10.0.0.1
R4(config-if)#tunnel mode ipv6ip
R4(config-if)#exit
```

Verify your tunnel configuration using the show interfaces command:

```
R4#show interfaces tunnel 0
Tunnel0 is up, line protocol is up
  Hardware is Tunnel
  MTU 1514 bytes, BW 9 Kbit/sec, DLY 500000 usec,
     reliability 255/255, txload 1/255, rxload 1/255
  Encapsulation TUNNEL, loopback not set
  Keepalive not set
  Tunnel source 10.0.0.14 (Serial0/0), destination 10.0.0.1
  Tunnel protocol/transport IPv6/IP
  Tunnel TTL 255
  Fast tunneling enabled
  Tunnel transmit bandwidth 8000 (kbps)
  Tunnel receive bandwidth 8000 (kbps)
  Last input never, output 00:00:41, output hang never
  Last clearing of "show interface" counters never
  Input queue: 0/75/0/0 (size/max/drops/flushes); Total output drops: 0
  Queueing strategy: fifo
  Output queue: 0/0 (size/max)
  5 minute input rate 0 bits/sec, 0 packets/sec
  5 minute output rate 0 bits/sec, 0 packets/sec
     0 packets input, 0 bytes, 0 no buffer
     Received 0 broadcasts, 0 runts, 0 giants, 0 throttles
     0 input errors, 0 CRC, 0 frame, 0 overrun, 0 ignored, 0 abort
     30 packets output, 2860 bytes, 0 underruns
     0 output errors, 0 collisions, 0 interface resets
     0 unknown protocol drops
     0 output buffer failures, 0 output buffers swapped out
```

Finally, verify that you can ping across the tunnel using a simple ping:

```
R4#ping 2001:abcd:1111:a::1 repeat 10 size 1500

Type escape sequence to abort.
Sending 10, 1500-byte ICMP Echos to 2001:ABCD:1111:A::1, timeout is 2 seconds:
!!!!!!!!!!
Success rate is 100 percent (10/10), round-trip min/avg/max = 404/407/408 ms
```

Task 4

The task OSPFv3 configuration requirements are straightforward. To advertise the LAN subnets that are connected as inter-area OSPF routes, you need to assign them to different areas. This task is completed as follows:

```
R1(config)#ipv6 router ospf 1
R1(config-rtr)#router-id 1.1.1.1
R1(config-rtr)#exit
R1(config)#interface tunnel 0
R1(config-if)#ipv6 ospf 1 area 0
R1(config-if)#exit
R1(config)#interface fastethernet 0/0
R1(config-if)#ipv6 ospf 1 area 1
R1(config-if)#exit

R4(config)#ipv6 router ospf 4
R4(config-rtr)#router-id 4.4.4.4
R4(config-rtr)#exit
R4(config)#interface tunnel 0
R4(config-if)#ipv6 ospf 4 area 0
R4(config-if)#exit
R4(config)#interface fastethernet 0/0
R4(config-if)#ipv6 ospf 4 area 4
R4(config-if)#exit
```

Verify your configuration using the `show ipv6 ospf neighbor` command on R1 and R4:

```
R1#show ipv6 ospf neighbor

Neighbor ID     Pri   State         Dead Time   Interface ID   Interface
4.4.4.4           1   FULL/ -       00:00:34    9              Tunnel0

R4#show ipv6 ospf neighbor

Neighbor ID     Pri   State         Dead Time   Interface ID   Interface
1.1.1.1           1   FULL/ -       00:00:38    9              Tunnel0
```

Following this, verify that the prefixes are advertised and received as required:

```
R1#show ipv6 route ospf
IPv6 Routing Table - 7 entries
Codes: C - Connected, L - Local, S - Static, R - RIP, B - BGP
       U - Per-user Static route
       I1 - ISIS L1, I2 - ISIS L2, IA - ISIS interarea, IS - ISIS summary
       O - OSPF intra, OI - OSPF inter, OE1 - OSPF ext 1, OE2 - OSPF ext 2
       ON1 - OSPF NSSA ext 1, ON2 - OSPF NSSA ext 2
OI  3FFE:ABCD:1111:4::/64 [110/11112]
      via FE80::A00:E, Tunnel0

R4#show ipv6 route ospf
IPv6 Routing Table - 7 entries
Codes: C - Connected, L - Local, S - Static, R - RIP, B - BGP
       U - Per-user Static route
       I1 - ISIS L1, I2 - ISIS L2, IA - ISIS interarea, IS - ISIS summary
       O - OSPF intra, OI - OSPF inter, OE1 - OSPF ext 1, OE2 - OSPF ext 2
       ON1 - OSPF NSSA ext 1, ON2 - OSPF NSSA ext 2
OI  3FFE:ABCD:1111:1::/64 [110/11112]
      via FE80::A00:1, Tunnel0
```

Finally, verify that R1 and R4 can ping each other LAN-to-LAN:

```
R1#ping 3FFE:ABCD:1111:4::4 source fastethernet 0/0 repeat 10

Type escape sequence to abort.
```

```
Sending 10, 100-byte ICMP Echos to 3FFE:ABCD:1111:4::4, timeout is 2 seconds:
Packet sent with a source address of 3FFE:ABCD:1111:1::1
!!!!!!!!!!
Success rate is 100 percent (10/10), round-trip min/avg/max = 36/36/40 ms

R4#ping 3FFE:ABCD:1111:1::1 source fastethernet 0/0 repeat 10

Type escape sequence to abort.
Sending 10, 100-byte ICMP Echos to 3FFE:ABCD:1111:1::1, timeout is 2 seconds:
Packet sent with a source address of 3FFE:ABCD:1111:4::4
!!!!!!!!!!
Success rate is 100 percent (10/10), round-trip min/avg/max = 36/37/40 ms
```

Task 5

OSPFv3 supports both authentication and encryption for security. To configure OSPFv3 area authentication, you need to use the area <area> authentication ipsec spi <size> [md5|sha1] <key> OSPFv3 configuration command. This task is completed as follows:

```
R1(config)#ipv6 router ospf 1
R1(config-rtr)#$ ipsec spi 256 sha1 1234567890abcdef1234567890abcdef12345678
R1(config-rtr)#exit

R4(config)#ipv6 router ospf 4
R4(config-rtr)#$ ipsec spi 256 sha1 1234567890abcdef1234567890abcdef12345678
R4(config-rtr)#exit
```

Verify OSPFv3 area authentication using the show ipv6 ospf command

```
R4#show ipv6 ospf
 Routing Process "ospfv3 4" with ID 4.4.4.4
 It is an area border router
 SPF schedule delay 5 secs, Hold time between two SPFs 10 secs
 Minimum LSA interval 5 secs. Minimum LSA arrival 1 secs
 LSA group pacing timer 240 secs
 Interface flood pacing timer 33 msecs
 Retransmission pacing timer 66 msecs
 Number of external LSA 0. Checksum Sum 0x000000
 Number of areas in this router is 2. 2 normal 0 stub 0 nssa
 Reference bandwidth unit is 100 mbps
    Area BACKBONE(0)
        Number of interfaces in this area is 1
        SHA-1 Authentication, SPI 256
        SPF algorithm executed 3 times
        Number of LSA 8. Checksum Sum 0x0462B5
        Number of DCbitless LSA 0
        Number of indication LSA 0
        Number of DoNotAge LSA 0
        Flood list length 0
    Area 4
        Number of interfaces in this area is 1
        SPF algorithm executed 2 times
        Number of LSA 5. Checksum Sum 0x016A26
        Number of DCbitless LSA 0
        Number of indication LSA 0
        Number of DoNotAge LSA 0
        Flood list length 0
```

By default, because IPv6 uses built-in IPsec functions, Cisco IOS software automatically creates IPsec policies for the configured authentication. The policy can be viewed using the show crypto ipsec sa [interface <name>] command on the router(s). Authentication Header (AH) is used. If you configure encryption, then Encapsulating Security Payload (ESP) will be used instead. Check the relevant SA states based on your configuration:

```
R4#show crypto ipsec sa interface tunnel 0

interface: Tunnel0
    Crypto map tag: (none), local addr FE80::A00:E
```

```
IPsecv6 policy name: OSPFv3-4-256
IPsecv6-created ACL name: Tunnel0-ipsecv6-ACL

protected vrf: (none)
local  ident (addr/mask/prot/port): (FE80::/10/89/0)
remote ident (addr/mask/prot/port): (::/0/89/0)
current_peer :: port 500
  PERMIT, flags={origin_is_acl,}
 #pkts encaps: 18, #pkts encrypt: 0, #pkts digest: 18
 #pkts decaps: 18, #pkts decrypt: 0, #pkts verify: 18
 #pkts compressed: 0, #pkts decompressed: 0
 #pkts not compressed: 0, #pkts compr. failed: 0
 #pkts not decompressed: 0, #pkts decompress failed: 0
 #send errors 0, #recv errors 0

  local crypto endpt.: FE80::A00:E, remote crypto endpt.: ::
  path mtu 1514, ip mtu 1514, ip mtu idb Tunnel0
  current outbound spi: 0x100(256)

  inbound esp sas:

  inbound ah sas:
   spi: 0x100(256)
     transform: ah-sha-hmac ,
     in use settings ={Transport, }
     conn id: 2001, flow_id: SW:1, crypto map: (none)
     no sa timing
     replay detection support: N
     Status: ACTIVE

  inbound pcp sas:

  outbound esp sas:

  outbound ah sas:
   spi: 0x100(256)
     transform: ah-sha-hmac ,
     in use settings ={Transport, }
     conn id: 2002, flow_id: SW:2, crypto map: (none)
     no sa timing
     replay detection support: N
     Status: ACTIVE

  outbound pcp sas:
```

Additionally, you can also view the configuration parameters for the applied policy using the show crypto ipsec policy command on the router. The policy name, by default, will be OSPFv3-<process ID>-<SPI>. For example, on R1, the applied policy name will be OSPFv3-4-256. This is validated and illustrated in the following output:

```
R4#show crypto ipsec policy
Crypto IPsec client security policy data

Policy name:      OSPFv3-4-256
Policy refcount:  1
Inbound  AH SPI:  256 (0x100)
Outbound AH SPI:  256 (0x100)
Inbound  AH Key:  1234567890ABCDEF1234567890ABCDEF12345678
Outbound AH Key:  1234567890ABCDEF1234567890ABCDEF12345678
Transform set:    ah-sha-hmac
```

FINAL ROUTER CONFIGURATIONS

R1

```
R1#term len 0
R1#sh run
Building configuration...
```

```
Current configuration : 1245 bytes
!
version 12.4
service timestamps debug datetime msec
service timestamps log datetime msec
no service password-encryption
!
hostname R1
!
boot-start-marker
boot-end-marker
!
no logging console
!
no aaa new-model
no network-clock-participate slot 1
no network-clock-participate wic 0
ip cef
!
no ip domain lookup
ip auth-proxy max-nodata-conns 3
ip admission max-nodata-conns 3
!
ipv6 unicast-routing
ipv6 cef
!
interface Tunnel0
 no ip address
 ipv6 address 2001:ABCD:1111:A::1/64
 ipv6 ospf 1 area 0
 tunnel source Serial0/0
 tunnel destination 10.0.0.14
 tunnel mode ipv6ip
!
interface FastEthernet0/0
 no ip address
 duplex auto
 speed auto
 ipv6 address 3FFE:ABCD:1111:1::1/64
 ipv6 ospf 1 area 1
!
interface Serial0/0
 ip address 10.0.0.1 255.255.255.252
 clock rate 2000000
!
interface Serial0/1
 no ip address
 shutdown
!
router eigrp 254
 network 10.0.0.0
 no auto-summary
!
ip forward-protocol nd
!
no ip http server
no ip http secure-server
!
ipv6 router ospf 1
 router-id 1.1.1.1
 log-adjacency-changes
 area 0 authentication ipsec spi 256 sha1 1234567890ABCDEF1234567890ABCDEF12345678
!
control-plane
!
line con 0
line aux 0
line vty 0 4
 login
!
end

R1#
```

R2

```
R2#term len 0
R2#sh run
Building configuration...

Current configuration : 847 bytes
!
version 12.4
service timestamps debug datetime msec
service timestamps log datetime msec
no service password-encryption
!
hostname R2
!
boot-start-marker
boot-end-marker
!
no logging console
!
no aaa new-model
no network-clock-participate slot 1
no network-clock-participate wic 0
ip cef
!
no ip domain lookup
ip auth-proxy max-nodata-conns 3
ip admission max-nodata-conns 3
!
interface FastEthernet0/0
 no ip address
 shutdown
 duplex auto
 speed auto
!
interface Serial0/0
 ip address 10.0.0.2 255.255.255.252
!
interface Serial0/1
 ip address 10.0.0.9 255.255.255.252
!
router eigrp 254
 network 10.0.0.0
 no auto-summary
!
ip forward-protocol nd
!
no ip http server
no ip http secure-server
!
control-plane
!
line con 0
line aux 0
line vty 0 4
 login
!
end

R2#
```

R3

```
R3#term len 0
R3#sh run
Building configuration...

Current configuration : 1188 bytes
!
version 12.4
service timestamps debug datetime msec
service timestamps log datetime msec
no service password-encryption
```

```
!
hostname R3
!
boot-start-marker
boot-end-marker
!
no logging console
!
no aaa new-model
no network-clock-participate slot 1
no network-clock-participate wic 0
ip cef
!
no ip domain lookup
ip auth-proxy max-nodata-conns 3
ip admission max-nodata-conns 3
!
interface FastEthernet0/0
 no ip address
 shutdown
 duplex auto
 speed auto
!
interface Serial1/0
 no ip address
 shutdown
 clock rate 128000
!
interface Serial1/1
 ip address 10.0.0.10 255.255.255.252
 clock rate 128000
!
interface Serial1/2
 ip address 10.0.0.13 255.255.255.252
 clock rate 128000
!
interface Serial1/3
 no ip address
 shutdown
!
interface Serial1/4
 no ip address
 shutdown
!
interface Serial1/5
 no ip address
 shutdown
!
interface Serial1/6
 no ip address
 shutdown
!
interface Serial1/7
 no ip address
 shutdown
!
router eigrp 254
 network 10.0.0.0
 no auto-summary
!
ip forward-protocol nd
!
no ip http server
no ip http secure-server
!
control-plane
!
line con 0
line aux 0
line vty 0 4
 login
!
end

R3#
```

R4

```
R4#term len 0
R4#sh run
Building configuration...

Current configuration : 1225 bytes
!
version 12.4
service timestamps debug datetime msec
service timestamps log datetime msec
no service password-encryption
!
hostname R4
!
boot-start-marker
boot-end-marker
!
no logging console
!
no aaa new-model
no network-clock-participate slot 1
no network-clock-participate wic 0
ip cef
!
no ip domain lookup
ip auth-proxy max-nodata-conns 3
ip admission max-nodata-conns 3
!
ipv6 unicast-routing
ipv6 cef
!
interface Tunnel0
 no ip address
 ipv6 address 2001:ABCD:1111:A::4/64
 ipv6 ospf 4 area 0
 tunnel source Serial0/0
 tunnel destination 10.0.0.1
 tunnel mode ipv6ip
!
interface FastEthernet0/0
 no ip address
 duplex auto
 speed auto
 ipv6 address 3FFE:ABCD:1111:4::4/64
 ipv6 ospf 4 area 4
!
interface Serial0/0
 ip address 10.0.0.14 255.255.255.252
!
interface Serial0/1
 no ip address
 shutdown
!
router eigrp 254
 network 10.0.0.0
 no auto-summary
!
ip forward-protocol nd
!
no ip http server
no ip http secure-server
!
ipv6 router ospf 4
 router-id 4.4.4.4
 log-adjacency-changes
 area 0 authentication ipsec spi 256 sha1 1234567890ABCDEF1234567890ABCDEF12345678
!
control-plane
!
line con 0
line aux 0
line vty 0 4
 login
!
end

R4#
```

CCNP LAB 47

Internet Protocol Version 6 Lab

Lab Objective:

The focus of this lab is to understand tunneling implementation and configuration in Cisco IOS routers. Additional technologies include tunnel security.

Lab Topology:

The lab network topology is illustrated below:

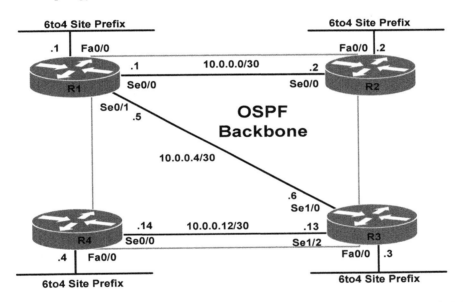

IMPORTANT NOTE: If you are using the www.howtonetwork.net racks, please bring up the LAN interfaces connected to the routers by issuing the no shutdown command on the connected switches. If you are using a home lab with no Switches, you can bring up the LAN interfaces using the following configurations on your routers:

```
interface fastethernet 0/0
  no keepalive
  loopback
  no shutdown
```

Alternately, you can simply connect the interfaces to a hub or switch if you have one available in your own lab.

Task 1

Configure hostnames, IP addressing on the all routers as illustrated in the network topology.

Task 2

In preparation for 6to4 tunnel, configure the following Loopback 0 interfaces on all routers:

- R1: Loopback 0 - IP Address 1.1.1.1/32
- R2: Loopback 0 - IP Address 2.2.2.2/32
- R3: Loopback 0 - IP Address 3.3.3.3/32
- R4: Loopback 0 - IP Address 4.4.4.4/32

Task 3

Enable OSPF on all router WAN and Loopback interfaces. Verify your OSPF configuration using the appropriate commands.

Task 4

Configure 6to4 prefixes on the LAN interfaces of all routers. Use the Loopback 0 IP address to complete the 48-bit global prefix. The router number should complete the next 16-bits, for a complete 64-bit site prefix. Verify your IPv6 configuration using the appropriate commands.

Task 5

Configure 6to4 tunnels on all routers. Ensure that all routers can ping each other LAN-to-LAN.

LAB VALIDATION

Task 1

Please refer to previous labs for basic IPv4, IPv6 addressing and hostname configuration. This will not be included in this section to avoid being redundant.

Task 2

Please refer to previous labs for basic IPv4 and Loopback interface configuration. This will not be included in this section to avoid being redundant.

Task 3

```
R1(config)#router ospf 1
R1(config-router)#network 0.0.0.0 255.255.255.255 area 0
R1(config-router)#exit

R2(config)#router ospf 2
R2(config-router)#network 0.0.0.0 255.255.255.255 area 0
R2(config-router)#exit

R3(config)#router ospf 3
R3(config-router)#network 0.0.0.0 255.255.255.255 area 0
R3(config-router)#exit

R4(config)#router ospf 4
R4(config-router)#network 0.0.0.0 255.255.255.255 area 0
R4(config-router)#exit
```

Verify basic OSPF configuration using the show ip ospf neighbor command:

```
R1#show ip ospf neighbor

Neighbor ID     Pri   State       Dead Time   Address     Interface
3.3.3.3           0   FULL/   -   00:00:34    10.0.0.6    Serial0/1
2.2.2.2           0   FULL/   -   00:00:39    10.0.0.2    Serial0/0

R2#show ip ospf neighbor

Neighbor ID     Pri   State       Dead Time   Address     Interface
1.1.1.1           0   FULL/   -   00:00:31    10.0.0.1    Serial0/0
```

```
R3#show ip ospf neighbor

Neighbor ID    Pri   State        Dead Time   Address      Interface
4.4.4.4          0   FULL/   -    00:00:31    10.0.0.14    Serial1/2
1.1.1.1          0   FULL/   -    00:00:38    10.0.0.5     Serial1/0

R4#show ip ospf neighbor

Neighbor ID    Pri   State        Dead Time   Address      Interface
3.3.3.3          0   FULL/   -    00:00:38    10.0.0.13    Serial0/0
```

Finally, verify that all routing information is correct using the show ip route command:

```
R1#show ip route ospf
      2.0.0.0/32 is subnetted, 1 subnets
O        2.2.2.2 [110/65] via 10.0.0.2, 00:02:19, Serial0/0
      3.0.0.0/32 is subnetted, 1 subnets
O        3.3.3.3 [110/65] via 10.0.0.6, 00:02:19, Serial0/1
      4.0.0.0/32 is subnetted, 1 subnets
O        4.4.4.4 [110/846] via 10.0.0.6, 00:02:19, Serial0/1
      10.0.0.0/30 is subnetted, 3 subnets
O        10.0.0.12 [110/845] via 10.0.0.6, 00:02:19, Serial0/1

R2#show ip route ospf
      1.0.0.0/32 is subnetted, 1 subnets
O        1.1.1.1 [110/65] via 10.0.0.1, 00:02:21, Serial0/0
      3.0.0.0/32 is subnetted, 1 subnets
O        3.3.3.3 [110/129] via 10.0.0.1, 00:02:21, Serial0/0
      4.0.0.0/32 is subnetted, 1 subnets
O        4.4.4.4 [110/910] via 10.0.0.1, 00:02:21, Serial0/0
      10.0.0.0/30 is subnetted, 3 subnets
O        10.0.0.12 [110/909] via 10.0.0.1, 00:02:21, Serial0/0
O        10.0.0.4 [110/128] via 10.0.0.1, 00:02:21, Serial0/0

R3#show ip route ospf
      1.0.0.0/32 is subnetted, 1 subnets
O        1.1.1.1 [110/782] via 10.0.0.5, 00:02:24, Serial1/0
      2.0.0.0/32 is subnetted, 1 subnets
O        2.2.2.2 [110/846] via 10.0.0.5, 00:02:24, Serial1/0
      4.0.0.0/32 is subnetted, 1 subnets
O        4.4.4.4 [110/782] via 10.0.0.14, 00:02:24, Serial1/2
      10.0.0.0/30 is subnetted, 3 subnets
O        10.0.0.0 [110/845] via 10.0.0.5, 00:02:24, Serial1/0

R4#show ip route ospf
      1.0.0.0/32 is subnetted, 1 subnets
O        1.1.1.1 [110/846] via 10.0.0.13, 00:02:16, Serial0/0
      2.0.0.0/32 is subnetted, 1 subnets
O        2.2.2.2 [110/910] via 10.0.0.13, 00:02:16, Serial0/0
      3.0.0.0/32 is subnetted, 1 subnets
O        3.3.3.3 [110/65] via 10.0.0.13, 00:02:16, Serial0/0
      10.0.0.0/30 is subnetted, 3 subnets
O        10.0.0.0 [110/909] via 10.0.0.13, 00:02:16, Serial0/0
O        10.0.0.4 [110/845] via 10.0.0.13, 00:02:16, Serial0/0
```

Task 4

Unlike static tunnel configuration, 6to4 tunneling has three main characteristics, which make it unique from static tunnel implementation. These characteristics are:

- Automatic or Dynamic Tunneling
- Automatic Prefix Assignment
- There is no IPv6 Route Propagation

6to4 automatic tunneling provides a dynamic method to deploy tunnels between IPv6 sites over IPv4 networks. Unlike with manually configured tunnels, there is no need to manually configure tunnel source and destination addresses to establish the tunnels. Instead, the tunneling of IPv6 packets between 6to4 sites is performed dynamically based on the destination IPv6 address of the packets originated by IPv6 hosts. These packets are then encapsulated in IPv4 and IPv4 routing protocols are used to transport the packets between the source and destination hosts.

Automatic prefix assignment provides a global aggregate IPv6 prefix to each 6to4 site which is based on the 2002::/16 prefix assigned by IANA for 6to4 sites. As stated earlier in this section, the tunnel endpoint, or destination is determined by the globally unique IPv4 address embedded in a 6to4 address. This address must be an address that is globally routable. In other words, RFC 191 (private IP addresses) cannot be used for 6to4 tunnels because they are not unique. This 32-bit IPv4 address is converted to Hexadecimal and the final representation is a 48-bit prefix. For example, if the IP address 1.1.1.1 was embedded into the IPv6 6to4 prefix, the final representation would be 2002:0101:0101::/48.

And finally, 6to4 tunneling uses special addresses which are a combination of the unique IPv6 routing prefix 2002::/16 and a globally unique 32-bit IPv4 address. With 6to4 tunneling, the tunnel endpoint (destination) is determined by the globally unique IPv4 address embedded in the 6to4 address. Because 6to4 prefixes are based on unique IPv4 address, the 48-bit IPv6 routes do not need to be propagated between 6to4 sites.

Given this understanding, this task is completed as follows:

```
R1(config)#interface fastethernet 0/0
R1(config-if)#ipv6 address 2002:101:101:1::1/64
R1(config-if)#exit

R2(config)#interface fastethernet 0/0
R2(config-if)#ipv6 address 2002:202:202:2::2/64
R2(config-if)#exit

R3(config)#interface fastethernet 0/0
R3(config-if)#ipv6 address 2002:303:303:3::3/64
R3(config-if)#exit

R4(config)#interface fastethernet 0/0
R4(config-if)#ipv6 address 2002:404:404:4::4/64
R4(config-if)#exit
```

Verify your configuration using the show ipv6 interface command on all routers:

```
R1#show ipv6 interface fastethernet 0/0
FastEthernet0/0 is up, line protocol is up
  IPv6 is enabled, link-local address is FE80::20F:23FF:FE5E:EC80
  Global unicast address(es):
    2002:101:101:1::1, subnet is 2002:101:101:1::/64
  Joined group address(es):
    FF02::1
    FF02::2
    FF02::1:FF00:1
    FF02::1:FF5E:EC80
  MTU is 1500 bytes

[Truncated Output]

R2#show ipv6 interface fastethernet 0/0
FastEthernet0/0 is up, line protocol is up
  IPv6 is enabled, link-local address is FE80::20D:28FF:FE9E:F940
  Global unicast address(es):
    2002:202:202:2::2, subnet is 2002:202:202:2::/64
  Joined group address(es):
    FF02::1
    FF02::2
    FF02::1:FF00:2
    FF02::1:FF9E:F940
  MTU is 1500 bytes

[Truncated Output]

R3#show ipv6 interface fastethernet 0/0
FastEthernet0/0 is up, line protocol is up
  IPv6 is enabled, link-local address is FE80::213:7FFF:FEAF:3E00
  Global unicast address(es):
    2002:303:303:3::3, subnet is 2002:303:303:3::/64
```

```
  Joined group address(es):
    FF02::1
    FF02::2
    FF02::1:FF00:3
    FF02::1:FFAF:3E00
  MTU is 1500 bytes

[Truncated Output]

R4#show ipv6 interface fastethernet 0/0
FastEthernet0/0 is up, line protocol is up
  IPv6 is enabled, link-local address is FE80::20F:23FF:FE5E:F120
  Global unicast address(es):
    2002:404:404:4::4, subnet is 2002:404:404:4::/64
    3FFE:ABCD:1111:4::4, subnet is 3FFE:ABCD:1111:4::/64
  Joined group address(es):
    FF02::1
    FF02::2
    FF02::1:FF00:4
    FF02::1:FF5E:F120
  MTU is 1500 bytes
```

Task 5

The configuration of 6to4 tunneling in Cisco IOS software is somewhat similar to that of static tunnels with the exception that no static tunnel destinations are configured. The following sequence of configuration steps is required to implement 6to4 tunneling in Cisco IOS software:

- Configure an IPv6 address on the internal (inside) 6to4 site interface. This is typically the LAN interface to which IPv6 hosts are connected. This is configured using the `ipv6 address [address/prefix-length]` interface configuration command. When you configure the site prefix, it must come from the 2002::/16 range

- Configure a static tunnel interface using the `interface tunnel [number]` global configuration command. The number range will vary depending on the version of Cisco IOS software that the router on which the tunnel is being configured is running

- Configure a tunnel source for the static tunnel using the `tunnel source [IPv4 address | interface]` interface configuration command. This is used as the tunnel source address. All packets sent across this tunnel will have this IPv4 address as the source address included in the IPv4 packet header. This is typically a Loopback interface but can be any interface with a globally routable IPv4 address

- Configure the tunnel interface as an unnumbered interface that will use the IPv6 address of the inside (internal) 6to4 site interface using the `ipv6 unnumbered [interface name]` interface configuration command

- Specify IPv6 as the passenger protocol and IPv4 as both the encapsulation and transport protocol for the dynamic IPv6 tunnel and specify 6to4 operation using the `tunnel mode ipv6ip 6to4` interface configuration command

- Configure a static route to remote 6to4 IPv6 subnets across the tunnel interface using the `ipv6 route <prefix/length> tunnel <number>` global configuration command

Following these guidelines, this task is completed as follows:

```
R1(config)#interface tunnel 0
R1(config-if)#ipv6 unnumbered fastethernet 0/0
R1(config-if)#tunnel source loopback 0
R1(config-if)#tunnel mode ipv6ip 6to4
R1(config-if)#exit
R1(config)#ipv6 route 2002::/16 tunnel 0
R1(config)#exit

R2(config)#interface tunnel 0
R2(config-if)#ipv6 unnumbered fastethernet 0/0
R2(config-if)#tunnel source loopback 0
```

```
R2(config-if)#tunnel mode ipv6ip 6to4
R2(config-if)#exit
R2(config)#ipv6 route 2002::/16 tunnel 0
R2(config)#exit

R3(config)#interface tunnel 0
R3(config-if)#ipv6 unnumbered fastethernet 0/0
R3(config-if)#tunnel source loopback 0
R3(config-if)#tunnel mode ipv6ip 6to4
R3(config-if)#exit
R3(config)#ipv6 route 2002::/16 tunnel 0
R3(config)#exit

R4(config)#interface tunnel 0
R4(config-if)#ipv6 unnumbered fastethernet 0/0
R4(config-if)#tunnel source loopback 0
R4(config-if)#tunnel mode ipv6ip 6to4
R4(config-if)#exit
R4(config)#ipv6 route 2002::/16 tunnel 0
R4(config)#exit
```

Following this, verify 6to4 tunnel configuration using the show interfaces command:

```
R1#show interfaces tunnel 0
Tunnel0 is up, line protocol is up
  Hardware is Tunnel
  MTU 1514 bytes, BW 9 Kbit/sec, DLY 500000 usec,
     reliability 255/255, txload 1/255, rxload 1/255
  Encapsulation TUNNEL, loopback not set
  Keepalive not set
  Tunnel source 1.1.1.1 (Loopback0), destination UNKNOWN
  Tunnel protocol/transport IPv6 6to4

  Fast tunneling enabled
  Tunnel transmit bandwidth 8000 (kbps)
  Tunnel receive bandwidth 8000 (kbps)
  Last input never, output 00:03:39, output hang never
  Last clearing of "show interface" counters never
  Input queue: 0/75/0/0 (size/max/drops/flushes); Total output drops: 0
  Queueing strategy: fifo
  Output queue: 0/0 (size/max)

[Truncated Output]
```

Finally, complete this task by pinging LAN-to-LAN between all routers:

```
R1#ping 2002:202:202:2::2 source fastethernet 0/0 repeat 10

Type escape sequence to abort.
Sending 10, 100-byte ICMP Echos to 2002:202:202:2::2, timeout is 2 seconds:
Packet sent with a source address of 2002:101:101:1::1
!!!!!!!!!!
Success rate is 100 percent (10/10), round-trip min/avg/max = 4/4/4 ms

R1#ping 2002:303:303:3::3 source fastethernet 0/0 repeat 10

Type escape sequence to abort.
Sending 10, 100-byte ICMP Echos to 2002:303:303:3::3, timeout is 2 seconds:
Packet sent with a source address of 2002:101:101:1::1
!!!!!!!!!!
Success rate is 100 percent (10/10), round-trip min/avg/max = 16/19/20 ms

R1#ping 2002:404:404:4::4 source fastethernet 0/0 repeat 10

Type escape sequence to abort.
Sending 10, 100-byte ICMP Echos to 2002:404:404:4::4, timeout is 2 seconds:
Packet sent with a source address of 2002:101:101:1::1
!!!!!!!!!!
Success rate is 100 percent (10/10), round-trip min/avg/max = 32/35/36 ms

R2#ping 2002:101:101:1::1 source fastethernet 0/0 repeat 10

Type escape sequence to abort.
Sending 10, 100-byte ICMP Echos to 2002:101:101:1::1, timeout is 2 seconds:
```

```
Packet sent with a source address of 2002:202:202:2::2
!!!!!!!!!!
Success rate is 100 percent (10/10), round-trip min/avg/max = 0/3/4 ms

R2#ping 2002:303:303:3::3 source fastethernet 0/0 repeat 10

Type escape sequence to abort.
Sending 10, 100-byte ICMP Echos to 2002:303:303:3::3, timeout is 2 seconds:
Packet sent with a source address of 2002:202:202:2::2
!!!!!!!!!!
Success rate is 100 percent (10/10), round-trip min/avg/max = 20/20/20 ms

R2#ping 2002:404:404:4::4 source fastethernet 0/0 repeat 10

Type escape sequence to abort.
Sending 10, 100-byte ICMP Echos to 2002:404:404:4::4, timeout is 2 seconds:
Packet sent with a source address of 2002:202:202:2::2
!!!!!!!!!!
Success rate is 100 percent (10/10), round-trip min/avg/max = 36/36/36 ms

R3#ping 2002:101:101:1::1 source fastethernet 0/0 repeat 10

Type escape sequence to abort.
Sending 10, 100-byte ICMP Echos to 2002:101:101:1::1, timeout is 2 seconds:
Packet sent with a source address of 2002:303:303:3::3
!!!!!!!!!!
Success rate is 100 percent (10/10), round-trip min/avg/max = 16/18/20 ms

R3#ping 2002:202:202:2::2 source fastethernet 0/0 repeat 10

Type escape sequence to abort.
Sending 10, 100-byte ICMP Echos to 2002:202:202:2::2, timeout is 2 seconds:
Packet sent with a source address of 2002:303:303:3::3
!!!!!!!!!!
Success rate is 100 percent (10/10), round-trip min/avg/max = 20/20/20 ms

R3#ping 2002:404:404:4::4 source fastethernet 0/0 repeat 10

Type escape sequence to abort.
Sending 10, 100-byte ICMP Echos to 2002:404:404:4::4, timeout is 2 seconds:
Packet sent with a source address of 2002:303:303:3::3
!!!!!!!!!!
Success rate is 100 percent (10/10), round-trip min/avg/max = 16/18/20 ms

R4#ping 2002:101:101:1::1 source fastethernet 0/0 repeat 10

Type escape sequence to abort.
Sending 10, 100-byte ICMP Echos to 2002:101:101:1::1, timeout is 2 seconds:
Packet sent with a source address of 2002:404:404:4::4
!!!!!!!!!!
Success rate is 100 percent (10/10), round-trip min/avg/max = 32/35/36 ms

R4#ping 2002:202:202:2::2 source fastethernet 0/0 repeat 10

Type escape sequence to abort.
Sending 10, 100-byte ICMP Echos to 2002:202:202:2::2, timeout is 2 seconds:
Packet sent with a source address of 2002:404:404:4::4
!!!!!!!!!!
Success rate is 100 percent (10/10), round-trip min/avg/max = 36/39/56 ms

R4#ping 2002:303:303:3::3 source fastethernet 0/0 repeat 10

Type escape sequence to abort.
Sending 10, 100-byte ICMP Echos to 2002:303:303:3::3, timeout is 2 seconds:
Packet sent with a source address of 2002:404:404:4::4
!!!!!!!!!!
Success rate is 100 percent (10/10), round-trip min/avg/max = 20/20/20 ms
```

FINAL ROUTER CONFIGURATIONS

R1

```
R1#term len 0
R1#sh run
Building configuration...
```

```
Current configuration : 1169 bytes
!
version 12.4
service timestamps debug datetime msec
service timestamps log datetime msec
no service password-encryption
!
hostname R1
!
boot-start-marker
boot-end-marker
!
no logging console
!
no aaa new-model
no network-clock-participate slot 1
no network-clock-participate wic 0
ip cef
!
no ip domain lookup
ip auth-proxy max-nodata-conns 3
ip admission max-nodata-conns 3
!
ipv6 unicast-routing
ipv6 cef
!
interface Loopback0
 ip address 1.1.1.1 255.255.255.255
!
interface Tunnel0
 no ip address
 no ip redirects
 ipv6 unnumbered FastEthernet0/0
 tunnel source Loopback0
 tunnel mode ipv6ip 6to4
!
interface FastEthernet0/0
 no ip address
 duplex auto
 speed auto
 ipv6 address 2002:101:101:1::1/64
!
interface Serial0/0
 ip address 10.0.0.1 255.255.255.252
 clock rate 2000000
!
interface Serial0/1
 ip address 10.0.0.5 255.255.255.252
!
router ospf 1
 log-adjacency-changes
 network 0.0.0.0 255.255.255.255 area 0
!
ip forward-protocol nd
!
no ip http server
no ip http secure-server
!
ipv6 route 2002::/16 Tunnel0
!
control-plane
!
line con 0
line aux 0
line vty 0 4
 login
!
end

R1#
```

R2

```
R2#term len 0
R2#sh run
Building configuration...

Current configuration : 1107 bytes
!
version 12.4
```

```
service timestamps debug datetime msec
service timestamps log datetime msec
no service password-encryption
!
hostname R2
!
boot-start-marker
boot-end-marker
!
no logging console
!
no aaa new-model
no network-clock-participate slot 1
no network-clock-participate wic 0
ip cef
!
no ip domain lookup
ip auth-proxy max-nodata-conns 3
ip admission max-nodata-conns 3
!
interface Loopback0
 ip address 2.2.2.2 255.255.255.255
!
interface Tunnel0
 no ip address
 no ip redirects
 ipv6 unnumbered FastEthernet0/0
 tunnel source Loopback0
 tunnel mode ipv6ip 6to4
!
interface FastEthernet0/0
 no ip address
 duplex auto
 speed auto
 ipv6 address 2002:202:202:2::2/64
!
interface Serial0/0
 ip address 10.0.0.2 255.255.255.252
!
interface Serial0/1
 no ip address
 shutdown
!
router ospf 2
 log-adjacency-changes
 network 0.0.0.0 255.255.255.255 area 0
!
ip forward-protocol nd
!
no ip http server
no ip http secure-server
!
ipv6 route 2002::/16 Tunnel0
!
control-plane
!
line con 0
line aux 0
line vty 0 4
 login
!
end

R2#
```

R3

```
R3#term len 0
R3#sh run
Building configuration...

Current configuration : 1459 bytes
!
version 12.4
service timestamps debug datetime msec
service timestamps log datetime msec
no service password-encryption
!
hostname R3
!
```

```
boot-start-marker
boot-end-marker
!
no logging console
!
no aaa new-model
no network-clock-participate slot 1
no network-clock-participate wic 0
ip cef
!
no ip domain lookup
ip auth-proxy max-nodata-conns 3
ip admission max-nodata-conns 3
!
interface Loopback0
 ip address 3.3.3.3 255.255.255.255
!
interface Tunnel0
 no ip address
 no ip redirects
 ipv6 unnumbered FastEthernet0/0
 tunnel source Loopback0
 tunnel mode ipv6ip 6to4
!
interface FastEthernet0/0
 no ip address
 duplex auto
 speed auto
 ipv6 address 2002:303:303:3::3/64
!
interface Serial1/0
 ip address 10.0.0.6 255.255.255.252
 clock rate 128000
!
interface Serial1/1
 no ip address
 shutdown
 clock rate 128000
!
interface Serial1/2
 ip address 10.0.0.13 255.255.255.252
 clock rate 128000
!
interface Serial1/3
 no ip address
 shutdown
!
interface Serial1/4
 no ip address
 shutdown
!
interface Serial1/5
 no ip address
 shutdown
!
interface Serial1/6
 no ip address
 shutdown
!
interface Serial1/7
 no ip address
 shutdown
!
router ospf 3
 log-adjacency-changes
 network 0.0.0.0 255.255.255.255 area 0
!
ip forward-protocol nd
!
no ip http server
no ip http secure-server
!
ipv6 route 2002::/16 Tunnel0
!
control-plane
!
line con 0
line aux 0
line vty 0 4
 login
!
end
R3#
```

R4

```
R4#term len 0
R4#sh run
Building configuration...

Current configuration : 1138 bytes
!
version 12.4
service timestamps debug datetime msec
service timestamps log datetime msec
no service password-encryption
!
hostname R4
!
boot-start-marker
boot-end-marker
!
no logging console
!
no aaa new-model
no network-clock-participate slot 1
no network-clock-participate wic 0
ip cef
!
no ip domain lookup
ip auth-proxy max-nodata-conns 3
ip admission max-nodata-conns 3
!
ipv6 unicast-routing
ipv6 cef
!
interface Loopback0
 ip address 4.4.4.4 255.255.255.255
!
interface Tunnel0
 no ip address
 no ip redirects
 ipv6 unnumbered FastEthernet0/0
 tunnel source Loopback0
 tunnel mode ipv6ip 6to4
!
interface FastEthernet0/0
 no ip address
 duplex auto
 speed auto
 ipv6 address 2002:404:404:4::4/64
!
interface Serial0/0
 ip address 10.0.0.14 255.255.255.252
!
interface Serial0/1
 no ip address
 shutdown
!
router ospf 4
 log-adjacency-changes
 network 0.0.0.0 255.255.255.255 area 0
!
ip forward-protocol nd
!
no ip http server
no ip http secure-server
!
ipv6 route 2002::/16 Tunnel0
!
control-plane
!
line con 0
line aux 0
line vty 0 4
 login
!
end
R4#
```

CCNP LAB 48

Internet Protocol Version 6 Lab

Lab Objective:

The focus of this lab is to understand tunneling implementation and configuration in Cisco IOS routers. Additional technologies include Multi Protocol Border Gateway Protocol (MP-BGP).

Lab Topology:

The lab network topology is illustrated below:

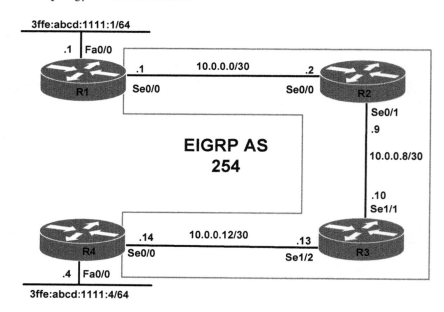

IMPORTANT NOTE: If you are using the www.howtonetwork.net racks, please bring up the LAN interfaces connected to the routers by issuing the no shutdown command on the connected switches. If you are using a home lab with no Switches, you can bring up the LAN interfaces using the following configurations on your routers:

```
interface fastethernet 0/0
  no keepalive
  loopback
  no shutdown
```

Alternately, you can simply connect the interfaces to a hub or switch if you have one available in your own lab.

Task 1

Configure hostnames, IP addressing on all routers as illustrated in the network topology.

Task 2

Enable EIGRP on all routers as illustrated in the topology. Verify your EIGRP configuration.

Task 3

Configure automatic IPv4-compatible tunnels on R1 and R4. The tunnel source interface should be configured as the WAN interface. Verify the configuration using the appropriate commands.

Task 4

Enable MP-BGP between R1 and R4 using AS 254 and advertise the LAN subnets connected to R1 and R4. Use the WAN interface addresses to complete the 128-bit IPv6 addresses that will be used for peering. Verify that you can ping LAN-to-LAN between R1 and R4.

LAB VALIDATION

Task 1

Please refer to previous labs for basic IPv4, IPv6 addressing and hostname configuration. This will not be included in this section to avoid being redundant.

Task 2

```
R1(config)#router eigrp 254
R1(config-router)#no auto-summary
R1(config-router)#network 10.0.0.0
R1(config-router)#exit

R2(config)#router eigrp 254
R2(config-router)#no auto-summary
R2(config-router)#network 10.0.0.0
R2(config-router)#exit

R3(config)#router eigrp 254
R3(config-router)#no auto-summary
R3(config-router)#network 10.0.0.0
R3(config-router)#exit

R4(config)#router eigrp 254
R4(config-router)#no auto-summary
R4(config-router)#network 10.0.0.0
R4(config-router)#exit
```

Verify your EIGRP configuration using the show ip eigrp neighbors command:

```
R1#show ip eigrp neighbors
IP-EIGRP neighbors for process 254
H   Address              Interface    Hold Uptime    SRTT   RTO  Q   Seq
                                      (sec)          (ms)        Cnt Num
0   10.0.0.2             Se0/0        12  00:01:31      5   200  0   8

R2#show ip eigrp neighbors
IP-EIGRP neighbors for process 254
H   Address              Interface    Hold Uptime    SRTT   RTO  Q   Seq
                                      (sec)          (ms)        Cnt Num
1   10.0.0.10            Se0/1        10  00:01:28      9   300  0   3
0   10.0.0.1             Se0/0        12  00:01:34      2   200  0   3

R3#show ip eigrp neighbors
IP-EIGRP neighbors for process 254
H   Address              Interface    Hold Uptime    SRTT   RTO  Q   Seq
                                      (sec)          (ms)        Cnt Num
1   10.0.0.14            Se1/2        13  00:01:26     12  1140  0   3
0   10.0.0.9             Se1/1        12  00:01:31     12  1140  0   7

R4#show ip eigrp neighbors
IP-EIGRP neighbors for process 254
H   Address              Interface    Hold Uptime    SRTT   RTO  Q   Seq
                                      (sec)          (ms)        Cnt Num
0   10.0.0.13            Se0/0        14  00:01:29     14   200  0   7
```

Task 3

Automatic IPv4-compatible tunnels use a tunnel mode of `ipv6ip auto-tunnel`. The tunnels are configured using only a source interface. The destination is automatically determined based on configured static routes or received MP-BGP updates. This task is completed as follows:

```
R1(config)#interface tunnel 0
R1(config-if)#tunnel source serial 0/0
R1(config-if)#tunnel mode ipv6ip auto-tunnel
R1(config-if)#exit

R4(config)#interface tunnel 0
R4(config-if)#tunnel source serial 0/0
R4(config-if)#tunnel mode ipv6ip auto-tunnel
R4(config-if)#exit
```

Verify your Tunnel status using the `show interfaces` command:

```
R1#show interfaces tunnel 0
Tunnel0 is up, line protocol is up
  Hardware is Tunnel
  MTU 1514 bytes, BW 9 Kbit/sec, DLY 500000 usec,
     reliability 255/255, txload 1/255, rxload 1/255
  Encapsulation TUNNEL, loopback not set
  Keepalive not set
  Tunnel source 10.0.0.1 (Serial0/0), destination UNKNOWN
  Tunnel protocol/transport IPv6 auto-tunnel

  Fast tunneling enabled
  Tunnel transmit bandwidth 8000 (kbps)
  Tunnel receive bandwidth 8000 (kbps)
  Last input 00:00:41, output 00:00:42, output hang never
  Last clearing of "show interface" counters never
  Input queue: 0/75/0/0 (size/max/drops/flushes); Total output drops: 0
  Queueing strategy: fifo
  Output queue: 0/0 (size/max)
  5 minute input rate 0 bits/sec, 0 packets/sec
  5 minute output rate 0 bits/sec, 0 packets/sec
     8 packets input, 983 bytes, 0 no buffer
     Received 0 broadcasts, 0 runts, 0 giants, 0 throttles
     0 input errors, 0 CRC, 0 frame, 0 overrun, 0 ignored, 0 abort
     14 packets output, 1375 bytes, 0 underruns
     0 output errors, 0 collisions, 0 interface resets
     0 unknown protocol drops
     0 output buffer failures, 0 output buffers swapped out
```

Task 4

Automatic IPv4-compatible tunnels enable IPv6 hosts to automatically enable tunnels to other IPv6 hosts across an IPv4 network infrastructure. Unlike 6to4 tunneling, automatic IPv4-compatible tunneling does use the IPv4-compatible IPv6 addresses. Automatic IPv4-compatible tunnels use the IPv6 prefix ::/96. To complete the 128-bit IPv6 address, the low order 32-bits are derived from the IPv4 address. These low-order 32-bits of the source and destination IPv6 addresses represent the source and destination IPv4 addresses of the tunnel endpoints. This task is completed as follows:

```
R1(config)#router bgp 254
R1(config-router)#bgp router-id 1.1.1.1
R1(config-router)#no bgp default ipv4-unicast
R1(config-router)#neighbor ::10.0.0.14 remote-as 254
R1(config-router)#address-family ipv6 unicast
R1(config-router-af)#neighbor ::10.0.0.14 activate
R1(config-router-af)#neighbor ::10.0.0.14 next-hop-self
R1(config-router-af)#network 3ffe:abcd:1111:1::/64
R1(config-router-af)#exit
R1(config-router)#exit

R4(config)#router bgp 254
R4(config-router)#bgp router-id 4.4.4.4
R4(config-router)#no bgp default ipv4-unicast
```

```
R4(config-router)#neighbor ::10.0.0.1 remote-as 254
R4(config-router)#address-family ipv6 unicast
R4(config-router-af)#neighbor ::10.0.0.1 activate
R4(config-router-af)#neighbor ::10.0.0.1 next-hop-self
R4(config-router-af)#network 3ffe:abcd:1111:4::/64
R4(config-router-af)#exit
R4(config-router)#exit
```

Verify MP-BGP configuration using the show bgp ipv6 unicast summary command:

```
R1#show bgp ipv6 unicast summary
BGP router identifier 1.1.1.1, local AS number 254
BGP table version is 3, main routing table version 3
2 network entries using 298 bytes of memory
2 path entries using 152 bytes of memory
3/2 BGP path/bestpath attribute entries using 372 bytes of memory
0 BGP route-map cache entries using 0 bytes of memory
0 BGP filter-list cache entries using 0 bytes of memory
BGP using 822 total bytes of memory
BGP activity 3/1 prefixes, 3/1 paths, scan interval 60 secs

Neighbor      V    AS MsgRcvd MsgSent TblVer  InQ OutQ Up/Down  State/PfxRcd
::10.0.0.14   4   254      4       4       3    0    0 00:00:36          1

R4#show bgp ipv6 unicast summary
BGP router identifier 4.4.4.4, local AS number 254
BGP table version is 3, main routing table version 3
2 network entries using 298 bytes of memory
2 path entries using 152 bytes of memory
3/2 BGP path/bestpath attribute entries using 372 bytes of memory
0 BGP route-map cache entries using 0 bytes of memory
0 BGP filter-list cache entries using 0 bytes of memory
BGP using 822 total bytes of memory
BGP activity 3/1 prefixes, 3/1 paths, scan interval 60 secs

Neighbor      V    AS MsgRcvd MsgSent TblVer  InQ OutQ Up/Down  State/PfxRcd
::10.0.0.1    4   254      5       5       3    0    0 00:01:24          1
```

Next, verify the BGP RIB entries using the show bgp ipv6 unicast command:

```
R1#show bgp ipv6 unicast
BGP table version is 3, local router ID is 1.1.1.1
Status codes: s suppressed, d damped, h history, * valid, > best, i - internal,
              r RIB-failure, S Stale
Origin codes: i - IGP, e - EGP, ? - incomplete

   Network          Next Hop            Metric LocPrf Weight Path
*> 3FFE:ABCD:1111:1::/64
                    ::                       0          32768 i
*>i3FFE:ABCD:1111:4::/64
                    ::10.0.0.14              0    100      0 i

R4#show bgp ipv6 unicast
BGP table version is 3, local router ID is 4.4.4.4
Status codes: s suppressed, d damped, h history, * valid, > best, i - internal,
              r RIB-failure, S Stale
Origin codes: i - IGP, e - EGP, ? - incomplete

   Network          Next Hop            Metric LocPrf Weight Path
*>i3FFE:ABCD:1111:1::/64
                    ::10.0.0.1               0    100      0 i
*> 3FFE:ABCD:1111:4::/64
                    ::                       0          32768 i
```

Finally, complete the task by pinging LAN-to-LAN between R1 and R4:

```
R1#ping 3FFE:ABCD:1111:4::4 source fastethernet 0/0 repeat 10 size 1500

Type escape sequence to abort.
Sending 10, 1500-byte ICMP Echos to 3FFE:ABCD:1111:4::4, timeout is 2 seconds:
Packet sent with a source address of 3FFE:ABCD:1111:1::1
!!!!!!!!!!
Success rate is 100 percent (10/10), round-trip min/avg/max = 404/407/408 ms

R4#ping 3FFE:ABCD:1111:1::1 source fastethernet 0/0 repeat 10 size 1500

Type escape sequence to abort.
```

```
Sending 10, 1500-byte ICMP Echos to 3FFE:ABCD:1111:1::1, timeout is 2 seconds:
Packet sent with a source address of 3FFE:ABCD:1111:4::4
!!!!!!!!!!
Success rate is 100 percent (10/10), round-trip min/avg/max = 404/407/412 ms
```

FINAL ROUTER CONFIGURATIONS

R1

```
R1#term len 0
R1#sh run
Building configuration...

Current configuration : 1298 bytes
!
version 12.4
service timestamps debug datetime msec
service timestamps log datetime msec
no service password-encryption
!
hostname R1
!
boot-start-marker
boot-end-marker
!
no logging console
!
no aaa new-model
no network-clock-participate slot 1
no network-clock-participate wic 0
ip cef
!
no ip domain lookup
ip auth-proxy max-nodata-conns 3
ip admission max-nodata-conns 3
!
ipv6 unicast-routing
ipv6 cef
!
interface Tunnel0
 no ip address
 no ip redirects
 tunnel source Serial0/0
 tunnel mode ipv6ip auto-tunnel
!
interface FastEthernet0/0
 no ip address
 duplex auto
 speed auto
 ipv6 address 3FFE:ABCD:1111:1::1/64
!
interface Serial0/0
 ip address 10.0.0.1 255.255.255.252
 clock rate 2000000
!
interface Serial0/1
 no ip address
 shutdown
!
router eigrp 254
 network 10.0.0.0
 no auto-summary
!
router bgp 254
 bgp router-id 1.1.1.1
 no bgp default ipv4-unicast
 bgp log-neighbor-changes
 neighbor ::10.0.0.14 remote-as 254
 !
 address-family ipv6
  neighbor ::10.0.0.14 activate
  neighbor ::10.0.0.14 next-hop-self
  network 3FFE:ABCD:1111:1::/64
 exit-address-family
!
ip forward-protocol nd
!
```

```
no ip http server
no ip http secure-server
!
control-plane
!
line con 0
line aux 0
line vty 0 4
 login
!
end
R1#
```

R2

```
R2#term len 0
R2#sh run
Building configuration...

Current configuration : 847 bytes
!
version 12.4
service timestamps debug datetime msec
service timestamps log datetime msec
no service password-encryption
!
hostname R2
!
boot-start-marker
boot-end-marker
!
no logging console
!
no aaa new-model
no network-clock-participate slot 1
no network-clock-participate wic 0
ip cef
!
no ip domain lookup
ip auth-proxy max-nodata-conns 3
ip admission max-nodata-conns 3
!
interface FastEthernet0/0
 no ip address
 shutdown
 duplex auto
 speed auto
!
interface Serial0/0
 ip address 10.0.0.2 255.255.255.252
!
interface Serial0/1
 ip address 10.0.0.9 255.255.255.252
!
router eigrp 254
 network 10.0.0.0
 no auto-summary
!
ip forward-protocol nd
!
no ip http server
no ip http secure-server
!
control-plane
!
line con 0
line aux 0
line vty 0 4
 login
!
end

R2#
```

R3

```
R3#term len 0
R3#sh run
Building configuration...
```

```
Current configuration : 1188 bytes
!
version 12.4
service timestamps debug datetime msec
service timestamps log datetime msec
no service password-encryption
!
hostname R3
!
boot-start-marker
boot-end-marker
!
no logging console
!
no aaa new-model
no network-clock-participate slot 1
no network-clock-participate wic 0
ip cef
!
no ip domain lookup
ip auth-proxy max-nodata-conns 3
ip admission max-nodata-conns 3
!
interface FastEthernet0/0
 no ip address
 shutdown
 duplex auto
 speed auto
!
interface Serial1/0
 no ip address
 shutdown
 clock rate 128000
!
interface Serial1/1
 ip address 10.0.0.10 255.255.255.252
 clock rate 128000
!
interface Serial1/2
 ip address 10.0.0.13 255.255.255.252
 clock rate 128000
!
interface Serial1/3
 no ip address
 shutdown
!
interface Serial1/4
 no ip address
 shutdown
!
interface Serial1/5
 no ip address
 shutdown
!
interface Serial1/6
 no ip address
 shutdown
!
interface Serial1/7
 no ip address
 shutdown
!
router eigrp 254
 network 10.0.0.0
 no auto-summary
!
ip forward-protocol nd
!
no ip http server
no ip http secure-server
!
control-plane
!
line con 0
line aux 0
line vty 0 4
 login
!
end

R3#
```

R4

```
R4#term len 0
R4#sh run
Building configuration...

Current configuration : 1276 bytes
!
version 12.4
service timestamps debug datetime msec
service timestamps log datetime msec
no service password-encryption
!
hostname R4
!
boot-start-marker
boot-end-marker
!
no logging console
!
no aaa new-model
no network-clock-participate slot 1
no network-clock-participate wic 0
ip cef
!
no ip domain lookup
ip auth-proxy max-nodata-conns 3
ip admission max-nodata-conns 3
!
ipv6 unicast-routing
ipv6 cef
!
interface Tunnel0
 no ip address
 no ip redirects
 tunnel source Serial0/0
 tunnel mode ipv6ip auto-tunnel
!
interface FastEthernet0/0
 no ip address
 duplex auto
 speed auto
 ipv6 address 3FFE:ABCD:1111:4::4/64
!
interface Serial0/0
 ip address 10.0.0.14 255.255.255.252
!
interface Serial0/1
 no ip address
 shutdown
!
router eigrp 254
 network 10.0.0.0
 no auto-summary
!
router bgp 254
 bgp router-id 4.4.4.4
 no bgp default ipv4-unicast
 bgp log-neighbor-changes
 neighbor ::10.0.0.1 remote-as 254
 !
 address-family ipv6
  neighbor ::10.0.0.1 activate
  neighbor ::10.0.0.1 next-hop-self
  network 3FFE:ABCD:1111:4::/64
 exit-address-family
!
ip forward-protocol nd
!
no ip http server
no ip http secure-server
!
control-plane
!
line con 0
line aux 0
line vty 0 4
 login
!
end

R4#
```

CCNP LAB 49

Internet Protocol Version 6 Lab

Lab Objective:

The focus of this lab is to understand tunneling implementation and configuration in Cisco IOS routers. Additional technologies include Multi Protocol Border Gateway Protocol (MP-BGP).

Lab Topology:

The lab network topology is illustrated below:

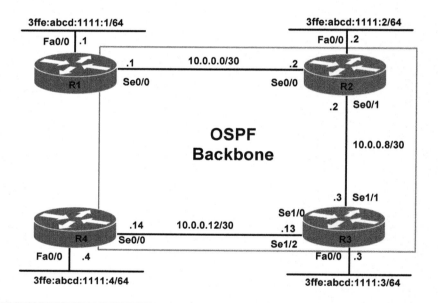

IMPORTANT NOTE: If you are using the www.howtonetwork.net racks, please bring up the LAN interfaces connected to the routers by issuing the `no shutdown` command on the connected switches. If you are using a home lab with no Switches, you can bring up the LAN interfaces using the following configurations on your routers:

```
interface fastethernet 0/0
  no keepalive
  loopback
  no shutdown
```

Alternately, you can simply connect the interfaces to a hub or switch if you have one available in your own lab.

Task 1

Configure hostnames, IP addressing on all routers as illustrated in the network topology. Next, configure the following Loopback 0 interfaces on all routers:
- R1: Loopback 0 - IP Address 1.1.1.1/32
- R2: Loopback 0 - IP Address 2.2.2.2/32

- R3: Loopback 0 - IP Address 3.3.3.3/32
- R4: Loopback 0 - IP Address 4.4.4.4/32

Task 2

Enable OSPF on all routers as illustrated in the topology. Advertise the Loopback 0 interfaces via OSPF as Type 2 External LSAs. Verify your OSPF configuration.

Task 3

Configure ISATAP tunnels on all routers. Use the Loopback 0 interface as the tunnel source. The tunnels should be configured using the fec0:abcd:1234:1::/64 subnet. Verify your configuration using the appropriate commands.

Task 4

Configure MP-BGP on all routers. All routers should use their ISATAP tunnel addresses for peering. Ensure that all routers advertise their LAN subnet via MP-BGP. MP-BGP peering should be configured on all routers as follows:

- R1 - Autonomous System 1: This router will peer with R2
- R2 - Autonomous System 2: This router will peer with R1 and R2
- R3 - Autonomous System 3: This router will peer with R2 and R4
- R4 - Autonomous System 4: This router will peer with R3

Verify your MP-BGP configuration using the appropriate commands.

Task 5

Ensure that all routers can ping each other LAN-to-LAN. Use the extended ping function for verification. Every router should be able to ping every other routers' LAN subnet without additional configuration. If not, check the configuration implemented in the previous lab tasks.

LAB VALIDATION

Task 1

Please refer to previous labs for basic IPv4, IPv6 addressing and hostname configuration. This will not be included in this section to avoid being redundant.

Task 2

Please refer to previous labs for basic OSPF configuration. Following this, verify your OSPF configuration using the show ip ospf neighbor command:

```
R1#show ip ospf neighbor

Neighbor ID     Pri   State        Dead Time   Address     Interface
2.2.2.2           0   FULL/   -    00:00:39    10.0.0.2    Serial0/0

R2#show ip ospf neighbor

Neighbor ID     Pri   State        Dead Time   Address     Interface
3.3.3.3           0   FULL/   -    00:00:35    10.0.0.10   Serial0/1
1.1.1.1           0   FULL/   -    00:00:35    10.0.0.1    Serial0/0

R3#show ip ospf neighbor

Neighbor ID     Pri   State        Dead Time   Address     Interface
4.4.4.4           0   FULL/   -    00:00:31    10.0.0.14   Serial1/2
2.2.2.2           0   FULL/   -    00:00:33    10.0.0.9    Serial1/1
```

```
R4#show ip ospf neighbor

Neighbor ID     Pri   State        Dead Time   Address       Interface
3.3.3.3           0   FULL/  -     00:00:38    10.0.0.13     Serial0/0
```

Next, verify that all routing information is correct using the show ip route command:

```
R1#show ip route ospf
        2.0.0.0/32 is subnetted, 1 subnets
O E2    2.2.2.2 [110/20] via 10.0.0.2, 00:01:32, Serial0/0
        3.0.0.0/32 is subnetted, 1 subnets
O E2    3.3.3.3 [110/20] via 10.0.0.2, 00:01:32, Serial0/0
        4.0.0.0/32 is subnetted, 1 subnets
O E2    4.4.4.4 [110/20] via 10.0.0.2, 00:01:32, Serial0/0
        10.0.0.0/30 is subnetted, 3 subnets
O       10.0.0.8 [110/128] via 10.0.0.2, 00:01:32, Serial0/0
O       10.0.0.12 [110/909] via 10.0.0.2, 00:01:32, Serial0/0

R2#show ip route ospf
        1.0.0.0/32 is subnetted, 1 subnets
O E2    1.1.1.1 [110/20] via 10.0.0.1, 00:01:35, Serial0/0
        3.0.0.0/32 is subnetted, 1 subnets
O E2    3.3.3.3 [110/20] via 10.0.0.10, 00:01:35, Serial0/1
        4.0.0.0/32 is subnetted, 1 subnets
O E2    4.4.4.4 [110/20] via 10.0.0.10, 00:01:35, Serial0/1
        10.0.0.0/30 is subnetted, 3 subnets
O       10.0.0.12 [110/845] via 10.0.0.10, 00:01:36, Serial0/1

R3#show ip route ospf
        1.0.0.0/32 is subnetted, 1 subnets
O E2    1.1.1.1 [110/20] via 10.0.0.9, 00:01:39, Serial1/1
        2.0.0.0/32 is subnetted, 1 subnets
O E2    2.2.2.2 [110/20] via 10.0.0.9, 00:01:39, Serial1/1
        4.0.0.0/32 is subnetted, 1 subnets
O E2    4.4.4.4 [110/20] via 10.0.0.14, 00:01:39, Serial1/2
        10.0.0.0/30 is subnetted, 3 subnets
O       10.0.0.0 [110/845] via 10.0.0.9, 00:01:39, Serial1/1

R4#show ip route ospf
        1.0.0.0/32 is subnetted, 1 subnets
O E2    1.1.1.1 [110/20] via 10.0.0.13, 00:01:42, Serial0/0
        2.0.0.0/32 is subnetted, 1 subnets
O E2    2.2.2.2 [110/20] via 10.0.0.13, 00:01:42, Serial0/0
        3.0.0.0/32 is subnetted, 1 subnets
O E2    3.3.3.3 [110/20] via 10.0.0.13, 00:01:42, Serial0/0
        10.0.0.0/30 is subnetted, 3 subnets
O       10.0.0.8 [110/845] via 10.0.0.13, 00:01:42, Serial0/0
O       10.0.0.0 [110/909] via 10.0.0.13, 00:01:42, Serial0/0
```

Task 3

```
R1(config)#interface tunnel 0
R1(config-if)#tunnel source loopback 0
R1(config-if)#ipv6 address fec0:abcd:1234:1::/64 eui-64
R1(config-if)#tunnel mode ipv6ip isatap
R1(config-if)#no ipv6 nd suppress-ra
R1(config-if)#exit

R2(config)#interface tunnel 0
R2(config-if)#tunnel source loopback 0
R2(config-if)#ipv6 address fec0:abcd:1234:1::/64 eui-64
R2(config-if)#tunnel mode ipv6ip isatap
R2(config-if)#no ipv6 nd suppress-ra
R2(config-if)#exit

R3(config)#interface tunnel 0
R3(config-if)#tunnel source loopback 0
R3(config-if)#ipv6 address fec0:abcd:1234:1::/64 eui-64
R3(config-if)#tunnel mode ipv6ip isatap
R3(config-if)#no ipv6 nd suppress-ra
R3(config-if)#exit
```

```
R4(config)#interface tunnel 0
R4(config-if)#tunnel source loopback 0
R4(config-if)#ipv6 address fec0:abcd:1234:1::/64 eui-64
R4(config-if)#tunnel mode ipv6ip isatap
R4(config-if)#no ipv6 nd suppress-ra
R4(config-if)#exit
```

Verify ISATAP tunnel status and configuration using the show interfaces command:

```
R1#show interfaces tunnel 0
Tunnel0 is up, line protocol is up
  Hardware is Tunnel
  MTU 1514 bytes, BW 9 Kbit/sec, DLY 500000 usec,
     reliability 255/255, txload 1/255, rxload 1/255
  Encapsulation TUNNEL, loopback not set
  Keepalive not set
  Tunnel source 1.1.1.1 (Loopback0), destination UNKNOWN
  Tunnel protocol/transport IPv6 ISATAP

  Fast tunneling enabled
  Tunnel transmit bandwidth 8000 (kbps)
  Tunnel receive bandwidth 8000 (kbps)
  Last input never, output 00:05:21, output hang never
  Last clearing of "show interface" counters never
  Input queue: 0/75/0/0 (size/max/drops/flushes); Total output drops: 0
  Queueing strategy: fifo
  Output queue: 0/0 (size/max)
  5 minute input rate 0 bits/sec, 0 packets/sec
  5 minute output rate 0 bits/sec, 0 packets/sec
     0 packets input, 0 bytes, 0 no buffer
     Received 0 broadcasts, 0 runts, 0 giants, 0 throttles
     0 input errors, 0 CRC, 0 frame, 0 overrun, 0 ignored, 0 abort
     4 packets output, 384 bytes, 0 underruns
     0 output errors, 0 collisions, 0 interface resets
     0 unknown protocol drops
     0 output buffer failures, 0 output buffers swapped out
```

Verify ISATAP IPv6 addressing using the show ipv6 interface command:

```
R1#show ipv6 interface tunnel 0
Tunnel0 is up, line protocol is up
  IPv6 is enabled, link-local address is FE80::5EFE:101:101
  Global unicast address(es):
    FEC0:ABCD:1234:1:0:5EFE:101:101, subnet is FEC0:ABCD:1234:1::/64 [EUI]
  Joined group address(es):
    FF02::1
    FF02::2
    FF02::1:FF01:101
  MTU is 1480 bytes
  ICMP error messages limited to one every 100 milliseconds
  ICMP redirects are enabled
  ND DAD is not supported
  ND reachable time is 30000 milliseconds
  ND advertised reachable time is 0 milliseconds
  ND advertised retransmit interval is 0 milliseconds
  ND router advertisements live for 1800 seconds
  Hosts use stateless autoconfig for addresses.
```

Task 4

```
R1(config)#router bgp 1
R1(config-router)#bgp router-id 1.1.1.1
R1(config-router)#address-family ipv6
R1(config-router-af)#neighbor FEC0:ABCD:1234:1:0:5EFE:202:202 remote-as 2
R1(config-router-af)#neighbor FEC0:ABCD:1234:1:0:5EFE:202:202 activate
R1(config-router-af)#network 3FFE:ABCD:1111:1::/64
R1(config-router-af)#exit-address-family
R1(config-router)#exit

R2(config)#router bgp 2
R2(config-router)#bgp router-id 2.2.2.2
```

```
R2(config-router)#address-family ipv6
R2(config-router-af)#neighbor FEC0:ABCD:1234:1:0:5EFE:101:101 remote-as 1
R2(config-router-af)#neighbor FEC0:ABCD:1234:1:0:5EFE:101:101 activate
R2(config-router-af)#neighbor FEC0:ABCD:1234:1:0:5EFE:303:303 remote-as 3
R2(config-router-af)#neighbor FEC0:ABCD:1234:1:0:5EFE:303:303 activate
R2(config-router-af)#network 3FFE:ABCD:1111:2::/64
R2(config-router-af)#exit-address-family
R2(config-router)#exit

R3(config)#router bgp 3
R3(config-router)#bgp router-id 3.3.3.3
R3(config-router)#address-family ipv6
R3(config-router-af)#neighbor FEC0:ABCD:1234:1:0:5EFE:202:202 remote-as 2
R3(config-router-af)#neighbor FEC0:ABCD:1234:1:0:5EFE:202:202 activate
R3(config-router-af)#neighbor FEC0:ABCD:1234:1:0:5EFE:404:404 remote-as 4
R3(config-router-af)#neighbor FEC0:ABCD:1234:1:0:5EFE:404:404 activate
R3(config-router-af)#network 3FFE:ABCD:1111:3::/64
R3(config-router-af)#exit-address-family
R3(config-router)#exit

R4(config)#router bgp 4
R4(config-router)#bgp router-id 4.4.4.4
R4(config-router)#address-family ipv6
R4(config-router-af)#neighbor FEC0:ABCD:1234:1:0:5EFE:303:303 remote-as 3
R4(config-router-af)#neighbor FEC0:ABCD:1234:1:0:5EFE:303:303 activate
R4(config-router-af)#network 3FFE:ABCD:1111:4::/64
R4(config-router-af)#exit-address-family
R4(config-router)#exit
```

Verify MP-BGP configuration using the show bgp ipv6 unicast summary command:

```
R1#show bgp ipv6 unicast summary
BGP router identifier 1.1.1.1, local AS number 1
BGP table version is 5, main routing table version 5
4 network entries using 596 bytes of memory
4 path entries using 304 bytes of memory
5/4 BGP path/bestpath attribute entries using 620 bytes of memory
3 BGP AS-PATH entries using 72 bytes of memory
0 BGP route-map cache entries using 0 bytes of memory
0 BGP filter-list cache entries using 0 bytes of memory
BGP using 1592 total bytes of memory
BGP activity 4/0 prefixes, 4/0 paths, scan interval 60 secs

Neighbor        V    AS MsgRcvd MsgSent   TblVer  InQ OutQ Up/Down  State/PfxRcd
FEC0:ABCD:1234:1:0:5EFE:202:202
                4     2    16      14        5    0    0 00:10:15        3

R2#show bgp ipv6 unicast summary
BGP router identifier 2.2.2.2, local AS number 2
BGP table version is 6, main routing table version 6
4 network entries using 596 bytes of memory
4 path entries using 304 bytes of memory
5/4 BGP path/bestpath attribute entries using 620 bytes of memory
3 BGP AS-PATH entries using 72 bytes of memory
0 BGP route-map cache entries using 0 bytes of memory
0 BGP filter-list cache entries using 0 bytes of memory
BGP using 1592 total bytes of memory
BGP activity 4/0 prefixes, 4/0 paths, scan interval 60 secs

Neighbor        V    AS MsgRcvd MsgSent   TblVer  InQ OutQ Up/Down  State/PfxRcd
FEC0:ABCD:1234:1:0:5EFE:101:101
                4     1    14      16        6    0    0 00:10:19        1
FEC0:ABCD:1234:1:0:5EFE:303:303
                4     3    10      10        6    0    0 00:02:32        2

R3#show bgp ipv6 unicast summary
BGP router identifier 3.3.3.3, local AS number 3
BGP table version is 6, main routing table version 6
4 network entries using 596 bytes of memory
4 path entries using 304 bytes of memory
5/4 BGP path/bestpath attribute entries using 620 bytes of memory
3 BGP AS-PATH entries using 72 bytes of memory
0 BGP route-map cache entries using 0 bytes of memory
```

```
0 BGP filter-list cache entries using 0 bytes of memory
BGP using 1592 total bytes of memory
BGP activity 4/0 prefixes, 4/0 paths, scan interval 60 secs

Neighbor            V    AS MsgRcvd MsgSent   TblVer  InQ OutQ Up/Down   State/PfxRcd
FEC0:ABCD:1234:1:0:5EFE:202:202
                    4     2     10      10       6    0    0 00:02:37       2
FEC0:ABCD:1234:1:0:5EFE:404:404
                    4     4      5       8       6    0    0 00:00:58       1

R4#show bgp ipv6 unicast summary
BGP router identifier 4.4.4.4, local AS number 4
BGP table version is 5, main routing table version 5
4 network entries using 596 bytes of memory
4 path entries using 304 bytes of memory
5/4 BGP path/bestpath attribute entries using 620 bytes of memory
3 BGP AS-PATH entries using 72 bytes of memory
0 BGP route-map cache entries using 0 bytes of memory
0 BGP filter-list cache entries using 0 bytes of memory
BGP using 1592 total bytes of memory
BGP activity 4/0 prefixes, 4/0 paths, scan interval 60 secs

Neighbor            V    AS MsgRcvd MsgSent   TblVer  InQ OutQ Up/Down   State/PfxRcd
FEC0:ABCD:1234:1:0:5EFE:303:303
                    4     3      9       6       5    0    0 00:01:02       3
```

Finally, verify that all routers have the LAN subnets in their MP-BGP RIB Tables:

```
R1#show bgp ipv6 unicast
BGP table version is 5, local router ID is 1.1.1.1
Status codes: s suppressed, d damped, h history, * valid, > best, i - internal,
              r RIB-failure, S Stale
Origin codes: i - IGP, e - EGP, ? - incomplete

   Network          Next Hop            Metric LocPrf Weight Path
*> 3FFE:ABCD:1111:1::/64
                    ::                        0         32768 i
*> 3FFE:ABCD:1111:2::/64
                    FEC0:ABCD:1234:1:0:5EFE:202:202
                                              0            0 2 i
*> 3FFE:ABCD:1111:3::/64
                    FEC0:ABCD:1234:1:0:5EFE:303:303
                                                           0 2 3 i
*> 3FFE:ABCD:1111:4::/64
                    FEC0:ABCD:1234:1:0:5EFE:404:404
                                                           0 2 3 4 i

R2#show bgp ipv6 unicast
BGP table version is 6, local router ID is 2.2.2.2
Status codes: s suppressed, d damped, h history, * valid, > best, i - internal,
              r RIB-failure, S Stale
Origin codes: i - IGP, e - EGP, ? - incomplete

   Network          Next Hop            Metric LocPrf Weight Path
*> 3FFE:ABCD:1111:1::/64
                    FEC0:ABCD:1234:1:0:5EFE:101:101
                                              0            0 1 i
*> 3FFE:ABCD:1111:2::/64
                    ::                        0         32768 i
*> 3FFE:ABCD:1111:3::/64
                    FEC0:ABCD:1234:1:0:5EFE:303:303
                                              0            0 3 i
*> 3FFE:ABCD:1111:4::/64
                    FEC0:ABCD:1234:1:0:5EFE:404:404
                                                           0 3 4 i

R3#show bgp ipv6 unicast
BGP table version is 6, local router ID is 3.3.3.3
Status codes: s suppressed, d damped, h history, * valid, > best, i - internal,
              r RIB-failure, S Stale
Origin codes: i - IGP, e - EGP, ? - incomplete
```

```
          Network          Next Hop            Metric LocPrf Weight Path
 *> 3FFE:ABCD:1111:1::/64
                           FECO:ABCD:1234:1:0:5EFE:101:101
                                                             0 2 1 i
 *> 3FFE:ABCD:1111:2::/64
                           FECO:ABCD:1234:1:0:5EFE:202:202
                                              0              0 2 i
 *> 3FFE:ABCD:1111:3::/64
                           ::                 0          32768 i
 *> 3FFE:ABCD:1111:4::/64
                           FECO:ABCD:1234:1:0:5EFE:404:404
                                              0              0 4 i

R4#show bgp ipv6 unicast
BGP table version is 5, local router ID is 4.4.4.4
Status codes: s suppressed, d damped, h history, * valid, > best, i - internal,
              r RIB-failure, S Stale
Origin codes: i - IGP, e - EGP, ? - incomplete

          Network          Next Hop            Metric LocPrf Weight Path
 *> 3FFE:ABCD:1111:1::/64
                           FECO:ABCD:1234:1:0:5EFE:101:101
                                                             0 3 2 1 i
 *> 3FFE:ABCD:1111:2::/64
                           FECO:ABCD:1234:1:0:5EFE:202:202
                                                             0 3 2 i
 *> 3FFE:ABCD:1111:3::/64
                           FECO:ABCD:1234:1:0:5EFE:303:303
                                              0              0 3 i
 *> 3FFE:ABCD:1111:4::/64
                           ::                 0          32768 i
```

Task 5

If you have completed all task as required, this step will be completed with no issues. Use the extended ping function to ping LAN-to-LAN between routers. With the implemented configuration, all prefixes are advertised and received via BGP, as illustrated in the output of the IPv6 routing table on any one of the routers; the example below showing R1s IPv6 RIB:

```
R1#show ipv6 route 3FFE:ABCD:1111:2::/64
IPv6 Routing Table - 9 entries
Codes: C - Connected, L - Local, S - Static, R - RIP, B - BGP
       U - Per-user Static route
       I1 - ISIS L1, I2 - ISIS L2, IA - ISIS interarea, IS - ISIS summary
       O - OSPF intra, OI - OSPF inter, OE1 - OSPF ext 1, OE2 - OSPF ext 2
       ON1 - OSPF NSSA ext 1, ON2 - OSPF NSSA ext 2
B   3FFE:ABCD:1111:2::/64 [20/0]
     via FECO:ABCD:1234:1:0:5EFE:202:202
```

However, notice that the NEXT_HOP addresses are the ISATAP tunnel interfaces, which means that the packets are forwarded out of these tunnels across the IPv4 infrastructure:

```
R1#show ipv6 route FECO:ABCD:1234:1:0:5EFE:202:202
IPv6 Routing Table - 9 entries
Codes: C - Connected, L - Local, S - Static, R - RIP, B - BGP
       U - Per-user Static route
       I1 - ISIS L1, I2 - ISIS L2, IA - ISIS interarea, IS - ISIS summary
       O - OSPF intra, OI - OSPF inter, OE1 - OSPF ext 1, OE2 - OSPF ext 2
       ON1 - OSPF NSSA ext 1, ON2 - OSPF NSSA ext 2
C   FECO:ABCD:1234:1::/64 [0/0]
     via ::, Tunnel0
```

Complete this last task by using the extended ping function on all routers as follows:

```
R1#ping 3FFE:ABCD:1111:2::2 source fastethernet 0/0 repeat 10 size 1500

Type escape sequence to abort.
Sending 10, 1500-byte ICMP Echos to 3FFE:ABCD:1111:2::2, timeout is 2 seconds:
Packet sent with a source address of 3FFE:ABCD:1111:1::1
!!!!!!!!!!
```

```
Success rate is 100 percent (10/10), round-trip min/avg/max = 16/17/20 ms

R1#ping 3FFE:ABCD:1111:3::3 source fastethernet 0/0 repeat 10 size 1500

Type escape sequence to abort.
Sending 10, 1500-byte ICMP Echos to 3FFE:ABCD:1111:3::3, timeout is 2 seconds:
Packet sent with a source address of 3FFE:ABCD:1111:1::1
!!!!!!!!!!
Success rate is 100 percent (10/10), round-trip min/avg/max = 212/215/216 ms

R1#ping 3FFE:ABCD:1111:4::4 source fastethernet 0/0 repeat 10 size 1500

Type escape sequence to abort.
Sending 10, 1500-byte ICMP Echos to 3FFE:ABCD:1111:4::4, timeout is 2 seconds:
Packet sent with a source address of 3FFE:ABCD:1111:1::1
!!!!!!!!!!
Success rate is 100 percent (10/10), round-trip min/avg/max = 404/407/408 ms

R2#ping 3FFE:ABCD:1111:1::1 source fastethernet 0/0 repeat 10 size 1500

Type escape sequence to abort.
Sending 10, 1500-byte ICMP Echos to 3FFE:ABCD:1111:1::1, timeout is 2 seconds:
Packet sent with a source address of 3FFE:ABCD:1111:2::2
!!!!!!!!!!
Success rate is 100 percent (10/10), round-trip min/avg/max = 16/18/20 ms

R2#ping 3FFE:ABCD:1111:3::3 source fastethernet 0/0 repeat 10 size 1500

Type escape sequence to abort.
Sending 10, 1500-byte ICMP Echos to 3FFE:ABCD:1111:3::3, timeout is 2 seconds:
Packet sent with a source address of 3FFE:ABCD:1111:2::2
!!!!!!!!!!
Success rate is 100 percent (10/10), round-trip min/avg/max = 208/208/212 ms

R2#ping 3FFE:ABCD:1111:4::4 source fastethernet 0/0 repeat 10 size 1500

Type escape sequence to abort.
Sending 10, 1500-byte ICMP Echos to 3FFE:ABCD:1111:4::4, timeout is 2 seconds:
Packet sent with a source address of 3FFE:ABCD:1111:2::2
!!!!!!!!!!
Success rate is 100 percent (10/10), round-trip min/avg/max = 400/400/400 ms

R3#ping 3FFE:ABCD:1111:1::1 source fastethernet 0/0 repeat 10 size 1500

Type escape sequence to abort.
Sending 10, 1500-byte ICMP Echos to 3FFE:ABCD:1111:1::1, timeout is 2 seconds:
Packet sent with a source address of 3FFE:ABCD:1111:3::3
!!!!!!!!!!
Success rate is 100 percent (10/10), round-trip min/avg/max = 212/215/220 ms

R3#ping 3FFE:ABCD:1111:2::2 source fastethernet 0/0 repeat 10 size 1500

Type escape sequence to abort.
Sending 10, 1500-byte ICMP Echos to 3FFE:ABCD:1111:2::2, timeout is 2 seconds:
Packet sent with a source address of 3FFE:ABCD:1111:3::3
!!!!!!!!!!
Success rate is 100 percent (10/10), round-trip min/avg/max = 208/208/208 ms

R3#ping 3FFE:ABCD:1111:4::4 source fastethernet 0/0 repeat 10 size 1500

Type escape sequence to abort.
Sending 10, 1500-byte ICMP Echos to 3FFE:ABCD:1111:4::4, timeout is 2 seconds:
Packet sent with a source address of 3FFE:ABCD:1111:3::3
!!!!!!!!!!
Success rate is 100 percent (10/10), round-trip min/avg/max = 208/208/208 ms

R4#ping 3FFE:ABCD:1111:1::1 source fastethernet 0/0 repeat 10 size 1500

Type escape sequence to abort.
Sending 10, 1500-byte ICMP Echos to 3FFE:ABCD:1111:1::1, timeout is 2 seconds:
Packet sent with a source address of 3FFE:ABCD:1111:4::4
!!!!!!!!!!
Success rate is 100 percent (10/10), round-trip min/avg/max = 404/407/408 ms

R4#ping 3FFE:ABCD:1111:2::2 source fastethernet 0/0 repeat 10 size 1500

Type escape sequence to abort.
Sending 10, 1500-byte ICMP Echos to 3FFE:ABCD:1111:2::2, timeout is 2 seconds:
Packet sent with a source address of 3FFE:ABCD:1111:4::4
!!!!!!!!!!
```

```
Success rate is 100 percent (10/10), round-trip min/avg/max = 400/400/404 ms

R4#ping 3FFE:ABCD:1111:3::3 source fastethernet 0/0 repeat 10 size 1500

Type escape sequence to abort.
Sending 10, 1500-byte ICMP Echos to 3FFE:ABCD:1111:3::3, timeout is 2 seconds:
Packet sent with a source address of 3FFE:ABCD:1111:4::4
!!!!!!!!!!
Success rate is 100 percent (10/10), round-trip min/avg/max = 208/208/208 ms
```

FINAL ROUTER CONFIGURATIONS

R1

```
R1#term len 0
R1#sh run
Building configuration...

Current configuration : 1535 bytes
!
version 12.4
service timestamps debug datetime msec
service timestamps log datetime msec
no service password-encryption
!
hostname R1
!
boot-start-marker
boot-end-marker
!
no logging console
!
no aaa new-model
no network-clock-participate slot 1
no network-clock-participate wic 0
ip cef
!
no ip domain lookup
ip auth-proxy max-nodata-conns 3
ip admission max-nodata-conns 3
!
ipv6 unicast-routing
ipv6 cef
!
interface Loopback0
 ip address 1.1.1.1 255.255.255.255
!
interface Tunnel0
 no ip address
 no ip redirects
 ipv6 address FEC0:ABCD:1234:1::/64 eui-64
 no ipv6 nd suppress-ra
 tunnel source Loopback0
 tunnel mode ipv6ip isatap
!
interface FastEthernet0/0
 no ip address
 duplex auto
 speed auto
 ipv6 address 3FFE:ABCD:1111:1::1/64
!
interface Serial0/0
 ip address 10.0.0.1 255.255.255.252
 clock rate 2000000
!
interface Serial0/1
 no ip address
 shutdown
!
router ospf 1
 log-adjacency-changes
 redistribute connected subnets
 network 10.0.0.0 0.255.255.255 area 0
!
router bgp 1
 no synchronization
 bgp router-id 1.1.1.1
 bgp log-neighbor-changes
```

```
 neighbor FEC0:ABCD:1234:1:0:5EFE:202:202 remote-as 2
 no neighbor FEC0:ABCD:1234:1:0:5EFE:202:202 activate
 no auto-summary
 !
 address-family ipv6
  neighbor FEC0:ABCD:1234:1:0:5EFE:202:202 activate
  network 3FFE:ABCD:1111:1::/64
 exit-address-family
!
ip forward-protocol nd
!
no ip http server
no ip http secure-server
!
control-plane
!
line con 0
line aux 0
line vty 0 4
 login
!
end

R1#
```

R2

```
R2#term len 0
R2#sh run
Building configuration...

Current configuration : 1687 bytes
!
version 12.4
service timestamps debug datetime msec
service timestamps log datetime msec
no service password-encryption
!
hostname R2
!
boot-start-marker
boot-end-marker
!
no logging console
!
no aaa new-model
no network-clock-participate slot 1
no network-clock-participate wic 0
ip cef
!
no ip domain lookup
ip auth-proxy max-nodata-conns 3
ip admission max-nodata-conns 3
!
ipv6 unicast-routing
ipv6 cef
!
interface Loopback0
 ip address 2.2.2.2 255.255.255.255
!
interface Tunnel0
 no ip address
 no ip redirects
 ipv6 address FEC0:ABCD:1234:1::/64 eui-64
 no ipv6 nd suppress-ra
 tunnel source Loopback0
 tunnel mode ipv6ip isatap
!
interface FastEthernet0/0
 no ip address
 duplex auto
 speed auto
 ipv6 address 3FFE:ABCD:1111:2::2/64
!
interface Serial0/0
 ip address 10.0.0.2 255.255.255.252
!
interface Serial0/1
 ip address 10.0.0.9 255.255.255.252
!
router ospf 2
```

```
   log-adjacency-changes
   redistribute connected subnets
   network 10.0.0.0 0.255.255.255 area 0
!
router bgp 2
 no synchronization
 bgp router-id 2.2.2.2
 bgp log-neighbor-changes
 neighbor FEC0:ABCD:1234:1:0:5EFE:101:101 remote-as 1
 no neighbor FEC0:ABCD:1234:1:0:5EFE:101:101 activate
 neighbor FEC0:ABCD:1234:1:0:5EFE:303:303 remote-as 3
 no neighbor FEC0:ABCD:1234:1:0:5EFE:303:303 activate
 no auto-summary
 !
 address-family ipv6
  neighbor FEC0:ABCD:1234:1:0:5EFE:101:101 activate
  neighbor FEC0:ABCD:1234:1:0:5EFE:303:303 activate
  network 3FFE:ABCD:1111:2::/64
 exit-address-family
!
ip forward-protocol nd
!
no ip http server
no ip http secure-server
!
control-plane
!
line con 0
line aux 0
line vty 0 4
 login
!
end

R2#
```

R3

```
R3#term len 0
R3#sh run
Building configuration...

Current configuration : 2028 bytes
!
version 12.4
service timestamps debug datetime msec
service timestamps log datetime msec
no service password-encryption
!
hostname R3
!
boot-start-marker
boot-end-marker
!
no logging console
!
no aaa new-model
no network-clock-participate slot 1
no network-clock-participate wic 0
ip cef
!
no ip domain lookup
ip auth-proxy max-nodata-conns 3
ip admission max-nodata-conns 3
!
ipv6 unicast-routing
ipv6 cef
!
interface Loopback0
 ip address 3.3.3.3 255.255.255.255
!
interface Tunnel0
 no ip address
 no ip redirects
 ipv6 address FEC0:ABCD:1234:1::/64 eui-64
 no ipv6 nd suppress-ra
 tunnel source Loopback0
 tunnel mode ipv6ip isatap
!
interface FastEthernet0/0
 no ip address
```

```
 duplex auto
 speed auto
 ipv6 address 3FFE:ABCD:1111:3::3/64
!
interface Serial1/0
 no ip address
 shutdown
 clock rate 128000
!
interface Serial1/1
 ip address 10.0.0.10 255.255.255.252
 clock rate 128000
!
interface Serial1/2
 ip address 10.0.0.13 255.255.255.252
 clock rate 128000
!
interface Serial1/3
 no ip address
 shutdown
!
interface Serial1/4
 no ip address
 shutdown
!
interface Serial1/5
 no ip address
 shutdown
!
interface Serial1/6
 no ip address
 shutdown
!
interface Serial1/7
 no ip address
 shutdown
!
router ospf 3
 log-adjacency-changes
 redistribute connected subnets
 network 10.0.0.0 0.255.255.255 area 0
!
router bgp 3
 no synchronization
 bgp router-id 3.3.3.3
 bgp log-neighbor-changes
 neighbor FEC0:ABCD:1234:1:0:5EFE:202:202 remote-as 2
 no neighbor FEC0:ABCD:1234:1:0:5EFE:202:202 activate
 neighbor FEC0:ABCD:1234:1:0:5EFE:404:404 remote-as 4
 no neighbor FEC0:ABCD:1234:1:0:5EFE:404:404 activate
 no auto-summary
 !
 address-family ipv6
  neighbor FEC0:ABCD:1234:1:0:5EFE:202:202 activate
  neighbor FEC0:ABCD:1234:1:0:5EFE:404:404 activate
  network 3FFE:ABCD:1111:3::/64
 exit-address-family
!
ip forward-protocol nd
!
no ip http server
no ip http secure-server
!
control-plane
!
line con 0
line aux 0
line vty 0 4
 login
!
end

R3#
```

R4

```
R4#term len 0
R4#sh run
Building configuration...

Current configuration : 1516 bytes
```

```
!
version 12.4
service timestamps debug datetime msec
service timestamps log datetime msec
no service password-encryption
!
hostname R4
!
boot-start-marker
boot-end-marker
!
no logging console
!
no aaa new-model
no network-clock-participate slot 1
no network-clock-participate wic 0
ip cef
!
no ip domain lookup
ip auth-proxy max-nodata-conns 3
ip admission max-nodata-conns 3
!
ipv6 unicast-routing
ipv6 cef
!
interface Loopback0
 ip address 4.4.4.4 255.255.255.255
!
interface Tunnel0
 no ip address
 no ip redirects
 ipv6 address FEC0:ABCD:1234:1::/64 eui-64
 no ipv6 nd suppress-ra
 tunnel source Loopback0
 tunnel mode ipv6ip isatap
!
interface FastEthernet0/0
 no ip address
 duplex auto
 speed auto
 ipv6 address 3FFE:ABCD:1111:4::4/64
!
interface Serial0/0
 ip address 10.0.0.14 255.255.255.252
!
interface Serial0/1
 no ip address
 shutdown
!
router ospf 4
 log-adjacency-changes
 redistribute connected subnets
 network 10.0.0.0 0.255.255.255 area 0
!
router bgp 4
 no synchronization
 bgp router-id 4.4.4.4
 bgp log-neighbor-changes
 neighbor FEC0:ABCD:1234:1:0:5EFE:303:303 remote-as 3
 no neighbor FEC0:ABCD:1234:1:0:5EFE:303:303 activate
 no auto-summary
 !
 address-family ipv6
  neighbor FEC0:ABCD:1234:1:0:5EFE:303:303 activate
  network 3FFE:ABCD:1111:4::/64
 exit-address-family
!
ip forward-protocol nd
!
no ip http server
no ip http secure-server
!
control-plane
!
line con 0
line aux 0
line vty 0 4
 login
!
end

R4#
```

CCNP LAB 50

Internet Protocol Version 6 Lab

Lab Objective:

The focus of this lab is to understand tunneling implementation and configuration in Cisco IOS routers. Additional technologies include RIPng convergence and tunnel operation parameters.

Lab Topology:

The lab network topology is illustrated below:

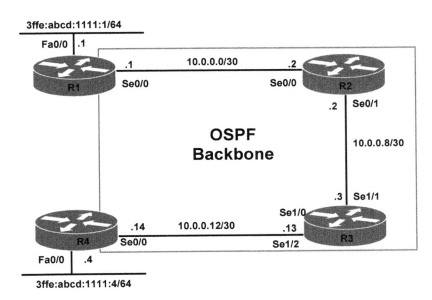

IMPORTANT NOTE: If you are using the www.howtonetwork.net racks, please bring up the LAN interfaces connected to the routers by issuing the no shutdown command on the connected switches. If you are using a home lab with no Switches, you can bring up the LAN interfaces using the following configurations on your routers:

```
interface fastethernet 0/0
  no keepalive
  loopback
  no shutdown
```

Alternately, you can simply connect the interfaces to a hub or switch if you have one available in your own lab.

Task 1

Configure hostnames, IP addressing on all routers as illustrated in the network topology. Next, configure the following Loopback 0 interfaces on R1 and R4:

- R1: Loopback 0 - IP Address 1.1.1.1/32
- R4: Loopback 0 - IP Address 4.4.4.4/32

Task 2

Enable OSPF on all routers as illustrated in the topology. Advertise the Loopback 0 interfaces via OSPF as Type 1 External LSAs. Verify your OSPF configuration.

Task 3

Configure GRE tunnels on all R1 and R4. Use the Loopback 0 interfaces as the tunnel source and destination addresses. Use an IPv6 subnet of your choosing for the GRE tunnel addressing. Verify your configuration using the appropriate commands and pinging across the GRE tunnel.

Task 4

Configure RIPng across the tunnel interfaces between R1 and R4. Advertise the LAN subnets connected to these routers via RIPng. These prefixes should be received with a metric of 10. You are NOT allowed to use offset lists when completing this task. Verify your configuration using the appropriate commands.

Task 5

To prevent incorrect configuration or injection of packets from a foreign source, secure the GRE tunnel between R1 and R4 using the password '1234'. Additionally, ensure that datagrams received out of sequence are dropped and that checksumming is enabled for both of the tunnel interfaces. Verify your configuration using the appropriate commands.

Task 6

To improve RIPng convergence, configure protocol timers so that updates are sent out every 5 seconds. The updates should expire after 10 seconds and the RIPng garbage collection period should happen after 15 seconds. There should be no hold down interval. Verify your configuration using the appropriate commands.

LAB VALIDATION

Task 1

Please refer to previous labs for basic IPv4, IPv6 addressing and hostname configuration. This will not be included in this section to avoid being redundant.

Task 2

Please refer to previous labs for basic OSPF configuration. Following this, verify your OSPF configuration using the show ip ospf neighbor command:

```
R1#show ip ospf neighbor

Neighbor ID     Pri   State           Dead Time   Address         Interface
2.2.2.2           0   FULL/   -       00:00:39    10.0.0.2        Serial0/0

R2#show ip ospf neighbor

Neighbor ID     Pri   State           Dead Time   Address         Interface
3.3.3.3           0   FULL/   -       00:00:35    10.0.0.10       Serial0/1
1.1.1.1           0   FULL/   -       00:00:35    10.0.0.1        Serial0/0

R3#show ip ospf neighbor

Neighbor ID     Pri   State           Dead Time   Address         Interface
4.4.4.4           0   FULL/   -       00:00:31    10.0.0.14       Serial1/2
2.2.2.2           0   FULL/   -       00:00:33    10.0.0.9        Serial1/1

R4#show ip ospf neighbor

Neighbor ID     Pri   State           Dead Time   Address         Interface
3.3.3.3           0   FULL/   -       00:00:38    10.0.0.13       Serial0/0
```

Next, verify that all routing information is correct using the show ip route command:

```
R1#show ip route ospf
     4.0.0.0/32 is subnetted, 1 subnets
O E1    4.4.4.4 [110/929] via 10.0.0.2, 00:00:41, Serial0/0
     10.0.0.0/30 is subnetted, 3 subnets
O        10.0.0.8 [110/128] via 10.0.0.2, 00:05:42, Serial0/0
O        10.0.0.12 [110/909] via 10.0.0.2, 00:05:42, Serial0/0

R2#show ip route ospf
     1.0.0.0/32 is subnetted, 1 subnets
O E1    1.1.1.1 [110/84] via 10.0.0.1, 00:01:07, Serial0/0
     4.0.0.0/32 is subnetted, 1 subnets
O E1    4.4.4.4 [110/865] via 10.0.0.10, 00:01:14, Serial0/1
     10.0.0.0/30 is subnetted, 3 subnets
O        10.0.0.12 [110/845] via 10.0.0.10, 00:06:08, Serial0/1

R3#show ip route ospf
     1.0.0.0/32 is subnetted, 1 subnets
O E1    1.1.1.1 [110/865] via 10.0.0.9, 00:01:22, Serial1/1
     4.0.0.0/32 is subnetted, 1 subnets
O E1    4.4.4.4 [110/801] via 10.0.0.14, 00:01:29, Serial1/2
     10.0.0.0/30 is subnetted, 3 subnets
O        10.0.0.0 [110/845] via 10.0.0.9, 00:06:19, Serial1/1

R4#show ip route ospf
     1.0.0.0/32 is subnetted, 1 subnets
O E1    1.1.1.1 [110/929] via 10.0.0.13, 00:01:34, Serial0/0
     10.0.0.0/30 is subnetted, 3 subnets
O        10.0.0.8 [110/845] via 10.0.0.13, 00:06:27, Serial0/0
O        10.0.0.0 [110/909] via 10.0.0.13, 00:06:27, Serial0/0
```

Task 3

NOTE: Because RIPng uses Link Local addresses as the NEXT HOP address, like other IPv6 IGPs, you do NOT need to actually configure a global Unicast IPv6 address on the tunnel. However, this is included only as recommended practice.

```
R1(config)#interface tunnel 0
R1(config-if)#ipv6 address 2002:abcd:1111:a::1/64
R1(config-if)#tunnel source loopback 0
R1(config-if)#tunnel destination 4.4.4.4
R1(config-if)#tunnel mode gre ip
R1(config-if)#exit

R4(config)#interface tunnel 0
R4(config-if)#ipv6 address 2002:abcd:1111:a::4/64
R4(config-if)#tunnel source loopback 0
R4(config-if)#tunnel destination 1.1.1.1
R4(config-if)#tunnel mode gre ip
R4(config-if)#exit
```

Verify the tunnel configuration using the show interfaces command:

```
R1#show interfaces tunnel 0
Tunnel0 is up, line protocol is up
  Hardware is Tunnel
  MTU 1514 bytes, BW 9 Kbit/sec, DLY 500000 usec,
     reliability 255/255, txload 1/255, rxload 1/255
  Encapsulation TUNNEL, loopback not set
  Keepalive not set
  Tunnel source 1.1.1.1 (Loopback0), destination 4.4.4.4
  Tunnel protocol/transport GRE/IP
    Key disabled, sequencing disabled
    Checksumming of packets disabled
  Tunnel TTL 255
  Fast tunneling enabled
  Tunnel transmit bandwidth 8000 (kbps)
```

```
  Tunnel receive bandwidth 8000 (kbps)

[Truncated Output]
R4#show interfaces tunnel 0
Tunnel0 is up, line protocol is up
  Hardware is Tunnel
  MTU 1514 bytes, BW 9 Kbit/sec, DLY 500000 usec,
     reliability 255/255, txload 1/255, rxload 1/255
  Encapsulation TUNNEL, loopback not set
  Keepalive not set
  Tunnel source 4.4.4.4 (Loopback0), destination 1.1.1.1
  Tunnel protocol/transport GRE/IP
    Key disabled, sequencing disabled
    Checksumming of packets disabled
  Tunnel TTL 255
  Fast tunneling enabled
  Tunnel transmit bandwidth 8000 (kbps)
  Tunnel receive bandwidth 8000 (kbps)
```

Complete the task by pinging across the tunnel interface:

```
R4#ping 2002:abcd:1111:a::1 repeat 10

Type escape sequence to abort.
Sending 10, 100-byte ICMP Echos to 2002:ABCD:1111:A::1, timeout is 2 seconds:
!!!!!!!!!!
Success rate is 100 percent (10/10), round-trip min/avg/max = 36/37/40 ms
```

Task 4

To complete this task you must redistribute the connected LAN interfaces and assign a route metric of 9. This will ensure that the prefixes are received with a metric of 10 by the remote router. Because only a single interface exists, you do not necessarily need to use a route map when configuring redistribution. This task is completed as follows:

```
R1(config)#ipv6 router rip R1-RIP
R1(config-rtr)#redistribute connected metric 9
R1(config-rtr)#exit
R1(config)#interface tunnel 0
R1(config-if)#ipv6 rip R1-RIP enable
R1(config-if)#exit

R4(config)#ipv6 router rip R4-RIP
R4(config-rtr)#redistribute connected metric 9
R4(config-rtr)#exit
R4(config)#interface tunnel 0
R4(config-if)#ipv6 rip R4-RIP enable
R4(config-if)#exit
```

NOTE: The RIPng Tag is locally significant and does NOT need to be the same on all routers. The only parameters that need be the same are the UDP port number and Multicast group.

Verify RIPng routing configuration using the `show ipv6 route` command:

```
R1#show ipv6 route rip
IPv6 Routing Table - 7 entries
Codes: C - Connected, L - Local, S - Static, R - RIP, B - BGP
       U - Per-user Static route
       I1 - ISIS L1, I2 - ISIS L2, IA - ISIS interarea, IS - ISIS summary
       O - OSPF intra, OI - OSPF inter, OE1 - OSPF ext 1, OE2 - OSPF ext 2
       ON1 - OSPF NSSA ext 1, ON2 - OSPF NSSA ext 2
R    3FFE:ABCD:1111:4::/64 [120/10]
     via FE80::20F:23FF:FE5E:F120, Tunnel0

R4#show ipv6 route rip
IPv6 Routing Table - 7 entries
Codes: C - Connected, L - Local, S - Static, R - RIP, B - BGP
       U - Per-user Static route
```

```
        I1 - ISIS L1, I2 - ISIS L2, IA - ISIS interarea, IS - ISIS summary
        O - OSPF intra, OI - OSPF inter, OE1 - OSPF ext 1, OE2 - OSPF ext 2
        ON1 - OSPF NSSA ext 1, ON2 - OSPF NSSA ext 2
R    3FFE:ABCD:1111:1::/64 [120/10]
     via FE80::20F:23FF:FE5E:EC80, Tunnel0
```

Finally, verify that R1 and R4 can ping each other LAN-to-LAN using an extended ping:

```
R1#ping 3FFE:ABCD:1111:4::4 source fastethernet 0/0 repeat 10 size 1500

Type escape sequence to abort.
Sending 10, 1500-byte ICMP Echos to 3FFE:ABCD:1111:4::4, timeout is 2 seconds:
Packet sent with a source address of 3FFE:ABCD:1111:1::1
!!!!!!!!!!
Success rate is 100 percent (10/10), round-trip min/avg/max = 404/406/408 ms

R4#ping 3FFE:ABCD:1111:1::1 source fastethernet 0/0 repeat 10 size 1500

Type escape sequence to abort.
Sending 10, 1500-byte ICMP Echos to 3FFE:ABCD:1111:1::1, timeout is 2 seconds:
Packet sent with a source address of 3FFE:ABCD:1111:4::4
!!!!!!!!!!
Success rate is 100 percent (10/10), round-trip min/avg/max = 404/407/412 ms
```

Task 5

To complete this task, you must configure a tunnel ID key. The tunnel ID keys can be used as a form of weak security to prevent incorrect configuration or injection of packets from a foreign source. The tunnel ID key has to be the same on both ends. This task is completed as follows:

```
R1(config)#interface tunnel 0
R1(config-if)#tunnel key 1234
R1(config-if)#tunnel sequence-datagrams
R1(config-if)#tunnel checksum
R1(config-if)#exit

R4(config)#interface tunnel 0
R4(config-if)#tunnel key 1234
R4(config-if)#tunnel sequence-datagrams
R4(config-if)#tunnel checksum
R4(config-if)#exit
```

Verify your configuration using the show interfaces command:

```
R1#show interfaces tunnel 0
Tunnel0 is up, line protocol is up
  Hardware is Tunnel
  MTU 1514 bytes, BW 9 Kbit/sec, DLY 500000 usec,
     reliability 255/255, txload 1/255, rxload 1/255
  Encapsulation TUNNEL, loopback not set
  Keepalive not set
  Tunnel source 1.1.1.1 (Loopback0), destination 4.4.4.4
  Tunnel protocol/transport GRE/IP
    Key 0x4D2, Order sequence numbers 49/36 (tx/rx)
    Checksumming of packets enabled

[Truncated Output]

R4#show interfaces tunnel 0
Tunnel0 is up, line protocol is up
  Hardware is Tunnel
  MTU 1514 bytes, BW 9 Kbit/sec, DLY 500000 usec,
     reliability 255/255, txload 1/255, rxload 1/255
  Encapsulation TUNNEL, loopback not set
  Keepalive not set
  Tunnel source 4.4.4.4 (Loopback0), destination 1.1.1.1
  Tunnel protocol/transport GRE/IP
    Key 0x4D2, Order sequence numbers 35/46 (tx/rx)
    Checksumming of packets enabled

[Truncated Output]
```

Task 6

```
R1(config)#ipv6 router rip R1-RIP
R1(config-rtr)#timers 5 10 0 15
R1(config-rtr)#exit

R4(config)#ipv6 router rip R4-RIP
R4(config-rtr)#timers 5 10 0 15
R4(config-rtr)#exit
```

Verify your configuration using the **show ipv6 rip \<tag>** command:

```
1#show ipv6 rip R1-RIP
RIP process "R1-RIP", port 521, multicast-group FF02::9, pid 192
     Administrative distance is 120. Maximum paths is 16
     Updates every 5 seconds, expire after 10
     Holddown lasts 0 seconds, garbage collect after 15
     Split horizon is on; poison reverse is off
     Default routes are not generated
     Periodic updates 50, trigger updates 2
  Interfaces:
    Tunnel0
  Redistribution:
    Redistributing protocol connected with metric 9
```

FINAL ROUTER CONFIGURATIONS

R1

```
R1#term len 0
R1#sh run
Building configuration...

Current configuration : 1327 bytes
!
version 12.4
service timestamps debug datetime msec
service timestamps log datetime msec
no service password-encryption
!
hostname R1
!
boot-start-marker
boot-end-marker
!
no logging console
!
no aaa new-model
no network-clock-participate slot 1
no network-clock-participate wic 0
ip cef
!
no ip domain lookup
ip auth-proxy max-nodata-conns 3
ip admission max-nodata-conns 3
!
ipv6 unicast-routing
ipv6 cef
!
interface Loopback0
 ip address 1.1.1.1 255.255.255.255
!
interface Tunnel0
 no ip address
 ipv6 address 2002:ABCD:1111:A::1/64
 ipv6 rip R1-RIP enable
 tunnel source Loopback0
 tunnel destination 4.4.4.4
 tunnel key 1234
 tunnel sequence-datagrams
```

```
 tunnel checksum
!
interface FastEthernet0/0
 no ip address
 duplex auto
 speed auto
 ipv6 address 3FFE:ABCD:1111:1::1/64
!
interface Serial0/0
 ip address 10.0.0.1 255.255.255.252
 clock rate 2000000
!
interface Serial0/1
 no ip address
 shutdown
!
router ospf 1
 log-adjacency-changes
 redistribute connected metric-type 1 subnets
 network 10.0.0.0 0.255.255.255 area 0
!
ip forward-protocol nd
!
no ip http server
no ip http secure-server
!
ipv6 router rip R1-RIP
  timers 5 10 0 15
 redistribute connected metric 9
!
control-plane
!
line con 0
line aux 0
line vty 0 4
 login
!
end

R1#
```

R2

```
R2#term len 0
R2#sh run
Building configuration...

Current configuration : 903 bytes
!
version 12.4
service timestamps debug datetime msec
service timestamps log datetime msec
no service password-encryption
!
hostname R2
!
boot-start-marker
boot-end-marker
!
no logging console
!
no aaa new-model
no network-clock-participate slot 1
no network-clock-participate wic 0
ip cef
!
no ip domain lookup
ip auth-proxy max-nodata-conns 3
ip admission max-nodata-conns 3
!
interface FastEthernet0/0
 no ip address
 shutdown
 duplex auto
```

```
 speed auto
!
interface Serial0/0
 ip address 10.0.0.2 255.255.255.252
!
interface Serial0/1
 ip address 10.0.0.9 255.255.255.252
!
router ospf 2
 log-adjacency-changes
 redistribute connected subnets
 network 10.0.0.0 0.255.255.255 area 0
!
ip forward-protocol nd
!
no ip http server
no ip http secure-server
!
control-plane
!
line con 0
line aux 0
line vty 0 4
 login
!
end

R2#
```

R3

```
R3#term len 0
R3#sh run
Building configuration...

Current configuration : 1244 bytes
!
version 12.4
service timestamps debug datetime msec
service timestamps log datetime msec
no service password-encryption
!
hostname R3
!
boot-start-marker
boot-end-marker
!
no logging console
!
no aaa new-model
no network-clock-participate slot 1
no network-clock-participate wic 0
ip cef
!
no ip domain lookup
ip auth-proxy max-nodata-conns 3
ip admission max-nodata-conns 3
!
interface FastEthernet0/0
 no ip address
 shutdown
 duplex auto
 speed auto
!
interface Serial1/0
 no ip address
 shutdown
 clock rate 128000
!
interface Serial1/1
 ip address 10.0.0.10 255.255.255.252
 clock rate 128000
!
```

```
interface Serial1/2
 ip address 10.0.0.13 255.255.255.252
 clock rate 128000
!
interface Serial1/3
 no ip address
 shutdown
!
interface Serial1/4
 no ip address
 shutdown
!
interface Serial1/5
 no ip address
 shutdown
!
interface Serial1/6
 no ip address
 shutdown
!
interface Serial1/7
 no ip address
 shutdown
!
router ospf 3
 log-adjacency-changes
 redistribute connected subnets
 network 10.0.0.0 0.255.255.255 area 0
!
ip forward-protocol nd
!
no ip http server
no ip http secure-server
!
control-plane
!
line con 0
line aux 0
line vty 0 4
 login
!
end

R3#
```

R4

```
R4#term len 0
R4#sh run
Building configuration...

Current configuration : 1308 bytes
!
version 12.4
service timestamps debug datetime msec
service timestamps log datetime msec
no service password-encryption
!
hostname R4
!
boot-start-marker
boot-end-marker
!
no logging console
!
no aaa new-model
no network-clock-participate slot 1
no network-clock-participate wic 0
ip cef
!
no ip domain lookup
ip auth-proxy max-nodata-conns 3
ip admission max-nodata-conns 3
```

```
!
ipv6 unicast-routing
ipv6 cef
!
interface Loopback0
 ip address 4.4.4.4 255.255.255.255
!
interface Tunnel0
 no ip address
 ipv6 address 2002:ABCD:1111:A::4/64
 ipv6 rip R4-RIP enable
 tunnel source Loopback0
 tunnel destination 1.1.1.1
 tunnel key 1234
 tunnel sequence-datagrams
 tunnel checksum
!
interface FastEthernet0/0
 no ip address
 duplex auto
 speed auto
 ipv6 address 3FFE:ABCD:1111:4::4/64
!
interface Serial0/0
 ip address 10.0.0.14 255.255.255.252
!
interface Serial0/1
 no ip address
 shutdown
!
router ospf 4
 log-adjacency-changes
 redistribute connected metric-type 1 subnets
 network 10.0.0.0 0.255.255.255 area 0
!
ip forward-protocol nd
!
no ip http server
no ip http secure-server
!
ipv6 router rip R4-RIP
  timers 5 10 0 15
 redistribute connected metric 9
!
control-plane
!
line con 0
line aux 0
line vty 0 4
 login
!
end

R4#
```

CCNP LAB 51

Cisco IOS IP SLA and FHRP Lab

Lab Objective:

The focus of this lab is to understand Cisco IOS IP SLA Operations and FHRP implementation and configuration in Cisco IOS routers. Additional technologies include EOT and preemption.

Lab Topology:

The lab network topology is illustrated below:

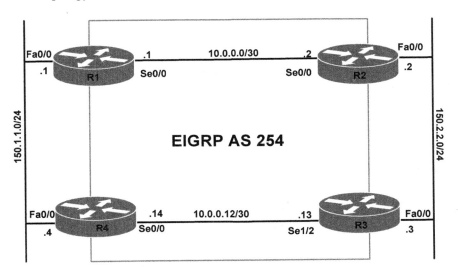

IMPORTANT NOTE: If you are using the www.howtonetwork.net racks, please bring up the LAN interfaces connected to the routers by issuing the no shutdown command on the connected switches. If you are using a home lab with no Switches, you can bring up the LAN interfaces using the following configurations on your routers:

```
interface fastethernet 0/0
  no keepalive
  loopback
  no shutdown
```

Alternately, you can simply connect the interfaces to a hub or switch if you have one available in your own lab.

Task 1

Configure hostnames, IP addressing on all routers as illustrated in the network topology. Next, configure the following Loopback 0 interfaces on R2 R2: Loopback 0 - IP Address 2.2.2.2/32

Task 2

Enable EIGRP on the WAN interfaces of all routers as illustrated in the topology. Advertise the FastEthernet 0/0 and Loopback 0 subnet as External routes. Verify your EIGRP configuration.

Task 3

Configure HSRP on the LAN segment between R1 and R4. Use a VIP of 150.1.1.254. Configure R1 with a priority of 200 and R4 with a priority of 150. Verify your HSRP configuration.

Task 4

Configure Cisco IOS IP SLA Operations so that when R1 loses the route to the 2.2.2.2/32 prefix, it reduces its HSRP priority such that R4 becomes primary gateway for the HSRP group. This solution should be configured as follows:

- R1 should open an HTTP (port 80) session to the IP address 2.2.2.2/32 only every 5 seconds
- The connection should be sourced from Serial 0/0
- The IP SLA Operation should have a timeout of 10 seconds
- R1 should wait for 6 secs after a failed Operation to lower the configured HSRP priority
- R1 should wait for 10 secs after the 2.2.2.2/32 prefix is reachable again to become active
- Do NOT use HSRP-specific commands to influence preemption timers
- Use any Cisco IP SLA Operation number and Cisco EOT number of your choice

Verify your configuration using the appropriate commands. Test your solution by disabling the link between R1 and R2 and verify IP SLA and HSRP operation and functionality.

Task 5

Configure VRRP on the LAN segment between R2 and R3. Use a VIP of 150.2.2.254. Configure R2 with a priority of 200 and R3 with a priority of 150. Verify your VRRP configuration.

Task 6

Configure VRRP on R2 so that when the Serial 0/0 interface goes down, the priority will then be lowered so that R4 can become master router. Verify and test your VRRP configuration.

LAB VALIDATION

Task 1

Please refer to previous labs for basic IPv4, IPv6 addressing and hostname configuration. This will not be included in this section to avoid being redundant.

Task 2

Please refer to previous labs for basic EIGRP configuration. Following this, verify your EIGRP configuration using the `show ip eigrp neighbors` command:

```
R1#show ip eigrp neighbors
IP-EIGRP neighbors for process 254
H   Address              Interface      Hold Uptime   SRTT   RTO  Q  Seq
                                        (sec)         (ms)        Cnt Num
0   10.0.0.2             Se0/0           14 00:00:47    4    200  0  6

R2#show ip eigrp neighbors
IP-EIGRP neighbors for process 254
H   Address              Interface      Hold Uptime   SRTT   RTO  Q  Seq
                                        (sec)         (ms)        Cnt Num
0   10.0.0.1             Se0/0           11 00:00:49    3    200  0  3

R3#show ip eigrp neighbors
IP-EIGRP neighbors for process 254
H   Address              Interface      Hold Uptime   SRTT   RTO  Q  Seq
                                        (sec)         (ms)        Cnt Num
0   10.0.0.14            Se1/2           14 00:00:20    9   1140  0  5

R4#show ip eigrp neighbors
IP-EIGRP neighbors for process 254
```

```
H    Address              Interface         Hold Uptime   SRTT    RTO   Q  Seq
                                            (sec)         (ms)          Cnt Num
0    10.0.0.13            Se0/0             10  00:00:22   13     200   0  3
```

Next, verify that all routing information is correct using the show ip route command:

```
R1#show ip route eigrp
       2.0.0.0/32 is subnetted, 1 subnets
D        2.2.2.2 [90/2297856] via 10.0.0.2, 00:03:43, Serial0/0
       150.2.0.0/24 is subnetted, 1 subnets
D EX    150.2.2.0 [170/2172416] via 10.0.0.2, 00:03:41, Serial0/0

R2#show ip route eigrp
       150.1.0.0/24 is subnetted, 1 subnets
D EX    150.1.1.0 [170/2172416] via 10.0.0.1, 00:03:52, Serial0/0

R3#show ip route eigrp
       150.1.0.0/24 is subnetted, 1 subnets
D EX    150.1.1.0 [170/20514560] via 10.0.0.14, 00:03:20, Serial1/2
R4#show ip route eigrp
       150.2.0.0/24 is subnetted, 1 subnets
D EX    150.2.2.0 [170/2172416] via 10.0.0.13, 00:03:25, Serial0/0
```

Task 3

```
R1(config)#interface fastethernet 0/0
R1(config-if)#standby 1 ip 150.1.1.254
R1(config-if)#standby 1 priority 200
R1(config-if)#exit

R4(config)#interface fastethernet 0/0
R4(config-if)#standby 1 ip 150.1.1.254
R4(config-if)#standby 1 priority 150
R4(config-if)#exit
```

Verify HSRP using the show standby <group> [brief] command on the two routers. You should keep in mind that, by default, preemption is not enabled for HSRP:

```
R1#show stand brief
                      P indicates configured to preempt.
                      |
Interface  Grp Prio P State    Active    Standby       Virtual IP
Fa0/0      1   200  Active    local     150.1.1.4     150.1.1.254

R4#show stand brief
                      P indicates configured to preempt.
                      |
Interface  Grp Prio P State     Active     Standby      Virtual IP
Fa0/0      1   150   Standby  150.1.1.1  local        150.1.1.254
```

Task 4

The requirements of this task are three-fold. First, you need to configure the Cisco IOS IP SLA Operation to ping the 2.2.2.2/32 address every 2 seconds. It is important to remember that the default timeout value is 5 seconds (5000 milliseconds). Therefore, you specify a frequency of 2 seconds, you first need to lower the timeout value to a value less than 5000 milliseconds otherwise Cisco IOS software will print out the following error message on the device console:

```
R1(config-sla-monitor-echo)#frequency 2
%Illegal Value: Cannot set Frequency to be less than Timeout
```

This first part of this task, i.e. the IP SLA Operation configuration, is completed as follows:

```
R1(config)#ip sla monitor 1
R1(config-sla-monitor)#$ipaddr 2.2.2.2 dest-port 80 source-ipaddr 10.0.0.1
R1(config-sla-monitor-tcp)#timeout 10
```

```
R1(config-sla-monitor-tcp)#frequency 5
R1(config-sla-monitor-tcp)#exit
R1(config)#ip sla monitor schedule 1 start-time now life forever
R1(config)#exit
```

Because R2 is a Cisco IOS device, you must enable RTR | IP SLA Responder on this device:

```
R2(config)#ip sla monitor responder type tcpConnect ipaddress 2.2.2.2 port 80
```

Verify the operation statistics using the show ip sla monitor statistics command:

```
R1#show ip sla monitor statistics 1
Round trip time (RTT)    Index 1
        Latest RTT: 8 ms
Latest operation start time: 21:39:36.295 CST Tue May 31 2011
Latest operation return code: OK
Number of successes: 22
Number of failures: 0
Operation time to live: Forever
```

Verify the responder state using the show ip sla monitor responder command:

```
R2#show ip sla monitor responder
IP SLA Monitor Responder is: Enabled
Number of control message received: 29 Number of errors: 0
Recent sources:
        10.0.0.1 [12:02:07.595 UTC Sun May 15 2011]
        10.0.0.1 [12:02:02.595 UTC Sun May 15 2011]
        10.0.0.1 [12:01:57.595 UTC Sun May 15 2011]
        10.0.0.1 [12:01:52.595 UTC Sun May 15 2011]
        10.0.0.1 [12:01:47.595 UTC Sun May 15 2011]
Recent error sources:

tcpConnect Responder:
  IP Address            Port
  2.2.2.2                80
```

The second part of this task requires that you configure Enhanced Object Tracking or EOT. Here is where you specify the up and down delay values. Complete this task as follows:

```
R1(config)#track 1 rtr 1 reachability
R1(config-track)#delay down 6
R1(config-track)#delay up 10
R1(config-track)#exit
```

Verify your configuration using the show track <object number> command:

```
R1#show track 1
Track 1
  Response Time Reporter 1 reachability
  Reachability is Up
   7 changes, last change 00:05:00
  Delay up 10 secs, down 6 secs
  Latest operation return code: OK
  Latest RTT (millisecs) 8
```

The final requirement of this configuration is to configure HSRP so that preemption is enabled and that the priority of R1 is lowered enough to allow R4 to become active gateway. This last task is completed as follows:

```
R1(config)#interface fastethernet 0/0
R1(config-if)#standby 1 preempt
R1(config-if)#standby 1 track 1 decrement 51
R1(config-if)#exit

R4(config)#interface fastethernet 0/0
R4(config-if)#standby 1 preempt
R4(config-if)#exit
```

Verify your configuration using the show standby command on both routers:

```
R1#show standby fastethernet 0/0 1
FastEthernet0/0 - Group 1
  State is Active
    2 state changes, last state change 00:28:58
  Virtual IP address is 150.1.1.254
  Active virtual MAC address is 0000.0c07.ac01
    Local virtual MAC address is 0000.0c07.ac01 (v1 default)
  Hello time 3 sec, hold time 10 sec
    Next hello sent in 1.456 secs
  Preemption enabled
  Active router is local
  Standby router is 150.1.1.4, priority 150 (expires in 7.152 sec)
  Priority 200 (configured 200)
    Track object 1 state Up decrement 51
  IP redundancy name is "hsrp-Fa0/0-1" (default)

R4#show standby fastethernet 0/0 1
FastEthernet0/0 - Group 1
  State is Standby
    1 state change, last state change 00:29:12
  Virtual IP address is 150.1.1.254
  Active virtual MAC address is 0000.0c07.ac01
    Local virtual MAC address is 0000.0c07.ac01 (v1 default)
  Hello time 3 sec, hold time 10 sec
    Next hello sent in 0.000 secs
  Preemption enabled
  Active router is 150.1.1.1, priority 200 (expires in 8.288 sec)
  Standby router is local
  Priority 150 (configured 150)
  IP redundancy name is "hsrp-Fa0/0-1" (default)
```

Finally, test your solution by enabling logging and shutting down the R1-R2 link:

```
R1(config)#logging consol debugging
R1(config)#interface serial 0/0
R1(config-if)#shutdown
R1(config-if)#
R1(config-if)#
R1(config-if)#
Jun  1 02:46:51.175: %DUAL-5-NBRCHANGE: IP-EIGRP(0) 254: Neighbor 10.0.0.2
(Serial0/0) is down: interface down
Jun  1 02:46:53.151: %LINK-5-CHANGED: Interface Serial0/0, changed state to
administratively down
Jun  1 02:46:54.151: %LINEPROTO-5-UPDOWN: Line protocol on Interface Serial0/0,
changed state to down
Jun  1 02:47:13.495: %TRACKING-5-STATE: 1 rtr 1 reachability Up->Down
Jun  1 02:47:15.551: %HSRP-5-STATECHANGE: FastEthernet0/0 Grp 1 state Active -> Speak
Jun  1 02:47:25.551: %HSRP-5-STATECHANGE: FastEthernet0/0 Grp 1 state Speak ->
Standby
```

Next, check the HSRP gateway states using the show standby command on both routers:

```
R1#show standby fastethernet 0/0 1
FastEthernet0/0 - Group 1
  State is Standby
    16 state changes, last state change 00:00:31
  Virtual IP address is 150.1.1.254
  Active virtual MAC address is 0000.0c07.ac01
    Local virtual MAC address is 0000.0c07.ac01 (v1 default)
  Hello time 3 sec, hold time 10 sec
    Next hello sent in 1.808 secs
  Preemption enabled
  Active router is 150.1.1.4, priority 150 (expires in 7.808 sec)
  Standby router is local
  Priority 149 (configured 200)
    Track object 1 state Down decrement 51
  IP redundancy name is "hsrp-Fa0/0-1" (default)

R4#show standby fastethernet 0/0 1
FastEthernet0/0 - Group 1
```

```
State is Active
  14 state changes, last state change 00:00:49
Virtual IP address is 150.1.1.254
Active virtual MAC address is 0000.0c07.ac01
  Local virtual MAC address is 0000.0c07.ac01 (v1 default)
Hello time 3 sec, hold time 10 sec
  Next hello sent in 1.076 secs
Preemption enabled
Active router is local
Standby router is 150.1.1.1, priority 149 (expires in 9.072 sec)
Priority 150 (configured 150)
IP redundancy name is "hsrp-Fa0/0-1" (default)
```

Finally, verify your configuration in the reverse direction by bringing up the Serial 0/0 interface:

```
R1(config)#logging console debugging
R1(config)#interface serial 0/0
R1(config-if)#no shutdown
R1(config-if)#
R1(config-if)#
R1(config-if)#
Jun  1 02:49:50.243: %LINK-3-UPDOWN: Interface Serial0/0, changed state to up
Jun  1 02:49:51.163: %DUAL-5-NBRCHANGE: IP-EIGRP(0) 254: Neighbor 10.0.0.2
(Serial0/0) is up: new adjacency
Jun  1 02:49:51.243: %LINEPROTO-5-UPDOWN: Line protocol on Interface Serial0/0,
changed state to up
Jun  1 02:50:02.495: %TRACKING-5-STATE: 1 rtr 1 reachability Down->Up
Jun  1 02:50:03.551: %HSRP-5-STATECHANGE: FastEthernet0/0 Grp 1 state Standby ->
Active
```

Task 5

```
R2(config)#interface fastethernet 0/0
R2(config-if)#vrrp 1 ip 150.2.2.254
R2(config-if)#vrrp 1 priority 200
R2(config-if)#exit

R3(config)#interface fastethernet 0/0
R3(config-if)#vrrp 1 ip 150.2.2.254
R3(config-if)#vrrp 1 priority 150
R3(config-if)#exit
```

Verify VRRP configuration using the show vrrp command on both routers:

```
R2#show vrrp interface fastethernet 0/0 group 1
FastEthernet0/0 - Group 1
  State is Master
  Virtual IP address is 150.2.2.254
  Virtual MAC address is 0000.5e00.0101
  Advertisement interval is 1.000 sec
  Preemption enabled
  Priority is 200
  Master Router is 150.2.2.2 (local), priority is 200
  Master Advertisement interval is 1.000 sec
  Master Down interval is 3.218 sec

R3#show vrrp interface fastethernet 0/0 group 1
FastEthernet0/0 - Group 1
  State is Backup
  Virtual IP address is 150.2.2.254
  Virtual MAC address is 0000.5e00.0101
  Advertisement interval is 1.000 sec
  Preemption enabled
  Priority is 150
  Master Router is 150.2.2.2, priority is 200
  Master Advertisement interval is 1.000 sec
  Master Down interval is 3.414 sec (expires in 3.190 sec)
```

Task 6

To complete this task, you need to configure EOT to track Serial0/0s line protocol. This tracked object should then be referenced under the VRRP interface configuration. By default, VRRP preemption is enabled and no explicit configuration is required. The only other thing required is that the priority be decremented sufficiently to allow R3 to become virtual router master:

```
R2(config)#track 1 interface serial 0/0 line-protocol
R2(config-track)#exit
R2(config)#interface fastethernet 0/0
R2(config-if)#vrrp 1 track 1 decrement 51
R2(config-if)#exit
```

Next, verify your configuration using the show vrrp command:

```
R2#show vrrp interface fastethernet 0/0 group 1
FastEthernet0/0 - Group 1
  State is Master
  Virtual IP address is 150.2.2.254
  Virtual MAC address is 0000.5e00.0101
  Advertisement interval is 1.000 sec
  Preemption enabled
  Priority is 200
    Track object 1 state Up decrement 51
  Master Router is 150.2.2.2 (local), priority is 200
  Master Advertisement interval is 1.000 sec
  Master Down interval is 3.218 sec
```

Next, test your configuration by enabling logging and shutting down the Serial0/0 interface:

```
R2(config)#logging console debugging
R2(config)#interface serial 0/0
R2(config-if)#shutdown
R2(config-if)#
*May 15 12:36:47.011: %TRACKING-5-STATE: 1 interface Se0/0 line-protocol Up->Down
*May 15 12:36:47.039: %DUAL-5-NBRCHANGE: IP-EIGRP(0) 254: Neighbor 10.0.0.1
(Serial0/0) is down: interface down
*May 15 12:36:49.011: %LINK-5-CHANGED: Interface Serial0/0, changed state to
administratively down
*May 15 12:36:50.011: %LINEPROTO-5-UPDOWN: Line protocol on Interface Serial0/0,
changed state to down
*May 15 12:36:50.183: %VRRP-6-STATECHANGE: Fa0/0 Grp 1 state Master -> Backup
```

Use the show vrrp command again to verify the VRRP states on both routers:

```
R2#show vrrp interface fastethernet 0/0 group 1
FastEthernet0/0 - Group 1
  State is Backup
  Virtual IP address is 150.2.2.254
  Virtual MAC address is 0000.5e00.0101
  Advertisement interval is 1.000 sec
  Preemption enabled
  Priority is 149 (cfgd 200)
    Track object 1 state Down decrement 51
  Master Router is 150.2.2.3, priority is 150
  Master Advertisement interval is 1.000 sec
  Master Down interval is 3.218 sec (expires in 3.026 sec)

R3#show vrrp interface fastethernet 0/0 group 1
FastEthernet0/0 - Group 1
  State is Master
  Virtual IP address is 150.2.2.254
  Virtual MAC address is 0000.5e00.0101
  Advertisement interval is 1.000 sec
  Preemption enabled
  Priority is 150
  Master Router is 150.2.2.3 (local), priority is 150
  Master Advertisement interval is 1.000 sec
  Master Down interval is 3.414 sec
```

Finally, test your configuration in the reverse order by bringing up the Serial0/0 interface:

```
R2(config)#interface serial 0/0
R2(config-if)#no shutdown
R2(config-if)#
R2(config-if)#
*May 15 12:38:42.939: %LINK-3-UPDOWN: Interface Serial0/0, changed state to up
*May 15 12:38:42.939: %TRACKING-5-STATE: 1 interface Se0/0 line-protocol Down->Up
*May 15 12:38:43.939: %LINEPROTO-5-UPDOWN: Line protocol on Interface Serial0/0,
changed state to up
*May 15 12:38:44.731: %DUAL-5-NBRCHANGE: IP-EIGRP(0) 254: Neighbor 10.0.0.1
(Serial0/0) is up: new adjacency
*May 15 12:38:45.327: %VRRP-6-STATECHANGE: Fa0/0 Grp 1 state Backup -> Master
```

FINAL ROUTER CONFIGURATIONS

R1

```
R1#term len 0
R1#sh run
Building configuration...

Current configuration : 1293 bytes
!
! Last configuration change at 22:13:55 CST Tue May 31 2011
!
version 12.4
service timestamps debug datetime msec
service timestamps log datetime msec
no service password-encryption
!
hostname R1
!
boot-start-marker
boot-end-marker
!
no logging console
!
no aaa new-model
clock timezone CST -5
no network-clock-participate slot 1
no network-clock-participate wic 0
ip cef
!
no ip domain lookup
ip auth-proxy max-nodata-conns 3
ip admission max-nodata-conns 3
ip sla monitor 1
 type tcpConnect dest-ipaddr 2.2.2.2 dest-port 80 source-ipaddr 10.0.0.1
 timeout 10
 frequency 5
ip sla monitor schedule 1 life forever start-time now
!
track 1 rtr 1 reachability
 delay down 6 up 10
!
interface FastEthernet0/0
 ip address 150.1.1.1 255.255.255.0
 duplex auto
 speed auto
 standby 1 ip 150.1.1.254
 standby 1 priority 200
 standby 1 preempt
 standby 1 track 1 decrement 51
!
interface Serial0/0
 ip address 10.0.0.1 255.255.255.252
 clock rate 2000000
!
interface Serial0/1
```

```
 no ip address
 shutdown
!
router eigrp 254
 redistribute connected
 network 10.0.0.0
 no auto-summary
!
ip forward-protocol nd
!
no ip http server
no ip http secure-server
!
control-plane
!
line con 0
line aux 0
line vty 0 4
 login
!
end

R1#
```

R2

```
R2#term len 0
R2#sh run
Building configuration...

Current configuration : 1154 bytes
!
version 12.4
service timestamps debug datetime msec
service timestamps log datetime msec
no service password-encryption
!
hostname R2
!
boot-start-marker
boot-end-marker
!
no logging console
!
no aaa new-model
no network-clock-participate slot 1
no network-clock-participate wic 0
ip cef
!
no ip domain lookup
ip auth-proxy max-nodata-conns 3
ip admission max-nodata-conns 3
ip sla monitor responder
ip sla monitor responder type tcpConnect ipaddress 2.2.2.2 port 80
!
track 1 interface Serial0/0 line-protocol
!
interface Loopback0
 ip address 2.2.2.2 255.255.255.255
!
interface FastEthernet0/0
 ip address 150.2.2.2 255.255.255.0
 duplex auto
 speed auto
 vrrp 1 ip 150.2.2.254
 vrrp 1 priority 200
 vrrp 1 track 1 decrement 51
!
interface Serial0/0
 ip address 10.0.0.2 255.255.255.252
!
interface Serial0/1
 no ip address
```

```
 shutdown
!
router eigrp 254
 redistribute connected
 network 2.0.0.0
 network 10.0.0.0
 no auto-summary
!
ip forward-protocol nd
!
no ip http server
no ip http secure-server
!
control-plane
!
line con 0
line aux 0
line vty 0 4
 login
!
end

R2#
```

R3

```
R3#term len 0
R3#sh run
Building configuration...

Current configuration : 1254 bytes
!
version 12.4
service timestamps debug datetime msec
service timestamps log datetime msec
no service password-encryption
!
hostname R3
!
boot-start-marker
boot-end-marker
!
no logging console
!
no aaa new-model
no network-clock-participate slot 1
no network-clock-participate wic 0
ip cef
!
no ip domain lookup
ip auth-proxy max-nodata-conns 3
ip admission max-nodata-conns 3
!
interface FastEthernet0/0
 ip address 150.2.2.3 255.255.255.0
 duplex auto
 speed auto
 vrrp 1 ip 150.2.2.254
 vrrp 1 priority 150
!
interface Serial1/0
 no ip address
 shutdown
 clock rate 128000
!
interface Serial1/1
 no ip address
 shutdown
 clock rate 128000
!
interface Serial1/2
 ip address 10.0.0.13 255.255.255.252
 clock rate 128000
```

```
!
interface Serial1/3
 no ip address
 shutdown
!
interface Serial1/4
 no ip address
 shutdown
!
interface Serial1/5
 no ip address
 shutdown
!
interface Serial1/6
 no ip address
 shutdown
!
interface Serial1/7
 no ip address
 shutdown
!
router eigrp 254
 redistribute connected
 network 10.0.0.0
 no auto-summary
!
ip forward-protocol nd
!
no ip http server
no ip http secure-server
!
control-plane
!
line con 0
line aux 0
line vty 0 4
 login
!
end

R3#
```

R4

```
R4#term len 0
R4#sh run
Building configuration...

Current configuration : 940 bytes
!
version 12.4
service timestamps debug datetime msec
service timestamps log datetime msec
no service password-encryption
!
hostname R4
!
boot-start-marker
boot-end-marker
!
no logging console
!
no aaa new-model
no network-clock-participate slot 1
no network-clock-participate wic 0
ip cef
!
no ip domain lookup
ip auth-proxy max-nodata-conns 3
ip admission max-nodata-conns 3
!
interface FastEthernet0/0
 ip address 150.1.1.4 255.255.255.0
```

```
 duplex auto
 speed auto
 standby 1 ip 150.1.1.254
 standby 1 priority 150
 standby 1 preempt
!
interface Serial0/0
 ip address 10.0.0.14 255.255.255.252
!
interface Serial0/1
 no ip address
 shutdown
!
router eigrp 254
 redistribute connected
 network 10.0.0.0
 no auto-summary
!
ip forward-protocol nd
!
no ip http server
no ip http secure-server
!
control-plane
!
line con 0
line aux 0
line vty 0 4
 login
!
end

R4#
```

CCNP LAB 52

Cisco IOS EOT and FHRP Lab

Lab Objective:

The focus of this lab is to understand Enhanced Object Tracking and FHRP implementation and configuration in Cisco IOS routers. Additional technologies include IRDP.

Lab Topology:

The lab network topology is illustrated below:

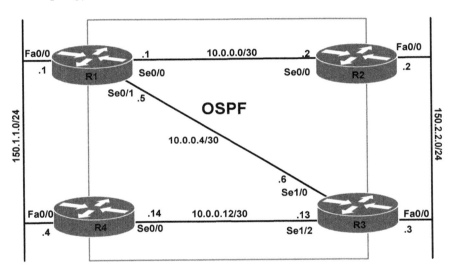

IMPORTANT NOTE: If you are using the **www.howtonetwork.net racks**, please bring up the LAN interfaces connected to the routers by issuing the no shutdown command on the connected switches. If you are using a home lab with no Switches, you can bring up the LAN interfaces using the following configurations on your routers:

```
interface fastethernet 0/0
  no keepalive
  loopback
  no shutdown
```

Alternately, you can simply connect the interfaces to a hub or switch if you have one available in your own lab.

Task 1

Configure hostnames, IP addressing on all routers as illustrated in the network topology.

Task 2

Enable OSPF on the WAN interfaces of all routers as illustrated in the topology. Use OSPF area 0 in your configuration. Advertise the FastEthernet 0/0 subnets as Type 1 OSPF External routes. Verify your OSPF configuration using the appropriate commands.

Task 3

Configure VRRP on the LAN segment between R1 and R4. Use a VIP of 150.1.1.254. Configure R1 with a priority of 110 and R4 with a priority of 100. Verify your VRRP configuration.

Task 4

Configure Enhanced Object Tracking so that when BOTH the Serial 0/0 and Serial 0/1 interfaces on R1 fail, R4 assumes the route of virtual router master.

Verify your configuration using the appropriate commands. Test your solution by disabling the R1-R2 and R1-R3 links and verify EOT and VRRP operation and functionality.

Task 5

Configure IRDP on the LAN segment between R2 and R3. R2 should be the preferred gateway for devices residing on this subnet. IRDP Broadcasts should be sent only when the routers are solicited by clients. These advertisements should be valid for no more than 10 seconds. Verify your configuration using the appropriate commands.

LAB VALIDATION

Task 1

Please refer to previous labs for basic IPv4, IPv6 addressing and hostname configuration. This will not be included in this section to avoid being redundant.

Task 2

Please refer to previous labs for basic OSPF configuration. Following this, verify your OSPF configuration using the show ip ospf neighbor and show ip route commands.

Task 3

By default, the VRRP priority is 100; therefore, no explicit configuration is required to specify this value of R4. This task is completed as follows:

```
R1(config)#interface fastethernet 0/0
R1(config-if)#vrrp 1 priority 110
R1(config-if)#vrrp 1 ip 150.1.1.254
R1(config-if)#exit

R4(config)#interface fastethernet 0/0
R4(config-if)#vrrp 1 ip 150.1.1.254
R4(config-if)#exit
```

Following this configuration, verify VRRP status using the show vrrp command:

```
R1#show vrrp interface fastethernet 0/0 group 1
FastEthernet0/0 - Group 1
  State is Master
  Virtual IP address is 150.1.1.254
  Virtual MAC address is 0000.5e00.0101
  Advertisement interval is 1.000 sec
  Preemption enabled
  Priority is 110
  Master Router is 150.1.1.1 (local), priority is 110
  Master Advertisement interval is 1.000 sec
  Master Down interval is 3.570 sec

R4#show vrrp interface fastethernet 0/0 group 1
FastEthernet0/0 - Group 1
  State is Backup
```

```
Virtual IP address is 150.1.1.254
Virtual MAC address is 0000.5e00.0101
Advertisement interval is 1.000 sec
Preemption enabled
Priority is 100
Master Router is 150.1.1.1, priority is 110
Master Advertisement interval is 1.000 sec
Master Down interval is 3.609 sec (expires in 2.869 sec)
```

Task 4

This task requires the use of BOOLEAN logic in conjunction with EOT. Cisco IOS supports the Boolean 'AND' and Boolean 'OR' functions. When a tracked list has been assigned a Boolean 'AND' function, it means that each object defined within a subset must be in an up state so that the tracked object can become up. However, when the tracked list has been assigned a Boolean 'OR' function, it means that at least one object defined within a subset must be in an up state so that the tracked object can become up.

Because this task requires that R1 decrement its priority such that R4 becomes virtual router master only after BOTH the Serial0/0 and Serial0/1 interfaces are down, we need to use a Boolean 'OR' function. In other words, as long as one of the interfaces is up, the tracked object, the router should not decrement its VRRP priority. This task is completed as follows:

```
R1(config)#track 100 interface serial 0/0 line-protocol
R1(config-track)#exit
R1(config)#track 101 interface serial 0/1 line-protocol
R1(config-track)#exit
R1(config)#track 102 list boolean or
R1(config-track)#object 100
R1(config-track)#object 101
R1(config-track)#exit
R1(config)#interface fastethernet 0/0
R1(config-if)#vrrp 1 track 102 decrement 20
R1(config-if)#exit
```

Following this, verify the EOT configuration using the show track command:

```
R1#show track
Track 100
  Interface Serial0/0 line-protocol
  Line protocol is Up
    3 changes, last change 00:04:43
  Tracked by:
    Track-list 102

Track 101
  Interface Serial0/1 line-protocol
  Line protocol is Up
    3 changes, last change 00:04:30
  Tracked by:
    Track-list 102

Track 102
  List boolean or
  Boolean OR is Up
    2 changes, last change 00:05:22
    object 100 Up
    object 101 Up
  Tracked by:
    VRRP FastEthernet0/0 1
```

Next, verify VRRP status using the show vrrp command:

```
R1#show vrrp interface fastethernet 0/0 group 1
FastEthernet0/0 - Group 1
  State is Master
  Virtual IP address is 150.1.1.254
  Virtual MAC address is 0000.5e00.0101
  Advertisement interval is 1.000 sec
```

```
  Preemption enabled
  Priority is 110
    Track object 102 state Up decrement 20
  Master Router is 150.1.1.1 (local), priority is 110
  Master Advertisement interval is 1.000 sec
  Master Down interval is 3.570 sec
```

Following this, test your configuration by first shutting down the Serial 0/0 interface on R1. Due to the EOT configuration, this will NOT cause the router to decrement its priority:

```
R1(config)#interface serial 0/0
R1(config-if)#shut
R1(config-if)#exit
R1(config)#do show track
Track 100
  Interface Serial0/0 line-protocol
  Line protocol is Down (hw admin-down)
    4 changes, last change 00:00:06
  Tracked by:
    Track-list 102

Track 101
  Interface Serial0/1 line-protocol
  Line protocol is Up
    3 changes, last change 00:05:16
  Tracked by:
    Track-list 102

Track 102
  List boolean or
  Boolean OR is Up
    2 changes, last change 00:06:08
    object 100 Down
    object 101 Up
  Tracked by:
    VRRP FastEthernet0/0 1
R1(config)#do show vrrp interface fastethernet 0/0 group 1
FastEthernet0/0 - Group 1
  State is Master
  Virtual IP address is 150.1.1.254
  Virtual MAC address is 0000.5e00.0101
  Advertisement interval is 1.000 sec
  Preemption enabled
  Priority is 110
    Track object 102 state Up decrement 20
  Master Router is 150.1.1.1 (local), priority is 110
  Master Advertisement interval is 1.000 sec
  Master Down interval is 3.570 sec
```

However, if you also shut down the Serial 0/1 interface, then the tracked object is considered down because BOTH interfaces are down. This, in turn, causes the router to decrement the configured VRRP priority by 20 as specified in the configuration:

```
R1(config)#do show track
Track 100
  Interface Serial0/0 line-protocol
  Line protocol is Down (hw admin-down)
    4 changes, last change 00:02:01
  Tracked by:
    Track-list 102

Track 101
  Interface Serial0/1 line-protocol
  Line protocol is Down (hw admin-down)
    4 changes, last change 00:00:04
  Tracked by:
    Track-list 102

Track 102
  List boolean or
  Boolean OR is Down
    3 changes, last change 00:00:03
```

```
   object 100 Down
   object 101 Down
  Tracked by:
   VRRP FastEthernet0/0 1
R1(config)#do show vrrp interface fastethernet 0/0 group 1
FastEthernet0/0 - Group 1
 State is Backup
 Virtual IP address is 150.1.1.254
 Virtual MAC address is 0000.5e00.0101
 Advertisement interval is 1.000 sec
 Preemption enabled
 Priority is 90  (cfgd 110)
   Track object 102 state Down decrement 20
 Master Router is 150.1.1.4, priority is 100
 Master Advertisement interval is 1.000 sec
 Master Down interval is 3.570 sec (expires in 2.938 sec)
```

Task 5

The ICMP Router Discovery Protocol (IRDP) uses ICMP router advertisements and router solicitation messages to allow a network host to discover the addresses of operational gateways on the subnet. IRDP is an alternative gateway discovery method that eliminates the need for manual configuration of gateway addresses on network hosts and is independent of any specific routing protocol.

It is important to remember that ICMP router discovery messages do not constitute a routing protocol. Instead, they enable hosts to discover the existence of neighboring gateways, but do not determine which gateway is best to reach a particular destination. However, this process can be influenced by specifying a priority for each gateway.

By default, ICMP router advertisements are sent out as Broadcast packets to the destination address 255.255.255.255. However, Cisco IOS allows administrators to configure the gateways to send IRDP messages using IP Multicast, to the destination address 224.0.0.1. By default, Cisco IOS software sends out IRDP advertisements between every 450 and 600 seconds. However, issuing the `ip irdp maxadvertinterval 0` interface configuration command causes the router to advertise only when solicited by clients. This task is completed as follows:

```
R2(config)#interface fastethernet 0/0
R2(config-if)#ip irdp
R2(config-if)#ip irdp preference 1
R2(config-if)#ip irdp maxadvertinterval 0
R2(config-if)#ip irdp holdtime 10
R2(config-if)#exit

R3(config)#interface fastethernet 0/0
R3(config-if)#ip irdp
R3(config-if)#ip irdp maxadvertinterval 0
R3(config-if)#ip irdp holdtime 10
R3(config-if)#exit
```

Following this configuration, verify IRDP using the `show ip irdp` command:

```
R3#show ip irdp fastethernet 0/0
FastEthernet0/0 has router discovery enabled

Advertisements will not be sent except upon solicitation.
Advertisements are valid for 10 seconds.
Default preference will be 1.

R4#show ip irdp fastethernet 0/0
FastEthernet0/0 has router discovery enabled

Advertisements will not be sent except upon solicitation.
Advertisements are valid for 10 seconds.
Default preference will be 0.
```

FINAL ROUTER CONFIGURATIONS

R1

```
R1#term len 0
R1#sh run
Building configuration...

Current configuration : 1213 bytes
!
version 12.4
service timestamps debug datetime msec
service timestamps log datetime msec
no service password-encryption
!
hostname R1
!
boot-start-marker
boot-end-marker
!
no logging console
!
no aaa new-model
no network-clock-participate slot 1
no network-clock-participate wic 0
ip cef
!
no ip domain lookup
ip auth-proxy max-nodata-conns 3
ip admission max-nodata-conns 3
!
track 100 interface Serial0/0 line-protocol
!
track 101 interface Serial0/1 line-protocol
!
track 102 list boolean or
 object 100
 object 101
!
interface FastEthernet0/0
 ip address 150.1.1.1 255.255.255.0
 duplex auto
 speed auto
 vrrp 1 ip 150.1.1.254
 vrrp 1 priority 110
 vrrp 1 track 102 decrement 20
!
interface Serial0/0
 ip address 10.0.0.1 255.255.255.252
 clock rate 2000000
!
interface Serial0/1
 ip address 10.0.0.5 255.255.255.252
!
router ospf 1
 router-id 1.1.1.1
 log-adjacency-changes
 redistribute connected metric-type 1 subnets
 network 10.0.0.1 0.0.0.0 area 0
 network 10.0.0.5 0.0.0.0 area 0
!
ip forward-protocol nd
!
no ip http server
no ip http secure-server
!
control-plane
!
line con 0
line aux 0
line vty 0 4
 login
!
end

R1#
```

R2

```
R2#term len 0
R2#sh run
Building configuration...

Current configuration : 1020 bytes
!
version 12.4
service timestamps debug datetime msec
service timestamps log datetime msec
no service password-encryption
!
hostname R2
!
boot-start-marker
boot-end-marker
!
no aaa new-model
no network-clock-participate slot 1
no network-clock-participate wic 0
ip cef
!
no ip domain lookup
ip auth-proxy max-nodata-conns 3
ip admission max-nodata-conns 3
!
interface FastEthernet0/0
 ip address 150.2.2.2 255.255.255.0
 ip irdp
 ip irdp maxadvertinterval 0
 ip irdp minadvertinterval 0
 ip irdp holdtime 10
 ip irdp preference 1
 duplex auto
 speed auto
!
interface Serial0/0
 ip address 10.0.0.2 255.255.255.252
!
interface Serial0/1
 no ip address
 shutdown
!
router ospf 2
 router-id 2.2.2.2
 log-adjacency-changes
 redistribute connected metric-type 1 subnets
 network 10.0.0.2 0.0.0.0 area 0
!
ip forward-protocol nd
!
no ip http server
no ip http secure-server
!
control-plane
!
line con 0
line aux 0
line vty 0 4
 login
!
end

R2#
```

R3

```
R3#term len 0
R3#sh run
Building configuration...

Current configuration : 1403 bytes
!
version 12.4
```

```
service timestamps debug datetime msec
service timestamps log datetime msec
no service password-encryption
!
hostname R3
!
boot-start-marker
boot-end-marker
!
no logging console
!
no aaa new-model
no network-clock-participate slot 1
no network-clock-participate wic 0
ip cef
!
no ip domain lookup
ip auth-proxy max-nodata-conns 3
ip admission max-nodata-conns 3
!
interface FastEthernet0/0
 ip address 150.2.2.3 255.255.255.0
 ip irdp
 ip irdp maxadvertinterval 0
 ip irdp minadvertinterval 0
 ip irdp holdtime 10
 duplex auto
 speed auto
!
interface Serial1/0
 ip address 10.0.0.6 255.255.255.252
 clock rate 128000
!
interface Serial1/1
 no ip address
 shutdown
 clock rate 128000
!
interface Serial1/2
 ip address 10.0.0.13 255.255.255.252
 clock rate 128000
!
interface Serial1/3
 no ip address
 shutdown
!
interface Serial1/4
 no ip address
 shutdown
!
interface Serial1/5
 no ip address
 shutdown
!
interface Serial1/6
 no ip address
 shutdown
!
interface Serial1/7
 no ip address
 shutdown
!
router ospf 3
 router-id 3.3.3.3
 log-adjacency-changes
 redistribute connected metric-type 1 subnets
 network 10.0.0.6 0.0.0.0 area 0
 network 10.0.0.13 0.0.0.0 area 0
!
ip forward-protocol nd
!
no ip http server
no ip http secure-server
!
control-plane
```

```
!
line con 0
line aux 0
line vty 0 4
 login
!

R3#
```

R4

```
R4#term len 0
R4#sh run
Building configuration...

Current configuration : 954 bytes
!
version 12.4
service timestamps debug datetime msec
service timestamps log datetime msec
no service password-encryption
!
hostname R4
!
boot-start-marker
boot-end-marker
!
no logging console
!
no aaa new-model
no network-clock-participate slot 1
no network-clock-participate wic 0
ip cef
!
no ip domain lookup
ip auth-proxy max-nodata-conns 3
ip admission max-nodata-conns 3
!
interface FastEthernet0/0
 ip address 150.1.1.4 255.255.255.0
 duplex auto
 speed auto
 vrrp 1 ip 150.1.1.254
!
interface Serial0/0
 ip address 10.0.0.14 255.255.255.252
!
interface Serial0/1
 no ip address
 shutdown
!
router ospf 4
 router-id 4.4.4.4
 log-adjacency-changes
 redistribute connected metric-type 1 subnets
 network 10.0.0.14 0.0.0.0 area 0
!
ip forward-protocol nd
!
no ip http server
no ip http secure-server
!
control-plane
!
line con 0
line aux 0
line vty 0 4
 login
!

R4#
```

CCNP LAB 53

Cisco IOS IP SLA and BGP Lab

Lab Objective:

The focus of this lab is to understand Cisco IOS IP SLA Operations and BGP implementation and configuration in Cisco IOS routers. Additional technologies include EOT.

Lab Topology:

The lab network topology is illustrated below:

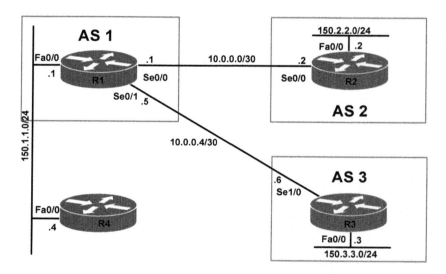

IMPORTANT NOTE: If you are using the **www.howtonetwork.net racks**, please bring up the LAN interfaces connected to the routers by issuing the no shutdown command on the connected switches. If you are using a home lab with no Switches, you can bring up the LAN interfaces using the following configurations on your routers:

```
interface fastethernet 0/0
 no keepalive
 loopback
 no shutdown
```

Alternately, you can simply connect the interfaces to a hub or switch if you have one available in your own lab.

Task 1

Configure hostnames, IP addressing on all routers as illustrated in the network topology.

Task 2

Enable BGP on R1, R2 and R3 as illustrated in the topology. Use the physical interfaces for the BGP peering. Advertise the LAN subnets on R2 and R3 via BGP. Do NOT advertise the LAN subnet between R1 and R4 via BGP. Verify the configuration using the appropriate commands.

Task 3

Configure R1 so that R2 and R3 are able to reach the LAN subnet between R1 and R4. You must adhere to the following restrictions when completing this task:

1. Do NOT advertise the 150.1.1.0/24 subnet via BGP
2. Do NOT redistribute the connected subnet into BGP
3. Do NOT advertise a default route via BGP
4. Do NOT configure static routes on either R2 or R3

You are allowed one static route, which can NOT be a default route, on R1. This route can be advertised via BGP using the `network x.x.x.x mask y.y.y.y` command. This route should have a network mask no longer than a /16, i.e. a mask no longer than 255.255.0.0. Verify the configuration using the appropriate commands.

Task 4

Configure R4 so that it is able to ping the 150.2.2.0/24 and 150.3.3.0/24 subnets and vice-versa. Verify your configuration using standard and extended pings.

Task 5

Configure a Cisco IOS IP SLA Operation on R1 so that when the LAN connection between R1 and R4 is down, the route advertised in Task 3 is withdrawn and is no longer advertised. Test your solution by disabling the LAN interface on R1.

LAB VALIDATION

Task 1

Please refer to previous labs for basic IPv4, IPv6 addressing and hostname configuration. This will not be included in this section to avoid being redundant.

Task 2

Please refer to previous labs for basic BGP configuration. Following this, verify your BGP configuration using the `show ip bgp neighbor` and `show ip route` commands. Following this configuration, your BGP RIBs should show the following path information:

```
R1#show ip bgp
BGP table version is 3, local router ID is 1.1.1.1
Status codes: s suppressed, d damped, h history, * valid, > best, i - internal,
              r RIB-failure, S Stale
Origin codes: i - IGP, e - EGP, ? - incomplete

   Network          Next Hop            Metric LocPrf Weight Path
*> 150.2.2.0/24     10.0.0.2                 0             0 2 i
*> 150.3.3.0/24     10.0.0.6                 0             0 3 i

R2#show ip bgp
BGP table version is 3, local router ID is 2.2.2.2
Status codes: s suppressed, d damped, h history, * valid, > best, i - internal,
              r RIB-failure, S Stale
Origin codes: i - IGP, e - EGP, ? - incomplete

   Network          Next Hop            Metric LocPrf Weight Path
*> 150.2.2.0/24     0.0.0.0                  0         32768 i
*> 150.3.3.0/24     10.0.0.1                           0 1 3 i

R3#show ip bgp
BGP table version is 3, local router ID is 3.3.3.3
Status codes: s suppressed, d damped, h history, * valid, > best, i - internal,
              r RIB-failure, S Stale
Origin codes: i - IGP, e - EGP, ? - incomplete

   Network          Next Hop            Metric LocPrf Weight Path
```

```
*> 150.2.2.0/24    10.0.0.5                            0 1 2 i
*> 150.3.3.0/24    0.0.0.0                    0    32768 i
```

Finally, verify that R2 and R3 can ping each other LAN-to-LAN using an extended ping:

```
R2#ping 150.3.3.3 source 150.2.2.2 repeat 10 size 1500

Type escape sequence to abort.
Sending 10, 1500-byte ICMP Echos to 150.3.3.3, timeout is 2 seconds:
Packet sent with a source address of 150.2.2.2
!!!!!!!!!!
Success rate is 100 percent (10/10), round-trip min/avg/max = 204/204/204 ms

R3#ping 150.2.2.2 source 150.3.3.3 repeat 10 size 1500

Type escape sequence to abort.
Sending 10, 1500-byte ICMP Echos to 150.2.2.2, timeout is 2 seconds:
Packet sent with a source address of 150.3.3.3
!!!!!!!!!!
Success rate is 100 percent (10/10), round-trip min/avg/max = 204/204/204 ms
```

Task 3

To complete this task, you need to configure a static route pointing to Null0. Given the task requirements, feel free to use any static route between 150.0.0.0/8 and 150.1.0.0/16. When complete, this prefix should be advertised via BGP using the network command. This will allow R2 and R3 to reach the 150.1.1.0/24 prefix. This task is completed as follows:

```
R1(config)#ip route 150.1.0.0 255.255.0.0 null 0
R1(config)#router bgp 1
R1(config-router)#network 150.1.0.0 mask 255.255.0.0
R1(config-router)#exit
```

Following this, verify the BGP RIB on R1, R2 and R3 using the show ip bgp command:

```
R1#show ip bgp
BGP table version is 4, local router ID is 1.1.1.1
Status codes: s suppressed, d damped, h history, * valid, > best, i - internal,
              r RIB-failure, S Stale
Origin codes: i - IGP, e - EGP, ? - incomplete

   Network          Next Hop         Metric LocPrf Weight Path
*> 150.1.0.0        0.0.0.0               0        32768 i
*> 150.2.2.0/24     10.0.0.2              0            0 2 i
*> 150.3.3.0/24     10.0.0.6              0            0 3 i

R2#show ip bgp
BGP table version is 4, local router ID is 2.2.2.2
Status codes: s suppressed, d damped, h history, * valid, > best, i - internal,
              r RIB-failure, S Stale
Origin codes: i - IGP, e - EGP, ? - incomplete

   Network          Next Hop         Metric LocPrf Weight Path
*> 150.1.0.0        10.0.0.1              0            0 1 i
*> 150.2.2.0/24     0.0.0.0               0        32768 i
*> 150.3.3.0/24     10.0.0.1                           0 1 3 i

R3#show ip bgp
BGP table version is 4, local router ID is 3.3.3.3
Status codes: s suppressed, d damped, h history, * valid, > best, i - internal,
              r RIB-failure, S Stale
Origin codes: i - IGP, e - EGP, ? - incomplete

   Network          Next Hop         Metric LocPrf Weight Path
*> 150.1.0.0        10.0.0.5              0            0 1 i
*> 150.2.2.0/24     10.0.0.5                           0 1 2 i
*> 150.3.3.0/24     0.0.0.0               0        32768 i
```

CCNP LAB 53: CISCO IOS IP SLA AND BGP LAB

Complete this task by ensuring that R2 and R3 can ping the 150.1.1.0/24 prefix LAN-to-LAN:

```
R2#ping 150.1.1.1 source 150.2.2.2 repeat 10 size 1500

Type escape sequence to abort.
Sending 10, 1500-byte ICMP Echos to 150.1.1.1, timeout is 2 seconds:
Packet sent with a source address of 150.2.2.2
!!!!!!!!!!
Success rate is 100 percent (10/10), round-trip min/avg/max = 12/15/16 ms

R3#ping 150.1.1.1 source 150.3.3.3 repeat 10 size 1500

Type escape sequence to abort.
Sending 10, 1500-byte ICMP Echos to 150.1.1.1, timeout is 2 seconds:
Packet sent with a source address of 150.3.3.3
!!!!!!!!!!
Success rate is 100 percent (10/10), round-trip min/avg/max = 192/192/192 ms
```

Task 4

To complete this task, you simply need to configure a static default route on R4 pointing to R1:

```
R4(config)#ip route 0.0.0.0 0.0.0.0 fastethernet 0/0 150.1.1.1
```

Following this, use ping to verify LAN-to-LAN connectivity between R4 and routers R2 and R3:

```
R2#ping 150.1.1.4 source 150.2.2.2 repeat 10 size 1500

Type escape sequence to abort.
Sending 10, 1500-byte ICMP Echos to 150.1.1.4, timeout is 2 seconds:
Packet sent with a source address of 150.2.2.2
!!!!!!!!!!
Success rate is 100 percent (10/10), round-trip min/avg/max = 12/15/16 ms

R3#ping 150.1.1.4 source 150.3.3.3 repeat 10 size 1500

Type escape sequence to abort.
Sending 10, 1500-byte ICMP Echos to 150.1.1.4, timeout is 2 seconds:
Packet sent with a source address of 150.3.3.3
!!!!!!!!!!
Success rate is 100 percent (10/10), round-trip min/avg/max = 192/192/192 ms
```

Task 5

To complete this task, you need to configure an IP SLA Operation to ping the LAN IP address of R4 - since IP SLA Operations cannot monitor interface states. Next, you need to configure EOT to track the IP SLA Operation. And finally, your need to configure the static route to use EOT such that it will be removed if the tracked object is down. This is completed as follows:

```
R1(config)#ip sla monitor 1
R1(config-sla-monitor)#$rotocol ipIcmpEcho 150.1.1.4 source-ipaddr 150.1.1.1
R1(config-sla-monitor-echo)#exit
R1(config)#ip sla monitor schedule 1 start-time now life forever
R1(config)#track 1 rtr 1 state
R1(config-track)#exit
R1(config)#ip route 150.1.0.0 255.255.0.0 null 0 track 1
R1(config)#exit
```

Verify your Cisco IP SLA Operation statistics using the show ip sla monitor command:

```
R1#show ip sla monitor statistics 1
Round trip time (RTT)   Index 1
        Latest RTT: 1 ms
Latest operation start time: *19:41:43.345 UTC Thu Jun 2 2011
Latest operation return code: OK
Number of successes: 4
Number of failures: 0
Operation time to live: Forever
```

Next, verify your tracking configuration using the show track command:

```
R1#show track
Track 1
  Response Time Reporter 1 state
  State is Up
    1 change, last change 00:03:36
  Latest operation return code: OK
  Latest RTT (millisecs) 1
  Tracked by:
    STATIC-IP-ROUTING 0
```

Finally, verify static routing EOT using the show ip route command:

```
R1#show ip route 150.1.0.0 255.255.0.0
Routing entry for 150.1.0.0/16
  Known via "static", distance 1, metric 0 (connected)
  Advertised by bgp 1
  Routing Descriptor Blocks:
  * directly connected, via Null0
      Route metric is 0, traffic share count is 1
```

To complete this task, you need to test this solution by disabling the LAN interface on R1:

```
R1(config)#interface fastethernet 0/0
R1(config-if)#shut
R1(config-if)#do show ip sla monitor statistics 1
Round trip time (RTT)    Index 1
      Latest RTT: NoConnection/Busy/Timeout
Latest operation start time: *19:46:43.345 UTC Thu Jun 2 2011
Latest operation return code: Timeout
Number of successes: 8
Number of failures: 1
Operation time to live: Forever

R1(config-if)#do show track
Track 1
  Response Time Reporter 1 state
  State is Down
    2 changes, last change 00:00:25
  Latest operation return code: Timeout
  Tracked by:
    STATIC-IP-ROUTING 0

R1(config-if)#do show ip route 150.1.0.0 255.255.0.0
% Network not in table

R1(config-if)#do show ip bgp
BGP table version is 7, local router ID is 1.1.1.1
Status codes: s suppressed, d damped, h history, * valid, > best, i - internal,
              r RIB-failure, S Stale
Origin codes: i - IGP, e - EGP, ? - incomplete

   Network          Next Hop         Metric LocPrf Weight Path
*> 150.2.2.0/24     10.0.0.2              0             0 2 i
*> 150.3.3.0/24     10.0.0.6              0             0 3 i
```

FINAL ROUTER CONFIGURATIONS

R1

```
R1#term len 0
R1#sh run
Building configuration...

Current configuration : 1203 bytes
!
version 12.4
```

```
service timestamps debug datetime msec
service timestamps log datetime msec
no service password-encryption
!
hostname R1
!
boot-start-marker
boot-end-marker
!
no logging console
!
no aaa new-model
no network-clock-participate slot 1
no network-clock-participate wic 0
ip cef
!
no ip domain lookup
ip auth-proxy max-nodata-conns 3
ip admission max-nodata-conns 3
ip sla monitor 1
 type echo protocol ipIcmpEcho 150.1.1.4 source-ipaddr 150.1.1.1
ip sla monitor schedule 1 life forever start-time now
!
track 1 rtr 1
!
interface FastEthernet0/0
 ip address 150.1.1.1 255.255.255.0
 duplex auto
 speed auto
!
interface Serial0/0
 ip address 10.0.0.1 255.255.255.252
 clock rate 2000000
!
interface Serial0/1
 ip address 10.0.0.5 255.255.255.252
!
router bgp 1
 no synchronization
 bgp router-id 1.1.1.1
 bgp log-neighbor-changes
 network 150.1.0.0
 neighbor 10.0.0.2 remote-as 2
 neighbor 10.0.0.6 remote-as 3
 no auto-summary
!
ip forward-protocol nd
ip route 150.1.0.0 255.255.0.0 Null0 track 1
!
no ip http server
no ip http secure-server
!
control-plane
!
line con 0
line aux 0
line vty 0 4
 login
!
end

R1#
```

R2

```
R2#term len 0
R2#sh run
Building configuration...

Current configuration : 962 bytes
!
version 12.4
service timestamps debug datetime msec
```

```
service timestamps log datetime msec
no service password-encryption
!
hostname R2
!
boot-start-marker
boot-end-marker
!
no logging console
!
no aaa new-model
no network-clock-participate slot 1
no network-clock-participate wic 0
ip cef
!
no ip domain lookup
ip auth-proxy max-nodata-conns 3
ip admission max-nodata-conns 3
!
interface FastEthernet0/0
 ip address 150.2.2.2 255.255.255.0
 duplex auto
 speed auto
!
interface Serial0/0
 ip address 10.0.0.2 255.255.255.252
!
interface Serial0/1
 no ip address
 shutdown
!
router bgp 2
 no synchronization
 bgp router-id 2.2.2.2
 bgp log-neighbor-changes
 network 150.2.2.0 mask 255.255.255.0
 neighbor 10.0.0.1 remote-as 1
 no auto-summary
!
ip forward-protocol nd
!
no ip http server
no ip http secure-server
!
control-plane
!
line con 0
line aux 0
line vty 0 4
 login
!
end

R2#
```

R3

```
R3#term len 0
R3#sh run
Building configuration...

Current configuration : 1301 bytes
!
version 12.4
service timestamps debug datetime msec
service timestamps log datetime msec
no service password-encryption
!
hostname R3
!
boot-start-marker
boot-end-marker
!
```

```
no logging console
!
no aaa new-model
no network-clock-participate slot 1
no network-clock-participate wic 0
ip cef
!
no ip domain lookup
ip auth-proxy max-nodata-conns 3
ip admission max-nodata-conns 3
!
interface FastEthernet0/0
 ip address 150.3.3.3 255.255.255.0
 duplex auto
 speed auto
!
interface Serial1/0
 ip address 10.0.0.6 255.255.255.252
 clock rate 128000
!
interface Serial1/1
 no ip address
 shutdown
 clock rate 128000
!
interface Serial1/2
 no ip address
 shutdown
 clock rate 128000
!
interface Serial1/3
 no ip address
 shutdown
!
interface Serial1/4
 no ip address
 shutdown
!
interface Serial1/5
 no ip address
 shutdown
!
interface Serial1/6
 no ip address
 shutdown
!
interface Serial1/7
 no ip address
 shutdown
!
router bgp 3
 no synchronization
 bgp router-id 3.3.3.3
 bgp log-neighbor-changes
 network 150.3.3.0 mask 255.255.255.0
 neighbor 10.0.0.5 remote-as 1
 no auto-summary
!
ip forward-protocol nd
!
no ip http server
no ip http secure-server
!
control-plane
!
line con 0
line aux 0
line vty 0 4
 login
!
end

R3#
```

R4

```
R4#term len 0
R4#sh run
Building configuration...

Current configuration : 831 bytes
!
version 12.4
service timestamps debug datetime msec
service timestamps log datetime msec
no service password-encryption
!
hostname R4
!
boot-start-marker
boot-end-marker
!
no logging console
!
no aaa new-model
no network-clock-participate slot 1
no network-clock-participate wic 0
ip cef
!
no ip domain lookup
ip auth-proxy max-nodata-conns 3
ip admission max-nodata-conns 3
!
interface FastEthernet0/0
 ip address 150.1.1.4 255.255.255.0
 duplex auto
 speed auto
!
interface Serial0/0
 no ip address
 shutdown
!
interface Serial0/1
 no ip address
 shutdown
!
ip forward-protocol nd
ip route 0.0.0.0 0.0.0.0 FastEthernet0/0 150.1.1.1
!
no ip http server
no ip http secure-server
!
control-plane
!
!
line con 0
line aux 0
line vty 0 4
 login
!
end

R4#
```

CCNP LAB 54

Cisco Policy Based Routing Lab

Lab Objective:

The focus of this lab is to understand Cisco Policy Based Routing (PBR) implementation and configuration in Cisco IOS routers. Additional technologies include path control.

Lab Topology:

The lab network topology is illustrated below:

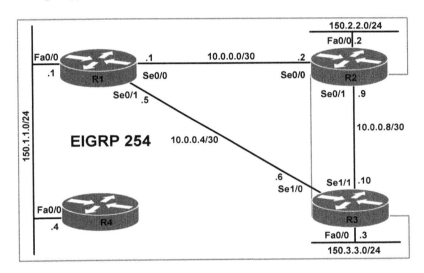

IMPORTANT NOTE: If you are using the www.howtonetwork.net racks, please bring up the LAN interfaces connected to the routers by issuing the `no shutdown` command on the connected switches. If you are using a home lab with no Switches, you can bring up the LAN interfaces using the following configurations on your routers:

```
interface fastethernet 0/0
  no keepalive
  loopback
  no shutdown
```

Alternately, you can simply connect the interfaces to a hub or switch if you have one available in your own lab.

Task 1

Configure hostnames, IP addressing on all routers as illustrated in the network topology.

Task 2

Enable EIGRP using AS 254 on all routers as illustrated in the topology. Do NOT enable EIGRP on the link between R2 and R3. EIGRP packets should not be sent out of the FastEthernet 0/0 interfaces of either R2 or R3. Verify the EIGRP configuration using the appropriate commands.

Task 3

Management has requested that traffic sourced from the 150.1.1.0/24 subnet that has a packet size between 0 and 500 bytes and between 1000 and 1500 bytes and is destined to the 150.3.3.0/24 subnet be sent via R2. All other traffic should following the normal routing path. Verify and test your configuration using the appropriate commands.

Task 4

Management has requested that in the event that the R1-R3 link fails, all traffic sourced from the 150.3.3.0/24 subnet destined to the 150.1.1.0/24 and 150.2.2.0/24 subnets be forwarded via the R2-R3 link. This should ONLY happen when the R1-R2 link is down. Ensure that the 150.3.3.0/24 subnet can reach the 150.1.1.0/24 and 150.2.2.0/24 subnets and vice-versa when you complete this task. You are NOT allowed to configure static routes on R3 to complete this task. Additionally, to minimize device configuration, you MUST use a single ACL with a single entry or line. Verify and test your configuration using the appropriate commands.

LAB VALIDATION

Task 1

Please refer to previous labs for basic IPv4, IPv6 addressing and hostname configuration. This will not be included in this section to avoid being redundant.

Task 2

Please refer to previous labs for basic EIGRP configuration. Following this, verify your EIGRP configuration using the show ip eigrp neighbors and show ip route commands. Following this configuration, your route tables should show the following path information:

```
R1#show ip route eigrp
     150.2.0.0/24 is subnetted, 1 subnets
D       150.2.2.0 [90/2172416] via 10.0.0.2, 00:03:31, Serial0/0
     150.3.0.0/24 is subnetted, 1 subnets
D       150.3.3.0 [90/2172416] via 10.0.0.6, 00:02:50, Serial0/1

R2#show ip route eigrp
     10.0.0.0/30 is subnetted, 3 subnets
D       10.0.0.4 [90/2681856] via 10.0.0.1, 00:03:16, Serial0/0
     150.1.0.0/24 is subnetted, 1 subnets
D       150.1.1.0 [90/2172416] via 10.0.0.1, 00:03:36, Serial0/0
     150.3.0.0/24 is subnetted, 1 subnets
D       150.3.3.0 [90/2684416] via 10.0.0.1, 00:02:55, Serial0/0

R3#show ip route eigrp
     10.0.0.0/30 is subnetted, 3 subnets
D       10.0.0.0 [90/21024000] via 10.0.0.5, 00:02:57, Serial1/0
     150.1.0.0/24 is subnetted, 1 subnets
D       150.1.1.0 [90/20514560] via 10.0.0.5, 00:02:57, Serial1/0
     150.2.0.0/24 is subnetted, 1 subnets
D       150.2.2.0 [90/21026560] via 10.0.0.5, 00:02:57, Serial1/0
R4#show ip route eigrp
     10.0.0.0/30 is subnetted, 2 subnets
D       10.0.0.0 [90/2172416] via 150.1.1.1, 00:01:15, FastEthernet0/0
D       10.0.0.4 [90/2172416] via 150.1.1.1, 00:01:15, FastEthernet0/0
     150.2.0.0/24 is subnetted, 1 subnets
D       150.2.2.0 [90/2174976] via 150.1.1.1, 00:01:15, FastEthernet0/0
     150.3.0.0/24 is subnetted, 1 subnets
D       150.3.3.0 [90/2174976] via 150.1.1.1, 00:01:15, FastEthernet0/0
```

Task 3

Several steps are required to complete this task. The first step is that you need to configure an ACL that matches traffic that is sourced from the 150.1.1.0/24 subnet and is destined to the 150.3.3.0/24 subnet. Next, you will need to configure a route map with at least two permit statements. The first permit statement will match traffic in specified in the ACL as long as the packets are between 0 and 500 bytes. The second permit statement will match traffic in the specified ACL as long as the packets are between 1000 and 1500 bytes. Optionally, you can also configure an explicit deny statement for the route map to prevent all other traffic from being policy routed (default behavior). This task is completed as follows:

```
R1(config)#access-list 100 permit ip 150.1.1.0 0.0.0.255 150.3.3.0 0.0.0.255
R1(config)#route-map LAN-PBR permit 10
R1(config-route-map)#match ip address 100
R1(config-route-map)#match length 0 500
R1(config-route-map)#set ip next-hop 10.0.0.2
R1(config-route-map)#exit
R1(config)#route-map LAN-PBR permit 20
R1(config-route-map)#match length 1000 1500
R1(config-route-map)#match ip address 100
R1(config-route-map)#set ip next-hop 10.0.0.2
R1(config-route-map)#exit
R1(config)#route-map LAN-PBR deny 30
R1(config-route-map)#exit
R1(config)#interface fastethernet 0/0
R1(config-if)#ip policy route-map LAN-PBR
R1(config-if)#exit
```

NOTE: You can also use the set interface command when configuring the route map. This is because an explicit route to 150.3.3.0/24 exists in the routing table. If no there is no explicit, or if only a default route is present in the routing table, the command will be ignored.

Verify your route map configuration using the show route-map <name> command:

```
R1#show route-map
route-map LAN-PBR, permit, sequence 10
  Match clauses:
    ip address (access-lists): 100
    length 0 500
  Set clauses:
    ip next-hop 10.0.0.2
  Policy routing matches: 0 packets, 0 bytes

route-map LAN-PBR, permit, sequence 20
  Match clauses:
    ip address (access-lists): 100
    length 1000 1500
  Set clauses:
    ip next-hop 10.0.0.2
  Policy routing matches: 0 packets, 0 bytes

route-map LAN-PBR, deny, sequence 30
  Match clauses:
  Set clauses:
  Policy routing matches: 0 packets, 0 bytes
```

Next, test your configuration by pinging the 150.3.3.0/24 subnet from R4 using different packet sizes. The following illustrates a 300 byte ping from R4 to R3s LAN interface address:

```
R4#ping 150.3.3.3 size 300

Type escape sequence to abort.
Sending 5, 300-byte ICMP Echos to 150.3.3.3, timeout is 2 seconds:
!!!!!
```

Using the show route-map command, we can see matches against the first permit statement:

```
R1#show route-map
route-map LAN-PBR, permit, sequence 10
  Match clauses:
    ip address (access-lists): 100
    length 0 500
  Set clauses:
```

```
      ip next-hop 10.0.0.2
    Policy routing matches: 5 packets, 1570 bytes

route-map LAN-PBR, permit, sequence 20
  Match clauses:
    ip address (access-lists): 100
    length 1000 1500
  Set clauses:
    ip next-hop 10.0.0.2
  Policy routing matches: 0 packets, 0 bytes

route-map LAN-PBR, deny, sequence 30
  Match clauses:
  Set clauses:
  Policy routing matches: 0 packets, 0 bytes
```

Next, a 700 byte ping is sent from R4 to the LAN interface of R3:

```
R4#ping 150.3.3.3 size 700

Type escape sequence to abort.
Sending 5, 700-byte ICMP Echos to 150.3.3.3, timeout is 2 seconds:
!!!!!
Success rate is 100 percent (5/5), round-trip min/avg/max = 92/92/92 ms
```

This time, there will be no matches against the PBR configuration. Only the five packets from the previous ping test will have matched the configuration applied to R1:

```
R1#show route-map
route-map LAN-PBR, permit, sequence 10
  Match clauses:
    ip address (access-lists): 100
    length 0 500
  Set clauses:
    ip next-hop 10.0.0.2
  Policy routing matches: 5 packets, 1570 bytes

route-map LAN-PBR, permit, sequence 20
  Match clauses:
    ip address (access-lists): 100
    length 1000 1500
  Set clauses:
    ip next-hop 10.0.0.2
  Policy routing matches: 0 packets, 0 bytes

route-map LAN-PBR, deny, sequence 30
  Match clauses:
  Set clauses:
  Policy routing matches: 0 packets, 0 bytes
```

Finally, to complete our validation, a 1300 byte ping is sent from R4 to the LAN interface of R3.

```
R4#ping 150.3.3.3 size 1300

Type escape sequence to abort.
Sending 5, 1300-byte ICMP Echos to 150.3.3.3, timeout is 2 seconds:
!!!!!

Success rate is 100 percent (5/5), round-trip min/avg/max = 176/179/180 ms
```

This time the traffic will match the second permit statement in the route map. The only matches will therefore be 5 packets from the 300 byte ping (permit statement 10) and 5 packets from the 1300 byte ping (permit statement 20). This is validated using the show route-map command:

```
R1#show route-map
route-map LAN-PBR, permit, sequence 10
  Match clauses:
    ip address (access-lists): 100
    length 0 500
  Set clauses:
```

```
        ip next-hop 10.0.0.2
    Policy routing matches: 5 packets, 1570 bytes

  route-map LAN-PBR, permit, sequence 20
    Match clauses:
      ip address (access-lists): 100
      length 1000 1500
    Set clauses:
      ip next-hop 10.0.0.2
    Policy routing matches: 5 packets, 6570 bytes

  route-map LAN-PBR, deny, sequence 30
    Match clauses:
    Set clauses:
    Policy routing matches: 0 packets, 0 bytes
```

NOTE: You can also verify your configuration using the debug `ip policy` command while sending pings with varying sizes from the 150.1.1.0/24 subnet to the 150.3.3.0/23 subnet.

Task 4

The requirements of this task are two-fold: the first is PBR implementation and the second is IP routing implementation. The PBR requirement is that traffic is only sent across the R2-R3 link when the R1-R3 is down. This means that you must use either the default next hop or default interface route map 'set' statements. Either option is acceptable when completing this task. The first requirement of this task is completed as follows:

```
R3(config)#access-list 100 permit ip 150.3.3.0 0.0.0.255 150.0.0.0 0.1.1.255
R3(config)#route-map LAN-PBR permit 10
R3(config-route-map)#set ip default next-hop 10.0.0.9
R3(config-route-map)#match ip address 100
R3(config-route-map)#exit
R3(config)#route-map LAN-PBR deny 20
R3(config-route-map)#exit
R3(config)#interface fastethernet 0/0
R3(config-if)#ip policy route-map LAN-PBR
R3(config-if)#exit
```

Following this, you can test PBR while dynamic routing information is still available for use by R3. The output below shows a ping from 150.3.3.254 to 150.1.1.1 while the EIGRP route for the destination network is still in the IP routing table:

```
R3#show ip route 150.1.1.0 255.255.255.0
Routing entry for 150.1.1.0/24
  Known via "eigrp 254", distance 90, metric 20514560, type internal
  Redistributing via eigrp 254
  Last update from 10.0.0.5 on Serial1/0, 00:09:47 ago
  Routing Descriptor Blocks:
  * 10.0.0.5, from 10.0.0.5, 00:09:47 ago, via Serial1/0
      Route metric is 20514560, traffic share count is 1
      Total delay is 20100 microseconds, minimum bandwidth is 128 Kbit
      Reliability 255/255, minimum MTU 1500 bytes
      Loading 1/255, Hops 1
R3#
R3#debug ip policy
Policy routing debugging is on
R3#
R3#
*May 16 17:51:01.863: IP: s=150.3.3.254 (FastEthernet0/0), d=150.1.1.1, len 100, FIB
policy match
*May 16 17:51:01.863: IP: s=150.3.3.254 (FastEthernet0/0), d=150.1.1.1, len 100, FIB
policy rejected(explicit route) - normal forwarding
*May 16 17:51:01.879: IP: s=150.3.3.254 (FastEthernet0/0), d=150.1.1.1, len 100, FIB
policy match
*May 16 17:51:01.879: IP: s=150.3.3.254 (FastEthernet0/0), d=150.1.1.1, len 100, FIB
policy rejected(explicit route) - normal forwarding
*May 16 17:51:01.899: IP: s=150.3.3.254 (FastEthernet0/0), d=150.1.1.1, len 100, FIB
policy match
*May 16 17:51:01.899: IP: s=150.3.3.254 (FastEthernet0/0), d=150.1.1.1, len 100, FIB
policy rejected(explicit route) - normal forwarding
*May 16 17:51:01.919: IP: s=150.3.3.254 (FastEthernet0/0), d=150.1.1.1, len 100, FIB
```

```
policy match
*May 16 17:51:01.919: IP: s=150.3.3.254 (FastEthernet0/0), d=150.1.1.1, len 100, FIB
policy rejected(explicit route) - normal forwarding
*May 16 17:51:01.935: IP: s=150.3.3.254 (FastEthernet0/0), d=150.1.1.1, len 100, FIB
policy match
*May 16 17:51:01.935: IP: s=150.3.3.254 (FastEthernet0/0), d=150.1.1.1, len 100, FIB
policy rejected(explicit route) - normal forwarding
```

The second requirement of this task is to ensure that routing between the 150.3.3.0/24 and the 150.1.1.0/24 and 150.2.2.0/24 subnets works when the R1-R3 link is no longer available. While the task requirements stipulate that no static routes can be configured on R3, there is no such restriction imposed on R1 or R2. The simplest solution is therefore to configure a floating static route on R2 which is then redistributed into EIGRP. This will be used to reach the 150.3.3.0/24 subnet when the R1-R3 link is unavailable. This task is completed as follows:

```
R2(config)#ip route 150.3.3.0 255.255.255.0 10.0.0.10 254
R2(config)#router eigrp 254
R2(config-router)#redistribute static
R2(config-router)#exit
```

The following illustrates the same ping when the dynamic routing information is no longer available because, for example, the WAN interface has been disabled:

```
R3(config)#interface serial 1/0
R3(config-if)#shutdown
*May 16 18:12:13.147: %DUAL-5-NBRCHANGE: IP-EIGRP(0) 254: Neighbor 10.0.0.5
(Serial1/0) is down: interface down
*May 16 18:12:15.123: %LINK-5-CHANGED: Interface Serial1/0, changed state to
administratively down
*May 16 18:12:16.123: %LINEPROTO-5-UPDOWN: Line protocol on Interface Serial1/0,
changed state to down
R3(config-if)#do show ip route 150.1.1.0 255.255.255.0
% Network not in table
R3(config-if)#do show ip route 150.2.2.0 255.255.255.0
% Network not in table
R3(config-if)#
*May 16 18:12:52.171: IP: s=150.3.3.254 (FastEthernet0/0), d=150.1.1.1, len 100, FIB
policy match
*May 16 18:12:52.171: IP: s=150.3.3.254 (FastEthernet0/0), d=150.1.1.1, g=10.0.0.9,
len 100, FIB policy routed
*May 16 18:12:52.191: IP: s=150.3.3.254 (FastEthernet0/0), d=150.1.1.1, len 100, FIB
policy match
*May 16 18:12:52.191: IP: s=150.3.3.254 (FastEthernet0/0), d=150.1.1.1, g=10.0.0.9,
len 100, FIB policy routed
*May 16 18:12:52.251: IP: s=150.3.3.254 (FastEthernet0/0), d=150.1.1.1, len 100, FIB
policy match
*May 16 18:12:52.251: IP: s=150.3.3.254 (FastEthernet0/0), d=150.1.1.1, g=10.0.0.9,
len 100, FIB policy routed
*May 16 18:12:52.271: IP: s=150.3.3.254 (FastEthernet0/0), d=150.1.1.1, len 100, FIB
policy match
*May 16 18:12:52.271: IP: s=150.3.3.254 (FastEthernet0/0), d=150.1.1.1, g=10.0.0.9,
len 100, FIB policy routed
*May 16 18:12:52.291: IP: s=150.3.3.254 (FastEthernet0/0), d=150.1.1.1, len 100, FIB
policy match
*May 16 18:12:52.291: IP: s=150.3.3.254 (FastEthernet0/0), d=150.1.1.1, g=10.0.0.9,
len 100, FIB policy routed
```

The successful ping is possible because of the redistributed static route on R2 which is installed into the EIGRP Topology Table and IP routing table on R1 as follows:

```
R1#show ip eigrp 254 topology 150.3.3.0 255.255.255.0
IP-EIGRP (AS 254): Topology entry for 150.3.3.0/24
  State is Passive, Query origin flag is 1, 1 Successor(s), FD is 2681856
  Routing Descriptor Blocks:
  10.0.0.2 (Serial0/0), from 10.0.0.2, Send flag is 0x0
      Composite metric is (2681856/2169856), Route is External
      Vector metric:
        Minimum bandwidth is 1544 Kbit
        Total delay is 40000 microseconds
```

```
            Reliability is 255/255
            Load is 1/255
            Minimum MTU is 1500
            Hop count is 1
       External data:
            Originating router is 150.2.2.2
            AS number of route is 0
            External protocol is Static, external metric is 0
            Administrator tag is 0 (0x00000000)
```

FINAL ROUTER CONFIGURATIONS

R1

```
R1#term len 0
R1#sh run
Building configuration...

Current configuration : 1303 bytes
!
version 12.4
service timestamps debug datetime msec
service timestamps log datetime msec
no service password-encryption
!
hostname R1
!
boot-start-marker
boot-end-marker
!
no logging console
!
no aaa new-model
no network-clock-participate slot 1
no network-clock-participate wic 0
ip cef
!
no ip domain lookup
ip auth-proxy max-nodata-conns 3
ip admission max-nodata-conns 3
!
interface FastEthernet0/0
 ip address 150.1.1.1 255.255.255.0
 ip policy route-map LAN-PBR
 duplex auto
 speed auto
!
interface Serial0/0
 ip address 10.0.0.1 255.255.255.252
 clock rate 2000000
!
interface Serial0/1
 ip address 10.0.0.5 255.255.255.252
!
router eigrp 254
 network 10.0.0.1 0.0.0.0
 network 10.0.0.5 0.0.0.0
 network 150.1.1.1 0.0.0.0
 no auto-summary
!
ip forward-protocol nd
!
no ip http server
no ip http secure-server
!
access-list 100 permit ip 150.1.1.0 0.0.0.255 150.3.3.0 0.0.0.255
!
route-map LAN-PBR permit 10
 match ip address 100
 match length 0 500
 set ip next-hop 10.0.0.2
!
route-map LAN-PBR permit 20
 match ip address 100
 match length 1000 1500
```

```
 set ip next-hop 10.0.0.2
!
route-map LAN-PBR deny 30
!
control-plane
!
line con 0
line aux 0
line vty 0 4
 login
!
end

R1#
```

R2

```
R2#term len 0
R2#sh run
Building configuration...

Current configuration : 996 bytes
!
version 12.4
service timestamps debug datetime msec
service timestamps log datetime msec
no service password-encryption
!
hostname R2
!
boot-start-marker
boot-end-marker
!
no logging console
!
no aaa new-model
no network-clock-participate slot 1
no network-clock-participate wic 0
ip cef
!
no ip domain lookup
ip auth-proxy max-nodata-conns 3
ip admission max-nodata-conns 3
!
interface FastEthernet0/0
 ip address 150.2.2.2 255.255.255.0
 duplex auto
 speed auto
!
interface Serial0/0
 ip address 10.0.0.2 255.255.255.252
!
interface Serial0/1
 ip address 10.0.0.9 255.255.255.252
!
router eigrp 254
 redistribute static
 passive-interface FastEthernet0/0
 network 10.0.0.2 0.0.0.0
 network 150.2.2.2 0.0.0.0
 no auto-summary
!
ip forward-protocol nd
ip route 150.3.3.0 255.255.255.0 10.0.0.10 254
!
no ip http server
no ip http secure-server
!
control-plane
!
line con 0
line aux 0
line vty 0 4
 login
!
end

R2#
```

R3

```
R3#term len 0
R3#sh run
Building configuration...

Current configuration : 1477 bytes
!
version 12.4
service timestamps debug datetime msec
service timestamps log datetime msec
no service password-encryption
!
hostname R3
!
boot-start-marker
boot-end-marker
!
no logging console
!
no aaa new-model
no network-clock-participate slot 1
no network-clock-participate wic 0
ip cef
!
no ip domain lookup
ip auth-proxy max-nodata-conns 3
ip admission max-nodata-conns 3
!
interface FastEthernet0/0
 ip address 150.3.3.3 255.255.255.0
 ip policy route-map LAN-PBR
 duplex auto
 speed auto
!
interface Serial1/0
 ip address 10.0.0.6 255.255.255.252
 clock rate 128000
!
interface Serial1/1
 ip address 10.0.0.10 255.255.255.252
 clock rate 128000
!
interface Serial1/2
 no ip address
 shutdown
 clock rate 128000
!
interface Serial1/3
 no ip address
 shutdown
!
interface Serial1/4
 no ip address
 shutdown
!
interface Serial1/5
 no ip address
 shutdown
!
interface Serial1/6
 no ip address
 shutdown
!
interface Serial1/7
 no ip address
 shutdown
!
router eigrp 254
 passive-interface FastEthernet0/0
 network 10.0.0.6 0.0.0.0
 network 150.3.3.3 0.0.0.0
 no auto-summary
!
ip forward-protocol nd
!
no ip http server
no ip http secure-server
!
access-list 100 permit ip 150.3.3.0 0.0.0.255 150.0.0.0 0.1.1.255
```

```
!
route-map LAN-PBR permit 10
 match ip address 100
 set ip default next-hop 10.0.0.9
!
route-map LAN-PBR deny 20
!
control-plane
!
line con 0
line aux 0
line vty 0 4
 login
!
end

R3#
```

R4

```
R4#term len 0
R4#sh run
Building configuration...

Current configuration : 843 bytes
!
version 12.4
service timestamps debug datetime msec
service timestamps log datetime msec
no service password-encryption
!
hostname R4
!
boot-start-marker
boot-end-marker
!
no logging console
!
no aaa new-model
no network-clock-participate slot 1
no network-clock-participate wic 0
ip cef
!
no ip domain lookup
ip auth-proxy max-nodata-conns 3
ip admission max-nodata-conns 3
!
interface FastEthernet0/0
 ip address 150.1.1.4 255.255.255.0
 duplex auto
 speed auto
!
interface Serial0/0
 no ip address
 shutdown
!
interface Serial0/1
 no ip address
 shutdown
!
router eigrp 254
 network 150.1.1.4 0.0.0.0
 no auto-summary
!
ip forward-protocol nd
!
no ip http server
no ip http secure-server
!
control-plane
!
line con 0
line aux 0
line vty 0 4
 login
!
end

R4#
```

CCNP LAB 55

Cisco Policy Based Routing Lab

Lab Objective:

The focus of this lab is to understand Cisco Policy Based Routing (PBR) implementation and configuration in Cisco IOS routers. Additional technologies include traffic filtering.

Lab Topology:

The lab network topology is illustrated below:

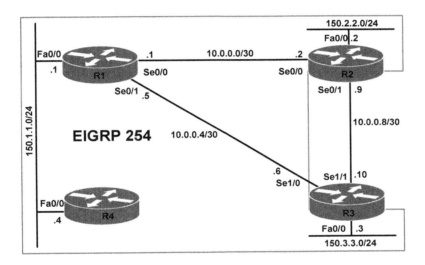

IMPORTANT NOTE: If you are using the www.howtonetwork.net racks, please bring up the LAN interfaces connected to the routers by issuing the no shutdown command on the connected switches. If you are using a home lab with no Switches, you can bring up the LAN interfaces using the following configurations on your routers:

```
interface fastethernet 0/0
  no keepalive
  loopback
  no shutdown
```

Alternately, you can simply connect the interfaces to a hub or switch if you have one available in your own lab.

Task 1

Configure hostnames, IP addressing on all routers as illustrated in the network topology.

Task 2

Enable EIGRP using AS 254 on all routers as illustrated in the topology. Do NOT enable EIGRP on the link between R2 and R3. EIGRP packets should NOT be sent out of the LAN interfaces of R2 or R3. Verify the configuration using the appropriate commands.

Task 3

Management is concerned about network security and using the default Telnet port of 23. All routers are configured to accept Telnet connections on port 3023 instead as a result. Management would like to ensure that all Telnet traffic received ingressing R1s LAN interface be discarded. However, Telnet traffic using port 3023 should be forwarded via Serial 0/1 with an IP Precedence value of 4. You are NOT allowed to use inbound or bound ACLs to complete this task - you MUST use PBR. Implement the solution required to complete this task on R1 and verify and test your configuration.

Task 4

For security purposes, Management has requested that locally originated Telnet connections from R2 or R3 to R4 only be discarded. However, these routers should be able to Telnet to other devices or subnets. You are NOT allowed to use inbound or outbound ACLs to complete this task - you MUST use PBR. Implement the solution required to complete this task on both R2 and R3 then verify and test your configuration.

LAB VALIDATION

Task 1

Please refer to previous labs for basic IPv4, IPv6 addressing and hostname configuration. This will not be included in this section to avoid being redundant.

Task 2

Please refer to previous labs for basic EIGRP configuration. Following this, verify your EIGRP configuration using the show ip eigrp neighbors and show ip route commands. Following this configuration, your route tables should show the following path information:

```
R1#show ip route eigrp
     150.2.0.0/24 is subnetted, 1 subnets
D       150.2.2.0 [90/2172416] via 10.0.0.2, 01:38:15, Serial0/0
     150.3.0.0/24 is subnetted, 1 subnets
D       150.3.3.0 [90/2172416] via 10.0.0.6, 00:07:58, Serial0/1

R2#show ip route eigrp
     10.0.0.0/30 is subnetted, 3 subnets
D       10.0.0.4 [90/2681856] via 10.0.0.1, 00:08:11, Serial0/0
     150.1.0.0/24 is subnetted, 1 subnets
D       150.1.1.0 [90/2172416] via 10.0.0.1, 01:38:28, Serial0/0
     150.3.0.0/24 is subnetted, 1 subnets
D       150.3.3.0 [90/2684416] via 10.0.0.1, 00:08:11, Serial0/0

R3#show ip route eigrp
     10.0.0.0/30 is subnetted, 3 subnets
D       10.0.0.0 [90/21024000] via 10.0.0.5, 00:08:15, Serial1/0
     150.1.0.0/24 is subnetted, 1 subnets
D       150.1.1.0 [90/20514560] via 10.0.0.5, 00:08:15, Serial1/0
     150.2.0.0/24 is subnetted, 1 subnets
D       150.2.2.0 [90/21026560] via 10.0.0.5, 00:08:15, Serial1/0

R4#show ip route eigrp
     10.0.0.0/30 is subnetted, 2 subnets
D       10.0.0.0 [90/2172416] via 150.1.1.1, 01:36:10, FastEthernet0/0
D       10.0.0.4 [90/2172416] via 150.1.1.1, 00:08:19, FastEthernet0/0
     150.2.0.0/24 is subnetted, 1 subnets
D       150.2.2.0 [90/2174976] via 150.1.1.1, 01:36:10, FastEthernet0/0
     150.3.0.0/24 is subnetted, 1 subnets
D       150.3.3.0 [90/2174976] via 150.1.1.1, 00:08:18, FastEthernet0/0
```

Task 3

The requirements of this task are quite straightforward. First, an ACL is required to match the Telnet traffic (port 23). This should be forwarded to the Null0 interface, which is a bit bucket. All traffic sent to the Null0 interface is discarded.

The second requirement is that Telnet traffic using port 3023 should be forwarded via Serial 0/1 with an IP Precedence value of 4. This task is completed as follows:

```
R1(config)#access-list 100 permit tcp any any eq telnet
R1(config)#access-list 101 permit tcp any any eq 3023
R1(config)#route-map LAN-PBR permit 10
R1(config-route-map)#match ip address 100
R1(config-route-map)#set interface null0
%Warning:Use P2P interface for routemap set
                interface clause

R1(config-route-map)#exit
R1(config)#route-map LAN-PBR permit 20
R1(config-route-map)#match ip address 101
R1(config-route-map)#set ip precedence 4
R1(config-route-map)#set interface serial 0/1
R1(config-route-map)#exit
R1(config)#route-map LAN-PBR deny 30
R1(config-route-map)#exit
R1(config)#interface fastethernet 0/0
R1(config-if)#ip policy route-map LAN-PBR
R1(config-if)#exit
```

Next, verify your route map configuration using the show `route-map <name>` command:

```
R1#show route-map LAN-PBR
route-map LAN-PBR, permit, sequence 10
  Match clauses:
    ip address (access-lists): 100
  Set clauses:
    interface Null0
  Policy routing matches: 0 packets, 0 bytes

route-map LAN-PBR, permit, sequence 20
  Match clauses:
    ip address (access-lists): 101
  Set clauses:
    ip precedence flash-override
    interface Serial0/1
  Policy routing matches: 0 packets, 0 bytes

route-map LAN-PBR, deny, sequence 30
  Match clauses:
  Set clauses:
  Policy routing matches: 0 packets, 0 bytes
```

Following this, test your configuration by attempting to Telnet from R4 to either R2 or R3 using first the default standard port number (23) and then the custom port number (3023). To configure Cisco IOS routers to accept connections on port xx23, e.g. 1023, 2023, 3023, 4023, etc, you simply add the `rotary 23` command under the VTY configuration as follows:

```
R2(config)#line vty 0 4
R2(config-line)#rotary 23
R2(config-line)#exit
```

You can then use the `show line vty <line number>` command to verify the configuration:

```
R2#show line vty 0
   Tty Typ    Tx/Rx   A Modem  Roty AccO AccI   Uses  Noise  Overruns  Int
    66 VTY             -    -     23    -    -      0      0     0/0      -

Line 66, Location: "", Type: ""
```

```
Length: 24 lines, Width: 80 columns
Baud rate (TX/RX) is 9600/9600
Status: No Exit Banner
Capabilities: none
Modem state: Idle
Group codes:     0
Special Chars: Escape  Hold  Stop  Start  Disconnect  Activation
               ^^x     none  -     -      none
Timeouts:      Idle EXEC    Idle Session   Modem Answer  Session    Dispatch
               00:10:00     never                        none       not set
                            Idle Session Disconnect Warning
                            never
                            Login-sequence User Response
                            00:00:30
                            Autoselect Initial Wait
                            not set
Modem type is unknown.
Session limit is not set.
Time since activation: never
Editing is enabled.
History is enabled, history size is 20.
DNS resolution in show commands is enabled
Full user help is disabled
Allowed input transports are lat pad telnet rlogin mop v120 ssh.
Allowed output transports are lat pad telnet rlogin mop v120 ssh.
Preferred transport is lat.
No output characters are padded
No special data dispatching characters
```

Next, test your configuration by attempting to first Telnet from R4 to either R2 or R3 while you are running PBR debugging:

```
R4#telnet 10.0.0.6
Trying 10.0.0.6 ...
% Connection timed out; remote host not responding

R1#debug ip policy
Policy routing debugging is on
R1#
R1#
R1#
*Jun  3 01:49:36.646: IP: s=150.1.1.4 (FastEthernet0/0), d=10.0.0.6, len 44, FIB
policy match
*Jun  3 01:49:36.646: IP: s=150.1.1.4 (FastEthernet0/0), d=10.0.0.6 (Null0), len 44,
FIB policy routed(drop)
*Jun  3 01:49:38.646: IP: s=150.1.1.4 (FastEthernet0/0), d=10.0.0.6, len 44, FIB
policy match
*Jun  3 01:49:38.646: IP: s=150.1.1.4 (FastEthernet0/0), d=10.0.0.6 (Null0), len 44,
FIB policy routed(drop)
*Jun  3 01:49:42.646: IP: s=150.1.1.4 (FastEthernet0/0), d=10.0.0.6, len 44, FIB
policy match
*Jun  3 01:49:42.646: IP: s=150.1.1.4 (FastEthernet0/0), d=10.0.0.6 (Null0), len 44,
FIB policy routed(drop)
*Jun  3 01:49:50.646: IP: s=150.1.1.4 (FastEthernet0/0), d=10.0.0.6, len 44, FIB
policy match
*Jun  3 01:49:50.646: IP: s=150.1.1.4 (FastEthernet0/0), d=10.0.0.6 (Null0), len 44,
FIB policy routed(drop)
```

Notice that in the output above the traffic is policy routed; however, because it is routed to the Null0 interface, the traffic is essentially dropped, hence the drop in parenthesis (brackets).

Next, initiate a Telnet connection from R4 to R2 or R3, this time using TCP port 3023 instead:

```
R4#telnet 10.0.0.6 3023
Trying 10.0.0.6, 3023 ... Open

Password required, but none set

R1#debug ip policy
Policy routing debugging is on
R1#
```

```
R1#
R1#
*Jun  3 01:47:44.138: IP: s=150.1.1.4 (FastEthernet0/0), d=10.0.0.6, len 44, FIB
policy match
*Jun  3 01:47:44.138: IP: s=150.1.1.4 (FastEthernet0/0), d=10.0.0.6 (Serial0/1), len
44, FIB policy routed
*Jun  3 01:47:44.150: IP: s=150.1.1.4 (FastEthernet0/0), d=10.0.0.6, len 40, FIB
policy match
*Jun  3 01:47:44.150: IP: s=150.1.1.4 (FastEthernet0/0), d=10.0.0.6 (Serial0/1), len
40, FIB policy routed
*Jun  3 01:47:44.154: IP: s=150.1.1.4 (FastEthernet0/0), d=10.0.0.6, len 40, FIB
policy match
*Jun  3 01:47:44.154: IP: s=150.1.1.4 (FastEthernet0/0), d=10.0.0.6 (Serial0/1), len
40, FIB policy routed
*Jun  3 01:47:44.170: IP: s=150.1.1.4 (FastEthernet0/0), d=10.0.0.6, len 43, FIB
policy match
*Jun  3 01:47:44.170: IP: s=150.1.1.4 (FastEthernet0/0), d=10.0.0.6 (Serial0/1), len
43, FIB policy routed
*Jun  3 01:47:44.170: IP: s=150.1.1.4 (FastEthernet0/0), d=10.0.0.6, len 43, FIB
policy match
*Jun  3 01:47:44.170: IP: s=150.1.1.4 (FastEthernet0/0), d=10.0.0.6 (Serial0/1), len
43, FIB policy routed
```

Task 4

To complete this task, the PBR configuration must be applied globally using the `ip local policy <route-map-name>` global configuration command, otherwise it will not match traffic originated by the router. This task is completed as follows:

```
R2(config)#ip access-list extended NO-TELNET-TO-R4-ONLY
R2(config-ext-nacl)#permit tcp any host 150.1.1.4 eq 23
R2(config-ext-nacl)#exit
R2(config)#route-map LOCAL-PBR-POLICY permit 10
R2(config-route-map)#match ip address NO-TELNET-TO-R4-ONLY
R2(config-route-map)#set interface null 0
%Warning:Use P2P interface for routemap set
                interface clause

R2(config-route-map)#exit
R2(config)#route-map LOCAL-PBR-POLICY deny 20
R2(config-route-map)#exit
R2(config)#ip local policy route-map LOCAL-PBR-POLICY
R2(config)#exit

R3(config)#ip access-list extended NO-TELNET-TO-R4-ONLY
R3(config-ext-nacl)#permit tcp any host 150.1.1.4 eq telnet
R3(config-ext-nacl)#exit
R3(config)#route-map LOCAL-PBR-POLICY permit 10
R3(config-route-map)#match ip address NO-TELNET-TO-R4-ONLY
R3(config-route-map)#set interface null 0
%Warning:Use P2P interface for routemap set
                interface clause

R3(config-route-map)#exit
R3(config)#route-map LOCAL-PBR-POLICY deny 20
R3(config-route-map)#exit
R3(config)#ip local policy route-map LOCAL-PBR-POLICY
R3(config)#exit
```

Next, verify your route map configuration using the `show route-map <name>` command:

```
R2#show route-map LOCAL-PBR-POLICY
route-map LOCAL-PBR-POLICY, permit, sequence 10
  Match clauses:
    ip address (access-lists): NO-TELNET-TO-R4-ONLY
  Set clauses:
    interface Null0
  Policy routing matches: 0 packets, 0 bytes

route-map LOCAL-PBR-POLICY, deny, sequence 20
  Match clauses:
  Set clauses:
  Policy routing matches: 0 packets, 0 bytes
```

```
R3#show route-map LOCAL-PBR-POLICY
route-map LOCAL-PBR-POLICY, permit, sequence 10
  Match clauses:
    ip address (access-lists): NO-TELNET-TO-R4-ONLY
  Set clauses:
    interface Null0
  Policy routing matches: 0 packets, 0 bytes

route-map LOCAL-PBR-POLICY, deny, sequence 20
  Match clauses:
  Set clauses:
  Policy routing matches: 0 packets, 0 bytes
```

Finally, test your solution by attempting to Telnet from R2 or R3 to R4 using the standard TCP port number (23). Use the debug ip policy command to view PBR operation real-time:

```
R2#debug ip policy
Policy routing debugging is on
R2#
R2#
R2#
R2#telnet 150.1.1.4
Trying 150.1.1.4 ...

*May 17 08:26:14.323: IP: route map LOCAL-PBR-POLICY, item 10, permit
*May 17 08:26:14.327: IP: s=10.0.0.2 (local), d=150.1.1.4 (Null0), len 44, policy
routed
*May 17 08:26:14.327: IP: local to Null0 150.1.1.4
*May 17 08:26:16.327: IP: s=10.0.0.2 (local), d=150.1.1.4, len 44, policy match
*May 17 08:26:16.327: IP: route map LOCAL-PBR-POLICY, item 10, permit
*May 17 08:26:16.327: IP: s=10.0.0.2 (local), d=150.1.1.4 (Null0), len 44, policy
routed
*May 17 08:26:16.327: IP: local to Null0 150.1.1.4
*May 17 08:26:20.327: IP: s=10.0.0.2 (local), d=150.1.1.4, len 44, policy match
*May 17 08:26:20.327: IP: route map LOCAL-PBR-POLICY, item 10, permit
*May 17 08:26:20.327: IP: s=10.0.0.2 (local), d=150.1.1.4 (Null0), len 44, policy
routed
*May 17 08:26:20.327: IP: local to Null0 150.1.1.4
*May 17 08:26:28.327: IP: s=10.0.0.2 (local), d=150.1.1.4, len 44, policy match
*May 17 08:26:28.327: IP: route map LOCAL-PBR-POLICY, item 10, permit
*May 17 08:26:28.327: IP: s=10.0.0.2 (local), d=150.1.1.4 (Null0), len 44, policy
routed
*May 17 08:26:28.327: IP: local to Null0 150.1.1.4

% Connection timed out; remote host not responding
```

Next, attempt to Telnet to R4 using any other port number, for example, using TCP port 3023:

```
R2#telnet 150.1.1.4 3023
Trying 150.1.1.4, 3023 ... Open

Password required, but none set

*May 17 08:28:09.635: IP: s=10.0.0.2 (local), d=150.1.1.4, len 44, policy match
*May 17 08:28:09.635: IP: route map LOCAL-PBR-POLICY, item 20, deny
*May 17 08:28:09.635: IP: s=10.0.0.2 (local), d=150.1.1.4, len 44, policy rejected --
normal forwarding
*May 17 08:28:09.639: IP: s=10.0.0.2 (local), d=150.1.1.4, len 40, policy match
*May 17 08:28:09.643: IP: route map LOCAL-PBR-POLICY, item 20, deny
*May 17 08:28:09.643: IP: s=10.0.0.2 (local), d=150.1.1.4, len 40, policy rejected --
normal forwarding
*May 17 08:28:09.643: IP: s=10.0.0.2 (local), d=150.1.1.4, len 40, policy match
*May 17 08:28:09.647: IP: route map LOCAL-PBR-POLICY, item 20, deny
*May 17 08:28:09.647: IP: s=10.0.0.2 (local), d=150.1.1.4, len 40, policy rejected --
normal forwarding
*May 17 08:28:09.651: IP: s=10.0.0.2 (local), d=150.1.1.4, len 43, policy match
*May 17 08:28:09.651: IP: route map LOCAL-PBR-POLICY, item 20, deny
*May 17 08:28:09.651: IP: s=10.0.0.2 (local), d=150.1.1.4, len 43, policy rejected --
normal forwarding

[Connection to 150.1.1.4 closed by foreign host]
```

FINAL ROUTER CONFIGURATIONS

R1

```
R1#term len 0
R1#sh run
Building configuration...

Current configuration : 1320 bytes
!
version 12.4
service timestamps debug datetime msec
service timestamps log datetime msec
no service password-encryption
!
hostname R1
!
boot-start-marker
boot-end-marker
!
no logging console
!
no aaa new-model
no network-clock-participate slot 1
no network-clock-participate wic 0
ip cef
!
no ip domain lookup
ip auth-proxy max-nodata-conns 3
ip admission max-nodata-conns 3
!
track 1 list boolean and
 object 2 not
!
interface FastEthernet0/0
 ip address 150.1.1.1 255.255.255.0
 ip policy route-map LAN-PBR
 duplex auto
 speed auto
!
interface Serial0/0
 ip address 10.0.0.1 255.255.255.252
 clock rate 2000000
!
interface Serial0/1
 ip address 10.0.0.5 255.255.255.252
!
router eigrp 254
 network 10.0.0.1 0.0.0.0
 network 10.0.0.5 0.0.0.0
 network 150.1.1.1 0.0.0.0
 no auto-summary
!
ip forward-protocol nd
!
no ip http server
no ip http secure-server
!
access-list 100 permit tcp any any eq telnet
access-list 101 permit tcp any any eq 3023
!
route-map LAN-PBR permit 10
 match ip address 100
 set interface Null0
!
route-map LAN-PBR permit 20
 match ip address 101
 set ip precedence flash-override
 set interface Serial0/1
!
route-map LAN-PBR deny 30
!
control-plane
!
line con 0
line aux 0
line vty 0 4
 login
 rotary 23
```

```
!
end

R1#
```

R2

```
R2#term len 0
R2#sh run
Building configuration...

Current configuration : 1187 bytes
!
version 12.4
service timestamps debug datetime msec
service timestamps log datetime msec
no service password-encryption
!
hostname R2
!
boot-start-marker
boot-end-marker
!
no aaa new-model
no network-clock-participate slot 1
no network-clock-participate wic 0
ip cef
!
no ip domain lookup
ip auth-proxy max-nodata-conns 3
ip admission max-nodata-conns 3
!
interface FastEthernet0/0
 ip address 150.2.2.2 255.255.255.0
 duplex auto
 speed auto
!
interface Serial0/0
 ip address 10.0.0.2 255.255.255.252
!
interface Serial0/1
 ip address 10.0.0.9 255.255.255.252
!
router eigrp 254
 passive-interface FastEthernet0/0
 network 10.0.0.2 0.0.0.0
 network 150.2.2.2 0.0.0.0
 no auto-summary
!
ip local policy route-map LOCAL-PBR-POLICY
ip forward-protocol nd
!
no ip http server
no ip http secure-server
!
ip access-list extended NO-TELNET-TO-R4-ONLY
 permit tcp any host 150.1.1.4 eq telnet
!
route-map LOCAL-PBR-POLICY permit 10
 match ip address NO-TELNET-TO-R4-ONLY
 set interface Null0
!
route-map LOCAL-PBR-POLICY deny 20
!
control-plane
!
line con 0
line aux 0
line vty 0 4
 login
 rotary 23
!
end

R2#
```

R3

```
R3#term len 0
R3#sh run
Building configuration...

Current configuration : 1546 bytes
!
version 12.4
service timestamps debug datetime msec
service timestamps log datetime msec
no service password-encryption
!
hostname R3
!
boot-start-marker
boot-end-marker
!
no logging console
!
no aaa new-model
no network-clock-participate slot 1
no network-clock-participate wic 0
ip cef
!
no ip domain lookup
ip auth-proxy max-nodata-conns 3
ip admission max-nodata-conns 3
!
interface FastEthernet0/0
 ip address 150.3.3.3 255.255.255.0
 duplex auto
 speed auto
!
interface Serial1/0
 ip address 10.0.0.6 255.255.255.252
 clock rate 128000
!
interface Serial1/1
 ip address 10.0.0.10 255.255.255.252
 clock rate 128000
!
interface Serial1/2
 no ip address
 shutdown
 clock rate 128000
!
interface Serial1/3
 no ip address
 shutdown
!
interface Serial1/4
 no ip address
 shutdown
!
interface Serial1/5
 no ip address
 shutdown
!
interface Serial1/6
 no ip address
 shutdown
!
interface Serial1/7
 no ip address
 shutdown
!
router eigrp 254
 passive-interface FastEthernet0/0
 network 10.0.0.6 0.0.0.0
 network 150.3.3.3 0.0.0.0
 no auto-summary
!
ip local policy route-map LOCAL-PBR-POLICY
ip forward-protocol nd
!
no ip http server
no ip http secure-server
!
ip access-list extended NO-TELNET-TO-R4-ONLY
 permit tcp any host 150.1.1.4 eq telnet
!
```

```
route-map LOCAL-PBR-POLICY permit 10
 match ip address NO-TELNET-TO-R4-ONLY
 set interface Null0
!
route-map LOCAL-PBR-POLICY deny 20
!
control-plane
!
line con 0
line aux 0
line vty 0 4
 login
 rotary 23
!
end

R3#
```

R4

```
R4#term len 0
R4#sh run
Building configuration...

Current configuration : 854 bytes
!
version 12.4
service timestamps debug datetime msec
service timestamps log datetime msec
no service password-encryption
!
hostname R4
!
boot-start-marker
boot-end-marker
!
no logging console
!
no aaa new-model
no network-clock-participate slot 1
no network-clock-participate wic 0
ip cef
!
no ip domain lookup
ip auth-proxy max-nodata-conns 3
ip admission max-nodata-conns 3
!
interface FastEthernet0/0
 ip address 150.1.1.4 255.255.255.0
 duplex auto
 speed auto
!
interface Serial0/0
 no ip address
 shutdown
!
interface Serial0/1
 no ip address
 shutdown
!
router eigrp 254
 network 150.1.1.4 0.0.0.0
 no auto-summary
!
ip forward-protocol nd
!
no ip http server
no ip http secure-server
!
control-plane
!
line con 0
line aux 0
line vty 0 4
 login
 rotary 23
!
end
R4#
```

CCNP LAB 56

Cisco Policy Based Routing Lab

Lab Objective:

The focus of this lab is to understand Cisco Policy Based Routing (PBR) implementation and configuration in Cisco IOS routers. Additional technologies include EOT and path control.

Lab Topology:

The lab network topology is illustrated below:

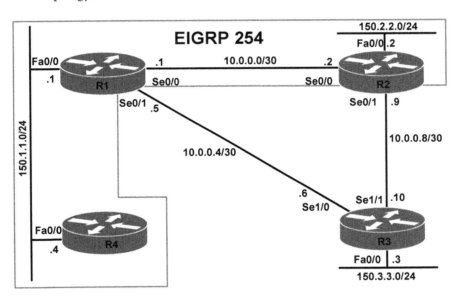

IMPORTANT NOTE: If you are using the www.howtonetwork.net racks, please bring up the LAN interfaces connected to the routers by issuing the no shutdown command on the connected switches. If you are using a home lab with no Switches, you can bring up the LAN interfaces using the following configurations on your routers:

```
interface fastethernet 0/0
 no keepalive
 loopback
 no shutdown
```

Alternately, you can simply connect the interfaces to a hub or switch if you have one available in your own lab.

Task 1

Configure hostnames, IP addressing on all routers as illustrated in the network topology. In addition, configure a Loopback 0 interface on R1 with the IP address 1.1.1.1/32.

Task 2

Configure EIGRP as illustrated in the topology. Do NOT enable EIGRP on the R1-R3 link or the R2-R3 link. You should ensure that no EIGRP packets are sent out of the FastEthernet0/0 interface on R2. R1 should advertise a default route to R4. Configure a static default route on R2 pointing to R3. Configure three static routes on R3: two static routes for the 150.1.1.0/24 subnet should point to R1; two static routes for 150.2.2.0/24 and 0.0.0.0/0 should point to R2. Verify your configuration using the appropriate commands.

Task 3

Configure IOS PBR on R1 so that all TCP and ICMP traffic from the 150.1.1.0/24 subnet to any subnet is forwarded to 10.0.0.2 (R2). In the event that the path via R2 is unavailable, configure PBR so that the router forwards this traffic to 10.0.0.6 (R3). However, this alternate path should ONLY be used based on Cisco Discovery Protocol (CDP) reachability information. Finally, ensure that all other traffic from the 150.1.1.0/24 subnet to any subnet should be forwarded via 10.0.0.3 (R3). If this path is down, this traffic should be discarded. Verify your configuration using the appropriate show commands and/or debugging commands.

Task 4

Configure IOS PBR with EOT on R2 and R3 such that when either of the routers' WAN links to R1 is down, all traffic from the local LAN is sent across the R2-R3 link. When the WAN link is up, traffic from the LAN segments should be forwarded to R1. Verify your PBR configuration using the appropriate show and/or debugging commands.

LAB VALIDATION

Task 1

Please refer to previous labs for basic IPv4, IPv6 addressing and hostname configuration. This will not be included in this section to avoid being redundant.

Task 2

Please refer to previous labs for basic EIGRP configuration. Following this, verify your EIGRP configuration using the `show ip eigrp neighbors` and `show ip route` commands. Following this configuration, your route tables should show the following route information:

```
R1#show ip route
Codes: C - connected, S - static, R - RIP, M - mobile, B - BGP
       D - EIGRP, EX - EIGRP external, O - OSPF, IA - OSPF inter area
       N1 - OSPF NSSA external type 1, N2 - OSPF NSSA external type 2
       E1 - OSPF external type 1, E2 - OSPF external type 2
       i - IS-IS, su - IS-IS summary, L1 - IS-IS level-1, L2 - IS-IS level-2
       ia - IS-IS inter area, * - candidate default, U - per-user static route
       o - ODR, P - periodic downloaded static route

Gateway of last resort is not set

     1.0.0.0/32 is subnetted, 1 subnets
C       1.1.1.1 is directly connected, Loopback0
     10.0.0.0/30 is subnetted, 2 subnets
C       10.0.0.0 is directly connected, Serial0/0
C       10.0.0.4 is directly connected, Serial0/1
     150.1.0.0/24 is subnetted, 1 subnets
C       150.1.1.0 is directly connected, FastEthernet0/0
     150.2.0.0/24 is subnetted, 1 subnets
D       150.2.2.0 [90/2172416] via 10.0.0.2, 00:01:17, Serial0/0

R2#show ip route
Codes: C - connected, S - static, R - RIP, M - mobile, B - BGP
       D - EIGRP, EX - EIGRP external, O - OSPF, IA - OSPF inter area
       N1 - OSPF NSSA external type 1, N2 - OSPF NSSA external type 2
       E1 - OSPF external type 1, E2 - OSPF external type 2
       i - IS-IS, su - IS-IS summary, L1 - IS-IS level-1, L2 - IS-IS level-2
       ia - IS-IS inter area, * - candidate default, U - per-user static route
       o - ODR, P - periodic downloaded static route
```

```
Gateway of last resort is 10.0.0.10 to network 0.0.0.0

        10.0.0.0/30 is subnetted, 2 subnets
C          10.0.0.8 is directly connected, Serial0/1
C          10.0.0.0 is directly connected, Serial0/0
        150.1.0.0/24 is subnetted, 1 subnets
D          150.1.1.0 [90/2172416] via 10.0.0.1, 00:00:24, Serial0/0
        150.2.0.0/24 is subnetted, 1 subnets
C          150.2.2.0 is directly connected, FastEthernet0/0
S*      0.0.0.0/0 [1/0] via 10.0.0.10

R3#show ip route
Codes: C - connected, S - static, R - RIP, M - mobile, B - BGP
       D - EIGRP, EX - EIGRP external, O - OSPF, IA - OSPF inter area
       N1 - OSPF NSSA external type 1, N2 - OSPF NSSA external type 2
       E1 - OSPF external type 1, E2 - OSPF external type 2
       i - IS-IS, su - IS-IS summary, L1 - IS-IS level-1, L2 - IS-IS level-2
       ia - IS-IS inter area, * - candidate default, U - per-user static route
       o - ODR, P - periodic downloaded static route

Gateway of last resort is 10.0.0.9 to network 0.0.0.0

        10.0.0.0/30 is subnetted, 2 subnets
C          10.0.0.8 is directly connected, Serial1/1
C          10.0.0.4 is directly connected, Serial1/0
        150.1.0.0/24 is subnetted, 1 subnets
S          150.1.1.0 [1/0] via 10.0.0.5
        150.2.0.0/24 is subnetted, 1 subnets
S          150.2.2.0 [1/0] via 10.0.0.9
        150.3.0.0/24 is subnetted, 1 subnets
C          150.3.3.0 is directly connected, FastEthernet0/0
S*      0.0.0.0/0 [1/0] via 10.0.0.9

R4#show ip route
Codes: C - connected, S - static, R - RIP, M - mobile, B - BGP
       D - EIGRP, EX - EIGRP external, O - OSPF, IA - OSPF inter area
       N1 - OSPF NSSA external type 1, N2 - OSPF NSSA external type 2
       E1 - OSPF external type 1, E2 - OSPF external type 2
       i - IS-IS, su - IS-IS summary, L1 - IS-IS level-1, L2 - IS-IS level-2
       ia - IS-IS inter area, * - candidate default, U - per-user static route
       o - ODR, P - periodic downloaded static route

Gateway of last resort is 150.1.1.1 to network 0.0.0.0

        150.1.0.0/24 is subnetted, 1 subnets
C          150.1.1.0 is directly connected, FastEthernet0/0
D*      0.0.0.0/0 [90/30720] via 150.1.1.1, 00:00:50, FastEthernet0/0
```

Task 3

The requirements of this task are three-fold. First, all TCP and ICMP traffic should be policy routed via 10.0.0.2 (R2). This can be completed by specifying the next hop or interface for this type of traffic. The second requirement is that in the event that the path to R2 is not available, the same traffic should then be sent via R3; however, this should only be done based on CDP reachability information. In other words, if CDP determines that R3 is unavailable, the traffic should not be sent to this router.

To satisfy this second requirement, we need to use the verify-availability keyword. The verify-availability keyword is used to force the router to check the Cisco Discovery Protocol (CDP) database to determine if an entry is available for the next hop that is specified by the set ip default next-hop command. This command prevents traffic from being black holed in situations where the specified next hop IP address is not directly connected to the router, for example. In such cases, if the specified next hop IP address does become unreachable, the router would never know and will continue sending packets to it, resulting in a black holing of traffic. This keyword is applied using a separate line in the route map.

Finally, the third requirement is that all other traffic be policy routed via R3. This can be done by specifying either the next hop address or specifying the egress interface. The requirements within this task are satisfied by configuring R1 as follows:

```
R1(config)#ip access-list extended TCP-AND-ICMP
R1(config-ext-nacl)#permit icmp 150.1.1.0 0.0.0.255 any
R1(config-ext-nacl)#permit tcp 150.1.1.0 0.0.0.255 any
R1(config-ext-nacl)#exit
R1(config)#route-map LAN-PBR permit 10
R1(config-route-map)#match ip address TCP-AND-ICMP
R1(config-route-map)#set ip next-hop 10.0.0.2
R1(config-route-map)#set ip next-hop verify-availability
R1(config-route-map)#set ip default next-hop 10.0.0.6
R1(config-route-map)#exit
R1(config)#route-map LAN-PBR permit 20
R1(config-route-map)#set ip next-hop 10.0.0.6
R1(config-route-map)#exit
R1(config)#interface fastethernet 0/0
R1(config-if)#ip policy route-map LAN-PBR
R1(config-if)#exit
```

Following this, verify your route map using the show route-map <name> command:

```
R1#show route-map LAN-PBR
route-map LAN-PBR, permit, sequence 10
  Match clauses:
    ip address (access-lists): TCP-AND-ICMP
  Set clauses:
    ip next-hop 10.0.0.2
    ip next-hop verify-availability
    ip default next-hop 10.0.0.6
  Policy routing matches: 0 packets, 0 bytes

route-map LAN-PBR, permit, sequence 20
  Match clauses:
  Set clauses:
    ip next-hop 10.0.0.6
  Policy routing matches: 0 packets, 0 bytes
```

Next, verify your solution by pinging or initiating a Telnet session to R3. You can also enable debugging for PBR to verify matches against the configured policy:

```
R4#ping 150.3.3.3

Type escape sequence to abort.
Sending 5, 100-byte ICMP Echos to 150.3.3.3, timeout is 2 seconds:
!!!!!
Success rate is 100 percent (5/5), round-trip min/avg/max = 16/18/20 ms

R1#debug ip policy
Policy routing debugging is on
R1#
R1#
R1#
R1#
*Jun  3 10:54:53.467: IP: s=150.1.1.4 (FastEthernet0/0), d=150.3.3.3, len 100, FIB
policy match
*Jun  3 10:54:53.467: IP: s=150.1.1.4 (FastEthernet0/0), d=150.3.3.3, g=10.0.0.2, len
100, FIB policy routed
*Jun  3 10:54:53.487: IP: s=150.1.1.4 (FastEthernet0/0), d=150.3.3.3, len 100, FIB
policy match
*Jun  3 10:54:53.487: IP: s=150.1.1.4 (FastEthernet0/0), d=150.3.3.3, g=10.0.0.2, len
100, FIB policy routed
*Jun  3 10:54:53.507: IP: s=150.1.1.4 (FastEthernet0/0), d=150.3.3.3, len 100, FIB
policy match
*Jun  3 10:54:53.507: IP: s=150.1.1.4 (FastEthernet0/0), d=150.3.3.3, g=10.0.0.2, len
100, FIB policy routed
*Jun  3 10:54:53.523: IP: s=150.1.1.4 (FastEthernet0/0), d=150.3.3.3, len 100, FIB
policy match
*Jun  3 10:54:53.527: IP: s=150.1.1.4 (FastEthernet0/0), d=150.3.3.3, g=10.0.0.2, len
100, FIB policy routed
*Jun  3 10:54:53.543: IP: s=150.1.1.4 (FastEthernet0/0), d=150.3.3.3, len 100, FIB
policy match
*Jun  3 10:54:53.543: IP: s=150.1.1.4 (FastEthernet0/0), d=150.3.3.3, g=10.0.0.2, len
100, FIB policy routed
```

Next, verify failover based on CDP reachability by disabling the R1-R2 link and performing the same ping test from R4 to the LAN IP address of R3:

```
R4#ping 150.3.3.3

Type escape sequence to abort.
Sending 5, 100-byte ICMP Echos to 150.3.3.3, timeout is 2 seconds:
!!!!!
Success rate is 100 percent (5/5), round-trip min/avg/max = 16/18/20 ms

R1(config)#interface serial 0/0
R1(config-if)#shut
R1(config-if)#
*Jun  3 11:23:40.587: IP: s=150.1.1.4 (FastEthernet0/0), d=150.3.3.3, g=10.0.0.6, len
100, FIB policy routed
*Jun  3 11:23:40.607: IP: s=150.1.1.4 (FastEthernet0/0), d=150.3.3.3, len 100, FIB
policy match
*Jun  3 11:23:40.607: CEF-IP-POLICY: fib for addr 10.0.0.2 is default; Nexthop
rejected
*Jun  3 11:23:40.607: IP: s=150.1.1.4 (FastEthernet0/0), d=150.3.3.3, g=10.0.0.6, len
100, FIB policy routed
*Jun  3 11:23:40.623: IP: s=150.1.1.4 (FastEthernet0/0), d=150.3.3.3, len 100, FIB
policy match
*Jun  3 11:23:40.623: CEF-IP-POLICY: fib for addr 10.0.0.2 is default; Nexthop
rejected
*Jun  3 11:23:40.623: IP: s=150.1.1.4 (FastEthernet0/0), d=150.3.3.3, g=10.0.0.6, len
100, FIB policy routed
*Jun  3 11:23:40.643: IP: s=150.1.1.4 (FastEthernet0/0), d=150.3.3.3, len 100, FIB
policy match
*Jun  3 11:23:40.643: CEF-IP-POLICY: fib for addr 10.0.0.2 is default; Nexthop
rejected
*Jun  3 11:23:40.643: IP: s=150.1.1.4 (FastEthernet0/0), d=150.3.3.3, g=10.0.0.6, len
100, FIB policy routed
*Jun  3 11:23:40.659: IP: s=150.1.1.4 (FastEthernet0/0), d=150.3.3.3, len 100, FIB
policy match
*Jun  3 11:23:40.663: CEF-IP-POLICY: fib for addr 10.0.0.2 is default; Nexthop
rejected
*Jun  3 11:23:40.663: IP: s=150.1.1.4 (FastEthernet0/0), d=150.3.3.3, g=10.0.0.6, len
100, FIB policy routed
```

Task 4

This task requires that Enhanced Object Tracking be used to track the status of each of the routers' WAN connections to R1. This task is completed as follows:

```
R2(config)#track 1 interface  serial 0/0 line-protocol
R2(config-track)#exit
R2(config)#route-map LAN-PBR permit 10
R2(config-route-map)#set ip next-hop verify-availability 10.0.0.1 1 track 1
R2(config-route-map)#set ip next-hop 10.0.0.10
R2(config-route-map)#exit
R2(config)#interface fastethernet 0/0
R2(config-if)#ip policy route-map LAN-PBR
R2(config-if)#exit

R3(config)#track 1 interface serial 1/0 line-protocol
R3(config-track)#exit
R3(config)#route-map LAN-PBR permit 10
R3(config-route-map)#set ip next-hop verify-availability 10.0.0.5 1 track 1
R3(config-route-map)#set ip next-hop 10.0.0.9
R3(config-route-map)#exit
R3(config)#interface fastethernet 0/0
R3(config-if)#ip policy route-map LAN-PBR
R3(config-if)#exit
```

Following this, first verify your EOT configuration using the show track command:

```
R2#show track
Track 1
  Interface Serial0/0 line-protocol
  Line protocol is Up
```

```
       1 change, last change 00:00:26
    Tracked by:
      ROUTE-MAP 0

R3#show track
Track 1
  Interface Serial1/0 line-protocol
  Line protocol is Up
    1 change, last change 00:00:32
  Tracked by:
    ROUTE-MAP 0
```

Next, verify route map configuration using the show route-map <name> command:

```
R2#show route-map LAN-PBR
route-map LAN-PBR, permit, sequence 10
  Match clauses:
  Set clauses:
    ip next-hop verify-availability 10.0.0.1 1 track 1  [up]
    ip next-hop 10.0.0.10
  Policy routing matches: 0 packets, 0 bytes

R3#show route-map LAN-PBR
route-map LAN-PBR, permit, sequence 10
  Match clauses:
  Set clauses:
    ip next-hop verify-availability 10.0.0.5 1 track 1  [up]
    ip next-hop 10.0.0.9
  Policy routing matches: 0 packets, 0 bytes
```

To test your solution, first ping from the R2 or R3 LAN subnet to the R4. To view PBR operation in real time, enable PBR debugging while sending the pings. The following shows host 150.2.2.254 sending pings to 150.1.1.4 (R4s LAN IP) while PBR debugging is enabled on R2:

```
R2#debug ip policy
Policy routing debugging is on
R2#
R2#
R2#
R2#
*May 17 18:08:49.475: IP: s=150.2.2.254 (FastEthernet0/0), d=150.1.1.4, len 100, FIB
policy match
*May 17 18:08:49.475: IP: s=150.2.2.254 (FastEthernet0/0), d=150.1.1.4, g=10.0.0.1,
len 100, FIB policy routed
*May 17 18:08:49.479: IP: s=150.2.2.254 (FastEthernet0/0), d=150.1.1.4, len 100, FIB
policy match
*May 17 18:08:49.479: IP: s=150.2.2.254 (FastEthernet0/0), d=150.1.1.4, g=10.0.0.1,
len 100, FIB policy routed
*May 17 18:08:49.487: IP: s=150.2.2.254 (FastEthernet0/0), d=150.1.1.4, len 100, FIB
policy match
*May 17 18:08:49.487: IP: s=150.2.2.254 (FastEthernet0/0), d=150.1.1.4, g=10.0.0.1,
len 100, FIB policy routed
*May 17 18:08:49.491: IP: s=150.2.2.254 (FastEthernet0/0), d=150.1.1.4, len 100, FIB
policy match
*May 17 18:08:49.491: IP: s=150.2.2.254 (FastEthernet0/0), d=150.1.1.4, g=10.0.0.1,
len 100, FIB policy routed
*May 17 18:08:49.499: IP: s=150.2.2.254 (FastEthernet0/0), d=150.1.1.4, len 100, FIB
policy match
*May 17 18:08:49.499: IP: s=150.2.2.254 (FastEthernet0/0), d=150.1.1.4, g=10.0.0.1,
len 100, FIB policy routed
```

Next, verify redundancy by disabling the R1-R2 link and performing the same test:

```
R2(config)#interface serial 0/0
R2(config-if)#shut
R2(config-if)#
*May 17 18:10:48.739: %TRACKING-5-STATE: 1 interface Se0/0 line-protocol Up->Down
*May 17 18:10:48.763: %DUAL-5-NBRCHANGE: IP-EIGRP(0) 254: Neighbor 10.0.0.1
(Serial0/0) is down: interface down
```

```
*May 17 18:10:50.739: %LINK-5-CHANGED: Interface Serial0/0, changed state to
administratively down
*May 17 18:10:51.739: %LINEPROTO-5-UPDOWN: Line protocol on Interface Serial0/0,
changed state to down
R2(config-if)#
R2(config-if)#
*May 17 18:10:59.215: IP: s=150.2.2.254 (FastEthernet0/0), d=150.1.1.4, len 100, FIB
policy match
*May 17 18:10:59.215: IP: s=150.2.2.254 (FastEthernet0/0), d=150.1.1.4, g=10.0.0.10,
len 100, FIB policy routed
*May 17 18:10:59.251: IP: s=150.2.2.254 (FastEthernet0/0), d=150.1.1.4, len 100, FIB
policy match
*May 17 18:10:59.251: IP: s=150.2.2.254 (FastEthernet0/0), d=150.1.1.4, g=10.0.0.10,
len 100, FIB policy routed
*May 17 18:10:59.283: IP: s=150.2.2.254 (FastEthernet0/0), d=150.1.1.4, len 100, FIB
policy match
*May 17 18:10:59.283: IP: s=150.2.2.254 (FastEthernet0/0), d=150.1.1.4, g=10.0.0.10,
len 100, FIB policy routed
*May 17 18:10:59.315: IP: s=150.2.2.254 (FastEthernet0/0), d=150.1.1.4, len 100, FIB
policy match
*May 17 18:10:59.315: IP: s=150.2.2.254 (FastEthernet0/0), d=150.1.1.4, g=10.0.0.10,
len 100, FIB policy routed
*May 17 18:10:59.347: IP: s=150.2.2.254 (FastEthernet0/0), d=150.1.1.4, len 100, FIB
policy match
*May 17 18:10:59.351: IP: s=150.2.2.254 (FastEthernet0/0), d=150.1.1.4, g=10.0.0.10,
len 100, FIB policy routed
```

FINAL ROUTER CONFIGURATIONS

R1

```
R1#term len 0
R1#sh run
Building configuration...

Current configuration : 1316 bytes
!
version 12.4
service timestamps debug datetime msec
service timestamps log datetime msec
no service password-encryption
!
hostname R1
!
boot-start-marker
boot-end-marker
!
no logging console
!
no aaa new-model
no network-clock-participate slot 1
no network-clock-participate wic 0
ip cef
!
no ip domain lookup
ip auth-proxy max-nodata-conns 3
ip admission max-nodata-conns 3
!
interface FastEthernet0/0
 ip address 150.1.1.1 255.255.255.0
 ip summary-address eigrp 254 0.0.0.0 0.0.0.0 5
 ip policy route-map LAN-PBR
 duplex auto
 speed auto
!
interface Serial0/0
 ip address 10.0.0.1 255.255.255.252
 clock rate 2000000
!
interface Serial0/1
 ip address 10.0.0.5 255.255.255.252
!
```

```
router eigrp 254
 network 10.0.0.1 0.0.0.0
 network 150.1.1.1 0.0.0.0
 no auto-summary
!
ip forward-protocol nd
!
no ip http server
no ip http secure-server
!
ip access-list extended TCP-AND-ICMP
 permit tcp 150.1.1.0 0.0.0.255 any
 permit icmp 150.1.1.0 0.0.0.255 any
!
route-map LAN-PBR permit 10
 match ip address TCP-AND-ICMP
 set ip next-hop 10.0.0.2
 set ip next-hop verify-availability
 set ip default next-hop 10.0.0.6
!
route-map LAN-PBR permit 20
 set ip next-hop 10.0.0.6
!
control-plane
!
line con 0
line aux 0
line vty 0 4
 login
!
end

R1#
```

R2

```
R2#term len 0
R2#sh run
Building configuration...

Current configuration : 1149 bytes
!
version 12.4
service timestamps debug datetime msec
service timestamps log datetime msec
no service password-encryption
!
hostname R2
!
boot-start-marker
boot-end-marker
!
no logging console
!
no aaa new-model
no network-clock-participate slot 1
no network-clock-participate wic 0
ip cef
!
no ip domain lookup
ip auth-proxy max-nodata-conns 3
ip admission max-nodata-conns 3
!
track 1 interface Serial0/0 line-protocol
!
interface FastEthernet0/0
 ip address 150.2.2.2 255.255.255.0
 ip policy route-map LAN-PBR
 duplex auto
 speed auto
!
interface Serial0/0
 ip address 10.0.0.2 255.255.255.252
!
```

```
interface Serial0/1
 ip address 10.0.0.9 255.255.255.252
!
router eigrp 254
 passive-interface FastEthernet0/0
 network 10.0.0.2 0.0.0.0
 network 150.2.2.2 0.0.0.0
 no auto-summary
!
ip forward-protocol nd
ip route 0.0.0.0 0.0.0.0 10.0.0.10
!
!
no ip http server
no ip http secure-server
!
route-map LAN-PBR permit 10
 set ip next-hop verify-availability 10.0.0.1 1 track 1
 set ip next-hop 10.0.0.10
!
control-plane
!
line con 0
line aux 0
line vty 0 4
 login
!
end

R2#
```

R3

```
R3#term len 0
R3#sh run
Building configuration...

Current configuration : 1447 bytes
!
version 12.4
service timestamps debug datetime msec
service timestamps log datetime msec
no service password-encryption
!
hostname R3
!
boot-start-marker
boot-end-marker
!
no logging console
!
no aaa new-model
no network-clock-participate slot 1
no network-clock-participate wic 0
ip cef
!
no ip domain lookup
ip auth-proxy max-nodata-conns 3
ip admission max-nodata-conns 3
!
track 1 interface Serial1/0 line-protocol
!
interface FastEthernet0/0
 ip address 150.3.3.3 255.255.255.0
 ip policy route-map LAN-PBR
 duplex auto
 speed auto
!
interface Serial1/0
 ip address 10.0.0.6 255.255.255.252
 clock rate 128000
!
interface Serial1/1
```

```
  ip address 10.0.0.10 255.255.255.252
  clock rate 128000
!
interface Serial1/2
 no ip address
 shutdown
 clock rate 128000
!
interface Serial1/3
 no ip address
 shutdown
!
interface Serial1/4
 no ip address
 shutdown
!
interface Serial1/5
 no ip address
 shutdown
!
interface Serial1/6
 no ip address
 shutdown
!
interface Serial1/7
 no ip address
 shutdown
!
ip forward-protocol nd
ip route 0.0.0.0 0.0.0.0 10.0.0.9
ip route 150.1.1.0 255.255.255.0 10.0.0.5
ip route 150.2.2.0 255.255.255.0 10.0.0.9
!
no ip http server
no ip http secure-server
!
route-map LAN-PBR permit 10
 set ip next-hop verify-availability 10.0.0.5 1 track 1
 set ip next-hop 10.0.0.9
!
control-plane
!
line con 0
line aux 0
line vty 0 4
 login
!
end

R3#
```

R4

```
R4#term len 0
R4#sh run
Building configuration...

Current configuration : 833 bytes
!
version 12.4
service timestamps debug datetime msec
service timestamps log datetime msec
no service password-encryption
!
hostname R4
!
boot-start-marker
boot-end-marker
!
no logging console
!
no aaa new-model
no network-clock-participate slot 1
```

```
no network-clock-participate wic 0
ip cef
!
no ip domain lookup
ip auth-proxy max-nodata-conns 3
ip admission max-nodata-conns 3
!
interface FastEthernet0/0
 ip address 150.1.1.4 255.255.255.0
 duplex auto
 speed auto
!
interface Serial0/0
 no ip address
 shutdown
!
interface Serial0/1
 no ip address
 shutdown
!
router eigrp 254
 network 0.0.0.0
 no auto-summary
!
ip forward-protocol nd
!
no ip http server
no ip http secure-server
!
control-plane
!
line con 0
line aux 0
line vty 0 4
 login
!
end

R4#
```

CCNP LAB 57

Cisco IOS PBR, SLA and EOT Lab

Lab Objective:

The focus of this lab is to understand PBR implementation and configuration in Cisco IOS routers. Additional technologies include IP SLA Operations and Enhanced Object Tracking.

Lab Topology:

The lab network topology is illustrated below:

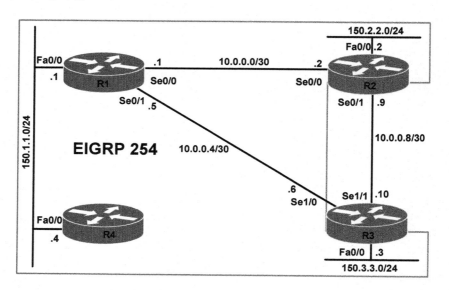

IMPORTANT NOTE: If you are using the **www.howtonetwork.net racks**, please bring up the LAN interfaces connected to the routers by issuing the `no shutdown` command on the connected switches. If you are using a home lab with no Switches, you can bring up the LAN interfaces using the following configurations on your routers:

```
interface fastethernet 0/0
  no keepalive
  loopback
  no shutdown
```

Alternately, you can simply connect the interfaces to a hub or switch if you have one available in your own lab.

Task 1

Configure hostnames, IP addressing on all routers as illustrated in the network topology. In addition, configure a Loopback 0 interface on R1 with the IP address 1.1.1.1/32.

Task 2

Configure EIGRP as illustrated in the topology. Ensure that no EIGRP packets are sent out of the LAN interfaces of R2 and R3. Do NOT enable EIGRP for the R2-R3 link. Ensure that R1 advertises a default route to R4.

Next, configure static default routes on R2 and R3 as follows:
* R2 should have a default static route pointing to R3
* R3 should have a default static route pointing to R2

Verify your configuration using the appropriate commands on all routers in the network.

Task 3

Configure IOS PBR on R1 so that when R1 loses the EIGRP route to the 150.2.2.0/24 subnet, all traffic sourced from the 150.1.1.0/24 subnet to this destination is sent via R3. In addition to this, configure IOS PBR on R1 so that when R1 loses the EIGRP route to the 150.3.3.0/24 subnet, all traffic sourced from the 150.1.1.0/24 subnet to this destination is sent via R2. To avoid black holing traffic, configure R1 to check the CDP database to determine if an entry is available for the specified next hop address. Verify your configuration using the appropriate commands.

Task 4

Configure PBR on R2 and R3 so that when either of their WAN connections to R1 are down, only HTTP and HTTPS should be permitted from the local LAN segment and sent across the R2-R3 WAN link. Assuming that QoS is enabled on the R2-R3 link, this traffic should be forwarded using an IP Precedence of 4. All other traffic from the LAN subnet of the router that lost its WAN connection to R1 should be forwarded with an IP Precedence of 2.

When the WAN link to R1 is up, all traffic should follow the EIGRP route through R1. When completing this task, you MUST adhere to the following restrictions:
* You MUST use Cisco Enhanced Object Tracking (EOT) in your solution
* You MUST use Cisco IOS IP SLA Operations and in your solution
* The Cisco IOS IP SLA Operation should ping the connected IP address of R1
* As long as EIGRP routing information is present, PBR should be inactive

Verify the PBR configuration using the appropriate show commands or debugging commands.

LAB VALIDATION

Task 1

Please refer to previous labs for basic IPv4, IPv6 addressing and hostname configuration. This will not be included in this section to avoid being redundant.

Task 2

Please refer to previous labs for basic EIGRP configuration. Following this, verify your EIGRP configuration using the show ip eigrp neighbors and show ip route commands. Following this configuration, your route tables should show the following route information:

```
R1#show ip route
Codes: C - connected, S - static, R - RIP, M - mobile, B - BGP
       D - EIGRP, EX - EIGRP external, O - OSPF, IA - OSPF inter area
       N1 - OSPF NSSA external type 1, N2 - OSPF NSSA external type 2
       E1 - OSPF external type 1, E2 - OSPF external type 2
       i - IS-IS, su - IS-IS summary, L1 - IS-IS level-1, L2 - IS-IS level-2
       ia - IS-IS inter area, * - candidate default, U - per-user static route
       o - ODR, P - periodic downloaded static route

Gateway of last resort is 0.0.0.0 to network 0.0.0.0

     10.0.0.0/30 is subnetted, 2 subnets
C       10.0.0.0 is directly connected, Serial0/0
C       10.0.0.4 is directly connected, Serial0/1
```

```
       150.1.0.0/24 is subnetted, 1 subnets
C         150.1.1.0 is directly connected, FastEthernet0/0
       150.2.0.0/24 is subnetted, 1 subnets
D         150.2.2.0 [90/2172416] via 10.0.0.2, 00:05:52, Serial0/0
       150.3.0.0/24 is subnetted, 1 subnets
D         150.3.3.0 [90/2172416] via 10.0.0.6, 00:03:51, Serial0/1
D*     0.0.0.0/0 is a summary, 00:00:05, Null0

R2#show ip route
Codes: C - connected, S - static, R - RIP, M - mobile, B - BGP
       D - EIGRP, EX - EIGRP external, O - OSPF, IA - OSPF inter area
       N1 - OSPF NSSA external type 1, N2 - OSPF NSSA external type 2
       E1 - OSPF external type 1, E2 - OSPF external type 2
       i - IS-IS, su - IS-IS summary, L1 - IS-IS level-1, L2 - IS-IS level-2
       ia - IS-IS inter area, * - candidate default, U - per-user static route
       o - ODR, P - periodic downloaded static route

Gateway of last resort is 10.0.0.10 to network 0.0.0.0

       10.0.0.0/30 is subnetted, 3 subnets
C         10.0.0.8 is directly connected, Serial0/1
C         10.0.0.0 is directly connected, Serial0/0
D         10.0.0.4 [90/2681856] via 10.0.0.1, 00:03:58, Serial0/0
       150.1.0.0/24 is subnetted, 1 subnets
D         150.1.1.0 [90/2172416] via 10.0.0.1, 00:05:58, Serial0/0
       150.2.0.0/24 is subnetted, 1 subnets
C         150.2.2.0 is directly connected, FastEthernet0/0
       150.3.0.0/24 is subnetted, 1 subnets
D         150.3.3.0 [90/2684416] via 10.0.0.1, 00:03:58, Serial0/0
S*     0.0.0.0/0 [1/0] via 10.0.0.10

R3#show ip route
Codes: C - connected, S - static, R - RIP, M - mobile, B - BGP
       D - EIGRP, EX - EIGRP external, O - OSPF, IA - OSPF inter area
       N1 - OSPF NSSA external type 1, N2 - OSPF NSSA external type 2
       E1 - OSPF external type 1, E2 - OSPF external type 2
       i - IS-IS, su - IS-IS summary, L1 - IS-IS level-1, L2 - IS-IS level-2
       ia - IS-IS inter area, * - candidate default, U - per-user static route
       o - ODR, P - periodic downloaded static route

Gateway of last resort is 10.0.0.9 to network 0.0.0.0

       10.0.0.0/30 is subnetted, 3 subnets
C         10.0.0.8 is directly connected, Serial1/1
D         10.0.0.0 [90/21024000] via 10.0.0.5, 00:04:00, Serial1/0
C         10.0.0.4 is directly connected, Serial1/0
       150.1.0.0/24 is subnetted, 1 subnets
D         150.1.1.0 [90/20514560] via 10.0.0.5, 00:04:00, Serial1/0
       150.2.0.0/24 is subnetted, 1 subnets
D         150.2.2.0 [90/21026560] via 10.0.0.5, 00:04:00, Serial1/0
       150.3.0.0/24 is subnetted, 1 subnets
C         150.3.3.0 is directly connected, FastEthernet0/0
S*     0.0.0.0/0 [1/0] via 10.0.0.9

R4#show ip route
Codes: C - connected, S - static, R - RIP, M - mobile, B - BGP
       D - EIGRP, EX - EIGRP external, O - OSPF, IA - OSPF inter area
       N1 - OSPF NSSA external type 1, N2 - OSPF NSSA external type 2
       E1 - OSPF external type 1, E2 - OSPF external type 2
       i - IS-IS, su - IS-IS summary, L1 - IS-IS level-1, L2 - IS-IS level-2
       ia - IS-IS inter area, * - candidate default, U - per-user static route
       o - ODR, P - periodic downloaded static route

Gateway of last resort is 150.1.1.1 to network 0.0.0.0

       150.1.0.0/24 is subnetted, 1 subnets
C         150.1.1.0 is directly connected, FastEthernet0/0
D*     0.0.0.0/0 [90/30720] via 150.1.1.1, 00:00:16, FastEthernet0/0
```

Task 3

In order to complete this task, we need to use the set ip default next-hop route map set clause. In order to ensure that CDP reachability is verified, we also need to use the set ip default next-hop verify-availability set clause. The verify-availability keyword forces the router to check the CDP database to determine if an entry is available for the next hop that is specified by the set ip default next-hop command. This command prevents traffic from being black holed in situations where the specified next hop IP address is not directly connected to the router, for example. In such cases, if the specified next hop IP address does become unreachable, the router would never know and will continue sending packets to it, resulting in a black holing of traffic. This keyword is applied using a separate line in the route map. This task is completed as follows:

```
R1(config)#ip access-list extended TO-R2-LAN
R1(config-ext-nacl)#permit ip 150.1.1.0 0.0.0.255 150.2.2.0 0.0.0.255
R1(config-ext-nacl)#exit
R1(config)#ip access-list extended TO-R3-LAN
R1(config-ext-nacl)#permit ip 150.1.1.0 0.0.0.255 150.3.3.0 0.0.0.255
R1(config-ext-nacl)#exit
R1(config)#route-map LAN-PBR permit 10
R1(config-route-map)#match ip address TO-R2-LAN
R1(config-route-map)#set ip next-hop verify-availability
R1(config-route-map)#set ip default next-hop 10.0.0.6
R1(config-route-map)#exit
R1(config)#route-map LAN-PBR permit 20
R1(config-route-map)#match ip address TO-R3-LAN
R1(config-route-map)#set ip next-hop verify-availability
R1(config-route-map)#set ip default next-hop 10.0.0.2
R1(config-route-map)#exit
R1(config)#route-map LAN-PBR deny 30
R1(config-route-map)#exit
R1(config)#interface fastethernet 0/0
R1(config-if)#ip policy route-map LAN-PBR
R1(config-if)#exit
```

Next, verify your PBR configuration using the **show route-map <name>** command:

```
R1#show route-map LAN-PBR
route-map LAN-PBR, permit, sequence 10
  Match clauses:
    ip address (access-lists): TO-R2-LAN
  Set clauses:
    ip next-hop verify-availability
    ip default next-hop 10.0.0.6
  Policy routing matches: 0 packets, 0 bytes

route-map LAN-PBR, permit, sequence 20
  Match clauses:
    ip address (access-lists): TO-R3-LAN
  Set clauses:
    ip next-hop verify-availability
    ip default next-hop 10.0.0.2
  Policy routing matches: 0 packets, 0 bytes

route-map LAN-PBR, deny, sequence 30
  Match clauses:
  Set clauses:
    Policy routing matches: 0 packets, 0 bytes
```

Test your solution by shutting first shutting down the R1-R2 link and then pinging 150.2.2.0/24 from R4. You can enable PBR debugging to view PBR operation in real time:

```
R4#ping 150.2.2.2

Type escape sequence to abort.
Sending 5, 100-byte ICMP Echos to 150.2.2.2, timeout is 2 seconds:
!!!!!
Success rate is 100 percent (5/5), round-trip min/avg/max = 32/32/32 ms

R1#debug ip policy
Policy routing debugging is on
R1#configure terminal
Enter configuration commands, one per line.  End with CNTL/Z.
R1(config)#interface serial 0/0
R1(config-if)#shutdown
R1(config-if)#end
R1#
```

```
R1#
*Jun  3 17:58:19.942: IP: s=150.1.1.4 (FastEthernet0/0), d=150.2.2.2, len 100, FIB
policy match
*Jun  3 17:58:19.942: IP: s=150.1.1.4 (FastEthernet0/0), d=150.2.2.2, g=10.0.0.6, len
100, FIB policy routed
*Jun  3 17:58:19.974: IP: s=150.1.1.4 (FastEthernet0/0), d=150.2.2.2, len 100, FIB
policy match
*Jun  3 17:58:19.974: IP: s=150.1.1.4 (FastEthernet0/0), d=150.2.2.2, g=10.0.0.6, len
100, FIB policy routed
*Jun  3 17:58:20.006: IP: s=150.1.1.4 (FastEthernet0/0), d=150.2.2.2, len 100, FIB
policy match
*Jun  3 17:58:20.006: IP: s=150.1.1.4 (FastEthernet0/0), d=150.2.2.2, g=10.0.0.6, len
100, FIB policy routed
*Jun  3 17:58:20.038: IP: s=150.1.1.4 (FastEthernet0/0), d=150.2.2.2, len 100, FIB
policy match
*Jun  3 17:58:20.038: IP: s=150.1.1.4 (FastEthernet0/0), d=150.2.2.2, g=10.0.0.6, len
100, FIB policy routed
*Jun  3 17:58:20.070: IP: s=150.1.1.4 (FastEthernet0/0), d=150.2.2.2, len 100, FIB
policy match
*Jun  3 17:58:20.070: IP: s=150.1.1.4 (FastEthernet0/0), d=150.2.2.2, g=10.0.0.6, len
100, FIB policy routed
```

Next, test the Policy Based Routing operation for the 150.3.3.0/24 subnet by shutting down the R1-R3 link and pinging R3s LAN IP address from R4:

```
R4#ping 150.3.3.3

Type escape sequence to abort.
Sending 5, 100-byte ICMP Echos to 150.3.3.3, timeout is 2 seconds:
!!!!!
Success rate is 100 percent (5/5), round-trip min/avg/max = 16/18/20 ms

R1#debug ip policy
Policy routing debugging is on
R1#configure terminal
Enter configuration commands, one per line.  End with CNTL/Z.
R1(config)#interface serial 0/1
R1(config-if)#shutdown
R1(config-if)#end
R1#
R1#
*Jun  3 18:04:25.286: IP: s=150.1.1.4 (FastEthernet0/0), d=150.3.3.3, len 100, FIB
policy match
*Jun  3 18:04:25.286: IP: s=150.1.1.4 (FastEthernet0/0), d=150.3.3.3, g=10.0.0.2, len
100, FIB policy routed
*Jun  3 18:04:25.302: IP: s=150.1.1.4 (FastEthernet0/0), d=150.3.3.3, len 100, FIB
policy match
*Jun  3 18:04:25.306: IP: s=150.1.1.4 (FastEthernet0/0), d=150.3.3.3, g=10.0.0.2, len
100, FIB policy routed
*Jun  3 18:04:25.322: IP: s=150.1.1.4 (FastEthernet0/0), d=150.3.3.3, len 100, FIB
policy match
*Jun  3 18:04:25.322: IP: s=150.1.1.4 (FastEthernet0/0), d=150.3.3.3, g=10.0.0.2, len
100, FIB policy routed
*Jun  3 18:04:25.342: IP: s=150.1.1.4 (FastEthernet0/0), d=150.3.3.3, len 100, FIB
policy match
*Jun  3 18:04:25.342: IP: s=150.1.1.4 (FastEthernet0/0), d=150.3.3.3, g=10.0.0.2, len
100, FIB policy routed
*Jun  3 18:04:25.362: IP: s=150.1.1.4 (FastEthernet0/0), d=150.3.3.3, len 100, FIB
policy match
*Jun  3 18:04:25.362: IP: s=150.1.1.4 (FastEthernet0/0), d=150.3.3.3, g=10.0.0.2, len
100, FIB policy routed
```

Task 4

This task requires the use of the set ip next-hop <address> and the set ip next-hop verify-availability <address> <sequence> track <object number>] route map mode subcommands. The issue is that this command supersedes dynamic routing as far as traffic forwarding goes. Therefore, to ensure that PBR is used ONLY when the dynamic routing information is no longer available, while still using the set ip next-hop [<address> | verify-availability <address> <sequence> track <object number>] route map mode subcommand, we need to use the NOT command with a Boolean tracked object.

The NOT keyword negates the state of the object, which means that when the object is up, the tracked list detects the object as down. In other words, what will happen is that when the tracked object (tracked via IP SLA Operation) is up, PBR will see it as down, therefore using the dynamic routing information. Inversely, when the tracked object is down, PBR will see it as up and therefore implement policy routing. This task is completed as follows:

```
R1(config)#ip sla monitor responder

R2(config)#ip sla monitor responder
R2(config)#ip access-list extended HTTP-AND-HTTPS
R2(config-ext-nacl)#permit tcp any any eq www
R2(config-ext-nacl)#permit tcp any any eq 443
R2(config-ext-nacl)#exit
R2(config)#ip sla monitor 1
R2(config-sla-monitor)#$rotocol ipIcmpEcho 10.0.0.1 source-ip 10.0.0.2
R2(config-sla-monitor-echo)#exit
R2(config)#ip sla monitor schedule 1 start-time now life forever
R2(config)#track 1 rtr 1
R2(config-track)#exit
R2(config)#track 2 list boolean or
R2(config-track)#object 1 not
R2(config-track)#exit
R2(config)#route-map LAN-PBR permit 10
R2(config-route-map)#match ip address HTTP-AND-HTTPS
R2(config-route-map)#set ip next-hop verify-availability 10.0.0.10 1 track 2
R2(config-route-map)#set ip precedence 4
R2(config-route-map)#exit
R2(config)#route-map LAN-PBR permit 20
R2(config-route-map)#set ip next-hop verify-availability 192.0.2.1 1 track 2
R2(config-route-map)#set ip precedence 2
R2(config-route-map)#exit
R2(config)#interface fastethernet 0/0
R2(config-if)#ip policy route-map LAN-PBR
R2(config-if)#exit

R3(config)#ip sla monitor responder
R3(config)#ip sla monitor 1
R3(config-sla-monitor)#$rotocol ipIcmpEcho 10.0.0.5 source-ipaddr 10.0.0.6
R3(config-sla-monitor-echo)#exit
R3(config)#ip sla monitor schedule 1 life forever start-time now
R3(config)#track 1 rtr 1
R3(config-track)#exit
R3(config)#track 2 list boolean or
R3(config-track)#object 1 not
R3(config-track)#exit
R3(config)#ip access-list extended HTTP-AND-HTTPS
R3(config-ext-nacl)#permit tcp any any eq www
R3(config-ext-nacl)#permit tcp any any eq 443
R3(config-ext-nacl)#route-map LAN-PBR permit 10
R3(config-route-map)#match ip address HTTP-AND-HTTPS
R3(config-route-map)#set ip next-hop verify-availability 10.0.0.9 1 track 2
R3(config-route-map)#set ip precedence 4
R3(config-route-map)#exit
R3(config)#route-map LAN-PBR permit 20
R3(config-route-map)#set ip next-hop verify-availability 192.0.2.1 1 track 2
R3(config-route-map)#set ip precedence 2
R3(config-route-map)#exit
R3(config)#interface fastethernet 0/0
R3(config-if)#ip policy route-map LAN-PBR
R3(config-if)#exit
```

Given this configuration, as long as the IP SLA Operation reports a success, the tracked object will show up as down, which in turn means that PBR will NOT be used. The IP SLA Operation has been configured to ping directly connected R1 WAN interface from both routers. The assumption here is that if R2 and R3 both cannot ping the WAN interfaces to which they are connected to R1, then it is safe to assume that EIGRP is also down between these two routers and R1. Following this configuration, first verify the IP SLA Operation state using the show ip sla monitor statistics command on both routers:

```
R2#show ip sla monitor statistics 1
Round trip time (RTT)    Index 1
```

```
              Latest RTT: 11 ms
Latest operation start time: *01:22:54.466 UTC Wed May 18 2011
Latest operation return code: OK
Number of successes: 9
Number of failures: 0
Operation time to live: Forever

R3#show ip sla monitor statistics 1
Round trip time (RTT)    Index 1
              Latest RTT: 12 ms
Latest operation start time: *12:21:00.694 UTC Tue May 17 2011
Latest operation return code: OK
Number of successes: 6
Number of failures: 0
Operation time to live: Forever
```

Next, verify the EOT configuration using the show track command on both routers:

```
R2#show track
Track 1
  Response Time Reporter 1 state
  State is Up
    4 changes, last change 00:09:25
  Latest operation return code: OK
  Latest RTT (millisecs) 11
  Tracked by:
    Track-list 2

Track 2
  List boolean or
  Boolean OR is Down
    5 changes, last change 00:09:25
    object 1 not Up
  Tracked by:
    ROUTE-MAP 0

R3#show track
Track 1
  Response Time Reporter 1 state
  State is Up
    2 changes, last change 00:06:45
  Latest operation return code: OK
  Latest RTT (millisecs) 12
  Tracked by:
    Track-list 2

Track 2
  List boolean or
  Boolean OR is Down
    3 changes, last change 00:06:45
    object 1 not Up
  Tracked by:
    ROUTE-MAP 0
```

Note in the output above that track list 2, which is tracking track list 1 and is also being tracked in the PBR configuration shows a down state. This is because of the Bolean NOT keyword in the EOT configuration which inverses the logic. As long as track list 1 shows up, track list 2 will show down. When track list 1 shows down, track list 2 will show up. This can be verified by looking at the route maps configured on both routers using the show route-map command:

```
R2#show route-map LAN-PBR
route-map LAN-PBR, permit, sequence 10
  Match clauses:
    ip address (access-lists): HTTP-AND-HTTPS
  Set clauses:
    ip precedence flash-override
    ip next-hop verify-availability 10.0.0.10 1 track 2  [down]
  Policy routing matches: 0 packets, 0 bytes

route-map LAN-PBR, permit, sequence 20
```

```
  Match clauses:
  Set clauses:
    ip precedence immediate
    ip next-hop verify-availability 10.0.0.10 1 track 2  [down]
  Policy routing matches: 0 packets, 0 bytes

R3#show route-map LAN-PBR
route-map LAN-PBR, permit, sequence 10
  Match clauses:
    ip address (access-lists): HTTP-AND-HTTPS
  Set clauses:
    ip precedence flash-override
    ip next-hop verify-availability 10.0.0.9 1 track 2  [down]
  Policy routing matches: 0 packets, 0 bytes

route-map LAN-PBR, permit, sequence 20
  Match clauses:
  Set clauses:
    ip next-hop verify-availability 10.0.0.9 1 track 2  [down]
  Policy routing matches: 0 packets, 0 bytes
```

To test our configuration, first initiate an HTTP or HTTPS session from LAN-to-LAN between R2 and R3. As long as the EIGRP is up and IP SLA Operations reports an OK, the PBR configuration will be ignored and normal forwarding will be used. You can enable HTTP and HTTPS functionality on Cisco IOS routers using the ip http server or ip http secure-server global configuration commands on the routers. The following shows forwarding for an HTTP connection from host 150.2.2.254 (connected to R2) to 150.3.3.3 (R3) while EIGRP is up and Policy Based Routing debugging is enabled on R2:

```
R2#debug ip policy
Policy routing debugging is on
R2#
R2#
*May 18 01:36:14.670: IP: s=150.2.2.254 (FastEthernet0/0), d=150.3.3.3, len 44, FIB
policy match
*May 18 01:36:14.670: IP: s=150.2.2.254 (FastEthernet0/0), d=150.3.3.3, len 44, FIB
policy rejected - normal forwarding
*May 18 01:36:14.686: IP: s=150.2.2.254 (FastEthernet0/0), d=150.3.3.3, len 40, FIB
policy match
*May 18 01:36:14.686: IP: s=150.2.2.254 (FastEthernet0/0), d=150.3.3.3, len 40, FIB
policy rejected - normal forwarding
*May 18 01:36:14.686: IP: s=150.2.2.254 (FastEthernet0/0), d=150.3.3.3, len 40, FIB
policy match
*May 18 01:36:14.686: IP: s=150.2.2.254 (FastEthernet0/0), d=150.3.3.3, len 40, FIB
policy rejected - normal forwarding
```

Next, shut down BOTH of the WAN interfaces on R1 and verify the route maps configured on R2 and R3 using the show route-map <name> command:

```
R1(config)#interface serial 0/0
R1(config-if)#shutdown
R1(config-if)#exit
R1(config)#interface serial 0/1
R1(config-if)#shutdown
R1(config-if)#exit

R2#show route-map LAN-PBR
route-map LAN-PBR, permit, sequence 10
  Match clauses:
    ip address (access-lists): HTTP-AND-HTTPS
  Set clauses:
    ip precedence flash-override
    ip next-hop verify-availability 10.0.0.10 1 track 2  [up]
  Policy routing matches: 0 packets, 0 bytes

route-map LAN-PBR, permit, sequence 20
  Match clauses:
  Set clauses:
    ip precedence immediate
```

```
      ip next-hop verify-availability 10.0.0.10 1 track 2  [up]
    Policy routing matches: 0 packets, 0 bytes

R3#show route-map LAN-PBR
route-map LAN-PBR, permit, sequence 10
  Match clauses:
    ip address (access-lists): HTTP-AND-HTTPS
  Set clauses:
    ip precedence flash-override
    ip next-hop verify-availability 10.0.0.9 1 track 2  [up]
  Policy routing matches: 0 packets, 0 bytes

route-map LAN-PBR, permit, sequence 20
  Match clauses:
  Set clauses:
    ip next-hop verify-availability 10.0.0.9 1 track 2  [up]
  Policy routing matches: 0 packets, 0 bytes
```

Next, an HTTP connection is again initiated from the 150.2.2.254 host to 150.3.3.3 while Policy Based Routing (PBR) debugging is enabled on R2:

```
R2#debug ip policy
Policy routing debugging is on
R2#
R2#
*May 18 02:28:12.477: IP: s=150.2.2.254 (FastEthernet0/0), d=150.3.3.3, len 44, FIB
policy match
*May 18 02:28:12.477: IP: s=150.2.2.254 (FastEthernet0/0), d=150.3.3.3, g=10.0.0.10,
len 44, FIB policy routed
*May 18 02:28:12.493: IP: s=150.2.2.254 (FastEthernet0/0), d=150.3.3.3, len 40, FIB
policy match
*May 18 02:28:12.493: IP: s=150.2.2.254 (FastEthernet0/0), d=150.3.3.3, g=10.0.0.10,
len 40, FIB policy routed
*May 18 02:28:12.493: IP: s=150.2.2.254 (FastEthernet0/0), d=150.3.3.3, len 40, FIB
policy match
*May 18 02:28:12.493: IP: s=150.2.2.254 (FastEthernet0/0), d=150.3.3.3, g=10.0.0.10,
len 40, FIB policy routed
```

FINAL ROUTER CONFIGURATIONS

R1

```
R1#term len 0
R1#sh run
Building configuration...

Current configuration : 1478 bytes
!
version 12.4
service timestamps debug datetime msec
service timestamps log datetime msec
no service password-encryption
!
hostname R1
!
boot-start-marker
boot-end-marker
!
no logging console
!
no aaa new-model
no network-clock-participate slot 1
no network-clock-participate wic 0
ip cef
!
no ip domain lookup
ip auth-proxy max-nodata-conns 3
ip admission max-nodata-conns 3
ip sla monitor responder
!
interface FastEthernet0/0
```

```
 ip address 150.1.1.1 255.255.255.0
 ip summary-address eigrp 254 0.0.0.0 0.0.0.0 5
 ip policy route-map LAN-PBR
 duplex auto
 speed auto
!
interface Serial0/0
 ip address 10.0.0.1 255.255.255.252
 shutdown
 clock rate 2000000
!
interface Serial0/1
 ip address 10.0.0.5 255.255.255.252
 shutdown
!
router eigrp 254
 network 0.0.0.0
 no auto-summary
!
ip forward-protocol nd
!
no ip http server
no ip http secure-server
!
ip access-list extended TO-R2-LAN
 permit ip 150.1.1.0 0.0.0.255 150.2.2.0 0.0.0.255
ip access-list extended TO-R3-LAN
 permit ip 150.1.1.0 0.0.0.255 150.3.3.0 0.0.0.255
!
route-map LAN-PBR permit 10
 match ip address TO-R2-LAN
 set ip next-hop verify-availability
 set ip default next-hop 10.0.0.6
!
route-map LAN-PBR permit 20
 match ip address TO-R3-LAN
 set ip next-hop verify-availability
 set ip default next-hop 10.0.0.2
!
route-map LAN-PBR deny 30
!
control-plane
!
line con 0
 logging synchronous
line aux 0
line vty 0 4
 login
!
end

R1#
```

R2

```
R2#term len 0
R2#sh run
Building configuration...

Current configuration : 1536 bytes
!
version 12.4
service timestamps debug datetime msec
service timestamps log datetime msec
no service password-encryption
!
hostname R2
!
boot-start-marker
boot-end-marker
!
no logging console
!
no aaa new-model
no network-clock-participate slot 1
no network-clock-participate wic 0
```

```
ip cef
!
no ip domain lookup
ip auth-proxy max-nodata-conns 3
ip admission max-nodata-conns 3
ip sla monitor 1
 type echo protocol ipIcmpEcho 10.0.0.1 source-ipaddr 10.0.0.2
ip sla monitor schedule 1 life forever start-time now
!
track 1 rtr 1
!
track 2 list boolean or
 object 1 not
!
interface FastEthernet0/0
 ip address 150.2.2.2 255.255.255.0
 ip policy route-map LAN-PBR
 duplex auto
 speed auto
!
interface Serial0/0
 ip address 10.0.0.2 255.255.255.252
!
interface Serial0/1
 ip address 10.0.0.9 255.255.255.252
!
router eigrp 254
 passive-interface FastEthernet0/0
 network 10.0.0.2 0.0.0.0
 network 150.2.0.0
 no auto-summary
!
ip forward-protocol nd
ip route 0.0.0.0 0.0.0.0 10.0.0.10
!
ip http server
no ip http secure-server
!
ip access-list extended HTTP-AND-HTTPS
 permit tcp any any eq www
 permit tcp any any eq 443
!
route-map LAN-PBR permit 10
 match ip address HTTP-AND-HTTPS
 set ip precedence flash-override
 set ip next-hop verify-availability 10.0.0.10 1 track 2
!
route-map LAN-PBR permit 20
 set ip precedence immediate
 set ip next-hop verify-availability 10.0.0.10 1 track 2
!
control-plane
!
line con 0
line aux 0
line vty 0 4
 login
!
end

R2#
```

R3

```
R3#term len 0
R3#sh run
Building configuration...

Current configuration : 1852 bytes
!
version 12.4
service timestamps debug datetime msec
service timestamps log datetime msec
no service password-encryption
!
hostname R3
!
```

```
boot-start-marker
boot-end-marker
!
no logging console
!
no aaa new-model
no network-clock-participate slot 1
no network-clock-participate wic 0
ip cef
!
no ip domain lookup
ip auth-proxy max-nodata-conns 3
ip admission max-nodata-conns 3
ip sla monitor 1
 type echo protocol ipIcmpEcho 10.0.0.5 source-ipaddr 10.0.0.6
ip sla monitor schedule 1 life forever start-time now
!
track 1 rtr 1
!
track 2 list boolean or
 object 1 not
!
interface FastEthernet0/0
 ip address 150.3.3.3 255.255.255.0
 ip policy route-map LAN-PBR
 duplex auto
 speed auto
!
interface Serial1/0
 ip address 10.0.0.6 255.255.255.252
 clock rate 128000
!
interface Serial1/1
 ip address 10.0.0.10 255.255.255.252
 clock rate 128000
!
interface Serial1/2
 no ip address
 shutdown
 clock rate 128000
!
interface Serial1/3
 no ip address
 shutdown
!
interface Serial1/4
 no ip address
 shutdown
!
interface Serial1/5
 no ip address
 shutdown
!
interface Serial1/6
 no ip address
 shutdown
!
interface Serial1/7
 no ip address
 shutdown
!
router eigrp 254
 passive-interface FastEthernet0/0
 network 10.0.0.6 0.0.0.0
 network 150.3.3.3 0.0.0.0
 no auto-summary
!
ip forward-protocol nd
ip route 0.0.0.0 0.0.0.0 10.0.0.9
!
ip http server
no ip http secure-server
!
ip access-list extended HTTP-AND-HTTPS
 permit tcp any any eq www
 permit tcp any any eq 443
!
!
route-map LAN-PBR permit 10
```

```
 match ip address HTTP-AND-HTTPS
 set ip precedence flash-override
 set ip next-hop verify-availability 10.0.0.9 1 track 2
!
route-map LAN-PBR permit 20
 set ip next-hop verify-availability 10.0.0.9 1 track 2
!
control-plane
!
line con 0
line aux 0
line vty 0 4
 login
!
end

R3#
```

R4

```
R4#term len 0
R4#sh run
Building configuration...

Current configuration : 833 bytes
!
version 12.4
service timestamps debug datetime msec
service timestamps log datetime msec
no service password-encryption
!
hostname R4
!
boot-start-marker
boot-end-marker
!
no logging console
!
no aaa new-model
no network-clock-participate slot 1
no network-clock-participate wic 0
ip cef
!
no ip domain lookup
ip auth-proxy max-nodata-conns 3
ip admission max-nodata-conns 3
!
interface FastEthernet0/0
 ip address 150.1.1.4 255.255.255.0
 duplex auto
 speed auto
!
interface Serial0/0
 no ip address
 shutdown
!
interface Serial0/1
 no ip address
 shutdown
!
router eigrp 254
 network 0.0.0.0
 no auto-summary
!
ip forward-protocol nd
!
no ip http server
no ip http secure-server
!
control-plane
!
line con 0
line aux 0
line vty 0 4
 login
!
end
R4#
```

CCNP LAB 58

Cisco IOS GLBP Lab

Lab Objective:

The focus of this lab is to understand Gateway Load Balancing Protocol (GLBP) implementation and configuration in Cisco IOS routers. Additional technologies include security and timers.

Lab Topology:

The lab network topology is illustrated below:

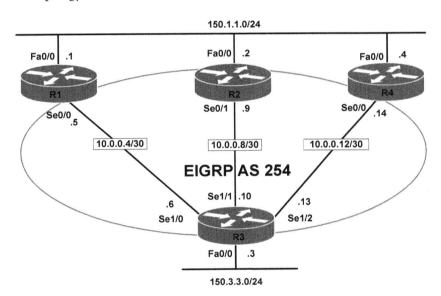

IMPORTANT NOTE: If you are using the www.howtonetwork.net racks, please bring up the LAN interfaces connected to the routers by issuing the no shutdown command on the connected switches. If you are using a home lab with no Switches, you can bring up the LAN interfaces using the following configurations on your routers:

```
interface fastethernet 0/0
  no keepalive
  loopback
  no shutdown
```

Alternately, you can simply connect the interfaces to a hub or switch if you have one available in your own lab.

Task 1

Configure hostnames, IP addressing on all routers as illustrated in the network topology.

Task 2

Configure EIGRP as illustrated in the topology. Redistribute the LAN subnets into EIGRP.

Verify your configuration using the appropriate commands on all routers in the network.

Task 3

Configure GLBP on R1, R2, and R4. Ensure that R1 is elected AVG. R2 should be standby. The gateway IP should be 150.1.1.254. Verify your configuration using the appropriate commands.

Task 4

Configure MD5 authentication for GLBP. Use a password of 'CCNP' for authentication and a key chain named GLBP. Verify your configuration using the appropriate commands.

Task 5

In the future, NAT will be implemented on R1, R2, and R3. In preparation for this, configure GLBP so that a host will be guaranteed to use the same virtual MAC address as long as the number of Virtual Forwarders (VFs) in the GLBP group is constant. Verify your configuration using the appropriate commands.

Task 6

To allow for faster failover of GLBP, configure R1, R2 and R4 so that the gateways send five Hellos every second. If four Hellos are missed, then GLBP should be declared down. Verify your configuration using the appropriate commands.

LAB VALIDATION

Task 1

Please refer to previous labs for basic IPv4, IPv6 addressing and hostname configuration. This will not be included in this section to avoid being redundant.

Task 2

Please refer to previous labs for basic EIGRP configuration. Following this, verify your EIGRP configuration using the `show ip eigrp neighbors` and `show ip route` commands. Following this configuration, your route tables should show the following route information:

```
R1#show ip route eigrp
     10.0.0.0/30 is subnetted, 3 subnets
D       10.0.0.8 [90/21024000] via 10.0.0.6, 00:03:06, Serial0/1
D       10.0.0.12 [90/21024000] via 10.0.0.6, 00:02:11, Serial0/1
     150.3.0.0/24 is subnetted, 1 subnets
D EX    150.3.3.0 [170/2172416] via 10.0.0.6, 00:03:06, Serial0/1

R2#show ip route eigrp
     10.0.0.0/30 is subnetted, 3 subnets
D       10.0.0.12 [90/21024000] via 10.0.0.10, 00:02:15, Serial0/1
D       10.0.0.4 [90/21024000] via 10.0.0.10, 00:03:10, Serial0/1
     150.3.0.0/24 is subnetted, 1 subnets
D EX    150.3.3.0 [170/2172416] via 10.0.0.10, 00:03:10, Serial0/1

R3#show ip route eigrp
     150.1.0.0/24 is subnetted, 1 subnets
D EX    150.1.1.0 [170/20514560] via 10.0.0.14, 00:02:16, Serial1/2
                  [170/20514560] via 10.0.0.9, 00:02:16, Serial1/1
                  [170/20514560] via 10.0.0.5, 00:02:16, Serial1/0

R4#show ip route eigrp
     10.0.0.0/30 is subnetted, 3 subnets
D       10.0.0.8 [90/21024000] via 10.0.0.13, 00:02:22, Serial0/0
D       10.0.0.4 [90/21024000] via 10.0.0.13, 00:02:22, Serial0/0
     150.3.0.0/24 is subnetted, 1 subnets
D EX    150.3.3.0 [170/2172416] via 10.0.0.13, 00:02:22, Serial0/0
```

Task 3

To complete this task, you need to configure R1 with the highest priority. In order to ensure that R2 is elected standby, this router should be assigned the second highest priority. By default, GLBP assigns a priority of 100. Finally, you need to explicitly enable preemption as it is disabled by default. This task is completed as follows:

```
R1(config)#interface fastethernet 0/0
R1(config-if)#glbp 1 priority 110
R1(config-if)#glbp 1 ip 150.1.1.254
R1(config-if)#glbp 1 preempt
R1(config-if)#exit

R2(config)#interface fastethernet 0/0
R2(config-if)#glbp 1 priority 105
R2(config-if)#glbp 1 ip 150.1.1.254
R2(config-if)#glbp 1 preempt
R2(config-if)#exit

R4(config)#interface fastethernet 0/0
R4(config-if)#glbp 1 preempt
R4(config-if)#glbp 1 ip 150.1.1.254
R4(config-if)#exit
```

Following this, verify your configuration using the show glbp command:

```
R1#show glbp fastethernet 0/0 1 brief
Interface  Grp  Fwd  Pri  State    Address         Active router   Standby router
Fa0/0      1    -    110  Active   150.1.1.254     local           150.1.1.2
Fa0/0      1    1    -    Active   0007.b400.0101  local           -
Fa0/0      1    2    -    Listen   0007.b400.0102  150.1.1.2       -
Fa0/0      1    3    -    Listen   0007.b400.0103  150.1.1.4       -

R2#show glbp fastethernet 0/0 1 brief
Interface  Grp  Fwd  Pri  State    Address         Active router   Standby router
Fa0/0      1    -    105  Standby  150.1.1.254     150.1.1.1       local
Fa0/0      1    1    -    Listen   0007.b400.0101  150.1.1.1       -
Fa0/0      1    2    -    Active   0007.b400.0102  local           -
Fa0/0      1    3    -    Listen   0007.b400.0103  150.1.1.4       -

R4#show glbp fastethernet 0/0 1 brief
Interface  Grp  Fwd  Pri  State    Address         Active router   Standby router
Fa0/0      1    -    100  Listen   150.1.1.254     150.1.1.1       150.1.1.2
Fa0/0      1    1    -    Listen   0007.b400.0101  150.1.1.1       -
Fa0/0      1    2    -    Listen   0007.b400.0102  150.1.1.2       -
Fa0/0      1    3    -    Active   0007.b400.0103  local           -
```

Task 4

```
R1(config)#key chain GLBP
R1(config-keychain)#key 1
R1(config-keychain-key)#key-string CCNP
R1(config-keychain-key)#exit
R1(config-keychain)#exit
R1(config)#interface fastethernet 0/0
R1(config-if)#glbp 1 authentication md5 key-chain GLBP
R1(config-if)#exit
R1(config)#end

R2(config)#key chain GLBP
R2(config-keychain)#key 1
R2(config-keychain-key)#key-string CCNP
R2(config-keychain-key)#exit
R2(config-keychain)#exit
R2(config)#interface fastethernet 0/0
R2(config-if)#glbp 1 authentication md5 key-chain GLBP
R2(config-if)#exit
R2(config)#end

R4(config)#key chain GLBP
R4(config-keychain)#key 1
```

```
R4(config-keychain-key)#key-string CCNP
R4(config-keychain-key)#exit
R4(config-keychain)#exit
R4(config)#interface fastethernet 0/0
R4(config-if)#glbp 1 authentication md5 key-chain GLBP
R4(config-if)#exit
R4(config)#end
```

Next, verify your configuration using the show key chain and show glbp commands:

```
R1#show key chain GLBP
Key-chain GLBP:
    key 1 -- text "CCNP"
        accept lifetime (always valid) - (always valid) [valid now]
        send lifetime (always valid) - (always valid) [valid now]

R1#show glbp fastethernet 0/0 1
FastEthernet0/0 - Group 1
  State is Active
    2 state changes, last state change 00:11:27
  Virtual IP address is 150.1.1.254
  Hello time 3 sec, hold time 10 sec
    Next hello sent in 2.780 secs
  Redirect time 600 sec, forwarder time-out 14400 sec
  Authentication MD5, key-chain "GLBP"
  Preemption enabled, min delay 0 sec
  Active is local
  Standby is 150.1.1.2, priority 105 (expires in 8.620 sec)
  Priority 110 (configured)
  Weighting 100 (default 100), thresholds: lower 1, upper 100
  Load balancing: round-robin
  Group members:
    000d.289e.f940 (150.1.1.2) authenticated
    000f.235e.ec80 (150.1.1.1) local
    000f.235e.f120 (150.1.1.4) authenticated
  There are 3 forwarders (1 active)
```

[Truncated Output]

Task 5

Stateful applications such as Network Address Translation (NAT) require that state information be maintained for each connection. It is therefore important to ensure that a host will use the same gateway as this is where the NAT translations will exist. By default, GLBP will use round robin load balancing. This can cause issues when NATing. To ensure that a host will be guaranteed to use the same virtual MAC address as long as the number of Virtual Forwaders (VFs) in the GLBP group is constant we need to configure GLBP to use host dependent load balancing. This task is completed on R1 and R2. The only reason R4 would ever become GLBP AVG would be when R1 and R2 are down. In this case, there is no need to implement any type of load balancing as it will be the only gateway.

The reason that this command is required on R2 is that if R1 fails, it assumes roles of AVG. It should therefore be configured to use this load balancing method for itself and R4:

```
R1(config)#interface fastethernet 0/0
R1(config-if)#glbp 1 load-balancing host-dependent
R1(config-if)#exit

R2(config)#interface fastethernet 0/0
R2(config-if)#glbp 1 load-balancing host-dependent
R2(config-if)#exit
```

Verify the adjusted load balancing method using the show glbp command:

```
R1#show glbp fastethernet 0/0 1
FastEthernet0/0 - Group 1
  State is Active
    2 state changes, last state change 00:19:44
  Virtual IP address is 150.1.1.254
```

```
Hello time 3 sec, hold time 10 sec
    Next hello sent in 0.888 secs
Redirect time 600 sec, forwarder time-out 14400 sec
Authentication MD5, key-chain "GLBP"
Preemption enabled, min delay 0 sec
Active is local
Standby is 150.1.1.2, priority 105 (expires in 9.740 sec)
Priority 110 (configured)
Weighting 100 (default 100), thresholds: lower 1, upper 100
Load balancing: host-dependent
Group members:
    000d.289e.f940 (150.1.1.2) authenticated
    000f.235e.ec80 (150.1.1.1) local
    000f.235e.f120 (150.1.1.4) authenticated
There are 3 forwarders (1 active)

[Truncated Output]

R2#show glbp fastethernet 0/0 1
FastEthernet0/0 - Group 1
  State is Standby
    1 state change, last state change 00:16:48
  Virtual IP address is 150.1.1.254
  Hello time 3 sec, hold time 10 sec
    Next hello sent in 0.000 secs
  Redirect time 600 sec, forwarder time-out 14400 sec
  Authentication MD5, key-chain "GLBP"
  Preemption enabled, min delay 0 sec
  Active is 150.1.1.1, priority 110 (expires in 8.096 sec)
  Standby is local
  Priority 105 (configured)
  Weighting 100 (default 100), thresholds: lower 1, upper 100
  Load balancing: host-dependent
  Group members:
    000d.289e.f940 (150.1.1.2) local
    000f.235e.ec80 (150.1.1.1) authenticated
    000f.235e.f120 (150.1.1.4) authenticated
  There are 3 forwarders (1 active)

[Truncated Output]
```

Task 6

The requirements of this task are straightforward. To ensure that routers send five Hellos every two seconds, we need to perform basic mathematical calculations. First, there are 1000 milliseconds in a second, therefore, GLBP should be configured to send Hellos every 200 ms. Next, if four Hellos are missed, GLBP should be declared down. This means we need to configure a hold time of 800 ms. This task is completed on all four GLBP routers as follows:

```
R1(config)#interface fastethernet 0/0
R1(config-if)#glbp 1 timers msec 200 msec 800
R1(config-if)#exit

R2(config)#interface fastethernet 0/0
R2(config-if)#glbp 1 timers msec 200 msec 800
R2(config-if)#exit

R3(config)#interface fastethernet 0/0
R3(config-if)#glbp 1 timers msec 200 msec 800
R3(config-if)#exit
```

Next, verify your GLBP configuration using the show glbp command:

```
R1#show glbp fastethernet 0/0
FastEthernet0/0 - Group 1
  State is Active
    2 state changes, last state change 01:15:11
  Virtual IP address is 150.1.1.254
  Hello time 200 msec, hold time 800 msec
    Next hello sent in 0.004 secs
  Redirect time 600 sec, forwarder time-out 14400 sec
  Authentication MD5, key-chain "GLBP"
```

```
  Preemption enabled, min delay 0 sec
  Active is local
  Standby is 150.1.1.2, priority 105 (expires in 0.744 sec)
  Priority 110 (configured)
  Weighting 100 (default 100), thresholds: lower 1, upper 100
  Load balancing: host-dependent
  Group members:
    000d.289e.f940 (150.1.1.2) authenticated
    000f.235e.ec80 (150.1.1.1) local
    000f.235e.f120 (150.1.1.4) authenticated
  There are 3 forwarders (1 active)

[Truncated Output]

R2#show glbp fastethernet 0/0
FastEthernet0/0 - Group 1
  State is Standby
    4 state changes, last state change 00:08:54
  Virtual IP address is 150.1.1.254
  Hello time 200 msec, hold time 800 msec
    Next hello sent in 0.000 secs
  Redirect time 600 sec, forwarder time-out 14400 sec
  Authentication MD5, key-chain "GLBP"
  Preemption enabled, min delay 0 sec
  Active is 150.1.1.1, priority 110 (expires in 0.608 sec)
  Standby is local
  Priority 105 (configured)
  Weighting 100 (default 100), thresholds: lower 1, upper 100
  Load balancing: host-dependent
  Group members:
    000d.289e.f940 (150.1.1.2) local
    000f.235e.ec80 (150.1.1.1) authenticated
    000f.235e.f120 (150.1.1.4) authenticated
  There are 3 forwarders (1 active)

[Truncated Output]

R4#show glbp fastethernet 0/0
FastEthernet0/0 - Group 1
  State is Listen
    2 state changes, last state change 00:08:57
  Virtual IP address is 150.1.1.254
  Hello time 200 msec, hold time 800 msec
    Next hello sent in 0.056 secs
  Redirect time 600 sec, forwarder time-out 14400 sec
  Authentication MD5, key-chain "GLBP"
  Preemption enabled, min delay 0 sec
  Active is 150.1.1.1, priority 110 (expires in 0.568 sec)
  Standby is 150.1.1.2, priority 105 (expires in 0.560 sec)
  Priority 100 (default)
  Weighting 100 (default 100), thresholds: lower 1, upper 100
  Load balancing: round-robin
  Group members:
    000d.289e.f940 (150.1.1.2) authenticated
    000f.235e.ec80 (150.1.1.1) authenticated
    000f.235e.f120 (150.1.1.4) local
  There are 3 forwarders (1 active)

[Truncated Output]
```

FINAL ROUTER CONFIGURATIONS

R1

```
R1#term len 0
R1#sh run
Building configuration...

Current configuration : 1106 bytes
!
version 12.4
service timestamps debug datetime msec
```

```
service timestamps log datetime msec
no service password-encryption
!
hostname R1
!
boot-start-marker
boot-end-marker
!
no logging console
!
no aaa new-model
no network-clock-participate slot 1
no network-clock-participate wic 0
ip cef
!
no ip domain lookup
ip auth-proxy max-nodata-conns 3
ip admission max-nodata-conns 3
!
key chain GLBP
 key 1
   key-string CCNP
!
interface FastEthernet0/0
 ip address 150.1.1.1 255.255.255.0
 duplex auto
 speed auto
 glbp 1 ip 150.1.1.254
 glbp 1 timers msec 200 msec 800
 glbp 1 priority 110
 glbp 1 preempt
 glbp 1 load-balancing host-dependent
 glbp 1 authentication md5 key-chain GLBP
!
interface Serial0/0
 no ip address
 shutdown
 clock rate 2000000
!
interface Serial0/1
 ip address 10.0.0.5 255.255.255.252
!
router eigrp 254
 redistribute connected
 network 10.0.0.0
 no auto-summary
!
ip forward-protocol nd
!
no ip http server
no ip http secure-server
!
control-plane
!
line con 0
line aux 0
line vty 0 4
 login
!
end

R1#
```

R2

```
R2#term len 0
R2#sh run
Building configuration...

Current configuration : 1086 bytes
!
version 12.4
service timestamps debug datetime msec
service timestamps log datetime msec
```

```
no service password-encryption
!
hostname R2
!
boot-start-marker
boot-end-marker
!
no logging console
!
no aaa new-model
no network-clock-participate slot 1
no network-clock-participate wic 0
ip cef
!
no ip domain lookup
ip auth-proxy max-nodata-conns 3
ip admission max-nodata-conns 3
!
key chain GLBP
 key 1
   key-string CCNP
!
interface FastEthernet0/0
 ip address 150.1.1.2 255.255.255.0
 duplex auto
 speed auto
 glbp 1 ip 150.1.1.254
 glbp 1 timers msec 200 msec 800
 glbp 1 priority 105
 glbp 1 preempt
 glbp 1 load-balancing host-dependent
 glbp 1 authentication md5 key-chain GLBP
!
interface Serial0/0
 no ip address
 shutdown
!
interface Serial0/1
 ip address 10.0.0.9 255.255.255.252
!
router eigrp 254
 redistribute connected
 network 10.0.0.0
 no auto-summary
!
ip forward-protocol nd
!
no ip http server
no ip http secure-server
!
control-plane
!
line con 0
line aux 0
line vty 0 4
 login
!
end

R2#
```

R3

```
R3#term len 0
R3#sh run
Building configuration...

Current configuration : 1235 bytes
!
version 12.4
service timestamps debug datetime msec
service timestamps log datetime msec
no service password-encryption
!
```

```
hostname R3
!
boot-start-marker
boot-end-marker
!
no logging console
!
no aaa new-model
no network-clock-participate slot 1
no network-clock-participate wic 0
ip cef
!
no ip domain lookup
ip auth-proxy max-nodata-conns 3
ip admission max-nodata-conns 3
!
interface FastEthernet0/0
 ip address 150.3.3.3 255.255.255.0
 duplex auto
 speed auto
!
interface Serial1/0
 ip address 10.0.0.6 255.255.255.252
 clock rate 128000
!
interface Serial1/1
 ip address 10.0.0.10 255.255.255.252
 clock rate 128000
!
interface Serial1/2
 ip address 10.0.0.13 255.255.255.252
 clock rate 128000
!
interface Serial1/3
 no ip address
 shutdown
!
interface Serial1/4
 no ip address
 shutdown
!
interface Serial1/5
 no ip address
 shutdown
!
interface Serial1/6
 no ip address
 shutdown
!
interface Serial1/7
 no ip address
 shutdown
!
router eigrp 254
 redistribute connected
 network 10.0.0.0
 no auto-summary
!
ip forward-protocol nd
!
no ip http server
no ip http secure-server
!
control-plane
!
line con 0
line aux 0
line vty 0 4
 login
!
end

R3#
```

R4

```
R4#term len 0
R4#sh run
Building configuration...

Current configuration : 1028 bytes
!
version 12.4
service timestamps debug datetime msec
service timestamps log datetime msec
no service password-encryption
!
hostname R4
!
boot-start-marker
boot-end-marker
!
no logging console
!
no aaa new-model
no network-clock-participate slot 1
no network-clock-participate wic 0
ip cef
!
no ip domain lookup
ip auth-proxy max-nodata-conns 3
ip admission max-nodata-conns 3
!
key chain GLBP
 key 1
   key-string CCNP
!
interface FastEthernet0/0
 ip address 150.1.1.4 255.255.255.0
 duplex auto
 speed auto
 glbp 1 ip 150.1.1.254
 glbp 1 timers msec 200 msec 800
 glbp 1 preempt
 glbp 1 authentication md5 key-chain GLBP
!
interface Serial0/0
 ip address 10.0.0.14 255.255.255.252
!
interface Serial0/1
 no ip address
 shutdown
!
router eigrp 254
 redistribute connected
 network 10.0.0.0
 no auto-summary
!
ip forward-protocol nd
!
no ip http server
no ip http secure-server
!
control-plane
!
line con 0
line aux 0
line vty 0 4
 login
!
end

R4#
```

CCNP LAB 59

Cisco IOS GLBP Lab

Lab Objective:

The focus of this lab is to understand Gateway Load Balancing Protocol (GLBP) implementation and configuration in Cisco IOS routers. Additional technologies include GLBP load balancing.

Lab Topology:

The lab network topology is illustrated below:

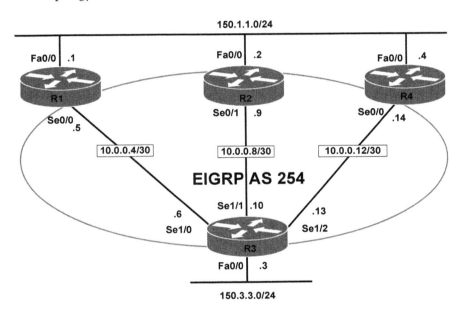

IMPORTANT NOTE: If you are using the www.howtonetwork.net racks, please bring up the LAN interfaces connected to the routers by issuing the no shutdown command on the connected switches. If you are using a home lab with no Switches, you can bring up the LAN interfaces using the following configurations on your routers:

```
interface fastethernet 0/0
  no keepalive
  loopback
  no shutdown
```

Alternately, you can simply connect the interfaces to a hub or switch if you have one available in your own lab.

Task 1

Configure hostnames, IP addressing on all routers as illustrated in the network topology.

Task 2

Configure EIGRP as illustrated in the topology. Redistribute the LAN subnets into EIGRP.

Verify your configuration using the appropriate commands on all routers in the network.

Task 3

Configure GLBP on R1, R2, and R4. Ensure that R1 is elected AVG. R2 should be standby. The gateway IP should be 150.1.1.254. Verify your configuration using the appropriate commands.

Task 4

Configure load balancing for GLBP so that traffic is distributed between R1, R2 and R4 using a ratio of 50:30:20. In the event that R1 fails, R2 should use the default load balancing method. Verify your configuration using the appropriate commands.

Task 5

Management has requested that when R2 becomes AVG, old forwarder MAC address that was assigned to R1 ceases being used and hosts are migrated away from this address as soon as possible. Configure GLBP so that when R2 becomes AVG, it stops using the old virtual forwarder MAC address in ARP replies within one minute.

To allow for dynamic host ARP cache timeout, ensure that R2 continues to forward packets that were sent to the old virtual forwarder MAC address for no more than five hours. Verify your configuration using the appropriate commands.

Task 6

In the future, multiple GLBP groups will be configured on the LAN segment connecting routers R1, R2, and R5. To allow for easier identification as to what these groups are for, configure the current GLBP group with a group name of 'SERVER-GLBP-GROUP'. Verify your configuration using the appropriate commands.

LAB VALIDATION

Task 1

Please refer to previous labs for basic IPv4, IPv6 addressing and hostname configuration. This will not be included in this section to avoid being redundant.

Task 2

Please refer to previous labs for basic EIGRP configuration. Following this, verify your EIGRP configuration using the `show ip eigrp neighbors` and `show ip route` commands. Following this configuration, your route tables should show the following route information:

```
R1#show ip route eigrp
     10.0.0.0/30 is subnetted, 3 subnets
D       10.0.0.8 [90/21024000] via 10.0.0.6, 00:03:06, Serial0/1
D       10.0.0.12 [90/21024000] via 10.0.0.6, 00:02:11, Serial0/1
     150.3.0.0/24 is subnetted, 1 subnets
D EX    150.3.3.0 [170/2172416] via 10.0.0.6, 00:03:06, Serial0/1

R2#show ip route eigrp
     10.0.0.0/30 is subnetted, 3 subnets
D       10.0.0.12 [90/21024000] via 10.0.0.10, 00:02:15, Serial0/1
D       10.0.0.4 [90/21024000] via 10.0.0.10, 00:03:10, Serial0/1
     150.3.0.0/24 is subnetted, 1 subnets
D EX    150.3.3.0 [170/2172416] via 10.0.0.10, 00:03:10, Serial0/1

R3#show ip route eigrp
     150.1.0.0/24 is subnetted, 1 subnets
D EX    150.1.1.0 [170/20514560] via 10.0.0.14, 00:02:16, Serial1/2
                  [170/20514560] via 10.0.0.9, 00:02:16, Serial1/1
                  [170/20514560] via 10.0.0.5, 00:02:16, Serial1/0

R4#show ip route eigrp
```

```
      10.0.0.0/30 is subnetted, 3 subnets
D        10.0.0.8 [90/21024000] via 10.0.0.13, 00:02:22, Serial0/0
D        10.0.0.4 [90/21024000] via 10.0.0.13, 00:02:22, Serial0/0
      150.3.0.0/24 is subnetted, 1 subnets
D EX   150.3.3.0 [170/2172416] via 10.0.0.13, 00:02:22, Serial0/0
```

Task 3

To complete this task, you need to configure R1 with the highest priority. In order to ensure that R2 is elected standby, this router should be assigned the second highest priority. By default, GLBP assigns a priority of 100. Finally, you need to explicitly enable preemption as it is disabled by default. This task is completed as follows:

```
R1(config)#interface fastethernet 0/0
R1(config-if)#glbp 1 priority 110
R1(config-if)#glbp 1 ip 150.1.1.254
R1(config-if)#glbp 1 preempt
R1(config-if)#exit

R2(config)#interface fastethernet 0/0
R2(config-if)#glbp 1 priority 105
R2(config-if)#glbp 1 ip 150.1.1.254
R2(config-if)#glbp 1 preempt
R2(config-if)#exit

R4(config)#interface fastethernet 0/0
R4(config-if)#glbp 1 preempt
R4(config-if)#glbp 1 ip 150.1.1.254
R4(config-if)#exit
```

Following this, verify your configuration using the show glbp command:

```
R1#show glbp fastethernet 0/0 1 brief
Interface  Grp  Fwd  Pri  State     Address         Active router   Standby router
Fa0/0      1    -    110  Active    150.1.1.254     local           150.1.1.2
Fa0/0      1    1    -    Active    0007.b400.0101  local           -
Fa0/0      1    2    -    Listen    0007.b400.0102  150.1.1.2       -
Fa0/0      1    3    -    Listen    0007.b400.0103  150.1.1.4       -

R2#show glbp fastethernet 0/0 1 brief
Interface  Grp  Fwd  Pri  State     Address         Active router   Standby router
Fa0/0      1    -    105  Standby   150.1.1.254     150.1.1.1       local
Fa0/0      1    1    -    Listen    0007.b400.0101  150.1.1.1       -
Fa0/0      1    2    -    Active    0007.b400.0102  local           -
Fa0/0      1    3    -    Listen    0007.b400.0103  150.1.1.4       -

R4#show glbp fastethernet 0/0 1 brief
Interface  Grp  Fwd  Pri  State     Address         Active router   Standby router
Fa0/0      1    -    100  Listen    150.1.1.254     150.1.1.1       150.1.1.2
Fa0/0      1    1    -    Listen    0007.b400.0101  150.1.1.1       -
Fa0/0      1    2    -    Listen    0007.b400.0102  150.1.1.2       -
Fa0/0      1    3    -    Active    0007.b400.0103  local           -
```

Task 4

GLBP uses a weighting scheme to determine the forwarding capacity of each gateway that is in the GLBP group. The weighting assigned to a gateway in the GLBP group can be used to determine whether it will forward packets and, if so, the proportion of hosts in the LAN for which it will forward packets.

By default, each gateway is assigned a weight of 100. Administrators can additionally configure the gateways to make dynamic weighting adjustments by configuring object tracking, such as for interfaces and IP prefixes, in conjunction with GLBP. If an interface fails, the weighting is dynamically decreased by the specified value, allowing gateways with higher weighting values to be used to forward more traffic than those with lower weighting values.

In addition to this, thresholds can be set to disable forwarding when the weighting for a GLBP group falls below a certain value, and then when it rises above another threshold, forwarding is automatically re-enabled.

A backup virtual forwarder can become the AVF if the current AVF weighting falls below the low weighting threshold for 30 seconds. This is the ability GLBP to place a weight on each device when calculating the amount of load sharing that will occur through MAC assignment. Each GLBP router in the group will advertise its weighting and assignment; the AVG will act based on that value.

To complete this task, we need to change the load balancing method from round robin (default) to weighted. Next, we need to specify the ratios on the AVG (R1). This is completed as follows:

```
R1(config)#interface fastethernet 0/0
R1(config-if)#glbp 1 weighting 50
R1(config-if)#glbp 1 load-balancing weighted
R1(config-if)#exit

R2(config)#interface fastethernet 0/0
R2(config-if)#glbp 1 weighting 30
R2(config-if)#exit

R4(config)#interface fastethernet 0/0
R4(config-if)#glbp 1 weighting 20
R4(config-if)#exit
```

Following this, verify your configuration using the show glbp command:

```
R1#show glbp fastethernet 0/0
FastEthernet0/0 - Group 1
  State is Active
    2 state changes, last state change 01:57:27
  Virtual IP address is 150.1.1.254
  Hello time 3 sec, hold time 10 sec
    Next hello sent in 1.716 secs
  Redirect time 600 sec, forwarder time-out 14400 sec
  Preemption enabled, min delay 0 sec
  Active is local
  Standby is 150.1.1.2, priority 105 (expires in 9.656 sec)
  Priority 110 (configured)
  Weighting 50 (configured 50), thresholds: lower 1, upper 50
  Load balancing: weighted
  Group members:
    000d.289e.f940 (150.1.1.2)
    000f.235e.ec80 (150.1.1.1) local
    000f.235e.f120 (150.1.1.4)
  There are 3 forwarders (1 active)
  Forwarder 1
    State is Active
      1 state change, last state change 01:57:17
    MAC address is 0007.b400.0101 (default)
    Owner ID is 000f.235e.ec80
    Redirection enabled
    Preemption enabled, min delay 30 sec
    Active is local, weighting 50
  Forwarder 2
    State is Listen
      8 state changes, last state change 00:32:27
    MAC address is 0007.b400.0102 (learnt)
    Owner ID is 000d.289e.f940
    Redirection enabled, 57.128 sec remaining (maximum 60 sec)
    Time to live: 17997.124 sec (maximum 18000 sec)
    Preemption enabled, min delay 30 sec
    Active is 150.1.1.2 (primary), weighting 30 (expires in 7.124 sec)
  Forwarder 3
    State is Listen
      4 state changes, last state change 00:32:20
    MAC address is 0007.b400.0103 (learnt)
    Owner ID is 000f.235e.f120
    Redirection enabled, 599.192 sec remaining (maximum 600 sec)
    Time to live: 14399.192 sec (maximum 14400 sec)
    Preemption enabled, min delay 30 sec
    Active is 150.1.1.4 (primary), weighting 20 (expires in 9.188 sec)

R2#show glbp fastethernet 0/0
FastEthernet0/0 - Group 1
  State is Standby
```

```
    7 state changes, last state change 00:34:18
Virtual IP address is 150.1.1.254
Hello time 3 sec, hold time 10 sec
   Next hello sent in 0.012 secs
Redirect time 60 sec, forwarder time-out 18000 sec
Preemption enabled, min delay 0 sec
Active is 150.1.1.1, priority 110 (expires in 9.048 sec)
Standby is local
Priority 105 (configured)
Weighting 30 (configured 30), thresholds: lower 1, upper 30
Load balancing: round-robin
Group members:
   000d.289e.f940 (150.1.1.2) local
   000f.235e.ec80 (150.1.1.1)
   000f.235e.f120 (150.1.1.4)
There are 3 forwarders (1 active)
Forwarder 1
   State is Listen
     6 state changes, last state change 00:34:48
   MAC address is 0007.b400.0101 (learnt)
   Owner ID is 000f.235e.ec80
   Time to live: 14399.000 sec (maximum 14400 sec)
   Preemption enabled, min delay 30 sec
   Active is 150.1.1.1 (primary), weighting 50 (expires in 8.996 sec)
Forwarder 2
   State is Active
     1 state change, last state change 01:56:41
   MAC address is 0007.b400.0102 (default)
   Owner ID is 000d.289e.f940
   Preemption enabled, min delay 30 sec
   Active is local, weighting 30
Forwarder 3
   State is Listen
     8 state changes, last state change 00:34:13
   MAC address is 0007.b400.0103 (learnt)
   Owner ID is 000f.235e.f120
   Time to live: 14399.004 sec (maximum 14400 sec)
   Preemption enabled, min delay 30 sec
   Active is 150.1.1.4 (primary), weighting 20 (expires in 9.000 sec)

R4#show glbp fastethernet 0/0
FastEthernet0/0 - Group 1
   State is Listen
     7 state changes, last state change 00:36:37
   Virtual IP address is 150.1.1.254
   Hello time 3 sec, hold time 10 sec
     Next hello sent in 1.904 secs
   Redirect time 600 sec, forwarder time-out 14400 sec
   Preemption enabled, min delay 0 sec
   Active is 150.1.1.1, priority 110 (expires in 8.892 sec)
   Standby is 150.1.1.2, priority 105 (expires in 9.852 sec)
   Priority 100 (default)
   Weighting 20 (configured 20), thresholds: lower 1, upper 20
   Load balancing: round-robin
   Group members:
     000d.289e.f940 (150.1.1.2)
     000f.235e.ec80 (150.1.1.1)
     000f.235e.f120 (150.1.1.4) local
   There are 3 forwarders (1 active)
   Forwarder 1
     State is Listen
       4 state changes, last state change 00:36:37
     MAC address is 0007.b400.0101 (learnt)
     Owner ID is 000f.235e.ec80
     Time to live: 14399.596 sec (maximum 14400 sec)
     Preemption enabled, min delay 30 sec
     Active is 150.1.1.1 (primary), weighting 50 (expires in 9.592 sec)
   Forwarder 2
     State is Listen
       8 state changes, last state change 00:36:38
     MAC address is 0007.b400.0102 (learnt)
     Owner ID is 000d.289e.f940
     Time to live: 17997.552 sec (maximum 18000 sec)
     Preemption enabled, min delay 30 sec
     Active is 150.1.1.2 (primary), weighting 30 (expires in 7.552 sec)
   Forwarder 3
     State is Active
```

```
     1 state change, last state change 01:58:08
   MAC address is 0007.b400.0103 (default)
   Owner ID is 000f.235e.f120
   Preemption enabled, min delay 30 sec
   Active is local, weighting 20
```

Task 5

Within the GLBP group, a single gateway is elected as the AVG, and another gateway is elected as the standby virtual gateway. All other remaining gateways in the group are placed in a listen state. If an AVG fails, the standby virtual gateway will assume responsibility for the virtual IP address. At the same time, an election is held and a new standby virtual gateway is then elected from the gateways currently in the listen state.

In the event the AVF fails, one of the secondary virtual forwarders in the listen state assumes responsibility for the virtual MAC address. However, because the new AVF is already a forwarder using another virtual MAC address, GLBP needs to ensure that the old forwarder MAC address ceases being used and hosts are migrated away from this address. This is achieved using two timers:

* The redirect timer
* The timeout timer

The redirect time is the interval during which the AVG continues to redirect hosts to the old virtual forwarder MAC address. When this timer expires, the AVG stops using the old virtual forwarder MAC address in ARP replies, although the virtual forwarder will continue to forward packets that were sent to the old virtual forwarder MAC address.

When the timeout timer expires, the virtual forwarder is removed from all the gateways in the GLBP group. Any clients still using the old MAC address within their ARP caches must refresh the entry to obtain the new virtual MAC address. GLBP uses the hello messages to communicate the current state of these two timers. This task is completed on R2 as follows:

```
R2(config)#interface fastethernet 0/0
R2(config-if)#glbp 1 timers redirect 60 18000
R2(config-if)#exit
```

Next, verify your configuration using the **show glbp** command:

```
R2#show glbp fastethernet 0/0
FastEthernet0/0 - Group 1
  State is Standby
    7 state changes, last state change 00:21:39
  Virtual IP address is 150.1.1.254
  Hello time 3 sec, hold time 10 sec
    Next hello sent in 2.360 secs
  Redirect time 60 sec (active 600 sec), forwarder time-out 18000 sec (active 14400
sec)
  Preemption enabled, min delay 0 sec
  Active is 150.1.1.1, priority 110 (expires in 8.328 sec)
  Standby is local

[Truncated Output]
```

Task 6

The requirement of this task is straightforward and is completed as follows:

```
R1(config)#interface fastethernet 0/0
R1(config-if)#glbp 1 name SERVER-GLBP-GROUP
R1(config-if)#exit

R2(config)#interface fastethernet 0/0
R2(config-if)#glbp 1 name SERVER-GLBP-GROUP
R2(config-if)#exit
```

```
R4(config)#interface fastethernet 0/0
R4(config-if)#glbp 1 name SERVER-GLBP-GROUP
R4(config-if)#exit
```

Following this, verify your configuration using the show glbp command:

```
R1#show glbp fastethernet 0/0
FastEthernet0/0 - Group 1
  State is Active
    2 state changes, last state change 01:52:39
  Virtual IP address is 150.1.1.254
  Hello time 3 sec, hold time 10 sec
    Next hello sent in 2.096 secs
  Redirect time 600 sec, forwarder time-out 14400 sec
  Preemption enabled, min delay 0 sec
  Active is local
  Standby is 150.1.1.2, priority 105 (expires in 7.124 sec)
  Priority 110 (configured)
  Weighting 50 (configured 50), thresholds: lower 1, upper 50
  Load balancing: weighted
  IP redundancy name is "SERVER-GLBP-GROUP"
  Group members:
    000d.289e.f940 (150.1.1.2)
    000f.235e.ec80 (150.1.1.1) local
    000f.235e.f120 (150.1.1.4)

[Truncated Output]

R2#show glbp fastethernet 0/0
FastEthernet0/0 - Group 1
  State is Standby
    7 state changes, last state change 00:27:53
  Virtual IP address is 150.1.1.254
  Hello time 3 sec, hold time 10 sec
    Next hello sent in 0.980 secs
  Redirect time 60 sec (active 600 sec), forwarder time-out 18000 sec (active 14400
sec)
  Preemption enabled, min delay 0 sec
  Active is 150.1.1.1, priority 110 (expires in 6.944 sec)
  Standby is local
  Priority 105 (configured)
  Weighting 30 (configured 30), thresholds: lower 1, upper 30
  Load balancing: round-robin
  IP redundancy name is "SERVER-GLBP-GROUP"
  Group members:
    000d.289e.f940 (150.1.1.2) local
    000f.235e.ec80 (150.1.1.1)
    000f.235e.f120 (150.1.1.4)

[Truncated Output]

R4#show glbp fastethernet 0/0
FastEthernet0/0 - Group 1
  State is Listen
    7 state changes, last state change 00:27:49
  Virtual IP address is 150.1.1.254
  Hello time 3 sec, hold time 10 sec
    Next hello sent in 1.564 secs
  Redirect time 600 sec, forwarder time-out 14400 sec
  Preemption enabled, min delay 0 sec
  Active is 150.1.1.1, priority 110 (expires in 8.460 sec)
  Standby is 150.1.1.2, priority 105 (expires in 9.488 sec)
  Priority 100 (default)
  Weighting 20 (configured 20), thresholds: lower 1, upper 20
  Load balancing: round-robin
  IP redundancy name is "SERVER-GLBP-GROUP"
  Group members:
    000d.289e.f940 (150.1.1.2)
    000f.235e.ec80 (150.1.1.1)
    000f.235e.f120 (150.1.1.4) local

[Truncated Output]
```

FINAL ROUTER CONFIGURATIONS

R1

```
R1#term len 0
R1#sh run
Building configuration...

Current configuration : 1034 bytes
!
version 12.4
service timestamps debug datetime msec
service timestamps log datetime msec
no service password-encryption
!
hostname R1
!
boot-start-marker
boot-end-marker
!
no logging console
!
no aaa new-model
no network-clock-participate slot 1
no network-clock-participate wic 0
ip cef
!
no ip domain lookup
ip auth-proxy max-nodata-conns 3
ip admission max-nodata-conns 3
!
interface FastEthernet0/0
 ip address 150.1.1.1 255.255.255.0
 duplex auto
 speed auto
 glbp 1 ip 150.1.1.254
 glbp 1 priority 110
 glbp 1 preempt
 glbp 1 weighting 50
 glbp 1 load-balancing weighted
 glbp 1 name SERVER-GLBP-GROUP
!
interface Serial0/0
 no ip address
 shutdown
 clock rate 2000000
!
interface Serial0/1
 ip address 10.0.0.5 255.255.255.252
!
router eigrp 254
 redistribute connected
 network 10.0.0.0
 no auto-summary
!
ip forward-protocol nd
!
no ip http server
no ip http secure-server
!
control-plane
!
line con 0
line aux 0
line vty 0 4
 login
!
end

R1#
```

R2

```
R2#term len 0
R2#sh run
Building configuration...

Current configuration : 1015 bytes
!
version 12.4
service timestamps debug datetime msec
service timestamps log datetime msec
no service password-encryption
!
hostname R2
!
boot-start-marker
boot-end-marker
!
no logging console
!
no aaa new-model
no network-clock-participate slot 1
no network-clock-participate wic 0
ip cef
!
no ip domain lookup
ip auth-proxy max-nodata-conns 3
ip admission max-nodata-conns 3
!
!
interface FastEthernet0/0
 ip address 150.1.1.2 255.255.255.0
 duplex auto
 speed auto
 glbp 1 ip 150.1.1.254
 glbp 1 timers redirect 60 18000
 glbp 1 priority 105
 glbp 1 preempt
 glbp 1 weighting 30
 glbp 1 name SERVER-GLBP-GROUP
!
interface Serial0/0
 no ip address
 shutdown
!
interface Serial0/1
 ip address 10.0.0.9 255.255.255.252
!
router eigrp 254
 redistribute connected
 network 10.0.0.0
 no auto-summary
!
ip forward-protocol nd
!
no ip http server
no ip http secure-server
!
control-plane
!
line con 0
line aux 0
line vty 0 4
 login
!
end

R2#
```

R3

```
R3#sh run
Building configuration...

Current configuration : 1235 bytes
!
version 12.4
service timestamps debug datetime msec
service timestamps log datetime msec
no service password-encryption
!
hostname R3
!
boot-start-marker
boot-end-marker
!
no logging console
!
no aaa new-model
no network-clock-participate slot 1
no network-clock-participate wic 0
ip cef
!
no ip domain lookup
ip auth-proxy max-nodata-conns 3
ip admission max-nodata-conns 3
!
interface FastEthernet0/0
 ip address 150.3.3.3 255.255.255.0
 duplex auto
 speed auto
!
interface Serial1/0
 ip address 10.0.0.6 255.255.255.252
 clock rate 128000
!
interface Serial1/1
 ip address 10.0.0.10 255.255.255.252
 clock rate 128000
!
interface Serial1/2
 ip address 10.0.0.13 255.255.255.252
 clock rate 128000
!
interface Serial1/3
 no ip address
 shutdown
!
interface Serial1/4
 no ip address
 shutdown
!
interface Serial1/5
 no ip address
 shutdown
!
interface Serial1/6
 no ip address
 shutdown
!
interface Serial1/7
 no ip address
 shutdown
!
router eigrp 254
 redistribute connected
 network 10.0.0.0
 no auto-summary
!
ip forward-protocol nd
!
no ip http server
no ip http secure-server
!
```

```
control-plane
!
line con 0
line aux 0
line vty 0 4
 login
!
end
```

R4

```
R4#term len 0
R4#sh run
Building configuration...

Current configuration : 962 bytes
!
version 12.4
service timestamps debug datetime msec
service timestamps log datetime msec
no service password-encryption
!
hostname R4
!
boot-start-marker
boot-end-marker
!
no logging console
!
no aaa new-model
no network-clock-participate slot 1
no network-clock-participate wic 0
ip cef
!
no ip domain lookup
ip auth-proxy max-nodata-conns 3
ip admission max-nodata-conns 3
!
interface FastEthernet0/0
 ip address 150.1.1.4 255.255.255.0
 duplex auto
 speed auto
 glbp 1 ip 150.1.1.254
 glbp 1 preempt
 glbp 1 weighting 20
 glbp 1 name SERVER-GLBP-GROUP
!
interface Serial0/0
 ip address 10.0.0.14 255.255.255.252
!
interface Serial0/1
 no ip address
 shutdown
!
router eigrp 254
 redistribute connected
 network 10.0.0.0
 no auto-summary
!
ip forward-protocol nd
!
no ip http server
no ip http secure-server
!
control-plane
!
line con 0
line aux 0
line vty 0 4
 login
!
end

R4#
```

CCNP LAB 60

Cisco IOS IP SLA and GLBP Lab

Lab Objective:

The focus of this lab is to understand Gateway Load Balancing Protocol (GLBP) implementation and configuration in Cisco IOS routers. Additional technologies include GLBP load balancing.

Lab Topology:

The lab network topology is illustrated below:

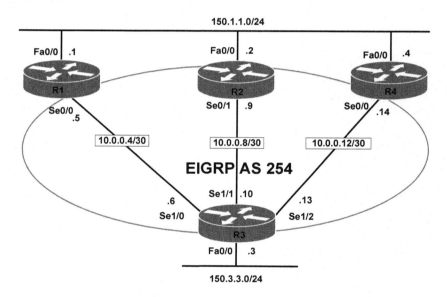

IMPORTANT NOTE: If you are using the www.howtonetwork.net racks, please bring up the LAN interfaces connected to the routers by issuing the no shutdown command on the connected switches. If you are using a home lab with no Switches, you can bring up the LAN interfaces using the following configurations on your routers:

```
interface fastethernet 0/0
  no keepalive
  loopback
  no shutdown
```

Alternately, you can simply connect the interfaces to a hub or switch if you have one available in your own lab.

Task 1

Configure hostnames, IP addressing on all routers as illustrated in the network topology.

Task 2

Configure EIGRP as illustrated in the topology. Redistribute the LAN subnets into EIGRP.

Verify your configuration using the appropriate commands on all routers in the network.

Task 3

Configure GLBP on R1, R2, and R4. Ensure that R1 is elected AVG. R2 should be standby. The gateway IP should be 150.1.1.254. Verify your configuration using the appropriate commands.

Task 4

Configure load balancing for GLBP so that traffic is distributed between R1, R2 and R4 using a ratio of 50:30:20. Configure weighting thresholds on R1 as follows:
- Should R1s weighting value fall below 30, it should give up its role as a Virtual Forwarder
- When R1s weighting value rises above 45, it should assume its role as a Virtual Forwarder
- Should R1s weighting value fall below 20, it should give up its role as a Virtual Forwarder
- When R1s weighting value rises above 25, it should assume its role as a Virtual Forwarder

R4 should use default thresholds. Verify your configuration using the appropriate commands.

Task 5

Configure Cisco IOS IP SLA Operations on R1 and R2 that ping the connected WAN interface to R3. Should R1s WAN link go down, its weight should be reduced to 25. Should R2s WAN link go down, its weighting value should be reduced to 15. Verify your configuration using the appropriate commands. Next, test the configuration by shutting down R1s WAN link and then checking the GLBP status on R1, R2 and R3. Next, with R1s WAN interface still disabled, shut R2s WAN interface and check the GLBP status on R2 and R4.

LAB VALIDATION

Task 1

Please refer to previous labs for basic IPv4, IPv6 addressing and hostname configuration. This will not be included in this section to avoid being redundant.

Task 2

Please refer to previous labs for basic EIGRP configuration. Following this, verify your EIGRP configuration using the show ip eigrp neighbors and show ip route commands. Following this configuration, your route tables should show the following route information:

```
R1#show ip route eigrp
       10.0.0.0/30 is subnetted, 3 subnets
D         10.0.0.8 [90/21024000] via 10.0.0.6, 00:03:06, Serial0/1
D         10.0.0.12 [90/21024000] via 10.0.0.6, 00:02:11, Serial0/1
       150.3.0.0/24 is subnetted, 1 subnets
D EX      150.3.3.0 [170/2172416] via 10.0.0.6, 00:03:06, Serial0/1

R2#show ip route eigrp
       10.0.0.0/30 is subnetted, 3 subnets
D         10.0.0.12 [90/21024000] via 10.0.0.10, 00:02:15, Serial0/1
D         10.0.0.4 [90/21024000] via 10.0.0.10, 00:03:10, Serial0/1
       150.3.0.0/24 is subnetted, 1 subnets
D EX      150.3.3.0 [170/2172416] via 10.0.0.10, 00:03:10, Serial0/1

R3#show ip route eigrp
       150.1.0.0/24 is subnetted, 1 subnets
D EX      150.1.1.0 [170/20514560] via 10.0.0.14, 00:02:16, Serial1/2
                    [170/20514560] via 10.0.0.9, 00:02:16, Serial1/1
                    [170/20514560] via 10.0.0.5, 00:02:16, Serial1/0

R4#show ip route eigrp
       10.0.0.0/30 is subnetted, 3 subnets
D         10.0.0.8 [90/21024000] via 10.0.0.13, 00:02:22, Serial0/0
D         10.0.0.4 [90/21024000] via 10.0.0.13, 00:02:22, Serial0/0
       150.3.0.0/24 is subnetted, 1 subnets
D EX      150.3.3.0 [170/2172416] via 10.0.0.13, 00:02:22, Serial0/0
```

Task 3

To complete this task, you need to configure R1 with the highest priority. In order to ensure that R2 is elected standby, this router should be assigned the second highest priority. By default, GLBP assigns a priority of 100. Finally, you need to explicitly enable preemption as it is disabled by default. This task is completed as follows:

```
R1(config)#interface fastethernet 0/0
R1(config-if)#glbp 1 priority 110
R1(config-if)#glbp 1 ip 150.1.1.254
R1(config-if)#glbp 1 preempt
R1(config-if)#exit

R2(config)#interface fastethernet 0/0
R2(config-if)#glbp 1 priority 105
R2(config-if)#glbp 1 ip 150.1.1.254
R2(config-if)#glbp 1 preempt
R2(config-if)#exit

R4(config)#interface fastethernet 0/0
R4(config-if)#glbp 1 preempt
R4(config-if)#glbp 1 ip 150.1.1.254
R4(config-if)#exit
```

Following this, verify your configuration using the show glbp command:

```
R1#show glbp fastethernet 0/0 1 brief
Interface  Grp  Fwd  Pri  State    Address         Active router  Standby router
Fa0/0      1    -    110  Active   150.1.1.254     local          150.1.1.2
Fa0/0      1    1    -    Active   0007.b400.0101  local          -
Fa0/0      1    2    -    Listen   0007.b400.0102  150.1.1.2      -
Fa0/0      1    3    -    Listen   0007.b400.0103  150.1.1.4      -

R2#show glbp fastethernet 0/0 1 brief
Interface  Grp  Fwd  Pri  State    Address         Active router  Standby router
Fa0/0      1    -    105  Standby  150.1.1.254     150.1.1.1      local
Fa0/0      1    1    -    Listen   0007.b400.0101  150.1.1.1      -
Fa0/0      1    2    -    Active   0007.b400.0102  local          -
Fa0/0      1    3    -    Listen   0007.b400.0103  150.1.1.4      -

R4#show glbp fastethernet 0/0 1 brief
Interface  Grp  Fwd  Pri  State    Address         Active router  Standby router
Fa0/0      1    -    100  Listen   150.1.1.254     150.1.1.1      150.1.1.2
Fa0/0      1    1    -    Listen   0007.b400.0101  150.1.1.1      -
Fa0/0      1    2    -    Listen   0007.b400.0102  150.1.1.2      -
Fa0/0      1    3    -    Active   0007.b400.0103  local          -
```

Task 4

To complete this task, we need to configure weighted load balancing. When configuring this the method, Cisco IOS software allows you to specify upper and lower thresholds. If the weighting of a router falls from the specified maximum threshold to a value below the lower threshold, the router gives up its role as a Virtual Forwarder. When the weighting value of the router rises above the upper threshold, the router can resume its active Virtual Forwarder role. This task is completed by implementing the following configuration on all routers:

```
R1(config)#interface fastethernet 0/0
R1(config-if)#glbp 1 weighting 50 lower 30 upper 45
R1(config-if)#glbp 1 load-balancing weighted
R1(config-if)#exit

R2(config)#interface fastethernet 0/0
R2(config-if)#glbp 1 weighting 30 lower 10 upper 25
R2(config-if)#glbp 1 load-balancing weighted
R2(config-if)#exit

R4(config)#interface fastethernet 0/0
R4(config-if)#glbp 1 weighting 20
R4(config-if)#exit
```

Next, verify your configuration on all routers using the show glbp command:

```
R1#show glbp fastethernet 0/0
FastEthernet0/0 - Group 1
  State is Active
    2 state changes, last state change 00:00:25
  Virtual IP address is 150.1.1.254
  Hello time 3 sec, hold time 10 sec
    Next hello sent in 1.972 secs
  Redirect time 600 sec, forwarder time-out 14400 sec
  Preemption enabled, min delay 0 sec
  Active is local
  Standby is 150.1.1.2, priority 105 (expires in 7.972 sec)
  Priority 110 (configured)
  Weighting 50 (configured 50), thresholds: lower 30, upper 45
  Load balancing: weighted
  Group members:
    000d.289e.f940 (150.1.1.2)
    000f.235e.ec80 (150.1.1.1) local
    000f.235e.f120 (150.1.1.4)
  There are 3 forwarders (1 active)
  Forwarder 1
    State is Active
      1 state change, last state change 00:00:15
    MAC address is 0007.b400.0101 (default)
    Owner ID is 000f.235e.ec80
    Redirection enabled
    Preemption enabled, min delay 30 sec
    Active is local, weighting 50
  Forwarder 2
    State is Listen
    MAC address is 0007.b400.0102 (learnt)
    Owner ID is 000d.289e.f940
    Redirection enabled, 598.112 sec remaining (maximum 600 sec)
    Time to live: 14398.112 sec (maximum 14400 sec)
    Preemption enabled, min delay 30 sec
    Active is 150.1.1.2 (primary), weighting 30 (expires in 8.112 sec)
  Forwarder 3
    State is Listen
    MAC address is 0007.b400.0103 (learnt)
    Owner ID is 000f.235e.f120
    Redirection enabled, 599.008 sec remaining (maximum 600 sec)
    Time to live: 14399.008 sec (maximum 14400 sec)
    Preemption enabled, min delay 30 sec
    Active is 150.1.1.4 (primary), weighting 20 (expires in 9.004 sec)

R2#show glbp fastethernet 0/0
FastEthernet0/0 - Group 1
  State is Standby
    1 state change, last state change 00:00:30
  Virtual IP address is 150.1.1.254
  Hello time 3 sec, hold time 10 sec
    Next hello sent in 2.424 secs
  Redirect time 600 sec, forwarder time-out 14400 sec
  Preemption enabled, min delay 0 sec
  Active is 150.1.1.1, priority 110 (expires in 7.424 sec)
  Standby is local
  Priority 105 (configured)
  Weighting 30 (configured 30), thresholds: lower 20, upper 25
  Load balancing: weighted
  Group members:
    000d.289e.f940 (150.1.1.2) local
    000f.235e.ec80 (150.1.1.1)
    000f.235e.f120 (150.1.1.4)
  There are 3 forwarders (1 active)
  Forwarder 1
    State is Listen
    MAC address is 0007.b400.0101 (learnt)
    Owner ID is 000f.235e.ec80
    Time to live: 14397.420 sec (maximum 14400 sec)
    Preemption enabled, min delay 30 sec
    Active is 150.1.1.1 (primary), weighting 50 (expires in 9.628 sec)
  Forwarder 2
    State is Active
      1 state change, last state change 00:00:35
    MAC address is 0007.b400.0102 (default)
    Owner ID is 000d.289e.f940
    Preemption enabled, min delay 30 sec
    Active is local, weighting 30
```

```
Forwarder 3
  State is Listen
  MAC address is 0007.b400.0103 (learnt)
  Owner ID is 000f.235e.f120
  Time to live: 14399.520 sec (maximum 14400 sec)
  Preemption enabled, min delay 30 sec
  Active is 150.1.1.4 (primary), weighting 20 (expires in 9.520 sec)

R4#show glbp fastethernet 0/0
FastEthernet0/0 - Group 1
  State is Listen
  Virtual IP address is 150.1.1.254
  Hello time 3 sec, hold time 10 sec
    Next hello sent in 1.100 secs
  Redirect time 600 sec, forwarder time-out 14400 sec
  Preemption enabled, min delay 0 sec
  Active is 150.1.1.1, priority 110 (expires in 8.204 sec)
  Standby is 150.1.1.2, priority 105 (expires in 7.200 sec)
  Priority 100 (default)
  Weighting 20 (configured 20), thresholds: lower 1, upper 20
  Load balancing: round-robin
  Group members:
    000d.289e.f940 (150.1.1.2)
    000f.235e.ec80 (150.1.1.1)
    000f.235e.f120 (150.1.1.4) local
  There are 3 forwarders (1 active)
  Forwarder 1
    State is Listen
    MAC address is 0007.b400.0101 (learnt)
    Owner ID is 000f.235e.ec80
    Time to live: 14398.200 sec (maximum 14400 sec)
    Preemption enabled, min delay 30 sec
    Active is 150.1.1.1 (primary), weighting 50 (expires in 7.228 sec)
  Forwarder 2
    State is Listen
    MAC address is 0007.b400.0102 (learnt)
    Owner ID is 000d.289e.f940
    Time to live: 14399.228 sec (maximum 14400 sec)
    Preemption enabled, min delay 30 sec
    Active is 150.1.1.2 (primary), weighting 30 (expires in 9.228 sec)
  Forwarder 3
    State is Active
      1 state change, last state change 00:00:37
    MAC address is 0007.b400.0103 (default)
    Owner ID is 000f.235e.f120
    Preemption enabled, min delay 30 sec
    Active is local, weighting 20
```

Task 5

This task requires the configuration of Cisco IOS IP SLA Operations on R1 and R2. In addition to this, Enhanced Object Tracking (EOT) should also be configured. The EOT configuration should track the configured Cisco IOS IP SLA Operation and should be used to decrement the GLBP weight as specified on both R1 and R2. This task is completed as follows:

```
R1(config)#ip sla monitor 1
R1(config-sla-monitor)#$IcmpEcho 10.0.0.6 source-interface serial 0/1
R1(config-sla-monitor-echo)#exit
R1(config)#ip sla monitor schedule 1 start-time now life forever
R1(config)#track 1 rtr 1
R1(config-track)#exit
R1(config)#interface fastethernet 0/0
R1(config-if)#glbp 1 weighting track 1 decrement 35
R1(config-if)#exit

R2(config)#ip sla monitor 1
R2(config-sla-monitor)#$rotocol ipIcmpEcho 10.0.0.10 source-ipaddr 10.0.0.9
R2(config-sla-monitor-echo)#exit
R2(config)#ip sla monitor schedule 1 start-time now life forever
R2(config)#track 1 rtr 1
R2(config-track)#exit
R2(config)#interface fastethernet 0/0
R2(config-if)#glbp 1 weighting track 1 decrement 15
R2(config-if)#exit
```

Next, verify Cisco IOS IP SLA Operations using the show ip sla monitor command:

```
R1#show ip sla monitor statistics 1
Round trip time (RTT)    Index 1
        Latest RTT: 8 ms
Latest operation start time: *06:29:12.561 UTC Sat Jun 4 2011
Latest operation return code: OK
Number of successes: 6
Number of failures: 0
Operation time to live: Forever

R2#show ip sla monitor statistics 1
Round trip time (RTT)    Index 1
        Latest RTT: 8 ms
Latest operation start time: *19:56:26.883 UTC Wed May 18 2011
Latest operation return code: OK
Number of successes: 3
Number of failures: 0
Operation time to live: Forever
```

Next, verify your EOT configuration on R1 and R2 using the show track command:

```
R1#show track
Track 1
  Response Time Reporter 1 state
  State is Up
    2 changes, last change 00:06:00
  Latest operation return code: OK
  Latest RTT (millisecs) 8
  Tracked by:
    GLBP FastEthernet0/0 1

R2#show track
Track 1
  Response Time Reporter 1 state
  State is Up
    1 change, last change 00:03:24
  Latest operation return code: OK
  Latest RTT (millisecs) 8
  Tracked by:
    GLBP FastEthernet0/0 1
```

Finally, before you begin testing, verify GLBP using the show glbp command:

```
R1#show glbp fastethernet 0/0
FastEthernet0/0 - Group 1
  State is Active
    2 state changes, last state change 00:17:56
  Virtual IP address is 150.1.1.254
  Hello time 3 sec, hold time 10 sec
    Next hello sent in 0.016 secs
  Redirect time 600 sec, forwarder time-out 14400 sec
  Preemption enabled, min delay 0 sec
  Active is local
  Standby is 150.1.1.2, priority 105 (expires in 9.036 sec)
  Priority 110 (configured)
  Weighting 50 (configured 50), thresholds: lower 30, upper 45
    Track object 1 state Up decrement 25
  Load balancing: weighted
  Group members:
    000d.289e.f940 (150.1.1.2)
    000f.235e.ec80 (150.1.1.1) local
    000f.235e.f120 (150.1.1.4)

[Truncated Output]

R2#show glbp fastethernet 0/0
FastEthernet0/0 - Group 1
  State is Standby
    1 state change, last state change 00:18:11
  Virtual IP address is 150.1.1.254
  Hello time 3 sec, hold time 10 sec
```

```
    Next hello sent in 0.168 secs
  Redirect time 600 sec, forwarder time-out 14400 sec
  Preemption enabled, min delay 0 sec
  Active is 150.1.1.1, priority 110 (expires in 8.144 sec)
  Standby is local
  Priority 105 (configured)
  Weighting 30 (configured 30), thresholds: lower 20, upper 25
    Track object 1 state Up decrement 15
  Load balancing: weighted
  Group members:
    000d.289e.f940 (150.1.1.2) local
    000f.235e.ec80 (150.1.1.1)
    000f.235e.f120 (150.1.1.4)
  There are 3 forwarders (1 active)

[Truncated Output]
```

At this point, we can begin testing GLBP. First, as requested, shut down the WAN link on R1 and verify the GLBP status on R1, R2 and R4 using the show glbp command:

```
R1(config)#interface serial 0/1
R1(config-if)#shutdown
R1(config-if)#exit
R1(config)#exit
R1#show glbp fastethernet 0/0
FastEthernet0/0 - Group 1
  State is Active
    2 state changes, last state change 00:29:55
  Virtual IP address is 150.1.1.254
  Hello time 3 sec, hold time 10 sec
    Next hello sent in 1.116 secs
  Redirect time 600 sec, forwarder time-out 14400 sec
  Preemption enabled, min delay 0 sec
  Active is local
  Standby is 150.1.1.2, priority 105 (expires in 7.164 sec)
  Priority 110 (configured)
  Weighting 25, low (configured 50), thresholds: lower 30, upper 45
    Track object 1 state Down decrement 25
  Load balancing: weighted
  Group members:
    000d.289e.f940 (150.1.1.2)
    000f.235e.ec80 (150.1.1.1) local
    000f.235e.f120 (150.1.1.4)
  There are 3 forwarders (0 active)
  Forwarder 1
    State is Listen
      2 state changes, last state change 00:04:10
    MAC address is 0007.b400.0101 (default)
    Owner ID is 000f.235e.ec80
    Redirection enabled
    Preemption enabled, min delay 30 sec
    Active is 150.1.1.4 (secondary), weighting 20 (expires in 7.144 sec)
  Forwarder 2
    State is Listen
    MAC address is 0007.b400.0102 (learnt)
    Owner ID is 000d.289e.f940
    Redirection enabled, 599.232 sec remaining (maximum 600 sec)
    Time to live: 14399.228 sec (maximum 14400 sec)
    Preemption enabled, min delay 30 sec
    Active is 150.1.1.2 (primary), weighting 30 (expires in 9.228 sec)
  Forwarder 3
    State is Listen
    MAC address is 0007.b400.0103 (learnt)
    Owner ID is 000f.235e.f120
    Redirection enabled, 597.140 sec remaining (maximum 600 sec)
    Time to live: 14397.140 sec (maximum 14400 sec)
    Preemption enabled, min delay 30 sec
    Active is 150.1.1.4 (primary), weighting 20 (expires in 7.136 sec)
```

Notice in the output above that R1 is no longer being used as a Virtual Forwarder. Next, check that the same is also depicted on routers R2 and R4:

```
R2#show glbp fastethernet 0/0
FastEthernet0/0 - Group 1
  State is Standby
    1 state change, last state change 00:31:40
  Virtual IP address is 150.1.1.254
  Hello time 3 sec, hold time 10 sec
    Next hello sent in 1.424 secs
  Redirect time 600 sec, forwarder time-out 14400 sec
  Preemption enabled, min delay 0 sec
  Active is 150.1.1.1, priority 110 (expires in 9.404 sec)
  Standby is local
  Priority 105 (configured)
  Weighting 30 (configured 30), thresholds: lower 20, upper 25
    Track object 1 state Up decrement 15
  Load balancing: weighted
  Group members:
    000d.289e.f940 (150.1.1.2) local
    000f.235e.ec80 (150.1.1.1)
    000f.235e.f120 (150.1.1.4)
  There are 3 forwarders (1 active)
  Forwarder 1
    State is Listen
    MAC address is 0007.b400.0101 (learnt)
    Owner ID is 000f.235e.ec80
    Time to live: 14398.760 sec (maximum 14400 sec)
    Preemption enabled, min delay 30 sec
    Active is 150.1.1.4 (secondary), weighting 25 (expires in 8.728 sec)
  Forwarder 2
    State is Active
    1 state change, last state change 00:31:45
    MAC address is 0007.b400.0102 (default)
    Owner ID is 000d.289e.f940
    Preemption enabled, min delay 30 sec
    Active is local, weighting 30
  Forwarder 3
    State is Listen
    MAC address is 0007.b400.0103 (learnt)
    Owner ID is 000f.235e.f120
    Time to live: 14398.724 sec (maximum 14400 sec)
    Preemption enabled, min delay 30 sec
    Active is 150.1.1.4 (primary), weighting 20 (expires in 8.724 sec)

R4#show glbp fastethernet 0/0
FastEthernet0/0 - Group 1
  State is Listen
  Virtual IP address is 150.1.1.254
  Hello time 3 sec, hold time 10 sec
    Next hello sent in 0.544 secs
  Redirect time 600 sec, forwarder time-out 14400 sec
  Preemption enabled, min delay 0 sec
  Active is 150.1.1.1, priority 110 (expires in 7.524 sec)
  Standby is 150.1.1.2, priority 105 (expires in 9.548 sec)
  Priority 100 (default)
  Weighting 20 (configured 20), thresholds: lower 1, upper 20
  Load balancing: round-robin
  Group members:
    000d.289e.f940 (150.1.1.2)
    000f.235e.ec80 (150.1.1.1)
    000f.235e.f120 (150.1.1.4) local
  There are 3 forwarders (2 active)
  Forwarder 1
    State is Active
    1 state change, last state change 00:07:05
    MAC address is 0007.b400.0101 (learnt)
    Owner ID is 000f.235e.ec80
    Time to live: 14397.520 sec (maximum 14400 sec)
    Preemption enabled, min delay 30 sec
    Active is local, weighting 20
  Forwarder 2
    State is Listen
    MAC address is 0007.b400.0102 (learnt)
    Owner ID is 000d.289e.f940
    Time to live: 14398.308 sec (maximum 14400 sec)
    Preemption enabled, min delay 30 sec
    Active is 150.1.1.2 (primary), weighting 30 (expires in 8.308 sec)
  Forwarder 3
    State is Active
```

```
  1 state change, last state change 00:32:32
  MAC address is 0007.b400.0103 (default)
  Owner ID is 000f.235e.f120
  Preemption enabled, min delay 30 sec
Active is local, weighting 20
```

Finally, shut down the WAN link on R2 and verify the GLBP status on routers R2 and R4:

```
R2(config)#interface serial 0/1
R2(config-if)#shutdown
R2(config-if)#exit
R2(config)#exit
R2#show glbp fastethernet 0/0
FastEthernet0/0 - Group 1
  State is Standby
    1 state change, last state change 00:38:21
  Virtual IP address is 150.1.1.254
  Hello time 3 sec, hold time 10 sec
    Next hello sent in 2.500 secs
  Redirect time 600 sec, forwarder time-out 14400 sec
  Preemption enabled, min delay 0 sec
  Active is 150.1.1.1, priority 110 (expires in 7.476 sec)
  Standby is local
  Priority 105 (configured)
  Weighting 15, low (configured 30), thresholds: lower 20, upper 25
    Track object 1 state Down decrement 15
  Load balancing: weighted
  Group members:
    000d.289e.f940 (150.1.1.2) local
    000f.235e.ec80 (150.1.1.1)
    000f.235e.f120 (150.1.1.4)
  There are 3 forwarders (0 active)
  Forwarder 1
    State is Listen
    MAC address is 0007.b400.0101 (learnt)
    Owner ID is 000f.235e.ec80
    Time to live: 14398.892 sec (maximum 14399 sec)
    Preemption enabled, min delay 30 sec
    Active is 150.1.1.4 (secondary), weighting 20 (expires in 9.892 sec)
  Forwarder 2
    State is Listen
      2 state changes, last state change 00:01:34
    MAC address is 0007.b400.0102 (default)
    Owner ID is 000d.289e.f940
    Preemption enabled, min delay 30 sec
    Active is 150.1.1.4 (secondary), weighting 20 (expires in 9.888 sec)
  Forwarder 3
    State is Listen
    MAC address is 0007.b400.0103 (learnt)
    Owner ID is 000f.235e.f120
    Time to live: 14399.888 sec (maximum 14400 sec)
    Preemption enabled, min delay 30 sec
    Active is 150.1.1.4 (primary), weighting 20 (expires in 9.888 sec)
```

Notice that R4 is not AVF for all three GLBP MAC addresses. Verify the same on R4:

```
R4#show glbp fastethernet 0/0
FastEthernet0/0 - Group 1
  State is Listen
  Virtual IP address is 150.1.1.254
  Hello time 3 sec, hold time 10 sec
    Next hello sent in 1.936 secs
  Redirect time 600 sec, forwarder time-out 14400 sec
  Preemption enabled, min delay 0 sec
  Active is 150.1.1.1, priority 110 (expires in 8.916 sec)
  Standby is 150.1.1.2, priority 105 (expires in 7.940 sec)
  Priority 100 (default)
  Weighting 20 (configured 20), thresholds: lower 1, upper 20
  Load balancing: round-robin
  Group members:
    000d.289e.f940 (150.1.1.2)
    000f.235e.ec80 (150.1.1.1)
    000f.235e.f120 (150.1.1.4) local
  There are 3 forwarders (3 active)
  Forwarder 1
```

```
   State is Active
     1 state change, last state change 00:14:01
   MAC address is 0007.b400.0101 (learnt)
   Owner ID is 000f.235e.ec80
   Time to live: 14398.912 sec (maximum 14400 sec)
   Preemption enabled, min delay 30 sec
   Active is local, weighting 20
 Forwarder 2
   State is Active
     1 state change, last state change 00:02:37
   MAC address is 0007.b400.0102 (learnt)
   Owner ID is 000d.289e.f940
   Time to live: 14398.256 sec (maximum 14400 sec)
   Preemption enabled, min delay 30 sec
   Active is local, weighting 20
 Forwarder 3
   State is Active
     1 state change, last state change 00:39:29
   MAC address is 0007.b400.0103 (default)
   Owner ID is 000f.235e.f120
   Preemption enabled, min delay 30 sec
   Active is local, weighting 20
```

FINAL ROUTER CONFIGURATIONS

R1

```
R1#term len 0
R1#sh run
Building configuration...

Current configuration : 1214 bytes
!
version 12.4
service timestamps debug datetime msec
service timestamps log datetime msec
no service password-encryption
!
hostname R1
!
boot-start-marker
boot-end-marker
!
no logging console
!
no aaa new-model
no network-clock-participate slot 1
no network-clock-participate wic 0
ip cef
!
no ip domain lookup
ip auth-proxy max-nodata-conns 3
ip admission max-nodata-conns 3
ip sla monitor 1
 type echo protocol ipIcmpEcho 10.0.0.6 source-interface Serial0/1
ip sla monitor schedule 1 life forever start-time now
!
track 1 rtr 1
!
interface FastEthernet0/0
 ip address 150.1.1.1 255.255.255.0
 duplex auto
 speed auto
 glbp 1 ip 150.1.1.254
 glbp 1 priority 110
 glbp 1 preempt
 glbp 1 weighting 50 lower 30 upper 45
 glbp 1 load-balancing weighted
 glbp 1 weighting track 1 decrement 25
!
interface Serial0/0
 no ip address
 shutdown
 clock rate 2000000
!
interface Serial0/1
```

```
 ip address 10.0.0.5 255.255.255.252
!
router eigrp 254
 redistribute connected
 network 10.0.0.0
 no auto-summary
!
ip forward-protocol nd
!
no ip http server
no ip http secure-server
!
control-plane
!
line con 0
line aux 0
line vty 0 4
 login
!
end

R1#
```

R2

```
R2#term len 0
R2#sh run
Building configuration...

Current configuration : 1191 bytes
!
version 12.4
service timestamps debug datetime msec
service timestamps log datetime msec
no service password-encryption
!
hostname R2
!
boot-start-marker
boot-end-marker
!
no logging console
!
no aaa new-model
no network-clock-participate slot 1
no network-clock-participate wic 0
ip cef
!
no ip domain lookup
ip auth-proxy max-nodata-conns 3
ip admission max-nodata-conns 3
ip sla monitor 1
 type echo protocol ipIcmpEcho 10.0.0.10 source-ipaddr 10.0.0.9
ip sla monitor schedule 1 life forever start-time now
!
track 1 rtr 1
!
interface FastEthernet0/0
 ip address 150.1.1.2 255.255.255.0
 duplex auto
 speed auto
 glbp 1 ip 150.1.1.254
 glbp 1 priority 105
 glbp 1 preempt
 glbp 1 weighting 30 lower 20 upper 25
 glbp 1 load-balancing weighted
 glbp 1 weighting track 1 decrement 15
!
interface Serial0/0
 no ip address
 shutdown
!
interface Serial0/1
 ip address 10.0.0.9 255.255.255.252
!
router eigrp 254
 redistribute connected
 network 10.0.0.0
 no auto-summary
!
ip forward-protocol nd
```

```
!
no ip http server
no ip http secure-server
!
control-plane
!
line con 0
line aux 0
line vty 0 4
 login
!
end

R2#
```

R3

```
R3#sh run
Building configuration...

Current configuration : 1235 bytes
!
version 12.4
service timestamps debug datetime msec
service timestamps log datetime msec
no service password-encryption
!
hostname R3
!
boot-start-marker
boot-end-marker
!
no logging console
!
no aaa new-model
no network-clock-participate slot 1
no network-clock-participate wic 0
ip cef
!
no ip domain lookup
ip auth-proxy max-nodata-conns 3
ip admission max-nodata-conns 3
!
interface FastEthernet0/0
 ip address 150.3.3.3 255.255.255.0
 duplex auto
 speed auto
!
interface Serial1/0
 ip address 10.0.0.6 255.255.255.252
 clock rate 128000
!
interface Serial1/1
 ip address 10.0.0.10 255.255.255.252
 clock rate 128000
!
interface Serial1/2
 ip address 10.0.0.13 255.255.255.252
 clock rate 128000
!
interface Serial1/3
 no ip address
 shutdown
!
interface Serial1/4
 no ip address
 shutdown
!
interface Serial1/5
 no ip address
 shutdown
!
interface Serial1/6
 no ip address
 shutdown
!
interface Serial1/7
 no ip address
 shutdown
!
router eigrp 254
```

```
 redistribute connected
 network 10.0.0.0
 no auto-summary
!
ip forward-protocol nd
!
no ip http server
no ip http secure-server
!
control-plane
!
line con 0
line aux 0
line vty 0 4
 login
!
end
```

R4

```
R4#term len 0
R4#sh run
Building configuration...

Current configuration : 931 bytes
!
version 12.4
service timestamps debug datetime msec
service timestamps log datetime msec
no service password-encryption
!
hostname R4
!
boot-start-marker
boot-end-marker
!
no logging console
!
no aaa new-model
no network-clock-participate slot 1
no network-clock-participate wic 0
ip cef
!
no ip domain lookup
ip auth-proxy max-nodata-conns 3
ip admission max-nodata-conns 3
!
interface FastEthernet0/0
 ip address 150.1.1.4 255.255.255.0
 duplex auto
 speed auto
 glbp 1 ip 150.1.1.254
 glbp 1 preempt
 glbp 1 weighting 20
!
interface Serial0/0
 ip address 10.0.0.14 255.255.255.252
!
interface Serial0/1
 no ip address
 shutdown
!
router eigrp 254
 redistribute connected
 network 10.0.0.0
 no auto-summary
!
ip forward-protocol nd
!
no ip http server
no ip http secure-server
!
control-plane
!
line con 0
line aux 0
line vty 0 4
 login
!
end
R4#
```

CCNP LAB 61

Embedded Event Manager Lab

Lab Objective:

The focus of this lab is to understand Embedded Event Manager (EEM) implementation and configuration in Cisco IOS routers. Additional technologies include SNMP security.

Lab Topology:

This lab requires only a single router running, at a minimum, Cisco IOS Software 12.4 Mainline. The router should have at least one Ethernet interface. The primary purpose of this lab is to reinforce configuration knowledge of the stated chapter.

> **IMPORTANT NOTE:** If you have multiple devices and servers / hosts in your home lab and you would like to test solutions for topics such as Syslog, SNMP and NetFlow by setting up host and viewing charts or logging information, for example, please feel free to do so. While these labs include logging to 'supposed' hosts, there are no SNMP or Syslog servers in the http://www.howtonetwork.net racks and so you will not be able to test the solutions in those racks. If you only have a single router, you can bring up the Ethernet interface by implementing the following configuration:
>
> ```
> !
> interface fastethernet 0/0
> loopback
> no keepalive
> no shut
> !
> ```

Task 1

Configure the router with a hostname of R1. Next, enable the LAN interface of the router and assign it the IP address 150.1.1.1/24. Ensure that this interface is in an up / up state.

Task 2

Configure an EEM applet on the router such that following any configuration change, the log message 'SAVING CONFIGURATION' is printed and the router automatically saves the configuration. The router should also send an SNMP trap to host 150.1.1.254 using an SNMPv2 community string of 'SECURITY'. This trap should include the message 'CONFIG SAVED'. Verify your configuration using the appropriate commands.

Task 3

Management is concerned about the device being reloaded accidentally. Until they get an ACS server running TACACS+, which will be used to restrict commands at the user level, they have requested that the 'reload' command be ignored when executed on the router. They also request that the shortened form of this command, 'relo' is also ignored. Configure an EEM applet to satisfy this request. Ensure that the router prints the message 'NOT ALLOWED' whenever this command is attempted. Test and verify your configuration using the appropriate commands.

Task 4

In the future, assume that OSPF will be enabled on the router. To facilitate OSPF adjacency flap trouble-shooting, configure an EEM applet that captures the contents of the show processes cpu command to an existing file named PROC_UTIL that is stored in Flash memory. It is important to ensure that this file is not overwritten, but instead, additional data is simply added to it. Next, configure the same applet so that the output of the show interface serial 0/0 command. This information should be added to an existing file named SERIAL_STATS that is stored in Flash memory. Verify your configuration.

LAB VALIDATION

Task 1

If your routers interface is not connected to a switch or hub, you need to complete this task as is shown below. If you do have a hub or switch, you can omit the loopback and no keepalive commands under the LAN interface. This example assumes a standalone router.

```
Router(config)#hostname R1
R1(config)#interface fastethernet 0/0
R1(config-if)#ip address 150.1.1.1 255.255.255.0
R1(config-if)#loopback
Loopback is a traffic-affecting operation
R1(config-if)#no keepalive
R1(config-if)#no shutdown
R1(config-if)#exit
```

Next, verify your configuration using the show ip interface brief command:

```
R1#show ip interface brief
Interface          IP-Address   OK? Method Status                 Protocol
FastEthernet0/0    150.1.1.1    YES manual up                     up
Serial0/0          unassigned   YES unset  administratively down  down
Serial0/1          unassigned   YES unset  administratively down  down
```

Task 2

In order to complete this task we need to configure both EEM and SNMP on the router. Ensure that the EEM applet matches the Syslog message '%SYS-5-CONFIG_I:' which indicates that the router has been configured. Next, specify the actions the EEM applet should take. These will include logging a message and sending an SNMP trap which includes the string or data stated in the task. This task is completed as follows:

```
R1(config)#event manager applet CONFIGURATION-CHANGE-APPLET
R1(config-applet)#event syslog pattern %SYS-5-CONFIG_I:
R1(config-applet)#action 1.0 syslog msg "SAVING CONFIGURATION"
R1(config-applet)#action 1.1 snmp-trap strdata "CONFIG SAVED"
R1(config-applet)#action 1.2 cli command "enable"
R1(config-applet)#action 1.3 cli command "write memory"
R1(config-applet)#exit
R1(config)#snmp-server community SECURITY RO
R1(config)#snmp-server host 150.1.1.254 traps SECURITY event-manager
R1(config)#snmp-server enable traps event-manager
R1(config)#exit
```

Next, verify EEM configuration using the show event manager command:

```
R1(config)#do show event manager policy registered
No.  Class   Type   Event Type   Trap  Time Registered           Name
1    applet  user   syslog       Off   Sat Jun 4 07:10:40 2011
CONFIGURATION-CHANGE-APPLET
 pattern {%SYS-5-CONFIG_I:}
 action 1.0 syslog msg "SAVING CONFIGURATION"
 action 1.1 snmp-trap strdata "CONFIG SAVED"
 action 1.2 cli command "enable"
 action 1.3 cli command "write memory"
```

Following this, verify SNMP configuration using the show snmp command:

```
R1(config)#do show snmp
Chassis: JAE08020Z7T
0 SNMP packets input
    0 Bad SNMP version errors
    0 Unknown community name
    0 Illegal operation for community name supplied
    0 Encoding errors
    0 Number of requested variables
    0 Number of altered variables
    0 Get-request PDUs
    0 Get-next PDUs
    0 Set-request PDUs
    0 Input queue packet drops (Maximum queue size 1000)
0 SNMP packets output
    0 Too big errors (Maximum packet size 1500)
    0 No such name errors
    0 Bad values errors
    0 General errors
    0 Response PDUs
    0 Trap PDUs

SNMP logging: enabled
    Logging to 150.1.1.254.162, 0/10, 0 sent, 0 dropped.
```

Next, test your Embedded Event Manager configuration by exiting configuration mode:

```
R1(config)#exit
R1#
*Jun  4 07:24:50.379: %SYS-5-CONFIG_I: Configured from console by console
*Jun  4 07:24:50.391: %HA_EM-6-LOG: CONFIGURATION-CHANGE-APPLET: SAVING CONFIGURATION
R1#
R1#
```

Finally, ensure that the router generated and sent an SNMP trap to host 150.1.1.254:

```
R1#show snmp
Chassis: JAE08020Z7T
0 SNMP packets input
    0 Bad SNMP version errors
    0 Unknown community name
    0 Illegal operation for community name supplied
    0 Encoding errors
    0 Number of requested variables
    0 Number of altered variables
    0 Get-request PDUs
    0 Get-next PDUs
    0 Set-request PDUs
    0 Input queue packet drops (Maximum queue size 1000)
2 SNMP packets output
    0 Too big errors (Maximum packet size 1500)
    0 No such name errors
    0 Bad values errors
    0 General errors
    0 Response PDUs
    2 Trap PDUs

SNMP logging: enabled
    Logging to 150.1.1.254.162, 0/10, 2 sent, 0 dropped.
```

Task 3

In order to complete this task, you need to configure EEM to skip the specified commands when they are issued on the router. This task is completed as follows:

```
R1(config)#event manager applet NO-RELOAD
R1(config-applet)#event cli pattern "relo*" sync no skip yes
R1(config-applet)#action 1.0 syslog msg "NOT ALLOWED"
R1(config-applet)#exit
```

Next, verify your EEM applet using the show event manager command:

```
R1#show event manager policy registered
No.  Class  Type    Event Type            Trap  Time Registered          Name
1    applet user    syslog                Off   Sat Jun 4 07:10:40 2011
CONFIGURATION-CHANGE-APPLET
 pattern {%SYS-5-CONFIG_I:}
 action 1.0 syslog msg "SAVING CONFIGURATION"
 action 1.1 snmp-trap strdata "CONFIG SAVED"
 action 1.2 cli command "enable"
 action 1.3 cli command "write memory"

2    applet user    cli                   Off   Sat Jun 4 07:32:20 2011   NO-RELOAD
 pattern {relo} sync no skip yes
 action 1.0 syslog msg "NOT ALLOWED"
```

Finally, test your configuration by attempting to reboot the router from the console using either the reload or relo commands. If you have completed this successfully, neither one will work:

```
R1#reload
R1#
*Jun  4 07:36:54.031: %HA_EM-6-LOG: NO-RELOAD: NOT ALLOWED

R1#
R1#relo
R1#
*Jun  4 07:37:01.567: %HA_EM-6-LOG: NO-RELOAD: NOT ALLOWED

R1#
```

Task 4

The requirements of this task are straightforward. To include the output of a command to an existing file, you need to use output redirection, specifically, the append keyword:

```
R1(config)#event manager applet OSPF
R1(config-applet)#event syslog pattern "Neighbor Down: Dead timer expired"
R1(config-applet)#action 1.0 cli command "enable"
R1(config-applet)#$cli command "show processes cpu | append flash:PROC_UTIL"
R1(config-applet)#$d "show interfaces serial 0/0 | append flash:SERIAL_STATS"
R1(config-applet)#exit
```

Next, verify your EEM applet using the show event manager command:

```
R1#show event manager policy registered
No.  Class  Type    Event Type            Trap  Time Registered          Name
1    applet user    syslog                Off   Sat Jun 4 07:10:40 2011
CONFIGURATION-CHANGE-APPLET
 pattern {%SYS-5-CONFIG_I:}
 action 1.0 syslog msg "SAVING CONFIGURATION"
 action 1.1 snmp-trap strdata "CONFIG SAVED"
 action 1.2 cli command "enable"
 action 1.3 cli command "write memory"

2    applet user    cli                   Off   Sat Jun 4 07:32:20 2011   NO-RELOAD
 pattern {relo} sync no skip yes
 action 1.0 syslog msg "NOT ALLOWED"

3    applet user    syslog                Off   Sat Jun 4 07:41:21 2011   OSPF
 pattern {Neighbor Down: Dead timer expired}
 action 1.0 cli command "enable"
 action 1.1 cli command "show processes cpu | append flash:PROC_UTIL"
 action 1.2 cli command "show interfaces serial 0/0 | append flash:SERIAL_STATS"
```

If you have more than one router, you can test the applet by enabling OSPF and then shutting down an interface so that the neighbor adjacency goes down.

FINAL ROUTER CONFIGURATIONS

R1

```
R1#term len 0
R1#sh run
Building configuration...

Current configuration : 1528 bytes
!
version 12.4
service timestamps debug datetime msec
service timestamps log datetime msec
no service password-encryption
!
hostname R1
!
boot-start-marker
boot-end-marker
!
no aaa new-model
no network-clock-participate slot 1
no network-clock-participate wic 0
ip cef
!
ip auth-proxy max-nodata-conns 3
ip admission max-nodata-conns 3
!
interface FastEthernet0/0
 ip address 150.1.1.1 255.255.255.0
 loopback
 duplex auto
 speed auto
 no keepalive
!
interface Serial0/0
 no ip address
 shutdown
!
interface Serial0/1
 no ip address
 shutdown
!
ip forward-protocol nd
!
no ip http server
no ip http secure-server
!
snmp-server community SECURITY RO
snmp-server enable traps event-manager
snmp-server host 150.1.1.254 SECURITY   event-manager
!
control-plane
!
line con 0
line aux 0
line vty 0 4
 login
!
event manager applet CONFIGURATION-CHANGE-APPLET
 event syslog pattern "%SYS-5-CONFIG_I:"
 action 1.0 syslog msg "SAVING CONFIGURATION"
 action 1.1 snmp-trap strdata "CONFIG SAVED"
 action 1.2 cli command "enable"
 action 1.3 cli command "write memory"
event manager applet NO-RELOAD
 event cli pattern "relo" sync no skip yes
 action 1.0 syslog msg "NOT ALLOWED"
event manager applet OSPF
 event syslog pattern "Neighbor Down: Dead timer expired"
 action 1.0 cli command "enable"
 action 1.1 cli command "show processes cpu | append flash:PROC_UTIL"
 action 1.2 cli command "show interfaces serial 0/0 | append flash:SERIAL_STATS"
!
end

R1#
```

CCNP LAB 62

Embedded Event Manager Lab

Lab Objective:

The focus of this lab is to understand Embedded Event Manager (EEM) implementation and configuration in Cisco IOS routers. Additional technologies include Cisco IOS ERM.

Lab Topology:

This lab requires only a single router running, at a minimum, Cisco IOS Software 12.4 Mainline. The router should have at least one Ethernet interface. The primary purpose of this lab is to reinforce configuration knowledge of the stated chapter.

> **IMPORTANT NOTE:** If you have multiple devices and servers / hosts in your home lab and you would like to test solutions for topics such as Syslog, SNMP and NetFlow by setting up host and viewing charts or logging information, for example, please feel free to do so. While these labs include logging to 'supposed' hosts, there are no SNMP or Syslog servers in the http://www.howtonetwork.net racks and so you will not be able to test the solutions in those racks. If you only have a single router, you can bring up the Ethernet interface by implementing the following configuration:
>
> ```
> !
> interface fastethernet 0/0
> loopback
> no keepalive
> no shut
> !
> ```

Task 1

Configure the router with a hostname of R1. Next, enable the LAN interface of the router and assign it the IP address 150.1.1.1/24. Ensure that this interface is in an up / up state.

Task 2

Configure a Cisco IOS Embedded Resource Manager (ERM) policy for critical CPU and memory utilization. The router should generate a critical Syslog message when the CPU and memory utilization exceeds 80% within a 15 second interval. Additionally, a Syslog message should also be generated when the CPU and memory utilization falls below 50% within a 15 second interval. Verify the Embedded Resource Manager configuration using appropriate commands.

Task 3

Management is worried about someone accidentally shutting down and interface and locking themselves (and every one) out of the router. They have requested that you configure an EEM script so that if the FastEthernet0/0 interface is shut down, the router will automatically re-enable the interface. Verify and testing your configuration using the appropriate commands.

Task 4

Configure the following static routes on the router (NOTE: ensure that interface Fa0/0 is up):

- 10.0.0.0/24 via 150.1.1.254
- 10.0.1.0/24 via 150.1.1.254

Management has requested that until they get the Cisco ACS server installed, the router should not allow anyone to delete the static routes. Write an EEM applet that prevents these, and any other, static routes from being deleted until AAA is configured on the router. The router should print the message 'ACTION NOT ALLOWED'. Verify your EEM configuration and test the applet by attempting to delete a static route.

LAB VALIDATION

Task 1

If your routers interface is not connected to a switch or hub, you need to complete this task as is shown below. If you do have a hub or switch, you can omit the loopback and no keepalive commands under the LAN interface. This example assumes a standalone router.

```
Router(config)#hostname R1
R1(config)#interface fastethernet 0/0
R1(config-if)#ip address 150.1.1.1 255.255.255.0
R1(config-if)#loopback
Loopback is a traffic-affecting operation
R1(config-if)#no keepalive
R1(config-if)#no shutdown
R1(config-if)#exit
```

Next, verify your configuration using the show ip interface brief command:

```
R1#show ip interface brief
Interface       IP-Address   OK? Method Status                 Protocol
FastEthernet0/0 150.1.1.1    YES manual up                     up
Serial0/0       unassigned   YES unset  administratively down  down
Serial0/1       unassigned   YES unset  administratively down  down
```

Task 2

Embedded Resource Manager (ERM), while technically beyond the scope of the CCNP course, is an important tool that can be used to leverage additional monitoring tools in the real world. ERM allows you to monitor internal system resource utilization for specific resources such as the buffer, memory, and CPU. ERM monitors resource utilization from the perspective of various subsystems within the Cisco IOS software such as resource owners (ROs) and resource users (RUs). Additionally, ERM allows you to configure threshold values for system resources which allows alarm or Syslog generation when these thresholds are exceeded or fall belong specified values. Additional information on ERM can be found on the Cisco website. The URL for this information is located below (at the time of the writing of this guide):

http://www.cisco.com/en/US/docs/ios/12_3t/12_3t14/feature/guide/gt_rmimg.html

This task is completed on the router as follows:

```
R1(config)#resource policy
R1(config-erm)#policy HIGH-CPU-AND-MEMORY global
R1(config-erm-policy)#system
R1(config-policy-node)#cpu total
R1(config-owner-cpu)#critical rising 80 interval 15 falling 50 interval 15
R1(config-owner-cpu)#exit
R1(config-policy-node)#memory processor
R1(config-owner-memory)#critical rising 80 interval 15 falling 50 interval 15
R1(config-owner-memory)#exit
R1(config-erm-policy)#exit
R1(config-erm)#user global HIGH-CPU-AND-MEMORY
R1(config-erm)#exit
```

Next, verify ERM configuration using the `show running-config` command:

```
R1#show run | section resource policy
resource policy
  policy HIGH-CPU-AND-MEMORY global
   system
     cpu total
      critical rising 80 interval 15 falling 50 interval 15
     !
     memory processor
      critical rising 80 interval 15 falling 50 interval 15
     !
  !
 !
user global HIGH-CPU-AND-MEMORY
 !
```

Task 3

```
R1(config)#event manager applet NO-SHUT
R1(config-applet)#$"FastEthernet0/0, changed state to administratively down"
R1(config-applet)#action 1.0 cli command "enable"
R1(config-applet)#action 1.1 cli command "configure terminal"
R1(config-applet)#action 1.2 cli command "interface fastethernet 0/0"
R1(config-applet)#action 1.3 cli command "no shutdown"
R1(config-applet)#action 1.4 cli command "end"
R1(config-applet)#exit
```

Following this, verify the EEM configuration using the `show event manager` command:

```
R1#show event manager policy registered
No.  Class   Type   Event Type       Trap  Time Registered        Name
1    applet  user   syslog           Off   Sat Jun 4 18:43:26 2011  NO-SHUT
 pattern {FastEthernet0/0, changed state to administratively down}
 action 1.0 cli command "enable"
 action 1.1 cli command "configure terminal"
 action 1.2 cli command "interface fastethernet 0/0"
 action 1.3 cli command "no shutdown"
 action 1.4 cli command "end"
```

Finally, test the applet by attempting to shut down the FastEthernet0/0 interface on the router:

```
R1(config)#interface fastethernet 0/0
R1(config-if)#shutdown
R1(config-if)#
*Jun  4 18:45:14.945: %LINK-5-CHANGED: Interface FastEthernet0/0, changed state to
administratively down
*Jun  4 18:45:15.133: %SYS-5-CONFIG_I: Configured from console by  on vty0 (EEM:NO-
SHUT)
*Jun  4 18:45:17.113: %LINK-3-UPDOWN: Interface FastEthernet0/0, changed state to up
R1(config-if)#do sh interfaces fastethernet 0/0
FastEthernet0/0 is up, line protocol is up
  Hardware is AmdFE, address is 000f.235e.ec80 (bia 000f.235e.ec80)
  Internet address is 150.1.1.1/24
  MTU 1500 bytes, BW 100000 Kbit/sec, DLY 100 usec,
     reliability 255/255, txload 1/255, rxload 1/255
  Encapsulation ARPA, loopback set
  Keepalive not set

[Truncated Output]
```

Task 4

```
R1(config)#ip route 10.0.0.0 255.255.255.0 fastethernet 0/0 150.1.1.254
R1(config)#ip route 10.0.1.0 255.255.255.0 fastethernet 0/0 150.1.1.254
R1(config)#event manager applet NO-DELETING-ROUTES
R1(config-applet)#event cli pattern "no ip route *" sync no skip yes
R1(config-applet)#action 1.0 syslog msg "ACTION NOT ALLOWED"
R1(config-applet)#exit
```

Next, verify the EEM applet configuration using the `show event manager` command:

```
R1#show event manager policy registered
No.  Class    Type    Event Type        Trap  Time Registered       Name
1    applet   user    syslog            Off   Sat Jun 4 18:43:26 2011  NO-SHUT
 pattern {FastEthernet0/0, changed state to administratively down}
 action 1.0 cli command "enable"
 action 1.1 cli command "configure terminal"
 action 1.2 cli command "interface fastethernet 0/0"
 action 1.3 cli command "no shutdown"
 action 1.4 cli command "end"

2    applet   user    cli               Off   Sat Jun 4 18:48:47 2011   NO-DELETING-
ROUTES
 pattern {no ip route *} sync no skip yes
 action 1.0 syslog msg "ACTION NOT ALLOWED"
```

Next, verify that the static routes are installed into the IP routing table:

```
R1#show ip route static
     10.0.0.0/24 is subnetted, 2 subnets
S       10.0.0.0 [1/0] via 150.1.1.254, FastEthernet0/0
S       10.0.1.0 [1/0] via 150.1.1.254, FastEthernet0/0
```

Finally, test your solution by attempting to delete a static route:

```
R1(config)#no ip route 10.0.1.0 255.255.255.0 fastethernet 0/0 150.1.1.254
R1(config)#
*Jun  4 18:51:52.113: %HA_EM-6-LOG: NO-DELETING-ROUTES: ACTION NOT ALLOWED

R1(config)#no ip route 10.0.0.0 255.255.255.0 fastethernet 0/0 150.1.1.254
R1(config)#
*Jun  4 18:52:08.205: %HA_EM-6-LOG: NO-DELETING-ROUTES: ACTION NOT ALLOWED

R1(config)#do show ip route static
     10.0.0.0/24 is subnetted, 2 subnets
S       10.0.0.0 [1/0] via 150.1.1.254, FastEthernet0/0
S       10.0.1.0 [1/0] via 150.1.1.254, FastEthernet0/0
R1(config)#
```

FINAL ROUTER CONFIGURATIONS

R1

```
R1#term len 0
R1#sh run
Building configuration...

Current configuration : 1607 bytes
!
version 12.4
service timestamps debug datetime msec
service timestamps log datetime msec
no service password-encryption
!
hostname R1
!
boot-start-marker
boot-end-marker
!
!
no aaa new-model
!
resource policy
  policy HIGH-CPU-AND-MEMORY global
    system
      cpu total
        critical rising 80 interval 15 falling 50 interval 15
      !
      memory processor
```

```
        critical rising 80 interval 15 falling 50 interval 15
    !
   user global HIGH-CPU-AND-MEMORY
   !
 !
 no network-clock-participate slot 1
 no network-clock-participate wic 0
 ip cef
 !
 ip auth-proxy max-nodata-conns 3
 ip admission max-nodata-conns 3
 !
 interface FastEthernet0/0
  ip address 150.1.1.1 255.255.255.0
  loopback
  duplex auto
  speed auto
  no keepalive
 !
 interface Serial0/0
  no ip address
  shutdown
 !
 interface Serial0/1
  no ip address
  shutdown
 !
 ip forward-protocol nd
 ip route 10.0.0.0 255.255.255.0 FastEthernet0/0 150.1.1.254
 ip route 10.0.1.0 255.255.255.0 FastEthernet0/0 150.1.1.254
 !
 no ip http server
 no ip http secure-server
 !
 control-plane
 !
 line con 0
 line aux 0
 line vty 0 4
  login
 !
 event manager applet NO-SHUT
  event syslog pattern "FastEthernet0/0, changed state to administratively down"
  action 1.0 cli command "enable"
  action 1.1 cli command "configure terminal"
  action 1.2 cli command "interface fastethernet 0/0"
  action 1.3 cli command "no shutdown"
  action 1.4 cli command "end"
 event manager applet NO-DELETING-ROUTES
  event cli pattern "no ip route *" sync no skip yes
  action 1.0 syslog msg "ACTION NOT ALLOWED"
 !
 end

 R1#
```

CCNP LAB 63

Syslog and NTP Lab

Lab Objective:

The focus of this lab is to understand Syslog implementation and configuration in Cisco IOS routers. Additional technologies include Network Time Protocol.

Lab Topology:

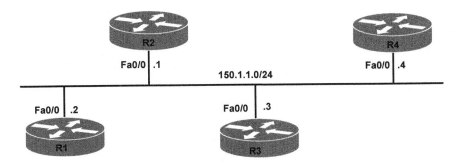

Task 1

Configure hostnames and IP address on all routers as illustrated in the topology.

Task 2

To ensure that all logg messages have the correct timestamps, configure R1 as a Network Time Protocol (NTP) server. R1 should have a stratum of 5. All routers should synchronize their time with R1..Assume that all routers reside in the Central Standard (CST) time zone - 6 hours behind Greenwich Mean Time (GMT). Verify your configuration using appropriate commands.

Task 3

Configure all routers so that all logging messages contain the following pertinent information:
- All messages should include date and time information, up to the millisecond
- The local time zone should be used for time stamps

In the future, multiple subinterfaces will be configured off the FastEthernet0/0 interface. These subinterfaces will be used for critical test networks and it is important that any transitions be logged. Therefore, configure the routers so that subinterface up/down transitions are logged. All routers should log to 150.1.1.254. Verify the configuration using the appropriate commands.

Task 4

Management has requested messages also be logged to an NMS with the IP address 150.1.1.254. Only log messages with a severity level of 3 and below should be logged and sent to the NMS. The SNMP NMS is using RO community 'LOGGING'. Next, verify your configuration using the appropriate commands.

LAB VALIDATION

Task 1

This task is straightforward and is completed as follows:

```
Router(config)#hostname R1
R1(config)#interface fastethernet 0/0
R1(config-if)#ip address 150.1.1.1 255.255.255.0
R1(config-if)#no shutdown
R1(config-if)#exit

Router(config)#hostname R2
R2(config)#interface fastethernet 0/0
R2(config-if)#ip address 150.1.1.2 255.255.255.0
R2(config-if)#no shutdown
R2(config-if)#exit

Router(config)#hostname R3
R3(config)#interface fastethernet 0/0
R3(config-if)#ip address 150.1.1.3 255.255.255.0
R3(config-if)#no shutdown
R3(config-if)#exit

Router(config)#hostname R4
R4(config)#interface fastethernet 0/0
R4(config-if)#ip address 150.1.1.4 255.255.255.0
R4(config-if)#no shutdown
R4(config-if)#exit
```

Task 2

This task requires that R1 and R2 be configured as both NTP masters (servers) and NTP clients. R3 and R4 should only be configured as NTP clients. This task is completed as follows:

```
R1(config)#clock timezone CST -6
R1(config)#ntp master 5
R1(config)#ntp server 150.1.1.2
R1(config)#exit

R2(config)#clock timezone CST -6
R2(config)#ntp master 8
R2(config)#ntp server 150.1.1.1
R2(config)#exit

R3(config)#clock timezone CST -6
R3(config)#ntp server 150.1.1.1
R3(config)#ntp server 150.1.1.2
R3(config)#exit

R4(config)#clock timezone CST -6
R4(config)#ntp server 150.1.1.1
R4(config)#ntp server 150.1.1.2
R4(config)#exit
```

Next, verify your NTP configuration using the `show ntp status` command:

```
R1#show ntp status
Clock is synchronized, stratum 5, reference is 127.127.7.1
nominal freq is 250.0000 Hz, actual freq is 250.0000 Hz, precision is 2**16
reference time is D1A2BDD7.1DBB5D77 (23:12:55.116 CST Tue Jun 14 2011)
clock offset is 0.0000 msec, root delay is 0.00 msec
root dispersion is 7875.02 msec, peer dispersion is 7875.02 msec

R2#show ntp status
Clock is synchronized, stratum 6, reference is 150.1.1.1
nominal freq is 250.0000 Hz, actual freq is 250.0000 Hz, precision is 2**18
reference time is D1A2BEDE.F4959A1C (23:17:18.955 CST Tue Jun 14 2011)
clock offset is 0.1005 msec, root delay is 2.59 msec
```

```
root dispersion is 375.15 msec, peer dispersion is 0.03 msec

R3#show ntp status
Clock is synchronized, stratum 6, reference is 150.1.1.1
nominal freq is 250.0000 Hz, actual freq is 250.0000 Hz, precision is 2**18
reference time is D1A2BEE4.10F17933 (23:17:24.066 CST Tue Jun 14 2011)
clock offset is 0.0323 msec, root delay is 2.61 msec
root dispersion is 375.09 msec, peer dispersion is 0.03 msec

R4#show ntp status
Clock is synchronized, stratum 6, reference is 150.1.1.1
nominal freq is 250.0000 Hz, actual freq is 250.0000 Hz, precision is 2**18
reference time is D1A2BEE9.9B64AC3B (23:17:29.607 CST Tue Jun 14 2011)
clock offset is -0.0265 msec, root delay is 2.49 msec
root dispersion is 1250.08 msec, peer dispersion is 875.02 msec
```

Task 3

This task requires that you use the service timestamps command. Additionally, to allow the logging of subinterface transitions, you need to enable logging for such events under the FastEthernet0/0 interface of all routers. Finally, enable logging and specify the destination host:

```
R1(config)#service timestamps log datetime msec localtime show-timezone
R1(config)#interface fastethernet 0/0
R1(config-if)#logging event subif-link-status
R1(config-if)#exit
R1(config)#logging on
R1(config)#logging 150.1.1.254
R1(config)#exit

R2(config)#service timestamps log datetime msec localtime show-timezone
R2(config)#interface fastethernet 0/0
R2(config-if)#logging event subif-link-status
R2(config-if)#exit
R2(config)#logging on
R2(config)#logging 150.1.1.254
R2(config)#exit

R3(config)#service timestamps log datetime msec localtime show-timezone
R3(config)#interface fastethernet 0/0
R3(config-if)#logging event subif-link-status
R3(config-if)#exit
R3(config)#logging on
R3(config)#logging 150.1.1.254
R3(config)#exit

R4(config)#service timestamps log datetime msec localtime show-timezone
R4(config)#interface fastethernet 0/0
R4(config-if)#logging event subif-link-status
R4(config-if)#exit
R4(config)#logging on
R4(config)#logging 150.1.1.254
R4(config)#exit
```

Next, verify your configuration using the show logging command on any of the routers:

```
R4#show logging
Syslog logging: enabled (11 messages dropped, 0 messages rate-limited,
                0 flushes, 0 overruns, xml disabled, filtering disabled)
    Console logging: disabled
    Monitor logging: level debugging, 0 messages logged, xml disabled,
                filtering disabled
    Buffer logging: level debugging, 1 messages logged, xml disabled,
                filtering disabled
    Logging Exception size (4096 bytes)
    Count and timestamp logging messages: disabled

No active filter modules.

    Trap logging: level informational, 35 message lines logged
        Logging to 150.1.1.254(global) (udp port 514, audit disabled,  link up), 3
message lines logged, xml disabled,
                filtering disabled
```

```
Log Buffer (4096 bytes):

Jun 14 23:41:40.294 CST: %SYS-5-CONFIG_I: Configured from console by console
```

To verify logging parameters under the FastEthernet0/0 interface, view the configuration:

```
R4#more system:running-config | section FastEthernet0/0
interface FastEthernet0/0
 ip address 150.1.1.4 255.255.255.0
 logging event subif-link-status
 duplex auto
 speed auto
```

Task 4

To complete this task, you need to configure basic SNMP parameters and then configure SNMP to send Syslog traps. To specify the severity level of messages sent to the history table on the router and an SNMP NMS, you need to use the logging history <severity> command. This task is completed on all routers as follows:

```
R1(config)#snmp-server enable traps syslog
R1(config)#logging history 3
R1(config)#snmp-server host 150.1.1.254 traps LOGGING syslog
R1(config)#snmp-server community LOGGING RO
R1(config)#exit

R2(config)#snmp-server enable traps syslog
R2(config)#logging history 3
R2(config)#snmp-server host 150.1.1.254 traps LOGGING syslog
R2(config)#snmp-server community LOGGING RO
R2(config)#exit

R3(config)#snmp-server enable traps syslog
R3(config)#logging history 3
R3(config)#snmp-server host 150.1.1.254 traps LOGGING syslog
R3(config)#snmp-server community LOGGING RO
R3(config)#exit

R4(config)#snmp-server enable traps syslog
R4(config)#logging history 3
R4(config)#snmp-server host 150.1.1.254 traps LOGGING syslog
R4(config)#snmp-server community LOGGING RO
R1(config)#exit
```

FINAL ROUTER CONFIGURATIONS

R1

```
R1#term len 0
R1#sh run
Building configuration...

Current configuration : 1067 bytes
!
! Last configuration change at 00:23:19 CST Wed Jun 15 2011
!
version 12.4
service timestamps debug datetime msec
service timestamps log datetime msec localtime show-timezone
no service password-encryption
!
hostname R1
!
boot-start-marker
boot-end-marker
!
no logging console
!
no aaa new-model
clock timezone CST -6
```

```
no network-clock-participate slot 1
no network-clock-participate wic 0
ip cef
!
ip auth-proxy max-nodata-conns 3
ip admission max-nodata-conns 3
!
interface FastEthernet0/0
 ip address 150.1.1.1 255.255.255.0
 logging event subif-link-status
 duplex auto
 speed auto
!
interface Serial0/0
 no ip address
 shutdown
!
interface Serial0/1
 no ip address
 shutdown
!
ip forward-protocol nd
!
no ip http server
no ip http secure-server
!
logging history errors
logging 150.1.1.254
snmp-server community LOGGING RO
snmp-server enable traps syslog
snmp-server host 150.1.1.254 LOGGING  syslog
!
control-plane
!
line con 0
line aux 0
line vty 0 4
 login
!
ntp master 5
!
end

R1#
```

R2

```
R2#term len 0
R2#sh run
Building configuration...

Current configuration : 1101 bytes
!
! Last configuration change at 00:07:37 CST Wed Jun 15 2011
!
version 12.4
service timestamps debug datetime msec
service timestamps log datetime msec localtime show-timezone
no service password-encryption
!
hostname R2
!
boot-start-marker
boot-end-marker
!
no logging console
!
no aaa new-model
clock timezone CST -6
no network-clock-participate slot 1
no network-clock-participate wic 0
ip cef
!
ip auth-proxy max-nodata-conns 3
```

```
ip admission max-nodata-conns 3
!
interface FastEthernet0/0
 ip address 150.1.1.2 255.255.255.0
 logging event subif-link-status
 duplex auto
 speed auto
!
interface Serial0/0
 no ip address
 shutdown
!
interface Serial0/1
 no ip address
 shutdown
!
ip forward-protocol nd
!
no ip http server
no ip http secure-server
!
logging history errors
logging 150.1.1.254
snmp-server community LOGGING RO
snmp-server enable traps syslog
snmp-server host 150.1.1.254 LOGGING  syslog
!
control-plane
!
line con 0
line aux 0
line vty 0 4
 login
!
ntp clock-period 17179916
ntp server 150.1.1.1
!
end

R2#
```

R3

```
R3#term len 0
R3#sh run
Building configuration...

Current configuration : 1383 bytes
!
! Last configuration change at 00:07:40 CST Wed Jun 15 2011
!
version 12.4
service timestamps debug datetime msec
service timestamps log datetime msec localtime show-timezone
no service password-encryption
!
hostname R3
!
boot-start-marker
boot-end-marker
!
no logging console
!
no aaa new-model
clock timezone CST -6
no network-clock-participate slot 1
no network-clock-participate wic 0
ip cef
!
ip auth-proxy max-nodata-conns 3
ip admission max-nodata-conns 3
!
interface FastEthernet0/0
 ip address 150.1.1.3 255.255.255.0
 logging event subif-link-status
```

```
 duplex auto
 speed auto
!
interface Serial1/0
 no ip address
 shutdown
!
interface Serial1/1
 no ip address
 shutdown
!
interface Serial1/2
 no ip address
 shutdown
!
interface Serial1/3
 no ip address
 shutdown
!
interface Serial1/4
 no ip address
 shutdown
!
interface Serial1/5
 no ip address
 shutdown
!
interface Serial1/6
 no ip address
 shutdown
!
interface Serial1/7
 no ip address
 shutdown
!
ip forward-protocol nd
!
no ip http server
no ip http secure-server
!
logging history errors
logging 150.1.1.254
snmp-server community LOGGING RO
snmp-server enable traps syslog
snmp-server host 150.1.1.254 LOGGING  syslog
!
control-plane
!
line con 0
line aux 0
line vty 0 4
 login
!
ntp clock-period 17179889
ntp server 150.1.1.1
!
end
R3#
```

R4

```
R4#term len 0
R4#sh run
Building configuration...

Current configuration : 1133 bytes
!
! Last configuration change at 00:07:41 CST Wed Jun 15 2011
!
version 12.4
service timestamps debug datetime msec
service timestamps log datetime msec localtime show-timezone
no service password-encryption
!
```

```
hostname R4
!
boot-start-marker
boot-end-marker
!
logging buffered 4096 debugging
no logging console
!
no aaa new-model
clock timezone CST -6
no network-clock-participate slot 1
no network-clock-participate wic 0
ip cef
!
ip auth-proxy max-nodata-conns 3
ip admission max-nodata-conns 3
!
interface FastEthernet0/0
 ip address 150.1.1.4 255.255.255.0
 logging event subif-link-status
 duplex auto
 speed auto
!
interface Serial0/0
 no ip address
 shutdown
!
interface Serial0/1
 no ip address
 shutdown
!
ip forward-protocol nd
!
no ip http server
no ip http secure-server
!
logging history errors
logging 150.1.1.254
snmp-server community LOGGING RO
snmp-server enable traps syslog
snmp-server host 150.1.1.254 LOGGING  syslog
!
control-plane
!
line con 0
line aux 0
line vty 0 4
 login
!
ntp clock-period 17179877
ntp server 150.1.1.1
!
end

R4#
```

CCNP LAB 64

SNMP Traps and Informs Lab

Lab Objective:

The focus of this lab is to understand Simple Network Management Protocol implementation and configuration in Cisco IOS routers. Additional technologies include security.

Lab Topology:

This lab requires only a single router running, at a minimum, Cisco IOS Software 12.4 Mainline. The router should have at least one Ethernet interface. The primary purpose of this lab is to reinforce configuration knowledge of the stated chapter.

IMPORTANT NOTE: If you have multiple devices and servers / hosts in your home lab and you would like to test solutions for topics such as Syslog, SNMP and NetFlow by setting up host and viewing charts or logging information, for example, please feel free to do so. While these labs include logging to 'supposed' hosts, there are no SNMP or Syslog servers in the http://www.howtonetwork.net racks and so you will not be able to test the solutions in those racks. If you only have a single router, you can bring up the Ethernet interface by implementing the following configuration:

```
!
interface fastethernet 0/0
loopback
no keepalive
no shut
!
```

Task 1

Configure two SNMP communities on the device: one RO community named STANDARD and one RW community named ADVANCED. The RO community should be accessible only by NMSs 150.2.2.253 and 150.2.2.254. The RW community should be accessible only by NMSs 150.3.3.253 and 150.3.3.254. Verify your SNMP configuration using the appropriate commands.

Task 2

Management recently purchased a CiscoWorks LMS solution. They would to use RME for device configuration file and software image management. This will be performed via the Trivial File Transfer Protocol (TFTP). Configure the device so that only host 150.1.1.254 is allowed TFTP access to perform these actions.

Task 3

Management has requested that, for easier identification, SNMP traps and informs be sent from the device using a source IP address of 1.1.1.1. In addition to this, Management has also requested that CiscoWorks be allowed to initiate a remote reload (reboot) of this device. This is important as this tool will be used for software upgrades in the future. Configure the device as requested. Verify your configuration using the appropriate commands.

Task 4

Configure the router to send SNMPv2 traps to hosts 150.2.2.253 and 150.2.2.254. These should be sent with the community string STANDARD. Verify your configuration using the appropriate commands. The device should only send environmental monitor traps to host 150.2.2.253 and Syslog traps to host 150.2.2.254. Verify your SNMP configuration using the appropriate commands.

Task 5

Configure the router to send SNMPv2 informs to hosts 150.3.3.253 and 150.3.3.254. These should be sent with the community string ADVANCED. To ensure that informs are received, the router should be configured to resend an inform at least 10 time while waiting at least 60 seconds between retries. And finally, to prevent the premature discarding of pending informs due to a lack of acknowledgement, configure the router to store up to 50 unacknowledged informs. Verify your configuration using the appropriate commands.

LAB VALIDATION

Task 1

This task is straightforward and requires ACLs with SNMP. This is completed as follows:

```
R1(config)#access-list 1 permit host 150.2.2.253
R1(config)#access-list 1 permit host 150.2.2.254
R1(config)#access-list 2 permit host 150.3.3.253
R1(config)#access-list 2 permit host 150.3.3.254
R1(config)#snmp-server community STANDARD RO 1
R1(config)#snmp-server community ADVANCED RW 2
```

Verify your configuration using the **show snmp community** command on the router:

```
R1#show snmp community

Community name: ILMI
Community Index: cisco0
Community SecurityName: ILMI
storage-type: read-only   active

Community name: STANDARD
Community Index: cisco1
Community SecurityName: STANDARD
storage-type: nonvolatile        active access-list: 1

Community name: ADVANCED
Community Index: cisco2
Community SecurityName: ADVANCED
storage-type: nonvolatile        active access-list: 2
```

Task 2

The CiscoWorks LAN Management Solution (LMS) is comprised of several individual software applications that can be used for the configuration and administration of campus networks. LMS also provides monitoring, and troubleshooting capabilities. The following applications are included in the CiscoWorks LAN Management Solution suite:

*   Resource Manager Essentials (RME)
*   CiscoWorks Health and Utilization Monitor
*   Device Fault Manager (DFM)
*   Internetwork Performance Monitor (IPM)

Resource Manager can also be used for network monitoring and fault information for tracking devices that are critical to network uptime. RME can also be used for device configuration and software image management via TFTP. This task is completed in one of two ways. The legacy methods of implementing this configuration is shown below:

```
R1(config)#access-list 3 permit host 150.3.3.254
R1(config)#snmp-server tftp-server-list 3
R1(config)#exit
```

In current versions of software, this task would be completed as follows:

```
R1(config)#access-list 3 permit host 150.3.3.254
R1(config)#snmp-server file-transfer access-group 3 protocol tftp
R1(config)#exit
```

While there is no explicit command to view the configured parameters, you can always view the device configuration file to verify your configuration:

```
R1#more system:running-config | section snmp
snmp-server community STANDARD RO 1
snmp-server community ADVANCED RW 2
snmp-server file-transfer access-group 3 protocol tftp
```

Task 3

In order to specify a source IP address, you must configure an interface with this IP address and then specify that as the SNMP source interface. To complete the second requirement, you need to use the `system-shutdown` SNMP command. This command allows a certain SNMP set operation to trigger a router reboot and can be used by CiscoWorks LMS Resource Manager Essentials (RME). This task is completed as follows:

```
R1(config)#interface loopback 0
R1(config-if)#ip address 1.1.1.1 255.255.255.255
R1(config-if)#exit
R1(config)#snmp-server trap-source loopback 0
R1(config)#snmp-server source-interface informs loopback 0
R1(config)#snmp-server system-shutdown
R1(config)#exit
```

Again, view the device configuration to verify your solution:

```
R1#more system:running-config | section snmp
snmp-server community STANDARD RO 1
snmp-server community ADVANCED RW 2
snmp-server trap-source Loopback0
snmp-server source-interface informs Loopback0
snmp-server system-shutdown
snmp-server file-transfer access-group 3 protocol tftp
```

Task 4

The requirements of this task are straightforward and are completed as follows:

```
R1(config)#snmp-server host 150.2.2.253 traps version 2c STANDARD envmon
R1(config)#snmp-server host 150.2.2.254 traps version 2c STANDARD syslog
R1(config)#snmp-server enable traps envmon
R1(config)#snmp-server enable traps syslog
```

Next, verify your configuration using the `show snmp host` command:

```
R1#show snmp host

Notification host: 150.2.2.253  udp-port: 162   type: trap
user: STANDARD  security model: v2c

Notification host: 150.2.2.254  udp-port: 162   type: trap
user: STANDARD  security model: v2c
```

Task 5

The requirements of this task are straightforward. To configure SNMP inform parameters, we need to use the `snmp-server inform` command. This task is completed as follows:

```
R1(config)#snmp-server host 150.3.3.253 informs version 2c ADVANCED
R1(config)#snmp-server host 150.3.3.254 informs version 2c ADVANCED
R1(config)#snmp-server inform retries 10
R1(config)#snmp-server inform timeout 60
R1(config)#snmp-server inform pending 50
```

Following this, verify your configuration using the `show snmp` command:

```
R1#show snmp
Chassis: JAE08020Z7T
0 SNMP packets input
    0 Bad SNMP version errors
    0 Unknown community name
    0 Illegal operation for community name supplied
    0 Encoding errors
    0 Number of requested variables
    0 Number of altered variables
    0 Get-request PDUs
    0 Get-next PDUs
    0 Set-request PDUs
    0 Input queue packet drops (Maximum queue size 1000)
0 SNMP packets output
    0 Too big errors (Maximum packet size 1500)
    0 No such name errors
    0 Bad values errors
    0 General errors
    0 Response PDUs
    0 Trap PDUs

SNMP logging: enabled
    Logging to 150.2.2.253.162, 0/10, 0 sent, 0 dropped.
    Logging to 150.2.2.254.162, 0/10, 0 sent, 0 dropped.

SNMP Manager-role output packets
    0 Get-request PDUs
    0 Get-next PDUs
    0 Get-bulk PDUs
    0 Set-request PDUs
    0 Inform-request PDUs
    0 Timeouts
    0 Drops
SNMP Manager-role input packets
    0 Inform request PDUs
    0 Trap PDUs
    0 Response PDUs
    0 Responses with errors

SNMP informs: enabled
    Informs in flight 0/50 (current/max)
    Logging to 150.3.3.253.162
        0 sent, 0 in-flight, 0 retries, 0 failed, 0 dropped
    Logging to 150.3.3.254.162
        0 sent, 0 in-flight, 0 retries, 0 failed, 0 dropped
```

You can also use the `show snmp host` command for verification:

```
R1#show snmp host

Notification host: 150.3.3.253  udp-port: 162    type: inform
user: ADVANCED  security model: v2c

Notification host: 150.3.3.254  udp-port: 162    type: inform
user: ADVANCED  security model: v2c

Notification host: 150.2.2.253  udp-port: 162    type: trap
user: STANDARD  security model: v2c

Notification host: 150.2.2.254  udp-port: 162    type: trap
user: STANDARD  security model: v2c
```

Finally, you can also verify your configuration by looking at the device configuration file:

```
R1#show running-config | section include inform
snmp-server source-interface informs Loopback0
snmp-server host 150.3.3.253 inform version 2c ADVANCED
snmp-server host 150.3.3.254 inform version 2c ADVANCED
snmp-server inform retries 10 timeout 60 pending 50
```

FINAL ROUTER CONFIGURATIONS

R1

```
R1#term len 0
R1#sh run
Building configuration...

Current configuration : 1563 bytes
!
version 12.4
service timestamps debug datetime msec
service timestamps log datetime msec
no service password-encryption
!
hostname R1
!
boot-start-marker
boot-end-marker
!
no logging console
!
no aaa new-model
no network-clock-participate slot 1
no network-clock-participate wic 0
ip cef
!
ip auth-proxy max-nodata-conns 3
ip admission max-nodata-conns 3
!
interface Loopback0
 ip address 1.1.1.1 255.255.255.255
!
interface FastEthernet0/0
 ip address 150.1.1.1 255.255.255.0
 duplex auto
 speed auto
!
interface Serial0/0
 no ip address
 shutdown
!
interface Serial0/1
 no ip address
 shutdown
!
ip forward-protocol nd
!
no ip http server
no ip http secure-server
!
access-list 1 permit 150.2.2.254
access-list 1 permit 150.2.2.253
access-list 2 permit 150.3.3.254
access-list 2 permit 150.3.3.253
access-list 3 permit 150.3.3.254
snmp-server community STANDARD RO 1
snmp-server community ADVANCED RW 2
snmp-server trap-source Loopback0
snmp-server source-interface informs Loopback0
snmp-server system-shutdown
snmp-server enable traps envmon
snmp-server enable traps syslog
snmp-server host 150.3.3.253 inform version 2c ADVANCED
snmp-server host 150.3.3.254 inform version 2c ADVANCED
snmp-server host 150.2.2.253 version 2c STANDARD  envmon
snmp-server host 150.2.2.254 version 2c STANDARD  syslog
snmp-server file-transfer access-group 3 protocol tftp
snmp-server inform retries 10 timeout 60 pending 50
!
control-plane
!
line con 0
line aux 0
line vty 0 4
 login
!
end

R1#
```

CCNP LAB 65

NetFlow and Accounting Lab

Lab Objective:

The focus of this lab is to understand Cisco IOS NetFlow implementation and configuration in Cisco IOS routers. Additional technologies include Cisco IOS IP Accounting.

Lab Topology:

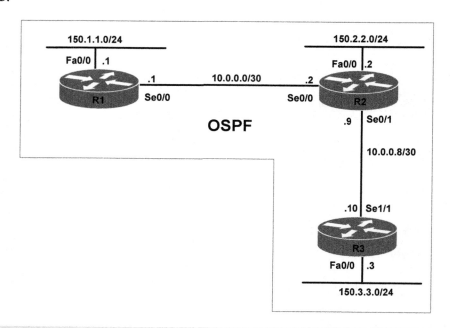

IMPORTANT NOTE: If you are using the www.howtonetwork.net racks, please bring up the LAN interfaces connected to the routers by issuing the no shutdown command on the connected switches. If you are using a home lab with no Switches, you can bring up the LAN interfaces using the following configurations on your routers:

```
interface fastethernet 0/0
  no keepalive
  loopback
  no shutdown
```

Alternately, you can simply connect the interfaces to a hub or switch if you have one available in your own lab.

Task 1

Configure hostnames and IP address on all routers as illustrated in the topology.

Task 2

Configure OSPF on all routers as illustrated in the topology. Verify your configuration using the appropriate commands.

Task 3

Configure Cisco IOS IP accounting on all router WAN interfaces. All routers should store IP accounting information for all packets egressing the WAN interfaces. Verify your IP accounting configuration using the appropriate commands.

Task 4

Configure Cisco IOS NetFlow on all routers. All routers should collect forward statistics for all ingress flows to host 192.168.1.254 using NetFlow version 5 and a destination port of 8000. This traffic should be sourced from the FastEthernet 0/0 interface of all routers.

Task 5

Assume that R1 is a core Internet router. To ensure that as much NetFlow information is stored, configure the router to store up to 128K (131072) entries in the cache. Additionally, configure Cisco IOS NetFlow on this router so that export statistics include the originating autonomous system (AS) for the source and destination. And finally, because R1 will be receiving traffic from multiple hosts on the LAN subnet, configure Cisco IOS NetFlow so that the router captures the MAC addresses of the incoming source and the outgoing destination from the first Layer 2 frame in the flow. Verify your configuration.

LAB VALIDATION

Task 1

Please refer to previous labs for basic IPv4, IPv6 addressing and hostname configuration. This will not be included in this section to avoid being redundant.

Task 2

Please refer to previous labs for basic EIGRP configuration. Following this, verify your OSPF configuration using the `show ip ospf neighbor` and `show ip route` commands. Following this configuration, your route tables should show the following route information:

```
R1#show ip route ospf
     10.0.0.0/30 is subnetted, 2 subnets
O       10.0.0.8 [110/128] via 10.0.0.2, 00:14:34, Serial0/0
     150.2.0.0/24 is subnetted, 1 subnets
O       150.2.2.0 [110/65] via 10.0.0.2, 00:14:34, Serial0/0
     150.3.0.0/24 is subnetted, 1 subnets
O       150.3.3.0 [110/129] via 10.0.0.2, 00:14:34, Serial0/0

R2#show ip route ospf
     150.1.0.0/24 is subnetted, 1 subnets
O       150.1.1.0 [110/65] via 10.0.0.1, 00:14:39, Serial0/0
     150.3.0.0/24 is subnetted, 1 subnets
O       150.3.3.0 [110/65] via 10.0.0.10, 00:14:39, Serial0/1

R3#show ip route ospf
     10.0.0.0/30 is subnetted, 2 subnets
O       10.0.0.0 [110/845] via 10.0.0.9, 00:14:36, Serial1/1
     150.1.0.0/24 is subnetted, 1 subnets
O       150.1.1.0 [110/846] via 10.0.0.9, 00:14:36, Serial1/1
     150.2.0.0/24 is subnetted, 1 subnets
O       150.2.2.0 [110/782] via 10.0.0.9, 00:14:36, Serial1/1
```

Task 3

While not as granular and detailed as Cisco IOS NetFlow, Cisco IOS IP accounting can be a very powerful troubleshooting tool. IP accounting allows administrators to configure the router to record the number of bytes (IP header and data) and packets switched through the system on a source and destination IP address basis. Only transit IP traffic is measured and only on an outbound basis; traffic generated by the router access server or terminating in this device is not included in the accounting statistics. This task is completed as follows:

```
R1(config)#interface serial 0/0
R1(config-if)#ip accounting output-packets
R1(config-if)#exit

R2(config)#interface serial 0/0
R2(config-if)#ip accounting output-packets
R2(config-if)#exit
R2(config)#interface serial 0/1
R2(config-if)#ip accounting output-packets
R2(config-if)#exit

R3(config)#interface serial 1/1
R3(config-if)#ip accounting output-packets
R3(config-if)#exit
```

Next, verify your configuration using the show ip accounting command. Keep in mind that IP accounting does not capture traffic generated by the local router. Only transit traffic statistics are kept. Therefore, to test, you can ping and Telnet, etc, between R1 and R3 and then verify the statistics on R2 as the traffic will transit that router.

```
R2#show ip accounting output-packets
     Source           Destination        Packets          Bytes
   150.1.1.1          10.0.0.10            100            150000
   10.0.0.10          150.1.1.1            100            150000
   150.3.3.3          10.0.0.1             105             50500
   10.0.0.1           150.3.3.3            105             50500
```

Task 4

This task is straightforward and is completed as follows:

```
R1(config)#interface fastethernet 0/0
R1(config-if)#ip flow ingress
R1(config-if)#exit
R1(config)#ip flow-export destination 192.168.1.254 8000
R1(config)#ip flow-export version 5
R1(config)#ip flow-export source fastethernet 0/0

R2(config)#interface fastethernet 0/0
R2(config-if)#ip flow ingress
R2(config-if)#exit
R2(config)#ip flow-export destination 192.168.1.254 8000
R2(config)#ip flow-export version 5
R2(config)#ip flow-export source fastethernet 0/0

R3(config)#interface fastethernet 0/0
R3(config-if)#ip flow ingress
R3(config-if)#exit
R3(config)#ip flow-export destination 192.168.1.254 8000
R3(config)#ip flow-export version 5
R3(config)#ip flow-export source fastethernet 0/0
```

Next, verify your configuration using the show ip cache flow command. If you have hosts that are connected to one of the LAN subnets on any of the routers, you can generate some traffic, e.g. pings, Telnet, HTTP, etc, to view information on traffic statistics that will be sent to the NetFlow Collector specified in the previous lab tasks:

```
R1#show ip cache flow
IP packet size distribution (322 total packets):
   1-32   64    96   128   160   192   224   256   288   320   352   384   416   448   480
   .000  .183  .000  .099  .000  .000  .000  .000  .000  .000  .000  .000  .000  .000  .000

    512   544   576  1024  1536  2048  2560  3072  3584  4096  4608
   .000  .000  .000  .717  .000  .000  .000  .000  .000  .000  .000

IP Flow Switching Cache, 278544 bytes
  1 active, 4095 inactive, 12 added
  462 ager polls, 0 flow alloc failures
  Active flows timeout in 30 minutes
  Inactive flows timeout in 15 seconds
```

```
IP Sub Flow Cache, 21640 bytes
  1 active, 1023 inactive, 12 added, 12 added to flow
  0 alloc failures, 0 force free
  1 chunk, 1 chunk added
  last clearing of statistics never
Protocol         Total    Flows  Packets Bytes  Packets Active(Sec) Idle(Sec)
--------         Flows    /Sec   /Flow   /Pkt   /Sec    /Flow       /Flow
TCP-Telnet       4        0.0    13      42     0.0     1.8         4.9
TCP-WWW          1        0.0    1       44     0.0     0.0         15.0
UDP-other        1        0.0    231     604    0.0     312.0       15.5
ICMP             5        0.0    6       100    0.0     0.7         15.7
Total:           11       0.0    29      454    0.0     29.4        11.7

SrcIf     SrcIPaddress   DstIf   DstIPaddress   Pr SrcP DstP Pkts
Fa0/0     150.1.1.252    Se0/0   10.0.0.10      06 2AFA 0017 24
Fa0/0     150.1.1.252    Se0/0   10.0.0.2       06 2AFC 0050 3
```

Task 5

The requirements in this task are straightforward. In order to change the default cache size from 65535 (64K) to a new value, you need to disable NetFlow on all interfaces first or reboot the router following the change. If not, the router will print the following message on the console:

```
R1(config)#ip flow-cache entries 131072
%The change in number of entries will take effect after either
    the next reboot or when netflow is turned off on all interfaces.
```

By default, with Cisco IOS NetFlow, values from Layer 2 and Layer 3 fields are not captured. This default behavior, however, can be changed by using the ip flow-capture <option> command in global configuration mode. This task is completed as follows:

```
R1(config)#interface fastethernet 0/0
R1(config-if)#no ip flow ingress
R1(config-if)#exit
R1(config)#ip flow-cache entries 131072
R1(config)#ip flow-export version 5 origin-as
R1(config)#ip flow-capture mac-addresses
R1(config)#interface fastethernet 0/0
R1(config-if)#ip flow ingress
R1(config-if)#exit
```

Next, verify your configuration using the show ip cache verbose flow command:

```
R1#show ip cache verbose flow
IP packet size distribution (342 total packets):
   1-32   64   96  128  160  192  224  256  288  320  352  384  416  448  480
   .000 .230 .000 .093 .000 .000 .000 .000 .000 .000 .000 .000 .000 .000 .000

   512  544  576 1024 1536 2048 2560 3072 3584 4096 4608
   .000 .000 .000 .675 .000 .000 .000 .000 .000 .000 .000

IP Flow Switching Cache, 8913408 bytes
  1 active, 131071 inactive, 19 added
  551 ager polls, 0 flow alloc failures
  Active flows timeout in 30 minutes
  Inactive flows timeout in 15 seconds
IP Sub Flow Cache, 672392 bytes
  2 active, 32766 inactive, 23 added, 19 added to flow
  0 alloc failures, 0 force free
  1 chunk, 2 chunks added
  last clearing of statistics never
Protocol         Total    Flows  Packets Bytes  Packets Active(Sec) Idle(Sec)
--------         Flows    /Sec   /Flow   /Pkt   /Sec    /Flow       /Flow
TCP-Telnet       4        0.0    13      42     0.0     1.8         4.9
TCP-WWW          8        0.0    2       41     0.0     0.6         11.9
UDP-other        1        0.0    231     604    0.0     312.0       15.5
ICMP             5        0.0    6       100    0.0     0.7         15.7
Total:           18       0.0    18      428    0.0     18.2        11.6

SrcIf          SrcIPaddress   DstIf          DstIPaddress   Pr TOS Flgs  Pkts
Port Msk AS                   Port Msk AS    NextHop            B/Pk     Active
Fa0/0          150.1.1.252    Se0/0          10.0.0.2       06 C0  10    1
2AFE /24 0                    0050 /30 0     10.0.0.0           40       0.0
MAC:           0007.8432.dd00                0000.0000.0000
```

FINAL ROUTER CONFIGURATIONS

R1

```
R1#term len 0
R1#sh run
Building configuration...

Current configuration : 1135 bytes
!
version 12.4
service timestamps debug datetime msec
service timestamps log datetime msec
no service password-encryption
!
hostname R1
!
boot-start-marker
boot-end-marker
!
no logging console
!
no aaa new-model
no network-clock-participate slot 1
no network-clock-participate wic 0
ip cef
!
ip flow-cache entries 131072
no ip domain lookup
ip auth-proxy max-nodata-conns 3
ip admission max-nodata-conns 3
!
interface FastEthernet0/0
 ip address 150.1.1.1 255.255.255.0
 ip flow ingress
 duplex auto
 speed auto
!
interface Serial0/0
 ip address 10.0.0.1 255.255.255.252
 ip accounting output-packets
 clock rate 2000000
!
interface Serial0/1
 no ip address
 shutdown
!
router ospf 1
 router-id 1.1.1.1
 log-adjacency-changes
 network 0.0.0.0 255.255.255.255 area 0
!
ip forward-protocol nd
!
ip flow-capture mac-addresses
ip flow-export source FastEthernet0/0
ip flow-export version 5 origin-as
ip flow-export destination 192.168.1.254 8000
!
no ip http server
no ip http secure-server
!
control-plane
!
line con 0
line aux 0
line vty 0 4
 login
!
end

R1#
```

R2

```
R2#term len 0
R2#sh run
Building configuration...

Current configuration : 1101 bytes
!
version 12.4
service timestamps debug datetime msec
service timestamps log datetime msec
no service password-encryption
!
hostname R2
!
boot-start-marker
boot-end-marker
!
no logging console
!
no aaa new-model
no network-clock-participate slot 1
no network-clock-participate wic 0
ip cef
!
no ip domain lookup
ip auth-proxy max-nodata-conns 3
ip admission max-nodata-conns 3
!
interface FastEthernet0/0
 ip address 150.2.2.2 255.255.255.0
 ip flow ingress
 duplex auto
 speed auto
!
interface Serial0/0
 ip address 10.0.0.2 255.255.255.252
 ip accounting output-packets
!
interface Serial0/1
 ip address 10.0.0.9 255.255.255.252
 ip accounting output-packets
!
router ospf 2
 router-id 2.2.2.2
 log-adjacency-changes
 network 0.0.0.0 255.255.255.255 area 0
!
ip forward-protocol nd
!
ip flow-export source FastEthernet0/0
ip flow-export version 5
ip flow-export destination 192.168.1.254 8000
!
ip http server
no ip http secure-server
!
control-plane
!
line con 0
line aux 0
line vty 0 4
 password cisco
 login
!
end

R2#
```

R3

```
R3#term len 0
R3#sh run
Building configuration...

Current configuration : 1402 bytes
!
version 12.4
service timestamps debug datetime msec
service timestamps log datetime msec
no service password-encryption
```

```
!
hostname R3
!
boot-start-marker
boot-end-marker
!
no logging console
!
no aaa new-model
no network-clock-participate slot 1
no network-clock-participate wic 0
ip cef
!
no ip domain lookup
ip auth-proxy max-nodata-conns 3
ip admission max-nodata-conns 3
!
interface FastEthernet0/0
 ip address 150.3.3.3 255.255.255.0
 ip flow ingress
 duplex auto
 speed auto
!
interface Serial1/0
 no ip address
 shutdown
 clock rate 128000
!
interface Serial1/1
 ip address 10.0.0.10 255.255.255.252
 ip accounting output-packets
 clock rate 128000
!
interface Serial1/2
 no ip address
 shutdown
 clock rate 128000
!
interface Serial1/3
 no ip address
 shutdown
!
interface Serial1/4
 no ip address
 shutdown
!
interface Serial1/5
 no ip address
 shutdown
!
interface Serial1/6
 no ip address
 shutdown
!
interface Serial1/7
 no ip address
 shutdown
!
router ospf 3
 router-id 3.3.3.3
 log-adjacency-changes
 network 0.0.0.0 255.255.255.255 area 0
!
ip forward-protocol nd
!
ip flow-export source FastEthernet0/0
ip flow-export version 5
ip flow-export destination 192.168.1.254 8000
!
no ip http server
no ip http secure-server
!
control-plane
!
line con 0
line aux 0
line vty 0 4
 password cisco
 login
!
end
R3#
```

CCNP LAB 66

Cisco IOS NBAR Lab

Lab Objective:

The focus of this lab is to understand Network Based Application Recognition implementation and configuration in Cisco IOS routers.

Lab Topology:

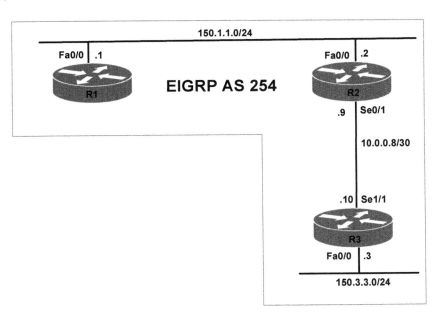

IMPORTANT NOTE: If you are using the www.howtonetwork.net racks, please bring up the LAN interfaces connected to the routers by issuing the no shutdown command on the connected switches. If you are using a home lab with no Switches, you can bring up the LAN interfaces using the following configurations on your routers:

```
interface fastethernet 0/0
  no keepalive
  loopback
  no shutdown
```

Alternately, you can simply connect the interfaces to a hub or switch if you have one available in your own lab.

Task 1

Configure hostnames and IP address on all routers as illustrated in the topology.

Task 2

Configure OSPF on all routers as illustrated in the topology. Verify your configuration using the appropriate commands.

Task 3

Configure R2 to discover traffic for all protocols known to NBAR on FastEthernet0/0. Verify your configuration using the appropriate commands.

Task 4

Management has decided that, for security purposes, some protocols be configured to use non-default port numbers in addition to their standard port numbers. These protocols and their non-default port numbers are listed below:

- File Transfer Protocol - TCP port 2021
- Telnet - TCP port 3023
- Hypertext Transfer Protocol - TCP port 8080

Configure NBAR so that statistics for these non-default port numbers are correctly collected.

Task 5

You are troubleshooting router performance issues on R2 and observer the following errors:

```
%NBAR-2-NOMEMORY: No memory available for StILE lmalloc -Traceback= 0x604EFEEC
0x6044AD40 0x6044AE64 0x6044D540 0x60445D28 0x6044E47C 0x6046F858 0x60454BCC
0x6045575C 0x60456748 0x60F1201C 0x6052F44C 0x6054DE80 0x605F4
%NBAR-2-RMNORESOURCE : NBAR resources exhausted
%NBAR-2-NOSTATEMEM : Memory for maintaining state used up
%NBAR-2-RMINVALIDCONFIG: NBAR resource manager : too many buckets
```

Given this, management has requested that you decrease the idle time to 60 seconds, increase the initial memory size to 2M and allow up to 68K expansion. Verify your configuration using the appropriate commands.

Task 6

Your company is running a custom, in-house application that uses TCP ports 6700 and 6705 as well as UDP port between 6800 and 6900. Configure R2 so that the router monitors and correctly classifies this traffic. Assume the application is named OOMPALOOMPA.

LAB VALIDATION

Task 1

Please refer to previous labs for basic IPv4, IPv6 addressing and hostname configuration. This will not be included in this section to avoid being redundant.

Task 2

Please refer to previous labs for basic EIGRP configuration. Following this, verify your EIGRP configuration using the and commands. Following this configuration, your route tables should show the following route information:

```
R1#     10.0.0.0/30 is subnetted, 1 subnets
D       10.0.0.8 [90/2172416] via 150.1.1.2, 00:18:09, FastEthernet0/0
     150.3.0.0/24 is subnetted, 1 subnets
D       150.3.3.0 [90/2174976] via 150.1.1.2, 00:17:54, FastEthernet0/0

R2#
     150.3.0.0/24 is subnetted, 1 subnets
D       150.3.3.0 [90/2172416] via 10.0.0.10, 00:18:00, Serial0/1

R3#     150.1.0.0/24 is subnetted, 1 subnets
D       150.1.1.0 [90/20514560] via 10.0.0.9, 00:18:02, Serial1/1
```

Task 3

The requirements of this task are straightforward. Prior to configuring NBAR, it is important to remember that you must also enable CEF on the router. This task is completed as follows:

```
R2(config)#R2(config)#R2(config-if)#
R2(config-if)#
```

Verify your configuration using the command. This command can be used to view statistics for a single protocol, all known protocols, etc. You can generate additional traffic, e.g. Telnet, HTTP, HTTPS, etc in your lab to view statistics about those protocols. Assuming only EIGRP is running on the LAN segment between R1 and R2, use the following command to view the EIGRP protocol statistics:

```
R2# FastEthernet0/0
                        Input                    Output
                        -----                    ------
        Protocol        Packet Count             Packet Count
                        Byte Count               Byte Count
                        5min Bit Rate (bps)      5min Bit Rate (bps)
                        5min Max Bit Rate (bps)  5min Max Bit Rate (bps)
        ----------------------------------------------------------------
        eigrp           526                      265
                        38790                    19580
                        0                        0
                        0                        0
        unknown         0                        0
                        0                        0
                        0                        0
                        0                        0
        Total           2604                     291
                        1308854                  22052
                        7000                     0
                        7000                     0
```

Task 4

The requirements of this task are straightforward. To configure NBAR to search for a protocol or protocol name using a port number other than the well-known port, use the global configuration command. This task is completed as follows on router R2:

```
R2(config)#R2(config)#R2(config)#
```

Next, verify the configuration using the command:

```
R2#
port-map bgp              udp 179
port-map bgp              tcp 179
port-map citrix           udp 1604
port-map citrix           tcp 1494
port-map cuseeme          udp 7648 7649 24032
port-map cuseeme          tcp 7648 7649
port-map dhcp             udp 67 68
port-map dns              udp 53
port-map dns              tcp 53
port-map edonkey          tcp 4662
port-map exchange         tcp 135
port-map fasttrack        tcp 1214
port-map finger           tcp 79
port-map gnutella         tcp 6346 6347 6348 6349 6355 5634
port-map gopher           udp 70
port-map gopher           tcp 70
port-map h323             udp 1300 1718 1719 1720 11720
port-map h323             tcp 1300 1718 1719 1720 11000 - 11999
port-map imap             udp 143 220
port-map imap             tcp 143 220
port-map irc              udp 194
port-map irc              tcp 194
port-map kerberos         udp 88 749
port-map kerberos         tcp 88 749
port-map l2tp             udp 1701
port-map ldap             udp 389
port-map ldap             tcp 389
port-map mgcp             udp 2427 2727
port-map mgcp             tcp 2427 2428 2727
port-map netbios          udp 137 138
port-map netbios          tcp 137 139
port-map netshow          tcp 1755
port-map nfs              udp 2049
port-map nfs              tcp 2049
port-map nntp             udp 119
```

```
port-map nntp                 tcp 119
port-map notes                udp 1352
port-map notes                tcp 1352
port-map novadigm             udp 3460 3461 3462 3463 3464 3465
port-map novadigm             tcp 3460 3461 3462 3463 3464 3465
port-map ntp                  udp 123
port-map ntp                  tcp 123
port-map pcanywhere           udp 22 5632
port-map pcanywhere           tcp 65301 5631
port-map pop3                 udp 110
port-map pop3                 tcp 110
port-map pptp                 tcp 1723
port-map printer              udp 515
port-map printer              tcp 515
port-map rcmd                 tcp 512 513 514
port-map rip                  udp 520
port-map rsvp                 udp 1698 1699
port-map rtsp                 tcp 554
port-map secure-ftp           tcp 990
port-map secure-http          tcp 443
port-map secure-imap          udp 585 993
port-map secure-imap          tcp 585 993
port-map secure-irc           udp 994
port-map secure-irc           tcp 994
port-map secure-ldap          udp 636
port-map secure-ldap          tcp 636
port-map secure-nntp          udp 563
port-map secure-nntp          tcp 563
port-map secure-pop3          udp 995
port-map secure-pop3          tcp 995
port-map secure-telnet        tcp 992
port-map sip                  udp 5060
port-map sip                  tcp 5060
port-map skinny               tcp 2000 2001 2002
port-map smtp                 tcp 25
port-map snmp                 udp 161 162
port-map snmp                 tcp 161 162
port-map socks                tcp 1080
port-map sqlnet               tcp 1521
port-map sqlserver            tcp 1433
port-map ssh                  tcp 22
port-map streamwork           udp 1558
port-map sunrpc               udp 111
port-map sunrpc               tcp 111
port-map syslog               udp 514
port-map tftp                 udp 69
port-map vdolive              tcp 7000
port-map winmx                tcp 6699
port-map xwindows             tcp 6000 6001 6002 6003
```

Task 5

NBAR consumes a lot of memory, which may cause adverse performance issues on the router. It is always important to understand the platform on which you are going to be implementing NBAR on prior to doing so—especially in production environments with a lot of traffic. The NBAR resource allocations and idle time-out values can be viewed using the command, the output of which is shown below:

```
R2#
NBAR memory usage for tracking Stateful sessions
    Max-age              : 120 secs
    Initial memory       : 1369 KBytes
    Max initial memory   : 4566 KBytes
    Memory expansion     : 68 KBytes
    Max memory expansion : 68 KBytes
    Memory in use        : 1369 KBytes
    Max memory allowed   : 9132 KBytes
    Active links         : 0
    Total links          : 20144
```

To complete this task, you need to use the global configuration command on R2. This task is completed as follows:

```
R2(config)#
```

Next, use the command to verify the modified NBAR allocations:

```
2#
NBAR memory usage for tracking Stateful sessions
   Max-age             : 60 secs
   Initial memory      : 2048 KBytes
   Max initial memory  : 4566 KBytes
   Memory expansion    : 68 KBytes
   Max memory expansion : 68 KBytes
   Memory in use       : 2047 KBytes
   Max memory allowed  : 9132 KBytes
   Active links        : 0
   Total links         : 30117
```

Task 6

To complete this task, you must use the command to classify the TCP and the UDP ports to be used by the OOMPALOOMPA application. Because you cannot create a custom map for two unlike protocols, you must configure two custom maps - one for TCP and the other for UDP. This is completed as follows:

```
R2(config)#R2(config)#
```

Next, verify your configuration using the command:

```
R2#port-map OOMPALOOMPA_TCP        tcp 6701 6705
R2#
R2#port-map OOMPALOOMPA_UDP        udp 6800 - 6900
R2#
```

FINAL ROUTER CONFIGURATIONS

R1

```
R1#term len 0
R1#sh run
Building configuration...

Current configuration : 813 bytes
!
version 12.4
service timestamps debug datetime msec
service timestamps log datetime msec
no service password-encryption
!
hostname R1
!
boot-start-marker
boot-end-marker
!
no logging console
!
no aaa new-model
no network-clock-participate slot 1
no network-clock-participate wic 0
ip cef
!
ip auth-proxy max-nodata-conns 3
ip admission max-nodata-conns 3
!
interface FastEthernet0/0
 ip address 150.1.1.1 255.255.255.0
 duplex auto
 speed auto
!
interface Serial0/0
 no ip address
 shutdown
!
interface Serial0/1
 no ip address
 shutdown
!
router eigrp 254
 network 0.0.0.0
 no auto-summary
!
ip forward-protocol nd
!
no ip http server
```

```
no ip http secure-server
!
control-plane
!
line con 0
line aux 0
line vty 0 4
 login
!
end

R1#
```

R2

```
R2#term len 0
R2#sh run
Building configuration...

Current configuration : 1086 bytes
!
version 12.4
service timestamps debug datetime msec
service timestamps log datetime msec
no service password-encryption
!
hostname R2
!
boot-start-marker
boot-end-marker
!
no logging console
!
no aaa new-model
no network-clock-participate slot 1
no network-clock-participate wic 0
ip cef
!
ip nbar resources 60 2048 2000
ip nbar port-map http tcp 80 8080
ip nbar port-map telnet tcp 23 2023
ip nbar port-map ftp tcp 21 2021
ip nbar custom OOMPALOOMPA_TCP tcp 6701 6705
ip nbar custom OOMPALOOMPA_UDP udp range 6800 6900
!
ip auth-proxy max-nodata-conns 3
ip admission max-nodata-conns 3
!
interface FastEthernet0/0
 ip address 150.1.1.2 255.255.255.0
 ip nbar protocol-discovery
 duplex auto
 speed auto
!
interface Serial0/0
 no ip address
 shutdown
!
interface Serial0/1
 ip address 10.0.0.9 255.255.255.252
!
router eigrp 254
 network 0.0.0.0
 no auto-summary
!
ip forward-protocol nd
!
no ip http server
no ip http secure-server
!
control-plane
!
line con 0
line aux 0
line vty 0 4
 login
!
end

R2#
```

R3

```
R3#term len 0
R3#sh run
Building configuration...

Current configuration : 1127 bytes
!
version 12.4
service timestamps debug datetime msec
service timestamps log datetime msec
no service password-encryption
!
hostname R3
!
boot-start-marker
boot-end-marker
!
no logging console
!
no aaa new-model
no network-clock-participate slot 1
no network-clock-participate wic 0
ip cef
!
ip auth-proxy max-nodata-conns 3
ip admission max-nodata-conns 3
!
interface FastEthernet0/0
 ip address 150.3.3.3 255.255.255.0
 duplex auto
 speed auto
!
interface Serial1/0
 no ip address
 shutdown
!
interface Serial1/1
 ip address 10.0.0.10 255.255.255.252
 clock rate 128000
!
interface Serial1/2
 no ip address
 shutdown
!
interface Serial1/3
 no ip address
 shutdown
!
interface Serial1/4
 no ip address
 shutdown
!
interface Serial1/5
 no ip address
 shutdown
!
interface Serial1/6
 no ip address
 shutdown
!
interface Serial1/7
 no ip address
 shutdown
!
router eigrp 254
 network 0.0.0.0
 no auto-summary
!
ip forward-protocol nd
!
no ip http server
no ip http secure-server
!
control-plane
!
line con 0
line aux 0
line vty 0 4
 login
!
end
R3#
```

CCNP LAB 67

Cisco Configuration Archive Lab

Lab Objective:

The focus of this lab is to understand Cisco IOS Configuration Archive implementation and configuration in Cisco IOS routers. Additional technologies include KRON.

Lab Topology:

This lab requires only a single router running, at a minimum, Cisco IOS Software 12.4 Mainline. The router should have at least one Ethernet interface. The primary purpose of this lab is to reinforce configuration knowledge of the stated chapter.

> **IMPORTANT NOTE:** If you have multiple devices and servers / hosts in your home lab and you would like to test solutions for topics such as Syslog, SNMP and NetFlow by setting up host and viewing charts or logging information, for example, please feel free to do so. While these labs include logging to 'supposed' hosts, there are no SNMP or Syslog servers in the http://www.howtonetwork.net racks and so you will not be able to test the solutions in those racks. If you only have a single router, you can bring up the Ethernet interface by implementing the following configuration:
>
> ```
> !
> interface fastethernet 0/0
> loopback
> no keepalive
> no shut
> !
> ```

Task 1

Configure Cisco IOS Configuration Archive feature on the router. The router should store the archived configuration on an FTP server with the IP address 150.1.1.254. The router should include its hostname and timestamp in the configuration archive. The FTP server allows connections from user 'secureconfig' with a password of 'h2n3tw0rk'. In addition to this, enables automatic generation of a configuration backup prior to a `write memory` or `copy running-config startup-config` operation; however, scheduled backups should occur every 8 hours. Verify your configuration using the appropriate commands.

Task 2

To provide some redundancy to the IOS Configuration Archive feature, configure a Cisco IOS Command Scheduler (KRON) policy that will run the `archive config` command every 24 hours. Verify your configuration using the appropriate commands.

Task 3

In the future, management would like QoS implemented. In the interim, they are considering implementing NBAR to determine what types of traffic and how much is received from the LAN. The network team has a daily 10AM meeting. Users typically come into the office between 8 and 8:30 AM. It is as this time that there will be a lot of traffic coming into the router from the LAN. To ensure that this data is not lost, configure the router to redirect to TFTP server 150.1.1.254 the output of the `show ip nbar protocol` discovery command every day at 8:30AM using KRON. Verify your configuration using the appropriate commands.

LAB VALIDATION

Task 1

While the core tasks of this lab are straightforward, there is an additional element that has yet to be discussed. The Cisco IOS Configuration Archive feature supports the $h and $t variables which allow the device hostname ($h) and timestamp information ($t) to be used as the filename. For example, if the device is called R1 and these variables are used, the archived file would be named R1- Jun-15-19:09:41.264 for example. This task is completed as follows:

```
Router(config)#hostname R1
R1(config)#interface fastethernet 0/0
R1(config-if)#ip address 150.1.1.1 255.255.255.0
R1(config-if)#exit
R1(config)#ip ftp username secureconfig
R1(config)#ip ftp password h2n3tw0rk
R1(config)#archive
R1(config-archive)#path ftp://150.1.1.254/$h$t
R1(config-archive)#write-memory
R1(config-archive)#time-period 480
R1(config-archive)#exit
R1(config)#exit
```

Next, verify your configuration using the `show running-config` command:

```
R1#show running-config | section archive|ftp
archive
 path ftp://150.1.1.254/$h$t
 write-memory
 time-period 480
ip ftp username secureconfig
ip ftp password h2n3tw0rk
```

Finally, verify archive operation using the `show archive` command. Notice the filename has is using the device hostname (R1) plus the timestamp (R1-Jun-15-19:39:26.191). The (-1) indicates that this will be the first file. If you have an FTP server connected to the router, you can set up an account and verify and test the Configuration Archive feature:

```
R1#show archive
The next archive file will be named ftp://150.1.1.254/R1-Jun-15-19:41:19.367-1
 Archive #  Name
   0
   1

[Truncated Output]
```

Task 2

The `archive config` command allows you to manually archive the configuration file to the specified destination. To automate this process, we can leverage the Cisco IOS Command Scheduler (KRON) so that the router automatically performs this action. The same could also be performed using the Embedded Event Manager (EEM). This task is completed as follows:

```
R1(config)#kron policy-list RUN-ARCHIVE-DAILY
R1(config-kron-policy)#cli archive config
R1(config-kron-policy)#exit
R1(config)#kron occurrence BACKUP in 1440 recurring
R1(config-kron-occurrence)#policy-list RUN-ARCHIVE-DAILY
R1(config-kron-occurrence)#exit
```

Next, verify your solution by viewing the router configuration:

```
R1#more system:running-config | section kron
kron occurrence BACKUP in 1:0:0 recurring
 policy-list RUN-ARCHIVE-DAILY
kron policy-list RUN-ARCHIVE-DAILY
 cli archive config
```

Finally, use the show kron command to verify policy occurrence schedule configuration:

```
R1#show kron schedule
Kron Occurrence Schedule
backup inactive, will run again in 0 days 23:57:49
```

Task 3

The requirements of this task are fairly straightforward. This task is completed as follows:

```
R1(config)#kron policy-list NBAR-STATISTICS
R1(config-kron-policy)#$l-discovery | redirect tftp://150.1.1.254//NBAR.txt
R1(config-kron-policy)#exit
R1(config)#kron occurrence DAILY-NBAR-STATISTICS at 08:30 recurring
R1(config-kron-occurrence)#exit
```

Next, verify your configuration using the show running-config command:

```
R1#more system:running-config | section kron
kron occurrence BACKUP in 1:0:0 recurring
 policy-list RUN-ARCHIVE-DAILY
kron occurrence DAILY-NBAR-STATISTICS at 8:30 recurring
kron policy-list RUN-ARCHIVE-DAILY
 cli archive config
kron policy-list NBAR-STATISTICS
cli show ip nbar protocol-discovery | redirect tftp://150.1.1.254//NBAR.txt
```

Next, verify KRON occurrence scheduling using the show kron schedule command:

```
R1#show kron schedule
Kron Occurrence Schedule
BACKUP inactive, will run again in 0 days 23:23:33
DAILY-NBAR-STATISTICS inactive, will run again in 0 days 23:47:18 at 8 :30 on
```

FINAL ROUTER CONFIGURATIONS

R1

```
R1#term len 0
R1#sh run
Building configuration...

Current configuration : 1235 bytes
!
! Last configuration change at 08:41:44 UTC Wed Jun 15 2011
!
version 12.4
service timestamps debug datetime msec
service timestamps log datetime msec
no service password-encryption
!
hostname R1
!
boot-start-marker
boot-end-marker
!
no aaa new-model
no network-clock-participate slot 1
no network-clock-participate wic 0
ip cef
!
```

```
ip auth-proxy max-nodata-conns 3
ip admission max-nodata-conns 3
!
archive
 path ftp://150.1.1.254/$h$t
 write-memory
 time-period 480
!
ip ftp username secureconfig
ip ftp password h2n3tw0rk
!
interface FastEthernet0/0
 ip address 150.1.1.1 255.255.255.0
 shutdown
 duplex auto
 speed auto
!
interface Serial0/0
 no ip address
 shutdown
!
interface Serial0/1
 no ip address
 shutdown
!
ip forward-protocol nd
!
no ip http server
no ip http secure-server
!
kron occurrence BACKUP in 1:0:0 recurring
 policy-list RUN-ARCHIVE-DAILY
!
kron occurrence DAILY-NBAR-STATISTICS at 8:30 recurring
!
kron policy-list RUN-ARCHIVE-DAILY
 cli archive config
!
kron policy-list NBAR-STATISTICS
 cli show ip nbar protocol-discovery | redirect tftp://10.1.1.1//NBAR.txt
!
control-plane
!
line con 0
line aux 0
line vty 0 4
 login
!
end

R1#
```

CCNP LAB 68

Cisco IOS RITE and SPAN Lab

Lab Objective:

The focus of this lab is to understand Router IP Traffic Export (RITE) and Switched Port Analyzer (SPAN) implementation and configuration in Cisco IOS routers.

Lab Topology:

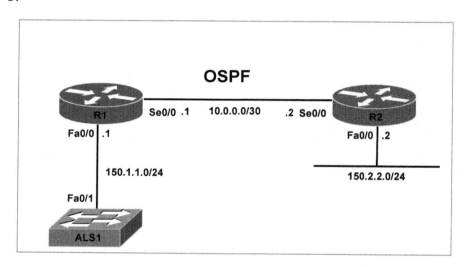

IMPORTANT NOTE: If you are using the www.howtonetwork.net racks, please bring up the LAN interfaces connected to the routers by issuing the no shutdown command on the connected switches. If you are using a home lab with no Switches, you can bring up the LAN interfaces using the following configurations on your routers:

```
interface fastethernet 0/0
  no keepalive
  loopback
  no shutdown
```

Alternately, you can simply connect the interfaces to a hub or switch if you have one available in your own lab.

Task 1

Configure hostnames and IP addresses on all devices as illustrated in the topology. In addition, configure VLAN 100 on switch ALS1. Assign R1s FastEthernet0/0 to this VLAN and configure a VLAN interface (SVI) with the IP address 150.1.1.254 on switch ALS1. Following this, confirm that switch ALS1 pings router R1.

Task 2

Configure OSPF on R1 and R2 as illustrated in the topology. Ensure that R2 can ping switch ALS1. Verify your configuration using the appropriate commands.

Task 3

There have been some network issues experienced on the LAN segment between R1 and ALS1. Configure SPAN on ALS1 so that all ingress and egress traffic from R1s LAN interface is mirrored to FastEthernet 0/8. FastEthernet 0/8 will have an administrator workstation running Wire Shark. In addition to being used for monitoring, this workstation will also need to reach other network devices and all received frames should be assigned to VLAN 100. Verify your configuration using the appropriate commands.

Task 4

R2 is connected to a hub, which makes implementing SPAN impossible. However, users that are connected to this hub are also complaining of network latency. Configure RITE on R2 so that all ingress and egress traffic from the LAN interface is sent to a host with the MAC address 00-24-E7-47-32-40. R1 should only capture inbound and outbound HTTP traffic. All other type should be ignored. Ensure that one in two packets are exported. Verify your configuration.

LAB VALIDATION

Task 1

Please refer to previous tasks for basic VLAN and IP addressing configuration. These will not be included in this section for brevity and to avoid being redundant. Following your configuration, switch ALS1 should be able to ping R1. This is illustrated in the output below:

```
ALS1#ping 150.1.1.1

Type escape sequence to abort.
Sending 5, 100-byte ICMP Echos to 150.1.1.1, timeout is 2 seconds:
!!!!!
Success rate is 100 percent (5/5), round-trip min/avg/max = 1/202/1000 ms
```

Task 2

Please refer to previous labs for basic OSPF configuration. Following this, verify your OSPF configuration using the show ip ospf neighbors and show ip route commands. Following this configuration, your route tables should show the following route information:

```
R1#show ip route ospf
     150.2.0.0/24 is subnetted, 1 subnets
O       150.2.2.0 [110/65] via 10.0.0.2, 00:00:00, Serial0/0

R2#show ip route ospf
     150.1.0.0/24 is subnetted, 1 subnets
O       150.1.1.0 [110/65] via 10.0.0.1, 00:00:21, Serial0/0
```

In order to allow R2 to ping ALS1, you need to configure a default gateway on switch ALS1:

```
ALS1(config)#ip default-gateway 150.1.1.1
```

Following this, R2 will be able to ping switch ALS1 and vice-versa:

```
R2#ping 150.1.1.254 repeat 10 size 1500 source fastethernet 0/0

Type escape sequence to abort.
Sending 10, 1500-byte ICMP Echos to 150.1.1.254, timeout is 2 seconds:
Packet sent with a source address of 150.2.2.2
!!!!!!!!!!
Success rate is 100 percent (10/10), round-trip min/avg/max = 16/16/20 ms
```

Task 3

While the core requirements of this task are simple, it is important to remember that when a port is specified as a SPAN destination port, by default, it is a receive-only port and cannot transmit data. The state of the SPAN destination port is up/down by design. This state is used in order to make it evident that the port is currently not usable as a production port. To allow ingress traffic, you must use the `ingress, encapsulation <isl|dot1q>` and `vlan <tag>` keywords. These keywords enable ingress traffic forwarding on the SPAN destination port, specify the ingress encapsulation and type and VLAN ID respectively. Keep in mind, however, that most Cisco IOS switches now only support 802.1Q; therefore, you do not necessarily need to specify this default encapsulation type. This task is completed as follows:

```
ALS1(config)#monitor session 1 source interface fastethernet 0/1 both
ALS1(config)#$nterface fastethernet 0/8 encapsulation dot1q ingress vlan 100
```

Next, verify your configuration using the show monitor session command:

```
ALS1#show monitor session 1
Session 1
---------
Type              : Local Session
Source Ports      :
    Both          : Fa0/1
Destination Ports : Fa0/8
    Encapsulation : DOT1Q
          Ingress: Enabled, default VLAN = 100
    Ingress encapsulation: DOT1Q
```

You can also append the `detail` keyword for additional information on the session:

```
ALS1#show monitor session 1 detail
Session 1
---------
Type              : Local Session
Source Ports      :
    RX Only       : None
    TX Only       : None
    Both          : Fa0/1
Source VLANs      :
    RX Only       : None
    TX Only       : None
    Both          : None
Source RSPAN VLAN : None
Destination Ports : Fa0/8
    Encapsulation : DOT1Q
          Ingress: Enabled, default VLAN = 100
    Ingress encapsulation: DOT1Q
Reflector Port    : None
Filter VLANs      : None
Dest RSPAN VLAN   : None
```

Task 4

While the core requirements of this task are straightforward, it is important to remember that you can use ACLs with RITE. The requirement that all ingress and egress HTTP traffic be mirrored means that you must use ACLs that matches both ingress and egress HTTP traffic. You cannot accomplish this with a single ACL. This is completed as follows:

```
R2(config)#ip access-list extended INBOUND-HTTP-TRAFFIC
R2(config-ext-nacl)#permit tcp any any eq www
R2(config-ext-nacl)#exit
R2(config)#ip access-list extended OUTBOUND-HTTP-TRAFFIC
R2(config-ext-nacl)#permit tcp any eq www any
R2(config-ext-nacl)#exit
R2(config)#ip traffic-export profile IOS-RITE
R2(conf-rite)#bidirectional
R2(conf-rite)#incoming access-list INBOUND-HTTP-TRAFFIC
R2(conf-rite)#outgoing access-list OUTBOUND-HTTP-TRAFFIC
R2(conf-rite)#mac-address 0024.E747.3240
R2(conf-rite)#incoming sample one-in-every 2
R2(conf-rite)#outgoing sample one-in-every 2
R2(conf-rite)#interface fastethernet 0/0
R2(conf-rite)#exit
R2(conf-rite)#interface fastethernet 0/0
R2(conf-rite)#exit
R2(config)#interface fastethernet 0/0
R2(config-if)#ip traffic-export apply IOS-RITE
```

```
*Jun 15 21:48:53.999: %RITE-5-ACTIVATE: Activated IP traffic export on interface
FastEthernet0/0
R2(config-if)#exit
```

Next, view the router configuration to verify that you solution is configured correctly:

```
R2#more system:running-config | section traffic-export
ip traffic-export profile IOS-RITE
  interface FastEthernet0/0
  bidirectional
  incoming access-list INBOUND-HTTP-TRAFFIC
  outgoing access-list OUTBOUND-HTTP-TRAFFIC
  mac-address 0024.e747.3240
  incoming sample one-in-every 2
  outgoing sample one-in-every 2
 ip traffic-export apply IOS-RITE
```

Following this, use the show ip traffic-export command to verify statistics:

```
R2#show ip traffic-export interface fastethernet 0/0
Router IP Traffic Export Parameters
Monitored Interface              FastEthernet0/0
      Export Interface               FastEthernet0/0
      Destination MAC address 0024.e747.3240
      bi-directional traffic export is on
Output IP Traffic Export Information    Packets/Bytes Exported    0/0
      Packets Dropped             0
      Sampling Rate             one-in-every 2 packets
      Access List        OUTBOUND-HTTP-TRAFFIC [named extended IP]
Input IP Traffic Export Information     Packets/Bytes Exported    0/0
      Packets Dropped             119
      Sampling Rate             one-in-every 2 packets
      Access List        INBOUND-HTTP-TRAFFIC [named extended IP]
      Profile IOS-RITE is Active
```

To test RITE, assuming you have a device connected to the same segment as R2, you can use the traffic-export interface <interface> start and traffic-export interface <interface> stop privileged EXEC commands.

FINAL ROUTER CONFIGURATIONS

R1

```
R1#term len 0
R1#sh run
Building configuration...

Current configuration : 910 bytes
!
version 12.4
service timestamps debug datetime msec
service timestamps log datetime msec
no service password-encryption
!
hostname R1
!
boot-start-marker
boot-end-marker
!
no logging console
!
no aaa new-model
no network-clock-participate slot 1
no network-clock-participate wic 0
ip cef
!
no ip domain lookup
ip auth-proxy max-nodata-conns 3
```

```
 ip admission max-nodata-conns 3
 !
 interface FastEthernet0/0
  ip address 150.1.1.1 255.255.255.0
  duplex auto
  speed auto
 !
 interface Serial0/0
  ip address 10.0.0.1 255.255.255.252
  clock rate 2000000
 !
 interface Serial0/1
  no ip address
  shutdown
 !
 router ospf 1
  router-id 1.1.1.1
  log-adjacency-changes
  network 0.0.0.0 255.255.255.255 area 0
 !
 ip forward-protocol nd
 !
 no ip http server
 no ip http secure-server
 !
 control-plane
 !
 line con 0
 line aux 0
 line vty 0 4
  login
 !
 end

 R1#
```

R2

```
R2#term len 0
R2#sh run
Building configuration...

Current configuration : 1358 bytes
!
version 12.4
service timestamps debug datetime msec
service timestamps log datetime msec
no service password-encryption
!
hostname R2
!
boot-start-marker
boot-end-marker
!
no logging console
no logging cns-events
!
no aaa new-model
no network-clock-participate slot 1
no network-clock-participate wic 0
!
ip traffic-export profile IOS-RITE
  interface FastEthernet0/0
  bidirectional
  incoming access-list INBOUND-HTTP-TRAFFIC
  outgoing access-list OUTBOUND-HTTP-TRAFFIC
  mac-address 0024.e747.3240
  incoming sample one-in-every 2
  outgoing sample one-in-every 2
ip cef
!
no ip domain lookup
ip auth-proxy max-nodata-conns 3
ip admission max-nodata-conns 3
```

```
!
interface FastEthernet0/0
 ip address 150.2.2.2 255.255.255.0
 ip traffic-export apply IOS-RITE
 duplex auto
 speed auto
!
interface Serial0/0
 ip address 10.0.0.2 255.255.255.252
!
interface Serial0/1
 no ip address
 shutdown
!
router ospf 2
 router-id 2.2.2.2
 log-adjacency-changes
 network 0.0.0.0 255.255.255.255 area 0
!
ip forward-protocol nd
!
no ip http server
no ip http secure-server
!
ip access-list extended INBOUND-HTTP-TRAFFIC
 permit tcp any any eq www
ip access-list extended OUTBOUND-HTTP-TRAFFIC
 permit tcp any eq www any
!
control-plane
!
line con 0
line aux 0
line vty 0 4
 login
!
!
end

R2#
```

FINAL SWITCH CONFIGURATION

ALS1

```
ALS1#term len 0
ALS1#sh run
Building configuration...

Current configuration : 1054 bytes
!
version 12.1
no service pad
service timestamps debug uptime
service timestamps log uptime
no service password-encryption
!
hostname ALS1
!
ip subnet-zero
!
vtp domain hard
vtp mode transparent
!
spanning-tree mode pvst
no spanning-tree optimize bpdu transmission
spanning-tree extend system-id
!
vlan 100
!
interface FastEthernet0/1
```

```
 switchport access vlan 100
 switchport mode access
!
interface FastEthernet0/2
!
interface FastEthernet0/3
!
interface FastEthernet0/4
!
interface FastEthernet0/5
!
interface FastEthernet0/6
!
interface FastEthernet0/7
!
interface FastEthernet0/8
!
interface FastEthernet0/9
!
interface FastEthernet0/10
!
interface FastEthernet0/11
!
interface FastEthernet0/12
!
interface Vlan1
 no ip address
 no ip route-cache
 shutdown
!
interface Vlan100
 ip address 150.1.1.254 255.255.255.0
 no ip route-cache
!
ip default-gateway 150.1.1.1
ip http server
!
line con 0
line vty 5 15
!
monitor session 1 source interface Fa0/1
monitor session 1 destination interface Fa0/8 encapsulation dot1q ingress vlan 100
end

ALS1#
```

CCNP LAB 69

Cisco IOS RITE and RSPAN Lab

Lab Objective:

The focus of this lab is to understand Router IP Traffic Export (RITE) and Remote Switched Port Analyzer (SPAN) implementation and configuration in Cisco IOS routers.

Lab Topology:

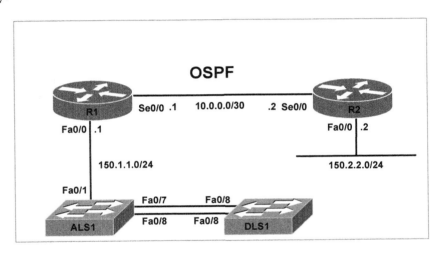

> **IMPORTANT NOTE:** If you are using the **www.howtonetwork.net racks,** please bring up the LAN interfaces connected to the routers by issuing the `no shutdown` command on the connected switches. If you are using a home lab with no Switches, you can bring up the LAN interfaces using the following configurations on your routers:
>
> ```
> interface fastethernet 0/0
>   no keepalive
>   loopback
>   no shutdown
> ```
>
> Alternately, you can simply connect the interfaces to a hub or switch if you have one available in your own lab.

Task 1

Configure hostnames and IP addresses on all devices as illustrated in the topology. In addition, configure VLAN 100 on switches ALS1 and DLS1. Assign R1s FastEthernet0/0 to this VLAN and configure a VLAN interface (SVI) with the IP address 150.1.1.253 on DLS1 and a VLAN interface (SVI) with the IP address 150.1.1.254 on ALS2. Verify that switches ALS1 and DLS1 can ping each other as well as router R1.

Task 2

Configure OSPF on R1 and R2 as illustrated in the topology. Ensure that R2 can ping switch ALS1 and DLS1. Verify your configuration using the appropriate commands.

Task 3

In the future, switch DLS1 will have a FastEthernet0/1 configured as a trunk link. There will be multiple VLANs traversing this trunk link. Management has requested that you configure an RSPAN session to monitor ingress and egress traffic received from FastEthernet0/1. However, in the interim, they have requested that the captured traffic be restricted to that from VLANs 200, 400, and 600. This traffic should be sent to FastEthernet0/5 on switch ALS1. The RSPAN session should be configured to use VLAN 456. Implement this solution and verify the RSPAN configuration using the appropriate commands on both switches.

Task 4

VLAN 100 is used as a transit VLAN to the rest of the network. The security team has an NIPS (Network-based Intrusion Prevention System) connected to port FastEthernet 0/3 on switch DLS1. The request that all traffic in VLAN 100 (receive) be mirrored to this port. To allow the IPS to be able to reset sessions, ensure that ingress traffic is permitted on this port. This traffic should be assigned to VLAN 200. Configure a local SPAN session on switch DLS1 to satisfy this requirement. Verify your configuration using the appropriate commands.

Task 5

In the future, R2 will have several WAN links turned up. Serial 0/0 will be the only link that will be connected to the Internet. The other WAN links will be used for spoke connectivity across a private Frame Relay network. Management has requested that you monitor all bidirectional traffic coming into and leaving out of the Serial 0/0 interface on R2. This traffic should be sent to a Network-based Intrusion Prevention System (NIPS) residing on the LAN segment of R2. This NIPS has the MAC address 00-24-E7-47-32-40. To ensure as much traffic is captured as possible, configure R2 so that every other packet is sent to the NIPS. Assume that all ICMP traffic is denied. Configure R2 so that only TCP and UDP traffic is exported. Verify your configuration using the appropriate commands.

LAB VALIDATION

Task 1

Please refer to previous tasks for basic VLAN and IP addressing configuration. These will not be included in this section for brevity and to avoid being redundant. Following your configuration, switch ALS1 should be able to ping R1. This is illustrated in the output below:

```
ALS1#ping 150.1.1.0

Type escape sequence to abort.
Sending 5, 100-byte ICMP Echos to 150.1.1.0, timeout is 2 seconds:

Reply to request 0 from 150.1.1.1, 1 ms
Reply to request 1 from 150.1.1.254, 1 ms
Reply to request 1 from 150.1.1.1, 1 ms
Reply to request 2 from 150.1.1.254, 1 ms
Reply to request 2 from 150.1.1.1, 1 ms
Reply to request 3 from 150.1.1.254, 4 ms
Reply to request 3 from 150.1.1.1, 4 ms
Reply to request 4 from 150.1.1.254, 4 ms
Reply to request 4 from 150.1.1.1, 4 ms

DLS1#ping 150.1.1.0

Type escape sequence to abort.
Sending 5, 100-byte ICMP Echos to 150.1.1.0, timeout is 2 seconds:

Reply to request 0 from 150.1.1.1, 4 ms
Reply to request 1 from 150.1.1.1, 1 ms
Reply to request 1 from 150.1.1.253, 1 ms
Reply to request 2 from 150.1.1.1, 1 ms
Reply to request 2 from 150.1.1.253, 1 ms
Reply to request 3 from 150.1.1.1, 1 ms
Reply to request 3 from 150.1.1.253, 1 ms
Reply to request 4 from 150.1.1.1, 1 ms
Reply to request 4 from 150.1.1.253, 1 ms
```

Task 2

Please refer to previous labs for basic OSPF configuration. Following this, verify your OSPF configuration using the `show ip ospf neighbors` and `show ip route` commands. Following this configuration, your route tables should show the following route information:

```
R1#show ip route ospf
     150.2.0.0/24 is subnetted, 1 subnets
O       150.2.2.0 [110/65] via 10.0.0.2, 00:03:57, Serial0/0

R2#show ip route ospf
     150.1.0.0/24 is subnetted, 1 subnets
O       150.1.1.0 [110/65] via 10.0.0.1, 00:04:08, Serial0/0
```

In order to allow R2 to ping ALS1 and DLS1, you need to configure a default gateway on switch ALS1 as well as on DLS1:

```
ALS1(config)#ip default-gateway 150.1.1.1

DLS1(config)#ip default-gateway 150.1.1.1
```

Following this, R2 will be able to ping switch ALS1 and vice-versa:

```
R2#ping 150.1.1.253 source fastethernet 0/0 size 1500 repeat 10

Type escape sequence to abort.
Sending 10, 1500-byte ICMP Echos to 150.1.1.253, timeout is 2 seconds:
Packet sent with a source address of 150.2.2.2
.!!!!!!!!!
Success rate is 90 percent (9/10), round-trip min/avg/max = 16/16/20 ms

R2#ping 150.1.1.254 source fastethernet 0/0 size 1500 repeat 10

Type escape sequence to abort.
Sending 10, 1500-byte ICMP Echos to 150.1.1.254, timeout is 2 seconds:
Packet sent with a source address of 150.2.2.2
.!!!!!!!!!
Success rate is 90 percent (9/10), round-trip min/avg/max = 12/12/16 ms
```

Task 3

The core requirements of this task are straightforward. Basically, what is required is an RSPAN session between DLS1 and ALS1 using VLAN 456. The source port should be FastEthernernt0/1 on switch DLS1 and the destination port should be FastEthernet0/5 on switch ALS1. The caveat here is that when monitoring a trunk link, ALL traffic, i.e. for all VLANs, will be monitored. The task, however, requests that only traffic for VLANs 200, 400, and 600 be monitored. To do this, we need to filter the VLANs that will be monitored in the RSPAN session configured on switch DLS1 using the `monitor session <session> filter vlan <list>` command on switch DLS1. This task is completed as follows:

```
DLS1(config)#vlan 456
DLS1(config-vlan)#remote-span
DLS1(config-vlan)#exit
DLS1(config)#monitor session 1 source interface fastethernet 0/1 both
DLS1(config)#monitor session 1 destination remote vlan 456
DLS1(config)#$ - 199 , 201 - 399 , 401 - 455 , 457 - 599 , 601 - 4094
```

IMPORTANT NOTE: If you are using the **www.howtonetwork.net** racks, the current switches, as of the time of the writing of this guide, are 3550 series switches. Therefore, when completing this lab, you must configure a reflector port for the RSPAN destination. A reflector port is the mechanism that copies packets onto an RSPAN VLAN. The reflector port forwards only the traffic from the RSPAN source session with which it is affiliated. Any device connected to a port set as a reflector port loses connectivity until the RSPAN source session is disabled. Any unused port can be specified as a reflector port. This port will simply loop back untagged traffic to the switch.

The traffic is then placed on the RSPAN VLAN and flooded to any trunk ports that carry the RSPAN VLAN. The Catalyst 2970, 3560, 3750, 4500 and 6500 series switches do not require the configuration of a reflector port when you configure an RSPAN session. If you are completing this lab on one of these switches, omit the reflector-port keyword. If configured on a 2950 / 3550, use the following configuration to complete this task:

```
vlan 456
remote-span
!
monitor ses 1 source interface fastethenet 0/1 both
monitor ses 1 dest rem vl 456 reflector-port fa 0/2
!
```

```
ALS1(config)#vlan 456
ALS1(config-vlan)#remote-span
ALS1(config-vlan)#exit
ALS1(config)#monitor session 1 source remote vlan 456
ALS1(config)#monitor session 1 destination interface fastethernet 0/5
```

Next, verify your RSPAN configuration using the show monitor session command:

```
ALS1#show monitor session 1
Session 1
---------
Type              : Remote Destination Session
Source RSPAN VLAN : 456
Destination Ports : Fa0/5
    Encapsulation : Native
          Ingress: Disabled

DLS1#show monitor session 1
Session 1
---------
Type                  : Remote Source Session
Source Ports          :
    Both              : Fa0/1
Reflector Port        : Fa0/2
Filter VLANs          : 1-199,201-399,401-455,457-599,601-4094
Dest RSPAN VLAN       : 456
```

Additionally, you can append the detail keyword for more information:

```
DLS1#show monitor session 1 detail
Session 1
---------
Type                  : Remote Source Session
Description           : -
Source Ports          :
    RX Only           : None
    TX Only           : None
    Both              : Fa0/1
Source VLANs          :
    RX Only           : None
    TX Only           : None
    Both              : None
Source RSPAN VLAN     : None
Destination Ports     : None
Reflector Port        : Fa0/2
Filter VLANs          : 1-199,201-399,401-455,457-599,601-4094
Dest RSPAN VLAN       : 456
```

Task 4

The requirements of this task are straightforward. This task is completed as follows on DLS1:

```
DLS1(config)#monitor session 2 source vlan 100 rx
DLS1(config)#$nterface fastethernet 0/3 encapsulation dot1q ingress vlan 200
DLS1(config)#exit
```

Next, verify your configuration using the show monitor session command:

```
DLS1#show monitor session 2 detail
Session 2
---------
Type                     : Local Session
Description              : -
Source Ports             :
    RX Only              : None
    TX Only              : None
    Both                 : None
Source VLANs             :
    RX Only              : 100
    TX Only              : None
    Both                 : None
Source RSPAN VLAN        : None
Destination Ports        : Fa0/3
    Encapsulation        : DOT1Q
           Ingress       : Enabled, default VLAN = 200
Reflector Port           : None
Filter VLANs             : None
Dest RSPAN VLAN          : None
```

Task 5

The core requirements of this task are straightforward. However, in order to monitor traffic that is received and sent via Serial 0/0, we need to apply the RITE profile to this interface. Within the RITE profile, we need to specify FastEthernet0/0 as the egress interface as this is where the Network-based Intrusion Prevention System be connected. This task is completed as follows:

```
R2(config)#access-list 100 permit tcp any any
R2(config)#access-list 100 permit udp any any
R2(config)#access-list 101 permit tcp any any
R2(config)#access-list 101 permit udp any any
R2(config)#ip traffic-export profile INTERNET-MONITORING
R2(conf-rite)#bidirectional
R2(conf-rite)#incoming access-list 100
R2(conf-rite)#incoming sample one-in-every 2
R2(conf-rite)#outgoing access-list 101
R2(conf-rite)#outgoing sample one-in-every 2
R2(conf-rite)#mac-address 0024.E747.3240
R2(conf-rite)#interface fastethernet 0/0
R2(conf-rite)#exit
R2(config)#interface s0/0
R2(config-if)#ip traffic-export apply INTERNET-MONITORING
R2(config-if)#
*Jun 15 11:31:47.843: %RITE-5-ACTIVATE: Activated IP traffic export on interface
Serial0/0
R2(config-if)#exit
```

Following this, use the show ip traffic-export command to verify statistics:

```
R2#show ip traffic-export interface serial 0/0
Router IP Traffic Export Parameters
Monitored Interface            Serial0/0
        Export Interface               FastEthernet0/0
        Destination MAC address 0024.e747.3240
        bi-directional traffic export is on
Output IP Traffic Export Information    Packets/Bytes Exported    0/0
        Packets Dropped           0
        Sampling Rate             one-in-every 2 packets
        Access List             101 [extended IP]
Input IP Traffic Export Information    Packets/Bytes Exported    0/0
        Packets Dropped           0
        Sampling Rate             one-in-every 2 packets
        Access List             100 [extended IP]
        Profile INTERNET-MONITORING is Active
```

To test RITE, assuming you have a device connected to the same segment as R2, you can use the traffic-export interface <interface> start and traffic-export interface <interface> stop privileged EXEC commands.

FINAL ROUTER CONFIGURATIONS

R1

```
R1#term len 0
R1#sh run
Building configuration...

Current configuration : 910 bytes
!
version 12.4
service timestamps debug datetime msec
service timestamps log datetime msec
no service password-encryption
!
hostname R1
!
boot-start-marker
boot-end-marker
!
no logging console
!
no aaa new-model
no network-clock-participate slot 1
no network-clock-participate wic 0
ip cef
!
no ip domain lookup
ip auth-proxy max-nodata-conns 3
ip admission max-nodata-conns 3
!
interface FastEthernet0/0
 ip address 150.1.1.1 255.255.255.0
 duplex auto
 speed auto
!
interface Serial0/0
 ip address 10.0.0.1 255.255.255.252
 clock rate 2000000
!
interface Serial0/1
 no ip address
 shutdown
!
router ospf 1
 router-id 1.1.1.1
 log-adjacency-changes
 network 0.0.0.0 255.255.255.255 area 0
!
ip forward-protocol nd
!
no ip http server
no ip http secure-server
!
control-plane
!
line con 0
line aux 0
line vty 0 4
 login
!
end

R1#
```

R2

```
R2#term len 0
R2#sh run
Building configuration...

Current configuration : 1319 bytes
!
version 12.4
service timestamps debug datetime msec
service timestamps log datetime msec
```

```
no service password-encryption
!
hostname R2
!
boot-start-marker
boot-end-marker
!
no logging cns-events
!
no aaa new-model
no network-clock-participate slot 1
no network-clock-participate wic 0
!
ip traffic-export profile INTERNET-MONITORING
  interface FastEthernet0/0
  bidirectional
  incoming access-list 100
  outgoing access-list 101
  mac-address 0024.e747.3240
  incoming sample one-in-every 2
  outgoing sample one-in-every 2
ip cef
!
no ip domain lookup
ip auth-proxy max-nodata-conns 3
ip admission max-nodata-conns 3
!
interface FastEthernet0/0
 ip address 150.2.2.2 255.255.255.0
 duplex auto
 speed auto
!
interface Serial0/0
 ip address 10.0.0.2 255.255.255.252
 ip traffic-export apply INTERNET-MONITORING
!
interface Serial0/1
 no ip address
 shutdown
!
router ospf 2
 router-id 2.2.2.2
 log-adjacency-changes
 network 0.0.0.0 255.255.255.255 area 0
!
ip forward-protocol nd
!
no ip http server
no ip http secure-server
!
access-list 100 permit tcp any any
access-list 100 permit udp any any
access-list 101 permit tcp any any
access-list 101 permit udp any any
!
control-plane
!
line con 0
line aux 0
line vty 0 4
 login
!
end

R2#
```

FINAL SWITCH CONFIGURATIONS

ALS1

```
ALS1#term len 0
ALS1#sh run
Building configuration...

Current configuration : 1042 bytes
```

```
!
version 12.1
no service pad
service timestamps debug uptime
service timestamps log uptime
no service password-encryption
!
hostname ALS1
!
ip subnet-zero
!
vtp domain hard
vtp mode transparent
!
spanning-tree mode pvst
no spanning-tree optimize bpdu transmission
spanning-tree extend system-id
!
vlan 100
!
vlan 456
 remote-span
!
interface FastEthernet0/1
 switchport access vlan 100
 switchport mode access
!
interface FastEthernet0/2
!
interface FastEthernet0/3
!
interface FastEthernet0/4
!
interface FastEthernet0/5
!
interface FastEthernet0/6
!
interface FastEthernet0/7
!
interface FastEthernet0/8
!
interface FastEthernet0/9
!
interface FastEthernet0/10
!
interface FastEthernet0/11
!
interface FastEthernet0/12
!
interface Vlan1
 no ip address
 no ip route-cache
 shutdown
!
interface Vlan100
 ip address 150.1.1.253 255.255.255.0
 no ip route-cache
!
ip default-gateway 150.1.1.1
ip http server
!
line con 0
line vty 5 15
!
monitor session 1 destination interface Fa0/5
monitor session 1 source remote vlan 456
end
ALS1#
```

DLS1

```
DLS1#term len 0
DLS1#sh run
Building configuration...

Current configuration : 4138 bytes
!
version 12.2
no service pad
service timestamps debug datetime msec
service timestamps log datetime msec
no service password-encryption
!
```

```
hostname DLS1
!
no aaa new-model
ip subnet-zero
!
vtp domain hard
vtp mode transparent
!
spanning-tree mode pvst
spanning-tree extend system-id
!
vlan internal allocation policy ascending
!
vlan 100,200
!
vlan 456
 remote-span
!
interface FastEthernet0/1
 switchport mode dynamic desirable
!
interface FastEthernet0/2
 switchport mode dynamic desirable
!
interface FastEthernet0/3
 switchport mode dynamic desirable
!
interface FastEthernet0/4
 switchport mode dynamic desirable
!
interface FastEthernet0/5
 switchport mode dynamic desirable
!
interface FastEthernet0/6
 switchport mode dynamic desirable
!
interface FastEthernet0/7
 switchport mode dynamic desirable
!
interface FastEthernet0/8
 switchport mode dynamic desirable
!
interface FastEthernet0/9
 switchport mode dynamic desirable
!
interface FastEthernet0/10
 switchport mode dynamic desirable
!
interface FastEthernet0/11
 switchport mode dynamic desirable
!
interface FastEthernet0/12
 switchport mode dynamic desirable

[Truncated Output]

interface Vlan1
 no ip address
 shutdown
!
interface Vlan100
 ip address 150.1.1.254 255.255.255.0
!
ip default-gateway 150.1.1.1
ip classless
ip http server
ip http secure-server
!
control-plane
!
line con 0
line vty 5 15
!
monitor session 1 source interface Fa0/1
monitor session 1 filter vlan 1 - 199 , 201 - 399 , 401 - 455 , 457 - 599 , 601 -
4094
monitor session 1 destination remote vlan 456 reflector-port Fa0/2
monitor session 2 source vlan 100 rx
monitor session 2 destination interface Fa0/3 encapsulation dot1q ingress vlan 200
end

DLS1#
```

CCNP LAB 70

Syslog and SNMP Lab

Lab Objective:

The focus of this lab is to understand Syslog and Simple Network Management Protocol implementation and configuration in Cisco IOS routers.

Lab Topology:

This lab requires only a single router running, at a minimum, Cisco IOS Software 12.4 Mainline. The router should have at least one Ethernet interface. The primary purpose of this lab is to reinforce configuration knowledge of the stated chapter.

IMPORTANT NOTE: If you have multiple devices and servers / hosts in your home lab and you would like to test solutions for topics such as Syslog, SNMP and NetFlow by setting up host and viewing charts or logging information, for example, please feel free to do so. While these labs include logging to 'supposed' hosts, there are no SNMP or Syslog servers in the http://www.howtonetwork.net racks and so you will not be able to test the solutions in those racks. If you only have a single router, you can bring up the Ethernet interface by implementing the following configuration:

```
!
interface fastethernet 0/0
loopback
no keepalive
no shut
!
```

Task 1

Configure local login for the Console port on the router. Next, configure two user accounts on the router. The first user account should be for user STANDARD with a password of CCNP1. The second user account should be for user ADVANCED with a password of CCNP2. User STANDARD should be assigned the lowest privilege level, while user ADVANCED should be assigned the highest privilege level. Verify and test your configuration appropriately.

Task 2

Configure the router so that all informational messages are sent to Syslog server 150.1.1.254. These messages should include user information. Verify and test your configuration using the appropriate commands.

Task 3

In the future, multiple devices will be added to the network and they will all be logging to the 150.1.1.254 host. Management has requested Syslog messages contain the actual hostname of the device, as well as the location, e.g. Dallas, TX or Atlanta, GA for easier identification. Assuming that this device resides in Dallas, TX, configure the router to include its hostname as well as the location Dallas, TX is Sylog messages. Verify your configuration.

Task 4

Management has requested that you implement SNMPv3 on the router. Configure the router for SNMPv3 using the following guidelines:

- Using a view named NOC that includes all MIB objects within the system group
- A group named SWITCH which uses no authentication and has read-only access
- A remote engine ID of 1a2b3c4d5e for host 150.1.1.254
- A user named PASS in group SWITCH using MD5 and with a password of h@rd!

Verify your configuration using the appropriate commands.

Task 5

Configure the router to send SNMP traps to host 150.1.1.254 as follows:

- Use the SNMPv3 authNoPriv Security Level and the SNMPv3 username PASS
- Send only the environmental monitor traps and send traps from Fasthernet 0/0

Verify your configuration using the appropriate commands.

LAB VALIDATION

Task 1

The requirements of this task are straightforward and should be very well known at this level. This task is completed as follows:

```
R1(config)#username STANDARD privilege 0 password CCNP1
R1(config)#username ADVANCED privilege 15 password CCNP2
R1(config)#line console 0
R1(config-line)#login local
R1(config-line)#exit
```

You can verify your configuration by looking at the router configuration file:

```
R1#more system:running-config | section username|line
username STANDARD privilege 0 password 0 CCNP1
username ADVANCED privilege 15 password 0 CCNP2
line con 0
 login local
line aux 0
line vty 0 4
 login
```

Next, test your solution by exiting an logging in first as user STANDARD:

```
R1#exit

R1 con0 is now available

Press RETURN to get started.

User Access Verification

Username: STANDARD
Password:
R1>
```

Finally , test your solution by exiting an logging in as user ADVANCED:

```
R1#exit

R1 con0 is now available
```

```
Press RETURN to get started.

User Access Verification
Username: ADVANCED
Password:
R1#
```

Task 2

The requirements of this task are straightforward and have been described in previous labs. The only exception is the logging of user events. In current versions of Cisco IOS Software, you can use the logging userinfo command to enable the logging of user information. This command allows for the logging of user information when the user invokes the enable privilege mode or when the user changes the privilege level. The information logged includes username, line and privileged level. This task is completed as follows:

```
R1(config)#logging on
R1(config)#logging trap informational
R1(config)#logging host 150.1.1.254
R1(config)#logging userinfo
R1(config)#exit
```

Following this, assuming you are consoled in and console logging is also enabled on the router, you will see a message similar to the following printed on the console:

```
*Jun 15 12:19:02.463: %SYS-5-CONFIG_I: Configured from console by ADVANCED on console
*Jun 15 12:19:03.463: %SYS-6-LOGGINGHOST_STARTSTOP: Logging to host 150.1.1.254
started - CLI initiated
```

Notice that the output includes the username (ADVANCED) as well as the line from which the configuration was performed (Console). A similar message would also be printed if, for example, the STANDARD user navigated from user EXEC to privileged EXEC mode on R1:

```
R1 con0 is now available

Press RETURN to get started.

User Access Verification

Username: STANDARD
Password:
R1>enable
R1#
*Jun 15 12:21:38.451: %SYS-5-PRIV_AUTH_PASS: Privilege level set to 15 by STANDARD on
console
R1#
R1#
R1#disable
R1>
*Jun 15 12:22:51.555: %SYS-5-PRIV_AUTH_PASS: Privilege level set to 1 by STANDARD on
console
R1>
```

Task 3

In most cases, when configuring logging, a source-interface is specified. This allows network administrators to determine which host sent the information - based on the IP address of the source interface. Cisco IOS Software enhances this functionality even further by allowing an identifier to be added to the beginning of all Syslog messages sent to remote hosts.

This identifier is specified using the logging origin-id string <identifier> global configuration command. The identifier can be the hostname, the IPv4 address, the IPv6 address, or any custom text. When specifying a custom text, you must use an underscore (_) if using multiple words. For example, howtonetwork_rack1, as spaces are not allowed. If you need to specify a custom string or text that will have spaces, you need to use parenthesis (brackets), for example "howtonetwork rack 1". When using this feature, it is important to remember that the specified custom text is only sent to remote destinations. It will NOT be included for local destinations, such as the Console or local buffer, for example. This task is completed as follows:

```
R1(config)#logging origin-id string "R1 - Dallas, TX"
```

You can verify your configuration by looking at the device configuration:

```
R1#more system:running-config | section logging
logging userinfo
logging origin-id string "R1 - Dallas, TX"
logging 150.1.1.254
```

Task 4

Because SNMPv3 configuration is technically beyond the scope of the current CCNP course, the same example used in the SWITCH certification guide is used here. If you read the section, you would have no problem completing this task. This task is completed as follows:

```
R1(config)#snmp-server view NOC system included
R1(config)#snmp-server group SWITCH v3 noauth read NOC
R1(config)#snmp-server engineID remote 150.1.1.254 1a2b3c4d5e
R1(config)#snmp-server user PASS SWITCH v3 auth md5 h@rd!

*Jun 15 12:50:36.331: Configuring snmpv3 USM user, persisting snmpEngineBoots. Please
Wait...

R1(config)#
```

You can view configured and default SNMP views using the show snmp view command:

```
R1#show snmp view
NOC system - included nonvolatile active
*ilmi system - included permanent active
*ilmi atmForumUni - included permanent active
v1default iso - included permanent active
v1default internet.6.3.15 - excluded permanent active
v1default internet.6.3.16 - excluded permanent active
v1default internet.6.3.18 - excluded permanent active
v1default ciscoMgmt.394 - excluded permanent active
v1default ciscoMgmt.395 - excluded permanent active
v1default ciscoMgmt.399 - excluded permanent active
v1default ciscoMgmt.400 - excluded permanent active
```

You can view configured groups using the show snmp group command:

```
R1#show snmp group
groupname: ILMI                            security model:v1
readview : *ilmi                           writeview: *ilmi
notifyview: <no notifyview specified>
row status: active

groupname: ILMI                            security model:v2c
readview : *ilmi                           writeview: *ilmi
notifyview: <no notifyview specified>
row status: active

groupname: SWITCH                          security model:v3 noauth
readview : NOC                             writeview: <no writeview specified>
notifyview: <no notifyview specified>
row status: active
```

Task 5

The requirements of this task are straightforward. This task is completed as follows:

```
R1(config)#snmp-server host 150.1.1.254 version 3 auth PASS envmon
R1(config)#snmp-server enable traps envmon
R1(config)#snmp-server source-interface traps fastethernet 0/0
```

Next, verify your configuration using the show snmp commands:

```
R1#show snmp
Chassis: JAE08020Z7T
0 SNMP packets input
    0 Bad SNMP version errors
    0 Unknown community name
    0 Illegal operation for community name supplied
    0 Encoding errors
    0 Number of requested variables
    0 Number of altered variables
    0 Get-request PDUs
    0 Get-next PDUs
    0 Set-request PDUs
    0 Input queue packet drops (Maximum queue size 1000)
0 SNMP packets output
    0 Too big errors (Maximum packet size 1500)
    0 No such name errors
    0 Bad values errors
    0 General errors
    0 Response PDUs
    0 Trap PDUs

SNMP logging: enabled
    Logging to 150.1.1.254.162, 0/10, 0 sent, 0 dropped.
```

To view host configuration parameters, use the show snmp host command:

```
R1#show snmp host
Notification host: 150.1.1.254  udp-port: 162   type: trap
user: PASS        security model: v3 auth
```

FINAL ROUTE CONFIGURATIONS

R1

```
R1#term len 0
R1#sh run
Building configuration...

Current configuration : 1249 bytes
!
version 12.4
service timestamps debug datetime msec
service timestamps log datetime msec
no service password-encryption
!
hostname R1
!
boot-start-marker
boot-end-marker
!
logging userinfo
!
no aaa new-model
no network-clock-participate slot 1
no network-clock-participate wic 0
ip cef
!
ip auth-proxy max-nodata-conns 3
ip admission max-nodata-conns 3
!
username STANDARD privilege 0 password 0 CCNP1
username ADVANCED privilege 15 password 0 CCNP2
!
interface FastEthernet0/0
 ip address 150.1.1.1 255.255.255.0
 duplex auto
 speed auto
```

```
!
interface Serial0/0
 no ip address
 shutdown
!
interface Serial0/1
 no ip address
 shutdown
!
ip forward-protocol nd
!
no ip http server
no ip http secure-server
!
logging origin-id string "R1 - Dallas, TX"
logging 150.1.1.254
snmp-server engineID remote 10.1.1.254 1A2B3C4D5E
snmp-server group SWITCH v3 noauth match exact read NOC
snmp-server group SWITCH v3 auth match exact
snmp-server view NOC system included
snmp-server trap-source FastEthernet0/0
snmp-server enable traps envmon
snmp-server host 150.1.1.254 version 3 auth PASS  envmon
!
control-plane
!
line con 0
 login local
line aux 0
line vty 0 4
 login
!
end

R1#
```

CCNP LAB 71

Multicast—PIM Dense Mode Lab

Lab Objective:

The focus of this lab is to understand IP Multicast Dense Mode forwarding in Cisco IOS routers. Additional technologies include Internet Group Management Protocol (IGMP).

Lab Topology:

The lab network topology is illustrated below:

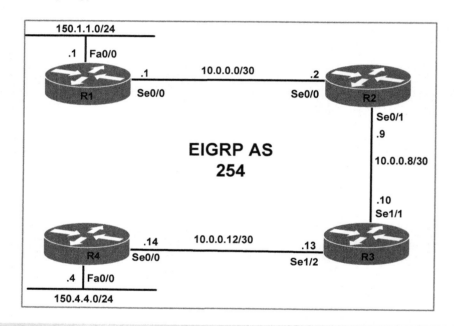

IMPORTANT NOTE: If you are using the www.howtonetwork.net racks, please bring up the LAN interfaces connected to the routers by issuing the `no shutdown` command on the connected switches. If you are using a home lab with no Switches, you can bring up the LAN interfaces using the following configurations on your routers:

```
interface fastethernet 0/0
  no keepalive
  loopback
  no shutdown
```

Alternately, you can simply connect the interfaces to a hub or switch if you have one available in your own lab.

Task 1

Configure the hostnames, IP addressing on all routers as illustrated in the network topology.

Task 2

Enable EIGRP on all routers as illustrated in the topology. Verify your EIGRP configuration.

Task 3

Enable Internet Group Management Protocol on the LAN interfaces of R1 and R4. Ensure that the configuration allows the host to request traffic from a specific host in the network. Next, enable Dense Mode forwarding on the interfaces. Verify your solution using the appropriate commands.

Task 4

Enable Dense Mode forwarding on all router WAN interfaces. Verify your configuration using the appropriate commands.

Task 5

Configure R1 so that its LAN interface is joined to Multicast group 227.1.1.1. Configure R4 so that its LAN interface is joined to Multicast group 227.4.4.4. Verify that R1 can ping R4s Multicast group and that R4 can ping R1s Multicast group.

LAB VALIDATION

Task 1

Please refer to previous tasks for basic VLAN and IP addressing configuration. These will not be included in this section for brevity and to avoid being redundant.

Task 2

Please refer to previous labs for basic EIGRP configuration. Following this, verify your EIGRP configuration using the `show ip eigrp neighbors` and `show ip route` commands. Following this configuration, your route tables should show the following route information:

```
R1#show ip route eigrp
     10.0.0.0/30 is subnetted, 3 subnets
D       10.0.0.8 [90/2681856] via 10.0.0.2, 00:00:12, Serial0/0
D       10.0.0.12 [90/21536000] via 10.0.0.2, 00:00:12, Serial0/0
     150.4.0.0/24 is subnetted, 1 subnets
D       150.4.4.0 [90/21538560] via 10.0.0.2, 00:00:12, Serial0/0

R2#show ip route eigrp
     10.0.0.0/30 is subnetted, 3 subnets
D       10.0.0.12 [90/21024000] via 10.0.0.10, 00:00:22, Serial0/1
     150.1.0.0/24 is subnetted, 1 subnets
D       150.1.1.0 [90/2172416] via 10.0.0.1, 00:00:17, Serial0/0
     150.4.0.0/24 is subnetted, 1 subnets
D       150.4.4.0 [90/21026560] via 10.0.0.10, 00:00:22, Serial0/1

R3#show ip route eigrp
     10.0.0.0/30 is subnetted, 3 subnets
D       10.0.0.0 [90/21024000] via 10.0.0.9, 00:00:25, Serial1/1
     150.1.0.0/24 is subnetted, 1 subnets
D       150.1.1.0 [90/21026560] via 10.0.0.9, 00:00:20, Serial1/1
     150.4.0.0/24 is subnetted, 1 subnets
D       150.4.4.0 [90/20514560] via 10.0.0.14, 00:00:31, Serial1/2

R4#show ip route eigrp
     10.0.0.0/30 is subnetted, 3 subnets
D       10.0.0.8 [90/21024000] via 10.0.0.13, 00:00:34, Serial0/0
D       10.0.0.0 [90/21536000] via 10.0.0.13, 00:00:28, Serial0/0
     150.1.0.0/24 is subnetted, 1 subnets
D       150.1.1.0 [90/21538560] via 10.0.0.13, 00:00:23, Serial0/0
```

Task 3

The core requirement of this task is straightforward. However, in order to complete this task as required you need to understand, from the wording, what version of IGMP is required. Specifically, the task is requiring that IGMPv3 be enabled. IGMP version 3, the most recent modification of the IGMP specification, is defined in RFC 3376. This version now allows the host to request traffic from a specific host in the network. Hosts can also specify a list of sources that they should not receive Multicast traffic from. These changes provide support for the use of Source Specific Multicast within the 232.0.0.0 /8 Multicast group address range. Given this understanding, this task is completed as follows:

```
R1(config)#ip multicast-routing
R1(config)#interface fastethernet 0/0
R1(config-if)#ip igmp version 3
R1(config-if)#ip pim dense-mode
R1(config-if)#exit

R4(config)#ip multicast-routing
R4(config)#interface fastethernet 0/0
R4(config-if)#ip igmp version 3
R4(config-if)#ip pim dense-mode
R4(config-if)#exit
```

Next, verify your configuration using the show ip igmp interface command:

```
R1#show ip igmp interface fastethernet 0/0
FastEthernet0/0 is up, line protocol is up
  Internet address is 150.1.1.1/24
  IGMP is enabled on interface
  Current IGMP host version is 3
  Current IGMP router version is 3
  IGMP query interval is 60 seconds
  IGMP querier timeout is 120 seconds
  IGMP max query response time is 10 seconds
  Last member query count is 2
  Last member query response interval is 1000 ms
  Inbound IGMP access group is not set
  IGMP activity: 1 joins, 0 leaves
  Multicast routing is enabled on interface
  Multicast TTL threshold is 0
  Multicast designated router (DR) is 150.1.1.1 (this system)
  IGMP querying router is 150.1.1.1 (this system)
  Multicast groups joined by this system (number of users):
    224.0.1.40(1)

R4#show ip igmp interface fastethernet 0/0
FastEthernet0/0 is up, line protocol is up
  Internet address is 150.4.4.4/24
  IGMP is enabled on interface
  Current IGMP host version is 3
  Current IGMP router version is 3
  IGMP query interval is 60 seconds
  IGMP querier timeout is 120 seconds
  IGMP max query response time is 10 seconds
  Last member query count is 2
  Last member query response interval is 1000 ms
  Inbound IGMP access group is not set
  IGMP activity: 1 joins, 0 leaves
  Multicast routing is enabled on interface
  Multicast TTL threshold is 0
  Multicast designated router (DR) is 150.4.4.4 (this system)
  IGMP querying router is 150.1.1.1
  Multicast groups joined by this system (number of users):
    224.0.1.40(1)
```

Notice in the last line of the output that the interface is automatically joined to group 224.0.1.40. This group is for Cisco RP Discovery messages. The interface is automatically joined to this group because Dense mode assumes that all hosts wants to receive Multicast traffic, unless they explicitly state that they do not. This group is enabled by default; however, it is not applicable in this section because there is no RP when PIM dense mode is enabled. It simply indicates that the interface is listening for packets that may be sent to this group address.

Task 4

The requirements of this task are straightforward. This task is completed as follows:

```
R1(config)#interface serial 0/0
R1(config-if)#ip pim dense-mode
R1(config-if)#exit

R2(config)#ip multicast-routing
```

```
R2(config)#interface serial 0/0
R2(config-if)#ip pim dense-mode
R2(config-if)#exit
R2(config)#interface serial 0/1
R2(config-if)#ip pim dense-mode
R2(config-if)#exit

R3(config)#ip multicast-routing
R3(config)#interface serial 1/1
R3(config-if)#ip pim dense-mode
R3(config-if)#exit
R3(config)#interface serial 1/2
R3(config-if)#ip pim dense-mode
R3(config-if)#exit

R4(config)#interface serial 0/0
R4(config-if)#ip pim dense-mode
R4(config-if)#exit
```

Next, verify PIM Dense Mode parameters using the show ip pim interface command:

```
R4#show ip pim interface serial 0/0 detail
Serial0/0 is up, line protocol is up
  Internet address is 10.0.0.14/30
  Multicast switching: fast
  Multicast packets in/out: 254/0
  Multicast TTL threshold: 0
  PIM: enabled
    PIM version: 2, mode: dense
    PIM DR: 0.0.0.0
    PIM neighbor count: 1
    PIM Hello/Query interval: 30 seconds
    PIM Hello packets in/out: 4/5
    PIM State-Refresh processing: enabled
    PIM State-Refresh origination: disabled
    PIM NBMA mode: disabled
    PIM ATM multipoint signalling: disabled
    PIM domain border: disabled
  Multicast Tagswitching: disabled
```

Task 5

To configure a router interface to join a Multicast group, a technique commonly used to test the Multicast configuration, use the ip igmp join-group <group> interface command:

```
R1(config)#interface fastethernet 0/0
R1(config-if)#ip igmp join-group 227.1.1.1
R1(config-if)#exit

R4(config)#interface fastethernet 0/0
R4(config-if)#ip igmp join-group 227.4.4.4
R4(config-if)#exit
```

Next, verify your configuration using the show ip igmp interface command:

```
R1#show ip igmp interface fastethernet 0/0
FastEthernet0/0 is up, line protocol is up
  Internet address is 150.1.1.1/24
  IGMP is enabled on interface
  Current IGMP host version is 3
  Current IGMP router version is 3
  IGMP query interval is 60 seconds
  IGMP querier timeout is 120 seconds
  IGMP max query response time is 10 seconds
  Last member query count is 2
  Last member query response interval is 1000 ms
  Inbound IGMP access group is not set
  IGMP activity: 3 joins, 0 leaves
  Multicast routing is enabled on interface
  Multicast TTL threshold is 0
  Multicast designated router (DR) is 150.4.4.4
  IGMP querying router is 150.1.1.1 (this system)
  Multicast groups joined by this system (number of users):
      224.0.1.40(1)  227.1.1.1(1)
```

```
R4#show ip igmp interface fastethernet 0/0
FastEthernet0/0 is up, line protocol is up
  Internet address is 150.4.4.4/24
  IGMP is enabled on interface
  Current IGMP host version is 3
  Current IGMP router version is 3
  IGMP query interval is 60 seconds
  IGMP querier timeout is 120 seconds
  IGMP max query response time is 10 seconds
  Last member query count is 2
  Last member query response interval is 1000 ms
  Inbound IGMP access group is not set
  IGMP activity: 2 joins, 0 leaves
  Multicast routing is enabled on interface
  Multicast TTL threshold is 0
  Multicast designated router (DR) is 150.4.4.4 (this system)
  IGMP querying router is 150.1.1.1
  Multicast groups joined by this system (number of users):
      224.0.1.40(1)  227.4.4.4(1)
```

Finally, complete the task by pinging the Multicast groups from routers R1 and R4:

```
R1#ping 227.4.4.4

Type escape sequence to abort.
Sending 1, 100-byte ICMP Echos to 227.4.4.4, timeout is 2 seconds:

Reply to request 0 from 10.0.0.14, 40 ms

R4#ping 227.1.1.1

Type escape sequence to abort.
Sending 1, 100-byte ICMP Echos to 227.1.1.1, timeout is 2 seconds:

Reply to request 0 from 10.0.0.1, 40 ms
```

FINAL ROUTER CONFIGURATIONS

R1

```
R1#term len 0
R1#sh run
Building configuration...

Current configuration : 986 bytes
!
version 12.4
service timestamps debug datetime msec
service timestamps log datetime msec
no service password-encryption
!
hostname R1
!
boot-start-marker
boot-end-marker
!
no logging console
!
no aaa new-model
no network-clock-participate slot 1
no network-clock-participate wic 0
ip cef
!
no ip domain lookup
ip multicast-routing
ip auth-proxy max-nodata-conns 3
ip admission max-nodata-conns 3
!
interface FastEthernet0/0
 ip address 150.1.1.1 255.255.255.0
 ip pim dense-mode
 ip igmp join-group 227.1.1.1
 ip igmp version 3
 duplex auto
 speed auto
```

```
!
interface Serial0/0
 ip address 10.0.0.1 255.255.255.252
 ip pim dense-mode
 clock rate 2000000
!
interface Serial0/1
 no ip address
!
router eigrp 254
 network 0.0.0.0
 no auto-summary
!
ip forward-protocol nd
!
no ip http server
no ip http secure-server
!
control-plane
!
line con 0
line aux 0
line vty 0 4
 login
!
end
R1#
```

R2

```
R2#term len 0
R2#sh run
Building configuration...

Current configuration : 906 bytes
!
version 12.4
service timestamps debug datetime msec
service timestamps log datetime msec
no service password-encryption
!
hostname R2
!
boot-start-marker
boot-end-marker
!
no logging console
!
no aaa new-model
no network-clock-participate slot 1
no network-clock-participate wic 0
ip cef
!
no ip domain lookup
ip multicast-routing
ip auth-proxy max-nodata-conns 3
ip admission max-nodata-conns 3
!
interface FastEthernet0/0
 no ip address
 shutdown
 duplex auto
 speed auto
!
interface Serial0/0
 ip address 10.0.0.2 255.255.255.252
 ip pim dense-mode
!
interface Serial0/1
 ip address 10.0.0.9 255.255.255.252
 ip pim dense-mode
!
router eigrp 254
 network 0.0.0.0
 no auto-summary
!
ip forward-protocol nd
!
no ip http server
no ip http secure-server
!
control-plane
```

```
!
line con 0
line aux 0
line vty 0 4
 login
!
end

R2#
```

R3

```
R3#term len 0
R3#sh run
Building configuration...

Current configuration : 1247 bytes
!
version 12.4
service timestamps debug datetime msec
service timestamps log datetime msec
no service password-encryption
!
hostname R3
!
boot-start-marker
boot-end-marker
!
no logging console
!
no aaa new-model
no network-clock-participate slot 1
no network-clock-participate wic 0
ip cef
!
no ip domain lookup
ip multicast-routing
ip auth-proxy max-nodata-conns 3
ip admission max-nodata-conns 3
!
interface FastEthernet0/0
 no ip address
 shutdown
 duplex auto
 speed auto
!
interface Serial1/0
 no ip address
 shutdown
 clock rate 128000
!
interface Serial1/1
 ip address 10.0.0.10 255.255.255.252
 ip pim dense-mode
 clock rate 128000
!
interface Serial1/2
 ip address 10.0.0.13 255.255.255.252
 ip pim dense-mode
 clock rate 128000
!
interface Serial1/3
 no ip address
 shutdown
!
interface Serial1/4
 no ip address
 shutdown
!
interface Serial1/5
 no ip address
 shutdown
!
interface Serial1/6
 no ip address
 shutdown
!
interface Serial1/7
 no ip address
 shutdown
!
router eigrp 254
```

```
 network 0.0.0.0
 no auto-summary
!
ip forward-protocol nd
!
no ip http server
no ip http secure-server
!
control-plane
!
line con 0
line aux 0
line vty 0 4
 login
!
end
R3#
```

R4

```
R4#term len 0
R4#sh run
Building configuration...

Current configuration : 955 bytes
!
version 12.4
service timestamps debug datetime msec
service timestamps log datetime msec
no service password-encryption
!
hostname R4
!
boot-start-marker
boot-end-marker
!
no logging console
!
no aaa new-model
no network-clock-participate slot 1
no network-clock-participate wic 0
ip cef
!
no ip domain lookup
ip multicast-routing
ip auth-proxy max-nodata-conns 3
ip admission max-nodata-conns 3
!
interface FastEthernet0/0
 ip address 150.4.4.4 255.255.255.0
 ip pim dense-mode
 ip igmp join-group 227.4.4.4
 ip igmp version 3
 duplex auto
 speed auto
!
interface Serial0/0
 ip address 10.0.0.14 255.255.255.252
 ip pim dense-mode
!
interface Serial0/1
 no ip address
 shutdown
!
router eigrp 254
 network 0.0.0.0
 no auto-summary
!
ip forward-protocol nd
!
no ip http server
no ip http secure-server
!
control-plane
!
line con 0
line aux 0
line vty 0 4
 login
!
end
R4#
```

CCNP LAB 72

Multicast—PIM Sparse Mode Lab

Lab Objective:

The focus of this lab is to understand IP Multicast Sparse Mode forwarding in Cisco IOS routers. Additional technologies include Internet Group Management Protocol (IGMP).

Lab Topology:

The lab network topology is illustrated below:

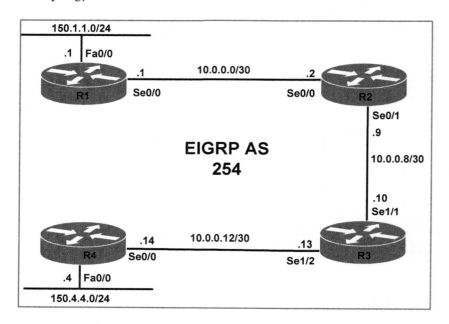

IMPORTANT NOTE: If you are using the www.howtonetwork.net racks, please bring up the LAN interfaces connected to the routers by issuing the no shutdown command on the connected switches. If you are using a home lab with no Switches, you can bring up the LAN interfaces using the following configurations on your routers:

```
interface fastethernet 0/0
  no keepalive
  loopback
  no shutdown
```

Alternately, you can simply connect the interfaces to a hub or switch if you have one available in your own lab.

Task 1

Configure the hostnames, IP addressing on all routers as illustrated in the network topology.

Task 2

Enable EIGRP on all routers as illustrated in the topology. Verify your EIGRP configuration.

Task 3

Enable Internet Group Management Protocol on the LAN interfaces of R1 and R4. These LAN interfaces are connected to legacy hosts that only understand basic IGMP. Configure the version that provides the most basic services. Finally, enable Sparse Mode forwarding on the router LAN interfaces. Verify your solution using the appropriate commands.

Task 4

Enable Sparse Mode forwarding on all router WAN interfaces. Verify your configuration using the appropriate commands.

Task 5

Configure R1 so that its LAN interface is joined to Multicast group 227.1.1.1. Configure R4 so that its LAN interface is joined to Multicast group 227.4.4.4. Verify that R1 can ping R4s Multicast group and that R4 can ping R1s Multicast group.

Task 6

Given that the network will be running Sparse Mode, configure R2 as the Rendezvous Point, or RP. Configure a Loopback 0 interface with the IP address 2.2.2.2/32 on this router. This Loopback address should be configured as the RP for all routers in the network. HINT: Use the `ip pim rp-address <address>` command on all routers. Verify your configuration and test you solution by pinging 227.4.4.4 from R1 and 227.1.1.1 from R4.

LAB VALIDATION

Task 1

Please refer to previous tasks for basic VLAN and IP addressing configuration. These will not be included in this section for brevity and to avoid being redundant.

Task 2

Please refer to previous labs for basic EIGRP configuration. Following this, verify your EIGRP configuration using the `show ip eigrp neighbors` and `show ip route` commands. Following this configuration, your route tables should show the following route information:

```
R1#show ip route eigrp
     10.0.0.0/30 is subnetted, 3 subnets
D       10.0.0.8 [90/2681856] via 10.0.0.2, 00:00:12, Serial0/0
D       10.0.0.12 [90/21536000] via 10.0.0.2, 00:00:12, Serial0/0
     150.4.0.0/24 is subnetted, 1 subnets
D       150.4.4.0 [90/21538560] via 10.0.0.2, 00:00:12, Serial0/0

R2#show ip route eigrp
     10.0.0.0/30 is subnetted, 3 subnets
D       10.0.0.12 [90/21024000] via 10.0.0.10, 00:00:22, Serial0/1
     150.1.0.0/24 is subnetted, 1 subnets
D       150.1.1.0 [90/2172416] via 10.0.0.1, 00:00:17, Serial0/0
     150.4.0.0/24 is subnetted, 1 subnets
D       150.4.4.0 [90/21026560] via 10.0.0.10, 00:00:22, Serial0/1

R3#show ip route eigrp
     10.0.0.0/30 is subnetted, 3 subnets
D       10.0.0.0 [90/21024000] via 10.0.0.9, 00:00:25, Serial1/1
     150.1.0.0/24 is subnetted, 1 subnets
D       150.1.1.0 [90/21026560] via 10.0.0.9, 00:00:20, Serial1/1
     150.4.0.0/24 is subnetted, 1 subnets
D       150.4.4.0 [90/20514560] via 10.0.0.14, 00:00:31, Serial1/2

R4#show ip route eigrp
     10.0.0.0/30 is subnetted, 3 subnets
D       10.0.0.8 [90/21024000] via 10.0.0.13, 00:00:34, Serial0/0
```

```
D        10.0.0.0 [90/21536000] via 10.0.0.13, 00:00:28, Serial0/0
     150.1.0.0/24 is subnetted, 1 subnets
D        150.1.1.0 [90/21538560] via 10.0.0.13, 00:00:23, Serial0/0
```

Task 3

The core requirement of this task is straightforward. IGMPv1 provides the most basic services. Given this understanding, this task is completed as follows:

```
R1(config)#ip multicast-routing
R1(config)#interface fastethernet 0/0
R1(config-if)#ip igmp version 1
R1(config-if)#ip pim sparse-mode
R1(config-if)#exit

R4(config)#ip multicast-routing
R4(config)#interface fastethernet 0/0
R4(config-if)#ip igmp version 1
R4(config-if)#ip pim sparse-mode
R4(config-if)#exit
```

Next, verify your configuration using the show ip igmp interface command:

```
R1#show ip igmp interface fastethernet 0/0
FastEthernet0/0 is up, line protocol is up
  Internet address is 150.1.1.1/24
  IGMP is enabled on interface
  Current IGMP host version is 1
  Current IGMP router version is 1
  IGMP query interval is 60 seconds
  Inbound IGMP access group is not set
  IGMP activity: 0 joins, 0 leaves
  Multicast routing is enabled on interface
  Multicast TTL threshold is 0
  Multicast designated router (DR) is 150.4.4.4
  IGMP querying router is 150.4.4.4 (this system)
  No multicast groups joined by this system

R4#show ip igmp interface fastethernet 0/0
FastEthernet0/0 is up, line protocol is up
  Internet address is 150.4.4.4/24
  IGMP is enabled on interface
  Current IGMP host version is 1
  Current IGMP router version is 1
  IGMP query interval is 60 seconds
  Inbound IGMP access group is not set
  IGMP activity: 0 joins, 0 leaves
  Multicast routing is enabled on interface
  Multicast TTL threshold is 0
  Multicast designated router (DR) is 150.4.4.4 (this system)
  IGMP querying router is 150.4.4.4 (this system)
  No multicast groups joined by this system
```

Notice that unlike Dense Mode, the interfaces are NOT automatically joined to any Multicast groups. This is because Sparse mode forwarding operates in a manner that is opposite to dense mode forwarding. That is, while dense mode assumes that all Multicast-enabled interfaces are interested in receiving Multicast packets unless explicitly configured otherwise, sparse mode assumes that no Multicast interfaces are interested in receiving Multicast packets unless explicitly configured otherwise; that is to say, unless a PIM join message is received on the interface. As such, routers in a sparse-mode network must explicitly request that the data stream be forwarded to them.

Task 4

The requirements of this task are straightforward. This task is completed as follows:

```
R1(config)#interface serial 0/0
R1(config-if)#ip pim sparse-mode
R1(config-if)#exit
```

```
R2(config)#ip multicast-routing
R2(config)#interface serial 0/0
R2(config-if)#ip pim sparse-mode
R2(config-if)#exit
R2(config)#interface serial 0/1
R2(config-if)#ip pim sparse-mode
R2(config-if)#exit

R3(config)#ip multicast-routing
R3(config)#interface serial 1/1
R3(config-if)#ip pim sparse-mode
R3(config-if)#exit
R3(config)#interface serial 1/2
R3(config-if)#ip pim sparse-mode
R3(config-if)#exit

R4(config)#interface serial 0/0
R4(config-if)#ip pim sparse-mode
R4(config-if)#exit
```

Next, verify PIM Sparse Mode parameters using the `show ip pim` interface command:

```
R1#show ip pim interface serial 0/0 detail
Serial0/0 is up, line protocol is up
  Internet address is 10.0.0.1/30
  Multicast switching: fast
  Multicast packets in/out: 667/1
  Multicast TTL threshold: 0
  PIM: enabled
    PIM version: 2, mode: sparse
    PIM DR: 0.0.0.0
    PIM neighbor count: 1
    PIM Hello/Query interval: 30 seconds
    PIM Hello packets in/out: 61/63
    PIM State-Refresh processing: enabled
    PIM State-Refresh origination: disabled
    PIM NBMA mode: disabled
    PIM ATM multipoint signalling: disabled
    PIM domain border: disabled
  Multicast Tagswitching: disabled
```

Task 5

To configure a router interface to join a Multicast group, a technique commonly used to test the Multicast configuration, use the `ip igmp join-group <group>` interface command:

```
R1(config)#interface fastethernet 0/0
R1(config-if)#ip igmp join-group 227.1.1.1
R1(config-if)#exit

R4(config)#interface fastethernet 0/0
R4(config-if)#ip igmp join-group 227.4.4.4
R4(config-if)#exit
```

Next, verify your configuration using the `show ip igmp interface` command:

```
R1#show ip igmp interface fastethernet 0/0
FastEthernet0/0 is up, line protocol is up
  Internet address is 150.1.1.1/24
  IGMP is enabled on interface
  Current IGMP host version is 1
  Current IGMP router version is 1
  IGMP query interval is 60 seconds
  Inbound IGMP access group is not set
  IGMP activity: 2 joins, 0 leaves
  Multicast routing is enabled on interface
  Multicast TTL threshold is 0
  Multicast designated router (DR) is 150.4.4.4
  IGMP querying router is 150.4.4.4
  Multicast groups joined by this system (number of users):
      227.1.1.1(1)

R4#show ip igmp interface fastethernet 0/0
```

```
FastEthernet0/0 is up, line protocol is up
  Internet address is 150.4.4.4/24
  IGMP is enabled on interface
  Current IGMP host version is 1
  Current IGMP router version is 1
  IGMP query interval is 60 seconds
  Inbound IGMP access group is not set
  IGMP activity: 3 joins, 0 leaves
  Multicast routing is enabled on interface
  Multicast TTL threshold is 0
  Multicast designated router (DR) is 150.4.4.4 (this system)
  IGMP querying router is 150.4.4.4 (this system)
  Multicast groups joined by this system (number of users):
      227.4.4.4(1)
```

Task 6

When sparse-mode is enabled, one of the routers in the network performs a special function as a connection point between the source and the receiver. This router is referred to as the Rendezvous Point, or RP. The RP combines knowledge of the group source with the requests from the receiver. The RP is where the sender and the receiver first meet before the shortest-path tree is established. In other words, once the sender and receiver are aware of each other via the use of the RP, they use the shortest path between sender and receiver, based on routing protocol metric, to send and receive Multicast packets.

Once the Multicast traffic from the source and the requests from the receivers connect at the RP, the traffic is forwarded through the network. This shared tree has the RP at the top of the forwarding tree with the network segments and receivers as the branches and leaves, respectively. This is often referred to as the Rendezvous Point Tree (RPT). The shared-tree used by sparse mode is represented with the (*, G) notation. The * is used as a wildcard because the actual source of the Multicast stream is never known until registered with the RP.

In Cisco IOS Software, there are three ways in which the location of the RP can be specified:
* By statically configuring the router or switch with the RP IP address
* Automatically, using the Cisco Auto-RP mechanism
* Automatically, using the Bootstrap Router mechanism with PIMv2

This task requires that you statically configure the RP address on all routers using the `ip pim rp-address <address>` command. This task is completed as follows:

```
R1(config)#ip pim rp-address 2.2.2.2

R2(config)#interface loopback 0
R2(config-if)#ip address 2.2.2.2 255.255.255.255
R2(config-if)#ip pim sparse-mode
R2(config-if)#exit
R2(config)#ip pim rp-address 2.2.2.2
R2(config)#exit
```

NOTE: You MUST advertise the Loopback 0 interface via EIGRP. If you enabled EIGRP for all networks using the `network 0.0.0.0` command, no additional configuration is necessary. However, if you explicitly enabled EIGRP for specific subnets, you need to also advertise the configured Loopback 0 interface via EIGRP; otherwise, no other router can reach this address.

```
R3(config)#ip pim rp-address 2.2.2.2

R4(config)#ip pim rp-address 2.2.2.2
```

Next, verify static RP configuration using the `show ip pim rp` command:

```
R1#show ip pim rp
Group: 227.4.4.4, RP: 2.2.2.2, uptime 00:02:09, expires never
Group: 227.1.1.1, RP: 2.2.2.2, uptime 00:00:47, expires never
Group: 224.0.1.40, RP: 2.2.2.2, uptime 00:02:09, expires never
```

```
R2#show ip pim rp
Group: 227.4.4.4, RP: 2.2.2.2, next RP-reachable in 00:00:52
Group: 227.1.1.1, RP: 2.2.2.2, next RP-reachable in 00:00:16
Group: 224.0.1.40, RP: 2.2.2.2, next RP-reachable in 00:01:21

R3#show ip pim rp
Group: 227.4.4.4, RP: 2.2.2.2, uptime 00:02:18, expires never
Group: 227.1.1.1, RP: 2.2.2.2, uptime 00:01:24, expires never
Group: 224.0.1.40, RP: 2.2.2.2, uptime 00:02:21, expires never

R4#show ip pim rp
Group: 227.4.4.4, RP: 2.2.2.2, uptime 00:02:30, expires never
Group: 227.1.1.1, RP: 2.2.2.2, uptime 00:01:36, expires never
Group: 224.0.1.40, RP: 2.2.2.2, uptime 00:02:30, expires never
```

In addition to the two statically defined Multicast groups, also notice that group 224.0.1.40 is also listed in the output of this command. This is the group address used for RP Discovery messages. This group is enabled by default as is used for RP Discovery. Finally, complete the task by pinging 227.4.4.4 from R1 and 227.1.1.1 from R4:

```
R1#ping 227.4.4.4

Type escape sequence to abort.
Sending 1, 100-byte ICMP Echos to 227.4.4.4, timeout is 2 seconds:

Reply to request 0 from 10.0.0.14, 32 ms

R4#ping 227.1.1.1

Type escape sequence to abort.
Sending 1, 100-byte ICMP Echos to 227.1.1.1, timeout is 2 seconds:

Reply to request 0 from 10.0.0.1, 48 ms
```

FINAL ROUTER CONFIGURATIONS

R1

```
R1#term len 0
R1#sh run
Building configuration...

Current configuration : 1014 bytes
!
version 12.4
service timestamps debug datetime msec
service timestamps log datetime msec
no service password-encryption
!
hostname R1
!
boot-start-marker
boot-end-marker
!
no logging console
!
no aaa new-model
no network-clock-participate slot 1
no network-clock-participate wic 0
ip cef
!
no ip domain lookup
ip multicast-routing
ip auth-proxy max-nodata-conns 3
ip admission max-nodata-conns 3
!
interface FastEthernet0/0
 ip address 150.1.1.1 255.255.255.0
 ip pim sparse-mode
```

```
    ip igmp join-group 227.1.1.1
    ip igmp version 1
    duplex auto
    speed auto
   !
   interface Serial0/0
    ip address 10.0.0.1 255.255.255.252
    ip pim sparse-mode
    clock rate 2000000
   !
   interface Serial0/1
    no ip address
   !
   router eigrp 254
    network 0.0.0.0
    no auto-summary
   !
   ip forward-protocol nd
   !
   no ip http server
   no ip http secure-server
   ip pim rp-address 2.2.2.2
   !
   control-plane
   !
   line con 0
   line aux 0
   line vty 0 4
    login
   !
   end

   R1#
```

R2

```
   R2#term len 0
   R2#sh run
   Building configuration...

   Current configuration : 1012 bytes
   !
   version 12.4
   service timestamps debug datetime msec
   service timestamps log datetime msec
   no service password-encryption
   !
   hostname R2
   !
   boot-start-marker
   boot-end-marker
   !
   no logging console
   !
   no aaa new-model
   no network-clock-participate slot 1
   no network-clock-participate wic 0
   ip cef
   !
   no ip domain lookup
   ip multicast-routing
   ip auth-proxy max-nodata-conns 3
   ip admission max-nodata-conns 3
   !
   interface Loopback0
    ip address 2.2.2.2 255.255.255.255
    ip pim sparse-mode
   !
   interface FastEthernet0/0
    no ip address
    shutdown
    duplex auto
    speed auto
```

```
!
interface Serial0/0
 ip address 10.0.0.2 255.255.255.252
 ip pim sparse-mode
!
interface Serial0/1
 ip address 10.0.0.9 255.255.255.252
 ip pim sparse-mode
!
router eigrp 254
 network 0.0.0.0
 no auto-summary
!
ip forward-protocol nd
!
no ip http server
no ip http secure-server
ip pim rp-address 2.2.2.2
!
control-plane
!
line con 0
line aux 0
line vty 0 4
 login
!
end

R2#
```

R3

```
R3#term len 0
R3#sh run
Building configuration...

Current configuration : 1275 bytes
!
version 12.4
service timestamps debug datetime msec
service timestamps log datetime msec
no service password-encryption
!
hostname R3
!
boot-start-marker
boot-end-marker
!
no logging console
!
no aaa new-model
no network-clock-participate slot 1
no network-clock-participate wic 0
ip cef
!
no ip domain lookup
ip multicast-routing
ip auth-proxy max-nodata-conns 3
ip admission max-nodata-conns 3
!
interface FastEthernet0/0
 no ip address
 shutdown
 duplex auto
 speed auto
!
interface Serial1/0
 no ip address
 shutdown
 clock rate 128000
!
interface Serial1/1
 ip address 10.0.0.10 255.255.255.252
 ip pim sparse-mode
 clock rate 128000
```

```
!
interface Serial1/2
 ip address 10.0.0.13 255.255.255.252
 ip pim sparse-mode
 clock rate 128000
!
interface Serial1/3
 no ip address
 shutdown
!
interface Serial1/4
 no ip address
 shutdown
!
interface Serial1/5
 no ip address
 shutdown
!
interface Serial1/6
 no ip address
 shutdown
!
interface Serial1/7
 no ip address
 shutdown
!
router eigrp 254
 network 0.0.0.0
 no auto-summary
!
ip forward-protocol nd
!
no ip http server
no ip http secure-server
ip pim rp-address 2.2.2.2
!
control-plane
!
line con 0
line aux 0
line vty 0 4
 login
!
end

R3#
```

R4

```
R4#term len 0
R4#sh run
Building configuration...

Current configuration : 983 bytes
!
version 12.4
service timestamps debug datetime msec
service timestamps log datetime msec
no service password-encryption
!
hostname R4
!
boot-start-marker
boot-end-marker
!
no logging console
!
no aaa new-model
no network-clock-participate slot 1
no network-clock-participate wic 0
ip cef
!
no ip domain lookup
ip multicast-routing
```

```
ip auth-proxy max-nodata-conns 3
ip admission max-nodata-conns 3
!
interface FastEthernet0/0
 ip address 150.4.4.4 255.255.255.0
 ip pim sparse-mode
 ip igmp join-group 227.4.4.4
 ip igmp version 1
 duplex auto
 speed auto
!
interface Serial0/0
 ip address 10.0.0.14 255.255.255.252
 ip pim sparse-mode
!
interface Serial0/1
 no ip address
 shutdown
!
router eigrp 254
 network 0.0.0.0
 no auto-summary
!
ip forward-protocol nd
!
no ip http server
no ip http secure-server
ip pim rp-address 2.2.2.2
!
control-plane
!
line con 0
line aux 0
line vty 0 4
 login
!
end

R4#
```

CCNP LAB 73

Multicast—PIM Auto RP Lab

Lab Objective:

The focus of this lab is to understand IP Multicast Auto RP implementation Cisco IOS routers. Additional technologies include Internet Group Management Protocol (IGMP).

Lab Topology:

The lab network topology is illustrated below:

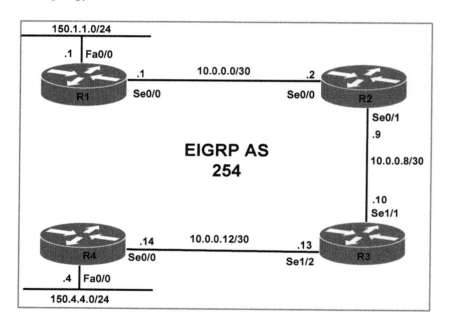

IMPORTANT NOTE: If you are using the www.howtonetwork.net racks, please bring up the LAN interfaces connected to the routers by issuing the `no shutdown` command on the connected switches. If you are using a home lab with no Switches, you can bring up the LAN interfaces using the following configurations on your routers:

```
interface fastethernet 0/0
  no keepalive
  loopback
  no shutdown
```

Alternately, you can simply connect the interfaces to a hub or switch if you have one available in your own lab.

Task 1

Configure the hostnames, IP addressing on all routers as illustrated in the network topology.

Task 2

Enable EIGRP on all routers as illustrated in the topology. Verify your EIGRP configuration.

Task 3

Enable Internet Group Management Protocol version 2 on the LAN interfaces of routers R1 and R4. Next, enable Sparse-Dense Mode forwarding on the interfaces. Verify your solution using the appropriate commands.

Task 4

Enable Sparse-Dense Mode forwarding on all router WAN interfaces. Verify your configuration using the appropriate commands.

Task 5

Configure R1 so that its LAN interface is joined to Multicast group 227.1.1.1. Configure R4 so that its LAN interface is joined to Multicast group 227.4.4.4. Verify that R1 can ping R4s Multicast group and that R4 can ping R1s Multicast group.

Task 6

Configure Cisco Auto RP functionality on all routers. Use the following guidelines:
- R2 should be configured with a Loopback 0 interface of 2.2.2.2/32
- R2 should be configured to announce Loopback 0 as the candidate RP for all groups
- R3 should be configured with a Loopback 0 interface of 3.3.3.3/32
- R3 should be configured to advertise the RP information to all other routers
- R3 should use its Loopback 0 interface to send these advertisements
- R1 and R4 should be configured to listen to advertised RP Discovery messages

To complete this task, use the following commands on the routers. It will be up to you to determine which command(s) will need to be enabled on which router.
- The ip pim send-rp-discovery command
- The ip pim send-rp-announce command
- The ip pim accept-rp auto-rp command

Finally, complete this task by pinging from R1 to 227.4.4.4 and from R4 to 227.1.1.1.

LAB VALIDATION

Task 1

Please refer to previous tasks for basic VLAN and IP addressing configuration. These will not be included in this section for brevity and to avoid being redundant.

Task 2

Please refer to previous labs for basic EIGRP configuration. Following this, verify your EIGRP configuration using the show ip eigrp neighbors and show ip route commands. Following this configuration, your route tables should show the following route information:

```
R1#show ip route eigrp
     10.0.0.0/30 is subnetted, 3 subnets
D       10.0.0.8 [90/2681856] via 10.0.0.2, 00:00:12, Serial0/0
D       10.0.0.12 [90/21536000] via 10.0.0.2, 00:00:12, Serial0/0
     150.4.0.0/24 is subnetted, 1 subnets
D       150.4.4.0 [90/21538560] via 10.0.0.2, 00:00:12, Serial0/0

R2#show ip route eigrp
     10.0.0.0/30 is subnetted, 3 subnets
D       10.0.0.12 [90/21024000] via 10.0.0.10, 00:00:22, Serial0/1
     150.1.0.0/24 is subnetted, 1 subnets
D       150.1.1.0 [90/2172416] via 10.0.0.1, 00:00:17, Serial0/0
     150.4.0.0/24 is subnetted, 1 subnets
D       150.4.4.0 [90/21026560] via 10.0.0.10, 00:00:22, Serial0/1
```

```
R3#show ip route eigrp
     10.0.0.0/30 is subnetted, 3 subnets
D       10.0.0.0 [90/21024000] via 10.0.0.9, 00:00:25, Serial1/1
     150.1.0.0/24 is subnetted, 1 subnets
D       150.1.1.0 [90/21026560] via 10.0.0.9, 00:00:20, Serial1/1
     150.4.0.0/24 is subnetted, 1 subnets
D       150.4.4.0 [90/20514560] via 10.0.0.14, 00:00:31, Serial1/2

R4#show ip route eigrp
     10.0.0.0/30 is subnetted, 3 subnets
D       10.0.0.8 [90/21024000] via 10.0.0.13, 00:00:34, Serial0/0
D       10.0.0.0 [90/21536000] via 10.0.0.13, 00:00:28, Serial0/0
     150.1.0.0/24 is subnetted, 1 subnets
D       150.1.1.0 [90/21538560] via 10.0.0.13, 00:00:23, Serial0/0
```

Task 3

The requirement of this task is straightforward. This task is completed as follows:

```
R1(config)#ip multicast-routing
R1(config)#interface fastethernet 0/0
R1(config-if)#ip igmp version 2
R1(config-if)#ip pim sparse-dense-mode
R1(config-if)#exit

R4(config)#ip multicast-routing
R4(config)#interface fastethernet 0/0
R4(config-if)#ip igmp version 2
R4(config-if)#ip pim sparse-dense-mode
R4(config-if)#exit
```

Next, verify your configuration using the show ip igmp interface command:

```
R1#show ip igmp interface fastethernet 0/0
FastEthernet0/0 is up, line protocol is up
  Internet address is 150.1.1.1/24
  IGMP is enabled on interface
  Current IGMP host version is 2
  Current IGMP router version is 2
  IGMP query interval is 60 seconds
  IGMP querier timeout is 120 seconds
  IGMP max query response time is 10 seconds
  Last member query count is 2
  Last member query response interval is 1000 ms
  Inbound IGMP access group is not set
  IGMP activity: 1 joins, 0 leaves
  Multicast routing is enabled on interface
  Multicast TTL threshold is 0
  Multicast designated router (DR) is 150.1.1.4
  IGMP querying router is 150.1.1.1 (this system)
  Multicast groups joined by this system (number of users):
      224.0.1.40(1)
```

Notice in the last line of the output that the interface is automatically joined to group 224.0.1.40. This group is for Cisco RP Discovery messages. The interface is automatically joined to this group because Dense mode assumes that all hosts wants to receive Multicast traffic, unless they explicitly state that they do not. This group is enabled by default; it simply indicates that the interface is listening for packets that may be sent to this group address. You can verify the PIM operational mode using the show ip pim interface command:

```
R1#show ip pim interface fastethernet 0/0 detail
FastEthernet0/0 is up, line protocol is up
  Internet address is 150.1.1.1/24
  Multicast switching: fast
  Multicast packets in/out: 326/0
  Multicast TTL threshold: 0
  PIM: enabled
    PIM version: 2, mode: sparse-dense
    PIM DR: 150.1.1.4
    PIM neighbor count: 0
    PIM Hello/Query interval: 30 seconds
```

```
      PIM Hello packets in/out: 19/21
      PIM State-Refresh processing: enabled
      PIM State-Refresh origination: disabled
      PIM NBMA mode: disabled
      PIM ATM multipoint signalling: disabled
      PIM domain border: disabled
   Multicast Tagswitching: disabled
```

Task 4

The requirements of this task are straightforward. This task is completed as follows:

```
R1(config)#interface serial 0/0
R1(config-if)#ip pim sparse-dense-mode
R1(config-if)#exit

R2(config)#ip multicast-routing
R2(config)#interface serial 0/0
R2(config-if)#ip pim sparse-dense-mode
R2(config-if)#exit
R2(config)#interface serial 0/1
R2(config-if)#ip pim sparse-dense-mode
R2(config-if)#exit

R3(config)#ip multicast-routing
R3(config)#interface serial 1/1
R3(config-if)#ip pim sparse-dense-mode
R3(config-if)#exit
R3(config)#interface serial 1/2
R3(config-if)#ip pim sparse-dense-mode
R3(config-if)#exit

R4(config)#interface serial 0/0
R4(config-if)#ip pim sparse-dense-mode
R4(config-if)#exit
```

Next, verify PIM Sparse-Dense Mode parameters using the show ip pim interface command:

```
R4#show ip pim interface serial 0/0 detail
Serial0/0 is up, line protocol is up
   Internet address is 10.0.0.14/30
   Multicast switching: fast
   Multicast packets in/out: 332/0
   Multicast TTL threshold: 0
   PIM: enabled
      PIM version: 2, mode: sparse-dense
      PIM DR: 0.0.0.0
      PIM neighbor count: 1
      PIM Hello/Query interval: 30 seconds
      PIM Hello packets in/out: 2/3
      PIM State-Refresh processing: enabled
      PIM State-Refresh origination: disabled
      PIM NBMA mode: disabled
      PIM ATM multipoint signalling: disabled
      PIM domain border: disabled
   Multicast Tagswitching: disabled
```

Task 5

To configure a router interface to join a Multicast group, a technique commonly used to test the Multicast configuration, use the ip igmp join-group <group> interface command:

```
R1(config)#interface fastethernet 0/0
R1(config-if)#ip igmp join-group 227.1.1.1
R1(config-if)#exit

R4(config)#interface fastethernet 0/0
R4(config-if)#ip igmp join-group 227.4.4.4
R4(config-if)#exit
```

Next, verify your configuration using the show ip igmp interface command:

```
R1#show ip igmp interface fastethernet 0/0
FastEthernet0/0 is up, line protocol is up
  Internet address is 150.1.1.1/24
  IGMP is enabled on interface
  Current IGMP host version is 2
  Current IGMP router version is 2
  IGMP query interval is 60 seconds
  IGMP querier timeout is 120 seconds
  IGMP max query response time is 10 seconds
  Last member query count is 2
  Last member query response interval is 1000 ms
  Inbound IGMP access group is not set
  IGMP activity: 3 joins, 0 leaves
  Multicast routing is enabled on interface
  Multicast TTL threshold is 0
  Multicast designated router (DR) is 150.4.4.4
  IGMP querying router is 150.1.1.1 (this system)
  Multicast groups joined by this system (number of users):
      224.0.1.40(1)  227.1.1.1(1)

R4#show ip igmp interface fastethernet 0/0
FastEthernet0/0 is up, line protocol is up
  Internet address is 150.4.4.4/24
  IGMP is enabled on interface
  Current IGMP host version is 2
  Current IGMP router version is 2
  IGMP query interval is 60 seconds
  IGMP querier timeout is 120 seconds
  IGMP max query response time is 10 seconds
  Last member query count is 2
  Last member query response interval is 1000 ms
  Inbound IGMP access group is not set
  IGMP activity: 3 joins, 0 leaves
  Multicast routing is enabled on interface
  Multicast TTL threshold is 0
  Multicast designated router (DR) is 150.4.4.4 (this system)
  IGMP querying router is 150.1.1.1
  Multicast groups joined by this system (number of users):
      224.0.1.40(1)  227.4.4.4(1)
```

Task 6

This task requires the configuration of auto RP. As stated in the TSHOOT guide, in Cisco IOS Software, there are three ways in which the location of the RP can be specified:
- By statically configuring the router or switch with the RP IP address
- Automatically, using the Cisco Auto-RP mechanism
- Automatically, using the Bootstrap Router mechanism with PIMv2

While the concept of Auto-RP seems very complex, the operation of auto RP is actually fairly straightforward. Each router that you configure to be an RP begins generating Cisco-RP-Announce messages addressed to the 224.0.1.39 group address. These announce messages are flooded through the network in a dense-mode fashion, ensuring that each router receives a copy. Next, the mapping agent for the network listens for the various announce messages and makes a decision as to which router is the RP.

In the event that there are multiple RPs (for redundancy), the candidate RP with the highest IP address is chosen as the RP for the network. The mapping agent then advertises this decision to the network in a Cisco-RP-Discovery message addressed to the 224.0.1.40 group address. Like the announce message, the discovery message is propagated in a dense-mode fashion throughout the network. Once all routers in the network receive the RP, Multicast operates using sparse-mode. This is the reason we need to enable Sparse-Dense mode forwarding. To complete this task, use the `ip pim accept-rp auto-rp` command on R1 and R4. This command configures these routers to accept join and register messages only for RPs that are in the Auto-RP cache. These cache entries are created after the RP information is flooded:

```
R1(config)#ip pim accept-rp auto-rp

R4(config)#ip pim accept-rp auto-rp
```

Next, use the `ip pim send-rp-announce` command on the router you want to become the RP. In this lab, that would be R1. This command causes the router to send an Auto-RP announcement message to the well-known group CISCO-RP-ANNOUNCE (224.0.1.39). This message announces the router as a candidate RP for all or specified Multicast groups:

```
R2(config)#interface loopback 0
R2(config-if)#ip address 2.2.2.2 255.255.255.255
R2(config-if)#ip pim sparse-dense-mode
R2(config-if)#exit
R2(config)#ip pim send-rp-announce loopback 0 scope 255
```

NOTE: You MUST advertise the Loopback 0 interface via EIGRP. If you enabled EIGRP for all networks using the `network 0.0.0.0` command, no additional configuration is necessary. However, if you explicitly enabled EIGRP for specific subnets, you need to also advertise the configured Loopback 0 interface via EIGRP; otherwise, no other router can reach this address.

When using this command, the scope specifies the TTL of these announcements. For example, if you specified a scope of 1, the packet would be sent out with a TTL of 1.

Finally, use the `ip pim send-rp-discovery` command on the router you want to become the RP mapping agent. In this lab, that would be R3. When Auto-RP is used, the following sequence of events occur:

The RP mapping agent (R3) listens on well-known group address CISCO-RP-ANNOUNCE (224.0.1.39), which candidate RPs (R2) send announcements to.

The RP mapping agent (R3) sends RP-to-group mappings in an Auto-RP discovery message to the well-known group CISCO-RP-DISCOVERY (224.0.1.40). The TTL value (determined by the scope) limits how many hops the message can take.

PIM designated routers (R1 and R4) listen to this group and use the RPs they learn about from the discovery message. This task is completed on R3 as follows:

```
R3(config)#interface loopback 0
R3(config-if)#ip address 3.3.3.3 255.255.255.255
R3(config-if)#ip pim sparse-dense-mode
R3(config-if)#exit
R3(config)#ip pim send-rp-discovery loopback 0 scope 255
```

NOTE: You MUST advertise the Loopback 0 interface via EIGRP. If you enabled EIGRP for all networks using the `network 0.0.0.0` command, no additional configuration is necessary. However, if you explicitly enabled EIGRP for specific subnets, you need to also advertise the configured Loopback 0 interface via EIGRP; otherwise, no other router can reach this address.

Next, use the `show ip pim autorp` command to view auto RP received and sent packets:

```
R1#show ip pim autorp
AutoRP Information:
  AutoRP is enabled.

PIM AutoRP Statistics: Sent/Received
  RP Announce: 0/0, RP Discovery: 0/3
```

Notice that R1 has received RP-Discovery messages. It has not sent out any other RP messages:

```
R2#show ip pim autorp
AutoRP Information:
  AutoRP is enabled.

PIM AutoRP Statistics: Sent/Received
  RP Announce: 24/0, RP Discovery: 0/3
```

Notice that R2 has sent out RP-Announce packets. It has also received RP-Discovery packets.

```
R3#show ip pim autorp
AutoRP Information:
  AutoRP is enabled.

PIM AutoRP Statistics: Sent/Received
  RP Announce: 0/6, RP Discovery: 9/0
```

Notice that R3 has received RP-Announce messages, and has sent out RP-Discovery messages:

```
R4#show ip pim autorp
AutoRP Information:
  AutoRP is enabled.

PIM AutoRP Statistics: Sent/Received
  RP Announce: 0/0, RP Discovery: 0/3
```

And finally, notice that R4 has only received RP-Discovery messages and sent out none:

Following this, verify RP-to-Group mappings using the `show ip pim rp` command:

```
R1#show ip pim rp
Group: 227.4.4.4, RP: 2.2.2.2, v2, v1, uptime 00:07:19, expires 00:02:40
Group: 227.1.1.1, RP: 2.2.2.2, v2, v1, uptime 00:07:19, expires 00:02:40

R2#show ip pim rp
Group: 227.4.4.4, RP: 2.2.2.2, v2, v1, next RP-reachable in 00:00:14
Group: 227.1.1.1, RP: 2.2.2.2, v2, v1, next RP-reachable in 00:00:14

R3#show ip pim rp
Group: 227.4.4.4, RP: 2.2.2.2, v2, v1, uptime 00:07:12, expires 00:02:43
Group: 227.1.1.1, RP: 2.2.2.2, v2, v1, uptime 00:07:12, expires 00:02:43

R4#show ip pim rp
Group: 227.4.4.4, RP: 2.2.2.2, v2, v1, uptime 00:07:07, expires 00:02:47
Group: 227.1.1.1, RP: 2.2.2.2, v2, v1, uptime 00:07:07, expires 00:02:47
```

Finally, complete this task by pinging from R1 to 227.4.4.4 and from R4 to 227.1.1.1

```
R1#ping 227.4.4.4

Type escape sequence to abort.
Sending 1, 100-byte ICMP Echos to 227.4.4.4, timeout is 2 seconds:

Reply to request 0 from 10.0.0.14, 32 ms

R4#ping 227.1.1.1

Type escape sequence to abort.
Sending 1, 100-byte ICMP Echos to 227.1.1.1, timeout is 2 seconds:

Reply to request 0 from 10.0.0.1, 48 ms
```

FINAL ROUTER CONFIGURATIONS

R1

```
R1#term len 0
R1#sh run
Building configuration...

Current configuration : 994 bytes
!
version 12.4
service timestamps debug datetime msec
service timestamps log datetime msec
no service password-encryption
```

```
!
hostname R1
!
boot-start-marker
boot-end-marker
!
no logging console
!
no aaa new-model
no network-clock-participate slot 1
no network-clock-participate wic 0
ip cef
!
no ip domain lookup
ip multicast-routing
ip auth-proxy max-nodata-conns 3
ip admission max-nodata-conns 3
!
interface FastEthernet0/0
 ip address 150.1.1.1 255.255.255.0
 ip pim sparse-dense-mode
 ip igmp join-group 227.1.1.1
 duplex auto
 speed auto
!
interface Serial0/0
 ip address 10.0.0.1 255.255.255.252
 ip pim sparse-dense-mode
 clock rate 2000000
!
interface Serial0/1
 no ip address
 shutdown
!
router eigrp 254
 network 0.0.0.0
 no auto-summary
!
ip forward-protocol nd
!
no ip http server
no ip http secure-server
ip pim accept-rp auto-rp
!
control-plane
!
line con 0
line aux 0
line vty 0 4
 login
!
end

R1#
```

R2

```
R2#term len 0
R2#sh run
Building configuration...

Current configuration : 1059 bytes
!
version 12.4
service timestamps debug datetime msec
service timestamps log datetime msec
no service password-encryption
!
hostname R2
!
boot-start-marker
boot-end-marker
!
no logging console
```

```
!
no aaa new-model
no network-clock-participate slot 1
no network-clock-participate wic 0
ip cef
!
no ip domain lookup
ip multicast-routing
ip auth-proxy max-nodata-conns 3
ip admission max-nodata-conns 3
!
interface Loopback0
 ip address 2.2.2.2 255.255.255.255
 ip pim sparse-dense-mode
!
interface FastEthernet0/0
 ip address 150.2.2.2 255.255.255.0
 duplex auto
 speed auto
!
interface Serial0/0
 ip address 10.0.0.2 255.255.255.252
 ip pim sparse-dense-mode
!
interface Serial0/1
 ip address 10.0.0.9 255.255.255.252
 ip pim sparse-dense-mode
!
router eigrp 254
 network 0.0.0.0
 no auto-summary
!
ip forward-protocol nd
!
no ip http server
no ip http secure-server
ip pim send-rp-announce Loopback0 scope 255
!
control-plane
!
line con 0
line aux 0
line vty 0 4
 login
!
end

R2#
```

R3

```
R3#term len 0
R3#sh run
Building configuration...

Current configuration : 1401 bytes
!
version 12.4
service timestamps debug datetime msec
service timestamps log datetime msec
no service password-encryption
!
hostname R3
!
boot-start-marker
boot-end-marker
!
no logging console
!
no aaa new-model
no network-clock-participate slot 1
no network-clock-participate wic 0
ip cef
!
```

```
no ip domain lookup
ip multicast-routing
ip auth-proxy max-nodata-conns 3
ip admission max-nodata-conns 3
!
interface Loopback0
 ip address 3.3.3.3 255.255.255.255
 ip pim sparse-dense-mode
!
interface FastEthernet0/0
 ip address 150.3.3.3 255.255.255.0
 duplex auto
 speed auto
!
interface Serial1/0
 no ip address
 shutdown
 clock rate 128000
!
interface Serial1/1
 ip address 10.0.0.10 255.255.255.252
 ip pim sparse-dense-mode
 clock rate 128000
!
interface Serial1/2
 ip address 10.0.0.13 255.255.255.252
 ip pim sparse-dense-mode
 clock rate 128000
!
interface Serial1/3
 no ip address
 shutdown
!
interface Serial1/4
 no ip address
 shutdown
!
interface Serial1/5
 no ip address
 shutdown
!
interface Serial1/6
 no ip address
 shutdown
!
interface Serial1/7
 no ip address
 shutdown
!
router eigrp 254
 network 0.0.0.0
 no auto-summary
!
ip forward-protocol nd
!
no ip http server
no ip http secure-server
ip pim send-rp-discovery Loopback0 scope 255
!
control-plane
!
line con 0
line aux 0
line vty 0 4
 login
!
end

R3#
```

R4

```
R4#term len 0
R4#sh run
Building configuration...

Current configuration : 975 bytes
!
version 12.4
service timestamps debug datetime msec
service timestamps log datetime msec
no service password-encryption
!
hostname R4
!
boot-start-marker
boot-end-marker
!
no logging console
!
no aaa new-model
no network-clock-participate slot 1
no network-clock-participate wic 0
ip cef
!
no ip domain lookup
ip multicast-routing
ip auth-proxy max-nodata-conns 3
ip admission max-nodata-conns 3
!
interface FastEthernet0/0
 ip address 150.4.4.4 255.255.255.0
 ip pim sparse-dense-mode
 ip igmp join-group 227.4.4.4
 duplex auto
 speed auto
!
interface Serial0/0
 ip address 10.0.0.14 255.255.255.252
 ip pim sparse-dense-mode
!
interface Serial0/1
 no ip address
 shutdown
!
router eigrp 254
 network 0.0.0.0
 no auto-summary
!
ip forward-protocol nd
!
no ip http server
no ip http secure-server
ip pim accept-rp auto-rp
!
control-plane
!
line con 0
line aux 0
line vty 0 4
 login
!
end

R4#
```

CCNP LAB 74

Branch Office Connectivity Lab

Lab Objective:

The focus of this lab is to understand branch office connectivity implementation and configuration. Additional technologies include IP routing, FHRPs, and IPsec VPNs.

Lab Topology:

The lab network topology is illustrated below:

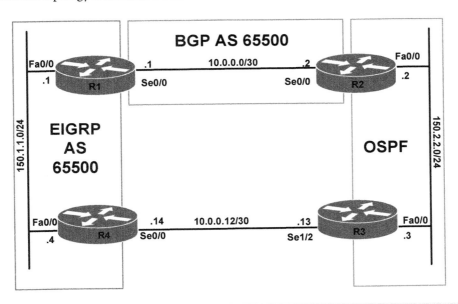

IMPORTANT NOTE: If you are using the www.howtonetwork.net racks, please bring up the LAN interfaces connected to the routers by issuing the no shutdown command on the connected switches. If you are using a home lab with no Switches, you can bring up the LAN interfaces using the following configurations on your routers:

```
interface fastethernet 0/0
  no keepalive
  loopback
  no shutdown
```

Alternately, you can simply connect the interfaces to a hub or switch if you have one available in your own lab.

Task 1

Configure hostnames, IP addressing on all routers as illustrated in the network topology.

Task 2

Configure IP routing as illustrated in the topology. Use AS 65500 for both BGP and EIGRP. Use OSPF process

ID 1 for OSPF. Do NOT enable any dynamic routing protocols on the R3-R4 link. However, ensure that R1 and R2 know about this subnet.

Ensure that all routers can each other. Implement the necessary route redistribution so that all routers can ping each other. However, you are NOT allowed to redistribute anything into BGP.
Verify the solution using the appropriate commands on all routers.

Task 3

Configure HSRP on the LAN segment between R1 and R4. Use a VIP of 150.1.1.254. Configure R1 with a priority of 105 and R4 with a priority of 100. Ensure that R4 becomes active gateway when R1s Serial 0/0 interface goes down. When R1s Serial0/0 interface comes up, R1 should wait 30 seconds before it assumes the role of active gateway. Verify your HSRP configuration.

Task 4

Assume that the link between R1 and R2 is secure; however, the link between R3 and R4 is not. Management requests that you configure an IPsec tunnel so that when the R1-R2 link is down, traffic between the 150.1.1.0/24 and 150.2.2.0/24 subnets is encrypted and sent across the R3-R4 link. Do NOT configure a GRE Tunnel. Configure the IPsec solution as follows:
- Use Advanced Encryption Standard (AES) as the encryption algorithm
- Use a 256-bit AES encryption key
- Use pre-shared key authentication with a shared key of CCNP2011
- Use Diffie-Hellman group 5

Test your solution and verify that R1 and R2 can ping each other from their LAN interfaces.

LAB VALIDATION

Task 1

Please refer to previous labs for basic IPv4, IPv6 addressing and hostname configuration. This will not be included in this section to avoid being redundant.

Task 2

The requirements of this task are straightforward. OSPF, EIGRP and BGP configuration as well as redistribution have been illustrated in previous labs. This task is completed as follows:

```
R1(config)#router eigrp 65500
R1(config-router)#no auto-summary
R1(config-router)#network 150.1.1.1 0.0.0.0
R1(config-router)#redistribute connected
R1(config-router)#redistribute bgp 65500
R1(config-router)#default-metric 1544 2000 255 1 1500
R1(config-router)#exit
R1(config)#router bgp 65500
R1(config-router)#bgp router-id 1.1.1.1
R1(config-router)#neighbor 10.0.0.2 remote-as 65500
R1(config-router)#network 150.1.1.0 mask 255.255.255.0
R1(config-router)#bgp redistribute-internal
R1(config-router)#exit

R2(config)#router ospf 1
R2(config-router)#router-id 2.2.2.2
R2(config-router)#network 150.2.2.2 0.0.0.0 area 0
R2(config-router)#redistribute connected subnets
R2(config-router)#redistribute bgp 65500 subnets
R2(config-router)#exit
R2(config)#router bgp 65500
R2(config-router)#bgp router-id 2.2.2.2
```

```
R2(config-router)#neighbor 10.0.0.1 remote-as 65500
R2(config-router)#bgp redistribute-internal
R2(config-router)#network 150.2.2.0 mask 255.255.255.0
R2(config-router)#exit

R3(config)#router ospf 1
R3(config-router)#router-id 3.3.3.3
R3(config-router)#network 150.2.2.3 0.0.0.0 area 0
R3(config-router)#redistribute connected subnets
R3(config-router)#exit

R4(config)#router eigrp 65500
R4(config-router)#no auto-summary
R4(config-router)#network 150.1.1.4 0.0.0.0
R4(config-router)#redistribute connected
R4(config-router)#exit
```

Following this, verify IP routing using the **show ip route** command on all routers:

```
R1#show ip route
Codes: C - connected, S - static, R - RIP, M - mobile, B - BGP
       D - EIGRP, EX - EIGRP external, O - OSPF, IA - OSPF inter area
       N1 - OSPF NSSA external type 1, N2 - OSPF NSSA external type 2
       E1 - OSPF external type 1, E2 - OSPF external type 2
       i - IS-IS, su - IS-IS summary, L1 - IS-IS level-1, L2 - IS-IS level-2
       ia - IS-IS inter area, * - candidate default, U - per-user static route
       o - ODR, P - periodic downloaded static route

Gateway of last resort is not set

     10.0.0.0/30 is subnetted, 2 subnets
D EX    10.0.0.12 [170/2172416] via 150.1.1.4, 00:01:28, FastEthernet0/0
C       10.0.0.0 is directly connected, Serial0/0
     150.1.0.0/24 is subnetted, 1 subnets
C       150.1.1.0 is directly connected, FastEthernet0/0
     150.2.0.0/24 is subnetted, 1 subnets
B       150.2.2.0 [200/0] via 10.0.0.2, 00:04:33

R2#show ip route
Codes: C - connected, S - static, R - RIP, M - mobile, B - BGP
       D - EIGRP, EX - EIGRP external, O - OSPF, IA - OSPF inter area
       N1 - OSPF NSSA external type 1, N2 - OSPF NSSA external type 2
       E1 - OSPF external type 1, E2 - OSPF external type 2
       i - IS-IS, su - IS-IS summary, L1 - IS-IS level-1, L2 - IS-IS level-2
       ia - IS-IS inter area, * - candidate default, U - per-user static route
       o - ODR, P - periodic downloaded static route

Gateway of last resort is not set

     10.0.0.0/30 is subnetted, 2 subnets
O E2    10.0.0.12 [110/20] via 150.2.2.3, 00:02:41, FastEthernet0/0
C       10.0.0.0 is directly connected, Serial0/0
     150.1.0.0/24 is subnetted, 1 subnets
B       150.1.1.0 [200/0] via 10.0.0.1, 00:04:36
     150.2.0.0/24 is subnetted, 1 subnets
C       150.2.2.0 is directly connected, FastEthernet0/0

R3#show ip route
Codes: C - connected, S - static, R - RIP, M - mobile, B - BGP
       D - EIGRP, EX - EIGRP external, O - OSPF, IA - OSPF inter area
       N1 - OSPF NSSA external type 1, N2 - OSPF NSSA external type 2
       E1 - OSPF external type 1, E2 - OSPF external type 2
       i - IS-IS, su - IS-IS summary, L1 - IS-IS level-1, L2 - IS-IS level-2
       ia - IS-IS inter area, * - candidate default, U - per-user static route
       o - ODR, P - periodic downloaded static route

Gateway of last resort is not set

     10.0.0.0/30 is subnetted, 2 subnets
C       10.0.0.12 is directly connected, Serial1/2
O E2    10.0.0.0 [110/20] via 150.2.2.2, 00:02:43, FastEthernet0/0
     150.1.0.0/24 is subnetted, 1 subnets
O E2    150.1.1.0 [110/1] via 150.2.2.2, 00:02:43, FastEthernet0/0
     150.2.0.0/24 is subnetted, 1 subnets
C       150.2.2.0 is directly connected, FastEthernet0/0
```

```
R4#show ip route
Codes: C - connected, S - static, R - RIP, M - mobile, B - BGP
       D - EIGRP, EX - EIGRP external, O - OSPF, IA - OSPF inter area
       N1 - OSPF NSSA external type 1, N2 - OSPF NSSA external type 2
       E1 - OSPF external type 1, E2 - OSPF external type 2
       i - IS-IS, su - IS-IS summary, L1 - IS-IS level-1, L2 - IS-IS level-2
       ia - IS-IS inter area, * - candidate default, U - per-user static route
       o - ODR, P - periodic downloaded static route

Gateway of last resort is not set

     10.0.0.0/30 is subnetted, 2 subnets
C       10.0.0.12 is directly connected, Serial0/0
D EX    10.0.0.0 [170/2172416] via 150.1.1.1, 00:01:38, FastEthernet0/0
     150.1.0.0/24 is subnetted, 1 subnets
C       150.1.1.0 is directly connected, FastEthernet0/0
     150.2.0.0/24 is subnetted, 1 subnets
D EX    150.2.2.0 [170/2172416] via 150.1.1.1, 00:01:38, FastEthernet0/0
```

Finally, ping from all routers to every other router to verify your solution. For brevity, the solution will show pings from R4 to every other router in the network:

```
R4#ping 150.1.1.1

Type escape sequence to abort.
Sending 5, 100-byte ICMP Echos to 150.1.1.1, timeout is 2 seconds:
!!!!!
Success rate is 100 percent (5/5), round-trip min/avg/max = 1/2/4 ms

R4#ping 10.0.0.2

Type escape sequence to abort.
Sending 5, 100-byte ICMP Echos to 10.0.0.2, timeout is 2 seconds:
!!!!!
Success rate is 100 percent (5/5), round-trip min/avg/max = 1/3/4 ms

R4#ping 150.2.2.3

Type escape sequence to abort.
Sending 5, 100-byte ICMP Echos to 150.2.2.3, timeout is 2 seconds:
!!!!!
Success rate is 100 percent (5/5), round-trip min/avg/max = 1/3/4 ms
```

Task 3

The core requirements of this task are straightforward. To ensure that R1 re-assumes its role as the primary gateway after its Serial0/0 link comes up, you can specify this parameter in the Enhanced Object Tracking configuration or using HSRP commands. This lab solution shows the delay value being specified using HSRP commands:

```
R1(config)#track 1 interface serial 0/0 line-protocol
R1(config-track)#exit
R1(config)#interface fastethernet 0/0
R1(config-if)#standby 1 ip 150.1.1.254
R1(config-if)#standby 1 priority 105
R1(config-if)#standby 1 preempt
R1(config-if)#standby 1 preempt delay minimum 30
R1(config-if)#standby 1 track 1 decrement 10
R1(config-if)#exit
```

If you wanted to use EOT, you could also complete this section as follows:

```
R1(config)#track 1 interface serial 0/0 line-protocol
R1(config-track)#delay up 30
R1(config-track)#exit
```

Complete this task on R4 as follows:

```
R4(config)#interface fastethernet 0/0
R4(config-if)#standby 1 ip 150.1.1.254
R4(config-if)#standby 1 preempt
R4(config-if)#exit
```

Verify your HSRP configuration using the show standby commands:

```
R1#show standby fastethernet 0/0
FastEthernet0/0 - Group 1
  State is Active
    2 state changes, last state change 00:03:08
  Virtual IP address is 150.1.1.254
  Active virtual MAC address is 0000.0c07.ac01
    Local virtual MAC address is 0000.0c07.ac01 (v1 default)
  Hello time 3 sec, hold time 10 sec
    Next hello sent in 0.820 secs
  Preemption enabled, delay min 30 secs
  Active router is local
  Standby router is 150.1.1.4, priority 100 (expires in 9.916 sec)
  Priority 105 (configured 105)
    Track object 1 state Up decrement 10
  IP redundancy name is "hsrp-Fa0/0-1" (default)

R4#show standby fastethernet 0/0
FastEthernet0/0 - Group 1
  State is Standby
    1 state change, last state change 00:00:34
  Virtual IP address is 150.1.1.254
  Active virtual MAC address is 0000.0c07.ac01
    Local virtual MAC address is 0000.0c07.ac01 (v1 default)
  Hello time 3 sec, hold time 10 sec
    Next hello sent in 1.484 secs
  Preemption enabled
  Active router is 150.1.1.1, priority 105 (expires in 9.384 sec)
  Standby router is local
  Priority 100 (default 100)
  IP redundancy name is "hsrp-Fa0/0-1" (default)
```

Task 4

The requirements of this task are two-fold. First, you need to configure a site-to-site IPsec VPN between R3 and R4. Second, you need to ensure that traffic is sent across this tunnel when the WAN link between R1 and R2 is down. Additionally, because the subnets are advertised by internal BGP, they will have an administrative distance of 200. To ensure that this path is only used as a backup, you need to modify the default administrative distance values on R1 and R2 as well. This task is completed as follows:

```
R1(config)#router eigrp 65500
R1(config-router)#distance eigrp 90 210
R1(config-router)#exit

R2(config)#router ospf 1
R2(config-router)#distance ospf external 210
R2(config-router)#exit

R3(config)#ip route 150.1.1.0 255.255.255.0 10.0.0.14 254
R3(config)#router ospf 1
R3(config-router)#redistribute static subnets
R3(config-router)#exit
R3(config)#ip access-list extended SECURE-TRAFFIC
R3(config-ext-nacl)#permit ip 150.2.2.0 0.0.0.255 150.1.1.0 0.0.0.255
R3(config-ext-nacl)#exit
R3(config)#crypto isakmp policy 1
R3(config-isakmp)#encryption aes 256
R3(config-isakmp)#authentication pre-share
R3(config-isakmp)#group 5
R3(config-isakmp)#exit
R3(config)#crypto isakmp key CCNP2011 address 10.0.0.14
R3(config)#crypto ipsec transform-set AES-SECURE esp-aes 256
R3(cfg-crypto-trans)#exit
R3(config)#crypto map BACKUP-SOLUTION 1 ipsec-isakmp
% NOTE: This new crypto map will remain disabled until a peer
        and a valid access list have been configured.
R3(config-crypto-map)#set peer 10.0.0.14
R3(config-crypto-map)#set transform-set AES-SECURE
R3(config-crypto-map)#match address SECURE-TRAFFIC
R3(config-crypto-map)#exit
R3(config)#interface serial 1/2
R3(config-if)#crypto map BACKUP-SOLUTION
R3(config-if)#exit
```

```
R4(config)#ip route 150.2.2.0 255.255.255.0 10.0.0.13 254
R4(config)#router eigrp 65500
R4(config-router)#redistribute static
R4(config-router)#exit
R4(config)#ip access-list extended SECURE-TRAFFIC
R4(config-ext-nacl)#permit ip 150.1.1.0 0.0.0.255 150.2.2.0 0.0.0.255
R4(config-ext-nacl)#exit
R4(config)#crypto isakmp policy 1
R4(config-isakmp)#encryption aes 256
R4(config-isakmp)#authentication pre-share
R4(config-isakmp)#group 5
R4(config-isakmp)#exit
R4(config)#crypto isakmp key CCNP2011 address 10.0.0.13
R4(config)#crypto ipsec transform-set AES-SECURE esp-aes 256
R4(cfg-crypto-trans)#exit
R4(config)#crypto map BACKUP-SOLUTION 1 ipsec-isakmp
% NOTE: This new crypto map will remain disabled until a peer
        and a valid access list have been configured.
R4(config-crypto-map)#set peer 10.0.0.13
R4(config-crypto-map)#set transform-set AES-SECURE
R4(config-crypto-map)#match address SECURE-TRAFFIC
R4(config-crypto-map)#exit
R4(config)#interface serial 0/0
R4(config-if)#crypto map BACKUP-SOLUTION
R4(config-if)#exit
```

Next, verify your configuration using the show crypto commands:

```
R4#show crypto isakmp policy

Global IKE policy
Protection suite of priority 1
   encryption algorithm:   AES - Advanced Encryption Standard (256 bit keys).
   hash algorithm:         Secure Hash Standard
   authentication method:  Pre-Shared Key
   Diffie-Hellman group:   #5 (1536 bit)
   lifetime:               86400 seconds, no volume limit
Default protection suite
   encryption algorithm:   DES - Data Encryption Standard (56 bit keys).
   hash algorithm:         Secure Hash Standard
   authentication method:  Rivest-Shamir-Adleman Signature
   Diffie-Hellman group:   #1 (768 bit)
   lifetime:               86400 seconds, no volume limit

R4#show crypto map
Crypto Map "BACKUP-SOLUTION" 1 ipsec-isakmp
        Peer = 10.0.0.13
        Extended IP access list SECURE-TRAFFIC
            access-list SECURE-TRAFFIC permit ip 150.1.1.0 0.0.0.255 150.2.2.0
0.0.0.255
        Current peer: 10.0.0.13
        Security association lifetime: 4608000 kilobytes/3600 seconds
        PFS (Y/N): N
        Transform sets={
                AES-SECURE,
        }
        Interfaces using crypto map BACKUP-SOLUTION:
                Serial0/0
```

Finally, test your solution by disabling the R1-R2 link and checking routing on R1 and R2 for the 150.2.2.0/24 and 150.1.1.0/24 subnets. Prior to this, the routing for the subnets is as follows:

```
R1#show ip route 150.2.2.0 255.255.255.0
Routing entry for 150.2.2.0/24
  Known via "bgp 65500", distance 200, metric 0, type internal
  Redistributing via eigrp 65500
  Advertised by eigrp 65500
  Last update from 10.0.0.2 00:02:10 ago
  Routing Descriptor Blocks:
  * 10.0.0.2, from 10.0.0.2, 00:02:10 ago
      Route metric is 0, traffic share count is 1
      AS Hops 0

R2#show ip route 150.1.1.0 255.255.255.0
```

```
Routing entry for 150.1.1.0/24
  Known via "bgp 65500", distance 200, metric 0, type internal
  Redistributing via ospf 1
  Advertised by ospf 1 subnets
  Last update from 10.0.0.1 00:01:30 ago
  Routing Descriptor Blocks:
  * 10.0.0.1, from 10.0.0.1, 00:01:30 ago
      Route metric is 0, traffic share count is 1
      AS Hops 0

R3#show ip route 150.1.1.0 255.255.255.0
Routing entry for 150.1.1.0/24
  Known via "ospf 1", distance 110, metric 1, type extern 2, forward metric 1
  Last update from 150.2.2.2 on FastEthernet0/0, 00:01:45 ago
  Routing Descriptor Blocks:
  * 150.2.2.2, from 2.2.2.2, 00:01:45 ago, via FastEthernet0/0
      Route metric is 1, traffic share count is 1

R4#show ip route 150.2.2.0 255.255.255.0
Routing entry for 150.2.2.0/24
  Known via "eigrp 65500", distance 170, metric 2172416, type external
  Redistributing via eigrp 65500
  Last update from 150.1.1.1 on FastEthernet0/0, 00:03:48 ago
  Routing Descriptor Blocks:
  * 150.1.1.1, from 150.1.1.1, 00:03:48 ago, via FastEthernet0/0
      Route metric is 2172416, traffic share count is 1
      Total delay is 20100 microseconds, minimum bandwidth is 1544 Kbit
      Reliability 255/255, minimum MTU 1500 bytes
      Loading 1/255, Hops 1
```

Next, shut down the WAN link that connects routers R1 and R2:

```
R1(config)#interface serial 0/0
R1(config-if)#shutdown
```

After this, verify that routing information is correct:

```
R1#show ip route 150.2.2.0 255.255.255.0
Routing entry for 150.2.2.0/24
  Known via "eigrp 65500", distance 170, metric 2172416, type external
  Redistributing via eigrp 65500
  Last update from 150.1.1.4 on FastEthernet0/0, 00:00:09 ago
  Routing Descriptor Blocks:
  * 150.1.1.4, from 150.1.1.4, 00:00:09 ago, via FastEthernet0/0
      Route metric is 2172416, traffic share count is 1
      Total delay is 20100 microseconds, minimum bandwidth is 1544 Kbit
      Reliability 255/255, minimum MTU 1500 bytes
      Loading 1/255, Hops 1

R2#show ip route 150.1.1.0 255.255.255.0
Routing entry for 150.1.1.0/24
  Known via "ospf 1", distance 110, metric 20, type extern 2, forward metric 1
  Last update from 150.2.2.3 on FastEthernet0/0, 00:00:56 ago
  Routing Descriptor Blocks:
  * 150.2.2.3, from 3.3.3.3, 00:00:56 ago, via FastEthernet0/0
      Route metric is 20, traffic share count is 1
```

Next, ping between R1 and R2:

```
R1#ping 150.2.2.2 repeat 20 size 1500

Type escape sequence to abort.
Sending 20, 1500-byte ICMP Echos to 150.2.2.2, timeout is 2 seconds:
!!!!!!!!!!!!!!!!!!!!
Success rate is 100 percent (20/20), round-trip min/avg/max = 220/222/224 ms

R2#ping 150.1.1.1 repeat 20 size 1500

Type escape sequence to abort.
Sending 20, 1500-byte ICMP Echos to 150.1.1.1, timeout is 2 seconds:
!!!!!!!!!!!!!!!!!!!!
Success rate is 100 percent (20/20), round-trip min/avg/max = 220/222/224 ms
```

Finally, view encryption status and statistics using the show crypto commands:

R3#show crypto ipsec sa

```
interface: Serial1/2
    Crypto map tag: BACKUP-SOLUTION, local addr 10.0.0.13

   protected vrf: (none)
   local  ident (addr/mask/prot/port): (150.2.2.0/255.255.255.0/0/0)
   remote ident (addr/mask/prot/port): (150.1.1.0/255.255.255.0/0/0)
   current_peer 10.0.0.14 port 500
     PERMIT, flags={origin_is_acl,}
   #pkts encaps: 80, #pkts encrypt: 80, #pkts digest: 80
   #pkts decaps: 80, #pkts decrypt: 80, #pkts verify: 80
   #pkts compressed: 0, #pkts decompressed: 0
   #pkts not compressed: 0, #pkts compr. failed: 0
   #pkts not decompressed: 0, #pkts decompress failed: 0
   #send errors 0, #recv errors 0

    local crypto endpt.: 10.0.0.13, remote crypto endpt.: 10.0.0.14
    path mtu 1500, ip mtu 1500, ip mtu idb Serial1/2
    current outbound spi: 0x8E8C5624(2391561764)

    inbound esp sas:
     spi: 0x127922C2(309928642)
       transform: esp-256-aes ,
       in use settings ={Tunnel, }
       conn id: 2001, flow_id: SW:1, crypto map: BACKUP-SOLUTION
       sa timing: remaining key lifetime (k/sec): (4607493/3273)
       IV size: 16 bytes
       replay detection support: N
       Status: ACTIVE

    inbound ah sas:

    inbound pcp sas:

    outbound esp sas:
     spi: 0x8E8C5624(2391561764)
       transform: esp-256-aes ,
       in use settings ={Tunnel, }
       conn id: 2002, flow_id: SW:2, crypto map: BACKUP-SOLUTION
       sa timing: remaining key lifetime (k/sec): (4607495/3265)
       IV size: 16 bytes
       replay detection support: N
       Status: ACTIVE

    outbound ah sas:

    outbound pcp sas:
```

R4#show crypto ipsec sa

```
interface: Serial0/0
    Crypto map tag: BACKUP-SOLUTION, local addr 10.0.0.14

   protected vrf: (none)
   local  ident (addr/mask/prot/port): (150.1.1.0/255.255.255.0/0/0)
   remote ident (addr/mask/prot/port): (150.2.2.0/255.255.255.0/0/0)
   current_peer 10.0.0.13 port 500
     PERMIT, flags={origin_is_acl,}
   #pkts encaps: 80, #pkts encrypt: 80, #pkts digest: 80
   #pkts decaps: 80, #pkts decrypt: 80, #pkts verify: 80
   #pkts compressed: 0, #pkts decompressed: 0
   #pkts not compressed: 0, #pkts compr. failed: 0
   #pkts not decompressed: 0, #pkts decompress failed: 0
   #send errors 0, #recv errors 0

    local crypto endpt.: 10.0.0.14, remote crypto endpt.: 10.0.0.13
    path mtu 1500, ip mtu 1500, ip mtu idb Serial0/0
    current outbound spi: 0x127922C2(309928642)

    inbound esp sas:
     spi: 0x8E8C5624(2391561764)
       transform: esp-256-aes ,
       in use settings ={Tunnel, }
       conn id: 2001, flow_id: SW:1, crypto map: BACKUP-SOLUTION
       sa timing: remaining key lifetime (k/sec): (4482975/3270)
       IV size: 16 bytes
```

```
           replay detection support: N
           Status: ACTIVE

       inbound ah sas:

       inbound pcp sas:

       outbound esp sas:
        spi: 0x127922C2(309928642)
           transform: esp-256-aes ,
           in use settings ={Tunnel, }
           conn id: 2002, flow_id: SW:2, crypto map: BACKUP-SOLUTION
           sa timing: remaining key lifetime (k/sec): (4482973/3269)
           IV size: 16 bytes
           replay detection support: N
           Status: ACTIVE

       outbound ah sas:

       outbound pcp sas:

R3#show crypto session detail
Crypto session current status

Code: C - IKE Configuration mode, D - Dead Peer Detection
K - Keepalives, N - NAT-traversal, X - IKE Extended Authentication

Interface: Serial1/2
Session status: UP-ACTIVE
Peer: 10.0.0.14 port 500 fvrf: (none) ivrf: (none)
        Phase1_id: 10.0.0.14
        Desc: (none)
   IKE SA: local 10.0.0.13/500 remote 10.0.0.14/500 Active
           Capabilities:(none) connid:1 lifetime:23:53:37
   IPSEC FLOW: permit ip 150.2.2.0/255.255.255.0 150.1.1.0/255.255.255.0
        Active SAs: 2, origin: crypto map
        Inbound:  #pkts dec'ed 80 drop 0 life (KB/Sec) 4607493/3219
        Outbound: #pkts enc'ed 80 drop 0 life (KB/Sec) 4607495/3219

R4#show crypto session detail
Crypto session current status

Code: C - IKE Configuration mode, D - Dead Peer Detection
K - Keepalives, N - NAT-traversal, X - IKE Extended Authentication

Interface: Serial0/0
Session status: UP-ACTIVE
Peer: 10.0.0.13 port 500 fvrf: (none) ivrf: (none)
        Phase1_id: 10.0.0.13
        Desc: (none)
   IKE SA: local 10.0.0.14/500 remote 10.0.0.13/500 Active
           Capabilities:(none) connid:1 lifetime:23:53:49
   IPSEC FLOW: permit ip 150.1.1.0/255.255.255.0 150.2.2.0/255.255.255.0
        Active SAs: 2, origin: crypto map
        Inbound:  #pkts dec'ed 80 drop 0 life (KB/Sec) 4482975/3230
        Outbound: #pkts enc'ed 80 drop 0 life (KB/Sec) 4482973/3230
```

FINAL ROUTER CONFIGURATIONS

R1

```
R1#term len 0
R1#sh run
Building configuration...

Current configuration : 1339 bytes
!
version 12.4
service timestamps debug datetime msec
service timestamps log datetime msec
no service password-encryption
!
hostname R1
!
boot-start-marker
boot-end-marker
```

```
!
no logging console
!
no aaa new-model
no network-clock-participate slot 1
no network-clock-participate wic 0
ip cef
!
no ip domain lookup
ip auth-proxy max-nodata-conns 3
ip admission max-nodata-conns 3
!
track 1 interface Serial0/0 line-protocol
!
interface FastEthernet0/0
 ip address 150.1.1.1 255.255.255.0
 duplex auto
 speed auto
 standby 1 ip 150.1.1.254
 standby 1 priority 105
 standby 1 preempt delay minimum 30
 standby 1 track 1
!
interface Serial0/0
 ip address 10.0.0.1 255.255.255.252
 clock rate 2000000
!
interface Serial0/1
 no ip address
 shutdown
!
router eigrp 65500
 redistribute connected
 redistribute bgp 65500
 network 150.1.1.1 0.0.0.0
 default-metric 1544 2000 255 1 1500
 distance eigrp 90 210
 no auto-summary
!
router bgp 65500
 no synchronization
 bgp router-id 1.1.1.1
 bgp log-neighbor-changes
 bgp redistribute-internal
 network 150.1.1.0 mask 255.255.255.0
 neighbor 10.0.0.2 remote-as 65500
 no auto-summary
!
ip forward-protocol nd
!
no ip http server
no ip http secure-server
!
control-plane
!
line con 0
line aux 0
line vty 0 4
 login
!
end

R1#
```

R2

```
R2#term len 0
R2#sh run
Building configuration...

Current configuration : 1181 bytes
!
version 12.4
service timestamps debug datetime msec
service timestamps log datetime msec
no service password-encryption
!
hostname R2
!
boot-start-marker
```

```
boot-end-marker
!
no logging console
!
no aaa new-model
no network-clock-participate slot 1
no network-clock-participate wic 0
ip cef
!
no ip domain lookup
ip auth-proxy max-nodata-conns 3
ip admission max-nodata-conns 3
!
interface FastEthernet0/0
 ip address 150.2.2.2 255.255.255.0
 duplex auto
 speed auto
!
interface Serial0/0
 ip address 10.0.0.2 255.255.255.252
!
interface Serial0/1
 no ip address
 shutdown
!
router ospf 1
 router-id 2.2.2.2
 log-adjacency-changes
 redistribute connected subnets
 redistribute bgp 65500 subnets
 network 150.2.2.2 0.0.0.0 area 0
 distance ospf external 210
!
router bgp 65500
 no synchronization
 bgp router-id 2.2.2.2
 bgp log-neighbor-changes
 bgp redistribute-internal
 network 150.2.2.0 mask 255.255.255.0
 neighbor 10.0.0.1 remote-as 65500
 no auto-summary
!
ip forward-protocol nd
!
no ip http server
no ip http secure-server
!
control-plane
!
line con 0
line aux 0
line vty 0 4
 login
!
end

R2#
```

R3

```
R3#term len 0
R3#sh run
Building configuration...

Current configuration : 1752 bytes
!
version 12.4
service timestamps debug datetime msec
service timestamps log datetime msec
no service password-encryption
!
hostname R3
!
boot-start-marker
boot-end-marker
!
no logging console
!
no aaa new-model
no network-clock-participate slot 1
no network-clock-participate wic 0
```

```
 ip cef
!
no ip domain lookup
ip auth-proxy max-nodata-conns 3
ip admission max-nodata-conns 3
!
crypto isakmp policy 1
 encr aes 256
 authentication pre-share
 group 5
crypto isakmp key CCNP2011 address 10.0.0.14
!
crypto ipsec transform-set AES-SECURE esp-aes 256
!
crypto map BACKUP-SOLUTION 1 ipsec-isakmp
 set peer 10.0.0.14
 set transform-set AES-SECURE
 match address SECURE-TRAFFIC
!
interface FastEthernet0/0
 ip address 150.2.2.3 255.255.255.0
 duplex auto
 speed auto
!
interface Serial1/0
 no ip address
 shutdown
 clock rate 128000
!
interface Serial1/1
 no ip address
 shutdown
 clock rate 128000
!
interface Serial1/2
 ip address 10.0.0.13 255.255.255.252
 clock rate 128000
 crypto map BACKUP-SOLUTION
!
interface Serial1/3
 no ip address
 shutdown
!
interface Serial1/4
 no ip address
 shutdown
!
interface Serial1/5
 no ip address
 shutdown
!
interface Serial1/6
 no ip address
 shutdown
!
interface Serial1/7
 no ip address
 shutdown
!
router ospf 1
 router-id 3.3.3.3
 log-adjacency-changes
 redistribute connected subnets
 redistribute static subnets
 network 150.2.2.3 0.0.0.0 area 0
!
ip forward-protocol nd
ip route 150.1.1.0 255.255.255.0 10.0.0.14 254
!
no ip http server
no ip http secure-server
!
ip access-list extended SECURE-TRAFFIC
 permit ip 150.2.2.0 0.0.0.255 150.1.1.0 0.0.0.255
!
control-plane
!
line con 0
line aux 0
line vty 0 4
 login
!
end
R3#
```

R4

```
R4#term len 0
R4#sh run
Building configuration...

Current configuration : 1415 bytes
!
version 12.4
service timestamps debug datetime msec
service timestamps log datetime msec
no service password-encryption
!
hostname R4
!
boot-start-marker
boot-end-marker
!
no logging console
!
no aaa new-model
no network-clock-participate slot 1
no network-clock-participate wic 0
ip cef
!
no ip domain lookup
ip auth-proxy max-nodata-conns 3
ip admission max-nodata-conns 3
!
crypto isakmp policy 1
 encr aes 256
 authentication pre-share
 group 5
crypto isakmp key CCNP2011 address 10.0.0.13
!
crypto ipsec transform-set AES-SECURE esp-aes 256
!
crypto map BACKUP-SOLUTION 1 ipsec-isakmp
 set peer 10.0.0.13
 set transform-set AES-SECURE
 match address SECURE-TRAFFIC
!
interface FastEthernet0/0
 ip address 150.1.1.4 255.255.255.0
 duplex auto
 speed auto
 standby 1 ip 150.1.1.254
 standby 1 preempt
!
interface Serial0/0
 ip address 10.0.0.14 255.255.255.252
 crypto map BACKUP-SOLUTION
!
interface Serial0/1
 no ip address
 shutdown
!
router eigrp 65500
 redistribute connected
 redistribute static
 network 150.1.1.4 0.0.0.0
 no auto-summary
!
ip forward-protocol nd
ip route 150.2.2.0 255.255.255.0 10.0.0.13 254
!
no ip http server
no ip http secure-server
!
ip access-list extended SECURE-TRAFFIC
 permit ip 150.1.1.0 0.0.0.255 150.2.2.0 0.0.0.255
!
control-plane
!
line con 0
line aux 0
line vty 0 4
 login
!
end

R4#
```

CCNP LAB 75

Branch Office Connectivity Lab

Lab Objective:

The focus of this lab is to understand branch office connectivity implementation and configuration. Additional technologies include IP routing, tunnels, and IPsec VPNs.

Lab Topology:

The lab network topology is illustrated below:

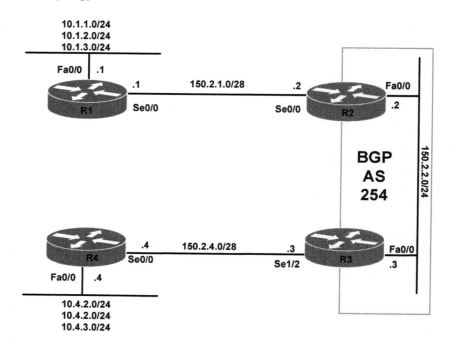

> **IMPORTANT NOTE:** If you are using the www.howtonetwork.net racks, please bring up the LAN interfaces connected to the routers by issuing the `no shutdown` command on the connected switches. If you are using a home lab with no Switches, you can bring up the LAN interfaces using the following configurations on your routers:
>
> ```
> interface fastethernet 0/0
>   no keepalive
>   loopback
>   no shutdown
> ```
>
> Alternately, you can simply connect the interfaces to a hub or switch if you have one available in your own lab.

Task 1

Configure hostnames, IP addressing on all routers as illustrated in the network topology.

Task 2

Configure BGP on R2 and R3 as illustrated in the topology. Ensure that the R1-R2 and the R3-R3 WAN subnets are advertised. Verify your configuration using the appropriate commands.

Task 3

Configure a GRE tunnel between R1 and R4. Enable OSPF and advertise the LAN subnets that are connected to these routers. Verify your configuration using the appropriate commands.

Task 4

Management is concerned about security over the GRE tunnel. They have requested that the GRE tunnel itself be encrypted using IPsec to allow for secure connectivity between the R1 and R4 subnets across this tunnel. Configure the IPsec solution as follows:
*   Use Triple Digital Encryption Standard (3DES) as the encryption algorithm
*   Use pre-shared key authentication with a shared key of CCNP2011
*   Use Diffie-Hellman group 2

Due to the relatively complex nature of this task, the following section includes a bank of commands that you can use to completed this task. Your task is to figure out which of these commands to apply where. The bank of available commands is as follows:
*   The `crypto isakmp policy` command
*   The `crypto isakmp key` command
*   The `crypto ipsec transform-set` command and `mode transport` subcommand
*   The `crypto ipsec profile` command and `set transform-set` subcommand
*   The `tunnel mode ipsec ipv4` command
*   The `tunnel protection ipsec profile` command

Test your solution and verify that R1 and R2 can ping each other from their LAN interfaces.

LAB VALIDATION

Task 1

Please refer to previous labs for basic IPv4, IPv6 addressing and hostname configuration. This will not be included in this section to avoid being redundant.

Task 2

The requirements in this task are straightforward. Because basic BGP configuration has been illustrated in detail in previous labs, this configuration is omitted for brevity. Following the configuration, your routing tables on R2 and R3 should show the following IP route entries:

```
R2#show ip route bgp
     150.2.0.0/16 is variably subnetted, 3 subnets, 2 masks
B       150.2.4.0/28 [200/0] via 150.2.2.3, 00:00:14

R3#show ip route bgp
     150.2.0.0/16 is variably subnetted, 3 subnets, 2 masks
B       150.2.1.0/28 [200/0] via 150.2.2.2, 00:00:26
```

Task 3

In order to complete this task, several actions are required. First, to allow for the configuration of a GRE tunnel between R1 and R4, you need to configure static routes for these routers' links to R2 and R3, i.e. their WAN links. Next, configure the GRE tunnel and enable OSPF for all the connected subnets. This task is completed as follows:

```
R1(config)#ip route 150.2.4.4 255.255.255.255 serial 0/0
R1(config)#router ospf 1
R1(config-router)#router-id 1.1.1.1
R1(config-router)#exit
R1(config)#interface tunnel 0
R1(config-if)#ip address 192.168.1.1 255.255.255.0
R1(config-if)#tunnel source serial 0/0
R1(config-if)#tunnel destination 150.2.4.4
R1(config-if)#ip ospf 1 area 0
R1(config-if)#exit
R1(config)#interface fastethernet 0/0
R1(config-if)#ip ospf 1 area 1
R1(config-if)#exit

R4(config)#ip route 150.2.1.1 255.255.255.255 serial 0/0
R4(config)#router ospf 4
R4(config-router)#router-id 4.4.4.4
R4(config-router)#exit
R4(config)#interface tunnel 0
R4(config-if)#ip address 192.168.1.4 255.255.255.0
R4(config-if)#tunnel source serial 0/0
R4(config-if)#tunnel destination 150.2.1.1
R4(config-if)#ip ospf 4 area 0
R4(config-if)#exit
R4(config)#interface fastethernet 0/0
R4(config-if)#ip ospf 4 area 4
R4(config-if)#exit
```

Next, verify your configuration by checking OSPF adjacency states. This also confirms whether the GRE tunnel between R1 and R4 is up and operational as well:

```
R1#show ip ospf neighbor

Neighbor ID     Pri   State         Dead Time   Address        Interface
4.4.4.4           0   FULL/  -      00:00:35    192.168.1.4    Tunnel0

R4#show ip ospf neighbor

Neighbor ID     Pri   State         Dead Time   Address        Interface
1.1.1.1           0   FULL/  -      00:00:32    192.168.1.1    Tunnel0
```

Finally, verify that the LAN subnets are advertised as configured:

```
R1#show ip route ospf
      10.0.0.0/24 is subnetted, 6 subnets
O IA    10.4.2.0 [110/11112] via 192.168.1.4, 00:03:40, Tunnel0
O IA    10.4.3.0 [110/11112] via 192.168.1.4, 00:03:40, Tunnel0
O IA    10.4.1.0 [110/11112] via 192.168.1.4, 00:03:40, Tunnel0

R4#show ip route ospf
      10.0.0.0/24 is subnetted, 6 subnets
O IA    10.1.3.0 [110/11112] via 192.168.1.1, 00:03:52, Tunnel0
O IA    10.1.2.0 [110/11112] via 192.168.1.1, 00:03:52, Tunnel0
O IA    10.1.1.0 [110/11112] via 192.168.1.1, 00:03:52, Tunnel0
```

Additionally, ping between the LAN subnets to confirm LAN-to-LAN reachability:

```
R1#ping 10.4.1.4 source 10.1.1.1 repeat 10 size 1500
Type escape sequence to abort.
Sending 10, 1500-byte ICMP Echos to 10.4.1.4, timeout is 2 seconds:
Packet sent with a source address of 10.1.1.1
!!!!!!!!!!
Success rate is 100 percent (10/10), round-trip min/avg/max = 208/212/216 ms
```

Task 4

The requirements of this task are a little complex; however, you have the bank of commands to use to complete this task. Using this bank, this task is completed as follows:

```
R1(config)#crypto isakmp policy 1
R1(config-isakmp)#encryption 3des
R1(config-isakmp)#authentication pre-share
```

```
R1(config-isakmp)#group 2
R1(config-isakmp)#exit
R1(config)#crypto isakmp key CCNP2011 address 150.2.4.4
R1(config)#crypto ipsec transform-set TRIPLE-DES esp-3des
R1(cfg-crypto-trans)#mode transport
R1(cfg-crypto-trans)#exit
R1(config)#crypto ipsec profile ENCRYPT-GRE
R1(ipsec-profile)#set transform-set TRIPLE-DES
R1(ipsec-profile)#exit
R1(config)#interface tunnel 0
R1(config-if)#tunnel mode ipsec ipv4
R1(config-if)#tunnel protection ipsec profile ENCRYPT-GRE
R1(config-if)#exit

R4(config)#crypto isakmp policy 1
R4(config-isakmp)#encryption 3des
R4(config-isakmp)#authentication pre-share
R4(config-isakmp)#group 2
R4(config-isakmp)#exit
R4(config)#crypto isakmp key CCNP2011 address 150.2.1.1
R4(config)#crypto ipsec transform-set TRIPLE-DES esp-3des
R4(cfg-crypto-trans)#mode transport
R4(cfg-crypto-trans)#exit
R4(config)#crypto ipsec profile ENCRYPT-GRE
R4(ipsec-profile)#set transform-set TRIPLE-DES
R4(ipsec-profile)#exit
R4(config)#interface tunnel 0
R4(config-if)#tunnel mode ipsec ipv4
R4(config-if)#tunnel protection ipsec profile ENCRYPT-GRE
R4(config-if)#exit
```

Following this, verify your configuration using the show crypto commands:

```
R1#show crypto ipsec profile
IPSEC profile ENCRYPT-GRE
        Security association lifetime: 4608000 kilobytes/3600 seconds
        PFS (Y/N): N
        Transform sets={
                TRIPLE-DES,
        }

R1#show crypto isakmp policy

Global IKE policy
Protection suite of priority 1
        encryption algorithm:    Three key triple DES
        hash algorithm:          Secure Hash Standard
        authentication method:   Pre-Shared Key
        Diffie-Hellman group:    #2 (1024 bit)
        lifetime:                86400 seconds, no volume limit
Default protection suite
        encryption algorithm:    DES - Data Encryption Standard (56 bit keys).
        hash algorithm:          Secure Hash Standard
        authentication method:   Rivest-Shamir-Adleman Signature
        Diffie-Hellman group:    #1 (768 bit)
        lifetime:                86400 seconds, no volume limit

R1#show crypto session detail
Crypto session current status

Code: C - IKE Configuration mode, D - Dead Peer Detection
K - Keepalives, N - NAT-traversal, X - IKE Extended Authentication

Interface: Tunnel0
Session status: UP-ACTIVE
Peer: 150.2.4.4 port 500 fvrf: (none) ivrf: (none)
        Phase1_id: 150.2.4.4
        Desc: (none)
  IKE SA: local 150.2.1.1/500 remote 150.2.4.4/500 Active
          Capabilities:(none) connid:1 lifetime:23:55:37
  IPSEC FLOW: permit ip 0.0.0.0/0.0.0.0 0.0.0.0/0.0.0.0
        Active SAs: 2, origin: crypto map
        Inbound:  #pkts dec'ed 37 drop 0 life (KB/Sec) 4536717/3338
        Outbound: #pkts enc'ed 37 drop 0 life (KB/Sec) 4536717/3338
```

Next, verify that the Tunnel interface is up following the modified configuration parameters:

```
R1#show interfaces tunnel 0
Tunnel0 is up, line protocol is up
  Hardware is Tunnel
  Internet address is 192.168.1.1/24
  MTU 1514 bytes, BW 9 Kbit/sec, DLY 500000 usec,
    reliability 255/255, txload 1/255, rxload 1/255
  Encapsulation TUNNEL, loopback not set
  Keepalive not set
  Tunnel source 150.2.1.1 (Serial0/0), destination 150.2.4.4
  Tunnel protocol/transport IPSEC/IP
  Tunnel TTL 255
  Fast tunneling enabled
  Tunnel transmit bandwidth 8000 (kbps)
  Tunnel receive bandwidth 8000 (kbps)
  Tunnel protection via IPSec (profile "ENCRYPT-GRE")
  Last input 00:19:17, output 00:19:18, output hang never
  Last clearing of "show interface" counters never
  Input queue: 0/75/0/0 (size/max/drops/flushes); Total output drops: 0
  Queueing strategy: fifo
  Output queue: 0/0 (size/max)
  5 minute input rate 0 bits/sec, 0 packets/sec
  5 minute output rate 0 bits/sec, 0 packets/sec
     174 packets input, 31060 bytes, 0 no buffer
     Received 0 broadcasts, 0 runts, 0 giants, 0 throttles
     0 input errors, 0 CRC, 0 frame, 0 overrun, 0 ignored, 0 abort
     188 packets output, 32492 bytes, 0 underruns
     0 output errors, 0 collisions, 0 interface resets
     0 unknown protocol drops
     0 output buffer failures, 0 output buffers swapped out
```

Following that, verify your OSPF neighbor adjacencies and dynamic routing information:

```
R1#show ip ospf neighbor

Neighbor ID     Pri   State           Dead Time   Address         Interface
4.4.4.4           0   FULL/  -        00:00:31    192.168.1.4     Tunnel0

R1#show ip route ospf
     10.0.0.0/24 is subnetted, 6 subnets
O IA    10.4.2.0 [110/11112] via 192.168.1.4, 00:07:07, Tunnel0
O IA    10.4.3.0 [110/11112] via 192.168.1.4, 00:07:07, Tunnel0
O IA    10.4.1.0 [110/11112] via 192.168.1.4, 00:07:07, Tunnel0
```

Next, ping between router R1 and router R4s LAN subnets using an extended ping:

```
R1#ping 10.4.1.4 source 10.1.1.1 repeat 10 size 1500

Type escape sequence to abort.
Sending 10, 1500-byte ICMP Echos to 10.4.1.4, timeout is 2 seconds:
Packet sent with a source address of 10.1.1.1
!!!!!!!!!!
Success rate is 100 percent (10/10), round-trip min/avg/max = 244/246/248 ms
```

Finally, verify encryption statistics (and configuration) on the router(s):

```
R1#show crypto ipsec sa

interface: Tunnel0
    Crypto map tag: Tunnel0-head-0, local addr 150.2.1.1

   protected vrf: (none)
   local  ident (addr/mask/prot/port): (0.0.0.0/0.0.0.0/0/0)
   remote ident (addr/mask/prot/port): (0.0.0.0/0.0.0.0/0/0)
   current_peer 150.2.4.4 port 500
     PERMIT, flags={origin_is_acl,}
    #pkts encaps: 122, #pkts encrypt: 122, #pkts digest: 122
    #pkts decaps: 102, #pkts decrypt: 102, #pkts verify: 102
    #pkts compressed: 0, #pkts decompressed: 0
    #pkts not compressed: 0, #pkts compr. failed: 0
    #pkts not decompressed: 0, #pkts decompress failed: 0
    #send errors 0, #recv errors 0
```

```
  local crypto endpt.: 150.2.1.1, remote crypto endpt.: 150.2.4.4
  path mtu 1500, ip mtu 1500, ip mtu idb Serial0/0
  current outbound spi: 0xD1D1D721(3520190241)

  inbound esp sas:
   spi: 0x4CE1DAD9(1289870041)
     transform: esp-3des ,
     in use settings ={Tunnel, }
     conn id: 2001, flow_id: SW:1, crypto map: Tunnel0-head-0
     sa timing: remaining key lifetime (k/sec): (4536696/2881)
     IV size: 8 bytes
     replay detection support: N
     Status: ACTIVE

  inbound ah sas:

  inbound pcp sas:

  outbound esp sas:
   spi: 0xD1D1D721(3520190241)
     transform: esp-3des ,
     in use settings ={Tunnel, }
     conn id: 2002, flow_id: SW:2, crypto map: Tunnel0-head-0
     sa timing: remaining key lifetime (k/sec): (4536680/2879)
     IV size: 8 bytes
     replay detection support: N
     Status: ACTIVE

  outbound ah sas:

  outbound pcp sas:
```

Finally, you can use the `show crypto isakmp sa [detail]` command to verify SA status:

```
R1#show crypto isakmp sa detail
Codes: C - IKE configuration mode, D - Dead Peer Detection
       K - Keepalives, N - NAT-traversal
       X - IKE Extended Authentication
       psk - Preshared key, rsig - RSA signature
       renc - RSA encryption

C-id  Local       Remote    I-VRF    Status Encr Hash Auth DH Lifetime Cap.
1     150.2.1.1   150.2.4.4          ACTIVE 3des sha  psk  2  23:27:11
         Connection-id:Engine-id =  1:1(software)
```

This solution is commonly used in branch office solutions where you need to enable dynamic IP routing protocols over a GRE tunnel across the Internet. If you were to debug IP traffic traversing either R2 or R3, for example, while traffic was traversing the LAN subnets of R1 and R4, you would see ESP packets going back and forth. In other words, the GRE packets are encapsulation using IPsec in a manner that would be similar to encapsulating and transporting voice packets using IP, i.e. VoIP. Alternatively, you could also configure an ACL and enable logging and view the matches against the ACL as illustrated below on R3:

```
R3(config)#access-list 100 permit ip any any log-input
R3(config)#interface serial 1/2
R3(config-if)#ip access-group 100 out
R3(config-if)#ip access-group 100 in
*Jun 15 20:19:51.427: %SEC-6-IPACCESSLOGNP: list 100 permitted 50 150.2.4.4 ->
150.2.1.1, 1 packet
*Jun 15 20:21:32.351: %SEC-6-IPACCESSLOGNP: list 100 permitted 50 150.2.1.1 ->
150.2.4.4, 1 packet
```

If you were to send multiple pings or transfer data between the LAN subnets connected to R1 and R4, you would see multiple packets being sent instead of just the single packet:

```
*Jun 15 20:25:37.139: %SEC-6-IPACCESSLOGNP: list 100 permitted 50 150.2.4.4 ->
150.2.1.1, 135 packets
*Jun 15 20:26:37.139: %SEC-6-IPACCESSLOGNP: list 100 permitted 50 150.2.1.1 ->
150.2.4.4, 138 packets
```

In the output above, IP protocol 50 is being permitted between R1 and R4. IP protocol number 50 is Encapsulating Security Payload (ESP). In both transport and tunnel mode, IPsec adds a new header to all the IP packets to provide the required information for securing the data within the original IP datagram. This header may either be an Encapsulating Security Payload (ESP) or Authentication Header (AH) header.

ESP is an IP-based protocol that uses IP port 50 for communication between IPsec peers. ESP is used to provide confidentiality, integrity, and authenticity of the data, i.e. secure data via encryption and authentication. Additionally, ESP also provides anti-replay protection services. ESP does not provide any kind of protection for the outer IP header

AH, is an IP-based protocol that uses IP port 51 for communication between IPsec peers. AH is used to protect the integrity and authenticity of data, and also offers anti-replay protection; however, AH does not provide confidentiality protection. In other words, AH does not provide encryption like ESP. AH does provide protection to the IP header; however, it should be noted that not all fields in the IP header, e.g. TTL, are protected.

FINAL ROUTER CONFIGURATIONS

R1

```
R1#term len 0
R1#sh run
Building configuration...

Current configuration : 1475 bytes
!
version 12.4
service timestamps debug datetime msec
service timestamps log datetime msec
no service password-encryption
!
hostname R1
!
boot-start-marker
boot-end-marker
!
no logging console
!
no aaa new-model
no network-clock-participate slot 1
no network-clock-participate wic 0
ip cef
!
no ip domain lookup
ip auth-proxy max-nodata-conns 3
ip admission max-nodata-conns 3
!
crypto isakmp policy 1
 encr 3des
 authentication pre-share
 group 2
crypto isakmp key CCNP2011 address 150.2.4.4
!
crypto ipsec transform-set TRIPLE-DES esp-3des
 mode transport
!
crypto ipsec profile ENCRYPT-GRE
 set transform-set TRIPLE-DES
!
interface Tunnel0
 ip address 192.168.1.1 255.255.255.0
 ip ospf 1 area 0
 tunnel source Serial0/0
 tunnel destination 150.2.4.4
 tunnel mode ipsec ipv4
 tunnel protection ipsec profile ENCRYPT-GRE
!
interface FastEthernet0/0
```

```
 ip address 10.1.2.1 255.255.255.0 secondary
 ip address 10.1.3.1 255.255.255.0 secondary
 ip address 10.1.1.1 255.255.255.0
 ip ospf 1 area 1
 duplex auto
 speed auto
!
interface Serial0/0
 ip address 150.2.1.1 255.255.255.240
 clock rate 2000000
!
interface Serial0/1
 no ip address
 shutdown
!
router ospf 1
 router-id 1.1.1.1
 log-adjacency-changes
!
ip forward-protocol nd
ip route 150.2.4.4 255.255.255.255 Serial0/0
!
no ip http server
no ip http secure-server
!
!
control-plane
!
line con 0
line aux 0
line vty 0 4
 login
!
end

R1#
```

R2

```
R2#term len 0
R2#sh run
Building configuration...

Current configuration : 973 bytes
!
version 12.4
service timestamps debug datetime msec
service timestamps log datetime msec
no service password-encryption
!
hostname R2
!
boot-start-marker
boot-end-marker
!
no aaa new-model
no network-clock-participate slot 1
no network-clock-participate wic 0
ip cef
!
no ip domain lookup
ip auth-proxy max-nodata-conns 3
ip admission max-nodata-conns 3
!
interface FastEthernet0/0
 ip address 150.2.2.2 255.255.255.0
 duplex auto
 speed auto
!
interface Serial0/0
 ip address 150.2.1.2 255.255.255.240
!
interface Serial0/1
 ip address 10.0.0.9 255.255.255.252
 shutdown
```

```
!
router bgp 254
 no synchronization
 bgp router-id 2.2.2.2
 bgp log-neighbor-changes
 network 150.2.1.0 mask 255.255.255.240
 neighbor 150.2.2.3 remote-as 254
 no auto-summary
!
ip forward-protocol nd
!
no ip http server
no ip http secure-server
!
control-plane
!
line con 0
line aux 0
line vty 0 4
 login
!
end

R2#
```

R3

```
R3#term len 0
R3#sh run
Building configuration...

Current configuration : 1290 bytes
!
version 12.4
service timestamps debug datetime msec
service timestamps log datetime msec
no service password-encryption
!
hostname R3
!
boot-start-marker
boot-end-marker
!
no aaa new-model
no network-clock-participate slot 1
no network-clock-participate wic 0
ip cef
!
no ip domain lookup
ip auth-proxy max-nodata-conns 3
ip admission max-nodata-conns 3
!
interface FastEthernet0/0
 ip address 150.2.2.3 255.255.255.0
 duplex auto
 speed auto
!
interface Serial1/0
 no ip address
 shutdown
 clock rate 128000
!
interface Serial1/1
 no ip address
 shutdown
 clock rate 128000
!
interface Serial1/2
 ip address 150.2.4.3 255.255.255.240
 clock rate 128000
!
interface Serial1/3
 no ip address
 shutdown
!
```

```
interface Serial1/4
 no ip address
 shutdown
!
interface Serial1/5
 no ip address
 shutdown
!
interface Serial1/6
 no ip address
 shutdown
!
interface Serial1/7
 no ip address
 shutdown
!
router bgp 254
 no synchronization
 bgp router-id 3.3.3.3
 bgp log-neighbor-changes
 network 150.2.4.0 mask 255.255.255.240
 neighbor 150.2.2.2 remote-as 254
 no auto-summary
!
ip forward-protocol nd
!
no ip http server
no ip http secure-server
!
control-plane
!
line con 0
line aux 0
line vty 0 4
 login
!
end

R3#
```

R4

```
R4#term len 0
R4#sh run
Building configuration...

Current configuration : 1545 bytes
!
version 12.4
service timestamps debug datetime msec
service timestamps log datetime msec
no service password-encryption
!
hostname R4
!
boot-start-marker
boot-end-marker
!
no logging console
!
no aaa new-model
no network-clock-participate slot 1
no network-clock-participate wic 0
ip cef
!
no ip domain lookup
ip auth-proxy max-nodata-conns 3
ip admission max-nodata-conns 3
!
crypto isakmp policy 1
 encr 3des
 authentication pre-share
 group 2
crypto isakmp key CCNP2011 address 150.2.1.1
!
```

```
crypto ipsec transform-set TRIPLE-DES esp-3des
 mode transport
!
crypto ipsec profile ENCRYPT-GRE
 set transform-set TRIPLE-DES
!
interface Tunnel0
 ip address 192.168.1.4 255.255.255.0
 ip ospf 4 area 0
 tunnel source Serial0/0
 tunnel destination 150.2.1.1
 tunnel mode ipsec ipv4
 tunnel protection ipsec profile ENCRYPT-GRE
!
interface FastEthernet0/0
 ip address 10.4.2.1 255.255.255.0 secondary
 ip address 10.4.3.1 255.255.255.0 secondary
 ip address 10.4.2.4 255.255.255.0 secondary
 ip address 10.4.3.4 255.255.255.0 secondary
 ip address 10.4.1.4 255.255.255.0
 ip ospf 4 area 4
 duplex auto
 speed auto
!
interface Serial0/0
 ip address 150.2.4.4 255.255.255.240
!
interface Serial0/1
 no ip address
 shutdown
!
router ospf 4
 router-id 4.4.4.4
 log-adjacency-changes
!
ip forward-protocol nd
ip route 150.2.1.1 255.255.255.255 Serial0/0
!
no ip http server
no ip http secure-server
!
control-plane
!
line con 0
line aux 0
line vty 0 4
 login
!
end

R4#
```

CCNP LAB 76

WAN IP Quality of Service Lab

Lab Objective:

The focus of this lab is to understand WAN IP Quality of Service(QoS) implementation and configuration. Additional technologies include Cisco IOS DHCP Server configuration.

Lab Topology:

The lab network topology is illustrated below:

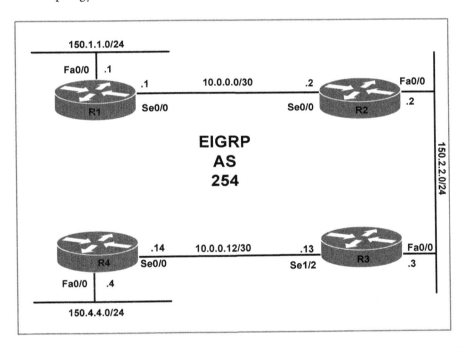

IMPORTANT NOTE: If you are using the www.howtonetwork.net racks, please bring up the LAN interfaces connected to the routers by issuing the `no shutdown` command on the connected switches. If you are using a home lab with no Switches, you can bring up the LAN interfaces using the following configurations on your routers:

```
interface fastethernet 0/0
  no keepalive
  loopback
  no shutdown
```

Alternately, you can simply connect the interfaces to a hub or switch if you have one available in your own lab.

Task 1

Configure hostnames, IP addressing on all routers as illustrated in the network topology.

Task 2

Configure EIGRP using Autonomous System number 254 as illustrated in the topology. Verify your configuration using the appropriate commands.

Task 3

In the future, a network module with an additional LAN interface will be installed on R1 and R4. Following this, Cisco IP phones will be connected to the 150.1.2.0/24 and 150.4.5.0/24 subnets that will be provisioned on the LAN interfaces of R1 and R4, respectively. These phones will register with a Cisco Unified Communications Manager server with the IP address 150.1.1.254. Configure Cisco IOS DHCP Server on R1 and R4 for the data (150.1.1.0/24 and 150.4.4.0/24) and voice (150.1.2.0/24 and 150.4.5.0/24) subnets. The data pool should assign clients DNS servers 150.1.1.200 and 150.1.1.201. The domain name should be howtonetwork.net.

Verify your configuration using the appropriate commands.

Task 4

Users have complained about bad voice quality issues. To address this, configure LLQ on R1 and R4 so that all traffic between the voice subnets is allocated 256Kbps bandwidth during periods of congestion. This traffic should be transmitted via a DSCP value of EF. Verify your configuration using the appropriate commands.

Task 5

There are applications that reside on R1 and R4s data VLANs that use HTTP and HTTPS. These applications are business critical and management has requested that all HTTP and HTTPS traffic between the 150.1.1.0/24 and 150.4.4.0/24 subnets be allocated a bandwidth of 512K and be sent across the WAN with a DSCP value of AF 21. Verify your configuration.

Task 6

In the future, management wants QoS configured on the WAN interfaces of R2 and R3. Before this is done, however, management tasks you with configuring the routers so as to determine what QoS policy should be applied to these interfaces, assuming that the DSCP markings of packets are trusted. Configure R2 and R3 to meet these requirements, then verify your solution using the appropriate commands on these routers.

LAB VALIDATION

Task 1

Please refer to previous labs for basic IPv4, IPv6 addressing and hostname configuration. This will not be included in this section to avoid being redundant.

Task 2

Please refer to previous labs for basic EIGRP configuration. Following this, verify your EIGRP configuration using the show ip eigrp neighbors and show ip route commands. Following this configuration, your route tables should show the following route information:

```
R1#show ip route eigrp
     10.0.0.0/30 is subnetted, 2 subnets
D       10.0.0.12 [90/21026560] via 10.0.0.2, 00:05:17, Serial0/0
     150.2.0.0/24 is subnetted, 1 subnets
D       150.2.2.0 [90/2172416] via 10.0.0.2, 00:05:17, Serial0/0
     150.4.0.0/24 is subnetted, 1 subnets
D       150.4.4.0 [90/21029120] via 10.0.0.2, 00:05:17, Serial0/0

R2#show ip route eigrp
     10.0.0.0/30 is subnetted, 2 subnets
D       10.0.0.12 [90/20514560] via 150.2.2.3, 00:05:15, FastEthernet0/0
     150.1.0.0/24 is subnetted, 1 subnets
D       150.1.1.0 [90/2172416] via 10.0.0.1, 00:05:15, Serial0/0
     150.4.0.0/24 is subnetted, 1 subnets
```

```
D        150.4.4.0 [90/20517120] via 150.2.2.3, 00:05:15, FastEthernet0/0

R3#show ip route eigrp
     10.0.0.0/30 is subnetted, 2 subnets
D        10.0.0.0 [90/2172416] via 150.2.2.2, 00:05:16, FastEthernet0/0
     150.1.0.0/24 is subnetted, 1 subnets
D        150.1.1.0 [90/2174976] via 150.2.2.2, 00:05:16, FastEthernet0/0
     150.4.0.0/24 is subnetted, 1 subnets
D        150.4.4.0 [90/20514560] via 10.0.0.14, 00:05:16, Serial1/2

R4#show ip route eigrp
     10.0.0.0/30 is subnetted, 2 subnets
D        10.0.0.0 [90/2684416] via 10.0.0.13, 00:05:16, Serial0/0
     150.1.0.0/24 is subnetted, 1 subnets
D        150.1.1.0 [90/2686976] via 10.0.0.13, 00:05:16, Serial0/0
     150.2.0.0/24 is subnetted, 1 subnets
D        150.2.2.0 [90/2172416] via 10.0.0.13, 00:05:16, Serial0/0
```

Task 3

The requirements of this task are straightforward. The only thing to remember is that you must specify the CUCM IP address using DHCP option 150. This task is completed as follows:

```
R1(config)#ip dhcp pool DATA
R1(dhcp-config)#network 150.1.1.0 /24
R1(dhcp-config)#default-router 150.1.1.1
R1(dhcp-config)#dns-server 150.1.1.200 150.1.1.201
R1(dhcp-config)#domain-name howtonetwork.net
R1(dhcp-config)#exit
R1(config)#ip dhcp pool VOICE
R1(dhcp-config)#network 150.1.2.0 /24
R1(dhcp-config)#option 150 ip 150.1.1.254
R1(dhcp-config)#default-router 150.1.2.1
R1(dhcp-config)#exit

R4(config)#ip dhcp pool DATA
R4(dhcp-config)#network 150.4.4.0 /24
R4(dhcp-config)#default-router 150.4.4.4
R4(dhcp-config)#dns-server 150.1.1.200 150.1.1.201
R4(dhcp-config)#domain-name howtonetwork.net
R4(dhcp-config)#exit
R4(config)#ip dhcp pool VOICE
R4(dhcp-config)#network 150.4.5.0 /24
R4(dhcp-config)#option 150 ip 150.1.1.254
R4(dhcp-config)#default-router 150.4.5.4
R4(dhcp-config)#exit
```

Next, verify your configuration by viewing the device configuration files on R1 and R4:

```
R1#more system:running-config | section dhcp
no ip dhcp use vrf connected
ip dhcp pool DATA
   network 150.1.1.0 255.255.255.0
   default-router 150.1.1.1
   dns-server 150.1.1.200 150.1.1.201
   domain-name howtonetwork.net
ip dhcp pool VOICE
   network 150.1.2.0 255.255.255.0
   default-router 150.1.2.1
   option 150 ip 150.1.1.254

R4#more system:running-config | section dhcp
no ip dhcp use vrf connected
ip dhcp pool DATA
   network 150.4.4.0 255.255.255.0
   default-router 150.4.4.4
   dns-server 150.1.1.200 150.1.1.201
   domain-name howtonetwork.net
ip dhcp pool VOICE
   network 150.4.5.0 255.255.255.0
   option 150 ip 150.1.1.254
   default-router 150.4.5.4
```

Optionally, you can verify DHCP pool statistics using the `show ip dhcp pool` command:

```
R4#show ip dhcp pool

Pool DATA :
 Utilization mark (high/low)    : 100 / 0
 Subnet size (first/next)       : 0 / 0
 Total addresses                : 254
 Leased addresses               : 0
 Pending event                  : none
 1 subnet is currently in the pool :
 Current index        IP address range                  Leased addresses
 150.4.4.1            150.4.4.1      - 150.4.4.254       0

Pool VOICE :
 Utilization mark (high/low)    : 100 / 0
 Subnet size (first/next)       : 0 / 0
 Total addresses                : 254
 Leased addresses               : 0
 Pending event                  : none
 1 subnet is currently in the pool :
 Current index        IP address range                  Leased addresses
 150.4.5.1            150.4.5.1      - 150.4.5.254       0
```

Task 4

This task requires that you enable Low Latency Queuing. LLQ is configured in conjunction with CBWFQ. CBWFQ is implemented using the Cisco IOS Modular QoS CLI (MQC). MQC configuration in Cisco IOS software requires three steps to be performed. These steps are:

Define a class map, which is used to identify the 'interesting traffic' using the `class-map [match-any|match-all] <name>` global configuration command. In class map configuration mode, match packets against an ACL, protocol, or other QoS parameters such as DSCP values, for example. To ensure successful matches, it is important that traffic is marked and classified and the network edge.

The `match-any` and `match-all` keywords allow you to specify whether to match any one of the parameters matched in the class-map (if more than one is specified) or match all parameters in the class map. Using the `match-all` keyword means that all specified conditions must be met for an actual match to be made.

Define a policy-map, which is used to determine what to do with the different class-maps once the traffic has been matched. The policy map can be used to implement LLQ (strict priority queuing), WRED, and other actions, such as re-marking packets before they are transmitted across the WAN. The policy-map is configured using the `policy-map <name>` global configuration command.

In policy-map configuration mode, explicitly configured class-maps are matched using the `class <class-map-name>` command. The default class, which is used for all other traffic types that are not included in the explicitly configured class-maps is configured using the `class class-default` policy-map configuration command.

Apply the policy-map to interfaces, subinterfaces, PVCs, or DLCIs using the `service-policy output <policy-map-name>` configuration command.

Following these guidelines, this task is completed as follows:

```
R1(config)#access-list 100 permit ip 150.1.2.0 0.0.0.255 150.4.5.0 0.0.0.255
R1(config)#class-map VOICE
R1(config-cmap)#match access-group 100
R1(config-cmap)#exit
R1(config)#policy-map WAN-QoS-POLICY
R1(config-pmap)#class VOICE
```

```
R1(config-pmap-c)#priority 256
R1(config-pmap-c)#set ip dscp ef
R1(config-pmap-c)#exit
R1(config-pmap)#exit
R1(config)#interface serial 0/0
R1(config-if)#service-policy output WAN-QoS-POLICY
R1(config-if)#exit

R4(config)#access-list 100 permit ip 150.4.5.0 0.0.0.255 150.1.2.0 0.0.0.255
R4(config)#class-map VOICE
R4(config-cmap)#match access-group 100
R4(config-cmap)#exit
R4(config)#policy-map WAN-QoS-POLICY
R4(config-pmap)#class VOICE
R4(config-pmap-c)#priority 256
R4(config-pmap-c)#set ip dscp ef
R4(config-pmap-c)#exit
R4(config-pmap)#exit
R4(config)#interface serial 0/0
R4(config-if)#service-policy output WAN-QoS-POLICY
R4(config-if)#exit
```

Next, verify your configuration using the show policy-map command on the routers:

```
R1#show policy-map interface serial 0/0
 Serial0/0

  Service-policy output: WAN-QoS-POLICY

    Class-map: VOICE (match-all)
      0 packets, 0 bytes
      5 minute offered rate 0 bps, drop rate 0 bps
      Match: access-group 100
      Queueing
        Strict Priority
        Output Queue: Conversation 264
        Bandwidth 256 (kbps) Burst 6400 (Bytes)
        (pkts matched/bytes matched) 0/0
        (total drops/bytes drops) 0/0
      QoS Set
        dscp ef
          Packets marked 0

    Class-map: class-default (match-any)
      49 packets, 3316 bytes
      5 minute offered rate 0 bps, drop rate 0 bps
      Match: any
```

Task 5

The requirements of this task are straightforward. All that is required is an ACL that matches the specified traffic types and then a class-map to match this traffic. This class-map is then inserted in the existing policy map with the desired parameters. This is completed as follows:

```
R1(config)#access-list 101 permit tcp any any eq www
R1(config)#access-list 101 permit tcp any any eq 443
R1(config)#class-map WEB
R1(config-cmap)#match access-group 101
R1(config-cmap)#exit
R1(config)#policy-map WAN-QoS-POLICY
R1(config-pmap)#class WEB
R1(config-pmap-c)#bandwidth 512
R1(config-pmap-c)#set ip dscp af21
R1(config-pmap-c)#exit
R1(config-pmap)#exit

R4(config)#access-list 101 permit tcp any any eq www
R4(config)#access-list 101 permit tcp any any eq 443
R4(config)#class-map WEB
R4(config-cmap)#match access-group 101
R4(config-cmap)#exit
R4(config)#policy-map WAN-QoS-POLICY
R4(config-pmap)#class WEB
R4(config-pmap-c)#bandwidth 512
R4(config-pmap-c)#set ip dscp af21
```

```
R4(config-pmap-c)#exit
R4(config-pmap)#exit
```

Next, use the show policy-map command to verify your configuration and solution:

```
R1#show policy-map interface serial 0/0 output
 Serial0/0

  Service-policy output: WAN-QoS-POLICY

    Class-map: VOICE (match-all)
      0 packets, 0 bytes
      5 minute offered rate 0 bps, drop rate 0 bps
      Match: access-group 100
      Queueing
        Strict Priority
        Output Queue: Conversation 264
        Bandwidth 256 (kbps) Burst 6400 (Bytes)
        (pkts matched/bytes matched) 0/0
        (total drops/bytes drops) 0/0
      QoS Set
        dscp ef
          Packets marked 0

    Class-map: WEB (match-all)
      0 packets, 0 bytes
      5 minute offered rate 0 bps, drop rate 0 bps
      Match: access-group 101
      Queueing
        Output Queue: Conversation 265
        Bandwidth 512 (kbps)Max Threshold 64 (packets)
        (pkts matched/bytes matched) 0/0
        (depth/total drops/no-buffer drops) 0/0/0
      QoS Set
        dscp af21
          Packets marked 0

    Class-map: class-default (match-any)
      209 packets, 13716 bytes
      5 minute offered rate 0 bps, drop rate 0 bps
      Match: any
```

You can test your solution by Telnetting between R1 and R4 using port 80 or 443 and then checking the policy map for matches against this type of traffic:

```
R1#telnet 150.4.4.4 www
Trying 150.4.4.4, 80 ...
% Connection refused by remote host

R1#telnet 150.4.4.4 443
Trying 150.4.4.4, 443 ...
% Connection refused by remote host

R1#show policy-map interface serial 0/0 output
 Serial0/0

  Service-policy output: WAN-QoS-POLICY

    Class-map: VOICE (match-all)
      0 packets, 0 bytes
      5 minute offered rate 0 bps, drop rate 0 bps
      Match: access-group 100
      Queueing
        Strict Priority
        Output Queue: Conversation 264
        Bandwidth 256 (kbps) Burst 6400 (Bytes)
        (pkts matched/bytes matched) 0/0
        (total drops/bytes drops) 0/0
      QoS Set
        dscp ef
          Packets marked 0

    Class-map: WEB (match-all)
      2 packets, 96 bytes
      5 minute offered rate 0 bps, drop rate 0 bps
      Match: access-group 101
```

```
Queueing
  Output Queue: Conversation 265
  Bandwidth 512 (kbps)Max Threshold 64 (packets)
  (pkts matched/bytes matched) 2/96
  (depth/total drops/no-buffer drops) 0/0/0
QoS Set
  dscp af21
    Packets marked 2

Class-map: class-default (match-any)
  251 packets, 16444 bytes
  5 minute offered rate 0 bps, drop rate 0 bps
  Match: any
```

Task 6

This task requires that you enable the AutoQoS for the Enterprise feature. This is enabled using the `auto discover qos <trust>` interface configuration command. The `<trust>` keyword indicates that the DSCP markings of packets are trusted, or are used for classification of the voice, video, and data traffic. If this keyword is omitted, then the voice, video, and data traffic is classified using NBAR, and the matched packets are marked with the appropriate DSCP value prior to being transmitted by the router. This task is completed as follows:

```
R2(config)#interface serial 0/0
R2(config-if)#auto discovery qos trust
R2(config-if)#exit
R2(config)#interface serial 0/1
R2(config-if)#auto discovery qos trust
R2(config-if)#exit

R3(config)#interface serial 1/1
R3(config-if)#auto discovery qos trust
R3(config-if)#exit
R3(config)#interface serial 1/2
R3(config-if)#auto discovery qos trust
R3(config-if)#exit
```

Next, verify your configuring using the `show auto discovery qos` command. Keep in mind that you may have to wait quite a while for statistics to be gathered:

```
R2#show auto discovery qos
Serial0/0
 AutoQoS Discovery enabled for trusted DSCP
 Discovery up time: 9 minutes, 37 seconds
 AutoQoS Class information:
 No AutoQoS data discovered

Serial0/1
 AutoQoS Discovery enabled for trusted DSCP
 Discovery up time: 9 minutes, 30 seconds
 AutoQoS Class information:
 No AutoQoS data discovered

R3#show auto discovery qos
Serial1/1
 AutoQoS Discovery enabled for trusted DSCP
 Discovery up time: 7 minutes, 16 seconds
 AutoQoS Class information:
 No AutoQoS data discovered

Serial1/2
 AutoQoS Discovery enabled for trusted DSCP
 Discovery up time: 7 minutes, 8 seconds
 AutoQoS Class information:
 No AutoQoS data discovered
```

FINAL ROUTER CONFIGURATIONS

R1

```
R1#term len 0
R1#sh run
Building configuration...

Current configuration : 1572 bytes
!
version 12.4
service timestamps debug datetime msec
service timestamps log datetime msec
no service password-encryption
!
hostname R1
!
boot-start-marker
boot-end-marker
!
no logging console
!
no aaa new-model
no network-clock-participate slot 1
no network-clock-participate wic 0
ip cef
!
no ip dhcp use vrf connected
!
ip dhcp pool DATA
   network 150.1.1.0 255.255.255.0
   default-router 150.1.1.1
   dns-server 150.1.1.200 150.1.1.201
   domain-name howtonetwork.net
!
ip dhcp pool VOICE
   network 150.1.2.0 255.255.255.0
   default-router 150.1.2.1
   option 150 ip 150.1.1.254
!
!
no ip domain lookup
ip auth-proxy max-nodata-conns 3
ip admission max-nodata-conns 3
!
class-map match-all WEB
 match access-group 101
class-map match-all VOICE
 match access-group 100
!
policy-map WAN-QoS-POLICY
 class VOICE
  priority 256
  set ip dscp ef
 class WEB
  bandwidth 512
  set ip dscp af21
!
interface FastEthernet0/0
 ip address 150.1.1.1 255.255.255.0
 duplex auto
 speed auto
!
interface Serial0/0
 ip address 10.0.0.1 255.255.255.252
 clock rate 2000000
 service-policy output WAN-QoS-POLICY
!
interface Serial0/1
 no ip address
 shutdown
!
router eigrp 254
 network 0.0.0.0
```

```
 no auto-summary
!
ip forward-protocol nd
!
ip http server
no ip http secure-server
!
access-list 100 permit ip 150.1.2.0 0.0.0.255 150.4.5.0 0.0.0.255
access-list 101 permit tcp any any eq www
access-list 101 permit tcp any any eq 443
!
control-plane
!
line con 0
line aux 0
line vty 0 4
 login
!
end

R1#
```

R2

```
R2#term len 0
R2#sh run
Building configuration...

Current configuration : 899 bytes
!
version 12.4
service timestamps debug datetime msec
service timestamps log datetime msec
no service password-encryption
!
hostname R2
!
boot-start-marker
boot-end-marker
!
no logging console
!
no aaa new-model
no network-clock-participate slot 1
no network-clock-participate wic 0
ip cef
!
no ip domain lookup
ip auth-proxy max-nodata-conns 3
ip admission max-nodata-conns 3
!
interface FastEthernet0/0
 ip address 150.2.2.2 255.255.255.0
 duplex auto
 speed auto
!
interface Serial0/0
 ip address 10.0.0.2 255.255.255.252
 auto discovery qos trust
!
interface Serial0/1
 no ip address
 shutdown
 auto discovery qos trust
!
router eigrp 254
 network 0.0.0.0
 no auto-summary
!
ip forward-protocol nd
!
no ip http server
no ip http secure-server
```

```
!
control-plane
!
line con 0
line aux 0
line vty 0 4
 login
!
end

R2#
```

R3

```
R3#term len 0
R3#sh run
Building configuration...

Current configuration : 1239 bytes
!
version 12.4
service timestamps debug datetime msec
service timestamps log datetime msec
no service password-encryption
!
hostname R3
!
boot-start-marker
boot-end-marker
!
no logging console
!
no aaa new-model
no network-clock-participate slot 1
no network-clock-participate wic 0
ip cef
!
no ip domain lookup
ip auth-proxy max-nodata-conns 3
ip admission max-nodata-conns 3
!
interface FastEthernet0/0
 ip address 150.2.2.3 255.255.255.0
 duplex auto
 speed auto
!
interface Serial1/0
 no ip address
 shutdown
 clock rate 128000
!
interface Serial1/1
 no ip address
 shutdown
 auto discovery qos trust
 clock rate 128000
!
interface Serial1/2
 ip address 10.0.0.13 255.255.255.252
 auto discovery qos trust
 clock rate 128000
!
interface Serial1/3
 no ip address
 shutdown
!
interface Serial1/4
 no ip address
 shutdown
!
interface Serial1/5
 no ip address
 shutdown
```

```
!
interface Serial1/6
 no ip address
 shutdown
!
interface Serial1/7
 no ip address
 shutdown
!
router eigrp 254
 network 0.0.0.0
 no auto-summary
!
ip forward-protocol nd
!
no ip http server
no ip http secure-server
!
control-plane
!
n 0
line aux 0
line vty 0 4
 login
!
end

R3#
```

R4

```
R4#term len 0
R4#sh run
Building configuration...

Current configuration : 1553 bytes
!
version 12.4
service timestamps debug datetime msec
service timestamps log datetime msec
no service password-encryption
!
hostname R4
!
boot-start-marker
boot-end-marker
!
no logging console
!
no aaa new-model
no network-clock-participate slot 1
no network-clock-participate wic 0
ip cef
!
no ip dhcp use vrf connected
!
ip dhcp pool DATA
   network 150.4.4.0 255.255.255.0
   default-router 150.4.4.4
   dns-server 150.1.1.200 150.1.1.201
   domain-name howtonetwork.net
!
ip dhcp pool VOICE
   network 150.4.5.0 255.255.255.0
   option 150 ip 150.1.1.254
   default-router 150.4.5.4
!
no ip domain lookup
ip auth-proxy max-nodata-conns 3
ip admission max-nodata-conns 3
!
class-map match-all WEB
 match access-group 101
```

```
class-map match-all VOICE
 match access-group 100
!
policy-map WAN-QoS-POLICY
 class VOICE
  priority 256
  set ip dscp ef
 class WEB
  bandwidth 512
  set ip dscp af21
!
interface FastEthernet0/0
 ip address 150.4.4.4 255.255.255.0
 duplex auto
 speed auto
!
interface Serial0/0
 ip address 10.0.0.14 255.255.255.252
 service-policy output WAN-QoS-POLICY
!
interface Serial0/1
 no ip address
 shutdown
!
router eigrp 254
 network 0.0.0.0
 no auto-summary
!
ip forward-protocol nd
!
ip http server
no ip http secure-server
!
access-list 100 permit ip 150.4.5.0 0.0.0.255 150.1.2.0 0.0.0.255
access-list 101 permit tcp any any eq www
access-list 101 permit tcp any any eq 443
!
control-plane
!
line con 0
line aux 0
line vty 0 4
 login
!
end

R4#
```

CCNP LAB 77

WAN IP Quality of Service Lab

Lab Objective:

The focus of this lab is to understand WAN IP Quality of Service(QoS) implementation and configuration. Additional technologies Network-based Application Recognition (NBAR).

Lab Topology:

The lab network topology is illustrated below:

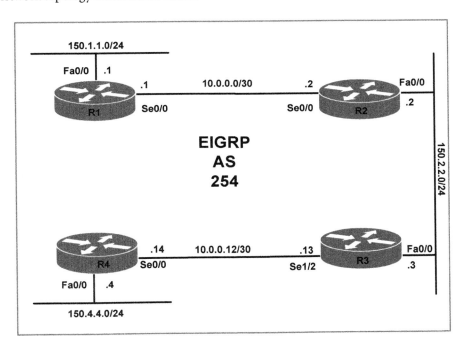

IMPORTANT NOTE: If you are using the www.howtonetwork.net racks, please bring up the LAN interfaces connected to the routers by issuing the no shutdown command on the connected switches. If you are using a home lab with no Switches, you can bring up the LAN interfaces using the following configurations on your routers:

```
interface fastethernet 0/0
  no keepalive
  loopback
  no shutdown
```

Alternately, you can simply connect the interfaces to a hub or switch if you have one available in your own lab.

Task 1

Configure hostnames, IP addressing on all routers as illustrated in the network topology.

Task 2

Configure EIGRP using Autonomous System number 254 as illustrated in the topology. Verify your configuration using the appropriate commands.

Task 3

Assuming that the QoS has been correctly implemented on the LAN subnets connected to R1 and R4, enable the Auto QoS feature on these routers such that they trust the DSCP values of VoIP packets. These WAN links have a bandwidth of 256Kbps. Verify your Auto QoS configuration using the appropriate commands.

Task 4

Management has requested that Auto QoS be enabled on the R2-R3 link. They are concerned that there may be some transit traffic that has not been properly classified and therefore requested that the routers be configured to match VoIP packets using NBAR. Implement this configuration and verify your solution using the appropriate commands.

Task 5

In the future, there will be video traffic traversing the R2-R3 link. Management has requested that this traffic be assigned 30% of the bandwidth. The voice traffic should be using 40% of the bandwidth instead of the current specified value. Modify the QoS policy applied to the LAN interfaces of R2 and R3 to do this. Verify your configuration using the appropriate commands.

LAB VALIDATION

Task 1

Please refer to previous labs for basic IPv4, IPv6 addressing and hostname configuration. This will not be included in this section to avoid being redundant.

Task 2

Please refer to previous labs for basic EIGRP configuration. Following this, verify your EIGRP configuration using the `show ip eigrp neighbors` and `show ip route` commands. Following this configuration, your route tables should show the following route information:

```
R1#show ip route eigrp
     10.0.0.0/30 is subnetted, 2 subnets
D       10.0.0.12 [90/21026560] via 10.0.0.2, 00:00:07, Serial0/0
     150.2.0.0/24 is subnetted, 1 subnets
D       150.2.2.0 [90/2172416] via 10.0.0.2, 00:01:37, Serial0/0
     150.4.0.0/24 is subnetted, 1 subnets
D       150.4.4.0 [90/21029120] via 10.0.0.2, 00:00:07, Serial0/0

R2#show ip route eigrp
     10.0.0.0/30 is subnetted, 2 subnets
D       10.0.0.12 [90/20514560] via 150.2.2.3, 00:00:13, FastEthernet0/0
     150.1.0.0/24 is subnetted, 1 subnets
D       150.1.1.0 [90/2172416] via 10.0.0.1, 00:01:43, Serial0/0
     150.4.0.0/24 is subnetted, 1 subnets
D       150.4.4.0 [90/20517120] via 150.2.2.3, 00:00:13, FastEthernet0/0

R3#show ip route eigrp
     10.0.0.0/30 is subnetted, 2 subnets
D       10.0.0.0 [90/2172416] via 150.2.2.2, 00:00:29, FastEthernet0/0
     150.1.0.0/24 is subnetted, 1 subnets
D       150.1.1.0 [90/2174976] via 150.2.2.2, 00:00:29, FastEthernet0/0
     150.4.0.0/24 is subnetted, 1 subnets
D       150.4.4.0 [90/20514560] via 10.0.0.14, 00:00:45, Serial1/2

R4#show ip route eigrp
     10.0.0.0/30 is subnetted, 2 subnets
D       10.0.0.0 [90/2684416] via 10.0.0.13, 00:00:33, Serial0/0
     150.1.0.0/24 is subnetted, 1 subnets
```

```
D       150.1.1.0 [90/2686976] via 10.0.0.13, 00:00:33, Serial0/0
     150.2.0.0/24 is subnetted, 1 subnets
D       150.2.2.0 [90/2172416] via 10.0.0.13, 00:00:49, Serial0/0
```

Task 3

The core requirement of this task is straightforward. There caveat however, is that the Auto QoS feature must be enabled on both ends of the link. Therefore, the same configuration will be required on the WAN interfaces of R2 and R3 that are connected to R1 and R4, respectively. The task is therefore completed on all four routers as follows:

```
R1(config)#ip cef
R1(config)#interface serial 0/0
R1(config-if)#bandwidth 256
R1(config-if)#auto qos voip trust
R1(config-if)#exit

R2(config)#ip cef
R2(config)#interface serial 0/0
R2(config-if)#bandwidth 256
R2(config-if)#auto qos voip trust
R2(config-if)#exit

R3(config)#ip cef
R3(config)#interface serial 1/2
R3(config-if)#bandwidth 256
R3(config-if)#auto qos voip trust
R3(config-if)#exit

R4(config)#ip cef
R4(config)#interface serial 0/0
R4(config-if)#bandwidth 256
R4(config-if)#auto qos voip trust
R4(config-if)#exit
```

When enabling the Cisco IOS Auto QoS feature, it is important to remember that the bandwidth of the Serial interface determines the speed of the link and the speed of the link in turn determines the configurations generated by the AutoQoS feature. By default, all links with a bandwidth value of 768Kbps and below are considered low bandwidth links. When Auto QoS is enabled on these interfaces, the router converts the link to a PPP Multilink configuration, allowing for better utilization of bandwidth. However, if the link speed is above 768Kbps, then the Auto QoS feature does not use PPP Multilink. Instead, the configuration is implemented for high bandwidth links, i.e. no Multilink interface is created on the router.

Next, verify the applied Auto QoS configuration using the `show auto qos` command:

```
R1#show auto qos
 !
 policy-map AutoQoS-Policy-Trust
  class AutoQoS-VoIP-RTP-Trust
   priority percent 70
  class AutoQoS-VoIP-Control-Trust
   bandwidth percent 5
  class class-default
   fair-queue
 !
 class-map match-any AutoQoS-VoIP-RTP-Trust
  match ip dscp ef
 !
 class-map match-any AutoQoS-VoIP-Control-Trust
  match ip dscp cs3
  match ip dscp af31
 !
 rmon event 33333 log trap AutoQoS description "AutoQoS SNMP traps for Voice Drops"
owner AutoQoS
 rmon alarm 33335 cbQosCMDropBitRate.1175.1177 30 absolute rising-threshold 1 33333
falling-threshold 0 owner AutoQoS

 Serial0/0 -
 !
 interface Serial0/0
  no ip address
```

```
 encapsulation ppp
 no fair-queue
 ppp multilink
 ppp multilink group 2001100115
!
interface Multilink2001100115
 bandwidth 256
 ip address 10.0.0.1 255.255.255.252
 ppp multilink
 ppp multilink fragment delay 10
 ppp multilink interleave
 ppp multilink group 2001100115
 service-policy output AutoQoS-Policy-Trust
 ip rtp header-compression iphc-format
```

To view statistics for Auto QoS, use the show policy-map interface command:

```
R1#show policy-map interface multilink 2001100115
 Multilink2001100115

  Service-policy output: AutoQoS-Policy-Trust

    Class-map: AutoQoS-VoIP-RTP-Trust (match-any)
      0 packets, 0 bytes
      5 minute offered rate 0 bps, drop rate 0 bps
      Match: ip dscp ef (46)
        0 packets, 0 bytes
        5 minute rate 0 bps
      Queueing
        Strict Priority
        Output Queue: Conversation 72
        Bandwidth 70 (%)
        Bandwidth 179 (kbps) Burst 4475 (Bytes)
        (pkts matched/bytes matched) 0/0
        (total drops/bytes drops) 0/0

    Class-map: AutoQoS-VoIP-Control-Trust (match-any)
      0 packets, 0 bytes
      5 minute offered rate 0 bps, drop rate 0 bps
      Match: ip dscp cs3 (24)
        0 packets, 0 bytes
        5 minute rate 0 bps
      Match: ip dscp af31 (26)
        0 packets, 0 bytes
        5 minute rate 0 bps
      Queueing
        Output Queue: Conversation 73
        Bandwidth 5 (%)
        Bandwidth 12 (kbps)Max Threshold 64 (packets)
        (pkts matched/bytes matched) 0/0
        (depth/total drops/no-buffer drops) 0/0/0

    Class-map: class-default (match-any)
      172 packets, 13985 bytes
      5 minute offered rate 0 bps, drop rate 0 bps
      Match: any
      Queueing
        Flow Based Fair Queueing
        Maximum Number of Hashed Queues 64
        (total queued/total drops/no-buffer drops) 0/0/0
```

Task 4

Prior to configuring the Auto QoS Feature, ensure that you are familiar with the following prerequisites and restrictions:

- Cisco Express Forwarding (CEF) is required and must be globally enabled on the router
- Remove any policy-maps currently applied to the interface
- Ensure that the correct bandwidth has been configured for the interface
- Ensure that the interface is configured with an IP address
- The auto qos voip command is not supported on subinterfaces or gigabit interfaces
- The auto qos voip command is supported with Frame Relay DLCIs
- If the trust is not specified, a policy-map named AutoQoS-Policy-UnTrust is created
- If the trust keyword is used, a policy-map named AutoQoS-Policy-Trust is created

Because the Auto QoS for VoIP feature is supported for FastEthernet interfaces, this task is completed by issuing the following commands on R2 and R3:

```
R2(config)#interface fastethernet 0/0
R2(config-if)#auto qos voip
R2(config-if)#exit

R3(config)#interface fastethernet 0/0
R3(config-if)#auto qos voip
R3(config-if)#exit
```

Next, verify your configuration using the show auto qos command:

```
R2#show auto qos
!
policy-map AutoQoS-Policy-UnTrust
 class AutoQoS-VoIP-RTP-UnTrust
  priority percent 70
  set dscp ef
 class AutoQoS-VoIP-Control-UnTrust
  bandwidth percent 5
  set dscp af31
 class AutoQoS-VoIP-Remark
  set dscp default
 class class-default
  fair-queue
!
policy-map AutoQoS-Policy-Trust
 class AutoQoS-VoIP-RTP-Trust
  priority percent 70
 class AutoQoS-VoIP-Control-Trust
  bandwidth percent 5
 class class-default
  fair-queue
!
class-map match-any AutoQoS-VoIP-Remark
 match ip dscp ef
 match ip dscp cs3
 match ip dscp af31
!
class-map match-any AutoQoS-VoIP-RTP-Trust
 match ip dscp ef
!
class-map match-any AutoQoS-VoIP-Control-Trust
 match ip dscp cs3
 match ip dscp af31
!
class-map match-any AutoQoS-VoIP-Control-UnTrust
 match access-group name AutoQoS-VoIP-Control
!
class-map match-any AutoQoS-VoIP-RTP-UnTrust
 match protocol rtp audio
 match access-group name AutoQoS-VoIP-RTCP
!
ip access-list extended AutoQoS-VoIP-RTCP
 permit udp any any range 16384 32767
!
ip access-list extended AutoQoS-VoIP-Control
 permit tcp any any eq 1720
 permit tcp any any range 11000 11999
 permit udp any any eq 2427
 permit tcp any any eq 2428
 permit tcp any any range 2000 2002
 permit udp any any eq 1719
 permit udp any any eq 5060
 rmon event 33333 log trap AutoQoS description "AutoQoS SNMP traps for Voice Drops"
owner AutoQoS
 rmon alarm 33334 cbQosCMDropBitRate.1117.1119 30 absolute rising-threshold 1 33333
falling-threshold 0 owner AutoQoS
 rmon alarm 33335 cbQosCMDropBitRate.1197.1199 30 absolute rising-threshold 1 33333
falling-threshold 0 owner AutoQoS

FastEthernet0/0 -
 !
```

```
 interface FastEthernet0/0
  service-policy output AutoQoS-Policy-UnTrust

Serial0/0 -
 !
 interface Serial0/0
  no ip address
  encapsulation ppp
  no fair-queue
  ppp multilink
  ppp multilink group 2001100115
 !
 interface Multilink2001100115
  bandwidth 256
  ip address 10.0.0.2 255.255.255.252
  ppp multilink
  ppp multilink fragment delay 10
  ppp multilink interleave
  ppp multilink group 2001100115
  service-policy output AutoQoS-Policy-Trust
  ip rtp header-compression iphc-format
```

To view statistics for Auto QoS, use the show policy-map interface command:

```
R2#show policy-map interface fastethernet 0/0
 FastEthernet0/0

  Service-policy output: AutoQoS-Policy-UnTrust

    Class-map: AutoQoS-VoIP-RTP-UnTrust (match-any)
      0 packets, 0 bytes
      5 minute offered rate 0 bps, drop rate 0 bps
      Match: protocol rtp audio
        0 packets, 0 bytes
        5 minute rate 0 bps
      Match: access-group name AutoQoS-VoIP-RTCP
        0 packets, 0 bytes
        5 minute rate 0 bps
      Queueing
        Strict Priority
        Output Queue: Conversation 264
        Bandwidth 70 (%)
        Bandwidth 70000 (kbps) Burst 1750000 (Bytes)
        (pkts matched/bytes matched) 0/0
        (total drops/bytes drops) 0/0
      QoS Set
        dscp ef
          Packets marked 0

    Class-map: AutoQoS-VoIP-Control-UnTrust (match-any)
      0 packets, 0 bytes
      5 minute offered rate 0 bps, drop rate 0 bps
      Match: access-group name AutoQoS-VoIP-Control
        0 packets, 0 bytes
        5 minute rate 0 bps
      Queueing
        Output Queue: Conversation 265
        Bandwidth 5 (%)
        Bandwidth 5000 (kbps)Max Threshold 64 (packets)
        (pkts matched/bytes matched) 0/0
        (depth/total drops/no-buffer drops) 0/0/0
      QoS Set
        dscp af31
          Packets marked 0

    Class-map: AutoQoS-VoIP-Remark (match-any)
      0 packets, 0 bytes
      5 minute offered rate 0 bps, drop rate 0 bps
      Match: ip dscp ef (46)
        0 packets, 0 bytes
        5 minute rate 0 bps
      Match: ip dscp cs3 (24)
        0 packets, 0 bytes
        5 minute rate 0 bps
      Match: ip dscp af31 (26)
        0 packets, 0 bytes
        5 minute rate 0 bps
```

```
QoS Set
  dscp default
    Packets marked 0

Class-map: class-default (match-any)
  481 packets, 40280 bytes
  5 minute offered rate 0 bps, drop rate 0 bps
  Match: any
  Queueing
    Flow Based Fair Queueing
    Maximum Number of Hashed Queues 256
    (total queued/total drops/no-buffer drops) 0/0/0
```

Task 5

This task requires that you create a class map that matches IP video traffic, i.e. RTP Video, and then include it in the existing policy-map applied to the FastEthernet interfaces of routers R2 and R3. Within policy-map configuration mode, you also need to modify the default bandwidth that is assigned to VoIP traffic. This task is therefore completed as follows:

```
R2(config)#class-map Untrusted-Video
R2(config-cmap)#match protocol rtp video
R2(config-cmap)#exit
R2(config)#policy-map AutoQoS-Policy-UnTrust
R2(config-pmap)#class AutoQoS-VoIP-RTP-UnTrust
R2(config-pmap-c)#priority percent 40
R2(config-pmap-c)#exit
R2(config-pmap)#class Untrusted-Video
R2(config-pmap-c)#bandwidth percent 30
R2(config-pmap-c)#exit

R3(config)#class-map Untrusted-Video
R3(config-cmap)#match protocol rtp video
R3(config-cmap)#exit
R3(config)#policy-map AutoQoS-Policy-UnTrust
R3(config-pmap)#class AutoQoS-VoIP-RTP-UnTrust
R3(config-pmap-c)#priority percent 40
R3(config-pmap-c)#exit
R3(config-pmap)#class Untrusted-Video
R3(config-pmap-c)#bandwidth percent 30
R3(config-pmap-c)#exit
```

Verify your configuration using the show policy-map interface command:

```
R2#show policy-map interface fastethernet 0/0
 FastEthernet0/0

  Service-policy output: AutoQoS-Policy-UnTrust

    Class-map: AutoQoS-VoIP-RTP-UnTrust (match-any)
      0 packets, 0 bytes
      5 minute offered rate 0 bps, drop rate 0 bps
      Match: protocol rtp audio
        0 packets, 0 bytes
        5 minute rate 0 bps
      Match: access-group name AutoQoS-VoIP-RTCP
        0 packets, 0 bytes
        5 minute rate 0 bps
      Queueing
        Strict Priority
        Output Queue: Conversation 264
        Bandwidth 40 (%)
        Bandwidth 40000 (kbps) Burst 1000000 (Bytes)
        (pkts matched/bytes matched) 0/0
        (total drops/bytes drops) 0/0
      QoS Set
        dscp ef
          Packets marked 0

    Class-map: AutoQoS-VoIP-Control-UnTrust (match-any)
      0 packets, 0 bytes
      5 minute offered rate 0 bps, drop rate 0 bps
      Match: access-group name AutoQoS-VoIP-Control
        0 packets, 0 bytes
```

```
      5 minute rate 0 bps
  Queueing
    Output Queue: Conversation 265
    Bandwidth 5 (%)
    Bandwidth 5000 (kbps)Max Threshold 64 (packets)
    (pkts matched/bytes matched) 0/0
    (depth/total drops/no-buffer drops) 0/0/0
  QoS Set
    dscp af31
      Packets marked 0

Class-map: AutoQoS-VoIP-Remark (match-any)
  0 packets, 0 bytes
  5 minute offered rate 0 bps, drop rate 0 bps
  Match: ip dscp ef (46)
    0 packets, 0 bytes
    5 minute rate 0 bps
  Match: ip dscp cs3 (24)
    0 packets, 0 bytes
    5 minute rate 0 bps
  Match: ip dscp af31 (26)
    0 packets, 0 bytes
    5 minute rate 0 bps
  QoS Set
    dscp default
      Packets marked 0

Class-map: Untrusted-Video (match-all)
  0 packets, 0 bytes
  5 minute offered rate 0 bps, drop rate 0 bps
  Match: protocol rtp video
  Queueing
    Output Queue: Conversation 266
    Bandwidth 30 (%)
    Bandwidth 30000 (kbps)Max Threshold 64 (packets)
    (pkts matched/bytes matched) 0/0
    (depth/total drops/no-buffer drops) 0/0/0

Class-map: class-default (match-any)
  823 packets, 68909 bytes
  5 minute offered rate 0 bps, drop rate 0 bps
  Match: any
  Queueing
    Flow Based Fair Queueing
    Maximum Number of Hashed Queues 256
    (total queued/total drops/no-buffer drops) 0/0/0
```

FINAL ROUTER CONFIGURATIONS

R1

```
R1#term len 0
R1#sh run
Building configuration...

Current configuration : 1829 bytes
!
version 12.4
service timestamps debug datetime msec
service timestamps log datetime msec
no service password-encryption
!
hostname R1
!
boot-start-marker
boot-end-marker
!
no logging console
!
no aaa new-model
no network-clock-participate slot 1
no network-clock-participate wic 0
ip cef
```

```
!
no ip domain lookup
ip auth-proxy max-nodata-conns 3
ip admission max-nodata-conns 3
!
class-map match-any AutoQoS-VoIP-RTP-Trust
 match ip dscp ef
class-map match-any AutoQoS-VoIP-Control-Trust
 match ip dscp cs3
 match ip dscp af31
!
policy-map AutoQoS-Policy-Trust
 class AutoQoS-VoIP-RTP-Trust
  priority percent 70
 class AutoQoS-VoIP-Control-Trust
  bandwidth percent 5
 class class-default
  fair-queue
!
interface Multilink2001100115
 bandwidth 256
 ip address 10.0.0.1 255.255.255.252
 ip tcp header-compression iphc-format
 ppp multilink
 ppp multilink fragment delay 10
 ppp multilink interleave
 ppp multilink group 2001100115
 service-policy output AutoQoS-Policy-Trust
 ip rtp header-compression iphc-format
!
interface FastEthernet0/0
 ip address 150.1.1.1 255.255.255.0
 duplex auto
 speed auto
!
interface Serial0/0
 bandwidth 256
 no ip address
 encapsulation ppp
 auto qos voip trust
 no fair-queue
 clock rate 2000000
 ppp multilink
 ppp multilink group 2001100115
!
interface Serial0/1
 no ip address
 shutdown
!
router eigrp 254
 network 0.0.0.0
 no auto-summary
!
ip forward-protocol nd
!
no ip http server
no ip http secure-server
!
control-plane
!
rmon event 33333 log trap AutoQoS description "AutoQoS SNMP traps for Voice Drops"
owner AutoQoS
rmon alarm 33340 cbQosCMDropBitRate.1769.1771 30 absolute rising-threshold 1 33333
falling-threshold 0 owner AutoQoS
!
line con 0
line aux 0
line vty 0 4
 login
 length 0
!
end

R1#
```

R2

```
R2#term len 0
R2#sh run
Building configuration...

Current configuration : 2544 bytes
!
version 12.4
service timestamps debug datetime msec
service timestamps log datetime msec
no service password-encryption
!
hostname R2
!
boot-start-marker
boot-end-marker
!
no logging console
!
no aaa new-model
no network-clock-participate slot 1
no network-clock-participate wic 0
ip cef
!
no ip domain lookup
ip auth-proxy max-nodata-conns 3
ip admission max-nodata-conns 3
!
class-map match-all Untrusted-Video
 match protocol rtp video
!
policy-map AutoQoS-Policy-UnTrust
 class AutoQoS-VoIP-RTP-UnTrust
  priority percent 40
  set dscp ef
 class AutoQoS-VoIP-Control-UnTrust
  bandwidth percent 5
  set dscp af31
 class AutoQoS-VoIP-Remark
  set dscp default
 class Untrusted-Video
  bandwidth percent 30
 class class-default
  fair-queue
policy-map AutoQoS-Policy-Trust
 class AutoQoS-VoIP-RTP-Trust
  priority percent 70
 class AutoQoS-VoIP-Control-Trust
  bandwidth percent 5
 class class-default
  fair-queue
!
interface Multilink2001100115
 bandwidth 256
 ip address 10.0.0.2 255.255.255.252
 ip tcp header-compression iphc-format
 ppp multilink
 ppp multilink fragment delay 10
 ppp multilink interleave
 ppp multilink group 2001100115
 service-policy output AutoQoS-Policy-Trust
 ip rtp header-compression iphc-format
!
interface FastEthernet0/0
 ip address 150.2.2.2 255.255.255.0
 duplex auto
 speed auto
 auto qos voip
 service-policy output AutoQoS-Policy-UnTrust
!
interface Serial0/0
 bandwidth 256
 no ip address
 encapsulation ppp
 auto qos voip trust
```

```
 no fair-queue
 ppp multilink
 ppp multilink group 2001100115
!
interface Serial0/1
 no ip address
 shutdown
!
router eigrp 254
 network 0.0.0.0
 no auto-summary
!
ip forward-protocol nd
!
no ip http server
no ip http secure-server
!
ip access-list extended AutoQoS-VoIP-Control
 permit tcp any any eq 1720
 permit tcp any any range 11000 11999
 permit udp any any eq 2427
 permit tcp any any eq 2428
 permit tcp any any range 2000 2002
 permit udp any any eq 1719
 permit udp any any eq 5060
ip access-list extended AutoQoS-VoIP-RTCP
 permit udp any any range 16384 32767
!
control-plane
!
rmon event 33333 log trap AutoQoS description "AutoQoS SNMP traps for Voice Drops"
owner AutoQoS
rmon alarm 33334 cbQosCMDropBitRate.1117.1119 30 absolute rising-threshold 1 33333
falling-threshold 0 owner AutoQoS
rmon alarm 33335 cbQosCMDropBitRate.1197.1199 30 absolute rising-threshold 1 33333
falling-threshold 0 owner AutoQoS
!
line con 0
line aux 0
line vty 0 4
 login
 length 0
!
end

R2#
```

R3

```
R3#term len 0
R3#sh run
Building configuration...

Current configuration : 3344 bytes
!
version 12.4
service timestamps debug datetime msec
service timestamps log datetime msec
no service password-encryption
!
hostname R3
!
boot-start-marker
boot-end-marker
!
no logging console
!
no aaa new-model
no network-clock-participate slot 1
no network-clock-participate wic 0
ip cef
!
no ip domain lookup
ip auth-proxy max-nodata-conns 3
ip admission max-nodata-conns 3
!
```

```
class-map match-all Untrusted-Video
 match protocol rtp video
class-map match-any AutoQoS-VoIP-Remark
 match ip dscp ef
 match ip dscp cs3
 match ip dscp af31
class-map match-any AutoQoS-VoIP-RTP-Trust
 match ip dscp ef
class-map match-any AutoQoS-VoIP-Control-Trust
 match ip dscp cs3
 match ip dscp af31
class-map match-any AutoQoS-VoIP-Control-UnTrust
 match access-group name AutoQoS-VoIP-Control
class-map match-any AutoQoS-VoIP-RTP-UnTrust
 match protocol rtp audio
 match access-group name AutoQoS-VoIP-RTCP
!
policy-map AutoQoS-Policy-UnTrust
 class AutoQoS-VoIP-RTP-UnTrust
  priority percent 40
  set dscp ef
 class AutoQoS-VoIP-Control-UnTrust
  bandwidth percent 5
  set dscp af31
 class AutoQoS-VoIP-Remark
  set dscp default
 class Untrusted-Video
  bandwidth percent 30
 class class-default
  fair-queue
policy-map AutoQoS-Policy-Trust
 class AutoQoS-VoIP-RTP-Trust
  priority percent 70
 class AutoQoS-VoIP-Control-Trust
  bandwidth percent 5
 class class-default
  fair-queue
!
interface Multilink2001100117
 bandwidth 256
 ip address 10.0.0.13 255.255.255.252
 ip tcp header-compression iphc-format
 ppp multilink
 ppp multilink fragment delay 10
 ppp multilink interleave
 ppp multilink group 2001100117
 service-policy output AutoQoS-Policy-Trust
 ip rtp header-compression iphc-format
!
interface FastEthernet0/0
 ip address 150.2.2.3 255.255.255.0
 duplex auto
 speed auto
 auto qos voip
 service-policy output AutoQoS-Policy-UnTrust
!
interface Serial1/0
 no ip address
 shutdown
 clock rate 128000
!
interface Serial1/1
 no ip address
 shutdown
 clock rate 128000
!
interface Serial1/2
 bandwidth 256
 no ip address
 encapsulation ppp
 auto qos voip trust
 no fair-queue
 clock rate 128000
 ppp multilink
 ppp multilink group 2001100117
!
interface Serial1/3
```

```
 no ip address
 shutdown
!
interface Serial1/4
 no ip address
 shutdown
!
interface Serial1/5
 no ip address
 shutdown
!
interface Serial1/6
 no ip address
 shutdown
!
interface Serial1/7
 no ip address
 shutdown
!
router eigrp 254
 network 0.0.0.0
 no auto-summary
!
ip forward-protocol nd
!
no ip http server
no ip http secure-server
!
ip access-list extended AutoQoS-VoIP-Control
 permit tcp any any eq 1720
 permit tcp any any range 11000 11999
 permit udp any any eq 2427
 permit tcp any any eq 2428
 permit tcp any any range 2000 2002
 permit udp any any eq 1719
 permit udp any any eq 5060
ip access-list extended AutoQoS-VoIP-RTCP
 permit udp any any range 16384 32767
!
control-plane
!
rmon event 33333 log trap AutoQoS description "AutoQoS SNMP traps for Voice Drops"
owner AutoQoS
rmon alarm 33334 cbQosCMDropBitRate.1123.1125 30 absolute rising-threshold 1 33333
falling-threshold 0 owner AutoQoS
rmon alarm 33335 cbQosCMDropBitRate.1203.1205 30 absolute rising-threshold 1 33333
falling-threshold 0 owner AutoQoS
!
line con 0
line aux 0
line vty 0 4
 login
 length 0
!
end

R3#
```

R4

```
R4#term len 0
R4#sh run
Building configuration...

Current configuration : 1810 bytes
!
version 12.4
service timestamps debug datetime msec
service timestamps log datetime msec
no service password-encryption
!
hostname R4
!
boot-start-marker
boot-end-marker
```

```
!
no logging console
!
no aaa new-model
no network-clock-participate slot 1
no network-clock-participate wic 0
ip cef
!
no ip domain lookup
ip auth-proxy max-nodata-conns 3
ip admission max-nodata-conns 3
!
class-map match-any AutoQoS-VoIP-RTP-Trust
 match ip dscp ef
class-map match-any AutoQoS-VoIP-Control-Trust
 match ip dscp cs3
 match ip dscp af31
!
policy-map AutoQoS-Policy-Trust
 class AutoQoS-VoIP-RTP-Trust
  priority percent 70
 class AutoQoS-VoIP-Control-Trust
  bandwidth percent 5
 class class-default
  fair-queue
!
interface Multilink2001100115
 bandwidth 256
 ip address 10.0.0.14 255.255.255.252
 ip tcp header-compression iphc-format
 ppp multilink
 ppp multilink fragment delay 10
 ppp multilink interleave
 ppp multilink group 2001100115
 service-policy output AutoQoS-Policy-Trust
 ip rtp header-compression iphc-format
!
interface FastEthernet0/0
 ip address 150.4.4.4 255.255.255.0
 duplex auto
 speed auto
!
interface Serial0/0
 bandwidth 256
 no ip address
 encapsulation ppp
 auto qos voip trust
 no fair-queue
 ppp multilink
 ppp multilink group 2001100115
!
interface Serial0/1
 no ip address
 shutdown
!
router eigrp 254
 network 0.0.0.0
 no auto-summary
!
ip forward-protocol nd
!
no ip http server
no ip http secure-server
!
control-plane
!
rmon event 33333 log trap AutoQoS description "AutoQoS SNMP traps for Voice Drops"
owner AutoQoS
rmon alarm 33334 cbQosCMDropBitRate.1117.1119 30 absolute rising-threshold 1 33333
falling-threshold 0 owner AutoQoS
!
line con 0
line aux 0
line vty 0 4
 login
 length 0
!
end
R4#
```

CCNP LAB 78

PPP over Ethernet (PPPoE) Lab

Lab Objective:

The focus of this lab is to understand PPP over Ethernet (PPPoE) implementation and configuration. Additional technologies tested include PAP authentication and security.

Lab Topology:

The lab network topology is illustrated below:

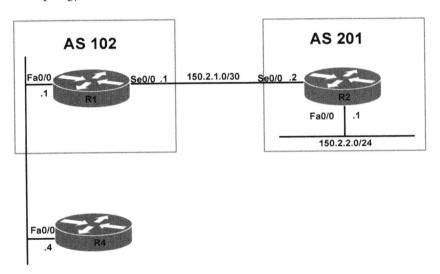

IMPORTANT NOTE: If you are using the **www.howtonetwork.net racks**, please bring up the LAN interfaces connected to the routers by issuing the `no shutdown` command on the connected switches. If you are using a home lab with no Switches, you can bring up the LAN interfaces using the following configurations on your routers:

```
interface fastethernet 0/0
 no keepalive
 loopback
 no shutdown
```

Alternately, you can simply connect the interfaces to a hub or switch if you have one available in your own lab.

Task 1

Configure hostnames, IP addressing on all routers as illustrated in the network topology. Configure an IP address of 150.1.1.1/24 on the LAN interface of R1. Do NOT configure an address on the LAN interface of R4.

Task 2

Configure BGP between R1 and R2 as illustrated in the topology. Advertise the 150.2.2.0/24 subnet via BGP and verify that R1 can reach this subnet. Advertise the 150.1.1.0/24 subnet connected to R1 via BGP and verify that R2 can reach this subnet.

Task 3

Assume that router R1 is an ISP router. This router will be a 'server' for client router R4. This router should have the following PPPoE configuration applied to it:

NOTE: This task is provided to you because these configurations are beyond the scope of the current CCNP curriculum. Simple copy and paste this configuration or manually type it in to complete the task. There are no additional configurations required to complete this task.

```
username ROUTER4 password CCNP2011
!
bba-group pppoe global
 virtual-template 1
!
interface fastethernet0/0
 pppoe enable group global
!
interface virtual-template1
 mtu 1492
 ip unnumbered fastethernet0/0
 peer default ip address pool CLIENT-POOL
 ppp authentication pap
!
ip local pool CLIENT-POOL 150.1.1.100 150.1.1.254
```

Task 4

Given the configuration above on R1 (ISP Router), implement PPPoE on R4. Next, verify your configuration using the appropriate commands. Test your solution by ensuring that R4 is able to ping the LAN subnet of R2 and vice-versa.

LAB VALIDATION

Task 1

Please refer to previous labs for basic IPv4 addressing and hostname configuration. This will not be included in this section to avoid being redundant.

Task 2

Please refer to previous labs for basic BGP configuration. Next, verify your BGP configuration using the show ip bgp summary and show ip route commands. Following this configuration, your routing tables on R1 and R2 should show the following route information:

```
R1#show ip route bgp
     150.2.0.0/16 is variably subnetted, 2 subnets, 2 masks
B       150.2.2.0/24 [20/0] via 150.2.1.2, 00:02:10

R2#show ip route bgp
     150.1.0.0/24 is subnetted, 1 subnets
B       150.1.1.0 [20/0] via 150.2.1.1, 00:00:09
```

Next, verify LAN-to-LAN connectivity between the subnets using an extended ping:

```
R1#ping 150.2.2.2 source 150.1.1.1 repeat 10 size 1500

Type escape sequence to abort.
Sending 10, 1500-byte ICMP Echos to 150.2.2.2, timeout is 2 seconds:
Packet sent with a source address of 150.1.1.1
!!!!!!!!!!
Success rate is 100 percent (10/10), round-trip min/avg/max = 12/15/16 ms
```

Task 3

The requirements of this task are straightforward. Simply paste the configuration into the router as specified. No additional configuration is required to complete this task.

CCNP LAB 78: PPP OVER ETHERNET (PPPOE) LAB

Task 4

This task requires a fair amount of configuration; however, all necessary commands can be found in the ROUTE guide. This task is completed as follows:

```
R4(config)#interface fastfthernet0/0
R4(config-if)#no shutdown
R4(config-if)#no ip address
R4(config-if)#pppoe enable
R4(config-if)#pppoe-client dial-pool-number 1
R4(config-if)#exit
R4(config)#interface dialer 1
R4(config-if)#ip mtu 1492
R4(config-if)#ip address negotiated
R4(config-if)#encapsulation ppp
R4(config-if)#dialer pool 1
R4(config-if)#dialer-group 1
R4(config-if)#ppp authentication pap callin
R4(config-if)#ppp pap sent-username ROUTER4 password CCNP2011
R4(config-if)#ppp ipcp route default
R4(config-if)#exit
```

Following this, verify that R4 has received an IP address from the pool configured on R1:

```
R4#show ip interface brief
Interface          IP-Address      OK? Method Status                  Protocol
FastEthernet0/0    unassigned      YES manual up                      up
Serial0/0          unassigned      YES manual administratively down   down
Serial0/1          unassigned      YES TFTP   administratively down   down
Virtual-Access1    unassigned      YES unset  up                      up
Virtual-Access2    unassigned      YES unset  up                      up
Dialer1            150.1.1.100     YES IPCP   up                      up
```

When PPPoE is enabled, the router automatically creates one or more Virtual-Access interfaces. You can view which Virtual-Access interface is associated with the Dialer interface using the `show interfaces dialer <number>` command as follows:

```
R4#show interfaces dialer 1
Dialer1 is up, line protocol is up (spoofing)
  Hardware is Unknown
  Internet address is 150.1.1.100/32
  MTU 1500 bytes, BW 56 Kbit/sec, DLY 20000 usec,
     reliability 255/255, txload 1/255, rxload 1/255
  Encapsulation PPP, loopback not set
  Keepalive set (10 sec)
  DTR is pulsed for 1 seconds on reset
  Interface is bound to Vi2
  Last input never, output never, output hang never
  Last clearing of "show interface" counters 00:15:06
  Input queue: 0/75/0/0 (size/max/drops/flushes); Total output drops: 0
  Queueing strategy: weighted fair
  Output queue: 0/1000/64/0 (size/max total/threshold/drops)
     Conversations  0/0/16 (active/max active/max total)
     Reserved Conversations 0/0 (allocated/max allocated)
     Available Bandwidth 42 kilobits/sec
  5 minute input rate 0 bits/sec, 0 packets/sec
  5 minute output rate 0 bits/sec, 0 packets/sec
     146 packets input, 2044 bytes
     148 packets output, 2072 bytes
Bound to:
Virtual-Access2 is up, line protocol is up
  Hardware is Virtual Access interface
  MTU 1500 bytes, BW 56 Kbit/sec, DLY 20000 usec,
     reliability 255/255, txload 1/255, rxload 1/255
  Encapsulation PPP, LCP Open
  Listen: CDPCP
  Open: IPCP
  PPPoE vaccess, cloned from Dialer1
  Vaccess status 0x44, loopback not set
  Keepalive set (10 sec)
  Interface is bound to Di1 (Encapsulation PPP)
  Last input 00:07:24, output never, output hang never
  Last clearing of "show interface" counters 00:08:13
```

```
Input queue: 0/75/0/0 (size/max/drops/flushes); Total output drops: 0
Queueing strategy: fifo
Output queue: 0/40 (size/max)
5 minute input rate 0 bits/sec, 0 packets/sec
5 minute output rate 0 bits/sec, 0 packets/sec
   96 packets input, 1339 bytes, 0 no buffer
   Received 0 broadcasts, 0 runts, 0 giants, 0 throttles
   0 input errors, 0 CRC, 0 frame, 0 overrun, 0 ignored, 0 abort
   96 packets output, 1339 bytes, 0 underruns
   0 output errors, 0 collisions, 0 interface resets
   0 unknown protocol drops
   0 output buffer failures, 0 output buffers swapped out
   0 carrier transitions
```

Next, verify that the default route is installed. In the solution example, the ppp ipcp route default interface configuration command is applied under the Dialer interface. This command instructs router to add a default route to the routing table during PPP negotiation. This command is NOT supported in older IOS versions; therefore, you would complete the same solution using the ip route 0.0.0.0 0.0.0.0 dialer [number] global configuration command instead. Keep in mind that these commands are mutually exclusive. Use one or the other. You can NOT use both! Use the show ip route command to verify the default route:

```
R4#show ip route
Codes: C - connected, S - static, R - RIP, M - mobile, B - BGP
       D - EIGRP, EX - EIGRP external, O - OSPF, IA - OSPF inter area
       N1 - OSPF NSSA external type 1, N2 - OSPF NSSA external type 2
       E1 - OSPF external type 1, E2 - OSPF external type 2
       i - IS-IS, su - IS-IS summary, L1 - IS-IS level-1, L2 - IS-IS level-2
       ia - IS-IS inter area, * - candidate default, U - per-user static route
       o - ODR, P - periodic downloaded static route

Gateway of last resort is 150.1.1.1 to network 0.0.0.0

     150.1.0.0/32 is subnetted, 2 subnets
C       150.1.1.1 is directly connected, Dialer1
C       150.1.1.100 is directly connected, Dialer1
S*   0.0.0.0/0 [1/0] via 150.1.1.1
```

Notice that the static route is installed into the routing table with a metric of 1, which is the same metric that would be assigned to a manually configured static route. Finally, complete task requirements by pinging from R4 to R2s LAN subnet address of 150.2.2.2/24:

```
R4#ping 150.2.2.2 repeat 10 size 1500

Type escape sequence to abort.
Sending 10, 1500-byte ICMP Echos to 150.2.2.2, timeout is 2 seconds:
!!!!!!!!!!
Success rate is 100 percent (10/10), round-trip min/avg/max = 16/18/24 ms
```

NOTE: You can perform additional checks using the show pppoe commands. The options that are available with these commands include:

```
R4#show pppoe ?
  derived    Cached PPPoE configuration information
  relay      PPPoE relay information
  session    PPPoE Session information
  summary    PPPoE sessions summary
  throttled  PPPoE Throttled information
```

For example, to view session information, append the session keyword to this command:

```
R4#show pppoe session
    1 client session

Uniq ID  PPPoE  RemMAC          Port                      Source  VA        State
         SID    LocMAC                                            VA-st
   N/A     6    000f.235e.ec80  Fa0/0                     Di1     Vi2       UP
                000f.235e.f120                                    UP
```

And to view detailed statistics, including byte and packet counts, append the all keyword:

```
R4#show pppoe session all
Total PPPoE sessions 1


session id: 6
local MAC address: 000f.235e.f120, remote MAC address: 000f.235e.ec80
virtual access interface: Vi2, outgoing interface: Fa0/0
    403 packets sent, 401 received
    20788 bytes sent, 21324 received
```

FINAL ROUTER CONFIGURATIONS

R1

```
R1>en
R1#term len 0
R1#sh run
Building configuration...

Current configuration : 1395 bytes
!
version 12.4
service timestamps debug datetime msec
service timestamps log datetime msec
no service password-encryption
!
hostname R1
!
boot-start-marker
boot-end-marker
!
no logging console
!
no aaa new-model
no network-clock-participate slot 1
no network-clock-participate wic 0
ip cef
!
no ip dhcp use vrf connected
!
no ip domain lookup
ip auth-proxy max-nodata-conns 3
ip admission max-nodata-conns 3
!
username ROUTER4 password 0 CCNP2011
!
bba-group pppoe global
 virtual-template 1
!
interface FastEthernet0/0
 ip address 150.1.1.1 255.255.255.0
 duplex auto
 speed auto
 pppoe enable group global
!
interface Serial0/0
 ip address 150.2.1.1 255.255.255.252
 clock rate 2000000
!
interface Serial0/1
 no ip address
 shutdown
!
interface Virtual-Template1
 mtu 1492
 ip unnumbered FastEthernet0/0
 peer default ip address pool CLIENT-POOL
 ppp authentication pap
!
router bgp 102
 no synchronization
 bgp router-id 1.1.1.1
 bgp log-neighbor-changes
```

```
  network 150.1.1.0 mask 255.255.255.0
  neighbor 150.2.1.2 remote-as 201
  no auto-summary
 !
 ip local pool CLIENT-POOL 150.1.1.100 150.1.1.254
 ip forward-protocol nd
 !
 no ip http server
 no ip http secure-server
 !
 control-plane
 !
 line con 0
 line aux 0
 line vty 0 4
  login
 !
 end

 R1#
```

R2

```
 R2#term len 0
 R2#sh run
 Building configuration...

 Current configuration : 1107 bytes
 !
 version 12.4
 service timestamps debug datetime msec
 service timestamps log datetime msec
 no service password-encryption
 !
 hostname R2
 !
 boot-start-marker
 boot-end-marker
 !
 no logging console
 !
 no aaa new-model
 no network-clock-participate slot 1
 no network-clock-participate wic 0
 ip cef
 !
 no ip domain lookup
 ip auth-proxy max-nodata-conns 3
 ip admission max-nodata-conns 3
 !
 interface FastEthernet0/0
  ip address 150.2.2.2 255.255.255.0
  duplex auto
  speed auto
 !
 interface Serial0/0
  ip address 150.2.1.2 255.255.255.252
 !
 interface Serial0/1
  no ip address
  shutdown
 !
 router bgp 201
  no synchronization
  bgp router-id 2.2.2.2
  bgp log-neighbor-changes
  network 150.2.2.0 mask 255.255.255.0
  neighbor 150.2.1.1 remote-as 102
  no auto-summary
 !
 ip forward-protocol nd
 !
 no ip http server
 no ip http secure-server
 !
 control-plane
 !
 line con 0
```

```
line aux 0
line vty 0 4
 login
!
end

R2#
```

R4

```
R4#term len 0
R4#sh run
Building configuration...

Current configuration : 1031 bytes
!
version 12.4
service timestamps debug datetime msec
service timestamps log datetime msec
no service password-encryption
!
hostname R4
!
boot-start-marker
boot-end-marker
!
no logging console
!
no aaa new-model
no network-clock-participate slot 1
no network-clock-participate wic 0
ip cef
!
no ip domain lookup
ip auth-proxy max-nodata-conns 3
ip admission max-nodata-conns 3
!
interface FastEthernet0/0
 no ip address
 duplex auto
 speed auto
 pppoe enable group global
 pppoe-client dial-pool-number 1
!
interface Serial0/0
 no ip address
 shutdown
!
interface Serial0/1
 no ip address
 shutdown
!
interface Dialer1
 ip address negotiated
 ip mtu 1492
 encapsulation ppp
 dialer pool 1
 dialer-group 1
 ppp authentication pap callin
 ppp pap sent-username ROUTER4 password 0 CCNP2011
 ppp ipcp route default
!
ip forward-protocol nd
!
no ip http server
no ip http secure-server
!
control-plane
!
line con 0
line aux 0
line vty 0 4
 login
!
end

R4#
```

CCNP LAB 79

PPP over Ethernet (PPPoE) Lab

Lab Objective:

The focus of this lab is to understand PPP over Ethernet (PPPoE) implementation and configuration. Additional technologies tested include CHAP authentication and NAT.

Lab Topology:

The lab network topology is illustrated below:

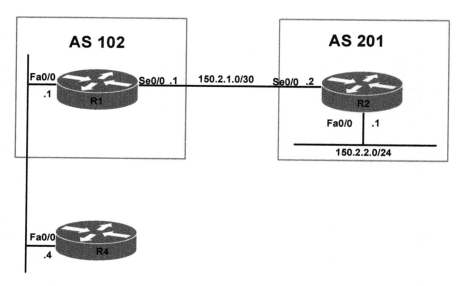

IMPORTANT NOTE: If you are using the www.howtonetwork.net racks, please bring up the LAN interfaces connected to the routers by issuing the `no shutdown` command on the connected switches. If you are using a home lab with no Switches, you can bring up the LAN interfaces using the following configurations on your routers:

```
interface fastethernet 0/0
  no keepalive
  loopback
  no shutdown
```

Alternately, you can simply connect the interfaces to a hub or switch if you have one available in your own lab.

Task 1

Configure hostnames, IP addressing on all routers as illustrated in the network topology. Configure an IP address of 150.1.1.1/24 on the LAN interface of R1. Do NOT configure an address on the LAN interface of R4.

Task 2

Configure BGP between R1 and R2 as illustrated in the topology. Advertise the 150.2.2.0/24 subnet via BGP and verify that R1 can reach this subnet. Do NOT advertise the 150.1.1.0/24 subnet connected to R1 via BGP. Verify the configuration using the appropriate commands.

Task 3

Assume that router R1 is an ISP router. This router will be a 'server' for client router R4. This router should have the following PPPoE configuration applied to it:

NOTE: This task is provided to you because these configurations are beyond the scope of the current CCNP curriculum. Simple copy and paste this configuration or manually type it in to complete the task. There are no additional configurations required to complete this task.

```
username ROUTER4 password CCNP2011
!
bba-group pppoe global
 virtual-template 1
!
interface fastethernet0/0
 pppoe enable group global
!
interface virtual-template1
 mtu 1492
 ip unnumbered fastethernet0/0
 peer default ip address pool CLIENT-POOL
 ppp authentication chap
!
ip local pool CLIENT-POOL 150.1.1.100 150.1.1.254
```

Task 4

Given the configuration above on R1 (ISP Router), implement PPPoE on R4. Next, verify your configuration using the appropriate commands. Test your solution by ensuring that R4 is able to ping 150.1.1.1 (R1), which should be its default gateway.

Task 5

Configure R1 so that R4 is able to reach R2s LAN subnet; however, R2 should never be able to initiate a connection to R4. Verify your configuration using the appropriate commands. When completing this task, you MUST adhere to the following restrictions:

- You are NOT allowed to use any static routes on any routers
- You are NOT allowed to advertise a default via BGP
- You are NOT allowed to advertise the 150.1.1.0/24 subnet via BGP
- You are NOT allowed to redistribute any routes

Following completion, ensure that R1 can ping R2s LAN subnet, but not vice-versa.

LAB VALIDATION

Task 1

Please refer to previous labs for basic IPv4 addressing and hostname configuration. This will not be included in this section to avoid being redundant.

Task 2

Please refer to previous labs for basic BGP configuration. Next, verify your BGP configuration using the show ip bgp summary and show ip route commands. Following this configuration, the BTP routing tables on R1 and R2 should show the following route entries:

```
R1#show ip bgp
BGP table version is 4, local router ID is 1.1.1.1
Status codes: s suppressed, d damped, h history, * valid, > best, i - internal,
```

```
            r RIB-failure, S Stale
Origin codes: i - IGP, e - EGP, ? - incomplete

    Network          Next Hop          Metric LocPrf Weight Path
*> 150.2.2.0/24      150.2.1.2              0             0 201 i

R2#show ip bgp
BGP table version is 5, local router ID is 2.2.2.2
Status codes: s suppressed, d damped, h history, * valid, > best, i - internal,
              r RIB-failure, S Stale
Origin codes: i - IGP, e - EGP, ? - incomplete

    Network          Next Hop          Metric LocPrf Weight Path
*> 150.2.2.0/24      0.0.0.0                0         32768 i
```

Task 3

The requirements of this task are straightforward. Simply paste the configuration into the router as specified. No additional configuration is required to complete this task.

Task 4

The requirements of this task are similar to those of the previous lab with the only difference being that this time CHAP security is used instead of PAP This task is completed as follows:

```
R4(config)#interface fastethernet 0/0
R4(config-if)#no shutdown
R4(config-if)#no ip address
R4(config-if)#pppoe enable
R4(config-if)#pppoe-client dial-pool-number 1
R4(config-if)#exit
R4(config)#interface dialer 1
R4(config-if)#ip mtu 1492
R4(config-if)#ip address negotiated
R4(config-if)#encapsulation ppp
R4(config-if)#dialer pool 1
R4(config-if)#dialer-group 1
R4(config-if)#ppp authentication pap callin
R4(config-if)#ppp chap hostname ROUTER4
R4(config-if)#ppp chap password CCNP2011
R4(config-if)#ppp ipcp route default
R4(config-if)#exit
```

Following this, verify that R4 has received an IP address from the pool configured on R1:

```
R4#show ip interface brief
Interface          IP-Address      OK? Method Status                Protocol
FastEthernet0/0    unassigned      YES manual up                    up
Serial0/0          unassigned      YES manual administratively down down
Serial0/1          unassigned      YES TFTP   administratively down down
Virtual-Access1    unassigned      YES unset  up                    up
Virtual-Access2    unassigned      YES unset  up                    up
Dialer1            150.1.1.100     YES IPCP   up                    up
```

When PPPoE is enabled, the router automatically creates one or more Virtual-Access interfaces. You can view which Virtual-Access interface is associated with the Dialer interface using the show interfaces dialer <number> command as follows:

```
R4#show interfaces dialer 1
Dialer1 is up, line protocol is up (spoofing)
  Hardware is Unknown
  Internet address is 150.1.1.100/32
  MTU 1500 bytes, BW 56 Kbit/sec, DLY 20000 usec,
     reliability 255/255, txload 1/255, rxload 1/255
  Encapsulation PPP, loopback not set
  Keepalive set (10 sec)
  DTR is pulsed for 1 seconds on reset
  Interface is bound to Vi2
  Last input never, output never, output hang never
  Last clearing of "show interface" counters 00:03:48
  Input queue: 0/75/0/0 (size/max/drops/flushes); Total output drops: 0
  Queueing strategy: weighted fair
```

```
   Output queue: 0/1000/64/0 (size/max total/threshold/drops)
      Conversations  0/0/16 (active/max active/max total)
      Reserved Conversations 0/0 (allocated/max allocated)
      Available Bandwidth 42 kilobits/sec
   5 minute input rate 0 bits/sec, 0 packets/sec
   5 minute output rate 0 bits/sec, 0 packets/sec
      44 packets input, 616 bytes
      44 packets output, 616 bytes
Bound to:
Virtual-Access2 is up, line protocol is up
  Hardware is Virtual Access interface
  MTU 1500 bytes, BW 56 Kbit/sec, DLY 20000 usec,
     reliability 255/255, txload 1/255, rxload 1/255
  Encapsulation PPP, LCP Open
  Listen: CDPCP
  Open: IPCP
  PPPoE vaccess, cloned from Dialer1
  Vaccess status 0x44, loopback not set
  Keepalive set (10 sec)
  DTR is pulsed for 5 seconds on reset
  Interface is bound to Di1 (Encapsulation PPP)
  Last input 00:03:43, output never, output hang never
  Last clearing of "show interface" counters 00:03:44
  Input queue: 0/75/0/0 (size/max/drops/flushes); Total output drops: 0
  Queueing strategy: fifo
  Output queue: 0/40 (size/max)
  5 minute input rate 0 bits/sec, 0 packets/sec
  5 minute output rate 0 bits/sec, 0 packets/sec
     53 packets input, 749 bytes, 0 no buffer
     Received 0 broadcasts, 0 runts, 0 giants, 0 throttles
     0 input errors, 0 CRC, 0 frame, 0 overrun, 0 ignored, 0 abort
     52 packets output, 731 bytes, 0 underruns
     0 output errors, 0 collisions, 0 interface resets
     0 unknown protocol drops
     0 output buffer failures, 0 output buffers swapped out
     0 carrier transitions
```

Next, verify that the default route is installed. In the solution example, the `ppp ipcp route default` interface configuration command is applied under the Dialer interface. This command instructs router to add a default route to the routing table during PPP negotiation. This command is NOT supported in older IOS versions; therefore, you would complete the same solution using the `ip route 0.0.0.0 0.0.0.0 dialer [number]` global configuration command instead. Keep in mind that these commands are mutually exclusive. Use one or the other. You can NOT use both! Use the `show ip route` command to verify the default route:

```
R4#show ip route
Codes: C - connected, S - static, R - RIP, M - mobile, B - BGP
       D - EIGRP, EX - EIGRP external, O - OSPF, IA - OSPF inter area
       N1 - OSPF NSSA external type 1, N2 - OSPF NSSA external type 2
       E1 - OSPF external type 1, E2 - OSPF external type 2
       i - IS-IS, su - IS-IS summary, L1 - IS-IS level-1, L2 - IS-IS level-2
       ia - IS-IS inter area, * - candidate default, U - per-user static route
       o - ODR, P - periodic downloaded static route

Gateway of last resort is 150.1.1.1 to network 0.0.0.0

     150.1.0.0/32 is subnetted, 2 subnets
C       150.1.1.1 is directly connected, Dialer1
C       150.1.1.100 is directly connected, Dialer1
S*   0.0.0.0/0 [1/0] via 150.1.1.1
```

Notice that the static route is installed into the routing table with a metric of 1, which is the same metric that would be assigned to a manually configured static route. Finally, complete task requirements by pinging from R4 to 150.1.1.1 (R1):

```
R4#ping 150.1.1.1 repeat 10 size 1500

Type escape sequence to abort.
Sending 10, 1500-byte ICMP Echos to 150.1.1.1, timeout is 2 seconds:
!!!!!!!!!!
Success rate is 100 percent (10/10), round-trip min/avg/max = 4/6/12 ms
```

Task 5

If you ignore the unnecessary banter, you will notice that this task requires that Port Address Translation, or NAT Overload, is required. This will allow R4 to ping R2, but not allow R2 to initiate inbound connections destined to R4. This task is completed as follows:

```
R1(config)#interface virtual-template 1
R1(config-if)#ip nat inside
R1(config-if)#exit
R1(config)#interface serial 0/0
R1(config-if)#ip nat outside
R1(config-if)#exit
R1(config)#ip nat inside source list 100 interface serial 0/0 overload
R1(config)#access-list 100 permit ip 150.1.1.0 0.0.0.255 any
R1(config)#exit
```

Following this configuration, test your solution by pinging between R4 and R2:

```
R4#ping 150.2.2.2 repeat 10

Type escape sequence to abort.
Sending 10, 100-byte ICMP Echos to 150.2.2.2, timeout is 2 seconds:
!!!!!!!!!!
Success rate is 100 percent (10/10), round-trip min/avg/max = 4/4/4 ms
```

Next, verify NAT / PAT operation using the `show ip nat translations` command on R1:

```
R1#show ip nat translations
Pro Inside global      Inside local      Outside local      Outside global
icmp 150.2.1.1:1       150.1.1.100:1     150.2.2.2:1        150.2.2.2:1
```

Additional Information

To test or verify the PPP authentication method, simply enable PPP debugging on the router and the disable and re-enable the Dialer interface on R1, for example:

```
R4(config)#logging console
R4(config)#interface dialer 1
R4(config-if)#shutdown
*Jun 16 05:04:26.099: Di1 DDR: dialer shutdown complete
R4(config-if)#do debug ppp negotiation
PPP protocol negotiation debugging is on
R4(config-if)#do debug ppp authentication
PPP authentication debugging is on
R4(config-if)#no shutdown
*Jun 16 05:04:59.271: %LINK-3-UPDOWN: Interface Dialer1, changed state to up
*Jun 16 05:05:11.359: %DIALER-6-BIND: Interface Vi2 bound to profile Di1
*Jun 16 05:05:11.363: Vi2 PPP: Phase is DOWN, Setup
*Jun 16 05:05:11.363: Vi2 PPP: Using dialer call direction
*Jun 16 05:05:11.363: Vi2 PPP: Treating connection as a callout
*Jun 16 05:05:11.363: Vi2 PPP: Session handle[71000007] Session id[0]
*Jun 16 05:05:11.363: Vi2 PPP: Phase is ESTABLISHING, Active Open
*Jun 16 05:05:11.363: Vi2 PPP: Authorization required
*Jun 16 05:05:11.363: Vi2 PPP: No remote authentication for call-out
*Jun 16 05:05:11.363: Vi2 LCP: O CONFREQ [Closed] id 1 len 10
*Jun 16 05:05:11.367: Vi2 LCP:    MagicNumber 0x0F516A40 (0x05060F516A40)
*Jun 16 05:05:11.367: %LINK-3-UPDOWN: Interface Virtual-Access2, changed state to up
*Jun 16 05:05:11.367: Vi2 LCP: I CONFREQ [REQsent] id 1 len 19
*Jun 16 05:05:11.371: Vi2 LCP:    MRU 1492 (0x010405D4)
*Jun 16 05:05:11.371: Vi2 LCP:    AuthProto CHAP (0x0305C22305)
*Jun 16 05:05:11.371: Vi2 LCP:    MagicNumber 0x0F515128 (0x05060F515128)
*Jun 16 05:05:11.371: Vi2 LCP: O CONFNAK [REQsent] id 1 len 8
*Jun 16 05:05:11.371: Vi2 LCP:    MRU 1500 (0x010405DC)
*Jun 16 05:05:11.371: Vi2 LCP: I CONFACK [REQsent] id 1 len 10
*Jun 16 05:05:11.371: Vi2 LCP:    MagicNumber 0x0F516A40 (0x05060F516A40)
*Jun 16 05:05:11.375: Vi2 LCP: I CONFREQ [ACKrcvd] id 2 len 19
*Jun 16 05:05:11.375: Vi2 LCP:    MRU 1500 (0x010405DC)
*Jun 16 05:05:11.375: Vi2 LCP:    AuthProto CHAP (0x0305C22305)
*Jun 16 05:05:11.375: Vi2 LCP:    MagicNumber 0x0F515128 (0x05060F515128)
*Jun 16 05:05:11.375: Vi2 LCP: O CONFACK [ACKrcvd] id 2 len 19
*Jun 16 05:05:11.375: Vi2 LCP:    MRU 1500 (0x010405DC)
*Jun 16 05:05:11.375: Vi2 LCP:    AuthProto CHAP (0x0305C22305)
*Jun 16 05:05:11.375: Vi2 LCP:    MagicNumber 0x0F515128 (0x05060F515128)
```

```
*Jun 16 05:05:11.379: Vi2 LCP: State is Open
*Jun 16 05:05:11.379: Vi2 PPP: No authorization without authentication
*Jun 16 05:05:11.379: Vi2 PPP: Phase is AUTHENTICATING, by the peer
*Jun 16 05:05:11.379: Vi2 CHAP: I CHALLENGE id 1 len 23 from "R1"
*Jun 16 05:05:11.383: Vi2 CHAP: Using hostname from interface CHAP
*Jun 16 05:05:11.383: Vi2 CHAP: Using password from interface CHAP
*Jun 16 05:05:11.383: Vi2 CHAP: O RESPONSE id 1 len 28 from "ROUTER4"
*Jun 16 05:05:11.411: Vi2 CHAP: I SUCCESS id 1 len 4
*Jun 16 05:05:11.415: Vi2 PPP: Phase is FORWARDING, Attempting Forward
*Jun 16 05:05:11.415: Vi2 PPP: Queue IPCP code[1] id[1]
*Jun 16 05:05:11.415: Vi2 PPP SSS: Receive SSS-Mgr Connect-Local
*Jun 16 05:05:11.419: Vi2 PPP: Phase is ESTABLISHING, Finish LCP
*Jun 16 05:05:11.419: Vi2 PPP: Phase is UP
*Jun 16 05:05:11.419: Vi2 IPCP: O CONFREQ [Closed] id 1 len 10
*Jun 16 05:05:11.419: Vi2 IPCP:    Address 0.0.0.0 (0x030600000000)
*Jun 16 05:05:11.423: Vi2 CDPCP: O CONFREQ [Closed] id 1 len 4
*Jun 16 05:05:11.423: Vi2 PPP: Process pending ncp packets
*Jun 16 05:05:11.423: Vi2 IPCP: Redirect packet to Vi2
*Jun 16 05:05:11.423: Vi2 IPCP: I CONFREQ [REQsent] id 1 len 10
*Jun 16 05:05:11.423: Vi2 IPCP:    Address 150.1.1.1 (0x030696010101)
*Jun 16 05:05:11.423: Vi2 IPCP: O CONFACK [REQsent] id 1 len 10
*Jun 16 05:05:11.423: Vi2 IPCP:    Address 150.1.1.1 (0x030696010101)
*Jun 16 05:05:11.427: Vi2 LCP: I PROTREJ [Open] id 3 len 10 protocol CDPCP
(0x820701010004)
*Jun 16 05:05:11.427: Vi2 CDPCP: State is Closed
*Jun 16 05:05:11.427: Vi2 CDPCP: State is Listen
*Jun 16 05:05:11.427: Vi2 IPCP: I CONFNAK [ACKsent] id 1 len 10
*Jun 16 05:05:11.427: Vi2 IPCP:    Address 150.1.1.100 (0x030696010164)
*Jun 16 05:05:11.427: Vi2 IPCP: O CONFREQ [ACKsent] id 2 len 10
*Jun 16 05:05:11.431: Vi2 IPCP:    Address 150.1.1.100 (0x030696010164)
*Jun 16 05:05:11.431: Vi2 IPCP: I CONFACK [ACKsent] id 2 len 10
*Jun 16 05:05:11.431: Vi2 IPCP:    Address 150.1.1.100 (0x030696010164)
*Jun 16 05:05:11.431: Vi2 IPCP: State is Open
*Jun 16 05:05:11.435: Di1 IPCP: Install negotiated IP interface address 150.1.1.100
*Jun 16 05:05:11.439: Di1 IPCP: Install default route thru 150.1.1.1
*Jun 16 05:05:11.439: Di1 IPCP: Install route to 150.1.1.1
*Jun 16 05:05:11.443: Vi2 IPCP: Add link info for cef entry 150.1.1.1
*Jun 16 05:05:12.419: %LINEPROTO-5-UPDOWN: Line protocol on Interface Virtual-
Access2, changed state to up
```

To test or verify PPPoE operation, simply perform the same actions and instead enable PPPoE debugging on the router, for example:

```
R4(config)#logging console
R4(config)#interface dialer 1
R4(config-if)#shut
*Jun 16 05:09:19.015: %DIALER-6-UNBIND: Interface Vi2 unbound from profile Di1
*Jun 16 05:09:19.015: Di1 DDR: dialer shutdown complete
*Jun 16 05:09:19.047: %LINK-3-UPDOWN: Interface Virtual-Access2, changed state to
down
*Jun 16 05:09:20.011: %LINEPROTO-5-UPDOWN: Line protocol on Interface Virtual-
Access2, changed state to down
*Jun 16 05:09:21.015: %LINK-5-CHANGED: Interface Dialer1, changed state to
administratively down
R4(config-if)#do debug pppoe events
PPPoE protocol events debugging is on
R4(config-if)#do debug pppoe packets
PPPoE control packets debugging is on
R4(config-if)#no shut
R4(config-if)#
*Jun 16 05:09:58.183: %LINK-3-UPDOWN: Interface Dialer1, changed state to up
*Jun 16 05:09:59.511:   Sending PADI: Interface = FastEthernet0/0
*Jun 16 05:09:59.511: pppoe_send_padi:
        FF FF FF FF FF FF 00 0F 23 5E F1 20 88 63 11 09
        00 00 00 0C 01 01 00 00 01 03 00 04 85 06 8D 4C ...
*Jun 16 05:09:59.511: PPPoE 0: I PADO  R:000f.235e.ec80 L:000f.235e.f120 Fa0/0
        00 0F 23 5E F1 20 00 0F 23 5E EC 80 88 63 11 07
        00 00 00 26 01 01 00 00 01 03 00 04 85 06 8D 4C ...
*Jun 16 05:10:01.559:   PPPOE: we've got our pado and the pado timer went off
*Jun 16 05:10:01.559: OUT PADR from PPPoE Session
        00 0F 23 5E EC 80 00 0F 23 5E F1 20 88 63 11 19
        00 00 00 26 01 01 00 00 01 03 00 04 85 06 8D 4C ...
*Jun 16 05:10:01.563: PPPoE 4: I PADS  R:000f.235e.ec80 L:000f.235e.f120 Fa0/0
        00 0F 23 5E F1 20 00 0F 23 5E EC 80 88 63 11 65
        00 04 00 26 01 01 00 00 01 03 00 04 85 06 8D 4C ...
*Jun 16 05:10:01.563: IN PADS from PPPoE Session
```

```
*Jun 16 05:10:01.567: %DIALER-6-BIND: Interface Vi2 bound to profile Di1
*Jun 16 05:10:01.567: PPPoE: Virtual Access interface obtained.
*Jun 16 05:10:01.571: PPPoE : encap string prepared
*Jun 16 05:10:01.571: [O]PPPoE 4: data path set to Virtual Acess
*Jun 16 05:10:01.575: %LINK-3-UPDOWN: Interface Virtual-Access2, changed state to up
*Jun 16 05:10:02.575: %LINEPROTO-5-UPDOWN: Line protocol on Interface Virtual-
Access2, changed state to up
```

FINAL ROUTER CONFIGURATIONS

R1

```
R1#term len 0
R1#sh run
Building configuration...

Current configuration : 1433 bytes
!
version 12.4
service timestamps debug datetime msec
service timestamps log datetime msec
no service password-encryption
!
hostname R1
!
boot-start-marker
boot-end-marker
!
no logging console
!
no aaa new-model
no network-clock-participate slot 1
no network-clock-participate wic 0
ip cef
!
no ip domain lookup
ip auth-proxy max-nodata-conns 3
ip admission max-nodata-conns 3
!
username ROUTER4 password 0 CCNP2011
!
bba-group pppoe global
 virtual-template 1
!
interface FastEthernet0/0
 ip address 150.1.1.1 255.255.255.0
 duplex auto
 speed auto
 pppoe enable group global
!
interface Serial0/0
 ip address 150.2.1.1 255.255.255.252
 ip nat outside
 ip virtual-reassembly
 clock rate 2000000
!
interface Serial0/1
 no ip address
 shutdown
!
interface Virtual-Template1
 mtu 1492
 ip unnumbered FastEthernet0/0
 ip nat inside
 ip virtual-reassembly
 peer default ip address pool CLIENT-POOL
 ppp authentication chap
!
router bgp 102
 no synchronization
 bgp router-id 1.1.1.1
 bgp log-neighbor-changes
 neighbor 150.2.1.2 remote-as 201
 no auto-summary
!
```

```
ip local pool CLIENT-POOL 150.1.1.100 150.1.1.254
ip forward-protocol nd
!
no ip http server
no ip http secure-server
ip nat inside source list 100 interface Serial0/0 overload
!
access-list 100 permit ip 150.1.1.0 0.0.0.255 any
!
control-plane
!
line con 0
line aux 0
line vty 0 4
 login
!
end

R1#
```

R2

```
R2#term len 0
R2#sh run
Building configuration...

Current configuration : 968 bytes
!
version 12.4
service timestamps debug datetime msec
service timestamps log datetime msec
no service password-encryption
!
hostname R2
!
boot-start-marker
boot-end-marker
!
no logging console
!
no aaa new-model
no network-clock-participate slot 1
no network-clock-participate wic 0
ip cef
!
no ip domain lookup
ip auth-proxy max-nodata-conns 3
ip admission max-nodata-conns 3
!
interface FastEthernet0/0
 ip address 150.2.2.2 255.255.255.0
 duplex auto
 speed auto
!
interface Serial0/0
 ip address 150.2.1.2 255.255.255.252
!
interface Serial0/1
 no ip address
 shutdown
!
router bgp 201
 no synchronization
 bgp router-id 2.2.2.2
 bgp log-neighbor-changes
 network 150.2.2.0 mask 255.255.255.0
 neighbor 150.2.1.1 remote-as 102
 no auto-summary
!
ip forward-protocol nd
!
no ip http server
no ip http secure-server
!
control-plane
!
line con 0
```

```
 line aux 0
 line vty 0 4
  login
 !
 end

 R2#
```

R4

```
R4#term len 0
R4#sh run
Building configuration...

Current configuration : 1037 bytes
!
version 12.4
service timestamps debug datetime msec
service timestamps log datetime msec
no service password-encryption
!
hostname R4
!
boot-start-marker
boot-end-marker
!
no logging console
!
no aaa new-model
no network-clock-participate slot 1
no network-clock-participate wic 0
ip cef
!
no ip domain lookup
ip auth-proxy max-nodata-conns 3
ip admission max-nodata-conns 3
!
interface FastEthernet0/0
 no ip address
 duplex auto
 speed auto
 pppoe enable group global
 pppoe-client dial-pool-number 1
!
interface Serial0/0
 no ip address
 shutdown
!
interface Serial0/1
 no ip address
 shutdown
!
interface Dialer1
 ip address negotiated
 ip mtu 1492
 encapsulation ppp
 dialer pool 1
 dialer-group 1
 ppp authentication pap callin
 ppp chap hostname ROUTER4
 ppp chap password 0 CCNP2011
 ppp ipcp route default
!
ip forward-protocol nd
!
no ip http server
no ip http secure-server
!
control-plane
!
line con 0
line aux 0
line vty 0 4
 login
!
end

R4#
```

CCNP LAB 80

Branch Office Connectivity Lab

___

Lab Objective:

The focus of this lab is to understand branch office connectivity solutions, implementation and configuration. Additional technologies tested include NAT, PAT and network security.

Lab Topology:

The lab network topology is illustrated below:

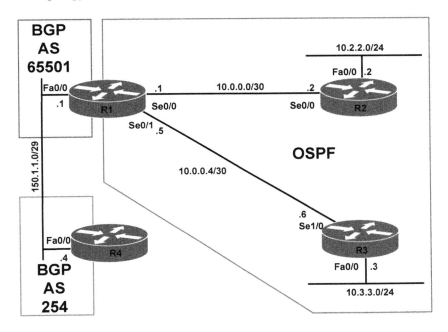

IMPORTANT NOTE: If you are using the www.howtonetwork.net racks, please bring up the LAN interfaces connected to the routers by issuing the `no shutdown` command on the connected switches. If you are using a home lab with no Switches, you can bring up the LAN interfaces using the following configurations on your routers:

```
interface fastethernet 0/0
  no keepalive
  loopback
  no shutdown
```

Alternately, you can simply connect the interfaces to a hub or switch if you have one available in your own lab.

Task 1

Configure hostnames, IP addressing on all routers as illustrated in the network topology. In addition to this, configure Loopback 0 with an IP Address of 160.0.0.4/32 on R4.

Task 2

Configure IP routing as illustrated in the topology. Management has requested that only a default route be advertised to R1 from the ISP (R4). Management has requested that redistribution NOT be performed on R1. Additionally, they do not want any non-private IP addresses within the OSPF domain. Configure routing so that R2 and R4 have reachability to all unknown (external) destinations. This should only happen if R1 is receiving the default route from the ISP (R4). Verify the configuration using appropriate commands.

Task 3

Configure Internet access for the spoke subnets connected to routers R2 and R3 as follows:
- All traffic from the 10.2.2.0/24 subnet should appear to originate from 150.1.1.2
- All traffic from the 10.3.3.0/24 subnet should appear to originate from 150.1.1.3

Following this configuration, verify that both R2 and R3 can ping the 160.0.0.4/32 address.

Task 4

Management has advised that they would some of the business' customers on the Internet to access a web server that is connected to the R3 LAN. This server has yet to be turned up, but they request that you implement a solution so that all HTTP traffic ONLY destined to address 150.1.1.5 is forwarded to a Loopback 0 interface with the IP address 3.3.3.3 on R3. Implement this solution and test it by connecting to 150.1.1.5, using port 80, from R4.

Task 5

Management is concerned about Internet security, they have compiled a list of activities that they would like you to implement on the Internet-facing router (R1). The list is as follows:
- Router R1 should be configured to discard messages that can be used to inform the source host that the destination Unicast address is unreachable
- Router R1 should be configured so that all IP packets that contain IP options should be discarded by the router
- Router R1 should be configured so that the source of an IP packet is not allowed to specify the network path a packet takes
- Router R1 should be configured so that it is not possible to send an IP broadcast packet to a remote IP subnet

LAB VALIDATION

Task 1

Please refer to previous labs for basic IPv4 addressing and hostname configuration. This will not be included in this section to avoid being redundant.

Task 2

While the requirements of this task are straightforward, and OSPF and BGP configuration has been described in detail in previous labs. This task is completed as follows:

```
R1(config)#router ospf 1
R1(config-router)#router-id 1.1.1.1
R1(config-router)#network 10.0.0.0 0.255.255.255 area 0
R1(config-router)#default-information originate
R1(config-router)#exit
R1(config)#router bgp 65501
R1(config-router)#bgp router-id 1.1.1.1
R1(config-router)#neighbor 150.1.1.4 remote-as 254
R1(config-router)#exit

R2(config)#router ospf 2
R2(config-router)#router-id 2.2.2.2
```

```
R2(config-router)#network 10.0.0.0 0.255.255.255 area 0
R2(config-router)#exit

R3(config)#router ospf 3
R3(config-router)#router-id 3.3.3.3
R3(config-router)#network 10.0.0.0 0.255.255.255 area 0
R3(config-router)#exit

R4(config)#router bgp 254
R4(config-router)#bgp router-id 4.4.4.4
R4(config-router)#neighbor 150.1.1.1 remote-as 65501
R4(config-router)#neighbor 150.1.1.1 default-originate
R4(config-router)#exit
```

Next, verify your configurations using the show ip route command on R1, R2, and R3:

```
R1#show ip route
Codes: C - connected, S - static, R - RIP, M - mobile, B - BGP
       D - EIGRP, EX - EIGRP external, O - OSPF, IA - OSPF inter area
       N1 - OSPF NSSA external type 1, N2 - OSPF NSSA external type 2
       E1 - OSPF external type 1, E2 - OSPF external type 2
       i - IS-IS, su - IS-IS summary, L1 - IS-IS level-1, L2 - IS-IS level-2
       ia - IS-IS inter area, * - candidate default, U - per-user static route
       o - ODR, P - periodic downloaded static route

Gateway of last resort is 150.1.1.4 to network 0.0.0.0

     10.0.0.0/8 is variably subnetted, 4 subnets, 2 masks
O       10.3.3.0/24 [110/65] via 10.0.0.6, 00:02:32, Serial0/1
O       10.2.2.0/24 [110/65] via 10.0.0.2, 00:02:32, Serial0/0
C       10.0.0.0/30 is directly connected, Serial0/0
C       10.0.0.4/30 is directly connected, Serial0/1
     150.1.0.0/29 is subnetted, 1 subnets
C       150.1.1.0 is directly connected, FastEthernet0/0
B*   0.0.0.0/0 [20/0] via 150.1.1.4, 00:01:10

R2#show ip route
Codes: C - connected, S - static, R - RIP, M - mobile, B - BGP
       D - EIGRP, EX - EIGRP external, O - OSPF, IA - OSPF inter area
       N1 - OSPF NSSA external type 1, N2 - OSPF NSSA external type 2
       E1 - OSPF external type 1, E2 - OSPF external type 2
       i - IS-IS, su - IS-IS summary, L1 - IS-IS level-1, L2 - IS-IS level-2
       ia - IS-IS inter area, * - candidate default, U - per-user static route
       o - ODR, P - periodic downloaded static route

Gateway of last resort is 10.0.0.1 to network 0.0.0.0

     10.0.0.0/8 is variably subnetted, 4 subnets, 2 masks
O       10.3.3.0/24 [110/129] via 10.0.0.1, 00:02:40, Serial0/0
C       10.2.2.0/24 is directly connected, FastEthernet0/0
C       10.0.0.0/30 is directly connected, Serial0/0
O       10.0.0.4/30 [110/128] via 10.0.0.1, 00:02:40, Serial0/0
O*E2 0.0.0.0/0 [110/1] via 10.0.0.1, 00:01:18, Serial0/0

R3#show ip route
Codes: C - connected, S - static, R - RIP, M - mobile, B - BGP
       D - EIGRP, EX - EIGRP external, O - OSPF, IA - OSPF inter area
       N1 - OSPF NSSA external type 1, N2 - OSPF NSSA external type 2
       E1 - OSPF external type 1, E2 - OSPF external type 2
       i - IS-IS, su - IS-IS summary, L1 - IS-IS level-1, L2 - IS-IS level-2
       ia - IS-IS inter area, * - candidate default, U - per-user static route
       o - ODR, P - periodic downloaded static route

Gateway of last resort is 10.0.0.5 to network 0.0.0.0

     10.0.0.0/8 is variably subnetted, 4 subnets, 2 masks
C       10.3.3.0/24 is directly connected, FastEthernet0/0
O       10.2.2.0/24 [110/846] via 10.0.0.5, 00:02:44, Serial1/0
O       10.0.0.0/30 [110/845] via 10.0.0.5, 00:02:44, Serial1/0
C       10.0.0.4/30 is directly connected, Serial1/0
O*E2 0.0.0.0/0 [110/1] via 10.0.0.5, 00:01:22, Serial1/0
```

Because R4 is not receiving any routes, you can simply verify the BGP status:

```
R4#show ip bgp summary
BGP router identifier 4.4.4.4, local AS number 254
```

```
BGP table version is 1, main routing table version 1

Neighbor     V    AS MsgRcvd MsgSent  TblVer  InQ OutQ Up/Down  State/PfxRcd
150.1.1.1    4 65501       6       7       1    0    0 00:03:08            0
```

Task 3

The requirements of this task are straightforward and require that Port Address Translation, PAT or NAT Overload, be implemented on R1. This task is completed as follows:

```
R1(config)#ip nat pool SITE-2-POOL 150.1.1.2 150.1.1.2 prefix-length 29
R1(config)#ip nat pool SITE-3-POOL 150.1.1.3 150.1.1.3 prefix-length 29
R1(config)#ip access-list extended SITE-2-ONLY
R1(config-ext-nacl)#permit ip 10.2.2.0 0.0.0.255 any
R1(config-ext-nacl)#exit
R1(config)#ip access-list extended SITE-3-ONLY
R1(config-ext-nacl)#permit ip 10.3.3.0 0.0.0.255 any
R1(config-ext-nacl)#exit
R1(config)#ip nat inside source list SITE-2-ONLY pool SITE-2-POOL overload
R1(config)#ip nat inside source list SITE-3-ONLY pool SITE-3-POOL overload
R1(config)#interface serial 0/0
R1(config-if)#ip nat inside
R1(config-if)#exit
R1(config)#interface serial 0/1
R1(config-if)#ip nat inside
R1(config-if)#exit
R1(config)#interface fastethernet 0/0
R1(config-if)#ip nat outside
R1(config-if)#exit
```

Following this configuration, test connectivity from R2s LAN to the 160.0.0.4/32 address:

```
R2#ping 160.0.0.4 source fastethernet 0/0 repeat 10 size 1500

Type escape sequence to abort.
Sending 10, 1500-byte ICMP Echos to 160.0.0.4, timeout is 2 seconds:
Packet sent with a source address of 10.2.2.2
.!!!!!!!!!
Success rate is 90 percent (9/10), round-trip min/avg/max = 16/22/76 ms
```

Next, perform the same test - this time, however, from R3s LAN:

```
R3#ping 160.0.0.4 source fastethernet 0/0 size 1500 repeat 10

Type escape sequence to abort.
Sending 10, 1500-byte ICMP Echos to 160.0.0.4, timeout is 2 seconds:
Packet sent with a source address of 10.3.3.3
.!!!!!!!!!
Success rate is 90 percent (9/10), round-trip min/avg/max = 192/192/196 ms
```

Finally, verify PAT operation using the show ip nat translations command on R1:

```
R1#show ip nat translations
Pro Inside global    Inside local     Outside local    Outside global
icmp 150.1.1.2:1     10.2.2.2:1       160.0.0.4:1      160.0.0.4:1
icmp 150.1.1.3:2     10.3.3.3:2       160.0.0.4:2      160.0.0.4:2
```

Task 4

The requirements of this task are straightforward. All that is required in that you create a static NAT for TCP port 80 on R1. On R3, simply configure a Loopback interface with IP address 3.3.3.3/32 and advertise it via OSPF. To test, enable Cisco IOS HTTP server functionality on R3 using the ip http server global configuration command. This task is completed as follows:

```
R3(config)#interface loopback 0
R3(config-if)#ip address 3.3.3.3 255.255.255.255
R3(config-if)#exit
```

```
R3(config)#router ospf 3
R3(config-router)#network 3.3.3.3 0.0.0.0 area 0
R3(config-router)#exit
R3(config)#ip http server
R3(config)#exit

R1(config)#ip nat inside source static tcp 3.3.3.3 80 150.1.1.5 80
```

Verify your configuration on R1 using the show ip nat translations command:

```
R1#show ip nat translations verbose
Pro Inside global      Inside local      Outside local      Outside global
tcp 150.1.1.5:80       3.3.3.3:80        ---                ---
    create 00:00:16, use 00:00:16 timeout:0,
    flags:
static, extended, extendable, use_count: 0, entry-id: 6, lc_entries: 0
```

Finally, test your solution by connecting to 150.1.1.5 from R4 using TCP port 80:

```
R4#telnet 150.1.1.5 www
Trying 150.1.1.5, 80 ... Open

quit
HTTP/1.1 400 Bad Request
Date: Thu, 16 Jun 2011 11:59:42 GMT
Server: cisco-IOS
Accept-Ranges: none

400 Bad Request

[Connection to 150.1.1.5 closed by foreign host]
```

You can use the show ip nat translations verbose command to view detailed connection information while the session is in progress:

```
R1#show ip nat translations verbose
Pro Inside global      Inside local      Outside local      Outside global
tcp 150.1.1.5:80       3.3.3.3:80        150.1.1.4:12028    150.1.1.4:12028
    create 00:00:04, use 00:00:04 timeout:86400000, left 23:59:55,
    flags:
extended, use_count: 0, entry-id: 8, lc_entries: 0

tcp 150.1.1.5:80       3.3.3.3:80        150.1.1.4:15989    150.1.1.4:15989
    create 00:00:25, use 00:00:18 timeout:86400000, left 00:00:41,
    flags:
extended, timing-out, use_count: 0, entry-id: 7, lc_entries: 0

tcp 150.1.1.5:80       3.3.3.3:80        ---                ---
    create 00:00:56, use 00:00:04 timeout:0,
    flags:
static, extended, extendable, use_count: 2, entry-id: 6, lc_entries: 0
```

Task 5

The requirements of this task are straightforward. To complete it, you need to disable ICMP unreachables, drop packets with IP options, disable source-routing, and disable the directed Broadcast feature. This task is completed as follows:

```
R1(config)#interface fastethernet 0/0
R1(config-if)#no ip unreachables
R1(config-if)#no ip directed-broadcast
R1(config-if)#exit
R1(config)#ip options drop
R1(config)#no ip source-route
```

FINAL ROUTER CONFIGURATIONS

R1

```
R1#term len 0
R1#sh run
Building configuration...

Current configuration : 1722 bytes
!
version 12.4
service timestamps debug datetime msec
service timestamps log datetime msec
no service password-encryption
!
hostname R1
!
boot-start-marker
boot-end-marker
!
no logging console
!
no aaa new-model
no network-clock-participate slot 1
no network-clock-participate wic 0
no ip source-route
ip options drop
ip cef
!
no ip domain lookup
ip auth-proxy max-nodata-conns 3
ip admission max-nodata-conns 3
!
interface FastEthernet0/0
 ip address 150.1.1.1 255.255.255.248
 no ip unreachables
 ip nat outside
 ip virtual-reassembly
 duplex auto
 speed auto
!
interface Serial0/0
 ip address 10.0.0.1 255.255.255.252
 ip nat inside
 ip virtual-reassembly
 clock rate 2000000
!
interface Serial0/1
 ip address 10.0.0.5 255.255.255.252
 ip nat inside
 ip virtual-reassembly
!
router ospf 1
 router-id 1.1.1.1
 log-adjacency-changes
 network 10.0.0.0 0.255.255.255 area 0
 default-information originate
!
router bgp 65501
 no synchronization
 bgp router-id 1.1.1.1
 bgp log-neighbor-changes
 neighbor 150.1.1.4 remote-as 254
 no auto-summary
!
ip forward-protocol nd
!
no ip http server
no ip http secure-server
ip nat pool SITE-2-POOL 150.1.1.2 150.1.1.2 prefix-length 29
ip nat pool SITE-3-POOL 150.1.1.3 150.1.1.3 prefix-length 29
ip nat inside source list SITE-2-ONLY pool SITE-2-POOL overload
ip nat inside source list SITE-3-ONLY pool SITE-3-POOL overload
ip nat inside source static tcp 3.3.3.3 80 150.1.1.5 80 extendable
!
ip access-list extended SITE-2-ONLY
 permit ip 10.2.2.0 0.0.0.255 any
ip access-list extended SITE-3-ONLY
```

```
 permit ip 10.3.3.0 0.0.0.255 any
!
control-plane
!
line con 0
line aux 0
line vty 0 4
 login
!
end

R1#
```

R2

```
R2#term len 0
R2#sh run
Building configuration...

Current configuration : 903 bytes
!
version 12.4
service timestamps debug datetime msec
service timestamps log datetime msec
no service password-encryption
!
hostname R2
!
boot-start-marker
boot-end-marker
!
no logging console
!
no aaa new-model
no network-clock-participate slot 1
no network-clock-participate wic 0
ip cef
!
no ip domain lookup
ip auth-proxy max-nodata-conns 3
ip admission max-nodata-conns 3
!
interface FastEthernet0/0
 ip address 10.2.2.2 255.255.255.0
 duplex auto
 speed auto
!
interface Serial0/0
 ip address 10.0.0.2 255.255.255.252
!
interface Serial0/1
 no ip address
 shutdown
!
router ospf 2
 router-id 2.2.2.2
 log-adjacency-changes
 network 10.0.0.0 0.255.255.255 area 0
!
ip forward-protocol nd
!
no ip http server
no ip http secure-server
!
control-plane
!
line con 0
line aux 0
line vty 0 4
 password CCNP
 login
!
end

R2#
```

R3

```
R3#term len 0
R3#sh run
Building configuration...

Current configuration : 1329 bytes
!
version 12.4
service timestamps debug datetime msec
service timestamps log datetime msec
no service password-encryption
!
hostname R3
!
boot-start-marker
boot-end-marker
!
no logging console
!
no aaa new-model
no network-clock-participate slot 1
no network-clock-participate wic 0
ip cef
!
no ip domain lookup
ip auth-proxy max-nodata-conns 3
ip admission max-nodata-conns 3
!
interface Loopback0
 ip address 3.3.3.3 255.255.255.255
!
interface FastEthernet0/0
 ip address 10.3.3.3 255.255.255.0
 duplex auto
 speed auto
!
interface Serial1/0
 ip address 10.0.0.6 255.255.255.252
 clock rate 128000
!
interface Serial1/1
 no ip address
 shutdown
 clock rate 128000
!
interface Serial1/2
 no ip address
 shutdown
 clock rate 128000
!
interface Serial1/3
 no ip address
 shutdown
!
interface Serial1/4
 no ip address
 shutdown
!
interface Serial1/5
 no ip address
 shutdown
!
interface Serial1/6
 no ip address
 shutdown
!
interface Serial1/7
 no ip address
 shutdown
!
router ospf 3
 router-id 3.3.3.3
 log-adjacency-changes
 network 3.3.3.3 0.0.0.0 area 0
 network 10.0.0.0 0.255.255.255 area 0
!
ip forward-protocol nd
!
ip http server
no ip http secure-server
```

```
!
control-plane
!
line con 0
line aux 0
line vty 0 4
 password CCNP
 login
!
end
R3#
```

R4

```
R4#term len 0
R4#sh run
Building configuration...

Current configuration : 1019 bytes
!
version 12.4
service timestamps debug datetime msec
service timestamps log datetime msec
no service password-encryption
!
hostname R4
!
boot-start-marker
boot-end-marker
!
no logging console
!
no aaa new-model
no network-clock-participate slot 1
no network-clock-participate wic 0
ip cef
!
no ip domain lookup
ip auth-proxy max-nodata-conns 3
ip admission max-nodata-conns 3
!
interface Loopback0
 ip address 160.0.0.4 255.255.255.255
!
interface FastEthernet0/0
 ip address 150.1.1.4 255.255.255.248
 duplex auto
 speed auto
!
interface Serial0/0
 no ip address
 shutdown
!
interface Serial0/1
 no ip address
 shutdown
!
router bgp 254
 no synchronization
 bgp router-id 4.4.4.4
 bgp log-neighbor-changes
 neighbor 150.1.1.1 remote-as 65501
 neighbor 150.1.1.1 default-originate
 no auto-summary
!
ip forward-protocol nd
!
no ip http server
no ip http secure-server
!
control-plane
!
line con 0
line aux 0
line vty 0 4
 login
!
end

R4#
```

CCNP LAB 81

CCNP Multi-Technology Lab

Lab Objective:

The objective of this lab is to cover all relevant CCNP ROUTE and SWITCH theory. These labs will include topics from each of these guides. It should be noted that not all topics will be included in all labs. Additionally, not all solutions will be illustrated in detail. You can refer to previous labs for assistance with some basic configurations.

Lab Topology:

The lab network topology is illustrated below:

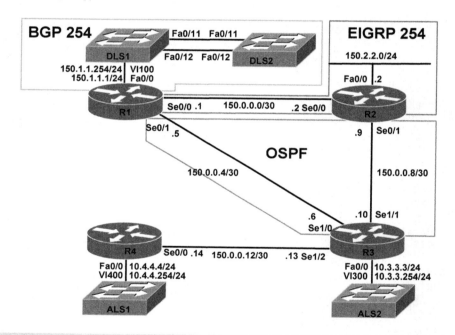

IMPORTANT NOTE: If you are using the www.howtonetwork.net racks, please implement the following pre-lab configurations. This is required because of the manner in which the routers and switches are physically cabled to each other. The following configuration should be applied to switch ALS1:

```
!
hostname ALS1
!
vtp mode transparent
!
vlan 100
 name R1-VLAN
!
vlan 300
 name R3-VLAN
!
```

```
vlan 400
 name R4-VLAN
!
interface fastethernet 0/1
 switchport access vlan 100
 switchport mode access
!
interface fastethernet 0/2
shutdown
!
interface fastethernet 0/3
 switchport access vlan 300
 switchport mode access
!
interface fastethernet 0/4
 switchport access vlan 400
 switchport mode access
!
interface range fastethernet 0/5 - 6
shutdown
!
interface fastethernet0/7
 switchport mode trunk
!
interface fastethernet 0/8
 switchport mode trunk
!
interface range fastethernet 0/9 - 10
 shutdown
!
interface range fastethernet 0/11 - 12
 switchport mode trunk
!
interface vlan 400
 ip address 10.4.4.254 255.255.255.0
 no shutdown
!
ip default-gateway 10.4.4.4
!
line vty 0 4
 privilege level 15
 password cisco
 login
!
end
!
hostname ALS2
!
vtp mode transparent
!
vlan 300
 name R3-VLAN
!
interface range fastethernet 0/1 - 10
 shutdown
!
interface fastethernet 0/11
 switchport mode trunk
!
interface fastethernet 0/12
 switchport mode trunk
!
interface vlan 300
 ip address 10.3.3.254 255.255.255.0
 no shutdown
!
ip default-gateway 10.3.3.3
!
line vty 0 4
 privilege level 15
 password cisco
 login
 !
end
!
hostname DLS1
!
ip routing
```

```
!
vtp mode transparent
!
vlan 100
 name R1-VLAN
!
interface range fastethernet 0/1 - 6
 shutdown
!
interface range fastethernet 0/7 - 8
 switchport trunk encapsulation dot1q
 switchport mode trunk
!
interface range fastethernet 0/9 - 10
 shutdown
!
interface fastethernet 0/11
 switchport mode dynamic desirable
!
interface fastethernet 0/12
 switchport mode dynamic desirable
!
interface range fastethernet 0/13 - 48
 shutdown
!
interface vlan 100
 ip address 150.1.1.254 255.255.255.0
 no shutdown
!
line vty 0 4
 privilege level 15
 password cisco
 login
!
end


!
hostname DLS2
!
ip routing
!
vtp mode transparent
!
interface range fastethernet 0/1 - 10
 shutdown
!
interface fastethernet 0/11
 switchport mode dynamic desirable
!
interface fastethernet 0/12
 switchport mode dynamic desirable
!
interface range fastethernet 0/13 - 48
 shutdown
!
line vty 0 4
 privilege level 15
 password cisco
 login
!
end
!
interface fastethernet 0/12
 switchport mode trunk
!
interface vlan 300
 ip address 10.3.3.254 255.255.255.0
 no shutdown
!
ip default-gateway 10.3.3.3
!
line vty 0 4
 privilege level 15
 password cisco
 login
!
end
```

If you are using the www.howtonetwork.net racks, please bring up the LAN interface connected to R2 by the following configuration:

```
interface fastethernet 0/0
  ip address 150.2.2.2 255.255.255.0
  no keepalive
  loopback
  no shutdown
```

Alternatively, you can simply connect the interface to a hub or one of the switches and bring up the interface in the standard manner.

Task 1

Configure hostnames, IP addressing on all routers as illustrated in the network topology.

Task 2

Configure an LACP EtherChannel between DLS1 and DLS2. Assign this EtherChannel the IP subnet 192.168.0.0/30. Verify that DLS1 and DLS2 can ping each other across this link.

Task 3

In the future, multiple links will be added to the EtherChannel between DLS1 and DLS2. To mitigate against any potential issues cause my mismatched configurations, ensure that the switches disable the links if such an event happened. Verify your configuration.

Task 4

Management wants to ensure that if any other devices other than R1, R3, and R4 are connected to switch ALS1, the ports should drop packets with unknown MAC addresses, the switch should send out an SNMP trap and a Syslog message, and the violation counter is incremented. The Syslog should and SNMP traps should be sent to host 150.2.2.254. An SNMP read-only community string of CCNP should be used. This configuration should survive a reboot of the switch. Verify your configuration using the appropriate commands.

Task 5

Configure BGP between DLS1 and DLS2. Use the Layer 3 EtherChannel for peering. Configure and advertise the following Loopback interfaces on DLS2 via BGP:

* Loopback 10: IP Address 172.16.10.2/32
* Loopback 11: IP Address 172.16.11.2/32
* Loopback 12: IP Address 172.16.11.2/32

Next, configure BGP between DLS1 and R1. Ensure that R1 is able to receive all of the prefixes advertised by DLS2 and vice-versa. Finally, ensure that R1 is able to ping all of the prefixes advertised by DLS2. You are NOT allowed to use the `neighbor <address> next-hop-self` command in your solution. Also, you are NOT allowed to use static routes. Verify your solution using the appropriate commands.

Task 6

Configure EIGRP between R1 and R2 as illustrated in the topology. Next, configure OSPF area 0 on R1, R2 and R3 as illustrated in the topology. Do NOT enable OSPF for R3s LAN subnet or between R3 and R4. Verify your configuration using the appropriate commands.

Task 7

Configure your network so that R2 and R3 can reach the IP subnets advertised by DLS2 and all devices can reach each other. You are NOT allowed to redistribute any routes into OSPF or EIGRP when completing this task. You can, however, redistribute routes into BGP. You are only allowed to configure R1. Verify your solution using the appropriate commands.

Task 8

Configure your network so that if either R2 or R3 loses its link to R1, all other devices are still able to reach the local router. When you implement your solution, keep in mind that when either the R1-R2 or R1-R3 links are up, your solution should ensure that R2 prefers the path via R1 to reach the DLS2 subnets, while R3 prefers the path via R1 to reach the DLS2 subnets.

Test your solution by first disabling the R1-R2 link and pinging from the LAN subnet of R2 to one of the Loopbacks on DLS2. Next, test your solution by disabling the R1-R3 link and pinging from R3 to one of the Loopback subnets on switch DLS2.

Task 9

Configure your network so that the 10.x.x.x subnets connected to R3 and R4 are able to ping all other subnets. You are NOT allowed to advertise these subnets via OSPF. In addition to this, you are NOT allowed to configure any static routes when completing this task. These devices should be able to ping all other devices even if the R1-R3 link fails. Verify your solution by pinging from ALS1 and ALS2 to one of the Loopback subnets on switch DLS2. Finally, disable the R1-R3 link and verify that the switches are still able to ping other devices, e.g. DLS2.

LAB VALIDATION

Task 1

Please refer to previous labs for basic IPv4 addressing and hostname configuration. This will not be included in this section to avoid being redundant.

Task 2

Please refer to previous labs for basic EtherChannel configuration. This will not be included in this section to avoid being redundant. Following your implementation, verify your solution using the show etherchannel commands to view the configuration parameters and also the operating mode (channel protocol) being used:

```
DLS1#show etherchannel summary
Flags:  D - down         P - bundled in port-channel
        I - stand-alone  s - suspended
        H - Hot-standby (LACP only)
        R - Layer3       S - Layer2
        U - in use       f - failed to allocate aggregator

        M - not in use, minimum links not met
        u - unsuitable for bundling
        w - waiting to be aggregated
        d - default port


Number of channel-groups in use: 1
Number of aggregators:            1

Group  Port-channel  Protocol    Ports
------+-------------+-----------+-----------------------------------------------
10     Po10(RU)      LACP        Fa0/11(P)   Fa0/12(P)
```

You can verify LACP information using the show lacp commands:

```
DLS1#show lacp neighbor
Flags:  S - Device is requesting Slow LACPDUs
        F - Device is requesting Fast LACPDUs
        A - Device is in Active mode          P - Device is in Passive mode

Channel group 10 neighbors

Partner's information:

                      LACP port                    Admin  Oper  Port    Port
Port        Flags     Priority  Dev ID        Age   key    Key   Number  State
```

```
Fa0/11    SA    32768    000b.fd67.6500  15s  0x0  0xA  0x36  0x3D
Fa0/12    SA    32768    000b.fd67.6500  12s  0x0  0xA  0x37  0x3D
```

Finally, complete this task by pinging between DLS1 and DLS2 across the EtherChannel.

```
DLS1#ping 192.168.0.2

Type escape sequence to abort.
Sending 5, 100-byte ICMP Echos to 192.168.0.2, timeout is 2 seconds:
!!!!!
Success rate is 100 percent (5/5), round-trip min/avg/max = 4/4/4 ms
```

Task 3

To complete this task, you need to enable the EtherChannel Guard feature on both switches:

```
DLS1(config)#spanning-tree etherchannel guard misconfig

DLS2(config)#spanning-tree etherchannel guard misconfig
```

Verify your configuration using the show spanning-tree summary command:

```
DLS1#show spanning-tree summary
Switch is in pvst mode
Root bridge for: none
Extended system ID           is enabled
Portfast Default             is disabled
PortFast BPDU Guard Default  is disabled
Portfast BPDU Filter Default is disabled
Loopguard Default            is disabled
EtherChannel misconfig guard is enabled
UplinkFast                   is disabled
BackboneFast                 is disabled
Configured Pathcost method used is short

Name               Blocking Listening Learning Forwarding STP Active
------------------ -------- --------- -------- ---------- ----------
VLAN0001                1        0        0         1          2
VLAN0100                1        0        0         1          2
------------------ -------- --------- -------- ---------- ----------
2 vlans                 2        0        0         2          4

DLS2#show spanning-tree summary
Switch is in pvst mode
Root bridge for: none
Extended system ID           is enabled
Portfast Default             is disabled
PortFast BPDU Guard Default  is disabled
Portfast BPDU Filter Default is disabled
Loopguard Default            is disabled
EtherChannel misconfig guard is enabled
UplinkFast                   is disabled
BackboneFast                 is disabled
Configured Pathcost method used is short

Name               Blocking Listening Learning Forwarding STP Active
------------------ -------- --------- -------- ---------- ----------
Total                   0        0        0         0          0
```

Task 4

To complete this task, you need to enable sticky learning and specify a maximum of one MAC address for these ports (default). In addition, change the violation mode to restrict. Finally, you also need to configure Syslogging and SNMP on switch ALS1. This is completed as follows:

```
ALS1(config)#interface range fastethernet 0/1 , fastethernet 0/3 - 4
ALS1(config-if-range)#switchport port-security
ALS1(config-if-range)#switchport port-security mac-address sticky
ALS1(config-if-range)#switchport port-security violation restrict
ALS1(config-if-range)#exit
ALS1(config)#logging on
ALS1(config)#logging 150.2.2.254
```

```
ALS1(config)#logging trap informational
ALS1(config)#snmp-server community CCNP RO
ALS1(config)#snmp-server host 150.2.2.254 traps CCNP port-security
ALS1(config)#snmp-server enable traps port-security
```

Verify your port security configuration using the show port-security commands:

```
ALS1#show port-security
Secure Port  MaxSecureAddr  CurrentAddr  SecurityViolation  Security Action
                (Count)        (Count)        (Count)
---------------------------------------------------------------------------
      Fa0/1            1            1                  0         Restrict
      Fa0/3            1            1                  0         Restrict
      Fa0/4            1            1                  0         Restrict
---------------------------------------------------------------------------
Total Addresses in System (excluding one mac per port)    : 0
Max Addresses limit in System (excluding one mac per port) : 1024
```

To view security sticky learned MAC addresses, append the address keyword:

```
ALS1#show port-security address
            Secure Mac Address Table
-------------------------------------------------------------------------
Vlan    Mac Address       Type          Ports     Remaining Age
                                                      (mins)
----    -----------       ----          -----     -------------
100    000f.235e.ec80    SecureSticky    Fa0/1         -
300    0013.7faf.3e00    SecureSticky    Fa0/3         -
400    000f.235e.f120    SecureSticky    Fa0/4         -
-------------------------------------------------------------------------
Total Addresses in System (excluding one mac per port)    : 0
Max Addresses limit in System (excluding one mac per port) : 1024
```

Verify logging using the **show logging** command:

```
ALS1#show logging
Syslog logging: enabled (0 messages dropped, 0 messages rate-limited, 0 flushes, 0
overruns)
    Console logging: disabled
    Monitor logging: level debugging, 0 messages logged
    Buffer logging: level debugging, 112 messages logged
    Exception Logging: size (4096 bytes)
    File logging: disabled
    Trap logging: level informational, 116 message lines logged
        Logging to 150.2.2.254, 1 message lines logged

[Truncated Output]
```

Finally, verify SNMP using the show snmp commands:

```
ALS1#show snmp
Chassis: FAB0540Y20Z
0 SNMP packets input
    0 Bad SNMP version errors
    0 Unknown community name
    0 Illegal operation for community name supplied
    0 Encoding errors
    0 Number of requested variables
    0 Number of altered variables
    0 Get-request PDUs
    0 Get-next PDUs
    0 Set-request PDUs
0 SNMP packets output
    0 Too big errors (Maximum packet size 1500)
    0 No such name errors
    0 Bad values errors
    0 General errors
    0 Response PDUs
    0 Trap PDUs
SNMP global trap: disabled

SNMP logging: enabled
```

```
    Logging to 150.2.2.254.162, 0/10, 0 sent, 0 dropped.
SNMP agent enabled
```

Task 5

The basic BGP peering configuration to complete this task is straightforward. There are, some caveats, however, to be aware of. First, to complete this task, you will need to configure switch DLS1 as a Route Reflector. This will allow DLS2 and R1 to receive each others' advertised prefixes. This is configuration is completed as follows:

```
DLS1(config)#router bgp 254
DLS1(config-router)#neighbor 192.168.0.2 route-reflector-client
DLS1(config-router)#neighbor 150.1.1.1 remote-as 254
DLS1(config-router)#neighbor 150.1.1.1 route-reflector-client
DLS1(config-router)#exit
```

Next, to complete the specified task without using the neighbor <address> next-hop-self command, you need to configure an outbound route map on DLS1 to change the NEXT_HOP attribute. This is the recommended method of changing the NEXT_HOP attribute on a Route Reflector. This is the only supported method when the same command has been applied to clients of the Route Reflector. The neighbor <address> next-hop-self is applicable on a Route Reflector from routes received from an external peer. This task is completed as follows:

```
DLS1(config)#route-map CHANGE-R1-NEXT-HOP
DLS1(config-route-map)#set ip next
DLS1(config-route-map)#set ip next-hop 150.1.1.254
% Warning: Next hop address is our address
DLS1(config-route-map)#exit
DLS1(config)#router bgp 254
DLS1(config-router)#neighbor 150.1.1.1 route-map CHANGE-R1-NEXT-HOP out
DLS1(config-router)#exit
```

Finally, to complete this task, you need to advertise a default route from DLS1 to DLS2:

```
DLS1(config)#router bgp 254
DLS1(config-router)#neighbor 192.168.0.2 default-originate
DLS1(config-router)#exit
```

Verify your solution by looking at the BGP RIBs of all devices within Autonomous System 254:

```
DLS1#show ip bgp
BGP table version is 10, local router ID is 1.1.1.1
Status codes: s suppressed, d damped, h history, * valid, > best, i - internal,
              r RIB-failure, S Stale
Origin codes: i - IGP, e - EGP, ? - incomplete

   Network          Next Hop            Metric LocPrf Weight Path
*>i172.16.10.1/32   192.168.0.2              0    100      0 i
*>i172.16.11.1/32   192.168.0.2              0    100      0 i
*>i172.16.12.1/32   192.168.0.2              0    100      0 i

DLS2#show ip bgp
BGP table version is 5, local router ID is 2.2.2.2
Status codes: s suppressed, d damped, h history, * valid, > best, i - internal,
              r RIB-failure, S Stale
Origin codes: i - IGP, e - EGP, ? - incomplete

   Network          Next Hop            Metric LocPrf Weight Path
*>i0.0.0.0          192.168.0.1              0    100      0 i
*>  172.16.10.1/32  0.0.0.0                  0           32768 i
*>  172.16.11.1/32  0.0.0.0                  0           32768 i
*>  172.16.12.1/32  0.0.0.0                  0           32768 i

R1#show ip bgp
BGP table version is 7, local router ID is 1.0.1.1
Status codes: s suppressed, d damped, h history, * valid, > best, i - internal,
              r RIB-failure, S Stale
Origin codes: i - IGP, e - EGP, ? - incomplete

   Network          Next Hop            Metric LocPrf Weight Path
```

```
*>i172.16.10.1/32    150.1.1.254             0        100     0 i
*>i172.16.11.1/32    150.1.1.254             0        100     0 i
*>i172.16.12.1/32    150.1.1.254             0        100     0 i
```

Finally, verify that R1 can ping the Loopback subnets advertised by switch DLS2:

```
R1#ping 172.16.10.1

Type escape sequence to abort.
Sending 5, 100-byte ICMP Echos to 172.16.10.1, timeout is 2 seconds:
!!!!!
Success rate is 100 percent (5/5), round-trip min/avg/max = 1/2/4 ms

R1#ping 172.16.11.1

Type escape sequence to abort.
Sending 5, 100-byte ICMP Echos to 172.16.11.1, timeout is 2 seconds:
!!!!!
Success rate is 100 percent (5/5), round-trip min/avg/max = 1/2/4 ms

R1#ping 172.16.12.1

Type escape sequence to abort.
Sending 5, 100-byte ICMP Echos to 172.16.12.1, timeout is 2 seconds:
!!!!!
Success rate is 100 percent (5/5), round-trip min/avg/max = 1/2/4 ms
```

Task 6

Please refer to previous labs for basic OSPF and EIGRP configuration. Following configuration, the routing tables on your routers should show the following entries:

```
R1#show ip route
Codes: C - connected, S - static, R - RIP, M - mobile, B - BGP
       D - EIGRP, EX - EIGRP external, O - OSPF, IA - OSPF inter area
       N1 - OSPF NSSA external type 1, N2 - OSPF NSSA external type 2
       E1 - OSPF external type 1, E2 - OSPF external type 2
       i - IS-IS, su - IS-IS summary, L1 - IS-IS level-1, L2 - IS-IS level-2
       ia - IS-IS inter area, * - candidate default, U - per-user static route
       o - ODR, P - periodic downloaded static route

Gateway of last resort is not set

     172.16.0.0/32 is subnetted, 3 subnets
B       172.16.12.1 [200/0] via 150.1.1.254, 00:18:00
B       172.16.11.1 [200/0] via 150.1.1.254, 00:18:00
B       172.16.10.1 [200/0] via 150.1.1.254, 00:18:00
     150.0.0.0/30 is subnetted, 3 subnets
C       150.0.0.4 is directly connected, Serial0/1
C       150.0.0.0 is directly connected, Serial0/0
O       150.0.0.8 [110/845] via 150.0.0.6, 00:02:39, Serial0/1
     150.1.0.0/24 is subnetted, 1 subnets
C       150.1.1.0 is directly connected, FastEthernet0/0
     150.2.0.0/24 is subnetted, 1 subnets
D       150.2.2.0 [90/2172416] via 150.0.0.2, 00:03:44, Serial0/0

R2#show ip route
Codes: C - connected, S - static, R - RIP, M - mobile, B - BGP
       D - EIGRP, EX - EIGRP external, O - OSPF, IA - OSPF inter area
       N1 - OSPF NSSA external type 1, N2 - OSPF NSSA external type 2
       E1 - OSPF external type 1, E2 - OSPF external type 2
       i - IS-IS, su - IS-IS summary, L1 - IS-IS level-1, L2 - IS-IS level-2
       ia - IS-IS inter area, * - candidate default, U - per-user static route
       o - ODR, P - periodic downloaded static route

Gateway of last resort is not set

     150.0.0.0/30 is subnetted, 3 subnets
O       150.0.0.4 [110/845] via 150.0.0.10, 00:02:49, Serial0/1
C       150.0.0.0 is directly connected, Serial0/0
C       150.0.0.8 is directly connected, Serial0/1
     150.2.0.0/24 is subnetted, 1 subnets
C       150.2.2.0 is directly connected, FastEthernet0/0

R3#show ip route
Codes: C - connected, S - static, R - RIP, M - mobile, B - BGP
```

```
        D - EIGRP, EX - EIGRP external, O - OSPF, IA - OSPF inter area
        N1 - OSPF NSSA external type 1, N2 - OSPF NSSA external type 2
        E1 - OSPF external type 1, E2 - OSPF external type 2
        i - IS-IS, su - IS-IS summary, L1 - IS-IS level-1, L2 - IS-IS level-2
        ia - IS-IS inter area, * - candidate default, U - per-user static route
        o - ODR, P - periodic downloaded static route

Gateway of last resort is not set

     10.0.0.0/24 is subnetted, 1 subnets
C       10.3.3.0 is directly connected, FastEthernet0/0
     150.0.0.0/30 is subnetted, 3 subnets
C       150.0.0.4 is directly connected, Serial1/0
C       150.0.0.12 is directly connected, Serial1/2
C       150.0.0.8 is directly connected, Serial1/1
```

Task 7

To complete this task, you need to redistribute OSPF and EIGRP into BGP. Because we are NOT allowed to redistribute into OSPF or EIGRP, you need to use default routing. This task is completed by implementing the following configuration on R1:

```
R1(config)#router bgp 254
R1(config-router)#redistribute ospf 1 match
R1(config-router)#redistribute eigrp 254
R1(config-router)#exit
R1(config)#router ospf 1
R1(config-router)#default-information originate always
R1(config-router)#exit
R1(config)#interface serial 0/0
R1(config-if)#ip summary-address eigrp 254 0.0.0.0 0.0.0.0
R1(config-if)#exit
```

Next, verify the IP routing tables on all devices using the show ip route command:

```
R1#show ip route
Codes: C - connected, S - static, R - RIP, M - mobile, B - BGP
        D - EIGRP, EX - EIGRP external, O - OSPF, IA - OSPF inter area
        N1 - OSPF NSSA external type 1, N2 - OSPF NSSA external type 2
        E1 - OSPF external type 1, E2 - OSPF external type 2
        i - IS-IS, su - IS-IS summary, L1 - IS-IS level-1, L2 - IS-IS level-2
        ia - IS-IS inter area, * - candidate default, U - per-user static route
        o - ODR, P - periodic downloaded static route

Gateway of last resort is 0.0.0.0 to network 0.0.0.0

     172.16.0.0/32 is subnetted, 3 subnets
B       172.16.12.1 [200/0] via 150.1.1.254, 00:29:25
B       172.16.11.1 [200/0] via 150.1.1.254, 00:29:25
B       172.16.10.1 [200/0] via 150.1.1.254, 00:29:25
     150.0.0.0/30 is subnetted, 3 subnets
C       150.0.0.4 is directly connected, Serial0/1
C       150.0.0.0 is directly connected, Serial0/0
O       150.0.0.8 [110/845] via 150.0.0.6, 00:01:23, Serial0/1
     150.1.0.0/24 is subnetted, 1 subnets
C       150.1.1.0 is directly connected, FastEthernet0/0
     150.2.0.0/24 is subnetted, 1 subnets
D       150.2.2.0 [90/2172416] via 150.0.0.2, 00:15:09, Serial0/0
D*   0.0.0.0/0 is a summary, 00:01:13, Null0

R2#show ip route
Codes: C - connected, S - static, R - RIP, M - mobile, B - BGP
        D - EIGRP, EX - EIGRP external, O - OSPF, IA - OSPF inter area
        N1 - OSPF NSSA external type 1, N2 - OSPF NSSA external type 2
        E1 - OSPF external type 1, E2 - OSPF external type 2
        i - IS-IS, su - IS-IS summary, L1 - IS-IS level-1, L2 - IS-IS level-2
        ia - IS-IS inter area, * - candidate default, U - per-user static route
        o - ODR, P - periodic downloaded static route

Gateway of last resort is 150.0.0.1 to network 0.0.0.0

     150.0.0.0/30 is subnetted, 3 subnets
O       150.0.0.4 [110/845] via 150.0.0.10, 00:01:31, Serial0/1
C       150.0.0.0 is directly connected, Serial0/0
C       150.0.0.8 is directly connected, Serial0/1
```

```
        150.2.0.0/24 is subnetted, 1 subnets
C          150.2.2.0 is directly connected, FastEthernet0/0
D*     0.0.0.0/0 [90/2681856] via 150.0.0.1, 00:01:20, Serial0/0

R3#show ip route
Codes: C - connected, S - static, R - RIP, M - mobile, B - BGP
       D - EIGRP, EX - EIGRP external, O - OSPF, IA - OSPF inter area
       N1 - OSPF NSSA external type 1, N2 - OSPF NSSA external type 2
       E1 - OSPF external type 1, E2 - OSPF external type 2
       i - IS-IS, su - IS-IS summary, L1 - IS-IS level-1, L2 - IS-IS level-2
       ia - IS-IS inter area, * - candidate default, U - per-user static route
       o - ODR, P - periodic downloaded static route

Gateway of last resort is 150.0.0.5 to network 0.0.0.0

        10.0.0.0/24 is subnetted, 1 subnets
C          10.3.3.0 is directly connected, FastEthernet0/0
        150.0.0.0/30 is subnetted, 3 subnets
C          150.0.0.4 is directly connected, Serial1/0
C          150.0.0.12 is directly connected, Serial1/2
C          150.0.0.8 is directly connected, Serial1/1
O*E2 0.0.0.0/0 [110/1] via 150.0.0.5, 00:01:34, Serial1/0

DLS1#show ip route
Codes: C - connected, S - static, R - RIP, M - mobile, B - BGP
       D - EIGRP, EX - EIGRP external, O - OSPF, IA - OSPF inter area
       N1 - OSPF NSSA external type 1, N2 - OSPF NSSA external type 2
       E1 - OSPF external type 1, E2 - OSPF external type 2
       i - IS-IS, su - IS-IS summary, L1 - IS-IS level-1, L2 - IS-IS level-2
       ia - IS-IS inter area, * - candidate default, U - per-user static route
       o - ODR, P - periodic downloaded static route

Gateway of last resort is not set

        172.16.0.0/32 is subnetted, 3 subnets
B          172.16.12.1 [200/0] via 192.168.0.2, 00:41:41
B          172.16.11.1 [200/0] via 192.168.0.2, 00:41:41
B          172.16.10.1 [200/0] via 192.168.0.2, 00:41:41
        192.168.0.0/30 is subnetted, 1 subnets
C          192.168.0.0 is directly connected, Port-channel10
        150.0.0.0/30 is subnetted, 3 subnets
B          150.0.0.4 [200/0] via 150.1.1.1, 00:02:20
B          150.0.0.0 [200/0] via 150.1.1.1, 00:02:11
B          150.0.0.8 [200/845] via 150.0.0.6, 00:02:15
        150.1.0.0/24 is subnetted, 1 subnets
C          150.1.1.0 is directly connected, Vlan100
        150.2.0.0/24 is subnetted, 1 subnets
B          150.2.2.0 [200/2172416] via 150.0.0.2, 00:03:30

DLS2#show ip route
Codes: C - connected, S - static, R - RIP, M - mobile, B - BGP
       D - EIGRP, EX - EIGRP external, O - OSPF, IA - OSPF inter area
       N1 - OSPF NSSA external type 1, N2 - OSPF NSSA external type 2
       E1 - OSPF external type 1, E2 - OSPF external type 2
       i - IS-IS, su - IS-IS summary, L1 - IS-IS level-1, L2 - IS-IS level-2
       ia - IS-IS inter area, * - candidate default, U - per-user static route
       o - ODR, P - periodic downloaded static route

Gateway of last resort is 192.168.0.1 to network 0.0.0.0

        172.16.0.0/32 is subnetted, 3 subnets
C          172.16.12.1 is directly connected, Loopback12
C          172.16.11.1 is directly connected, Loopback11
C          172.16.10.1 is directly connected, Loopback10
        192.168.0.0/30 is subnetted, 1 subnets
C          192.168.0.0 is directly connected, Port-channel10
        150.0.0.0/30 is subnetted, 3 subnets
B          150.0.0.4 [200/0] via 150.1.1.1, 00:02:01
B          150.0.0.0 [200/0] via 150.1.1.1, 00:01:52
B          150.0.0.8 [200/845] via 150.0.0.6, 00:01:56
        150.2.0.0/24 is subnetted, 1 subnets
B          150.2.2.0 [200/2172416] via 150.0.0.2, 00:01:47
B*     0.0.0.0/0 [200/0] via 192.168.0.1, 00:25:14
```

Task 8

To complete this task, you need to redistribute between EIGRP and OSPF on R2. In addition to this, you must modify the BGP configuration on R1 so that external OSPF routes are also redistributed. By default, only internal OSPF routes are redistributed. This configuration must be modified on R1 and R2 as follows:

```
R1(config)#router bgp 254
R1(config-router)#redistribute ospf 1 match internal external 2
R1(config-router)#exit

R2(config)#router eigrp 254
R2(config-router)#redistribute ospf 2 metric 1544 20000 255 1 1500
R2(config-router)#exit
R2(config)#router ospf 2
R2(config-router)#redistribute eigrp 254 subnets
R2(config-router)#default-information originate metric 10
R2(config-router)#exit
```

When redistributing into OSPF, a default route is not redistribute automatically. Therefore, you must use the `default-information originate <always>` command. The `default-information origi-nate` command used by itself will configure the router to advertise a default route if a default route is already present in the routing table. The `always` keyword can be appended to this command to force the router to generate a default route even when one does not exist in the routing table. This keyword should be used with caution as it may result in the black-holing of traffic within the OSPF domain or the forwarding of packets for all unknown destinations to the configured router.

The metric is appended to this command so that when the R1-R3 link is up, R3 will always use the R1-R3 link to reach the DLS2 subnets. No additional configuration is required for EIGRP.

Following this, perform the first task validation task by disabling the R1-R2 link, verifying the routing information and pinging from the LAN subnet of R2 to one of the Loopbacks on DLS2:

```
R2#show ip route
Codes: C - connected, S - static, R - RIP, M - mobile, B - BGP
       D - EIGRP, EX - EIGRP external, O - OSPF, IA - OSPF inter area
       N1 - OSPF NSSA external type 1, N2 - OSPF NSSA external type 2
       E1 - OSPF external type 1, E2 - OSPF external type 2
       i - IS-IS, su - IS-IS summary, L1 - IS-IS level-1, L2 - IS-IS level-2
       ia - IS-IS inter area, * - candidate default, U - per-user static route
       o - ODR, P - periodic downloaded static route

Gateway of last resort is 150.0.0.10 to network 0.0.0.0

     150.0.0.0/30 is subnetted, 2 subnets
O       150.0.0.4 [110/845] via 150.0.0.10, 00:00:46, Serial0/1
C       150.0.0.8 is directly connected, Serial0/1
     150.2.0.0/24 is subnetted, 1 subnets
C       150.2.2.0 is directly connected, FastEthernet0/0
O*E2 0.0.0.0/0 [110/1] via 150.0.0.10, 00:00:12, Serial0/1

R2#ping 172.16.10.1 source 150.2.2.2 size 1500 repeat 10

Type escape sequence to abort.
Sending 10, 1500-byte ICMP Echos to 172.16.10.1, timeout is 2 seconds:
Packet sent with a source address of 150.2.2.2
!!!!!!!!!!
Success rate is 100 percent (10/10), round-trip min/avg/max = 380/382/384 ms
```

Perform the second validation test by disabling the R1-R3 link, verifying the routing information and pinging from R3 to one of the Loopbacks on DLS2:

```
R3#show ip route
Codes: C - connected, S - static, R - RIP, M - mobile, B - BGP
       D - EIGRP, EX - EIGRP external, O - OSPF, IA - OSPF inter area
       N1 - OSPF NSSA external type 1, N2 - OSPF NSSA external type 2
       E1 - OSPF external type 1, E2 - OSPF external type 2
       i - IS-IS, su - IS-IS summary, L1 - IS-IS level-1, L2 - IS-IS level-2
       ia - IS-IS inter area, * - candidate default, U - per-user static route
       o - ODR, P - periodic downloaded static route

Gateway of last resort is 150.0.0.9 to network 0.0.0.0

     10.0.0.0/24 is subnetted, 1 subnets
C       10.3.3.0 is directly connected, FastEthernet0/0
     150.0.0.0/30 is subnetted, 3 subnets
```

```
O E2     150.0.0.0 [110/20] via 150.0.0.9, 00:00:05, Serial1/1
C        150.0.0.12 is directly connected, Serial1/2
C        150.0.0.8 is directly connected, Serial1/1
      150.2.0.0/24 is subnetted, 1 subnets
O E2     150.2.2.0 [110/20] via 150.0.0.9, 00:00:05, Serial1/1
O*E2  0.0.0.0/0 [110/10] via 150.0.0.9, 00:00:05, Serial1/1

R3#ping 172.16.10.1 size 1500 repeat 10

Type escape sequence to abort.
Sending 10, 1500-byte ICMP Echos to 172.16.10.1, timeout is 2 seconds:
!!!!!!!!!!
Success rate is 100 percent (10/10), round-trip min/avg/max = 204/205/208 ms
```

Task 9

While seemingly complex, the task itself is very simple. First, you need to think outside the box. R4 needs some type of default route to reach the rest of the network, otherwise neither it nor ALS1 will be able to each any other subnets. The task states we cannot use static routes or even enable a dynamic routing protocol. This leave ODR available. ODR is NOT a dynamic routing protocol. It is a CDP extension. This first part is completed as follows:

```
R3(config)#router odr
R3(config-router)#exit
R3(config)#interface serial 1/2
R3(config-if)#cdp enable
R3(config-if)#exit

R4(config)#interface serial 0/0
R4(config-if)#cdp enable
R4(config-if)#exit
```

Following this, verify IP routing information using the show ip route command:

```
R3#show ip route odr
     10.0.0.0/24 is subnetted, 2 subnets
o        10.4.4.0 [160/1] via 150.0.0.14, 00:00:54, Serial1/2

R4#show ip route
Codes: C - connected, S - static, R - RIP, M - mobile, B - BGP
       D - EIGRP, EX - EIGRP external, O - OSPF, IA - OSPF inter area
       N1 - OSPF NSSA external type 1, N2 - OSPF NSSA external type 2
       E1 - OSPF external type 1, E2 - OSPF external type 2
       i - IS-IS, su - IS-IS summary, L1 - IS-IS level-1, L2 - IS-IS level-2
       ia - IS-IS inter area, * - candidate default, U - per-user static route
       o - ODR, P - periodic downloaded static route

Gateway of last resort is 150.0.0.13 to network 0.0.0.0

     10.0.0.0/24 is subnetted, 1 subnets
C        10.4.4.0 is directly connected, FastEthernet0/0
     150.0.0.0/30 is subnetted, 1 subnets
C        150.0.0.12 is directly connected, Serial0/0
o*   0.0.0.0/0 [160/1] via 150.0.0.13, 00:00:42, Serial0/0
```

The second requirement is that we cannot advertise any of the 10.x.x.x subnets; however, they should be able to reach all other subnets. Again, thinking outside the box, we can use NAT to satisfy this requirement. The simplest solution would be to PAT everything to a configured IP address, e.g. a Loopback interface on R3. Therefore, even if the R1-R3 link were to fail, the solution would still work. This solution is completed as follows:

```
R3(config)#interface loopback 100
R3(config-if)#ip address 150.0.0.254 255.255.255.255
R3(config-if)#exit
R3(config)#router ospf 3
R3(config-router)#network 150.0.0.254 0.0.0.0 area 0
R3(config-router)#exit
R3(config)#access-list 100 permit ip 10.3.3.0 0.0.0.255 any
R3(config)#access-list 100 permit ip 10.4.4.0 0.0.0.255 any
R3(config)#interface fastethernet 0/0
```

```
R3(config-if)#ip nat inside
R3(config-if)#interface serial 1/2
R3(config-if)#exit
R3(config-if)#ip nat inside
R3(config-if)#exit
R3(config)#interface serial 1/0
R3(config-if)#ip nat outside
R3(config-if)#exit
R3(config)#interface serial 1/1
R3(config-if)#ip nat outside
R3(config-if)#exit
R3(config)#ip nat inside source list 100 interface loopback 100 overload
```

Verify your configuration by pinging from ALS1 and ALS2 to a Loopback subnet on DLS2:

```
ALS1#ping 172.16.10.1

Type escape sequence to abort.
Sending 5, 100-byte ICMP Echos to 172.16.10.1, timeout is 2 seconds:
!!!!!
Success rate is 100 percent (5/5), round-trip min/avg/max = 28/30/32 ms
```

```
ALS2#ping 172.16.10.1

Type escape sequence to abort.
Sending 5, 100-byte ICMP Echos to 172.16.10.1, timeout is 2 seconds:
!!!!!
Success rate is 100 percent (5/5), round-trip min/avg/max = 16/16/20 ms
```

```
R3#show ip nat translations
Pro Inside global      Inside local       Outside local       Outside global
icmp 150.0.0.254:1491  10.3.3.254:1491    172.16.10.1:1491    172.16.10.1:1491
icmp 150.0.0.254:1492  10.3.3.254:1492    172.16.10.1:1492    172.16.10.1:1492
icmp 150.0.0.254:1493  10.3.3.254:1493    172.16.10.1:1493    172.16.10.1:1493
icmp 150.0.0.254:1494  10.3.3.254:1494    172.16.10.1:1494    172.16.10.1:1494
icmp 150.0.0.254:1495  10.3.3.254:1495    172.16.10.1:1495    172.16.10.1:1495
icmp 150.0.0.254:6585  10.4.4.254:6585    172.16.10.1:6585    172.16.10.1:6585
icmp 150.0.0.254:6586  10.4.4.254:6586    172.16.10.1:6586    172.16.10.1:6586
icmp 150.0.0.254:6587  10.4.4.254:6587    172.16.10.1:6587    172.16.10.1:6587
icmp 150.0.0.254:6588  10.4.4.254:6588    172.16.10.1:6588    172.16.10.1:6588
icmp 150.0.0.254:6589  10.4.4.254:6589    172.16.10.1:6589    172.16.10.1:6589
```

Finally, test redundancy by disabling the R1-R3 link and performing the same test:

```
R3(config)#interface serial 1/0
R3(config-if)#shut
R3#show ip route ospf
      150.0.0.0/16 is variably subnetted, 4 subnets, 2 masks
O E2    150.0.0.0/30 [110/20] via 150.0.0.9, 00:00:22, Serial1/1
      150.2.0.0/24 is subnetted, 1 subnets
O E2    150.2.2.0 [110/20] via 150.0.0.9, 00:00:22, Serial1/1
O*E2 0.0.0.0/0 [110/10] via 150.0.0.9, 00:00:22, Serial1/1
```

```
ALS2#ping 172.16.12.1

Type escape sequence to abort.
Sending 5, 100-byte ICMP Echos to 172.16.12.1, timeout is 2 seconds:
!!!!!
Success rate is 100 percent (5/5), round-trip min/avg/max = 16/17/20 ms
```

```
ALS1#ping 172.16.11.1

Type escape sequence to abort.
Sending 5, 100-byte ICMP Echos to 172.16.10.1, timeout is 2 seconds:
!!!!!
Success rate is 100 percent (5/5), round-trip min/avg/max = 32/32/32 ms
```

Verify NAT translations on R3 using the show ip nat translations command:

```
R3#show ip nat translations
Pro Inside global      Inside local       Outside local       Outside global
icmp 150.0.0.254:5221  10.3.3.254:5221    172.16.12.1:5221    172.16.12.1:5221
icmp 150.0.0.254:5222  10.3.3.254:5222    172.16.12.1:5222    172.16.12.1:5222
icmp 150.0.0.254:5223  10.3.3.254:5223    172.16.12.1:5223    172.16.12.1:5223
```

```
icmp 150.0.0.254:5224   10.3.3.254:5224   172.16.12.1:5224   172.16.12.1:5224
icmp 150.0.0.254:5225   10.3.3.254:5225   172.16.12.1:5225   172.16.12.1:5225
icmp 150.0.0.254:2534   10.4.4.254:2534   172.16.11.1:2534   172.16.11.1:2534
icmp 150.0.0.254:2535   10.4.4.254:2535   172.16.11.1:2535   172.16.11.1:2535
icmp 150.0.0.254:2536   10.4.4.254:2536   172.16.11.1:2536   172.16.11.1:2536
icmp 150.0.0.254:2537   10.4.4.254:2537   172.16.11.1:2537   172.16.11.1:2537
icmp 150.0.0.254:2538   10.4.4.254:2538   172.16.11.1:2538   172.16.11.1:2538
```

FINAL SWITCH CONFIGURATIONS

DLS1

```
DLS1#term len 0
DLS1#sh run
Building configuration...

Current configuration : 4938 bytes
!
version 12.2
no service pad
service timestamps debug datetime msec
service timestamps log datetime msec
no service password-encryption
!
hostname DLS1
!
no logging console
!
no aaa new-model
ip subnet-zero
ip routing
no ip domain-lookup
!
vtp domain null
vtp mode transparent
!
spanning-tree mode pvst
spanning-tree extend system-id
!
vlan internal allocation policy ascending
!
vlan 100
 name R1-VLAN
!
interface Port-channel10
 no switchport
 ip address 192.168.0.1 255.255.255.252
!
interface FastEthernet0/1
 switchport mode dynamic desirable
 shutdown
!
interface FastEthernet0/2
 switchport mode dynamic desirable
 shutdown
!
interface FastEthernet0/3
 switchport mode dynamic desirable
 shutdown
!
interface FastEthernet0/4
 switchport mode dynamic desirable
 shutdown
!
interface FastEthernet0/5
 switchport mode dynamic desirable
 shutdown
!
interface FastEthernet0/6
 switchport mode dynamic desirable
 shutdown
!
interface FastEthernet0/7
 switchport trunk encapsulation dot1q
 switchport mode trunk
!
```

```
interface FastEthernet0/8
 switchport trunk encapsulation dot1q
 switchport mode trunk
!
interface FastEthernet0/9
 switchport mode dynamic desirable
 shutdown
!
interface FastEthernet0/10
 switchport mode dynamic desirable
 shutdown
!
interface FastEthernet0/11
 no switchport
 no ip address
 channel-group 10 mode active
!
interface FastEthernet0/12
 no switchport
 no ip address
 channel-group 10 mode active

[Truncated Output]

interface Vlan1
 no ip address
 shutdown
!
interface Vlan100
 ip address 150.1.1.254 255.255.255.0
!
router bgp 254
 no synchronization
 bgp router-id 1.1.1.1
 bgp log-neighbor-changes
 neighbor 150.1.1.1 remote-as 254
 neighbor 150.1.1.1 route-reflector-client
 neighbor 150.1.1.1 route-map CHANGE-R1-NEXT-HOP out
 neighbor 192.168.0.2 remote-as 254
 neighbor 192.168.0.2 route-reflector-client
 neighbor 192.168.0.2 default-originate
 no auto-summary
!
ip classless
ip http server
ip http secure-server
!
route-map CHANGE-R1-NEXT-HOP permit 10
 set ip next-hop 150.1.1.254
!
control-plane
!
line con 0
line vty 0 4
 privilege level 15
 password cisco
 login
line vty 5 15
 login
!
end
DLS1#
```

DLS2

```
DLS2#term len 0
DLS2#sh run
Building configuration...

Current configuration : 4893 bytes
!
version 12.2
no service pad
service timestamps debug datetime msec
service timestamps log datetime msec
no service password-encryption
!
hostname DLS2
!
```

```
no logging console
!
no aaa new-model
ip subnet-zero
ip routing
no ip domain-lookup
!
vtp domain null
vtp mode transparent
!
spanning-tree mode pvst
spanning-tree extend system-id
!
vlan internal allocation policy ascending
!
interface Loopback10
 ip address 172.16.10.1 255.255.255.255
!
interface Loopback11
 ip address 172.16.11.1 255.255.255.255
!
interface Loopback12
 ip address 172.16.12.1 255.255.255.255
!
interface Port-channel10
 no switchport
 ip address 192.168.0.2 255.255.255.252
!
interface FastEthernet0/1
 switchport mode dynamic desirable
 shutdown
!
interface FastEthernet0/2
 switchport mode dynamic desirable
 shutdown
!
interface FastEthernet0/3
 switchport mode dynamic desirable
 shutdown
!
interface FastEthernet0/4
 switchport mode dynamic desirable
 shutdown
!
interface FastEthernet0/5
 switchport mode dynamic desirable
 shutdown
!
interface FastEthernet0/6
 switchport mode dynamic desirable
 shutdown
!
interface FastEthernet0/7
 switchport mode dynamic desirable
 shutdown
!
interface FastEthernet0/8
 switchport mode dynamic desirable
 shutdown
!
interface FastEthernet0/9
 switchport mode dynamic desirable
 shutdown
!
interface FastEthernet0/10
 switchport mode dynamic desirable
 shutdown
!
interface FastEthernet0/11
 no switchport
 no ip address
 channel-group 10 mode active
!
interface FastEthernet0/12
 no switchport
 no ip address
 channel-group 10 mode active

[Truncated Output]

interface Vlan1
```

```
 no ip address
 shutdown
!
router bgp 254
 no synchronization
 bgp router-id 2.2.2.2
 bgp log-neighbor-changes
 network 172.16.10.1 mask 255.255.255.255
 network 172.16.11.1 mask 255.255.255.255
 network 172.16.12.1 mask 255.255.255.255
 neighbor 192.168.0.1 remote-as 254
 no auto-summary
!
ip classless
ip http server
ip http secure-server
!
control-plane
!
line con 0
line vty 0 4
 privilege level 15
 password cisco
 login
line vty 5 15
 login
!
end

DLS2#
```

ALS1

```
ALS1#term len 0
ALS1#sh run
Building configuration...

Current configuration : 2003 bytes
!
version 12.1
no service pad
service timestamps debug uptime
service timestamps log uptime
no service password-encryption
!
hostname ALS1
!
no logging console
!
ip subnet-zero
!
no ip domain-lookup
vtp domain null
vtp mode transparent
!
spanning-tree mode pvst
no spanning-tree optimize bpdu transmission
spanning-tree extend system-id
!
vlan 100
 name R1-VLAN
!
vlan 300
 name R3-VLAN
!
vlan 400
 name R4-VLAN
!
interface FastEthernet0/1
 switchport access vlan 100
 switchport mode access
 switchport port-security
 switchport port-security violation restrict
 switchport port-security mac-address sticky
 switchport port-security mac-address sticky 000f.235e.ec80
!
interface FastEthernet0/2
 shutdown
!
interface FastEthernet0/3
```

```
  switchport access vlan 300
  switchport mode access
  switchport port-security
  switchport port-security violation restrict
  switchport port-security mac-address sticky
  switchport port-security mac-address sticky 0013.7faf.3e00
 !
 interface FastEthernet0/4
  switchport access vlan 400
  switchport mode access
  switchport port-security
  switchport port-security violation restrict
  switchport port-security mac-address sticky
  switchport port-security mac-address sticky 000f.235e.f120
 !
 interface FastEthernet0/5
  shutdown
 !
 interface FastEthernet0/6
  shutdown
 !
 interface FastEthernet0/7
  switchport mode trunk
 !
 interface FastEthernet0/8
  switchport mode trunk
 !
 interface FastEthernet0/9
  shutdown
 !
 interface FastEthernet0/10
  shutdown
 !
 interface FastEthernet0/11
  switchport mode trunk
 !
 interface FastEthernet0/12
  switchport mode trunk
 !
 interface Vlan1
  no ip address
  no ip route-cache
  shutdown
 !
 interface Vlan400
  ip address 10.4.4.254 255.255.255.0
  no ip route-cache
 !
 ip default-gateway 10.4.4.4
 ip http server
 logging 150.2.2.254
 snmp-server community CCNP RO
 snmp-server enable traps port-security
 snmp-server host 150.2.2.254 CCNP  port-security
 !
 line con 0
 line vty 0 4
  privilege level 15
  password cisco
  login
 line vty 5 15
  login
 !
 end
 ALS1#
```

ALS2

```
ALS2#term len 0
ALS2#sh run
Building configuration...

Current configuration : 1135 bytes
!
version 12.1
no service pad
service timestamps debug uptime
service timestamps log uptime
no service password-encryption
```

```
!
hostname ALS2
!
no logging console
!
ip subnet-zero
!
no ip domain-lookup
vtp domain null
vtp mode transparent
!
spanning-tree mode pvst
no spanning-tree optimize bpdu transmission
spanning-tree extend system-id
!
vlan 300
 name R3-VLAN
!
interface FastEthernet0/1
 shutdown
!
interface FastEthernet0/2
 shutdown
!
interface FastEthernet0/3
 shutdown
!
interface FastEthernet0/4
 shutdown
!
interface FastEthernet0/5
 shutdown
!
interface FastEthernet0/6
 shutdown
!
interface FastEthernet0/7
 shutdown
!
interface FastEthernet0/8
 shutdown
!
interface FastEthernet0/9
 shutdown
!
interface FastEthernet0/10
 shutdown
!
interface FastEthernet0/11
 switchport mode trunk
!
interface FastEthernet0/12
 switchport mode trunk
!
interface Vlan1
 no ip address
 no ip route-cache
 shutdown
!
interface Vlan300
 ip address 10.3.3.254 255.255.255.0
 no ip route-cache
!
ip default-gateway 10.3.3.3
ip http server
!
line con 0
line vty 0 4
 privilege level 15
 password cisco
 login
line vty 5 15
 login
!
end

ALS2#
```

FINAL ROUTER CONFIGURATIONS

R1

```
R1#term len 0
R1#sh run
Building configuration...

Current configuration : 1293 bytes
!
version 12.4
service timestamps debug datetime msec
service timestamps log datetime msec
no service password-encryption
!
hostname R1
!
boot-start-marker
boot-end-marker
!
no logging console
!
no aaa new-model
no network-clock-participate slot 1
no network-clock-participate wic 0
ip cef
!

no ip domain lookup
ip auth-proxy max-nodata-conns 3
ip admission max-nodata-conns 3
!
interface FastEthernet0/0
 ip address 150.1.1.1 255.255.255.0
 duplex auto
 speed auto
!
interface Serial0/0
 ip address 150.0.0.1 255.255.255.252
 ip summary-address eigrp 254 0.0.0.0 0.0.0.0 5
 clock rate 2000000
!
interface Serial0/1
 ip address 150.0.0.5 255.255.255.252
!
router eigrp 254
 network 150.0.0.1 0.0.0.0
 no auto-summary
!
router ospf 1
 router-id 1.0.1.1
 log-adjacency-changes
 network 150.0.0.5 0.0.0.0 area 0
 default-information originate always
!
router bgp 254
 no synchronization
 bgp router-id 1.0.1.1
 bgp log-neighbor-changes
 redistribute eigrp 254
 redistribute ospf 1 match internal external 2
 neighbor 150.1.1.254 remote-as 254
 no auto-summary
!
ip forward-protocol nd
!
no ip http server
no ip http secure-server
!
control-plane
!
line con 0
line aux 0
line vty 0 4
 password cisco
 login
!
end

R1#
```

R2

```
R2#term len 0
R2#sh run
Building configuration...

Current configuration : 1151 bytes
!
version 12.4
service timestamps debug datetime msec
service timestamps log datetime msec
no service password-encryption
!
hostname R2
!
boot-start-marker
boot-end-marker
!
no logging console
!
no aaa new-model
no network-clock-participate slot 1
no network-clock-participate wic 0
ip cef
!
no ip domain lookup
ip auth-proxy max-nodata-conns 3
ip admission max-nodata-conns 3
!
interface FastEthernet0/0
 ip address 150.2.2.2 255.255.255.0
 loopback
 duplex auto
 speed auto
 no keepalive
!
interface Serial0/0
 ip address 150.0.0.2 255.255.255.252
!
interface Serial0/1
 ip address 150.0.0.9 255.255.255.252
!
router eigrp 254
 redistribute ospf 2 metric 1544 20000 255 1 1500
 network 150.0.0.2 0.0.0.0
 network 150.2.2.2 0.0.0.0
 no auto-summary
!
router ospf 2
 router-id 2.2.2.2
 log-adjacency-changes
 redistribute eigrp 254 subnets
 network 150.0.0.9 0.0.0.0 area 0
 default-information originate metric 10
!
ip forward-protocol nd
!
no ip http server
no ip http secure-server
!
control-plane
!
line con 0
line aux 0
line vty 0 4
 password cisco
 login
!
end
R2#
```

R3

```
R3#term len 0
R3#sh run
Building configuration...

Current configuration : 1728 bytes
!
version 12.4
```

```
service timestamps debug datetime msec
service timestamps log datetime msec
no service password-encryption
!
hostname R3
!
boot-start-marker
boot-end-marker
!
no logging console
!
no aaa new-model
no network-clock-participate slot 1
no network-clock-participate wic 0
ip cef
!
no ip domain lookup
ip auth-proxy max-nodata-conns 3
ip admission max-nodata-conns 3
!
interface Loopback100
 ip address 150.0.0.254 255.255.255.255
!
interface FastEthernet0/0
 ip address 10.3.3.3 255.255.255.0
 ip nat inside
 ip virtual-reassembly
 duplex auto
 speed auto
!
interface Serial1/0
 ip address 150.0.0.6 255.255.255.252
 ip nat outside
 ip virtual-reassembly
 clock rate 128000
!
interface Serial1/1
 ip address 150.0.0.10 255.255.255.252
 ip nat outside
 ip virtual-reassembly
 clock rate 128000
!
interface Serial1/2
 ip address 150.0.0.13 255.255.255.252
 ip nat inside
 ip virtual-reassembly
 clock rate 128000
!
interface Serial1/3
 no ip address
 shutdown
!
interface Serial1/4
 no ip address
 shutdown
!
interface Serial1/5
 no ip address
 shutdown
!
interface Serial1/6
 no ip address
 shutdown
!
interface Serial1/7
 no ip address
 shutdown
!
router odr
!
router ospf 3
 router-id 3.3.3.3
 log-adjacency-changes
 network 150.0.0.6 0.0.0.0 area 0
 network 150.0.0.10 0.0.0.0 area 0
 network 150.0.0.254 0.0.0.0 area 0
!
ip forward-protocol nd
!
no ip http server
no ip http secure-server
```

```
ip nat inside source list 100 interface Loopback100 overload
!
access-list 100 permit ip 10.3.3.0 0.0.0.255 any
access-list 100 permit ip 10.4.4.0 0.0.0.255 any
!
control-plane
!
line con 0
line aux 0
line vty 0 4
 password cisco
 login
!
end
R3#
```

R4

```
R4#term len 0
R4#sh run
Building configuration...

Current configuration : 809 bytes
!
version 12.4
service timestamps debug datetime msec
service timestamps log datetime msec
no service password-encryption
!
hostname R4
!
boot-start-marker
boot-end-marker
!
no logging console
!
no aaa new-model
no network-clock-participate slot 1
no network-clock-participate wic 0
ip cef
!
no ip domain lookup
ip auth-proxy max-nodata-conns 3
ip admission max-nodata-conns 3
!
interface FastEthernet0/0
 ip address 10.4.4.4 255.255.255.0
 duplex auto
 speed auto
!
interface Serial0/0
 ip address 150.0.0.14 255.255.255.252
!
interface Serial0/1
 no ip address
 shutdown
!
ip forward-protocol nd
!
no ip http server
no ip http secure-server
!
control-plane
!
line con 0
line aux 0
line vty 0 4
 password cisco
 login
!
end

R4#
```

CCNP LAB 82

CCNP Multi-Technology Lab

Lab Objective:

The objective of this lab is to cover all relevant CCNP ROUTE and SWITCH theory. These labs will include topics from each of these guides. It should be noted that not all topics will be included in all labs. Additionally, not all solutions will be illustrated in detail. You can refer to previous labs for assistance with some basic configurations.

Lab Topology:

The lab network topology is illustrated below:

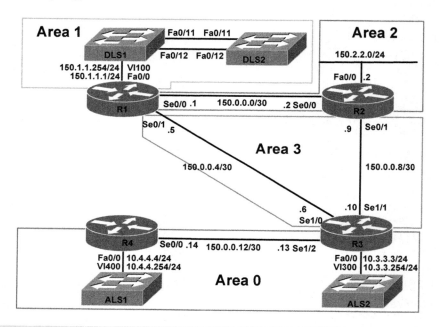

IMPORTANT NOTE: If you are using the www.howtonetwork.net racks, please implement the following pre-lab configurations. This is required because of the manner in which the routers and switches are physically cabled to each other. The following configuration should be applied to switch ALS1:

```
!
hostname ALS1
!
vtp mode transparent
!
vlan 100
 name R1-VLAN
!
vlan 300
 name R3-VLAN
!
```

```
vlan 400
 name R4-VLAN
!
interface fastethernet 0/1
 switchport access vlan 100
 switchport mode access
!
interface fastethernet 0/2
shutdown
!
interface fastethernet 0/3
 switchport access vlan 300
 switchport mode access
!
interface fastethernet 0/4
 switchport access vlan 400
 switchport mode access
!
interface range fastethernet 0/5 - 6
shutdown
!
interface fastethernet0/7
 switchport mode trunk
!
interface fastethernet 0/8
 switchport mode trunk
!
interface range fastethernet 0/9 - 10
 shutdown
!
interface range fastethernet 0/11 - 12
 switchport mode trunk
!
!
interface vlan 400
 ip address 10.4.4.254 255.255.255.0
 no shutdown
!
ip default-gateway 10.4.4.4
!
line vty 0 4
 privilege level 15
 password cisco
 login
!
end

hostname ALS2
!
vtp mode transparent
!
vlan 300
 name R3-VLAN
!
interface range fastethernet 0/1 - 10
 shutdown
!
interface fastethernet 0/11
 switchport mode trunk
!
interface fastethernet 0/12
 switchport mode trunk
!
interface vlan 300
 ip address 10.3.3.254 255.255.255.0
 no shutdown
!
ip default-gateway 10.3.3.3
!
line vty 0 4
 privilege level 15
 password cisco
 login
!
end

!
hostname DLS1
!
ip routing
!
vtp mode transparent
```

```
!
vlan 100
 name R1-VLAN
!
interface range fastethernet 0/1 - 6
 shutdown
!
interface range fastethernet 0/7 - 8
 switchport trunk encapsulation dot1q
 switchport mode trunk
!
interface range fastethernet 0/9 - 10
 shutdown
!
interface fastethernet 0/11
 switchport mode dynamic desirable
!
interface fastethernet 0/12
 switchport mode dynamic desirable
!
interface range fastethernet 0/13 - 48
 shutdown
!
interface vlan 100
 ip address 150.1.1.254 255.255.255.0
 no shutdown
!
line vty 0 4
 privilege level 15
 password cisco
 login
!
end
!
hostname DLS2
!
ip routing
!
vtp mode transparent
!
interface range fastethernet 0/1 - 10
 shutdown
!
interface fastethernet 0/11
 switchport mode dynamic desirable
!
interface fastethernet 0/12
 switchport mode dynamic desirable
!
interface range fastethernet 0/13 - 48
 shutdown
!
line vty 0 4
 privilege level 15
 password cisco
 login
!
end
```

If you are using the www.howtonetwork.net racks, please bring up the LAN interface connected to R2 by the following configuration:

```
interface fastethernet 0/0
 ip address 150.2.2.2 255.255.255.0
 no keepalive
 loopback
 no shutdown
```

Alternatively, you can simply connect the interface to a hub or one of the switches and bring up the interface in the standard manner.

Task 1

Configure hostnames, IP addressing on all routers as illustrated in the network topology.

Task 2

Configure VTP on DLS1 and DLS2 so that DLS2 automatically receives VLAN information from DLS1. Both switches should reside in domain 2011. Secure VTP messages with a password of CCNP2011. Configure an

SVI in VLAN 100 for DLS2. Assign this SVI the IP address 150.1.1.253/24. Verify your configuration using the appropriate commands. Also, verify that all devices on the 150.1.1.0/24 subnet can ping each other.

Task 3

Configure switches DLS1 and DLS2 to use the 802.1w and 802.1t standards. In addition to this, configure the switches to use 32 bit based values for default port path costs Verify the solution and configuration using the appropriate commands.

Task 4

In the future, Cisco IP phones will be connected to ports Fa0/1 to Fa0/5 on switches DLS1 and DSL2. Implement QoS so that markings sent by Cisco phones are trusted. In addition to this, configure QoS so that all user data received on these ports is assigned a CoS value of 2. Verify your configuration using the appropriate commands.

Task 5

In the future, non-Cisco IP phones will be connected to ports Fa0/1 to Fa0/5 on switch ALS2. Implement QoS so that the switch rewrites the CoS value for all incoming frames to a configured default value of 1, regardless of any existing CoS value. Verify your configuration using the appropriate commands.

Task 6

Configure OSPF on all routers as illustrated in the topology. You must adhere to the following guidelines and restrictions when implementing OSPF:
* Ensure that no switches will ever participate in the DR/BDR election process
* Ensure that area 1 supports Type 7 LSAs
* Ensure that no Type 3 LSAs are flooded into area 1
* Ensure that no Hellos are sent out the LAN interfaces of R2, R3, and R4

Your solution should take into account a possible R1-R3 or R2-R3 link failure. Routing should work in the event that either one of these links fails. Verify your solution by checking the routing tables of all devices. Next, test your solution by disabling the R1-R3 link and verifying that you can ping from R4 to DLS2. Finally, test your solution by disabling the R2-R3 link and verifying that you can ping from R4 to R2s LAN interface.

Task 7

Authenticate the OSPF backbone using the plaintext password CCNP2011. Verify your configuration using the appropriate commands.

Task 8

IP version 6 needs to be integrated into the network. Enable RIPng between switches DLS1 and DSL2 as well as router R1. Use the 3ffe:abcd:1111:1/64 subnet. Verify your configuration.

Task 9

Configure ISATAP tunnels on all routers. Use Loopback interfaces as the tunnel source. These Loopback interfaces should use the router number; for example, the Loopback interface on R1 should be assigned IP address 1.1.1.1/32, the Loopback interface on R2 should be assigned IP address 2.2.2.2/32, etc. The tunnels should be configured using the fec0:abcd:1234:1::/64 subnet. Verify your configuration using the appropriate commands.

Task 10

Configure the following IP version 6 (IPv6) LAN subnets on the following routers:
* R2: IPv6 LAN subnet 3ffe:abcd:1111:2/64
* R3: IPv6 LAN subnet 3ffe:abcd:1111:3/64
* R4: IPv6 LAN subnet 3ffe:abcd:1111:4/64

Next, configure MP-BGP on all routers. All routers should use their ISATAP tunnel addresses for peering. Ensure that all routers advertise their LAN subnet via MP-BGP. MP-BGP peering should be configured on all routers as follows:
- R1 - Autonomous System 1: This router will peer with R2
- R2 - Autonomous System 2: This router will peer with R1 and R3
- R3 - Autonomous System 3: This router will peer with R2 and R4
- R4 - Autonomous System 4: This router will peer with R3

Verify your MP-BGP configuration using the appropriate commands.

Task 11

Configure the following IPv6 subnets on routers R2, R3, and R4. These should be advertised via MP-BGP. The subnet allocations are as follows:
- R2 LAN subnet: 3ffe:abcd:1111:1/64
- R3 LAN subnet: 3ffe:abcd:1111:3/64
- R4 LAN subnet: 3ffe:abcd:1111:4/64

Verify your configuration using the appropriate commands. Finally, complete this task by also ensuring that all IPv6 subnets can ping each other. You do not need to be able to ping the switches from the subnets connected to R2, R3, or R4 when completing this task verification.

LAB VALIDATION

Task 1

Please refer to previous labs for basic IPv4 addressing and hostname configuration. This will not be included in this section to avoid being redundant.

Task 2

Please refer to previous labs for basic VTP configuration. This will not be included in this section to avoid being redundant. Verify your solution using the `show vtp` commands:

```
DLS1#show vtp status
VTP Version                     : running VTP2
Configuration Revision          : 1
Maximum VLANs supported locally : 1005
Number of existing VLANs        : 6
VTP Operating Mode              : Server
VTP Domain Name                 : 2011
VTP Pruning Mode                : Disabled
VTP V2 Mode                     : Enabled
VTP Traps Generation            : Disabled
MD5 digest                      : 0xA5 0xC3 0x7F 0x1D 0x9F 0xA2 0xA6 0xC8
Configuration last modified by 150.1.1.254 at 3-1-93 05:53:51
Local updater ID is 150.1.1.254 on interface Vl100 (lowest numbered VLAN interface found)

DLS2#show vtp status
VTP Version                     : running VTP2
Configuration Revision          : 1
Maximum VLANs supported locally : 1005
Number of existing VLANs        : 6
VTP Operating Mode              : Client
VTP Domain Name                 : 2011
VTP Pruning Mode                : Disabled
VTP V2 Mode                     : Enabled
VTP Traps Generation            : Disabled
MD5 digest                      : 0xA5 0xC3 0x7F 0x1D 0x9F 0xA2 0xA6 0xC8
Configuration last modified by 150.1.1.254 at 3-1-93 05:53:51

DLS1#show vtp password
VTP Password: CCNP2011

DLS2#show vtp password
VTP Password: CCNP2011
```

Next, following the SVI configuration on DLS2, verify connectivity with the 150.1.1.0/24 subnet:

```
DLS2#ping 150.1.1.0

Type escape sequence to abort.
Sending 5, 100-byte ICMP Echos to 150.1.1.0, timeout is 2 seconds:
.
Reply to request 1 from 150.1.1.254, 1 ms
Reply to request 1 from 150.1.1.1, 1 ms
Reply to request 2 from 150.1.1.254, 1 ms
Reply to request 2 from 150.1.1.1, 1 ms
Reply to request 3 from 150.1.1.254, 1 ms
Reply to request 3 from 150.1.1.1, 1 ms
Reply to request 4 from 150.1.1.254, 1 ms
Reply to request 4 from 150.1.1.1, 1 ms
```

Task 3

The requirements of this task are straightforward, assuming you remember your Spanning Tree standards from the SWITCH guide. IEEE 802.1w is Rapid STP. The 802.1t standard introduced the extended system ID to conserve MAC addresses and reduces the Bridge Priority to 4 bits and adds a 12-bit Extended System ID. No explicit configuration is required on current Cisco IOS Catalyst switches to enable this functionality. In addition to this, the 802.1t standard assigns 32-bit (long) default port cost values to each port. However, this feature must be explicitly enabled in Cisco IOS Catalyst switches. This task is therefore completed as follows:

```
DLS1(config)#spanning-tree pathcost method long
DLS1(config)#spanning-tree mode rapid-pvst

DLS2(config)#spanning-tree pathcost method long
DLS2(config)#spanning-tree mode rapid-pvst
```

Verify your configuration using the show spanning-tree commands:

```
DLS1#show spanning-tree summary
Switch is in rapid-pvst mode
Root bridge for: none
Extended system ID           is enabled
Portfast Default             is disabled
PortFast BPDU Guard Default  is disabled
Portfast BPDU Filter Default is disabled
Loopguard Default            is disabled
EtherChannel misconfig guard is enabled
UplinkFast                   is disabled
BackboneFast                 is disabled
Configured Pathcost method used is long

Name                    Blocking Listening Learning Forwarding STP Active
----------------------- -------- --------- -------- ---------- ----------
VLAN0001                    1        0         0         3          4
VLAN0100                    1        0         0         3          4
----------------------- -------- --------- -------- ---------- ----------
2 vlans                     2        0         0         6          8

DLS1#show spanning-tree pathcost method
Spanning tree default pathcost method used is long

DLS1#show spanning-tree interface fastethernet 0/11

Vlan             Role Sts Cost       Prio.Nbr Type
---------------- ---- --- ---------  -------- ------------------------------
VLAN0001         Desg FWD 200000     128.11   P2p
VLAN0100         Desg FWD 200000     128.11   P2p
```

Task 4

To complete this task, the trust boundary needs to be extended to the switch port on the Cisco IP phone. However, instead of trusting the CoS values, specify a default value to be assigned instead. This task is completed on switches DSL1 and DLS2 as follows:

```
DLS1(config)#mls qos
QoS: ensure flow-control on all interfaces are OFF for proper operation.
DLS1(config)#interface range fastethernet 0/1 - 5
DLS1(config-if-range)#mls qos trust cos
DLS1(config-if-range)#mls qos trust device cisco-phone
DLS1(config-if-range)#switchport priority extend cos 2
DLS1(config-if-range)#exit

DLS2(config)#mls qos
QoS: ensure flow-control on all interfaces are OFF for proper operation.
DLS2(config)#interface range fastethernet 0/1 - 5
DLS2(config-if-range)#mls qos trust cos
DLS2(config-if-range)#mls qos trust device cisco-phone
DLS2(config-if-range)#switchport priority extend cos 2
DLS2(config-if-range)#exit
```

Verify your configuration using the show mls qos commands:

```
DLS2#show mls qos interface fastethernet 0/1
FastEthernet0/1
trust state: not trusted
trust mode: trust cos
COS override: dis
default COS: 0
DSCP Mutation Map: Default DSCP Mutation Map
Trust device: cisco-phone
```

To verify the appliance trust, i.e. the trust settings for the device connected to the Cisco IP phone switch port, use the show interfaces <name> switchport command:

```
DLS2#show interfaces fastethernet 0/1 switchport
Name: Fa0/1
Switchport: Enabled
Administrative Mode: dynamic desirable
Operational Mode: down
Administrative Trunking Encapsulation: negotiate
Negotiation of Trunking: On
Access Mode VLAN: 1 (default)
Trunking Native Mode VLAN: 1 (default)
Administrative Native VLAN tagging: enabled
Voice VLAN: none
Administrative private-vlan host-association: none
Administrative private-vlan mapping: none
Administrative private-vlan trunk native VLAN: none
Administrative private-vlan trunk Native VLAN tagging: enabled
Administrative private-vlan trunk encapsulation: dot1q
Administrative private-vlan trunk normal VLANs: none
Administrative private-vlan trunk associations: none
Administrative private-vlan trunk mappings: none
Operational private-vlan: none
Trunking VLANs Enabled: ALL
Pruning VLANs Enabled: 2-1001
Capture Mode Disabled
Capture VLANs Allowed: ALL

Protected: false
Unknown unicast blocked: disabled
Unknown multicast blocked: disabled
Appliance trust: 2
```

Task 5

To complete this task on switch ALS2, you need to override the CoS value for all received incoming frames to the specified or desired value. This task is completed as follows:

```
ALS2(config)#interface range fastethernet 0/1 - 5
ALS2(config-if-range)#mls qos cos 1
ALS2(config-if-range)#mls qos cos override
ALS2(config-if-range)#exit
```

Verify your configuration using the show mls qos commands:

```
ALS2#show mls qos interface fastethernet 0/1
FastEthernet0/1
```

```
trust state: not trusted
trust mode: not trusted
COS override: ena
default COS: 1
pass-through: none
trust device: none
```

Task 6

The requirements of this task are verify straightforward. To disable the DR/BDR election on the switches, ensure that they have a priority of 0. Second, OSPF area 1 will need to be configured as a totally stubby NSSA. All other areas follow normal OSPF configuration rules. Keep in mind that you will need to configure virtual links to allow for full IP connectivity. This consideration should factor in a possible R1-R3 link failure, as well as an R2-R3 link failure. Following your configuration, the OSPF Neighbor Tables on all of the routers should show the adjacency states that are printed in the output below:

```
R1#show ip ospf neighbor

Neighbor ID     Pri    State         Dead Time    Address       Interface
2.2.2.2          0     FULL/  -        -           150.0.0.2     OSPF_VL1
3.3.3.3          0     FULL/  -        -           150.0.0.10    OSPF_VL0
150.1.1.253      0     FULL/DROTHER  00:00:33      150.1.1.253   FastEthernet0/0
150.1.1.254      0     FULL/DROTHER  00:00:35      150.1.1.254   FastEthernet0/0
2.2.2.2          0     FULL/  -      00:00:38       150.0.0.2     Serial0/0
3.3.3.3          0     FULL/  -      00:00:36       150.0.0.6     Serial0/1

R2#show ip ospf neighbor

Neighbor ID     Pri    State         Dead Time    Address       Interface
1.1.1.1          0     FULL/  -        -           150.0.0.1     OSPF_VL1
3.3.3.3          0     FULL/  -        -           150.0.0.10    OSPF_VL0
1.1.1.1          0     FULL/  -      00:00:38       150.0.0.1     Serial0/0
3.3.3.3          0     FULL/  -      00:00:30       150.0.0.10    Serial0/1

R3#show ip ospf neighbor

Neighbor ID     Pri    State         Dead Time    Address       Interface
4.4.4.4          0     FULL/  -      00:00:34       150.0.0.14    Serial1/2
2.2.2.2          0     FULL/  -        -           150.0.0.9     OSPF_VL1
1.1.1.1          0     FULL/  -        -           150.0.0.5     OSPF_VL0
2.2.2.2          0     FULL/  -      00:00:35       150.0.0.9     Serial1/1
1.1.1.1          0     FULL/  -      00:00:37       150.0.0.5     Serial1/0

R4#show ip ospf neighbor

Neighbor ID     Pri    State         Dead Time    Address       Interface
3.3.3.3          0     FULL/  -      00:00:32       150.0.0.13    Serial0/0

DLS1#show ip ospf neighbor

Neighbor ID     Pri    State         Dead Time    Address       Interface
1.1.1.1          1     FULL/DR       00:00:34      150.1.1.1     Vlan100
150.1.1.253      0     2WAY/DROTHER  00:00:30      150.1.1.253   Vlan100

DLS2#show ip ospf neighbor

Neighbor ID     Pri    State         Dead Time    Address       Interface
1.1.1.1          1     FULL/DR       00:00:32      150.1.1.1     Vlan100
150.1.1.254      0     2WAY/DROTHER  00:00:31      150.1.1.254   Vlan100
```

Verify the IP routing tables on all routers and switches using the `show ip route` command:

```
DLS1#show ip route ospf
O*IA 0.0.0.0/0 [110/2] via 150.1.1.1, 00:10:37, Vlan100

DLS2#show ip route ospf
O*IA 0.0.0.0/0 [110/2] via 150.1.1.1, 00:10:42, Vlan100
R1#show ip route ospf
     10.0.0.0/24 is subnetted, 2 subnets
O       10.4.4.0 [110/846] via 150.0.0.6, 00:15:04, Serial0/1
O       10.3.3.0 [110/65] via 150.0.0.6, 00:15:04, Serial0/1
     150.0.0.0/30 is subnetted, 4 subnets
O       150.0.0.12 [110/845] via 150.0.0.6, 00:15:04, Serial0/1
O       150.0.0.8 [110/845] via 150.0.0.6, 00:15:04, Serial0/1
```

```
          150.2.0.0/24 is subnetted, 1 subnets
O            150.2.2.0 [110/65] via 150.0.0.2, 00:15:04, Serial0/0

R2#show ip route ospf
          10.0.0.0/24 is subnetted, 2 subnets
O            10.4.4.0 [110/846] via 150.0.0.10, 00:15:15, Serial0/1
O            10.3.3.0 [110/65] via 150.0.0.10, 00:15:15, Serial0/1
          150.0.0.0/30 is subnetted, 4 subnets
O            150.0.0.4 [110/845] via 150.0.0.10, 00:15:15, Serial0/1
O            150.0.0.12 [110/845] via 150.0.0.10, 00:15:15, Serial0/1
          150.1.0.0/24 is subnetted, 1 subnets
O IA         150.1.1.0 [110/65] via 150.0.0.1, 00:15:15, Serial0/0

R3#show ip route ospf
          10.0.0.0/24 is subnetted, 2 subnets
O            10.4.4.0 [110/782] via 150.0.0.14, 00:15:19, Serial1/2
          150.0.0.0/30 is subnetted, 4 subnets
O IA         150.0.0.0 [110/845] via 150.0.0.9, 00:15:19, Serial1/1
                       [110/845] via 150.0.0.5, 00:15:19, Serial1/0
          150.1.0.0/24 is subnetted, 1 subnets
O IA         150.1.1.0 [110/782] via 150.0.0.5, 00:15:19, Serial1/0
          150.2.0.0/24 is subnetted, 1 subnets
O IA         150.2.2.0 [110/782] via 150.0.0.9, 00:15:19, Serial1/1

R4#show ip route ospf
          10.0.0.0/24 is subnetted, 2 subnets
O            10.3.3.0 [110/65] via 150.0.0.13, 00:15:21, Serial0/0
          150.0.0.0/30 is subnetted, 4 subnets
O IA         150.0.0.4 [110/845] via 150.0.0.13, 00:15:21, Serial0/0
O IA         150.0.0.0 [110/909] via 150.0.0.13, 00:15:21, Serial0/0
O IA         150.0.0.8 [110/845] via 150.0.0.13, 00:15:21, Serial0/0
          150.1.0.0/24 is subnetted, 1 subnets
O IA         150.1.1.0 [110/846] via 150.0.0.13, 00:15:21, Serial0/0
          150.2.0.0/24 is subnetted, 1 subnets
O IA         150.2.2.0 [110/846] via 150.0.0.13, 00:15:21, Serial0/0
```

Prior to any testing, verify end-to-end connectivity by pinging from the LAN subnet on R4 to the IP address configured on DLS2:

```
R4#ping 150.1.1.253 source 10.4.4.4 repeat 10 size 1500

Type escape sequence to abort.
Sending 10, 1500-byte ICMP Echos to 150.1.1.253, timeout is 2 seconds:
Packet sent with a source address of 10.4.4.4
!!!!!!!!!!
Success rate is 100 percent (10/10), round-trip min/avg/max = 380/382/388 ms
```

Next, test your redundant solution by disabling the R1-R3 link and performing the same test:

```
R1(config)#interface serial 0/1
R1(config-if)#shut
```

```
R4#ping 150.1.1.253 source 10.4.4.4 repeat 10 size 1500

Type escape sequence to abort.
Sending 10, 1500-byte ICMP Echos to 150.1.1.253, timeout is 2 seconds:
Packet sent with a source address of 10.4.4.4
!!!!!!!!!!
Success rate is 100 percent (10/10), round-trip min/avg/max = 392/394/396 ms
```

Optionally, use a Traceroute to verify the path the traffic is taking:

```
R4#traceroute ip

Target IP address: 150.1.1.253
Source address: 10.4.4.4
Numeric display [n]: y
Timeout in seconds [3]:
Probe count [3]:
Minimum Time to Live [1]:
Maximum Time to Live [30]:
```

```
Port Number [33434]:
Loose, Strict, Record, Timestamp, Verbose[none]:
Type escape sequence to abort.
Tracing the route to 150.1.1.253

  1 150.0.0.13 8 msec 8 msec 8 msec <<<<<<<<<<<<< R3s Serial1/2 Interface
  2 150.0.0.9 16 msec 16 msec 16 msec <<<<<<<<<<< R2s Serial0/1 Interface
  3 150.0.0.1 16 msec 16 msec 16 msec <<<<<<<<<< R1s Serial0/0 Interface
  4 150.1.1.253 16 msec *  24 msec <<<<<<<<<< DLS2s VLAN 100 Interface
```

Perform a second failover test by disabling the R2-R3 link and pinging R2s LAN subnet. Prior to this test, verify that R4s LAN subnet can ping R2s LAN subnet:

```
R4#ping 150.2.2.2 source 10.4.4.4 repeat 10 size 1500

Type escape sequence to abort.
Sending 10, 1500-byte ICMP Echos to 150.2.2.2, timeout is 2 seconds:
Packet sent with a source address of 10.4.4.4
!!!!!!!!!!
Success rate is 100 percent (10/10), round-trip min/avg/max = 380/380/384 ms

R2(config)#interface serial 0/1
R2(config-if)#shut

R4#ping 150.2.2.2 source 10.4.4.4 repeat 10 size 1500

Type escape sequence to abort.
Sending 10, 1500-byte ICMP Echos to 150.2.2.2, timeout is 2 seconds:
Packet sent with a source address of 10.4.4.4
!!!!!!!!!!
Success rate is 100 percent (10/10), round-trip min/avg/max = 392/393/396 ms
```

Optionally, use a Traceroute to verify the path the traffic is taking:

```
R4#traceroute ip

Target IP address: 150.2.2.2
Source address: 10.4.4.4
Numeric display [n]: y
Timeout in seconds [3]:
Probe count [3]:
Minimum Time to Live [1]:
Maximum Time to Live [30]:
Port Number [33434]:
Loose, Strict, Record, Timestamp, Verbose[none]:
Type escape sequence to abort.
Tracing the route to 150.2.2.2

  1 150.0.0.13 8 msec 8 msec 8 msec <<<<<<<<<<<<< R3s Serial1/2 Interface
  2 150.0.0.5 12 msec 16 msec 16 msec <<<<<<<<<<< R1s Serial0/1 Interface
  3 150.0.0.2 16 msec *  20 msec <<<<<<<<<< R2s Serial0/0 Interface
```

Task 7

When completing this task, it is important to remember that virtual links are a logical extension of the OSPF backbone. Therefore, all routers that have virtual links configured must also have authentication configured for the backbone. This task is completed as follows:

```
R1(config)#router ospf 1
R1(config-router)#area 0 authentication
R1(config-router)#area 2 virtual-link 2.2.2.2 authentication-key CCNP2011
R1(config-router)#area 3 virtual-link 3.3.3.3 authentication-key CCNP2011

R2(config)#router ospf 2
R2(config-router)#area 0 authentication
R2(config-router)#area 2 virtual-link 1.1.1.1 authentication-key CCNP2011
R2(config-router)#area 3 virtual-link 3.3.3.3 authentication-key CCNP2011

R3(config)#router ospf 3
R3(config-router)#area 0 authentication
R3(config-router)#area 3 virtual-link 2.2.2.2 authentication-key CCNP2011
R3(config-router)#area 3 virtual-link 1.1.1.1 authentication-key CCNP2011
R3(config-router)#exit
R3(config)#interface serial 1/2
R3(config-if)#ip ospf authentication-key CCNP2011
```

```
R4(config)#router ospf 4
R4(config-router)#area 0 authentication
R4(config-router)#exit
R4(config)#interface serial 0/0
R4(config-if)#ip ospf authentication-key CCNP2011
```

Next, verify OSPF virtual link states on R1, R2 and R3. Additionally, verify OSPF adjacency states between routers R3 and R4:

```
R1#show ip ospf virtual-links
Virtual Link OSPF_VL1 to router 2.2.2.2 is up
  Run as demand circuit
  DoNotAge LSA allowed.
  Transit area 2, via interface Serial0/0, Cost of using 64
  Transmit Delay is 1 sec, State POINT_TO_POINT,
  Timer intervals configured, Hello 10, Dead 40, Wait 40, Retransmit 5
    Hello due in 00:00:02
    Adjacency State FULL (Hello suppressed)
    Index 1/4, retransmission queue length 0, number of retransmission 0
    First 0x0(0)/0x0(0) Next 0x0(0)/0x0(0)
    Last retransmission scan length is 0, maximum is 0
    Last retransmission scan time is 0 msec, maximum is 0 msec
  Simple password authentication enabled

Virtual Link OSPF_VL0 to router 3.3.3.3 is up
  Run as demand circuit
  DoNotAge LSA allowed.
  Transit area 3, via interface Serial0/1, Cost of using 64
  Transmit Delay is 1 sec, State POINT_TO_POINT,
  Timer intervals configured, Hello 10, Dead 40, Wait 40, Retransmit 5
    Hello due in 00:00:00
    Adjacency State FULL (Hello suppressed)
    Index 2/5, retransmission queue length 0, number of retransmission 7
    First 0x0(0)/0x0(0) Next 0x0(0)/0x0(0)
    Last retransmission scan length is 1, maximum is 2
    Last retransmission scan time is 0 msec, maximum is 0 msec
  Simple password authentication enabled

R2#show ip ospf virtual-links
Virtual Link OSPF_VL1 to router 1.1.1.1 is up
  Run as demand circuit
  DoNotAge LSA allowed.
  Transit area 2, via interface Serial0/0, Cost of using 64
  Transmit Delay is 1 sec, State POINT_TO_POINT,
  Timer intervals configured, Hello 10, Dead 40, Wait 40, Retransmit 5
    Hello due in 00:00:01
    Adjacency State FULL (Hello suppressed)
    Index 1/3, retransmission queue length 0, number of retransmission 0
    First 0x0(0)/0x0(0) Next 0x0(0)/0x0(0)
    Last retransmission scan length is 0, maximum is 0
    Last retransmission scan time is 0 msec, maximum is 0 msec
  Simple password authentication enabled

Virtual Link OSPF_VL0 to router 3.3.3.3 is up
  Run as demand circuit
  DoNotAge LSA allowed.
  Transit area 3, via interface Serial0/1, Cost of using 64
  Transmit Delay is 1 sec, State POINT_TO_POINT,
  Timer intervals configured, Hello 10, Dead 40, Wait 40, Retransmit 5
    Hello due in 00:00:06
    Adjacency State FULL (Hello suppressed)
    Index 2/4, retransmission queue length 0, number of retransmission 0
    First 0x0(0)/0x0(0) Next 0x0(0)/0x0(0)
    Last retransmission scan length is 0, maximum is 0
    Last retransmission scan time is 0 msec, maximum is 0 msec
  Simple password authentication enabled

R3#show ip ospf virtual-links
Virtual Link OSPF_VL1 to router 2.2.2.2 is up
  Run as demand circuit
  DoNotAge LSA allowed.
  Transit area 3, via interface Serial1/1, Cost of using 781
  Transmit Delay is 1 sec, State POINT_TO_POINT,
  Timer intervals configured, Hello 10, Dead 40, Wait 40, Retransmit 5
    Hello due in 00:00:05
    Adjacency State FULL (Hello suppressed)
    Index 3/5, retransmission queue length 0, number of retransmission 0
    First 0x0(0)/0x0(0) Next 0x0(0)/0x0(0)
```

```
    Last retransmission scan length is 0, maximum is 0
    Last retransmission scan time is 0 msec, maximum is 0 msec
  Simple password authentication enabled

Virtual Link OSPF_VL0 to router 1.1.1.1 is up
  Run as demand circuit
  DoNotAge LSA allowed.
  Transit area 3, via interface Serial1/0, Cost of using 781
  Transmit Delay is 1 sec, State POINT_TO_POINT,
  Timer intervals configured, Hello 10, Dead 40, Wait 40, Retransmit 5
    Hello due in 00:00:08
    Adjacency State FULL (Hello suppressed)
    Index 2/4, retransmission queue length 0, number of retransmission 3
    First 0x0(0)/0x0(0) Next 0x0(0)/0x0(0)
    Last retransmission scan length is 1, maximum is 1
    Last retransmission scan time is 0 msec, maximum is 0 msec
  Simple password authentication enabled

R3#show ip ospf interface serial 1/2
Serial1/2 is up, line protocol is up
  Internet Address 150.0.0.13/30, Area 0
  Process ID 3, Router ID 3.3.3.3, Network Type POINT_TO_POINT, Cost: 781
  Transmit Delay is 1 sec, State POINT_TO_POINT
  Timer intervals configured, Hello 10, Dead 40, Wait 40, Retransmit 5
    oob-resync timeout 40
    Hello due in 00:00:06
  Supports Link-local Signaling (LLS)
  Index 4/6, flood queue length 0
  Next 0x0(0)/0x0(0)
  Last flood scan length is 1, maximum is 4
  Last flood scan time is 0 msec, maximum is 4 msec
  Neighbor Count is 1, Adjacent neighbor count is 1
    Adjacent with neighbor 4.4.4.4
  Suppress hello for 0 neighbor(s)
  Simple password authentication enabled

R4#show ip ospf interface serial 0/0
Serial0/0 is up, line protocol is up
  Internet Address 150.0.0.14/30, Area 0
  Process ID 4, Router ID 4.4.4.4, Network Type POINT_TO_POINT, Cost: 64
  Transmit Delay is 1 sec, State POINT_TO_POINT
  Timer intervals configured, Hello 10, Dead 40, Wait 40, Retransmit 5
    oob-resync timeout 40
    Hello due in 00:00:08
  Supports Link-local Signaling (LLS)
  Index 2/2, flood queue length 0
  Next 0x0(0)/0x0(0)
  Last flood scan length is 1, maximum is 1
  Last flood scan time is 0 msec, maximum is 0 msec
  Neighbor Count is 1, Adjacent neighbor count is 1
    Adjacent with neighbor 3.3.3.3
  Suppress hello for 0 neighbor(s)
  Simple password authentication enabled
```

Task 8

The requirements of this task are straightforward. This is completed as follows:

```
R1(config)#ip cef
R1(config)#ipv6 unicast-routing
R1(config)#ipv6 router rip CCNP
R1(config-rtr)#exit
R1(config)#interface fastethernet 0/0
R1(config-if)#ipv6 address 3ffe:abcd:1111:1::1/64
R1(config-if)#ipv6 rip CCNP enable
R1(config-if)#exit

DLS1(config)#ip cef
DLS1(config)#ipv6 unicast-routing
DLS1(config)#ipv6 router rip CCNP
DLS1(config-rtr)#exit
DLS1(config)#interface vlan 100
DLS1(config-if)#ipv6 address 3ffe:abcd:1111:1::254/64
DLS1(config-if)#ipv6 rip CCNP enable
DLS1(config-if)#exit

DLS2(config)#ip cef
```

```
DLS2(config)#ipv6 unicast-routing
DLS2(config)#ipv6 router rip CCNP
DLS2(config-rtr)#exit
DLS2(config)#interface vlan 100
DLS2(config-if)#ipv6 address 3ffe:abcd:1111:1::253/64
DLS2(config-if)#ipv6 rip CCNP enable
DLS2(config-if)#exit
```

Verify your configuration using the show ipv6 rip commands on any of the devices:

```
R1#show ipv6 rip database
RIP process "CCNP", local RIB
 3FFE:ABCD:1111:1::/64, metric 2
     FastEthernet0/0/FE80::20B:FDFF:FE67:6500, expires in 164 secs
     FastEthernet0/0/FE80::20F:23FF:FE03:2D80, expires in 160 secs
```

Task 9

To complete this task, you first need to configure Loopback interfaces on all routers and advertise these subnets via OSPF. Verify your configuration using the show ip ospf interfaces or show ip route command on all routers:

```
R1#show ip ospf interface brief
Interface    PID   Area      IP Address/Mask    Cost   State  Nbrs F/C
VL1          1     0         150.0.0.1/30       64     P2P    1/1
VL0          1     0         150.0.0.5/30       64     P2P    1/1
Fa0/0        1     1         150.1.1.1/24       1      DR     2/2
Se0/0        1     2         150.0.0.1/30       64     P2P    1/1
Lo0          1     3         1.1.1.1/32         1      LOOP   0/0
Se0/1        1     3         150.0.0.5/30       64     P2P    1/1

R2#show ip ospf interface brief
Interface    PID   Area      IP Address/Mask    Cost   State  Nbrs F/C
VL1          2     0         150.0.0.2/30       64     P2P    1/1
VL0          2     0         150.0.0.9/30       64     P2P    1/1
Lo0          2     2         2.2.2.2/32         1      LOOP   0/0
Fa0/0        2     2         150.2.2.2/24       1      DR     0/0
Se0/0        2     2         150.0.0.2/30       64     P2P    1/1
Se0/1        2     3         150.0.0.9/30       64     P2P    1/1

R3#show ip ospf interface brief
Interface    PID   Area      IP Address/Mask    Cost   State  Nbrs F/C
Fa0/0        3     0         10.3.3.3/24        1      DR     0/0
Se1/2        3     0         150.0.0.13/30      781    P2P    1/1
VL1          3     0         150.0.0.10/30      781    P2P    1/1
VL0          3     0         150.0.0.6/30       781    P2P    1/1
Lo0          3     3         3.3.3.3/32         1      LOOP   0/0
Se1/1        3     3         150.0.0.10/30      781    P2P    1/1
Se1/0        3     3         150.0.0.6/30       781    P2P    1/1

R4#show ip ospf interface brief
Interface    PID   Area      IP Address/Mask    Cost   State  Nbrs F/C
Lo0          4     0         4.4.4.4/32         1      LOOP   0/0
Se0/0        4     0         150.0.0.14/30      64     P2P    1/1
Fa0/0        4     0         10.4.4.4/24        1      DR     0/0
```

Following this, configure your ISATAP tunnels using the Loopback interfaces as sources:

```
R1(config)#interface tunnel 0
R1(config-if)#tunnel source loopback 0
R1(config-if)#ipv6 address fec0:abcd:1234:1::/64 eui-64
R1(config-if)#tunnel mode ipv6ip isatap
R1(config-if)#no ipv6 nd suppress-ra
R1(config-if)#exit

R2(config)#interface tunnel 0
R2(config-if)#tunnel source loopback 0
R2(config-if)#ipv6 address fec0:abcd:1234:1::/64 eui-64
R2(config-if)#tunnel mode ipv6ip isatap
R2(config-if)#no ipv6 nd suppress-ra
R2(config-if)#exit

R3(config)#interface tunnel 0
R3(config-if)#tunnel source loopback 0
```

```
R3(config-if)#ipv6 address fec0:abcd:1234:1::/64 eui-64
R3(config-if)#tunnel mode ipv6ip isatap
R3(config-if)#no ipv6 nd suppress-ra
R3(config-if)#exit

R4(config)#interface tunnel 0
R4(config-if)#tunnel source loopback 0
R4(config-if)#ipv6 address fec0:abcd:1234:1::/64 eui-64
R4(config-if)#tunnel mode ipv6ip isatap
R4(config-if)#no ipv6 nd suppress-ra
R4(config-if)#exit
```

Verify your tunnel status using the show interfaces tunnel <number> command:

```
R1#show interfaces tunnel 0
Tunnel0 is up, line protocol is up
  Hardware is Tunnel
  MTU 1514 bytes, BW 9 Kbit/sec, DLY 500000 usec,
     reliability 255/255, txload 1/255, rxload 1/255
  Encapsulation TUNNEL, loopback not set
  Keepalive not set
  Tunnel source 1.1.1.1 (Loopback0), destination UNKNOWN
  Tunnel protocol/transport IPv6 ISATAP

  Fast tunneling enabled
  Tunnel transmit bandwidth 8000 (kbps)
  Tunnel receive bandwidth 8000 (kbps)
  Last input never, output 00:00:35, output hang never
  Last clearing of "show interface" counters never
  Input queue: 0/75/0/0 (size/max/drops/flushes); Total output drops: 0
  Queueing strategy: fifo
  Output queue: 0/0 (size/max)
  5 minute input rate 0 bits/sec, 0 packets/sec
  5 minute output rate 0 bits/sec, 0 packets/sec
     0 packets input, 0 bytes, 0 no buffer
     Received 0 broadcasts, 0 runts, 0 giants, 0 throttles
     0 input errors, 0 CRC, 0 frame, 0 overrun, 0 ignored, 0 abort
     4 packets output, 384 bytes, 0 underruns
     0 output errors, 0 collisions, 0 interface resets
     0 unknown protocol drops
     0 output buffer failures, 0 output buffers swapped out
```

Next, configure MP-BGP on the routers as requested in the task. This is completed as follows:

```
R1(config)#router bgp 1
R1(config-router)#bgp router-id 1.1.1.1
R1(config-router)#address-family ipv6
R1(config-router-af)#neighbor FEC0:ABCD:1234:1:0:5EFE:202:202 remote-as 2
R1(config-router-af)#neighbor FEC0:ABCD:1234:1:0:5EFE:202:202 activate
R1(config-router-af)#network 3FFE:ABCD:1111:1::/64
R1(config-router-af)#exit-address-family
R1(config-router)#exit

R2(config)#ip cef
R2(config)#ipv6 unicast-routing
R2(config)#router bgp 2
R2(config-router)#bgp router-id 2.2.2.2
R2(config-router)#address-family ipv6
R2(config-router-af)#neighbor FEC0:ABCD:1234:1:0:5EFE:101:101 remote-as 1
R2(config-router-af)#neighbor FEC0:ABCD:1234:1:0:5EFE:101:101 activate
R2(config-router-af)#neighbor FEC0:ABCD:1234:1:0:5EFE:303:303 remote-as 3
R2(config-router-af)#neighbor FEC0:ABCD:1234:1:0:5EFE:303:303 activate
R2(config-router-af)#network 3FFE:ABCD:1111:2::/64
R2(config-router-af)#exit-address-family
R2(config-router)#exit

R3(config)#ip cef
R3(config)#ipv6 unicast-routing
R3(config)#router bgp 3
R3(config-router)#bgp router-id 3.3.3.3
R3(config-router)#address-family ipv6
R3(config-router-af)#neighbor FEC0:ABCD:1234:1:0:5EFE:202:202 remote-as 2
R3(config-router-af)#neighbor FEC0:ABCD:1234:1:0:5EFE:202:202 activate
R3(config-router-af)#neighbor FEC0:ABCD:1234:1:0:5EFE:404:404 remote-as 4
R3(config-router-af)#neighbor FEC0:ABCD:1234:1:0:5EFE:404:404 activate
R3(config-router-af)#network 3FFE:ABCD:1111:3::/64
R3(config-router-af)#exit-address-family
R3(config-router)#exit
```

```
R4(config)#ip cef
R4(config)#ipv6 unicast-routing
R4(config)#router bgp 4
R4(config-router)#bgp router-id 4.4.4.4
R4(config-router)#address-family ipv6
R4(config-router-af)#neighbor FEC0:ABCD:1234:1:0:5EFE:303:303 remote-as 3
R4(config-router-af)#neighbor FEC0:ABCD:1234:1:0:5EFE:303:303 activate
R4(config-router-af)#network 3FFE:ABCD:1111:4::/64
R4(config-router-af)#exit-address-family
R4(config-router)#exit
```

Verify MP-BGP configuration using the show bgp ipv6 unicast commands:

```
R1#show bgp ipv6 unicast
BGP table version is 5, local router ID is 1.1.1.1
Status codes: s suppressed, d damped, h history, * valid, > best, i - internal,
              r RIB-failure, S Stale
Origin codes: i - IGP, e - EGP, ? - incomplete

   Network          Next Hop            Metric LocPrf Weight Path
*> 3FFE:ABCD:1111:1::/64
                    ::                       0         32768 i
*> 3FFE:ABCD:1111:2::/64
                    FEC0:ABCD:1234:1:0:5EFE:202:202
                                             0             0 2 i
*> 3FFE:ABCD:1111:3::/64
                    FEC0:ABCD:1234:1:0:5EFE:303:303
                                                           0 2 3 i
*> 3FFE:ABCD:1111:4::/64
                    FEC0:ABCD:1234:1:0:5EFE:404:404
                                                           0 2 3 4 i

R2#show bgp ipv6 unicast
BGP table version is 6, local router ID is 2.2.2.2
Status codes: s suppressed, d damped, h history, * valid, > best, i - internal,
              r RIB-failure, S Stale
Origin codes: i - IGP, e - EGP, ? - incomplete

   Network          Next Hop            Metric LocPrf Weight Path
*> 3FFE:ABCD:1111:1::/64
                    FEC0:ABCD:1234:1:0:5EFE:101:101
                                             0             0 1 i
*> 3FFE:ABCD:1111:2::/64
                    ::                       0         32768 i
*> 3FFE:ABCD:1111:3::/64
                    FEC0:ABCD:1234:1:0:5EFE:303:303
                                             0             0 3 i
*> 3FFE:ABCD:1111:4::/64
                    FEC0:ABCD:1234:1:0:5EFE:404:404
                                                           0 3 4 i

3#show bgp ipv6 unicast
BGP table version is 6, local router ID is 3.3.3.3
Status codes: s suppressed, d damped, h history, * valid, > best, i - internal,
              r RIB-failure, S Stale
Origin codes: i - IGP, e - EGP, ? - incomplete

   Network          Next Hop            Metric LocPrf Weight Path
*> 3FFE:ABCD:1111:1::/64
                    FEC0:ABCD:1234:1:0:5EFE:101:101
                                                           0 2 1 i
*> 3FFE:ABCD:1111:2::/64
                    FEC0:ABCD:1234:1:0:5EFE:202:202
                                             0             0 2 i
*> 3FFE:ABCD:1111:3::/64
                    ::                       0         32768 i
*> 3FFE:ABCD:1111:4::/64
                    FEC0:ABCD:1234:1:0:5EFE:404:404
                                             0             0 4 i

R4#show bgp ipv6 unicast
BGP table version is 6, local router ID is 4.4.4.4
Status codes: s suppressed, d damped, h history, * valid, > best, i - internal,
              r RIB-failure, S Stale
Origin codes: i - IGP, e - EGP, ? - incomplete

   Network          Next Hop            Metric LocPrf Weight Path
*> 3FFE:ABCD:1111:1::/64
                    FEC0:ABCD:1234:1:0:5EFE:101:101
```

```
                                                                   0 3 2 1 i
*> 3FFE:ABCD:1111:2::/64
                 FECO:ABCD:1234:1:0:5EFE:202:202
                                                                   0 3 2 i
*> 3FFE:ABCD:1111:3::/64
                 FECO:ABCD:1234:1:0:5EFE:303:303
                                                     0             0 3 i
*> 3FFE:ABCD:1111:4::/64
                 ::                                  0         32768 i
```

Optionally, verify connectivity using extended LAN-to-LAN pings:

```
R1#ping 3FFE:ABCD:1111:2::2 source fastethernet 0/0 repeat 10 size 1500

Type escape sequence to abort.
Sending 10, 1500-byte ICMP Echos to 3FFE:ABCD:1111:2::2, timeout is 2 seconds:
Packet sent with a source address of 3FFE:ABCD:1111:1::1
!!!!!!!!!!
Success rate is 100 percent (10/10), round-trip min/avg/max = 208/208/212 ms

R1#ping 3FFE:ABCD:1111:3::3 source fastethernet 0/0 repeat 10 size 1500

Type escape sequence to abort.
Sending 10, 1500-byte ICMP Echos to 3FFE:ABCD:1111:3::3, timeout is 2 seconds:
Packet sent with a source address of 3FFE:ABCD:1111:1::1
!!!!!!!!!!
Success rate is 100 percent (10/10), round-trip min/avg/max = 208/208/212 ms

R1#ping 3FFE:ABCD:1111:4::4 source fastethernet 0/0 repeat 10 size 1500

Type escape sequence to abort.
Sending 10, 1500-byte ICMP Echos to 3FFE:ABCD:1111:4::4, timeout is 2 seconds:
Packet sent with a source address of 3FFE:ABCD:1111:1::1
!!!!!!!!!!
Success rate is 100 percent (10/10), round-trip min/avg/max = 396/399/400 ms
```

NOTE: Perform the same tests on R2, R3 and R4 if so desired.

FINAL ROUTER CONFIGURATIONS

R1

```
R1#sh run
Building configuration...

Current configuration : 1931 bytes
!
version 12.4
service timestamps debug datetime msec
service timestamps log datetime msec
no service password-encryption
!
hostname R1
!
boot-start-marker
boot-end-marker
!
no logging console
!
no aaa new-model
no network-clock-participate slot 1
no network-clock-participate wic 0
ip cef
!
no ip domain lookup
ip auth-proxy max-nodata-conns 3
ip admission max-nodata-conns 3
!
ipv6 unicast-routing
!
interface Loopback0
  ip address 1.1.1.1 255.255.255.255
```

```
!
interface Tunnel0
 no ip address
 no ip redirects
 ipv6 address FEC0:ABCD:1234:1::/64 eui-64
 no ipv6 nd suppress-ra
 tunnel source Loopback0
 tunnel mode ipv6ip isatap
!
interface FastEthernet0/0
 ip address 150.1.1.1 255.255.255.0
 duplex auto
 speed auto
 ipv6 address 3FFE:ABCD:1111:1::1/64
 ipv6 rip CCNP enable
 ipv6 rip CCNP default-information originate
!
interface Serial0/0
 ip address 150.0.0.1 255.255.255.252
 clock rate 2000000
!
interface Serial0/1
 ip address 150.0.0.5 255.255.255.252
!
router ospf 1
 router-id 1.1.1.1
 log-adjacency-changes
 area 0 authentication
 area 1 nssa no-summary
 area 2 virtual-link 2.2.2.2 authentication-key CCNP2011
 area 3 virtual-link 3.3.3.3 authentication-key CCNP2011
 network 1.1.1.1 0.0.0.0 area 3
 network 150.0.0.1 0.0.0.0 area 2
 network 150.0.0.5 0.0.0.0 area 3
 network 150.1.1.1 0.0.0.0 area 1
!
router bgp 1
 no synchronization
 bgp router-id 1.1.1.1
 bgp log-neighbor-changes
 neighbor FEC0:ABCD:1234:1:0:5EFE:202:202 remote-as 2
 no neighbor FEC0:ABCD:1234:1:0:5EFE:202:202 activate
 no auto-summary
 !
 address-family ipv6
  neighbor FEC0:ABCD:1234:1:0:5EFE:202:202 activate
  network 3FFE:ABCD:1111:1::/64
  no synchronization
 exit-address-family
!
ip forward-protocol nd
!
no ip http server
no ip http secure-server
!
ipv6 router rip CCNP
!
control-plane
!
line con 0
line aux 0
line vty 0 4
 password cisco
 login
!
end
```

R2

```
R2#term len 0
R2#sh run
Building configuration...

Current configuration : 1995 bytes
!
```

```
version 12.4
service timestamps debug datetime msec
service timestamps log datetime msec
no service password-encryption
!
hostname R2
!
boot-start-marker
boot-end-marker
!
no logging console
!
no aaa new-model
no network-clock-participate slot 1
no network-clock-participate wic 0
ip cef
!
no ip domain lookup
ip auth-proxy max-nodata-conns 3
ip admission max-nodata-conns 3
!
ipv6 unicast-routing
!
interface Loopback0
 ip address 2.2.2.2 255.255.255.255
!
interface Tunnel0
 no ip address
 no ip redirects
 ipv6 address FEC0:ABCD:1234:1::/64 eui-64
 no ipv6 nd suppress-ra
 tunnel source Loopback0
 tunnel mode ipv6ip isatap
!
interface FastEthernet0/0
 ip address 150.2.2.2 255.255.255.0
 loopback
 duplex auto
 speed auto
 ipv6 address 3FFE:ABCD:1111:2::2/64
 no keepalive
!
interface Serial0/0
 ip address 150.0.0.2 255.255.255.252
!
interface Serial0/1
 ip address 150.0.0.9 255.255.255.252
!
router ospf 2
 router-id 2.2.2.2
 log-adjacency-changes
 area 0 authentication
 area 2 virtual-link 1.1.1.1 authentication-key CCNP2011
 area 3 virtual-link 3.3.3.3 authentication-key CCNP2011
 passive-interface FastEthernet0/0
 network 2.2.2.2 0.0.0.0 area 2
 network 150.0.0.2 0.0.0.0 area 2
 network 150.0.0.9 0.0.0.0 area 3
 network 150.2.2.2 0.0.0.0 area 2
!
router bgp 2
 no synchronization
 bgp router-id 2.2.2.2
 bgp log-neighbor-changes
 neighbor FEC0:ABCD:1234:1:0:5EFE:101:101 remote-as 1
 no neighbor FEC0:ABCD:1234:1:0:5EFE:101:101 activate
 neighbor FEC0:ABCD:1234:1:0:5EFE:303:303 remote-as 3
 no neighbor FEC0:ABCD:1234:1:0:5EFE:303:303 activate
 no auto-summary
 !
 address-family ipv6
  neighbor FEC0:ABCD:1234:1:0:5EFE:101:101 activate
  neighbor FEC0:ABCD:1234:1:0:5EFE:303:303 activate
  network 3FFE:ABCD:1111:2::/64
 exit-address-family
!
ip forward-protocol nd
!
```

```
no ip http server
no ip http secure-server
!
control-plane
!
line con 0
line aux 0
line vty 0 4
 password cisco
 login
!
end

R2#
```

R3

```
R3#term len 0
R3#sh run
Building configuration...

Current configuration : 2396 bytes
!
version 12.4
service timestamps debug datetime msec
service timestamps log datetime msec
no service password-encryption
!
hostname R3
!
boot-start-marker
boot-end-marker
!
no logging console
!
no aaa new-model
no network-clock-participate slot 1
no network-clock-participate wic 0
ip cef
!
no ip domain lookup
ip auth-proxy max-nodata-conns 3
ip admission max-nodata-conns 3
!
ipv6 unicast-routing
!
interface Loopback0
 ip address 3.3.3.3 255.255.255.255
!
interface Tunnel0
 no ip address
 no ip redirects
 ipv6 address FECO:ABCD:1234:1::/64 eui-64
 no ipv6 nd suppress-ra
 tunnel source Loopback0
 tunnel mode ipv6ip isatap
!
interface FastEthernet0/0
 ip address 10.3.3.3 255.255.255.0
 duplex auto
 speed auto
 ipv6 address 3FFE:ABCD:1111:3::3/64
!
interface Serial1/0
 ip address 150.0.0.6 255.255.255.252
 clock rate 128000
!
interface Serial1/1
 ip address 150.0.0.10 255.255.255.252
 clock rate 128000
!
interface Serial1/2
 ip address 150.0.0.13 255.255.255.252
 ip ospf authentication-key CCNP2011
 clock rate 128000
!
```

```
interface Serial1/3
 no ip address
 shutdown
!
interface Serial1/4
 no ip address
 shutdown
!
interface Serial1/5
 no ip address
 shutdown
!
interface Serial1/6
 no ip address
 shutdown
!
interface Serial1/7
 no ip address
 shutdown
!
router ospf 3
 router-id 3.3.3.3
 log-adjacency-changes
 area 0 authentication
 area 3 virtual-link 2.2.2.2 authentication-key CCNP2011
 area 3 virtual-link 1.1.1.1 authentication-key CCNP2011
 passive-interface FastEthernet0/0
 network 3.3.3.3 0.0.0.0 area 3
 network 10.3.3.3 0.0.0.0 area 0
 network 150.0.0.6 0.0.0.0 area 3
 network 150.0.0.10 0.0.0.0 area 3
 network 150.0.0.13 0.0.0.0 area 0
!
router bgp 3
 no synchronization
 bgp router-id 3.3.3.3
 bgp log-neighbor-changes
 neighbor FEC0:ABCD:1234:1:0:5EFE:202:202 remote-as 2
 no neighbor FEC0:ABCD:1234:1:0:5EFE:202:202 activate
 neighbor FEC0:ABCD:1234:1:0:5EFE:404:404 remote-as 4
 no neighbor FEC0:ABCD:1234:1:0:5EFE:404:404 activate
 no auto-summary
 !
 address-family ipv6
  neighbor FEC0:ABCD:1234:1:0:5EFE:202:202 activate
  neighbor FEC0:ABCD:1234:1:0:5EFE:404:404 activate
  network 3FFE:ABCD:1111:3::/64
 exit-address-family
!
ip forward-protocol nd
!
no ip http server
no ip http secure-server
!
control-plane
!
line con 0
line aux 0
line vty 0 4
 password cisco
 login
!
end

R3#
```

R4

```
R4#term len 0
R4#sh run
Building configuration...

Current configuration : 1687 bytes
!
version 12.4
service timestamps debug datetime msec
```

```
 service timestamps log datetime msec
 no service password-encryption
 !
 hostname R4
 !
 boot-start-marker
 boot-end-marker
 !
 no logging console
 !
 no aaa new-model
 no network-clock-participate slot 1
 no network-clock-participate wic 0
 ip cef
 !
 no ip domain lookup
 ip auth-proxy max-nodata-conns 3
 ip admission max-nodata-conns 3
 !
 ipv6 unicast-routing
 !
 interface Loopback0
  ip address 4.4.4.4 255.255.255.255
 !
 interface Tunnel0
  no ip address
  no ip redirects
  ipv6 address FEC0:ABCD:1234:1::/64 eui-64
  no ipv6 nd suppress-ra
  tunnel source Loopback0
  tunnel mode ipv6ip isatap
 !
 interface FastEthernet0/0
  ip address 10.4.4.4 255.255.255.0
  duplex auto
  speed auto
  ipv6 address 3FFE:ABCD:1111:4::4/64
 !
 interface Serial0/0
  ip address 150.0.0.14 255.255.255.252
  ip ospf authentication-key CCNP2011
 !
 interface Serial0/1
  no ip address
  shutdown
 !
 router ospf 4
  router-id 4.4.4.4
  log-adjacency-changes
  area 0 authentication
  passive-interface FastEthernet0/0
  network 4.4.4.4 0.0.0.0 area 0
  network 10.4.4.4 0.0.0.0 area 0
  network 150.0.0.14 0.0.0.0 area 0
 !
 router bgp 4
  no synchronization
  bgp router-id 4.4.4.4
  bgp log-neighbor-changes
  neighbor FEC0:ABCD:1234:1:0:5EFE:303:303 remote-as 3
  no neighbor FEC0:ABCD:1234:1:0:5EFE:303:303 activate
  no auto-summary
  !
  address-family ipv6
   neighbor FEC0:ABCD:1234:1:0:5EFE:303:303 activate
   network 3FFE:ABCD:1111:4::/64
  exit-address-family
 !
 ip forward-protocol nd
 !
 no ip http server
 no ip http secure-server
 !
 control-plane
 !
 line con 0
 line aux 0
```

```
line vty 0 4
 password cisco
 login
!
end

R4#
```

FINAL SWITCH CONFIGURATIONS

DLS1

```
DLS1#term len 0
DLS1#sh run
Building configuration...

Current configuration : 5021 bytes
!
version 12.2
no service pad
service timestamps debug datetime msec
service timestamps log datetime msec
no service password-encryption
!
hostname DLS1
!
no logging console
!
no aaa new-model
mls qos
ipv6 unicast-routing
ip subnet-zero
ip routing
no ip domain-lookup
!
spanning-tree mode rapid-pvst
spanning-tree extend system-id
spanning-tree pathcost method long
!
vlan internal allocation policy ascending
!
interface FastEthernet0/1
 switchport mode dynamic desirable
 switchport priority extend cos 2
 shutdown
 mls qos trust device cisco-phone
 mls qos trust cos
!
interface FastEthernet0/2
 switchport mode dynamic desirable
 switchport priority extend cos 2
 shutdown
 mls qos trust device cisco-phone
 mls qos trust cos
!
interface FastEthernet0/3
 switchport mode dynamic desirable
 switchport priority extend cos 2
 shutdown
 mls qos trust device cisco-phone
 mls qos trust cos
!
interface FastEthernet0/4
 switchport mode dynamic desirable
 switchport priority extend cos 2
 shutdown
 mls qos trust device cisco-phone
 mls qos trust cos
!
interface FastEthernet0/5
 switchport mode dynamic desirable
 switchport priority extend cos 2
 shutdown
 mls qos trust device cisco-phone
```

```
 mls qos trust cos
!
interface FastEthernet0/6
 switchport mode dynamic desirable
 shutdown
!
interface FastEthernet0/7
 switchport trunk encapsulation dot1q
 switchport mode trunk
!
interface FastEthernet0/8
 switchport trunk encapsulation dot1q
 switchport mode trunk
!
interface FastEthernet0/9
 switchport mode dynamic desirable
 shutdown
!
interface FastEthernet0/10
 switchport mode dynamic desirable
 shutdown
!
interface FastEthernet0/11
 switchport mode dynamic desirable
!
interface FastEthernet0/12
 switchport mode dynamic desirable

[Truncated Output]

interface Vlan1
 no ip address
 shutdown
!
interface Vlan100
 ip address 150.1.1.254 255.255.255.0
 ip ospf priority 0
 ipv6 address 3FFE:ABCD:1111:1::254/64
 ipv6 rip CCNP enable
!
router ospf 254
 log-adjacency-changes
 area 1 nssa
 network 150.1.1.254 0.0.0.0 area 1
!
ip classless
ip http server
ip http secure-server
!
ipv6 router rip CCNP
!
control-plane
!
line con 0
line vty 0 4
 privilege level 15
 password cisco
 login
line vty 5 15
 login
!
end
DLS1#
```

DLS2

```
DLS2#term len 0
DLS2#sh run
Building configuration...

Current configuration : 4989 bytes
!
version 12.2
no service pad
service timestamps debug datetime msec
service timestamps log datetime msec
no service password-encryption
```

```
!
hostname DLS2
!
no logging console
!
no aaa new-model
mls qos
ipv6 unicast-routing
ip subnet-zero
ip routing
no ip domain-lookup
!
spanning-tree mode rapid-pvst
spanning-tree extend system-id
spanning-tree pathcost method long
!
vlan internal allocation policy ascending
!
interface FastEthernet0/1
 switchport mode dynamic desirable
 switchport priority extend cos 2
 shutdown
 mls qos trust device cisco-phone
 mls qos trust cos
!
interface FastEthernet0/2
 switchport mode dynamic desirable
 switchport priority extend cos 2
 shutdown
 mls qos trust device cisco-phone
 mls qos trust cos
!
interface FastEthernet0/3
 switchport mode dynamic desirable
 switchport priority extend cos 2
 shutdown
 mls qos trust device cisco-phone
 mls qos trust cos
!
interface FastEthernet0/4
 switchport mode dynamic desirable
 switchport priority extend cos 2
 shutdown
 mls qos trust device cisco-phone
 mls qos trust cos
!
interface FastEthernet0/5
 switchport mode dynamic desirable
 switchport priority extend cos 2
 shutdown
 mls qos trust device cisco-phone
 mls qos trust cos
!
interface FastEthernet0/6
 switchport mode dynamic desirable
 shutdown
!
interface FastEthernet0/7
 switchport mode dynamic desirable
 shutdown
!
interface FastEthernet0/8
 switchport mode dynamic desirable
 shutdown
!
interface FastEthernet0/9
 switchport mode dynamic desirable
 shutdown
!
interface FastEthernet0/10
 switchport mode dynamic desirable
 shutdown
!
interface FastEthernet0/11
 switchport mode dynamic desirable
!
interface FastEthernet0/12
 switchport mode dynamic desirable
```

```
[Truncated Output]

interface Vlan1
 no ip address
 shutdown
!
interface Vlan100
 ip address 150.1.1.253 255.255.255.0
 ip ospf priority 0
 ipv6 address 3FFE:ABCD:1111:1::253/64
 ipv6 rip CCNP enable
!
router ospf 253
 log-adjacency-changes
 area 1 nssa
 network 150.1.1.253 0.0.0.0 area 1
!
ip classless
ip http server
ip http secure-server
!
ipv6 router rip CCNP
!
control-plane
!
line con 0
line vty 0 4
 privilege level 15
 password cisco
 login
line vty 5 15
 login
!
end

DLS2#
```

ALS1

```
ALS1#term len 0
ALS1#sh run
Building configuration...

Current configuration : 1337 bytes
!
version 12.1
no service pad
service timestamps debug uptime
service timestamps log uptime
no service password-encryption
!
hostname ALS1
!
no logging console
!
ip subnet-zero
!
no ip domain-lookup
vtp domain fhrp
vtp mode transparent
!
spanning-tree mode pvst
no spanning-tree optimize bpdu transmission
spanning-tree extend system-id
!
vlan 100
 name R1-VLAN
!
vlan 300
 name R3-VLAN
!
vlan 400
 name R4-VLAN
!
interface FastEthernet0/1
 switchport access vlan 100
 switchport mode access
```

```
!
interface FastEthernet0/2
 shutdown
!
interface FastEthernet0/3
 switchport access vlan 300
 switchport mode access
!
interface FastEthernet0/4
 switchport access vlan 400
 switchport mode access
!
interface FastEthernet0/5
 shutdown
!
interface FastEthernet0/6
 shutdown
!
interface FastEthernet0/7
 switchport mode trunk
!
interface FastEthernet0/8
 switchport mode trunk
!
interface FastEthernet0/9
 shutdown
!
interface FastEthernet0/10
 shutdown
!
interface FastEthernet0/11
 switchport mode trunk
!
interface FastEthernet0/12
 switchport mode trunk
!
interface Vlan1
 no ip address
 no ip route-cache
 shutdown
!
interface Vlan400
 ip address 10.4.4.254 255.255.255.0
 no ip route-cache
!
ip default-gateway 10.4.4.4
ip http server
!
line con 0
line vty 0 4
 privilege level 15
 password cisco
 login
line vty 5 15
 login
!
end
ALS1#
```

ALS2

```
ALS2#term len 0
ALS2#sh run
Building configuration...

Current configuration : 1320 bytes
!
version 12.1
no service pad
service timestamps debug uptime
service timestamps log uptime
no service password-encryption
!
hostname ALS2
!
no logging console
!
ip subnet-zero
!
no ip domain-lookup
```

```
vtp domain fhrp
vtp mode transparent
!
spanning-tree mode pvst
no spanning-tree optimize bpdu transmission
spanning-tree extend system-id
!
vlan 300
 name R3-VLAN
!
interface FastEthernet0/1
 shutdown
 mls qos cos 1
 mls qos cos override
!
interface FastEthernet0/2
 shutdown
 mls qos cos 1
 mls qos cos override
!
interface FastEthernet0/3
 shutdown
 mls qos cos 1
 mls qos cos override
!
interface FastEthernet0/4
 shutdown
 mls qos cos 1
 mls qos cos override
!
interface FastEthernet0/5
 shutdown
 mls qos cos 1
 mls qos cos override
!
interface FastEthernet0/6
 shutdown
!
interface FastEthernet0/7
 shutdown
!
interface FastEthernet0/8
 shutdown
!
interface FastEthernet0/9
 shutdown
!
interface FastEthernet0/10
 shutdown
!
interface FastEthernet0/11
 switchport mode trunk
!
interface FastEthernet0/12
 switchport mode trunk
!
interface Vlan1
 no ip address
 no ip route-cache
 shutdown
!
interface Vlan300
 ip address 10.3.3.254 255.255.255.0
 no ip route-cache
!
ip default-gateway 10.3.3.3
ip http server
!
line con 0
line vty 0 4
 privilege level 15
 password cisco
 login
line vty 5 15
 login
!
end

ALS2#
```

CCNP LAB 83

CCNP Multi-Technology Lab

Lab Objective:

The objective of this lab is to cover all relevant CCNP ROUTE and SWITCH theory. These labs will include topics from each of these guides. It should be noted that not all topics will be included in all labs. Additionally, not all solutions will be illustrated in detail. You can refer to previous labs for assistance with some basic configurations.

Lab Topology:

The lab network topology is illustrated below:

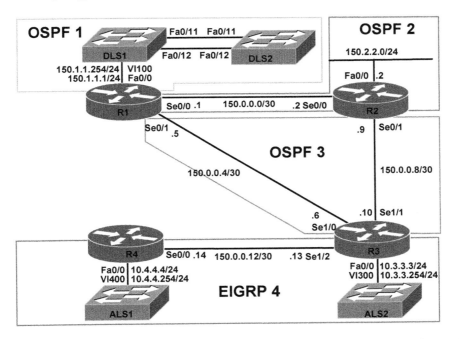

IMPORTANT NOTE: If you are using the www.howtonetwork.net racks, please implement the following pre-lab configurations. This is required because of the manner in which the routers and switches are physically cabled to each other. The following configuration should be applied to switch ALS1:

```
!
hostname ALS1
!
vtp mode transparent
!
vlan 100
 name R1-VLAN
!
vlan 300
 name R3-VLAN
!
```

```
vlan 400
 name R4-VLAN
!
interface fastethernet 0/1
 switchport access vlan 100
 switchport mode access
!
interface fastethernet 0/2
shutdown
!
interface fastethernet 0/3
 switchport access vlan 300
 switchport mode access
!
interface fastethernet 0/4
 switchport access vlan 400
 switchport mode access
!
interface range fastethernet 0/5 - 6
shutdown
!
interface fastethernet0/7
 switchport mode trunk
!
interface fastethernet 0/8
 switchport mode trunk
!
interface range fastethernet 0/9 - 10
 shutdown
!
interface range fastethernet 0/11 - 12
 switchport mode trunk
!
interface vlan 400
 ip address 10.4.4.254 255.255.255.0
 no shutdown
!
ip default-gateway 10.4.4.4
!
line vty 0 4
 privilege level 15
 password cisco
 login
!
end

hostname ALS2
!
vtp mode transparent
!
vlan 300
 name R3-VLAN
!
!
interface range fastethernet 0/1 - 10
 shutdown
!
interface fastethernet 0/11
 switchport mode trunk
!
interface fastethernet 0/12
 switchport mode trunk
!
interface vlan 300
 ip address 10.3.3.254 255.255.255.0
 no shutdown
!
ip default-gateway 10.3.3.3
!
line vty 0 4
 privilege level 15
 password cisco
 login
!
end

!
hostname DLS1
!
ip routing
!
vtp mode transparent
```

```
!
vlan 100
 name R1-VLAN
!
interface range fastethernet 0/1 - 6
 shutdown
!
interface range fastethernet 0/7 - 8
 switchport trunk encapsulation dot1q
 switchport mode trunk
!
interface range fastethernet 0/9 - 10
 shutdown
!
interface fastethernet 0/11
 switchport mode dynamic desirable
!
interface fastethernet 0/12
 switchport mode dynamic desirable
!
interface range fastethernet 0/13 - 48
 shutdown
!
interface vlan 100
 ip address 150.1.1.254 255.255.255.0
 no shutdown
!
line vty 0 4
 privilege level 15
 password cisco
 login
!
end

hostname DLS2
!
ip routing
!
vtp mode transparent
!
vlan 100
 name R1-VLAN
!
interface range fastethernet 0/1 - 10
 shutdown
!
interface fastethernet 0/11
 switchport mode dynamic desirable
!
interface fastethernet 0/12
 switchport mode dynamic desirable
!
interface range fastethernet 0/13 - 48
 shutdown
!
line vty 0 4
 privilege level 15
 password cisco
 login
!
end
```

If you are using the www.howtonetwork.net racks, please bring up the LAN interface connected to R2 by the following configuration:

```
interface fastethernet 0/0
 ip address 150.2.2.2 255.255.255.0
 no keepalive
 loopback
 no shutdown
```

Alternatively, you can simply connect the interface to a hub or one of the switches and bring up the interface in the standard manner.

Task 1

Configure hostnames, IP addressing on all routers as illustrated in the network topology.

Task 2

Configure an EtherChannel between DLS1 and DLS2. This should be a Layer 2 trunk link that is unconditionally bonded. Configure an SVI with the IP address 150.1.1.253/24 on DLS2. Verify that all devices on the 150.1.1.0/24 subnet can ping each other.

Task 3

Configure OSPF using process ID 1 on R1, DLS1 and DLS2. Ensure that no DR/BDR election will occur on the 150.1.1.0/24 subnet. All devices should peer with each other. Verify your configuration using the appropriate commands.

Task 4

Configure OSPF using process ID 2 between R1 and R2. Ensure that no OSPF Hellos are sent out the LAN interface of R2. Verify your configuration using the appropriate commands.

Task 5

Configure OSPF using process ID 3 between R1, R2 and R3. Do NOT enable OSPF on the LAN interface of R3. Verify your configuration using the appropriate commands.

Task 6

Configure EIGRP using AS 4 between R3 and R4. No EIGRP Hello packets should be sent out of the LAN interfaces of R3 or R4. R4 should be configured as a stub router. This router should advertise only connected subnets. R3 should advertise only a default route to R4. Verify EIGRP routing configuration using the appropriate commands.

Task 7

Redistribute between the OSPF processes on R1 and R2. Ensure that routes from one process will never be redistributed back into the same process. You are NOT allowed to modify the default administrative distance when completing this task. When completing this task, ensure that the cost of the routes to reflect the entire path. Verify your configuration using the appropriate commands on all routers and ensure that there are no routing loops when done.

Task 8

Configure one-way redistribution of EIGRP into OSPF on R3. Ensure that only a single prefix is advertised to the OSPF domain for the 10.3.3.0/24 and 10.4.4.0/24 subnets. The 150.0.0.12/30 subnet connecting R3 to R4 should never be advertised to the rest of the OSPF domain. You are NOT allowed to use a distribute list to complete this task. Verify that all other routers are able to reach the R3 and R4 LAN subnets and vice-versa.

Task 9

Management has advised that a new video solution will be implemented in the network. The IP Multicast server will reside on R1s LAN and clients will reside on R4s LAN. Configure PIM Dense Mode and assign R1s LAN interface to the 227.1.1.1 group and verify that you can ping this from R4s LAN interface. This should work even if the R1-R3 or the R2-R3 link is down.

LAB VALIDATION

Task 1

Please refer to previous labs for basic IPv4 addressing and hostname configuration. This will not be included in this section to avoid being redundant.

Task 2

Please refer to previous labs for EtherChannel configuration. This will not be included in this section to avoid being redundant. Verify your solution using the `show etherchannel` commands on both switches:

```
DLS1#show etherchannel summary
Flags:  D - down         P - bundled in port-channel
        I - stand-alone  s - suspended
        H - Hot-standby (LACP only)
        R - Layer3       S - Layer2
        U - in use       f - failed to allocate aggregator

        M - not in use, minimum links not met
        u - unsuitable for bundling
        w - waiting to be aggregated
        d - default port

Number of channel-groups in use: 1
Number of aggregators:           1

Group  Port-channel  Protocol    Ports
------+-------------+-----------+-----------------------------------------------
10     Po10(SU)         -        Fa0/11(P)   Fa0/12(P)

DLS2#show etherchannel summary
Flags:  D - down         P - bundled in port-channel
        I - stand-alone  s - suspended
        H - Hot-standby (LACP only)
        R - Layer3       S - Layer2
        U - in use       f - failed to allocate aggregator

        M - not in use, minimum links not met
        u - unsuitable for bundling
        w - waiting to be aggregated
        d - default port


Number of channel-groups in use: 1
Number of aggregators:           1

Group  Port-channel  Protocol    Ports
------+-------------+-----------+-----------------------------------------------
10     Po10(SU)         -        Fa0/11(P)   Fa0/12(P)
```

After configuring the SVI on switch DLS2, verify reachability on the 150.1.1.0/24 subnet:

```
DLS2#ping 150.1.1.0

Type escape sequence to abort.
Sending 5, 100-byte ICMP Echos to 150.1.1.0, timeout is 2 seconds:
.
Reply to request 1 from 150.1.1.254, 1 ms
Reply to request 1 from 150.1.1.1, 1 ms
Reply to request 2 from 150.1.1.254, 1 ms
Reply to request 2 from 150.1.1.1, 1 ms
Reply to request 3 from 150.1.1.254, 1 ms
Reply to request 3 from 150.1.1.1, 1 ms
Reply to request 4 from 150.1.1.254, 1 ms
Reply to request 4 from 150.1.1.1, 1 ms
```

Task 3

To complete this task, you need to configure an OSPF point-to-multipoint network type. All of the devices should reside in OSPF area 0. Verify OSPF using the show ip ospf commands:

```
R1#show ip ospf neighbor

Neighbor ID    Pri  State    Dead Time   Address        Interface
150.1.1.253     0   FULL/ -  00:01:43    150.1.1.253    FastEthernet0/0
150.1.1.254     0   FULL/ -  00:01:43    150.1.1.254    FastEthernet0/0

DLS1#show ip ospf neighbor

Neighbor ID    Pri  State    Dead Time   Address        Interface
150.1.1.253     0   FULL/ -  00:01:47    150.1.1.253    Vlan100
11.11.11.11     0   FULL/ -  00:01:47    150.1.1.1      Vlan100

DLS2#show ip ospf neighbor

Neighbor ID    Pri  State    Dead Time   Address        Interface
150.1.1.254     0   FULL/ -  00:01:56    150.1.1.254    Vlan100
11.11.11.11     0   FULL/ -  00:01:57    150.1.1.1      Vlan100
```

To view the network type, use the show ip ospf interface command:

```
DLS2#show ip ospf interface vlan 100
Vlan100 is up, line protocol is up
  Internet Address 150.1.1.253/24, Area 0
  Process ID 1, Router ID 150.1.1.253, Network Type POINT_TO_MULTIPOINT, Cost: 1
  Transmit Delay is 1 sec, State POINT_TO_MULTIPOINT
  Timer intervals configured, Hello 30, Dead 120, Wait 120, Retransmit 5
    oob-resync timeout 120
    Hello due in 00:00:28
  Supports Link-local Signaling (LLS)
  Cisco NSF helper support enabled
  IETF NSF helper support enabled
  Index 1/1, flood queue length 0
  Next 0x0(0)/0x0(0)
  Last flood scan length is 1, maximum is 1
  Last flood scan time is 0 msec, maximum is 0 msec
  Neighbor Count is 2, Adjacent neighbor count is 2
    Adjacent with neighbor 11.11.11.11
    Adjacent with neighbor 150.1.1.254
  Suppress hello for 0 neighbor(s)
```

Task 4

The same logic applied in the previous task should also be used to complete this task. Following this, verify OSPF configuration using the show ip ospf commands:

```
R1#show ip ospf neighbor

Neighbor ID     Pri   State        Dead Time   Address       Interface
22.22.22.11      0    FULL/  -     00:00:34    150.0.0.2     Serial0/0
150.1.1.253      0    FULL/  -     00:01:47    150.1.1.253   FastEthernet0/0
150.1.1.254      0    FULL/  -     00:01:51    150.1.1.254   FastEthernet0/0

R2#show ip ospf neighbor

Neighbor ID     Pri   State        Dead Time   Address       Interface
11.11.11.22      0    FULL/  -     00:00:32    150.0.0.1     Serial0/0
```

Task 5

The same logic applied in the previous task should also be used to complete this task. Following this, verify OSPF configuration using the show ip ospf commands:

```
R1#show ip ospf neighbor

Neighbor ID     Pri   State        Dead Time   Address       Interface
33.33.33.33      0    FULL/  -     00:00:37    150.0.0.6     Serial0/1
22.22.22.11      0    FULL/  -     00:00:34    150.0.0.2     Serial0/0
150.1.1.253      0    FULL/  -     00:01:31    150.1.1.253   FastEthernet0/0
150.1.1.254      0    FULL/  -     00:01:35    150.1.1.254   FastEthernet0/0

R2#show ip ospf neighbor

Neighbor ID     Pri   State        Dead Time   Address       Interface
33.33.33.33      0    FULL/  -     00:00:35    150.0.0.10    Serial0/1
11.11.11.22      0    FULL/  -     00:00:35    150.0.0.1     Serial0/0

R3#show ip ospf neighbor

Neighbor ID     Pri   State        Dead Time   Address       Interface
22.22.22.33      0    FULL/  -     00:00:39    150.0.0.9     Serial1/1
11.11.11.33      0    FULL/  -     00:00:39    150.0.0.5     Serial1/0
```

To verify which interfaces are enabled under which process, use the show ip ospf interface brief command on the router or switch:

```
R1#show ip ospf interface brief
Interface    PID   Area            IP Address/Mask     Cost   State  Nbrs F/C
Se0/1        3     0               150.0.0.5/30        64     P2P    1/1
Se0/0        2     0               150.0.0.1/30        64     P2P    1/1
Fa0/0        1     0               150.1.1.1/24        1      P2MP   2/2
```

Task 6

The configuration requirements of this task are straightforward. To ensure that R3 sends only a default route to R4, you need to enable filtering and configure the router to generate and advertise a default. Once complete, verify the solution using the show ip eigrp commands:

```
R3#show ip eigrp neighbors detail
IP-EIGRP neighbors for process 4
H   Address                 Interface       Hold Uptime    SRTT   RTO  Q  Seq
                                            (sec)          (ms)        Cnt Num
0   150.0.0.14              Se1/2            10 00:01:00    11   1140  0  8
    Restart time 00:00:08
    Version 12.4/1.2, Retrans: 1, Retries: 0, Prefixes: 1
    Stub Peer Advertising ( CONNECTED ) Routes
    Suppressing queries
```

On R4, use the show ip route command to ensure that only a default is received from R3:

```
R4#show ip route eigrp
D*   0.0.0.0/0 [90/2172416] via 150.0.0.13, 00:00:28, Serial0/0
```

Task 7

This task requires some thought. You need to implement route filtering when redistributing between the OSPF processes. EIGRP is great in such situations because external routes are assigned a higher administrative distance than internal routes - meaning that the likelihood of routing loops in such scenarios is very slim. The same concept could also be applied to OSPF; however, the task explicitly states that we should not modify default administrative distance values. Therefore, we must use filtering. This task is completed as follows:

```
R1(config)#ip prefix-list PROCESS-1-FILTER seq 5 permit 150.1.1.0/24
R1(config)#ip prefix-list PROCESS-2-FILTER seq 5 permit 150.0.0.0/30
R1(config)#ip prefix-list PROCESS-2-FILTER seq 7 permit 150.2.2.0/24
R1(config)#ip prefix-list PROCESS-3-FILTER seq 5 permit 150.0.0.4/30
R1(config)#ip prefix-list PROCESS-3-FILTER seq 7 permit 150.0.0.8/30
R1(config)#route-map PROCESS-1-FILTER deny 10
R1(config-route-map)#match ip address prefix-list PROCESS-1-FILTER
R1(config-route-map)#exit
R1(config)#route-map PROCESS-1-FILTER permit 20
R1(config-route-map)#exit
R1(config)#route-map PROCESS-2-FILTER deny 10
R1(config-route-map)#match ip address prefix-list PROCESS-2-FILTER
R1(config-route-map)#exit
R1(config)#route-map PROCESS-2-FILTER permit 20
R1(config-route-map)#exit
R1(config)#route-map PROCESS-3-FILTER deny 10
R1(config-route-map)#match ip address prefix-list PROCESS-3-FILTER
R1(config-route-map)#exit
R1(config)#route-map PROCESS-3-FILTER permit 20
R1(config-route-map)#exit
R1(config)#router ospf 1
R1(config-router)#redistribute ospf 2 subnets route-map PROCESS-1-FILTER
R1(config-router)#redistribute ospf 3 subnets route-map PROCESS-1-FILTER
R1(config-router)#exit
R1(config)#router ospf 2
R1(config-router)#redistribute ospf 1 subnets route-map PROCESS-2-FILTER
R1(config-router)#redistribute ospf 3 subnets route-map PROCESS-2-FILTER
R1(config-router)#exit
R1(config)#router ospf 3
R1(config-router)#redistribute ospf 1 subnets route-map PROCESS-3-FILTER
R1(config-router)#redistribute ospf 2 subnets route-map PROCESS-3-FILTER
```

The redistribution configuration on R2 would be implemented similar to the following:

```
R2(config)#ip prefix-list PROCESS-2-FILTER seq 5 permit 150.0.0.0/30
R2(config)#ip prefix-list PROCESS-2-FILTER seq 7 permit 150.2.2.0/24
R2(config)#ip prefix-list PROCESS-3-FILTER seq 5 permit 150.0.0.4/30
R2(config)#ip prefix-list PROCESS-3-FILTER seq 7 permit 150.0.0.8/30
R2(config)#route-map PROCESS-2-FILTER deny 10
R2(config-route-map)#match ip address prefix-list PROCESS-2-FILTER
R2(config-route-map)#exit
R2(config)#route-map PROCESS-2-FILTER permit 20
R2(config-route-map)#exit
R2(config)#route-map PROCESS-3-FILTER deny 10
```

```
R2(config-route-map)#match ip address prefix-list PROCESS-3-FILTER
R2(config-route-map)#exit
R2(config)#route-map PROCESS-3-FILTER permit 20
R2(config-route-map)#exit
R2(config)#router ospf 2
R2(config-router)#redistribute ospf 3 subnets route-map PROCESS-2-FILTER
R2(config-router)#exit
R2(config)#router ospf 3
R2(config-router)#redistribute ospf 2 subnets route-map PROCESS-3-FILTER
R2(config-router)#exit
```

Next, verify the Link State Databases of all devices using the show ip ospf commands:

DLS1#show ip ospf database

```
        OSPF Router with ID (150.1.1.254) (Process ID 1)

            Router Link States (Area 0)

Link ID          ADV Router       Age        Seq#        Checksum Link count
11.11.11.11      11.11.11.11      173        0x80000003 0x00EFCD 3
150.1.1.253      150.1.1.253      90         0x80000008 0x00ADAB 3
150.1.1.254      150.1.1.254      1935       0x80000007 0x00D382 3

            Type-5 AS External Link States

Link ID          ADV Router       Age        Seq#        Checksum Tag
150.0.0.0        11.11.11.11      510        0x80000001 0x009E16 0
150.0.0.4        11.11.11.11      500        0x80000001 0x00763A 0
150.0.0.8        11.11.11.11      500        0x80000001 0x00EBB0 0
150.2.2.0        11.11.11.11      510        0x80000001 0x008C20 0
```

DLS2#show ip ospf database

```
        OSPF Router with ID (150.1.1.253) (Process ID 1)

            Router Link States (Area 0)

Link ID          ADV Router       Age        Seq#        Checksum Link count
11.11.11.11      11.11.11.11      163        0x80000003 0x00EFCD 3
150.1.1.253      150.1.1.253      79         0x80000008 0x00ADAB 3
150.1.1.254      150.1.1.254      1926       0x80000007 0x00D382 3

            Type-5 AS External Link States

Link ID          ADV Router       Age        Seq#        Checksum Tag
150.0.0.0        11.11.11.11      501        0x80000001 0x009E16 0
150.0.0.4        11.11.11.11      491        0x80000001 0x00763A 0
150.0.0.8        11.11.11.11      491        0x80000001 0x00EBB0 0
150.2.2.0        11.11.11.11      501        0x80000001 0x008C20 0
```

R1#show ip ospf database

```
        OSPF Router with ID (11.11.11.33) (Process ID 3)

            Router Link States (Area 0)

Link ID          ADV Router       Age        Seq#        Checksum Link count
11.11.11.33      11.11.11.33      921        0x80000003 0x00FB68 2
22.22.22.33      22.22.22.33      689        0x80000003 0x00F524 2
33.33.33.33      33.33.33.33      2008       0x80000002 0x00C1E4 4

            Type-5 AS External Link States

Link ID          ADV Router       Age        Seq#        Checksum Tag
150.0.0.0        11.11.11.33      118        0x80000002 0x009489 0
150.0.0.0        22.22.22.33      106        0x80000002 0x008B71 0
150.1.1.0        11.11.11.33      128        0x80000002 0x001741 0
150.1.1.0        22.22.22.33      106        0x80000003 0x008E67 0
150.1.1.253      11.11.11.33      128        0x80000002 0x002B2F 0
150.1.1.253      22.22.22.33      106        0x80000003 0x00A255 0
150.1.1.254      11.11.11.33      128        0x80000002 0x002138 0
150.1.1.254      22.22.22.33      106        0x80000003 0x00985E 0
150.2.2.0        11.11.11.33      119        0x80000002 0x008293 0
150.2.2.0        22.22.22.33      107        0x80000002 0x00F63E 0

        OSPF Router with ID (11.11.11.22) (Process ID 2)

            Router Link States (Area 0)
```

```
Link ID         ADV Router      Age       Seq#       Checksum Link count
11.11.11.22     11.11.11.22     993       0x80000004 0x003484 2
22.22.22.11     22.22.22.11     731       0x80000002 0x0042B5 3

                Type-5 AS External Link States

Link ID         ADV Router      Age       Seq#       Checksum Tag
150.0.0.4       11.11.11.22     173       0x80000002 0x00AE76 0
150.0.0.4       22.22.22.11     154       0x80000002 0x008579 0
150.0.0.8       11.11.11.22     173       0x80000002 0x0024EC 0
150.0.0.8       22.22.22.11     154       0x80000002 0x00BF4B 0
150.1.1.0       11.11.11.22     183       0x80000002 0x00590A 0
150.1.1.253     11.11.11.22     183       0x80000002 0x006DF7 0
150.1.1.254     11.11.11.22     183       0x80000002 0x006301 0

          OSPF Router with ID (11.11.11.11) (Process ID 1)

                Router Link States (Area 0)

Link ID         ADV Router      Age       Seq#       Checksum Link count
11.11.11.11     11.11.11.11     678       0x80000003 0x00EFCD 3
150.1.1.253     150.1.1.253     599       0x80000008 0x00ADAB 3
150.1.1.254     150.1.1.254     403       0x80000008 0x00D183 3

                Type-5 AS External Link States

Link ID         ADV Router      Age       Seq#       Checksum Tag
150.0.0.0       11.11.11.11     200       0x80000002 0x00191B 0
150.0.0.4       11.11.11.11     190       0x80000002 0x00F03F 0
150.0.0.8       11.11.11.11     190       0x80000002 0x0066B5 0
150.2.2.0       11.11.11.11     200       0x80000002 0x000725 0
```

R2#show ip ospf database

```
          OSPF Router with ID (22.22.22.33) (Process ID 3)

                Router Link States (Area 0)

Link ID         ADV Router      Age       Seq#       Checksum Link count
11.11.11.33     11.11.11.33     914       0x80000003 0x00FB68 2
22.22.22.33     22.22.22.33     678       0x80000003 0x00F524 2
33.33.33.33     33.33.33.33     1998      0x80000002 0x00C1E4 4

                Type-5 AS External Link States

Link ID         ADV Router      Age       Seq#       Checksum Tag
150.0.0.0       11.11.11.33     111       0x80000002 0x009489 0
150.0.0.0       22.22.22.33     95        0x80000002 0x008B71 0
150.1.1.0       11.11.11.33     121       0x80000002 0x001741 0
150.1.1.0       22.22.22.33     95        0x80000003 0x008E67 0
150.1.1.253     11.11.11.33     121       0x80000003 0x002B2F 0
150.1.1.253     22.22.22.33     95        0x80000003 0x00A255 0
150.1.1.254     11.11.11.33     121       0x80000002 0x002138 0
150.1.1.254     22.22.22.33     95        0x80000003 0x00985E 0
150.2.2.0       11.11.11.33     112       0x80000002 0x008293 0
150.2.2.0       22.22.22.33     96        0x80000002 0x00F63E 0

          OSPF Router with ID (22.22.22.11) (Process ID 2)

                Router Link States (Area 0)

Link ID         ADV Router      Age       Seq#       Checksum Link count
11.11.11.22     11.11.11.22     945       0x80000004 0x003484 2
22.22.22.11     22.22.22.11     681       0x80000002 0x0042B5 3

                Type-5 AS External Link States

Link ID         ADV Router      Age       Seq#       Checksum Tag
150.0.0.4       11.11.11.22     125       0x80000002 0x00AE76 0
150.0.0.4       22.22.22.11     104       0x80000002 0x008579 0
150.0.0.8       11.11.11.22     125       0x80000002 0x0024EC 0
150.0.0.8       22.22.22.11     104       0x80000002 0x00BF4B 0
150.1.1.0       11.11.11.22     135       0x80000002 0x00590A 0
150.1.1.253     11.11.11.22     135       0x80000002 0x006DF7 0
150.1.1.254     11.11.11.22     135       0x80000002 0x006301 0
```

R3#show ip ospf database

```
          OSPF Router with ID (33.33.33.33) (Process ID 3)
```

```
                 Router Link States (Area 0)

Link ID        ADV Router       Age     Seq#         Checksum Link count
11.11.11.33    11.11.11.33      928     0x80000003 0x00FB68 2
22.22.22.33    22.22.22.33      694     0x80000003 0x00F524 2
33.33.33.33    33.33.33.33      2012    0x80000002 0x00C1E4 4

                 Type-5 AS External Link States

Link ID        ADV Router       Age     Seq#         Checksum Tag
150.0.0.0      11.11.11.33      125     0x80000002 0x009489 0
150.0.0.0      22.22.22.33      110     0x80000002 0x008B71 0
150.1.1.0      11.11.11.33      135     0x80000002 0x001741 0
150.1.1.0      22.22.22.33      110     0x80000003 0x008E67 0
150.1.1.253    11.11.11.33      135     0x80000002 0x002B2F 0
150.1.1.253    22.22.22.33      110     0x80000003 0x00A255 0
150.1.1.254    11.11.11.33      135     0x80000002 0x002138 0
150.1.1.254    22.22.22.33      110     0x80000003 0x00985E 0
150.2.2.0      11.11.11.33      126     0x80000002 0x008293 0
150.2.2.0      22.22.22.33      111     0x80000002 0x00F63E 0
```

Verify your IP routing tables using the show ip route commands:

```
R1#show ip route ospf
      150.0.0.0/30 is subnetted, 3 subnets
O        150.0.0.8 [110/845] via 150.0.0.6, 00:12:59, Serial0/1
      150.1.0.0/16 is variably subnetted, 3 subnets, 2 masks
O        150.1.1.254/32 [110/1] via 150.1.1.254, 00:17:46, FastEthernet0/0
O        150.1.1.253/32 [110/1] via 150.1.1.253, 00:17:46, FastEthernet0/0
      150.2.0.0/24 is subnetted, 1 subnets
O        150.2.2.0 [110/65] via 150.0.0.2, 00:13:00, Serial0/0

R2#show ip route ospf
      150.0.0.0/30 is subnetted, 3 subnets
O        150.0.0.4 [110/845] via 150.0.0.10, 00:13:04, Serial0/1
      150.1.0.0/16 is variably subnetted, 3 subnets, 2 masks
O E1     150.1.1.254/32 [110/65] via 150.0.0.1, 00:04:02, Serial0/0
O E1     150.1.1.253/32 [110/65] via 150.0.0.1, 00:04:02, Serial0/0
O E1     150.1.1.0/24 [110/65] via 150.0.0.1, 00:04:02, Serial0/0

R3#show ip route ospf
      150.0.0.0/30 is subnetted, 4 subnets
O E1     150.0.0.0 [110/845] via 150.0.0.9, 00:03:28, Serial1/1
                   [110/845] via 150.0.0.5, 00:03:28, Serial1/0
      150.1.0.0/16 is variably subnetted, 3 subnets, 2 masks
O E1     150.1.1.254/32 [110/782] via 150.0.0.5, 00:03:28, Serial1/0
O E1     150.1.1.253/32 [110/782] via 150.0.0.5, 00:03:28, Serial1/0
O E1     150.1.1.0/24 [110/782] via 150.0.0.5, 00:03:28, Serial1/0
      150.2.0.0/24 is subnetted, 1 subnets
O E1     150.2.2.0 [110/782] via 150.0.0.9, 00:03:28, Serial1/1
```

NOTE: Keep in mind that your output may vary slightly from what is printed above depending on the solution you implemented and the manner in which routes were received.

Task 8

To complete this task, you need to first use the summary-address OSPF command on R3:

```
R3(config)#router ospf 3
R3(config-router)#summary-address 10.0.0.0 255.0.0.0
R3(config-router)#summary-address 150.0.0.12 255.255.255.252 not-advertise
R3(config-router)#redistribute eigrp 4 subnets
R3(config-router)#exit
```

Next, you need to update the redistribution configuration so that this route is not redistributed back into OSPF process ID 3 on either R1 or R2:

```
R1(config)#ip prefix-list PROCESS-3-FILTER seq 9 deny 10.0.0.0/8
R1(config)#end
R1#clear ip ospf redistribution

R2(config)#ip prefix-list PROCESS-3-FILTER seq 9 permit 10.0.0.0/8
R2(config)#end
R2#clear ip ospf redistribution
```

Verify your configuration using the show ip ospf commands:

```
R3#show ip ospf database

            OSPF Router with ID (33.33.33.33) (Process ID 3)

              Router Link States (Area 0)

Link ID         ADV Router      Age      Seq#       Checksum Link count
11.11.11.33     11.11.11.33     126      0x80000004 0x00F969 2
22.22.22.33     22.22.22.33     1737     0x80000003 0x00F524 2
33.33.33.33     33.33.33.33     476      0x80000004 0x00C3DE 4

              Type-5 AS External Link States

Link ID         ADV Router      Age      Seq#       Checksum Tag
10.0.0.0        33.33.33.33     241      0x80000001 0x00838E 0

[Truncated Output]
```

Use the show ip route command to ensure that the 150.0.0.12/30 subnet is not advertised:

```
R1#show ip route ospf
O E2 10.0.0.0/8 [110/20] via 150.0.0.6, 00:06:49, Serial0/1
        150.0.0.0/30 is subnetted, 3 subnets
O       150.0.0.8 [110/845] via 150.0.0.6, 00:10:39, Serial0/1
        150.1.0.0/16 is variably subnetted, 3 subnets, 2 masks
O       150.1.1.254/32 [110/1] via 150.1.1.254, 00:36:27, FastEthernet0/0
O       150.1.1.253/32 [110/1] via 150.1.1.253, 00:36:27, FastEthernet0/0
        150.2.0.0/24 is subnetted, 1 subnets
O       150.2.2.0 [110/65] via 150.0.0.2, 00:31:41, Serial0/0

R2#show ip route ospf
O E2 10.0.0.0/8 [110/20] via 150.0.0.10, 00:07:36, Serial0/1
        150.0.0.0/30 is subnetted, 3 subnets
O       150.0.0.4 [110/845] via 150.0.0.10, 00:11:25, Serial0/1
        150.1.0.0/16 is variably subnetted, 3 subnets, 2 masks
O E1    150.1.1.254/32 [110/65] via 150.0.0.1, 00:04:29, Serial0/0
O E1    150.1.1.253/32 [110/65] via 150.0.0.1, 00:04:29, Serial0/0
O E1    150.1.1.0/24 [110/65] via 150.0.0.1, 00:04:29, Serial0/0
```

Finally, verify your configurations using simple pings between all routers. For example, ping from switch DLS2 to all other routers, and work through each router:

```
DLS2#ping 150.2.2.2

Type escape sequence to abort.
Sending 5, 100-byte ICMP Echos to 150.2.2.2, timeout is 2 seconds:
!!!!!
Success rate is 100 percent (5/5), round-trip min/avg/max = 1/3/4 ms

DLS2#ping 10.3.3.3

Type escape sequence to abort.
Sending 5, 100-byte ICMP Echos to 10.3.3.3, timeout is 2 seconds:
!!!!!
Success rate is 100 percent (5/5), round-trip min/avg/max = 16/16/16 ms

DLS2#ping 10.4.4.4

Type escape sequence to abort.
Sending 5, 100-byte ICMP Echos to 10.4.4.4, timeout is 2 seconds:
!!!!!
Success rate is 100 percent (5/5), round-trip min/avg/max = 28/28/32 ms
```

Repeat the same exercise for all other routers in the network.

Task 9

To complete this task, you need to enable Dense Mode forwarding on ALL interfaces along the path. Next, verify using the show ip pim commands:

```
R1#show ip pim interface

Address           Interface        Ver/   Nbr    Query  DR     DR
                                   Mode   Count  Intvl  Prior
150.0.0.1         Serial0/0        v2/D   1      30     1      0.0.0.0
150.0.0.5         Serial0/1        v2/D   1      30     1      0.0.0.0
150.1.1.1         FastEthernet0/0  v2/D   0      30     1      150.1.1.1

R2#show ip pim interface

Address           Interface        Ver/   Nbr    Query  DR     DR
                                   Mode   Count  Intvl  Prior
150.0.0.2         Serial0/0        v2/D   1      30     1      0.0.0.0
150.0.0.9         Serial0/1        v2/D   1      30     1      0.0.0.0

R3#show ip pim interface

Address           Interface        Ver/   Nbr    Query  DR     DR
                                   Mode   Count  Intvl  Prior
150.0.0.6         Serial1/0        v2/D   1      30     1      0.0.0.0
150.0.0.10        Serial1/1        v2/D   1      30     1      0.0.0.0
150.0.0.13        Serial1/2        v2/D   1      30     1      0.0.0.0

R4#show ip pim interface

Address           Interface        Ver/   Nbr    Query  DR     DR
                                   Mode   Count  Intvl  Prior
150.0.0.14        Serial0/0        v2/D   1      30     1      0.0.0.0
10.4.4.4          FastEthernet0/0  v2/D   0      30     1      10.4.4.4
```

You can also use the show ip pim neighbor command for detailed neighbor information:

```
R2#show ip pim neighbor
PIM Neighbor Table
Mode: B - Bidir Capable, DR - Designated Router, N - Default DR Priority,
      S - State Refresh Capable
Neighbor          Interface        Uptime/Expires      Ver    DR
Address                                                       Prio/Mode
150.0.0.1         Serial0/0        00:03:39/00:01:31 v2     1 / S
150.0.0.10        Serial0/1        00:03:54/00:01:16 v2     1 / S
```

To view Multicast group(s) information, use the show ip igmp commands:

```
R1#show ip igmp groups detail

Flags: L - Local, U - User, SG - Static Group, VG - Virtual Group,
       SS - Static Source, VS - Virtual Source,
       Ac - Group accounted towards access control limit

Interface:      FastEthernet0/0
Group:          227.1.1.1
Flags:          L U
Uptime:         00:04:54
Group mode:     EXCLUDE (Expires: 00:02:34)
Last reporter:  150.1.1.1
Source list is empty

Interface:      Serial0/0
Group:          224.0.1.40
Flags:          L U
Uptime:         00:06:02
Group mode:     INCLUDE
Last reporter:  150.0.0.1
Source list is empty
```

Finally, test your solution by pinging group 227.1.1.1 from the LAN interface of R4:

```
R4#ping 227.1.1.1 source fastethernet 0/0

Type escape sequence to abort.
Sending 1, 100-byte ICMP Echos to 227.1.1.1, timeout is 2 seconds:
Packet sent with a source address of 10.4.4.4

Reply to request 0 from 150.0.0.5, 36 ms
```

FINAL ROUTER CONFIGURATIONS

R1

```
R1#term len 0
R1#sh run
Building configuration...

Current configuration : 2417 bytes
!
version 12.4
service timestamps debug datetime msec
service timestamps log datetime msec
no service password-encryption
!
hostname R1
!
boot-start-marker
boot-end-marker
!
no logging console
!
no aaa new-model
no network-clock-participate slot 1
no network-clock-participate wic 0
ip cef
!
no ip domain lookup
ip multicast-routing
ip auth-proxy max-nodata-conns 3
ip admission max-nodata-conns 3
!
interface FastEthernet0/0
 ip address 150.1.1.1 255.255.255.0
 ip pim dense-mode
 ip igmp join-group 227.1.1.1
 ip ospf network point-to-multipoint
 duplex auto
 speed auto
!
interface Serial0/0
 ip address 150.0.0.1 255.255.255.252
 ip pim dense-mode
 clock rate 2000000
!
interface Serial0/1
 ip address 150.0.0.5 255.255.255.252
 ip pim dense-mode
!
router ospf 1
 router-id 11.11.11.11
 log-adjacency-changes
 redistribute ospf 2 metric-type 1 subnets route-map PROCESS-1-FILTER
 redistribute ospf 3 metric-type 1 subnets route-map PROCESS-1-FILTER
 network 150.1.1.1 0.0.0.0 area 0
!
router ospf 2
 router-id 11.11.11.22
 log-adjacency-changes
 redistribute ospf 1 metric-type 1 subnets route-map PROCESS-2-FILTER
 redistribute ospf 3 metric-type 1 subnets route-map PROCESS-2-FILTER
 network 150.0.0.1 0.0.0.0 area 0
!
router ospf 3
 router-id 11.11.11.33
 log-adjacency-changes
 redistribute ospf 1 metric-type 1 subnets route-map PROCESS-3-FILTER
 redistribute ospf 2 metric-type 1 subnets route-map PROCESS-3-FILTER
 network 150.0.0.5 0.0.0.0 area 0
!
ip forward-protocol nd
!
no ip http server
no ip http secure-server
!
ip prefix-list PROCESS-1-FILTER seq 5 permit 150.1.1.0/24
!
ip prefix-list PROCESS-2-FILTER seq 5 permit 150.0.0.0/30
```

```
ip prefix-list PROCESS-2-FILTER seq 7 permit 150.2.2.0/24
!
ip prefix-list PROCESS-3-FILTER seq 5 permit 150.0.0.4/30
ip prefix-list PROCESS-3-FILTER seq 7 permit 150.0.0.8/30
ip prefix-list PROCESS-3-FILTER seq 9 permit 10.0.0.0/8
!
route-map PROCESS-3-FILTER deny 10
 match ip address prefix-list PROCESS-3-FILTER
!
route-map PROCESS-3-FILTER permit 20
!
route-map PROCESS-2-FILTER deny 10
 match ip address prefix-list PROCESS-2-FILTER
!
route-map PROCESS-2-FILTER permit 20
!
route-map PROCESS-1-FILTER deny 10
 match ip address prefix-list PROCESS-1-FILTER
!
route-map PROCESS-1-FILTER permit 20
!
control-plane
!
line con 0
line aux 0
line vty 0 4
 password cisco
 login
!
end

R1#
```

R2

```
R2#term len 0
R2#sh run
Building configuration...

Current configuration : 1845 bytes
!
version 12.4
service timestamps debug datetime msec
service timestamps log datetime msec
no service password-encryption
!
hostname R2
!
boot-start-marker
boot-end-marker
!
no logging console
!
no aaa new-model
no network-clock-participate slot 1
no network-clock-participate wic 0
ip cef
!
no ip domain lookup
ip multicast-routing
ip auth-proxy max-nodata-conns 3
ip admission max-nodata-conns 3
!
interface FastEthernet0/0
 ip address 150.2.2.2 255.255.255.0
 loopback
 duplex auto
 speed auto
 no keepalive
!
interface Serial0/0
 ip address 150.0.0.2 255.255.255.252
 ip pim dense-mode
!
interface Serial0/1
 ip address 150.0.0.9 255.255.255.252
 ip pim dense-mode
!
```

```
router ospf 2
 router-id 22.22.22.11
 log-adjacency-changes
 redistribute ospf 3 metric-type 1 subnets route-map PROCESS-2-FILTER
 passive-interface FastEthernet0/0
 network 150.0.0.2 0.0.0.0 area 0
 network 150.2.2.2 0.0.0.0 area 0
!
router ospf 3
 router-id 22.22.22.33
 log-adjacency-changes
 redistribute ospf 2 metric-type 1 subnets route-map PROCESS-3-FILTER
 network 150.0.0.9 0.0.0.0 area 0
!
ip forward-protocol nd
!
no ip http server
no ip http secure-server
!
ip prefix-list PROCESS-2-FILTER seq 5 permit 150.0.0.0/30
ip prefix-list PROCESS-2-FILTER seq 7 permit 150.2.2.0/24
!
ip prefix-list PROCESS-3-FILTER seq 5 permit 150.0.0.4/30
ip prefix-list PROCESS-3-FILTER seq 7 permit 150.0.0.8/30
ip prefix-list PROCESS-3-FILTER seq 9 permit 10.0.0.0/8
!
route-map PROCESS-3-FILTER deny 10
 match ip address prefix-list PROCESS-3-FILTER
!
route-map PROCESS-3-FILTER permit 20
!
route-map PROCESS-2-FILTER deny 10
 match ip address prefix-list PROCESS-2-FILTER
!
route-map PROCESS-2-FILTER permit 20
!
control-plane
!
line con 0
line aux 0
line vty 0 4
 password cisco
 login
!
end

R2#
```

R3

```
R3#term len 0
R3#sh run
Building configuration...

Current configuration : 1747 bytes
!
version 12.4
service timestamps debug datetime msec
service timestamps log datetime msec
no service password-encryption
!
hostname R3
!
boot-start-marker
boot-end-marker
!
no logging console
!
no aaa new-model
no network-clock-participate slot 1
no network-clock-participate wic 0
ip cef
!
no ip domain lookup
ip multicast-routing
ip auth-proxy max-nodata-conns 3
ip admission max-nodata-conns 3
!
```

```
interface FastEthernet0/0
 ip address 10.3.3.3 255.255.255.0
 duplex auto
 speed auto
!
interface Serial1/0
 ip address 150.0.0.6 255.255.255.252
 ip pim dense-mode
 clock rate 128000
!
interface Serial1/1
 ip address 150.0.0.10 255.255.255.252
 ip pim dense-mode
 clock rate 128000
!
interface Serial1/2
 ip address 150.0.0.13 255.255.255.252
 ip pim dense-mode
 ip summary-address eigrp 4 0.0.0.0 0.0.0.0 5
 clock rate 128000
!
interface Serial1/3
 no ip address
 shutdown
!
interface Serial1/4
 no ip address
 shutdown
!
interface Serial1/5
 no ip address
 shutdown
!
interface Serial1/6
 no ip address
 shutdown
!
interface Serial1/7
 no ip address
 shutdown
!
router eigrp 4
 network 10.3.3.3 0.0.0.0
 network 150.0.0.13 0.0.0.0
 distribute-list prefix DEFAULT-ONLY out Serial1/2
 no auto-summary
!
router ospf 3
 router-id 33.33.33.33
 log-adjacency-changes
 summary-address 150.0.0.12 255.255.255.252 not-advertise
 summary-address 10.0.0.0 255.0.0.0
 redistribute eigrp 4 subnets
 network 150.0.0.6 0.0.0.0 area 0
 network 150.0.0.10 0.0.0.0 area 0
!
ip forward-protocol nd
!
no ip http server
no ip http secure-server
!
ip prefix-list DEFAULT-ONLY seq 5 permit 0.0.0.0/0
!
control-plane
!
line con 0
line aux 0
line vty 0 4
 password cisco
 login
!
end

R3#
```

R4

```
R4#term len 0
R4#sh run
Building configuration...

Current configuration : 1014 bytes
!
version 12.4
service timestamps debug datetime msec
service timestamps log datetime msec
no service password-encryption
!
hostname R4
!
boot-start-marker
boot-end-marker
!
no logging console
!
no aaa new-model
no network-clock-participate slot 1
no network-clock-participate wic 0
ip cef
!
no ip domain lookup
ip multicast-routing
ip auth-proxy max-nodata-conns 3
ip admission max-nodata-conns 3
!
interface FastEthernet0/0
 ip address 10.4.4.4 255.255.255.0
 ip pim dense-mode
 duplex auto
 speed auto
!
interface Serial0/0
 ip address 150.0.0.14 255.255.255.252
 ip pim dense-mode
!
interface Serial0/1
 no ip address
 shutdown
!
router eigrp 4
 passive-interface FastEthernet0/0
 network 10.4.4.4 0.0.0.0
 network 150.0.0.14 0.0.0.0
 no auto-summary
 eigrp stub connected
!
ip forward-protocol nd
!
no ip http server
no ip http secure-server
!
control-plane
!
line con 0
line aux 0
line vty 0 4
 password cisco
 login
!
end

R4#
```

FINAL SWITCH CONFIGURATIONS

DLS1

```
DLS1#term len 0
DLS1#sh run
Building configuration...
```

```
Current configuration : 6345 bytes
!
version 12.2
no service pad
service timestamps debug datetime msec
service timestamps log datetime msec
no service password-encryption
!
hostname DLS1
!
no logging console
!
no aaa new-model
ip subnet-zero
ip routing
no ip domain-lookup
!
vtp domain null
vtp mode transparent
!
crypto pki trustpoint TP-self-signed-587410816
 enrollment selfsigned
 subject-name cn=IOS-Self-Signed-Certificate-587410816
 revocation-check none
 rsakeypair TP-self-signed-587410816
!
crypto pki certificate chain TP-self-signed-587410816
 certificate self-signed 01
  3082023B 308201A4 A0030201 02020101 300D0609 2A864886 F70D0101 04050030
  30312E30 2C060355 04031325 494F532D 53656C66 2D536967 6E65642D 43657274
  69666963 6174652D 35383734 31303831 36301E17 0D393330 33303130 30313532
  345A170D 32303031 30313030 30303030 5A303031 2E302C06 03550403 1325494F
  532D5365 6C662D53 69676E65 642D4365 72746966 69636174 652D3538 37343130
  38313630 819F300D 06092A86 4886F70D 01010105 0003818D 00308189 02818100
  B2DDE221 AD572F9E DDD50554 60BAA44A 3991B35A EBA97247 E99A000E DFD77BA6
  1EDA2260 A901B109 5ABD3E6B 84733F17 EC5E00AB 8DE92E71 DF767259 CDE4406A
  870E15B2 8D344042 D89CE1FE 2F1587C0 8BE15003 ADD8C995 5787F957 6CB5383E
  72C8A31B 5C084D04 7463090E 7162ED0C 6511026B B6753693 A54DD0CE 956855F5
  02030100 01A36530 63300F06 03551D13 0101FF04 05300301 01FF3010 0603551D
  11040930 07820544 4C53312E 301F0603 551D2304 18301680 14DBED5D DCA7E850
  482C7A6E 75E9701A 881C0083 72301D06 03551D0E 04160414 DBED5DDC A7E85048
  2C7A6E75 E9701A88 1C008372 300D0609 2A864886 F70D0101 04050003 8181005B
  68CD2952 004AC7C4 5FB8D144 7F914EE9 D83463A4 FAFD1ACE D1EC1B58 011903D4
  DEB27CE2 4644638F 0C883AAC B434C2D2 2AD7AD8E 4A8E3C48 1C24E2C1 381FEBD1
  A1638C0B A4A2CCC7 69DC51FE 1785DF24 6B9E13F5 89A4AE07 07376633 C51155D2
  0CD6EA2E D894C280 2E26454D 9C6CC1D3 6F6D1C69 040A876A FBB52209 020637
  quit
!
spanning-tree mode pvst
spanning-tree extend system-id
!
vlan internal allocation policy ascending
!
vlan 100
 name R1-VLAN
!
vlan 200,300,400,500,600,700,800
!
interface Port-channel10
 switchport trunk encapsulation dot1q
 switchport mode trunk
!
interface FastEthernet0/1
 switchport mode dynamic desirable
 shutdown
!
interface FastEthernet0/2
 switchport mode dynamic desirable
 shutdown
!
interface FastEthernet0/3
 switchport mode dynamic desirable
 shutdown
!
interface FastEthernet0/4
 switchport mode dynamic desirable
 shutdown
!
```

```
interface FastEthernet0/5
 switchport mode dynamic desirable
 shutdown
!
interface FastEthernet0/6
 switchport mode dynamic desirable
 shutdown
!
interface FastEthernet0/7
 switchport trunk encapsulation dot1q
 switchport mode trunk
!
interface FastEthernet0/8
 switchport trunk encapsulation dot1q
 switchport mode trunk
!
interface FastEthernet0/9
 switchport mode dynamic desirable
 shutdown
!
interface FastEthernet0/10
 switchport mode dynamic desirable
 shutdown
!
interface FastEthernet0/11
 switchport trunk encapsulation dot1q
 switchport mode trunk
 channel-group 10 mode on
!
interface FastEthernet0/12
 switchport trunk encapsulation dot1q
 switchport mode trunk
 channel-group 10 mode on

[Truncated Output]

interface Vlan1
 no ip address
 shutdown
!
interface Vlan100
 ip address 150.1.1.254 255.255.255.0
 ip ospf network point-to-multipoint
!
router ospf 1
 log-adjacency-changes
 network 150.1.1.254 0.0.0.0 area 0
!
ip classless
ip http server
ip http secure-server
!
control-plane
!
line con 0
line vty 0 4
 privilege level 15
 password cisco
 login
line vty 5 15
 login
!
end
DLS1#
```

DLS2

```
DLS2#term len 0
DLS2#sh run
Building configuration...

Current configuration : 4654 bytes
!
version 12.2
no service pad
service timestamps debug datetime msec
service timestamps log datetime msec
no service password-encryption
```

```
!
hostname DLS2
!
no logging console
!
no aaa new-model
ip subnet-zero
ip routing
no ip domain-lookup
!
vtp domain 2011
vtp mode transparent
!
spanning-tree mode pvst
spanning-tree extend system-id
!
vlan internal allocation policy ascending
!
vlan 100
 name R1-VLAN
!
interface Port-channel10
 switchport trunk encapsulation dot1q
 switchport mode trunk
!
interface FastEthernet0/1
 switchport mode dynamic desirable
 shutdown
!
interface FastEthernet0/2
 switchport mode dynamic desirable
 shutdown
!
interface FastEthernet0/3
 switchport mode dynamic desirable
 shutdown
!
interface FastEthernet0/4
 switchport mode dynamic desirable
 shutdown
!
interface FastEthernet0/5
 switchport mode dynamic desirable
 shutdown
!
interface FastEthernet0/6
 switchport mode dynamic desirable
 shutdown
!
interface FastEthernet0/7
 switchport mode dynamic desirable
 shutdown
!
interface FastEthernet0/8
 switchport mode dynamic desirable
 shutdown
!
interface FastEthernet0/9
 switchport mode dynamic desirable
 shutdown
!
interface FastEthernet0/10
 switchport mode dynamic desirable
 shutdown
!
interface FastEthernet0/11
 switchport trunk encapsulation dot1q
 switchport mode trunk
 channel-group 10 mode on
!
interface FastEthernet0/12
 switchport trunk encapsulation dot1q
 switchport mode trunk
 channel-group 10 mode on

[Truncated Output]

interface Vlan1
 no ip address
```

```
 shutdown
!
interface Vlan100
 ip address 150.1.1.253 255.255.255.0
 ip ospf network point-to-multipoint
!
router ospf 1
 log-adjacency-changes
 network 150.1.1.253 0.0.0.0 area 0
!
ip classless
ip http server
ip http secure-server
!
control-plane
!
line con 0
line vty 0 4
 privilege level 15
 password cisco
 login
line vty 5 15
 login
!
end

DLS2#
```

ALS1

```
ALS1#term len 0
ALS1#sh run
Building configuration...

Current configuration : 1337 bytes
!
version 12.1
no service pad
service timestamps debug uptime
service timestamps log uptime
no service password-encryption
!
hostname ALS1
!
no logging console
!
ip subnet-zero
!
no ip domain-lookup
vtp domain fhrp
vtp mode transparent
!
spanning-tree mode pvst
no spanning-tree optimize bpdu transmission
spanning-tree extend system-id
!
vlan 100
 name R1-VLAN
!
vlan 300
 name R3-VLAN
!
vlan 400
 name R4-VLAN
!
interface FastEthernet0/1
 switchport access vlan 100
 switchport mode access
!
interface FastEthernet0/2
 shutdown
!
interface FastEthernet0/3
 switchport access vlan 300
 switchport mode access
!
interface FastEthernet0/4
 switchport access vlan 400
```

```
 switchport mode access
!
interface FastEthernet0/5
 shutdown
!
interface FastEthernet0/6
 shutdown
!
interface FastEthernet0/7
 switchport mode trunk
!
interface FastEthernet0/8
 switchport mode trunk
!
interface FastEthernet0/9
 shutdown
!
interface FastEthernet0/10
 shutdown
!
interface FastEthernet0/11
 switchport mode trunk
!
interface FastEthernet0/12
 switchport mode trunk
!
interface Vlan1
 no ip address
 no ip route-cache
 shutdown
!
interface Vlan400
 ip address 10.4.4.254 255.255.255.0
 no ip route-cache
!
ip default-gateway 10.4.4.4
ip http server
!
line con 0
line vty 0 4
 privilege level 15
 password cisco
 login
line vty 5 15
 login
!
end

ALS1#
```

ALS2

```
ALS2#term len 0
ALS2#sh run
Building configuration...

Current configuration : 1135 bytes
!
version 12.1
no service pad
service timestamps debug uptime
service timestamps log uptime
no service password-encryption
!
hostname ALS2
!
no logging console
!
ip subnet-zero
!
no ip domain-lookup
vtp domain fhrp
vtp mode transparent
!
spanning-tree mode pvst
no spanning-tree optimize bpdu transmission
spanning-tree extend system-id
!
```

```
vlan 300
 name R3-VLAN
!
interface FastEthernet0/1
 shutdown
!
interface FastEthernet0/2
 shutdown
!
interface FastEthernet0/3
 shutdown
!
interface FastEthernet0/4
 shutdown
!
interface FastEthernet0/5
 shutdown
!
interface FastEthernet0/6
 shutdown
!
interface FastEthernet0/7
 shutdown
!
interface FastEthernet0/8
 shutdown
!
interface FastEthernet0/9
 shutdown
!
interface FastEthernet0/10
 shutdown
!
interface FastEthernet0/11
 switchport mode trunk
!
interface FastEthernet0/12
 switchport mode trunk
!
interface Vlan1
 no ip address
 no ip route-cache
 shutdown
!
interface Vlan300
 ip address 10.3.3.254 255.255.255.0
 no ip route-cache
!
ip default-gateway 10.3.3.3
ip http server
!
line con 0
line vty 0 4
 privilege level 15
 password cisco
 login
line vty 5 15
 login
!
end

ALS2#
```

CCNP LAB 84

CCNP Multi-Technology Lab

Lab Objective:

The objective of this lab is to cover all relevant CCNP ROUTE and SWITCH theory. These labs will include topics from each of these guides. It should be noted that not all topics will be included in all labs. Additionally, not all solutions will be illustrated in detail. You can refer to previous labs for assistance with some basic configurations.

Lab Topology:

The lab network topology is illustrated below:

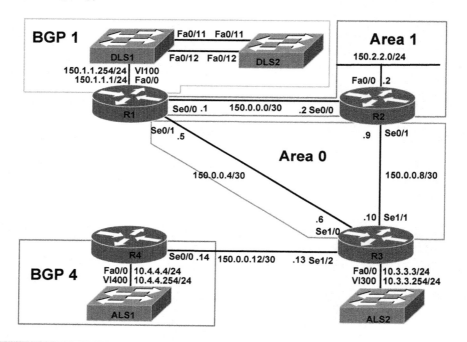

IMPORTANT NOTE: If you are using the www.howtonetwork.net racks, please implement the following pre-lab configurations. This is required because of the manner in which the routers and switches are physically cabled to each other. The following configuration should be applied to switch ALS1:

```
!
hostname ALS1
!
vtp mode transparent
!
vlan 100
 name R1-VLAN
!
vlan 300
 name R3-VLAN
!
```

```
vlan 400
 name R4-VLAN
!
interface fastethernet 0/1
 switchport access vlan 100
 switchport mode access
!
interface fastethernet 0/2
shutdown
!
interface fastethernet 0/3
 switchport access vlan 300
 switchport mode access
!
interface fastethernet 0/4
 switchport access vlan 400
 switchport mode access
!
interface range fastethernet 0/5 - 6
shutdown
!
interface fastethernet0/7
 switchport mode trunk
!
interface fastethernet 0/8
 switchport mode trunk
!
interface range fastethernet 0/9 - 10
 shutdown
!
interface range fastethernet 0/11 - 12
 switchport mode trunk
!
interface vlan 400
 ip address 10.4.4.254 255.255.255.0
 no shutdown
!
ip default-gateway 10.4.4.4
!
line vty 0 4
 privilege level 15
 password cisco
 login
!
end

hostname ALS2
!
vtp mode transparent
!
vlan 300
 name R3-VLAN
!
interface range fastethernet 0/1 - 10
 shutdown
!
interface fastethernet 0/11
 switchport mode trunk
!
interface fastethernet 0/12
 switchport mode trunk
!
interface vlan 300
 ip address 10.3.3.254 255.255.255.0
 no shutdown
!
ip default-gateway 10.3.3.3
!
line vty 0 4
 privilege level 15
 password cisco
 login
!
end

!
hostname DLS1
!
ip routing
!
vtp mode transparent
!
```

```
vlan 100
 name R1-VLAN
!
interface range fastethernet 0/1 - 6
 shutdown
!
interface range fastethernet 0/7 - 8
 switchport trunk encapsulation dot1q
 switchport mode trunk
!
interface range fastethernet 0/9 - 10
 shutdown
!
interface fastethernet 0/11
 switchport mode dynamic desirable
!
interface fastethernet 0/12
 switchport mode dynamic desirable
!
interface range fastethernet 0/13 - 48
 shutdown
!
interface vlan 100
 ip address 150.1.1.254 255.255.255.0
 no shutdown
!
line vty 0 4
 privilege level 15
 password cisco
 login
!
end

hostname DLS2
!
ip routing
!
vtp mode transparent
!
vlan 100
 name R1-VLAN
!
interface vlan 100
 ip address 150.1.1.253 255.255.255.0
 no shutdown
!
interface range fastethernet 0/1 - 10
 shutdown
!
interface fastethernet 0/11
 switchport mode dynamic desirable
!
interface fastethernet 0/12
 switchport mode dynamic desirable
!
interface range fastethernet 0/13 - 48
 shutdown
!
line vty 0 4
 privilege level 15
 password cisco
 login
!
end
```

If you are using the www.howtonetwork.net racks, please bring up the LAN interface connected to R2 by the following configuration:

```
interface fastethernet 0/0
 ip address 150.2.2.2 255.255.255.0
 no keepalive
 loopback
 no shutdown
```

Alternatively, you can simply connect the interface to a hub or one of the switches and bring up the interface in the standard manner.

Task 1

Configure hostnames, IP addressing on all routers as illustrated in the network topology.

Task 2

Configure an EtherChannel between DLS1 and DLS2. This should be a Layer 2 trunk link that uses PAgP. Assign IP address 150.1.1.253/24 to switch DLS2. Finally, verify that all devices on the 150.1.1.0/24 subnet can ping each other.

Task 3

To ensure a consistent Spanning Tree topology, ensure that ALS1 will be the root for all of the configured VLANs. Should a superior BPDU be received, the port should be disabled. Verify your configuration using the appropriate commands.

Task 4

Configure the EtherChannel between DLS1 and DLS2 to load distribution based on the destination MAC address. Verify your configuration.

Next, management has requested that all ports on ALS1 that are connected to the routers be configured in such a manner that if a BPDU is received, the ports are disabled. These ports should be re-enabled after 10 minutes. Implement this solution and verify your configuration.

Task 5

Configure BGP using AS 1 on R1, DLS1 and DLS2. Ensure that Non-Stop Forwarding (NSF) for BGP is enabled and all routers are peered with each other. Verify your configuration using the appropriate commands.

Task 6

Configure OSPF between R1, R2, and R3 as illustrated in the topology. Ensure that OSPF Hellos are not sent out the LAN interfaces of R2. Do NOT enable OSPF for the LAN segments connected to R1 or R3. Verify your OSPF configuration using the appropriate commands.

Task 7

Configure BGP on router R4. This router should peer with R1. Use Loopback interfaces that are comprised of the router numbers, i.e. 1.1.1.1/32 on R1 and 4.4.4.4/32 on R4. Verify your configuration using the appropriate commands. When completing this task, you MUST adhere to these restrictions and guidelines:
- You are allowed only ONE static route on R3 - this route can NOT be a default route
- You are allowed only ONE static route on R4 - this route can NOT be a default route
- You are NOT allowed any static routes on R1 - you can NOT originate a default route

Ensure that the Loopback interfaces are advertised as EXTERNAL routes. Do NOT redistribute any other connected subnets into OSPF when completing this task. Verify your configuration using the appropriate commands.

Task 8

Configure and then advertise the following prefixes via BGP on switches DLS1 and DLS2:
- DLS1: Loopback 0 - IP Address 100.1.1.1/24
- DLS2: Loopback 0 - IP Address 200.2.2.2/24

Next, advertise the 10.4.4.4/24 subnet connected to router R4 via BGP. Do NOT advertise the 150.1.1.0/24 prefix via OSPF or BGP. Verify that the prefixes are received by all BGP speakers.

Task 9

Configure your network so that the 150.1.1.0/24 , 100.1.1.0/24, and 200.2.2.0/24 subnets can ping the 10.4.4.0/24 subnet and vice-versa. Complete this task while adhering to the following:
- You are allowed to use only ONE static route . This can either be on R1 or R3
- You are NOT allowed to use any static or default routes on R4
- You are NOT allowed to advertise the 150.1.1.0/24 subnet via OSPF or BGP

Next, test your configuration by pinging from the 150.1.1.0/24 , 100.1.1.0/24, and 200.2.2.0/24 subnets to the 10.4.4.0/24 subnet and vice-versa. All pings should be successful.

Task 10

Configure Loopback interfaces with the IP addresses 2.2.2.2/32 and 3.3.3.3/32 respectively on R2 and R3. Next, configure 6to4 prefixes on the LAN interfaces of all routers. Use the Loopback addresses to complete the 48-bit global prefix. The router number should complete the next 16-bits, for a complete site prefix. Verify your configuration using the appropriate commands.

Finally, configure 6to4 tunnels on R2 and R3. Ensure that these two routers can ping each other LAN-to-LAN across the 6to4 tunnels. Use the extended ping function for verification.

Task 11

At this point, the 10.3.3.0/24 subnet connected to R3s LAN interface should not be known to any other router, i.e. should not be advertised by OSPF. Management has requested that this subnet remain anonymous. However, they would like devices residing on this subnet to be able to reach the LAN subnets on R2 and R3 only. These devices should appear to be coming from the 150.3.3.0/24 subnet. When completing this task, you MUST adhere to the following restrictions:
- You are NOT allowed to configure any additional interfaces on R3, i.e. Loopbacks
- There should be a one-to-one translation for the 10.3.3.0/24 subnet
- Your configuration should NOT 'break' the current OSPF or BGP routing in place

Verify your configuration by pinging the 150.1.1.0/24 and 150.2.2.0/24 subnets from ALS2

LAB VALIDATION

Task 1

Please refer to previous labs for basic IPv4 addressing and hostname configuration. This will not be included in this section to avoid being redundant.

Task 2

Please refer to previous labs for EtherChannel configuration. This will not be included in this section to avoid being redundant. Verify your solution using the show etherchannel commands on both switches:

```
DLS1#show etherchannel summary
Flags:  D - down        P - bundled in port-channel
        I - stand-alone s - suspended
        H - Hot-standby (LACP only)
        R - Layer3       S - Layer2
        U - in use       f - failed to allocate aggregator

        M - not in use, minimum links not met
        u - unsuitable for bundling
        w - waiting to be aggregated
        d - default port


Number of channel-groups in use: 1
Number of aggregators:           1

Group  Port-channel  Protocol    Ports
------+-------------+-----------+-----------------------------------------------
10     Po10(SU)      PAgP        Fa0/11(P)   Fa0/12(P)

DLS2#show etherchannel summary
Flags:  D - down        P - bundled in port-channel
        I - stand-alone s - suspended
        H - Hot-standby (LACP only)
        R - Layer3       S - Layer2
        U - in use       f - failed to allocate aggregator
```

```
         M - not in use, minimum links not met
         u - unsuitable for bundling
         w - waiting to be aggregated
         d - default port

Number of channel-groups in use: 1
Number of aggregators:            1

Group  Port-channel  Protocol    Ports
------+-------------+-----------+-----------------------------------------------
10     Po10(SU)       PAgP        Fa0/11(P)    Fa0/12(P)
```

After configuring the SVI on switch DLS2, verify reachability on the 150.1.1.0/24 subnet:

```
LS2#ping 150.1.1.0

Type escape sequence to abort.
Sending 5, 100-byte ICMP Echos to 150.1.1.0, timeout is 2 seconds:
.
Reply to request 1 from 150.1.1.254, 1 ms
Reply to request 1 from 150.1.1.1, 1 ms
Reply to request 2 from 150.1.1.254, 1 ms
Reply to request 2 from 150.1.1.1, 1 ms
Reply to request 3 from 150.1.1.254, 1 ms
Reply to request 3 from 150.1.1.1, 1 ms
Reply to request 4 from 150.1.1.254, 1 ms
Reply to request 4 from 150.1.1.1, 1 ms
```

Task 3

To complete this task you need to configure the Root Guard feature on the switch. The Root Guard feature prevents a Designated Port from becoming a Root Port. If a port on which the Root Guard feature receives a superior BPDU, it moves the port into a root-inconsistent state, thus maintaining the current Root Bridge status quo.

Unlike other STP enhancements, which can also be enabled on a global basis, Root Guard must be manually enabled on all ports where the Root Bridge should not appear. To complete this task successfully, first ensure that switch ALS1 is the root for all VLANs and then enable Root Guard on all designated ports. The first part of this task is completed as follows:

```
ALS1(config)#spanning-tree vlan 1 priority 0
ALS1(config)#spanning-tree vlan 100 priority 0
ALS1(config)#spanning-tree vlan 300 priority 0
ALS1(config)#spanning-tree vlan 400 priority 0

ALS1#show spanning-tree summary
Switch is in pvst mode
Root bridge for: VLAN0001, VLAN0100, VLAN0300, VLAN0400

[Truncated Output]
```

Next, to determine which ports are designated and actively forwarding, use the `show spanning-tree [vlan <number> active [detail]` command:

```
ALS1#show spanning-tree vlan 100 active

VLAN0100
  Spanning tree enabled protocol ieee
  Root ID    Priority    100
             Address     0007.8432.dd00
             This bridge is the root
             Hello Time   2 sec  Max Age 20 sec  Forward Delay 15 sec

  Bridge ID  Priority    100   (priority 0 sys-id-ext 100)
             Address     0007.8432.dd00
             Hello Time   2 sec  Max Age 20 sec  Forward Delay 15 sec
             Aging Time 300

Interface        Role Sts Cost      Prio.Nbr Type
---------------- ---- --- --------- -------- --------------------------------
```

965

```
Fa0/1          Desg FWD 19          128.1      P2p
Fa0/7          Desg FWD 19          128.7      P2p
Fa0/8          Desg FWD 19          128.8      P2p
Fa0/11         Desg FWD 19          128.11     P2p
Fa0/12         Desg FWD 19          128.12     P2p
```

Port Fa0/1 is irrelevent because it is connected to R1. To complete this task, simply enable the Root Guard feature on the remaining trunk ports:

```
ALS1(config)#interface range fastethernet 0/7 - 8 , fastethernet 0/11 - 12
ALS1(config-if-range)#spanning-tree guard root
ALS1(config-if-range)#exit
```

To test Root Guard, you can increase the priority on ALS1 to 4096, for example, and configure a priority of 0 on either DLS1 or ALS2. This will result in the following error message:

```
06:00:49: %SPANTREE-2-ROOTGUARD_BLOCK: Root guard blocking port FastEthernet0/7 on
VLAN0100.
```

Also, use the `show spanning-tree inconsistentports` to determine which switch the ports have been placed into an inconsistent state (Root Guard or Loop Guard) by the switch:

```
ALS1#show spanning-tree inconsistentports

Name                   Interface              Inconsistency
-------------------    -------------------    -------------------
VLAN0100               FastEthernet0/7        Root Inconsistent
VLAN0100               FastEthernet0/8        Root Inconsistent

Number of inconsistent ports (segments) in the system : 2
```

Task 4

To complete this task, you need to use the port-channel load-balance command on switches DLS1 and DLS2. Next, implement BPDU Guard on the ports that routers are connected to switch ALS1. Finally, enable the err-disable recovery for BPDU Guard and specify the timer. Complete the first part of this task by configuring switches DLS1 and DLS2 as follows:

```
DLS1(config)#port-channel load-balance dst-mac
```

```
DLS2(config)#port-channel load-balance dst-mac
```

Verify load balancing using the `show etherchannel load-balance` command:

```
DLS1#show etherchannel load-balance
EtherChannel Load-Balancing Configuration:
        dst-mac

EtherChannel Load-Balancing Addresses Used Per-Protocol:
Non-IP: Destination MAC address
  IPv4: Destination MAC address
```

Complete the second part of this task by configuring switch ALS1 as follows:

```
ALS1(config)#interface range fastethernet 0/1 , fastethernet 0/3 - 4
ALS1(config-if-range)#spanning-tree bpduguard enable
ALS1(config-if-range)#exit
ALS1(config)#errdisable recovery cause bpduguard
ALS1(config)#errdisable recovery interval 600
```

Verify BPDU Guard configuration using the `show spanning-tree interface <name> detail` command on switch ALS1:

```
ALS1#show spanning-tree interface fastethernet 0/1 detail
 Port 1 (FastEthernet0/1) of VLAN0100 is forwarding
   Port path cost 19, Port priority 128, Port Identifier 128.1.
   Designated root has priority 100, address 0007.8432.dd00
```

```
Designated bridge has priority 100, address 0007.8432.dd00
Designated port id is 128.1, designated path cost 0
Timers: message age 0, forward delay 0, hold 0
Number of transitions to forwarding state: 1
Link type is point-to-point by default
Bpdu guard is enabled
BPDU: sent 3148, received 0
```

Use the show errdisable commands to verify the errdisable recovery reasons and intervals:

```
ALS1#show errdisable recovery
ErrDisable Reason      Timer Status
----------------       -------------
udld                   Disabled
bpduguard              Enabled
security-violatio      Disabled
channel-misconfig      Disabled
vmps                   Disabled
pagp-flap              Disabled
dtp-flap               Disabled
link-flap              Disabled
psecure-violation      Disabled
gbic-invalid           Disabled
dhcp-rate-limit        Disabled
unicast-flood          Disabled
loopback               Disabled

Timer interval: 600 seconds

Interfaces that will be enabled at the next timeout:
```

Task 5

The requirements of this task are straightforward. To enable NSF for BGP, you need to enable the bgp graceful-restart command on all devices under BGP configuration:

```
R1(config)#router bgp 1
R1(config-router)#bgp router-id 1.1.1.1
R1(config-router)#neighbor 150.1.1.253 remote-as 1
R1(config-router)#neighbor 150.1.1.254 remote-as 1
R1(config-router)#bgp graceful-restart
R1(config-router)#exit

DLS1(config)#router bgp 1
DLS1(config-router)#bgp router-id 150.1.1.254
DLS1(config-router)#neighbor 150.1.1.1 remote-as 1
DLS1(config-router)#neighbor 150.1.1.253 remote-as 1
DLS1(config-router)#bgp graceful-restart
DLS1(config-router)#exit

DLS2(config)#router bgp 1
DLS2(config-router)#bgp router-id 150.1.1.253
DLS2(config-router)#neighbor 150.1.1.1 remote-as 1
DLS2(config-router)#neighbor 150.1.1.254 remote-as 1
DLS2(config-router)#bgp graceful-restart
DLS2(config-router)#exit
```

Verify the BGP peering configuration using the show ip bgp summary command:

```
R1#show ip bgp summary
BGP router identifier 1.1.1.1, local AS number 1
BGP table version is 1, main routing table version 1

Neighbor       V    AS MsgRcvd MsgSent    TblVer  InQ OutQ Up/Down  State/PfxRcd
150.1.1.253    4     1       4       5         1    0    0 00:01:24            0
150.1.1.254    4     1       5       6         1    0    0 00:03:04            0

DLS1#show ip bgp summary
BGP router identifier 150.1.1.254, local AS number 1
BGP table version is 1, main routing table version 1

Neighbor       V    AS MsgRcvd MsgSent    TblVer  InQ OutQ Up/Down  State/PfxRcd
150.1.1.1      4     1       5       4         1    0    0 00:02:45            0
```

```
 150.1.1.253  4     1      3        3          1    0    0 00:00:47          0

DLS2#show ip bgp summary
BGP router identifier 150.1.1.253, local AS number 1
BGP table version is 1, main routing table version 1

Neighbor      V    AS MsgRcvd MsgSent   TblVer  InQ OutQ Up/Down  State/PfxRcd
150.1.1.1     4    1      4       3          1    0    0 00:00:34          0
150.1.1.254   4    1      3       3          1    0    0 00:00:17          0
```

Verify BGP NSF configuration using the show ip bgp neighbors <address> command:

```
R1#show ip bgp neighbors
BGP neighbor is 150.1.1.253,  remote AS 1, internal link
  BGP version 4, remote router ID 150.1.1.253
  BGP state = Established, up for 00:02:26
  Last read 00:00:23, last write 00:00:26, hold time is 180, keepalive interval is 60
seconds
  Neighbor capabilities:
    Route refresh: advertised and received(old & new)
    Address family IPv4 Unicast: advertised and received
    Graceful Restart Capability: advertised
  Message statistics:
    InQ depth is 0
    OutQ depth is 0
                    Sent      Rcvd
    Opens:           1         1
    Notifications:   0         0
    Updates:         0         0
    Keepalives:      5         4
    Route Refresh:   0         0
    Total:           6         5
  Default minimum time between advertisement runs is 0 seconds

[Truncated Output]
```

Task 6

Please refer to previous tasks for basic OSPF configuration. Following this, use the show ip ospf neighbor command to verify adjacencies:

```
R1#show ip ospf neighbor

Neighbor ID      Pri   State           Dead Time   Address        Interface
3.3.3.3            0   FULL/   -       00:00:36    150.0.0.6      Serial0/1
2.2.2.2            0   FULL/   -       00:00:38    150.0.0.2      Serial0/0

R2#show ip ospf neighbor

Neighbor ID      Pri   State           Dead Time   Address        Interface
3.3.3.3            0   FULL/   -       00:00:31    150.0.0.10     Serial0/1
1.1.1.1            0   FULL/   -       00:00:33    150.0.0.1      Serial0/0

R3#show ip ospf neighbor

Neighbor ID      Pri   State           Dead Time   Address        Interface
2.2.2.2            0   FULL/   -       00:00:37    150.0.0.9      Serial1/1
1.1.1.1            0   FULL/   -       00:00:34    150.0.0.5      Serial1/0
```

Next, verify routing using the show ip route command on all three routers:

```
R1#show ip route ospf
     150.0.0.0/30 is subnetted, 3 subnets
O       150.0.0.8 [110/845] via 150.0.0.6, 00:00:11, Serial0/1
     150.2.0.0/24 is subnetted, 1 subnets
O       150.2.2.0 [110/65] via 150.0.0.2, 00:00:11, Serial0/0

R2#show ip route ospf
     150.0.0.0/30 is subnetted, 3 subnets
O       150.0.0.4 [110/845] via 150.0.0.10, 00:00:23, Serial0/1

R3#show ip route ospf
     150.0.0.0/30 is subnetted, 4 subnets
O IA    150.0.0.0 [110/845] via 150.0.0.9, 00:00:34, Serial1/1
                  [110/845] via 150.0.0.5, 00:00:34, Serial1/0
```

```
       150.2.0.0/24 is subnetted, 1 subnets
O IA     150.2.2.0 [110/782] via 150.0.0.9, 00:00:34, Serial1/1
```

Task 7

This task has several requirements. First, you must configure the specified Loopback interfaces and advertise them via BGP. Next, you need to configure BGP between R1 and R4. You must include the `neighbor <address> ebgp-multihop` command in addition to specifying the Loopback interfaces as update sources. Following that, you need to adhere to the restrictions while ensuring that the BGP session can also be established. This task is completed as follows:

```
R1(config)#interface loopback 0
R1(config-if)#ip address 1.1.1.1 255.255.255.255
R1(config-if)#exit
R1(config)#router bgp 1
R1(config-router)#neighbor 4.4.4.4 remote-as 4
R1(config-router)#neighbor 4.4.4.4 update-source loopback 0
R1(config-router)#neighbor 4.4.4.4 ebgp-multihop
R1(config-router)#exit
R1(config-router)#route-map LOOPBACK0 permit 10
R1(config-route-map)#match interface loopback 0
R1(config-route-map)#exit
R1(config)#router ospf 1
R1(config-router)#redistribute connected subnets route-map LOOPBACK0
R1(config-router)#exit

R3(config)#ip route 4.4.4.4 255.255.255.255 serial 1/2
R3(config)#router ospf 3
R3(config-router)#redistribute static subnets
R3(config-router)#exit

R4(config)#interface loopback 0
R4(config-if)#ip address 4.4.4.4 255.255.255.255
R4(config-if)#exit
R4(config)#ip route 1.1.1.1 255.255.255.255 serial 0/0
R4(config)#router bgp 4
R4(config-router)#bgp router-id 4.4.4.4
R4(config-router)#neighbor 1.1.1.1 remote-as 1
R4(config-router)#neighbor 1.1.1 update-source loopback 0
R4(config-router)#neighbor 1.1.1.1 ebgp-multihop
R4(config-router)#exit
```

Following this, verify BGP peering using the `show ip bgp summary` command:

```
R1#show ip bgp summary
BGP router identifier 1.1.1.1, local AS number 1
BGP table version is 1, main routing table version 1

Neighbor      V   AS MsgRcvd MsgSent  TblVer  InQ OutQ Up/Down  State/PfxRcd
4.4.4.4       4    4       5       5       1    0    0 00:01:01            0
150.1.1.253   4    1      82      84       1    0    0 01:20:05            0
150.1.1.254   4    1      83      84       1    0    0 01:21:45            0

R4#show ip bgp summary
BGP router identifier 4.4.4.4, local AS number 4
BGP table version is 1, main routing table version 1

Neighbor      V   AS MsgRcvd MsgSent  TblVer  InQ OutQ Up/Down  State/PfxRcd
1.1.1.1       4    1       5       5       1    0    0 00:01:19            0
```

Task 8

This task is straightforward. Verify your BGP RIBs using the `show ip bgp` command:

```
DLS1#show ip bgp
BGP table version is 24, local router ID is 150.1.1.254
Status codes: s suppressed, d damped, h history, * valid, > best, i - internal,
              r RIB-failure, S Stale
Origin codes: i - IGP, e - EGP, ? - incomplete

   Network          Next Hop          Metric LocPrf Weight Path
* i10.4.4.0/24      4.4.4.4                0    100      0 4 i
*> 100.1.1.0/24     0.0.0.0                0         32768 i
*>i200.2.2.0        150.1.1.253            0    100      0 i

DLS2#show ip bgp
```

```
BGP table version is 8, local router ID is 150.1.1.253
Status codes: s suppressed, d damped, h history, * valid, > best, i - internal,
              r RIB-failure, S Stale
Origin codes: i - IGP, e - EGP, ? - incomplete

   Network          Next Hop            Metric LocPrf Weight Path
*  i10.4.4.0/24     4.4.4.4                  0    100      0 4 i
*>i100.1.1.0/24     150.1.1.254              0    100      0 i
*> 200.2.2.0        0.0.0.0                  0         32768 i

R1#show ip bgp
BGP table version is 10, local router ID is 1.1.1.1
Status codes: s suppressed, d damped, h history, * valid, > best, i - internal,
              r RIB-failure, S Stale
Origin codes: i - IGP, e - EGP, ? - incomplete

   Network          Next Hop            Metric LocPrf Weight Path
*> 10.4.4.0/24      4.4.4.4                  0             0 4 i
*>i100.1.1.0/24     150.1.1.254              0    100      0 i
*>i200.2.2.0        150.1.1.253              0    100      0 i

R4#show ip bgp
BGP table version is 6, local router ID is 4.4.4.4
Status codes: s suppressed, d damped, h history, * valid, > best, i - internal,
              r RIB-failure, S Stale
Origin codes: i - IGP, e - EGP, ? - incomplete

   Network          Next Hop            Metric LocPrf Weight Path
*> 10.4.4.0/24      0.0.0.0                  0         32768 i
*> 100.1.1.0/24     1.1.1.1                            0 1 i
*> 200.2.2.0        1.1.1.1                            0 1 i
```

Task 9

This task is not as complex as it might appear if you have a good understanding of BGP and IP routing in general. First, because switches DLS1 and DLS2 do not know about the 4.4.4.4/32 prefix, they will show the route received from R4 as inaccessible. This can be verified as follows:

```
DLS1#show ip bgp 10.4.4.0 255.255.255.0
BGP routing table entry for 10.4.4.0/24, version 24
Paths: (1 available, no best path)
  Not advertised to any peer
  4
    4.4.4.4 (inaccessible) from 150.1.1.1 (1.1.1.1)
      Origin IGP, metric 0, localpref 100, valid, internal

DLS2#show ip bgp 10.4.4.0 255.255.255.0
BGP routing table entry for 10.4.4.0/24, version 8
Paths: (1 available, no best path)
  Not advertised to any peer
  4
    4.4.4.4 (inaccessible) from 150.1.1.1 (1.1.1.1)
      Origin IGP, metric 0, localpref 100, valid, internal
```

To resolve this, you will need to modify the BGP NEXT_HOP attribute on R1 so that this field is updated to reflect R1 as the NEXT_HOP instead.

Second, while BOTH the 100.1.1.0/24 and 200.2.2.0/24 prefixes are advertised by R1 to R4, the 150.1.1.0/24 prefix is not. This means that we will instead need to advertise a default route to router R2 and R3 via OSPF. This will allow these routers to forward packets destined to this subnet to R1 - where the subnet resides.

Third, we also need to advertise a default route via BGP to R4. This will allow R4 to reach the 150.1.1.0/24 subnet (via R3). And finally, we are allowed to use a single static route on either R1 or R3. We will choose to use this on R3 and configure a static route for the 10.1.1.0/24 prefix. This prefix will then be redistributed into OSPF, allowing all routers to know about the location of this subnet. This task is therefore completed as follows:

```
R1(config)#router bgp 1
R1(config-router)#neighbor 150.1.1.253 next-hop-self
R1(config-router)#neighbor 150.1.1.254 next-hop-self
R1(config-router)#neighbor 4.4.4.4 default-originate
R1(config-router)#exit
```

```
R1(config)#router ospf 1
R1(config-router)#default-information originate always
R1(config-router)#exit

R3(config)#ip route 10.4.4.0 255.255.255.0 serial 1/2
R3(config)#end
R3#clear ip ospf redistribution
```

Following this, verify the routing tables of all devices using the show ip route command:

```
R1#show ip route
Codes: C - connected, S - static, R - RIP, M - mobile, B - BGP
       D - EIGRP, EX - EIGRP external, O - OSPF, IA - OSPF inter area
       N1 - OSPF NSSA external type 1, N2 - OSPF NSSA external type 2
       E1 - OSPF external type 1, E2 - OSPF external type 2
       i - IS-IS, su - IS-IS summary, L1 - IS-IS level-1, L2 - IS-IS level-2
       ia - IS-IS inter area, * - candidate default, U - per-user static route
       o - ODR, P - periodic downloaded static route

Gateway of last resort is not set

        1.0.0.0/32 is subnetted, 1 subnets
C          1.1.1.1 is directly connected, Loopback0
        100.0.0.0/24 is subnetted, 1 subnets
B          100.1.1.0 [200/0] via 150.1.1.254, 00:21:26
        4.0.0.0/32 is subnetted, 1 subnets
O E2    4.4.4.4 [110/20] via 150.0.0.6, 00:00:27, Serial0/1
B       200.2.2.0/24 [200/0] via 150.1.1.253, 00:20:59
        10.0.0.0/24 is subnetted, 1 subnets
B          10.4.4.0 [20/0] via 4.4.4.4, 00:00:22
        150.0.0.0/30 is subnetted, 3 subnets
C          150.0.0.4 is directly connected, Serial0/1
C          150.0.0.0 is directly connected, Serial0/0
O          150.0.0.8 [110/845] via 150.0.0.6, 00:17:23, Serial0/1
        150.1.0.0/24 is subnetted, 1 subnets
C          150.1.1.0 is directly connected, FastEthernet0/0
        150.2.0.0/24 is subnetted, 1 subnets
O          150.2.2.0 [110/65] via 150.0.0.2, 00:17:25, Serial0/0

R2#show ip route ospf
        1.0.0.0/32 is subnetted, 1 subnets
O E2    1.1.1.1 [110/20] via 150.0.0.1, 00:18:22, Serial0/0
        4.0.0.0/32 is subnetted, 1 subnets
O E2    4.4.4.4 [110/20] via 150.0.0.10, 00:01:27, Serial0/1
        10.0.0.0/24 is subnetted, 1 subnets
O E2    10.4.4.0 [110/20] via 150.0.0.10, 00:01:27, Serial0/1
        150.0.0.0/30 is subnetted, 3 subnets
O          150.0.0.4 [110/845] via 150.0.0.10, 00:18:22, Serial0/1
O*E2 0.0.0.0/0 [110/1] via 150.0.0.1, 00:03:20, Serial0/0

R3#show ip route ospf
        1.0.0.0/32 is subnetted, 1 subnets
O E2    1.1.1.1 [110/20] via 150.0.0.5, 00:20:38, Serial1/0
        150.0.0.0/30 is subnetted, 4 subnets
O IA    150.0.0.0 [110/845] via 150.0.0.9, 00:20:48, Serial1/1
                   [110/845] via 150.0.0.5, 00:20:48, Serial1/0
        150.2.0.0/24 is subnetted, 1 subnets
O IA    150.2.2.0 [110/782] via 150.0.0.9, 00:20:48, Serial1/1
O*E2 0.0.0.0/0 [110/1] via 150.0.0.5, 00:05:46, Serial1/0

R4#show ip route
Codes: C - connected, S - static, R - RIP, M - mobile, B - BGP
       D - EIGRP, EX - EIGRP external, O - OSPF, IA - OSPF inter area
       N1 - OSPF NSSA external type 1, N2 - OSPF NSSA external type 2
       E1 - OSPF external type 1, E2 - OSPF external type 2
       i - IS-IS, su - IS-IS summary, L1 - IS-IS level-1, L2 - IS-IS level-2
       ia - IS-IS inter area, * - candidate default, U - per-user static route
       o - ODR, P - periodic downloaded static route

Gateway of last resort is 1.1.1.1 to network 0.0.0.0

        1.0.0.0/32 is subnetted, 1 subnets
S          1.1.1.1 is directly connected, Serial0/0
        100.0.0.0/24 is subnetted, 1 subnets
B          100.1.1.0 [20/0] via 1.1.1.1, 00:25:01
        4.0.0.0/32 is subnetted, 1 subnets
C          4.4.4.4 is directly connected, Loopback0
B       200.2.2.0/24 [20/0] via 1.1.1.1, 00:24:31
```

```
      10.0.0.0/24 is subnetted, 1 subnets
C        10.4.4.0 is directly connected, FastEthernet0/0
      150.0.0.0/30 is subnetted, 1 subnets
C        150.0.0.12 is directly connected, Serial0/0
B*    0.0.0.0/0 [20/0] via 1.1.1.1, 00:06:12
```

Following this, verify end-to-end connectivity using the extended ping function on all devices:

```
R1#ping 10.4.4.4 source 150.1.1.1 size 1500 repeat 10

Type escape sequence to abort.
Sending 10, 1500-byte ICMP Echos to 10.4.4.4, timeout is 2 seconds:
Packet sent with a source address of 150.1.1.1
!!!!!!!!!!
Success rate is 100 percent (10/10), round-trip min/avg/max = 380/380/384 ms

DLS1#ping 10.4.4.4 source 100.1.1.1 size 1500 repeat 10

Type escape sequence to abort.
Sending 10, 1500-byte ICMP Echos to 10.4.4.4, timeout is 2 seconds:
Packet sent with a source address of 100.1.1.1
!!!!!!!!!!
Success rate is 100 percent (10/10), round-trip min/avg/max = 380/380/384 ms

DLS2#ping 10.4.4.4 source 200.2.2.2 size 1500 repeat 10

Type escape sequence to abort.
Sending 10, 1500-byte ICMP Echos to 10.4.4.4, timeout is 2 seconds:
Packet sent with a source address of 200.2.2.2
!!!!!!!!!!
Success rate is 100 percent (10/10), round-trip min/avg/max = 380/381/384 ms
```

Task 10

Unlike static tunnel configuration, 6to4 tunneling has three main characteristics, which make it unique from static tunnel implementation. These characteristics are:
- Automatic or Dynamic Tunneling
- Automatic Prefix Assignment
- There is no IPv6 Route Propagation

6to4 automatic tunneling provides a dynamic method to deploy tunnels between IPv6 sites over IPv4 networks. Unlike with manually configured tunnels, there is no need to manually configure tunnel source and destination addresses to establish the tunnels. Instead, the tunneling of IPv6 packets between 6to4 sites is performed dynamically based on the destination IPv6 address of the packets originated by IPv6 hosts. These packets are then encapsulated in IPv4 and IPv4 routing protocols are used to transport the packets between the source and destination hosts.

Automatic prefix assignment provides a global aggregate IPv6 prefix to each 6to4 site which is based on the 2002::/16 prefix assigned by IANA for 6to4 sites. As stated earlier in this section, the tunnel endpoint, or destination is determined by the globally unique IPv4 address embedded in a 6to4 address. This address must be an address that is globally routable. In other words, RFC 191 (private IP addresses) cannot be used for 6to4 tunnels because they are not unique. This 32-bit IPv4 address is converted to Hexadecimal and the final representation is a 48-bit prefix. For example, if the IP address 1.1.1.1 was embedded into the IPv6 6to4 prefix, the final representation would be 2002:0101:0101::/48.

And finally, 6to4 tunneling uses special addresses which are a combination of the unique IPv6 routing prefix 2002::/16 and a globally unique 32-bit IPv4 address. With 6to4 tunneling, the tunnel endpoint (destination) is determined by the globally unique IPv4 address embedded in the 6to4 address. Because 6to4 prefixes are based on unique IPv4 address, the 48-bit IPv6 routes do not need to be propagated between 6to4 sites. This task is completed as follows:

```
R2(config)#interface loopback 0
R2(config-if)#ip address 2.2.2.2 255.255.255.255
```

```
R2(config-if)#exit
R2(config)#router ospf 2
R2(config-router)#redistribute connected subnets
R2(config-router)#exit
R2(config)#ipv6 unicast-routing
R2(config)#ip cef
R2(config)#interface fastethernet 0/0
R2(config-if)#ipv6 address 2002:202:202:2::2/64
R2(config-if)#exit
R2(config)#interface tunnel 0
R2(config-if)#ipv6 unnumbered fastethernet 0/0
R2(config-if)#tunnel source loopback 0
R2(config-if)#tunnel mode ipv6ip 6to4
R2(config-if)#exit
R2(config)#ipv6 route 2002::/16 tunnel 0
R2(config)#exit

R3(config)#interface loopback 0
R3(config-if)#ip address 3.3.3.3 255.255.255.255
R3(config-if)#exit
R3(config)#router ospf 3
R3(config-router)#network 3.3.3.3 0.0.0.0 area 0
R3(config-router)#exit
R3(config)#ipv6 unicast-routing
R3(config)#ip cef
R3(config)#interface fastethernet 0/0
R3(config-if)#ipv6 address 2002:303:303:3::3/64
R3(config-if)#exit
R3(config)#interface tunnel 0
R3(config-if)#ipv6 unnumbered fastethernet 0/0
R3(config-if)#tunnel source loopback 0
R3(config-if)#tunnel mode ipv6ip 6to4
R3(config-if)#exit
R3(config)#ipv6 route 2002::/16 tunnel 0
R3(config)#exit
```

Verify your IPv6 addressing using the show ipv6 interface command on both routers:

```
R2#show ipv6 interface fastethernet 0/0
FastEthernet0/0 is up, line protocol is up
  IPv6 is enabled, link-local address is FE80::20D:28FF:FE9E:F940
  Global unicast address(es):
    2002:202:202:2::2, subnet is 2002:202:202:2::/64
  Joined group address(es):
    FF02::1
    FF02::2
    FF02::1:FF00:2
    FF02::1:FF9E:F940
  MTU is 1500 bytes

[Truncated Output]

R3#show ipv6 interface fastethernet 0/0
FastEthernet0/0 is up, line protocol is up
  IPv6 is enabled, link-local address is FE80::213:7FFF:FEAF:3E00
  Global unicast address(es):
    2002:303:303:3::3, subnet is 2002:303:303:3::/64
  Joined group address(es):
    FF02::1
    FF02::2
    FF02::1:FF00:3
    FF02::1:FFAF:3E00
  MTU is 1500 bytes

[Truncated Output]

R2#show ipv6 interface tunnel 0
Tunnel0 is up, line protocol is up
  IPv6 is enabled, link-local address is FE80::202:202
  Interface is unnumbered. Using address of FastEthernet0/0
  No global unicast address is configured
  Joined group address(es):
    FF02::1
    FF02::2
    FF02::1:FF02:202
  MTU is 1480 bytes
```

```
[Truncated Output]

R3#show ipv6 interface tunnel 0
Tunnel0 is up, line protocol is up
  IPv6 is enabled, link-local address is FE80::303:303
  Interface is unnumbered. Using address of FastEthernet0/0
  No global unicast address is configured
  Joined group address(es):
    FF02::1
    FF02::2
    FF02::1:FF03:303
  MTU is 1480 bytes

[Truncated Output]
```

Next, verify IPv6 routing using the show ipv6 route command on both routers:

```
R2#show ipv6 route
IPv6 Routing Table - 5 entries
Codes: C - Connected, L - Local, S - Static, R - RIP, B - BGP
       U - Per-user Static route
       I1 - ISIS L1, I2 - ISIS L2, IA - ISIS interarea, IS - ISIS summary
       O - OSPF intra, OI - OSPF inter, OE1 - OSPF ext 1, OE2 - OSPF ext 2
       ON1 - OSPF NSSA ext 1, ON2 - OSPF NSSA ext 2
S   2002::/16 [1/0]
     via ::, Tunnel0
C   2002:202:202:2::/64 [0/0]
     via ::, FastEthernet0/0
L   2002:202:202:2::2/128 [0/0]
     via ::, FastEthernet0/0
L   FE80::/10 [0/0]
     via ::, Null0
L   FF00::/8 [0/0]
     via ::, Null0
```

Finally, verify LAN-to-LAN connectivity between the IPv6 subnets using an extended ping:

```
R2#ping 2002:303:303:3::3 source fastethernet 0/0 repeat 10 size 1500

Type escape sequence to abort.
Sending 10, 1500-byte ICMP Echos to 2002:303:303:3::3, timeout is 2 seconds:
Packet sent with a source address of 2002:202:202:2::2
!!!!!!!!!!
Success rate is 100 percent (10/10), round-trip min/avg/max = 204/207/208 ms

R3#ping 2002:202:202:2::2 source fastethernet 0/0 repeat 10 size 1500

Type escape sequence to abort.
Sending 10, 1500-byte ICMP Echos to 2002:202:202:2::2, timeout is 2 seconds:
Packet sent with a source address of 2002:303:303:3::3
!!!!!!!!!!
Success rate is 100 percent (10/10), round-trip min/avg/max = 204/207/208 ms
```

Task 11

To complete this task, you need to configure a NAT pool using the 150.1.1.0/24 subnet. In order to allow reachability to this subnet, without creating an additional interface, you need to configure a static route pointing to Null0 and advertise it via OSPF. Complete this as follows:

```
R3(config)#ip route 150.3.3.0 255.255.255.0 null 0
R3(config)#$at pool R3-LAN-POOL 150.3.3.1 150.3.3.254 netmask 255.255.255.0
R3(config)#access-list 100 permit ip 10.3.3.0 0.0.0.255 150.1.1.0 0.0.0.255
R3(config)#access-list 100 permit ip 10.3.3.0 0.0.0.255 150.2.2.0 0.0.0.255
R3(config)#ip nat inside source list 100 pool R3-LAN-POOL
R3(config)#interface fastethernet 0/0
R3(config-if)#ip nat inside
R3(config-if)#exit
R3(config)#interface serial 1/0
R3(config-if)#ip nat outside
R3(config-if)#exit
R3(config)#interface serial 1/1
R3(config-if)#ip nat outside
R3(config-if)#exit
R3(config)#end
R3#clear ip ospf redistribution
```

Following this configuration, ping from R3s LAN subnet to 150.1.1.0/24 and 150.2.2.0/24:

```
ALS2#ping 150.1.1.1

Type escape sequence to abort.
Sending 5, 100-byte ICMP Echos to 150.1.1.1, timeout is 2 seconds:
.!!!!
Success rate is 80 percent (4/5), round-trip min/avg/max = 16/17/20 ms

ALS2#ping 150.2.2.2

Type escape sequence to abort.
Sending 5, 100-byte ICMP Echos to 150.2.2.2, timeout is 2 seconds:
!!!!!
Success rate is 100 percent (5/5), round-trip min/avg/max = 16/16/20 ms
```

Finally, verify NAT operation using the show ip nat translations command on R3:

```
R3#show ip nat translations
Pro Inside global      Inside local       Outside local      Outside global
icmp 150.3.3.1:4484    10.3.3.254:4484    150.1.1.1:4484     150.1.1.1:4484
icmp 150.3.3.1:4485    10.3.3.254:4485    150.1.1.1:4485     150.1.1.1:4485
icmp 150.3.3.1:4486    10.3.3.254:4486    150.1.1.1:4486     150.1.1.1:4486
icmp 150.3.3.1:4487    10.3.3.254:4487    150.1.1.1:4487     150.1.1.1:4487
icmp 150.3.3.1:4488    10.3.3.254:4488    150.1.1.1:4488     150.1.1.1:4488
icmp 150.3.3.1:7980    10.3.3.254:7980    150.2.2.2:7980     150.2.2.2:7980
icmp 150.3.3.1:7981    10.3.3.254:7981    150.2.2.2:7981     150.2.2.2:7981
icmp 150.3.3.1:7982    10.3.3.254:7982    150.2.2.2:7982     150.2.2.2:7982
icmp 150.3.3.1:7983    10.3.3.254:7983    150.2.2.2:7983     150.2.2.2:7983
icmp 150.3.3.1:7984    10.3.3.254:7984    150.2.2.2:7984     150.2.2.2:7984
```

FINAL ROUTER CONFIGURATIONS

R1

```
R1#term len 0
R1#sh run
Building configuration...

Current configuration : 1662 bytes
!
version 12.4
service timestamps debug datetime msec
service timestamps log datetime msec
no service password-encryption
!
hostname R1
!
boot-start-marker
boot-end-marker
!
no logging console
!
no aaa new-model
no network-clock-participate slot 1
no network-clock-participate wic 0
ip cef
!
no ip domain lookup
ip auth-proxy max-nodata-conns 3
ip admission max-nodata-conns 3
!
interface Loopback0
 ip address 1.1.1.1 255.255.255.255
!
interface FastEthernet0/0
 ip address 150.1.1.1 255.255.255.0
 duplex auto
 speed auto
!
interface Serial0/0
 ip address 150.0.0.1 255.255.255.252
 clock rate 2000000
```

```
!
interface Serial0/1
 ip address 150.0.0.5 255.255.255.252
!
router ospf 1
 router-id 1.1.1.1
 log-adjacency-changes
 redistribute connected subnets route-map LOOPBACK0
 network 150.0.0.1 0.0.0.0 area 1
 network 150.0.0.5 0.0.0.0 area 0
 default-information originate always
!
router bgp 1
 no synchronization
 bgp router-id 1.1.1.1
 bgp log-neighbor-changes
 bgp graceful-restart restart-time 120
 bgp graceful-restart stalepath-time 360
 bgp graceful-restart
 neighbor 4.4.4.4 remote-as 4
 neighbor 4.4.4.4 ebgp-multihop 255
 neighbor 4.4.4.4 update-source Loopback0
 neighbor 4.4.4.4 default-originate
 neighbor 150.1.1.253 remote-as 1
 neighbor 150.1.1.253 next-hop-self
 neighbor 150.1.1.254 remote-as 1
 neighbor 150.1.1.254 next-hop-self
 no auto-summary
!
ip forward-protocol nd
!
no ip http server
no ip http secure-server
!
route-map LOOPBACK0 permit 10
 match interface Loopback0
!
control-plane
!
line con 0
line aux 0
line vty 0 4
 password cisco
 login
!
end

R1#
```

R2

```
R2#term len 0
R2#sh run
Building configuration...

Current configuration : 1351 bytes
!
version 12.4
service timestamps debug datetime msec
service timestamps log datetime msec
no service password-encryption
!
hostname R2
!
boot-start-marker
boot-end-marker
!
no logging console
!
no aaa new-model
no network-clock-participate slot 1
no network-clock-participate wic 0
ip cef
!
no ip domain lookup
ip auth-proxy max-nodata-conns 3
ip admission max-nodata-conns 3
!
ipv6 unicast-routing
```

```
!
interface Loopback0
 ip address 2.2.2.2 255.255.255.255
!
interface Tunnel0
 no ip address
 no ip redirects
 ipv6 unnumbered FastEthernet0/0
 tunnel source Loopback0
 tunnel mode ipv6ip 6to4
!
interface FastEthernet0/0
 ip address 150.2.2.2 255.255.255.0
 loopback
 duplex auto
 speed auto
 ipv6 address 2002:202:202:2::2/64
 no keepalive
!
interface Serial0/0
 ip address 150.0.0.2 255.255.255.252
!
interface Serial0/1
 ip address 150.0.0.9 255.255.255.252
!
router ospf 2
 router-id 2.2.2.2
 log-adjacency-changes
 redistribute connected subnets
 passive-interface FastEthernet0/0
 network 150.0.0.2 0.0.0.0 area 1
 network 150.0.0.9 0.0.0.0 area 0
 network 150.2.2.2 0.0.0.0 area 1
!
ip forward-protocol nd
!
no ip http server
no ip http secure-server
!
ipv6 route 2002::/16 Tunnel0
!
control-plane
!
line con 0
line aux 0
line vty 0 4
 password cisco
 login
!
end

R2#
```

R3

```
R3#term len 0
R3#sh run
Building configuration...

Current configuration : 2126 bytes
!
version 12.4
service timestamps debug datetime msec
service timestamps log datetime msec
no service password-encryption
!
hostname R3
!
boot-start-marker
boot-end-marker
!
no logging console
!
no aaa new-model
no network-clock-participate slot 1
no network-clock-participate wic 0
ip cef
!
no ip domain lookup
ip auth-proxy max-nodata-conns 3
```

```
  ip admission max-nodata-conns 3
 !
 ipv6 unicast-routing
 !
 interface Loopback0
  ip address 3.3.3.3 255.255.255.255
 !
 interface Tunnel0
  no ip address
  no ip redirects
  ipv6 unnumbered FastEthernet0/0
  tunnel source Loopback0
  tunnel mode ipv6ip 6to4
 !
 interface FastEthernet0/0
  ip address 10.3.3.3 255.255.255.0
  ip nat inside
  ip virtual-reassembly
  duplex auto
  speed auto
  ipv6 address 2002:303:303:3::3/64
 !
 interface Serial1/0
  ip address 150.0.0.6 255.255.255.252
  ip nat outside
  ip virtual-reassembly
  clock rate 128000
 !
 interface Serial1/1
  ip address 150.0.0.10 255.255.255.252
  ip nat outside
  ip virtual-reassembly
  clock rate 128000
 !
 interface Serial1/2
  ip address 150.0.0.13 255.255.255.252
  clock rate 128000
 !
 interface Serial1/3
  no ip address
  shutdown
 !
 interface Serial1/4
  no ip address
  shutdown
 !
 interface Serial1/5
  no ip address
  shutdown
 !
 interface Serial1/6
  no ip address
  shutdown
 !
 interface Serial1/7
  no ip address
  shutdown
 !
 router ospf 3
  router-id 3.3.3.3
  log-adjacency-changes
  redistribute static subnets
  network 3.3.3.3 0.0.0.0 area 0
  network 150.0.0.6 0.0.0.0 area 0
  network 150.0.0.10 0.0.0.0 area 0
 !
 ip forward-protocol nd
 ip route 4.4.4.4 255.255.255.255 Serial1/2
 ip route 10.4.4.0 255.255.255.0 Serial1/2
 ip route 150.3.3.0 255.255.255.0 Null0
 !
 !
 no ip http server
 no ip http secure-server
 ip nat pool R3-LAN-POOL 150.3.3.1 150.3.3.254 netmask 255.255.255.0
 ip nat inside source list 100 pool R3-LAN-POOL
 !
 access-list 100 permit ip 10.3.3.0 0.0.0.255 150.1.1.0 0.0.0.255
 access-list 100 permit ip 10.3.3.0 0.0.0.255 150.2.2.0 0.0.0.255
 ipv6 route 2002::/16 Tunnel0
 !
```

```
control-plane
!
line con 0
line aux 0
line vty 0 4
 password cisco
 login
!
end

R3#
```

R4

```
R4#term len 0
R4#sh run
Building configuration...

Current configuration : 1146 bytes
!
version 12.4
service timestamps debug datetime msec
service timestamps log datetime msec
no service password-encryption
!
hostname R4
!
boot-start-marker
boot-end-marker
!
no logging console
!
no aaa new-model
no network-clock-participate slot 1
no network-clock-participate wic 0
ip cef
!
no ip domain lookup
ip auth-proxy max-nodata-conns 3
ip admission max-nodata-conns 3
!
interface Loopback0
 ip address 4.4.4.4 255.255.255.255
!
interface FastEthernet0/0
 ip address 10.4.4.4 255.255.255.0
 duplex auto
 speed auto
!
interface Serial0/0
 ip address 150.0.0.14 255.255.255.252
!
interface Serial0/1
 no ip address
!
router bgp 4
 no synchronization
 bgp router-id 4.4.4.4
 bgp log-neighbor-changes
 network 10.4.4.0 mask 255.255.255.0
 neighbor 1.1.1.1 remote-as 1
 neighbor 1.1.1.1 ebgp-multihop 255
 neighbor 1.1.1.1 update-source Loopback0
 no auto-summary
!
ip forward-protocol nd
ip route 1.1.1.1 255.255.255.255 Serial0/0
!
no ip http server
no ip http secure-server
!
control-plane
!
line con 0
line aux 0
line vty 0 4
 password cisco
 login
!
end
R4#
```

FINAL SWITCH CONFIGURATIONS

DLS1

```
DLS1#term len 0
DLS1#sh run
Building configuration...

Current configuration : 4993 bytes
!
version 12.2
no service pad
service timestamps debug datetime msec
service timestamps log datetime msec
no service password-encryption
!
hostname DLS1
!
no logging console
!
no aaa new-model
ip subnet-zero
ip routing
no ip domain-lookup
!
vtp domain secure
vtp mode transparent
!
port-channel load-balance dst-mac
!
spanning-tree mode pvst
spanning-tree extend system-id
!
vlan internal allocation policy ascending
!
vlan 100
 name R1-VLAN
!
interface Loopback0
 ip address 100.1.1.1 255.255.255.0
!
interface Port-channel10
 switchport trunk encapsulation dot1q
 switchport mode trunk
!
interface FastEthernet0/1
 switchport mode dynamic desirable
 shutdown
!
interface FastEthernet0/2
 switchport mode dynamic desirable
 shutdown
!
interface FastEthernet0/3
 switchport mode dynamic desirable
 shutdown
!
interface FastEthernet0/4
 switchport mode dynamic desirable
 shutdown
!
interface FastEthernet0/5
 switchport mode dynamic desirable
 shutdown
!
interface FastEthernet0/6
 switchport mode dynamic desirable
 shutdown
!
interface FastEthernet0/7
 switchport trunk encapsulation dot1q
 switchport mode trunk
!
interface FastEthernet0/8
 switchport trunk encapsulation dot1q
 switchport mode trunk
!
interface FastEthernet0/9
```

```
 switchport mode dynamic desirable
 shutdown
!
interface FastEthernet0/10
 switchport mode dynamic desirable
 shutdown
!
interface FastEthernet0/11
 switchport trunk encapsulation dot1q
 switchport mode trunk
 channel-group 10 mode desirable
!
interface FastEthernet0/12
 switchport trunk encapsulation dot1q
 switchport mode trunk
 channel-group 10 mode desirable

[Truncated Output]

interface Vlan1
 no ip address
 shutdown
!
interface Vlan100
 ip address 150.1.1.254 255.255.255.0
!
router bgp 1
 no synchronization
 bgp router-id 150.1.1.254
 bgp log-neighbor-changes
 bgp graceful-restart restart-time 120
 bgp graceful-restart stalepath-time 360
 bgp graceful-restart
 network 100.1.1.0 mask 255.255.255.0
 neighbor 150.1.1.1 remote-as 1
 neighbor 150.1.1.253 remote-as 1
 no auto-summary
!
ip classless
ip http server
ip http secure-server
!
control-plane
!
line con 0
line vty 0 4
 privilege level 15
 password cisco
 login
line vty 5 15
 login
!
end

DLS1#
```

DLS2

```
DLS2#term len 0
DLS2#sh run
Building configuration...

Current configuration : 6603 bytes
!
version 12.2
no service pad
service timestamps debug datetime msec
service timestamps log datetime msec
no service password-encryption
!
hostname DLS2
!
no logging console
!
no aaa new-model
ip subnet-zero
ip routing
no ip domain-lookup
```

```
!
vtp domain secure
vtp mode transparent
!
crypto pki trustpoint TP-self-signed-4251411712
 enrollment selfsigned
 subject-name cn=IOS-Self-Signed-Certificate-4251411712
 revocation-check none
 rsakeypair TP-self-signed-4251411712
!
crypto pki certificate chain TP-self-signed-4251411712
 certificate self-signed 01
  3082023D 308201A6 A0030201 02020101 300D0609 2A864886 F70D0101 04050030
  31312F30 2D060355 04031326 494F532D 53656C66 2D536967 6E65642D 43657274
  69666963 6174652D 34323531 34313137 3132301E 170D3933 30333031 30343531
  35395A17 0D323030 31303130 30303030 305A3031 312F302D 06035504 03132649
  4F532D53 656C662D 5369676E 65642D43 65727469 66696361 74652D34 32353134
  31313731 3230819F 300D0609 2A864886 F70D0101 01050003 818D0030 81890281
  8100BAAA AC1C8450 0918BF5B 07DDB633 31E10D67 9D935C85 5206A584 FB17895D
  465EEC05 DE6CEA88 26147436 C847AA81 2094418D 9EDFC438 64035547 DCA6048C
  EA050417 E676476F 7644C154 DA454939 F0309634 8DAA5D54 FABE7282 3E785059
  4D05944B 3F9FF266 3F909618 E52F918C 69BE861E CAB5311B D599AD96 82B62A39
  CC6D0203 010001A3 65306330 0F060355 1D130101 FF040530 030101FF 30100603
  551D1104 09300782 05444C53 322E301F 0603551D 23041830 168014F4 E1F78348
  24047B46 3BD162F0 5A28DE61 7C592A30 1D060355 1D0E0416 0414F4E1 F7834824
  047B463B D162F05A 28DE617C 592A300D 06092A86 4886F70D 01010405 00038181
  00781FE8 D6D94AD9 85DDFAF4 5FEEF04B 7476260C C94EFB39 3FA7A6CB DB38B85F
  3F318479 41E7FA4B 457A02D2 CBABB831 992F4A9E E1CDDABF 77BD0B5D D717F924
  6C72C7A8 25F84154 A6381F55 90A14F8A 34713CF0 933CB4E5 B4C9E65D 1CB63F9C
  696619AC 22D8DB37 6D2A9B56 AA5A4111 0CCB9CBD 62FA571C 6F044F5A 38977D98 E7
  quit
port-channel load-balance dst-mac
!
spanning-tree mode pvst
spanning-tree extend system-id
!
vlan internal allocation policy ascending
!
vlan 100
 name R1-VLAN
!
vlan 192
 name secure-vlan
!
interface Loopback0
 ip address 200.2.2.2 255.255.255.0
!
interface Port-channel10
 switchport trunk encapsulation dot1q
 switchport mode trunk
!
interface FastEthernet0/1
 switchport mode dynamic desirable
 shutdown
!
interface FastEthernet0/2
 switchport mode dynamic desirable
 shutdown
!
interface FastEthernet0/3
 switchport mode dynamic desirable
 shutdown
!
interface FastEthernet0/4
 switchport mode dynamic desirable
 shutdown
!
interface FastEthernet0/5
 switchport mode dynamic desirable
 shutdown
!
interface FastEthernet0/6
 switchport mode dynamic desirable
 shutdown
!
interface FastEthernet0/7
 switchport mode dynamic desirable
 shutdown
!
```

```
interface FastEthernet0/8
 switchport mode dynamic desirable
 shutdown
!
interface FastEthernet0/9
 switchport mode dynamic desirable
 shutdown
!
interface FastEthernet0/10
 switchport mode dynamic desirable
 shutdown
!
interface FastEthernet0/11
 switchport trunk encapsulation dot1q
 switchport mode trunk
 channel-group 10 mode desirable
!
interface FastEthernet0/12
 switchport trunk encapsulation dot1q
 switchport mode trunk
 channel-group 10 mode desirable

[Truncated Output]

interface Vlan1
 no ip address
 shutdown
!
interface Vlan100
 ip address 150.1.1.253 255.255.255.0
!
router bgp 1
 no synchronization
 bgp router-id 150.1.1.253
 bgp log-neighbor-changes
 bgp graceful-restart restart-time 120
 bgp graceful-restart stalepath-time 360
 bgp graceful-restart
 network 200.2.2.0
 neighbor 150.1.1.1 remote-as 1
 neighbor 150.1.1.254 remote-as 1
 no auto-summary
!
ip classless
ip http server
ip http secure-server
!
control-plane
!
line con 0
line vty 0 4
 privilege level 15
 password cisco
 login
line vty 5 15
 login
!
end

DLS2#
```

ALS1

```
ALS1#term len 0
ALS1#sh run
Building configuration...

Current configuration : 1654 bytes
!
version 12.1
no service pad
service timestamps debug uptime
service timestamps log uptime
no service password-encryption
!
hostname ALS1
!
no logging console
!
```

```
errdisable recovery cause bpduguard
errdisable recovery interval 600
ip subnet-zero
!
no ip domain-lookup
vtp domain secure
vtp mode transparent
!
spanning-tree mode pvst
no spanning-tree optimize bpdu transmission
spanning-tree extend system-id
spanning-tree vlan 1,100,300,400 priority 0
!
vlan 100
 name R1-VLAN
!
vlan 300
 name R3-VLAN
!
vlan 400
 name R4-VLAN
!
interface FastEthernet0/1
 switchport access vlan 100
 switchport mode access
 spanning-tree bpduguard enable
!
interface FastEthernet0/2
 shutdown
!
interface FastEthernet0/3
 switchport access vlan 300
 switchport mode access
 spanning-tree bpduguard enable
!
interface FastEthernet0/4
 switchport access vlan 400
 switchport mode access
 spanning-tree bpduguard enable
!
interface FastEthernet0/5
 shutdown
!
interface FastEthernet0/6
 shutdown
!
interface FastEthernet0/7
 switchport mode trunk
 spanning-tree guard root
!
interface FastEthernet0/8
 switchport mode trunk
 spanning-tree guard root
!
interface FastEthernet0/9
 shutdown
!
interface FastEthernet0/10
 shutdown
!
interface FastEthernet0/11
 switchport mode trunk
 spanning-tree guard root
!
interface FastEthernet0/12
 switchport mode trunk
 spanning-tree guard root
!
interface Vlan1
 no ip address
 no ip route-cache
 shutdown
!
interface Vlan400
 ip address 10.4.4.254 255.255.255.0
 no ip route-cache
!
ip default-gateway 10.4.4.4
ip http server
```

```
!
line con 0
line vty 0 4
 privilege level 15
 password cisco
 login
line vty 5 15
 login
!
end

ALS1#
```

ALS2

```
ALS2#term len 0
ALS2#sh run
Building configuration...

Current configuration : 1135 bytes
!
version 12.1
no service pad
service timestamps debug uptime
service timestamps log uptime
no service password-encryption
!
hostname ALS2
!
no logging console
!
ip subnet-zero
!
no ip domain-lookup
vtp domain fhrp
vtp mode transparent
!
spanning-tree mode pvst
no spanning-tree optimize bpdu transmission
spanning-tree extend system-id
!
vlan 300
 name R3-VLAN
!
interface FastEthernet0/1
 shutdown
!
interface FastEthernet0/2
 shutdown
!
interface FastEthernet0/3
 shutdown
!
interface FastEthernet0/4
 shutdown
!
interface FastEthernet0/5
 shutdown
!
interface FastEthernet0/6
 shutdown
!
interface FastEthernet0/7
 shutdown
!
interface FastEthernet0/8
 shutdown
!
interface FastEthernet0/9
 shutdown
!
interface FastEthernet0/10
 shutdown
!
interface FastEthernet0/11
 switchport mode trunk
!
interface FastEthernet0/12
```

```
 switchport mode trunk
!
interface Vlan1
 no ip address
 no ip route-cache
 shutdown
!
interface Vlan300
 ip address 10.3.3.254 255.255.255.0
 no ip route-cache
!
ip default-gateway 10.3.3.3
ip http server
!
line con 0
line vty 0 4
 privilege level 15
 password cisco
 login
line vty 5 15
 login
!
end

ALS2#
```

CCNP LAB 85

CCNP Multi-Technology Lab

Lab Objective:

The objective of this lab is to cover all relevant CCNP ROUTE and SWITCH theory. These labs will include topics from each of these guides. It should be noted that not all topics will be included in all labs. Additionally, not all solutions will be illustrated in detail. You can refer to previous labs for assistance with some basic configurations.

Lab Topology:

The lab network topology is illustrated below:

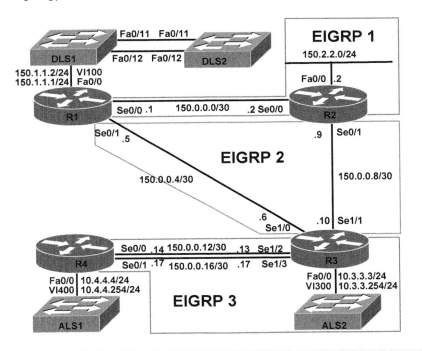

IMPORTANT NOTE: If you are using the www.howtonetwork.net racks, please implement the following pre-lab configurations. This is required because of the manner in which the routers and switches are physically cabled to each other. The following configuration should be applied to switch ALS1:

```
!
hostname ALS1
!
vtp mode transparent
!
vlan 100
 name R1-VLAN
!
vlan 300
 name R3-VLAN
!
```

```
vlan 400
 name R4-VLAN
!
interface fastethernet 0/1
 switchport access vlan 100
 switchport mode access
!
interface fastethernet 0/2
 shutdown
!
interface fastethernet 0/3
 switchport access vlan 300
 switchport mode access
!
interface fastethernet 0/4
 switchport access vlan 400
 switchport mode access
!
interface range fastethernet 0/5 - 6
 shutdown
!
interface fastethernet0/7
 switchport mode trunk
!
interface fastethernet 0/8
 switchport mode trunk
!
interface range fastethernet 0/9 - 10
 shutdown
!
interface range fastethernet 0/11 - 12
 switchport mode trunk
!
interface vlan 400
 ip address 10.4.4.254 255.255.255.0
 no shutdown
!
ip default-gateway 10.4.4.4
!
line vty 0 4
 privilege level 15
 password cisco
 login
!
end

hostname ALS2
!
vtp mode transparent
!
vlan 300
 name R3-VLAN
!
interface range fastethernet 0/1 - 10
 shutdown
!
interface fastethernet 0/11
 switchport mode trunk
!
interface fastethernet 0/12
 switchport mode trunk
!
interface vlan 300
 ip address 10.3.3.254 255.255.255.0
 no shutdown
!
ip default-gateway 10.3.3.3
!
line vty 0 4
 privilege level 15
 password cisco
 login
!
end

hostname DLS1
!
ip routing
!
vtp mode transparent
!
vlan 100
 name R1-VLAN
interface range fastethernet 0/1 - 6
 shutdown
```

```
!
interface range fastethernet 0/7 - 8
 switchport trunk encapsulation dot1q
 switchport mode trunk
!
interface range fastethernet 0/9 - 10
 shutdown
!
interface fastethernet 0/11
 switchport mode dynamic desirable
!
interface fastethernet 0/12
 switchport mode dynamic desirable
!
interface range fastethernet 0/13 - 48
 shutdown
!
interface vlan 100
 ip address 150.1.1.2 255.255.255.0
 no shutdown
!
line vty 0 4
 privilege level 15
 password cisco
 login
!
end

hostname DLS2
!
ip routing
!
vtp mode transparent
!
interface range fastethernet 0/1 - 10
 shutdown
!
interface fastethernet 0/11
 switchport mode dynamic desirable
!
interface fastethernet 0/12
 switchport mode dynamic desirable
!
interface range fastethernet 0/13 - 48
 shutdown
!
line vty 0 4
 privilege level 15
 password cisco
 login
!
end
```

If you are using the www.howtonetwork.net racks, please bring up the LAN interface connected to R2 by the following configuration:

```
ip address 150.2.2.2 255.255.255.0
 no keepalive
 loopback
 no shutdown
```

Alternatively, you can simply connect the interface to a hub or one of the switches and bring up the interface in the standard manner.

Task 1

Configure hostnames, IP addressing on all routers as illustrated in the network topology.

Task 2

Configure an EtherChannel between DLS1 and DLS2. This should be a Layer 2 access link that uses LACP. Configure interface VLAN 100 on switch DLS2. This interface should receive its IP address information via DHCP. Verify your configuration using the appropriate commands.

Task 3

Configure Cisco IOS DHCP Snooping for all VLANs on switch DLS1. For additional security, configure switch DLS1 to prevent IP spoofing attacks by filtering the traffic based on the DHCP Snooping Binding Database. Finally, ensure that Option 82 is not used. Verify the Cisco IOS DHCP Snooping configuration using the appropriate commands.

Task 4

Configure Cisco IOS DHCP server on R1. Configure the following DHCP parameters:
- A default gateway of 192.168.1.1 should be configured for this subnet
- Addresses 192.168.1.1 to 10 should never be assigned by R1
- R1 should ping a pool address 10 times before assigning it to a requesting client
- The lease should last for 4 hours
- Switch DLS2 should reside in the howtonetwork.net domain
- Switch DLS2 should use DNS server 150.1.1.1

Verify your configuration using the appropriate commands.

Task 5

Configure EIGRP illustrated in the topology. You must adhere to the following guidelines:
- R2 should NEVER be used as a transit router, even in the event that the R1-R3 link fails
- R4 should only RECEIVE routes but should be reachable from all other routers
- Switches DLS1 and DLS2 should be reachable from all other devices in the network
- No EIGRP Hello's should be sent out the LAN interfaces of any router
- Do NOT advertise the 150.1.1.0/24 subnet via EIGRP; this subnet should not be reachable
- Do NOT advertise the 10.4.4.0/24 subnet via EIGRP; however, ensure that it is reachable
- The 10.3.3.0/24 subnet should be advertised as an EXTERNAL EIGRP route

Task 5

Redistribute between the different EIGRP instances on R1, R2, and R3. Do NOT redistribute the 150.1.1.0/24 subnet into EIGRP; however, ensure that all routers are able to reach this subnet. You are NOT allowed to configure static routes or redistribute or advertise this subnet via EIGRP when completing this task. Verify your solution by pinging DLS2 from any other router.

Task 6

In the future, an IP videos solution will be implemented. This video solution will use Multicast. Configure IP Multicast so that R2 is the RP. The RP address should be 2.2.2.2/32. To test Multicast operation, configure R1s LAN interface to join group 227.1.1.1. Enable IP Multicast support on R1, R2, R3, DLS1 and DLS2. Do NOT enable IP Multicast on R4. Ensure that all other devices can ping this Multicast group.

Task 7

In order to ensure that video traffic is protected in the event of network congestion, configure QoS on R1's WAN interfaces so that this type of traffic is allocated 40% of interface bandwidth. You are NOT allowed to use ACLs in your solution. Verify your configuration using the appropriate commands.

Task 8

In the future, a new application will be integrated into the network. This new application will use TCP ports 2023, 3023, 4023 and 5023. Modify the existing QoS policy on R1 so that this traffic is allocated 10% of interface bandwidth. You are NOT allowed to use Access Lists to complete this task. Verify your configuration using the appropriate commands.

Task 9

Management would like to integrate IPv6 into the network. Configure the following IPv6 subnets on the LAN interfaces of R2 and R3:
- R2 LAN IPv6 Subnet: 3FFE:2222:2222:2222::/64
- R3 LAN IPv6 Subnet: 3FFE:3333:3333:3333::/64

Next, enable OSPFv3 between R2 and R3 and ensure that these two subnets are reachable from all the two routers. You are NOT allowed to enable IPv6 or OSPFv3 routing on the WAN interfaces of R2 and R3. Ensure that the R2 LAN subnet is assigned to area 2, while the R3 LAN subnet is assigned to area 3. Verify your solution using the extended ping function.

Task 10

For security, configure area authentication for OSPFv3s backbone. Use the following parameters when you are configuring the authentication parameters:
- Use a Security Parameters Index (SPI) of 678
- Use Message Digest 5 (MD5) authentication
- Use a key of 1234567890abcdef1234567890abcdef

Task 11

For security, Management has requested that all ports on switch ALS1 that are not trunk links or connected to routers be configured to adhere to the following restrictions:
- The ports should NOT be able to communicate directly with each other at Layer 2
- All ports should be dynamically allocated to VLANs by server 150.1.1.254

You are NOT allowed to use Private VLANs to complete this task.

Task 12

For security, Management has requested that all ports on switch ALS2 that are not trunk links be configured so that Broadcast traffic should never exceed 5%, Multicast traffic should never exceed 20% and Unicast traffic should never exceed 80%. In the event that these thresholds are exceeded, the switch should send out an SNMP trap to server 150.1.1.254. This server is expecting the switch to use an SNMP community string of CCNP2011. Verify the configuration using the appropriate commands.

LAB VALIDATION

Task 1

Please refer to previous labs for basic IPv4, IPv6 addressing and hostname configuration. This will not be included in this section to avoid being redundant.

Task 2

Please refer to previous labs for basic EtherChannel configuration. This will not be included in this section to avoid being redundant. Following your configuration, verify EtherChannel operational status using the show etherchannel commands:

```
DLS1#show etherchannel summary
Flags:  D - down         P - bundled in port-channel
        I - stand-alone  s - suspended
        H - Hot-standby (LACP only)
        R - Layer3       S - Layer2
        U - in use       f - failed to allocate aggregator

        M - not in use, minimum links not met
        u - unsuitable for bundling
        w - waiting to be aggregated
        d - default port


Number of channel-groups in use: 1
Number of aggregators:           1

Group  Port-channel  Protocol    Ports
------+-------------+-----------+-----------------------------------------
10     Po10(SU)       LACP        Fa0/11(P)    Fa0/12(P)
```

```
DLS2#show etherchannel summary
Flags:  D - down         P - bundled in port-channel
        I - stand-alone  s - suspended
        H - Hot-standby (LACP only)
        R - Layer3       S - Layer2
        U - in use       f - failed to allocate aggregator

        M - not in use, minimum links not met
        u - unsuitable for bundling
        w - waiting to be aggregated
        d - default port

Number of channel-groups in use: 1
Number of aggregators:            1

Group  Port-channel  Protocol    Ports
------+-------------+-----------+-----------------------------------------------
10     Po10(SU)      LACP        Fa0/11(P)   Fa0/12(P)
```

You can verify Layer 2 configuration parameters using the show interfaces <name> switchport command on either one or both of the switches:

```
DLS2#show interfaces port-channel 10 switchport
Name: Po10
Switchport: Enabled
Administrative Mode: static access
Operational Mode: static access
Administrative Trunking Encapsulation: negotiate
Operational Trunking Encapsulation: native
Negotiation of Trunking: Off
Access Mode VLAN: 100 (R1-VLAN)
Trunking Native Mode VLAN: 1 (default)
Administrative Native VLAN tagging: enabled
Voice VLAN: none
Administrative private-vlan host-association: none
Administrative private-vlan mapping: none
Administrative private-vlan trunk native VLAN: none
Administrative private-vlan trunk Native VLAN tagging: enabled
Administrative private-vlan trunk encapsulation: dot1q
Administrative private-vlan trunk normal VLANs: none
Administrative private-vlan trunk associations: none
Administrative private-vlan trunk mappings: none
Operational private-vlan: none
Trunking VLANs Enabled: ALL
Pruning VLANs Enabled: 2-1001

Protected: false
Unknown unicast blocked: disabled
Unknown multicast blocked: disabled
Appliance trust: none
```

On switch DLS2, use the show interfaces command to verify DHCP client configuration:

```
DLS2#show interfaces vlan 100
Vlan100 is up, line protocol is up
  Hardware is EtherSVI, address is 000b.fd67.6500 (bia 000b.fd67.6500)
  Internet address will be negotiated using DHCP
  MTU 1500 bytes, BW 1000000 Kbit, DLY 10 usec,
     reliability 255/255, txload 1/255, rxload 1/255
  Encapsulation ARPA, loopback not set
  Keepalive not supported
  ARP type: ARPA, ARP Timeout 04:00:00
  Last input never, output 00:00:00, output hang never
  Last clearing of "show interface" counters never
  Input queue: 0/75/0/0 (size/max/drops/flushes); Total output drops: 0
  Queueing strategy: fifo
  Output queue: 0/40 (size/max)
  5 minute input rate 0 bits/sec, 0 packets/sec
  5 minute output rate 0 bits/sec, 0 packets/sec
     0 packets input, 0 bytes, 0 no buffer
     Received 0 broadcasts (0 IP multicasts)
     0 runts, 0 giants, 0 throttles
     0 input errors, 0 CRC, 0 frame, 0 overrun, 0 ignored
     1 packets output, 618 bytes, 0 underruns
     0 output errors, 0 interface resets
     0 output buffer failures, 0 output buffers swapped out
```

Task 3

The requirements of this task are straightforward. In addition to configuring DHCP Snooping, you also need to configure the IP Source Guard feature. This task is completed as follows:

```
DLS1(config)#ip dhcp snooping
DLS1(config)#ip dhcp snooping vlan 100
DLS1(config)#no ip dhcp snooping information option
DLS1(config)#interface range fastethernet 0/7 - 8
DLS1(config-if-range)#ip dhcp snooping trust
DLS1(config-if-range)#exit
DLS1(config)#interface port-channel 10
DLS1(config-if)#ip verify source
DLS1(config-if)#exit
```

Following this, verify your configuration using the show ip dhcp snooping command:

```
DLS1(config)#do show ip dhcp snooping
Switch DHCP snooping is enabled
DHCP snooping is configured on following VLANs:
100
DHCP snooping is operational on following VLANs:
100
DHCP snooping is configured on the following L3 Interfaces:

Insertion of option 82 is disabled
   circuit-id format: vlan-mod-port
   remote-id format: MAC
Option 82 on untrusted port is not allowed
Verification of hwaddr field is enabled
Verification of giaddr field is enabled
DHCP snooping trust/rate is configured on the following Interfaces:

Interface                   Trusted    Rate limit (pps)
------------------------    -------    ----------------
FastEthernet0/7             yes        unlimited
FastEthernet0/8             yes        unlimited
```

Task 4

The requirements of this task are straightforward. This task is completed as follows:

```
R1(config)#ip dhcp excluded-address 150.1.1.1 150.1.1.10
R1(config)#ip dhcp ping packets 10
R1(config)#ip dhcp pool VLAN-100-DHCP-POOL
R1(dhcp-config)#network 150.1.1.0 /24
R1(dhcp-config)#default-router 150.1.1.1
R1(dhcp-config)#lease 0 4 0
R1(dhcp-config)#domain-name howtonetwork.net
R1(dhcp-config)#dns-server 150.1.1.1
R1(dhcp-config)#exit
```

Following your configuration, DLS2 should receive an IP address via DHCP from R1. Verify the DHCP configuration and bindings using the show ip dhcp commands:

```
R1#show ip dhcp pool VLAN-100-DHCP-POOL

Pool VLAN-100-DHCP-POOL :
 Utilization mark (high/low)    : 100 / 0
 Subnet size (first/next)       : 0 / 0
 Total addresses                : 254
 Leased addresses               : 1
 Pending event                  : none
 1 subnet is currently in the pool :
 Current index       IP address range                    Leased addresses
 150.1.1.12          150.1.1.1       - 150.1.1.254        1

R1#show ip dhcp binding
Bindings from all pools not associated with VRF:
IP address          Client-ID/              Lease expiration        Type
                    Hardware address/
                    User name
150.1.1.11          0063.6973.636f.2d30.    Jun 19 2011 02:07 AM    Automatic
                    3030.622e.6664.3637.
```

```
                         2e36.3530.302d.566c.
                         3130.30
DLS1#show ip dhcp snooping binding vlan 100
MacAddress            IpAddress         Lease(sec)  Type            VLAN  Interface
-----------------     ----------------  ----------  -------------   ----  ---------------
-----
00:0B:FD:67:65:00     150.1.1.11        14070       dhcp-snooping   100   Port-channel10
Total number of bindings: 1

DLS1#show ip source binding dhcp-snooping vlan 100
MacAddress            IpAddress         Lease(sec)  Type            VLAN  Interface
-----------------     ----------------  ----------  -------------   ----  ---------------
-----
00:0B:FD:67:65:00     150.1.1.11        14149       dhcp-snooping   100   Port-channel10
Total number of bindings: 1
```

Task 5

The requirements of this task are straightforward. In order to prevent R2 from being a transit router, even in the event of an R1-R3 link failure, you need to configure this router as a stub router. Additionally, R4 should also be configured as a stub router that will receive routes but never advertise any. This task is completed as follows:

```
R1(config)#router eigrp 1
R1(config-router)#no auto-summary
R1(config-router)#network 150.0.0.1 0.0.0.0
R1(config-router)#exit
R1(config)#router eigrp 2
R1(config-router)#no auto-summary
R1(config-router)#network 150.0.0.5 0.0.0.0
R1(config-router)#exit

R2(config)#router eigrp 1
R2(config-router)#no auto-summary
R2(config-router)#network 150.2.2.2 0.0.0.0
R2(config-router)#network 150.0.0.2 0.0.0.0
R2(config-router)#passive-interface fastethernet 0/0
R2(config-router)#eigrp stub
R2(config-router)#exit
R2(config)#router eigrp 2
R2(config-router)#no auto-summary
R2(config-router)#network 150.0.0.9 0.0.0.0
R2(config-router)#eigrp stub
R2(config-router)#exit

R3(config)#router eigrp 2
R3(config-router)#no auto-summary
R3(config-router)#network 150.0.0.6 0.0.0.0
R3(config-router)#network 150.0.0.10 0.0.0.0
R3(config-router)#exit
R3(config)#ip route 10.4.4.0 255.255.255.0 serial 1/2
R3(config)#ip route 10.4.4.0 255.255.255.0 serial 1/3
R3(config)#router eigrp 3
R3(config-router)#no auto-summary
R3(config-router)#network 150.0.0.13 0.0.0.0
R3(config-router)#network 150.0.0.17 0.0.0.0
R3(config-router)#redistribute static
R3(config-router)#redistribute connected
R3(config-router)#exit

R4(config)#router eigrp 3
R4(config-router)#no auto-summary
R4(config-router)#network 150.0.0.14 0.0.0.0
R4(config-router)#network 150.0.0.18 0.0.0.0
R4(config-router)#eigrp stub receive-only
R4(config-router)#exit
```

Following this, verify EIGRP configuration using the show ip eigrp commands:

```
R1#show ip eigrp neighbors
IP-EIGRP neighbors for process 1
H   Address               Interface       Hold Uptime    SRTT  RTO  Q   Seq
                                          (sec)          (ms)       Cnt Num
0   150.0.0.2             Se0/0            12  00:17:26    2    200  0   6
```

```
IP-EIGRP neighbors for process 2
H   Address                    Interface      Hold Uptime     SRTT    RTO  Q  Seq
                                              (sec)           (ms)         Cnt Num
0   150.0.0.6                  Se0/1            14 00:16:04     10     200  0  4

R2#show ip eigrp neighbors
IP-EIGRP neighbors for process 1
H   Address                    Interface      Hold Uptime     SRTT    RTO  Q  Seq
                                              (sec)           (ms)         Cnt Num
0   150.0.0.1                  Se0/0            10 00:17:32      2     200  0  7

IP-EIGRP neighbors for process 2
H   Address                    Interface      Hold Uptime     SRTT    RTO  Q  Seq
                                              (sec)           (ms)         Cnt Num
0   150.0.0.10                 Se0/1            13 00:16:06     13     200  0  7

R3#show ip eigrp neighbors
IP-EIGRP neighbors for process 2
H   Address                    Interface      Hold Uptime     SRTT    RTO  Q  Seq
                                              (sec)           (ms)         Cnt Num
1   150.0.0.9                  Se1/1            11 00:16:08     11    1710  0  3
0   150.0.0.5                  Se1/0            12 00:16:14     10    1140  0  3

IP-EIGRP neighbors for process 3
H   Address                    Interface      Hold Uptime     SRTT    RTO  Q  Seq
                                              (sec)           (ms)         Cnt Num
1   150.0.0.18                 Se1/3            11 00:05:43     14    1140  0  17
0   150.0.0.14                 Se1/2            10 00:13:14     13    1140  0  18

R4#show ip eigrp neighbors
IP-EIGRP neighbors for process 3
H   Address                    Interface      Hold Uptime     SRTT    RTO  Q  Seq
                                              (sec)           (ms)         Cnt Num
1   150.0.0.17                 Se0/1            10 00:05:46     14     200  0  20
0   150.0.0.13                 Se0/0            11 00:13:17     15     200  0  21
```

Task 6

When completing this task, keep in mind that you should NOT configure redistribution on R2 as this is a sub router under both EIGRP autonomous systems:

```
R1(config)#router eigrp 1
R1(config-router)#redistribute eigrp 2
R1(config-router)#exit
R1(config)#router eigrp 2
R1(config-router)#redistribute eigrp 1
R1(config-router)#exit
R1(config)#interface serial 0/0
R1(config-if)#ip summary-address eigrp 1 0.0.0.0 0.0.0.0
R1(config-if)#exit
R1(config)#interface serial 0/1
R1(config-if)#ip summary-address eigrp 2 0.0.0.0 0.0.0.0
R1(config-if)#exit

R3(config)#router eigrp 2
R3(config-router)#redistribute connected
R3(config-router)#redistribute static
R3(config-router)#exit
R3(config)#router eigrp 3
R3(config-router)#redistribute eigrp 2
R3(config-router)#exit
```

Finally, configure a static default route on DLS1 to ensure that this is reachable from all the other devices. DLS2 has a default received via DHCP so this step in not necessary:

```
DLS1(config)#ip route 0.0.0.0 0.0.0.0 vlan 100 150.1.1.1
```

Next, verify routing using the show ip route command on all routers:

```
R1#show ip route eigrp
     10.0.0.0/24 is subnetted, 2 subnets
D EX   10.4.4.0 [170/21024000] via 150.0.0.6, 00:01:41, Serial0/1
D EX   10.3.3.0 [170/2172416] via 150.0.0.6, 00:01:49, Serial0/1
     150.0.0.0/30 is subnetted, 5 subnets
D EX   150.0.0.16 [170/21024000] via 150.0.0.6, 00:01:49, Serial0/1
D EX   150.0.0.12 [170/21024000] via 150.0.0.6, 00:01:49, Serial0/1
D      150.0.0.8 [90/21024000] via 150.0.0.6, 00:21:14, Serial0/1
```

```
         150.2.0.0/24 is subnetted, 1 subnets
D          150.2.2.0 [90/2172416] via 150.0.0.2, 00:22:40, Serial0/0
D*      0.0.0.0/0 is a summary, 00:01:49, Null0

R2#show ip route eigrp
         10.0.0.0/24 is subnetted, 2 subnets
D EX     10.4.4.0 [170/21024000] via 150.0.0.10, 00:01:49, Serial0/1
D EX     10.3.3.0 [170/2172416] via 150.0.0.10, 00:01:58, Serial0/1
         150.0.0.0/30 is subnetted, 5 subnets
D EX     150.0.0.16 [170/21024000] via 150.0.0.10, 00:01:58, Serial0/1
D        150.0.0.4 [90/21024000] via 150.0.0.10, 00:21:22, Serial0/1
D EX     150.0.0.12 [170/21024000] via 150.0.0.10, 00:01:58, Serial0/1
D*      0.0.0.0/0 [90/2681856] via 150.0.0.1, 00:01:58, Serial0/0

R3#show ip route eigrp
D*EX 0.0.0.0/0 [170/21024000] via 150.0.0.5, 00:03:25, Serial1/0

R4#show ip route eigrp
         10.0.0.0/24 is subnetted, 2 subnets
D EX     10.3.3.0 [170/2172416] via 150.0.0.17, 00:09:06, Serial0/1
                  [170/2172416] via 150.0.0.13, 00:09:06, Serial0/0
         150.0.0.0/30 is subnetted, 4 subnets
D EX     150.0.0.4 [170/21024000] via 150.0.0.17, 00:09:06, Serial0/1
                   [170/21024000] via 150.0.0.13, 00:09:06, Serial0/0
D EX     150.0.0.8 [170/21024000] via 150.0.0.17, 00:09:06, Serial0/1
                   [170/21024000] via 150.0.0.13, 00:09:06, Serial0/0
D*EX 0.0.0.0/0 [170/21536000] via 150.0.0.17, 00:01:42, Serial0/1
                   [170/21536000] via 150.0.0.13, 00:01:42, Serial0/0
```

Complete this task by pinging DLS2 from any other device; for example, the ping from router R4 should be successful as illustrated below:

```
R4#ping 150.1.1.11 source fastethernet 0/0 size 1500 repeat 10

Type escape sequence to abort.
Sending 10, 1500-byte ICMP Echos to 150.1.1.11, timeout is 2 seconds:
Packet sent with a source address of 10.4.4.4
!!!!!!!!!!
Success rate is 100 percent (10/10), round-trip min/avg/max = 380/382/384 ms
```

Task 6

To complete this task, you need to configure a Loopback interface on R2 and advertise it via EIGRP. Next, enable PIM Sparse-Mode on all interfaces in the path. Finally, join R1s LAN interface to Multicast group 227.1.1.1 and verify your solution by pinging this group from all other devices within the network. This task is completed as follows:

```
R1(config)#ip multicast-routing
R1(config)#interface fastethernet 0/0
R1(config-if)#ip pim sparse-mode
R1(config-if)#ip igmp join-group 227.1.1.1
R1(config-if)#exit
R1(config)#interface serial 0/0
R1(config-if)#ip pim sparse-mode
R1(config-if)#exit
R1(config)#interface serial 0/1
R1(config-if)#ip pim sparse-mode
R1(config-if)#exit
R1(config)#ip pim rp-address 2.2.2.2

R2(config)#ip multicast-routing
R2(config)#interface loopback 0
R2(config-if)#ip address 2.2.2.2 255.255.255.255
R2(config-if)#ip pim sparse-mode
R2(config-if)#exit
R2(config)#router eigrp 1
R2(config-router)#network 2.2.2.2 0.0.0.0
R2(config-router)#exit
R2(config)#router eigrp 2
R2(config-router)#network 2.2.2.2 0.0.0.0
R2(config-router)#exit
R2(config-if)#exit
R2(config)#interface serial 0/0
```

```
R2(config-if)#ip pim sparse-mode
R2(config-if)#exit
R2(config)#interface serial 0/1
R2(config-if)#ip pim sparse-mode
R2(config-if)#exit
R2(config)#ip pim rp-address 2.2.2.2

R3(config)#ip multicast-routing
R3(config)#interface serial 1/0
R3(config-if)#ip pim sparse-mode
R3(config-if)#exit
R3(config)#interface serial 1/1
R3(config-if)#ip pim sparse-mode
R3(config-if)#exit
R3(config)#interface serial 1/2
R3(config-if)#ip pim sparse-mode
R3(config-if)#exit
R3(config)#interface serial 1/3
R3(config-if)#ip pim sparse-mode
R3(config-if)#exit
R3(config)#interface fastethernet 0/0
R3(config-if)#ip pim sparse-mode
R3(config-if)#exit
R3(config)#ip pim rp-address 2.2.2.2
R3(config)#exit

DLS1(config)#ip multicast-routing
DLS1(config)#interface vlan 100
DLS1(config-if)#ip pim sparse-mode
DLS1(config-if)#exit
DLS1(config)#ip pim rp-address 2.2.2.2
DLS1(config)#exit

DLS2(config)#ip multicast-routing
DLS2(config)#interface vlan 100
DLS2(config-if)#ip pim sparse-mode
DLS2(config-if)#exit
DLS2(config)#ip pim rp-address 2.2.2.2
DLS2(config)#exit
```

Verify your configuration using the show ip igmp and show ip pim commands:

```
R1#show ip igmp interface fastethernet 0/0
FastEthernet0/0 is up, line protocol is up
  Internet address is 150.1.1.1/24
  IGMP is enabled on interface
  Current IGMP host version is 2
  Current IGMP router version is 2
  IGMP query interval is 60 seconds
  IGMP querier timeout is 120 seconds
  IGMP max query response time is 10 seconds
  Last member query count is 2
  Last member query response interval is 1000 ms
  Inbound IGMP access group is not set
  IGMP activity: 2 joins, 0 leaves
  Multicast routing is enabled on interface
  Multicast TTL threshold is 0
  Multicast designated router (DR) is 150.1.1.11
  IGMP querying router is 150.1.1.1 (this system)
  Multicast groups joined by this system (number of users):
      224.0.1.40(1)   227.1.1.1(1)

DLS1#show ip pim rp
Group: 227.1.1.1, RP: 2.2.2.2, uptime 00:06:27, expires never
Group: 224.0.1.40, RP: 2.2.2.2, uptime 00:06:27, expires never

DLS2#show ip pim rp
Group: 227.1.1.1, RP: 2.2.2.2, uptime 00:01:13, expires never
Group: 224.0.1.40, RP: 2.2.2.2, uptime 00:01:13, expires never

R2#show ip pim rp
Group: 227.1.1.1, RP: 2.2.2.2, next RP-reachable in 00:00:21
Group: 224.0.1.40, RP: 2.2.2.2, next RP-reachable in 00:00:21

R3#show ip pim rp
Group: 227.1.1.1, RP: 2.2.2.2, v2, uptime 00:00:32, expires never
Group: 224.0.1.40, RP: 2.2.2.2, v2, uptime 00:05:56, expires never
```

Finally, verify reachability to the Multicast group using a simple ping:

```
R2#ping 227.1.1.1

Type escape sequence to abort.
Sending 1, 100-byte ICMP Echos to 227.1.1.1, timeout is 2 seconds:

Reply to request 0 from 150.0.0.1, 4 ms
Reply to request 0 from 150.0.0.1, 36 ms
Reply to request 0 from 150.0.0.1, 8 ms

R3#ping 227.1.1.1

Type escape sequence to abort.
Sending 1, 100-byte ICMP Echos to 227.1.1.1, timeout is 2 seconds:

Reply to request 0 from 150.0.0.5, 20 ms

DLS1#ping 227.1.1.1

Type escape sequence to abort.
Sending 1, 100-byte ICMP Echos to 227.1.1.1, timeout is 2 seconds:

Reply to request 0 from 150.1.1.1, 8 ms

DLS2#ping 227.1.1.1

Type escape sequence to abort.
Sending 1, 100-byte ICMP Echos to 227.1.1.1, timeout is 2 seconds:

Reply to request 0 from 150.1.1.1, 8 ms
```

Task 7

In order to complete this task without using ACLs for classification, you need to use NBAR on the router. This task is completed as follows:

```
R1(config)#ip cef
R1(config)#class-map VIDEO
R1(config-cmap)#match protocol rtp video
R1(config-cmap)#exit
R1(config)#policy-map WAN-QoS-Outbound
R1(config-pmap)#class VIDEO
R1(config-pmap-c)#bandwidth percent 40
R1(config-pmap-c)#exit
R1(config-pmap)#exit
R1(config)#interface serial 0/0
R1(config-if)#service-policy output WAN-QoS-Outbound
R1(config-if)#exit
R1(config)#interface serial 0/1
R1(config-if)#service-policy output WAN-QoS-Outbound
R1(config-if)#exit
```

Verify your configuration using the show policy-map commands:

```
R1#show policy-map WAN-QoS-Outbound
  Policy Map WAN-QoS-Outbound
    Class VIDEO
      Bandwidth 40 (%) Max Threshold 64 (packets)

R1#show policy-map interface serial 0/0 output
 Serial0/0

  Service-policy output: WAN-QoS-Outbound

    Class-map: VIDEO (match-all)
      0 packets, 0 bytes
      5 minute offered rate 0 bps, drop rate 0 bps
      Match: protocol rtp video
      Queueing
        Output Queue: Conversation 265
        Bandwidth 40 (%)
        Bandwidth 617 (kbps)Max Threshold 64 (packets)
        (pkts matched/bytes matched) 0/0
        (depth/total drops/no-buffer drops) 0/0/0
```

```
    Class-map: class-default (match-any)
      45 packets, 2880 bytes
      5 minute offered rate 0 bps, drop rate 0 bps
      Match: any
```

Task 8

To complete this task, you need to use NBAR and define a custom application for which you will modify the existing QoS policy. This task is completed as follows:

```
R1(config)#ip nbar port-map custom-01 tcp 2023 3023 4023 5023
R1(config)#class-map APPLICATION
R1(config-cmap)#match protocol custom-01
R1(config-cmap)#exit
R1(config)#policy-map WAN-QoS-Outbound
R1(config-pmap)#class APPLICATION
R1(config-pmap-c)#bandwidth percent 10
R1(config-pmap-c)#exit
```

Verify your NBAR configuration using the show ip nbar commands:

```
R1#show ip nbar port-map custom-01
port-map custom-01                    tcp 2023 3023 4023 5023
```

Verify QoS configuration using the show policy-map commands:

```
R1#show policy-map WAN-QoS-Outbound
  Policy Map WAN-QoS-Outbound
    Class VIDEO
      Bandwidth 40 (%) Max Threshold 64 (packets)
    Class APPLICATION
      Bandwidth 10 (%) Max Threshold 64 (packets)

R1#show policy-map interface serial 0/1 output
 Serial0/1

  Service-policy output: WAN-QoS-Outbound

    Class-map: VIDEO (match-all)
      0 packets, 0 bytes
      5 minute offered rate 0 bps, drop rate 0 bps
      Match: protocol rtp video
      Queueing
        Output Queue: Conversation 265
        Bandwidth 40 (%)
        Bandwidth 617 (kbps)Max Threshold 64 (packets)
        (pkts matched/bytes matched) 0/0
        (depth/total drops/no-buffer drops) 0/0/0

    Class-map: APPLICATION (match-all)
      0 packets, 0 bytes
      5 minute offered rate 0 bps, drop rate 0 bps
      Match: protocol custom-01
      Queueing
        Output Queue: Conversation 266
        Bandwidth 10 (%)
        Bandwidth 154 (kbps)Max Threshold 64 (packets)
        (pkts matched/bytes matched) 0/0
        (depth/total drops/no-buffer drops) 0/0/0

    Class-map: class-default (match-any)
      235 packets, 15208 bytes
      5 minute offered rate 0 bps, drop rate 0 bps
      Match: any
```

Task 9

Please refer to previous tasks for basic IPv6 addressing. Following completion, verify your configuration using the show ipv6 commands:

```
R2#show ipv6 interface fastethernet 0/0
FastEthernet0/0 is up, line protocol is up
  IPv6 is enabled, link-local address is FE80::20D:28FF:FE9E:F940
```

```
 Global unicast address(es):
   3FFE:2222:2222:2222::2, subnet is 3FFE:2222:2222:2222::/64
 Joined group address(es):
   FF02::1
   FF02::2
   FF02::1:FF00:2
   FF02::1:FF9E:F940
 MTU is 1500 bytes

[Truncated Output]

R3#show ipv6 interface fastethernet 0/0
FastEthernet0/0 is up, line protocol is up
  IPv6 is enabled, link-local address is FE80::213:7FFF:FEAF:3E00
  Global unicast address(es):
    3FFE:3333:3333:3333::3, subnet is 3FFE:3333:3333:3333::/64
  Joined group address(es):
    FF02::1
    FF02::2
    FF02::1:FF00:3
    FF02::1:FFAF:3E00
  MTU is 1500 bytes

[Truncated Output]
```

To complete the second part of this task, you need to configure a static Tunnel and then enable OSPFv3 across this tunnel. Keep in mind that because IPv6 IGPs use the Link Local address as the NEXT-HOP IPv6 address, you do not necessarily need to assign a global IPv6 subnet to the tunnel. This is completed as follows:

```
R2(config)#interface tunnel 0
R2(config-if)#tunnel source loopback 0
R2(config-if)#tunnel destination 3.3.3.3
R2(config-if)#tunnel mode ipv6ip
R2(config-if)#ipv6 enable
R2(config-if)#ipv6 ospf 2 area 0
R2(config)#interface fastethernet 0/0
R2(config-if)#ipv6 ospf 2 area 2
R2(config-if)#exit
R2(config)#ipv6 router ospf 2
R2(config-rtr)#router-id 2.2.2.2
R2(config-rtr)#exit

R3(config)#interface loopback 0
R3(config-if)#ip address 3.3.3.3 255.255.255.255
R3(config-if)#exit
R3(config)#router eigrp 2
R3(config-router)#network 3.3.3.3 0.0.0.0
R3(config-router)#exit
R3(config)#router eigrp 3
R3(config-router)#network 3.3.3.3 0.0.0.0
R3(config-router)#exit

R3(config)#interface tunnel 0
R3(config-if)#tunnel source loopback 0
R3(config-if)#tunnel destination 2.2.2.2
R3(config-if)#tunnel mode ipv6ip
R3(config-if)#ipv6 enable
R3(config-if)#ipv6 ospf 3 area 0
R3(config-if)#exit
R3(config)#interface fastethernet 0/0
R3(config-if)#ipv6 ospf 3 area 3
R3(config-if)#exit
R3(config)#ipv6 router ospf 3
R3(config-rtr)#router-id 3.3.3.3
R3(config-rtr)#exit
```

Following this, verify your Tunnel states using the show interfaces and show ipv6 interface commands on both of the routers:

```
R2#show interfaces tunnel 0
Tunnel0 is up, line protocol is up
  Hardware is Tunnel
  MTU 1514 bytes, BW 9 Kbit/sec, DLY 500000 usec,
     reliability 255/255, txload 1/255, rxload 1/255
  Encapsulation TUNNEL, loopback not set
  Keepalive not set
```

```
Tunnel source 2.2.2.2 (Loopback0), destination 3.3.3.3
Tunnel protocol/transport IPv6/IP
Tunnel TTL 255
Fast tunneling enabled
Tunnel transmit bandwidth 8000 (kbps)
Tunnel receive bandwidth 8000 (kbps)

[Truncated Output]

R2#show ipv6 interface tunnel 0
Tunnel0 is up, line protocol is up
  IPv6 is enabled, link-local address is FE80::202:202
  No global unicast address is configured
  Joined group address(es):
    FF02::1
    FF02::2
    FF02::5
    FF02::1:FF02:202
  MTU is 1480 bytes
  ICMP error messages limited to one every 100 milliseconds
  ICMP redirects are enabled
  ND DAD is enabled, number of DAD attempts: 1
  ND reachable time is 30000 milliseconds
  Hosts use stateless autoconfig for addresses.
```

Verify OSPFv3 adjacency states using the show ipv6 ospf neighbor command:

```
R2#show ipv6 ospf neighbor

Neighbor ID     Pri   State         Dead Time   Interface ID    Interface
3.3.3.3           1   FULL/  -      00:00:39    24              Tunnel0

R3#show ipv6 ospf neighbor

Neighbor ID     Pri   State         Dead Time   Interface ID    Interface
2.2.2.2           1   FULL/  -      00:00:37    10              Tunnel0
```

Verify IPv6 routing using the show ipv6 route commands:

```
R2#show ipv6 route ospf
IPv6 Routing Table - 5 entries
Codes: C - Connected, L - Local, S - Static, R - RIP, B - BGP
       U - Per-user Static route
       I1 - ISIS L1, I2 - ISIS L2, IA - ISIS interarea, IS - ISIS summary
       O - OSPF intra, OI - OSPF inter, OE1 - OSPF ext 1, OE2 - OSPF ext 2
       ON1 - OSPF NSSA ext 1, ON2 - OSPF NSSA ext 2
OI  3FFE:3333:3333:3333::/64 [110/11112]
     via FE80::303:303, Tunnel0

R3#show ipv6 route ospf
IPv6 Routing Table - 5 entries
Codes: C - Connected, L - Local, S - Static, R - RIP, B - BGP
       U - Per-user Static route
       I1 - ISIS L1, I2 - ISIS L2, IA - ISIS interarea, IS - ISIS summary
       O - OSPF intra, OI - OSPF inter, OE1 - OSPF ext 1, OE2 - OSPF ext 2
       ON1 - OSPF NSSA ext 1, ON2 - OSPF NSSA ext 2
OI  3FFE:2222:2222:2222::/64 [110/11112]
     via FE80::202:202, Tunnel0
```

Finally, verify LAN-to-LAN connectivity between the IPv6 subnets using an extended ping:

```
R2#$333:3333:3333::3 source 3FFE:2222:2222:2222::2 repeat 10 size 1500

Type escape sequence to abort.
Sending 10, 1500-byte ICMP Echos to 3FFE:3333:3333:3333::3, timeout is 2 seconds:
Packet sent with a source address of 3FFE:2222:2222:2222::2
!!!!!!!!!!
Success rate is 100 percent (10/10), round-trip min/avg/max = 208/208/212 ms
```

Task 10

OSPFv3 supports both authentication and encryption for security. To configure OSPFv3 area authentication, you need to use the area <area> authentication ipsec spi <size> [md5|sha1] <key> OSPFv3 configuration command. This task is completed as follows:

```
R2(config)#ipv6 router ospf 2
R2(config-rtr)#$entication ipsec spi 678 md5 1234567890abcdef1234567890abcdef
R2(config-rtr)#exit

R3(config)#ipv6 router ospf 3
R3(config-rtr)#$entication ipsec spi 678 md5 1234567890abcdef1234567890abcdef
R3(config-rtr)#exit
```

Verify OSPFv3 area authentication using the **show ipv6 ospf** command:

```
R3#show ipv6 ospf
 Routing Process "ospfv3 3" with ID 3.3.3.3
 It is an area border router
 SPF schedule delay 5 secs, Hold time between two SPFs 10 secs
 Minimum LSA interval 5 secs. Minimum LSA arrival 1 secs
 LSA group pacing timer 240 secs
 Interface flood pacing timer 33 msecs
 Retransmission pacing timer 66 msecs
 Number of external LSA 0. Checksum Sum 0x000000
 Number of areas in this router is 2. 2 normal 0 stub 0 nssa
 Reference bandwidth unit is 100 mbps
    Area BACKBONE(0)
        Number of interfaces in this area is 1
        MD5 Authentication, SPI 678
        SPF algorithm executed 3 times
        Number of LSA 6. Checksum Sum 0x032E78
        Number of DCbitless LSA 0
        Number of indication LSA 0
        Number of DoNotAge LSA 0
        Flood list length 0
    Area 3
        Number of interfaces in this area is 1
        SPF algorithm executed 2 times
        Number of LSA 4. Checksum Sum 0x01CA07
        Number of DCbitless LSA 0
        Number of indication LSA 0
        Number of DoNotAge LSA 0
        Flood list length 0
```

By default, because IPv6 uses built-in IPsec functions, Cisco IOS software automatically creates IPsec policies for the configured authentication. The policy can be viewed using the show crypto ipsec sa [interface <name>] command on the router(s). Authentication Header (AH) is used. If you configure encryption, then Encapsulating Security Payload (ESP) will be used instead. Check the relevant SA states based on your configuration:

```
R3#show crypto ipsec sa interface tunnel 0

interface: Tunnel0
    Crypto map tag: (none), local addr FE80::303:303

    IPsecv6 policy name: OSPFv3-3-678
    IPsecv6-created ACL name: Tunnel0-ipsecv6-ACL

    protected vrf: (none)
    local  ident (addr/mask/prot/port): (FE80::/10/89/0)
    remote ident (addr/mask/prot/port): (::/0/89/0)
    current_peer :: port 500
      PERMIT, flags={origin_is_acl,}
     #pkts encaps: 12, #pkts encrypt: 0, #pkts digest: 12
     #pkts decaps: 12, #pkts decrypt: 0, #pkts verify: 12
     #pkts compressed: 0, #pkts decompressed: 0
     #pkts not compressed: 0, #pkts compr. failed: 0
     #pkts not decompressed: 0, #pkts decompress failed: 0
     #send errors 0, #recv errors 0

      local crypto endpt.: FE80::303:303, remote crypto endpt.: ::
      path mtu 1514, ip mtu 1514, ip mtu idb Tunnel0
      current outbound spi: 0x2A6(678)

      inbound esp sas:

      inbound ah sas:
       spi: 0x2A6(678)
         transform: ah-md5-hmac ,
```

```
        in use settings ={Transport, }
        conn id: 2001, flow_id: SW:1, crypto map: (none)
        no sa timing
        replay detection support: N
        Status: ACTIVE

   inbound pcp sas:

   outbound esp sas:

   outbound ah sas:
    spi: 0x2A6(678)
        transform: ah-md5-hmac ,
        in use settings ={Transport, }
        conn id: 2002, flow_id: SW:2, crypto map: (none)
        no sa timing
        replay detection support: N
        Status: ACTIVE

   outbound pcp sas:
```

Additionally, you can also view the configuration parameters for the applied policy using the `show crypto ipsec policy` command on the router. The policy name, by default, will be OSPFv3-<process ID>-<SPI>. For example, on R1, the applied policy name will be OSPFv3-R1-678. This is validated and illustrated in the following output:

```
R3#show crypto ipsec policy
Crypto IPsec client security policy data

Policy name:       OSPFv3-3-678
Policy refcount:   1
Inbound  AH SPI:   678 (0x2A6)
Outbound AH SPI:   678 (0x2A6)
Inbound  AH Key:   1234567890ABCDEF1234567890ABCDEF
Outbound AH Key:   1234567890ABCDEF1234567890ABCDEF
Transform set:     ah-md5-hmac
```

Task 11

To complete this task, you need to enable the protected port feature on these ports. In addition, VMPS on the switch. This task is completed as follows:

```
ALS1(config)#vmps server 150.1.1.254
ALS1(config)#$thernet 0/2 , fastethernet 0/5 - 6, fastethernet 0/9 - 10
ALS1(config-if-range)#switchport mode access
ALS1(config-if-range)#switchport access vlan dynamic
ALS1(config-if-range)#switchport protected
ALS1(config-if-range)#exit
```

Verify basic Layer 2 parameters using the `show interfaces switchport` command:

```
ALS1#show interfaces fastethernet 0/2 switchport
Name: Fa0/2
Switchport: Enabled
Administrative Mode: dynamic access
Operational Mode: down
Administrative Trunking Encapsulation: dot1q
Negotiation of Trunking: Off
Access Mode VLAN: unassigned
Trunking Native Mode VLAN: 1 (default)
Voice VLAN: none
Administrative private-vlan host-association: none
Administrative private-vlan mapping: none
Administrative private-vlan trunk native VLAN: none
Administrative private-vlan trunk encapsulation: dot1q
Administrative private-vlan trunk normal VLANs: none
Administrative private-vlan trunk private VLANs: none
Operational private-vlan: none
Trunking VLANs Enabled: ALL
Pruning VLANs Enabled: 2-1001
Capture Mode Disabled
Capture VLANs Allowed: ALL
Protected: true
Appliance trust: none
```

Verify VMPS configuration and operation using the show vmps commands:

```
ALS1#show vmps
VQP Client Status:
---------------------
VMPS VQP Version:   1
Reconfirm Interval: 60 min
Server Retry Count: 3
VMPS domain server: 150.1.1.254 (primary, current)

Reconfirmation status
---------------------
VMPS Action:        other
```

Task 12

To complete this task, you need to enable storm control (port-based traffic control) and then enable SNMP so that traps are sent to server 150.1.1.254. This task is completed as follows:

```
ALS2(config)#interface range fastethernet 0/1 - 9
ALS2(config-if-range)#storm-control broadcast level 5
ALS2(config-if-range)#storm-control multicast level 20
ALS2(config-if-range)#storm-control unicast level 80
ALS2(config-if-range)#storm-control action trap
ALS2(config-if-range)#exit
ALS2(config)#snmp-server community CCNP2011 RO
ALS2(config)#snmp-server host 150.1.1.254 traps CCNP2011
ALS2(config)#snmp-server enable traps
```

Verify storm control configuration using the show storm-control commands:

```
ALS2#show storm-control
Interface  Filter State   Trap State    Upper    Lower    Current  Traps Sent
---------  ------------   -----------   -------  -------   -------  ----------
Fa0/1      Forwarding     Below rising   5.00%    5.00%    0.00%        0
Fa0/2      Forwarding     Below rising   5.00%    5.00%    0.00%        0
Fa0/3      Forwarding     Below rising   5.00%    5.00%    0.00%        0
Fa0/4      Forwarding     Below rising   5.00%    5.00%    0.00%        0
Fa0/5      Forwarding     Below rising   5.00%    5.00%    0.00%        0
Fa0/6      Forwarding     Below rising   5.00%    5.00%    0.00%        0
Fa0/7      Forwarding     Below rising   5.00%    5.00%    0.00%        0
Fa0/8      Forwarding     Below rising   5.00%    5.00%    0.00%        0
Fa0/9      Forwarding     Below rising   5.00%    5.00%    0.00%        0
Fa0/10     inactive       inactive     100.00%  100.00%    N/A          0
Fa0/11     inactive       inactive     100.00%  100.00%    N/A          0
Fa0/12     inactive       inactive     100.00%  100.00%    N/A          0
```

Verify SNMP configuration using the show snmp commands:

```
ALS2#show snmp
Chassis: FOC0620Y1FR
0 SNMP packets input
    0 Bad SNMP version errors
    0 Unknown community name
    0 Illegal operation for community name supplied
    0 Encoding errors
    0 Number of requested variables
    0 Number of altered variables
    0 Get-request PDUs
    0 Get-next PDUs
    0 Set-request PDUs
0 SNMP packets output
    0 Too big errors (Maximum packet size 1500)
    0 No such name errors
    0 Bad values errors
    0 General errors
    0 Response PDUs
    0 Trap PDUs
SNMP global trap: enabled

SNMP logging: enabled
    Logging to 150.1.1.254.162, 0/10, 0 sent, 0 dropped.
SNMP agent enabled
```

FINAL ROUTER CONFIGURATIONS

R1

```
R1#term len 0
R1#sh run
Building configuration...

Current configuration : 1862 bytes
!
version 12.4
service timestamps debug datetime msec
service timestamps log datetime msec
no service password-encryption
!
hostname R1
!
boot-start-marker
boot-end-marker
!
no logging console
!
no aaa new-model
no network-clock-participate slot 1
no network-clock-participate wic 0
ip cef
!
ip nbar port-map custom-01 tcp 2023 3023 4023 5023
no ip dhcp use vrf connected
ip dhcp excluded-address 150.1.1.1 150.1.1.10
ip dhcp ping packets 10
!
ip dhcp pool VLAN-100-DHCP-POOL
   network 150.1.1.0 255.255.255.0
   default-router 150.1.1.1
   domain-name howtonetwork.net
   dns-server 150.1.1.1
   lease 0 4
!
no ip domain lookup
ip multicast-routing
ip auth-proxy max-nodata-conns 3
ip admission max-nodata-conns 3
!
class-map match-all VIDEO
 match protocol rtp video
class-map match-all APPLICATION
 match protocol custom-01
!
policy-map WAN-QoS-Outbound
 class VIDEO
  bandwidth percent 40
 class APPLICATION
  bandwidth percent 10
!
interface FastEthernet0/0
 ip address 150.1.1.1 255.255.255.0
 ip pim sparse-mode
 ip igmp join-group 227.1.1.1
 duplex auto
 speed auto
!
interface Serial0/0
 ip address 150.0.0.1 255.255.255.252
 ip pim sparse-mode
 ip summary-address eigrp 1 0.0.0.0 0.0.0.0 5
 clock rate 2000000
 service-policy output WAN-QoS-Outbound
!
interface Serial0/1
 ip address 150.0.0.5 255.255.255.252
 ip pim sparse-mode
 ip summary-address eigrp 2 0.0.0.0 0.0.0.0 5
 service-policy output WAN-QoS-Outbound
!
router eigrp 1
 redistribute eigrp 2
 network 150.0.0.1 0.0.0.0
```

```
 no auto-summary
!
router eigrp 2
 redistribute eigrp 1
 network 150.0.0.5 0.0.0.0
 no auto-summary
!
ip forward-protocol nd
!
no ip http server
no ip http secure-server
ip pim rp-address 2.2.2.2
!
control-plane
!
line con 0
line aux 0
line vty 0 4
 password cisco
 login
!
end

R1#
```

R2

```
R2#term len 0
R2#sh run
Building configuration...

Current configuration : 1665 bytes
!
version 12.4
service timestamps debug datetime msec
service timestamps log datetime msec
no service password-encryption
!
hostname R2
!
boot-start-marker
boot-end-marker
!
no logging console
!
no aaa new-model
no network-clock-participate slot 1
no network-clock-participate wic 0
ip cef
!
no ip domain lookup
ip multicast-routing
ip auth-proxy max-nodata-conns 3
ip admission max-nodata-conns 3
!
ipv6 unicast-routing
!
interface Loopback0
 ip address 2.2.2.2 255.255.255.255
 ip pim sparse-mode
!
interface Tunnel0
 no ip address
 ipv6 enable
 ipv6 ospf 2 area 0
 tunnel source Loopback0
 tunnel destination 3.3.3.3
 tunnel mode ipv6ip
!
interface FastEthernet0/0
 ip address 150.2.2.2 255.255.255.0
 loopback
 duplex auto
 speed auto
 ipv6 address 3FFE:2222:2222:2222::2/64
 ipv6 ospf 2 area 2
 no keepalive
!
```

```
interface Serial0/0
 ip address 150.0.0.2 255.255.255.252
 ip pim sparse-mode
!
interface Serial0/1
 ip address 150.0.0.9 255.255.255.252
 ip pim sparse-mode
!
router eigrp 1
 passive-interface FastEthernet0/0
 network 2.2.2.2 0.0.0.0
 network 150.0.0.2 0.0.0.0
 network 150.2.2.2 0.0.0.0
 no auto-summary
 eigrp stub connected summary
!
router eigrp 2
 network 2.2.2.2 0.0.0.0
 network 150.0.0.9 0.0.0.0
 no auto-summary
 eigrp stub connected summary
!
ip forward-protocol nd
!
no ip http server
no ip http secure-server
ip pim rp-address 2.2.2.2
!
ipv6 router ospf 2
 router-id 2.2.2.2
 log-adjacency-changes
 area 0 authentication ipsec spi 678 md5 1234567890ABCDEF1234567890ABCDEF
!
control-plane
!
line con 0
line aux 0
line vty 0 4
 password cisco
 login
!

R2#
```

R3

```
R3#term len 0
R3#sh run
Building configuration...

Current configuration : 2198 bytes
!
version 12.4
service timestamps debug datetime msec
service timestamps log datetime msec
no service password-encryption
!
hostname R3
!
boot-start-marker
boot-end-marker
!
no logging console
!
no aaa new-model
no network-clock-participate slot 1
no network-clock-participate wic 0
ip cef
!
no ip domain lookup
ip multicast-routing
ip auth-proxy max-nodata-conns 3
ip admission max-nodata-conns 3
!
ipv6 unicast-routing
!
interface Loopback0
 ip address 3.3.3.3 255.255.255.255
```

```
!
interface Tunnel0
 no ip address
 ipv6 enable
 ipv6 ospf 3 area 0
 tunnel source Loopback0
 tunnel destination 2.2.2.2
 tunnel mode ipv6ip
!
interface FastEthernet0/0
 ip address 10.3.3.3 255.255.255.0
 ip pim sparse-mode
 duplex auto
 speed auto
 ipv6 address 3FFE:3333:3333:3333::3/64
 ipv6 ospf 3 area 3
!
interface Serial1/0
 ip address 150.0.0.6 255.255.255.252
 ip pim sparse-mode
 clock rate 128000
!
interface Serial1/1
 ip address 150.0.0.10 255.255.255.252
 ip pim sparse-mode
 clock rate 128000
!
interface Serial1/2
 ip address 150.0.0.13 255.255.255.252
 ip pim sparse-mode
 clock rate 128000
!
interface Serial1/3
 ip address 150.0.0.17 255.255.255.252
 ip pim sparse-mode
 clock rate 128000
!
interface Serial1/4
 no ip address
 shutdown
!
interface Serial1/5
 no ip address
 shutdown
!
interface Serial1/6
 no ip address
 shutdown
!
interface Serial1/7
 no ip address
 shutdown
!
router eigrp 2
 redistribute connected
 redistribute static
 network 3.3.3.3 0.0.0.0
 network 150.0.0.6 0.0.0.0
 network 150.0.0.10 0.0.0.0
 no auto-summary
!
router eigrp 3
 redistribute connected
 redistribute static
 redistribute eigrp 2
 network 3.3.3.3 0.0.0.0
 network 150.0.0.13 0.0.0.0
 network 150.0.0.17 0.0.0.0
 no auto-summary
!
ip forward-protocol nd
ip route 10.4.4.0 255.255.255.0 Serial1/2
ip route 10.4.4.0 255.255.255.0 Serial1/3
!
no ip http server
no ip http secure-server
ip pim rp-address 2.2.2.2
!
ipv6 router ospf 3
 router-id 3.3.3.3
```

```
 log-adjacency-changes
 area 0 authentication ipsec spi 678 md5 1234567890ABCDEF1234567890ABCDEF
!
control-plane
!
line con 0
line aux 0
line vty 0 4
 password cisco
 login
!
end

R3#
```

R4

```
R4#term len 0
R4#sh run
Building configuration...

Current configuration : 938 bytes
!
version 12.4
service timestamps debug datetime msec
service timestamps log datetime msec
no service password-encryption
!
hostname R4
!
boot-start-marker
boot-end-marker
!
no logging console
!
no aaa new-model
no network-clock-participate slot 1
no network-clock-participate wic 0
ip cef
!
no ip domain lookup
ip auth-proxy max-nodata-conns 3
ip admission max-nodata-conns 3
!
interface FastEthernet0/0
 ip address 10.4.4.4 255.255.255.0
 duplex auto
 speed auto
!
interface Serial0/0
 ip address 150.0.0.14 255.255.255.252
!
interface Serial0/1
 ip address 150.0.0.18 255.255.255.252
!
router eigrp 3
 network 150.0.0.14 0.0.0.0
 network 150.0.0.18 0.0.0.0
 no auto-summary
 eigrp stub receive-only
!
ip forward-protocol nd
!
no ip http server
no ip http secure-server
!
control-plane
!
line con 0
line aux 0
line vty 0 4
 password cisco
 login
!
end

R4#
```

FINAL SWITCH CONFIGURATIONS

DLS1

```
DLS1#term len 0
DLS1#sh run
Building configuration...

Current configuration : 4814 bytes
!
version 12.2
no service pad
service timestamps debug datetime msec
service timestamps log datetime msec
no service password-encryption
!
hostname DLS1
!
no logging console
!
no aaa new-model
ip subnet-zero
ip routing
no ip domain-lookup
!
ip dhcp snooping vlan 100
no ip dhcp snooping information option
ip dhcp snooping
ip multicast-routing
vtp domain switch
vtp mode transparent
!
spanning-tree mode pvst
spanning-tree extend system-id
!
vlan internal allocation policy ascending
!
vlan 100
 name R1-VLAN
!
interface Port-channel10
 switchport access vlan 100
 switchport mode access
 ip verify source
!
interface FastEthernet0/1
 switchport mode dynamic desirable
 shutdown
!
interface FastEthernet0/2
 switchport mode dynamic desirable
 shutdown
!
interface FastEthernet0/3
 switchport mode dynamic desirable
 shutdown
!
interface FastEthernet0/4
 switchport mode dynamic desirable
 shutdown
!
interface FastEthernet0/5
 switchport mode dynamic desirable
 shutdown
!
interface FastEthernet0/6
 switchport mode dynamic desirable
 shutdown
!
interface FastEthernet0/7
 switchport trunk encapsulation dot1q
 switchport mode trunk
 ip dhcp snooping trust
!
interface FastEthernet0/8
 switchport trunk encapsulation dot1q
 switchport mode trunk
```

```
 ip dhcp snooping trust
!
interface FastEthernet0/9
 switchport mode dynamic desirable
 shutdown
!
interface FastEthernet0/10
 switchport mode dynamic desirable
 shutdown
!
interface FastEthernet0/11
 switchport access vlan 100
 switchport mode access
 channel-group 10 mode active
!
interface FastEthernet0/12
 switchport access vlan 100
 switchport mode access
 channel-group 10 mode active

[Truncated Output]

interface Vlan1
 no ip address
 shutdown
!
interface Vlan100
 ip address 150.1.1.2 255.255.255.0
 ip pim sparse-mode
!
ip classless
ip route 0.0.0.0 0.0.0.0 Vlan100 150.1.1.1
ip http server
ip http secure-server
!
ip pim rp-address 2.2.2.2
!
control-plane
!
line con 0
line vty 0 4
 privilege level 15
 password cisco
 login
line vty 5 15
 login
!
end

DLS1#
```

DLS2

```
DLS2#term len 0
DLS2#sh run
Building configuration...

Current configuration : 4572 bytes
!
version 12.2
no service pad
service timestamps debug datetime msec
service timestamps log datetime msec
no service password-encryption
!
hostname DLS2
!
no logging console
!
no aaa new-model
ip subnet-zero
ip routing
no ip domain-lookup
!
ip multicast-routing
vtp domain SWITCH
vtp mode transparent
!
```

```
spanning-tree mode pvst
spanning-tree extend system-id
!
vlan internal allocation policy ascending
!
vlan 100
 name R1-VLAN
!
interface Port-channel10
 switchport access vlan 100
 switchport mode access
!
interface FastEthernet0/1
 switchport mode dynamic desirable
 shutdown
!
interface FastEthernet0/2
 switchport mode dynamic desirable
 shutdown
!
interface FastEthernet0/3
 switchport mode dynamic desirable
 shutdown
!
interface FastEthernet0/4
 switchport mode dynamic desirable
 shutdown
!
interface FastEthernet0/5
 switchport mode dynamic desirable
 shutdown
!
interface FastEthernet0/6
 switchport mode dynamic desirable
 shutdown
!
interface FastEthernet0/7
 switchport mode dynamic desirable
 shutdown
!
interface FastEthernet0/8
 switchport mode dynamic desirable
 shutdown
!
interface FastEthernet0/9
 switchport mode dynamic desirable
 shutdown
!
interface FastEthernet0/10
 switchport mode dynamic desirable
 shutdown
!
interface FastEthernet0/11
 switchport access vlan 100
 switchport mode access
 channel-group 10 mode active
!
interface FastEthernet0/12
 switchport access vlan 100
 switchport mode access
 channel-group 10 mode active

[Truncated Output]

interface Vlan1
 no ip address
 shutdown
!
interface Vlan100
 ip address dhcp
 ip pim sparse-mode
!
ip classless
ip http server
ip http secure-server
!
ip pim rp-address 2.2.2.2
!
control-plane
```

```
!
line con 0
line vty 0 4
 privilege level 15
 password cisco
 login
line vty 5 15
 login
!
end

DLS2#
```

ALS1

```
ALS1#term len 0
ALS1#sh run
Building configuration...

Current configuration : 1909 bytes
!
version 12.1
no service pad
service timestamps debug uptime
service timestamps log uptime
no service password-encryption
!
hostname ALS1
!
no logging console
!
ip subnet-zero
!
no ip domain-lookup
vtp domain switch
vtp mode transparent
!
vmps server 150.1.1.254 primary
spanning-tree mode pvst
no spanning-tree optimize bpdu transmission
spanning-tree extend system-id
!
vlan 100
 name R1-VLAN
!
vlan 300
 name R3-VLAN
!
vlan 400
 name R4-VLAN
!
interface FastEthernet0/1
 switchport access vlan dynamic
 switchport mode access
 spanning-tree portfast
!
interface FastEthernet0/2
 switchport access vlan dynamic
 switchport mode access
 switchport protected
 shutdown
 spanning-tree portfast
!
interface FastEthernet0/3
 switchport access vlan 300
 switchport mode access
!
interface FastEthernet0/4
 switchport access vlan 400
 switchport mode access
!
interface FastEthernet0/5
 switchport access vlan dynamic
 switchport mode access
 switchport protected
 shutdown
 spanning-tree portfast
!
```

```
 interface FastEthernet0/6
  switchport access vlan dynamic
  switchport mode access
  switchport protected
  shutdown
  spanning-tree portfast
 !
 interface FastEthernet0/7
  switchport mode trunk
 !
 interface FastEthernet0/8
  switchport mode trunk
 !
 interface FastEthernet0/9
  switchport access vlan dynamic
  switchport mode access
  switchport protected
  shutdown
  spanning-tree portfast
 !
 interface FastEthernet0/10
  switchport access vlan dynamic
  switchport mode access
  switchport protected
  shutdown
  spanning-tree portfast
 !
 interface FastEthernet0/11
  switchport mode trunk
 !
 interface FastEthernet0/12
  switchport mode trunk
 !
 interface Vlan1
  no ip address
  no ip route-cache
  shutdown
 !
 interface Vlan400
  ip address 10.4.4.254 255.255.255.0
  no ip route-cache
 !
 ip default-gateway 10.4.4.4
 ip http server
 !
 line con 0
 line vty 0 4
  privilege level 15
  password cisco
  login
 line vty 5 15
  login
 !
 end

ALS1#
```

ALS2

```
R3#term len 0
R3#sh run
Building configuration...

Current configuration : 2198 bytes
!
version 12.4
service timestamps debug datetime msec
service timestamps log datetime msec
no service password-encryption
!
hostname R3
!
boot-start-marker
boot-end-marker
!
no logging console
!
no aaa new-model
```

```
no network-clock-participate slot 1
no network-clock-participate wic 0
ip cef
!
no ip domain lookup
ip multicast-routing
ip auth-proxy max-nodata-conns 3
ip admission max-nodata-conns 3
!
ipv6 unicast-routing
!
interface Loopback0
 ip address 3.3.3.3 255.255.255.255
!
interface Tunnel0
 no ip address
 ipv6 enable
 ipv6 ospf 3 area 0
 tunnel source Loopback0
 tunnel destination 2.2.2.2
 tunnel mode ipv6ip
!
interface FastEthernet0/0
 ip address 10.3.3.3 255.255.255.0
 ip pim sparse-mode
 duplex auto
 speed auto
 ipv6 address 3FFE:3333:3333:3333::3/64
 ipv6 ospf 3 area 3
!
interface Serial1/0
 ip address 150.0.0.6 255.255.255.252
 ip pim sparse-mode
 clock rate 128000
!
interface Serial1/1
 ip address 150.0.0.10 255.255.255.252
 ip pim sparse-mode
 clock rate 128000
!
interface Serial1/2
 ip address 150.0.0.13 255.255.255.252
 ip pim sparse-mode
 clock rate 128000
!
interface Serial1/3
 ip address 150.0.0.17 255.255.255.252
 ip pim sparse-mode
 clock rate 128000
!
interface Serial1/4
 no ip address
 shutdown
!
interface Serial1/5
 no ip address
 shutdown
!
interface Serial1/6
 no ip address
 shutdown
!
interface Serial1/7
 no ip address
 shutdown
!
router eigrp 2
 redistribute connected
 redistribute static
 network 3.3.3.3 0.0.0.0
 network 150.0.0.6 0.0.0.0
 network 150.0.0.10 0.0.0.0
 no auto-summary
!
router eigrp 3
 redistribute connected
 redistribute static
 redistribute eigrp 2
 network 3.3.3.3 0.0.0.0
```

```
 network 150.0.0.13 0.0.0.0
 network 150.0.0.17 0.0.0.0
 no auto-summary
!
ip forward-protocol nd
ip route 10.4.4.0 255.255.255.0 Serial1/2
ip route 10.4.4.0 255.255.255.0 Serial1/3
!
no ip http server
no ip http secure-server
ip pim rp-address 2.2.2.2
!
ipv6 router ospf 3
 router-id 3.3.3.3
 log-adjacency-changes
 area 0 authentication ipsec spi 678 md5 1234567890ABCDEF1234567890ABCDEF
!
control-plane
!
line con 0
line aux 0
line vty 0 4
 password cisco
 login
!
end

R3#
R3#10.3.3.254
Trying 10.3.3.254 ... Open


User Access Verification

Password:
ALS2#

ALS2#term len 0
ALS2#sh run
Building configuration...

Current configuration : 3167 bytes
!
version 12.1
no service pad
service timestamps debug uptime
service timestamps log uptime
no service password-encryption
!
hostname ALS2
!
no logging console
!
ip subnet-zero
!
no ip domain-lookup
vtp domain switch
vtp mode transparent
!
spanning-tree mode pvst
no spanning-tree optimize bpdu transmission
spanning-tree extend system-id
!
vlan 300
 name R3-VLAN
!
interface FastEthernet0/1
 shutdown
 storm-control broadcast level 5.00
 storm-control multicast level 20.00
 storm-control unicast level 80.00
 storm-control action trap
!
interface FastEthernet0/2
 shutdown
 storm-control broadcast level 5.00
 storm-control multicast level 20.00
 storm-control unicast level 80.00
 storm-control action trap
```

```
!
interface FastEthernet0/3
 shutdown
 storm-control broadcast level 5.00
 storm-control multicast level 20.00
 storm-control unicast level 80.00
 storm-control action trap
!
interface FastEthernet0/4
 shutdown
 storm-control broadcast level 5.00
 storm-control multicast level 20.00
 storm-control unicast level 80.00
 storm-control action trap
!
interface FastEthernet0/5
 shutdown
 storm-control broadcast level 5.00
 storm-control multicast level 20.00
 storm-control unicast level 80.00
 storm-control action trap
!
interface FastEthernet0/6
 shutdown
 storm-control broadcast level 5.00
 storm-control multicast level 20.00
 storm-control unicast level 80.00
 storm-control action trap
!
interface FastEthernet0/7
 shutdown
 storm-control broadcast level 5.00
 storm-control multicast level 20.00
 storm-control unicast level 80.00
 storm-control action trap
!
interface FastEthernet0/8
 shutdown
 storm-control broadcast level 5.00
 storm-control multicast level 20.00
 storm-control unicast level 80.00
 storm-control action trap
!
interface FastEthernet0/9
 shutdown
 storm-control broadcast level 5.00
 storm-control multicast level 20.00
 storm-control unicast level 80.00
 storm-control action trap
!
interface FastEthernet0/10
 shutdown
!
interface FastEthernet0/11
 switchport mode trunk
!
interface FastEthernet0/12
 switchport mode trunk
!
interface Vlan1
 no ip address
 no ip route-cache
 shutdown
!
interface Vlan300
 ip address 10.3.3.254 255.255.255.0
 no ip route-cache
!
ip default-gateway 10.3.3.3
ip http server
snmp-server community CCNP2011 RO
snmp-server enable traps snmp authentication warmstart linkdown linkup coldstart
snmp-server enable traps config
snmp-server enable traps copy-config
snmp-server enable traps syslog
snmp-server enable traps entity
snmp-server enable traps flash insertion removal
snmp-server enable traps bridge
snmp-server enable traps stpx
```

```
snmp-server enable traps rtr
snmp-server enable traps c2900
snmp-server enable traps vtp
snmp-server enable traps vlancreate
snmp-server enable traps vlandelete
snmp-server enable traps port-security
snmp-server enable traps MAC-Notification
snmp-server enable traps envmon fan shutdown supply temperature status
snmp-server enable traps hsrp
snmp-server enable traps cluster
snmp-server enable traps vlan-membership
snmp-server host 150.1.1.254 CCNP2011
!
line con 0
line vty 0 4
 privilege level 15
 password cisco
 login
line vty 5 15
 login
!
end

ALS2#
```

CCNP LAB 86

Troubleshooting Lab

Lab Objective:

The focus of this lab is to hone your trouble isolation and resolution skills. This lab will include Layer 2 and Layer 3 technologies which fall within the scope of the current CCNP curriculum.

Lab Topology:

The lab network topology is illustrated below:

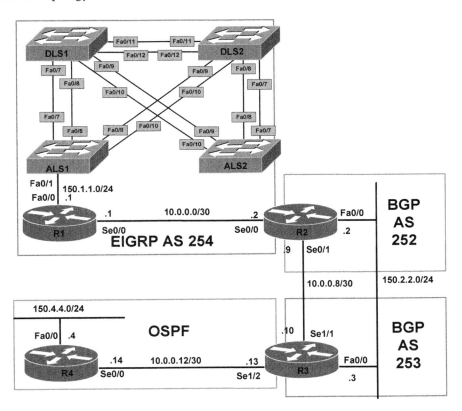

IMPORTANT NOTE: If you are using the www.howtonetwork.net racks, please download and paste the troubleshooting lab configurations. If you are using your own rack or lab, please modify this configuration to reflect the actual interface types, etc, that you have on your devices. Prior to beginning all labs, apply the pre-lab configuration for each individual device.

When completing these labs, it is important to resolve the trouble tickets in the order in which they are listed because they build on each other. For example, if you begin with Trouble Ticket # 3, you might not get the expected resolution or result if you have not completed Trouble Ticket # 1 and Trouble Ticket # 2. It is very important to follow the order listed.

Trouble Ticket # 1

You have received a problem report indicating that switch DLS2 is unable to reach any other device within VLAN 100. Troubleshoot and resolve this issue. Verify your solution using a simple ping from switch DLS2 to any other device within this VLAN.

Trouble Ticket # 2

You have received a problem report indicating that switch DLS2 is not receiving any routing information for external networks. Troubleshoot and resolve this issue. You can NOT modify the configurations on any routers when resolving this issue. Following resolution, verify that DLS2 has external EIGRP routes in its routing table.

Trouble Ticket # 3

You have received a problem report indicating that users on the 150.4.4.0/24 subnet are unable to reach the 150.1.1.0/24 and 172.16.1.0/24 subnets. Troubleshoot and resolve this issue. Verify your solution using a ping from the 150.4.4.0/24 subnets to the 150.1.1.0/24 and 172.16.1.0/24 subnets. You are only allowed to change the configuration on ONE device when implementing a resolution for this issue. Verify by pinging between the subnets.

Trouble Ticket # 4

You have received a problem report indicating that the corporate NOC is unable to ping half of the devices that reside on the 172.16.1.0/24 subnet from the 150.4.4.0/24 subnet. Troubleshoot and resolve this issue. Validate your resolution by pinging all of the devices that reside on the subnet from the 150.4.4.0/24 subnet.

LAB SOLUTIONS

Solution # 1

The VLAN Access Control List (VACL) on switch DLS2 is mis-configured as follows:

```
vlan access-map FORWARD-ALL 10
 action drop
```

The result of this configuration is all packets and frames within this VLAN will be dropped by the switch. To resolve this issue, the switch VACL needs to be re-configured as follows:

```
DLS2(config)#vlan access-map FORWARD-ALL 10
DLS2(config-access-map)#action forward
```

Solution # 2

Switch DLS1 has been configured with a duplicate EIGRP router ID (the same as R2):

```
DLS1#show run | begin router eigrp
router eigrp 254
 no auto-summary
 eigrp router-id 1.0.0.2
 network 0.0.0.0
```

By default, a router running EIGRP will NOT accept external routes from another router that has the same router ID. This is designed to prevent loops. In order to resolve this issue, the EIGRP router ID needs to be configured as follows:

```
DLS1(config)#router eigrp 254
DLS1(config-router)#eigrp router-id 1.0.0.3
DLS1(config-router)#end
```

NOTE: You can use any other value or completely remove the RID to complete this task.

Solution # 3

R2 has been configured to redistribute an EIGRP process that does not exist:

```
R2#show running-config | section bgp
 no synchronization
 bgp router-id 2.2.2.2
 bgp log-neighbor-changes
 redistribute eigrp 252
 neighbor 10.0.0.10 remote-as 253
 no auto-summary
```

To resolve this issue, you need to configure BGP to redistribute EIGRP AS 254 instead:

```
R2(config)#router bgp 252
R2(config-router)#redistribute eigrp 254
```

Solution # 4

The issue is that switches ALS1 and ALS2 have no default gateway, which prevents them from forwarding packets beyond their local subnet. Configure a default gateway as follows:

```
ALS1(config)#ip default-gateway 172.16.1.1
ALS2(config)#ip default-gateway 172.16.1.1
```

FINAL WORKING ROUTER CONFIGURATIONS

R1

```
R1#term len 0
R1#sh run
Building configuration...

Current configuration : 901 bytes
!
version 12.4
service timestamps debug datetime msec
service timestamps log datetime msec
no service password-encryption
!
hostname R1
!
boot-start-marker
boot-end-marker
!
no logging console
!
no aaa new-model
no network-clock-participate slot 1
no network-clock-participate wic 0
ip cef
!
no ip domain lookup
ip auth-proxy max-nodata-conns 3
ip admission max-nodata-conns 3
!
interface FastEthernet0/0
 ip address 150.1.1.1 255.255.255.0
 duplex auto
 speed auto
!
interface Serial0/0
 ip address 10.0.0.1 255.255.255.252
 clock rate 2000000
!
interface Serial0/1
 no ip address
 shutdown
!
router eigrp 254
 network 10.0.0.1 0.0.0.0
 network 150.1.1.1 0.0.0.0
```

```
 no auto-summary
 eigrp router-id 1.0.0.1
!
ip forward-protocol nd
!
no ip http server
no ip http secure-server
!
control-plane
!
line con 0
line aux 0
line vty 0 4
 login
!
end

R1#
```

R2

```
R2#term len 0
R2#sh run
Building configuration...

Current configuration : 1136 bytes
!
version 12.4
service timestamps debug datetime msec
service timestamps log datetime msec
no service password-encryption
!
hostname R2
!
boot-start-marker
boot-end-marker
!
no logging console
!
no aaa new-model
no network-clock-participate slot 1
no network-clock-participate wic 0
ip cef
!
no ip domain lookup
ip auth-proxy max-nodata-conns 3
ip admission max-nodata-conns 3
!
interface FastEthernet0/0
 ip address 150.2.2.2 255.255.255.0
 duplex auto
 speed auto
!
interface Serial0/0
 ip address 10.0.0.2 255.255.255.252
!
interface Serial0/1
 ip address 10.0.0.9 255.255.255.252
!
router eigrp 254
 redistribute connected
 redistribute bgp 252
 network 10.0.0.2 0.0.0.0
 default-metric 1544 20000 255 1 1500
 no auto-summary
 eigrp router-id 1.0.0.2
!
router bgp 252
 no synchronization
 bgp router-id 2.2.2.2
 bgp log-neighbor-changes
 redistribute eigrp 254
 neighbor 10.0.0.10 remote-as 253
 no auto-summary
!
ip forward-protocol nd
!
no ip http server
```

```
no ip http secure-server
!
control-plane
!
line con 0
line aux 0
line vty 0 4
 login
!
end

R2#
```

R3

```
R3#term len 0
R3#sh run
Building configuration...

Current configuration : 1482 bytes
!
version 12.4
service timestamps debug datetime msec
service timestamps log datetime msec
no service password-encryption
!
hostname R3
!
boot-start-marker
boot-end-marker
!
no logging console
!
no aaa new-model
no network-clock-participate slot 1
no network-clock-participate wic 0
ip cef
!
no ip domain lookup
ip auth-proxy max-nodata-conns 3
ip admission max-nodata-conns 3
!
interface FastEthernet0/0
 ip address 150.2.2.3 255.255.255.0
 duplex auto
 speed auto
!
interface Serial1/0
 no ip address
 shutdown
 clock rate 128000
!
interface Serial1/1
 ip address 10.0.0.10 255.255.255.252
 clock rate 128000
!
interface Serial1/2
 ip address 10.0.0.13 255.255.255.252
 clock rate 128000
!
interface Serial1/3
 no ip address
 shutdown
!
interface Serial1/4
 no ip address
 shutdown
!
interface Serial1/5
 no ip address
 shutdown
!
interface Serial1/6
 no ip address
 shutdown
!
interface Serial1/7
 no ip address
```

```
  shutdown
!
router ospf 3
 router-id 3.3.3.3
 log-adjacency-changes
 redistribute connected subnets
 redistribute bgp 253 subnets
 network 10.0.0.13 0.0.0.0 area 0
!
router bgp 253
 no synchronization
 bgp router-id 3.3.3.3
 bgp log-neighbor-changes
 redistribute ospf 3 match internal external 1
 neighbor 10.0.0.9 remote-as 252
 no auto-summary
!
ip forward-protocol nd
!
no ip http server
no ip http secure-server
!
control-plane
!
line con 0
line aux 0
line vty 0 4
 login
!
end

R3#
```

R4

```
R4#term len 0
R4#sh run
Building configuration...

Current configuration : 931 bytes
!
version 12.4
service timestamps debug datetime msec
service timestamps log datetime msec
no service password-encryption
!
hostname R4
!
boot-start-marker
boot-end-marker
!
no logging console
!
no aaa new-model
no network-clock-participate slot 1
no network-clock-participate wic 0
ip cef
!
no ip domain lookup
ip auth-proxy max-nodata-conns 3
ip admission max-nodata-conns 3
!
interface FastEthernet0/0
 ip address 150.4.4.4 255.255.255.0
 duplex auto
 speed auto
!
interface Serial0/0
 ip address 10.0.0.14 255.255.255.252
!
interface Serial0/1
 no ip address
 shutdown
!
router ospf 4
 router-id 4.4.4.4
 log-adjacency-changes
 redistribute connected metric-type 1 subnets
```

```
 network 10.0.0.14 0.0.0.0 area 0
!
ip forward-protocol nd
!
no ip http server
no ip http secure-server
!
control-plane
!
line con 0
line aux 0
line vty 0 4
 login
!
end
R4#
```

FINAL WORKING SWITCH CONFIGURATIONS

DLS1

```
DLS1#
DLS1#term len 0
DLS1#sh run
Building configuration...

Current configuration : 5345 bytes
!
version 12.2
no service pad
service timestamps debug datetime msec
service timestamps log datetime msec
no service password-encryption
!
hostname DLS1
!
no logging console
!
no aaa new-model
ip subnet-zero
ip routing
no ip domain-lookup
!
vtp domain CCNP2011
vtp mode transparent
!
mac access-list extended SECURE-HOSTS
 permit host 0007.8432.dd07 any
 permit host 000f.235e.ec80 any
 permit any host 000f.235e.ec80
 permit any host 0007.8432.dd07
!
spanning-tree mode pvst
spanning-tree extend system-id
spanning-tree vlan 172 priority 0
!
vlan internal allocation policy ascending
!
vlan access-map SECURE-VLAN-100 10
 action forward
 match ip address 100
vlan access-map SECURE-VLAN-100 20
 action drop
 match ip address 101
vlan access-map SECURE-VLAN-100 30
 action forward
 match mac address SECURE-HOSTS
!
vlan filter SECURE-VLAN-100 vlan-list 100
!
vlan 100
 name R1-VLAN
!
vlan 172
```

```
  name SWITCH-VLAN
!
interface Port-channel1
 switchport trunk encapsulation dot1q
 switchport mode trunk
 switchport nonegotiate
!
interface Port-channel2
 switchport trunk encapsulation dot1q
 switchport mode trunk
 switchport nonegotiate
!
interface FastEthernet0/1
 switchport mode dynamic desirable
!
interface FastEthernet0/2
 switchport mode dynamic desirable
!
interface FastEthernet0/3
 switchport mode dynamic desirable
!
interface FastEthernet0/4
 switchport mode dynamic desirable
!
interface FastEthernet0/5
 switchport mode dynamic desirable
!
interface FastEthernet0/6
 switchport mode dynamic desirable
!
interface FastEthernet0/7
 switchport trunk encapsulation dot1q
 switchport mode trunk
 switchport nonegotiate
 channel-group 1 mode on
!
interface FastEthernet0/8
 switchport trunk encapsulation dot1q
 switchport mode trunk
 switchport nonegotiate
 channel-group 1 mode on
!
interface FastEthernet0/9
 switchport trunk encapsulation dot1q
 switchport mode trunk
 switchport nonegotiate
 channel-group 2 mode on
!
interface FastEthernet0/10
 switchport trunk encapsulation dot1q
 switchport mode trunk
 switchport nonegotiate
 channel-group 2 mode on
!
interface FastEthernet0/11
 switchport mode dynamic desirable
!
interface FastEthernet0/12
 switchport mode dynamic desirable

[Truncated Output]

interface Vlan1
 no ip address
 shutdown
!
interface Vlan100
 ip address 150.1.1.2 255.255.255.0
!
interface Vlan172
 ip address 172.16.1.2 255.255.255.0
 standby 172 ip 172.16.1.1
 standby 172 priority 105
 standby 172 preempt
!
router eigrp 254
 no auto-summary
 eigrp router-id 1.0.0.3
 network 0.0.0.0
```

```
!
ip classless
ip http server
ip http secure-server
!
access-list 100 permit eigrp any any
access-list 100 permit tcp any any
access-list 100 permit icmp any any
access-list 101 permit ospf any any
access-list 101 permit udp any any
!
control-plane
!
line con 0
line vty 0 4
 privilege level 15
 password cisco
 login
line vty 5 15
 privilege level 15
 password cisco
 login
!
end

DLS1#
```

DLS2

```
DLS2#term len 0
DLS2#sh run
Building configuration...

Current configuration : 4711 bytes
!
version 12.2
no service pad
service timestamps debug datetime msec
service timestamps log datetime msec
no service password-encryption
!
hostname DLS2
!
no logging console
!
no aaa new-model
ip subnet-zero
ip routing
no ip domain-lookup
!
vtp domain CCNP2011
vtp mode transparent
!
spanning-tree mode pvst
spanning-tree extend system-id
spanning-tree vlan 172 priority 4096
!
vlan internal allocation policy ascending
!
vlan access-map FORWARD-ALL 10
 action forward
!
vlan filter FORWARD-ALL vlan-list 172
!
vlan 172
 name SWITCH-VLAN
!
interface Port-channel2
 switchport trunk encapsulation dot1q
 switchport mode trunk
 switchport nonegotiate
!
interface Port-channel1
 switchport trunk encapsulation dot1q
 switchport mode trunk
 switchport nonegotiate
!
interface FastEthernet0/1
 switchport mode dynamic desirable
```

```
!
interface FastEthernet0/2
 switchport mode dynamic desirable
!
interface FastEthernet0/3
 switchport mode dynamic desirable
!
interface FastEthernet0/4
 switchport mode dynamic desirable
!
interface FastEthernet0/5
 switchport mode dynamic desirable
!
interface FastEthernet0/6
 switchport mode dynamic desirable
!
interface FastEthernet0/7
 switchport trunk encapsulation dot1q
 switchport mode trunk
 switchport nonegotiate
 channel-group 1 mode on
!
interface FastEthernet0/8
 switchport trunk encapsulation dot1q
 switchport mode trunk
 switchport nonegotiate
 channel-group 1 mode on
!
interface FastEthernet0/9
 switchport trunk encapsulation dot1q
 switchport mode trunk
 switchport nonegotiate
 channel-group 2 mode on
!
interface FastEthernet0/10
 switchport trunk encapsulation dot1q
 switchport mode trunk
 switchport nonegotiate
 channel-group 2 mode on
!
interface FastEthernet0/11
 switchport mode dynamic desirable
!
interface FastEthernet0/12
 switchport mode dynamic desirable

[Truncated Output]

interface Vlan1
 no ip address
 shutdown
!
interface Vlan172
 ip address 172.16.1.3 255.255.255.0
 standby 172 ip 172.16.1.1
 standby 172 preempt
!
router eigrp 254
 no auto-summary
 eigrp router-id 1.0.0.4
 network 0.0.0.0
!
ip classless
ip http server
ip http secure-server
!
control-plane
!
line con 0
line vty 0 4
 privilege level 15
 password cisco
 login
line vty 5 15
 privilege level 15
 password cisco
 login
!
end
DLS2#
```

ALS1

```
ALS1#term len 0
ALS1#sh run
Building configuration...

Current configuration : 1611 bytes
!
version 12.1
no service pad
service timestamps debug uptime
service timestamps log uptime
no service password-encryption
!
hostname ALS1
!
no logging console
!
ip subnet-zero
!
no ip domain-lookup
vtp domain CCNP2011
vtp mode transparent
!
spanning-tree mode pvst
no spanning-tree optimize bpdu transmission
spanning-tree extend system-id
!
vlan 100
 name R1-VLAN
!
vlan 172
 name SWITCH-VLAN
!
interface Port-channel1
 switchport mode trunk
 switchport nonegotiate
 flowcontrol send off
!
interface Port-channel2
 switchport mode trunk
 switchport nonegotiate
 flowcontrol send off
!
interface FastEthernet0/1
 switchport access vlan 100
 switchport mode access
!
interface FastEthernet0/2
!
interface FastEthernet0/3
!
interface FastEthernet0/4
!
interface FastEthernet0/5
!
interface FastEthernet0/6
!
interface FastEthernet0/7
 switchport mode trunk
 switchport nonegotiate
 channel-group 1 mode on
!
interface FastEthernet0/8
 switchport mode trunk
 switchport nonegotiate
 channel-group 1 mode on
!
interface FastEthernet0/9
 switchport mode trunk
 switchport nonegotiate
 channel-group 2 mode on
!
interface FastEthernet0/10
 switchport mode trunk
 switchport nonegotiate
 channel-group 2 mode on
!
interface FastEthernet0/11
```

```
  shutdown
!
interface FastEthernet0/12
  shutdown
!
interface Vlan1
  no ip address
  no ip route-cache
  shutdown
!
interface Vlan172
  ip address 172.16.1.10 255.255.255.0
  no ip route-cache
!
ip default-gateway 172.16.1.1
ip http server
!
line con 0
line vty 0 4
  privilege level 15
  password cisco
  login
line vty 5 15
  privilege level 15
  password cisco
  login
!
end

ALS1#
```

ALS2

```
ALS2#term len 0
ALS2#sh run
Building configuration...

Current configuration : 1514 bytes
!
version 12.1
no service pad
service timestamps debug uptime
service timestamps log uptime
no service password-encryption
!
hostname ALS2
!
no logging console
!
ip subnet-zero
!
no ip domain-lookup
vtp domain CCNP2011
vtp mode transparent
!
spanning-tree mode pvst
no spanning-tree optimize bpdu transmission
spanning-tree extend system-id
!
vlan 172
  name SWITCH-VLAN
!
interface Port-channel1
  switchport mode trunk
  switchport nonegotiate
  flowcontrol send off
!
interface Port-channel2
  switchport mode trunk
  switchport nonegotiate
  flowcontrol send off
!
interface FastEthernet0/1
!
interface FastEthernet0/2
!
interface FastEthernet0/3
```

```
!
interface FastEthernet0/4
!
interface FastEthernet0/5
!
interface FastEthernet0/6
!
interface FastEthernet0/7
 switchport mode trunk
 switchport nonegotiate
 channel-group 1 mode on
!
interface FastEthernet0/8
 switchport mode trunk
 switchport nonegotiate
 channel-group 1 mode on
!
interface FastEthernet0/9
 switchport mode trunk
 switchport nonegotiate
 channel-group 2 mode on
!
interface FastEthernet0/10
 switchport mode trunk
 switchport nonegotiate
 channel-group 2 mode on
!
interface FastEthernet0/11
!
interface FastEthernet0/12
!
interface Vlan1
 no ip address
 no ip route-cache
 shutdown
!
interface Vlan172
 ip address 172.16.1.11 255.255.255.0
 no ip route-cache
!
ip default-gateway 172.16.1.1
ip http server
!
line con 0
line vty 0 4
 privilege level 15
 password cisco
 login
line vty 5 15
 privilege level 15
 password cisco
 login
!
end

ALS2#
```

CCNP LAB 87

Troubleshooting Lab

Lab Objective:

The focus of this lab is to hone your trouble isolation and resolution skills. This lab will include Layer 2 and Layer 3 technologies which fall within the scope of the current CCNP curriculum.

Lab Topology:

The lab network topology is illustrated below:

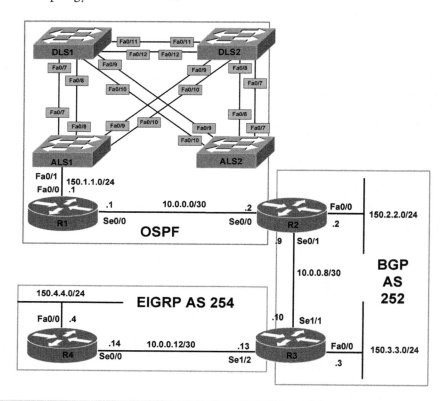

IMPORTANT NOTE: If you are using the www.howtonetwork.net racks, please download and paste the troubleshooting lab configurations. If you are using your own rack or lab, please modify this configuration to reflect the actual interface types, etc, that you have on your devices. Prior to beginning all labs, apply the pre-lab configuration for each individual device.

When completing these labs, it is important to resolve the trouble tickets in the order in which they are listed because they build on each other. For example, if you begin with Trouble Ticket # 3, you might not get the expected resolution or result if you have not completed Trouble Ticket # 1 and Trouble Ticket # 2. It is very important to follow the order listed.

Trouble Ticket # 1

You have received a problem report indicating that switch ALS2 is inaccessible and cannot be reached even from devices residing on the 172.16.1.0/24 subnet. Troubleshoot and resolve this issue. Verify your solution by pinging DLS2 from any device on the 172.16.1.0/24 subnet.

Trouble Ticket # 2

You have received a problem report indicating slow convergence on the switched network. A co-worker has recently implemented 802.1w to speed up convergence, but it appears that the change did not resolve this issue. Troubleshoot and resolve this issue.

Trouble Ticket # 3

You have received a problem report indicating that users connected to the 172.16.1.0/24 and the 150.1.1.0/24 subnets are unable to reach the 150.4.4.0/24 subnet. Troubleshoot and resolve this issue. You are allowed to use only ONE command on any two routers in the network. You are NOT allowed to use any static routes. Verify your solution by pinging between these subnets.

Trouble Ticket # 4

You have received a problem report indicating that users are unable to receive Multicast traffic being sent from R4s LAN subnet. The NOC has joined the LAN interface of this router to Multicast group 227.4.4.4 but you cannot ping it from any other router. Troubleshoot and resolve this issue. Test your solution by pinging this address from all other routers.

LAB SOLUTIONS

Solutionn # 1

Even though an SVI for VLAN 172 exists, VLAN 172 itself is not configured on switch ALS2.

```
ALS2#show vlan brief

VLAN Name                             Status    Ports
---- -------------------------------- --------- -------------------------------
1    default                          active    Fa0/1, Fa0/2, Fa0/3, Fa0/4
                                                Fa0/5, Fa0/6, Fa0/11, Fa0/12
1002 fddi-default                     act/unsup
1003 trcrf-default                    act/unsup
1004 fddinet-default                  act/unsup
1005 trbrf-default                    act/unsup
```

The result of this configuration is that the switch will be inaccessible from all other devices. To resolve this issue, configure VLAN 172 on switch ALS2:

```
ALS2(config)#vlan 172
ALS2(config-vlan)#name SWITCH-VLAN
```

Solution # 2

The issue is that all switches, EXCEPT for switch DLS1, are running Rapid STP. RSTP is an IEEE standard and is therefore able to interoperate with traditional STP. However, it is important to realize that RSTP loses its ability to provide sub-second re-convergence when implemented in a network that also contains switches that are only 802.1D capable. Verify the STP mode using the show spanning-tree summary command on all switches:

```
DLS1#show spanning-tree summary
Switch is in pvst mode

[Truncated Output]

DLS2#show spanning-tree summary
Switch is in rapid-pvst mode

[Truncated Output]
```

```
ALS1#show spanning-tree summary
Switch is in rapid-pvst mode

[Truncated Output]

ALS2#show spanning-tree summary
Switch is in rapid-pvst mode

[Truncated Output]
```

To resolve this issue, implement Rapid STP on switch DLS1:

```
DLS1(config)#spanning-tree mode rapid-pvst
```

Solution # 3

The issue is that iBGP has not been configured to redistribute routes into OSPF or EIGRP on routers R2 and R3 as can be seen in the configuration:

```
R2#show running-config | section bgp
 redistribute bgp 252 subnets
router bgp 252
 no synchronization
 bgp log-neighbor-changes
 network 150.2.2.0 mask 255.255.255.0
 redistribute ospf 2 match internal external 2
 neighbor 10.0.0.10 remote-as 252
 no auto-summary

R3#show running-config | section bgp
 redistribute bgp 252
router bgp 252
 no synchronization
 bgp router-id 3.3.3.3
 bgp log-neighbor-changes
 network 150.3.3.0 mask 255.255.255.0
 redistribute eigrp 254
 neighbor 10.0.0.9 remote-as 252
 no auto-summary
```

To resolve this issue, configure iBGP redistribution into IGPs using the **bgp redistribute-internal** command on routers R2 and R3:

```
R2(config)#router bgp 252
R2(config-router)#bgp redistribute-internal

R3(config)#router bgp 252
R3(config-router)#bgp redistribute-internal
```

Solution # 4

The issue is that R1 and R2 have IP Multicast interfaces configured for Sparse mode forwarding. In order to use Auto RP, you need to enable Sparse-Dense mode:

```
R1#show ip pim interface
```

Address	Interface	Ver/ Mode	Nbr Count	Query Intvl	DR Prior	DR
1.1.1.1	Loopback0	v2/S	0	30	1	1.1.1.1
10.0.0.1	Serial0/0	v2/S	1	30	1	0.0.0.0

```
R2#show ip pim interface
```

Address	Interface	Ver/ Mode	Nbr Count	Query Intvl	DR Prior	DR
10.0.0.2	Serial0/0	v2/S	1	30	1	0.0.0.0
10.0.0.9	Serial0/1	v2/S	1	30	1	0.0.0.0

To resolve this issue, you need to enable Sparse-Dense mode forwarding:

```
R1(config)#interface loopback 0
R1(config-if)#ip pim sparse-dense-mode
R1(config-if)#exit
```

```
R1(config)#interface serial 0/0
R1(config-if)#ip pim sparse-dense-mode

R2(config)#interface serial 0/0
R2(config-if)#ip pim sparse-dense-mode
R2(config-if)#exit
R2(config)#interface serial 0/1
R2(config-if)#ip pim sparse-dense-mode
```

FINAL WORKING ROUTER CONFIGURATIONS

R1

```
R1#term len 0
R1#sh run
Building configuration...

Current configuration : 1238 bytes
!
version 12.4
service timestamps debug datetime msec
service timestamps log datetime msec
no service password-encryption
!
hostname R1
!
boot-start-marker
boot-end-marker
!
no logging console
!
no aaa new-model
no network-clock-participate slot 1
no network-clock-participate wic 0
ip cef
!
no ip domain lookup
ip multicast-routing
ip auth-proxy max-nodata-conns 3
ip admission max-nodata-conns 3
!
interface Loopback0
 ip address 1.1.1.1 255.255.255.255
 ip pim sparse-dense-mode
!
interface FastEthernet0/0
 ip address 150.1.1.1 255.255.255.0
 duplex auto
 speed auto
!
interface Serial0/0
 ip address 10.0.0.1 255.255.255.252
 ip pim sparse-dense-mode
 clock rate 2000000
!
interface Serial0/1
 no ip address
 shutdown
!
router ospf 1
 router-id 1.1.1.1
 log-adjacency-changes
 area 1 nssa no-summary
 redistribute connected subnets
 network 10.0.0.1 0.0.0.0 area 0
 network 150.1.1.1 0.0.0.0 area 1
!
ip forward-protocol nd
!
no ip http server
no ip http secure-server
ip pim send-rp-announce Loopback0 scope 10
ip pim send-rp-discovery Loopback0 scope 10
!
control-plane
!
```

```
line con 0
line aux 0
line vty 0 4
 login
!
end

R1#
```

R2

```
R2#term len 0
R2#sh run
Building configuration...

Current configuration : 1282 bytes
!
version 12.4
service timestamps debug datetime msec
service timestamps log datetime msec
no service password-encryption
!
hostname R2
!
boot-start-marker
boot-end-marker
!
no logging console
!
no aaa new-model
no network-clock-participate slot 1
no network-clock-participate wic 0
ip cef
!
no ip domain lookup
ip multicast-routing
ip auth-proxy max-nodata-conns 3
ip admission max-nodata-conns 3
!
interface FastEthernet0/0
 ip address 150.2.2.2 255.255.255.0
 duplex auto
 speed auto
!
interface Serial0/0
 ip address 10.0.0.2 255.255.255.252
 ip pim sparse-dense-mode
!
interface Serial0/1
 ip address 10.0.0.9 255.255.255.252
 ip pim sparse-dense-mode
!
router ospf 2
 router-id 2.2.2.2
 log-adjacency-changes
 redistribute connected subnets
 redistribute bgp 252 subnets
 network 10.0.0.2 0.0.0.0 area 0
!
router bgp 252
 no synchronization
 bgp log-neighbor-changes
 bgp redistribute-internal
 network 150.2.2.0 mask 255.255.255.0
 redistribute ospf 2 match internal external 2
 neighbor 10.0.0.10 remote-as 252
 no auto-summary
!
ip forward-protocol nd
!
no ip http server
no ip http secure-server
ip pim accept-rp auto-rp
!
control-plane
!
line con 0
line aux 0
line vty 0 4
```

```
 login
!
end
R2#

```

R3

```
R3#term len 0
R3#sh run
Building configuration...

Current configuration : 1616 bytes
!
version 12.4
service timestamps debug datetime msec
service timestamps log datetime msec
no service password-encryption
!
hostname R3
!
boot-start-marker
boot-end-marker
!
no logging console
!
no aaa new-model
no network-clock-participate slot 1
no network-clock-participate wic 0
ip cef
!
no ip domain lookup
ip multicast-routing
ip auth-proxy max-nodata-conns 3
ip admission max-nodata-conns 3
!
interface FastEthernet0/0
 ip address 150.2.2.3 255.255.255.0
 duplex auto
 speed auto
!
interface Serial1/0
 no ip address
 shutdown
 clock rate 128000
!
interface Serial1/1
 ip address 10.0.0.10 255.255.255.252
 ip pim sparse-dense-mode
 clock rate 128000
!
interface Serial1/2
 ip address 10.0.0.13 255.255.255.252
 ip pim sparse-dense-mode
 clock rate 128000
!
interface Serial1/3
 no ip address
 shutdown
!
interface Serial1/4
 no ip address
 shutdown
!
interface Serial1/5
 no ip address
 shutdown
!
interface Serial1/6
 no ip address
 shutdown
!
interface Serial1/7
 no ip address
 shutdown
!
router eigrp 254
 redistribute connected
```

```
   redistribute bgp 252
   network 10.0.0.13 0.0.0.0
   default-metric 1544 20000 255 1 1500
   no auto-summary
!
router bgp 252
   no synchronization
   bgp router-id 3.3.3.3
   bgp log-neighbor-changes
   bgp redistribute-internal
   network 150.3.3.0 mask 255.255.255.0
   redistribute eigrp 254
   neighbor 10.0.0.9 remote-as 252
   no auto-summary
!
ip forward-protocol nd
!
no ip http server
no ip http secure-server
ip pim accept-rp auto-rp
!
control-plane
!
line con 0
line aux 0
line vty 0 4
   login
!
end

R3#
```

R4

```
R4#term len 0
R4#sh run
Building configuration...

Current configuration : 1031 bytes
!
version 12.4
service timestamps debug datetime msec
service timestamps log datetime msec
no service password-encryption
!
hostname R4
!
boot-start-marker
boot-end-marker
!
no logging console
!
no aaa new-model
no network-clock-participate slot 1
no network-clock-participate wic 0
ip cef
!
no ip domain lookup
ip multicast-routing
ip auth-proxy max-nodata-conns 3
ip admission max-nodata-conns 3
!
!
interface FastEthernet0/0
   ip address 150.4.4.4 255.255.255.0
   ip pim sparse-dense-mode
   ip igmp join-group 227.4.4.4
   duplex auto
   speed auto
!
interface Serial0/0
   ip address 10.0.0.14 255.255.255.252
   ip pim sparse-dense-mode
!
interface Serial0/1
   no ip address
   shutdown
!
router eigrp 254
```

```
 network 10.0.0.14 0.0.0.0
 network 150.4.4.4 0.0.0.0
 auto-summary
 eigrp stub connected
!
ip forward-protocol nd
!
no ip http server
no ip http secure-server
ip pim accept-rp auto-rp
!
control-plane
!
line con 0
line aux 0
line vty 0 4
 login
!
end

R4#
```

FINAL WORKING SWITCH CONFIGURATIONS

DLS1

```
DLS1#term len 0
DLS1#sh run
Building configuration...

Current configuration : 7042 bytes
!
version 12.2
no service pad
service timestamps debug datetime msec
service timestamps log datetime msec
no service password-encryption
!
hostname DLS1
!
no logging console
!
no aaa new-model
ip subnet-zero
ip routing
no ip domain-lookup
!
vtp domain CCNP2011
vtp mode transparent
!
mac access-list extended SECURE-HOSTS
 permit host 0007.8432.dd07 any
 permit host 000f.235e.ec80 any
 permit any host 000f.235e.ec80
 permit any host 0007.8432.dd07
!
spanning-tree mode rapid-pvst
spanning-tree extend system-id
spanning-tree vlan 172 priority 0
!
vlan internal allocation policy ascending
!
vlan access-map SECURE-VLAN-100 10
 action forward
 match ip address 100
vlan access-map SECURE-VLAN-100 20
 action drop
 match ip address 101
vlan access-map SECURE-VLAN-100 30
 action forward
 match mac address SECURE-HOSTS
!
vlan filter SECURE-VLAN-100 vlan-list 100
!
vlan 100
```

```
 name R1-VLAN
!
vlan 172
 name SWITCH-VLAN
!
interface Port-channel1
 switchport trunk encapsulation dot1q
 switchport mode trunk
 switchport nonegotiate
!
interface Port-channel2
 switchport trunk encapsulation dot1q
 switchport mode trunk
 switchport nonegotiate
!
interface FastEthernet0/1
 switchport mode dynamic desirable
!
interface FastEthernet0/2
 switchport mode dynamic desirable
!
interface FastEthernet0/3
 switchport mode dynamic desirable
!
interface FastEthernet0/4
 switchport mode dynamic desirable
!
interface FastEthernet0/5
 switchport mode dynamic desirable
!
interface FastEthernet0/6
 switchport mode dynamic desirable
!
interface FastEthernet0/7
 switchport trunk encapsulation dot1q
 switchport mode trunk
 switchport nonegotiate
 channel-group 1 mode on
!
interface FastEthernet0/8
 switchport trunk encapsulation dot1q
 switchport mode trunk
 switchport nonegotiate
 channel-group 1 mode on
!
interface FastEthernet0/9
 switchport trunk encapsulation dot1q
 switchport mode trunk
 switchport nonegotiate
 channel-group 2 mode on
!
interface FastEthernet0/10
 switchport trunk encapsulation dot1q
 switchport mode trunk
 switchport nonegotiate
 channel-group 2 mode on
!
interface FastEthernet0/11
 switchport mode dynamic desirable
!
interface FastEthernet0/12
 switchport mode dynamic desirable

[Truncated Output]

interface Vlan1
 no ip address
 shutdown
!
interface Vlan100
 ip address 150.1.1.2 255.255.255.0
!
interface Vlan172
 ip address 172.16.1.2 255.255.255.0
 standby 172 ip 172.16.1.1
 standby 172 priority 105
 standby 172 preempt
!
router ospf 1
```

```
 log-adjacency-changes
 area 1 nssa
 redistribute connected subnets
 network 150.1.1.2 0.0.0.0 area 1
!
ip classless
ip http server
ip http secure-server
!
access-list 100 permit eigrp any any
access-list 100 permit tcp any any
access-list 100 permit icmp any any
access-list 100 permit ospf any any
access-list 101 permit ospf any any
access-list 101 permit udp any any
!
control-plane
!
line con 0
line vty 0 4
 privilege level 15
 password cisco
 login
line vty 5 15
 privilege level 15
 password cisco
 login
!
end

DLS1#
```

DLS2

```
DLS2#term len 0
DLS2#sh run
Building configuration...

Current configuration : 6491 bytes
!
version 12.2
no service pad
service timestamps debug datetime msec
service timestamps log datetime msec
no service password-encryption
!
hostname DLS2
!
no logging console
!
no aaa new-model
ip subnet-zero
ip routing
no ip domain-lookup
!
vtp domain CCNP2011
vtp mode transparent
!
spanning-tree mode rapid-pvst
spanning-tree extend system-id
spanning-tree vlan 172 priority 4096
!
vlan internal allocation policy ascending
!
vlan access-map FORWARD-ALL 10
 action forward
!
vlan filter FORWARD-ALL vlan-list 172
!
vlan 172
 name SWITCH-VLAN
!
interface Port-channel2
 switchport trunk encapsulation dot1q
 switchport mode trunk
 switchport nonegotiate
!
interface Port-channel1
 switchport trunk encapsulation dot1q
 switchport mode trunk
```

```
 switchport nonegotiate
!
interface FastEthernet0/1
 switchport mode dynamic desirable
!
interface FastEthernet0/2
 switchport mode dynamic desirable
!
interface FastEthernet0/3
 switchport mode dynamic desirable
!
interface FastEthernet0/4
 switchport mode dynamic desirable
!
interface FastEthernet0/5
 switchport mode dynamic desirable
!
interface FastEthernet0/6
 switchport mode dynamic desirable
!
interface FastEthernet0/7
 switchport trunk encapsulation dot1q
 switchport mode trunk
 switchport nonegotiate
 channel-group 1 mode on
!
interface FastEthernet0/8
 switchport trunk encapsulation dot1q
 switchport mode trunk
 switchport nonegotiate
 channel-group 1 mode on
!
interface FastEthernet0/9
 switchport trunk encapsulation dot1q
 switchport mode trunk
 switchport nonegotiate
 channel-group 2 mode on
!
interface FastEthernet0/10
 switchport trunk encapsulation dot1q
 switchport mode trunk
 switchport nonegotiate
 channel-group 2 mode on
!
interface FastEthernet0/11
 switchport mode dynamic desirable
!
interface FastEthernet0/12
 switchport mode dynamic desirable

[Truncated Output]

interface Vlan1
 no ip address
 shutdown
!
interface Vlan172
 ip address 172.16.1.3 255.255.255.0
 standby 172 ip 172.16.1.1
 standby 172 preempt
!
ip classless
ip route 0.0.0.0 0.0.0.0 172.16.1.2
ip http server
ip http secure-server
!
control-plane
!
line con 0
line vty 0 4
 privilege level 15
 password cisco
 login
line vty 5 15
 privilege level 15
 password cisco
 login
!
end

DLS2#
```

ALS1

```
ALS1#term len 0
ALS1#sh run
Building configuration...

Current configuration : 1619 bytes
!
version 12.1
no service pad
service timestamps debug uptime
service timestamps log uptime
no service password-encryption
!
hostname ALS1
!
no logging console
!
ip subnet-zero
!
no ip domain-lookup
vtp domain CCNP2011
vtp mode transparent
!
spanning-tree mode rapid-pvst
no spanning-tree optimize bpdu transmission
spanning-tree extend system-id
!
vlan 100
 name R1-VLAN
!
vlan 172
 name SWITCH-VLAN
!
interface Port-channel1
 switchport mode trunk
 switchport nonegotiate
 flowcontrol send off
!
interface Port-channel2
 switchport mode trunk
 switchport nonegotiate
 flowcontrol send off
!
interface FastEthernet0/1
 switchport access vlan 100
 switchport mode access
!
interface FastEthernet0/2
!
interface FastEthernet0/3
!
interface FastEthernet0/4
!
interface FastEthernet0/5
!
interface FastEthernet0/6
!
interface FastEthernet0/7
 switchport mode trunk
 switchport nonegotiate
 channel-group 1 mode on
!
interface FastEthernet0/8
 switchport mode trunk
 switchport nonegotiate
 channel-group 1 mode on
!
interface FastEthernet0/9
 switchport mode trunk
 switchport nonegotiate
 channel-group 2 mode on
!
interface FastEthernet0/10
 switchport mode trunk
 switchport nonegotiate
 channel-group 2 mode on
!
interface FastEthernet0/11
```

```
 shutdown
!
interface FastEthernet0/12
 shutdown
!
interface Vlan1
 no ip address
 no ip route-cache
 shutdown
!
interface Vlan172
 ip address 172.16.1.10 255.255.255.0
 no ip route-cache
!
ip default-gateway 172.16.1.1
ip http server
!
line con 0
line vty 0 4
 privilege level 15
 password cisco
 login
line vty 5 15
 privilege level 15
 password cisco
 login
!
!
end
ALS1#
```

ALS2

```
ALS2#term len 0
ALS2#sh run
Building configuration...

Current configuration : 1522 bytes
!
version 12.1
no service pad
service timestamps debug uptime
service timestamps log uptime
no service password-encryption
!
hostname ALS2
!
no logging console
!
ip subnet-zero
!
no ip domain-lookup
vtp domain CCNP2011
vtp mode transparent
!
!
spanning-tree mode rapid-pvst
no spanning-tree optimize bpdu transmission
spanning-tree extend system-id
!
vlan 172
 name SWITCH-VLAN
!
interface Port-channel1
 switchport mode trunk
 switchport nonegotiate
 flowcontrol send off
!
interface Port-channel2
 switchport mode trunk
 switchport nonegotiate
 flowcontrol send off
!
interface FastEthernet0/1
!
interface FastEthernet0/2
!
```

```
interface FastEthernet0/3
!
interface FastEthernet0/4
!
interface FastEthernet0/5
!
interface FastEthernet0/6
!
interface FastEthernet0/7
 switchport mode trunk
 switchport nonegotiate
 channel-group 1 mode on
!
interface FastEthernet0/8
 switchport mode trunk
 switchport nonegotiate
 channel-group 1 mode on
!
interface FastEthernet0/9
 switchport mode trunk
 switchport nonegotiate
 channel-group 2 mode on
!
interface FastEthernet0/10
 switchport mode trunk
 switchport nonegotiate
 channel-group 2 mode on
!
interface FastEthernet0/11
!
interface FastEthernet0/12
!
interface Vlan1
 no ip address
 no ip route-cache
 shutdown
!
interface Vlan172
 ip address 172.16.1.11 255.255.255.0
 no ip route-cache
!
ip default-gateway 172.16.1.1
ip http server
!
line con 0
line vty 0 4
 privilege level 15
 password cisco
 login
line vty 5 15
 privilege level 15
 password cisco
 login
!
end

ALS2#
```

CCNP LAB 88

Troubleshooting Lab

Lab Objective:

The focus of this lab is to hone your trouble isolation and resolution skills. This lab will include Layer 2 and Layer 3 technologies which fall within the scope of the current CCNP curriculum.

Lab Topology:

The lab network topology is illustrated below:

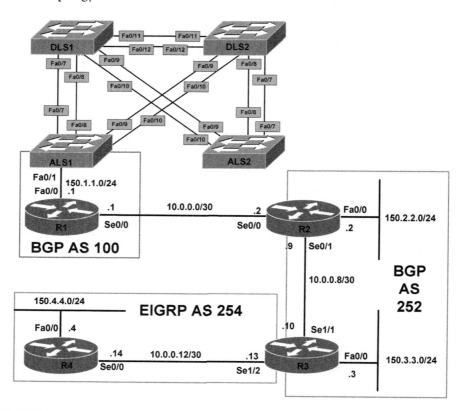

IMPORTANT NOTE: If you are using the www.howtonetwork.net racks, please download and paste the troubleshooting lab configurations. If you are using your own rack or lab, please modify this configuration to reflect the actual interface types, etc, that you have on your devices. Prior to beginning all labs, apply the pre-lab configuration for each individual device.

When completing these labs, it is important to resolve the trouble tickets in the order in which they are listed because they build on each other. For example, if you begin with Trouble Ticket # 3, you might not get the expected resolution or result if you have not completed Trouble Ticket # 1 and Trouble Ticket # 2. It is very important to follow the order listed.

Trouble Ticket # 1

You have received a problem report indicating that users on the 150.2.2.0/24 subnet are unable to reach users on the 172.16.1.0/24 subnet and vice-versa. Troubleshoot and resolve this issue. Verify your solution by pinging between these two subnets.

Trouble Ticket # 2

You have received a problem report indicating that users on the 150.3.3.0/24 subnet are also unable to reach users on the 172.16.1.0/24 subnet and vice-versa. Troubleshoot and resolve this issue. Verify your solution by pinging between these two subnets.

Trouble Ticket # 3

You have received a problem report indicating that users no users on the network can reach the 150.4.4.0/24 subnet. Troubleshoot and resolve this issue. Test your solution by pinging this subnet from any one of the other LAN subnets.

Trouble Ticket # 4

You have received a problem report indicating users connected to the 150.4.4.0/24 subnet are unable to receive IP addressing information via DHCP. Troubleshoot and resolve this issue.

LAB SOLUTIONS

Solution # 1

The static route on R1 has been mis-configured. It is pointing to 150.1.1.22 instead of 150.1.1.2:

```
R1#show ip route 172.16.1.0 255.255.255.0
Routing entry for 172.16.1.0/24
  Known via "static", distance 1, metric 0
  Advertised by bgp 100
  Routing Descriptor Blocks:
  * 150.1.1.22, via FastEthernet0/0
      Route metric is 0, traffic share count is 1
```

The result of this configuration is that the subnet will be inaccessible from all other devices. To resolve this issue, remove this static route and configure a correct next hop address:

```
R1(config)#no ip route 172.16.1.0 255.255.255.0 FastEthernet0/0 150.1.1.22
R1(config)#ip route 172.16.1.0 255.255.255.0 FastEthernet0/0 150.1.1.2
```

Solution # 2

By default, the NEXT_HOP attribute is not modified when routes are sent from a BGP speaker to an internal peer. This can be resolved in one of two ways:
*   Redistribute the 10.0.0.0/30 subnet into OSPF on R2
*   Change the NEXT_HOP attribute for BGP on R2

The following shows the latter solution. Either option is acceptable when completing this task.

```
R2(config)#router bgp 252
R2(config-router)#neighbor 10.0.0.10 next-hop-self
R2(config-router)#exit
```

Solution # 3

The issue is that R4 has been configured as a receive-only EIGRP stub router. This prevents the router from advertising the 150.4.4.0/24 subnet via EIGRP to R3:

```
R4#show running-config | section eigrp
router eigrp 254
```

```
network 0.0.0.0
no auto-summary
eigrp stub receive-only
```

To resolve this issue, configure R4 as an EIGRP stub. By default, this will cause the router to advertise connected subnets:

```
R4(config)#router eigrp 254
R4(config-router)#no eigrp stub receive-only
R4(config-router)#eigrp stub
```

Solution # 4

There are two issues here. First, the DHCP service is disabled on R2, the Cisco IOS DHCP Server. The second issue is that the Cisco IOS DHCP Relay Agent is not configured on R4. Resolve this issue by enabling Cisco IOS DHCP Server functionality on R2 and then also configuring the Cisco IOS DHCP Relay Agent on R4s LAN interface:

```
R2(config)#service dhcp

R4(config)#interface fastethernet 0/0
R4(config-if)#ip helper-address 10.0.0.9
R4(config-if)#exit
```

FINAL WORKING ROUTER CONFIGURATIONS

R1

```
R1#term len 0
R1#sh run
Building configuration...

Current configuration : 1085 bytes
!
version 12.4
service timestamps debug datetime msec
service timestamps log datetime msec
no service password-encryption
!
hostname R1
!
boot-start-marker
boot-end-marker
!
no logging console
!
no aaa new-model
no network-clock-participate slot 1
no network-clock-participate wic 0
ip cef
!
no ip domain lookup
ip auth-proxy max-nodata-conns 3
ip admission max-nodata-conns 3
!
interface FastEthernet0/0
 ip address 150.1.1.1 255.255.255.0
 duplex auto
 speed auto
!
interface Serial0/0
 ip address 10.0.0.1 255.255.255.252
 clock rate 2000000
!
interface Serial0/1
 no ip address
 shutdown
!
router bgp 100
 no synchronization
 bgp router-id 1.1.1.1
 bgp log-neighbor-changes
```

```
 network 150.1.1.0 mask 255.255.255.0
 network 172.16.1.0 mask 255.255.255.0
 neighbor 10.0.0.2 remote-as 252
 no auto-summary
!
ip forward-protocol nd
ip route 172.16.1.0 255.255.255.0 FastEthernet0/0 150.1.1.2
!
no ip http server
no ip http secure-server
!
control-plane
!
line con 0
line aux 0
line vty 0 4
 login
!
end
R1#
```

R2

```
R2#term len 0
R2#sh run
Building configuration...

Current configuration : 1391 bytes
!
version 12.4
service timestamps debug datetime msec
service timestamps log datetime msec
no service password-encryption
!
hostname R2
!
boot-start-marker
boot-end-marker
!
no logging console
!
no aaa new-model
no network-clock-participate slot 1
no network-clock-participate wic 0
ip cef
!
!
no ip dhcp use vrf connected
!
ip dhcp pool R4-SUBNET-POOL
   network 150.4.4.0 255.255.255.0
   update dns both
   default-router 150.4.4.4
   domain-name howtonetwork.net
   dns-server 172.16.1.254
   netbios-name-server 172.16.1.253
   lease 0 4
!
no ip domain lookup
ip auth-proxy max-nodata-conns 3
ip admission max-nodata-conns 3
!
interface FastEthernet0/0
 ip address 150.2.2.2 255.255.255.0
 duplex auto
 speed auto
!
interface Serial0/0
 ip address 10.0.0.2 255.255.255.252
!
interface Serial0/1
 ip address 10.0.0.9 255.255.255.252
!
router ospf 252
 router-id 2.2.2.2
 log-adjacency-changes
 network 10.0.0.9 0.0.0.0 area 0
!
router bgp 252
 no synchronization
```

```
 bgp router-id 2.2.2.2
 bgp log-neighbor-changes
 network 150.2.2.0 mask 255.255.255.0
 neighbor 10.0.0.1 remote-as 100
 neighbor 10.0.0.10 remote-as 252
 neighbor 10.0.0.10 next-hop-self
 no auto-summary
!
ip forward-protocol nd
!
no ip http server
no ip http secure-server
!
control-plane
!
line con 0
line aux 0
line vty 0 4
 login
!
end
R2#
```

R3

```
R3#term len 0
R3#sh run
Building configuration...

Current configuration : 1592 bytes
!
version 12.4
service timestamps debug datetime msec
service timestamps log datetime msec
no service password-encryption
!
hostname R3
!
boot-start-marker
boot-end-marker
!
no logging console
!
no aaa new-model
no network-clock-participate slot 1
no network-clock-participate wic 0
ip cef
!
no ip domain lookup
ip auth-proxy max-nodata-conns 3
ip admission max-nodata-conns 3
!
interface FastEthernet0/0
 ip address 150.3.3.3 255.255.255.0
 duplex auto
 speed auto
!
interface Serial1/0
 no ip address
 clock rate 128000
!
interface Serial1/1
 ip address 10.0.0.10 255.255.255.252
 clock rate 128000
!
interface Serial1/2
 ip address 10.0.0.13 255.255.255.252
 clock rate 128000
!
interface Serial1/3
 no ip address
 shutdown
!
interface Serial1/4
 no ip address
 shutdown
!
interface Serial1/5
 no ip address
 shutdown
```

```
!
interface Serial1/6
 no ip address
 shutdown
!
interface Serial1/7
 no ip address
 shutdown
!
router eigrp 254
 redistribute connected
 redistribute bgp 252 metric 1544 20000 255 1 1500
 network 10.0.0.13 0.0.0.0
 no auto-summary
!
router ospf 252
 router-id 3.3.3.3
 log-adjacency-changes
 network 10.0.0.10 0.0.0.0 area 0
!
router bgp 252
 no synchronization
 bgp router-id 3.3.3.3
 bgp log-neighbor-changes
 bgp redistribute-internal
 network 150.3.3.0 mask 255.255.255.0
 redistribute eigrp 254
 neighbor 10.0.0.9 remote-as 252
 no auto-summary
!
ip forward-protocol nd
!
no ip http server
no ip http secure-server
!
control-plane
!
line con 0
line aux 0
line vty 0 4
 login
!
end

R3#
```

R4

```
R4#term len 0
R4#sh run
Building configuration...

Current configuration : 868 bytes
!
version 12.4
service timestamps debug datetime msec
service timestamps log datetime msec
no service password-encryption
!
hostname R4
!
boot-start-marker
boot-end-marker
!
no logging console
!
no aaa new-model
no network-clock-participate slot 1
no network-clock-participate wic 0
ip cef
!
no ip domain lookup
ip auth-proxy max-nodata-conns 3
ip admission max-nodata-conns 3
!
interface FastEthernet0/0
 ip address 150.4.4.4 255.255.255.0
 ip helper-address 10.0.0.9
 duplex auto
 speed auto
```

```
!
interface Serial0/0
 ip address 10.0.0.14 255.255.255.252
!
interface Serial0/1
 no ip address
 shutdown
!
router eigrp 254
 network 0.0.0.0
 no auto-summary
 eigrp stub connected
!
ip forward-protocol nd
!
no ip http server
no ip http secure-server
!
control-plane
!
line con 0
line aux 0
line vty 0 4
 login
!
end

R4#
```

FINAL WORKING SWITCH CONFIGURATIONS

DLS1

```
DLS1#term len 0
DLS1#sh run
Building configuration...

Current configuration : 6958 bytes
!
version 12.2
no service pad
service timestamps debug datetime msec
service timestamps log datetime msec
no service password-encryption
!
hostname DLS1
!
no logging console
!
no aaa new-model
ip subnet-zero
ip routing
no ip domain-lookup
!
vtp domain CCNP2011
vtp mode transparent
!
mac access-list extended SECURE-HOSTS
 permit host 0007.8432.dd07 any
 permit host 000f.235e.ec80 any
 permit any host 000f.235e.ec80
 permit any host 0007.8432.dd07
!
spanning-tree mode rapid-pvst
spanning-tree extend system-id
spanning-tree vlan 172 priority 0
!
vlan internal allocation policy ascending
!
vlan access-map SECURE-VLAN-100 10
 action forward
 match ip address 100
vlan access-map SECURE-VLAN-100 20
 action drop
 match ip address 101
vlan access-map SECURE-VLAN-100 30
 action forward
```

```
 match mac address SECURE-HOSTS
!
vlan filter SECURE-VLAN-100 vlan-list 100
!
vlan 100
 name R1-VLAN
!
vlan 172
 name SWITCH-VLAN
!
interface Port-channel1
 switchport trunk encapsulation dot1q
 switchport mode trunk
 switchport nonegotiate
!
interface Port-channel2
 switchport trunk encapsulation dot1q
 switchport mode trunk
 switchport nonegotiate
!
interface FastEthernet0/1
 switchport mode dynamic desirable
!
interface FastEthernet0/2
 switchport mode dynamic desirable
!
interface FastEthernet0/3
 switchport mode dynamic desirable
!
interface FastEthernet0/4
 switchport mode dynamic desirable
!
interface FastEthernet0/5
 switchport mode dynamic desirable
!
interface FastEthernet0/6
 switchport mode dynamic desirable
!
interface FastEthernet0/7
 switchport trunk encapsulation dot1q
 switchport mode trunk
 switchport nonegotiate
 channel-group 1 mode on
!
interface FastEthernet0/8
 switchport trunk encapsulation dot1q
 switchport mode trunk
 switchport nonegotiate
 channel-group 1 mode on
!
interface FastEthernet0/9
 switchport trunk encapsulation dot1q
 switchport mode trunk
 switchport nonegotiate
 channel-group 2 mode on
!
interface FastEthernet0/10
 switchport trunk encapsulation dot1q
 switchport mode trunk
 switchport nonegotiate
 channel-group 2 mode on
!
interface FastEthernet0/11
 switchport mode dynamic desirable
!
interface FastEthernet0/12
 switchport mode dynamic desirable

[Truncated Output]

interface Vlan1
 no ip address
 shutdown
!
interface Vlan100
 ip address 150.1.1.2 255.255.255.0
!
interface Vlan172
 ip address 172.16.1.2 255.255.255.0
 standby 172 ip 172.16.1.1
 standby 172 priority 105
```

```
 standby 172 preempt
!
ip default-gateway 150.1.1.1
ip classless
ip route 0.0.0.0 0.0.0.0 150.1.1.1
ip http server
ip http secure-server
!
access-list 100 permit eigrp any any
access-list 100 permit tcp any any
access-list 100 permit icmp any any
access-list 101 permit ospf any any
access-list 101 permit udp any any
!
control-plane
!
line con 0
line vty 0 4
 privilege level 15
 password cisco
 login
line vty 5 15
 privilege level 15
 password cisco
 login
!
end
DLS1#
```

DLS2

```
DLS2#term len 0
DLS2#sh run
Building configuration...

Current configuration : 6326 bytes
!
version 12.2
no service pad
service timestamps debug datetime msec
service timestamps log datetime msec
no service password-encryption
!
hostname DLS2
!
no logging console
!
no aaa new-model
ip subnet-zero
no ip domain-lookup
!
vtp domain CCNP2011
vtp mode transparent
!
crypto pki trustpoint TP-self-signed-4251411712
 enrollment selfsigned
 subject-name cn=IOS-Self-Signed-Certificate-4251411712
 revocation-check none
 rsakeypair TP-self-signed-4251411712
!
crypto pki certificate chain TP-self-signed-4251411712
 certificate self-signed 01
  3082023D 308201A6 A0030201 02020101 300D0609 2A864886 F70D0101 04050030
  31312F30 2D060355 04031326 494F532D 53656C66 2D536967 6E65642D 43657274
  69666963 6174652D 34323531 34313137 3132301E 170D3933 30333031 30303038
  35315A17 0D323030 31303130 30303030 305A3031 312F302D 06035504 03132649
  4F532D53 656C662D 5369676E 65642D43 65727469 66696361 74652D34 32353134
  31313731 3230819F 300D0609 2A864886 F70D0101 01050003 818D0030 81890281
  8100AE94 C1F376F7 25FA8BF5 78952DDB D996311E BB88687C 159456EC 4DE8F593
  8F36B5F4 27371FCB 975F41A5 00644454 D6EE77CF D73A8C40 EFFB2C7F 23557F6D
  75074947 11683496 49E09EF8 4FD28F74 B728A9DA 6C581C3F E3B32D0F 6BE17264
  FB78B604 F32433BF AC42B45C 7D407F11 B8DBA748 78592994 04ADDA3C 63F9598D
  E14D0203 010001A3 65306330 0F060355 1D130101 FF040530 030101FF 30100603
  551D1104 09300782 05444C53 322E301F 0603551D 23041830 1680144E 29A5814C
  E971DC87 67B7A352 5285C959 17A7EC30 1D060355 1D0E0416 04144E29 A5814CE9
  71DC8767 B7A35252 85C95917 A7EC300D 06092A86 4886F70D 01010405 00038181
  004C710F D254C635 2CFEBAF3 DE561196 1AF7B3B0 6E93D731 21A0EB92 5C404468
  D093806C 8A91E8A5 CF832402 0D2155E0 7B6C00A1 69AA53D0 3F50A0D4 C2DCF183
  EEED7ED7 5B18BED4 6C1A5CE7 2EA11CB7 48A73B0D 4902A6B2 DB239A84 35A0AA01
  7241C7AE 6900881E 6300421E 7B37B01E 5A743362 9BC415F5 B0DA7453 C6932F93 79
```

```
 quit
!
spanning-tree mode rapid-pvst
spanning-tree extend system-id
spanning-tree vlan 172 priority 4096
!
vlan internal allocation policy ascending
!
vlan access-map FORWARD-ALL 10
 action forward
!
vlan filter FORWARD-ALL vlan-list 172
!
vlan 172
 name SWITCH-VLAN
!
interface Port-channel2
 switchport trunk encapsulation dot1q
 switchport mode trunk
 switchport nonegotiate
!
interface Port-channel1
 switchport trunk encapsulation dot1q
 switchport mode trunk
 switchport nonegotiate
!
interface FastEthernet0/1
 switchport mode dynamic desirable
!
interface FastEthernet0/2
 switchport mode dynamic desirable
!
interface FastEthernet0/3
 switchport mode dynamic desirable
!
interface FastEthernet0/4
 switchport mode dynamic desirable
!
interface FastEthernet0/5
 switchport mode dynamic desirable
!
interface FastEthernet0/6
 switchport mode dynamic desirable
!
interface FastEthernet0/7
 switchport trunk encapsulation dot1q
 switchport mode trunk
 switchport nonegotiate
 channel-group 1 mode on
!
interface FastEthernet0/8
 switchport trunk encapsulation dot1q
 switchport mode trunk
 switchport nonegotiate
 channel-group 1 mode on
!
interface FastEthernet0/9
 switchport trunk encapsulation dot1q
 switchport mode trunk
 switchport nonegotiate
 channel-group 2 mode on
!
interface FastEthernet0/10
 switchport trunk encapsulation dot1q
 switchport mode trunk
 switchport nonegotiate
 channel-group 2 mode on
!
interface FastEthernet0/11
 switchport mode dynamic desirable
!
interface FastEthernet0/12
 switchport mode dynamic desirable

[Truncated Output]

interface Vlan1
 no ip address
 no ip route-cache
 shutdown
!
```

```
  interface Vlan172
   ip address 172.16.1.3 255.255.255.0
   no ip route-cache
   standby 172 ip 172.16.1.1
   standby 172 preempt
  !
  ip default-gateway 172.16.1.2
  ip classless
  ip http server
  ip http secure-server
  !
  control-plane
  !
  line con 0
  line vty 0 4
   privilege level 15
   password cisco
   login
  line vty 5 15
   privilege level 15
   password cisco
   login
  !
  end
  DLS2#
```

ALS1

```
  ALS1#term len 0
  ALS1#sh run
  Building configuration...

  Current configuration : 1619 bytes
  !
  version 12.1
  no service pad
  service timestamps debug uptime
  service timestamps log uptime
  no service password-encryption
  !
  hostname ALS1
  !
  no logging console
  !
  ip subnet-zero
  !
  no ip domain-lookup
  vtp domain CCNP2011
  vtp mode transparent
  !
  spanning-tree mode rapid-pvst
  no spanning-tree optimize bpdu transmission
  spanning-tree extend system-id
  !
  vlan 100
   name R1-VLAN
  !
  vlan 172
   name SWITCH-VLAN
  !
  interface Port-channel1
   switchport mode trunk
   switchport nonegotiate
   flowcontrol send off
  !
  interface Port-channel2
   switchport mode trunk
   switchport nonegotiate
   flowcontrol send off
  !
  interface FastEthernet0/1
   switchport access vlan 100
   switchport mode access
  !
  interface FastEthernet0/2
  !
  interface FastEthernet0/3
  !
  interface FastEthernet0/4
  !
```

```
interface FastEthernet0/5
!
interface FastEthernet0/6
!
interface FastEthernet0/7
 switchport mode trunk
 switchport nonegotiate
 channel-group 1 mode on
!
interface FastEthernet0/8
 switchport mode trunk
 switchport nonegotiate
 channel-group 1 mode on
!
interface FastEthernet0/9
 switchport mode trunk
 switchport nonegotiate
 channel-group 2 mode on
!
interface FastEthernet0/10
 switchport mode trunk
 switchport nonegotiate
 channel-group 2 mode on
!
interface FastEthernet0/11
 shutdown
!
interface FastEthernet0/12
 shutdown
!
interface Vlan1
 no ip address
 no ip route-cache
 shutdown
!
interface Vlan172
 ip address 172.16.1.10 255.255.255.0
 no ip route-cache
!
ip default-gateway 172.16.1.1
ip http server
!
line con 0
line vty 0 4
 privilege level 15
 password cisco
 login
line vty 5 15
 privilege level 15
 password cisco
 login
!
end

ALS1#
```

ALS2

```
ALS2#term len 0
ALS2#sh run
Building configuration...

Current configuration : 1522 bytes
!
version 12.1
no service pad
service timestamps debug uptime
service timestamps log uptime
no service password-encryption
!
hostname ALS2
!
no logging console
!
ip subnet-zero
!
no ip domain-lookup
vtp domain CCNP2011
vtp mode transparent
!
```

```
spanning-tree mode rapid-pvst
no spanning-tree optimize bpdu transmission
spanning-tree extend system-id
!
vlan 172
 name SWITCH-VLAN
!
interface Port-channel1
 switchport mode trunk
 switchport nonegotiate
 flowcontrol send off
!
interface Port-channel2
 switchport mode trunk
 switchport nonegotiate
 flowcontrol send off
!
interface FastEthernet0/1
!
interface FastEthernet0/2
!
interface FastEthernet0/3
!
interface FastEthernet0/4
!
interface FastEthernet0/5
!
interface FastEthernet0/6
!
interface FastEthernet0/7
 switchport mode trunk
 switchport nonegotiate
 channel-group 1 mode on
!
interface FastEthernet0/8
 switchport mode trunk
 switchport nonegotiate
 channel-group 1 mode on
!
interface FastEthernet0/9
 switchport mode trunk
 switchport nonegotiate
 channel-group 2 mode on
!
interface FastEthernet0/10
 switchport mode trunk
 switchport nonegotiate
 channel-group 2 mode on
!
interface FastEthernet0/11
!
interface FastEthernet0/12
!
interface Vlan1
 no ip address
 no ip route-cache
 shutdown
!
interface Vlan172
 ip address 172.16.1.11 255.255.255.0
 no ip route-cache
!
ip default-gateway 172.16.1.1
ip http server
!
line con 0
line vty 0 4
 privilege level 15
 password cisco
 login
line vty 5 15
 privilege level 15
 password cisco
 login
!
end

ALS2#
```

CCNP LAB 89

Troubleshooting Lab

Lab Objective:

The focus of this lab is to hone your trouble isolation and resolution skills. This lab will include Layer 2 and Layer 3 technologies which fall within the scope of the current CCNP curriculum.

Lab Topology:

The lab network topology is illustrated below:

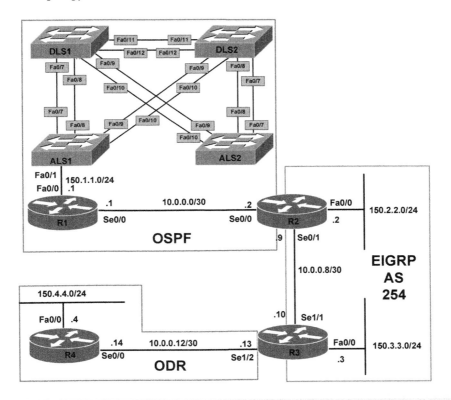

IMPORTANT NOTE: If you are using the www.howtonetwork.net racks, please download and paste the troubleshooting lab configurations. If you are using your own rack or lab, please modify this configuration to reflect the actual interface types, etc, that you have on your devices. Prior to beginning all labs, apply the pre-lab configuration for each individual device.

When completing these labs, it is important to resolve the trouble tickets in the order in which they are listed because they build on each other. For example, if you begin with Trouble Ticket # 3, you might not get the expected resolution or result if you have not completed Trouble Ticket # 1 and Trouble Ticket # 2. It is very important to follow the order listed.

Trouble Ticket # 1

You have received a problem report indicating that following a change on the 172.16.1.0/24 subnet, switches DLS1 and DLS2 are no longer able to establish an OSPF adjacency. Troubleshoot and resolve this issue. You are only allowed to makes changes to ONE of these devices, but not both.

Trouble Ticket # 2

You have received a problem report indicating that the Level 1 Network staff cannot see the OSPF neighbor adjacency between router R1 and switch DLS1. Troubleshoot and resolve this issue. You are only allowed to issue ONE command to resolve this issue.

Trouble Ticket # 3

Recently Quality of Service was implemented on the R2-R3 link. However, the NOC calls to report that packets are not getting marked as configured. Troubleshoot and resolve the issue.

Trouble Ticket # 4

You have received a problem report indicating that users on the 150.4.4.0/24 subnet are unable to reach any other subnet. Troubleshoot and resolve this issue.

Trouble Ticket # 5

Recently, IPv6 was integrated into the network. However, some test users connected to the 3FFE:ABCD:1111:1/64 (R1s LAN) and the 3FFE:ABCD:3333:3/64 (R4s LAN) subnets are complaining that they are unable to reach each other. Troubleshoot and resolve this issue.

Trouble Ticket # 6

You receive a call from the Level 1 NOC located on the 172.16.1.0/24 subnet stating that they have lost connectivity to R4. Troubleshoot and resolve this issue.

LAB SOLUTIONS

Solution # 1

The issue is that DLS1 (and all the other switches) are running MSTP. While switch DLS2 does have the MST configuration, it is actually running RSTP:

```
DLS1#show running-config | begin spanning-tree mode
spanning-tree mode mst
spanning-tree extend system-id
!
spanning-tree mst configuration
 name CCNP
 instance 1 vlan 172, 272
 instance 2 vlan 372, 472
 instance 3 vlan 572, 672
 instance 4 vlan 772, 872
!
spanning-tree mst 2 priority 0

DLS2#show running-config | begin spanning-tree mode
spanning-tree mode rapid-pvst
spanning-tree extend system-id
!
spanning-tree mst configuration
 name CCNP
 instance 1 vlan 172, 272
 instance 2 vlan 372, 472
 instance 3 vlan 572, 672
 instance 4 vlan 772, 872
!
spanning-tree mst 3 priority 0
```

To resolve this issue, configure DLS2 to also run MSTP:

```
DLS2(config)#spanning-tree mode mst
```

Solution # 2

The issue is NOT with the OSPF configuration itself. Again, keep in mind that OSPF will also form an adjacency as long as parameters, such as timers, are the same. The issue is actually because of the mismatched OSPF network statement and the IP address assigned to the SVI configured on switch DLS2. To resolve this issue, perform one of the following actions:

- Change the IP address on interface VLAN 100 to match the OSPF network statement
- Change the OSPF network statement to match the IP assigned to interface VLAN 100
- The solution below illustrates the first option:

```
DLS1(config-if)#interface vlan 100
DLS1(config-if)#ip add 150.1.1.2 255.255.255.0
```

Solution # 3

When implementing QoS, Class-Based Packet Marking changes values in a packet header with the set command. Cisco IOS confirms that your router runs CEF before you attach a service policy with the set command. To resolve this issue, configure you must enable IOS CEF on R2:

```
R2(config)#ip cef
```

Solution # 4

When implementing ODR, only the hub router should be configured with the router odr global configuration command. All that is required on the spoke(s) is that CDP be enabled. Correct this issue by disabling this command from router R4:

```
R4(config)#no router odr
```

Solution # 5

There are two issues here: first, the tunnel source and destination addresses on R1 are incorrect:

```
R1#show running-config interface tunnel 0
Building configuration...

Current configuration : 161 bytes
!
interface Tunnel0
 no ip address
 ipv6 address 2001:ABCD:1111:A::1/64
 ipv6 enable
 tunnel source 4.4.4.4
 tunnel destination 1.1.1.1
 tunnel mode ipv6ip
end
```

Second, the tunnel mode configured on R4 is incorrect:

```
R4#show running-config interface tunnel 0
Building configuration...

Current configuration : 161 bytes
!
interface Tunnel0
 no ip address
 ipv6 address 2001:ABCD:1111:A::4/64
 ipv6 enable
 tunnel source Loopback0
 tunnel destination 1.1.1.1
 tunnel mode ipip
end
```

Resolve this issue on R1 by implementing the following configuration:

```
R1(config)#interface tunnel 0
R1(config-if)#tunnel destination 4.4.4.4
R1(config-if)#tunnel source 1.1.1.1
```

Resolve this issue on R4 by implementing the following configuration:

```
R4(config)#interface tunnel 0
R4(config-if)#tunnel mode ipv6ip
```

Solution # 6

The issue is that the subnet between R3 and R4 is not advertised via EIGRP. This is the default behavior when running ODR.

```
R3#show running-config | section eigrp
router eigrp 254
 redistribute odr
 network 10.0.0.10 0.0.0.0
 network 150.3.3.3 0.0.0.0
 default-metric 1544 20000 255 1 1500
 no auto-summary
```

To resolve this issue, redistribute or advertise the connected subnet via EIGRP:

```
R3(config)#router eigrp 254
R3(config-router)#redistribute connected
```

FINAL WORKING ROUTER CONFIGURATIONS

R1

```
R1#term len 0
R1#sh run
Building configuration...

Current configuration : 1265 bytes
!
version 12.4
service timestamps debug datetime msec
service timestamps log datetime msec
no service password-encryption
!
hostname R1
!
boot-start-marker
boot-end-marker
!
no logging console
!
no aaa new-model
no network-clock-participate slot 1
no network-clock-participate wic 0
ip cef
!
no ip domain lookup
ip auth-proxy max-nodata-conns 3
ip admission max-nodata-conns 3
!
ipv6 unicast-routing
!
!
interface Loopback0
 ip address 1.1.1.1 255.255.255.255
!
interface Tunnel0
 no ip address
 ipv6 address 2001:ABCD:1111:A::1/64
 ipv6 enable
 tunnel source 1.1.1.1
 tunnel destination 4.4.4.4
 tunnel mode ipv6ip
!
interface FastEthernet0/0
 ip address 150.1.1.1 255.255.255.0
 ip ospf network point-to-multipoint
 duplex auto
 speed auto
 ipv6 address 3FFE:ABCD:1111:1::1/64
!
interface Serial0/0
```

```
 ip address 10.0.0.1 255.255.255.252
 clock rate 2000000
!
interface Serial0/1
 no ip address
 shutdown
!
router ospf 1
 router-id 1.1.1.1
 log-adjacency-changes
 network 1.1.1.1 0.0.0.0 area 0
 network 10.0.0.1 0.0.0.0 area 0
 network 150.1.1.1 0.0.0.0 area 0
!
ip forward-protocol nd
!
no ip http server
no ip http secure-server
!
ipv6 route ::/0 Tunnel0
!
control-plane
!
line con 0
line aux 0
line vty 0 4
 login
!
!
end

R1#
```

R2

```
R2#term len 0
R2#sh run
Building configuration...

Current configuration : 2609 bytes
!
version 12.4
service timestamps debug datetime msec
service timestamps log datetime msec
no service password-encryption
!
hostname R2
!
boot-start-marker
boot-end-marker
!
no logging console
!
no aaa new-model
no network-clock-participate slot 1
no network-clock-participate wic 0
ip cef
!
no ip domain lookup
ip auth-proxy max-nodata-conns 3
ip admission max-nodata-conns 3
!
class-map match-any AutoQoS-VoIP-Remark
 match ip dscp ef
 match ip dscp cs3
 match ip dscp af31
class-map match-any AutoQoS-VoIP-Control-UnTrust
 match access-group name AutoQoS-VoIP-Control
class-map match-any AutoQoS-VoIP-RTP-UnTrust
 match protocol rtp audio
 match access-group name AutoQoS-VoIP-RTCP
!
policy-map AutoQoS-Policy-UnTrust
 class AutoQoS-VoIP-RTP-UnTrust
  priority percent 70
  set dscp ef
 class AutoQoS-VoIP-Control-UnTrust
  bandwidth percent 5
  set dscp af31
 class AutoQoS-VoIP-Remark
  set dscp default
 class class-default
  fair-queue
```

```
!
interface Multilink2001100116
 bandwidth 512
 ip address 10.0.0.9 255.255.255.252
 ip tcp header-compression iphc-format
 ppp multilink
 ppp multilink fragment delay 10
 ppp multilink interleave
 ppp multilink group 2001100116
 service-policy output AutoQoS-Policy-UnTrust
 ip rtp header-compression iphc-format
!
interface FastEthernet0/0
 ip address 150.2.2.2 255.255.255.0
 duplex auto
 speed auto
!
interface Serial0/0
 ip address 10.0.0.2 255.255.255.252
!
interface Serial0/1
 bandwidth 512
 no ip address
 encapsulation ppp
 auto qos voip
 no fair-queue
 ppp multilink
 ppp multilink group 2001100116
!
router eigrp 254
 redistribute ospf 2 metric 1544 20000 255 1 1500
 network 10.0.0.9 0.0.0.0
 network 150.2.2.2 0.0.0.0
 no auto-summary
!
router ospf 2
 router-id 2.2.2.2
 log-adjacency-changes
 redistribute eigrp 254 subnets
 network 10.0.0.2 0.0.0.0 area 0
!
ip forward-protocol nd
!
no ip http server
no ip http secure-server
!
ip access-list extended AutoQoS-VoIP-Control
 permit tcp any any eq 1720
 permit tcp any any range 11000 11999
 permit udp any any eq 2427
 permit tcp any any eq 2428
 permit tcp any any range 2000 2002
 permit udp any any eq 1719
 permit udp any any eq 5060
ip access-list extended AutoQoS-VoIP-RTCP
 permit udp any any range 16384 32767
!
control-plane
!
rmon event 33333 log trap AutoQoS description "AutoQoS SNMP traps for Voice Drops"
owner AutoQoS
rmon alarm 33334 cbQosCMDropBitRate.1175.1177 30 absolute rising-threshold 1 33333
falling-threshold 0 owner AutoQoS
!
line con 0
line aux 0
line vty 0 4
 login
 length 0
!
end

R2#
```

R3

```
R3#term len 0
R3#sh run
Building configuration...

Current configuration : 3271 bytes
!
version 12.4
```

```
service timestamps debug datetime msec
service timestamps log datetime msec
no service password-encryption
!
hostname R3
!
boot-start-marker
boot-end-marker
!
no logging console
!
no aaa new-model
no network-clock-participate slot 1
no network-clock-participate wic 0
ip cef
!
no ip domain lookup
ip auth-proxy max-nodata-conns 3
ip admission max-nodata-conns 3
!
class-map match-any AutoQoS-VoIP-Remark
 match ip dscp ef
 match ip dscp cs3
 match ip dscp af31
class-map match-any AutoQoS-VoIP-Control-UnTrust
 match access-group name AutoQoS-VoIP-Control
class-map match-any AutoQoS-VoIP-RTP-UnTrust
 match protocol rtp audio
 match access-group name AutoQoS-VoIP-RTCP
!
!
policy-map AutoQoS-Policy-UnTrust
 class AutoQoS-VoIP-RTP-UnTrust
  priority percent 70
  set dscp ef
 class AutoQoS-VoIP-Control-UnTrust
  bandwidth percent 5
  set dscp af31
 class AutoQoS-VoIP-Remark
  set dscp default
 class class-default
  fair-queue
!
crypto isakmp policy 1
 encr aes 256
 authentication pre-share
 group 5
crypto isakmp key CCNP2011 address 10.0.0.14
!
crypto ipsec transform-set AES-SECURE esp-aes 256
!
crypto map SECURE 1 ipsec-isakmp
 set peer 10.0.0.14
 set transform-set AES-SECURE
 match address SECURE-TRAFFIC
!
interface Multilink2001100116
 bandwidth 128
 ip address 10.0.0.10 255.255.255.252
 ip tcp header-compression iphc-format
 ppp multilink
 ppp multilink fragment delay 10
 ppp multilink interleave
 ppp multilink group 2001100116
 service-policy output AutoQoS-Policy-UnTrust
 ip rtp header-compression iphc-format
!
interface FastEthernet0/0
 ip address 150.3.3.3 255.255.255.0
 duplex auto
 speed auto
!
interface Serial1/0
 no ip address
 shutdown
 clock rate 128000
!
interface Serial1/1
 bandwidth 512
 no ip address
 encapsulation ppp
 auto qos voip
 no fair-queue
 clock rate 128000
```

```
  ppp multilink
  ppp multilink group 2001100116
!
interface Serial1/2
 ip address 10.0.0.13 255.255.255.252
 clock rate 128000
 crypto map SECURE
!
interface Serial1/3
 no ip address
 shutdown
!
interface Serial1/4
 no ip address
 shutdown
!
interface Serial1/5
 no ip address
 shutdown
!
interface Serial1/6
 no ip address
 shutdown
!
interface Serial1/7
 no ip address
 shutdown
!
router odr
!
router eigrp 254
 redistribute connected
 redistribute odr
 network 10.0.0.10 0.0.0.0
 network 150.3.3.3 0.0.0.0
 default-metric 1544 20000 255 1 1500
 no auto-summary
!
ip forward-protocol nd
!
no ip http server
no ip http secure-server
!
ip access-list extended AutoQoS-VoIP-Control
 permit tcp any any eq 1720
 permit tcp any any range 11000 11999
 permit udp any any eq 2427
 permit tcp any any eq 2428
 permit tcp any any range 2000 2002
 permit udp any any eq 1719
 permit udp any any eq 5060
ip access-list extended AutoQoS-VoIP-RTCP
 permit udp any any range 16384 32767
ip access-list extended SECURE-TRAFFIC
 permit ip 150.3.3.0 0.0.0.255 150.4.4.0 0.0.0.255
!
control-plane
!
rmon event 33333 log trap AutoQoS description "AutoQoS SNMP traps for Voice Drops"
owner AutoQoS
rmon alarm 33333 cbQosCMDropBitRate.1081.1083 30 absolute rising-threshold 1 33333
falling-threshold 0 owner AutoQoS
!
line con 0
line aux 0
line vty 0 4
 login
 length 0
!
end
R3#
```

R4

```
R4#term len 0
R4#sh run
Building configuration...

Current configuration : 1493 bytes
!
version 12.4
service timestamps debug datetime msec
service timestamps log datetime msec
```

```
no service password-encryption
!
hostname R4
!
boot-start-marker
boot-end-marker
!
no logging console
!
no aaa new-model
no network-clock-participate slot 1
no network-clock-participate wic 0
ip cef
!
no ip domain lookup
ip auth-proxy max-nodata-conns 3
ip admission max-nodata-conns 3
!
ipv6 unicast-routing
!
crypto isakmp policy 1
 encr aes 256
 authentication pre-share
 group 5
crypto isakmp key CCNP2011 address 10.0.0.13
!
!
crypto ipsec transform-set AES-SECURE esp-aes 256
!
crypto map SECURE 1 ipsec-isakmp
 set peer 10.0.0.13
 set transform-set AES-SECURE
 match address SECURE-TRAFFIC
!
interface Loopback0
 ip address 4.4.4.4 255.255.255.255
!
interface Tunnel0
 no ip address
 ipv6 address 2001:ABCD:1111:A::4/64
 ipv6 enable
 tunnel source Loopback0
 tunnel destination 1.1.1.1
 tunnel mode ipv6ip
!
interface FastEthernet0/0
 ip address 150.4.4.4 255.255.255.0
 duplex auto
 speed auto
 ipv6 address 3FFE:ABCD:3333:3::3/64
!
interface Serial0/0
 ip address 10.0.0.14 255.255.255.252
 crypto map SECURE
!
interface Serial0/1
 no ip address
 shutdown
!
ip forward-protocol nd
!
no ip http server
no ip http secure-server
!
ip access-list extended SECURE-TRAFFIC
 permit ip 150.4.4.0 0.0.0.255 150.3.3.0 0.0.0.255
!
ipv6 route ::/0 Tunnel0
!
control-plane
!
line con 0
line aux 0
line vty 0 4
 login
!
end

R4#
```

FINAL WORKING SWITCH CONFIGURATIONS

DLS1

```
DLS1#term len 0
DLS1#sh run
Building configuration...

Current configuration : 7232 bytes
!
version 12.2
no service pad
service timestamps debug datetime msec
service timestamps log datetime msec
no service password-encryption
!
hostname DLS1
!
no logging console
!
no aaa new-model
ip subnet-zero
ip routing
no ip domain-lookup
!
vtp domain CCNP2011
vtp mode transparent
!
crypto pki trustpoint TP-self-signed-587410816
 enrollment selfsigned
 subject-name cn=IOS-Self-Signed-Certificate-587410816
 revocation-check none
 rsakeypair TP-self-signed-587410816
!
crypto pki certificate chain TP-self-signed-587410816
 certificate self-signed 01
  3082023B 308201A4 A0030201 02020101 300D0609 2A864886 F70D0101 04050030
  30312E30 2C060355 04031325 494F532D 53656C66 2D536967 6E65642D 43657274
  69666963 6174652D 35383734 31303831 36301E17 0D393330 33303231 35313435
  335A170D 32303031 30313030 30303030 5A303031 2E302C06 03550403 1325494F
  532D5365 6C662D53 69676E65 642D4365 72746966 69636174 652D3538 37343130
  38313630 819F300D 06092A86 4886F70D 01010105 0003818D 00308189 02818100
  AEBD2DC5 D3315DB6 238F0D95 29726BB6 F324D95A 78D837AF 2BDD9561 6A7FFA69
  ED7F4F3E 8E419C51 E30567A4 53F5D138 3A20D744 C9787252 707D7220 997ABCD1
  3D001AD5 7B85CF69 675C9414 9AF6668A EAB7D2F8 6812C4DF AD181C8B FD3017A8
  CCD7BBAC E699C736 A2E2BF53 42431705 AACD42D0 6560794D C912F167 C08F9F2B
  02030100 01A36530 63300F06 03551D13 0101FF04 05300301 01FF3010 0603551D
  11040930 07820544 4C53312E 301F0603 551D2304 18301680 142829C6 6CC38E29
  9C254177 B901013E 6A1CD5DA C2301D06 03551D0E 04160414 2829C66C C38E299C
  254177B9 01013E6A 1CD5DAC2 300D0609 2A864886 F70D0101 04050003 8181001C
  93ADE36D 021B3577 167C378B 958380EA 5901D61E CD4D09A4 57E61ADC 3106C207
  183213AD 6E0F1F00 2FFDC034 FD95CA1B 909B8341 F5336963 DA93A1E8 B967A50F
  57D81199 3E78342C DA628E2E 06318F0A D3E61004 784DFCDA B76BC726 05A616A3
  A47823FB 20D84774 37DBA61B 761AE8BE 6E977DAD B96028E9 78D2F4CF 2970A7
  quit
!
mac access-list extended SECURE-HOSTS
 permit host 0007.8432.dd07 any
 permit host 000f.235e.ec80 any
 permit any host 000f.235e.ec80
 permit any host 0007.8432.dd07
!
spanning-tree mode mst
spanning-tree extend system-id
!
spanning-tree mst configuration
 name CCNP
 instance 1 vlan 172, 272
 instance 2 vlan 372, 472
 instance 3 vlan 572, 672
 instance 4 vlan 772, 872
!
spanning-tree mst 2 priority 0
spanning-tree vlan 172 priority 0
!
vlan internal allocation policy ascending
!
vlan access-map SECURE-VLAN-100 10
```

```
 action forward
 match ip address 100
vlan access-map SECURE-VLAN-100 20
 action drop
 match ip address 101
vlan access-map SECURE-VLAN-100 30
 action forward
 match mac address SECURE-HOSTS
!
vlan filter SECURE-VLAN-100 vlan-list 100
!
vlan 100
 name R1-VLAN
!
vlan 172
 name SWITCH-VLAN
!
vlan 272,372,472,572,672,772,872
!
interface Port-channel1
 switchport trunk encapsulation dot1q
 switchport mode trunk
 switchport nonegotiate
!
interface Port-channel2
 switchport trunk encapsulation dot1q
 switchport mode trunk
 switchport nonegotiate
!
interface FastEthernet0/1
 switchport mode dynamic desirable
!
interface FastEthernet0/2
 switchport mode dynamic desirable
!
interface FastEthernet0/3
 switchport mode dynamic desirable
!
interface FastEthernet0/4
 switchport mode dynamic desirable
!
interface FastEthernet0/5
 switchport mode dynamic desirable
!
interface FastEthernet0/6
 switchport mode dynamic desirable
!
interface FastEthernet0/7
 switchport trunk encapsulation dot1q
 switchport mode trunk
 switchport nonegotiate
 channel-group 1 mode on
!
interface FastEthernet0/8
 switchport trunk encapsulation dot1q
 switchport mode trunk
 switchport nonegotiate
 channel-group 1 mode on
!
interface FastEthernet0/9
 switchport trunk encapsulation dot1q
 switchport mode trunk
 switchport nonegotiate
 channel-group 2 mode on
!
interface FastEthernet0/10
 switchport trunk encapsulation dot1q
 switchport mode trunk
 switchport nonegotiate
 channel-group 2 mode on
!
interface FastEthernet0/11
 switchport mode dynamic desirable
!
interface FastEthernet0/12
 switchport mode dynamic desirable

[Truncated Output]
```

```
interface Vlan1
 no ip address
 shutdown
!
interface Vlan100
 ip address 150.1.1.2 255.255.255.0
 ip ospf network point-to-point
 ip ospf hello-interval 30
!
interface Vlan172
 ip address 172.16.1.2 255.255.255.0
 standby 172 ip 172.16.1.1
 standby 172 priority 105
 standby 172 preempt
!
router ospf 1
 router-id 1.0.0.1
 log-adjacency-changes
 network 150.1.1.2 0.0.0.0 area 0
 network 172.16.1.2 0.0.0.0 area 1
!
ip classless
ip http server
ip http secure-server
!
access-list 100 permit eigrp any any
access-list 100 permit tcp any any
access-list 100 permit icmp any any
access-list 100 permit ospf any any
access-list 101 permit udp any any
!
control-plane
!
line con 0
line vty 0 4
 privilege level 15
 password cisco
 login
line vty 5 15
 privilege level 15
 password cisco
 login
!
end

DLS1#
```

DLS2

```
DLS2#term len 0
DLS2#sh run
Building configuration...

Current configuration : 6578 bytes
!
version 12.2
no service pad
service timestamps debug datetime msec
service timestamps log datetime msec
no service password-encryption
!
hostname DLS2
!
no logging console
!
no aaa new-model
ip subnet-zero
ip routing
no ip domain-lookup
!
vtp domain CCNP2011
vtp mode transparent
!
crypto pki trustpoint TP-self-signed-4251411712
 enrollment selfsigned
 subject-name cn=IOS-Self-Signed-Certificate-4251411712
 revocation-check none
 rsakeypair TP-self-signed-4251411712
```

```
!
crypto pki certificate chain TP-self-signed-4251411712
 certificate self-signed 01
  3082023D 308201A6 A0030201 02020101 300D0609 2A864886 F70D0101 04050030
  31312F30 2D060355 04031326 494F532D 53656C66 2D536967 6E65642D 43657274
  69666963 6174652D 34323531 34313137 3132301E 170D3933 30333032 31353135
  35335A17 0D323030 31303130 30303030 305A3031 312F302D 06035504 03132649
  4F532D53 656C662D 5369676E 65642D43 65727469 66696361 74652D34 32353134
  31313731 3230819F 300D0609 2A864886 F70D0101 01050003 818D0030 81890281
  8100E8D2 B354A3DC 3055D977 CA553215 F7B0EBDF AAF84ED5 C6BB5613 0B83D5D4
  4CB4109C 82A0E8F9 625B1DB6 24087AB5 49D97D41 F809DD90 21F1E0B0 3D551EB2
  3C58DFC2 37521AEA DB531AD8 0BE27076 51FD5BA0 87F5B809 BCFC0C2A E881003A
  FE98B44C DCC62189 BD0A7273 1C43B59E 4F0DAD7D 4621FEAA ECB2C187 1D4A0E7F
  00770203 010001A3 65306330 0F060355 1D130101 FF040530 030101FF 30100603
  551D1104 09300782 05444C53 322E301F 0603551D 23041830 168014AE 8DCC8DD6
  0B6A552D 2B3491A9 44B223D9 3D6B7A30 1D060355 1D0E0416 0414AE8D CC8DD60B
  6A552D2B 3491A944 B223D93D 6B7A300D 06092A86 4886F70D 01010405 00038181
  000AD56E 28479390 99FAC0B8 A0621A88 61A555DC 881D1262 F9330E1B E2E3952B
  2441BD11 428304AA C8BD6BAC 9678490F ADF93BDF 41307D7F EFA1FE8A 4DAAD9E0
  33CDDF57 0E4D869E 0B312D06 AD4F6C94 2C372FA1 950E98C0 8F59FE5A 75A3B725
  AFD49B7A 30172F31 B5E26235 30D82469 3B9DC438 C728E250 00B2BD34 BBB172B9 3E
  quit
!
spanning-tree mode mst
spanning-tree extend system-id
!
spanning-tree mst configuration
 name CCNP
 instance 1 vlan 172, 272
 instance 2 vlan 372, 472
 instance 3 vlan 572, 672
 instance 4 vlan 772, 872
!
spanning-tree mst 3 priority 0
spanning-tree vlan 172 priority 4096
!
vlan internal allocation policy ascending
!
vlan access-map FORWARD-ALL 10
 action forward
!
vlan filter FORWARD-ALL vlan-list 172
!
vlan 172
 name SWITCH-VLAN
!
vlan 272,372,472,572,672,772,872
!
interface Port-channel2
 switchport trunk encapsulation dot1q
 switchport mode trunk
 switchport nonegotiate
!
interface Port-channel1
 switchport trunk encapsulation dot1q
 switchport mode trunk
 switchport nonegotiate
!
interface FastEthernet0/1
 switchport mode dynamic desirable
!
interface FastEthernet0/2
 switchport mode dynamic desirable
!
interface FastEthernet0/3
 switchport mode dynamic desirable
!
interface FastEthernet0/4
 switchport mode dynamic desirable
!
interface FastEthernet0/5
 switchport mode dynamic desirable
!
interface FastEthernet0/6
 switchport mode dynamic desirable
!
interface FastEthernet0/7
 switchport trunk encapsulation dot1q
 switchport mode trunk
```

```
 switchport nonegotiate
 channel-group 1 mode on
!
interface FastEthernet0/8
 switchport trunk encapsulation dot1q
 switchport mode trunk
 switchport nonegotiate
 channel-group 1 mode on
!
interface FastEthernet0/9
 switchport trunk encapsulation dot1q
 switchport mode trunk
 switchport nonegotiate
 channel-group 2 mode on
!
interface FastEthernet0/10
 switchport trunk encapsulation dot1q
 switchport mode trunk
 switchport nonegotiate
 channel-group 2 mode on
!
interface FastEthernet0/11
 switchport mode dynamic desirable
!
interface FastEthernet0/12
 switchport mode dynamic desirable

[Truncated Output]

interface Vlan1
 no ip address
 shutdown
!
interface Vlan172
 ip address 172.16.1.3 255.255.255.0
 standby 172 ip 172.16.1.1
 standby 172 preempt
!
router ospf 2
 router-id 1.0.0.2
 log-adjacency-changes
 network 0.0.0.0 255.255.255.255 area 1
!
ip classless
ip http server
ip http secure-server
!
control-plane
!
line con 0
line vty 0 4
 privilege level 15
 password cisco
 login
line vty 5 15
 privilege level 15
 password cisco
 login
!
end
DLS2#
```

ALS1

```
ALS1#term len 0
ALS1#sh run
Building configuration...

Current configuration : 1830 bytes
!
version 12.1
no service pad
service timestamps debug uptime
service timestamps log uptime
no service password-encryption
!
hostname ALS1
!
```

```
no logging console
!
ip subnet-zero
!
no ip domain-lookup
vtp domain CCNP2011
vtp mode transparent
!
spanning-tree mode mst
no spanning-tree optimize bpdu transmission
spanning-tree extend system-id
!
spanning-tree mst configuration
 name CCNP
 instance 1 vlan 172, 272
 instance 2 vlan 372, 472
 instance 3 vlan 572, 672
 instance 4 vlan 772, 872
!
spanning-tree mst 1 priority 0
!
vlan 100
 name R1-VLAN
!
vlan 172
 name SWITCH-VLAN
!
vlan 272,372,472,572,672,772,872
!
interface Port-channel1
 switchport mode trunk
 switchport nonegotiate
 flowcontrol send off
!
interface Port-channel2
 switchport mode trunk
 switchport nonegotiate
 flowcontrol send off
!
interface FastEthernet0/1
 switchport access vlan 100
 switchport mode access
!
interface FastEthernet0/2
!
interface FastEthernet0/3
!
interface FastEthernet0/4
!
interface FastEthernet0/5
!
interface FastEthernet0/6
!
interface FastEthernet0/7
 switchport mode trunk
 switchport nonegotiate
 channel-group 1 mode on
!
interface FastEthernet0/8
 switchport mode trunk
 switchport nonegotiate
 channel-group 1 mode on
!
interface FastEthernet0/9
 switchport mode trunk
 switchport nonegotiate
 channel-group 2 mode on
!
interface FastEthernet0/10
 switchport mode trunk
 switchport nonegotiate
 channel-group 2 mode on
!
interface FastEthernet0/11
 shutdown
!
interface FastEthernet0/12
 shutdown
!
```

```
interface Vlan1
 no ip address
 no ip route-cache
 shutdown
!
interface Vlan172
 ip address 172.16.1.10 255.255.255.0
 no ip route-cache
!
ip default-gateway 172.16.1.1
ip http server
!
line con 0
line vty 0 4
 privilege level 15
 password cisco
 login
line vty 5 15
 privilege level 15
 password cisco
 login
!
end
ALS1#
```

ALS2

```
ALS2#term len 0
ALS2#sh run
Building configuration...

Current configuration : 1733 bytes
!
version 12.1
no service pad
service timestamps debug uptime
service timestamps log uptime
no service password-encryption
!
hostname ALS2
!
no logging console
!
ip subnet-zero
!
no ip domain-lookup
vtp domain CCNP2011
vtp mode transparent
!
spanning-tree mode mst
no spanning-tree optimize bpdu transmission
spanning-tree extend system-id
!
spanning-tree mst configuration
 name CCNP
 instance 1 vlan 172, 272
 instance 2 vlan 372, 472
 instance 3 vlan 572, 672
 instance 4 vlan 772, 872
!
spanning-tree mst 4 priority 0
!
vlan 172
 name SWITCH-VLAN
!
vlan 272,372,472,572,672,772,872
!
interface Port-channel1
 switchport mode trunk
 switchport nonegotiate
 flowcontrol send off
!
interface Port-channel2
 switchport mode trunk
 switchport nonegotiate
 flowcontrol send off
!
```

```
interface FastEthernet0/1
!
interface FastEthernet0/2
!
interface FastEthernet0/3
!
interface FastEthernet0/4
!
interface FastEthernet0/5
!
interface FastEthernet0/6
!
interface FastEthernet0/7
 switchport mode trunk
 switchport nonegotiate
 channel-group 1 mode on
!
interface FastEthernet0/8
 switchport mode trunk
 switchport nonegotiate
 channel-group 1 mode on
!
interface FastEthernet0/9
 switchport mode trunk
 switchport nonegotiate
 channel-group 2 mode on
!
interface FastEthernet0/10
 switchport mode trunk
 switchport nonegotiate
 channel-group 2 mode on
!
interface FastEthernet0/11
!
interface FastEthernet0/12
!
interface Vlan1
 no ip address
 no ip route-cache
 shutdown
!
interface Vlan172
 ip address 172.16.1.11 255.255.255.0
 no ip route-cache
!
ip default-gateway 172.16.1.1
ip http server
!
line con 0
line vty 0 4
 privilege level 15
 password cisco
 login
line vty 5 15
 privilege level 15
 password cisco
 login
!
end

ALS2#
```

CCNP LAB 90

Troubleshooting Lab

Lab Objective:

The focus of this lab is to hone your trouble isolation and resolution skills. This lab will include Layer 2 and Layer 3 technologies which fall within the scope of the current CCNP curriculum.

Lab Topology:

The lab network topology is illustrated below:

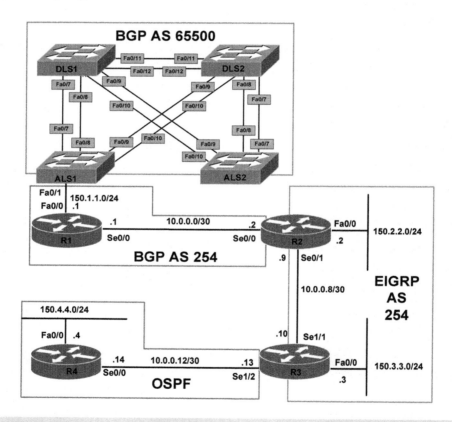

IMPORTANT NOTE: If you are using the www.howtonetwork.net racks, please download and paste the troubleshooting lab configurations. If you are using your own rack or lab, please modify this configuration to reflect the actual interface types, etc, that you have on your devices. Prior to beginning all labs, apply the pre-lab configuration for each individual device.

When completing these labs, it is important to resolve the trouble tickets in the order in which they are listed because they build on each other. For example, if you begin with Trouble Ticket # 3, you might not get the expected resolution or result if you have not completed Trouble Ticket # 1 and Trouble Ticket # 2. It is very important to follow the order listed.

Trouble Ticket # 1

You have received a problem report indicating that no one is able to reach switch DLS2. Troubleshoot and resolve this issue.

Trouble Ticket # 2

The NOC calls you to advise that they are unable to reach the 172.16.1.0/24 subnet from the 150.2.2.0/24 subnet. Troubleshoot and resolve this issue. However, ensure that your solution does NOT include advertising the 150.1.1.0/24 subnet via BGP or using static routes.

Trouble Ticket # 3

There is a secure tunnel between R1 and R4 that protects traffic between the 150.1.1.0/24 and 150.4.4.0/24 subnets. For some reason, this tunnel is not working and you are unable to ping between these subnets. Troubleshoot and resolve this issue.

Trouble Ticket # 4

A Multicast video solution is being tested between the 150.2.2.0/24 and the 150.3.3.0/24 subnets. However, the users are reporting that this is not working. Troubleshoot and resolve this issue. For proprietary reasons, the company does not allow RPs within the network.

LAB SOLUTIONS

Solution # 1

The issue is that DLS2 is running RIPv1 while switch DLS2 is running RIPv2. Switch DLS2 will therefore not receive any routing information from switch DLS1:

```
DLS2#show ip protocols
*** IP Routing is NSF aware ***

Routing Protocol is "rip"
  Outgoing update filter list for all interfaces is not set
  Incoming update filter list for all interfaces is not set
  Sending updates every 30 seconds, next due in 6 seconds
  Invalid after 180 seconds, hold down 180, flushed after 240
  Redistributing: rip
  Default version control: send version 1, receive version 1
    Interface                Send  Recv  Triggered RIP  Key-chain
    Vlan172                  1     1
  Automatic network summarization is not in effect
  Maximum path: 4
  Routing for Networks:
    172.16.0.0
  Routing Information Sources:
    Gateway          Distance      Last Update
  Distance: (default is 120)
```

To resolve this issue, configure switch DLS2 to also run RIPv2:

```
DLS2(config)#router rip
DLS2(config-router)#version 2
```

Solution # 2

There are two issues here: the first issue is that R1 has been configured with the incorrect AS number for its peer, switch DLS1:

```
R1#show ip bgp summary
BGP router identifier 1.1.1.1, local AS number 254
BGP table version is 12, main routing table version 12
6 network entries using 702 bytes of memory
6 path entries using 312 bytes of memory
5/4 BGP path/bestpath attribute entries using 620 bytes of memory
```

```
0 BGP route-map cache entries using 0 bytes of memory
0 BGP filter-list cache entries using 0 bytes of memory
BGP using 1634 total bytes of memory
BGP activity 7/1 prefixes, 7/1 paths, scan interval 60 secs

Neighbor     V    AS MsgRcvd MsgSent  TblVer  InQ OutQ Up/Down  State/PfxRcd
10.0.0.2     4   254      80      77      12    0    0 01:05:34           5
150.1.1.2    4 56500      74      88       0    0    0 00:01:13 Active
```

To resolve this issue, implement the following configuration on router R1:

```
R1(config)#router bgp 254
R1(config-router)#neighbor 150.1.1.2 remote-as 65500
```

The second issue is that the NEXT_HOP for this subnet will be unknown to R2. R2 will not be able to reach this subnet because of this. Resolve this issue on R1 as follows:

```
R1(config)#router bgp 254
R1(config-router)#neighbor 10.0.0.2 next-hop-self
```

Solution # 3

There issue actually resides on R2, which has an ACL applied in the inbound direction. This ACL needs to be modified to permit ESP (protocol number 50):

```
R2#show ip access-lists
Extended IP access list INTERNET-PROTECTION
    10 permit tcp any any eq bgp (27 matches)
    20 permit tcp any eq bgp any
    30 deny ospf any any
    40 deny eigrp any any
    50 deny udp any any eq rip
    60 deny 41 any any
    70 permit tcp any any eq www
    80 permit tcp any any eq 443
    90 deny tcp any any eq telnet
    100 deny tcp any eq telnet any
    110 permit icmp any any
    120 permit gre any any
    130 permit udp any eq 50 any
    140 permit udp any any eq 50
    150 permit udp any eq isakmp any
    160 permit udp any any eq isakmp
    200 deny ip any any (83 matches)
```

To resolve this issue, implement the following configuration on R2:

```
R2(config)#ip access-list extended INTERNET-PROTECTION
R2(config-ext-nacl)#170 permit esp any any
```

Solution # 4

The issue is that Sparse Mode forwarding is being used and there is no Rendezvous Point configured on the network:

```
R2#show ip pim interface

Address        Interface         Ver/   Nbr    Query  DR     DR
                                 Mode   Count  Intvl  Prior
150.2.2.2      FastEthernet0/0   v2/S   1      30     1      150.2.2.2
10.0.0.9       Serial0/1         v2/S   1      30     1      0.0.0.0

R3#show ip pim interface

Address        Interface         Ver/   Nbr    Query  DR     DR
                                 Mode   Count  Intvl  Prior
10.0.0.10      Serial1/1         v2/S   1      30     1      0.0.0.0
150.3.3.3      FastEthernet0/0   v2/S   1      30     1      150.3.3.3
```

To resolve this issue, without using an RP, configure Dense Mode forwarding instead:

```
R2(config)#int f0/0
R2(config-if)#ip pim dense-mode
R2(config-if)#exit
R2(config)#int s0/1
R2(config-if)#ip pim dense-mode

R3(config)#int f0/0
R3(config-if)#ip pim dense-mode
R3(config-if)#exit
R3(config)#int s1/1
R3(config-if)#ip pim dense-mode
```

FINAL WORKING ROUTER CONFIGURATIONS

R1

```
R1#ter len 0
R1#sh run
Building configuration...

Current configuration : 1641 bytes
!
version 12.4
service timestamps debug datetime msec
service timestamps log datetime msec
no service password-encryption
!
hostname R1
!
boot-start-marker
boot-end-marker
!
no logging console
!
no aaa new-model
no network-clock-participate slot 1
no network-clock-participate wic 0
ip cef
!
no ip domain lookup
ip auth-proxy max-nodata-conns 3
ip admission max-nodata-conns 3
!
crypto isakmp policy 1
 encr 3des
 authentication pre-share
 group 2
crypto isakmp key CCNP2011 address 10.0.0.14
!
!
crypto ipsec transform-set TRIPLE-DES esp-3des
 mode transport
!
crypto ipsec profile ENCRYPT-GRE
 set transform-set TRIPLE-DES
!
interface Loopback0
 ip address 1.1.1.1 255.255.255.255
!
interface Tunnel0
 ip address 192.168.1.1 255.255.255.248
 tunnel source Serial0/0
 tunnel destination 10.0.0.14
 tunnel mode ipsec ipv4
 tunnel protection ipsec profile ENCRYPT-GRE
!
interface FastEthernet0/0
 ip address 150.1.1.1 255.255.255.0
 duplex auto
 speed auto
!
interface Serial0/0
 ip address 10.0.0.1 255.255.255.252
 clock rate 2000000
!
interface Serial0/1
```

```
  no ip address
  shutdown
!
router eigrp 100
  network 150.1.1.1 0.0.0.0
  network 192.168.1.1 0.0.0.0
  no auto-summary
!
router bgp 254
  no synchronization
  bgp router-id 1.1.1.1
  bgp log-neighbor-changes
  network 1.1.1.1 mask 255.255.255.255
  neighbor 10.0.0.2 remote-as 254
  neighbor 10.0.0.2 next-hop-self
  neighbor 150.1.1.2 remote-as 65500
  neighbor 150.1.1.2 default-originate
  no auto-summary
!
ip forward-protocol nd
!
no ip http server
no ip http secure-server
!
control-plane
!
line con 0
line aux 0
line vty 0 4
  login
!
end

R1#
```

R2

```
R2#term len 0
R2#sh run
Building configuration...

Current configuration : 1278 bytes
!
version 12.4
service timestamps debug datetime msec
service timestamps log datetime msec
no service password-encryption
!
hostname R2
!
boot-start-marker
boot-end-marker
!
no logging console
!
no aaa new-model
no network-clock-participate slot 1
no network-clock-participate wic 0
ip cef
!
no ip domain lookup
ip multicast-routing
ip auth-proxy max-nodata-conns 3
ip admission max-nodata-conns 3
!
interface FastEthernet0/0
  ip address 150.2.2.2 255.255.255.0
  ip pim dense-mode
  ip igmp join-group 227.2.2.2
  duplex auto
  speed auto
!
interface Serial0/0
  ip address 10.0.0.2 255.255.255.252
  ip access-group INTERNET-PROTECTION in
!
interface Serial0/1
  ip address 10.0.0.9 255.255.255.252
  ip pim dense-mode
```

```
!
router eigrp 254
 redistribute connected
 redistribute bgp 254 metric 1544 20000 255 1 1500
 network 10.0.0.9 0.0.0.0
 network 150.2.2.2 0.0.0.0
 no auto-summary
!
router bgp 254
 no synchronization
 bgp router-id 2.2.2.2
 bgp log-neighbor-changes
 bgp redistribute-internal
 redistribute eigrp 254
 neighbor 10.0.0.1 remote-as 254
 neighbor 10.0.0.1 next-hop-self
 no auto-summary
!
ip forward-protocol nd
!
no ip http server
no ip http secure-server
!
ip access-list extended INTERNET-PROTECTION
 permit tcp any any eq bgp
 permit tcp any eq bgp any
 deny    ospf any any
 deny    eigrp any any
 deny    udp any any eq rip
 deny    41 any any
 permit tcp any any eq www
 permit tcp any any eq 443
 deny    tcp any any eq telnet
 deny    tcp any eq telnet any
 permit icmp any any
 permit gre any any
 permit udp any eq 50 any
 permit udp any any eq 50
 permit udp any eq isakmp any
 permit udp any any eq isakmp
 permit esp any any
 deny    ip any any
!
control-plane
!
line con 0
line aux 0
line vty 0 4
 login
!
end

R2#
```

R3

```
R3#term len 0
R3#sh run
Building configuration...

Current configuration : 1532 bytes
!
version 12.4
service timestamps debug datetime msec
service timestamps log datetime msec
no service password-encryption
!
hostname R3
!
boot-start-marker
boot-end-marker
!
no logging console
!
no aaa new-model
no network-clock-participate slot 1
no network-clock-participate wic 0
ip cef
!
```

```
 no ip domain lookup
 ip multicast-routing
 ip auth-proxy max-nodata-conns 3
 ip admission max-nodata-conns 3
 !
 interface FastEthernet0/0
  ip address 150.3.3.3 255.255.255.0
  ip pim dense-mode
  ip igmp join-group 227.3.3.3
  duplex auto
  speed auto
 !
 interface Serial1/0
  no ip address
  shutdown
  clock rate 128000
 !
 interface Serial1/1
  ip address 10.0.0.10 255.255.255.252
  ip pim dense-mode
  clock rate 128000
 !
 interface Serial1/2
  ip address 10.0.0.13 255.255.255.252
  clock rate 128000
 !
 interface Serial1/3
  no ip address
  shutdown
 !
 interface Serial1/4
  no ip address
  shutdown
 !
 interface Serial1/5
  no ip address
  shutdown
 !
 interface Serial1/6
  no ip address
  shutdown
 !
 interface Serial1/7
  no ip address
  shutdown
 !
 router eigrp 254
  redistribute ospf 3 metric 1544 20000 255 1 1500
  network 10.0.0.10 0.0.0.0
  network 150.3.3.3 0.0.0.0
  no auto-summary
 !
 router ospf 3
  router-id 3.3.3.3
  log-adjacency-changes
  redistribute eigrp 254 metric 10 metric-type 1 subnets tag 3333
  network 10.0.0.13 0.0.0.0 area 0
 !
 ip forward-protocol nd
 !
 no ip http server
 no ip http secure-server
 !
 control-plane
 !
 line con 0
 line aux 0
 line vty 0 4
  login
 !
 end
 R3#
```

R4

```
R4#term len 0
R4#sh run
Building configuration...

Current configuration : 1498 bytes
```

```
!
version 12.4
service timestamps debug datetime msec
service timestamps log datetime msec
no service password-encryption
!
hostname R4
!
boot-start-marker
boot-end-marker
!
no logging console
!
no aaa new-model
no network-clock-participate slot 1
no network-clock-participate wic 0
ip cef
!
no ip domain lookup
ip auth-proxy max-nodata-conns 3
ip admission max-nodata-conns 3
!
crypto isakmp policy 1
 encr 3des
 authentication pre-share
 group 2
crypto isakmp key CCNP2011 address 10.0.0.1
!
crypto ipsec transform-set TRIPLE-DES esp-3des
 mode transport
!
crypto ipsec profile ENCRYPT-GRE
 set transform-set TRIPLE-DES
!
interface Loopback0
 ip address 4.4.4.4 255.255.255.255
!
interface Tunnel0
 ip address 192.168.1.4 255.255.255.248
 tunnel source Serial0/0
 tunnel destination 10.0.0.1
 tunnel mode ipsec ipv4
 tunnel protection ipsec profile ENCRYPT-GRE
!
interface FastEthernet0/0
 ip address 150.4.4.4 255.255.255.0
 duplex auto
 speed auto
!
interface Serial0/0
 ip address 10.0.0.14 255.255.255.252
!
interface Serial0/1
 no ip address
 shutdown
!
router eigrp 100
 network 150.4.4.4 0.0.0.0
 network 192.168.1.4 0.0.0.0
 no auto-summary
!
router ospf 4
 router-id 4.4.4.4
 log-adjacency-changes
 network 4.4.4.4 0.0.0.0 area 1
 network 10.0.0.14 0.0.0.0 area 0
!
ip forward-protocol nd
!
no ip http server
no ip http secure-server
!
control-plane
!
line con 0
line aux 0
line vty 0 4
 login
!
end
R4#
```

FINAL WORKING SWITCH CONFIGURATIONS

DLS1

```
DLS1#term len 0
DLS1#sh run
Building configuration...

Current configuration : 7674 bytes
!
version 12.2
no service pad
service timestamps debug datetime msec
service timestamps log datetime msec
no service password-encryption
!
hostname DLS1
!
no logging console
!
no aaa new-model
ip subnet-zero
ip routing
no ip domain-lookup
!
vtp domain CCNP2011
vtp mode transparent
!
crypto pki trustpoint TP-self-signed-587410816
 enrollment selfsigned
 subject-name cn=IOS-Self-Signed-Certificate-587410816
 revocation-check none
 rsakeypair TP-self-signed-587410816
!
crypto pki certificate chain TP-self-signed-587410816
 certificate self-signed 01
  3082023B 308201A4 A0030201 02020101 300D0609 2A864886 F70D0101 04050030
  30312E30 2C060355 04031325 494F532D 53656C66 2D536967 6E65642D 43657274
  69666963 6174652D 35383734 31303831 36301E17 0D393330 33303130 30323631
  385A170D 32303031 30313030 30303030 5A303031 2E302C06 03550403 1325494F
  532D5365 6C662D53 69676E65 642D4365 72746966 69636174 652D3538 37343130
  38313630 819F300D 06092A86 4886F70D 01010105 0003818D 00308189 02818100
  C2CA4D89 D2218DFA EAB39F1C 78645163 09C4BD14 97BC6EA3 92478CE4 FECD51FD
  F0F4477D D2B855C0 656A5AC9 2B6D7676 3C6D6981 04DB47E0 8BE740A9 96F24892
  FC4E9A47 C597D9BF FC075C43 EF1D7B25 3E75F4A5 37242FA1 80234A62 CF2C2FAE
  9E1C4BE3 600197FA 7DD71965 379E6D6A 0E910A8F ADECD58C F7CAEE9F 9A2A021D
  02030100 01A36530 63300F06 03551D13 0101FF04 05300301 01FF3010 0603551D
  11040930 07820544 4C53312E 301F0603 551D2304 18301680 1492F5AF C5A0CB0D
  500DF95D 4B071EBE 121906D8 3A301D06 03551D0E 04160414 92F5AFC5 A0CB0D50
  0DF95D4B 071EBE12 1906D83A 300D0609 2A864886 F70D0101 04050003 8181005C
  5416F636 445BCB62 9F623BE0 9AE5021B D1A5C425 C34B7E53 32489192 280D6E70
  1FA0FF6D 007D1E8A 57EE5359 C5CAA22E 045A4E55 A7585A28 9AB8C144 2B8B3414
  87977DBA 703468C9 6C60ACCE C3D80BEB 9DADDB10 FCA96355 7406F0E3 F80831B8
  0401AFA9 ABFCE538 D95B9D3F EA84890C 0B420AC7 9E79ED91 FE040509 4A29E6
  quit
!
mac access-list extended SECURE-HOSTS
 permit host 0007.8432.dd07 any
 permit host 000f.235e.ec80 any
 permit any host 000f.235e.ec80
 permit any host 0007.8432.dd07
!
spanning-tree mode mst
spanning-tree extend system-id
!
spanning-tree mst configuration
 name CCNP
 instance 1 vlan 172, 272
 instance 2 vlan 372, 472
 instance 3 vlan 572, 672
 instance 4 vlan 772, 872
!
spanning-tree mst 2 priority 0
spanning-tree vlan 172 priority 0
!
vlan internal allocation policy ascending
!
vlan access-map SECURE-VLAN-100 10
 action forward
 match ip address 100
```

```
vlan access-map SECURE-VLAN-100 20
 action drop
 match ip address 101
vlan access-map SECURE-VLAN-100 30
 action forward
 match mac address SECURE-HOSTS
!
vlan filter SECURE-VLAN-100 vlan-list 100
!
vlan 100
 name R1-VLAN
!
vlan 172
 name SWITCH-VLAN
!
vlan 272,372,472,572,672,772,872
!
interface Port-channel1
 switchport trunk encapsulation dot1q
 switchport mode trunk
 switchport nonegotiate
!
interface Port-channel2
 switchport trunk encapsulation dot1q
 switchport mode trunk
 switchport nonegotiate
!
interface FastEthernet0/1
 switchport mode dynamic desirable
!
interface FastEthernet0/2
 switchport mode dynamic desirable
!
interface FastEthernet0/3
 switchport mode dynamic desirable
!
interface FastEthernet0/4
 switchport mode dynamic desirable
!
interface FastEthernet0/5
 switchport mode dynamic desirable
!
interface FastEthernet0/6
 switchport mode dynamic desirable
!
interface FastEthernet0/7
 switchport trunk encapsulation dot1q
 switchport mode trunk
 switchport nonegotiate
 channel-group 1 mode on
!
interface FastEthernet0/8
 switchport trunk encapsulation dot1q
 switchport mode trunk
 switchport nonegotiate
 channel-group 1 mode on
!
interface FastEthernet0/9
 switchport trunk encapsulation dot1q
 switchport mode trunk
 switchport nonegotiate
 channel-group 2 mode on
!
interface FastEthernet0/10
 switchport trunk encapsulation dot1q
 switchport mode trunk
 switchport nonegotiate
 channel-group 2 mode on
!
interface FastEthernet0/11
 switchport mode dynamic desirable
!
interface FastEthernet0/12
 switchport mode dynamic desirable

[Truncated Output]

interface Vlan1
 no ip address
 shutdown
!
```

```
interface Vlan100
 ip address 150.1.1.2 255.255.255.0
 ip ospf network point-to-point
 ip ospf hello-interval 30
!
interface Vlan172
 ip address 172.16.1.2 255.255.255.0
 standby 172 ip 172.16.1.1
 standby 172 priority 105
 standby 172 preempt
!
router rip
 version 2
 redistribute bgp 65500 metric 1 route-map SET-ADMIN-TAGS
 network 172.16.0.0
 no auto-summary
!
router bgp 65500
 no synchronization
 bgp router-id 1.0.0.1
 bgp log-neighbor-changes
 redistribute rip
 neighbor 150.1.1.1 remote-as 254
 no auto-summary
!
ip classless
ip http server
ip http secure-server
!
access-list 1 permit 0.0.0.0 255.254.255.255
access-list 2 permit 0.1.0.0 255.254.255.255
access-list 100 permit eigrp any any
access-list 100 permit tcp any any
access-list 100 permit icmp any any
access-list 100 permit ospf any any
access-list 101 permit udp any any
route-map SET-ADMIN-TAGS permit 10
 match ip address 1
 set tag 24680
!
route-map SET-ADMIN-TAGS permit 20
 match ip address 2
 set tag 13579
!
control-plane
!
line con 0
line vty 0 4
 privilege level 15
 password cisco
 login
line vty 5 15
 privilege level 15
 password cisco
 login
!
end

DLS1#
```

DLS2

```
DLS2#term len 0
DLS2#sh run
Building configuration...

Current configuration : 6541 bytes
!
version 12.2
no service pad
service timestamps debug datetime msec
service timestamps log datetime msec
no service password-encryption
!
hostname DLS2
!
no logging console
!
no aaa new-model
ip subnet-zero
```

```
ip routing
no ip domain-lookup
!
vtp domain CCNP2011
vtp mode transparent
!
crypto pki trustpoint TP-self-signed-4251411712
 enrollment selfsigned
 subject-name cn=IOS-Self-Signed-Certificate-4251411712
 revocation-check none
 rsakeypair TP-self-signed-4251411712
!
crypto pki certificate chain TP-self-signed-4251411712
 certificate self-signed 01
  3082023D 308201A6 A0030201 02020101 300D0609 2A864886 F70D0101 04050030
  31312F30 2D060355 04031326 494F532D 53656C66 2D536967 6E65642D 43657274
  69666963 6174652D 34323531 34313137 3132301E 170D3933 30333031 30303238
  33335A17 0D323030 31303130 30303030 305A3031 312F302D 06035504 03132649
  4F532D53 656C662D 5369676E 65642D43 65727469 66696361 74652D34 32353134
  31313731 3230819F 300D0609 2A864886 F70D0101 01050003 818D0030 81890281
  8100EBD7 58976F8B 96E9DA0E 2FAEA0A7 71A2CDE8 CEC02535 3D0D0E93 7D3C1C69
  A9518A67 96BC1E0A DF1DCE68 54C5A985 B3582306 3E92BF51 F09BCBAC 9FC50D10
  9E3E2787 B872D6EC 147D3096 DCD9C3B1 0D512DC0 602D588A 029480E8 495425E7
  93BEBF31 2FF0D42B C69504F2 A8C6646C 688B25FC F807119A 8929B5BD 4E1514DF
  51D10203 010001A3 65306330 0F060355 1D130101 FF040530 030101FF 30100603
  551D1104 09300782 05444C53 322E301F 0603551D 23041830 16801466 63F7CC4E
  9DF8BC0C CCFE20A4 A669AFBA 72BCF530 1D060355 1D0E0416 04146663 F7CC4E9D
  F8BC0CCC FE20A4A6 69AFBA72 BCF5300D 06092A86 4886F70D 01010405 00038181
  002F4C43 4EE3EC2C 6428D06D 977191FD 52CD28B6 3E79B7BA 64C27555 14C79758
  36746E04 A7748388 EE3A98A0 25101B73 A414F78A 4DAC2F1B C5BD20FC 1253D64A
  63189715 327F4070 B6D0161F 557CDEBB EE191035 520D8760 5EFC39F3 175D430E
  9F586D21 9EB21B77 5682BC90 DA4D2178 3AD7D0BB 74DF5A3E F13E3F60 55D6AE98 45
 quit
!
spanning-tree mode mst
spanning-tree extend system-id
!
spanning-tree mst configuration
 name CCNP
 instance 1 vlan 172, 272
 instance 2 vlan 372, 472
 instance 3 vlan 572, 672
 instance 4 vlan 772, 872
!
spanning-tree mst 3 priority 0
spanning-tree vlan 172 priority 4096
!
vlan internal allocation policy ascending
!
vlan access-map FORWARD-ALL 10
 action forward
!
vlan filter FORWARD-ALL vlan-list 172
!
vlan 172
 name SWITCH-VLAN
!
vlan 272,372,472,572,672,772,872
!
interface Port-channel2
 switchport trunk encapsulation dot1q
 switchport mode trunk
 switchport nonegotiate
!
interface Port-channel1
 switchport trunk encapsulation dot1q
 switchport mode trunk
 switchport nonegotiate
!
interface FastEthernet0/1
 switchport mode dynamic desirable
!
interface FastEthernet0/2
 switchport mode dynamic desirable
!
interface FastEthernet0/3
 switchport mode dynamic desirable
!
interface FastEthernet0/4
 switchport mode dynamic desirable
!
```

```
interface FastEthernet0/5
 switchport mode dynamic desirable
!
interface FastEthernet0/6
 switchport mode dynamic desirable
!
interface FastEthernet0/7
 switchport trunk encapsulation dot1q
 switchport mode trunk
 switchport nonegotiate
 channel-group 1 mode on
!
interface FastEthernet0/8
 switchport trunk encapsulation dot1q
 switchport mode trunk
 switchport nonegotiate
 channel-group 1 mode on
!
interface FastEthernet0/9
 switchport trunk encapsulation dot1q
 switchport mode trunk
 switchport nonegotiate
 channel-group 2 mode on
!
interface FastEthernet0/10
 switchport trunk encapsulation dot1q
 switchport mode trunk
 switchport nonegotiate
 channel-group 2 mode on
!
interface FastEthernet0/11
 switchport mode dynamic desirable
!
interface FastEthernet0/12
 switchport mode dynamic desirable

[Truncated Output]

interface Vlan1
 no ip address
 shutdown
!
interface Vlan172
 ip address 172.16.1.3 255.255.255.0
 standby 172 ip 172.16.1.1
 standby 172 preempt
!
router rip
 version 2
 network 172.16.0.0
 no auto-summary
!
ip classless
ip http server
ip http secure-server
!
control-plane
!
line con 0
line vty 0 4
 privilege level 15
 password cisco
 login
line vty 5 15
 privilege level 15
 password cisco
 login
!
end
DLS2#
```

ALS1

```
ALS1#term len 0
ALS1#sh run
Building configuration...

Current configuration : 1830 bytes
!
```

```
version 12.1
no service pad
service timestamps debug uptime
service timestamps log uptime
no service password-encryption
!
hostname ALS1
!
no logging console
!
ip subnet-zero
!
no ip domain-lookup
vtp domain CCNP2011
vtp mode transparent
!
spanning-tree mode mst
no spanning-tree optimize bpdu transmission
spanning-tree extend system-id
!
spanning-tree mst configuration
 name CCNP
 instance 1 vlan 172, 272
 instance 2 vlan 372, 472
 instance 3 vlan 572, 672
 instance 4 vlan 772, 872
!
spanning-tree mst 1 priority 0
!
vlan 100
 name R1-VLAN
!
vlan 172
 name SWITCH-VLAN
!
vlan 272,372,472,572,672,772,872
!
interface Port-channel1
 switchport mode trunk
 switchport nonegotiate
 flowcontrol send off
!
interface Port-channel2
 switchport mode trunk
 switchport nonegotiate
 flowcontrol send off
!
interface FastEthernet0/1
 switchport access vlan 100
 switchport mode access
!
interface FastEthernet0/2
!
interface FastEthernet0/3
!
interface FastEthernet0/4
!
interface FastEthernet0/5
!
interface FastEthernet0/6
!
interface FastEthernet0/7
 switchport mode trunk
 switchport nonegotiate
 channel-group 1 mode on
!
interface FastEthernet0/8
 switchport mode trunk
 switchport nonegotiate
 channel-group 1 mode on
!
interface FastEthernet0/9
 switchport mode trunk
 switchport nonegotiate
 channel-group 2 mode on
!
interface FastEthernet0/10
 switchport mode trunk
 switchport nonegotiate
 channel-group 2 mode on
!
```

```
interface FastEthernet0/11
 shutdown
!
interface FastEthernet0/12
 shutdown
!
interface Vlan1
 no ip address
 no ip route-cache
 shutdown
!
interface Vlan172
 ip address 172.16.1.10 255.255.255.0
 no ip route-cache
!
ip default-gateway 172.16.1.1
ip http server
!
line con 0
line vty 0 4
 privilege level 15
 password cisco
 login
line vty 5 15
 privilege level 15
 password cisco
 login
!
!
end
ALS1#
```

ALS2

```
ALS2#term len 0
ALS2#sh run
Building configuration...

Current configuration : 1733 bytes
!
version 12.1
no service pad
service timestamps debug uptime
service timestamps log uptime
no service password-encryption
!
hostname ALS2
!
no logging console
!
ip subnet-zero
!
no ip domain-lookup
vtp domain CCNP2011
vtp mode transparent
!
spanning-tree mode mst
no spanning-tree optimize bpdu transmission
spanning-tree extend system-id
!
spanning-tree mst configuration
 name CCNP
 instance 1 vlan 172, 272
 instance 2 vlan 372, 472
 instance 3 vlan 572, 672
 instance 4 vlan 772, 872
!
spanning-tree mst 4 priority 0
!
vlan 172
 name SWITCH-VLAN
!
vlan 272,372,472,572,672,772,872
!
interface Port-channel1
 switchport mode trunk
 switchport nonegotiate
 flowcontrol send off
!
interface Port-channel2
```

```
 switchport mode trunk
 switchport nonegotiate
 flowcontrol send off
!
interface FastEthernet0/1
!
interface FastEthernet0/2
!
interface FastEthernet0/3
!
interface FastEthernet0/4
!
interface FastEthernet0/5
!
interface FastEthernet0/6
!
interface FastEthernet0/7
 switchport mode trunk
 switchport nonegotiate
 channel-group 1 mode on
!
interface FastEthernet0/8
 switchport mode trunk
 switchport nonegotiate
 channel-group 1 mode on
!
interface FastEthernet0/9
 switchport mode trunk
 switchport nonegotiate
 channel-group 2 mode on
!
interface FastEthernet0/10
 switchport mode trunk
 switchport nonegotiate
 channel-group 2 mode on
!
interface FastEthernet0/11
!
interface FastEthernet0/12
!
interface Vlan1
 no ip address
 no ip route-cache
 shutdown
!
interface Vlan172
 ip address 172.16.1.11 255.255.255.0
 no ip route-cache
!
ip default-gateway 172.16.1.1
ip http server
!
line con 0
line vty 0 4
 privilege level 15
 password cisco
 login
line vty 5 15
 privilege level 15
 password cisco
 login
!
end

ALS2#
```

CCNP LAB 91

Troubleshooting Lab

Lab Objective:

The focus of this lab is to hone your trouble isolation and resolution skills. This lab will include Layer 2 and Layer 3 technologies which fall within the scope of the current CCNP curriculum.

Lab Topology:

The lab network topology is illustrated below:

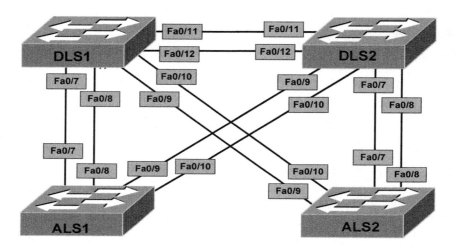

IMPORTANT NOTE: If you are using the www.howtonetwork.net racks, please download and paste the troubleshooting lab configurations. If you are using your own rack or lab, please modify this configuration to reflect the actual interface types, etc, that you have on your devices. Prior to beginning all labs, apply the pre-lab configuration for each individual device.

When completing these labs, it is important to resolve the trouble tickets in the order in which they are listed because they build on each other. For example, if you begin with Trouble Ticket # 3, you might not get the expected resolution or result if you have not completed Trouble Ticket # 1 and Trouble Ticket # 2. It is very important to follow the order listed.

Trouble Ticket # 1

You have received a problem report indicating that HSRP is not working between switches DLS1 and DLS1. Troubleshoot and resolve this issue.

Trouble Ticket # 2

The NOC has called you advising that they are unable to ping switch ALS1 from any of the devices. Troubleshoot and resolve this issue.

Trouble Ticket # 3

Users connected to the 150.100.1.0/24 subnet has complained that they are unable to reach devices on the 150.200.1.0/24 subnet and vice-versa. Troubleshoot and resolve this issue.

Trouble Ticket # 4

You have received an urgent call from the NOC stating that following some configuration changes on switches DLS1 and DLS2, their monitoring servers are no longer receiving any Spanning-Tree Protocol notifications from the devices. Troubleshoot and resolve this issue.

LAB SOLUTIONS

Solution # 1

The issue is that both switch DLS1 and DLS2 have been configured with the same IP addresses for the SVIs for VLANs 100 and 200:

```
DLS1#show running-config interface vlan 100
Building configuration...

Current configuration : 138 bytes
!
interface Vlan100
 ip address 150.100.1.2 255.255.255.0
 standby 100 ip 150.100.1.1
 standby 100 priority 105
 standby 100 preempt
end

DLS1#show running-config interface vlan 200
Building configuration...

Current configuration : 112 bytes
!
interface Vlan200
 ip address 150.200.1.2 255.255.255.0
 standby 200 ip 150.200.1.1
 standby 200 preempt
end

DLS2#show running-config interface vlan 100
Building configuration...

Current configuration : 112 bytes
!
interface Vlan100
 ip address 150.100.1.2 255.255.255.0
 standby 100 ip 150.100.1.1
 standby 100 preempt
end

DLS2#show running-config interface vlan 200
Building configuration...

Current configuration : 138 bytes
!
interface Vlan200
 ip address 150.200.1.2 255.255.255.0
 standby 200 ip 150.200.1.1
 standby 200 priority 105
 standby 200 preempt
end
```

To resolve this issue, change the configuration on switch DLS2s SVIs to a different IP address:

```
DLS2(config)#interface vlan 100
DLS2(config-if)#ip address 150.100.1.3 255.255.255.0
DLS2(config-if)#exit
DLS2(config)#interface vlan 200
DLS2(config-if)#ip address 150.200.1.3 255.255.255.0
DLS2(config-if)#exit
```

Solution # 2

The issue is that the EtherChannels between switch ALS1 and switches DLS1 and DLS2 are set to passive mode. This will prevent the LACP channel from forming.

```
DLS1#show etherchannel 1 port | include Mode
Channel group = 1              Mode = Passive          Gcchange = -
Channel group = 1              Mode = Passive          Gcchange = -

DLS2#show etherchannel 2 port | include Mode
Channel group = 2              Mode = Passive          Gcchange = -
Channel group = 2              Mode = Passive          Gcchange = -

ALS1#show etherchannel 1 port | include Mode
Channel group = 1              Mode = Passive          Gcchange = -
Channel group = 1              Mode = Passive          Gcchange = -

ALS1#show etherchannel 2 port | include Mode
Channel group = 2              Mode = Passive          Gcchange = -
Channel group = 2              Mode = Passive          Gcchange = -
```

To resolve this issue, configure at least one end of the EtherChannel in active mode:

```
DLS1(config)#interface range fastethernet 0/7 - 8
DLS1(config-if-range)#channel-group 1 mode active

DLS2(config)#interface range fastethernet 0/9 - 10
DLS2(config-if-range)#channel-group 2 mode active
```

Solution # 3

The issue is that both IP routing is disabled on both DLS1 and DLS2:

```
DLS1#show ip route
Default gateway is not set

Host                Gateway            Last Use    Total Uses   Interface
ICMP redirect cache is empty

DLS2#show ip route
Default gateway is not set

Host                Gateway            Last Use    Total Uses   Interface
ICMP redirect cache is empty
```

To resolve this issue, enable IP routing on both of the switches:

```
DLS1(config)#ip routing

DLS2(config)#ip routing
```

Solution # 4

The issue is that both Spanning Tree logging has been disabled (default) on both switches. To resolve this issue, enable logging globally and on all trunk links:

```
DLS1(config)#interface port-channel 1
DLS1(config-if)#logging event spanning-tree
DLS1(config-if)#exit
DLS1(config)#interface port-channel 2
DLS1(config-if)#logging event spanning-tree
DLS1(config-if)#exit
DLS1(config)#interface port-channel 5
DLS1(config-if)#logging event spanning-tree
DLS1(config-if)#exit
DLS1(config)#spanning-tree logging

DLS2(config)#interface port-channel 1
DLS2(config-if)#logging event spanning-tree
DLS2(config-if)#exit
DLS2(config)#interface port-channel 2
DLS2(config-if)#logging event spanning-tree
DLS2(config-if)#exit
DLS2(config)#interface port-channel 5
```

```
DLS2(config-if)#logging event spanning-tree
DLS2(config-if)#exit
DLS2(config)#spanning-tree logging
```

FINAL WORKING SWITCH CONFIGURATIONS

DLS1

```
DLS1#term len 0
DLS1#sh run
Building configuration...

Current configuration : 4839 bytes
!
version 12.2
no service pad
service timestamps debug datetime msec
service timestamps log datetime msec
no service password-encryption
!
hostname DLS1
!
no logging console
!
no aaa new-model
ip subnet-zero
ip routing
no ip domain-lookup
!
key chain HSRP-VLAN-100
 key 1
   key-string 7 133632313E3E216703171A03
!
spanning-tree mode pvst
spanning-tree logging
spanning-tree extend system-id
spanning-tree vlan 100 priority 0
spanning-tree vlan 200 priority 4096
!
vlan internal allocation policy ascending
!
interface Port-channel1
 switchport trunk encapsulation dot1q
 switchport trunk allowed vlan 1,100
 switchport mode trunk
 logging event spanning-tree
!
interface Port-channel2
 switchport trunk encapsulation dot1q
 switchport trunk allowed vlan 1,200
 switchport mode trunk
 logging event spanning-tree
!
interface Port-channel5
 switchport trunk encapsulation dot1q
 switchport mode trunk
 logging event spanning-tree
!
interface FastEthernet0/1
 switchport mode dynamic desirable
!
interface FastEthernet0/2
 switchport mode dynamic desirable
!
interface FastEthernet0/3
 switchport mode dynamic desirable
!
interface FastEthernet0/4
 switchport mode dynamic desirable
!
interface FastEthernet0/5
 switchport mode dynamic desirable
!
interface FastEthernet0/6
 switchport mode dynamic desirable
!
```

```
interface FastEthernet0/7
 switchport trunk encapsulation dot1q
 switchport trunk allowed vlan 1,100
 switchport mode trunk
 channel-group 1 mode active
!
interface FastEthernet0/8
 switchport trunk encapsulation dot1q
 switchport trunk allowed vlan 1,100
 switchport mode trunk
 channel-group 1 mode active
!
interface FastEthernet0/9
 switchport trunk encapsulation dot1q
 switchport trunk allowed vlan 1,200
 switchport mode trunk
 channel-group 2 mode active
!
interface FastEthernet0/10
 switchport trunk encapsulation dot1q
 switchport trunk allowed vlan 1,200
 switchport mode trunk
 channel-group 2 mode active
!
interface FastEthernet0/11
 switchport trunk encapsulation dot1q
 switchport mode trunk
 channel-group 5 mode desirable
!
interface FastEthernet0/12
 switchport trunk encapsulation dot1q
 switchport mode trunk
 channel-group 5 mode desirable

[Truncated Output]

interface Vlan1
 no ip address
 shutdown
!
interface Vlan100
 ip address 150.100.1.2 255.255.255.0
 standby version 2
 standby 100 ip 150.100.1.1
 standby 100 priority 105
 standby 100 preempt
 standby 100 authentication md5 key-chain HSRP-VLAN-100
!
interface Vlan200
 ip address 150.200.1.2 255.255.255.0
 standby version 2
 standby 200 ip 150.200.1.1
 standby 200 preempt
 standby 200 authentication md5 key-string 7 15212E2F31180E6900000712
!
ip classless
ip http server
ip http secure-server
!
logging 150.100.1.10
logging 150.200.1.10
!
control-plane
!
line con 0
line vty 5 15
!
end

DLS1#
```

DLS2

```
DLS2#term len 0
DLS2#sh run
Building configuration...

Current configuration : 4829 bytes
```

```
!
version 12.2
no service pad
service timestamps debug datetime msec
service timestamps log datetime msec
no service password-encryption
!
hostname DLS2
!
no logging console
!
no aaa new-model
ip subnet-zero
ip routing
no ip domain-lookup
!
key chain HSRP-VLAN-100
 key 1
   key-string 7 15212E2F31180E6900000712
!
spanning-tree mode pvst
spanning-tree logging
spanning-tree extend system-id
spanning-tree vlan 100 priority 4096
spanning-tree vlan 200 priority 0
!
vlan internal allocation policy ascending
!
interface Port-channel2
 switchport trunk encapsulation dot1q
 switchport trunk allowed vlan 1,100
 switchport mode trunk
 logging event spanning-tree
!
interface Port-channel1
 switchport trunk encapsulation dot1q
 switchport trunk allowed vlan 1,200
 switchport mode trunk
 logging event spanning-tree
!
interface Port-channel5
 switchport trunk encapsulation dot1q
 switchport mode trunk
 logging event spanning-tree
!
interface FastEthernet0/1
 switchport mode dynamic desirable
!
interface FastEthernet0/2
 switchport mode dynamic desirable
!
interface FastEthernet0/3
 switchport mode dynamic desirable
!
interface FastEthernet0/4
 switchport mode dynamic desirable
!
interface FastEthernet0/5
 switchport mode dynamic desirable
!
interface FastEthernet0/6
 switchport mode dynamic desirable
!
interface FastEthernet0/7
 switchport trunk encapsulation dot1q
 switchport trunk allowed vlan 1,200
 switchport mode trunk
 channel-group 1 mode active
!
interface FastEthernet0/8
 switchport trunk encapsulation dot1q
 switchport trunk allowed vlan 1,200
 switchport mode trunk
 channel-group 1 mode active
!
interface FastEthernet0/9
 switchport trunk encapsulation dot1q
 switchport trunk allowed vlan 1,100
 switchport mode trunk
```

```
 channel-group 2 mode active
!
interface FastEthernet0/10
 switchport trunk encapsulation dot1q
 switchport trunk allowed vlan 1,100
 switchport mode trunk
 channel-group 2 mode active
!
interface FastEthernet0/11
 switchport trunk encapsulation dot1q
 switchport mode trunk
 channel-group 5 mode auto
!
interface FastEthernet0/12
 switchport trunk encapsulation dot1q
 switchport mode trunk
 channel-group 5 mode auto

[Truncated Output]

interface Vlan1
 no ip address
 shutdown
!
interface Vlan100
 ip address 150.100.1.3 255.255.255.0
 standby version 2
 standby 100 ip 150.100.1.1
 standby 100 preempt
 standby 100 authentication md5 key-chain HSRP-VLAN-100
!
interface Vlan200
 ip address 150.200.1.3 255.255.255.0
 standby version 2
 standby 200 ip 150.200.1.1
 standby 200 priority 105
 standby 200 preempt
 standby 200 authentication md5 key-string 7 0812696D3C2B205A3A383E34
!
ip classless
ip http server
ip http secure-server
!
!
logging 150.100.1.10
logging 150.200.1.10
!
control-plane
!
line con 0
line vty 5 15
!
end

DLS2#
```

ALS1

```
ALS1#term len 0
ALS1#sh run
Building configuration...

Current configuration : 1304 bytes
!
version 12.1
no service pad
service timestamps debug uptime
service timestamps log uptime
no service password-encryption
!
hostname ALS1
!
no logging console
!
ip subnet-zero
!
no ip domain-lookup
!
```

```
spanning-tree mode pvst
no spanning-tree optimize bpdu transmission
spanning-tree extend system-id
!
interface Port-channel1
 switchport mode trunk
 flowcontrol send off
!
interface Port-channel2
 switchport mode trunk
 flowcontrol send off
!
interface FastEthernet0/1
 shutdown
!
interface FastEthernet0/2
 shutdown
!
interface FastEthernet0/3
 shutdown
!
interface FastEthernet0/4
 shutdown
!
interface FastEthernet0/5
 shutdown
!
interface FastEthernet0/6
 shutdown
!
interface FastEthernet0/7
 switchport mode trunk
 channel-group 1 mode passive
!
interface FastEthernet0/8
 switchport mode trunk
 channel-group 1 mode passive
!
interface FastEthernet0/9
 switchport mode trunk
 channel-group 2 mode passive
!
interface FastEthernet0/10
 switchport mode trunk
 channel-group 2 mode passive
!
interface FastEthernet0/11
 shutdown
!
interface FastEthernet0/12
 shutdown
!
interface Vlan1
 no ip address
 no ip route-cache
 shutdown
!
interface Vlan100
 ip address 150.100.1.254 255.255.255.0
 no ip route-cache
!
ip default-gateway 150.100.1.1
ip http server
!
line con 0
line vty 5 15
!
end

ALS1#
```

ALS2

```
ALS2#term len 0
ALS2#sh run
Building configuration...

Current configuration : 1224 bytes
```

```
!
version 12.1
no service pad
service timestamps debug uptime
service timestamps log uptime
no service password-encryption
!
hostname ALS2
!
no logging console
!
ip subnet-zero
!
no ip domain-lookup
!
spanning-tree mode pvst
no spanning-tree optimize bpdu transmission
spanning-tree extend system-id
!
interface Port-channel1
 switchport mode trunk
 flowcontrol send off
!
interface Port-channel2
 switchport mode trunk
 flowcontrol send off
!
interface FastEthernet0/1
!
interface FastEthernet0/2
!
interface FastEthernet0/3
!
interface FastEthernet0/4
!
interface FastEthernet0/5
!
interface FastEthernet0/6
!
interface FastEthernet0/7
 switchport mode trunk
 channel-group 1 mode passive
!
interface FastEthernet0/8
 switchport mode trunk
 channel-group 1 mode passive
!
interface FastEthernet0/9
 switchport mode trunk
 channel-group 2 mode passive
!
interface FastEthernet0/10
 switchport mode trunk
 channel-group 2 mode passive
!
interface FastEthernet0/11
!
interface FastEthernet0/12
!
interface Vlan1
 no ip address
 no ip route-cache
 shutdown
!
interface Vlan200
 ip address 150.200.1.254 255.255.255.0
 no ip route-cache
!
ip default-gateway 150.200.1.1
ip http server
!
line con 0
line vty 5 15
!
end

ALS2#
```

CCNP LAB 92

Troubleshooting Lab

Lab Objective:

The focus of this lab is to hone your trouble isolation and resolution skills. This lab will include Layer 2 and Layer 3 technologies which fall within the scope of the current CCNP curriculum.

Lab Topology:

The lab network topology is illustrated below:

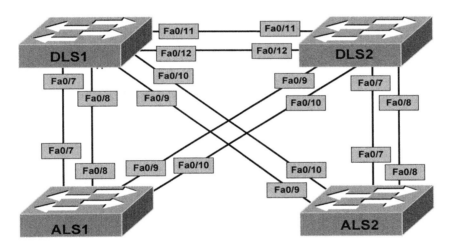

IMPORTANT NOTE: If you are using the www.howtonetwork.net racks, please download and paste the troubleshooting lab configurations. If you are using your own rack or lab, please modify this configuration to reflect the actual interface types, etc, that you have on your devices. Prior to beginning all labs, apply the pre-lab configuration for each individual device.

When completing these labs, it is important to resolve the trouble tickets in the order in which they are listed because they build on each other. For example, if you begin with Trouble Ticket # 3, you might not get the expected resolution or result if you have not completed Trouble Ticket # 1 and Trouble Ticket # 2. It is very important to follow the order listed.

Trouble Ticket # 1

The NOC has called to report that they are unable to see any prompts when they are trying to configure switches DLS1 and DLS2. Troubleshoot and resolve this issue.

Trouble Ticket # 2

You have received a problem report indicating that switch DLS1 is unable to ping any other device on the network, including its default gateway. Troubleshoot and resolve this issue.

Trouble Ticket # 3

The NOC has recently configured OSPF between switches DLS1 and DLS2. However, they advise that the OSPF adjacency is not coming up. Troubleshoot and resolve this issue.

Trouble Ticket # 4

The NOC has recently called you to advise that they are unable to ping between switches ALS1 and ALS2. Both switches can ping the HSRP VIPs. Troubleshoot and resolve this issue.

LAB SOLUTIONS

Solution # 1

The issue is that the prompt service for configuration mode has been disabled on the switches:

```
DLS1#show running-config | include service
no service pad
service timestamps debug datetime msec
service timestamps log datetime msec
no service password-encryption
no service prompt config
DLS1#configure terminal
Enter configuration commands, one per line.  End with CNTL/Z.
end
DLS1#

DLS2#show running-config | include service
no service pad
service timestamps debug datetime msec
service timestamps log datetime msec
no service password-encryption
no service prompt config
DLS2#configure terminal
Enter configuration commands, one per line.  End with CNTL/Z.
end
DLS2#
```

To resolve this issue, enable the configuration prompt service:

```
DLS1#config t
Configuring from terminal, memory, or network [terminal]?
Enter configuration commands, one per line.  End with CNTL/Z.
service prompt config
DLS1(config)#exit

DLS2#config t
Enter configuration commands, one per line.  End with CNTL/Z.
service prompt config
DLS2(config)#exit
```

Solution # 2

The issue is that switch DLS1 has a mis-configured VACL which is denying all ARP frames. ARP frames uses the Ethernet protocol type of value 0x806:

```
DLS1#show vlan access-map
Vlan access-map "SECURITY"  10
  Match clauses:
    mac address: ARP
  Action:
    drop

DLS1#show running-config | begin mac
mac access-list extended ARP
 permit any any 0x806 0x0
```

To resolve this issue, configure the VACL to forward ARP frames:

```
DLS1(config)#vlan access-map SECURITY 10
DLS1(config-access-map)#action forward
```

Solution # 3

The issue is that switch DLS2 has IP routing disabled even though OSPF has been configured.

```
DLS2#show ip route
Default gateway is not set

Host            Gateway         Last Use    Total Uses   Interface
ICMP redirect cache is empty
```

To resolve this issue, enable IP routing on switch DLS2:

```
DLS2(config)#ip routing
```

Solution # 4

The issue is that switch ALS2 has a mis-configured default gateway:

```
ALS2#show ip redirects
Default gateway is 150.100.1.1

Host            Gateway         Last Use    Total Uses   Interface
ICMP redirect cache is empty
```

To resolve this issue, configure the correct default gateway:

```
ALS2(config)#ip default-gateway 150.200.1.1
```

FINAL WORKING SWITCH CONFIGURATIONS

DLS1

```
term len 0
DLS1#term len 0
DLS1#sh run
Building configuration...

Current configuration : 6835 bytes
!
version 12.2
no service pad
service timestamps debug datetime msec
service timestamps log datetime msec
no service password-encryption
!
hostname DLS1
!
no logging console
!
no aaa new-model
ip subnet-zero
ip routing
no ip domain-lookup
!
key chain HSRP-VLAN-100
 key 1
  key-string 7 133632313E3E216703171A03
!
crypto pki trustpoint TP-self-signed-587410816
 enrollment selfsigned
 subject-name cn=IOS-Self-Signed-Certificate-587410816
 revocation-check none
 rsakeypair TP-self-signed-587410816
!
crypto pki certificate chain TP-self-signed-587410816
 certificate self-signed 01
  3082023B 308201A4 A0030201 02020101 300D0609 2A864886 F70D0101 04050030
  30312E30 2C060355 04031325 494F532D 53656C66 2D536967 6E65642D 43657274
  69666963 6174652D 35383734 31303831 36301E17 0D393330 33303130 30313235
  305A170D 32303031 30313030 30303030 5A303031 2E302C06 03550403 1325494F
  532D5365 6C662D53 69676E65 642D4365 72746966 69636174 652D3538 37343130
  38313630 819F300D 06092A86 4886F70D 01010105 0003818D 00308189 02818100
  A8486AF5 E11B3F65 B46B04BF E2FF48F8 25A735E7 78528E88 0DFE4EE7 F87628F3
  A039D5B8 580FF2F0 F5B71D91 268B171F 92BE8CCE E7BC3304 A14AFD2A 6C8AFE01
  B95C0842 5D44DDC8 137879C9 2F66B8AA A92690B6 399F7B81 771FFCF1 E1F9D80E
```

```
        66B7DDC0 197FAD86 79D45BBF 83057551 80BD8EF0 25B68184 49E6E660 DEA397DD
        02030100 01A36530 63300F06 03551D13 0101FF04 05300301 01FF3010 0603551D
        11040930 07820544 4C53312E 301F0603 551D2304 18301680 1491F4DC 1C0041E5
        D628FBBC 1F5E7CB2 4D7E13F8 0A301D06 03551D0E 04160414 91F4DC1C 0041E5D6
        28FBBC1F 5E7CB24D 7E13F80A 300D0609 2A864886 F70D0101 04050003 81810081
        5159E36D 96A4606F 7F0F5F7F F316F7C6 9DF02ACC 731FF2B0 53FF0835 B205D750
        0407AC83 73FF70B4 1972EDE6 B8840912 16A94A11 E2AC8082 66174F78 F76E9C06
        6A7AD303 A1376A6B 9676EDCA CA97F891 50930212 154DB265 0C3E8CBE 7BF77C6E
        F0F29808 213AD677 B21BEFE0 5121AA3F F4147857 F557AB7F 277A2B84 13A8C7
      quit
  !
  mac access-list extended ARP
   permit any any 0x806 0x0
  !
  spanning-tree mode pvst
  spanning-tree extend system-id
  spanning-tree vlan 100 priority 0
  spanning-tree vlan 200 priority 4096
  !
  vlan internal allocation policy ascending
  !
  vlan access-map SECURITY 10
   action drop
   match mac address ARP
  vlan access-map SECURITY 20
   action forward
  !
  vlan filter SECURITY vlan-list 100,200
  !
  interface Port-channel1
   switchport trunk encapsulation dot1q
   switchport trunk allowed vlan 1,100
   switchport mode trunk
   logging event spanning-tree
  !
  interface Port-channel2
   switchport trunk encapsulation dot1q
   switchport trunk allowed vlan 1,200
   switchport mode trunk
   logging event spanning-tree
  !
  interface Port-channel5
   switchport trunk encapsulation dot1q
   switchport mode trunk
   logging event spanning-tree
  !
  interface FastEthernet0/1
   switchport mode dynamic desirable
  !
  interface FastEthernet0/2
   switchport mode dynamic desirable
  !
  interface FastEthernet0/3
   switchport mode dynamic desirable
  !
  interface FastEthernet0/4
   switchport mode dynamic desirable
  !
  interface FastEthernet0/5
   switchport mode dynamic desirable
  !
  interface FastEthernet0/6
   switchport mode dynamic desirable
  !
  interface FastEthernet0/7
   switchport trunk encapsulation dot1q
   switchport trunk allowed vlan 1,100
   switchport mode trunk
   channel-group 1 mode active
  !
  interface FastEthernet0/8
   switchport trunk encapsulation dot1q
   switchport trunk allowed vlan 1,100
   switchport mode trunk
   channel-group 1 mode active
  !
  interface FastEthernet0/9
   switchport trunk encapsulation dot1q
   switchport trunk allowed vlan 1,200
   switchport mode trunk
   channel-group 2 mode active
  !
```

```
interface FastEthernet0/10
 switchport trunk encapsulation dot1q
 switchport trunk allowed vlan 1,200
 switchport mode trunk
 channel-group 2 mode active
!
interface FastEthernet0/11
 switchport trunk encapsulation dot1q
 switchport mode trunk
 channel-group 5 mode desirable
!
interface FastEthernet0/12
 switchport trunk encapsulation dot1q
 switchport mode trunk
 channel-group 5 mode desirable

[Truncated Output]

interface Vlan1
 no ip address
 shutdown
!
interface Vlan100
 ip address 150.100.1.2 255.255.255.0
 standby 100 ip 150.100.1.1
 standby 100 priority 105
 standby 100 preempt
 standby 100 authentication md5 key-chain HSRP-VLAN-100
!
interface Vlan200
 ip address 150.200.1.2 255.255.255.0
 standby 200 ip 150.200.1.1
 standby 200 preempt
 standby 200 authentication md5 key-string 7 15212E2F31180E6900000712
!
router ospf 1
 router-id 1.1.1.1
 log-adjacency-changes
 network 0.0.0.0 255.255.255.255 area 0
!
ip classless
ip http server
ip http secure-server
!
logging 150.100.1.10
logging 150.200.1.10
!
control-plane
!
line con 0
line vty 0 4
 login
line vty 5 15
 login
!
end
DLS1#
```

DLS2

```
DLS2#term len 0
DLS2#sh run
Building configuration...

Current configuration : 6881 bytes
!
version 12.2
no service pad
service timestamps debug datetime msec
service timestamps log datetime msec
no service password-encryption
!
hostname DLS2
!
no logging console
!
no aaa new-model
ip subnet-zero
ip routing
no ip domain-lookup
!
```

```
key chain HSRP-VLAN-100
 key 1
   key-string 7 15212E2F31180E6900000712
!
crypto pki trustpoint TP-self-signed-4251411712
 enrollment selfsigned
 subject-name cn=IOS-Self-Signed-Certificate-4251411712
 revocation-check none
 rsakeypair TP-self-signed-4251411712
!
crypto pki certificate chain TP-self-signed-4251411712
 certificate self-signed 01
  3082023D 308201A6 A0030201 02020101 300D0609 2A864886 F70D0101 04050030
  31312F30 2D060355 04031326 494F532D 53656C66 2D536967 6E65642D 43657274
  69666963 6174652D 34323531 34313137 3132301E 170D3933 30333031 30303131
  30315A17 0D323030 31303130 30303030 305A3031 312F302D 06035504 03132649
  4F532D53 656C662D 5369676E 65642D43 65727469 66696361 74652D34 32353134
  31313731 3230819F 300D0609 2A864886 F70D0101 01050003 818D0030 81890281
  8100DB95 774B86BB 26E28D61 CBE63593 9B31EA1D 73504689 3215E210 2E4238BB
  35C5ECDC AD7E63EF 317A8860 5BF2E3AD 6D0855F5 073F46D1 C0993E77 C0C88D30
  A77F042B 4153B855 548D86FF 472D48A7 E4FDFAFA 60F4368F EF295B56 A93C557C
  DEB812B4 A4DE3B28 EA54D80D 5E3AEBA5 9953A90E 00D7F1B8 7BED10DF 5DC6FE22
  89C30203 010001A3 65306330 0F060355 1D130101 FF040530 030101FF 30100603
  551D1104 09300782 05444C53 322E301F 0603551D 23041830 16801414 F59A78B2
  3C98DF37 1E06E466 F18015DA F7A84D30 1D060355 1D0E0416 041414F5 9A78B23C
  98DF371E 06E466F1 8015DAF7 A84D300D 06092A86 4886F70D 01010405 00038181
  00A429A1 01C7C8E0 0705EF59 9CC66374 0B37BB10 010D5ADD 7ABBB58B B4BCAA40
  D7FB35D1 447DF72B 4C15335E 760DCF40 3460F81B 76065B61 972F999B BBB9C5A0
  F9E250C2 192B8C16 4E208636 D2D5F064 57816D26 FE0549B3 0F854FED 5CBCA28E
  1BABB2CB 7A883BEF C2F08D17 40DEA9A2 057958E1 8F98B0A0 8C2894D6 2187F018 70
  quit
!
spanning-tree mode pvst
spanning-tree extend system-id
spanning-tree vlan 100 priority 4096
spanning-tree vlan 200 priority 0
!
vlan internal allocation policy ascending
!
interface Port-channel1
 switchport trunk encapsulation dot1q
 switchport trunk allowed vlan 1,200
 switchport mode trunk
 logging event spanning-tree
!
interface Port-channel2
 switchport trunk encapsulation dot1q
 switchport trunk allowed vlan 1,100
 switchport mode trunk
 logging event spanning-tree
!
interface Port-channel5
 switchport trunk encapsulation dot1q
 switchport mode trunk
 logging event spanning-tree
!
interface FastEthernet0/1
 switchport mode dynamic desirable
!
interface FastEthernet0/2
 switchport mode dynamic desirable
!
interface FastEthernet0/3
 switchport mode dynamic desirable
!
interface FastEthernet0/4
 switchport mode dynamic desirable
!
interface FastEthernet0/5
 switchport mode dynamic desirable
!
interface FastEthernet0/6
 switchport mode dynamic desirable
!
interface FastEthernet0/7
 switchport trunk encapsulation dot1q
 switchport trunk allowed vlan 1,200
 switchport mode trunk
 channel-group 1 mode active
!
interface FastEthernet0/8
 switchport trunk encapsulation dot1q
```

```
 switchport trunk allowed vlan 1,200
 switchport mode trunk
 channel-group 1 mode active
!
interface FastEthernet0/9
 switchport trunk encapsulation dot1q
 switchport trunk allowed vlan 1,100
 switchport mode trunk
 channel-group 2 mode active
!
interface FastEthernet0/10
 switchport trunk encapsulation dot1q
 switchport trunk allowed vlan 1,100
 switchport mode trunk
 channel-group 2 mode active
!
interface FastEthernet0/11
 switchport trunk encapsulation dot1q
 switchport mode trunk
 mac access-group SECURITY in
 channel-group 5 mode auto
!
interface FastEthernet0/12
 switchport trunk encapsulation dot1q
 switchport mode trunk
 mac access-group SECURITY in
 channel-group 5 mode auto

[Truncated Output]

interface Vlan1
 no ip address
 shutdown
!
interface Vlan100
 ip address 150.100.1.3 255.255.255.0
 standby 100 ip 150.100.1.1
 standby 100 priority 105
 standby 100 preempt
 standby 100 authentication md5 key-chain HSRP-VLAN-100
!
interface Vlan200
 ip address 150.200.1.3 255.255.255.0
 standby 200 ip 150.200.1.1
 standby 200 priority 105
 standby 200 preempt
 standby 200 authentication md5 key-string 7 0812696D3C2B205A3A383E34
!
router ospf 2
 router-id 2.2.2.2
 log-adjacency-changes
 network 0.0.0.0 255.255.255.255 area 0
!
ip classless
ip http server
ip http secure-server
!
logging 150.100.1.10
logging 150.200.1.10
!
control-plane
!
line con 0
line vty 0 4
 login
line vty 5 15
 login
!
end

DLS2#
```

ALS1

```
ALS1#sh run
Building configuration...

Current configuration : 1304 bytes
!
version 12.1
```

```
no service pad
service timestamps debug uptime
service timestamps log uptime
no service password-encryption
!
hostname ALS1
!
no logging console
!
ip subnet-zero
!
no ip domain-lookup
!
spanning-tree mode pvst
no spanning-tree optimize bpdu transmission
spanning-tree extend system-id
!
interface Port-channel1
 switchport mode trunk
 flowcontrol send off
!
interface Port-channel2
 switchport mode trunk
 flowcontrol send off
!
interface FastEthernet0/1
 shutdown
!
interface FastEthernet0/2
 shutdown
!
interface FastEthernet0/3
 shutdown
!
interface FastEthernet0/4
 shutdown
!
interface FastEthernet0/5
 shutdown
!
interface FastEthernet0/6
 shutdown
!
interface FastEthernet0/7
 switchport mode trunk
 channel-group 1 mode passive
!
interface FastEthernet0/8
 switchport mode trunk
 channel-group 1 mode passive
!
interface FastEthernet0/9
 switchport mode trunk
 channel-group 2 mode passive
!
interface FastEthernet0/10
 switchport mode trunk
 channel-group 2 mode passive
!
interface FastEthernet0/11
 shutdown
!
interface FastEthernet0/12
 shutdown
!
interface Vlan1
 no ip address
 no ip route-cache
 shutdown
!
interface Vlan100
 ip address 150.100.1.254 255.255.255.0
 no ip route-cache
!
ip default-gateway 150.100.1.1
ip http server
!
line con 0
line vty 5 15
!
end
ALS1#
```

ALS2

```
ALS2#term len 0
ALS2#sh run
Building configuration...

Current configuration : 1224 bytes
!
version 12.1
no service pad
service timestamps debug uptime
service timestamps log uptime
no service password-encryption
!
hostname ALS2
!
no logging console
!
ip subnet-zero
!
no ip domain-lookup
!
spanning-tree mode pvst
no spanning-tree optimize bpdu transmission
spanning-tree extend system-id
!
interface Port-channel1
 switchport mode trunk
 flowcontrol send off
!
interface Port-channel2
 switchport mode trunk
 flowcontrol send off
!
interface FastEthernet0/1
!
interface FastEthernet0/2
!
interface FastEthernet0/3
!
interface FastEthernet0/4
!
interface FastEthernet0/5
!
interface FastEthernet0/6
!
interface FastEthernet0/7
 switchport mode trunk
 channel-group 1 mode passive
!
interface FastEthernet0/8
 switchport mode trunk
 channel-group 1 mode passive
!
interface FastEthernet0/9
 switchport mode trunk
 channel-group 2 mode passive
!
interface FastEthernet0/10
 switchport mode trunk
 channel-group 2 mode passive
!
interface FastEthernet0/11
!
interface FastEthernet0/12
!
interface Vlan1
 no ip address
 no ip route-cache
 shutdown
!
interface Vlan200
 ip address 150.200.1.254 255.255.255.0
 no ip route-cache
!
ip default-gateway 150.200.1.1
ip http server
!
line con 0
line vty 5 15
!
end

ALS2#
```

CCNP LAB 93

Troubleshooting Lab

Lab Objective:

The focus of this lab is to hone your trouble isolation and resolution skills. This lab will include Layer 2 and Layer 3 technologies which fall within the scope of the current CCNP curriculum.

Lab Topology:

The lab network topology is illustrated below:

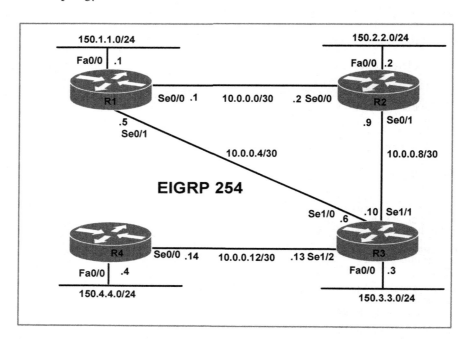

IMPORTANT NOTE: If you are using the www.howtonetwork.net racks, please download and paste the troubleshooting lab configurations. If you are using your own rack or lab, please modify this configuration to reflect the actual interface types, etc, that you have on your devices. Prior to beginning all labs, apply the pre-lab configuration for each individual device.

When completing these labs, it is important to resolve the trouble tickets in the order in which they are listed because they build on each other. For example, if you begin with Trouble Ticket # 3, you might not get the expected resolution or result if you have not completed Trouble Ticket # 1 and Trouble Ticket # 2. It is very important to follow the order listed.

Trouble Ticket # 1

You have received a call from Level 1 support indicating that following some scheduled changes, they have lost connectivity to router R2. Troubleshoot and resolve this issue.

Trouble Ticket # 2

Users are complaining about excessive latency between the 150.1.1.0/24 and 150.3.3.0/24 subnet. Previously, this traffic was load-shared across R2 because of the low-bandwidth 512Kbps connecting R1 and R3. Troubleshoot and resolve this issue.

Trouble Ticket # 3

You have received several complaints that the NOC is unable to reach some Loopback subnets configured on R1 from the other routers. Management has forbidden the modification of the EIGRP configuration on R1. With this restriction in mind, troubleshoot and resolve this issue.

Trouble Ticket # 4

You have received an urgent call from the NOC stating that while they were troubleshooting TCP connectivity issues between the 150.4.4.0/24 and 150.1.1.0/24 subnets they lost all connectivity to R4. Troubleshoot and resolve this issue.

LAB SOLUTIONS

Solution # 1

The issue is that R2 has been configured with all interfaces, except for FastEthernet0/0, as passive under EIGRP. This prevents the router from forming neighbor relationships with routers running EIGRP in the same autonomous system:

```
R2#show running-config | section eigrp
router eigrp 254
 passive-interface default
 no passive-interface FastEthernet0/0
 network 10.0.0.2 0.0.0.0
 network 10.0.0.9 0.0.0.0
 network 150.2.2.2 0.0.0.0
 no auto-summary
```

To resolve this issue, modify the configuration on R2 as follows:

```
R2(config)#router eigrp 254
R2(config-router)#passive-interface fastethernet 0/0
R2(config-router)#no passive-interface serial 0/0
R2(config-router)#no passive-interface serial 0/1
R2(config-router)#exit
```

Solution # 2

The issue is that while R1 and R3 have been configured to use unequal cost load sharing, they have been configured to forward packets using only the lowest metric (cost) path:

```
R3#show running-config | section eigrp
router eigrp 254
 variance 4
 traffic-share min across-interfaces
 passive-interface FastEthernet0/0
 network 10.0.0.6 0.0.0.0
 network 10.0.0.10 0.0.0.0
 network 10.0.0.13 0.0.0.0
 network 150.3.3.3 0.0.0.0
 no auto-summary

R1#show running-config | section eigrp
router eigrp 254
 variance 4
 traffic-share min across-interfaces
 redistribute static
 passive-interface FastEthernet0/0
 network 10.0.0.1 0.0.0.0
 network 10.0.0.5 0.0.0.0
 network 150.1.1.1 0.0.0.0
 no auto-summary
```

To resolve this issue, modify the configuration on these routers as follows:

```
R1(config)#router eigrp 254
R1(config-router)#no traffic-share min across-interfaces

R3(config)#router eigrp 254
R3(config-router)#no traffic-share min across-interfaces
```

Solution # 3

The issue is that the unreachable subnets are not covered in any of the advertised aggregate prefixes. To resolve this, without modifying the EIGRP configuration, do one of two things:

- Configure and advertise a summary route
- Configure and advertise a default route

```
R1(config)#ip route 172.30.48.0 255.255.240.0 null 0
OR
R1(config)#ip route 0.0.0.0 0.0.0.0 null 0
```

Solution # 4

The issue is that the clocking has been removed from the Serial1/2 interface on R3. The interface will therefore not come up:

```
R3#show controllers serial 1/2
CD2430 Slot 1, Port 2, Controller 0, Channel 2, Revision 19
Channel mode is synchronous serial
idb 0x84D4D7D8, buffer size 1524, V.35 DCE cable

R4#show controllers serial 0/0
Interface Serial0/0
Hardware is PowerQUICC MPC860
DTE V.35 clocks stopped.
```

To resolve this issue, configure R3s Serial1/2 interface to provide clocking:

```
R3(config)#interface serial 1/2
R3(config-if)#clock rate 128000
```

FINAL WORKING ROUTER CONFIGURATIONS

R1

```
R1#term len 0
R1#sh run
Building configuration...

Current configuration : 1567 bytes
!
version 12.4
service timestamps debug datetime msec
service timestamps log datetime msec
no service password-encryption
!
hostname R1
!
boot-start-marker
boot-end-marker
!
no logging console
!
no aaa new-model
no network-clock-participate slot 1
no network-clock-participate wic 0
ip cef
!
no ip domain lookup
ip auth-proxy max-nodata-conns 3
```

```
ip admission max-nodata-conns 3
!
interface Loopback100
 ip address 172.16.0.1 255.255.224.0
!
interface Loopback200
 ip address 172.16.32.1 255.255.224.0
!
interface Loopback300
 ip address 172.16.64.1 255.255.224.0
!
interface Loopback400
 ip address 172.16.96.1 255.255.224.0
!
interface Loopback700
 ip address 172.30.38.1 255.255.255.0
!
interface Loopback800
 ip address 172.30.48.1 255.255.255.0
!
interface Loopback900
 ip address 172.30.58.1 255.255.255.0
!
interface FastEthernet0/0
 ip address 150.1.1.1 255.255.255.0
 duplex auto
 speed auto
!
interface Serial0/0
 ip address 10.0.0.1 255.255.255.252
 clock rate 2000000
!
interface Serial0/1
 bandwidth 512
 ip address 10.0.0.5 255.255.255.252
!
router eigrp 254
 variance 4
 redistribute static
 passive-interface FastEthernet0/0
 network 10.0.0.1 0.0.0.0
 network 10.0.0.5 0.0.0.0
 network 150.1.1.1 0.0.0.0
 no auto-summary
!
ip forward-protocol nd
ip route 0.0.0.0 0.0.0.0 Null0
ip route 172.16.0.0 255.255.128.0 Null0
ip route 172.30.32.0 255.255.240.0 Null0
!
no ip http server
no ip http secure-server
!
control-plane
!
line con 0
line aux 0
line vty 0 4
 login
!
end
R1#
```

R2

```
R2#term len 0
R2#sh run
Building configuration...

Current configuration : 954 bytes
!
version 12.4
service timestamps debug datetime msec
service timestamps log datetime msec
no service password-encryption
!
hostname R2
!
```

```
boot-start-marker
boot-end-marker
!
no logging console
!
no aaa new-model
no network-clock-participate slot 1
no network-clock-participate wic 0
ip cef
!
no ip domain lookup
ip auth-proxy max-nodata-conns 3
ip admission max-nodata-conns 3
!
interface FastEthernet0/0
 ip address 150.2.2.2 255.255.255.0
 duplex auto
 speed auto
!
interface Serial0/0
 ip address 10.0.0.2 255.255.255.252
!
interface Serial0/1
 ip address 10.0.0.9 255.255.255.252
!
router eigrp 254
 passive-interface FastEthernet0/0
 network 10.0.0.2 0.0.0.0
 network 10.0.0.9 0.0.0.0
 network 150.2.2.2 0.0.0.0
 no auto-summary
!
ip forward-protocol nd
!
no ip http server
no ip http secure-server
!
control-plane
!
line con 0
line aux 0
line vty 0 4
 login
!
end

R2#
```

R3

```
R3#term len 0
R3#sh run
Building configuration...

Current configuration : 1362 bytes
!
version 12.4
service timestamps debug datetime msec
service timestamps log datetime msec
no service password-encryption
!
hostname R3
!
boot-start-marker
boot-end-marker
!
no logging console
!
no aaa new-model
no network-clock-participate slot 1
no network-clock-participate wic 0
ip cef
!
no ip domain lookup
ip auth-proxy max-nodata-conns 3
ip admission max-nodata-conns 3
!
interface FastEthernet0/0
```

```
 ip address 150.3.3.3 255.255.255.0
 duplex auto
 speed auto
!
interface Serial1/0
 bandwidth 512
 ip address 10.0.0.6 255.255.255.252
 clock rate 128000
!
interface Serial1/1
 ip address 10.0.0.10 255.255.255.252
 clock rate 128000
!
interface Serial1/2
 ip address 10.0.0.13 255.255.255.252
 clock rate 128000
!
interface Serial1/3
 no ip address
 shutdown
!
interface Serial1/4
 no ip address
 shutdown
!
interface Serial1/5
 no ip address
 shutdown
!
interface Serial1/6
 no ip address
 shutdown
!
interface Serial1/7
 no ip address
 shutdown
!
router eigrp 254
 variance 4
 passive-interface FastEthernet0/0
 network 10.0.0.6 0.0.0.0
 network 10.0.0.10 0.0.0.0
 network 10.0.0.13 0.0.0.0
 network 150.3.3.3 0.0.0.0
 no auto-summary
!
ip forward-protocol nd
!
no ip http server
no ip http secure-server
!
control-plane
!
line con 0
line aux 0
line vty 0 4
 login
!
end

R3#
```

R4

```
R4#term len 0
R4#sh run
Building configuration...

Current configuration : 883 bytes
!
version 12.4
service timestamps debug datetime msec
service timestamps log datetime msec
no service password-encryption
!
hostname R4
!
boot-start-marker
```

```
boot-end-marker
!
no logging console
!
no aaa new-model
no network-clock-participate slot 1
no network-clock-participate wic 0
ip cef
!
no ip domain lookup
ip auth-proxy max-nodata-conns 3
ip admission max-nodata-conns 3
!
interface FastEthernet0/0
 ip address 150.4.4.4 255.255.255.0
 duplex auto
 speed auto
!
interface Serial0/0
 ip address 10.0.0.14 255.255.255.252
!
interface Serial0/1
 no ip address
 shutdown
!
router eigrp 254
 passive-interface FastEthernet0/0
 network 10.0.0.14 0.0.0.0
 network 150.4.4.4 0.0.0.0
 no auto-summary
!
ip forward-protocol nd
!
no ip http server
no ip http secure-server
!
control-plane
!
line con 0
line aux 0
line vty 0 4
 login
!
end

R4#
```

CCNP LAB 94

Troubleshooting Lab

Lab Objective:

The focus of this lab is to hone your trouble isolation and resolution skills. This lab will include Layer 2 and Layer 3 technologies which fall within the scope of the current CCNP curriculum.

Lab Topology:

The lab network topology is illustrated below:

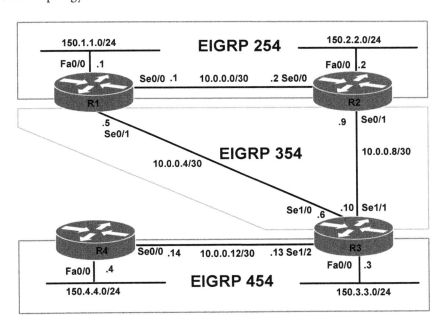

IMPORTANT NOTE: If you are using the www.howtonetwork.net racks, please download and paste the troubleshooting lab configurations. If you are using your own rack or lab, please modify this configuration to reflect the actual interface types, etc, that you have on your devices. Prior to beginning all labs, apply the pre-lab configuration for each individual device.

When completing these labs, it is important to resolve the trouble tickets in the order in which they are listed because they build on each other. For example, if you begin with Trouble Ticket # 3, you might not get the expected resolution or result if you have not completed Trouble Ticket # 1 and Trouble Ticket # 2. It is very important to follow the order listed.

Trouble Ticket # 1

You have received a call from Level 1 support indicating that following some scheduled WAN changes, connectivity from the 150.3.3.0/24 subnet to the 150.1.1.0/24 and 150.2.2.0/24 subnets has been lost. Troubleshoot and resolve this issue.

Trouble Ticket # 2

You have received a call from the NOC indicating that the EIGRP neighbor relationship between R3 and R4 failed following some scheduled routing configuration changes. Troubleshoot and resolve this issue.

Trouble Ticket # 3

You have received call from users connected to the 150.4.4.0/24 subnet advising that every time there is a report of a failed network link, they lose connectivity to the 150.1.1.0/24 and 150.2.2.0/24 subnets. Troubleshoot and resolve this issue.

Trouble Ticket # 4

You have received call from Level 1 support indicating that users connected to the 150.4.4.0/24 subnet cannot connect to a server with the IP address 150.3.3.254. The NOC has also stated that they are unable to ping R3s LAN interface IP address from R4. Troubleshoot and resolve this.

LAB SOLUTIONS

Solution # 1

The issue is that EIGRP authentication is mis-configured on R1 and R2. EIGRP authentication has been configured for AS 254 instead of AS 354:

```
R1#show running-config interface serial 0/1
Building configuration...

Current configuration : 148 bytes
!
interface Serial0/1
 ip address 10.0.0.5 255.255.255.252
 ip authentication mode eigrp 254 md5
 ip authentication key-chain eigrp 254 SECURE
end

R2#show running-config interface serial 0/1
Building configuration...

Current configuration : 148 bytes
!
interface Serial0/1
 ip address 10.0.0.9 255.255.255.252
 ip authentication mode eigrp 254 md5
 ip authentication key-chain eigrp 254 SECURE
end
```

To resolve this issue, implement authentication for AS 354 under these interfaces on R1 and R2:

```
R2(config-if)#interface serial 0/1
R2(config-if)#no ip authentication mode eigrp 254 md5
R2(config-if)#no ip authentication key-chain eigrp 254 SECURE
R2(config-if)#ip authentication mode eigrp 354 md5
R2(config-if)#ip authentication key-chain eigrp 354 SECURE

R3(config-if)#interface serial 0/1
R3(config-if)#no ip authentication mode eigrp 254 md5
R3(config-if)#no ip authentication key-chain eigrp 254 SECURE
R3(config-if)#ip authentication mode eigrp 354 md5
R3(config-if)#ip authentication key-chain eigrp 354 SECURE
```

Solution # 2

The issue is that the EIGRP K values are mismatched on routers R3 and R4:

```
R3#show running-config | section eigrp
redistribute eigrp 354
 network 10.0.0.13 0.0.0.0
 network 150.3.3.3 0.0.0.0
 metric weights 0 0 1 1 1 0
 no auto-summary
```

```
R4#show running-config | section eigrp
router eigrp 454
 network 10.0.0.14 0.0.0.0
 network 150.1.1.4 0.0.0.0
 metric weights 0 1 1 1 0 0
 no auto-summary
```

To resolve this issue, configure the K values using the same variables on both routers. This task can be completed by changing the K values on R3 to match those on R4, or vice-versa:

```
R3(config)#router eigrp 454
R3(config-router)#metric weights 0 1 1 1 0 0
```

Solution # 3

There are two issues here: the first is that the EIGRP 254 is not being redistributed by EIGRP 354 on R2. Therefore, if the R1-R3 link were to fail, the 150.1.1.0/24 and 150.2.2.0/24 subnets would never be advertised. The second issue is that EIGRP 254 is not redistributing EIGRP 354. Therefore, if either the R1-R3 or R2-R3 links failed, routers R1 or R2, respectively, would never have connectivity to the rest of the network:

```
R2#show running-config | section eigrp
 ip authentication mode eigrp 254 md5
 ip authentication key-chain eigrp 254 SECURE
router eigrp 254
 network 10.0.0.2 0.0.0.0
 network 150.2.2.2 0.0.0.0
 no auto-summary
router eigrp 354
 timers active-time 30
 network 10.0.0.9 0.0.0.0
 no auto-summary
```

To resolve this issue, implement route redistribution correctly on all routers:

```
R1(config)#router eigrp 254
R1(config-router)#redistribute eigrp 354

R2(config)#router eigrp 254
R2(config-router)#redistribute eigrp 354
R2(config-router)#exit
R2(config)#router eigrp 354
R2(config-router)#redistribute eigrp 254
```

Solution # 4

The issue here is that the 150.3.3.0/24 subnet has been configured as a secondary subnet on R4s LAN interface, which means that the received EIGRP route from R3 will be ignored:

```
R4#show running-config interface fastethernet 0/0
Building configuration...

Current configuration : 140 bytes
!
interface FastEthernet0/0
 ip address 150.3.3.4 255.255.255.0 secondary
 ip address 150.4.4.4 255.255.255.0
 duplex auto
 speed auto
end
```

To resolve this issue, remove this subnet from the LAN interface of R4:

```
R4(config)#interface fastethernet 0/0
R4(config-if)#no ip address 150.3.3.4 255.255.255.0 secondary
```

FINAL WORKING ROUTER CONFIGURATIONS

R1

```
R1#term len 0
R1#sh run
Building configuration...

Current configuration : 1157 bytes
!
version 12.4
service timestamps debug datetime msec
service timestamps log datetime msec
no service password-encryption
!
hostname R1
!
boot-start-marker
boot-end-marker
!
no logging console
!
no aaa new-model
no network-clock-participate slot 1
no network-clock-participate wic 0
ip cef
!
no ip domain lookup
ip auth-proxy max-nodata-conns 3
ip admission max-nodata-conns 3
!
key chain SECURE
 key 1
   key-string EIGRP-2011
!
interface FastEthernet0/0
 ip address 150.1.1.1 255.255.255.0
 duplex auto
 speed auto
!
interface Serial0/0
 ip address 10.0.0.1 255.255.255.252
 clock rate 2000000
!
interface Serial0/1
 ip address 10.0.0.5 255.255.255.252
 ip authentication mode eigrp 354 md5
 ip authentication key-chain eigrp 354 SECURE
!
router eigrp 254
 redistribute eigrp 354
 network 10.0.0.1 0.0.0.0
 network 150.1.1.1 0.0.0.0
 no auto-summary
!
router eigrp 354
 timers active-time 30
 redistribute eigrp 254
 network 10.0.0.5 0.0.0.0
 no auto-summary
!
ip forward-protocol nd
!
no ip http server
no ip http secure-server
!
control-plane
!
line con 0
line aux 0
line vty 0 4
 login
!
end

R1#
```

R2

```
R2#term len 0
R2#sh run
Building configuration...

Current configuration : 1137 bytes
!
version 12.4
service timestamps debug datetime msec
service timestamps log datetime msec
no service password-encryption
!
hostname R2
!
boot-start-marker
boot-end-marker
!
no logging console
!
no aaa new-model
no network-clock-participate slot 1
no network-clock-participate wic 0
ip cef
!
no ip domain lookup
ip auth-proxy max-nodata-conns 3
ip admission max-nodata-conns 3
!
key chain SECURE
 key 1
   key-string EIGRP-2011
!
interface FastEthernet0/0
 ip address 150.2.2.2 255.255.255.0
 duplex auto
 speed auto
!
interface Serial0/0
 ip address 10.0.0.2 255.255.255.252
!
interface Serial0/1
 ip address 10.0.0.9 255.255.255.252
 ip authentication mode eigrp 354 md5
 ip authentication key-chain eigrp 354 SECURE
!
router eigrp 254
 redistribute eigrp 354
 network 10.0.0.2 0.0.0.0
 network 150.2.2.2 0.0.0.0
 no auto-summary
!
router eigrp 354
 timers active-time 30
 redistribute eigrp 254
 network 10.0.0.9 0.0.0.0
 no auto-summary
!
ip forward-protocol nd
!
no ip http server
no ip http secure-server
!
control-plane
!
line con 0
line aux 0
line vty 0 4
 login
!
end

R2#
```

R3

```
R3#term len 0
R3#sh run
Building configuration...
```

```
Current configuration : 1654 bytes
!
version 12.4
service timestamps debug datetime msec
service timestamps log datetime msec
no service password-encryption
!
hostname R3
!
boot-start-marker
boot-end-marker
!
no logging console
!
no aaa new-model
no network-clock-participate slot 1
no network-clock-participate wic 0
ip cef
!
no ip domain lookup
ip auth-proxy max-nodata-conns 3
ip admission max-nodata-conns 3
!
key chain SECURE
 key 1
   key-string EIGRP-2011
!
interface FastEthernet0/0
 ip address 150.3.3.3 255.255.255.0
 duplex auto
 speed auto
!
interface Serial1/0
 ip address 10.0.0.6 255.255.255.252
 ip authentication mode eigrp 354 md5
 ip authentication key-chain eigrp 354 SECURE
 clock rate 128000
!
interface Serial1/1
 ip address 10.0.0.10 255.255.255.252
 ip authentication mode eigrp 354 md5
 ip authentication key-chain eigrp 354 SECURE
 clock rate 128000
!
interface Serial1/2
 ip address 10.0.0.13 255.255.255.252
 clock rate 128000
!
interface Serial1/3
 no ip address
 shutdown
!
interface Serial1/4
 no ip address
 shutdown
!
interface Serial1/5
 no ip address
 shutdown
!
interface Serial1/6
 no ip address
 shutdown
!
interface Serial1/7
 no ip address
 shutdown
!
router eigrp 354
 timers active-time 30
 redistribute eigrp 454
 network 10.0.0.6 0.0.0.0
 network 10.0.0.10 0.0.0.0
 no auto-summary
!
router eigrp 454
 redistribute eigrp 354
 network 10.0.0.13 0.0.0.0
 network 150.3.3.3 0.0.0.0
 metric weights 0 1 1 1 0 0
 no auto-summary
```

```
!
ip forward-protocol nd
!
no ip http server
no ip http secure-server
!
control-plane
!
line con 0
line aux 0
line vty 0 4
 login
!
end
R3#
```

R4

```
R4#term len 0
R4#sh run
Building configuration...

Current configuration : 911 bytes
!
version 12.4
service timestamps debug datetime msec
service timestamps log datetime msec
no service password-encryption
!
hostname R4
!
boot-start-marker
boot-end-marker
!
no logging console
!
no aaa new-model
no network-clock-participate slot 1
no network-clock-participate wic 0
ip cef
!
no ip domain lookup
ip auth-proxy max-nodata-conns 3
ip admission max-nodata-conns 3
!
interface FastEthernet0/0
 ip address 150.4.4.4 255.255.255.0
 duplex auto
 speed auto
!
interface Serial0/0
 ip address 10.0.0.14 255.255.255.252
!
interface Serial0/1
 no ip address
 shutdown
!
router eigrp 454
 network 10.0.0.14 0.0.0.0
 network 150.1.1.4 0.0.0.0
 metric weights 0 1 1 1 0 0
 no auto-summary
!
ip forward-protocol nd
!
no ip http server
no ip http secure-server
!
control-plane
!
line con 0
line aux 0
line vty 0 4
 login
!
end

R4#
```

CCNP LAB 95

Troubleshooting Lab

Lab Objective:

The focus of this lab is to hone your trouble isolation and resolution skills. This lab will include Layer 2 and Layer 3 technologies which fall within the scope of the current CCNP curriculum.

Lab Topology:

The lab network topology is illustrated below:

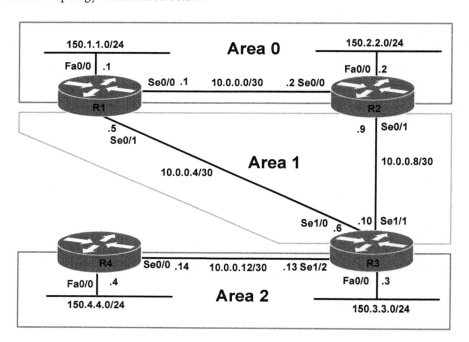

IMPORTANT NOTE: If you are using the www.howtonetwork.net racks, please download and paste the troubleshooting lab configurations. If you are using your own rack or lab, please modify this configuration to reflect the actual interface types, etc, that you have on your devices. Prior to beginning all labs, apply the pre-lab configuration for each individual device.

When completing these labs, it is important to resolve the trouble tickets in the order in which they are listed because they build on each other. For example, if you begin with Trouble Ticket # 3, you might not get the expected resolution or result if you have not completed Trouble Ticket # 1 and Trouble Ticket # 2. It is very important to follow the order listed.

Trouble Ticket # 1

You have received a call from Level 1 stating that following some configuration changes, the OSPF neighbor adjacency between R1 and R2 has failed. Troubleshoot and resolve this issue.

Trouble Ticket # 2

You have received a call stating that users connected R1 and R2 do not have any routing information for the 150.4.4.0/24 subnet. Troubleshoot and resolve this issue.

Trouble Ticket # 3

You have received a call from Level 1 support stating that while all of the users connected to the 150.3.3.0/24 subnets are able to reach the 150.4.4.0/24 subnet, and vice-versa, the support operatives are unable to ping the 150.4.4.4/24 address from any other device within the network. Troubleshoot and resolve this issue.

LAB SOLUTIONS

Solution # 1

The issue is that the routers are on different subnets. R1s Serial 0/0 interface is on the 10.0.0.0/30 subnet while R2s Serial0/0 interface is on the 10.0.0.0/29 subnet:

```
R1#show running-config interface serial 0/0
Building configuration...

Current configuration : 84 bytes
!
interface Serial0/0
 ip address 10.0.0.1 255.255.255.252
 ip ospf network point-to-multipoint
 ip ospf hello-interval 10
 clock rate 2000000
end

R2#show running-config interface serial 0/0
Building configuration...

Current configuration : 64 bytes
!
interface Serial0/0
 ip address 10.0.0.2 255.255.255.248
 ip ospf network point-to-multipoint
 ip ospf hello-interval 10
end
```

To resolve this issue, correct the IP addressing mis-configuration on R2s Serial 0/0 interface:

```
R2(config)#interface serial 0/0
R2(config-if)#ip address 10.0.0.2 255.255.255.252
```

Solution # 2

The issue is that OSPF virtual link configuration on all three routers is incorrect. On routers R1 and R2, the virtual links are using the link IP addresses instead of the RID of R3. On R3, the virtual links are using an incorrect transit area:

```
R1#show running-config | section ospf
 ip ospf network broadcast
 ip ospf hello-interval 5
router ospf 1
 router-id 1.1.1.1
 log-adjacency-changes
 area 1 virtual-link 10.0.0.6
 network 10.0.0.1 0.0.0.0 area 0
 network 10.0.0.5 0.0.0.0 area 1
 network 150.1.1.1 0.0.0.0 area 0

R2#show running-config | section ospf
 ip ospf network broadcast
 ip ospf hello-interval 5
router ospf 2
 router-id 2.2.2.2
 log-adjacency-changes
 area 1 virtual-link 10.0.0.10
 network 10.0.0.2 0.0.0.0 area 0
```

```
network 10.0.0.9 0.0.0.0 area 1
network 150.2.2.2 0.0.0.0 area 0

R3#show running-config | section ospf
 ip ospf authentication message-digest
 ip ospf message-digest-key 1 md5 CCNP2011
router ospf 3
 router-id 3.3.3.3
 log-adjacency-changes
 area 2 virtual-link 3.3.3.3
 area 2 virtual-link 2.2.2.2
 network 10.0.0.6 0.0.0.0 area 1
 network 10.0.0.10 0.0.0.0 area 1
 network 10.0.0.13 0.0.0.0 area 2
 network 150.3.3.3 0.0.0.0 area 2
```

To resolve this issue, implement the following configurations on these three routers:

```
R1(config-router)#router ospf 1
R1(config-router)#no area 1 virtual-link 10.0.0.6
R1(config-router)#area 1 virtual-link 3.3.3.3

R2(config)#router ospf 2
R2(config-router)#no area 1 virtual-link  10.0.0.10
R2(config-router)#area 1 virtual-link 3.3.3.3

R3(config)#router ospf 3
R3(config-router)#no area 2 virtual-link 2.2.2.2
R3(config-router)#no area 2 virtual-link 3.3.3.3
R3(config-router)#area 1 virtual-link 2.2.2.2
R3(config-router)#area 1 virtual-link 1.1.1.1
```

Solution # 3

The issue is the local PBR configuration, which is sending any ICMP packets originated by R4 to the Null0 interface - effectively sink-holing this type of traffic:

```
R4#show ip policy
Interface       Route map
local           LOCAL

R4#show route-map LOCAL
route-map LOCAL, permit, sequence 10
  Match clauses:
    ip address (access-lists): 100
  Set clauses:
    ip precedence immediate
    interface Null0
  Policy routing matches: 10 packets, 1040 bytes
route-map LOCAL, deny, sequence 20
  Match clauses:
  Set clauses:
  Policy routing matches: 0 packets, 0 bytes

R4#show ip access-lists 100
Extended IP access list 100
    10 permit icmp any any (10 matches)
```

To resolve this issue, remove the incorrect NEXT_HOP configuration from R4s PBR policy:

```
4(config)#route-map LOCAL permit 10
R4(config-route-map)#no set interface null 0
```

FINAL WORKING ROUTER CONFIGURATIONS

R1

```
R1#term len 0
R1#sh run
Building configuration...

Current configuration : 1011 bytes
```

```
!
version 12.4
service timestamps debug datetime msec
service timestamps log datetime msec
no service password-encryption
!
hostname R1
!
boot-start-marker
boot-end-marker
!
no logging console
!
no aaa new-model
no network-clock-participate slot 1
no network-clock-participate wic 0
ip cef
!
no ip domain lookup
ip auth-proxy max-nodata-conns 3
ip admission max-nodata-conns 3
!
interface FastEthernet0/0
 ip address 150.1.1.1 255.255.255.0
 duplex auto
 speed auto
!
interface Serial0/0
 ip address 10.0.0.1 255.255.255.252
 ip ospf network point-to-multipoint
 ip ospf hello-interval 10
 clock rate 2000000
!
interface Serial0/1
 ip address 10.0.0.5 255.255.255.252
!
router ospf 1
 router-id 1.1.1.1
 log-adjacency-changes
 area 1 virtual-link 3.3.3.3
 network 10.0.0.1 0.0.0.0 area 0
 network 10.0.0.5 0.0.0.0 area 1
 network 150.1.1.1 0.0.0.0 area 0
!
ip forward-protocol nd
!
no ip http server
no ip http secure-server
!
control-plane
!
line con 0
line aux 0
line vty 0 4
 login
!
end
R1#
```

R2

```
R2#term len 0
R2#sh run
Building configuration...

Current configuration : 991 bytes
!
version 12.4
service timestamps debug datetime msec
service timestamps log datetime msec
no service password-encryption
!
hostname R2
!
boot-start-marker
boot-end-marker
!
no logging console
```

```
!
no aaa new-model
no network-clock-participate slot 1
no network-clock-participate wic 0
ip cef
!
no ip domain lookup
ip auth-proxy max-nodata-conns 3
ip admission max-nodata-conns 3
!
interface FastEthernet0/0
 ip address 150.2.2.2 255.255.255.0
 duplex auto
 speed auto
!
interface Serial0/0
 ip address 10.0.0.2 255.255.255.252
 ip ospf network point-to-multipoint
 ip ospf hello-interval 10
!
interface Serial0/1
 ip address 10.0.0.9 255.255.255.252
!
router ospf 2
 router-id 2.2.2.2
 log-adjacency-changes
 area 1 virtual-link 3.3.3.3
 network 10.0.0.2 0.0.0.0 area 0
 network 10.0.0.9 0.0.0.0 area 1
 network 150.2.2.2 0.0.0.0 area 0
 !
ip forward-protocol nd
!
no ip http server
no ip http secure-server
!
control-plane
!
line con 0
line aux 0
line vty 0 4
 login
!
end

R2#
```

R3

```
R3#term len 0
R3#sh run
Building configuration...

Current configuration : 1490 bytes
!
version 12.4
service timestamps debug datetime msec
service timestamps log datetime msec
service password-encryption
!
hostname R3
!
boot-start-marker
boot-end-marker
!
no logging console
!
no aaa new-model
no network-clock-participate slot 1
no network-clock-participate wic 0
ip cef
!
no ip domain lookup
ip auth-proxy max-nodata-conns 3
ip admission max-nodata-conns 3
!
interface FastEthernet0/0
 ip address 150.3.3.3 255.255.255.0
```

```
 duplex auto
 speed auto
!
interface Serial1/0
 ip address 10.0.0.6 255.255.255.252
 clock rate 128000
!
interface Serial1/1
 ip address 10.0.0.10 255.255.255.252
 clock rate 128000
!
interface Serial1/2
 ip address 10.0.0.13 255.255.255.252
 ip ospf authentication message-digest
 ip ospf message-digest-key 1 md5 7 0130252A6B59565E70
 clock rate 128000
!
interface Serial1/3
 no ip address
 shutdown
!
interface Serial1/4
 no ip address
 shutdown
!
interface Serial1/5
 no ip address
 shutdown
!
interface Serial1/6
 no ip address
 shutdown
!
interface Serial1/7
 no ip address
 shutdown
!
router ospf 3
 router-id 3.3.3.3
 log-adjacency-changes
 area 1 virtual-link 2.2.2.2
 area 1 virtual-link 1.1.1.1
 network 10.0.0.6 0.0.0.0 area 1
 network 10.0.0.10 0.0.0.0 area 1
 network 10.0.0.13 0.0.0.0 area 2
 network 150.3.3.3 0.0.0.0 area 2
!
ip forward-protocol nd
!
no ip http server
no ip http secure-server
!
control-plane
!
line con 0
line aux 0
line vty 0 4
 login
!
end
R3#
```

R4

```
R4#term len 0
R4#sh run
Building configuration...

Current configuration : 1001 bytes
!
version 12.4
service timestamps debug datetime msec
service timestamps log datetime msec
service password-encryption
!
hostname R4
!
boot-start-marker
```

```
boot-end-marker
!
no logging console
!
no aaa new-model
no network-clock-participate slot 1
no network-clock-participate wic 0
ip cef
!
no ip domain lookup
ip auth-proxy max-nodata-conns 3
ip admission max-nodata-conns 3
!
interface FastEthernet0/0
 ip address 150.4.4.4 255.255.255.0
 duplex auto
 speed auto
!
interface Serial0/0
 ip address 10.0.0.14 255.255.255.252
 ip ospf authentication message-digest
 ip ospf message-digest-key 1 md5 7 1326343C3B5E547B7A
!
interface Serial0/1
 no ip address
 shutdown
!
router ospf 4
 router-id 4.4.4.4
 log-adjacency-changes
 network 10.0.0.14 0.0.0.0 area 2
 network 150.4.4.4 0.0.0.0 area 2
!
ip local policy route-map LOCAL
ip forward-protocol nd
!
no ip http server
no ip http secure-server
!
access-list 100 permit icmp any any
!
route-map LOCAL permit 10
 match ip address 100
 set ip precedence immediate
!
route-map LOCAL deny 20
!
control-plane
!
line con 0
line aux 0
line vty 0 4
 login
!
end

R4#
```

CCNP LAB 96

Troubleshooting Lab

Lab Objective:

The focus of this lab is to hone your trouble isolation and resolution skills. This lab will include Layer 2 and Layer 3 technologies which fall within the scope of the current CCNP curriculum.

Lab Topology:

The lab network topology is illustrated below:

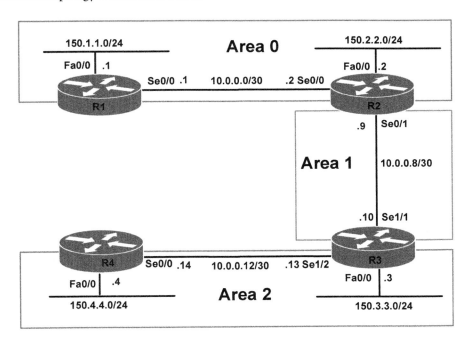

IMPORTANT NOTE: If you are using the www.howtonetwork.net racks, please download and paste the troubleshooting lab configurations. If you are using your own rack or lab, please modify this configuration to reflect the actual interface types, etc, that you have on your devices. Prior to beginning all labs, apply the pre-lab configuration for each individual device.

When completing these labs, it is important to resolve the trouble tickets in the order in which they are listed because they build on each other. For example, if you begin with Trouble Ticket # 3, you might not get the expected resolution or result if you have not completed Trouble Ticket # 1 and Trouble Ticket # 2. It is very important to follow the order listed.

Trouble Ticket # 1

You have received a call from Level 1 stating that following some configuration changes, the OSPF neighbor adjacency between R1 and R2 has failed. Troubleshoot and resolve this issue.

Trouble Ticket # 2

You have received a call from Level 1 stating that following some basic network configuration changes, the OSPF adjacency between R2 and R3 is down. Troubleshoot and resolve this issue.

Trouble Ticket # 3

You have received a call from Level 1 stating that the OSPF adjacency between R3 and R4 is down. Troubleshoot and resolve this issue.

Trouble Ticket # 4

You have received a call from Level 1 stating that there is intermittent connectivity between the 150.1.1.0/24 and 150.2.2.0/24 subnets and the 150.4.4.0/24 subnet. Due to a current configuration freeze on R3, Management allows you to only make changes to ONE device. With this restriction in mind, troubleshoot and resolve this issue.

LAB SOLUTIONS

Solution # 1

The issue is that there is no clocking on the WAN link between R1 and R2:

```
R1#show controllers serial 0/0
Interface Serial0/0
Hardware is PowerQUICC MPC860
DCE V.35, no clock

R2#show controllers serial 0/0
Interface Serial0/0
Hardware is PowerQUICC MPC860
DTE V.35 clocks stopped.
```

To resolve this issue, configure clocking on R1s WAN interface:

```
R1(config)#interface serial 0/0
R1(config-if)#clock rate 2000000
```

Solution # 2

The issue here is that there is an MTU mismatch between R2 and R3:

```
R2#show running-config interface serial 0/1
Building configuration...

Current configuration : 95 bytes
!
interface Serial0/1
 ip address 10.0.0.9 255.255.255.252
 ip mtu 1492
 ip ospf 2 area 1
end

R3#show running-config interface serial 1/1
Building configuration...

Current configuration : 102 bytes
!
interface Serial1/1
 ip address 10.0.0.10 255.255.255.252
 ip ospf 3 area 1
 clock rate 128000
end
```

To resolve this issue, you can do one of the following:
- Apply the same configuration to R3s WAN interface
- Remove this configuration on R2s WAN interface

This solution shows the latter of the acceptable solutions:

```
R2(config)#interface serial 0/0
R2(config-if)#no ip mtu 1492
```

Solution # 3

The issue here is that the interface configuration on R4 has been applied to the wrong interface. While R4 is connected to R3 via Serial 0/0, the configuration has been applied to Serial 0/1:

```
R4#show running-config interface serial 0/1
Building configuration...

Current configuration : 83 bytes
!
interface Serial0/1
 ip address 10.0.0.14 255.255.255.252
 ip ospf 4 area 2
end
```

To resolve this issue, remove this configuration from Serial 0/1 and apply it instead to Serial 0/0:

```
R4(config)#default interface serial 0/1
Building configuration...

Interface Serial0/1 set to default configuration
R4(config)#interface serial 0/0
R4(config-if)#ip address 10.0.0.14 255.255.255.252
R4(config-if)#ip ospf 4 area 2
R4(config-if)#exit
```

Solution # 4

The issue here is that the configuration applied to R2 causes a recursive routing issue because the tunnel source address is learned via the tunnel interface itself:

```
R2#show running-config interface loopback 0
Building configuration...

Current configuration : 81 bytes
!
interface Loopback0
 ip address 2.2.2.2 255.255.255.255
 ip ospf 2 area 0
end
```

This can be validated by looking at the contents of the routing table on R3:

```
R3#show ip route 2.2.2.2 255.255.255.255
Routing entry for 2.2.2.2/32
  Known via "ospf 3", distance 110, metric 11112, type intra area
  Last update from 192.168.1.2 on Tunnel0, 00:00:02 ago
  Routing Descriptor Blocks:
  * 192.168.1.2, from 2.2.2.2, 00:00:02 ago, via Tunnel0
      Route metric is 11112, traffic share count is 1
```

Given this issue, if logging was enabled, you would see the following printed on the console:

```
R3(config)#logging console
R3(config)#
*Jul 10 04:34:34.091: %OSPF-5-ADJCHG: Process 3, Nbr 2.2.2.2 on Serial1/1 from
LOADING to FULL, Loading Done
*Jul 10 04:34:49.955: %LINEPROTO-5-UPDOWN: Line protocol on Interface Tunnel0,
changed state to up
*Jul 10 04:34:50.067: %OSPF-5-ADJCHG: Process 3, Nbr 2.2.2.2 on Tunnel0 from LOADING
to FULL, Loading Done
*Jul 10 04:34:58.955: %TUN-5-RECURDOWN: Tunnel0 temporarily disabled due to recursive
routing
*Jul 10 04:34:59.955: %LINEPROTO-5-UPDOWN: Line protocol on Interface Tunnel0,
changed state to down
*Jul 10 04:34:59.955: %OSPF-5-ADJCHG: Process 3, Nbr 2.2.2.2 on Tunnel0 from FULL to
```

```
DOWN, Neighbor Down: Interface down or detached
*Jul 10 04:35:59.955: %LINEPROTO-5-UPDOWN: Line protocol on Interface Tunnel0,
changed state to up
*Jul 10 04:36:00.067: %OSPF-5-ADJCHG: Process 3, Nbr 2.2.2.2 on Tunnel0 from LOADING
to FULL, Loading Done
*Jul 10 04:36:08.955: %TUN-5-RECURDOWN: Tunnel0 temporarily disabled due to recursive
routing
*Jul 10 04:36:09.955: %LINEPROTO-5-UPDOWN: Line protocol on Interface Tunnel0,
changed state to down
*Jul 10 04:36:09.955: %OSPF-5-ADJCHG: Process 3, Nbr 2.2.2.2 on Tunnel0 from FULL to
DOWN, Neighbor Down: Interface down or detached
```

Recursive routing issues are common when implementing tunneling. It is important to have a solid understanding of routing to avoid these issues. To resolve this issue, assign the Loopback interface to area 1 on R2:

```
R2(config)#interface loopback 0
R2(config-if)#ip ospf 2 area 1
```

FINAL WORKING ROUTER CONFIGURATIONS

R1

```
R1#term len 0
R1#sh run
Building configuration...

Current configuration : 906 bytes
!
version 12.4
service timestamps debug datetime msec
service timestamps log datetime msec
no service password-encryption
!
hostname R1
!
boot-start-marker
boot-end-marker
!
no logging console
!
no aaa new-model
no network-clock-participate slot 1
no network-clock-participate wic 0
ip cef
!
no ip domain lookup
ip auth-proxy max-nodata-conns 3
ip admission max-nodata-conns 3
!
interface FastEthernet0/0
 ip address 150.1.1.1 255.255.255.0
 ip ospf 1 area 0
 duplex auto
 speed auto
!
interface Serial0/0
 ip address 10.0.0.1 255.255.255.252
 ip ospf 1 area 0
 clock rate 2000000
!
interface Serial0/1
 no ip address
 shutdown
!
router ospf 1
 router-id 1.1.1.1
 log-adjacency-changes
!
ip forward-protocol nd
!
no ip http server
no ip http secure-server
!
control-plane
!
line con 0
```

```
line aux 0
line vty 0 4
 login
!
end
R1#
```

R2

```
R2#term len 0
R2#sh run
Building configuration...

Current configuration : 1126 bytes
!
version 12.4
service timestamps debug datetime msec
service timestamps log datetime msec
no service password-encryption
!
hostname R2
!
boot-start-marker
boot-end-marker
!
no aaa new-model
no network-clock-participate slot 1
no network-clock-participate wic 0
ip cef
!
no ip domain lookup
ip auth-proxy max-nodata-conns 3
ip admission max-nodata-conns 3
!
interface Loopback0
 ip address 2.2.2.2 255.255.255.255
 ip ospf 2 area 1
!
interface Tunnel0
 ip address 192.168.1.2 255.255.255.254
 ip ospf 2 area 0
 tunnel source 2.2.2.2
 tunnel destination 3.3.3.3
!
interface FastEthernet0/0
 ip address 150.2.2.2 255.255.255.0
 ip ospf 2 area 0
 duplex auto
 speed auto
!
interface Serial0/0
 ip address 10.0.0.2 255.255.255.252
 ip ospf 2 area 0
!
interface Serial0/1
 ip address 10.0.0.9 255.255.255.252
 ip ospf 2 area 1
!
router ospf 2
 router-id 2.2.2.2
 log-adjacency-changes
 area 1 nssa no-summary
!
ip forward-protocol nd
!
no ip http server
no ip http secure-server
!
control-plane
!
line con 0
line aux 0
line vty 0 4
 login
!
end

R2#
```

R3

```
R3#term len 0
R3#sh run
Building configuration...

Current configuration : 1624 bytes
!
version 12.4
service timestamps debug datetime msec
service timestamps log datetime msec
no service password-encryption
!
hostname R3
!
boot-start-marker
boot-end-marker
!
no aaa new-model
no network-clock-participate slot 1
no network-clock-participate wic 0
ip cef
!
no ip domain lookup
ip auth-proxy max-nodata-conns 3
ip admission max-nodata-conns 3
!
interface Loopback0
 ip address 3.3.3.3 255.255.255.255
 ip ospf 3 area 1
!
interface Tunnel0
 ip address 192.168.1.3 255.255.255.254
 ip ospf 3 area 0
 tunnel source 3.3.3.3
 tunnel destination 2.2.2.2
!
interface FastEthernet0/0
 ip address 150.3.3.3 255.255.255.0
 duplex auto
 speed auto
!
interface Serial1/0
 no ip address
 shutdown
 clock rate 128000
!
interface Serial1/1
 ip address 10.0.0.10 255.255.255.252
 ip ospf 3 area 1
 clock rate 128000
!
interface Serial1/2
 ip address 10.0.0.13 255.255.255.252
 ip ospf 3 area 2
 clock rate 128000
!
interface Serial1/3
 no ip address
 shutdown
!
interface Serial1/4
 no ip address
 shutdown
!
interface Serial1/5
 no ip address
 shutdown
!
interface Serial1/6
 no ip address
 shutdown
!
interface Serial1/7
 no ip address
 shutdown
!
router ospf 3
 router-id 3.3.3.3
 log-adjacency-changes
 area 1 nssa
 redistribute connected metric-type 1 subnets route-map CONNECTED
!
ip forward-protocol nd
```

```
!
no ip http server
no ip http secure-server
!
route-map CONNECTED deny 10
 match interface Tunnel0
!
route-map CONNECTED permit 20
 match interface FastEthernet0/0
!
control-plane
!
line con 0
line aux 0
line vty 0 4
 login
!
end
R3#
```

R4

```
R4#term len 0
R4#sh run
Building configuration...

Current configuration : 887 bytes
!
version 12.4
service timestamps debug datetime msec
service timestamps log datetime msec
no service password-encryption
!
hostname R4
!
boot-start-marker
boot-end-marker
!
no logging console
!
no aaa new-model
no network-clock-participate slot 1
no network-clock-participate wic 0
ip cef
!
no ip domain lookup
ip auth-proxy max-nodata-conns 3
ip admission max-nodata-conns 3
!
interface FastEthernet0/0
 ip address 150.4.4.4 255.255.255.0
 ip ospf 4 area 2
 duplex auto
 speed auto
!
interface Serial0/0
 ip address 10.0.0.14 255.255.255.252
 ip ospf 4 area 2
!
interface Serial0/1
 no ip address
 shutdown
!
router ospf 4
 router-id 4.4.4.4
 log-adjacency-changes
!
ip forward-protocol nd
!
no ip http server
no ip http secure-server
!
control-plane
!
line con 0
line aux 0
line vty 0 4
 login
!
end
R4#
```

CCNP LAB 97

Troubleshooting Lab

Lab Objective:

The focus of this lab is to hone your trouble isolation and resolution skills. This lab will include Layer 2 and Layer 3 technologies which fall within the scope of the current CCNP curriculum.

Lab Topology:

The lab network topology is illustrated below:

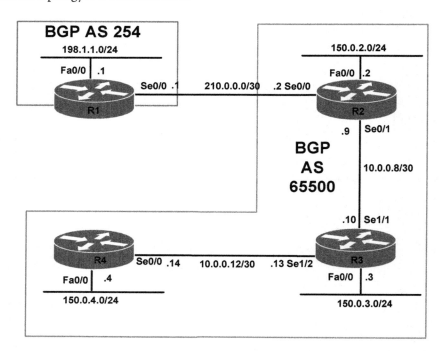

IMPORTANT NOTE: If you are using the www.howtonetwork.net racks, please download and paste the troubleshooting lab configurations. If you are using your own rack or lab, please modify this configuration to reflect the actual interface types, etc, that you have on your devices. Prior to beginning all labs, apply the pre-lab configuration for each individual device.

When completing these labs, it is important to resolve the trouble tickets in the order in which they are listed because they build on each other. For example, if you begin with Trouble Ticket # 3, you might not get the expected resolution or result if you have not completed Trouble Ticket # 1 and Trouble Ticket # 2. It is very important to follow the order listed.

Trouble Ticket # 1

You have received a call from the ISP indicating that the BGP adjacency between them and your edge router (R1) has gone down. Troubleshoot and resolve this issue.

Trouble Ticket # 2

You have received a call from the NOC indicating that users on all the 150.0.3.0/24 subnet are unable to reach the 198.1.1.0/24 subnet. At the moment, depart policy stipulates that IGP configurations cannot be modified until further notice. While adhering to the current restriction, troubleshoot and resolve this issue.

Trouble Ticket # 3

The NOC has called you to advise that after they enable BGP on R4, they failed to establish an adjacency with R3. Troubleshoot and resolve this issue.

Trouble Ticket # 4

You have received notification that users within AS 65500 are unable to reach the 150.4.4.0/24 subnet and vice-versa. Troubleshoot and resolve this issue.

LAB SOLUTIONS

Solution # 1

The issue is that the BGP peer IP address has been mis-configured on R2:

```
R2#show running-config | include neighbor
 bgp log-neighbor-changes
 neighbor 10.0.0.10 remote-as 65500
 neighbor 10.0.0.10 next-hop-self
 neighbor 201.0.0.1 remote-as 254
```

To resolve this issue, configure the correct BGP peer IP address on R2:

```
R2(config)#router bgp 65500
R2(config-router)#no neighbor 201.0.0.1 remote-as 254
R2(config-router)#neighbor 210.0.0.1 remote-as 254
```

Solution # 2

The issue is that the BGP NEXT_HOP attribute is unchanged when routes are advertised from an iBGP speaker to another iBGP speaker. Therefore, because the 210.0.0.0/30 subnet is unknown to the routers in AS 65500, the 198.1.1.0/24 prefix will be marked as inaccessible. To resolve this issue, while adhering to the restrictions, implement the following on R2:

```
R2(config)#router bgp 65500
R2(config-router)#neighbor 10.0.0.10 next-hop-self
```

Solution # 3

The issue is that there is a BGP password mismatch between R3 and R4:

```
R3#show running-config | section bgp
router bgp 65500
 no synchronization
 bgp router-id 3.3.3.3
 bgp log-neighbor-changes
 network 150.0.3.0 mask 255.255.255.0
 neighbor INTERNAL peer-group
 neighbor INTERNAL remote-as 65500
 neighbor INTERNAL password CCNP2011
 neighbor INTERNAL route-reflector-client
 neighbor 10.0.0.9 peer-group INTERNAL
 neighbor 10.0.0.14 peer-group INTERNAL
 no auto-summary

R4#show running-config | section bgp
router bgp 65500
 no synchronization
 bgp router-id 4.4.4.4
 bgp log-neighbor-changes
 network 150.0.4.0 mask 255.255.255.255
```

```
neighbor 10.0.0.13 remote-as 65500
neighbor 10.0.0.13 password CCNP2011
no auto-summary
```

This password mis-configuration will cause the following error messages on these routers:

```
R3#
*Jul 10 05:22:23.507: %TCP-6-BADAUTH: Invalid MD5 digest from 10.0.0.14(32321) to
10.0.0.13(179)
*Jul 10 05:22:25.507: %TCP-6-BADAUTH: Invalid MD5 digest from 10.0.0.14(32321) to
10.0.0.13(179)
*Jul 10 05:22:29.507: %TCP-6-BADAUTH: Invalid MD5 digest from 10.0.0.14(32321) to
10.0.0.13(179)

R4#
*Jul 10 04:01:39.919: %TCP-6-BADAUTH: Invalid MD5 digest from 10.0.0.13(14756) to
10.0.0.14(179)
*Jul 10 04:01:43.919: %TCP-6-BADAUTH: Invalid MD5 digest from 10.0.0.13(14756) to
10.0.0.14(179)
*Jul 10 04:01:51.919: %TCP-6-BADAUTH: Invalid MD5 digest from 10.0.0.13(14756) to
10.0.0.14(179)
```

To resolve this issue, configure the correct password on R4:

```
R4(config)#router bgp 65500
R4(config-router)#neighbor 10.0.0.13 password CCNP2011
```

Solution # 4

The issue is that the BGP network command configured on R4 is incorrect:

```
R4#show running-config | section bgp
router bgp 65500
 no synchronization
 bgp router-id 4.4.4.4
 bgp log-neighbor-changes
 network 150.0.4.0 mask 255.255.255.255
 neighbor 10.0.0.13 remote-as 65500
 no auto-summary
```

To resolve this issue, configure the correct network statement under BGP:

```
4(config)#router bgp 65500
R4(config-router)#no network 150.0.4.0 mask 255.255.255.255
R4(config-router)#network 150.0.4.0 mask 255.255.255.255
```

FINAL WORKING ROUTER CONFIGURATIONS

R1

```
R1#term len 0
R1#sh run
Building configuration...

Current configuration : 971 bytes
!
version 12.4
service timestamps debug datetime msec
service timestamps log datetime msec
no service password-encryption
!
hostname R1
!
boot-start-marker
boot-end-marker
!
no logging console
!
no aaa new-model
no network-clock-participate slot 1
no network-clock-participate wic 0
ip cef
```

```
!
no ip domain lookup
ip auth-proxy max-nodata-conns 3
ip admission max-nodata-conns 3
!
interface FastEthernet0/0
 ip address 198.1.1.1 255.255.255.0
 duplex auto
 speed auto
!
interface Serial0/0
 ip address 210.0.0.1 255.255.255.252
 clock rate 2000000
!
interface Serial0/1
 no ip address
 shutdown
!
router bgp 254
 no synchronization
 bgp router-id 1.1.1.1
 bgp log-neighbor-changes
 network 198.1.1.0
 neighbor 210.0.0.2 remote-as 65500
 no auto-summary
!
ip forward-protocol nd
!
no ip http server
no ip http secure-server
!
control-plane
!
line con 0
line aux 0
line vty 0 4
 login
!
end

R1#
```

R2

```
R2#term len 0
R2#sh run
Building configuration...

Current configuration : 1104 bytes
!
version 12.4
service timestamps debug datetime msec
service timestamps log datetime msec
no service password-encryption
!
hostname R2
!
boot-start-marker
boot-end-marker
!
no logging console
!
no aaa new-model
no network-clock-participate slot 1
no network-clock-participate wic 0
ip cef
!
no ip domain lookup
ip auth-proxy max-nodata-conns 3
ip admission max-nodata-conns 3
!
interface FastEthernet0/0
 ip address 150.0.2.2 255.255.255.0
 duplex auto
 speed auto
!
interface Serial0/0
 ip address 210.0.0.2 255.255.255.252
```

```
!
interface Serial0/1
 ip address 10.0.0.9 255.255.255.252
!
router eigrp 1
 network 10.0.0.0
 no auto-summary
!
router bgp 65500
 no synchronization
 bgp router-id 2.2.2.2
 bgp log-neighbor-changes
 network 150.0.2.0 mask 255.255.255.0
 neighbor 10.0.0.10 remote-as 65500
 neighbor 10.0.0.10 next-hop-self
 neighbor 10.0.0.10 password CCNP2011
 neighbor 210.0.0.1 remote-as 254
 no auto-summary
!
ip forward-protocol nd
!
no ip http server
no ip http secure-server
!
control-plane
!
line con 0
line aux 0
line vty 0 4
 login
!
end
R2#
```

R3

```
R3#term len 0
R3#sh run
Building configuration...

Current configuration : 1526 bytes
!
version 12.4
service timestamps debug datetime msec
service timestamps log datetime msec
no service password-encryption
!
hostname R3
!
boot-start-marker
boot-end-marker
!
no logging console
!
no aaa new-model
no network-clock-participate slot 1
no network-clock-participate wic 0
ip cef
!
no ip domain lookup
ip auth-proxy max-nodata-conns 3
ip admission max-nodata-conns 3
!
interface FastEthernet0/0
 ip address 150.0.3.3 255.255.255.0
 duplex auto
 speed auto
!
interface Serial1/0
 no ip address
 shutdown
 clock rate 128000
!
interface Serial1/1
 ip address 10.0.0.10 255.255.255.252
 clock rate 128000
!
interface Serial1/2
```

```
 ip address 10.0.0.13 255.255.255.252
 clock rate 128000
!
interface Serial1/3
 no ip address
 shutdown
!
interface Serial1/4
 no ip address
 shutdown
!
interface Serial1/5
 no ip address
 shutdown
!
interface Serial1/6
 no ip address
 shutdown
!
interface Serial1/7
 no ip address
 shutdown
!
router eigrp 1
 network 10.0.0.0
 no auto-summary
!
router bgp 65500
 no synchronization
 bgp router-id 3.3.3.3
 bgp log-neighbor-changes
 network 150.0.3.0 mask 255.255.255.0
 neighbor INTERNAL peer-group
 neighbor INTERNAL remote-as 65500
 neighbor INTERNAL password CCNP2011
 neighbor INTERNAL route-reflector-client
 neighbor 10.0.0.9 peer-group INTERNAL
 neighbor 10.0.0.14 peer-group INTERNAL
 no auto-summary
!
ip forward-protocol nd
!
no ip http server
no ip http secure-server
!
control-plane
!
line con 0
line aux 0
line vty 0 4
 login
!
end

R3#
```

R4

```
R4#term len 0
R4#sh run
Building configuration...

Current configuration : 1024 bytes
!
version 12.4
service timestamps debug datetime msec
service timestamps log datetime msec
no service password-encryption
!
hostname R4
!
boot-start-marker
boot-end-marker
!
no logging console
!
no aaa new-model
no network-clock-participate slot 1
```

```
no network-clock-participate wic 0
ip cef
!
no ip domain lookup
ip auth-proxy max-nodata-conns 3
ip admission max-nodata-conns 3
!
interface FastEthernet0/0
 ip address 150.0.4.4 255.255.255.0
 duplex auto
 speed auto
!
interface Serial0/0
 ip address 10.0.0.14 255.255.255.252
!
interface Serial0/1
 no ip address
 shutdown
!
router eigrp 1
 network 10.0.0.0
 no auto-summary
!
router bgp 65500
 no synchronization
 bgp router-id 4.4.4.4
 bgp log-neighbor-changes
 network 150.0.4.0 mask 255.255.255.0
 neighbor 10.0.0.13 remote-as 65500
 neighbor 10.0.0.13 password CCNP2011
 no auto-summary
!
ip forward-protocol nd
!
no ip http server
no ip http secure-server
!
control-plane
!
line con 0
line aux 0
line vty 0 4
 login
!
end

R4#
```

CCNP LAB 98

Troubleshooting Lab

Lab Objective:

The focus of this lab is to hone your trouble isolation and resolution skills. This lab will include Layer 2 and Layer 3 technologies which fall within the scope of the current CCNP curriculum.

Lab Topology:

The lab network topology is illustrated below:

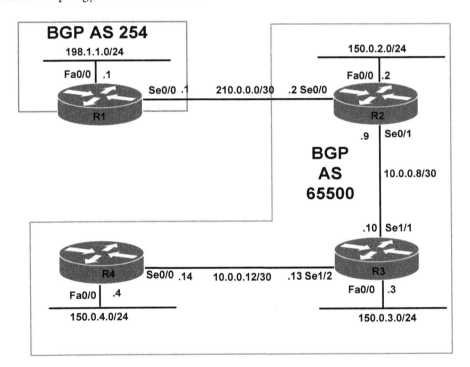

IMPORTANT NOTE: If you are using the www.howtonetwork.net racks, please download and paste the troubleshooting lab configurations. If you are using your own rack or lab, please modify this configuration to reflect the actual interface types, etc, that you have on your devices. Prior to beginning all labs, apply the pre-lab configuration for each individual device.

When completing these labs, it is important to resolve the trouble tickets in the order in which they are listed because they build on each other. For example, if you begin with Trouble Ticket # 3, you might not get the expected resolution or result if you have not completed Trouble Ticket # 1 and Trouble Ticket # 2. It is very important to follow the order listed.

Trouble Ticket # 1

You have configured BGP on R1 and R2 and notice that the adjacency is not established. Troubleshoot and resolve this issue.

Trouble Ticket # 2

You have received a call from the NOC stating that they are unable to reach the 198.1.1.0/24 subnet from the 150.3.3.0/24 subnet. Troubleshoot and resolve this issue.

Trouble Ticket # 3

You have received complaints stating that users connected to the 150.3.3.0/24 subnet are not able to communicate with users on the 150.2.2.0/24 subnet. Troubleshoot and resolve this.

Trouble Ticket # 4

The NOC has called you to advise that the 150.4.4.0/24 subnet is only able to reach devices on the 150.3.3.0/24 subnet, but nothing else. Troubleshoot and resolve this issue.

LAB SOLUTIONS

Solution # 1

When configuring indirectly connected external BGP peers, you need to modify the IP TTL of the BGP packets using the `neighbor <address> ebgp-multihop <1-254>` command:

```
R1#show running-config | section bgp
router bgp 254
 no synchronization
 bgp router-id 1.1.1.1
 bgp log-neighbor-changes
 network 198.1.1.0
 neighbor 2.2.2.2 remote-as 65500
 neighbor 2.2.2.2 update-source Loopback0
 no auto-summary

R2#show running-config | section bgp
router bgp 65500
 no synchronization
 bgp router-id 2.2.2.2
 bgp log-neighbor-changes
 network 150.0.2.0 mask 255.255.255.0
 neighbor 1.1.1.1 remote-as 254
 neighbor 1.1.1.1 update-source Loopback0
 neighbor 10.0.0.10 remote-as 65500
 neighbor 10.0.0.10 route-map NEXT_HOP out
 no auto-summary
```

To resolve this issue, implement the following configuration on R1 and R2:

```
R1(config)#router bgp 254
R1(config-router)#neighbor 2.2.2.2 ebgp-multihop 2

R2(config)#router bgp 65500
R2(config-router)#neighbor 1.1.1.1 ebgp-multihop 2
```

NOTE: You do NOT have to specify a value of '2' with this command to resolve this issue.

Solution # 2

The issue is that the outbound route-map configured on R2 is incorrect as it specifies a NEXT_HOP address of R3 instead of R2 for all advertised BGP prefixes:

```
R2#show route-map
route-map NEXT_HOP, permit, sequence 10
  Match clauses:
  Set clauses:
    ip next-hop 10.0.0.10
  Policy routing matches: 0 packets, 0 bytes
```

To resolve this issue, implement the following configuration on R2:

```
R2(config)#route-map NEXT_HOP permit 10
R2(config-route-map)#no set ip next-hop 10.0.0.10
R2(config-route-map)#set ip next-hop 10.0.0.9
```

Solution # 3

The issue is that the FastEthernet0/0 interface on R2 is shut down, which prevents this subnet from being advertised by R2 via BGP:

```
R2#show interfaces fastethernet 0/0
FastEthernet0/0 is administratively down, line protocol is down
  Hardware is AmdFE, address is 000d.289e.f940 (bia 000d.289e.f940)
  Internet address is 150.0.2.2/24
  MTU 1500 bytes, BW 100000 Kbit/sec, DLY 100 usec,
    reliability 255/255, txload 1/255, rxload 1/255
  Encapsulation ARPA, loopback not set
  Keepalive set (10 sec)
  Auto-duplex, Auto Speed, 100BaseTX/FX

[Truncated Output]
```

To resolve this issue, simply bring up the FastEthernet0/0 interface:

```
R2(config)#interface fastethernet 0/0
R2(config-if)#no shutdown
```

Solution # 4

The issue arises from the fact that R3 is not configured as a route reflector for R2 and R4:

```
R3#show running-config | section bgp
router bgp 65500
 no synchronization
 bgp router-id 3.3.3.3
 bgp log-neighbor-changes
 network 150.0.3.0 mask 255.255.255.0
 neighbor 10.0.0.9 remote-as 65500
 neighbor 10.0.0.9 route-map R2-NEXT-HOP out
 neighbor 10.0.0.14 remote-as 65500
 neighbor 10.0.0.14 route-map R4-NEXT-HOP out
 no auto-summary
```

To resolve this issue, configure R3 as a route reflector for R2 and R4:

```
R3(config)#router bgp 65500
R3(config-router)#neighbor 10.0.0.9 route-reflector-client
R3(config-router)#neighbor 10.0.0.14 route-reflector-client
```

FINAL WORKING ROUTER CONFIGURATIONS

R1

```
R1#term len 0
R1#sh run
Building configuration...

Current configuration : 1146 bytes
!
version 12.4
service timestamps debug datetime msec
service timestamps log datetime msec
no service password-encryption
!
hostname R1
!
boot-start-marker
boot-end-marker
!
no logging console
!
```

```
no aaa new-model
no network-clock-participate slot 1
no network-clock-participate wic 0
ip cef
!
no ip domain lookup
ip auth-proxy max-nodata-conns 3
ip admission max-nodata-conns 3
!
interface Loopback0
 ip address 1.1.1.1 255.255.255.255
!
interface FastEthernet0/0
 ip address 198.1.1.1 255.255.255.0
 duplex auto
 speed auto
!
interface Serial0/0
 ip address 210.0.0.1 255.255.255.252
 clock rate 2000000
!
interface Serial0/1
 no ip address
 shutdown
!
router bgp 254
 no synchronization
 bgp router-id 1.1.1.1
 bgp log-neighbor-changes
 network 198.1.1.0
 neighbor 2.2.2.2 remote-as 65500
 neighbor 2.2.2.2 ebgp-multihop 2
 neighbor 2.2.2.2 update-source Loopback0
 no auto-summary
!
ip forward-protocol nd
ip route 2.2.2.2 255.255.255.255 Serial0/0
!
no ip http server
no ip http secure-server
!
control-plane
!
line con 0
line aux 0
line vty 0 4
 login
!
end

R1#
```

R2

```
R2#term len 0
R2#sh run
Building configuration...

Current configuration : 1293 bytes
!
version 12.4
service timestamps debug datetime msec
service timestamps log datetime msec
no service password-encryption
!
hostname R2
!
boot-start-marker
boot-end-marker
!
no logging console
!
no aaa new-model
no network-clock-participate slot 1
no network-clock-participate wic 0
ip cef
```

```
!
no ip domain lookup
ip auth-proxy max-nodata-conns 3
ip admission max-nodata-conns 3
!
interface Loopback0
 ip address 2.2.2.2 255.255.255.255
!
interface FastEthernet0/0
 ip address 150.0.2.2 255.255.255.0
 duplex auto
 speed auto
!
interface Serial0/0
 ip address 210.0.0.2 255.255.255.252
!
interface Serial0/1
 ip address 10.0.0.9 255.255.255.252
!
router bgp 65500
 no synchronization
 bgp router-id 2.2.2.2
 bgp log-neighbor-changes
 network 150.0.2.0 mask 255.255.255.0
 neighbor 1.1.1.1 remote-as 254
 neighbor 1.1.1.1 ebgp-multihop 2
 neighbor 1.1.1.1 update-source Loopback0
 neighbor 10.0.0.10 remote-as 65500
 neighbor 10.0.0.10 route-map NEXT_HOP out
 no auto-summary
!
ip forward-protocol nd
ip route 1.1.1.1 255.255.255.255 Serial0/0
!
no ip http server
no ip http secure-server
!
route-map NEXT_HOP permit 10
 set ip next-hop 10.0.0.9
!
control-plane
!
line con 0
line aux 0
line vty 0 4
 login
!
end
R2#
```

R3

```
R3#term len 0
R3#sh run
Building configuration...

Current configuration : 1657 bytes
!
version 12.4
service timestamps debug datetime msec
service timestamps log datetime msec
no service password-encryption
!
hostname R3
!
boot-start-marker
boot-end-marker
!
no logging console
!
no aaa new-model
no network-clock-participate slot 1
no network-clock-participate wic 0
ip cef
!
no ip domain lookup
```

```
ip auth-proxy max-nodata-conns 3
ip admission max-nodata-conns 3
!
interface FastEthernet0/0
 ip address 150.0.3.3 255.255.255.0
 duplex auto
 speed auto
!
interface Serial1/0
 no ip address
 shutdown
 clock rate 128000
!
interface Serial1/1
 ip address 10.0.0.10 255.255.255.252
 clock rate 128000
!
interface Serial1/2
 ip address 10.0.0.13 255.255.255.252
 clock rate 128000
!
interface Serial1/3
 no ip address
 shutdown
!
interface Serial1/4
 no ip address
 shutdown
!
interface Serial1/5
 no ip address
 shutdown
!
interface Serial1/6
 no ip address
 shutdown
!
interface Serial1/7
 no ip address
 shutdown
!
router bgp 65500
 no synchronization
 bgp router-id 3.3.3.3
 bgp log-neighbor-changes
 network 150.0.3.0 mask 255.255.255.0
 neighbor 10.0.0.9 remote-as 65500
 neighbor 10.0.0.9 route-reflector-client
 neighbor 10.0.0.9 route-map R2-NEXT-HOP out
 neighbor 10.0.0.14 remote-as 65500
 neighbor 10.0.0.14 route-reflector-client
 neighbor 10.0.0.14 route-map R4-NEXT-HOP out
 no auto-summary
!
ip forward-protocol nd
!
no ip http server
no ip http secure-server
!
route-map R2-NEXT-HOP permit 10
 set ip next-hop 10.0.0.10
!
route-map R4-NEXT-HOP permit 10
 set ip next-hop 10.0.0.13
!
control-plane
!
line con 0
line aux 0
line vty 0 4
 login
!
end

R3#
```

R4

```
R4#term len 0
R4#s run
Building configuration...

Current configuration : 972 bytes
!
version 12.4
service timestamps debug datetime msec
service timestamps log datetime msec
no service password-encryption
!
hostname R4
!
boot-start-marker
boot-end-marker
!
no logging console
!
no aaa new-model
no network-clock-participate slot 1
no network-clock-participate wic 0
ip cef
!
no ip domain lookup
ip auth-proxy max-nodata-conns 3
ip admission max-nodata-conns 3
!
interface FastEthernet0/0
 ip address 150.0.4.4 255.255.255.0
 duplex auto
 speed auto
!
interface Serial0/0
 ip address 10.0.0.14 255.255.255.252
!
interface Serial0/1
 no ip address
 shutdown
!
router bgp 65500
 no synchronization
 bgp router-id 4.4.4.4
 bgp log-neighbor-changes
 network 150.0.4.0 mask 255.255.255.0
 neighbor 10.0.0.13 remote-as 65500
 no auto-summary
!
ip forward-protocol nd
!
no ip http server
no ip http secure-server
!
control-plane
!
line con 0
line aux 0
line vty 0 4
 login
!
end

R4#
```

CCNP LAB 99

Troubleshooting Lab

Lab Objective:

The focus of this lab is to hone your trouble isolation and resolution skills. This lab will include Layer 2 and Layer 3 technologies which fall within the scope of the current CCNP curriculum.

Lab Topology:

The lab network topology is illustrated below:

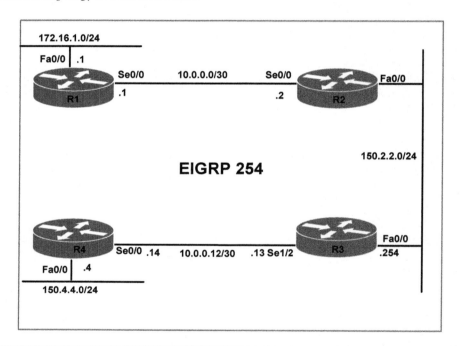

IMPORTANT NOTE: If you are using the www.howtonetwork.net racks, please download and paste the troubleshooting lab configurations. If you are using your own rack or lab, please modify this configuration to reflect the actual interface types, etc, that you have on your devices. Prior to beginning all labs, apply the pre-lab configuration for each individual device.

When completing these labs, it is important to resolve the trouble tickets in the order in which they are listed because they build on each other. For example, if you begin with Trouble Ticket # 3, you might not get the expected resolution or result if you have not completed Trouble Ticket # 1 and Trouble Ticket # 2. It is very important to follow the order listed.

Trouble Ticket # 1

You have received a call stating that users connected to the 172.16.1.0/24 subnet are unable to reach devices connected to the 150.4.4.0/24 subnet. Troubleshoot and resolve this issue.

Trouble Ticket # 2

You have received multiple complaints from the users on the 172.16.1.0/24 subnet that they commonly experience poor connectivity to a Web server with the IP address 150.4.4.254/24. Troubleshoot and resolve this issue.

Trouble Ticket # 3

Cisco IOS DHCP server has been configured on R3 to service clients located on the 150.4.4.0/24 subnet. However, you receive complaints that clients located on this subnet are unable to acquire IP addresses. Troubleshoot and resolve this issue.

LAB SOLUTIONS

Solution # 1

There are multiple issues that need to be addressed to resolve this problem: the first issue is that R1 has no routing (reachability) information for this subnet:

```
R1#show ip route
Codes: C - connected, S - static, R - RIP, M - mobile, B - BGP
       D - EIGRP, EX - EIGRP external, O - OSPF, IA - OSPF inter area
       N1 - OSPF NSSA external type 1, N2 - OSPF NSSA external type 2
       E1 - OSPF external type 1, E2 - OSPF external type 2
       i - IS-IS, su - IS-IS summary, L1 - IS-IS level-1, L2 - IS-IS level-2
       ia - IS-IS inter area, * - candidate default, U - per-user static route
       o - ODR, P - periodic downloaded static route

Gateway of last resort is not set

     172.16.0.0/24 is subnetted, 1 subnets
C       172.16.1.0 is directly connected, FastEthernet0/0
     10.0.0.0/30 is subnetted, 1 subnets
C       10.0.0.0 is directly connected, Serial0/0
```

The second issue is that the NAT configuration on R2 is incorrect in that NAT is applied to the FastEthernet interface instead of the Dialer interface:

```
R2#show ip nat statistics
Total active translations: 0 (0 static, 0 dynamic; 0 extended)
Outside interfaces:
  FastEthernet0/0
Inside interfaces:
  Serial0/0
Hits: 22  Misses: 3
CEF Translated packets: 25, CEF Punted packets: 0
Expired translations: 2
Dynamic mappings:
-- Inside Source
[Id: 3] access-list 100 interface FastEthernet0/0 refcount 0
Appl doors: 0
Normal doors: 0
Queued Packets: 0
```

And finally, the third issue that is causing this problem is that R2 is not advertising the 150.2.2.0/24 subnet, or even a default route, to router R4:

```
R3#show running-config | section eigrp
router eigrp 1
 network 10.0.0.13 0.0.0.0
 no auto-summary
```

To resolve the first issue, perform one of the following actions:
- Manually configure a static route on R1 pointing to R2
- Advertise a default route dynamically via OSPF on R2

The solution below shows the latter option:

```
R2(config)#router ospf 2
R2(config-router)#default-information originate
```

To resolve the second issue, reconfigure NAT on R2 as follows:

```
R2(config)#no ip nat inside source list 100 interface fastethernet0/0 over
R2(config)#ip nat inside source list 100 interface Dialer1 overload
R2(config)#interface dialer 1
R2(config-if)#ip nat outside
R2(config-if)#interface fastethernet 0/0
R2(config-if)#no ip nat outside
```

To resolve the third issue, perform one of the following actions on R3:
- Advertise the 150.2.2.0/24 subnet via EIGRP so R4 knows about this subnet
- Redistribute the 150.2.20/24 subnet into EIGRP so R4 knows about this subnet

The solution below shows the latter option:

```
R3(config)#router eigrp 1
R3(config-router)#redistribute connected
```

Solution # 2

While you may not have the hosts to perform such testing, from the description, you should be able to determine that this is a TCP issue - primarily due to MTU issues with the PPPoE implementation. MTU issues are a common cause for Layer 3 issues when using PPPoE. When a client attempts to connect to a web site, for example, the MTU size is negotiated during session negotiation between the client and server. Typically the client and server negotiate an MTU of 1500 bytes (Ethernet). To resolve this, you can use one of the following solutions:
- Adjust the workstation Maximum MTU Value
- Adjust the TCP MSS Size on the DSL Router

On the Cisco router, you can change the TCP MSS size via the `ip tcp adjust-mss <size>` interface configuration command. This command is used to specify maximum segment size (MSS) for transient packets that traverse a router, specifically TCP segments in the SYN bit set, when PPP over Ethernet (PPPoE) is being used in the network.

This command helps prevent TCP sessions from being dropped by adjusting the MSS value of the TCP SYN packets. It is effective only for TCP connections passing through the router. In most cases, the optimum value for the max-segment-size argument is 1452 bytes. This value plus the 20-byte IP header, the 20-byte TCP header, and the 8-byte PPPoE header add up to a 1500-byte packet that matches the MTU size for the Ethernet link.

It is important to remember that the TCP MSS command must specify a value of 1452 and not 1492, which is specified using the `ip mtu <size>` interface configuration command. To resolve this issue, implement the following configuration on R2:

```
R2(config)#interface serial 0/0
R2(config-if)#ip tcp adjust-mss 1452
```

Solution # 3

The issue is that R4 has been configured to NOT forward DHCP packets:

```
R4#show running-config | include forward
ip forward-protocol nd
no ip forward-protocol udp bootps
```

To resolve this issue, implement the following configuration on R4:

```
R4(config)#ip forward-protocol udp bootps
```

FINAL WORKING ROUTER CONFIGURATIONS

R1

```
R1#term len 0
R1#sh run
Building configuration...

Current configuration : 939 bytes
!
version 12.4
service timestamps debug datetime msec
service timestamps log datetime msec
no service password-encryption
!
hostname R1
!
boot-start-marker
boot-end-marker
!
no logging console
!
no aaa new-model
no network-clock-participate slot 1
no network-clock-participate wic 0
ip cef
!
no ip domain lookup
ip auth-proxy max-nodata-conns 3
ip admission max-nodata-conns 3
!
interface FastEthernet0/0
 ip address 172.16.1.1 255.255.255.0
 duplex auto
 speed auto
!
interface Serial0/0
 ip address 10.0.0.1 255.255.255.252
 clock rate 2000000
!
interface Serial0/1
 no ip address
 shutdown
!
router ospf 1
 router-id 1.1.1.1
 log-adjacency-changes
 network 10.0.0.1 0.0.0.0 area 0
 network 172.16.1.1 0.0.0.0 area 0
!
ip forward-protocol nd
!
no ip http server
no ip http secure-server
!
control-plane
!
line con 0
line aux 0
line vty 0 4
 login
!
end
R1#
```

R2

```
R2#term len 0
R2#sh run
Building configuration...

Current configuration : 1372 bytes
!
version 12.4
service timestamps debug datetime msec
service timestamps log datetime msec
no service password-encryption
!
hostname R2
!
```

```
boot-start-marker
boot-end-marker
!
no logging console
!
no aaa new-model
no network-clock-participate slot 1
no network-clock-participate wic 0
ip cef
!
no ip domain lookup
ip auth-proxy max-nodata-conns 3
ip admission max-nodata-conns 3
!
interface FastEthernet0/0
 no ip address
 duplex auto
 speed auto
 pppoe enable group global
 pppoe-client dial-pool-number 1
!
interface Serial0/0
 ip address 10.0.0.2 255.255.255.252
 ip nat inside
 ip virtual-reassembly
 ip tcp adjust-mss 1452
!
interface Serial0/1
 no ip address
 shutdown
!
interface Dialer1
 ip address negotiated
 ip mtu 1492
 ip nat outside
 ip virtual-reassembly
 encapsulation ppp
 dialer pool 1
 dialer-group 1
 ppp authentication pap callin
 ppp chap hostname ROUTER2
 ppp chap password 0 CCNP2011
 ppp ipcp route default
!
router ospf 2
 router-id 2.2.2.2
 log-adjacency-changes
 network 10.0.0.2 0.0.0.0 area 0
 default-information originate
!
ip forward-protocol nd
!
no ip http server
no ip http secure-server
ip nat inside source list 100 interface Dialer1 overload
!
access-list 100 permit ip 172.16.1.0 0.0.0.255 150.4.4.0 0.0.0.255
!
control-plane
!
line con 0
line aux 0
line vty 0 4
 login
!
end
R2#
```

R3

```
R3#term len 0
R3#sh run
Building configuration...

Current configuration : 1740 bytes
!
version 12.4
service timestamps debug datetime msec
service timestamps log datetime msec
no service password-encryption
!
```

```
hostname R3
!
boot-start-marker
boot-end-marker
!
no logging console
!
no aaa new-model
no network-clock-participate slot 1
no network-clock-participate wic 0
ip cef
!
no ip dhcp use vrf connected
!
ip dhcp pool R4-POOL
   network 150.4.4.0 255.255.255.0
   default-router 150.4.4.4
   dns-server 150.4.4.254
   netbios-name-server 150.4.4.254
   domain-name howtonetwork.net
   lease 0 8
!
no ip domain lookup
ip auth-proxy max-nodata-conns 3
ip admission max-nodata-conns 3
!
username ROUTER2 password 0 CCNP2011
!
bba-group pppoe global
 virtual-template 1
!
interface FastEthernet0/0
 ip address 150.2.2.254 255.255.255.0
 duplex auto
 speed auto
 pppoe enable group global
!
interface Serial1/0
 no ip address
 shutdown
 clock rate 128000
!
interface Serial1/1
 no ip address
 shutdown
 clock rate 128000
!
interface Serial1/2
 ip address 10.0.0.13 255.255.255.252
 clock rate 128000
!
interface Serial1/3
 no ip address
 shutdown
!
interface Serial1/4
 no ip address
 shutdown
!
interface Serial1/5
 no ip address
 shutdown
!
interface Serial1/6
 no ip address
 shutdown
!
interface Serial1/7
 no ip address
 shutdown
!
interface Virtual-Template1
 mtu 1492
 ip unnumbered FastEthernet0/0
 peer default ip address pool CLIENT-POOL
 ppp authentication chap
!
router eigrp 1
 redistribute connected
 network 10.0.0.13 0.0.0.0
 no auto-summary
!
ip local pool CLIENT-POOL 150.2.2.100 150.2.2.110
```

```
ip forward-protocol nd
!
no ip http server
no ip http secure-server
!
control-plane
!
line con 0
line aux 0
line vty 0 4
 login
!
end
R3#
```

R4

```
R4#term len 0
R4#sh run
Building configuration...

Current configuration : 910 bytes
!
version 12.4
service timestamps debug datetime msec
service timestamps log datetime msec
no service password-encryption
!
hostname R4
!
boot-start-marker
boot-end-marker
!
no logging console
!
no aaa new-model
no network-clock-participate slot 1
no network-clock-participate wic 0
ip cef
!
no ip domain lookup
ip auth-proxy max-nodata-conns 3
ip admission max-nodata-conns 3
!
interface FastEthernet0/0
 ip address 150.4.4.4 255.255.255.0
 ip helper-address 10.0.0.14
 duplex auto
 speed auto
!
interface Serial0/0
 ip address 10.0.0.14 255.255.255.252
!
interface Serial0/1
 no ip address
 shutdown
!
router eigrp 1
 network 10.0.0.14 0.0.0.0
 network 150.4.4.4 0.0.0.0
 no auto-summary
!
ip forward-protocol nd
!
no ip http server
no ip http secure-server
!
control-plane
!
line con 0
line aux 0
line vty 0 4
 login
!
end

R4#
```

CCNP LAB 100

Troubleshooting Lab

Lab Objective:

The focus of this lab is to hone your trouble isolation and resolution skills. This lab will include Layer 2 and Layer 3 technologies which fall within the scope of the current CCNP curriculum.

Lab Topology:

The lab network topology is illustrated below:

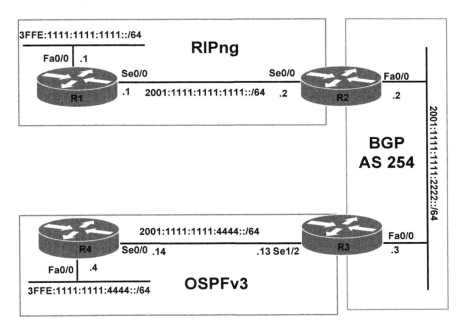

IMPORTANT NOTE: If you are using the www.howtonetwork.net racks, please download and paste the troubleshooting lab configurations. If you are using your own rack or lab, please modify this configuration to reflect the actual interface types, etc, that you have on your devices. Prior to beginning all labs, apply the pre-lab configuration for each individual device.

When completing these labs, it is important to resolve the trouble tickets in the order in which they are listed because they build on each other. For example, if you begin with Trouble Ticket # 3, you might not get the expected resolution or result if you have not completed Trouble Ticket # 1 and Trouble Ticket # 2. It is very important to follow the order listed.

Trouble Ticket # 1

Your co-worker has advised that after some configuration changes were made, they are now no longer able to reach any devices on the 3FFE:1111:1111:1111::/64 subnet from R2. Troubleshoot and resolve this issue.

Trouble Ticket # 2

Your co-worker has completed configuring MP-BGP on R2 and R3; however, they are unable to get the adjacency to be established. Troubleshoot and resolve this issue.

Trouble Ticket # 3

You have received a problem report that Level 1 is unable to reach the 3FFE:1111:1111:1111::/64 subnet from R3. Troubleshoot and resolve this issue.

Trouble Ticket # 4

You have received a problem report that the OSPF adjacency between R3 and R4 has gone down following some routine changes and will not re-establish. Troubleshoot and resolve.

LAB SOLUTIONS

Solution # 1

The issue is that RIPng has been configured to use different IPv6 Multicast groups:

```
R1#show running-config | section ipv6 router
ipv6 router rip CCNP2011
  port 521 multicast-group FF02::8

R2#show running-config | section ipv6 router
ipv6 router rip CCNP2011
  redistribute connected metric 2
  redistribute bgp 254 metric 2 include-connected
```

To resolve this issue, remove the configuration applied to R1 or implement the same configuration applied to R1 on R2. The solution below shows the former option:

```
R1(config)#ipv6 router rip CCNP2011
R1(config-rtr)#no port 521 multicast-group FF02::8
```

Solution # 2

The issue is that MP-BGP still requires an IPv4 RID. Because there are no interfaces configured with an IPv4 address, you must manually configure the MP-BGP RID:

```
R2#show running-config | section bgp
router bgp 254
 no bgp default ipv4-unicast
 bgp log-neighbor-changes
 neighbor 2001:1111:1111:2222::3 remote-as 254

R3#show running-config | section bgp
router bgp 254
 no bgp default ipv4-unicast
 bgp log-neighbor-changes
 neighbor 2001:1111:1111:2222::2 remote-as 254
```

To resolve this, manually configure a RID under MP-BGP on both R2 and R3:

```
R2(config)#router bgp 254
R2(config-router)#bgp router-id 2.2.2.2

R3(config)#router bgp 254
R3(config-router)#bgp router-id 3.3.3.3
```

Solution # 3

The issue is that the default route advertised via RIPng (from R1 to R2) is not automatically redistributed into MP-BGP. Instead, MP-BGP must be configured to advertise a default - allowing R3 to reach the 3FFE:1111:1111:1111::/64 subnet. To resolve this issue, you should implement the following configuration on R2:

```
R2(config)#router bgp 254
R2(config-router)#address-family ipv6
R2(config-router-af)#neighbor 2001:1111:1111:2222::3 default-originate
```

Solution # 4

The issue is that the Serial0/0 interface has been assigned to the incorrect OSPF area:

```
R4#show running-config interface serial 0/0
Building configuration...

Current configuration : 102 bytes
!
interface Serial0/0
 no ip address
 ipv6 address 2001:1111:1111:4444::4/64
 ipv6 ospf 4 area 1
end
```

To resolve this issue, assign the Serial0/0 interface to the correct OSPF area:

```
R4(config-if)#interface serial 0/0
R4(config-if)#ipv6 ospf 4 area 0
```

FINAL WORKING ROUTER CONFIGURATIONS

R1

```
R1#term len 0
R1#sh run
Building configuration...

Current configuration : 994 bytes
!
version 12.4
service timestamps debug datetime msec
service timestamps log datetime msec
no service password-encryption
!
hostname R1
!
boot-start-marker
boot-end-marker
!
no logging console
!
no aaa new-model
no network-clock-participate slot 1
no network-clock-participate wic 0
ip cef
!
no ip domain lookup
ip auth-proxy max-nodata-conns 3
ip admission max-nodata-conns 3
!
ipv6 unicast-routing
!
interface FastEthernet0/0
 no ip address
 duplex auto
 speed auto
 ipv6 address 3FFE:1111:1111:1111::1/64
!
interface Serial0/0
 no ip address
 ipv6 address 2001:1111:1111:1111::1/64
 ipv6 rip CCNP2011 enable
 ipv6 rip CCNP2011 default-information originate
 clock rate 2000000
!
interface Serial0/1
```

```
 no ip address
 shutdown
!
ip forward-protocol nd
!
no ip http server
no ip http secure-server
!
ipv6 route ::/0 Null0
ipv6 router rip CCNP2011
!
control-plane
!
line con 0
line aux 0
line vty 0 4
 login
!
end

R1#
```

R2

```
R2#term len 0
R2#sh run
Building configuration...

Current configuration : 1310 bytes
!
version 12.4
service timestamps debug datetime msec
service timestamps log datetime msec
no service password-encryption
!
hostname R2
!
boot-start-marker
boot-end-marker
!
no logging console
!
no aaa new-model
no network-clock-participate slot 1
no network-clock-participate wic 0
ip cef
!
no ip domain lookup
ip auth-proxy max-nodata-conns 3
ip admission max-nodata-conns 3
!
ipv6 unicast-routing
!
interface FastEthernet0/0
 no ip address
 duplex auto
 speed auto
 ipv6 address 2001:1111:1111:2222::2/64
!
interface Serial0/0
 no ip address
 ipv6 address 2001:1111:1111:1111::2/64
 ipv6 rip CCNP2011 enable
!
interface Serial0/1
 no ip address
 shutdown
!
router bgp 254
 bgp router-id 2.2.2.2
 no bgp default ipv4-unicast
 bgp log-neighbor-changes
 neighbor 2001:1111:1111:2222::3 remote-as 254
 !
 address-family ipv6
  neighbor 2001:1111:1111:2222::3 activate
  neighbor 2001:1111:1111:2222::3 default-originate
```

```
  bgp redistribute-internal
  redistribute rip CCNP2011 include-connected
  no synchronization
 exit-address-family
!
ip forward-protocol nd
!
no ip http server
no ip http secure-server
!
ipv6 router rip CCNP2011
 redistribute connected metric 2
 redistribute bgp 254 metric 2 include-connected
!
control-plane
!
line con 0
line aux 0
line vty 0 4
 login
!
end

R2#
```

R3

```
R3#term len 0
R3#sh run
Building configuration...

Current configuration : 1617 bytes
!
version 12.4
service timestamps debug datetime msec
service timestamps log datetime msec
no service password-encryption
!
hostname R3
!
boot-start-marker
boot-end-marker
!
no logging console
!
no aaa new-model
no network-clock-participate slot 1
no network-clock-participate wic 0
ip cef
!
no ip domain lookup
ip auth-proxy max-nodata-conns 3
ip admission max-nodata-conns 3
!
ipv6 unicast-routing
!
interface FastEthernet0/0
 no ip address
 duplex auto
 speed auto
 ipv6 address 2001:1111:1111:2222::3/64
!
interface Serial1/0
 no ip address
 shutdown
!
interface Serial1/1
 no ip address
 shutdown
!
interface Serial1/2
 no ip address
 ipv6 address 2001:1111:1111:4444::3/64
 ipv6 ospf 3 area 0
 clock rate 128000
!
interface Serial1/3
```

```
  no ip address
  shutdown
 !
 interface Serial1/4
  no ip address
  shutdown
 !
 interface Serial1/5
  no ip address
  shutdown
 !
 interface Serial1/6
  no ip address
  shutdown
 !
 interface Serial1/7
  no ip address
  shutdown
 !
 router bgp 254
  bgp router-id 3.3.3.3
  no bgp default ipv4-unicast
  bgp log-neighbor-changes
  neighbor 2001:1111:1111:2222::2 remote-as 254
  !
  address-family ipv6
   neighbor 2001:1111:1111:2222::2 activate
   bgp redistribute-internal
   redistribute ospf 3 include-connected
   no synchronization
  exit-address-family
 !
 ip forward-protocol nd
 !
 no ip http server
 no ip http secure-server
 !
 ipv6 router ospf 3
  router-id 3.3.3.3
  log-adjacency-changes
  default-information originate
  redistribute connected
  redistribute bgp 254 include-connected
 !
 control-plane
 !
 line con 0
 line aux 0
 line vty 0 4
  login
 !
 end

 R3#
```

R4

```
R4#term len 0
R4#sh run
Building configuration...

Current configuration : 953 bytes
!
version 12.4
service timestamps debug datetime msec
service timestamps log datetime msec
no service password-encryption
!
hostname R4
!
boot-start-marker
boot-end-marker
!
no logging console
!
no aaa new-model
no network-clock-participate slot 1
```

```
no network-clock-participate wic 0
ip cef
!
no ip domain lookup
ip auth-proxy max-nodata-conns 3
ip admission max-nodata-conns 3
!
ipv6 unicast-routing
!
interface FastEthernet0/0
 no ip address
 duplex auto
 speed auto
 ipv6 address 3FFE:1111:1111:4444::4/64
 ipv6 ospf 4 area 1
!
interface Serial0/0
 no ip address
 ipv6 address 2001:1111:1111:4444::4/64
 ipv6 ospf 4 area 0
!
interface Serial0/1
 no ip address
 shutdown
!
ip forward-protocol nd
!
no ip http server
no ip http secure-server
!
ipv6 router ospf 4
 router-id 4.4.4.4
 log-adjacency-changes
!
control-plane
!
line con 0
line aux 0
line vty 0 4
 login
!
end

R4#
```

CCNP LAB 101

EIGRP and OSPF VRF Lite Lab

Lab Objective:

The focus of this lab is to understand Virtual Routing and Forwarding Lite implementation and verification in Cisco IOS Software using EIGRP and OSPF. Additional technologies tested also include VRF-aware Network Address Translation (NAT).

Lab Topology:

The lab network topology is illustrated below:

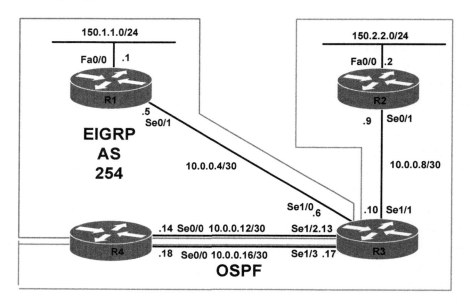

IMPORTANT NOTE: If you are using the www.howtonetwork.net racks, please bring up the LAN interfaces connected to the routers by issuing the no shutdown command on the connected switches. If you are using a home lab with no Switches, you can bring up the LAN interfaces using the following configurations on your routers:

```
interface fastethernet 0/0
  no keepalive
  loopback
  no shutdown
```

Alternately, you can simply connect the interfaces to a hub or switch if you have one available in your own lab.

Task 1

Configure hostnames, IP addressing on all routers as illustrated in the network topology.

Task 2

Configure the following VRFs on the devices in the network:

- R1: VRF Name - VRFONE: RD - 100:100
- R2: VRF Name - VRFTWO: RD - 200:200
- R3: VRF Name - VRFONE: RD - 100:100
- R3: VRF Name - VRFTWO: RD - 200:200
- R4: VRF Name - VRFONE: RD - 100:100
- R4: VRF Name - VRFTWO: RD - 200:200

Verify your configuration using the appropriate commands:

Task 3

Configure EIGRP using AS 254 on R1 and assign interface Serial0/1 and LAN interfaces to VRF VRFONE. Verify your configuration using the appropriate commands.

Task 4

Configure OSPF on R2 and assign interface Serial0/1 and LAN interfaces to VRF VRFTWO. Verify your configuration using the appropriate commands.

Task 5

Configure EIGRP and OSPF for VRFONE and VRFTWO on R3. Verify your configuration using the appropriate commands.

Task 6

Configure EIGRP and OSPF for VRFONE and VRFTWO on R4. Verify your configuration using the appropriate commands.

Task 7

Configure two additional Loopback interfaces on R4 as follows:
- Loopback 100: IP Address 100.4.4.4/32 - VRF: VRFONE
- Loopback 200: IP Address 100.4.4.4/32 - VRF: VRFTWO

Do NOT advertise these Loopbacks via OSPF or EIGRP. However, ensure that R4 is able to ping the 150.1.1.0/24 subnet in VRFONE from the Loopback100 interface and R4 is able to ping the 150.2.2.0/24 subnet in VRFTWO from the Loopback200 interface.

LAB VALIDATION

Task 1

Please refer to previous labs for basic IPv4 addressing and hostname configuration. This will not be included in this section to avoid being redundant.

Task 2

In Cisco IOS software, the configuration of VRF Lite is a simple and straightforward task. First, the VRF name must be defined using the `ip vrf [name]` global configuration command. Next, a route distinguisher is assigned to the VRF using the `rd [route distinguisher]` VRF configuration command. The route distinguisher is used to identify the VPN and is used to distinguish multiple VPN routes that have an identical prefix. The route distinguisher can be configured using either ASN:*nn* or IP-address:*nn* format.

NOTE: The *n* is simply represents and integer. You can use specify one integer or two integers.

This task is completed on all routers as follows:

```
R1(config)#ip vrf VRFONE
R1(config-vrf)#rd 100:100
R1(config-vrf)#exit

R2(config)#ip vrf VRFTWO
R2(config-vrf)#rd 200:200
R2(config-vrf)#exit

R3(config)#ip vrf VRFONE
R3(config-vrf)#rd 100:100
R3(config-vrf)#exit
R3(config)#ip vrf VRFTWO
R3(config-vrf)#rd 200:200
R3(config-vrf)#exit

R4(config)#ip vrf VRFONE
R4(config-vrf)#rd 100:100
R4(config-vrf)#exit
R4(config)#ip vrf VRFTWO
R4(config-vrf)#rd 200:200
R4(config-vrf)#exit
```

Following this, verify your solution using the `show ip vrf` command on all routers:

```
R1#show ip vrf
  Name                              Default RD          Interfaces

R2#show ip vrf
  Name                              Default RD          Interfaces
  VRFTWO                            200:200

R3#show ip vrf
  Name                              Default RD          Interfaces
  VRFONE                            100:100
  VRFTWO                            200:200

R4#show ip vrf
  Name                              Default RD          Interfaces
  VRFONE                            100:100
  VRFTWO                            200:200
```

Task 3

The requirements of this task are straightforward. For EIGRP and RIPv2, VRF configuration is implemented using the `address-family ipv4 vrf [name]` router configuration command. In addition, for EIGRP, the `autonomous-system [number]` VRF configuration subcommand must be used to specify the autonomous system number. Static routes for each VRF can be configured using the `ip route vrf [prefix] [mask] [interface | address]` global configuration command. This task is completed as follows:

```
R1(config)#interface fastethernet 0/0
R1(config-if)#ip vrf forwarding VRFONE
% Interface FastEthernet0/0 IP address 150.1.1.1 removed due to enabling VRF VRFONE
R1(config-if)#ip address 150.1.1.1 255.255.255.0
R1(config-if)#exit
R1(config)#interface serial 0/1
R1(config-if)#ip vrf forwarding VRFONE
% Interface Serial0/1 IP address 10.0.0.5 removed due to enabling VRF VRFONE
R1(config-if)#ip address 10.0.0.5 255.255.255.252
R1(config-if)#exit
R1(config)#router eigrp 1
R1(config-router)#address-family ipv4 vrf VRFONE
R1(config-router-af)#network 150.1.1.1 0.0.0.0
R1(config-router-af)#network 10.0.0.5 0.0.0.0
R1(config-router-af)#no auto-summary
R1(config-router-af)#autonomous-system 254
R1(config-router-af)#exit
```

Verify your configuration using the `show ip eigrp vrf <name>` commands:

```
R1#show ip eigrp vrf VRFONE interfaces
IP-EIGRP interfaces for process 254
                    Xmit Queue   Mean   Pacing Time   Multicast    Pending
Interface   Peers   Un/Reliable  SRTT   Un/Reliable   Flow Timer   Routes
Se0/1       0       0/0          0      0/1           0            0
Fa0/0       0       0/0          0      0/1           0            0
```

Task 4

The requirements of this task are straightforward. In Cisco IOS software VRF Lite using OSPF is configured using the `router ospf [process ID] vrf [name]` global configuration command followed by the `capability vrf-lite` router configuration command. The remainder of the configuration, e.g. `network` statements, is performed in a similar manner to when VRF Lite is not being used. This task is completed as follows:

```
R2(config)#interface fastethernet 0/0
R2(config-if)#ip vrf forwarding VRFTWO
% Interface FastEthernet0/0 IP address 150.2.2.2 removed due to enabling VRF VRFTWO
R2(config-if)#ip address 150.2.2.2 255.255.255.0
R2(config-if)#exit
R2(config)#interface serial 0/1
R2(config-if)#ip vrf forwarding VRFTWO
% Interface Serial0/1 IP address 10.0.0.9 removed due to enabling VRF VRFTWO
R2(config-if)#ip address 10.0.0.9 255.255.255.252
R2(config-if)#exit
R2(config)#router ospf 2
R2(config-router)#exit
R2(config)#router ospf 2 vrf VRFTWO
R2(config-router)#capability vrf-lite
R2(config-router)#router-id 2.2.2.2
R2(config-router)#network 150.2.2.2 0.0.0.0 area 0
R2(config-router)#network 10.0.0.9 0.0.0.0 area 0
R2(config-router)#exit
```

Verify your configuration using the `show ip ospf` commands:

```
R2#show ip ospf interface brief
Interface   PID   Area          IP Address/Mask   Cost   State   Nbrs F/C
Se0/1       2     0             10.0.0.9/30       64     P2P     0/0
Fa0/0       2     0             150.2.2.2/24      1      DR      0/0
```

Task 5

The requirements of this task are straightforward. Following the same logic used in the previous tasks, this task is completed as follows:

```
R3(config)#interface serial 1/0
R3(config-if)#ip vrf forwarding VRFONE
% Interface Serial1/0 IP address 10.0.0.6 removed due to enabling VRF VRFONE
R3(config-if)#ip address 10.0.0.6 255.255.255.252
R3(config-if)#exit
R3(config)#interface serial 1/1
R3(config-if)#ip vrf forwarding VRFTWO
% Interface Serial1/1 IP address 10.0.0.10 removed due to enabling VRF VRFTWO
R3(config-if)#ip address 10.0.0.10 255.255.255.252
R3(config-if)#exit
R3(config)#interface serial 1/2
R3(config-if)#ip vrf forwarding VRFONE
% Interface Serial1/2 IP address 10.0.0.13 removed due to enabling VRF VRFONE
R3(config-if)#ip address 10.0.0.13 255.255.255.252
R3(config-if)#exit
R3(config)#interface serial 1/3
R3(config-if)#ip vrf forwarding VRFTWO
% Interface Serial1/3 IP address 10.0.0.17 removed due to enabling VRF VRFTWO
R3(config-if)#ip address 10.0.0.17 255.255.255.252
R3(config-if)#exit
R3(config)#router eigrp 1
R3(config-router)#address-family ipv4 vrf VRFONE
R3(config-router-af)#no auto-summary
R3(config-router-af)#network 10.0.0.6 0.0.0.0
R3(config-router-af)#network 10.0.0.13 0.0.0.0
R3(config-router-af)#autonomous-system 254
R3(config-router-af)#exit
R3(config-router)#exit
R3(config)#router ospf 3 vrf VRFTWO
R3(config-router)#capability vrf-lite
R3(config-router)#router-id 3.3.3.3
R3(config-router)#network 10.0.0.10 0.0.0.0 area 0
R3(config-router)#network 10.0.0.17 0.0.0.0 area 0
R3(config-router)#exit
```

Verify your EIGRP configuration using the show ip eigrp vrf <name> commands:

```
R3#show ip eigrp vrf VRFONE interfaces
IP-EIGRP interfaces for process 254
                     Xmit Queue   Mean   Pacing Time   Multicast    Pending
Interface     Peers  Un/Reliable  SRTT   Un/Reliable   Flow Timer   Routes
Se1/0          1       0/0          9      5/190          226          0
Se1/2          0       0/0          0      5/5            0            0

R3#show ip eigrp vrf VRFONE neighbors
IP-EIGRP neighbors for process 254
H   Address                 Interface       Hold Uptime    SRTT   RTO   Q   Seq
                                            (sec)          (ms)         Cnt Num
0   10.0.0.5                Se1/0            11 00:03:07     9    1140   0   3
```

Verify your configuration using the show ip ospf commands:

```
R3#show ip ospf neighbor

Neighbor ID    Pri   State     Dead Time    Address      Interface
2.2.2.2         0    FULL/  -  00:00:31     10.0.0.9     Serial1/1
```

Task 6

Following the same logic applied in previous tasks, this task is completed as follows:

```
R4(config)#interface serial 0/0
R4(config-if)#ip vrf forwarding VRFONE
% Interface Serial0/0 IP address 10.0.0.14 removed due to enabling VRF VRFONE
R4(config-if)#ip address 10.0.0.14 255.255.255.252
R4(config-if)#exit
R4(config)#interface serial 0/1
R4(config-if)#ip vrf forwarding VRFTWO
% Interface Serial0/1 IP address 10.0.0.18 removed due to enabling VRF VRFTWO
R4(config-if)#ip address 10.0.0.18 255.255.255.252
R4(config-if)#exit
R4(config)#router eigrp 1
R4(config-router)#address-family ipv4 vrf VRFONE
R4(config-router-af)#no auto-summary
R4(config-router-af)#network 10.0.0.14 0.0.0.0
R4(config-router-af)#autonomous-system 254
R4(config-router-af)#exit
R4(config-router)#exit
R4(config)#router ospf 4 vrf VRFTWO
R4(config-router)#capability vrf-lite
R4(config-router)#router-id 4.4.4.4
R4(config-router)#network 10.0.0.18 0.0.0.0 area 0
R4(config-router)#exit
```

Verify your EIGRP configuration using the show ip eigrp vrf <name> commands:

```
R4#show ip eigrp vrf VRFONE interfaces
IP-EIGRP interfaces for process 254
                     Xmit Queue   Mean   Pacing Time   Multicast    Pending
Interface     Peers  Un/Reliable  SRTT   Un/Reliable   Flow Timer   Routes
Se0/0          1       0/0          23     0/15           127          0

R4#show ip eigrp vrf VRFONE neighbors
IP-EIGRP neighbors for process 254
H   Address                 Interface       Hold Uptime    SRTT   RTO   Q   Seq
                                            (sec)          (ms)         Cnt Num
0   10.0.0.13               Se0/0            13 00:02:19     23    200   0   8
```

Verify your configuration using the show ip ospf commands:

```
R4#show ip ospf neighbor

Neighbor ID    Pri   State     Dead Time    Address      Interface
3.3.3.3         0    FULL/  -  00:00:39     10.0.0.17    Serial0/1
```

At this point, verify VRF routing tables using the `show ip route vrf <name>` command:

```
R1#show ip route vrf VRFONE

Routing Table: VRFONE
Codes: C - connected, S - static, R - RIP, M - mobile, B - BGP
       D - EIGRP, EX - EIGRP external, O - OSPF, IA - OSPF inter area
       N1 - OSPF NSSA external type 1, N2 - OSPF NSSA external type 2
       E1 - OSPF external type 1, E2 - OSPF external type 2
       i - IS-IS, su - IS-IS summary, L1 - IS-IS level-1, L2 - IS-IS level-2
       ia - IS-IS inter area, * - candidate default, U - per-user static route
       o - ODR, P - periodic downloaded static route

Gateway of last resort is not set

     10.0.0.0/30 is subnetted, 2 subnets
D       10.0.0.12 [90/21024000] via 10.0.0.6, 00:10:26, Serial0/1
C       10.0.0.4 is directly connected, Serial0/1
     150.1.0.0/24 is subnetted, 1 subnets
C       150.1.1.0 is directly connected, FastEthernet0/0

R2#show ip route vrf VRFTWO

Routing Table: VRFTWO
Codes: C - connected, S - static, R - RIP, M - mobile, B - BGP
       D - EIGRP, EX - EIGRP external, O - OSPF, IA - OSPF inter area
       N1 - OSPF NSSA external type 1, N2 - OSPF NSSA external type 2
       E1 - OSPF external type 1, E2 - OSPF external type 2
       i - IS-IS, su - IS-IS summary, L1 - IS-IS level-1, L2 - IS-IS level-2
       ia - IS-IS inter area, * - candidate default, U - per-user static route
       o - ODR, P - periodic downloaded static route

Gateway of last resort is not set

     10.0.0.0/30 is subnetted, 2 subnets
C       10.0.0.8 is directly connected, Serial0/1
O       10.0.0.16 [110/845] via 10.0.0.10, 00:03:18, Serial0/1
     150.2.0.0/24 is subnetted, 1 subnets
C       150.2.2.0 is directly connected, FastEthernet0/0

R3#show ip route vrf VRFONE

Routing Table: VRFONE
Codes: C - connected, S - static, R - RIP, M - mobile, B - BGP
       D - EIGRP, EX - EIGRP external, O - OSPF, IA - OSPF inter area
       N1 - OSPF NSSA external type 1, N2 - OSPF NSSA external type 2
       E1 - OSPF external type 1, E2 - OSPF external type 2
       i - IS-IS, su - IS-IS summary, L1 - IS-IS level-1, L2 - IS-IS level-2
       ia - IS-IS inter area, * - candidate default, U - per-user static route
       o - ODR, P - periodic downloaded static route

Gateway of last resort is not set

     10.0.0.0/30 is subnetted, 2 subnets
C       10.0.0.12 is directly connected, Serial1/2
C       10.0.0.4 is directly connected, Serial1/0
     150.1.0.0/24 is subnetted, 1 subnets
D       150.1.1.0 [90/20514560] via 10.0.0.5, 00:10:49, Serial1/0

R3#show ip route vrf VRFTWO

Routing Table: VRFTWO
Codes: C - connected, S - static, R - RIP, M - mobile, B - BGP
       D - EIGRP, EX - EIGRP external, O - OSPF, IA - OSPF inter area
       N1 - OSPF NSSA external type 1, N2 - OSPF NSSA external type 2
       E1 - OSPF external type 1, E2 - OSPF external type 2
       i - IS-IS, su - IS-IS summary, L1 - IS-IS level-1, L2 - IS-IS level-2
       ia - IS-IS inter area, * - candidate default, U - per-user static route
       o - ODR, P - periodic downloaded static route

Gateway of last resort is not set

     10.0.0.0/30 is subnetted, 2 subnets
C       10.0.0.8 is directly connected, Serial1/1
C       10.0.0.16 is directly connected, Serial1/3
     150.2.0.0/24 is subnetted, 1 subnets
O       150.2.2.0 [110/782] via 10.0.0.9, 00:03:29, Serial1/1

R4#show ip route vrf VRFONE
```

```
Routing Table: VRFONE
Codes: C - connected, S - static, R - RIP, M - mobile, B - BGP
       D - EIGRP, EX - EIGRP external, O - OSPF, IA - OSPF inter area
       N1 - OSPF NSSA external type 1, N2 - OSPF NSSA external type 2
       E1 - OSPF external type 1, E2 - OSPF external type 2
       i - IS-IS, su - IS-IS summary, L1 - IS-IS level-1, L2 - IS-IS level-2
       ia - IS-IS inter area, * - candidate default, U - per-user static route
       o - ODR, P - periodic downloaded static route

Gateway of last resort is not set

     10.0.0.0/30 is subnetted, 2 subnets
C       10.0.0.12 is directly connected, Serial0/0
D       10.0.0.4 [90/21024000] via 10.0.0.13, 00:04:15, Serial0/0
     150.1.0.0/24 is subnetted, 1 subnets
D       150.1.1.0 [90/21026560] via 10.0.0.13, 00:04:15, Serial0/0

R4#show ip route vrf VRFTWO

Routing Table: VRFTWO
Codes: C - connected, S - static, R - RIP, M - mobile, B - BGP
       D - EIGRP, EX - EIGRP external, O - OSPF, IA - OSPF inter area
       N1 - OSPF NSSA external type 1, N2 - OSPF NSSA external type 2
       E1 - OSPF external type 1, E2 - OSPF external type 2
       i - IS-IS, su - IS-IS summary, L1 - IS-IS level-1, L2 - IS-IS level-2
       ia - IS-IS inter area, * - candidate default, U - per-user static route
       o - ODR, P - periodic downloaded static route

Gateway of last resort is not set

     10.0.0.0/30 is subnetted, 2 subnets
O       10.0.0.8 [110/845] via 10.0.0.17, 00:03:39, Serial0/1
C       10.0.0.16 is directly connected, Serial0/1
     150.2.0.0/24 is subnetted, 1 subnets
O       150.2.2.0 [110/846] via 10.0.0.17, 00:03:39, Serial0/1
```

Task 7

Simply because we have introduced VRF Lite into the network does not mean that the basic or core fundamentals do not apply. If VRF Lite was not used, we would use NAT to complete this task. Fortunately, Cisco IOS NAT is VRF-aware. This task is therefore completed as follows:

```
R4(config)#interface loopback 100
R4(config-if)#ip vrf forwarding VRFONE
R4(config-if)#ip address 100.4.4.4 255.255.255.255
R4(config-if)#ip nat inside
R4(config-if)#exit
R4(config)#interface loopback 200
R4(config-if)#ip vrf forwarding VRFTWO
R4(config-if)#ip address 100.4.4.4 255.255.255.255
R4(config-if)#ip nat inside
R4(config-if)#exit
R4(config)#interface serial 0/0
R4(config-if)#ip nat outside
R4(config-if)#exit
R4(config)#interface serial 0/1
R4(config-if)#ip nat outside
R4(config-if)#exit
R4(config)#access-list 100 permit ip host 100.4.4.4 any
R4(config)#$de source list 100 interface serial 0/0 vrf VRFONE overload
R4(config)#$de source list 100 interface serial 0/1 vrf VRFTWO overload
```

Following this configuration, test VRFONE NAT by pinging 150.1.1.1 from R4s Loopback100:

```
R4#ping vrf VRFONE 150.1.1.1 source loopback 100

Type escape sequence to abort.
Sending 5, 100-byte ICMP Echos to 150.1.1.1, timeout is 2 seconds:
Packet sent with a source address of 100.4.4.4
!!!!!
Success rate is 100 percent (5/5), round-trip min/avg/max = 28/30/32 ms
```

Verify VRFONE NAT translations using the show ip nat translations command:

```
R4#show ip nat translations vrf VRFONE verbose
Pro Inside global      Inside local      Outside local      Outside global
icmp 10.0.0.14:1       100.4.4.4:1       150.1.1.1:1        150.1.1.1:1
    create 00:00:20, use 00:00:20 timeout:60000, left 00:00:39, Map-Id(In): 1,
    flags:
extended, use_count: 0, VRF : VRFONE, entry-id: 1, lc_entries: 0
```

Next, test VRFONE NAT by pinging 150.2.2.2 from R4s Loopback100:

```
R4#ping vrf VRFTWO 150.2.2.2 source loopback 200

Type escape sequence to abort.
Sending 5, 100-byte ICMP Echos to 150.2.2.2, timeout is 2 seconds:
Packet sent with a source address of 100.4.4.4
!!!!!
Success rate is 100 percent (5/5), round-trip min/avg/max = 28/30/32 ms
```

Finally, verify VRFTWO NAT operation using the show ip nat translations command:

```
R4#show ip nat translations vrf VRFTWO verbose
Pro Inside global      Inside local      Outside local      Outside global
icmp 10.0.0.18:3       100.4.4.4:3       150.2.2.2:3        150.2.2.2:3
    create 00:00:09, use 00:00:09 timeout:60000, left 00:00:50, Map-Id(In): 2,
    flags:
extended, use_count: 0, VRF : VRFTWO, entry-id: 3, lc_entries: 0
```

FINAL ROUTER CONFIGURATIONS

R1

```
R1#term len 0
R1#sh run
Building configuration...

Current configuration : 1066 bytes
!
version 12.4
service timestamps debug datetime msec
service timestamps log datetime msec
no service password-encryption
!
hostname R1
!
boot-start-marker
boot-end-marker
!
no logging console
!
no aaa new-model
no network-clock-participate slot 1
no network-clock-participate wic 0
ip cef
!
ip vrf VRFONE
 rd 100:100
!
no ip domain lookup
ip auth-proxy max-nodata-conns 3
ip admission max-nodata-conns 3
!
interface FastEthernet0/0
 ip vrf forwarding VRFONE
 ip address 150.1.1.1 255.255.255.0
 duplex auto
 speed auto
!
interface Serial0/0
 no ip address
 clock rate 2000000
!
interface Serial0/1
```

```
  ip vrf forwarding VRFONE
  ip address 10.0.0.5 255.255.255.252
 !
 router eigrp 1
  auto-summary
  !
  address-family ipv4 vrf VRFONE
   network 10.0.0.5 0.0.0.0
   network 150.1.1.1 0.0.0.0
   no auto-summary
   autonomous-system 254
  exit-address-family
 !
 ip forward-protocol nd
 !
 no ip http server
 no ip http secure-server
 !
 control-plane
 !
 line con 0
 line aux 0
 line vty 0 4
  login
 !
 end
 R1#
```

R2

```
R2#term len 0
R2#sh run
Building configuration...

Current configuration : 1029 bytes
!
version 12.4
service timestamps debug datetime msec
service timestamps log datetime msec
no service password-encryption
!
hostname R2
!
boot-start-marker
boot-end-marker
!
no logging console
!
no aaa new-model
no network-clock-participate slot 1
no network-clock-participate wic 0
ip cef
!
ip vrf VRFTWO
 rd 200:200
!
no ip domain lookup
ip auth-proxy max-nodata-conns 3
ip admission max-nodata-conns 3
!
interface FastEthernet0/0
 ip vrf forwarding VRFTWO
 ip address 150.2.2.2 255.255.255.0
 duplex auto
 speed auto
!
interface Serial0/0
 no ip address
 shutdown
!
interface Serial0/1
 ip vrf forwarding VRFTWO
 ip address 10.0.0.9 255.255.255.252
!
router ospf 2 vrf VRFTWO
 router-id 2.2.2.2
 log-adjacency-changes
 capability vrf-lite
```

```
 network 10.0.0.9 0.0.0.0 area 0
 network 150.2.2.2 0.0.0.0 area 0
!
ip forward-protocol nd
!
no ip http server
no ip http secure-server
!
control-plane
!
line con 0
line aux 0
line vty 0 4
 login
!
end

R2#
```

R3

```
R3#term len 0
R3#sh run
Building configuration...

Current configuration : 1680 bytes
!
version 12.4
service timestamps debug datetime msec
service timestamps log datetime msec
no service password-encryption
!
hostname R3
!
boot-start-marker
boot-end-marker
!
no logging console
!
no aaa new-model
no network-clock-participate slot 1
no network-clock-participate wic 0
ip cef
!
ip vrf VRFONE
 rd 100:100
!
ip vrf VRFTWO
 rd 200:200
!
no ip domain lookup
ip auth-proxy max-nodata-conns 3
ip admission max-nodata-conns 3
!
interface FastEthernet0/0
 no ip address
 shutdown
 duplex auto
 speed auto
!
interface Serial1/0
 ip vrf forwarding VRFONE
 ip address 10.0.0.6 255.255.255.252
 clock rate 128000
!
interface Serial1/1
 ip vrf forwarding VRFTWO
 ip address 10.0.0.10 255.255.255.252
 clock rate 128000
!
interface Serial1/2
 ip vrf forwarding VRFONE
 ip address 10.0.0.13 255.255.255.252
 clock rate 128000
!
interface Serial1/3
 ip vrf forwarding VRFTWO
```

```
 ip address 10.0.0.17 255.255.255.252
 clock rate 128000
!
interface Serial1/4
 no ip address
 shutdown
!
interface Serial1/5
 no ip address
 shutdown
!
interface Serial1/6
 no ip address
 shutdown
!
interface Serial1/7
 no ip address
 shutdown
!
router eigrp 1
 auto-summary
 !
 address-family ipv4 vrf VRFONE
  network 10.0.0.6 0.0.0.0
  network 10.0.0.13 0.0.0.0
  no auto-summary
  autonomous-system 254
 exit-address-family
!
router ospf 3 vrf VRFTWO
 router-id 3.3.3.3
 log-adjacency-changes
 capability vrf-lite
 network 10.0.0.10 0.0.0.0 area 0
 network 10.0.0.17 0.0.0.0 area 0
!
ip forward-protocol nd
!
no ip http server
no ip http secure-server
!
control-plane
!
line con 0
line aux 0
line vty 0 4
 login
!
end
R3#
```

R4

```
R4#term len 0
R4#sh run
Building configuration...

Current configuration : 1699 bytes
!
version 12.4
service timestamps debug datetime msec
service timestamps log datetime msec
no service password-encryption
!
hostname R4
!
boot-start-marker
boot-end-marker
!
no logging console
!
no aaa new-model
no network-clock-participate slot 1
no network-clock-participate wic 0
ip cef
!
ip vrf VRFONE
 rd 100:100
```

```
!
ip vrf VRFTWO
 rd 200:200
!
no ip domain lookup
ip auth-proxy max-nodata-conns 3
ip admission max-nodata-conns 3
!
interface Loopback100
 ip vrf forwarding VRFONE
 ip address 100.4.4.4 255.255.255.255
 ip nat inside
 ip virtual-reassembly
!
interface Loopback200
 ip vrf forwarding VRFTWO
 ip address 100.4.4.4 255.255.255.255
 ip nat inside
 ip virtual-reassembly
!
interface FastEthernet0/0
 no ip address
 shutdown
 duplex auto
 speed auto
!
interface Serial0/0
 ip vrf forwarding VRFONE
 ip address 10.0.0.14 255.255.255.252
 ip nat outside
 ip virtual-reassembly
!
interface Serial0/1
 ip vrf forwarding VRFTWO
 ip address 10.0.0.18 255.255.255.252
 ip nat outside
 ip virtual-reassembly
!
router eigrp 1
 auto-summary
 !
 address-family ipv4 vrf VRFONE
  network 10.0.0.14 0.0.0.0
  no auto-summary
  autonomous-system 254
 exit-address-family
!
router ospf 4 vrf VRFTWO
 router-id 4.4.4.4
 log-adjacency-changes
 capability vrf-lite
 network 10.0.0.18 0.0.0.0 area 0
!
ip forward-protocol nd
!
no ip http server
no ip http secure-server
ip nat inside source list 100 interface Serial0/0 vrf VRFONE overload
ip nat inside source list 100 interface Serial0/1 vrf VRFTWO overload
!
access-list 100 permit ip host 100.4.4.4 any
!
control-plane
!
line con 0
line aux 0
line vty 0 4
 login
!
end

R4#
```

CPSIA information can be obtained
at www.ICGtesting.com
Printed in the USA
BVOW07s0849280617

488023BV00005B/70/P